Robert E. Wilcox

**THE PRENTICE HALL SERIES IN SECURITY AND INSURANCE**
**CONSULTING EDITOR: KENNETH BLACK, JR.**

# Life Insurance

# TWELFTH EDITION

# *Life Insurance*

## KENNETH BLACK, JR.

*Regents' Professor Emeritus of Insurance*
*College of Business Administration*
*Georgia State University*

## HAROLD D. SKIPPER, JR.

*C. V. Starr Distinguished Professor of International Insurance*
*College of Business Administration*
*Georgia State University*

Prentice Hall, Englewood Cliffs, NJ 07632

Library of Congress Cataloging-Publication Data
Black, Kenneth.
    Life insurance/Kenneth Black, Jr., Harold D. Skipper, Jr.—
  12th ed.
        p.       cm.
    Includes bibliographical references and index.
    ISBN 0-13-532995-7
      1. Insurance, Life. 2. Insurance, Life—United States
   3. Insurance, Health. 4. Insurance, Health—United States.
    I. Skipper, Harold D.             II. Title
HG8771.B55  1993
368.3'2—dc20                 92-31399

Acquisition editor:  Leah Jewell
Production editor:  Joanne Palmer
Prepress buyer:  Trudy Pisciotti
Manufacturing buyer:  Patrice Fraccio
Editorial assistant:  Renee Pelletier

 ©1994, 1987, 1982, 1976 by Prentice-Hall, Inc.
A Simon & Schuster company.
Englewood Cliffs, NJ  07632

Printed in the United States of America

10 9 8

ISBN 0-13-532995-7

Prentice-Hall International (UK) Limited, *London*
Prentice-Hall of Australia Pty. Limited, *Sydney*
Prentice-Hall Canada Inc., *Toronto*
Prentice-Hall Hispanoamericana, S.A., *Mexico*
Prentice-Hall of India Private Limited, *New Delhi*
Prentice-Hall of Japan, Inc., *Tokyo*
Simon & Schuster Asia Pte. Lit., *Singapore*
Editora Prentice-Hall do Brasil, Ltda., *Rio de Janeiro*

To
Kenneth Black, Sr.,
and the memory of Margaret Virginia Black


and
the memory of George W. Skipper, Jr.,
and Harold D. Skipper, Sr.

## SOLOMON STEPHEN HUEBNER

Dr. Solomon Stephen Huebner was a distinguished professor of Insurance at the Wharton School, University of Pennsylvania, and chairman of the Department of Insurance at that institution. He not only introduced the first university-level insurance courses in the United States but also wrote the first university-level insurance textbooks. Dr. Huebner wrote the first edition of this text, published in 1915, and since that time, succeeding editions have been in continuous use both at the university level and in professional designation programs. Through his strong leadership, he came to be known as the father of insurance education in the United States.

While at the University of Pennsylvania, Dr. Huebner was the moving force behind the establishment of both the American College and the American Institute for Property and Liability Underwriters. He served as the first president of the American College, using criteria of knowledge, character, and ethical practice to transform the distribution system of the life insurance business in the United States from the commercialism of the early twentieth century to the service-oriented professionalism a half-century later. This earned him the accolade "the teacher who changed an industry."

The authors are pleased to have been able to perpetuate this great educator's text. He built bridges of knowledge and understanding. The authors had the opportunity to cross one of his many bridges, moving from student to teacher, through the S. S. Huebner Foundation for Insurance Education at the University of Pennsylvania. We are grateful for the privilege that has been afforded us and hope that throughout this volume we have maintained the high standards of excellence and professionalism to which Dr. Huebner's entire career was committed.

# Contents

## PART II        TYPES OF LIFE INSURANCE PRODUCTS

### *Chapter 4*
### INTRODUCTION TO LIFE INSURANCE PRODUCTS AND THEIR ENVIRONMENT    74

### *Chapter 5*
### WHOLE LIFE INSURANCE POLICIES    98

### *Chapter 6*
### FLEXIBLE-PREMIUM LIFE INSURANCE POLICIES    124

### *Chapter 7*
### ANNUITY AND SPECIAL-PURPOSE POLICIES AND BENEFITS 147

## PART III       ASPECTS OF LIFE INSURANCE EVALUATION

### *Chapter 8*
### THE LIFE INSURANCE CONTRACT: I    177

## Chapter 9
# THE LIFE INSURANCE CONTRACT: II    210

## Chapter 10
# LIFE INSURANCE AND ANNUITY COST ANALYSIS AND DISCLOSURE    237

## Chapter 11
# INSURANCE ADVISOR AND COMPANY EVALUATION    275

# PART IV    USES OF LIFE INSURANCE IN PERSONAL FINANCIAL PLANNING    326

## Chapter 12
# LIFE INSURANCE PLANNING    326

# *Preface*

This book is a revision of its predecessors, the first of which was published in 1915, and contains major revisions to the last edition. We continued our effort to alter the book's emphasis on purely factual information about the life insurance industry, its products, and its operations to one that combines current information with its environment, theory and use in the life and health insurance marketplace. We sought to establish the treatise in an appropriate historical, international, economic, demographic, social, and political context through a liberal discussion of these environmental factors where appropriate. We have approached life and health insurance simultaneously from the viewpoint of the buyer, the advisor, and the insurer.

The turmoil experience by the financial services industry within recent years has called for a fresh, more detailed examination of life and health insurance and their uses and evaluations. We have attempted to respond to these demands not only by completely updating and rewriting many chapters but also by giving more depth to the subjects to provide the basis for a deeper understanding by college and university students as well as by insurance and other financial professionals.

A financial management perspective has been adopted to explain how life and health insurance products fit into a broad framework of financial planning. In this context, these products have both unique advantages and some disadvantages. We have endeavored to present a forthright appraisal of them and to suggest how they may be evaluated from contractual, cost, and performance viewpoints. With an increasingly competitive marketplace, the student and advisor will need to be armed with an appreciation of the means of making fair product and insurer comparisons and the shortcomings of these comparisons. The principles upon which life and health insurance are based are fundamental to understanding the industry, its products, and their use. For this reason, the volume contains an expanded treatment of life and health insurance fundamentals in Part I.

The discussion of life insurance planning has been substantially expanded to provide an environmental context and conceptual underpinning. The present process covers both inflation and a dynamic approach. Advancing computer technology makes this possible for students and practitioners alike.

As in the previous edition, entire chapters have been devoted to the tax treatment of life insurance, to estate and retirement planning, and to the business uses of life insurance. While these areas are subject to rapid obsolescence, we continue to believe that their inclusion is desirable for those students and practitioners who have had little exposure to the topics elsewhere and for those who need an easy summary of the materials.

Life insurance company management and the environment within which it operates are dealt with in the later chapters of the book. This edition introduces finance theory and concepts on which all financial service companies operate; this represents a major change in the text's approach to life insurer organization and financial management.

In sum, we have attempted to provide a comprehensive, unbiased treatise on individual and group life, health, and retirement products, their appropriate use and taxation, how to evaluate them and their supplier insurers, along with a thorough examination of life insurance company operations and regulation.

Whether this revision accomplishes the mission we sought to achieve can be judged only by its users. The authors invite critical comments in this regard.

## ACKNOWLEDGMENTS

The authors benefited greatly from the constructive advice and criticism of many individuals. These include:

Tony E. Holmes and Andrea T. Sellars, Alexander & Alexander Consulting; Peter Densen and Paul E. Rohner, Alexander & Alexander Services, Inc.; James B. Stradtner, Alexander Brown & Sons, Inc.; Larry Moews and Robert S. Seiler, Allstate Life Insurance Company; Mark C. Klopfenstein and J. R. Stainbrook, Arthur Andersen & Co.; Robert S. Littell, Brokers Resource Center; Inbum Cheong, Central Missouri State University; Donald Johnson, College for Financial Planning; James R. Fagan, Commonwealth Life Insurance Company; William B. Harman, Jr., Davis & Harman; Frank A. Bruni, H. W. Lentz, Jr., and Edward R. Morrissey, Deloitte Touche; Robert W. Cooper, Drake University; Adina Fleeger and Keith Smith, Equifax Services, Inc.; Mel Gregory and Brian S. O'Neil, The Equitable Financial Companies; Harry Garber and Calvert A. Jared, II, The Equitable Life Assurance Society of U.S.; Charles Bogen, H. Ray Eanes,

Steven C. Eldrige, Greg Hayes, Cliff Jones, Wayne Kauth, Paul E. Klein, and Martin Nissenbaum, Ernst & Young; Ronald M. Freres; Robert I. Damon, The Guardian Life Insurance Company of America; Margaret Lynch, Health Insurance Association of America; Fred C. Jackson, Fred Jackson & Associates; Anthony J. Del Tufo and Gary W. Roubinek, KPMG Peat Marwick; Morton E. Spitzer, Liberty Life Assurance Company of Boston; Archer L. Edgar and Elizabeth Tovian, Life Insurance Marketing and Research Association International; Carroll D. Burns, Life of Georgia; Stephen W. Forbes and Dani L. Long, Life Office Management Association; Herbert E. Lister; Robert E. Meeker, Meeker Associates; Kenneth K. Lau and Larry E. North, William M. Mercer, Inc.; Stephen T. Bow, Alan Knepper, John E. Reynolds and George B. Trotta, Metropolitan Life Insurance Company; Ernest J. Moorhead; Robert Klein and Carole J. Olson, National Association of Insurance Commissioners; H. Lee Cheney, III, National Financial Concepts; Charles B. Robinson, National Fraternal Congress of America; Frank A. Hacker, National Life of Vermont; Peter F. Frenzer and Doug Robinette, Nationwide Insurance Companies; William J. Clyne, John T. DeBardeleben, Dennis J. Flaherty, Thomas O. Jones, Robert J. O'Connell, Thomas J. O'Leary, Wilmer S. Poyner, Donald M. Rising, Lester L. Schoenberg, and James L. Wilkie, New York Life Insurance Company; Ronald J. McGinnity, Maureen B. Moreau, and Bob Ort, North American Reassurance Company; Daniel C. Doughety, John R. Filak, Robert K. Gleeson, William O. Goodwin, Richard Hall, Karen A. Holthe, Jon K. Magalska, Richard E. Moore, Ronald C. Nelson, John K. O'Meara and Gary V. Powell, Northwestern Mutual Life Insurance Comapny; F. O'Grady; Arthur J. Taylor, Paul Revere Life Insurance Company; Stanfield Hill and William B. Wallace, Phoenix Home Mutual Life Insurance Company; David Drury, Robert A. Stivers, and Larry D. Zimpleman, The Principal Financial Group; Stephen B. Bonner, Walter N. Miller, Paul E. Sarnoff, Louis Shuntich, and Richard A. Yorks, The Prudential Insurance Company of America; Dale R. Johnson, SAFECO Life Insurance Company; Richard M. Drury and Steven M. Meltzer, Scudder Variable Life Investment Fund; Floyd Watson, The Security Benefit Group of Companies; Linden N. Cole, Society of Actuaries; Stanley M. Hopp, Society of Insurance Research; Nancy Behrens and Hobart F. Meharg, State Farm Insurance Companies; William A. Ferguson, Andrew F. Giffin, and Phillip K. Polkinghorn, Towers Perrin/Tillinghast; Gary M. McCrite, Transamerica Life Companies; William Colby, TransKey; David Dunn, Eileen Gabriel, Thomas D. Hogan, and Christopher S. Ruisi, USLIFE Corporation; William W. Dotterwich, University of Tennessee.

Special acknowledgment is due Kenneth Black, III, for preparing the intial draft of Chapters 30, 31, and 32 on life insurer financial management and Stephen W. Forbes for his help in suggesting the conceptual outlines for these chapters. We are also indebted to several other Georgia State University colleagues, including Bruce A. Palmer, Martin F. Grace, Deborah J. Chollet, and Fred A. Tillman. Each of these persons read individual chapters and shared his/her criticism and judgment.

Finally the authors would like to record their appreciation of Jan Arnold, Susan Holliman Fuller, Tabitha Miller, and Nanette Cummings for their efforts and personal interest in helping with the many administrative duties associated with producing the manuscript.

Of course, none of those who reviewed the manuscript bears any responsibility for the deficiencies that may remain in the completed work.

Kenneth Black, Jr.
Harold D.Skipper, Jr.

# *Life Insurance*

# Chapter 1

# LIFE AND HEALTH INSURANCE IN PERSONAL FINANCIAL PLANNING

Life and health insurance have long been recognized as necessary and essential elements in an individual's or a family's financial program. The late Dr. S. S. Huebner is generally credited with being the catalyst behind this recognition through his logical and forceful arguments regarding the "duty" of family breadwinners to insure their lives for the benefit of those financially dependent upon them.[1] He observed that, in a modern society, a sense of family responsibility meant that life and health insurance would grow in importance. He argued that individuals' responsibilities to themselves and their families included both the years of survival (and, hence, included savings accumulation) and the years after death.

He also was among the earliest proponents of the need for a broad-based effort to plan and coordinate individuals' overall financial affairs. His early recommendation that the individual or family unit should be established and run on a sound business basis is now widely accepted and underpins the study of personal financial planning.[2] Life and health insurance continue to occupy an important role in the financial planning process. This chapter provides an introduction to this process and highlights the means by which life and health insurance can assist in accomplishing one's financial plans.

---

[1] See, generally, Solomon S. Huebner, *The Economics of Life Insurance* (New York: D. Appleton and Company, 1930).

[2] Ibid., pp. 14–17.

1

2    Chapter 1
**PERSONAL FINANCIAL PLANNING3**


## NATURE AND PURPOSE

While no universally accepted definition of **personal financial planning** exists, it can be considered as the process whereby an individual's or a family's overall financial objectives are used to develop and implement an integrated plan to accomplish their objectives. The essential elements of this financial planning concept are the identification of *overall* financial goals and objectives and then the development and implementation of an *integrated* plan to accomplish the objectives. The idea is to focus on the individual's (or family's) objectives as the starting point rather than starting with a particular financial instrument and determining how it may fit into a financial plan.

Financial planning in the past was far simpler than it is today—earn a little, save a little, educate the children, and then retire with reasonable comfort. However, planning today is more complex because of three factors: (1) greater economic uncertainty (e.g., greater fluctuations in interest rates and inflation), (2) constantly changing rules (e.g., frequent tax-law changes), and (3) a proliferation of new financial instruments (e.g., futures and variable universal life products). These factors combine to render sound planning more of a necessity than in past times.

Most persons use a variety of financial instruments to achieve their financial objectives. Thus such basic financial tools as life insurance, property and liability insurance, mutual funds, common stocks, bonds, annuities, savings accounts, wills, trusts, and real estate prove to be essential elements of many soundly conceived financial plans.

Unfortunately, many persons either fail to plan or do not follow a consistent, logical pattern in carrying out their financial plan. Failure to plan is not only foolish but often costly. It is easy, however, for busy persons to procrastinate. Many believe that their assets or incomes are not sufficient to justify a financial plan or they believe that the costs of planning services will be too high relative to benefits. Others either fail to plan or follow seemingly erratic patterns in accomplishing financial objectives because planning involves consideration of such unpleasant events as death, disability, unemployment, old age, destruction of property, and being sued.

Generally, these reasons, either alone or in combination, do not constitute valid objections to financial planning. This is not to suggest that the family

---

3 This and the following sections draw on G. Victor Hallman and Jerry S. Rosenbloom, *Personal Financial Planning*, 3rd ed. (New York: McGraw-Hill Book Company, 1983), chaps. 1 and 2; and C. Arthur Williams, Jr. and Richard M. Heins, *Risk Management and Insurance*, 5th ed. (New York: McGraw-Hill Book Company, 1985), chaps. 1 and 9.

earning $25,000 per year will utilize the same financial instruments or seek advice from the same financial advisors as a family earning $250,000 per year. However, each family should make plans to deal with death, disability, savings, and so on. Details vary, but the need for planning does not.

Within the financial planning process, life and health insurance can prove to be valuable and flexible financial instruments. Moreover, for many persons, the life insurance agent is the initiator of the financial planning process and may join other professionals, such as accountants, attorneys, tax consultants, and trust officers, in carrying out the financial planning process.

## THE PROCESS

The personal financial planning process might be considered a road map for accomplishing an individual's financial objectives. It provides an orderly, systematic approach to planning. The process itself involves six interrelated steps. While the steps are presented below as discrete actions to be taken, each step in fact blends into and complements those steps that precede and follow.

***Gather Information.*** The first step in the financial planning process is to assemble relevant quantitative and qualitative information. Relevant financial information varies from situation to situation but usually includes a listing of the individual's assets, liabilities, and net worth as well as information regarding the person's income and expenditures. Additionally, information is usually needed concerning the nature of the person's investments; life, health, and other insurance protection; employee benefits; tax situation; relevant estate planning documents such as wills and trusts; and inheritance prospects. This gathering of information about the client is usually accomplished with the aid of a fact-finding questionnaire or form, available from numerous sources.[4]

In addition to the preceding quantitative information, qualitative information is sought concerning the individual's interests, life-style, attitudes and desires, family situation, risk tolerance, and health and related information that will underlie the individual's goals and objectives. In fact, often at this stage the financial advisor assists the individual in establishing his or her objectives — the second step in the financial planning process.

***Establish Objectives.*** The process of setting goals and objectives is, in some ways, the most challenging aspect of the financial planning process. The competent financial planner is most helpful at this stage, for if an individual's goals and objectives are poorly conceived and formulated, any ensuing financial plan is likely to be faulty.

---

[4] The American College in Bryn Mawr, Pa., and the College for Financial Planning in Denver, Colo., publish such forms.

To aid the client in this endeavor, the advisor often must probe into aspects of the client's business and personal affairs and relationships that can be among an individual's most sensitive and confidential. This requires not only the necessity of establishing a keen bond of trust—and seeing to it that this trust bond is never broken—but it also involves the ability of the advisor to communicate and probe effectively and professionally.[5]

***Analyze Information.*** The third step in the personal financial planning process is to analyze the quantitative and qualitative information gathered and to do so in light of the client's objectives. Chapters 12 and 15 provide approaches for modeling a person's life insurance and retirement needs. Insurance policies would be reviewed carefully, as would all other financial, tax, and legal documents that the planner was competent to examine. Other financial and legal advisors may need to be consulted and advice sought from them at this stage. Deficiencies in the client's existing financial arrangement would be revealed by this analysis and the groundwork laid for the next stage in the process.

***Develop Plan.*** As the planner is analyzing the information gathered, probably in consultation with the client and other advisors, he or she probably already is formulating mentally the elements of a proposed financial plan. The plan should represent a coordinated, integrated effort to resolve problems and to help the client achieve his or her objectives in light of current financial and other constraints and limitations, with appropriate consideration concerning future possibilities.

***Implement Plan.*** With a proposed financial plan now available, the advisor holds further discussions with the client to help him or her understand how the plan can be implemented and how present financial and other constraints may affect the complete achievement of the earlier stated objectives. An outline plan showing implementation dates and types of actions to be taken and products to be purchased is often used. The proposal is often modified in light of further goal clarification resulting from continuing discussion. Implementation normally requires the services of other professionals, especially those in the legal and tax areas. Appropriate involvement of these professionals in the planning process smooths the implementation process.

***Monitor and Revise Plan.*** After the plan is implemented, the results should be monitored to ascertain the extent to which they are compatible with initial expectations. If they are not, changes may be needed. In addition to the need for revisions occasioned by results deviating from expectations or projections, revisions also will be necessitated by tax and other environmental changes and

---

[5] See, generally, G. Hugh Russell and Kenneth Black, Jr., *Human Behavior and Life Insurance* (Atlanta, Ga: Georgia State University Press, 1993), especially chaps. 4 and 5.

by the client's changing financial fortunes, family situation, and goals and objectives.

No plan is foolproof. Changes will occur and should be expected. Too often, the need for the planner to stress this simple yet important fact to the client is overlooked in the planning process.

## THE ELEMENTS OF A PERSONAL FINANCIAL PLAN

Personal financial plans should be just that: personal. They should be tailored to the individual, with no two plans being exactly alike. Even so, almost all financial plans have certain elements in common. This section presents an overview of the six common elements as well as an introduction as to how life and health insurance can be useful in helping to accomplish the individual's objectives.

### ESTABLISH RISK MANAGEMENT PLAN

*Nature of Personal Risk Management.* Most financial planning experts agree that the most basic element of each individual's financial plan is the establishment and maintenance of a sound program of personal risk management. The practice of risk management has been defined as the identification, measurement, and treatment of exposures to potential losses.[6] Risk management is concerned with losses that arise from damage to or destruction of property, from liability, and from loss of health and life. While historically the business enterprise has been the chief focus of risk management attention, the individual and family also should be subject to *personal* risk management.

As one authority has noted, the practice of risk management is not really an option. Individuals and families need merely to exist to face exposures to loss. Such exposures can be ignored altogether, but this is tantamount to selecting a risk management approach by default, and the approach selected often is not the best one. By managing properly one's exposures to loss, more acceptable results can be accomplished at minimum long-run costs.[7]

*The Risk Management Process.* Risk management involves the identification, measurement, and treatment of property, liability, and personal loss exposures. The risk management process tracks the six-step personal financial planning process.

*1. Gather Information.* One must first gather information to permit loss exposure identification. Individuals, families, and businesses face three classes of losses: property, liability, and personal. **Direct property exposures** are those that

6 Williams and Heins, *Risk Management and Insurance*, p. 4.
7 Ibid.

exist because of the possibility of damage to, destruction of, or disappearance of personal or real property. **Indirect property exposures** exist when an individual, family, or business can suffer a reduction in income (revenues less expenses) from the loss of use of property or when the value of property that is not damaged is lessened because of direct damage to other property. To illustrate: a family might have to live in a hotel until fire damage to their home is repaired. The possibility of extra living expenses would constitute an indirect property exposure to the family.

**Liability loss exposures** exist from "just living." One can be sued for numerous reasons, the most common cause being lawsuits from automobile accidents.

**Personal loss exposures** arise from the possibilities of death, illness or injury, and unemployment.[8] Such losses are associated with families, but businesses can and do suffer personal losses as well. For example, the death of a key employee in a small business could have a severe adverse financial impact on the business.

Of the three classes of loss exposures—property, liability, and personal—this book deals only with the personal category.[9]

*2. Establish Risk Management Objectives.* The second step in the risk management process is to establish objectives. These objectives should be consistent with and complement those established in connection with one's overall personal financial plan. In fact, the goals associated with the personal risk management program will probably already have been developed as a part of establishment of the personal financial goals. Often the overall goal may be stated as simply the family's avoiding financial catastrophe as a result of any of the three loss exposure classifications.

*3. Analyze Information.* The third step in the risk management process is to analyze the information gathered to permit estimation of the potential financial consequences of losses. This important step technically involves the determination of the probability or chance that a particular loss will occur and the impact that such a loss would have upon the financial affairs of the individual, family, or business.

The planner should appreciate the likelihood of the occurrence of personal losses. Therefore the probabilities of loss of life, health, and employment are presented below. These probabilities can be applied only to a large group of persons and have little or no meaning as applied to individuals.

---

8 Many authorities include old age financial dependency (superannuation) as a personal loss exposure. While this approach has merit, the area is separated from personal risk management for the purposes of this book. This treatment is justified because of the great importance of retirement planning.

9 For a discussion on property and liability loss exposure treatment, see Emmett Vaughan, *Fundamentals of Risk and Insurance*, 6th ed. (New York: John Wiley & Sons, 1992).

*(a) Loss of Life.* The major financial loss faced by most families as a result of death is loss of earning power, although death can also cause the family to incur additional expenses (e.g., funeral expenses and estate taxes). In measuring the financial consequences to a family (or a business) from the death of a family income earner (or profit producer in the case of an entrepreneur), one of several techniques could be adopted. These are discussed in Chapters 12 to 15. All techniques attempt to place an economic value on the financial loss suffered by the family (or business), and this value often is the basis upon which life insurance is purchased.

For selected ages, Table 1-1 shows probabilities of death within the next year and prior to attainment of age 65. The likelihood of death within one year for persons during their working years is small. However, the likelihood of death prior to age 65 is not insignificant. Indeed, approximately one in five persons now between the ages of 20 and 40 will die prior to age 65. Also, for many persons, death occurring after age 65 can create significant financial hardships, and death probabilities after age 65 are high. The key to planning for the death contingency is to focus on its financial consequences to the family or business, irrespective of its probability of occurring.

*(b) Loss of Health.* Poor health, like death, may cause two types of losses: (1) loss of earnings and (2) extra expenses. The dollar value of earnings lost because of a total disability may be estimated in a manner similar to that used in estimating the economic loss occasioned by death.

Unexpected extra expenses accompanying an injury, a sickness, or an impairment can take the form of hospital bills, surgical fees, drugs, or other medical expenses. Estimating the probability that a person will suffer a "morbidity condition" and the extent to which that condition will be disabling is difficult because (1) morbidity, unlike mortality, cannot be defined exactly, (2) morbidity varies in severity as well as frequency, and (3) morbidity conditions are not reported on a regular basis to public authorities.

**TABLE 1-1**       **PROBABILITIES OF DEATH**

| Age | Within a Year | Prior to Age 65 | | Age | Within a Year | Prior to Age 65 |
|---|---|---|---|---|---|---|
| 0 | 0.0100 | 0.21 | | 35 | 0.0017 | 0.18 |
| 5 | 0.0003 | 0.20 | | 40 | 0.0022 | 0.17 |
| 10 | 0.0002 | 0.20 | | 45 | 0.0032 | 0.16 |
| 15 | 0.0006 | 0.20 | | 50 | 0.0050 | 0.14 |
| 20 | 0.0011 | 0.19 | | 55 | 0.0081 | 0.12 |
| 25 | 0.0012 | 0.19 | | 60 | 0.0126 | 0.07 |
| 30 | 0.0014 | 0.18 | | | | |

*Source:* Derived from *Vital Statistics of the United States.* 1988, Vol. II, Part A, Sec. 6. Life Tables (Washington, D.C.: U.S. Department of Health and Human Services, Public Health Service, 1990), p. 10.

Even so, some information is available from insurance data. Table 1-2 shows the number of insured lives by gender and age that are disabled per 10,000 lives exposed. The table also shows the number disabled by durations of 1, 3 and 12 months. For example, out of 10,000 females, all age 32, it is estimated that 560 will suffer a total disability that lasts at least one month, 240 will suffer a total disability of at least three months' duration, and 30 will be disabled for at least one year.

By comparing the figures of Table 1-2 with those of Table 1-1, it can be observed that the probability of a total disability of three months duration or longer within the next year is significantly greater than the probability of death during the working years—by a factor of 10 or more for persons in their thirties. The rates of disablement are for insured lives, and such experience is more favorable than that found in the population as a whole. Thus, the Table 1-2 figures understate the rates of disablement for the average person.

*(c) Loss of Employment.* Involuntary unemployment caused by economic factors is another threat to a person's earning power. The potential loss can be estimated in a manner similar to that used for disability.

Unemployment rates of 5 to 10 percent have prevailed in the United States in recent years. Unemployment rates vary greatly over time. During 1983, the U.S. unemployment rate reached 11.4 percent. In 1933 about one-quarter of the labor force was unemployed in an average month. These data do not reveal the extent of partial unemployment.

One measure of the magnitude of unemployment loss is the duration of the unemployment. As one would expect, the average duration is related to the general state of the economy, but particular industries, areas, or persons can suffer substantial losses even when the economy is performing satisfactorily.

**TABLE 1-2     OUT OF 10,000 LIVES, NUMBER DISABLED**

| Age | Male Lives Duration of Disablement | | | Female Lives Duration of Disablement | | |
|---|---|---|---|---|---|---|
| | 1 Month | 3 Months | 1 Year | 1 Month | 3 Months | 1 Year |
| 17 | 240 | 110 | 30 | 340 | 80 | 10 |
| 22 | 370 | 170 | 40 | 430 | 130 | 10 |
| 27 | 400 | 190 | 50 | 530 | 190 | 20 |
| 32 | 500 | 170 | 30 | 560 | 240 | 30 |
| 37 | 430 | 170 | 50 | 650 | 300 | 50 |
| 42 | 560 | 200 | 50 | 870 | 340 | 50 |
| 47 | 500 | 220 | 70 | 930 | 380 | 60 |
| 52 | 600 | 240 | 80 | 880 | 380 | 80 |
| 57 | 770 | 340 | 130 | 850 | 410 | 110 |
| 62 | 1,060 | 490 | 180 | 850 | 430 | 130 |
| 67 | 1,060 | 430 | 220 | 940 | 490 | 160 |
| 72 | 1,220 | 560 | 280 | 880 | 520 | 200 |

*Source*: E. Paul Barnhart, "The 1982 Disability Tables," *Transactions of the Society of Actuaries*, Vol. XXXV (1983), pp. 784-787.

*4. Develop Risk Management Plan.* Once exposures have been identified and measured, the various tools of risk management should be considered and a decision made with respect to the best combination of tools to be used. The tools include primarily (1) **risk avoidance**: avoiding the risk altogether; (2) **risk reduction**: reducing the chance that a loss will occur or reducing the magnitude of a loss if it does occur; (3) **risk transfer**: transferring the financial consequences of any loss to some other party; and (4) **risk retention**: retaining or bearing the risk internally. Examples of each category include: (1) not purchasing a car for a college student, thus avoiding the liability and other exposures of auto ownership; (2) wellness programs adopted by employers or, from an individual's viewpoint, exercising regularly and adopting proper eating habits, thus reducing the risk of having a heart attack; (3) purchasing a medical expense policy from an insurance company, thereby transferring the financial consequences of incurring medical expenses because of loss of health; and (4) retaining any income losses that would result from a disability lasting three months or less.

*5. Implement Risk Management Plan.* The fifth step in the risk management process is to implement the risk management plan. For the average family, implementation may simply entail purchasing an insurance policy. If the personal risk management program involves such things as risk reduction through better eating and exercise habits, however, a major personal commitment is required from the individuals concerned.

*6. Monitor and Revise Risk Management Plan.* The sixth and final step in the risk management process involves monitoring the entire risk management plan and revising it as circumstances dictate. This means that the family should be aware that possible exposures to loss can be eliminated (e.g., by selling the beach house and eliminating the financial consequences to the family of its possible destruction), created (e.g., by buying a mountain cottage), and altered (e.g., leasing the newly acquired mountain cottage creates new possibilities for incurring liability). This step in the risk management process can be viewed as "completing the circle" in the sense that it represents a linkage with the first step in the process, that of loss exposure identification.

***Uses of Life and Health Insurance in Personal Risk Management.*** Life and health insurance have little relevance to the property and liability risk exposures of an individual, family, or business.[10] However, life and health insurance can and usually should be an element of the risk management program of the average individual and family.

Among private-sector financial instruments, life insurance is unique in that it is able immediately to provide funds with which to help replace the financial

---

[10]An important exception is that of estate conservation in connection with estate planning. See Chap. 14.

losses arising from an individual's death.[11] Life insurance alone guarantees that, for a relatively modest outlay, an individual's dependents or business will not have to suffer a major financial loss because of the individual's death. As discussed below, life insurance can be useful in other elements of a given individual's personal financial plan, although its providing of protection against the adverse financial consequences of death undoubtedly is its best-known function.

Since the elimination of the possibility of suffering a major sickness or injury is not possible, other means are required for dealing with the financial consequences that arise from loss of earnings and expenses caused by loss of health. In the majority of cases, health insurance is the method chosen and is essential in an individual's risk management plan. Most individuals need protection against both types of financial exposures: the risk of increased medical expenses and the risk of loss of earnings.

This protection usually is provided by one's employer, with limited protection provided to certain individuals through government plans. Even with such coverage, however, many persons discover upon close examination that they and their families remain unduly exposed to adverse financial risk from possible loss of health because employer and government-provided coverages leave major protection gaps.

## ESTABLISH SAVINGS/INVESTMENT PROGRAM

The second element of most persons' financial plans involves the establishment and maintenance of a savings and investment program. For some persons, especially those just entering the work force, this element can seem distant or even illusory. However, planners routinely encourage individuals to "pay themselves first" via a formalized savings program. Unfortunately, some families' incomes are such that their every dollar must be spent on current living expenses, with no surplus available for savings. Other persons, for various reasons (usually lack of discipline) spend all of their disposable income on current consumption, even though their total current needs could be met reasonably within their current income level and, at the same time, leave sufficient funds to establish a savings and investment program. Individuals want to accumulate wealth for a number of reasons; some of the more important reasons are discussed below.

*Emergency Fund.* An emergency fund is usually needed to meet unexpected expenses such as small disability losses, medical expenses, and

---

[11] Government benefits are made available to qualified individuals under certain conditions. See Chap. 25.

property losses that purposely are not covered by insurance, and to provide a financial cushion against such personal problems as prolonged unemployment. The size of the needed emergency fund varies greatly and depends upon such factors as family income, number of income earners, stability of employment, assets, debts, insurance deductibles, uncovered health and property insurance exposures, and the family's general attitudes toward risk and security. The size of the emergency fund often is expressed as so many months (such as three to six months) of a family income.

By its very nature, the emergency fund should be invested conservatively. There should be almost complete security of principal, marketability, and liquidity, although, of course, a reasonable rate of return is a desired objective. Within these constraints, logical investment outlets for emergency funds have included regular savings accounts in banks and other savings institutions, certain types of government securities, and life insurance policy cash values.

*Education Fund.* The cost of higher education in the United States and in other countries has increased dramatically over the last few years, particularly at private colleges and universities, but also at the high school level. These high costs can result in a tremendous financial drain for a family with college-age children, and, as a predictable drain, it can be prepared for in advance.

An educational investment fund, a relatively long-term objective, is set up with the hope that the fund will not be needed in the meantime. Therefore wider investment latitude is justified than in the case of the emergency fund, with the result that a more attractive investment yield often can be obtained.

Life insurance can be used as a vehicle for funding educational needs, at least in part. The cash value buildup in any cash value insurance policy can be tapped at the time of the need. In addition, a life insurance policy can ensure that the educational fund is completed even if the breadwinner of the family dies prematurely. Finally, some life insurance companies sell specific educational insurance policies, the purpose of which is to provide an amount of money at the time the child reaches college age.

*General Investment Fund.* Many persons desire to accumulate capital for general investment purposes. They want to obtain a better future standard of living, a second income in addition to the earnings from their employment or profession, greater financial security or a sense of personal self-reliance, the ability to retire early or to "take it easy" in their work in the future, or a capital fund to pass on to their children or grandchildren; or they may simply enjoy the investment process. In any event, individuals normally invest money with the view of maximizing their after-tax rates of return, consistent with their risk tolerances, and the investment constraints under which they must operate.

A wide variety of investment instruments exists for the purpose of accumulating capital. Generally, these instruments are classified as either fixed or variable investments. **Fixed-dollar investments** are those whose principal and/or income are contractually set in advance in terms of a specified or of a determinable value. **Variable-dollar investments** are those where neither the principal nor the income is contractually set in advance. In other words, both the value and income of variable-dollar investments can change, either up or down, with changes in economic conditions.

Common fixed-dollar investments include bonds, savings accounts, certificates of deposit, treasury bills and notes, preferred stock, and most life insurance and annuity cash values. Variable-dollar investments include home ownership, common stocks, mutual funds, certain tax-sheltered investments, ownership of business interests, commodities, fine artworks, precious metals, as well as variable annuities and variable life insurance.

*Retirement Fund.* For many persons, the objective of providing for retirement is of extreme importance. Because of the importance and unique characteristics of retirement planning, this subject is dealt with as a separate element within the overall financial plan and is discussed below.

### PROVIDE FOR RETIREMENT

Another element of most persons' financial plans is the provision for retirement. This element is typically of less concern to young working persons, but it increases greatly in importance as retirement age approaches. Although it is a subset of the general investment program discussed above, its importance argues for its being segregated, especially since several funding instruments and laws are oriented exclusively toward this specific purpose.

At advanced ages, a person's earnings usually stop or are considerably reduced, but his or her expenses continue. The person may prepare for this retirement period by saving and investing during his or her earning career but (1) saving is neither painless nor automatic, and the amounts needed may be great; furthermore, (2) the necessary amount is indefinite because it depends upon the length of the retirement period.

The probabilities that persons at selected ages will survive to age 65 are presented in Table 1-3. The table also indicates the average number of years that a person of each age will live beyond age 65. Consider a person who is now aged 35. The chances are about four in five that this person will live beyond age 65, the traditional retirement age. The average 35-year-old person will live over 12 years beyond age 65. Therefore if a 35-year-old man or woman is willing to be considered average, he or she will have to accumulate a sum that, invested at a reasonable rate of return, will produce enough income to meet his or her expenses over a period of 12.2 years. Of course, no way exists for a given individual to know whether he or she will live beyond age 65 for exactly 12.2 years, for 1 year, or for 30 years.

**TABLE 1-3**          **PROBABILITY OF SURVIVAL TO AGE 65 AND AVERAGE
REMAINING LIFE, 1988 (U.S.)**

| Age | Probability of Survival to Age 65 | Average Remaining Lifetime, in Years | Average Remaining Lifetime Beyond Age 65, in Years |
|-----|-----------------------------------|--------------------------------------|----------------------------------------------------|
| 0   | 0.79 | 74.9 | 9.9  |
| 10  | 0.80 | 65.9 | 10.9 |
| 20  | 0.81 | 56.3 | 11.3 |
| 30  | 0.82 | 46.9 | 11.9 |
| 35  | 0.82 | 42.2 | 12.2 |
| 40  | 0.83 | 37.6 | 12.6 |
| 45  | 0.84 | 33.0 | 13.0 |
| 50  | 0.86 | 28.6 | 13.6 |
| 55  | 0.88 | 24.4 | 14.4 |
| 60  | 0.93 | 20.5 | 15.5 |

*Source*: Derived from *Vital Statistics of the United States*, 1988, Vol. II, Part A.
Sec. 6. Life Tables (Washington, D.C.: U.S. Department of Health and Human
Services, Public Health Service, 1990), p. 11.

As the person grows older, the average number of years that he or she can expect to live beyond age 65 increases. If a person knew that he or she would live to be 100 years old and that his or her earning power would end completely at age 65, that person would have to accumulate over $245,600 by retirement age, assuming expenses of $15,000 a year, no inflation, and a 5 percent return after taxes on the balance of the accumulated sum. Few persons will live this long, but some will, and no one knows for certain whether he or she will be among them.

Unlike the probabilities associated with the other personal loss exposures, which have been declining over time, the probabilities associated with superannuation have been increasing. Much attention is now being devoted to this peril, particularly because of the increasing proportion of aged persons in the total population. In 1900, 54 percent of the U.S. population was under 25 years of age, 42 percent between 25 and 64, and 4 percent was aged 65 or more. In 1990 the corresponding percentages were 36 percent, 51 percent, and 13 percent.

Today a person can plan for retirement in many ways. Some of these ways involve government programs; others rely primarily on private insurance or other personal savings and investments. Some involve tax advantages; others do not. Although this aspect of personal financial planning is discussed in more detail in chapters 7, 14, 25, and 28, at this point it may be noted that typical sources of retirement income may include: Social Security retirement benefits, other government benefits, employer-provided pensions, individual retirement funds, deferred profit-sharing and other employee benefit plans, nonqualified deferred compensation plans, investments in other assets owned by the individual, and individually purchased fixed-dollar and variable-dollar annuities and life insurance cash values. The entrepreneur will usually rely on his or her business to provide retirement funds, either through the sale of the business or by continuing to receive income from the business.

## MINIMIZE TAXES

Because most families pay taxes of various sorts, the desire to minimize taxes is an understandable, logical, and laudable element of personal financial planning. Thus the tax implications of most financial transactions should be considered.

United States citizens are subject to a variety of taxes. These include sales taxes, property taxes, Social Security taxes, federal income taxes, state and local income taxes, federal estate taxes, state inheritance or estate taxes, and federal gift taxes. The relative importance of these taxes varies considerably among individuals, depending upon their circumstances and income levels. When engaging in tax planning, however, most persons are concerned primarily with income taxes, death taxes, and perhaps gift taxes.

That anyone would purchase life insurance or annuities solely to gain tax advantages is doubtful. Nonetheless, certain tax advantages, justified as sound social policy, accrue to these products. These tax advantages can make life insurance and annuities attractive for certain purposes within a broad personal financial plan.[12] Briefly stated, the tax advantages in the United States are:

   1. Exemption, in general, from income taxation of life insurance death proceeds, even though the proceeds received may greatly exceed the premiums paid for the insurance.

   2. Exemption (in whole or in part) from state inheritance taxation of life insurance death proceeds payable to certain named beneficiaries.

   3. Tax deferral on the interest credited to qualified life insurance and annuity cash values.

   4. Imposition of a moderate federal income tax on annuity income payments involving a favorable rule taxing the interest earnings of the principal sum being liquidated.

---

[12] See Chap. 13.

## ESTABLISH PROGRAM FOR HEIRS

Whether by design or default, all individuals have a plan as to how their assets will be distributed on their deaths. Either the individual prepares the plan or, failing that, state law imposes a plan. A sound personal financial plan does not leave this element to chance or to state law. It includes a conscientiously formulated and implemented program that comes into being upon the death of the individual, if not prior thereto.[13] The orderly and efficient transfer of property and the meeting of the objectives established for one's heirs constitute the heart of this plan element.

**Estate planning,** in the narrow sense of protecting an existing estate, has three objectives: (1) reduction of the estate transfer cost, (2) arrangement for the most economic method of paying transfer costs that cannot be eliminated, and (3) changes in the character of the estate property to make wise use of assets. Estate planning also includes the disposition of business interests and the use of pension and profit-sharing plans and other devices for individuals, to help them establish larger estates with tax-deferred dollars. Many techniques have been developed to achieve these objectives. Life insurance plays a vital role in a number of these techniques. The life insurance agent, the attorney who prepares the necessary legal documents, the accountant who gathers much of the needed information, and the trust officer who provides expert fiduciary services when needed—all of these individuals make up the estate planning team. Each provides a service or a particular expertise.

## MANAGE FAMILY CASH FLOW

The last element of the typical family's personal financial plan is management of the family's cash flow. This element permeates all others and, therefore, logically should not be viewed as the final element, but rather as providing the broad scheme that permits the accomplishment of all other elements.

Managing family cash flow means establishing a budget wherein periodic (e.g., monthly) income and expenditure patterns are projected, together with the system for keeping track of and analyzing actual income and expenditures. Clearly, all of the earlier elements of a person's financial plan would fit into the budget/analysis process.

As one would suspect, life and health insurance can assist in the cash flow management process only in indirect ways. For example, premium payment modes often can be varied to suit an individual's special income pattern, or policy loans or cash-value withdrawals can be used to overcome temporary cash flow shortages. Cash-value life insurance policies can be arranged so that premiums can be paid through policy loans or cash values where the need arises.

[13] See Chap. 14.

## THE FINANCIAL PLANNING TEAM

As alluded to previously, the financial planning process usually relies on the advice and services of several professionals. Historically, the life insurance agent has been the catalyst for the initiation of the process for most persons. Many agents today are broadening the scope of their financial planning activities to serve the role not only of catalyst but of manager as well. Increasingly, professionals in the securities, accounting, legal, and other areas are doing likewise.

Indeed, viewed from the standpoint of a team approach, comprehensive financial planning can be considered as the process that integrates and coordinates the expertise of specialized professionals in financial services for the benefit of the client.[14] In this team approach, each specialization assumes a definable and specific role in relation to the client's overall objectives. These experts' contributions of consultative advice and service and product implementation are more professional because they are directed toward satisfying needs and attaining objectives that have been clearly and comprehensively determined in the counseling sessions by the financial planner.

Comprehensive financial planners evolve and grow into their roles from a professional status that is nearly always initially grounded in a specialty, such as law, accounting, insurance, investments, and so on. As generalists, they are distinguished from other specialists not so much by greater intelligence or technical competence as by their adoption and practice of the financial planning process. The planning process itself thus becomes an *additional* specialized competence that the financial services professional brings to the service of client needs: it broadens knowledge, enables the professional to function as a peer of other specialists, and helps clients take fuller responsibility for their economic lives.

The financial planning process demands both a comprehensive financial planner to direct it and a team of other specialized professionals in financial services. All teams and organizations are characterized by pecking orders, and, on the financial planning team, the comprehensive financial planner who has the client's trust and confidence is the natural leader. In no sense, however, does this relationship belittle the positions of other team specialists. On the contrary, participation in a concerted planning effort for a client enhances the professionalism of specialists' contributions because their efforts are directed not only toward immediate problem solving, but also toward preventive strategies that contribute to the client's general well-being.

---

[14] This discussion draws from Dale S. Johnson, "Comprehensive Financial Planning: The Process and the Professionals," *The Journal of the American Society of CLU*, Vol. XXXVII (Oct. 1983), pp. 47–48.

## INTERRELATIONSHIP BETWEEN BUSINESS AND PERSONAL FINANCIAL PLANNING

The distinction between business financial planning and personal financial planning is essentially one of convenience, the chief difference being the entity for which the planning is performed. Even so, the principles, if not all of the details, are identical.

For most persons, moreover, a close relationship exists between the home and the business or vocation in which they are engaged. Indeed, the owner of a business, generally speaking, conducts the business primarily for the purpose of supporting a home, thus showing that the welfare of the home and the welfare of the business can be so intimately related as to be inseparable.

Therefore, for purposes of this book, it should be understood that references to *personal* financial planning extend to *business* financial planning, to the extent that an individual's personal financial affairs are influenced by or are derived from his or her business or vocation.

# Chapter 2

# LIFE AND HEALTH INSURANCE FUNDAMENTALS

## PRINCIPLES OF INSURANCE

As discussed in Chapter 1, humans are exposed to many serious perils, such as property losses from fire and windstorm, and personal losses from disability and death. Although individuals cannot predict or completely prevent the occurrence of these perils, they can provide against their financial effects. The function of insurance is to safeguard against such misfortunes by having the losses of the unfortunate few paid by the contributions of the many who are exposed to the same peril. This is the essence of insurance—the sharing of losses and, in the process, the substitution of a certain, small "loss" (the premium payment) for an uncertain, large loss. If the peril under consideration is that of death, the financial loss suffered can be reduced or even eliminated through life insurance. If the peril under consideration is disability, the financial loss can be indemnified through health insurance.

### INSURANCE DEFINED

Insurance may be defined from two perspectives: that of society and that of the individual. From society's viewpoint, life or health insurance may be defined as a social device whereby individuals transfer the financial risks associated with loss of life or health to the group of individuals, and which involves the accumulation of funds by the group from these individuals to meet the uncertain financial losses associated with loss of life or health. This definition has two key elements. First, for insurance to exist there must be a *transfer* of the risk from the individual to the group. Second, a *sharing of losses* by the group members must exist.

From the individual's point of view, life or health insurance may be defined as an agreement (insurance policy or certificate) whereby one party (the policyowner) pays a stipulated consideration (the premium) to the other party (the insurer), in return for which the insurer agrees to pay a defined amount of money if the person whose life is insured dies or suffers an illness or other disability during the term of the policy (or, in some cases, survives to a stated time). The emphasis here is legal and financial.

Every insurance organization is a mechanism for distributing losses. This is true whether a group of persons mutually insures each other (a mutual life insurance company) or an independent contractor (a stock life insurance company) assumes the risk and pays the resulting losses.

## LAW OF LARGE NUMBERS

To minimize the speculative element and reduce volatile fluctuations in year-to-year losses, the **law of large numbers** must be applicable to the insurance operation. This principle, applied to insurance, holds that the greater the number of similar exposures (e.g., lives insured) to a peril (e.g., death), the less the observed loss experience will deviate from the expected loss experience. Risk and uncertainty diminish as the number of exposure units increases.

The law of large numbers does not suggest that losses to particular individuals will become more predictable. Rather it states that the larger the group insured, the more predictable will be the loss experience for the group as a whole, other things being the same. (The fact that insurers issue policies of varying face amounts suggests that other things often are not the same.)

To insure a single life against death for $1,000 is clearly a gamble. If the number of persons insured is increased to 100, a large element of uncertainty as to observed results is still present. If 500,000 similar persons are insured, however observed death rates probably will vary from expected rates by less than 1 percent. Thus the insurer should be able to determine its anticipated death claims with a manageable degree of accuracy. *In theory*, if the number of lives insured was so large as to make the application of the law of large numbers virtually perfect, and if no possibility of a catastrophe existed (e.g., war or epidemic), practically all uncertainty as to the accuracy of the estimated losses during a given period would be removed.

## NATURE OF PERILS INSURED

Although all forms of insurance are alike in that they require a combination of many risks into a group, they differ with regard to the perils covered. A **peril** is a cause of loss, such as fire or windstorm with respect to property or an accident with respect to health. In the nonlife forms of insurance, perils insured against may or may not happen and, in the great majority of cases, do not happen. In life insurance, the event against which protection is granted—death—is an uncertainty for one year, but the probability of death generally increases with age until it becomes a virtual certainty. If a life insurance policy is to protect an insured during the whole of his or her life, an adequate fund must be accumulated to meet a claim that is certain to occur.

In the case of health insurance, not everyone becomes ill or suffers injury, and the risk does not follow as consistent a pattern as does the risk of dying. Under long-term health insurance contracts, however, the risk insured against increases over time, so it is necessary to accumulate an adequate fund to meet the relatively higher rates of claim that will develop as insureds in the group grow older.

## GAMBLING AND INSURANCE

Some persons allege that insurance is a gamble. One hears such remarks as, "The insurance company is betting you won't have a loss, and you're betting that you will." From the insured's point of view, insurance is the antithesis of gambling. Gambling creates a risk where none existed. Insurance transfers an already existing risk and, through the pooling of similar loss exposures of other insureds, actually reduces risk. Insurance companies, of course, would prefer that insureds not have losses. However, losses are inevitable and are planned for in insurers' rate structures.

## PRICING INDIVIDUAL LIFE AND HEALTH INSURANCE

The above insurance concepts and principles are fundamental to understanding how insurance functions. This section provides an overview of how life and health insurance are priced.

## LIFE AND HEALTH INSURANCE PRICING OBJECTIVES

The three life and health insurance pricing objectives are: (1) premium rates should be adequate, (2) they should be equitable, and (3) they should not be excessive.

*Rate Adequacy.* Insurance company rates must be adequate in light of the benefits promised under the company's insurance products. Rate inadequacy can lead to severe financial problems, if not insolvency.

Rate adequacy means that, for a given block of policies, total payments collected now and in the future by the insurer plus the investment earnings attributable to any net retained funds should be sufficient to fund the current and future benefits promised plus cover related expenses. A **block of policies** ordinarily constitutes all policies issued by the insurer under the same schedules of rates and values and on the same policy form.

An insurer cannot know with certainty the degree of rate adequacy until the final policy in the block has terminated. Because individually issued life insurance and many forms of health insurance are issued at rates and on terms and conditions that may be guaranteed for many years, the issue of rate adequacy is especially important in establishing initial premium levels. In fact, as shown below, life insurance companies conduct tests to ensure that rates charged are adequate (as well as equitable and not excessive).

Life insurance rates are not directly regulated to ensure adequacy, although the State of New York requires that premium rates be self-supporting on the basis of reasonable assumptions. However, state laws require life insurance companies to establish policy liabilities on their financial statements based on state-mandated assumptions.[1]

*Rate Equity.* Rates charged for life and health insurance should be equitable to policyowners. Equity means charging insureds amounts commensurate with the risks that they bring to the insurance process. Stated differently, no unfair subsidization should exist of any class of insureds by any other class of insureds.

The achievement of equity is a goal to be sought. In an imperfect world, it cannot be attained absolutely. Concepts of equity must give way to practical realities. These realities include the fact that the larger the number of separate classifications of insureds, the greater the expense in administering the plan. Also, a large enough group is necessary to permit reasonable prediction of losses within each classification. The assessment of the precise degree of risk that each proposed insured brings to a group is simply impossible.

As discussed later, the pursuit of equity is one of the goals of underwriting. **Underwriting** is the process by which insurers decide whether to issue insurance to a person and the terms and prices. Life insurers strive toward equitable treatment of insureds by varying life and health insurance rates by such factors as age, sex, plan, health, and benefits provided. Generally, a greater degree of refinement in rate classes — and therefore more actuarial equity — exists for life insurance than for health insurance. **Actuarial equity** is sometimes in conflict with concepts of **social equity**. For example, some persons believe it to be socially unacceptable to charge different life and health insurance rates to otherwise identically situated men and women.[2]

*Rates Not Excessive.* Life and health insurance rates should not be excessive in relation to the benefits provided. If the rate adequacy criterion can

[1] See Chap. 20.
[2] See Chap. 23.

be considered as establishing conceptually a minimum floor for rates, the "rates not excessive" criterion can be considered as establishing a ceiling.

Many states have defined excessiveness with respect to some health insurance policies. These states often provide that the insurer must reasonably expect to pay or actually pay in claims at least a certain minimum percentage (e.g., 50 percent) of the premiums collected.

While prices charged for life and health insurance in the United States do vary from company to company and with some companies, prices are high, competition today within the U.S. life insurance business is keener than in times past, thus largely militating against the possibility of excessive prices. Simply put, a life insurance company is not likely to sell much insurance if the rates it charges or the interest rates it credits to policy cash values are not competitive. Indeed, competition has been so severe with respect to some products that some industry observers are concerned that the objective of rate adequacy has been ignored by some companies.

## THE ELEMENTS OF LIFE AND HEALTH INSURANCE PRICING

A sound understanding of life and health insurance requires a sound understanding of the elements used in their pricing. The calculation of life and health insurance rates and values requires information and assumptions regarding five elements:

1. The probability of the event insured against occurring
2. The time value of money
3. The benefits promised
4. Expenses
5. Profits and contingencies

Insurance pricing is based on the concept of loss sharing. Loss sharing in turn involves the accumulation of a fund from amounts paid by insureds to provide benefits to the unfortunate few who suffer loss. To establish the amount to be charged, the insurer must start with some idea as to the likelihood of losses for the group.

The likelihood of losses in life and health insurance is shown by specially constructed tables. **Mortality tables** show yearly probabilities of death. **Morbidity tables** show yearly probabilities or other information on loss of health. These tables show incidences of death and loss of health for a given group of insureds over time—often from birth to the death of the final persons in the group. These tables constitute the foundation upon which the expected costs of life and health insurance are based.

Persons purchasing life insurance are not the same age. Generally, those insuring at the younger ages are less likely to die within the next year than those who purchase insurance at older ages. Equity therefore requires that the amounts charged be graded upward as the age at which the policy is issued increases. This is also true in health insurance, to the extent that the loss insured increases with increasing age.

Life and health insurance companies collect premiums in advance of providing insurance coverage. In longer-term coverage, that portion of amounts collected but not needed immediately to cover losses and expenses is invested and produces earnings that are used to supplement premium income to fund future expected benefits and ongoing expenses. In such cases, insurers discount (lower) premiums in advance in recognition of the fact that they will earn interest on the accumulated funds.

Besides the recognition of the time value of money, premium computation must take into account the period of coverage, the level of coverage, as well as all other factors related to the benefits promised the insured under the contract. Included here is the likelihood of policyowners voluntarily terminating their policies. With life insurance, the amount of any benefit payout is typically fixed and known in advance. With health insurance contracts, the total benefit payouts usually are not known in advance. This fact complicates health insurance pricing.

Many types of insurance policies are on the market. Some insure against death or disability for a limited number of years only, whereas others cover the whole of life; some call for the payment of premiums for a stated number of years only, others for the entire duration of the contract; for some, premiums are fixed, whereas with others the policyowner determines the level of premiums to be paid, within certain guidelines. Some promise the payment of policy benefits in one lump sum, whereas others provide for payment in a fixed number of installments, and so on. The rates for each coverage configuration are determined not only with reference to estimated probabilities of death, illness, or injury, but also according to the nature of the benefits promised and the expected premium payment pattern.

These complex conditions cannot be gauged appropriately by companies unless they follow scientific principles in rate computation. Life insurance typically provides a definite benefit amount in the event of death. Disability insurance typically promises a definite benefit in the event of disability. Other forms of health insurance provide benefits intended to finance needed long-term care or medical expenses because of a particular illness or injury. It is essential, therefore, that an accurate determination of the expected benefit cost be made and that an adequate amount be charged—an amount that is equitable as to age, sex, types of coverage, and other relevant factors. This is especially important because, unlike most other types of insurance, life and some health insurance contracts can extend for a long period of time or even throughout life and cannot be canceled by the company.

Later chapters will discuss the pricing of life and health insurance in detail. The following discussion is intended to provide an overview of the pricing process for the pure risk component only, as well as the principles involved, to facilitate a study of the evaluation and uses of individual life and health insurance.

Life and health insurance rates that are calculated to recognize (1) the probability of the event insured against occurring, (2) the time value of money, and (3) the benefits promised are referred to as **net rates**. They do not make allowance for the expenses the insurer incurs in selling, issuing, and maintaining the policy, nor do they make provision for profits or unforeseen contingencies. When loadings for expenses, contingencies, and profits are added to the net rate, the **gross rate**—the amount charged policyowners—is obtained. In computing net and gross rates, the company considers its objectives and its past experience for each factor involved.

The above procedure for deriving gross premium rates, followed in principle by many life insurers, is used in this chapter to illustrate insurance pricing concepts. However, a more common method of deriving a company's gross premium rate structure is for the insurer to select gross rates for pivotal ages (based on market and competitive considerations), and then to test these selected rates against its objectives and expectations as to realistic future experience. If the test rate does not produce the profit and desired results, the rate (or other policy elements) will be changed and the test repeated. With this procedure, the insurer does not calculate a net rate, then add amounts to cover expenses, profits and contingencies. Rather, the insurer simply selects a target gross rate to be tested. This amount, for example, may be the rate presently being charged by the company, or it may be the rate being charged by selected competitors for similar coverage.[3]

Still another approach to establishing a gross premium rate structure is to calculate gross premium rates directly through the use of realistic interest, mortality, expense and lapse assumptions, and a specific provision for contingencies and profit (or contribution to surplus). With cash values and a dividend scale assumed, the calculation of a gross premium rate structure is carried out by solving a mathematical equation.

No matter how the tentative gross rate is derived, it is tested against the company's anticipated future operating experience. The following discussion and examples focus on life insurance. However, the same principles and approaches apply to health insurance pricing.

## LIFE INSURANCE RATE COMPUTATION

The simplest form of life insurance protection is yearly renewable term (YRT) insurance. To illustrate the preceding principles, a brief explanation follows of the YRT plan, as well as of the single-premium and flexible-premium plans.

*Yearly Renewable Term Life Insurance.* Yearly renewable term life insurance provides coverage for a period of one year only, but guarantees the policyowner the right to renew (i.e., continue) the policy even if the insured

---

[3] See Chap. 21.

suffers poor health or otherwise becomes uninsurable.[4] Each year's premium pays the policy's share of mortality costs for the year. The renewal premium rate increases each year to reflect the annual rise in death rates as age advances.

The increasing probability of death may be seen in Table 2-1, which shows the annual male and female rates of mortality per 1,000 lives at various ages according to the **1980 Commissioners Standard Ordinary (CSO) Mortality Table**, the standard currently required by state regulatory authorities for the valuation (measurement) of certain policy liabilities.[5] For deriving life insurance premiums to be charged, insurers may use mortality rates that they judge to represent realistic expectations of future mortality experience for insured risks.

Table 2-1 shows that the rate of dying generally increases with age and at an increasing rate, rising ultimately to a certainty. Also, observe that female mortality experience is more favorable than that of males at every age. As a result of these mortality differences, all life insurers vary their premium charges by age, and the vast majority also vary them by the insured's gender, with females being charged lower rates for life insurance.

An example will illustrate YRT rate derivation. The mortality rate for males, age 30, according to the 1980 CSO Table, is 1.73 per 1,000. If 100,000 males age 30 are insured for $1,000 each, an insurer would expect to pay 173 death claims for a total payment of $173,000. Since 100,000 persons would be insured, the company would have to collect $1.73 from each insured individual to accumulate a fund sufficient to meet the 173 death claims. This rate is the same as the death rate.

This illustration includes only the mortality charge since investment income as well as allowances for contingencies, expenses, and profits are ignored. To derive a net rate, it is necessary to consider investment earnings.

Assume that the insurer credits a 5 percent annual return on all policyowner-related funds. To simplify the analysis, assume also that

| TABLE 2-1 | RATES OF MORTALITY PER 1,000 LIVES *(1980 CSO TABLE)* | |
|---|---|---|
| | Rate of Mortality | |
| Age | Male | Female |
| 10 | 0.73 | 0.68 |
| 20 | 1.90 | 1.05 |
| 30 | 1.73 | 1.38 |
| 40 | 3.02 | 2.42 |
| 50 | 6.71 | 4.96 |
| 60 | 16.08 | 9.47 |
| 70 | 39.51 | 22.11 |
| 80 | 98.84 | 65.99 |
| 90 | 221.77 | 190.75 |
| 99 | 1,000.00 | 1,000.00 |

[4] See Chap. 4.

[5] See Chap. 20.

policyowner payments to the insurer are made at the beginning of the policy year (a realistic assumption) and that death claims are paid only at year end (an unrealistic assumption) and that, therefore, the insurer has use of funds for a full year.

Ignoring other pricing components for now, the insurer need not now collect the full $173,000. In fact, the insurer need collect only $164,762. This amount, accumulated at 5 percent interest, will equal the $173,000 needed at the end of the year to honor all death claims ($164,762 x 1.05 = $173,000). Thus the insurer need not charge each insured the full $1.73 per $1,000 of insurance. It can charge $1.65 per $1,000, relying on its investment income to contribute the additional $0.08 per $1,000.

To this net rate would be added an amount necessary to provide reasonable allowances to cover expenses, contingencies, and profit. To keep the analysis simple, these elements will continue to be ignored.

Since death rates increase with age, the rate that policyowners must be charged each year increases proportionately. As surviving members of an insured group renew their insurance year after year, the increasing rate causes some to question the advisability of continuing the insurance. As the increases become more burdensome, those in good health tend to discontinue their coverage, whereas those in poor health have strong incentives to renew their policies even at the higher rates necessitated by advancing age. This tendency of insureds to use their superior knowledge of their own insurability to gain an advantage on the insurer is known as **adverse selection**, and if life insurers did not anticipate this phenomenon, eventually it would result in a continuing group of insureds whose mortality experience would exceed the mortality experience implicit within the rate schedule. The combination of increasing mortality rates caused by advancing age plus adverse selection produces abnormally high mortality rates; consequently, insurance companies commonly place a limit on the period during which yearly renewable term insurance can be renewed, or, alternatively, they provide premium levels for later years that are high enough to cover the anticipated adverse selection.[6]

***The Single-Premium Plan.*** Another method of purchasing insurance is to pay for the policy with a single premium. In contrast to the yearly renewable term net rate for a male aged 30 of $1.65 (followed by a series of rates each of which increases annually), the net premium for a single-premium whole life policy for a male aged 30, under the same mortality and interest assumptions as above, is $150.45 for each $1,000 of coverage. This amount, when increased for expenses, profits and contingencies, pays for the contract in full.

The single-premium whole life plan involves the payment of the policy's entire future mortality charges in a single sum. Since the insurer will on average

---

[6] The State of New York, in recognition of this phenomenon, prohibits renewal of such policies beyond age 70.

have use of these funds over an extended period of time, investment earnings constitute a major component from which benefits will be paid.

A highly simplified and admittedly unrealistic example will demonstrate the points made above. Assume that 100,000 males, all aged 95, purchase single-premium whole life policies whose face amounts are all $1,000. Assume further that the life insurer calculates its net rates based on the *1980 CSO Mortality Table*, with interest at 5 percent per year.[7] A modified version of the *1980 Mortality Table* is shown in Table 2-2.

Of the 100,000 males living at age 95, approximately 33,000 will die during the next year. These figures are based on a probability of death of 0.330 (i.e., 100,000 x 0.330 = 33,000), which is taken from the 1980 CSO Table. This means that 67,000 males will have survived to the age of 96.

Of the 67,000 who survived, an estimated 25,795 will die during the next year, based on the 1980 CSO Table death probability of 0.385 (i.e., 67,000 x 0.385 = 25,795). Thus 41,205 of the original group of 100,000 are estimated to survive to age 97, of which an estimated 19,778 will die during the next year, and so on. Note that during age 99 all 7,328 of the survivors will be considered to have died.

From these data one can calculate the total amount of money the insurer must collect today to be able to honor all future death claims in this group as they are incurred. Table 2-3 illustrates the calculation.

Column 4 gives present value factors that convert a given amount to be paid in the future to its present-day equivalent, assuming a time value of money of 5 percent. For example, $1,000 to be paid in five years is equivalent to $783.50 today ($1,000 x 0.7835). Stated differently, $783.50 today will accumulate to $1,000 in five years if invested to earn 5 percent per year.

During the first policy year (i.e., during age 95), 33,000 insureds of the original group of 100,000 are estimated to die, so the insurer will pay out a total

| TABLE 2-2 | MODIFIED VERSION OF | | |
|-----------|---------------------|---|---|
| | *1980 CSO MORTALITY TABLE* | | |
| (1) | (2) | (3) | (4) |
| Age | Number Living (Beginning of Year) | Probability of Death (During the Year) | Number Dying (During the Year) |
| 95 | 100,000 | 0.330 | 33,000 |
| 96 | 67,000 | 0.385 | 25,795 |
| 97 | 41,205 | 0.480 | 19,778 |
| 98 | 21,427 | 0.658 | 14,099 |
| 99 | 7,328 | 1.000 | 7,328 |
| 100 | 0 | | |

[7] The reader is reminded that actual rate computations involve the use of current company or industry experience.

TABLE 2-3          CALCULATION OF PRESENT VALUE OF CLAIMS
                   FOR 95-YEAR-OLD MALE

| (1) | (2) | (3) Total Death Claims | (4) | (5) |
|-----|-----|------|-----|-----|
| Policy Year | Number Dying During the Year | ($1,000 x No. Dying) For the Year | Present Value Factor at 5% | Present Value Total Death Claims |
| 1 | 33,000 | $33,000,000 | 0.9524 | $31,429,200 |
| 2 | 25,795 | 25,795,000 | 0.9070 | 23,396,065 |
| 3 | 19,778 | 19,778,000 | 0.8638 | 17,084,236 |
| 4 | 14,099 | 14,099,000 | 0.8227 | 11,599,247 |
| 5 | 7,328 | 7,328,000 | 0.7835 | 5,741,488 |
| | | Total present value | | $89,250,236 |

of $33,000,000 in death claims ($1,000 x 33,000 deaths) at the end of the first year. However, the insurer needs to have on hand today only $31,429,200, since this amount accumulated at 5 percent interest will equal $33,000,000 at the end of one year.[8]

During the second policy year, an estimated $25,795,000 is needed to honor the claims falling due during that year. However, those claims will not be paid for two years from the time of the issuance of the single-premium policy. Thus the insurer needs to collect only $23,396,065 in advance ($25,795,000 x 0.9070) to have available $25,795,000 in two years.

The process is continued for the other three policy years, with the present value factor becoming smaller (i.e., the discount being larger) the greater the time period involved. The result of this process is that the life insurer must collect $89,250,236 to be able to honor the $100,000,000 in claims as they occur; that is to say, the insurer needs to collect only $0.89 in premiums for each dollar of benefits to be paid out. The additional $0.11 is derived from investment income.

Since the initial number of insureds assumed was 100,000, the insurer would charge each insured a net single premium of $892.50 ($89,250,236 divided by 100,000) for each $1,000 of whole life insurance protection. To this net premium would be added amounts to cover expenses and so on, the result of which may yield a gross premium in excess of $1,000! No one would logically purchase insurance at such advanced ages since it is not economically feasible. As in the case of other risks that are insured, the administrative costs added to the value of the pure loss costs makes insurance practicable only when the probability of loss is relatively low. Good risk management suggests avoiding merely exchanging dollars with an insurance company.

This calculation also demonstrates clearly that a life insurance policy for the whole of life can be viewed as a series of yearly renewable term insurances continuing to the end of the mortality table. Note that the column 3 figures shown

---

[8] Remember that premiums were assumed to be paid in advance and death claims were assumed to be paid at the end of the year.

in Table 2-2, if multiplied by the policy face amounts of $1,000, give the year-by-year mortality charges, thus giving the yearly renewable term costs without the interest factor.

Since all mortality charges with single-premium life insurance are prepaid, the life insurance company cannot consider the full premium earned when paid. As is clear from Table 2-3, the initial premium plus interest earned thereon will, in essence, be utilized over the policy period to meet the claims. At any point in time, the insurer must show a liability on its balance sheet equal to the value of the unused fund. This value represents the present value of the future benefits promised under the life insurance policies and is the **policy reserve** referred to earlier.

Table 2-4 illustrates how these policy reserves evolve for this block of policies. The initial fund of $89,250,236 is developed from each of the 100,000 insureds, each age 95, paying a net single premium of $892.50 for $1,000 of insurance coverage. (Ignore the $236 excess.) This fund earns interest (at 5 percent) of $4,462,512 during the first policy year. Death claims of $33,000,000 are paid at the end of the first year, resulting in a fund balance or aggregate policy reserve of $60,712,747 at the end of the first policy year.

Although policy reserves for a block of policies are an aggregate concept, the portion applicable to each policy can be calculated. This portion is found by dividing the aggregate reserve by the number of insureds surviving the first policy year (in this case 67,000) to yield a reserve per policy of $906.

At the beginning of the second year, the aggregate reserve liability is the same as the previous year's ending balance ($60,712,747).[9] This fund is credited with $3,035,637 in interest, and $25,795,000 is paid out in death claims at year-end. The aggregate reserve has, therefore, fallen to $37,953,384, which represents the present value of the future benefits promised under the remaining policies. Note that the reserve per policy has increased to $921 even though the aggregate reserve has declined.

The above process is continued through the third, fourth, and fifth policy years. Note that the aggregate policy reserve (col. 6) continues to decline, but that the per-policy reserve must continue to grow, since, for a whole life policy, a death claim payment is a certainty. The per-policy reserve must equal the policy face amount the instant before the final policies mature as death claims at the end of age 99.

The last policy year deserves some comment. The number of insureds living at the beginning of the year is 7,328. Based on the mortality table used here, it is assumed that all of these remaining insureds will die during this year and that the full $1,000 face amount per policy will be paid to the beneficiaries at year-end.

The beginning reserve is $6,977,705. Interest of $348,885 is credited to the reserve. The $7,328,000 in death claims is paid even if, in reality, some insureds

---

[9] This assumes that all surviving policyowners choose to continue their participation.

**TABLE 2-4    DEVELOPMENT OF POLICY RESERVES FOR NET-SINGLE-PREMIUM WHOLE LIFE POLICY**

| (1) Policy Year | (2) Number Living at Beginning of Year | (3) Fund Balance at Beginning of Policy Year | (4) Interest Earned on Fund (at 5%) During Policy Year [(3)x5%] | (5) Death Claims Paid at End of Policy Year (See Table 2-3, Col. 3) | (6) Fund Balance at End of Policy Year [(3)+(4)-(5)] | (7) Fund Balance per Policy [(6)÷(2) Next] |
|---|---|---|---|---|---|---|
| 1 | 100,000 | $89,250.236 | $4,462.512 | $33,000.000 | $60,712.747 | $906 |
| 2 | 67,000 | 60,712.747 | 3,035.637 | 25,795.000 | 37,953.384 | 921 |
| 3 | 41,205 | 37,953.384 | 1,897.669 | 19,778.000 | 20,073.053 | 937 |
| 4 | 21,427 | 20,073.053 | 1,003.653 | 14,099.000 | 6,977.705 | 952 |
| 5 | 7,328 | 6,977.705 | 348.885 | 7,328.000 | 0[a] | - |

[a]Actually equals minus $1,410 instead of $0. The cumulative effect of rounding causes this slight relative difference.

survived the period. The assumption within the premium computation is that all insureds died, so the insurer would pay the face amount on all policies, even if all insureds did not die.

The aggregate reserve at the end of the fifth policy year (i.e., at age 100) would be exactly zero were all rounding errors eliminated. In theory, the aggregate policy reserve balance the instant before the 7,328 claims were paid would, of course, exactly equal the death claims and the per-policy reserve would be $1,000 per policy.[10]

In the preceding example, it was assumed that all 100,000 insureds paid their net single premiums for their $1,000 of insurance coverage and made no effort to terminate their policies prior to death. In fact, policyowners regularly decide for various reasons that they would prefer to voluntarily terminate (other than by dying!) their insurance policies. In these situations, the question arises as to what, if anything, the terminating policyowner should be entitled to in terms of a refund of all or a portion of the prepayments made toward future mortality charges. Should the policyowner be considered as having forfeited these prepayments or should the insurer be required to provide some "nonforfeiture" benefit?

This important question has been settled by state law and, before that, by industry practice. Current law in the United States requires that all life insurance policies that involve *significant* prepayments of future mortality charges provide for a type of partial refund of these prepayments to the terminating policyowner.[11] This refund is referred to as a life insurance policy's **cash surrender value** and is available to the policyowner upon termination of a life policy other than by death. This value is the savings element in every cash-value insurance policy, and it is different from the policy reserve, since the policy reserve is simply a pro-rata share of the balance sheet representation of the company's future obligations to policyowners as a group. Cash surrender values are those amounts that are available to the policyowner upon voluntary policy termination (surrender). More will be said on this point later.[12]

*The Level-Premium Plan.* Most persons do not have the resources for or do not wish to purchase their life insurance with a single-premium payment because of the relatively large initial outlay required. The practical difficulties arising from the single-premium plan and the fact that the mortality rate increases with age have been solved through the use of the level-premium plan.

[10] The reader is cautioned that the preceding examples as well as others in this chapter have been simplified purposely to illustrate the concepts involved and, in fact, do not represent actual insurance company practice. For example, minimum policy reserve standards are established by state law and may have little or no relationship to actual insurer results. The mortality and interest assumptions mandated by these laws coincide only rarely with those implicit within an insurer's gross premium rate structure — contrary to the one shown in the above example.

[11] What is "significant" is determined by law. See Chap. 20.

[12] See Chap. 9. Terminating policyowners may be afforded several options as to how to utilize the policy's cash value.

The fundamental idea of the level-premium plan is that the company can accept the same premium each year (a level premium), provided that the level premiums collected are the mathematical equivalent of the corresponding single premium. As a result, the level premiums paid in the early years of the contract will be more than sufficient to pay current death claims, but will be less than adequate to meet death claims that occur in later years. Life insurance was thus one of the first products marketed on the installment plan.

This leveling results in the creation of a fund from premiums paid in the early policy years, when mortality rates are low, just as a fund is created with single-premium policies. Naturally, the fund is smaller under level-premium plans than under single-premium plans, since the former involves less prefunding of future mortality charges. At any point in time, the fund, future interest, and future premiums together should be sufficient to enable the insurer to pay all death claims as they occur during the remaining coverage period provided by the class of policies.

The level-premium principle may be applied to a life policy of any duration, from short duration term policies to whole life policies. The level annual premium may amortize the single-premium cost of the insurance over the entire duration of the policy's coverage period or over any shorter period. For example, a whole life policy—referred to as an **ordinary life policy**—can have premiums paid over the entire policy duration—that is, the whole of life. Whole life policies can have level premiums paid over any shorter period, such as 10, 15, or 20 years or to a specified age—for example, to age 65. These policies are referred to as **10-, 15-,** and **20-payment whole life policies** and **life paid up at age 65 whole life policies**, respectively.

1. *Net-Level Premium Calculation.* A brief, if (again) unrealistic, example will illustrate how level premiums are calculated. Recall that the life insurer would charge each of our 100,000 males who are all 95 years old a net single premium of $892.50 per $1,000 of insurance for whole life coverage. In total, the insurer needed to collect $89,250,236 at date of issue.

If 100,000 insureds preferred to pay premiums on an annual basis, how much must the insurer charge each insured so that the insurer would be indifferent as to whether an insured paid for the whole life coverage with a single premium or a level premium (i.e., so that the two systems of payment were actuarially equivalent)? This is the fundamental question for beginning the analysis. Again, for simplicity, the illustration will ignore all allowances for expenses, profits, and contingencies as well as competitive aspects.

The problem can be solved using simple algebra. We know that the present value of death claims equals $89,250,236. The insurer must collect this amount, in total, as net *single* premiums. The insurer must, therefore, collect the mathematical equivalent in net *level* premiums if the insurer is to be indifferent as to method of premium payment. In other words, the present value of the net level premiums must be equal to the sum of the net single premiums, both of which, in turn, must equal the value of future death claims.

Table 2-5 illustrates the necessary calculation. The net level annual premium being sought is an unknown quantity, labeled "P" in column 2. It will be collected from each survivor each year. A total of 236,960 of these net level premiums (or 236,960P) is to be collected (the sum of col. 3). However, the value today of these premiums is 225,722P.

Note that the present value factors for column 4 of this table differ from those shown in column 4 of Table 2-3. This is because premiums (unlike claims) are assumed to be paid at the *beginning* of each year. Thus, the present value of each dollar in premiums to be collected the *first* policy year *is* a dollar.

It was mentioned above that the insurer must collect in net level premiums an amount equal, in present value terms, to the amount it expects to pay out in death claims. Thus the present value of net level premiums (225,722P) must equal the present value of future claims ($89,250,236). This is shown in Table 2-5. Dividing both sides of the equation by 225,722 yields the net level premium of $395.40. This would be the annualized equivalent of the single premium.[13]

The net level premium is considerably higher than one-fifth of the net single premium. This result should not be surprising, since, prior to the payment of the series of death claims, the insurer has use of far less money under the level-premium plan than under the single-premium plan and, therefore, interest

TABLE 2-5     ILLUSTRATIVE NET-LEVEL PREMIUM CALCULATION

| (1) Policy Year | (2) Net Level Premium to be Paid Annually by Each Survivor | (3) Number Living at the Beginning of Each Year | (4) Present Value Factor at 5% | (5) Present Value of Total Net Level Premiums [(2x3x4)] |
|---|---|---|---|---|
| 1 | P | 100,000 | 1.0000 | 100,000P |
| 2 | P | 67,000 | 0.9524 | 63,811P |
| 3 | P | 41,205 | 0.9070 | 37,373P |
| 4 | P | 21,427 | 0.8638 | 18,509P |
| 5 | P | 7,328 | 0.8227 | 6,029P |
| | | | Total present value | 225,722P |

*Since*  Present value of net level premiums (PVP) = 225,722P
     Present value of claims (see Table 2-3) (PVC) = $89,250,236
*And*      PVP = PVC
*Then*   225,722P = $89,250,236
*So*          P = $395.40

[13] An alternate but mathematically identical procedure to derive net level premiums is followed in Chap. 19. This alternative procedure relies on expected value concepts rather than on algebraic concepts.

income is not as large a factor in causing the premium to be lower. Also, note that the insurer will collect premiums only from those who survive. Although odd-sounding, this statement is highly important in explaining the level-premium concept. Under the level-premium plan, the insurer does not collect a full annual premium from 100,000 persons each year. It collects only from those who survive, thus necessitating a higher premium than would be the case otherwise. In other words, *the level-premium plan discounts for both interest and mortality.*[14] It can be demonstrated that the net level premium of $395.40 is exactly sufficient, when combined with interest, to pay all death claims and to end the last policy year with a balance of zero, as was illustrated in Table 2-4 with the net single premium.

   *2. Net Amount at Risk.* Policy reserves when stated on a per-policy basis can be considered as "vanishing" or ending with the insured's death. As a result, the insurer can be considered to have less than the policy's face amount at risk. Under this view of the reserve, therefore, the actual amount of pure life insurance protection at any point can be considered as the difference between the policy reserve at that point and the face amount of the contract. This difference is called the **net amount at risk**.

   Figure 2-1 shows a stylized whole life insurance policy of $1,000, which is payable on the death of the insured and may be purchased by a male aged 30 with a net level premium of $8.43 payable annually until death. The increasing reserve and the declining net amount risk reflected in this view of the life insurance contract are apparent.

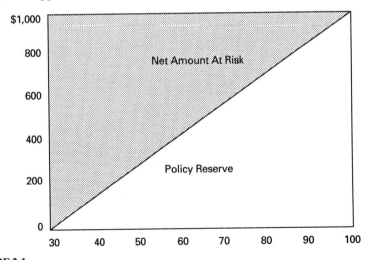

**FIGURE 2-1**

**PROPORTION OF PROTECTION (AMOUNT AT RISK) AND RESERVE IN A $1,000 ORDINARY LIFE CONTRACT ISSUED TO MALE AGED 30 (1980 CSO TABLE, 5%)**

---

[14] In practice, the level premium method also considers probabilities of policy terminations by other than death. See Chap. 21.

For example, at age 65, the reserve is $460 and the net amount at risk is $540. Remember that the sum of the net amount at risk and the reserve equals the face amount of the policy ($1,000 in the example). For all whole life policies, the net amount at risk declines as the reserve increases.

The foregoing analysis can be interpreted as dividing a life insurance policy into two parts: a decreasing amount of term insurance and an increasing savings element, which, when combined, are always just equal to the face of the policy. This can be a helpful way of viewing traditional cash-value insurance policies and is, in fact, an accurate way of viewing universal life policies, as discussed below.

*The Flexible-Premium Plan.* Many U.S. life insurers sell policies that permit the policyowner the flexibility of deciding the amount of the premium he or she would like to pay. **Universal life** (UL) policies are examples of such flexible plans.[15]

UL policy cash values are a function of the amount of the policyowner's past and present premium payments (and past and present expense and mortality charges as well as interest credits). Unlike the situation with traditional forms of cash-value insurance, the cash values of UL policies are not by-products of the leveling of premiums. Rather, they flow directly from the structure of the policy itself.

Subject to company rules regarding minimums and maximums, the policyowner may pay whatever premium during a policy year that he or she wishes. An amount to cover the insurer's expenses and mortality charges is subtracted from the cash value. The balance remaining, plus any premium payments and the previous period's fund balance, then forms the next period's cash value. A penalty for early policy termination—called a **surrender charge**—may be assessed against the policy's cash value. Mortality charges are based on the policy's net amount at risk calculated using the cash value instead of the reserve. Interest at the company's current rate is credited to the cash value. This process typically is repeated monthly.

No illustration is given here to demonstrate UL premium development, since the policyowner "develops" his or her own premium payment schedule. Of course, if the premium currently paid plus the current cash value is insufficient to cover fully all current mortality and expense charges, the UL policy will terminate.

## THE SAVINGS ASPECT OF LIFE INSURANCE

Many life insurance policies have cash values. Conceptually, all life insurance policy cash values can be derived in the same way and all evolve for the same

---

[15] See Chap. 6.

basic reason—prefunding of future mortality charges. As a practical matter, however, policies are usually viewed in different ways. Thus with traditional forms of life insurance, the savings element is considered a by-product of the level-premium method of payment. With universal life and some other newer forms of life insurance policies, the savings element is usually considered to be a more independent part of the policy, specifically designed to build a savings fund from which mortality and expense charges are withdrawn.

*The Savings Aspect of Traditional Cash-Value Insurance.* Life insurance premiums traditionally have been computed by making assumptions regarding all elements impinging on the policy and deriving an indivisible premium to be charged for the policy. Much misunderstanding about traditional forms of cash-value life insurance flows from ascribing to individual policies concepts that apply to insurance companies' financial operations. The per-policy reserve referred to earlier is a prime example. If the policy reserve (a liability) is translated into a fund held on behalf of an individual policyowner, it is possible to look on the death benefit as a combination of that fund plus term insurance. This model, unless used carefully, can lead to false conclusions and to a general misunderstanding of the underlying realities of the life insurance business.

Economists and marketing personnel tend to view a level-premium whole life contract as a divisible contract providing financial protection to the policyowner's beneficiaries, with other contract benefits available, including cash surrender and loan values. A policyowner may discontinue the insurance and surrender the policy for its cash value. Alternatively, a policyowner may borrow from the insurer an amount up to the cash value, at a contractually stated rate of interest, using the cash value as collateral. Despite these and other living benefits, the whole life policy is, theoretically, an *indivisible* contract. It is not partly "protection" and partly "savings," with the premiums divisible between these components, as evidenced by the fact that the policyowner cannot withdraw the cash value *without giving up the insurance protection.* Even though the idea that the whole life contract is an indivisible entity is legally and actuarially correct, some companies and individuals continue to explain it as a combination of decreasing term insurance protection and increasing savings.

*The Savings Aspect of Universal Life Insurance.* During the late 1970s, a new form of life insurance—universal life (UL) insurance—was introduced into the United States. This new form has since captured a major share of new life insurance sales to individuals.

The distinguishing features of universal life policies are their (1) flexibility and (2) transparency. UL policies are flexible in that they permit policyowners, within limits, to increase or decrease (even to zero) premium payments as they wish, and also, subject to certain constraints, to increase or decrease the policy face amount.

UL policies are transparent in the sense that the three key elements of life insurance product pricing—mortality, interest, and expenses—are identified and disclosed to the consumer. The savings component of UL policies is a direct function of the premium payments made by the policyowner. Other things being equal, the higher the premium payments, the higher will be the cash value.

With UL policies, the protection and savings components really are divisible and the methods used to derive each are apparent. The fact that one policy is technically indivisible and another is divisible does not change the fundamental nature of the policies. They simply constitute different ways of viewing the same thing.

## EXPERIENCE PARTICIPATION IN LIFE INSURANCE

A great proportion of the life insurance policies sold today provides that the policyowner will benefit (or suffer) from the favorable (or unfavorable) operating experience of the life insurance company. This "experience" is often based on the key elements of life insurance pricing—that is, mortality, interest, and expense, as well as profit and contingency allowances. Thus if the life insurance company experiences or expects to experience (1) lower mortality (morbidity), (2) greater investment earnings, or (3) lower expenses and taxes than the assumptions upon which its premiums are based, then it may pass along to the blocks or classes of policyowners producing or expected to produce such favorable deviations, the savings or a portion thereof accruing to the company. In other words, the policyowners can benefit from such favorable experience. Of course, the opposite can and does occur.

Some life insurance is sold on a guaranteed cost basis, meaning that all policy elements (i.e., the premium, the face amount, and the cash values, if any) are guaranteed and will not vary with the experience of the company. Such **guaranteed-cost, nonparticipating** policies can offer advantages and disadvantages to policyowners, as discussed more fully later. The chief drawback of such cash-value policies is that in periods of high investment return, they offer no means of passing excess returns to the policyowners, with the result that they become viewed as expensive policies and may even be replaced.

*Past Experience.* The oldest method of recognizing experience, **policy dividends**, has traditionally reflected the insurer's *past* experience. Policies that pay dividends are classified as **participating**. Policy dividends are paid on policies that base experience participation on deviations of actual from illustrated operating experience relative to the mortality, interest, and expense assumptions built into the premium.

Premiums for participating policies are usually—but not always—based on fairly conservative mortality, interest, and expense assumptions, and they include a specific allowance for some level of dividend payments, with the result that the payment of some level of dividends over a policy's life is reasonably assured. The actual amount to be paid is not known and is never guaranteed. If future results equal the assumptions implicit in the premium, the dividends illustrated to be paid when the policy was issued should be met. If future results are more favorable, dividends should be higher than were originally illustrated and vice versa. The term "dividend" as used in insurance should not be confused with the same term used to refer to earnings on shares of stock.

Dividends paid under participating insurance policies are, at least in the early policy years, mainly a return to the policyowner of a portion of his or her premium payment. This is the reason that policy dividends are not subjected to income taxation. Historically, the dividend allowance included has been fairly conservative, with the result that most insurers selling participating insurance policies have paid higher dividends than originally illustrated.[16] Today, however, many insurers illustrate dividends on a liberal basis, thus reducing the possibility that dividends actually paid will exceed illustrated dividends.

*Current and Expected Future Experience*. **Current assumption policies** permit policyowners to benefit from *current* and *expected* future experience. Some current assumption policies require the payment of periodic premiums while others permit the policyowner to pay premiums as desired. The former policies carry premiums that are based on current, realistic assumptions. Because of changed expectations, the insurer may raise premiums in future years, but always subject to a maximum premium computed using conservative assumptions—as in traditional participating insurance.

Universal life policies are current assumption policies, but with no required periodic payment. UL policy premiums are of whatever level the policyowner wishes to pay, subject to certain limits. The insurer applies its current or expected future mortality, interest, expense, and profit experience factors against the current cash value and any premium payment. The residual is the next period's cash value.

These current assumption policies—also sometimes referred to as **interest-sensitive policies**—are not participating in the sense of reflecting past experience. Most are, in fact, classified by state law as nonparticipating, but without guarantees of all policy elements.

## INTERACTION AMONG LIFE INSURANCE PRICING ELEMENTS

Earlier illustrations suggest that all a life insurance company needs to do to develop its gross premiums is to review its own experience carefully, calculate a net premium, and add allowances for expenses, profit, and contingencies. While

---

[16] See Chap. 21 for more detail on dividends and their calculation.

this can be a first step, many other facets enter into pricing in life insurance. For example, will the gross premium so developed be competitive? What proportion of the policyowners is expected voluntarily to terminate their policies, and when? What levels of cash value should be included (subject, of course, to state-imposed minimums)? What level of dividends should be included? How might inflation alter expected results? Are agent commissions sufficiently high to induce agents to sell the policy? What level of customer service is to be provided? The list of questions goes on and on, and the answers to them may suggest the need for further thought and change.

A life insurance company's raw materials—its operating experience in terms of mortality, interest, and expenses and its philosophy regarding profits and contingencies—can be changed only so much. However, the elements derived from these raw materials can be altered and rearranged. For example, a company offering a participating policy could have a lower gross premium if it lowered its policy dividends. A cash value higher than the required minimum necessitates a higher premium, other things being equal. Assuming a company has a very competitive price and liberal commissions, company market support costs may be significantly reduced. The marketing system(s) employed may permit adjustments in either agent or market support compensation.

The point is that an interaction exists among the various life insurance policy pricing elements. This section briefly explores this interaction to help the reader to understand better how a life insurance company functions from the standpoint of income and disbursements.

The following discussion can be considered a microcosm of a life insurance company. It focuses on a simulated test of a block of policies, even though a typical life insurance company may have many policy blocks. The reader is invited to notice, in particular, the sources of the company's income for this block of policies (i.e., premiums and investment income) and how they interact with the disbursements.

*The Asset-Share Calculation.* The testing of a tentative gross premium rate schedule and other policy elements is performed using the so-called **asset-share calculation**. It really is a simulation of the anticipated operating experience for a block of policies using the best estimates of what the individual factors will be for each future policy year. The purpose of the asset-share calculation is to determine, for a block of policies, whether the insurer's profit, reserving, and other objectives can be met based on the anticipated operating experience. The calculation derives an expected fund (per $1,000 of insurance) held by the company at the end of each policy year after payment of death claims, expenses, dividends or other nonguaranteed benefits or credits, cash surrender values, and allowance for actual interest earnings. The accumulated fund at the end of each policy year is divided by the number of surviving and persisting policyowners (lives exposed) to produce each policy's "share of assets" or asset share. Usually the test is for a maximum of 20 or 30 years.

Figure 2-2 shows, in simplified fashion, the mechanics of an asset-share calculation. Disbursements are netted against income. The balance represents the net addition to the insurer's assets. Of course, most of the accumulated assets will be required to fund future death claims, expenses, and so on. In other words, they are required to back policy reserves, and, to the extent the accumulated assets are not sufficient to do so, the insurer must, in essence, "loan" surplus to make good the deficit.

Asset-share calculations are made before the fact. Since future experience is not known, estimates must be made that are thought to be reasonable representations of that experience. Asset-share calculations seek to determine whether the individual elements of a policy result in a competitive product that is well balanced and produces acceptable results for both the insurance company and the policyowners.

If the asset shares produced by the tentative gross premiums are deficient in light of company objectives, the premiums may be increased or some specific policy benefit (i.e., death benefit, dividends, or cash values) decreased. Alternatively, the insurer could decide to avoid changes in the policy itself, instead focusing on operational economies to reduce expenses, a change in its investment philosophy to allow riskier and thus higher-yielding assets, or other operational changes. If the fund accumulation appears excessive, especially in light of competitive considerations, the premium rate can be reduced or benefits increased. Naturally, for participating insurance or nonparticipating insurance that has one or more nonguaranteed elements, the available asset share may also be adjusted by modifying the tentative dividend scale or other nonguaranteed policy elements.

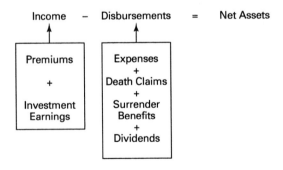

**FIGURE 2-2**

**INSURANCE COMPANY FUNDS FLOW**

*Illustrative Asset-Share Calculation.* The process by which a gross premium rate structure is tested can be explained most effectively by means of an illustrative asset-share calculation. Table 2-6 shows the results of such an asset-share calculation. For purposes of this illustration, all assumptions have been simplified and are somewhat arbitrary. (See pages 42–43.)

The tentative gross premium rate being tested is $15.00 per $1,000 for a participating ordinary life policy issued to males aged 35. Column 3 shows the expected number of deaths each year, based on an initial 100,000 insureds and on what the insurer believes to be the most reasonable expected future mortality experience. Column 4 provides the insurer's best estimate as to the number of insureds who will **lapse** (voluntarily terminate) their insurance policies each year.

The insurer's expected expenses over each of the next 20 years are listed in column 6, and columns 7 and 8 show cash surrender values and illustrated dividends that the insurer is also testing. The dividend scale shown in column 8 can be changed as the insurer judges appropriate, depending on test results. The dividend scale ultimately decided upon would be the one illustrated in all sales materials and advertisements and shown in the insurer's rate book.

Column 9 shows the total asset fund value carried over from the previous year. In the first year, it is, of course, equal to zero. Yearly premium income figures are shown in column 10; total yearly expense disbursements in column 11; total yearly death claim payouts in column 12; total yearly cash surrender value payouts in column 13; and total yearly dividend payments in column 14. Note that based on the cash-value schedule (shown in column 7) being tested, nothing would be paid to terminating policyowners until year 3.

Interest earned on net accumulated assets is shown in column 15, and the year-end fund balance is shown in column 16. Interest is earned (column 15) on the fund carried over from the previous year (column 9) plus premiums collected at the beginning of the year (column 10). However, from these two amounts one must subtract the expense disbursements (column 11)—assumed to be made at the beginning of each year—and one half of the year's death claim payouts. Why one half? Recall that the focus here is interest earned (or forgone) during the year on the funds on hand for the year. The assumption is that death claims are paid out uniformly throughout the year. Therefore the company, on average, has had use of only one half of the funds throughout the year; hence, the one-half factor applied to the column 12 figures.

The first year's negative figure in both columns 15 and 16 indicates that the insurer has spent more money than it has received from premiums and interest earnings from this block of policies. Finally, the entire process translates into assets accumulated on a per $1,000 basis, as shown in column 17.

The asset share fund for this block of policies is analogous to an income-outgo account. Each year premiums and interest earnings are credited to the account as income, and death claims, surrender and dividend payments, and

**TABLE 2-6  ASSET-SHARE CALCULATION FOR $1,000 ORDINARY LIFE ISSUED AT MALE AGE 35 ($15.00 RATE PER $1,000)**

| (1) Policy Year | (2) Number Paying Premiums at Beginning of Year | (3) Number Dying a | (4) Number Withdrawing b | (5) Number Alive at End of Year after Withdrawals [(2)-(3)-(4)] | (6) Expense Rate per $1,000 | (7) Cash Value per $1,000 on Withdrawal c | (8) Dividend per $1,000 | (9) Fund at Beginning of Year [(16) Prior Year] | (10) Premium Income [($15.00) x (2)] |
|---|---|---|---|---|---|---|---|---|---|
| 1 | 100,000 | 88 | 10,000 | 89,912 | $22.00 | $0.00 | $0.00 | $0 | $1,500,000 |
| 2 | 89,912 | 92 | 5,394 | 84,426 | 2.25 | 0.00 | 0.50 | -847,520 | 1,348,680 |
| 3 | 84,426 | 101 | 4,221 | 80,104 | 2.25 | 4.31 | 1.00 | 184,874 | 1,266,390 |
| 4 | 80,104 | 111 | 3,524 | 76,469 | 2.25 | 13.91 | 1.50 | 1,158,880 | 1,201,560 |
| 5 | 76,469 | 118 | 3,058 | 73,293 | 2.25 | 22.86 | 2.00 | 2,075,460 | 1,147,035 |
| 6 | 73,293 | 132 | 2,638 | 70,523 | 2.25 | 34.16 | 2.50 | 2,952,205 | 1,099,395 |
| 7 | 70,523 | 142 | 2,256 | 68,125 | 2.25 | 44.81 | 3.10 | 3,793,912 | 1,057,845 |
| 8 | 68,125 | 152 | 1,975 | 65,998 | 2.25 | 55.82 | 3.70 | 4,608,568 | 1,021,875 |
| 9 | 65,998 | 164 | 1,781 | 64,053 | 2.25 | 67.19 | 4.30 | 5,402,814 | 989,970 |
| 10 | 64,053 | 175 | 1,601 | 62,277 | 2.25 | 78.94 | 5.90 | 6,178,176 | 960,795 |
| 11 | 62,277 | 198 | 1,494 | 60,585 | 2.25 | 91.05 | 6.60 | 6,878,629 | 934,155 |
| 12 | 60,585 | 212 | 1,393 | 58,980 | 2.25 | 103.56 | 7.30 | 7,544,662 | 908,775 |
| 13 | 58,980 | 226 | 1,297 | 57,457 | 2.25 | 116.46 | 7.90 | 8,187,202 | 884,700 |
| 14 | 57,457 | 240 | 1,206 | 56,011 | 2.25 | 129.78 | 8.50 | 8,814,332 | 861,855 |
| 15 | 56,011 | 256 | 1,120 | 54,635 | 2.25 | 143.51 | 9.20 | 9,428,453 | 840,165 |
| 16 | 54,635 | 273 | 1,092 | 53,270 | 2.25 | 157.66 | 9.90 | 10,024,390 | 819,525 |
| 17 | 53,270 | 293 | 1,065 | 51,912 | 2.25 | 172.19 | 10.60 | 10,595,210 | 799,050 |
| 18 | 51,912 | 315 | 1,038 | 50,559 | 2.25 | 187.10 | 11.40 | 11,137,980 | 778,680 |
| 19 | 50,559 | 340 | 1,011 | 49,208 | 2.25 | 202.35 | 12.20 | 11,645,660 | 758,385 |
| 20 | 49,208 | 368 | 984 | 47,856 | 2.25 | 217.92 | 13.00 | 12,114,990 | 738,120 |

a Deaths based on select and ultimate experience mortality table. Deaths assumed to occur in middle of policy year on the average.

b Withdrawals based on Linton A Lapse Rates. Assumed to occur on anniversary at end of policy year.

c Case values; *1980 CSO Table*, 5 1/2 %.

**TABLE 2-6** (CONTINUED)

| Policy Year | (11) Expense Disbursements [(2) x (6)] | (12) Death Claims Paid [$1,000 x (3)] | (13) Amounts Paid on Surrender [(4) x (7)] | (14) Total Dividends Paid [(5) x (8)] | (15) Interest Earned During Year {[0.08 [(9)+(10) -(11)-1/2(12)] -(13)}] | (16) Fund at End of Year [(9)+(10)-(11)-(12) -(13)-(14)+(15)] | (17) Asset Share at End of Year [(16)÷(5)] | (18) Reserved at End of Year | (19) Surplus per $1,000 at End of Year [(17)-(18)] |
|---|---|---|---|---|---|---|---|---|---|
| 1 | $2,200,000 | $88,000 | $0 | $0 | $-59,520 | $-847,520 | $-9.43 | $9.15 | $-18.58 |
| 2 | 202,302 | 92,000 | 0 | 42,213 | 20,229 | 184.874 | 2.19 | 18.65 | -16.46 |
| 3 | 189,959 | 101,000 | 18,185 | 80,104 | 96,864 | 1,158.880 | 14.47 | 28.49 | -14.03 |
| 4 | 180,234 | 111,000 | 49,019 | 114,704 | 169,976 | 2,075,460 | 27.14 | 38.68 | -11.54 |
| 5 | 172,055 | 118,000 | 72,965 | 146,586 | 239,315 | 2,952,205 | 40.28 | 49.20 | -8.92 |
| 6 | 164,909 | 132,000 | 90,126 | 176,308 | 305,655 | 3,793,912 | 53.80 | 60.07 | -6.27 |
| 7 | 158,677 | 142,000 | 101,091 | 211,188 | 369,766 | 4,608,568 | 67.65 | 71.25 | -3.61 |
| 8 | 153,281 | 152,000 | 110,248 | 244,193 | 432,093 | 5,402.814 | 81.86 | 82.79 | -0.93 |
| 9 | 148,496 | 164,000 | 119,667 | 275,428 | 492,983 | 6,178.176 | 96.45 | 94.67 | 1.78 |
| 10 | 144,119 | 175,000 | 126,377 | 367,434 | 552,588 | 6,878.629 | 110.45 | 106.90 | 3.55 |
| 11 | 140,123 | 198,000 | 136,030 | 399,861 | 605,893 | 7,544.662 | 124.53 | 119.48 | 5.05 |
| 12 | 136,316 | 212,000 | 144,255 | 430,554 | 656,890 | 8,187.202 | 138.81 | 132.43 | 6.38 |
| 13 | 132,705 | 226,000 | 151,050 | 453,910 | 706,096 | 8,814.332 | 153.41 | 145.75 | 7.66 |
| 14 | 129,278 | 240,000 | 156,514 | 476,094 | 754,153 | 9,428.453 | 168.33 | 159.45 | 8.88 |
| 15 | 126,025 | 256,000 | 160,729 | 502,642 | 801,167 | 10,024.390 | 183.48 | 173.54 | 9.94 |
| 16 | 122,929 | 273,000 | 172,162 | 527,373 | 846,759 | 10,595.210 | 198.90 | 188.01 | 10.89 |
| 17 | 119,858 | 293,000 | 183,387 | 550,267 | 890,232 | 11,137.980 | 214.56 | 202.83 | 11.73 |
| 18 | 116,802 | 315,000 | 194,213 | 576,273 | 931,389 | 11,645.660 | 230.34 | 217.99 | 12.35 |
| 19 | 113,758 | 340,000 | 204,581 | 600,338 | 969,623 | 12,114.990 | 246.20 | 233.45 | 12.75 |
| 20 | 110,718 | 368,000 | 214,430 | 622,128 | 1,004,672 | 12,542.510 | 262.09 | 249.19 | 12.90 |

[d] Net-level-premium reserves, *1980 CSO Table, 5%.*

expense disbursements are charged against the account. The account balance at the end of each year (column 16) is divided by the number of surviving (i.e., those who did not die) *and* persisting (i.e., those who did not terminate) policyowners (column 5) to obtain the pro-rata share of the account for each surviving and persisting policyowner—the asset share (column 17). For example, at the end of the tenth year, $110.45 in assets is expected to have been accumulated for each of the 62,277 surviving and persisting policyowners.

Several significant facts are shown by the asset-share study. First, the asset share is negative at the end of the first policy year. This outcome reflects the high first-year expenses involved in selling, underwriting, and issuing new business and the use of a level premium.

A comparison of columns 7 and 17 for the first policy year shows that although terminating policyowners receive no cash value, the company nonetheless suffers an operating loss on each terminating policy. From the second year on, the company would experience a net gain on policies that are surrendered each year. Of course, future profits expected on such policies would be lost.

Column 18 shows the per-policy reserve that is assumed to be set up for this block of policies. Column 19 shows the year-by-year net accumulated effect on the company's surplus. Although policy reserves are not segregated on a company's balance sheet on a per-policy basis, they are shown on a per-policy basis here to illustrate better the concepts involved. Thus during the first policy year, a reserve of $9.15 per policy is established. This amount is obviously greater than the increase (actually a net decrease) in assets (-$9.43) that results from the first year's operations. As a result, company surplus is lowered to the extent of the difference (a total of -$18.58). This "surplus strain" continues through the eighth policy year. From the ninth policy year on, this block of policies, under the anticipated operating conditions, is expected to contribute positively to surplus, having "repaid" fully the amounts "borrowed" from surplus in the early policy years. After the eighth policy year, the increase in the asset side of the balance sheet more than offsets the increase in the reserve liability and does so increasingly as the years pass.

This example shows results for a single issue age. Blocks for other issue ages would also not show positive figures for several years under the assumptions used here.

As pointed out above, if the findings of the asset-share study do not develop satisfactory results for the company in terms of its objectives and the competitive environment, elements of the policy could be changed or the insurer could embark on a program to alter its expected mortality, lapse, or expense experience or to increase investment yields to achieve results judged acceptable. Asset shares are used to test premiums under various scenarios, including disaster conditions (i.e., extremely unfavorable investment earnings, mortality or lapse experience, or expense inflation). The computer has facilitated asset-share research, permitting prompt and economical analysis of the impact of proposed changes in any factor affecting the financial experience of a block of life insurance policies.

## RELATION OF CASH SURRENDER VALUES, RESERVES, AND ASSET SHARES

Previous discussions have attempted to delineate cash surrender values, reserves, and asset shares. To summarize: the **cash surrender value** represents the amount made available, contractually, to a withdrawing policyowner who is terminating his or her protection. This value is intended to represent an equitable distribution of the pro-rata share of the amount accumulated on behalf of the particular block of policies from which the policyowner is withdrawing.

The **policy reserve**, generally a higher value, represents a conservative measure of the company's liability for a given block of policies for financial statement purposes. Minimum liability values are mandated by regulation in the interest of solvency.[17]

The **asset share** is the pro-rata share of the assets accumulated on the basis of the company's anticipated operating experience, on behalf of the block of policies to which the particular policy belongs. In the case of a historical asset share, the assets accumulated would be based on the company's actual operating experience.

The asset share is typically less than the reserve in the early years, because of the uneven incidence of expense outlay as compared with the expense provision in premiums. The length of time it takes the asset share to exceed the reserve is a management decision that reflects how soon the company wishes to recover its excess first-year expenses. After the asset share equals the reserve, under most cash-value policies both continue to increase, but with the asset share normally growing at a slightly faster rate.

The cash surrender value must at least equal state-prescribed minimums and cannot be negative. In the early years, it usually lies somewhere between the asset share and the policy reserve.

[17] See Chap. 20.

# Chapter 3

# THE HISTORY, ROLE, AND IMPORTANCE OF LIFE AND HEALTH INSURANCE

Life and health insurance are of great importance throughout the world, as can be gleaned from Table 3-1. This table shows the ratio of life insurance in force to national income in selected countries. By this statistical measure, Japan leads all other nations shown. South Korea ranks second, and the United States ranks sixth. In general, the more economically developed a country, the greater the role of life insurance as an economic security device. Indeed, a United Nations' committee has formally recognized that life insurance "can play an important role in providing individual economic security and in national development efforts, including the mobilization of personal savings."[1]

This chapter presents a brief history of life insurance and an overview of its role in the U.S. economy. It also sets out the potential benefits of life insurance to individuals and to society as a whole.

## A BRIEF HISTORY OF LIFE INSURANCE

As Dr. Humbert O. Nelli wrote in his evaluation of the history of personal insurance, "History should explain the present and be a guide for the future."[2] As such, an understanding of the evolution of life insurance—with particular reference to the U.S.—should be required of all serious students of insurance.

---

[1] *Resolution 21(X), Life Insurance in Developing Countries.* Adopted at the tenth session of the Committee on Invisibles and Financing Related to Trade, United Nations Conference on Trade and Development, Dec. 1982.

[2] Humbert O. Nelli, "A New Look at the History of Personal Insurance," *Journal of the American Society of Chartered Life Underwriters*, Vol. XXIII (July 1969), p. 7. This historical overview is based on Humbert Nelli's work.

**TABLE 3-1    RATIO OF LIFE INSURANCE IN FORCE TO NATIONAL INCOME IN SELECTED COUNTRIES (PERCENT OF NATIONAL INCOME)**

| DEVELOPED COUNTRIES | 1982 | 1990 |
|---|---|---|
| Australia | 119 | 150 |
| Austria | 29 | 45 |
| Belgium | 51 | 115 |
| Canada | 172 | 202 |
| Denmark | 56 | 88 |
| Germany | 66 | 82 |
| Ireland | 105 | 217 |
| Italy | 8 | 15 |
| Japan | 297 | 494 |
| The Netherlands | 131 | 187 |
| Norway | 46 | 121 |
| Spain | 22 | 48 |
| United Kingdom | 85 | 124 |
| United States | 161 | 191 |
| **DEVELOPING COUNTRIES** | | |
| Costa Rica | 33 | 27 |
| Honduras | 33 | 43 |
| India | 22 | 25 |
| Indonesia | 3 | 8 |
| Pakistan | 16 | 17 |
| Philippines | 21 | 23 |
| South Africa | NA | 233 |
| South Korea | 91 | 235 |
| Thailand | 9 | 19 |
| Tunisia | 12[a] | 6 |
| Zambia | 11 | 9[a] |

*Sources:* American Council of Life Insurance (ACLI) and International Monetary Fund.
[a] 1983 data for Tunisia and 1989 data for Zambia.

## INTRODUCTION

A study of human history and civilization reveals a universal desire for security, and it indicates that the quest for security has been one of the most potent motivating forces in their material and cultural growth. Early societies relied on family and tribe cohesiveness for their security. With economic progress, however, this security source weakens. Insurance, in some form, has been a universal response to societies' quests for security.

Insurance, as it is known today, did not exist in ancient or medieval times, although practices having important elements of insurance existed. From the standpoint of the individual, the most important element of insurance is a total or partial relief from the potential burden of financial loss, commonly known as a *transfer of risk*. This is present to varying degrees in all instances presented in this section.

## EARLY MUTUAL INSURERS

*Greek Societies and Roman Collegia.* The beginnings of personal insurance are generally attributed to the Greeks (although the code of Hammurabi, c. 1750 b.c., provided for indemnity by the state for murder of a householder by a robber). The Greek societies—religious groups devoted to the observance and performance of prescribed feasts and sacrifices to their patron god—practiced elementary insurance. Those societies gained their greatest popularity during the Greek classical period, from about 500 to 200 b.c.

One of the most important social and religious rituals of ancient times, persisting today to a degree, was an elaborate funeral ceremony for the dead. The belief was that the soul of the departed could gain entrance into the special paradise of his or her faith only if the funeral was conducted with all required rituals, sacrifices, and feasts. The Greek societies assumed this risk for its members by assuring them of a proper burial.

The Roman collegia were associations patterned after the Greek societies. They were numerous during the period of the Roman republic, from about 400 to 44 B.C. The emperors, beginning with Caesar, feared the possibility that the collegia could become centers of revolt, so they suppressed most of them.[3] In time, the surviving collegia evolved into mutual benefit associations with stated benefits and regular membership contributions.[4] The dissolution of the Roman Empire brought an end to these societies, although similar organizations continued to exist in the Byzantine Empire.

*The Guilds of the Middle Ages.* The need for mutual protection and security not only continued but increased after the fall of Rome. The guilds evolved to meet this need. Although it would be wrong to state that the medieval guilds developed from the Roman collegia, the tradition and knowledge of the collegia are acknowledged to have had some influence on the guilds of England as well as on those of Italy. In England the guilds are believed to have been a combination of the old Germanic family relationship, the Roman collegia, and Christianity. Some of the merchant and craft guilds, which actually were trade associations, still exist today.

The guilds, particularly in England, provided mutual assistance to their members, as witnessed by the mentioning in most guild statutes of a host of perils for which members might qualify for relief (e.g., death, illness, capture by pirates, shipwreck, the burning of one's home, and the loss of the tools of one's trade). These medieval guilds, however, were not organized primarily for benevolent or relief purposes. Their primary purposes were religious, social, and economic. The benefits granted to guild members were neither a guarantee of aid nor an indemnity for accidental losses, but rather a system of organized charity. Even so, the risk transfer element was clearly present.

[3] See Terence O'Donnell, *History of Life Insurance in its Formative Years* (Chicago: American Conservation Co., 1936), pp. 52–53.

[4] Ibid., pp. 25 and 55–57.

*The English Friendly Societies.* If the guilds received more than their just share of attention from insurance writers, the Friendly Societies received too little, according to Nelli.[5] The Friendly Societies were the inheritors of the social and fraternal functions of the guilds, and some authorities believe that they formed an unbroken connection with the English guilds.[6]

Unlike the guilds, however, the societies were true mutual benefit groups. They were not concerned with trade, craft, or religion. These societies were operated by officers and a committee elected by the members, and they were governed by a set of rules adopted and amended by the membership as needed. They were of many diverse kinds, sizes, and membership composition. Hardly a hamlet in England did not have at least one Friendly Society. All societies had some form of death or burial fund benefit. In addition, benefits for a variety of other perils were provided by many of the societies. Unlike the guilds, however, the societies did not make benefit payments depend on the member's need, although they were often restricted by the amount of funds available.

The beginnings of Friendly Societies antedate, by some time, the first mortality tables, the laws of probability, and the mathematics of insurance. The societies operated on an **assessment basis** wherein the members were assessed as needed to provide the promised benefit payments. Contributions were not scaled according to the age or insurability of the members, so an unfair share of the burden was placed on the young, healthy members. As a result, many discontinued their membership. Mortality increased as the average age of the members increased,[7] placing a still heavier burden upon those of advancing years—the ones least able to afford it. High failure rates were inevitable under the circumstances.

The Friendly Societies pioneered the formation of private life insurance in England. They provided insurance protection in limited amounts to persons of meager or limited means in return for periodic (often weekly) contributions. They were the proving ground for various forms of insuring organizations and insurance services. Freedom from political control allowed them to improvise, try, fail, and try again.

*English Mutual Assurance Companies.* The first true mutual insurance company was The Life Assurance and Annuity Association established by the Mystery of the Mercers of London on October 4, 1699. It failed, deeply in debt, 46 years later.[8] Seven years later, The Amicable Society for a Perpetual Assurance Office was formed. It placed a limit of 2,000 to its membership, and it operated under a unique benefit system. The death benefit was not stated but

[5] Nelli, p. 12.

[6] J. M. Baernreither, *English Association of Working Men*, translated by Alice Taylor (London: Swan Sonnenschein and Company, 1889), p. 160.

[7] Whereas the guilds had an automatic, continuous turnover of members through apprenticeships and retirements, the societies had memberships that generally remained static.

[8] Hartley Withers, *Pioneers of British Life Assurance* (London: Staples Press, 1951), p. 27.

depended upon the number dying in any one year. Based upon calculations by Sir Thomas Allen, a sum was set aside each year that the year's claimants divided among themselves.[9]

By 1720 two English insurers, The Royal Exchange and The London (major stock companies), had managed to receive a monopoly on British insurance. Thus when the Equitable applied for a corporate charter in 1761, it met strong opposition. The Equitable founders, being refused a Royal Charter to form a stock life insurer, decided to form a mutual company that did not require a charter. Thus in 1765 The Society for Equitable Assurances on Lives and Survivorships was born. Management proved able and prudent, and it further assured its future by providing for assessment of policyowners if needed. The Equitable is said to be the first life insurer based on modern insurance principles.[10]

***Mutuals in the United States.*** The English Friendly Societies had no true counterpart in the United States. The English orders, such as the Odd Fellow and Foresters, had been introduced into the United States by English settlers before the Civil War, and they exerted a strong influence on the fraternal movement in the United States. Prior to that time, American associations were generally limited to political, literary, and commercial clubs.[11] Some authorities credit the predominantly middle-class outlook of America for the absence of true Friendly Societies.[12] The sparse population and wide expanse of territory in the eighteenth century may also have been a factor.

The first mutual life insurance corporation established in the United States was the Corporation for the Relief of the Poor and Distressed Presbyterian Ministers and for the Poor and Distressed Widows and Children of Presbyterian Ministers, organized in 1759 in Philadelphia by the synod of the Presbyterian Church. The insurer is the oldest life insurer in continued existence in the world, although known today by the (mercifully) shorter title of Presbyterian Ministers' Fund. Other well-known mutual life insurers founded during the early nineteenth century included The New England Mutual Life Insurance Company, founded in 1835 in Boston. It had difficulties with the Massachusetts legislature, however, which prevented it from writing insurance until 1843. In the meantime, in 1842, the Mutual Life Insurance Company of New York was founded, followed by the Mutual Benefit Life Insurance Company of New Jersey in 1845. Mutual companies were popular during this period, until the New York legislature, at the

---

[9] In 1866 the Amicable merged with the Norwich Union, which still exists today.

[10] Nelli, p. 17.

[11] After 1900 many small mutual benefit societies were formed among the millions of young immigrants from Germany, Russia, Italy, and the Balkan states. The youth of these new arrivals made assessment insurance attractive, but, in time, as their average age increased, these societies, too, fell prey to the ills of such organizations and failed, except for those that changed into fraternals with level premiums and reserves.

[12] O'Donnell, pp. 624–25.

prompting of the established mutuals in 1849,[13] required all insurers to place a $100,000 security deposit with the state. At that time such an amount was large enough effectively to preclude the creation of further mutual insurers.

## EARLY PROPRIETARY INSURERS

The right to receive rent from land, and to transfer this right to others, was well established before Roman times. A landowner, for a consideration, could transfer the rent or income from a designated farm or landholding to a beneficiary, who might receive this rent in money or in kind for life or for a specified time. It was but a short step from life rents based upon land to annuities based upon the grantor's solvency. Governments, as well as monasteries and other religious organizations, used the sale of annuities as fund-raising devices. The religious prohibition against usury made the annuity a favored device for borrowing large sums.

In fact, in 1689, Louis XIV of France used an annuity scheme devised by Lorenzo Tonti—hence the term **tontine**—to raise needed funds for the state. From the amounts contributed by the participants, a sum was set aside yearly to grant an annuity for life to the participants. As participants died and their attendant annuity obligations ceased, ever larger annuity amounts from the yearly sum became available to the survivors. The longer one lived, the larger grew the annuity payout. Other governments and private promoters continued this scheme almost into the twentieth century, when it was outlawed.

*Individual Underwriters.* The earliest proprietary insurers were individual underwriters who either alone or in concert with others assumed various life insurance risks. Contracts were of short duration; they were seldom as long as a year. Obviously, long-term life insurance contracts could not be satisfactorily underwritten by individuals. The insured could not be assured that he or she would outlive the insurer.

It was during this early time that the practice of individuals writing their names under the amount of risk that they were willing to bear arose. Hence, **underwriting** was born, and the person making the contract became known as the **underwriter**.

Some early underwriters apparently were not always eager to meet their obligations. A 1584 dispute, the earliest on record, illustrates how the meaning of words can be of critical importance in a life insurance contract. A life insurance contract was issued on June 15, 1583, by the office of insurance within the Royal Exchange, for £383 6s 9d on the life of William Gybbons for a term of 12 months. Thirteen individuals served as underwriters of the contract. The premium was £75. The insured died shortly before the expiration of one year. The insurers refused to pay on the grounds that *their* intended 12 months were the *shorter* lunar months, not the more common *calendar* months. On this basis, the policy

[13] Nelli, p. 20.

had expired. Mr. Gybbons' heirs brought suit against the underwriters. Not surprisingly, they prevailed.

*European Life Insurers.* Life insurance in the modern sense did not thrive until the capitalistic corporate device gained acceptance and mathematicians developed the theory of probability and actuarial science. In 1803, The Globe was organized as a stock company by Sir Richard Glyn, one of the promoters of The Equitable. The first life insurance company in France was founded in 1787, but it failed in 1792. The Compagnie d'Assurance Générales sur la Vie was founded December 29, 1819; it was followed by others, all of them stock companies and all successful. The first proprietary life insurer in Germany appears to have been the Deutsche Lebenversicherungs Gesellschaft, founded in 1828. It seems to have issued participating insurance. The Prudential (U.K.), formed in 1848, was the pioneer in industrial insurance, which it began to market about 1853.

*Asian Life Insurers.* It is interesting to note that the craftsmen's guilds developed in Japan during the Tokugawa period (1600–1868) evolved into organizations quite similar to the guilds of Western Europe. The first life insurance company to open for business in Japan was the Meiji Life Assurance Company, a stock corporation.[14] After seven years of monopoly by Meiji Life Assurance, two other modern life insurance companies were established. Teikoku Life Assurance Company was established in 1888 and Nippon Life Assurance Company Limited began in Oska in July, 1889.[15] Many other stock companies followed, and life insurance spread throughout Japan as a result of the impact of World War II and the postwar occupation policies of the Allied forces ordering the dissolution of the *zaibatsu*.[16] Most major companies converted to mutual life insurers.

Japanese and British insurers played a significant role in the development of life insurance in other Asian countries. In Korea, for example, British companies were most active in the insurance business until Japan gained complete control of Korea in 1905. The Cho-Sun Life Insurance Company, established in 1921, was the only company capitalized and owned by Koreans. The modern Korean life insurance industry really began in the 1960s.

In Singapore, British and other foreign companies played a major role in the development of the life insurance business. The domestic Singapore life insurance industry was born in 1908 with the establishment of the Great Eastern Life Assurance Company Limited to compete with the overseas companies.[17] The industry's major development has occurred since 1965.

[14] *The 100-Year History of Nippon Life* (Tokyo: The Nippon Life Insurance Company, 1991), p. 5.

[15] Ibid, p. 16.

[16] Conglomerates controlling vast amounts of capital and major parts of the Japanese economy, including financial institutions.

[17] Allen J. Pathmarajah, "Growth and Development of the Singapore Life Insurance Market and Its Future Outlook," *The Singapore Insurance Industry – Historical Perspective, Growth and Future Outlook* (Singapore:Singapore Insurance Training Centre, 1985), p. 195.

***Early U.S. Insurers.*** The growth of insurance in the American colonies was hampered by the earlier-mentioned monopoly on corporate insurers granted by the English Crown in 1720. This monopoly had a strong negative effect on insurance, since it prohibited the formation of new corporate insurers and few, if any, individuals in the colonies were knowledgeable or rich enough then to compete as individual underwriters with the London insurers.[18]

The earliest-located record of individual underwriters in the colonies was an advertisement of an insurance office opening that appeared in a 1721 edition of Philadelphia's *American Weekly Mercury*.[19] This insurance office is believed to have been for nonlife insurance.

The first corporate life insurer in the American colonies was the Presbyterian Minsters' Fund mentioned earlier. The first *proprietary* corporate insurer in the United States was founded after independence; it was the Insurance Company of North America, chartered in Pennsylvania on April 14, 1794. Originally organized to sell annuities, it changed its plans before applying for a charter. Its charter permitted it to do a general insurance business, including life. In five years only six life policies were issued, so the company discontinued its life insurance business in 1804.

The Pennsylvania Company for the Insurance on Lives and Granting Annuities, chartered in 1812, was the first North American insurer organized for the sole purpose of selling life insurance and annuities to the general public and the first that sold an appreciable volume of insurance.[20] The first policy was issued in 1813. In 1872 it discontinued its insurance business. The Massachusetts Hospital Life Insurance Company was founded in 1818, and the New York Life and Trust Company in 1830. The latter company is notable as the first insurer to employ agents. All three companies were stock companies that later discontinued their insurance business and continued as banks or trust companies.

The Girard Life Insurance, Annuity and Trust Company of Philadelphia, established in 1836, used a new principle of granting policyowners participation in its profits, although it was a stock company. The first policy dividends were allotted in 1844 as additions of insurance to policies in force three or more years.

As discussed above, the 1840s were marked by the rise and popularity of mutual insurers, but the New York deposit law hampered the formation of new mutuals. In the process, it opened the way for new stock companies. From 1853

---

[18] E. W. Patterson, *The Insurance Commissioner in the United States* (Cambridge: Harvard University Press, 1927), p. 522.

[19] In those days, a group of individual underwriters would form an **office of insurance**, where underwriters and applicants for insurance could meet and negotiate and where records of insurance transactions and contracts could be maintained. The name was retained after companies were formed as a designation of the company's main office. The name is still used today in many countries to designate an insurer, especially in the United Kingdom and its former colonies. The U.S. term **home office**—used to designate the insurer's main office—evolved from this usage.

[20] Gene A. Morton, *Principles of Life and Health Insurance* (Atlanta, Ga: Life Office Management Association, 1984), pp. 12–13.

until 1865, 41 new stock insurers were organized. Of these, only 11 survived. The Equitable Life Assurance Society of the United States, one of the survivors, was founded as a stock insurer in New York in 1859. In 1869 its president, Henry B. Hyde, revived the use of the tontine concept. The venture, highly successful for a time, is said to have precipitated one of the most competitive battles in U.S. life insurance history.[21]

## MILESTONES IN U.S. LIFE AND HEALTH INSURANCE

Numerous other historical events have influenced the shape today of the U.S. life insurance market; a few of the more important are highlighted below.

On the actuarial front, notable events include the preparation and publication in 1789 by Harvard Professor Edward Wigglesworth of a modified mortality table based on Massachusetts experience. This table permitted the first computation in the U.S. of premiums and reserves on a scientific basis.

Elizur Wright's 1853 publication of life policy valuation tables must also be considered a milestone in the progression of U.S. actuarial practice. Wright's early actuarial work undoubtedly helped shape U.S. life insurance practice, but the imprint he left on U.S. insurance regulation was perhaps even more important. He was the first insurance regulator of Massachusetts, and his progressive regulatory style led to numerous changes, including the use of nonforfeiture values.

Other significant actuarial events include the 1868 publication of the American Experience Table of Mortality. Developed from mortality experience from 1843 to 1858 and first used in 1861, this table was widely used until the 1940s.

Actuarial developments were a necessary precondition of life insurance product innovation. Product innovation, however, perhaps received its greatest impetus from an ever-expanding view of the role that life insurers could play in the provision of family economic security. The continued industrialization of the United States brought about a decreasing reliance on the family for economic security and more reliance on the individual's own, and his or her employer's, initiatives.

Indeed, it was during the industrializing nineteenth and early twentieth centuries that most of the principles that today underpin U.S. life insurance company practices and operations were developed and that witnessed the introduction of all of today's basic life insurance product forms. An early market catalyst dates from 1875 when the Prudential Insurance Company of America introduced industrial life insurance in the United States.[22] By 1879, the John Hancock Mutual Life Insurance Company and the Metropolitan Life Insurance

---

[21] O'Donnell, p. 174.

[22] The Prudential was incorporated as a stock company in 1873 as The Widows and Orphans Friendly Society. Its present name was assumed in 1877.

Company were also selling industrial life insurance. Although of little economic importance today, industrial life insurance and its debit marketing system can be credited with greatly enhancing public awareness of life insurance in the United States, and at one time industrial life comprised as much as one-fifth of all U.S. life insurance in force.

Details about the evolution of other individually issued life insurance products are provided in the chapters that follow. Group-based products evolved at a slower pace. Even so, the U.S. evolution may be contrasted with that in other countries where government-sponsored social insurance programs tended to be preferred to employer-sponsored programs.

Although the American Express Company established the first pension plan in U.S. industry in 1875, not until 1921 was the first insured pension plan issued—by the Metropolitan Life Insurance Company. The first group life insurance for employees was written in 1911 by The Equitable for Montgomery Ward and Company. The Prudential was a pioneer in credit life insurance and issued the first policy of this kind in 1928.

Government has had a significant role in shaping the U.S. life insurance business. Since early U.S. insurance was largely a local issue, it was natural that the states should have been more involved in insurance regulation than the U.S. federal government. At first, regulatory restrictions were incorporated into the charters that were granted to insurance companies by the state. Later, regulations on audits, investments, taxation, and licensing were by legislative action. Massachusetts and New York, leading regulatory states, enacted comprehensive insurance regulations in 1855 and 1859, respectively. Modern state regulation is usually associated with the appointment in 1858 of Elizur Wright as insurance commissioner of Massachusetts.[23]

The U.S. Supreme Court, in an 1869 case that challenged the rights of states to regulate insurance, confirmed the province of the states in insurance regulatory matters.[24] The Court held that since insurance was not commerce, it could not be subject to the prohibitions in the U.S. Constitution against states interfering with interstate commerce.

In the unrestrained climate of laissez-faire and frenzied finance of the late nineteenth century, life insurers found themselves accused of unscrupulous and unethical, if not illegal, practices. This led in 1905 to the so-called **Armstrong Investigation** in New York state. This investigation and its 1906 report are watershed events in U.S. insurance regulation. Other states were led to conduct similar investigations, resulting in massive changes in insurance laws throughout the United States. The report identified numerous life insurer practices deemed to be unsound and dishonest. First-year agents' commissions were judged to be often excessive; the remedy was a limitation on commissions (still in effect in New York). The practice of paying policy dividends only after five or 10 policy

[23] Nelli, p. 29.
[24] See *Paul v. Virginia* in Chap. 34.

years led to unrealistic policy illustrations and, so it was considered, to an inequitable distribution of surplus; the remedy was to outlaw such tontine-like dividends and to require an annual distribution of surplus and limitations on mutual insurer surplus accumulation (still the law in New York and in most other states). Exorbitant sums were spent on insurer lobbying activities and on executive salaries; greater disclosure via an annual statement and expense and salary limitations were the answers. Numerous other changes were required of companies, including a requirement that all policies contain certain standard provisions.

The Armstrong Investigation's repercussions were profound. The larger insurers, who bore the brunt of the report's criticisms, lost substantial market share. New insurers were created and benefited at the expense of the large insurers; growth of new insurers in the midwest United States was aided. The report's criticisms centered on stock life insurers. As a result, three of the then largest U.S. stock insurers—The Equitable, the Metropolitan, and the Prudential—converted to the mutual form of insurance shortly thereafter.

The 1930s were difficult years for the life insurance business. Numerous insurer real estate investments proved unsound during these difficult economic times. Bond defaults rose to new heights. Fewer favorable opportunities to reinvest rollover funds existed as interest rates fell to new contemporary lows. Despite the failure during this period of literally hundreds of depository institutions, relatively few failures occurred among life insurers. Dr. McCahan's detailed investigation, covering the 23-year period from 1909 to 1932, showed that "the average annual loss to policyowners during those 23 years did not exceed 29 cents for every $1,000 of net reserve."[25]

Besides its role as regulator, government also can be a competitor. The 1935 enactment of the Social Security Act and its subsequent amendments provided various life, health, and retirement benefits to the vast majority of U.S. citizens.[26] In doing so, the role of the private insurance mechanism in the United States was circumscribed.

The important role of the U.S. court system in affecting insurance regulation was perhaps most dramatically evidenced by the 1944 U.S. Supreme Court decision that reversed the 1869 view that had exempted insurance from federal government scrutiny.[27] By a one-vote majority, the court ruled that insurance was, indeed, commerce and, to the extent that transactions crossed state lines, it was interstate commerce. As such, the federal government had jurisdiction.

The prospects of the federal government substituting for the states was shocking to most in the insurance industry. Almost a century of relatively cozy

---

[25] S. S. Huebner and David McCahan, "The Solvency Record of Life Insurance," Chap. 7 in *Life Insurance as an Investment* (New York: Appleton-Century-Crofts, 1933).

[26] See Chap. 25.

[27] See *Southeastern Underwriters Association* case in Chap. 34.

state regulation could be swept away. The response was enactment by the U.S. Congress of the McCarran-Ferguson Act in 1945.[28] This act, while requiring a strengthening of the state regulatory system, provided that the states should continue to be the primary regulators of insurance and that insurance should remain generally exempt from federal antitrust laws. The states remain today the primary insurance regulators, although pressures exist for change and the federal government's regulatory role has expanded greatly since 1945.[29]

The 1950s and 1960s have been characterized as the Golden Age for U.S. life insurers.[30] The life insurance business had become a major supplier of funds to the U.S. capital markets. Whole life policies with high margins (by today's standards) were the backbone of the business. Relatively little price competition, coupled with a largely complacent insurance-buying public, ensured that even inefficient insurers could survive and make a profit.

The late 1960s witnessed the rise of consumerism. The Golden Age had ended. The realities of a changed environment crept slowly into life insurer managements and regulators throughout the 1970s. For those who may have questioned whether a new era had truly dawned, the 1980s and early 1990s removed all doubt.

## LIFE INSURERS AS FINANCIAL INSTITUTIONS

Life insurance companies have grown to be major financial institutions and play a correspondingly important role as financial intermediaries. This section provides an overview of that contemporary role.

### Nature of Life Insurance Company Investment Activity

As shown earlier, under cash-value life insurance the insurer, in effect, retains portions of the premiums paid during the early policy years and accumulates them, together with investment earnings on them, toward the payment of benefits in later years. As the rate of return on invested assets increases and other things being equal, the company can lower the premiums it charges for new or existing policies, increase the dividends or other nonguaranteed benefits it credits on existing policies, or both. Since premium rates and net costs are important competitive considerations, the investment function is a significant factor in a company's competitive position. This investment activity establishes the life insurance business as a significant factor in the capital markets.

*Sources of Investable Funds.* In a life insurance company, investable funds arise from both insurance and investment operations. The cash flow from insurance operations arises from the difference between cash receipts (premiums, annuity considerations, and other deposits) and cash disbursements (benefits and

---

[28] See Chap. 34.

[29] See Chap. 34.

[30] Buist M. Anderson, *Anderson on Life Insurance* (Boston: Little, Brown and Company, 1991), p. 16.

expenses). The cash flow from existing investments develops from current income (earnings from net interest, dividends, and realized capital gains), maturities, prepayments, redemptions, calls, and sales.

A close relationship exists between these two sources of investable funds. Part of each premium payment becomes available for investment in the economy. In calculating premiums, anticipated investment earnings are taken into account, thereby reducing the price of life insurance.

In 1991 total income of all U.S. life companies was $411.0 billion, with 64.2 percent from premium receipts and 28.9 percent from investment earnings. The remaining 6.9 percent was from other sources. As Figure 3-1 shows, the distribution of income for the U.S. life insurance business has shifted over the past three decades, with the investment income component growing relative to premium income.

Moreover, a significant shift has occurred within the premium category, as Figure 3-2 demonstrates. In 1960 life insurance premiums accounted for 69.1 percent of total premium income. By 1990 this proportion had dropped to 29.0 percent. As can be seen, annuity considerations have grown spectacularly.

***Magnitude of Investment Activity.*** The magnitude of life insurance company investment activity can best be illustrated by considering the figures in Table 3-2. On December 31, 1991, the assets of all U.S. life insurance companies approximated $1,551.2 billion, a 10.2 percent increase over the 1990 figure. The rapid growth of the annuity business (including guaranteed investment contracts —

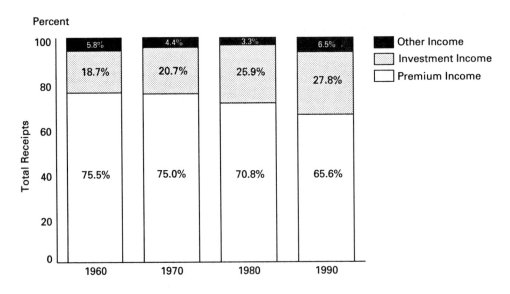

**FIGURE 3-1**

**THE MAJOR COMPONENTS OF U.S. LIFE INSURER INCOME: DISTRIBUTION OF TOTAL INCOME**

*Source:* ACLI

**FIGURE 3-2**

**THE CHANGING NATURE OF U.S. LIFE INSURER PREMIUM INCOME: DISTRIBUTION OF PREMIUM INCOME**

*Source:* ACLI

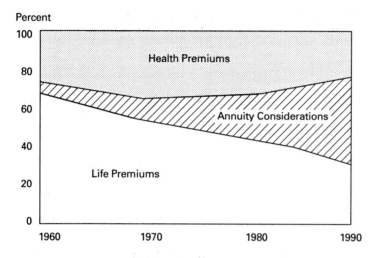

GICs) in recent years has been a major factor in recent asset growth. As large as the 1991 asset increase may seem, companies made investments far in excess of that figure because of rollovers (reinvestments at maturity) and funds flowing from the sale and redemption of securities and mortgage-loan principal amortization and prepayments.

Through life insurance company investment operations, another pooling arrangement comes into play. Millions of policyowners, contributing relatively

**TABLE 3-2**

**TOTAL ADMITTED ASSETS OF U.S. LIFE INSURANCE COMPANIES (MILLIONS)**

| Year | Amount |
| --- | --- |
| 1900 | $    1,742 |
| 1910 | 3,876 |
| 1920 | 7,320 |
| 1930 | 18,880 |
| 1940 | 30,802 |
| 1950 | 64,020 |
| 1960 | 119,576 |
| 1965 | 158,884 |
| 1970 | 207,254 |
| 1975 | 289,304 |
| 1980 | 479,210 |
| 1985 | 825,901 |
| 1991 | 1,551,201 |

*Source:* ACLI

small amounts of premiums annually, create a fund to be invested by professional investors. So invested, the funds provide the financial basis for more and better homes, utility systems, and schools, and for a more rapidly advancing technological base.

*Types of Life Insurer Investments.* Assets of life insurance companies back life and health insurance and annuity obligations and are built from policyowners' premiums and investment earnings. Figure 3-3 shows the magnitude and distribution of assets of U.S. life insurers for 1970 and 1990. The largest component of life insurance company assets in 1990 was corporate debt issues, whereas, in 1970, mortgages were the largest segment.

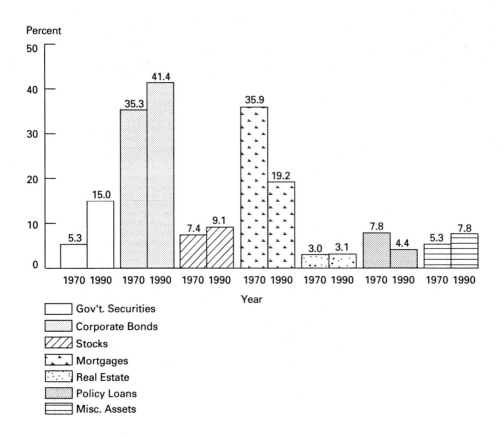

**FIGURE 3-3**

**DISTRIBUTION OF ASSETS OF U.S. LIFE INSURANCE COMPANIES**

*Source*: ACLI

## LIFE INSURANCE COMPANY INVESTMENT PERFORMANCE

The rate of return on invested assets is considered a key criterion in measuring life insurer performance. The **portfolio rate of return** is the weighted average of investments made over time at different rates of return. This composite rate is a summary measure of past and current investment results. Figure 3-4 illustrates the average net rates of return earned by U.S. life insurance companies over the years. These rates exclude income tax and, it is important to note, capital gains and losses. For some companies, such gains and losses have a material effect on overall investment performance. Individual company performance, naturally, varies both above and below the average for the industry.

Since the rate of return is a weighted average of returns on investments made in different time periods, the rate is clearly influenced by the timing of cash flows with respect to market interest rates. The portfolio rate of return is determined by factors that, in the short run, are largely out of the control of present investment officers; for this reason, the rate of return on new investments is an additional and important criterion for measuring investment performance.

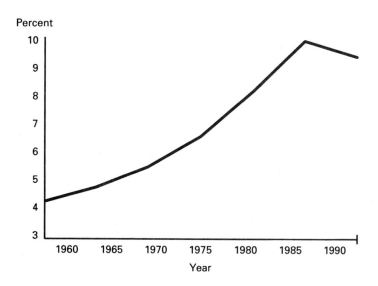

**FIGURE 3-4**

**NET INVESTMENT RETURNS FOR U.S. LIFE INSURANCE COMPANIES**

*Source*: ACLI

# LIFE AND HEALTH INSURANCE OWNERSHIP IN THE UNITED STATES

## LIFE INSURANCE OWNERSHIP

Life insurance in force in the United States reached a new high of $9,986.3 billion at the end of 1991—a 6.3 percent increase over 1990. Some 70 percent of adults in the United States own some form of life insurance; the overwhelming majority of them are insured through commercial life insurance companies.

If this amount were divided equally among all U.S. households, each would have had $102,700 of protection at year-end 1991. Excluding families without life insurance, the average for insured households was about $126,800. Despite significant increases in the amount of coverage, protection for all households equaled only about two years of disposable personal income per household.

The number of annuities in force with U.S. life insurance companies under individual and supplementary contracts totaled 18.4 million at the end of 1991. Individual annuities accounted for 17.3 million of this total.

## HEALTH INSURANCE OWNERSHIP

At the end of 1989, over 214 million U.S. citizens were protected by one or more forms of health care coverage. This figure includes over 189 million persons covered by some form of private health insurance. Approximately three in five in the 65-and-older population held private health insurance policies to supplement benefits available through Medicare. Regrettably, some 37 million U.S. citizens had neither private nor public health care financing available to them—a cause of great concern to public policymakers and insurers.[31]

Various forms of private health insurance coverage are available from different types of insurers: commercial insurance companies, hospital and medical service plans such as Blue Cross and Blue Shield, group medical plans operating on a prepayment basis such as health maintenance organizations, and others. Chapter 27 includes more information on the types and operations of health insurers.

Over 1,000 commercial insurance companies in the United States write individual or group health insurance coverage, or both. Health insurance coverage made available by insurance companies may be divided into two categories—medical expense insurance and disability income insurance. Medical expense insurance is reimbursement-type coverage that provides benefits that can cover virtually all expenses connected with medical care and related services. Disability income insurance provides periodic payments when the insured is unable to work as a result of sickness or injury.

Blue Cross and Blue Shield plans are nonprofit member plans that service statewide and other geographical areas, offering both individual and group

[31]See Chap. 27.

coverage. Blue Cross plans provide hospital care benefits on essentially a service-type basis, under which the organization, through a separate contract with member hospitals, reimburses the hospital for covered services provided to the insured. Blue Shield plans provide benefits for surgical and medical services performed by a physician. The typical Blue Shield plan provides benefits similar to those provided under the benefit provisions of hospital-surgical policies issued by insurance companies.

Health care coverage is also provided through health maintenance organizations (HMOs), which provide comprehensive health care services for their members for a fixed periodic payment. In such plans, health care professionals furnish needed care as specified in the contract to subscribers.[32]

## LIFE INSURANCE INTERNATIONALLY

Although this text's material is oriented toward U.S. life insurance, all of the principles and the great majority of the practices outlined herein are of universal application. Only details vary from culture to culture. As a consequence, U.S. readers are cautioned to avoid ascribing a "Made in the USA" label to this text's material.

The chapter introduction hinted at the relative economic importance of life insurance in national economies, and the section on life insurance history sets the evolution of life insurance in an international context. Even so, they fall short in terms of providing an overview of the importance of life insurance inter nationally.

### THE EXTENT AND IMPORTANCE OF LIFE INSURANCE WORLDWIDE

Figure 3-5 gives a world breakdown of the premium income for the life business. Thus, the Americas (both North America and Latin America) accounted for almost one-third of the total world life premium volume in 1990. The European share, at 31.4 percent, and the Asian share, at 33.8 percent, are growing at a more rapid rate than the North American (U.S. and Canada) share, with the European share expected to exceed that of the Americas in the future. The continued economic integration of the European Community countries has spurred economic development generally and, therefore, insurance development in particular.

Life insurance internationally behaves as a so-called **superior good**—a service or product whose sales expand at a rate greater than that of general economic expansion. In other words, for each one percent of economic growth, life insurance premium growth within an economy typically exceeds one percent. This observation is consistent with expectations that, as an economy develops, life insurance products are both more appreciated and needed.

---

[32] See Chap. 27 for more information about the various health care financing media.

**FIGURE 3-5**

**WORLDWIDE PREMIUM INCOME FROM THE LIFE BUSINESS BY CONTINENT FOR 1990.**

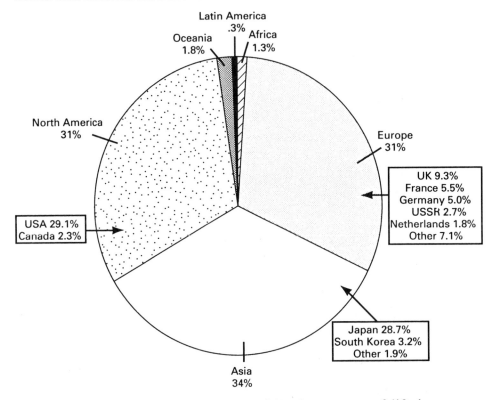

Life insurance density, as measured by the average of life insurance premiums paid per head of population, varies substantially, depending primarily on the absolute level of economic development. Thus the average Japanese citizen paid the equivalent of $1,645.45 in 1990 to life insurance companies. Switzerland was second, at $1,635.09 per capita, and Finland was third. Figure 3-6 shows the premiums per capita for 64 countries. Although the figures tend to increase each year, the relative positions of the countries do not change greatly from year to year.

## THE ROLE OF INTERGOVERNMENTAL ORGANIZATIONS

So important is insurance generally that several important intergovernmental organizations have permanent insurance-related mandates. Thus the **European Community (EC)** continues to adopt insurance directives, the intent of which is both to harmonize insurance regulation and to eliminate regulatory inefficiencies that hinder competition among the EC member countries.[33] The agreement in

---

[33] The EC, established in 1957 by the **Treaty of Rome**, had 12 members as of 1993. The 12 countries were Belgium, Denmark, France, Germany, Greece, Ireland, Italy, Luxembourg, The Netherlands, Portugal, Spain, and the United Kingdom. Austria, Finland, Sweden, and Turkey have applied for membership, and other countries are expected to do so.

**FIGURE 3-6**
**LIFE PREMIUMS PER CAPITA INTERNATIONALLY (IN U.S. DOLLARS)**

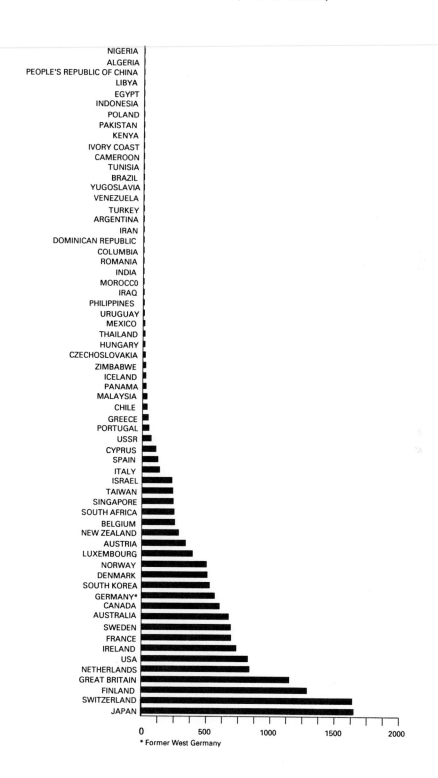

* Former West Germany

principle between the EC and the **European Free Trade Association** (EFTA) jointly to form a **European Economic Area** and for the EFTA countries to follow many EC directives, suggests the potential for an even more important role for the EC.[34] The EC countries write about 25 percent of the world's life insurance, with EFTA countries writing another 4 percent.[35]

Certain aspects of the codes of the **Organization for Economic Cooperation and Development (OECD)** set out obligations of member countries to liberalize their insurance markets progressively and to avoid discrimination against foreign insurers doing business within their markets.[36] The OECD's Insurance Committee conducts studies on and debates various regulatory issues of importance to life insurance. OECD countries, which are the most developed internationally, account for an estimated 90 percent of the world's life insurance premium volume.[37]

The **United Nations Conference on Trade and Development (UNCTAD)** assists developing countries through research, publications, seminars, and technical assistance. The UNCTAD is the only United Nations entity with a specific and permanent insurance mandate.

Negotiations under the auspices of the **General Agreement on Tariffs and Trade (GATT)** may produce an international agreement that covers financial services, including insurance. Such an agreement would bind signatory governments to have nondiscriminatory, clear, and publicly available regulatory rules and procedures. A successful outcome of these negotiations would undoubtedly cause numerous countries, including the United States, to change certain elements of insurance regulation.

With the growing internationalization of markets generally and financial services markets in particular, one can expect the role of intergovernmental organizations to grow. Just as national markets have agreed-upon rules and regulations, so too can international markets be expected to continue to evolve rules and regulations. No single country's government can reasonably be expected to establish and enforce international rules.

## THE ADVANTAGES OF AN INTERNATIONAL INSURANCE PERSPECTIVE[38]

The term **international insurance** traditionally is considered to encompass cross-border insurance transactions and ownership, insurance in connection with international transportation, and international reinsurance. Cross-border insurance transactions arise when an insurer is domiciled in a country different

---

[34] The seven EFTA countries are Austria, Finland, Iceland, Liechtenstein, Norway, Sweden, and Switzerland.

[35] *Sigma*, Swiss Reinsurance Company.

[36] The 24 OECD member countries include all EC and EFTA members, except Liechtenstein, plus Australia, Canada, Cyprus, Japan, New Zealand, and the United States.

[37] *Sigma*, Swiss Reinsurance Company.

[38] This section draws in part on the *International Insurance Society Value Statement*.

from that of the insured. Insurers and insureds not involved in international insurance as defined here (and the vast majority are not so involved) too often believe that understanding insurance practices and issues of other cultures is of little or no relevance to them. This view is myopic.

Life insurance products and the way they are sold in various markets naturally differ to suit each country's cultural, regulatory, tax, and economic environment. Yet term life insurance is still fundamentally limited-duration protection whether it is sold in Canada or Finland, and endowments are still high-value maturity instruments whether they are sold in Japan or Spain.

The operations of insurers around the world have numerous features in common. Although business environments vary dramatically, insurers in diverse markets often find themselves facing similar challenges. By exchanging ideas on how to meet these challenges, insurers can benefit themselves and their markets.

Insurance remains largely a local business, with nonlocal ownerships becoming increasingly common. Domestic companies and domestic subsidiaries of foreign-based insurers dominate many national insurance markets. Within any country market, products tend to be similar and distribution channels typically include some combination of exclusive agents, independent agents, direct response, and banks or securities firms. Insurers invest most of their funds domestically, yet lay off excess risk to reinsurers, many of whom are international. Governments set tax policy, approve policy forms (and, in some cases, rates), define the limits of the insurance activities of other financial institutions, and exercise surveillance over the financial condition and market conduct of insurers.

Notwithstanding these common features, each insurance market has evolved in its unique way. Many factors have shaped this evolution. For example:

- Variations in the importance of the concept of insurance in particular markets and the size of national economies have dictated how quickly local markets have grown and matured.

- Governments have shaped aspects of the industry through tax policies, financial requirements, social policies, and restrictions on other financial institutions.

- In some markets, cartels determine the rates (although their influence is steadily waning); in other markets, rate-making organizations prevail.

- The natural and social exposures within country markets—health care quality, life-style, litigation climate, exposure to catastrophes, quality of law enforcement—all shape a culture's security perceptions.

Any insurer concerned about trends in distribution channels, the potential role of banks and insurance companies, the erosion of cartels, or the impact of new products can invariably find country markets in which the change has already occurred and empirical evidence on the approaches that successful companies have used. Thus idea transfer across country markets represents a major opportunity for insurance companies interested in improving performance within their own markets.

Insurers around the world confront many of the same competitive threats. For example, insurers concerned with changes in tax laws affecting their products can look to the United States, where sales of single-premium life declined after some tax benefits ended, but where sales of retirement annuities consequently grew. In one European country, many expect the removal of tax benefits for single-premium products to boost sales of group and pension products.

Insurance companies can also learn from their international counterparts about strategies for lowering costs and improving productivity. One European company added a direct market channel to its branch office operations to spur new business development. A Japanese company creatively used technology to make its large sales force more productive. A U.S. company transformed its career agents into successful sellers of annuities. It took a new approach by targeting the middle-income market—rather than the traditional upper-income buyers of annuities—and markets that are less accessible to brokerage.

Terminology variations often create unnecessary barriers to understanding and, therefore, sometime inhibit one market from benefiting fully from the innovations of another. Variable life insurance in the United States is quite similar in functioning to unit-trust-linked life insurance in the United Kingdom. While British insurers provide **bonuses** on **with-profit policies**, U.S. and many non-Commonwealth country insurers pay **dividends** on **participating policies**. The ability of one market or insurer to benefit from the experience of other markets and other insurers is perhaps the greatest, if most overlooked, advantage of taking an international perspective of the business.

## LIFE INSURANCE AND THE INDIVIDUAL

The preceding section has highlighted the almost universal appreciation of life insurance. Aside from the advantage of providing financial protection for individuals, families, and businesses in each market, life and health insurance also benefit policyowners in other important ways.[39] The policyowner, in other words, can be considered a "beneficiary" under his or her own life and health insurance. A number of potential advantages deserve special mention in this respect.

### CAN ASSIST IN MAKING SAVINGS POSSIBLE

One occasionally hears those who argue that they prefer to save rather than purchase life insurance. Certainly, good savings habits should be encouraged, but

---

[39] Most of the advantages that follow were first taken from S. S. Huebner, *Economics of Life Insurance,* 3rd ed. (New York: Apppleton-Century-Crofts, 1959), pp. 143–240. As presented here, they represent modifications of the ones originally postulated by Dr. Huebner.

saving involves time, resources, and discipline. A savings program can yield only a small amount at the start, whereas an insurance policy guarantees the full face value or income benefit from its beginning, and, thus it can hedge the policyowner against failure through early death or disability to have sufficient working time to save adequately through other means. Thus if one is able to save $1,000 annually, it would take nearly 16 years to accumulate a fund of $25,000, assuming that the accumulations are safely invested annually at 6.0 percent compound interest. Even at that, an individual's ability to accumulate such a savings fund is contingent upon his or her survival for the full period and may be defeated by death or disability before the savings have reached any appreciable sum.

To depend entirely on saving as a means of providing for the future could prove disastrous financially. It is generally accepted that the first requisite in providing for the future support of dependents is reasonable certainty. Life and health insurance (or a rich and sharing relative!) serve as a hedge against the possible failure to continue the annual accumulations of the savings fund because of early death or disability. Through life and health insurance, a fund of $25,000 can be assured in any case.

## CAN FURNISH A SAFE AND PROFITABLE INVESTMENT

In addition to guaranteeing an immediate estate, some life insurance policies contain a savings element that can reach large proportions in later policy years. Life insurance policies and annuities are admirably adapted as accumulation devices and, with careful selection, can be reasonable, long-term savings instruments. The fact that interest credited to qualified policy cash values is tax deferred enhances the attractiveness of the contract as a savings vehicle.

Life insurance and annuities can furnish a profitable and safe investment service, but life insurance policies also make it possible for the policyowner to arrange for the safeguarding of the policy death proceeds for the benefit of the beneficiaries. Too often funds provided to heirs through life insurance death proceeds are lost by the beneficiary through speculation, unwise investments, or excessive, unnecessary expenditures. Sound financial planning suggests that such a contingency should be contemplated by the individual and can be discouraged or even prevented through judicious use of life insurance settlement options and trusts and in various other ways.

## CAN ENCOURAGE THRIFT

Life insurance can constitute an excellent means of encouraging thrift for many persons. Many persons who might not otherwise save regularly will nevertheless regularly pay premiums on a life insurance policy. If the policy is of the type that has a cash value, this can constitute a type of semicompulsory savings plan.

## CAN MINIMIZE WORRY AND INCREASE INITIATIVE

Writers have frequently asserted that life and health insurance can be regarded, not so much as producers of wealth, but as mechanisms for distributing funds from the fortunate to the unfortunate. In reality, life and health insurance can be important forces in the production of wealth, in that they can relieve the policyowner of worry and increase his or her efficiency. Constant worry can inhibit productivity. To the extent that concern about the financial consequences of loss of life or health causes an individual uncertainty and worry, life and health insurance could help reduce this concern.

## CAN AFFORD PROTECTION AGAINST CLAIMS OF CREDITORS

Most states have enacted exemption laws that protect life insurance cash values and death benefits from the claims of the insured's or beneficiary's creditors, or both. Frequently, the amount of such exempt insurance is limited to some reasonable amount. In some states, the exemption relates to all policies, without respect to amount or to policyowners' rights to change the beneficiary.

## CAN FURNISH AN ASSURED INCOME IN THE FORM OF ANNUITIES

Annuities can prove valuable to those older persons who have succeeded in saving only a limited amount of capital, and who have no one to whom they particularly care to transfer this sum on death. Assume that a person aged 65 has accumulated $100,000 and that this represents the entire funds available to the individual in his or her retirement years. Because of the limited size of the fund, the owner will be obliged to invest it in a most careful manner. Rates of return for such investments probably would not exceed 5 to 9 percent. Consequently, this individual would be limited to between $5,000 and $9,000 per year from the investment. Nor can he or she afford to take a portion of principal for living expenses, because this would reduce the available annual income in the future. The danger confronting this individual is just the opposite of that facing the person who wants insurance against premature death. The latter wants insurance because it is not known how long he or she will live; the former is confronted with the danger of living too long—that is, of outliving available income.

Just as the man or woman who felt that death or disability might intervene too soon could hedge against that risk, so the owner of the $100,000 fund who feels that the income is too limited or that he or she might outlive this income, can hedge against those risks by buying an annuity. A life annuity is a contract under which an insurance company promises to pay the owner a certain guaranteed minimum income every year for as long as the individual lives, with payment ceasing on death (unless a refund feature had been selected).[40] The life insurance company is able to liquidate both the capital sum and the interest thereon in making these payments. Applying the law of large numbers to the probabilities of survival—instead of probabilities of death as in the case of life insurance—the insurer can further discount the cost of providing an annuity (i.e., guarantee a larger income payment) and, at the same time, guarantee that the annuitant will not outlive the payments.

## CAN HELP PRESERVE AN ESTATE

Many persons will leave substantial estates on their death. In such instances, death taxes can be correspondingly substantial, with, for example, large estates being subject to as much as a 55 percent marginal tax rate in the United States. As explained in Chapter 13, the government expects taxes due to be paid in cash and within a reasonable time period. This payment often requires selling estate assets. Yet the heirs may prefer to retain these assets, either because of a depressed price occasioned by a down market or because of a desire to avoid loss of ownership.

Life insurance can be a natural means of providing funds to pay estate taxes. The heirs can be assured of having sufficient cash from the death proceeds to meet any tax obligations and thereby retain full ownership of estate assets. Chapter 14 outlines arrangements whereby the death proceeds themselves avoid taxation.

## CAN PROVIDE LIVING BENEFITS

Life insurance cash values have always been a source of policy flexibility and, like other savings, prove useful in family emergencies. The policyowner can borrow funds from the life insurance company on the security of the cash value, can surrender the policy for the full cash value, or, in some cases, can obtain portions of the cash value through a partial surrender.

Yet the cash value may not be sufficient to provide meaningful financial help. In recognition of the increased need for life insurance policies to provide enhanced **living benefits**, life insurers in the United States and elsewhere are including **accelerated death benefit** provisions within their policies. As explained in Chapter 7, these benefits permit the policyowner to obtain all or a portion of the death proceeds if the insured has a terminal illness or one of several specified dread diseases. Other such benefit provisions provide monthly long-term-care payments to the insured who, because of a medical condition, requires qualified long-time care. These living options render life insurance policies substantially more flexible today than in past times.

---

[40] See Chap. 7.

## LIFE INSURANCE AND SOCIETY

U.S. life insurance companies have undertaken many programs and projects to demonstrate that besides performing the worthwhile function of risk bearing and risk transfer, they are also good corporate citizens. Some of the programs and projects have involved efforts to improve housing, to create jobs, to hire and train more handicapped and disadvantaged persons, to promote and support community services, and a host of other programs. For example, the insurance industry, which perceives that it has both a social and business responsibility, remains the leading business funder of AIDS education, prevention, and services.

In a private enterprise economy, some would argue that life and health companies do not need to perform functions outside those related directly to the insurers' main corporate objectives. Life insurance companies' social responsibility can be considered as being met, according to some, if they provide fairly priced quality services to the public in an efficient manner. It is not the purpose of this volume to take sides in this debate. It is, however, noteworthy that studies conducted by the OECD and the UNCTAD have highlighted the broad economic and societal advantages that can accrue by having a strong and efficient life insurance market.[41] The UNCTAD study, prepared for developing countries, can help citizens of developed countries to appreciate the too-often neglected importance of life insurance and life insurers in their own economies.The study noted the classical advantages of life insurance:

> Life insurance can serve the interest of developing countries in numerous ways. Individual citizens who purchase life insurance policies provide their families with a measure of protection against the adverse financial consequences of premature death. This can provide individuals with a greater sense of security and can help minimize worry and distress both prior to and after death of a family breadwinner. Life insurance can also serve as a vehicle through which individuals can save money for emergencies and for retirement.[42]

The OECD study, after mentioning some of the same types of benefits, further observes:

> Life insurance is also a means whereby a person can make financial provision for...retirement by contributing regularly to a pension funded by a life insurance company. Private pension arrangements such as these therefore tend to supplement or even displace reliance on a state pension scheme, which many would agree is of benefit to a government.[43]

---

[41] Organization for Economic Cooperation and Development, *Consumers and Life Insurance* (Paris:OECD, 1987), and the United Nations Conference on Trade and Development, *The Promotion of Life Insurance in Developing Countries* (Geneva, Switzerland: UNCTAD, 1982).
[42] UNCTAD, p. iii.
[43] OECD, p. 10.

The study continues with this theme as follows:

> The fact that so many life insurance policies are purchased undoubtedly relieves pressure on the social welfare systems in many states. To that extent, life insurance is an advantage in the context of public finance, and, as a result, is generally viewed with favor by governments. A number of governments acknowledge this in tangible form by granting tax relief [deduction] to policyholders. . . . At this point, tax incentives for life insurance contributions are widespread among OECD member countries.[44]

Note the similarity between the above-listed advantages and those discussed earlier. The reference to developing countries could have as easily been redirected toward developed countries and the reference to OECD countries to non-OECD countries.

The UNCTAD study noted that, in addition to the above advantages, a strong and efficient life insurance market can aid in overall economic development. The following advantages were enumerated:

1. Life insurance can contribute to social stability by permitting individuals to minimize financial stress and worry.
2. Life insurance can reduce the financial burden on the State of caring for the aged and for those made financially destitute because of the death of a family breadwinner.
3. Through the accumulation from thousands of policyholders of small amounts of private savings, life insurers can accumulate sums to be invested in the public and private sectors. This can benefit an economy by creating a source of financing for new businesses, for new homeowners, and for farmers and their equipment.
4. The life insurance business generates employment.
5. Life insurance can permit more favorable credit terms to borrowers—both individuals and businesses—and can decrease the risk of default. Life insurance can also minimize the financial disruption to business caused by the death of key employees and owners.
6. By making available a variety of employee benefit plans...life insurance companies can promote better employee/employer relations and can provide low-cost benefits to a broad spectrum of persons who may otherwise have been unable to obtain such protection.[45]

The UNCTAD study introduction then notes: "Because of the foregoing reasons, the expansion and development of life insurance has been actively encouraged in many countries."[46]

Clearly, therefore, life and health insurance and life insurance companies play a critical role in developed and developing societies. Their importance will likely continue to grow worldwide.

[44] Ibid, p. 10.
[45] UNCTAD, pp. iii, 1–2.
[46] Ibid., p. 2.

# *Chapter 4*

# *INTRODUCTION TO LIFE INSURANCE PRODUCTS AND THEIR ENVIRONMENT*

This chapter and the three succeeding ones present the principal types of individual life insurance and annuity contracts sold in the United States. This chapter begins with an examination of recent life insurance product innovations. After a brief overview of the types of individual life insurance policies, a review of the nature and types of term life and endowment policies follows. Chapter 5 covers the nature and types of the various fixed-premium whole life policies, including variable life and current assumption whole life. Flexible-premium life insurance policies are presented in Chapter 6. Annuities and some special-purpose life insurance policies and benefits are reviewed in Chapter 7.

## RECENT LIFE INSURANCE PRODUCT INNOVATIONS

Before embarking on a presentation of the various types of life insurance policies, it will be instructive to review briefly the environmental influences causing recent and possibly future innovations in life insurance product design, as well as the general nature of innovations to date.

### ENVIRONMENTAL INFLUENCES

No single catalyst causes change within the life insurance business and in product design. Rather, several interrelated forces work simultaneously. Five of these are discussed below.

***Economic Developments***. Insurers in the 1980s witnessed a diversion of premium dollars as consumers perceived better financial opportunities through other savings and investment media. Cash flow problems were created for many insurers as dissatisfied policyowners either surrendered their policies or exercised their rights to obtain policy loans at below-market rates. High inflation rates, large continuing federal budget deficits, and resulting high and volatile interest rates caused existing and prospective policyowners to question whether many older insurance products offered sufficient value and flexibility.

Inflation causes insurance company operating expenses to rise, and, for many companies, this occurred at a time when premium income was static or even declining. In such situations, agency systems become more expensive to maintain and many companies seek alternative means for marketing their products. Additional marketing systems bring further competition to the industry.

In times of significant economic volatility, many consumers seek shorter-term, more liquid investments and avoid longer-term, fixed commitments. Traditional cash-value life insurance products often have been perceived as long-term, fixed commitments, and, therefore, demand for them often shrinks during volatile times.

The continuing internationalization of financial services adds new complexity to economic and regulatory matters. Countries, including the United States, can no longer view themselves as isolated economic islands. Important economic events in Asia and Europe cause economic fluctuations in the Americas, and vice versa. To appreciate this fact, one has but to witness the impact on the U.S. stock and bond markets of swings in interest rates and stock market values in Japan or the European Community.

With increasing internationalization can come increased capital from abroad, product and marketing innovations, and often a different way of managing companies. Increased capital strengthens the financial capacity of insurers and can result in more competition. Product and marketing innovations and different management styles can lead to greater consumer choice and value.

These various economic factors in combination have resulted in the development of new products and  benefits intended to meet the needs of both insurers and policyowners.

***Social and Demographic Change.*** Consumers today are better educated and more demanding. They are better able to discriminate between "good" and "poor" value, and increasingly they are demanding a dollar's worth of benefit for each dollar spent. These heightened expectations, spurred on by little or no growth in personal income for many consumers, have caused them to spend their dollars more carefully.

The net result is that existing and proposed policyowners examine more analytically the quality of existing and proposed policies, and sometimes they find them deficient in light of the new economic realities. Their heightened expectations lead them, quite naturally, to demand better value.

Along with changing consumer expectations has and will continue to come changes in demographics and consumer behavior that affect insurers. For example, the age of first marriage, for both men and women, is increasing in the United States and in many other countries, while the years of higher education lengthen. Married couples who have children—and many choose not to do so—are having fewer. Dual-income families are more common, as are single-parent families. The fitness trend results in healthier prospective insureds, but also sometimes in a perception of less need for life insurance. These trends alter life insurance demand, and insurers must respond appropriately or lose market share.

The U.S. population is aging. Persons in the 50-to-65 age category now represent 14 percent of the U.S. population, and this percentage will increase. More important, they already control one-third of the U.S. disposable income. This group's greatest financial need is for products to provide for old age, and they have the money to spend for these products. Much of the future success of the U.S. life insurance business will hinge on its response to this and to the over-65 age groups' demand.

Roughly one out of every eight persons in the United States is now 65 or older. By the year 2030, approximately one in five persons will be 65 or older—the same ratio as prevails today in the state of Florida. This aging trend, coupled with medical advances, will mean that the demand for nursing home and other types of extended care will grow enormously, for, according to the Health Insurance Association of America, approximately two out of five persons aged 65 or over may need nursing home care. The life insurance industry's response to this need for long-term care and its financing will continue to influence insurance product design and pricing.

*Government.* The role of government in influencing insurer product design, marketing, and other decisions continues to be critical. Governments, on the one hand, seem to support more strongly the notion of less regulatory involvement and to support regulation that promotes competition in the marketplace. This attitude and some concrete actions taken as a result of this attitude, have created a more competitive environment generally, with the life insurance business experiencing these same pressures.

On the other hand, new laws, regulations, and studies routinely render more complex the product design and other tasks of insurers. For example, a quick review of certain U.S. tax laws passed during the 1980s highlights how federal tax laws alone influence product design and marketing decisions:

- The Economic Recovery Tax Act of 1981 permitted workers to claim tax deductions, within limits, for retirement savings (thus increasing demand for life insurer savings products) and reduced or eliminated estate and gift taxes for most persons (thus decreasing demand for life insurance for estate liquidity).
- The Tax Equity and Fiscal Responsibility Act of 1982 imposed a penalty

tax on certain annuity withdrawals (thus decreasing the attractiveness of certain annuities as savings instruments).

- The Deficit Reduction Act of 1984, in addition to significantly changing the basis upon which life insurance companies were taxed, included for the first time a tax-law definition of life insurance for purposes of determining whether a policy qualified for favorable tax treatment. (High savings forms of life insurance generally could not qualify, with the result that most forms of endowment insurance disappeared.)

- The Tax Reform Act of 1986 (TRA '86) eliminated the tax deductibility of individual retirement account contributions for highly paid persons and eliminated the tax advantages of several classes of investments while retaining those for life insurance. (Some insurers designed products and marketing efforts explicitly to take advantage of this situation, thus both increasing sales and drawing congressional attention to a perceived tax abuse, which resulted in further congressional restrictions as embodied in the 1988 tax law cited below.) This Reform Act also phased out the deductibility of interest paid on personal policy loans (thus discouraging such loans, but also discouraging the design and sale of products intended to be financed via policy loans).

- The Technical and Miscellaneous Revenue Act of 1988 created a completely new class of life insurance contracts—so-called modified endowments—which are subject to less favorable taxation rules than those applying to tax-qualified life insurance via TRA'86, but more favorable ones than those applying to life insurance that failed the TRA'86 test. (Thus, insurers had to deal with life insurance policies that, for tax purposes, may be (1) life insurance, (2) almost life insurance, and (3) not life insurance—hence increasing the demand for both actuaries and tax accountants!)

Government studies can also affect insurers. Published studies by the U.S. General Accounting Office, the U.S. Internal Revenue Service, the National Association of Insurance Commissioners (NAIC), and other government organizations have had profound influences on insurance decision-making. For example, a controversial 1979 Federal Trade Commission (FTC) staff study on life insurance cost disclosure undoubtedly had a significant impact in terms of increasing consumer awareness.[1] This report, which received wide publicity, was highly critical of existing life insurance cost disclosure requirements and of various life insurance products and pricing. The life insurance industry took strong exception to the report's findings and conclusions,[2] but this very controversy added to consumer awareness about life insurance and the need to shop carefully.

[1] The Federal Trade Commission, *Life Insurance Cost Disclosure* (Washington, D.C.: U.S. Government Printing Office, 1979). See Chap. 10.

[2] See Blake T. Newton, Jr., "The Misleading Report on Life Insurance Cost Disclosure of the Federal Trade Commission Staff," *The Journal of the American Society of Chartered Life Underwriters*, Vol. XXXIII (Oct. 1979), p. 12.

Another regulatory factor that has brought about pressures for product innovation relates to the emphasis by regulators and others on mandated cost disclosure in life insurance. As discussed in Chapter 10, the NAIC model cost disclosure regulations probably have caused consumers to become more aware of cost differences in life insurance and annuities and to shop more competitively. Unfortunately, as will be discussed more fully later, increased price competitiveness has also caused many insurers and agents to illustrate future policy values that are unlikely to be realized.

Finally, government's role as a competitor of life insurers should not be omitted. Governmental social insurance programs impact insurers' product design and other decisions. Although this is not the direct subject of this chapter, the reader can perhaps best see how government's actions as an insurer can impact private insurers by considering the federal health insurance program for the elderly: Medicare. If Medicare paid all participants' medical expenses fully, little need would exist for insurer-provided Medicare supplemental policies. As Medicare benefits change, so too do insurers' Medicare supplemental policies.

As the tax burden for financing Social Security has grown over the years, pressures have been successfully mounted to decrease the system's relative benefit levels. Such actions in the United States and in numerous other countries can be expected to cause individuals to enhance their personal financial security programs against risks associated with loss of health and life, and for retirement. The products sold by life insurers can be expected to help fill this void in personal economic security.

*Technology.* Information and communication technology continue to make astounding progress. Increasingly, procedures and transactions can be mechanized. Use of artificial intelligence technology to aid in decision-making continues to appear in investments, claims settlement, underwriting, marketing, and other applications. Imaging technology is speeding policy issuance and data capture, and enhancing the quality of agent and customer service. Computers and peripheral equipment continue to be ever more powerful, more user-friendly, and lighter, thus permitting faster, more reliable marketing, product design, and service. Such improved technology has resulted in cost reductions, better service, more flexible products, better marketing approaches, and, in general, a more effective mobilization of corporate resources to help achieve a competitive advantage.

*Competition.* Increased consumer awareness has enhanced product competition. Not only has competition among life insurers increased, but competition from other, noninsurer financial services firms has raised the degree of competition to new levels. The news media seem more interested in life insurance; they find it to be a more appropriate topic for discussion and analysis than in times past.

All of the preceding catalysts have contributed to increasing competition among life insurance companies. Competition between life insurance companies and other savings and investment media also continues to grow, and there are expectations of even more vigorous competition ahead. In turn, insurers must "listen" better to consumer demands for better-valued, more flexible products.

## INSURANCE COMPANY REACTIONS

The net effect of the above environmental influences is that competition among financial service retailers is increasing, particularly in the middle- and upper-income markets. This increased competition emanates from consumers, as discussed above, and, within the life insurance business, from agents demanding lower-cost/higher-quality products and services for their customers.

In one sense, the old notion that "there isn't and can't be anything new in life insurance" is correct. The basics of life insurance do not change. In another sense, however, much is new.

Many consumers have demanded life insurance whose yields are competitive with returns on other investments. Some have stated a preference for flexible premium-payment schedules and the ability to alter other policy elements easily. Some have wanted transparent life insurance policies to show more clearly the various pricing components. Some have demanded greater disclosure and more up-to-date policy information. These are just a few of the types of "requests" that today's marketplace has made of insurers.

***Potentially Lower Cost Coverage.*** Life insurance coverage being offered today is potentially lower in cost than that offered in years past. This downward trend is attributable in part to the high investment returns earned by life insurers on money invested in the 1980s, and it is therefore expected. However, competition among life insurers (and agents), as well as between life insurers and other financial institutions, has put pressure on actuaries and insurer management to design and offer ever lower cost policies. This pressure, in turn, has forced insurers to place great emphasis on expense reduction and improved productivity. Many insurers, in an effort to gain a competitive advantage, have sought riskier investments for their portfolios with the expectation that they would generate higher yields. This shift may be a sound strategy if relatively small proportions of assets are invested in this way, but some insurers have found that their aggressiveness has backfired because of excessive investment defaults and consumer concern about these insurers' financial solidity.

Besides internal expense control and other efforts, insurers have adopted several innovative product design approaches in order to be able to offer potentially lower cost insurance. Four of these approaches are covered here: (1) indeterminate-premium plans, (2) more refined classification systems, (3) provision for direct recognition of policy loan activity and bonuses, and (4) provisions to encourage persistency.

*1. Indeterminate-Premium Plans.* **Indeterminate-premium** policies are technically classified as nonparticipating policies, but with nonguaranteed current premiums. A dual-premium structure is utilized whereby a scale of guaranteed maximum premiums is contained in the contract, but the insurance company reserves the right to and typically does charge lower premiums.

The lower current premium actually charged is subject to periodic change, but only on a class-wide basis. Changes may be made if anticipated future interest, mortality, or expense experience differs from that implicit in the current premium charged. Premiums can be raised or lowered by the company, but can never exceed the guaranteed maximum. The indeterminate-premium approach was first used with fixed-premium cash-value life policies, but has since been adapted to term life insurance policies, to flexible-premium policies, and to each pricing element of unbundled policies.

*2. More Refined Classification Systems.* In an effort to offer lower-priced insurance, insurers have adopted more highly refined risk-classification systems. Thus, whereas in the past otherwise similarly situated smokers and nonsmokers were charged the same premium, today most insurers charge smokers more than nonsmokers, in recognition of their higher average mortality.

Insurers have also provided lower rates for persons assessed to be **superstandard** or **preferred risks**. Preferred risks may be defined as nonsmokers whose health, life-style, family history, and other characteristics are such as to suggest that they will exhibit significantly better than average mortality experience. Additionally, many insurers offer products that permit insureds who demonstrate periodically that they are still in good health to pay lower premiums than otherwise. These "reentry" products are discussed later in this chapter.

*3. Provisions for Direct Recognition.* In an effort to refine life insurance pricing further and to offer lower cost insurance to select consumers, many companies now include an insurance policy provision that permits the company to recognize directly the extent of policy loan activity in policy benefits. Such provisions increase policy costs for those with policy loans and decrease costs for those without policy loans.[3]

*4. Provisions to Encourage Persistency.* The discussion on asset shares in Chapter 2 made it clear that lapse rates can have important implications for insurer product pricing. Other things being the same, the higher are early lapse rates, the greater are insurer losses, and, therefore, the more the insurer must charge for the policy. To discourage early lapses and thereby to be able to offer lower cost policies, insurers are designing products with high charges for early surrender and with prescribed bonuses for policies that remain in force for a certain minimum number of years.

***Increased Flexibility.*** Life insurance products offered today permit policyowners unprecedented flexibility. Many policies provide that the face amount may be decreased or increased (usually subject to insurability

---

[3] See Chap. 9.

requirements) at any time. Increased flexibility in premium payment is permitted, with some policies allowing the owner to pay premiums as desired, subject to tax and procedural limitations. With the increasing use of accelerated death benefit provisions, life insurance policies as living benefits assume even greater importance.

Life insurance products have always been flexible financial tools. Life insurance policy provisions permit the policyowner to alter various aspects of the policy.[4] Further flexibility was often accorded policyowners by allowing them by company practice to do what they wished even if the contract provisions did not make allowance for the action.

Even with these acknowledged contractual and extra-contractual opportunities, however, product flexibility today is superior to that which existed in the past. As stated earlier, pressure for this enhanced flexibility has come from several sources, but it has become feasible only because the needed technology support systems have been developed.

*Greater Disclosure.* Improved policy benefit and cost disclosure has been required by regulation in most states since the late 1970s. However, only in the 1980s did insurers begin to incorporate disclosure as a key element of policy design and operation.

This increased disclosure has two dimensions. First, some new products (e.g., universal life and current assumption whole life) disclose to the potential purchaser various elements that make up the product's pricing structure. This transparency permits the prospect to see clearly the portion of each premium payment applied toward mortality and expense charges and toward cash-value buildup. The interest credited to cash-value accumulations is also disclosed clearly in such products.[5]

In addition to disclosure of the pricing and benefit elements at the time of purchase, owners of these policies also receive, annually, up-to-date policy transaction summaries. They are thus able to monitor actual policy financial results and to compare these results against prevailing investment returns and other financial factors within the economy.

## INCREASED RISK TO CONSUMERS

The purchaser of a life insurance policy today stands to benefit in some or all of the above ways. The benefits, however, are not without their price. For one thing, enhanced flexibility within a contract is more costly, even in the face of significant technological advances and lower unit costs of production.

---

[4] See Chap. 9.

[5] However, neither the stated interest rate nor the other pricing elements may reflect accurately the policy's actual, internal pricing components. Companies may, for example, choose to assess an expense charge lower than that actually incurred; they may intend to make good the shortfall by assessing a somewhat higher mortality charge or by crediting a somewhat lower interest rate than they would otherwise.

Another highly important aspect of this "price" is that insurers cannot offer both lower cost, interest-sensitive policies on the one hand and liberal long-term, fixed-dollar guarantees on the other hand. Many life insurance products offer less liberal traditional insurance-type guarantees. Therefore, much of the investment, expense, and some of the mortality risk that traditionally has been borne almost exclusively by life insurers is shared increasingly by policyowners under these new products.

In fact, many individuals who purchased life insurance during the relatively high interest rate environment of the late 1970s and 1980s discovered at first hand the risks inherent in some of the newer, more interest-sensitive products. With policy values projected at double-digit interest rates, purchasers of these policies anticipated future cash-value accumulations substantial enough so that no further premiums needed be paid after a few years (so-called **vanish pay**). Actual policy crediting interest rates fell short of those illustrated, as prevailing market rates declined and insurers could not sustain the high investment returns necessary to support high cash-value interest rates.

Many policyowners apparently were not fully aware of the interest rate risks that they were assuming and became disillusioned with their policies. Many insurers, in an effort to minimize interest rate declines, undertook riskier investments to gain yield or they subsidized the credited policy interest rate through lower profits or drawing from surplus.

As a result of this era, recent times have witnessed an increased marketplace demand for products with more stable policy values and greater integrity. A parallel movement toward greater interest in insurer financial solidity has occurred as several insurers experienced financial difficulty because of their riskier portfolios.

## OVERVIEW OF TYPES OF LIFE INSURANCE

As suggested in Chapter 2, life insurance policies can be constructed and priced to fit a myriad of benefit and premium-payment patterns. Historically, however, life insurance benefit patterns have fit into one or a combination of three classes:

- Term Life Insurance
- Endowment Insurance
- Whole Life Insurance

**Term life insurance** pays a predetermined sum to the beneficiary if the insured's death occurs during a set number of years (the policy term) that is less than the whole of life. **Endowment insurance**, like term insurance, pays a predetermined sum to the beneficiary if the insured's death occurs during the policy term and, additionally, pays the (typically) same predetermined sum to the policyowner if the insured survives the policy term.

Finally, **whole life insurance** pays a predetermined sum to the beneficiary when the insured dies, regardless of when death occurs. Term policies typically have no cash values whereas endowment and whole life policies typically have cash values.

Another class of insurance issued by life insurers is annuities. An **annuity** pays a (typically) monthly benefit amount to a designated person (the annuitant) usually only if the annuitant is alive. Most annuities are savings instruments designed to first accumulate funds and then systematically to liquidate the funds, usually during one's retirement years.

The above life insurance classification scheme remains valid today, although it is not always possible to determine at policy issuance the exact class into which some types of policies fall. As discussed in Chapter 6, some policies permit the policyowner flexibility effectively to alter the type of insurance during the policy term, thus allowing the policy to be classified as to form only at a particular point. For presentation purposes, these flexible forms of life insurance are discussed as if they were an additional classification, even though all can properly be placed (at a given point in time) into one or a combination of the three traditional classes.

Figure 4-1 shows the changing U.S. market shares of individually issued life insurance. The rapid growth in the early 1980s of universal life is evident. New endowment insurance premiums during this period were uniformly less than 1 percent. Term's share, as measured by new premiums written, grew until the early 1980s, but declined somewhat thereafter.

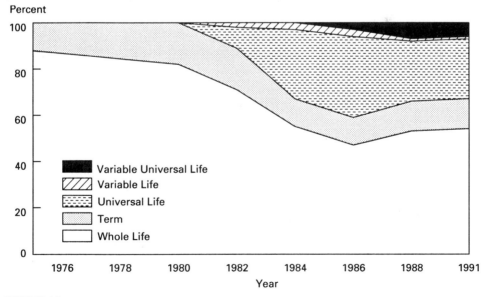

**FIGURE 4-1**

**THE CHANGING MIX OF NEW LIFE INSURANCE SALES IN THE UNITED STATES 1976–1991**
*Source*: Life Insurance Marketing and Research Association.

## TERM LIFE INSURANCE

Term life insurance sales, as measured by face amount, account for over one-third of all individual life insurance sold in the United States. While the proportion is higher in some countries (e.g., Canada) and lower in others (e.g., Japan), the vast majority of major international markets sells some type of term life insurance.

### NATURE OF TERM LIFE INSURANCE

Term life insurance furnishes life insurance protection for a limited number of years. The face amount of the policy is payable only if the insured's death occurs during the stipulated term, and nothing is paid in case of survival. The policy is said to **expire** at the end of the policy term. Term policies may be issued for as short a period as one year,[6] but customarily provide protection up to age 65, 70, or beyond.

Term insurance is more comparable to property and liability insurance contracts than to any other life insurance contract. If a building valued at $100,000 is insured for that amount under a five-year term property policy, the insurer will pay this amount only if total destruction occurs during the term. Similarly, if a person insures his or her life for $100,000 under a five-year term life policy, the insurer will pay $100,000 only if the insured's death occurs before the expiration of the five years; nothing is paid if death occurs after the expiration of the contract period.

Initial premium rates per $1,000 of coverage are lower for term life insurance than for other life products issued on the same basis, since the period of protection is limited. Premiums for term coverage, however, can escalate rapidly as the duration of the policy lengthens.

Term product prices are more easily compared than are prices of other life products, since term policies are structurally simpler than the other policies. They usually have no cash values or dividends, thus permitting policy comparisons on the basis of premiums. Because of this fact, more price competition has centered on term sales than on perhaps any other life insurance product. Some insurers and many buyers, in fact, treat term life insurance more as a commodity—an item that is essentially the same irrespective of the supplier and that, therefore, is sought at the lowest price.

Since commodity profit levels ordinarily are low, many insurers attempt to differentiate their term policies in some manner from those sold by other insurers, to avoid commodity "term wars." Even so, term insurance buyers as a group are price-sensitive and consider term policies to be easily replaceable, since few, if any, penalties attach to early termination. Consequently, term lapse rates are higher on average than are lapse rates for other policies.

---

[6] So-called "preliminary" or "initial" term insurance is available for periods as short as one month, but a maximum of 11 months. This insurance is usually restricted to situations in which protection is to start immediately, with the policy having a formal effective date of one or more months in the future.

High early lapse rates produce two types of losses for insurers. First, they may be unable to fully recoup underwriting and first-year commission expenses. Second, the policyowners who replace their term policies will tend to be those who are in good health; this possibly results in poorer than expected mortality from persisting policyowners. For these reasons, insurers have been seeking ways—via discounts for multi-year premium payments, more stringent underwriting for expected persistency, and other means—to minimize term lapse rates.

Four features common to many term life policies deserve special attention before discussing specific term products. These are the renewability, convertibility and reentry features as well as the interaction that exists between a term policy's conversion and waiver of premium features.

*Renewability.* Almost all one-year and five-year term policies and many 10-year and other duration policies contain an option that permits the policyowner to continue the policy for a limited number of additional periods of protection. This renewal option permits the policyowner, at the expiration of each term period, to continue the policy without reference to the insured's insurability status at renewal time. Usually, however, companies limit the age (generally to age 65 or 70) to which such term policies may be renewed.

The premium, although level for a given period, increases with each renewal and is based on the insured's attained age at renewal time. A scale of guaranteed future premium rates is contained in the contract, although for some types of term insurance the company charges a rate lower than that stated in the policy.

As the premium rate increases with each renewal, mortality experience increasingly reflects selection against the company. Resistance to the higher premiums and lower-cost product opportunities cause many insureds in good health to fail to renew, whereas the majority of those in poor health will renew even in the face of higher premiums. Insurers recognize this problem in their pricing structure or through other means such as the dividend scales, by limiting renewability to stipulated maximum ages or by product designs that encourage (or require) conversion.

From the policyowner's perspective, the term "renewability" means simply that the policy can be continued to the stipulated termination age. Renewal rates are fixed by contract and renewal is effected merely by the policyowner paying the billed premium. Therefore, renewable term policies can be viewed as increasing-premium, level-benefit term life insurance from the policyowner's perspective.

*Convertibility.* Most term insurance policies include a convertible feature. This feature permits the policyowner to exchange the term policy for a whole life or other cash-value insurance contract *without evidence of insurability*. Often, the period during which conversion is allowed is shorter than the maximum duration of the policy. About one in 12 term policies is converted in the United States.

The conversion privilege increases the flexibility of term life insurance. For example, at the time a term policy was purchased, a policyowner may not have selected the type of policy best adapted to his or her needs. He or she may have preferred another type but, because of budget considerations, decided on some form of low-premium term coverage. Following the issuance of the term policy, circumstances may have changed so as to enable the policyowner to purchase an adequate amount of other insurance. Alternatively, he or she may desire to utilize insurance as a means of accumulating funds rather than entirely for the purpose of protection against death. If, therefore, an individual concludes that term insurance does not meet present and future needs, this conclusion could be implemented by exchanging the term contract for a type of insurance that conforms better to his or her needs.

A significant percentage of insureds become uninsurable or insurable only at higher than standard rates. Under such circumstances, a term policy that cannot be renewed beyond a certain point may fail to protect the insured in the desired manner. If, however, the policy contains a conversion privilege, and if the time limit for making an exchange of the policy has not yet expired, the exercise of this privilege can be to the insured's advantage and thus protect against the possibility that insurance may expire before death occurs.

If the insured under a term policy is insurable at standard rates, there may be little or no financial advantage to exercising the conversion privilege, compared to reentering the marketplace and shopping carefully. The limited exception to this statement is if the insurer provides a **conversion credit**. Most U.S. insurers provide some type of conversion credit. The credit may apply only if the conversion takes place within a specified period (e.g., two years) from issue. The types of credits vary and include a dollar amount, such as $2 per $1,000 of insurance, a credit equal to the previous year's term premium paid, and a credit of a fixed percent of the new policy's premium.

Conversion may be permitted on an attained age or original age basis. The **attained-age method** of conversion involves the issuance of a whole life or other cash-value policy of a form currently being issued at the date of conversion. The premium rate for the new policy is that required at the insured's attained age and would be the same as that offered by the company to new insureds who could qualify for standard rates.

The **original-age method**, usually unavailable with universal life policies, involves a retroactive conversion, with the whole life or other cash-value policy bearing the date and premium rate that would have been paid had the whole life or other cash-value policy been taken out originally instead of the term policy. Most companies offering this option require that retroactive conversion take place within five years of the issue date of the term contract. The  policyowner is required to pay the difference between (1) the premiums (net of dividends or other credits) that would have been paid on the new policy had it been issued at the same time as the original policy, and (2) the premiums actually paid for the term policy, with interest on the difference at a stipulated annual rate (e.g., 6 or 8 percent).

It was said that the policyowner, in making a choice between the two bases of conversion, might prefer an original age conversion because he or she could obtain a lower premium rate and possibly more liberal contract provisions. However, with the trend toward lower premiums and better-valued products, it is far from clear that either potential benefit would necessarily materialize. Even if the premium rate for the original age conversion were less than the rate for current issues, the wisdom of making an original age conversion may be doubtful because of having to pay the back premiums plus interest.

*Reentry.* Many companies develop more competitive term rates by using the method of including a **reentry** feature. To understand better the mechanics of reentry term, an understanding of the three types of mortality tables used by insurers is necessary.[7] A **select mortality table** reflects the mortality experience of newly insured lives only. These persons exhibit superior (i.e., low) mortality relative to other people of the same age and sex, since to qualify for life insurance in the first place they must have been in good health and otherwise insurable at standard rates. This select period or "benefit of selection" usually lasts from 5 to 15 years.

An **ultimate mortality table** reflects the mortality experience beyond the select years (i.e., of those who already have been insured for several years). The benefit of selection has faded from the mortality experience of the ultimate group. Thus, a select table represents very favorable initial experience, whereas an ultimate table excludes this experience and, therefore, exhibits higher mortality. An **aggregate mortality table** includes data from both select and ultimate experience.

Traditional term premium scales are based on aggregate mortality experience. Reentry term premiums are based on a select/ultimate mortality split. This results in a scale of premium rates that varies not only by age but also by the duration since the insured last demonstrated insurability. Thus, three or more otherwise identically situated insureds each could be paying a different premium for the same coverage under the same policy form. The 30-year-old woman who just purchased a term policy using reentry (select and ultimate) pricing would be paying one rate; another woman, now aged 30, who purchased the same policy type last year (at age 29 and now age 30) would be paying a somewhat higher rate; a third woman, who purchased her policy two years ago (at age 28 and who is now 30), would be paying a still higher rate; and so on through from 2 to 12 more such situations, depending on the select mortality table used as the basis for the rates. Even though each insured would now be aged 30, the select/ultimate

[7] See Chap. 18.

dichotomy leads to a premium schedule that permits the person most recently insured to pay the lowest rate.

Such policies are referred to as **reentry term** because the insured may be able to reenter the select group periodically—often every five years—if the insured resubmits to the insurer satisfactory evidence of insurability at that time. For those insureds who fail to take advantage of the reentry provision or who fail to qualify for reentry because of insurability problems, ultimate rates are charged thereafter. These ultimate premiums are considerably higher than the select premiums, and higher than traditional aggregate term rates as well. A person who cannot qualify for select rates usually will be unable to qualify for a new policy based on aggregate rates and, therefore, must pay the higher ultimate rates.

*Interaction between Waiver of Premium and Conversion Features.* The majority of individual life insurance policies sold in the United States provide that if the insured becomes totally disabled (see Chapter 7), the insurer will waive (i.e., excuse) premium payments during the period of disability. This provision may be automatically included within the policy, or, more commonly, it is offered as an additional benefit for a specified additional charge.

When this **waiver of premium** (WP) feature is incorporated within a term policy, how the conversion feature interacts with the WP feature can be important. Three different provisions are available in the market. First, some contracts provide that if the insured becomes totally disabled, premiums for the term policy will be waived, but if the policyowner wishes to exercise the conversion option during this period, the company will not waive the premiums on the newly converted cash-value policy. In other words, full premiums must be paid by the policyowner for the new policy. Second, other companies permit the conversion *and* will waive premiums on the new cash-value policy. Clearly this approach is more valuable to the policyowner than the former.

Third, some companies provide for a waiver of premium on the term policy and on the new policy, but only if the conversion is delayed until the end of the period during which conversion is allowed. At that point an automatic conversion will take place *and* premiums on the new policy will be waived. This benefit provision falls between the two previously discussed provisions in terms of policyowner value.

Naturally, other things being equal, the more liberal the interaction of the WP and conversion features, the higher the additional premium for the WP feature should be, although actual pricing may not reflect this. This interaction can be a significant element of product evaluation, as can be the definition of disability.[8]

## TYPES OF TERM LIFE INSURANCE POLICIES

Term life policies have traditionally been issued on either a participating or guaranteed-cost, nonparticipating basis. As alluded to earlier, this is changing as

[8] See Chap. 9.

insurers seek ways of gaining a competitive edge. Term life insurance usually provides either a level or decreasing death benefit, with some increasing death benefit policy riders sold.

*Level Face Amount Policies.* The vast majority of term life insurance sold today in the United States provides for a level death benefit over the policy period. Premiums for such contracts either increase with age or remain level (the former is the more common).

*1. Increasing-Premium Policies.* Term policies with level death benefits and increasing premiums are commonly referred to as contracts that are "renewable," a term that is synonymous with "increasing premium," as alluded to earlier. Thus, **yearly renewable term** (YRT)—also called **annual renewable term** (ART)—and **five-year renewable term** policies are increasing-premium contracts. Some insurers offer renewable term policies of other durations, such as three, six, and ten years. YRT policies remain the most common form sold, although other duration renewable term policies have regained popularity recently, as insurers have sought ways of minimizing the commodity aspects of term, with its high lapse rates and low profitability.

YRT product design has been of considerable interest, as particularly intense price competition has centered around these products. The trend in YRT design over the past few years has been toward (1) lower premiums, (2) longer renewal periods (even to age 100), (3) a greater number of rate bands (e.g., different rates at $100,000, $250,000, $500,000, and $1 million amount bands), and (4) differentiated pricing categories.

Differential pricing can be accomplished in several ways. One common method is through the use of separate smoker/nonsmoker rates. Most major writers of YRT offer either nonsmoker rates or a preferred risk category.

YRT premium differences between smokers and nonsmokers can be substantial. Table 4-1 lists first-year YRT smoker and nonsmoker premiums for several companies.

**TABLE 4-1       SELECTED COMPANIES' YRT SMOKER AND NONSMOKER PREMIUMS ($100,000, FOR 35-YEAR-OLD MALE)**

|  | Premiums for: | |
|  | Smoker | Nonsmoker |
| --- | --- | --- |
| Company A | $ 204 | $ 192 |
| Company B | 207 | 137 |
| Company C | 225 | 194 |
| Company D | 236 | 177 |
| Company E | 241 | 150 |
| Company F | 282 | 185 |
| Company G | 319 | 192 |

*Source*: Best's Flitcraft Compend

**TABLE 4-2     TRADITIONAL YRT PREMIUMS AND REENTRY YRT PREMIUMS**
**(FOR 35-YEAR-OLD NONSMOKING MALE)**

| Policy Year | Age | Face Amount | Policy A Premiums Aggregrate | Policy B Premiums Current Reentry | Policy B Premiums Current Nonreentry | Policy B Premiums Failure to Reenter Maximum |
|---|---|---|---|---|---|---|
| 1 | 35 | $100,000 | $145 | $111 | $111 | $111 |
| 2 | 36 | 100,000 | 148 | 132 | 132 | 132 |
| 3 | 37 | 100,000 | 154 | 147 | 147 | 147 |
| 4 | 38 | 100,000 | 162 | 165 | 165 | 165 |
| 5 | 39 | 100,000 | 172 | 185 | 185 | 185 |
| 6 | 40 | 100,000 | 185 | 138 | 210 | 228 |
| 7 | 41 | 100,000 | 200 | 176 | 256 | 291 |
| 8 | 42 | 100,000 | 219 | 204 | 312 | 372 |
| 9 | 43 | 100,000 | 242 | 236 | 400 | 470 |
| 10 | 44 | 100,000 | 268 | 272 | 499 | 597 |
| 11 | 45 | 100,000 | 288 | 181 | 616 | 770 |
| 12 | 46 | 100,000 | 333 | 241 | 777 | 972 |
| 13 | 47 | 100,000 | 373 | 287 | 945 | 1,182 |
| 14 | 48 | 100,000 | 417 | 337 | 1,121 | 1,401 |
| 15 | 49 | 100,000 | 466 | 393 | 1,305 | 1,631 |
| 16 | 50 | 100,000 | 521 | 238 | 1,495 | 1,869 |
| 17 | 51 | 100,000 | 581 | 327 | 1,699 | 2,124 |
| 18 | 52 | 100,000 | 646 | 395 | 1,911 | 2,389 |
| 19 | 53 | 100,000 | 716 | 466 | 2,133 | 2,667 |
| 20 | 54 | 100,000 | 791 | 544 | 2,362 | 2,953 |

As mentioned earlier, companies increasingly utilize a reentry feature to differentiate pricing. Table 4-2 illustrates two companies' YRT products: Policy A is a traditional aggregate-based product, and Policy B is a reentry product with a five-year reentry feature and with indeterminate premiums.

The Policy B reentry premiums are indeed low. The second column under Policy B shows the premiums that the insurer anticipates charging if the insured does not qualify for the lower reentry premiums. The third column shows the maximum premiums that the insurer could charge if it chose to do so and if the insured did not qualify for reentry. Note that the first five years of premiums are the same for each of the three premium sets.

Many **graded-premium whole life** policies are, in effect, YRT policies that grade into level-premium whole life coverage after 20 years or at advanced ages (e.g., age 70). These policies are discussed in more detail in the following chapter.

Minimum issue ages for YRT policies range from 15 to 20 years old, with maximum issue ages of from 60 to 70. Many YRT contracts are now renewable to age 95 or 100 and convertible to age 65 or 70.

   *2. Policies with Other Premium Patterns.* A minority of term life insurance sold in the United States has premium payment patterns that do not fit into the increasing-premium category discussed above, although the face amount may remain level. Level-premium term contracts may be written for a set number of years or to cover the typical working lifetime. Contracts of the first type include 10-year and 20-year level-premium, nonrenewable policies. Contracts of the second type, providing essentially the same protection, are (1) life-expectancy term, and (2) term-to-age 65.

   The **life-expectancy term** policy provides protection for a number of years equal to the average life expectancy for a person of the proposed insured's age and sex, based on some specific mortality table. Although this contract is strictly a protection contract, the leveling of the premium over many years produces a cash value, which increases to a point and then declines to zero at the termination of the policy.

   The **term-to-age-65** (or **70**) policy provides protection for a somewhat shorter period than does the life-expectancy policy and consequently has a slightly lower premium. The policy's rationale is that it provides protection during the period of the individual's productive efforts, since 65 is usually considered retirement age. As with the life-expectancy contract, a cash value develops during the policy term. Neither of these contracts is very popular today. In fact, some companies have discontinued offering these long-term contracts altogether.

   Some life insurance companies sell what might most accurately be described as **front-end loaded term**, although they are also known by other names. These products have been designed by insurers principally to overcome one of the problems that has existed for agents in selling YRT and other low-premium term contracts: low commissions.

   A few insurers began designing what were basically ten-year or other duration level-premium term policies, but with a first-year premium that was higher than the other premiums, thus permitting higher agents' commissions and greater company profit. Obviously, the problem was to figure out how to sell the product, especially since YRT prices were considerably lower.

   This marketing problem was solved by providing a modest endowment (maturity value) feature at the end of the ten-year period. This differentiated the product from common ten-year term and obscured its higher cost. Companies purposely designed the endowment amount to be an exact multiple (usually two or three times) of the difference between the first- and second-year premiums. This difference they called a "deposit," and they sold the endowment feature not as an endowment, but as a return of the "deposit" doubled, or tripled, or any other relationship desired.

   This made for an attractive sales presentation that basically masked the high front-end load. The sales presentations also led to misleading and deceptive marketing practices that caused much regulatory concern.[9] Indeed, the name used for these policies—**"deposit" term**—was and is inherently misleading and its use has been outlawed in several states.

Other recent front-loaded term insurance variations have combined high first-year premiums or increasing-premium term policies with an annuity or mutual fund. They are sold as a package, with the result that what can be an expensive term policy is submerged into the sales presentation in which the two are offered as a package.

In theory, front-loaded term policies should result in lower long-run costs than the more traditional forms of term insurance, other things being equal. This is because the high first-year premium can cover most, if not all, of the high acquisition expenses, and (most important) those who terminate their policies during the initial period would have "paid their own way." Stated in terms of the example given in Chapter 2, the asset share for terminating policies should be positive from policy year one and should always be larger than the cash value paid (if any). Lapse rates should be lower, with the result that the insurer should be able to offer the policy at a price lower than that of other term life products. This theoretical promise has not materialized in the marketplace, although some insurers apparently are now designing products with more of a view to achieving this objective than for purposes of a misleading sales presentation.

***Nonlevel Face Amount Policies.*** A significant amount of term life insurance in the United States involves policies (or riders) whose face amounts decrease or increase with time. Decreasing term policies are commonly used to pay off an outstanding loan balance on the death of the debtor/insured, be it in connection with a home mortgage or a business or personal loan. Thus, **mortgage protection term** policies provide for face amount decreases that match the projected decreases in the principal amount owed under a mortgage loan. Since the larger proportion of each early mortgage loan payment is applied to pay interest, the initial decrease in a mortgage loan's outstanding balance is slight, with later declines being substantial. Mortgage protection policies' death benefits track this pattern and are available to cover a variety of mortgage loan durations (e.g, 10, 15, 20, 25, or 30 years) and amortization schedules. They also provide for a conversion right. Level premiums are sometimes limited to a somewhat shorter period than the policy duration.

Term insurance that decreases by a set amount each year is also available. Such policies are for durations of from 10 to 30 years and often decrease by the same amount each month.

A type of decreasing term, available as specialty coverage, is designed to ensure that premiums due on a juvenile's life insurance policy will be paid even if

[9] For a description of this product and marketing practices associated with it, see Harold Skipper, "Perspectives on Partial Endowment Type ("Deposit Term") Life Insurance: Implications for Regulation, *The Journal of the American Society of Chartered Life Underwriters*, Vol. XXXIII (July 1979).

the premium payor dies. In this case, the decreasing death benefit on the payor's life is exactly sufficient to pay all premiums due from the payor's death until the insured's age 21.

Another type of decreasing term life insurance is designed to appeal to young men and women whose family responsibilities call for a monthly income to be paid to the surviving spouse (typically) until a certain age or for a set period of usually 10, 15, or 20 years from the date of policy issuance. This **family income policy**, also available as a rider to other forms of insurance, is often sold to protect the family during the child-rearing years. Of course, if the insured lives beyond the specified age or beyond the set number of years from issue, no further coverage is provided by this benefit.

Term insurance whose death benefits increase with time is also sold, but virtually never as a separate policy. Insurers offer increasing term coverage as a **cost-of-living-adjustment** (COLA) rider to many policies. COLA riders provide for automatic increases in the policy death benefit in accordance with increases in the Consumer Price Index (CPI). The policyowner would be billed with the regular notice for the additional coverage. No evidence of insurability is required for these increases as long as the rider remains in force and is exercised fully each year. Declines in the CPI do not result in declines in amounts purchased. Rather the amount purchased in the previous year is simply carried forward to the current year.

Another type of increasing term insurance is provided by a **return-of-premium** feature (or rider). This feature provides that if the insured dies within a set number of years from the policy issue date (e.g., 20 years), the death benefit will include not only the basic policy face amount but also an amount equal to the sum of all the premiums paid to that point. This benefit is provided by increasing term insurance whose death benefit exactly equals the sum of the premiums paid. The feature can be useful in certain business situations (see Chapter 15), but it is also sometimes included in an attempt to differentiate the underlying policy from other similar contracts (thus making comparisons difficult) and to make the proposed policy seem more attractive to a prospect.

Increasing term insurance is also sometimes purchased through the use of policy dividends. This can be a valuable source of additional needed coverage and can render certain arrangements more flexible.[10]

## USES AND LIMITATIONS OF TERM INSURANCE

Term life insurance has long been the subject of debate. Some advocate the use of term insurance to the virtual exclusion of cash-value insurance and vice versa. Term life insurance's uses and limitations should be understood.

Term insurance can be useful for persons with low incomes and high insurance needs (a situation that often occurs because of family obligations).

---

[10] See, for example, Chap. 15, under "Nonqualified Deferred Compensation."

Good risk management principles suggest that the family unit should be protected against catastrophic losses. If the current income level does not permit the individual the option of purchasing whole life or other, higher-premium forms of cash-value life insurance in adequate amounts, the individual arguably has no choice but to purchase term, if adequate financial protection is to be provided.

Those who have a career to establish and have a temporarily limited income arguably should use their resources primarily to establish their careers. Investment in oneself for self-improvement during the early career development years clearly should have high priority.

Term life insurance can also prove useful for persons who have placed substantially all of their resources in a new business that is still in its formative stages; in such instances, death would result in serious loss to, if not destruction of, the invested capital. New enterprises are particularly speculative and become more settled only as time elapses. Term insurance can serve a useful hedging purpose, because of its low early-dollar outlay in the initial stages of these undertakings.

Related to the above are situations where life insurance is needed to indemnify the business for the death of one or more employees whose contributions to the firm are critical to its success. Also, owners of closely held businesses may wish to establish pre-death arrangements that ensure that their business interests will be sold at a fair price at their death so as to provide family liquidity. While cash-value policies are usually sold in each of the above two situations, term life insurance can also meet the need, especially if funds with which to pay premiums are not abundant.[11]

Many persons use term insurance as a supplement to an existing life insurance program during the child-rearing period. Term insurance can also be appropriate to use as a hedge against a financial loss already sustained, when a little time is required to repair the damage.

Term life insurance is naturally suited for ensuring that mortgages and other loans are paid off on the debtor/insured's death and as a vehicle for ensuring that education or other desired funds will be available if death were to cut short the period needed for the provider/insured to earn the needed funds. Term insurance is also a natural for all situations that call for temporary income protection needs.

Term insurance can be the basis for one's permanent insurance program *if* the program is well conceived and well executed. A well-conceived program is one that recognizes the increasing-premium nature of most term policies and devises a plan either to accommodate these increasing premiums or to minimize their impact (e.g., by having a program for reducing insurance needs over time). A well-conceived program realistically assesses the policyowner's willingness, ability, and commitment to follow through with the plan. A well-executed program is one that includes high-quality, reasonably priced coverage that provides the capability to adapt to changing circumstances. It involves the

[11] See Chap. 15.

faithful execution—usually on an annual basis—of the devised program. Thus, for example, if the decision is made to save through media other than life insurance, but the individual fails to set aside the planned amounts regularly, the program could be judged to have failed in its mission.

## ENDOWMENT INSURANCE

Unlike the situation in many other countries, in the United States, the amount of endowment insurance sold, relative to the other forms of life insurance, has been declining steadily for several years. Certain tax-law changes in the 1980s did not extend tax benefits to most newly sold endowment policies.[12] This hastened the decline of endowment sales in the United States. Even so, some of this type of insurance is still sold in tax-qualified retirement plans, many older endowment policies remain in force, and, from the reader's perspective, an understanding of the concepts that underlie endowments is essential.

### NATURE OF ENDOWMENT INSURANCE

Term policies provide for the payment of the full policy amount only in the event of the insured's death. Endowment policies, by contrast, provide not only for the payment of the policy face on the death of the insured during a fixed term of years, but also the payment of the full face amount at the end of the term if the insured is living. Whereas policies payable only in the event of death are purchased chiefly for the benefit of others, endowment policies, although affording protection to others against the death of the insured during the fixed term, usually pay to the insured if he or she survives the endowment period.

There are two ways of viewing endowment insurance: in terms of (1) the mathematical concept, and (2) the economic concept.

*Mathematical Concept.* The insurer makes two promises under endowment insurance: (1) to pay the face amount if the insured dies during the endowment period, and (2) to pay the face amount if the insured survives to the end of the endowment period. The first promise is identical with that made under a level term policy for an equivalent amount and period. The second introduces a new concept, the pure endowment. A **pure endowment** promises to pay the face amount *only* if the insured is living at the end of a specified period; nothing is paid in case of prior death. Pure endowment insurance is not sold as a separate contract in the United States. It is said that few people are willing to risk the apparent loss of all premiums paid in the event of death before the end of the endowment period.

[12] See Chap. 13.

Thus, to provide a death benefit during the endowment period, only term insurance for the same period need be added to the pure endowment. It can be seen that these two elements—(1) level term insurance, and (2) a pure endowment—will together meet the two promises made under endowment insurance.

***Economic Concept.*** Another analysis of endowment insurance, the economic concept, divides endowment insurance into two parts: decreasing term insurance and increasing savings. The savings part of the contract is available to the policyowner through surrender of or loan against the policy. This increasing "savings" feature is supplemented by decreasing term insurance, which, when added to the savings accumulation, equals the policy's face amount. This is the same analogy discussed in Chapter 2 with respect to whole life insurance policies.

Insurance contracts have not always fit the increasing savings, decreasing term insurance model.[13] In earlier times in the United States (and in some other countries), no guaranteed nonforfeiture values existed for life insurance contracts. If an individual was forced to cease premium payments, no return of any sort was available as a matter of contract. The contract promised to pay in the event of death or survival to a certain age, but if the contract was discontinued prior to the occurrence of these contingencies, all premiums were considered fully earned and the savings element was forfeited.[14]

## TYPES OF ENDOWMENT POLICIES

Many variations of endowment insurance exist. The policies are for set durations of 10 to 30 or more years, and others are arranged to mature at certain ages, such as 60, 65, 70 years, or older. In many Asian countries, endowment policies of from three to ten years' duration are common, and in some European countries, single-premium endowment policies are popular. Usually, contract premiums are due throughout the term, although limited-payment plans, such as an endowment at age 65 paid up in 20 years, have been available. In the United Kingdom, long-term endowment policies are commonly purchased as a mortgage-loan companion, the idea being that the endowment maturity value will pay off the outstanding loan balance at a preset time.

Besides the standard contracts, other applications of the endowment principle are sometimes made. With a **retirement income policy**, the amount payable at death is the face amount or cash value, whichever is greater. The

---

[13] See Institute of Life Insurance, *The Nature of the Whole Life Contract* (New York: ILI, 1974).

[14] Some companies did allow a cash value, but the policy usually contained no provision for them, so that the policyowner had no right to any surrender value. The values, when allowed, were small and generally were granted only if application was made within a short period after lapse. No regulatory requirement as to the allowance of a surrender value existed in any form until 1861, and no regulatory requirement existed for a cash surrender privilege until 1906.

contract is popularly used in insured pension plans utilizing individual contracts.[15] A **semiendowment policy** pays upon survival one-half the sum payable on death during the endowment period. The so-called "deposit" term policy discussed earlier provides a small endowment amount as its maturity value. Also, various kinds of **juvenile endowment policies** have been issued by certain companies. These include endowments maturing at specified ages for educational purposes. These educational endowment policies are particularly popular in Korea and certain other countries.

Since the company's liability under an endowment policy involves not only payment of the face upon death but also payment of the full amount upon survival of the term, it follows that the annual premium on these policies must be higher than that for whole life or term policies, except for the very long endowment periods, in which the rate is only slightly higher than that charged on an ordinary life policy.

## USES AND LIMITATIONS OF ENDOWMENT INSURANCE

At one time in the United States endowment insurance was considered an effective vehicle for accumulating savings. However, even before the 1984 tax-law changes effectively limited the endowment insurance market to various qualified retirement plans, endowment insurance was having great difficulty competing against whole life and term insurance.

Endowment policies issued prior to 1985 continue to enjoy the same tax treatment as other life insurance policies.[16] Thus, existing endowment policies could provide reasonable customer value. Endowments are still used in certain tax-qualified retirement plans, and the careful shopper in those circumstances can locate policies that provide good value.

Endowments remain popular savings instruments in numerous other countries. Favorable tax treatment coupled with a strong savings impetus has resulted in strong demand for such policies in these markets.

[15] See Chap. 28.
[16] See Chap. 13.

# Chapter 5

# WHOLE LIFE INSURANCE POLICIES

In contrast to term life insurance, whole life insurance is intended to provide insurance protection over one's entire lifetime. Whole life insurance has been the mainstay of the U.S. life insurance business for over a century and continues to be a significant component of new life insurance sales.

## THE NATURE OF WHOLE LIFE INSURANCE

The essence of **whole life insurance** is that it provides for the payment of the face amount upon the insured's death regardless of when death occurs. Its name describes its nature. It is insurance for the whole of life. As used in this text, the name does not refer to any specific type of whole life policy—of which there are many—but rather is generic and is used to describe any type of life insurance that can be maintained in effect indefinitely. By this definition, universal life policies can function as whole life insurance if they have sufficient cash value. However, with insufficient cash value, they function as term policies and provide protection for a limited period only.

Almost all whole life policies sold in the United States are based on mortality tables that assume that all insureds die by age 100. Since all insureds do not, in fact, die by age 100, but insurance companies price whole life insurance as if they do, it is only fair that the insurance company should pay the policy face amount to those few persons who live to age 100—as if they had died. This fact is the reason that whole life policies are sometimes referred to as endowment-at-age-100 policies. The age-100 "endowment" really is not an endowment in the usual sense, but rather it is paid by the insurer in recognition that the underlying reserve (and cash value) of the policy equals the policy face amount at age 100 and, therefore, no pure insurance protection exists beyond that point. Thus, the insurer should terminate the policy. Even if the company did not do so, the policyowner could surrender the policy for its cash value—which would equal the face amount.

Another equally valid viewpoint is that whole life policies are also term-to-age-100 policies. This view is justified by noting that the actuarial technique used for pricing whole life is the same, in concept, as that used to price any term policy. The age-100 payment, under this view, is a death benefit payment.

The face amounts payable under whole life policies typically remain at the same level throughout the policy duration unless the policy has a provision permitting or causing changes (e.g., a cost-of-living-adjustment rider). Also, through the use of dividends, participating policies' total death benefits can be increased over time.

In most whole life insurance policies, the premium remains at the same level throughout the premium payment period. Exceptions exist (e.g., graded premium whole life) wherein future premium changes are stipulated in the contract or by the insurer. With the indeterminate-premium approach, many whole life policies' future premium levels are unknown except that the maximum possible premium level is set by contract and near-term premiums may be guaranteed.

All whole life policies involve some prefunding of future mortality costs. The degree of prefunding is a function of the premium payment pattern and period. Because of this prefunding, all whole life policies sold in the United States are required to have cash values and, as mentioned earlier, the cash value must build to the policy face amount, usually by age 100.[1]

Whole life policy cash values are available to the policyowner at any time by the policyowner's surrendering (canceling) the policy. Alternatively, cash values can be used in other ways, providing flexibility to the policyowner.[2] Whole life policies must, by law, contain cash-value schedules that show for selected time periods the guaranteed minimum amounts that the policyowner could receive from the company on surrender of the policy.[3]

Owners of whole life insurance policies do not have to surrender their policies to have access to funds. Under participating whole life policies where dividends have purchased paid-up additional insurance, such additions may be surrendered for their then value with no impact on the policy proper. Also, policyowners normally can obtain a loan from the insurer for amounts up to that of the policy's cash value. Of course, interest is charged for this loan, and the loan is deducted from the gross cash value if the policy is surrendered or from

[1] Some policies endow at ages slightly less than 100 (e.g., at age 95). Any policy that matures at such a late age is, in effect, a whole life policy and is so considered here.

[2] See Chap. 9.

[3] Debate continues in regulatory, actuarial, and marketing circles regarding the desirability of permitting insurers to offer whole life policies without minimum required cash values.

the face amount if the insured dies and a death claim is payable. Policy loans may, but need not, be repaid at any time and are a source of policy flexibility.[4]

Most whole life insurance sold in the United States is participating, although a significant proportion is nonparticipating but with some nonguaranteed element. The amount of guaranteed-cost, nonpar whole life sold is small. This small share is understandable, since companies cannot afford to guarantee liberal pricing assumptions for decades into the future. As a result, conservatively priced products providing long-term guarantees do not compete well against those wherein the insurer does not guarantee every policy element.

The dividends paid under participating policies can provide an additional source of flexibility, since they may be used in several ways.[5] Some insurers have restructured the use of dividend payments to offer additional flexibility.

Insurance companies always provide **dividend illustrations** to prospective purchasers of participating policies. The illustration shows the insurer's **dividend scale** that would be expected to be paid under the policy if the mortality, expense, and interest experience implicit in the current scale of illustrated dividends were to be the actual basis for all future dividends. The dividend illustration is usually based on the recent past mortality, expense, and interest experience of the company. Important differences exist in the way insurers allocate amounts to be paid out as dividends, and these differences can have a major impact on the dividend levels illustrated as well as on the dividends that are actually paid.[6]

As mentioned in Chapter 2, dividends are not and cannot be guaranteed. **Dividends actually paid**, the schedule of which is a **dividend history**, will equal those illustrated only if the experience basis used to determine future dividends is the same as that implicit in the illustration. Future experience rarely tracks past experience exactly, and never over an extended period. On the other hand, some insurers have "frozen" their dividend scales (i.e., they pay dividends almost exactly as illustrated regardless of the developing experience). This practice treats dividends more as a series of nonguaranteed pure endowments and clearly is not in keeping with the principle of equity underpinning participating life insurance.[7]

Dividends actually paid generally have exceeded illustrated dividends for the majority of policies. This result is expected in periods where investment returns are generally higher during the period after policy issuance than they were during the period prior thereto. For example, a 1970 dividend illustration ordinarily would have been predicated largely on a company's pre-1970 experience. Dividends actually paid from 1970 to 1990 under a whole life policy would reasonably have been expected to be higher than illustrated, since post-

---

[4] See Chap. 9.

[5] See Chap. 9.

[6] See Chaps. 6 and 9.

[7] Insurers selling participating life insurance can be considered as implicitly agreeing to distribute surplus accumulated on behalf of a block of policies in a fair manner and in appropriate quantities. (See Chap. 9.)

1970 experience, especially as to interest, would have been better than pre-1970 experience. In fact, this was the situation for most companies.

Table 5-1 shows illustrated versus historical dividends for three life insurers' participating ordinary life policies. Companies A and B paid dividends that were greater than those illustrated, and, for both companies, dividends in later years were considerably higher than the ones illustrated at policy issuance. This was caused primarily by (1) the high investment returns insurers had been earning during the 1980s and (2) a 1985 change in the policy loan interest rate in these policies. This change, common among older participating policies, is discussed more fully later in this chapter.

Company C, on the other hand, had some difficulties. Until 1985, the year of a change in its policy loan interest rate, the insurer paid dividends exactly as illustrated—that is, it "froze" its dividend scale. One cannot deduce the reason for this action simply from viewing illustrated versus paid dividends. Either this insurer's actual investment and other operating experience failed to keep pace with improvements realized by other life insurers during this period, or

**TABLE 5-1    ILLUSTRATED VERSUS PAID DIVIDENDS ON THREE LIFE INSURERS' POLICIES (1971 ISSUES; PER $1,000 FOR $25,000 ORDINARY LIFE POLICIES FOR A 35-YEAR-OLD MALE)**

| Year | Company A | | Company B | | Company C | |
|------|-----------|------|-----------|------|-----------|------|
|      | Illustrated | Paid | Illustrated | Paid | Illustrated | Paid |
| 1972 | $0.00 | $0.00 | $1.32 | $1.32 | $1.16 | $1.16 |
| 1973 | 0.00 | 0.00 | 2.18 | 2.18 | 1.76 | 1.76 |
| 1974 | 3.04 | 3.10 | 3.05 | 3.20 | 2.39 | 2.39 |
| 1975 | 3.38 | 3.53 | 3.94 | 4.14 | 3.02 | 3.02 |
| 1976 | 3.74 | 4.04 | 4.74 | 4.99 | 3.65 | 3.65 |
| 1977 | 4.10 | 4.48 | 5.54 | 6.14 | 4.31 | 4.31 |
| 1978 | 4.47 | 4.94 | 6.33 | 7.07 | 4.94 | 4.94 |
| 1979 | 4.84 | 5.40 | 7.12 | 8.40 | 5.60 | 5.60 |
| 1980 | 5.19 | 6.22 | 7.90 | 9.59 | 6.26 | 6.26 |
| 1981 | 5.55 | 7.26 | 8.66 | 10.61 | 6.89 | 6.89 |
| 1982 | 6.27 | 8.48 | 9.07 | 11.19 | 7.52 | 7.52 |
| 1983 | 7.02 | 9.66 | 9.47 | 11.81 | 8.15 | 8.15 |
| 1984 | 7.80 | 12.78 | 9.89 | 21.98 | 8.81 | 8.81 |
| 1985 | 8.62 | 14.27 | 10.29 | 26.16 | 9.44 | 16.46 |
| 1986 | 9.44 | 15.61 | 10.73 | 27.88 | 10.10 | 17.66 |
| 1987 | 10.30 | 17.13 | 11.17 | 29.59 | 10.73 | 18.81 |
| 1988 | 11.19 | 21.86 | 11.66 | 30.19 | 11.39 | 20.01 |
| 1989 | 12.10 | 23.35 | 12.15 | 31.10 | 12.02 | 21.15 |
| 1990 | 13.03 | 25.13 | 12.67 | 30.16 | 12.68 | 21.28 |
| 1991 | 13.98 | 26.93 | 13.18 | 31.73 | 13.31 | 22.36 |

Gross Premium per $1,000:
Company A    $19.84
Company B    23.13
Company C    22.98

*Source*: A.M. Best Co.

management decided, for its own reasons, to pay significantly lower dividends than it should have based on the principle of equity underlying participating life insurance, or a combination of both reasons applies.

Some years ago, there were basically only two types of whole life insurance. One provided for level-premium payments to be made for the whole of life (ordinary life), and the other provided for premium payments to be made for a limited period of time only (limited payment whole life). Today, however, whole life policies come with a great variety of premium payment patterns and options and benefits. The most common types are presented below.

## TYPES OF WHOLE LIFE INSURANCE POLICIES

The discussion in Chapter 4 regarding life insurance product development applies particularly to whole life policies. Some companies' policies have been perceived by many persons, rightly or wrongly, as providing inadequate value for money spent and as not being responsive enough to changing economic conditions. As a result of the pressures discussed earlier, many innovations have developed in whole life insurance pricing and policy provisions. Because of the vast array of new whole life products and the even greater number of internal policy variations, the following discussion can highlight only the more important policies in terms of current interest.

### ORDINARY LIFE INSURANCE

**Ordinary life** provides whole life insurance with premiums that are payable for the whole of life. This oldest form of whole life may be referred to by several other names, including **straight life** and **continuous-premium whole life**, and often the term *whole life* itself is used to denote ordinary life insurance. The term *continuous-premium whole life* is logically more descriptive than *ordinary life*, but it enjoys little recognition.[8]

*Product Design*. Ordinary life policies are intended to afford permanent protection at a relatively modest annual outlay since the mortality costs are spread over the entire policy period. Table 5-2 lists gross premiums charged for several otherwise similar participating and guaranteed-cost, nonparticipating ordinary life insurance policies. Premium levels vary significantly. The premium paid for any cash-value policy, including whole life, is not a measure of the policy's *cost*. A policy can have a relatively high premium, yet be low in cost by having large dividends, cash values, or excess interest credits.[9]

---

[8] A further problem with the term *ordinary life* is that it easily can be confused with the term used to distinguish among the four classes of life insurance—i.e., group, credit, industrial and ordinary.

[9] See Chap. 10.

**TABLE 5-2    ORDINARY LIFE GROSS PREMIUMS CHARGED BY SELECTED INSURERS ($25,000 POLICY FOR A 35-YEAR-OLD MALE)**

| Type of Policy | Company | Gross Premium per $1,000 |
|---|---|---|
| Participating | A | $ 11.83 |
| | B | 13.95 |
| | C | 14.20 |
| | D | 15.66 |
| | E | 16.01 |
| | F | 21.68 |
| Nonparticipating | G | 10.70 |
| | H | 11.37 |
| | I | 12.22 |
| | J | 14.04 |
| | K | 17.00 |
| | L | 18.60 |

*Source*: A.M. Best Co.

Ordinary life policy cash values normally increase at a fairly constant rate, reaching the policy face amount at age 100. As discussed more fully in Chapter 9, cash values can be a source of policy flexibility. Early years' cash values are typically low, since the high costs associated with policy sale and issuance are charged off during the first years. These high costs result from the commission paid to the salesperson, which often is 40 to 80 percent or more of the first-year premium, as well as from underwriting and other administrative expenses.

Traditional whole life policies lost significant market share some years ago to universal life (UL). UL's flexibility and new-money interest-rate crediting mechanism, introduced at a time when interest rates were at historical highs, meant that projections of potential future policy values were attractive indeed to prospective buyers. Many were not well enough informed about the risks inherent in policy illustrations or they chose to believe that high rates would prevail. As interest rates fell, many discovered that new-money rates could fall as fast as they rose. Actual results did not meet expected results, and disillusionment by many policyowners ensued.

At the same time, insurers issuing traditional participating whole life policies, whose excess interest credits are realized through dividends, discovered that they could credit steadily higher rates of interest. Their interest rate crediting mechanism—the so-called portfolio average method (or variations thereon)—was predicated on their overall investment portfolio's return, which moved much more slowly than did new-money returns.

While new-money rates move quickly, portfolio rates change slowly. Traditional par products produce more attractive returns in a falling interest rate environment for the same reason that they produce less favorable returns—compared to new-money products—in a rising market. Thus, the advantage enjoyed by UL and other new-money-based products in a rising interest rate environment results in a disadvantage for them when interest rates fall—the very situation that prevailed during the later half of the 1980s and early 1990s. As interest rates stabilize, new money and portfolio yields should move closer together.

Hence the apparent cost advantage of UL over traditional par whole life evaporated or at least was greatly diminished. However, the flexibility that permits adjustment of premiums and death benefits and payment of large, single sums of money into the policy's cash value remained a strong selling point for UL compared with whole life.

To address those competitive dimensions, sellers of traditional whole life began creatively to introduce greater flexibility into their products. Many now offer prospective buyers the option of establishing their own level of future premium payments, subject to company-required minimum and tax-mandated maximum payments. This result is accomplished through several mechanisms. To enable the insured to pay a lower-than-usual premium, low-load term riders with face amounts of up to ten times the base contract amount were introduced. For example, a 35-year-old male buying $100,000 of ordinary life insurance might pay a $1,400 premium. A combination ordinary life/term rider can reduce the annual outlay to $400. By blending the whole life and term elements, any premium between $400 and $1,400 can be derived. Alternatively, combinations of a decreasing term rider and paid-up additions from dividends can produce a level death benefit, but with a lower-than-usual premium outlay, similar to that used with enhanced ordinary life policies (see later in this chapter).

Greater than usual premium payments—either periodic or single ones—can be accommodated through a policy rider that permits such payments to be used to purchase paid-up additions analogous to those purchased with dividends. When the cash value of the paid-up additions (both those purchased through dividends and by additional premium payments) is of sufficient size, an organized program of surrendering pieces of these additions, coupled with further policy dividends, can be used to pay the policy's premiums. This method of arranging to meet future premium payments with the possibility of no further payments by the policyowner is referred to as **vanish pay**. If future dividends and surrenders of paid-up additions are sufficient, the policy is, in effect, paid up. If such dividends and surrenders prove insufficient to meet further premium payments—for example, if dividends prove to be lower than initially anticipated—the policy will just as quickly become "unpaid-up," with the policyowner being required to resume payments to maintain the policy in force.

Finally, some insurers permit use of a **premium deposit rider** as a repository for excess policyowner payments. Under this rider, funds would be transferred, automatically as needed, to meet future premium payments, thus potentially relieving the policyowner of further policy payments at some point. Variations on each of the above mechanisms exist. For example, some companies use immediate annuities as a premium repository to minimize taxation, but in all cases the purpose is to provide the policyowner with greater flexibility.

*Policy Illustration.* Table 5-3 shows an illustration for a traditional participating $100,000 ordinary life policy issued to a 35-year-old male nonsmoker. Dividends are shown both as being netted against the premium payment and as purchasing paid-up additional insurance. Of course, only one option would be selected. The negative impact on early cash values of the front-end load is clear. The table shows that the guaranteed cash value at age 45 is to equal $11,411, and at age 55 it will be $29,486.

**TABLE 5-3     POLICY PREMIUMS AND VALUES FOR $100,000 ORDINARY LIFE PAR POLICY (FOR A 35-YEAR-OLD NONSMOKING MALE)**

| (1) | (2) | (3) | (4) | (5) | (6) | (7) | (8) |
|---|---|---|---|---|---|---|---|
| | | | | | If Dividends Used to Purchase Paid-Up Additions | | |
| End of Year | Gross Premium | Illustrated Dividends (Year-End)[a] | Premium Less Dividend (2-3 PreviousYr.) | Guaranteed Cash Surrender Value | Paid-Up Additional Insurance Purchased | Total Cash Value[b] | Total Death Benefit (Year-End)[c] |
| 1 | $ 1,533 | $16 | $1,533 | $0 | $78 | $15 | $100,078 |
| 2 | 1,533 | 100 | 1,517 | 1,078 | 550 | 1,195 | 100,550 |
| 3 | 1,533 | 187 | 1,433 | 2,201 | 1,410 | 2,515 | 101,410 |
| 4 | 1,533 | 277 | 1,346 | 3,371 | 2,655 | 3,991 | 102,655 |
| 5 | 1,533 | 371 | 1,256 | 4,588 | 4,285 | 5,634 | 104,285 |
| 6 | 1,533 | 465 | 1,162 | 5,852 | 6,286 | 7,456 | 106,286 |
| 7 | 1,533 | 563 | 1,068 | 7,165 | 8,661 | 9,476 | 108,661 |
| 8 | 1,533 | 660 | 970 | 8,528 | 11,393 | 11,704 | 111,393 |
| 9 | 1,533 | 762 | 873 | 9,942 | 14,491 | 14,163 | 114,491 |
| 10 | 1,533 | 862 | 771 | 11,411 | 17,938 | 16,870 | 117,938 |
| 11 | 1,533 | 967 | 671 | 12,933 | 21,743 | 19,843 | 121,743 |
| 12 | 1,533 | 1,063 | 566 | 14,515 | 25,869 | 23,100 | 125,869 |
| 13 | 1,533 | 1,163 | 470 | 16,156 | 30,325 | 26,664 | 130,325 |
| 14 | 1,533 | 1,237 | 370 | 17,860 | 35,033 | 30,534 | 135,033 |
| 15 | 1,533 | 1,313 | 296 | 19,629 | 39,997 | 34,733 | 139,997 |
| 16 | 1,533 | 1,389 | 220 | 21,466 | 45,215 | 39,287 | 145,215 |
| 17 | 1,533 | 1,470 | 144 | 23,370 | 50,700 | 44,224 | 150,700 |
| 18 | 1,533 | 1,552 | 63 | 25,341 | 56,454 | 49,571 | 156,454 |
| 19 | 1,533 | 1,637 | -19 | 27,380 | 62,486 | 55,359 | 162,486 |
| 20 | 1,533 | 1,726 | -104 | 29,486 | 68,807 | 61,621 | 168,807 |

[a] Dividends assume no policy loans. Loans will reduce dividends. Based on current dividend scale but not an estimate or guarantee of future results. Loan provision is at 8%.

[b] Guaranteed cash surrender value (col. 5) plus cash value of paid-up additional insurance.

[c] $100,000 plus col. 6.

*Uses of Ordinary Life*. In general, contemporary ordinary life insurance policies offer greater flexibility and value than did their earlier versions. For persons whose life insurance need is expected to extend over 10 to 15 or more years and who are interested in accumulating savings via life insurance, ordinary life may prove to be the insurance of choice. By leveling premium payments over the entire policy duration, outlays can be relatively modest. Interest credited on cash values enjoys favorable income tax treatment, thus rendering the policy a potentially attractive means of accumulating savings.

Most ordinary life policies prove costly for those whose life insurance need is less than 15 or so years, since the typically heavy front-end expenses result in lower medium-term value. Depending on the buyer's discipline and the availability of other, preferably tax-deferred, means of accumulating funds, a program of "buy term and invest the difference" can also prove to be an effective alternative for providing longer term economic security. It is not unusual, however, for a person to believe that he or she will "invest the difference," yet fail to do so. For some, ordinary life and other whole life policies can serve as a quasi-forced savings plan.

For many persons (especially young adults with children) whose careers are just beginning, the premium payment required for an adequate amount of ordinary life insurance may be too great, given other priorities. Rather than reduce the insurance amount to that with an affordable premium level, good risk management principles argue for placing primary emphasis on the insurance needed to cover the potential loss, with secondary emphasis on product type. The only effective choice, therefore, may be to purchase term insurance.

## LIMITED-PAYMENT WHOLE LIFE INSURANCE

Under the terms of **limited-payment whole life** policies, the face amount of the policy is payable at death, but premiums are charged for a limited number of years only, after which the policy becomes **paid-up** for its full face amount. The limitation may be expressed as a *number* of years of premium payments or an *age* to which premiums must be paid. A paid-up policy should not be confused with a matured policy. A policy is considered **matured** when the face amount becomes payable either as a death claim or because the policy cash value equals the face amount, as in an endowment policy. A paid-up policy is one that has not necessarily matured, but on which no further premium payments are due.

Although potentially identical in effect, a paid-up policy differs from a vanish pay policy. A paid-up policy is contractually guaranteed never to require premium payments beyond the stated premium payment period. No such guarantee exists with a vanish pay policy.

Premium payments may be fixed at almost any number of years—from 1 to 30, or even more. If premiums are limited to 20 years, for example, the policy is known as a **20-payment whole life** policy. The greater the number of premium payments, the more closely the contract resembles the ordinary life form.

Companies also make available contracts that limit premium payments to a certain age, such as to age 65, 70, or even higher. The objective typically would be to permit the owner to pay up the policy during his or her working lifetime. Thus, a policy that requires premiums to age 65 would be known as a **life-paid-up-at-age-65** policy (often abbreviated LP65). A 30-payment life and a LP65 policy both issued at age 35 (and based on the same pricing assumptions) would carry the same premium, since actually they would be the same policy.

As limited-payment policies require the payment of premiums for a period less than the contract term, it follows that the annual level premium under these plans must be larger than that necessary when premium payments continue throughout the life of the policy. Theoretically, the premiums payable under a limited-payment policy are the actuarial equivalent of the premiums payable for the insured's entire lifetime under an ordinary life plan.[10]

Because of the higher premiums, limited-payment plans are not well adapted to those whose income is small and whose need for insurance protection is great. Furthermore, many persons who may be able to pay premiums may choose an ordinary life policy, since it may afford greater flexibility via a vanish pay or other riders or they may be able to invest the difference in the premiums more profitably. For these and other reasons, sales in the United States of this class of whole life insurance are relatively small except in the juvenile and business insurance markets. Limited-payment policies fit the many business insurance situations in which it is desirable to ensure that the policy is fully paid for within a certain time period.[11]

Of course, the disadvantage of higher premiums is offset to some degree by the availability of larger policy values. Other things being the same, the higher the premium for a policy, the greater the cash values (due to the greater prefunding of future mortality charges). All limited-payment policies contain the same nonforfeiture, dividend, and settlement options as well as other standard features of ordinary life policies that provide policyowner flexibility.

The extreme form of limited-payment life insurance is the **single-premium whole life** policy. Such a policy has immediate substantial cash and loan value, and, of course, it is fully paid up from inception. Consequently, such a contract requires a substantial outlay. The other extreme of whole life is represented by the ordinary life insurance policy, for which the premiums are payable until the maturity of the contract. Limited-payment contracts vary between these extremes. Thus, five- and 10-pay life policies are close to single-premium policies, whereas a policy paid up at age 85 or beyond is, for all practical purposes, an ordinary life policy. Other things being the same, as the number of premium payments increases, the annual premium and, consequently, the rate of growth of policy values become correspondingly smaller.

---

[10] See Chap. 19.
[11] See Chap. 15.

Figure 5-1 shows illustrative cash surrender values for various whole life insurance policies for a male aged 35. As is clear, the size of the cash value varies inversely with the length of the premium-paying period. Thus, the ordinary life plan with payments for life has the lowest cash values, and the single-premium plan, which involves only one premium payment, has the highest. Note that after premium payments cease under the 10-payment and 20-payment whole life plans, the cash values in each instance equal those under the single-premium plan. For policies using the same underlying pricing assumptions, this must be the case, since after any limited-payment period expires, the value to the company of future premiums is zero and all future mortality costs must be covered from existing funds and interest earnings thereon.

## INDETERMINATE PREMIUM WHOLE LIFE INSURANCE

To increase their ability to compete effectively with participating products, several companies offer **indeterminate-premium whole life** policies. This concept, discussed in Chapter 4, applies to all forms of insurance but was first widely used with whole life.

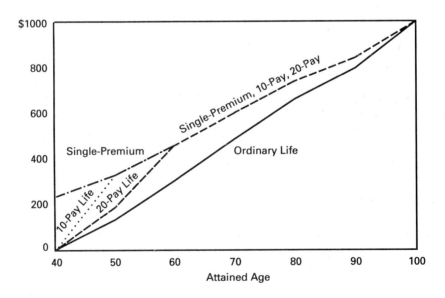

**FIGURE 5-1**

**ILLUSTRATIVE WHOLE LIFE POLICY CASH SURRENDER VALUES PER $1,000, FOR 40-YEAR-OLD MALE, BASED ON 1980 CSO TABLE, AT 5% INTEREST**

The key to this dual-premium nonpar contract is an actually payable premium that is lower than the maximum permissible contractual premium. In effect, a significant discount from the maximum premium is guaranteed for the first few contract years. Annually thereafter, the premium actually payable is set by the company, subject to the maximum constraint. The policy is designed to reflect, through its premium structure, up-to-date expectations as to future operating experience.

## CURRENT ASSUMPTION WHOLE LIFE

**Current assumption whole life** (CAWL) policies provide nonpar whole life insurance under a nontraditional, transparent format that relies on an indeterminate-premium structure. The policy typically uses new-money interest rates and current mortality charges in cash-value determination. This fact has led to the product also being referred to as **interest-sensitive whole life**.

Traditional whole life relies on dividends as the mechanism for passing through deviations of actual operational experience from that anticipated. CAWL, by contrast, relies on changes in the cash values and premiums to accommodate deviations in expected operational experience from that guaranteed in the contract.

Owners of CAWL policies are shown an allocation of the premium payments and interest earnings to cover the policy's pricing components: expenses, mortality charges, and interest earnings on cash-value buildups. Although this allocation may not faithfully reflect the company's actual internal pricing components, the owner, nonetheless, can visualize the unbundled, transparent functioning of the policy mechanism. By contrast, no allocation is visible with traditional whole life policies.

Figure 5-2 illustrates the funds flow pattern of a CAWL policy. The premium, determined in accordance with the procedure mentioned below, is paid to the insurer. Expense charges (if any) are then deducted. The contract sets out the maximum that can be charged, but companies may charge less. Many CAWL policies have no explicit expense charges; the charges are met through higher-than-needed mortality charges and through a margin in interest earnings.

The amount remaining is added to the previous year's accumulated fund balance (if any) to constitute a beginning-year balance. To this balance is added interest based on the insurer's current crediting rate. Rates over the past several years have ranged from 6 to 10 percent and even higher. Guaranteed minimum rates typically are 4.0, 4.5, or 5.0 percent.

Next, mortality charges are assessed. The calculations of these charges are based on the maximum permissible rates as set forth in the contract or, more often, on lower current rates. The rate is applied to the policy's net amount at risk (face amount less cash value).

**FIGURE 5-2**

**CURRENT ASSUMPTION WHOLE LIFE FUNDS FLOW**

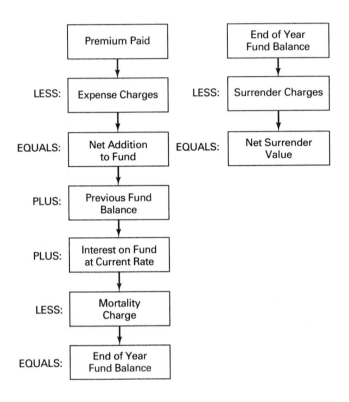

The remaining fund balance is the policy's cash value. Most contracts stipulate that surrender charges will be levied against the fund balance to derive the cash surrender value. This value is never less than that required by the standard nonforfeiture law.

Surrender charges are desirable from the perspective of the insurer and persisting policyowners. Of course, from the buyer's perspective, the lower the surrender charge the better the value, *ceteris paribus*. From the insurer's viewpoint, such charges permit a recoupment of some or all of the heavy policy-issuance expenses, thus minimizing the strain on surplus. Stated in terms of the discussion on assets shares in Chapter 2, surrender charges can permit a more equitable allocation of expenses between persisting and lapsing policyowners. In the absence of these charges and with other things being the same, terminating policyowners would depart with cash surrender values that, in all likelihood, greatly exceeded the corresponding asset share. The effect would be to require continuing policyowners to make good the deficit, thus reducing the long-term value of their policies.

***Product Design.*** CAWL products can be classified as falling into either a low-premium or high-premium category. Each category of products has characteristics in common:

1. Use of an accumulation account that is composed of the premium, less expense and mortality charges and credited with interest based on current rates.

2. Use of a surrender charge, fixed at issue, that is deducted from the accumulation account to derive the policy's cash surrender value.

3. Use of a fixed death benefit and maximum premium level at time of issue. (On the low-premium version, either of these may be subject to change.)

If there is a stated expense charge, it generally equals $20 to $50 per year. The surrender charge is usually expressed as some percentage of the first-year premium (often 100 percent) or of the accumulation account value. It usually grades down as a percentage of the accumulation account over a maximum of 15 or so years.

The low-premium version has several unique features. The initial (indeterminate) premium is low by traditional ordinary life insurance standards. The policy's **redetermination provision** generally states that after the initial guarantee period, the company can redetermine the premium using the same or new assumptions as to future interest and mortality. The policy contains specific quantitative guarantees as to the minimum interest rate to be credited and the maximum mortality charges to be levied. The premium is then redetermined, such that, together with the existing accumulation account value, it will be able to maintain a level death benefit to the end of life, if the new assumptions hold true. This will be recognized as a type of indeterminate-premium structure.

If the new assumptions are the same as those used at time of issue or previous redetermination, the premiums and death benefits are guaranteed for another period of years. However, if the assumptions have changed since the last redetermination, the new redetermined premium may be higher or lower than previously.

If the new premium is lower than the previous premium, the policyowner often may elect one of three options:

1. Pay the new lower premium and maintain the previous death benefit.

2. Continue to pay the previous premium, maintain the previous death benefit, and have the difference in the two premiums added to the accumulation fund.

3. Continue to pay the previous premium and use the difference to pay for an increased death benefit, subject to evidence of insurability.

Typically, the contract will stipulate one of these as the automatic option—often option 2 above—but the policyowner may elect a change at any time.

If the new premium is higher than the previous premium, the policyowner may elect one of three options:

1. Pay the new higher premium and maintain the previous death benefit.

2. Continue to pay the previous premium, but lower the policy death benefit to that which the new premium will sustain.

3. Continue to pay the previous premium and maintain the previous death benefit while using up some of the available cash value. (This option is not always available and, when available, requires the accumulation fund to be at or above a certain level for at least the next five policy years.)

Contracts typically stipulate option 1 as automatic, but the policyowner may direct otherwise at any time.

The high-premium version also has several unique aspects. The premium is relatively high but typically guaranteed never to increase. An optional pay-up or **vanishing-premium provision** is usually contained in the contract. This provision states that the policyowner may elect to cease paying premiums at a given point in time and essentially have a paid-up contract. The "point in time" is determined by comparing the accumulation account to a net single premium needed to pay up the contract, but with the net single premium based on current interest rates and mortality rates. Once the accumulation account exceeds this net single premium, the contract is essentially paid up. This typically occurs between the fifth and tenth policy years for most CAWL policies. It remains "paid up" *if and only if* the current or more favorable interest and mortality levels are maintained until maturity of the contract. This paid-up provision is not mandatory and the paid-up period is not guaranteed. The policy remains "paid up" only so long as the accumulation account exceeds the minimum required cash value. Once it falls below this level, premiums are required or the standard nonforfeiture options apply.

The low-premium and high-premium versions are simply two different approaches applied to the same basic product. With the low-premium version, current assumptions as to interest, mortality, and expenses are used to lower the current premium charged. With the high-premium version, these favorable anticipated deviations result in a far more rapid increase in cash values, with the result that the policy can be paid up quickly, although the contract is not guaranteed to remain paid up. Therefore, the vanishing premium version is not strictly comparable to the limited-payment whole life policies discussed previously.

Of course, variations in CAWL product design are found. For example, some insurers offer a death benefit that is equal to a level, stated face amount plus an additional amount equal to the accumulation fund balance. Some insurers make premium redeterminations every year or every three years instead of every five years, and some versions contain even longer guarantee periods. A few CAWL policies make adjustments based on interest alone and some index the policy's current interest rate to interest rates on money instruments, such as Treasury bills or certain bond indexes.

*Policy Illustration*. Table 5-4 shows illustrated premiums and policy values that are based on one company's low-premium and high-premium CAWL policies. Note that the difference between the two premium levels is significant ($6.18 versus $13.00 per $1,000) and that the charge for the low-premium version is considerably less than the premiums illustrated in Table 5-2 for ordinary life policies. Premiums are subject to a five-year redetermination period.

At current rates and assumptions, the high-premium policy could be tentatively paid up at the end of seven policy years, if the policy contained the vanishing premium provision. If premiums were stopped at that point, later-duration surrender values would be less than those shown in Table 5-4.

*Uses of CAWL*. Compared with universal life, current assumption whole life's level premium allows for easier company and policyowner administration. The level premium also gives the company greater control over the cash value buildup. The level premium/face amount combination may be more familiar to many persons than the universal life approach and therefore could be a more "comfortable" product. It is a blend of new and old.

Unlike the universal life policy, the CAWL policy will lapse if the premium is not paid.[12] This may provide some incentive for the policyowner to pay renewal premiums regularly and therefore could assist individuals who perceive themselves as not having the discipline to pay flexible premiums.

**TABLE 5-4    ILLUSTRATIVE PREMIUMS AND VALUES FOR TWO CURRENT ASSUMPTION WHOLE LIFE POLICIES (FOR 35-YEAR-OLD NONSMOKING MALE)**

| | | Low-Premium Version (per $1,000) | | | High-Premium Version (per $1,000) | | |
|---|---|---|---|---|---|---|---|
| Policy Year | Death Benefit | Current Premium | Guaranteed Surrender Value | Projected Surrender Value | Current Premium | Guaranteed Surrender Value | Projected Surrender Value[b] |
| 1 | $100,000 | $6.18 | $0 | $0 | $13.00 | $0 | $0 |
| 2 | 100,000 | 6.18 | 1 | 1 | 13.00 | 0 | 6 |
| 3 | 100,000 | 6.18 | 6 | 6 | 13.00 | 4 | 21 |
| 4 | 100,000 | 6.18 | 12 | 12 | 13.00 | 16 | 36 |
| 5[a] | 100,000 | 6.18 | 17 | 17 | 13.00 | 28 | 54 |
| 10[a] | 100,000 | 6.18 | 46 | 49 | 13.00 | 97 | 175 |
| 15[a] | 100,000 | 6.18 | 78 | 93 | 13.00 | 176 | 373 |
| 20[a] | 100,000 | 6.18 | 112 | 144 | 13.00 | 261 | 678 |

[a] Premium to be paid for next five years is redetermined by company.

[b] Assumes premiums continue to be paid each year and death benefit is kept at initial amount.

[12] Policies paid for under the vanish premium provision constitute an exception to this statement. Under these policies, the excess of the actual over the minimum required guaranteed cash value, if large enough, can be used to cover the premium due.

## VARIABLE LIFE INSURANCE[13]

**Variable life insurance** (VLI) is a type of whole life insurance whose values may vary directly with the performance of a set of earmarked investments. It was first offered for sale to the U.S. general public in 1976. Its success was initially quite limited, with only the Equitable Life Assurance Society involved in pioneering marketing efforts. Since that time, several insurers have begun offering traditional VLI or some version of it.

When VLI was introduced in this country—after being marketed successfully in The Netherlands, England, and Canada—it was thought of as a product that could help offset the adverse effects of inflation on life insurance policy death benefits. It was believed that over the long term the investment experience of common stocks supporting the policies would increase with inflation. Hence, it was anticipated that VLI benefits would increase with the value of the underlying stocks, thus providing a hedge against inflation.

Even if this were true in the long run, short-term variations are inevitable, with inflation heading in one direction and investment performance in the other. Increasingly, VLI investment funds have moved away from common stocks, and, as mentioned below, a variety of investment media are now available, many of which are more stable in the short run.

*Product Design.* A variable life insurance policy provides whole life insurance under which the death benefits and cash values vary to reflect the investment experience of a **separate account** (a separate pool of assets) supporting the reserves for such policies. Traditional VLI policies are of a fixed-premium nature, similar to traditional whole life insurance. A flexible-premium version of variable life, called variable universal life, is discussed in Chapter 6.

In VLI policies, premiums less an expense or sales load and a mortality charge are paid into a separate investment account. The policyowner may specify, within limits, where the assets backing the cash value are to be invested. Several options are generally available. Most companies offer money market funds, common stock funds, and bond funds, as well as other fund types. The policy death benefit ordinarily is directly related to the investment performance. However, regardless of the investment performance, the death benefit can never fall below a specified minimum amount. Cash values also vary with the investment performance of the underlying funds, but are not guaranteed. The cash value at any point in time is based on the market value of the assets backing the policy. The VLI contract passes all investment risk to the policyowner.

The death benefit is composed of two parts. The first is a guaranteed minimum death benefit that corresponds to the basic plan of insurance underlying

---

[13] This section draws on Gregory D. Jacobs, "Pricing Non-traditional Individual Life Products," *SOA Part 10 Study Note* (Itasca, Ill.: Society of Actuaries, 1984); Mary Jo Napoli, "Variable Annuities," ibid. (1985); and Frank L. Rainaldi, "Variable Life—An Investment Oriented Life Insurance Product with a Non-Investment Alternative," *The Journal of the American Society of CLU*, Vol. XXXVIII (January 1985).

the VLI contract. The second part of the death benefit is variable. Any positive excess interest credits (i.e., the excess of the return on the underlying funds over an assumed investment return) is used to buy additional "pieces" of insurance. These additional units of VLI are generally purchased at net premium rates on a daily, monthly, or annual basis. If the excess interest credits are negative, prior credited variable units will be surrendered and the total death benefit lowered. In no event will the total policy death benefit fall below the minimum guaranteed death benefit.

The cash value of a VLI policy varies daily. Unlike the variable insurance amounts, however, no minimum is guaranteed. At any point in time, the actual cash surrender value is based upon the market value of the policy's share of the separate account's underlying funds.

Variable life policies may be participating or nonparticipating. With participating VLI, the dividend is a function only of possible mortality and expense savings and includes no element of excess investment earnings. Excess investment earnings, less an asset management charge, are credited directly to policy cash values.

VLI should be distinguished from index-linked life insurance in which death benefits vary with an outside index such as the Consumer Price Index (CPI) or the Standard and Poor's 500 Stock Price Index. Funds backing indexed policies are invested in the insurer's general account, just as with traditional forms of whole life insurance. Index-linked policies' cash values do not vary with the underlying investment performance.

***Regulatory Developments***. VLI is influenced by regulation on more fronts than most insurance products. Issuers of VLI must, as with all insurance products, comply with state insurance laws and regulations. Variable contracts and their issuers are also subject to federal securities laws and are regulated by the Securities and Exchange Commission (SEC).

*1. Federal Securities Regulation.* Federal securities regulation of VLI has its basis principally in three laws and related regulations. The SEC administers these laws. The three laws are the Investment Company Act of 1940, the Securities Act of 1933, and the Securities Exchange Act of 1934.

Entities that invest VLI policyowner assets in securities are investment companies (mutual funds) as defined in the **Investment Company Act of 1940**. This act is the focal point of securities regulation of VLI. The act regulates investment company management and operation. It sets ground rules concerning security owners, maximum sales charges, investment management of contributions, and distribution of periodic financial reports.

The SEC provides limited exemptions from the sections of the 1940 Act that require management accountability to contractholders, that impose limitations on sales loads, and that require issuers to offer refunds under certain circumstances. SEC rules, for example, set out a definition and maximum for the sales load—currently 9 percent of premiums during the first 20 policy years, with some exceptions. A VLI policy must be funded by a life insurance company separate account and must provide death benefits and cash values that vary to reflect the account's investment experience. The policy must also provide a minimum death benefit guarantee and have the mortality and expense risk borne by the insurer.

The **Securities Act of 1933** sets registration, financial, and disclosure standards for securities. A VLI policy is a security. This act's main impact on VLI (and variable annuities—see Chapter 7) is the requirement that the potential purchaser be provided with a prospectus. This booklet includes the identity and nature of the insurer's business, the use to which the insurer will put the premiums, financial information on the insurer, the fees and expenses to be charged, and policyowner rights.

Whereas the 1933 Act deals principally with new securities issues, the **Securities Exchange Act of 1934** regulates the secondary securities market— i.e., the exchange of securities. Under the 1934 Act, the entity that distributes VLI—the insurance company or a sales company—usually must register as a broker-dealer. The act requires that **associated persons** pass an examination on the securities business. Associated persons include agents and many home office and agency employees. The 1934 Act regulates advertising, annual reports to shareholders, shareholder proxies, and financial reporting requirements.

The Maloney Act, an amendment to the Securities Exchange Act of 1934, made provision for the securities industry to form one or more bodies to regulate itself in accordance with the act's standards. The National Association of Securities Dealers (NASD) was established for this purpose in 1939. All broker-dealers, including agents who sell VLI, must register with the NASD and pass an examination.

*2. State Insurance Regulation.* VLI may be issued in all states, and all states make provision for separate accounts. Introduction of VLI in the states required legislative or regulatory authority. The basis for VLI regulation is the **Model Variable Life Insurance Regulation** adopted by the National Association of Insurance Commissioners.

The regulation establishes certain mandatory policy design characteristics and policy provisions. The regulation also covers the qualifications of a company to conduct a VLI business, operations of VLI separate account, and reserve requirements.

*Policy Provisions.* In most aspects, the VLI policy operates the same as a traditional whole life insurance policy. Fixed premiums are payable on regular due dates, and, if they are not paid, the policy lapses and goes under an option on lapse. Both reduced paid-up and extended term insurance on a fixed-dollar basis are available.

The policy may be reinstated subject to usual rules, except that the past-due premiums collected must not be less than 110 percent of the increase in cash value immediately available upon reinstatement. This condition is necessary because the reinstated policy reflects values associated with a policy that had never lapsed and thus would reflect any favorable investment experience during the period of lapse.

Loans of up to 90 percent of the cash value may be taken at a fixed (often 8 percent) or a variable interest rate. Loans against policy cash values have the effect of creating an additional investment fund. Under this approach, variable benefits are affected, since the return reflected in benefits is a blend of the separate account investment return and the net return earned on any policy loan. An interesting characteristic of this provision is that it presents an opportunity for a policyowner to influence the policy's variable benefits. In making a loan, the policyowner withdraws funds from the separate account and may make the policy less variable (up or down) while the policy loan is outstanding. This direct recognition feature was discussed in Chapter 4.

*Illustrations of Death Benefits and Cash Values.* Although it is relatively easy to describe how variable life insurance policy benefits will vary to reflect the investment experience of the underlying separate account, to describe the specific method of determining benefit variation is a challenge. To supplement the narrative descriptions in the policy and prospectus, illustrations of policy benefits (assuming hypothetical rates of return in the separate account) are developed. Currently, applicable regulations permit illustrations based on (1) annual gross rates of return (after any tax charges and before other deductions) of 0, 4, 6, 8, 10, and 12 percent and (2) the Standard and Poor's 500 Stock Price Index with dividends reinvested. Table 5-5 summarizes an illustration for a $100,000 level face amount policy issued to a male nonsmoker aged 35.

*The Appropriateness of VLI.* Variable life insurance should be appealing to those who desire whole life insurance at a fixed, level premium and also the potential for important equity-type gains (and losses). Obviously, since the investment risk rests with the policyowner, VLI is riskier than the more traditional forms of life insurance. As a result, it may not be appropriate as the centerpiece of many persons' insurance/savings programs. As discussed in Chapter 1, most sound financial plans have as one of their elements a savings program that is both highly liquid and relatively riskless. A VLI policy, at any point in time, may or may not meet this objective. Its cash value might be more appropriately considered as an element in one's long-term *investment* program.

## OTHER FORMS OF WHOLE LIFE INSURANCE

Five other forms of whole life insurance policies are covered here. The total market share of these five forms is not great, but they can be important products to individual buyers and they are an important part of the total sales of a number of companies.

**TABLE 5-5     ILLUSTRATION OF VARIABLE LIFE POLICY VALUES FOR $100,000 FACE AMOUNT (FOR 35-YEAR-OLD NONSMOKING MALE)**

Annual Premium: $1,570

| | Death Benefit Assuming Hypothetical Gross Annual Investment Return of: | | | | | Cash Surrender Value Assuming Hypothetical Gross Annual Investment Return of: | | | |
|---|---|---|---|---|---|---|---|---|---|
| Yr | 0% | 4% | 8% | 12% | Yr | 0% | 4% | 8% | 12% |
| 1 | $100,000 | $100,000 | $100,064 | $100,135 | 1 | $379 | $379 | $418 | $438 |
| 2 | 100,000 | 100,000 | 100,278 | 100,591 | 2 | 1,506 | 1,590 | 1,680 | 1,771 |
| 3 | 100,000 | 100,000 | 100,642 | 101,380 | 3 | 2,680 | 2,879 | 3,092 | 3,312 |
| 4 | 100,000 | 100,000 | 101,153 | 102,508 | 4 | 3,703 | 4,064 | 4,455 | 4,874 |
| 5 | 100,000 | 100,000 | 101,814 | 104,000 | 5 | 4,870 | 5,444 | 6,077 | 6,773 |
| 10 | 100,000 | 100,000 | 107,519 | 117,746 | 10 | 10,322 | 12,755 | 15,799 | 19,605 |
| 15 | 100,000 | 100,000 | 117,238 | 144,059 | 15 | 15,081 | 20,693 | 28,743 | 40,323 |
| 20 | 100,000 | 100,000 | 131,170 | 187,013 | 20 | 18,877 | 28,931 | 45,550 | 73,231 |
| 30 | 100,000 | 100,000 | 173,150 | 349,955 | 30 | 23,683 | 45,744 | 94,741 | 206,022 |

*Modified Life*. A **modified life** policy provides whole life insurance under which premiums are redistributed so that they are lower than an otherwise identical ordinary life policy during the first three or five years, and higher thereafter. Thus, one company under a "modified 5" may set the premium during the first five years so that it will double thereafter. Other redistributions are also used. During this preliminary period, the premium is more than the equivalent level-term premium for such a period, but less than the ordinary life premium at date of issue. Logically, after the preliminary period, the premium is somewhat larger than the ordinary life premium at the issue date, but less than the ordinary life premium at the insured's attained age at the end of the preliminary period. Regardless of the redistribution arrangement utilized, the company would expect to receive the actuarial equivalent of the regular ordinary life premiums, assuming, of course, that all underlying assumptions were equivalent.

*Enhanced Ordinary Life*. Several mutual companies offer a type of participating whole life policy that uses dividends to provide some form of level coverage at a lower-than-usual premium. The details, including the name given the plan, vary from company to company, but the purpose is basically the same: to provide a whole life participating policy with a low premium. Under these policies dividends are earmarked. Under one approach, the face amount of a special ordinary life policy is reduced after a few years. However, dividends are used to purchase deferred paid-up whole life additions, such that at the time the policy face amount is to be reduced, the paid-up additions fill the gap, with the result that the total death benefit is at least equal to the original face amount (based on illustrated dividends).

Under another approach, the actual policy face amount may be 60 to 80 percent of the initial death benefit, with the difference made up by the purchase of paid-up additions and term insurance in such proportions that the total death benefit is intended to remain equivalent to or greater than the initial death benefit. Under this approach, it is hoped that paid-up additions eventually are sufficient to require no further purchase of term insurance.

A guarantee period is used in all enhanced ordinary life policies to ensure that the total death benefit during the early policy years does not fall below the original level, even if dividends were to prove insufficient to meet the desired objectives. With most companies, if dividends actually paid exceeded those needed to purchase the requisite amount of additional coverage, the excess would be used to purchase paid-up additions. If dividends paid were lower than illustrated, the majority of plans require that one-year term be purchased.

*Graded Premium Whole Life.* The more traditional forms of **graded premium whole life** (GPWL) provide that premiums begin at a level that is 50 percent or lower than those for a comparable ordinary life policy. Premiums increase annually for a period of from 5 to 20 years and remain level thereafter. Cash values evolve much more slowly than with ordinary life, often not appearing for five or more years. Policies may be participating or nonparticipating and may have indeterminate premiums.

Many newer forms of GPWL are more akin to yearly renewable term (YRT) policies than whole life insurance. These types of GPWL begin with premiums that are comparable to those charged for YRT, and they have YRT-type increases for periods ranging from 15 to 40 years. The premium levels off thereafter. Typically, no cash values evolve until well after the tenth policy year. For some policies, there are no cash values at policy year 20, or even by age 70 for a few. Such products resemble and compete with YRT policies that automatically convert to ordinary life at later ages. Premiums are often indeterminate and smoker/nonsmoker rates are typically used. A few companies also have reentry provisions.

*Single-Premium Whole Life.* Until the 1980s, relatively few persons purchased a whole life policy with a single premium, in large measure because of the exceedingly high outlay required relative to the face amount—in the past often 40 to 50 percent of the face amount. However, by the late 1980s the "magic" of tax deferral of interest and creative product design by individual companies led to a great demand for an updated version of the product. As discussed in Chapter 13, however, abuses of the tax deferral aspect led to a corresponding demand for congressional action to close a tax loophole that permitted the abuse. As a result of a new tax law, therefore, demand for the product shrank. Even so, considerable premiums are still spent for such contracts.

**Single premium whole life** (SPWL) sold today uses the current assumption approach discussed earlier with respect to level premiums (see Figure 5-2). The purchaser pays a relatively large single premium to the insurer that credits current rates of interest to the fund value. Rather than mortality and expense charges being deducted annually from the cash value, they may be netted against the interest credited to the fund. Thus there may appear to be no specific deduction for these charges in the fund accumulation. Additional first-year policy expense charges might be levied against the premium.

Surrender charges are typically used. Some insurers also include **bailout provisions** that provide that if the credited interest rate falls below a certain level, the policyowner may surrender and incur no surrender charge. The usual range of policy options is available, including policy loans. Insurers usually impose high (e.g., $10,000) minimum premiums.

SPWL insurance can be useful for individuals who have the funds to purchase such coverage, although its appropriate usage is limited. Wealthy older persons often purchase it. The tax-preferred status accorded other forms of life insurance still accrues in part to the SPWL purchaser. Thus tax on interest earnings is deferred, if not avoided altogether, provided no withdrawals or policy loans are made. Death proceeds are tax-free and can easily avoid the publicity and expense of probate.[14]

*Indexed Whole Life.* Several companies offer a whole life policy whose face amount increases with increases in the CPI. In general, these policies have been classified as to whether the policyowner or the company assumes the inflation risk. Under the approach where the policyowner assumes the risk, the death benefit increases each year in accordance with the CPI and the insurance company bills the policyowner each year for the new, higher amount of insurance. The company agrees, by contract, not to require evidence of insurability for these increases, so long as each year's increase is exercised. If the policyowner declines in any year to purchase the increase, no further automatic increases are permitted.

The approach under which the insurer assumes the inflation risk is similar in effect to the preceding approach, except that the premium charged initially by the insurer is loaded in anticipation of future face amount increases. Thus increases in face amount do not alter the premium level paid. Such policies often have a cap as to the maximum total increase permitted.[15]

## RECENT EFFORTS TO ENHANCE VALUE WITHIN EXISTING POLICIES

Because of the various competitive and other forces impinging on U.S. life insurance companies, they began witnessing record numbers of surrenders in the high inflation period of the late 1970s and early 1980s. Policyowners often

---

[14] See Chap. 13.

[15] Many companies also offer a cost-of-living-adjustment rider similar in effect to that of indexed policies. (See Chap. 7.)

purchased replacement life insurance, and the new policy was frequently some form of fixed or flexible premium current assumption policy.

If the older policy was a guaranteed-cost, nonparticipating product, it had great difficulty competing with the new generation of products. These older products, which were priced on older, more conservative assumptions (by today's standards), did not make provision for the pass-through to policyowners of a share in favorable experience. These products were and remain susceptible to replacement.

In theory, older participating policies should offer sound value even in inflationary times and, therefore, should be far more resistive to replacement if the insurer's experience is at least average, and if the insurer distributes accumulated surplus in a reasonable and equitable manner. Regrettably, not all insurers have met these two tests.

A problem with many older whole life policies is that they often, by contract, permit the policyowner to exercise the loan option at interest rates that are below prevailing market rates. Naturally, when a person can borrow money at below market rates and invest the proceeds at or above prevailing market rates, he or she is wise to do so, other things being the same. This process, called **disintermediation**, is exactly what happened in the late 1970s and early 1980s, and, when combined with record numbers of policy surrenders, it led to massive reductions in insurer cash inflows. In fact, many life insurers actually experienced negative cash flows for the first time since the 1930s depression.

This fact meant that insurers had to liquidate bonds and other securities, usually at a significant discount from par. This action aggravated the problem. An additional important effect was that many insurers were forced to forgo investing in contemporary, high-yielding assets, since they needed the cash flow to fund not only the normal cash outflows, such as dividend payments, death claim payments, and expenses, but also to fund the greatly increased surrender value and policy loan outflows. When an insurer makes a policy loan at 5, 6, or 8 percent, it is "investing" its assets in that loan at that rate, much as if it had made a commercial mortgage loan. The critical difference, of course, is that the commercial loan would have earned a much higher rate of interest than that earned on policy loans.

As a result of these lost investment opportunities and the increased level of investments in policy loans (reaching 25 percent and higher of assets with some insurers), many companies' overall portfolio earnings rates did not grow as fast or to a level that they otherwise would have attained. Because of this, dividends paid at that time on many participating policies were not competitive with excess interest and other credits on current assumption policies.

Companies were keenly aware of these problems and many undertook efforts to enhance the value of their existing older policies, to render them less prone to surrender and replacement or to retain the policyowner as a client. These efforts generally fell into three categories:

1. Unilateral enhancements
2. Bilateral enhancements
3. Policy exchanges

## UNILATERAL ENHANCEMENTS

Several insurance companies have made unilateral changes in certain classes of older policies, the intended effects of which are to enhance the policy's value to its owner. Enhancements have been made with both participating and nonparticipating policies, although the exact extent of this activity is not known.

Some companies have unilaterally increased policy death benefits either on a permanent basis or on a year-to-year basis. One company, for example, provides an increase in the death benefit of pre-1974 issues of whole life policies equal to one-half of 1 percent of the policy face amount for each year the policy has been in force. This additional insurance is provided by one-year term additions at no additional charge to policyowners.

Other companies have effected a permanent increase in policy face amount by changing the reserve (and usually cash value) interest assumptions underpinning the policies. Insurers gained some tax advantage from following this approach, which they used to partially offset the cost of the enhancement. If the reserve/cash value bases are changed, cash values per $1,000 face amount can be less, but the total policy cash value is usually greater after the change.

## BILATERAL ENHANCEMENTS

Several insurers have embarked on bilateral update programs for older policies. These programs have involved the insurer offering to change—usually improve—some benefit in the policy, in return for the policyowner's agreement to change some aspect of the life insurance contract itself.

Many bilateral update programs have revolved around the policy loan clause. The first types were simply requests by some insurers to increase the guaranteed policy loan interest rate on certain older policies, in return for which the insurer would place the policy in a higher dividend classification. The amendment option typically was offered to those who owned policies that contained 5 and 6 percent loan clauses. The new loan rate was usually raised to 8 percent, although some companies opted to introduce a variable loan rate clause.

Another type of bilateral update program involved the direct recognition of policy loan activity within the policy's dividend formula. Under this approach, policyowners who borrowed heavily at low interest rates receive lower dividends than those who did not borrow as heavily. Most companies perceived the change to be of such significance as to warrant formal policyowner agreement.

Bilateral enhancements usually involve no change in premium or guaranteed cash values. The insurance coverage usually is unaffected. Dividends are usually the only item changed, besides the policy loan rate.

## POLICY EXCHANGES

Many—perhaps most—life insurance companies have addressed the problems of enhancement of older policies through exchanging old policies for new ones. This process may involve a formalized company procedure for a systematic internal replacement program; it may involve revised procedures to accommodate internal replacements that agents initiate but with no company sponsorship; or it may involve the insurer being uninformed while agents effect internal replacements of their clients' policies. From the policyowner's viewpoint, the net result can be the same.

Companies that have formalized exchange programs usually offer existing policyowners the opportunity to replace their older policies with newer versions under favorable terms or conditions. For example, many insurers will forgo or streamline evidence of insurability requirements. Reduced loadings may be offered on the new policy or increased policy face amounts may be offered.

Insurers' older policies are a major source of profits. As the asset share calculation in Chapter 2 illustrated, policies' contributions to surplus (profit) typically increase over time. Thus companies that undertake any meaningful enhancement programs usually forgo some current profit in hopes of future profit. This future profit is expected to be realized through existing improved policies because of higher earnings from higher loan interest rates. Increased profits may be expected to arise from increased business that flows from an improved company image among agents and the consumer. Tax savings might also partially offset current lost profits.

# Chapter 6

# *F*LEXIBLE-*P*REMIUM *L*IFE *I*NSURANCE *P*OLICIES

## GENERAL NATURE OF FLEXIBLE-PREMIUM LIFE INSURANCE POLICIES

Traditional life insurance policies have features that improve their ability to adapt to changing circumstances. The nonforfeiture and policy loan provisions, the dividend options of participating policies, and the renewable and convertible features of term insurance are all examples. Yet considerable rigidity exists in traditional life insurance products. It is usually not convenient to change either the face amount or the premium, except by lapsing or surrendering the old coverage and starting afresh.

Indeed, all life insurance policies sold in the United States prior to the 1970s were fixed-premium contracts issued on either a participating or guaranteed-cost, nonparticipating basis. With enhanced computer technology, flexible premium policies became feasible.

The first major U.S. life insurance industry change in policy flexibility occurred during this period when the **adjustable life** (AL) policy was introduced in 1971. The policy permitted the policyowner to select, within limits, whatever premium he or she wished, and later to adjust, within limits, the premium and/or policy face amount.

The introduction of **universal life** (UL) in 1979 built on the strengths of adjustable life, but also provided true flexibility in premium payments, contemporary interest rates, and an unbundling of the savings and pure protection elements and associated pricing. Increased disclosure to prospective purchasers and to existing policyowners accompanied the introduction of UL.

Some insurers, unsure whether UL policies were in their and their customers' best interest, sought a means of providing much of the UL flexibility, but within a traditional, fixed-premium context. Thus **flexible enhanced ordinary life** (FEOL) products, introduced as direct UL competitors in 1985, were born.

124

AL, UL, and FEOL are fixed-dollar contracts in the sense that they contain traditional insurance-type guarantees as to minimum cash values and death benefits. The marriage of flexibility and transparency with the equity-based potential of variable life insurance (VLI) was expected. With the introduction of **variable universal life** in early 1985, this was reality.

These four types of life insurance policies are distinguishable from the fixed-premium contracts discussed in chapters 4 and 5. Flexible-premium policies permit the policyowner—not the insurer—to decide, within limits, the premium level to be paid. Each of these policies also permits the policy death benefit to be adjusted.

## ADJUSTABLE LIFE INSURANCE

Adjustable life combines elements of traditional, fixed-premium life insurance and the ability, within limits, to alter (i.e., adjust) the policy plan, premium payments, and face amount.[1] Adjustable life is a level-premium, level-death benefit life insurance policy that can assume the form of any traditional term or whole life policy (within certain guidelines). It is thus a continuum of traditional level-premium life insurance, ranging from low-premium term through ordinary life to high-premium limited-payment whole life.

The **adjustment provision** that distinguishes AL from most other life-insurance contracts permits the policyowner to change the plan by requesting the insurer to change the policy configuration. Adjustments are made prospectively only. Premiums can be increased or decreased. The face amount can be increased (subject in most cases to evidence of insurability) or decreased. Some policies make allowance for an unscheduled or extra premium. Whenever any of these adjustments occur, the plan of insurance will usually also change.

An increase in premium increases future cash values and hence (1) lengthens the period of coverage if the policy is in the term portion of the adjustable life range, or (2) shortens the premium payment period if the policy is in the whole life range. A decrease in premium has the opposite effect.

The AL policy introduced a new concept to the life insurance business. The traditional approach to life insurance programming entailed first determining the face amount and plan of insurance; then, by entering a ratebook at the insured's age, the premium was calculated. If the resulting premium was not consistent with premium-paying ability, adjustments to the face amount or a change to another insurance plan were considered.

Under AL the process and the amount of insurance and premium is established first. Then the plan of insurance is determined by entering a modified ratebook at the insured's age.

---

[1] Minnesota Mutual, which pioneered this product, issued the first AL policies in 1971. The Bankers Life Company of Iowa entered the market in 1977. See Charles L. Trowbridge, "Adjustable Life—A New Solution to an Old Problem," *Journal of the American Society of Chartered Life Underwriters*, Vol. XXXI, No. 34 (Oct. 1977), pp. 12–20.

While AL introduced some important new concepts, it retained many aspects of traditional products. The AL policyowner may alter (adjust) the level of premiums paid, but premiums generally cannot be taken to zero without policy lapse. Therefore AL policies require certain minimum annual premium payments—usually equivalent to that for a five-year term policy. This is not the case with UL policies. Also, any change in the level of premium payments ordinarily requires formal notification of the company and a redefining of the resultant plan.

Once a particular premium payment level is decided upon, that premium is due at future due dates, unless the policyowner specifically requests a change. In this respect, AL is similar to fixed-premium policies. By contrast, UL policies require no implicit assumption regarding the level of future premium payments.

## UNIVERSAL LIFE INSURANCE

Universal life insurance policies are flexible-premium, adjustable-death benefit, unbundled life contracts. Their introduction in the late 1970s and early 1980s was the cause of as much debate and media attention as perhaps any other contemporary life insurance product.

UL was perceived by many as responding to consumer demands for low-cost, flexible life insurance. UL policies do offer great policyowner flexibility, but, as with all life insurance policies (both traditional and new), whether they are low-cost is a function of the manner in which the insurer has priced the product. Both of these important points are made clearer later in this chapter. First, however, it is worthwhile to develop an appreciation for the origins and growth of UL in the United States.

### THE ORIGINS AND GROWTH OF UNIVERSAL LIFE INSURANCE

The concepts upon which UL is based are as old as the concepts underlying level-premium payments and reserves—they are well over 100 years old. A key element—the use of the retrospective approach to cash value (and reserve) development—is analyzed and discussed, for example, in Spurgeon's 1922 authoritative book, *Life Contingencies*, long the standard for the study of this subject by U.S. actuarial students.[2] Jordan's 1952 and 1957 editions of *Life Contingencies* continued the analysis.[3]

It is said that the idea of universal life as a product was mentioned by H. L. Riedner in 1946 and by Alfred N. Guertin in 1964.[4] Ken E. Polk's 1974 article in the *Transactions of the Society of Actuaries*, along with the accompanying discussion papers, provided virtually all of the formulas needed for developing a workable UL policy. Polk referred to his hypothetical policy as variable premium life insurance.[5]

---

[2] See E. F. Spurgeon, *Life Contingencies* (London:Charles & Edward Layton, 1922), pp. 96–97.

[3] See, for example, C. W. Jordan, *Life Contingencies*, 2nd ed. (Chicago:The Society of Actuaries, 1957), Chap. 5.

[4] Stuart J. Kingston, "On Universal Life," *The National Underwriter*, Life/Health ed., Jan. 2, 1982, p. 25.

[5] Ken E. Polk, "Variable Premium Life Insurance," *Transactions of the Society of Actuaries*, Vol. XXVI (1974), pp. 449–465; and discussion, pp. 467–478.

It seems, however, that principal credit for conceiving of UL as a product goes to George R. Dinney of the Great-West Life, a Canadian insurer.[6] He appears to have conceived of the idea as early as 1962, although a written description of the product, which he dubbed *universal life plan*, apparently was made public only in 1971.[7]

James C. H. Anderson, then president of the actuarial consulting firm of Tillinghast, Nelson and Warren, Inc., probably did more than anyone to publicize UL as a viable product and to stimulate serious thinking about the possible need and wisdom for developing such a product. His paper, entitled "The Universal Life Insurance Policy"[8] and presented at the Seventh Pacific Insurance Conference in 1975, is considered by many to be the most important step along the road to UL.

In 1976 one insurer, American Agency Life, in fact developed and sold a UL policy of the type described in Anderson's paper. Because of adverse tax problems, the company soon discontinued sales. UL in its current form was not introduced and sold widely until its introduction by E.F. Hutton Life (then Life of California) in 1979.

The UL concept was at first not welcome by most persons in the U.S. life insurance business. It was perceived (and still is by some) as a threat to the orderly development of the industry, and as not being in consumers' or agents' best interests. Today few persons oppose UL. Most now see it simply as another, albeit important, life product that is available for consumers.

Universal life policy sales had a meteoric rise from an effective zero market share of new sales in 1979 to over 38 percent in 1985, its peak year. Since then, its share has declined to around a quarter of new individual life premiums—still a major proportion.

The initial high growth rate of UL was influenced by the high interest rate environment prevailing in the U.S. during the early to mid-1980s. During this time, interest rates on newly invested funds—those that backed UL products— were higher than those earned by established investment portfolios. In other words, new-money rates substantially exceeded portfolio rates.

Thus life products such as UL that were built on a new-money return had a competitive advantage over portfolio-based cash-value products—such as traditional participating whole life—because of the capability of displaying better values in their sales illustrations. When interest rates peaked and then declined, new money-based products no longer enjoyed this competitive advantage. This fact partially explains the relative decline in UL sales. Of course, over the longer term, otherwise similar new-money and portfolio products should perform similarly.

[6] George R. Dinney, "Universal Life," *The Actuary*, Vol. XV, supplement (Sept. 1981), p. 1, and J. Timothy Lynch, "Universal Life Insurance:A Primer," *The Journal of the American Society of Chartered Life Underwriters*, Vol. XXXVI (July 1982).

[7] Paper entitled "A Descent into the Maelstrom of the Insurance Future," presented in 1971 at the Canadian Institute of Actuaries.

[8] The paper was reproduced in the Tillinghast publication *Emphasis* (Nov. 1975).

## The Nature of Universal Life Insurance

UL policies offer flexibility in premium payment and adjustability in death benefits. After making an initial premium payment of at least some required minimum, policyowners may thereafter pay whatever amounts and at whatever times they wish, or even skip premium payments, provided the cash value will cover policy charges. Also, policyowners may raise (usually subject to evidence of insurability) or lower their policies' death benefits as they deem appropriate, with a minimum of difficulty.

When UL policies were first conceived and designed, the hope was that they would offer not only greater flexibility but also superior value. Superior value was to be realized through reduced distribution costs. Because of the products' flexibility and superior value, agents were expected to increase substantially their sales rates from the industry average of about one policy per week. If agents sold more policies, their commission rates could be lower, thus resulting in better policy value to the buyer.

While many products did provide lower commissions than those applicable to more traditional whole life policies, in reality distribution costs did not remain low for many insurers, since agents resisted the lower commission structures. Many companies that entered the UL field failed to provide adequate margins because of lower-than-expected sales. The administrative costs associated with UL flexibility are high by traditional standards, and the uncertainty associated with UL cash flows has proven a challenge for many insurers.

UL policies are transparent in their operation. The policyowner is able to see how the policy operates internally. An illustration is provided to prospective purchasers describing how policy elements—premiums, death benefits, interest credits, mortality charges, expenses, cash values—interact. Each year the policyowner receives similar information in the form of an annual report. Transparency does not mean that the policyowner can necessarily evaluate the adequacy of projected values; it means only that the policyowner will be able to see, after the fact, the disposition made of policy funds.

A key element of product transparency is that UL policies' cash values and pure insurance amounts are shown separately — that is, they are unbundled. The cash value changes each year in accordance with premium payments made, assessed expenses, and mortality charges and interest credits. The net amount at risk plus the cash value produces the total policy death benefit.

Figure 6-1 illustrates the operation of a typical UL policy. While similar in operation to current assumption whole life (CAWL) policies, UL policies differ from them in that neither the premium level nor the death benefit is fixed. Otherwise, the products are the same in concept. In fact, CAWL policies are sometimes referred to as fixed-premium UL policies.

Referring to Figure 6-1, the mechanics of a UL policy would be as follows: The policyowner pays a first premium of at least a certain required minimum

**FIGURE 6-1**

**UNIVERSAL LIFE FUNDS FLOW ILLUSTRATION**

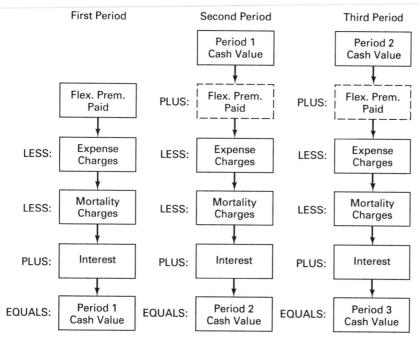

amount. From this initial premium would be subtracted first-period expense charges, although many UL policies have no identifiable front-end loadings.

Next, mortality charges based on the insured's attained age and the policy's net amount at risk and charges for any supplemental benefits (e.g., waiver of premium) would be subtracted. The mortality charges are usually indeterminate, the actual charge usually being less than the maximum rate contained within the policy.

After subtracting expense and mortality charges, the resulting fund is the initial policy cash value (not shown). This initial cash value is then credited with interest, usually at new-money rates, to arrive at the end-of-period cash value. Many UL policies levy high first-year surrender charges against the cash value of any terminating policy.

The second policy period (often a month) begins with the previous period's ending cash-value balance. To this amount the policyowner may add a further premium in an amount of his or her choosing. However, if the previous period's cash value is sufficient to cover the current expense and mortality charges, no premium need be paid. If the previous period's cash value is not sufficient, the policy will lapse in the absence of a further premium payment.

Expense and mortality charges would be subtracted from the sum of the previous period's ending cash-value balance and any premium payment, to arrive at the second-period initial cash value (not shown). Interest at the current rate would then be credited to this initial cash value to arrive at the end-of-period cash value for the second period.

The entire process would be repeated in the third, fourth, and later periods. If the cash value at any time were not sufficient to sustain the policy, the policy would lapse without further premium payments. No further premium need be paid, however, if the cash value is sufficient.

## UNIVERSAL LIFE PRODUCT DESIGN

Numerous UL product design variations exist. For example, joint life and second-to-die UL policies exist. This section does not attempt to address all variations. Rather, an effort is made to describe what seems to be the mainstream of product design.

*Death Benefit Patterns*. Universal life policies typically offer two death benefit patterns from which the purchaser selects one. Of course, the pattern may be changed at any time, but, in the absence of a change request, the selected pattern will be followed during the policy term.

The two patterns are usually labeled options A and B. **Option A** provides a level death benefit pattern, and **option B** provides a pattern that varies directly with cash-value variations.

Under option A, **the net amount at risk** (NAR) is adjusted each policy period (often monthly) so that the cash value and the NAR together always provide a level death benefit. Thus if the cash value increases over time, the NAR decreases by the exact amount and vice versa. This option can result in the same policy benefit pattern as that provided by traditional cash-value policies.

Option B stipulates that the policy death benefit at any time will be equal to the sum of a stated, level NAR and the then cash value. Thus if the cash value increases over time, the total policy death benefit increases exactly with the cash-value increase.

Figure 6-2 illustrates these two death benefit patterns both of which assume that the cash value increases over time. It can be seen that with option A the NAR decreases, whereas with option B it remains at a constant level.

The death benefit patterns provide for a **corridor** of NAR if the cash value becomes too large (as defined by tax law) relative to the NAR. This is illustrated in Figure 6-2 with option A. Without the corridor, a policy could effectively become an endowment and not qualify as life insurance under existing tax law. If a policy fails to meet the Internal Revenue Code (IRC) definition of life insurance, the policy is not accorded favorable tax treatment. (Chapter 13 discusses the important details of this IRC definition.)

Naturally, the greater the NAR, the higher will be the monthly mortality charges. Therefore, *ceteris paribus*, the option B pattern will result in higher mortality charges.

Decreases in the policy death benefit can be made by policyowner request at any time. Since the insurer's NAR is lowered, no evidence of insurability is required for decreases. A lowering of the death benefit naturally also lowers the mortality charges, assuming there is no cash-value withdrawal.

**FIGURE 6-2**

**UNIVERSAL LIFE DEATH BENEFIT PATTERNS**

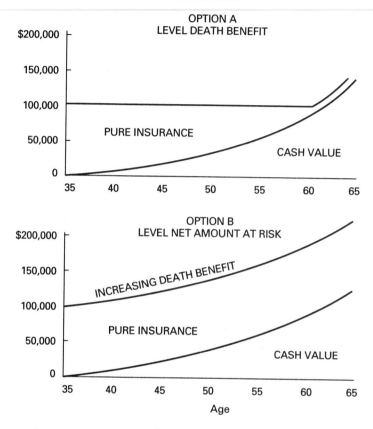

Increases in UL policy death benefits, other than those provided for automatically under option B or any cost of living rider, typically require evidence of insurability. Otherwise, insureds in poor health would have an incentive to increase their policy's death benefits (i.e., they would select against the company). Insurers often permit small increases without evidence, but this is usually done extra-contractually. Increases in policy death benefits result in higher monthly mortality charges, since the NAR increases.

Many companies permit policyowners to attach cost-of-living-adjustment (COLA) riders and future purchase options to their UL policies. COLA riders provide that the policy death benefit will be increased each year in accordance with the previous year's increase in the Consumer Price Index (CPI). Thus if the CPI increased 4 percent this year, a $100,000 policy would automatically increase next year to $104,000. No evidence of insurability would be required; the monthly mortality charges would simply reflect the higher NAR.

Future purchase options permit the increase of the NAR by up to a stipulated amount at designated future ages and events (see Chapter 7). No evidence of insurability is required. Future mortality charges would, of course, reflect the new, higher NAR.

*Premium Payments*. UL policyowners pay whatever premiums they desire and whenever they desire, subject to company rules regarding minimums and maximums. Most companies require only that the first premium be sufficient to cover the first month's expense and mortality charges, although most purchasers pay an amount that is well in excess of this minimum.

One of the potential disadvantages of UL is that policyowners might too easily allow their policies to lapse, since there are no "forced" savings—i.e., no required premium, as is the situation with the products discussed in chapters 4 and 5. To overcome this concern, at least partially, companies bill for a **planned** or **target premium** in accordance with the policyowner's stated preference.

Thus the buyer might agree to a monthly preauthorized draft of his or her bank account. Alternatively, the insurer might send a "bill" to the policyowner for the planned premium. The amount of the automatic bank draft or bill would be set by the policyowner, probably at the agent's suggestion.

Because of policyowners' concerns about not being well informed about their UL policies and especially about the uncertainty of future performance, many companies have introduced the concept of a **no lapse guarantee** based on a **minimum continuation premium**. Insurers applying this concept agree that the contract will remain in force even with no (or even with negative) cash value, provided the stipulated minimum continuation premium is paid. For example, a policy with a ten-year minimum continuation premium would guarantee that payment of this minimum premium would continue the policy in effect for up to 10 years, even if the insurer lowered interest credits or increased charges such that the policy would otherwise terminate at that premium level.

Figure 6-3 illustrates the flexible-premium feature of UL policies. In this illustration, Diane, a 35-year-old female policyowner, decides to pay $1,000 per year into her UL policy. She does this for five years, at which time she needs a lower outlay because she is sending her son to college. Diane, therefore, pays nothing for the next five policy years, with the cash value continuing to build based on the current interest rate net of mortality and expense charges.

At the end of the five-year period, she resumes premium payments but at a lower level ($500), since she is undertaking an important, costly expansion of her business. At age 55 she decides to increase payments to $1,500 per year.

The option A death benefit pattern is assumed, and the interest rate and expense and mortality scales are assumed to remain on their current bases (an admittedly unrealistic assumption). The initial $1,000 premium payment causes a constant rise in cash values, to almost $5,000 by age 40. The cash values continue to build even with no premium payment to age 45—although the rate of growth is far lower—at which time the cash value is less than $6,000. The $500 per year payment, combined with current interest credits, is more than enough to

**FIGURE 6-3**

**ILLUSTRATIVE UNIVERSAL LIFE PREMIUM AND CASH-VALUE PATTERNS**

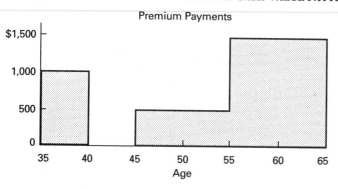

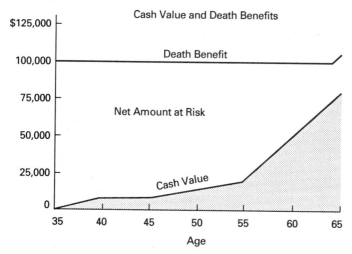

cover mortality and expense charges for the next ten years, so the age 55 cash value is about $20,000. The higher $1,500 premium causes a rapid buildup in cash values, so that by age 65 they stand at about $75,000.[9]

Naturally, any premium payment pattern could be assumed, subject only to company rules and the need to have a sufficient cash value to maintain the policy in force. If insufficient cash value exists to continue the policy, the policyowner is provided a 30 (or 60) day grace period in which to make a premium payment. Failure to do so results in the termination of coverage.

*Policy Loadings*. Figure 6-1 illustrated the nature of UL policy expense and other loading elements. Identifiable loadings are imposed on UL policies in one or both of two ways: (1) **front-end loads** and (2) **back-end loads**.

[9] If the insurer used the maximum permissible charges and the guaranteed minimum interest rate, this premium payment pattern would support the full $100,000 only until age 68, at which time the $1,500 premium would not be sufficient to sustain coverage.

The front-load approach was more prevalent with earlier UL policies. Newer UL products rely more heavily or totally on back-end loadings — so-called **surrender charges**. Some UL contracts are both back- and front-loaded, and a few have neither type of load.

The loading charges of a UL policy rarely, if ever, track a company's actual incurred expenses. Usually, the amount actually charged is insufficient to cover initial expenses, especially on policies with little or no front-end loadings.

These excess first-year expenses, it is hoped, will be recouped through renewal expense charges, through high early-surrender charges, through interest margins, through mortality margins, or through a combination of these. Indeed, for policies with little or no identifiable front-end load, it would be incorrect to contend that the policy had no loading. While no-load policies of all types do not have *identifiable* loading elements, a loading must somehow always be charged against the policy.

The margin between the actual investment earnings of the company and the rate it credits to UL policies is often an important source of income for covering excess expenses and for providing profits. Regrettably for insurers, however, consumers have grown to expect high interest rate credits on their cash values, so these margins have been less than many insurers expected, since they have strived to meet policyowner expectations. Mortality margins also can be important, and since policyowners are not as sensitive to the level of mortality charges as they are to the level of interest rates credited to their cash values, insurers increasingly have relied on mortality margins to cover incurred expenses.

Most UL policies with identifiable expense charges have higher first-year than renewal expense charges. Both initial and renewal expense charges can be on a per-policy basis, a per $1,000 of face amount basis, or on a percentage of premium. Some insurers use all three bases while others use two, one or none.

For example, one company's expense loading for the first policy year is composed of a flat $96 policy assessment plus a charge of $0.15 per $1,000 per month (i.e., $1.80 per $1,000 per year), plus a further charge of 10 percent of the premiums paid. Renewal expense charges are based solely on the 10 percent premium charge. This front-loaded policy has very low surrender charges.

Most companies assess a percentage premium charge, with the majority having the same first year and renewal percentage. Charges typically fall within the 2 1/2 to 20 percent range. Some insurers still assess a high first-year policy fee, with little or no fee thereafter, although the trend is to have the same policy fee for all years. Typical "high" first-year fees fall within the $200 to $400 range, with the newer levels falling in the $25 to $50 per year range.

There appears to be a trend toward companies discontinuing the use of fees based on each $1,000 face amount; the trend is especially pronounced for renewal years. Many insurers now assess only a percentage of premium load.

For companies with low or no identifiable front-end loads, the back-end loads—surrender charges—tend to be high, although they cannot exceed those permitted by law. Surrender charges may be expressed as a percentage of the first-year premium (most common for policies with no front loads), as a loss of excess interest for one year, as a flat dollar assessment per $1,000 face amount (e.g., $10 per $1,000), as a flat dollar assessment (e.g., $25), or as an amount equal to unpaid first-year expense charges. Policies that emphasize front loads usually have low or no back loads. In any event, surrender charges are highest during the first few policy years and grade downward with duration, often decreasing yearly after the first five policy years or sooner and typically reaching zero in from 5 to 12 years.

High back-end loads can create a so-called "tontine effect." This effect results whenever nonguaranteed death-related benefits (e.g., terminal dividends) or lapse-related benefits (e.g., cash surrender values) are low currently so as to afford higher values later. Thus if a policy's cash surrender value in the early policy years is less than the assets accumulated by the insurer on behalf of that policy (i.e., the policy's asset share), the surrender or lapse of the policy will result in an increase in insurer surplus. This surplus can be accumulated and used to enhance later cash values of persisting policies.

Policies (UL or otherwise) so constructed that their future values are in part dependent on the assumption of incurring gains from such high early lapses and surrenders are said to be **lapse-supported policies**. The danger of the practice to policyowners is that the expected rate of lapse or surrenders may fail to materialize, thus resulting in less early surplus from which to enhance future values. Additionally, questions of the equitable treatment of terminating versus persisting policyowners arise.

The extent to which insurers market lapse-supported policies is unknown. This issue relates principally to nonguaranteed policy elements and applies equally to all types of life insurance policies, not just to UL, although much concern is focused on the latter.

*Mortality and Other Benefit Charges*. Mortality charges are deducted each month from UL cash values. The total monthly mortality charge is derived by multiplying the applicable rate by the policy's NAR. The maximum rates per $1,000 are stated in the contract for all ages, and actual rates charged are guaranteed never to exceed these maximums. Most UL mortality charges are indeterminate, as mentioned previously, as well as differentiated according to cigarette smokers and nonsmokers and, in most states, according to gender. Some insurers vary mortality charges by policy size.

Insurers typically base their maximum mortality charges (printed in the policy) on those derived from the 1980 CSO mortality table, which is a conservative valuation table. Many insurers formerly used the 1958 CSO table, but its use is no longer permitted. The level of the current and anticipated actual mortality charges is of greater importance than the level of the guaranteed rates, because those are the fees actually charged.

Mortality rates actually charged by issuers of UL vary considerably. Table 6-1 lists mortality charges levied by six companies for three different ages. These

**TABLE 6-1     SELECTED COMPANIES' CURRENT MORTALITY CHARGES PER MONTH FOR $100,000 UL POLICY (MALE, NONSMOKER)**

|            | Age 25  | Age 40  | Age 55  |
|------------|---------|---------|---------|
| Company A  | $6.67   | $14.43  | $35.33  |
| Company B  | 9.17    | 12.08   | 25.83   |
| Company C  | 10.00   | 16.00   | 37.00   |
| Company D  | 14.00   | 21.00   | 46.00   |
| Company E  | 15.00   | 21.00   | 51.00   |
| Company F  | 16.00   | 31.00   | 73.00   |

are monthly charges and, therefore, a difference of only a few dollars can sum to a large amount over time. One could not conclude from these figures alone which of the various companies' policies might be a good buy. Interest credits and loadings also must be factored into the analysis. For example, Company F, with the highest mortality charges, has relatively low front-end loads and no surrender charges. Obviously, its mortality charges include provision for expense recovery.

Charges may exist for other policy benefits—for example, for policy riders. The COLA rider and the future purchase option rider were mentioned earlier. In addition, riders can be included that provide insurance on family members, provide waiver-of-premium (or waiver-of-mortality-charge) protection, offer accelerated death benefits, and afford additional insurance. None of these is unique to UL and they are discussed in Chapter 7.

Worth noting is the trend toward using the additional (term) insurance rider to lower overall mortality charges. Typically, these riders carry lower mortality charges than those of the UL policy itself and also lower commissions. By changing the mix of UL and such term insurance, policy cost and commissions can be made to vary.

*Cash Values*. The student will recall from looking at Figure 6-1 that the cash value is simply the residual of each period's funds flow. It results from taking the previous period's ending cash value balance (if any), adding to it any premium paid, subtracting expense and mortality charges, then adding current interest credits to the resulting fund balance. The result is the end-of-period cash value. All items except the current interest credit have been discussed above.

UL policies guarantee the crediting of at least some minimum contractually stated rate of interest to policy cash values. Guaranteed rates of 4 or 5 percent are most commonly found. During a high interest rate environment, these rates may seem low, but they are reasonable long-term guarantees and potentially of great value to the policyowner.

Some companies provide for a rolling interest rate guarantee. Under this approach, the insurer will guarantee to pay a rate of interest that is at least equal to a moving average rate (less some basis points) of an external index, such as five-year Treasury bills.

Companies currently credit interest rates in excess of their guaranteed rates. The first UL policies utilized a two-tiered interest approach wherein only the guaranteed rate was credited on the first $1,000 or so of cash values, with amounts in excess of $1,000 receiving the current rate. Most UL policies sold today do not make this distinction; they credit the entire cash value with the current rate, subject to a direct recognition feature.

Most UL policies provide that the current interest rate will be determined by the company. Others are indexed; these provide that the current interest rate will be set at a level slightly below that being credited on some external, well-recognized money instrument such as three-month or one-year Treasury bills.

Most nonindexed UL policies receive interest credits that are based on the companies' new-money rates of return. As discussed in Chapter 2, this rate represents what the company earns on its new investments. Many insurers, by contrast, use a portfolio rate of return, based on the earnings of the company's entire asset portfolio, or the assets backing a given block of policies.

New-money rates are more responsive to changing market interest rates, and this can work for or against the policyowner. If market rates are generally rising, cash values credited with interest on this basis should be higher than those credited with portfolio rates during the period. On the other hand, when market rates fall, portfolio rates could be — and at some point will be — higher than new-money rates. In such circumstances, the portfolio-based policy should outperform its new-money brother, other things being the same.

Like most cash-value policies, UL policies permit policyowners to obtain policy loans on the security of the policy's cash value. The direct recognition provision in UL policies is important in this regard. In most policies, it provides that interest at the current rates will be credited only to the portion of the cash value that is not used to secure a policy loan. The portion backing any policy loan may be credited only with the contractually guaranteed interest rate or at a rate that is one or two percentage points below the policy loan interest rate, thus producing a guaranteed spread for the insurer.

Not all UL issuers use a direct recognition provision. A few credit the current interest rate on the entire cash value, irrespective of policy loan activity. If the UL policy contains the variable loan rate now permitted in most states, little need exists for a direct recognition provision.[10]

With an increasing emphasis in sales presentation on later years' cash values, insurers have begun designing policies with certain **persistency bonuses**, the intent of which is to encourage policyowners to continue their policies. Two broad types of persistency bonuses, also called **enhancements**, are prevalent: an interest rate bonus and a mortality charge refund. The enhancement is credited to the policy's cash value after a minimum policy duration, after a minimum cash value has been attained, or after a minimum number of premiums has been paid. The interest rate bonus, stated as an additional interest rate, may be applied to the then accumulated cash value or it may be applied retroactively on a compound basis.

[10] See Chap. 9.

The mortality charge bonus may involve a total or partial credit to the cash value of previously assessed mortality charges. Both the mortality charge refund and the interest rate bonus enhancements may be applied more than once (e.g., once every five years).

Other types of persistency bonuses exist. For example, some companies will increase the death benefit, pay special dividends, or provide COLA increases. Terminal dividends, in use for decades, are also enhancements. Terminal dividends are paid by some insurers on policy termination as either a surrender or a death claim, after a participating policy has been in force for a minimum number of years (e.g., ten years).

Persistency bonuses can and do serve a legitimate purpose; they can encourage and reward policy persistency. On the other hand, they also can lend themselves to misuse, especially if the enhancement is credited in such a way as to lead customers to believe a policy offers better value than it truly does. This can occur, for example, if the enhancement is credited at durations typically used by consumers and agents for product evaluation (e.g., at policy year 20) and if that year's value is not representative of surrounding years' values.

Most UL policies permit partial cash-value surrenders. Usually, these surrenders must be for at least a minimum amount (e.g., $500) and may carry a processing charge (e.g., $25). The policy death benefit is reduced by the exact amount of any partial surrender. If it were not, the company would be inviting adverse selection. Total policy surrender, as discussed previously, often involves a surrender charge.

## USES AND LIMITATIONS OF UNIVERSAL LIFE INSURANCE

The universal life policy offers the possibility of being the only life insurance policy a person needs over his or her lifetime. Its flexibility in premium payments and death benefits renders it well-suited as an individual's "life cycle" policy.

*Simplified Life Cycle Illustration.* Figure 6-4 provides a simplified view of how this life cycle approach could work. This illustration ignores inflation and takes a simplistic view of insurance planning.[11] In it, Larry Townsend, aged 25, purchases a $50,000 UL policy using option A (level death benefit) and pays a premium of $500. The purpose of this policy is to pay off education debts incurred while he was obtaining a law degree. This starting situation is depicted at point A.

At point B Larry marries his long-time sweetheart, Nina, and, because of further obligations, believes the coverage amount under his UL policy should be increased to $75,000. At the same time, he increases the premium payment to $1,000. Cash values build slowly, as shown.

[11]See Chap. 12.

**FIGURE 6-4**

**HYPOTHETICAL LIFE CYCLE USING UNIVERSAL LIFE INSURANCE POLICY**

*Source*: Modified from Universal Life Basics (Indianapolis, Ind.: Pictorial Publishers, 1983), pp. 6–7D. Used with permission.

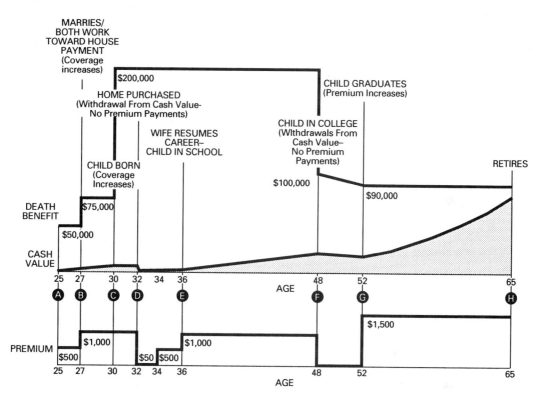

When Larry is 30, Nina has a child, Emily (point C). Because this life event has major implications for Larry and Nina, they increase the UL coverage amount to $200,000, but with no increase in premium. Larry again meets the insurability requirements.

Two years later, at point D, Larry and Nina withdraw $3,000 from the UL policy to help make a down payment on a new home. Such a cash withdrawal would normally reduce their death benefit by an equivalent amount, but they increase the coverage to maintain the previous amount. At this point, they also cease making premium payments to devote needed funds to the mortgage payment.

Two years later, they are able to resume $500 premium payments. Two years after that (point E), they are able to increase the payment to $1,000.

Life continues merrily for the happy family and when Larry is 48, Emily enters college (point F). They withdraw $2,500 per year for each of the next four years to help defray Emily's educational expenses, and they cease premium payments as well. They conclude that with the responsibilities of rearing Emily being essentially over, they can, simultaneously, decrease their total insurance amount to $100,000, although this amount will decrease each year by the amount of the $2,500 withdrawals.

Four years later, Emily graduates from college and goes into the world to make her mark, independent of Larry and Nina. The happy couple is now able to resume premium payments, and, with an eye toward accumulating a retirement fund, they make premium payments of $1,500 per year until Larry is 65, at which time (point H), they cease making premium payments and begin a systematic withdrawal program under their UL policy (and, of course, live happily ever after).

Notice that the single UL policy has served the needs of our hypothetical family well throughout their life cycle. The death benefit was altered as needed to suit the their current needs. Premium payments were similarly increased or decreased as financial circumstances dictated, and the cash values were a source of needed cash throughout life. This simplified example illustrates the flexibility of UL.

Although only one insured is shown in this figure, on close analysis (see Chapter 12), significant amounts of insurance may be needed on Nina's life also. A UL policy on her life, a joint life UL policy, or a spouse rider could have been illustrated, but, for simplicity, only one insured is considered here.

UL can be used in countless other ways as well, as can most other cash-value policies. A UL policy can be used in virtually every circumstance in which a whole life policy could be used. Like whole life, however, UL probably should not be purchased for short-term needs. Term will usually prove superior in such situations.

***Limitations on Illustrated Values.*** UL has helped the life insurance business regain consumers' savings dollars. UL is undoubtedly flexible and its operations are more transparent than most life products. As with other life policies that contain nonguaranteed elements, UL can be low in cost. However, whether it actually will be low cost can be determined only over time. An examination of how insurers have treated their past UL policyowners in terms of actual excess interest credits and actual mortality and expense charges can prove insightful.

Some argue that UL flexibility, especially with respect to premium payments, can lead to poor persistency, with the result that consumers lose money because of early UL policy terminations in the same way that they would with early whole life policy terminations. Results to date suggest that early UL policy persistency is roughly equivalent to that for whole life policies, but later persistency lags.

Concern exists that UL (and CAWL) policy advertisements and sales aids place undue emphasis on the current interest rate, to the exclusion of other potentially important elements such as expense loadings, mortality charges, and surrender charges. For example a $100,000 option B universal life policy that credits 9.0 percent has a projected 20-year cash surrender value of $46,191, based on a 45 year-old male nonsmoker, paying $1,500 per year, while another that credits 8.25 percent has a 20-year projected cash value of $56,617.

Consider also that the following policies, each of which advertises an 8.5 percent current interest credit and is based on similar policy and buyer profiles, have projected 10- and 20-year cash surrender values as follows:

| UL Policy | 10-Year Projected Cash Surrender Value | 20-Year Projected Cash Surrender Value |
|---|---|---|
| A | $14,488 | $41,379 |
| B | 15,541 | 46,916 |
| C | 16,826 | 52,054 |
| D | 18,742 | 68,134 |
| E | 19,862 | 56,131 |

Of course, these differences are all explainable to anyone who examines each element of these UL policies. To the great credit of UL policies, their operational transparency permits this examination; such an examination is not always easy with other cash-value products.

The concern does not rest with any deficiency related to transparency. Rather it rests with marketing approaches that place unwarranted emphasis on current interest rate credits, to the point that the average purchaser of the UL policy may be misled as to the product's future value.

Another concern results from the practice of projecting high interest rates for years and even decades into the future. These projections, unless carefully explained, can mislead and distort product value. While no one can know the "correct" rate to use for projections, everyone knows that the current rate is not correct. Rates will change.

The keys to avoiding deception (intended or otherwise) are carefully prepared illustrations and advertisements with appropriately worded caveats, illustrations that show policy value results using varying rates of interest, and, most important, well-informed agents and other financial advisors who very carefully guide the client through a potentially misleading morass. Of course, these concerns apply to other new-money products, including participating whole life policies.

Policy illustrations remain widely used as a basis for comparing prospective policy performance. Because of the highly speculative nature of long-term illustrations, many now argue against such comparisons. Instead, it is argued, the focus of comparison shopping should shift more to the performance characteristics of the insurers themselves and to an examination of actual historical policy values.

Another concern—again not just with UL policies but with all interest-sensitive products, including traditional participating whole life policies—is that in competition today one finds that the prospective purchaser is often shown noncomparable comparisons of two or more policies' future values. This "apples and oranges" problem has been alluded to earlier but warrants further comment.

Historically, dividend illustrations under participating policies were based on the company's average portfolio investment rate of return. Companies were loath to actually pay less dividends than those which were originally illustrated at the time the policy was sold. As a result, illustrations based on then current portfolio average returns were conservative. In effect, the purchaser of such a policy had reason to believe that these nonguaranteed illustrated dividends would, in fact, be paid—and probably at a higher level than illustrated.

Within the last few years, many companies selling participating insurance have shifted to new-money or investment generation approaches to investment income allocation within their dividend formulas. This was done at a time of rapidly rising interest rates, so the result was that dividends illustrated at new-money rates were higher than those illustrated on portfolio rates, since the portfolio rate is a weighted average of old and new investment returns. At this point, the two dividend illustrations became far less compatible.

The advent of nonparticipating new-money products such as UL and CAWL, which used not only current investment returns but also contained an element of anticipated favorable future results put further competitive pressure on illustrations. It was no longer sufficient, in such a competitive environment, in the judgment of many companies, to illustrate dividends by basing them on current and immediate past actual results, let alone portfolio results. It became necessary to build into dividend illustrations an element of anticipated future results not very dissimilar from that existing with the new-money nonparticipating products. Such illustrations began to take on the look of projections.

In one sense, this rendered some traditional-looking participating products more comparable to interest-sensitive nonparticipating products. Many companies, however, base dividend illustrations and interest rates for UL and CAWL policies on portfolio rates.

Therefore we are now faced with three sets of future value illustrations/projections: (1) portfolio average, (2) genuine investment generation method, and (3) new money with anticipated future projected experience. The likelihood of actual results being as favorable as those illustrated/projected varies with the current trend in interest rates. What is clear, however, is that the portfolio-based products' values should fluctuate the least, whereas the new money-product values can be expected to experience the greatest fluctuation, *ceteris paribus*.

The way in which the advisor factors these complex matters into his or her analysis is not easy. The financial analysis still must be conducted in many cases. The first step to an intelligent interpretation of results, however, is to gain an understanding of the assumptions underpinning the numbers. Chapter 10 picks up further on these points.

## VARIABLE UNIVERSAL LIFE INSURANCE

The next logical step in life insurance product evolution was to combine some of the flexible characteristics of universal life with the investment flexibility of variable life — the result was **variable universal life** (VUL).

VUL is subject to the same SEC and state regulations as variable life insurance (VLI). Thus under SEC interpretation of the laws discussed earlier, the VUL contract itself, the separate account, and the selling agent all must be registered.[12]

Some technical provisions of SEC regulation have been altered to accommodate the differences between the traditional, fixed-premium VLI contract and the VUL contract. These relate primarily to relief from SEC-mandated sales load limitations, which had been based on actual premium payments and had been oriented exclusively toward front-end-loaded contracts.

At the state level, the adoption by the states of the **Model Variable Life Insurance Regulation** of the National Association of Insurance Commissioners would have the effect of eliminating the early model regulation's restrictive product design criteria. Over 40 states have adopted a version of this regulation.

### NATURE OF VARIABLE UNIVERSAL LIFE INSURANCE

VUL tracks the UL model in that the policyowner decides, within limits, the premium to be paid each period, if any. The policyowner also has the option of increasing or decreasing the policy death benefit at will, subject only to policy minimums and, with respect to death benefit increases, evidence of insurability requirements.

Unlike the situation with UL, the assets backing the VUL policy are maintained in one or more separate accounts. In this respect, VUL is identical to VLI. The cash values of VUL are subject to fluctuation just like VLI cash values, and, like cash values of VLI, there also is no guarantee with respect to either a minimum rate of return or principal. In other words, cash values can decrease to zero.

The policyowner typically is offered a smorgasbord of funds into which he or she directs residual funds to be invested. These funds—in effect, mutual funds—have different investment characteristics, just as with a family of mutual funds. The policyowner has the option of periodically (e.g., quarterly) transferring funds from one account to another, often without a transaction fee. Since the transfer is within a life insurance policy, no taxable gain (or loss) is realizable because of the transaction.

The treatment of death benefits under most VUL policy designs differs from that under VLI; instead it follows the UL approach. VUL death benefits fluctuate with changes in the values of the underlying assets only under option

[12] See Chap. 5.

B. With the option A death benefit pattern, the face amount remains constant unless it is changed by the policyowner. As a result, all variations in investment returns are reflected solely in the policy's cash values, with no part used to fund changes in the policy's net amount at risk.

## USES AND LIMITATIONS OF VARIABLE UNIVERSAL LIFE

VUL policies are potentially useful for those persons who desire to treat their life insurance policy cash values more as an investment than a savings. The owner assumes the investment risk. The danger is that if separate account investment results are not favorable, the policy's cash value could be reduced to zero, at which point the policy would lapse without further premium payments. This risk should be considered most carefully. One of the strengths of the life insurance industry historically has been its investment guarantees. Whether many consumers will be willing to forgo these guarantees remains to be seen.

On the other hand, funds held in insurer separate accounts are earmarked to back the policies to which the funds apply and are separate from the insurer's general-account assets. In the event that the insurer experiences financial difficulty, this separation could afford an additional margin of safety for the VUL policyowner.

## FLEXIBLE ENHANCED ORDINARY LIFE

The enhanced ordinary life (EOL) policy, presented in Chapter 5, is a fixed-premium whole life policy that combines portions of ordinary life, term life, and paid-up additions. The mixture of whole life, term, and paid-up additions is fixed for the applicant of a given age/gender, as is the premium. As a response to the premium flexibility and death adjustability of universal life, some insurers have introduced an EOL-type policy with certain features of UL.

## CONCERNS ABOUT UNIVERSAL LIFE

Many companies perceived a need to offer products to compete with UL, but they did not believe that offering UL was the solution. They expressed concerns about the potential lack of premium commitment by the policyowner. In times of financial stringency, the policyowner might too easily cease paying the premium, thus endangering the life insurance program.

Additionally, because of a potentially unpredictable premium stream and the ease of cash value withdrawals from UL policies, insurers were compelled to adopt short-term investment strategies for the segment of the company's assets backing their UL policies. Shorter-duration investments are more volatile than longer-term investments and, over the long run, should produce lower returns. This perceived problem could be expected to result in less stable and lower policyowner returns, in returns being subsidized by profits from other products or from insurer surplus, or in the taking on of greater-than-normal investment risk (e.g., through junk bonds or risky mortgages) to enhance investment returns. The emphasis in UL marketing on its credited interest rate and on identifiable expense charges would only exacerbate the problem. To a degree, these companies' concerns proved to be valid.

## NATURE OF FLEXIBLE ENHANCED ORDINARY LIFE

Some companies thus decided to offer a product built on the traditional participating model, but with added flexibility.[13] **Flexible enhanced ordinary life** permits the combination of whole life, term, and paid-up additions in such proportions as to allow the policyowner to establish a comfortable premium level, within limits, and to adjust the policy face amount, within limits.

The product requires a certain minimum amount of whole life insurance, then permits the addition of whatever amount of term insurance is desired. By varying the mixture, the effective policy premium rate per $1,000 is varied, subject to a minimum required fixed premium.

Policy dividends, regular additional premiums, and "dump ins" all purchase paid-up insurance that can offset the term coverage dollar-for-dollar or can provide additional coverage. Thus a degree of flexibility in cash-value accumulation, mix of coverage, and premium is provided. Further flexibility is provided by allowing the policyowner to increase or decrease the amount of term insurance after issue and by allowing increases or decreases in the amount of additional premiums.

## LIFE INSURANCE POLICY COMPARISON CHART

The great variety of life insurance products available in today's marketplace can cause bewilderment. However, the vast majority of individual life insurance sold today is of one or more of six product types.

These six types are listed in Table 6-2 in the order in which they were presented in this book. Beside each type is a summary of its basic features and a listing of its advantages and disadvantages, both to the buyer and to the seller. The table is intended to highlight key points only and is to be interpreted only with the corresponding area of the book that presents the product. As with all such shorthand charts, exceptions to the general statements exist. Therefore the chart should be used only with great caution and only as a reminder to the reader of essential product features.

[13] See James J. Murphy and Linda S. Need, "Beyond Universal Life," *Journal of the American Society of Chartered Life Underwriters*, Vol. 40 (March 1986).

# TABLE 6-2

## LIFE INSURANCE POLICY COMPARISON CHART

| Product | Death Benefit | Premium | Cash Value | Cash Value or Dividends Use Current Interest? | Partial Surrenders Permitted? | Policy Elements Unbundled? | Direct Borrowing Recognition | Advantages To Buyer | Advantages To Seller | Disadvantages To Buyer | Disadvantages To Seller | Risks To Buyer |
|---|---|---|---|---|---|---|---|---|---|---|---|---|
| Annual Renewable Term | Fixed, Level | Fixed, Increasing | No cash value | N.A. | N.A. | No | N.A. | Low outlay. Can purchase large am'ts. Buyer can develop outside investment program. | May be easier to sell. | Increasing outlay. Buyer may not invest difference or may realize lower return. | Low commission. Little profit. High lapse rates. | • Increasing premium. • Can buyer earn more on investments than insurer? |
| Par-Ordinary Life | Fixed, Level | Fixed, Level | Fixed with minimum interest rate guaranteed. Excess through dividends. | Yes | Yes, but through paid-up additions only. | No | Yes, with many policies. | Familiar product. Predictable. Helps buyer discipline. Interest, mortality, and expense experience can be recognized. | Same as buyer. Traditional commissions. Greater margins. | Costly if lapsed early. Lack of flexibility. Can be more costly. | Can be less attractive to buyer. | • Failure to meet premium commitment. |
| Current Assumption Whole Life | Fixed, Level | May change based on insurer's experience. CV has guaranteed min. % / Maximum guaranteed, but insurer may charge less. | Minimum guaranteed. Excess interest lowers prem. or increases CV. | Yes | Yes | No | Yes | Takes advantage of high current interest rates and improved mortality. | Same as buyer. Traditional WL commissions. Responds to "buy term invest difference." | Premiums can increase or CV be lower than projected. Buyer takes risk on high premium version; policy can become unpaid-up. | If projections not met, can be negative client reaction. | If assumptions change adversely, • Premiums can be higher than with traditional products. • Cash value can be lower than with traditional products. |
| Variable Life | Guaranteed minimum can increase based on investment performance | Fixed, Level | Based on investment performance. Not guaranteed. | Yes | No | No, but to some degree shown in prospectus | Yes | Takes advantage of growth in economy. More in control of growth. | Responds to inflation objection. Traditional WL commissions. Shifts investment risk to buyer. | Buyer must decide on underlying investments & monitor them for change. Few guarantees. | Needs securities license. Older agents not used to selling. Rules of SEC & could get in trouble. | • Investment risk is great. • Can be higher in cost than traditional products. |
| Universal Life | Adjustable | Flexible | Varies depending on face am't. & premium Minimum guaranteed interest. Excess increases CV. | Yes | Yes | Yes | Yes | Greater transparency and more flexibility. | Consumer accepted. Widely publicized. May be easier to sell. | Flexibility places greater responsibility on buyer. Buyer assumes greater investment and mortality risks. | Generally, lower commissions. Renewals uncertain. Computer backup essential. Readily lapsable. | If assumption change adversely, • Investment performance can affect satisfaction of long-term goals. • Cash value can be lower than with traditional products. |
| Variable Universal Life | Adjustable | Flexible | Based on investment performance. Not guaranteed. | Yes | Yes | Yes | Yes | Takes advantage of growth of economy. More control of growth. Flexibility. | Shifts investment risk to buyer | Fewer guarantees. | Same as VLI, but more costly to administer. | • Will need to pay more if investment experiences are negative. |

# Chapter 7

# ANNUITY AND SPECIAL-PURPOSE POLICIES AND BENEFITS

## ANNUITIES

Annuities remain exceedingly popular as a means of personal savings in the United States, as revealed by a steadily increasing proportion of personal disposable income spent each year for them. This enhanced popularity reflects the continuing aging of the U.S. population and the concomitant desire to increase savings through a tax-favored vehicle in anticipation of retirement financial needs. The Figure 7-1 projections suggest the possibility of still greater annuity demand as today's baby boom generation (those who will begin retiring around the year 2010) allocates further amounts to retirement savings. It is worth noting that this same population aging phenomenon is occurring in other developed countries to varying degrees, as Figure 7-2 suggests.

### NATURE OF ANNUITIES

In the broadest sense, an annuity is simply a series of periodic payments. An annuity contract, then, is an insurance policy that promises to make a series of payments for a fixed period or over someone's lifetime. A **life annuity** is one wherein payments are contingent upon the continued existence of one or more lives, in contrast with an **annuity certain**, wherein payments are not contingent on the annuitant's being alive. Life annuities may be either **temporary** (payable for a fixed period or until the death of the annuitant, whichever is earlier) or **whole** (payable for the whole of the annuitant's life).

**FIGURE 7-1**

**PROPORTION OF U.S. POPULATION AGE 65 AND OLDER AT SELECTED YEARS**

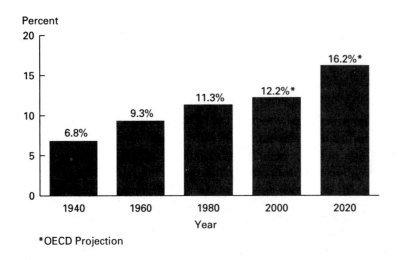

\*OECD Projection

*Purpose of Annuities*. Life insurance has as its principal mission the *creation* of a fund. The annuity, on the contrary, has as its basic function the systematic *liquidation* of a fund. Of course, most annuities are also accumulation instruments, but this is the mechanism for developing the fund to be liquidated. In its pure form, a whole life annuity may be defined as a contract whereby for a consideration (the premium), one party (the insurer) agrees to pay the other (the annuitant) a stipulated amount (the annuity) periodically throughout life. The understanding is that no portion of the consideration paid for the annuity need be refunded upon the annuitant's death. The purpose of the annuity is to protect against the possibility of outliving one's income—just the opposite purpose of that confronting a person who desires life insurance as protection against the loss of income through premature death.

Each payment under an annuity may be considered to represent a combination of principal and interest income and a survivorship element. Although not completely accurate (since insurers do not base calculations on life expectancy), one can view the operation of an annuity as follows: if a person exactly lives out his or her life expectancy, he or she would have neither gained nor lost through utilizing an annuity contract. If a person outlives his or her life expectancy under the contract, the additional payments would be derived from the funds contributed by those who failed to survive to their expectancy. On the other hand, if a person dies in advance of his or her life expectancy, the entire contributions (and interest forgone) would not have been recovered, and the excess provides income for those who outlive their expectancy. Since no one knows into which category he or she will fall, the arrangement is equitable and can succeed, from the company's point of view, through the operation of the law

**FIGURE 7-2**

**PROPORTION OF POPULATION PROJECTED TO BE AGE 65 AND OLDER FOR SELECTEDCOUNTRIES BY THE YEAR 2000**

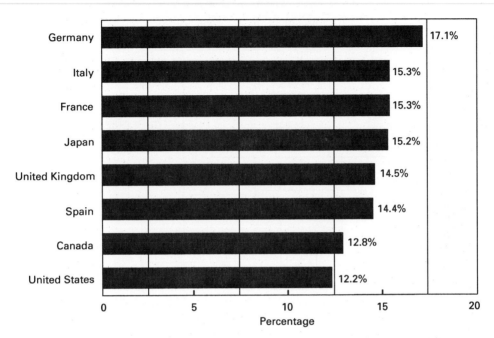

of large numbers. Only a life insurance company can guarantee that a given sum can be scientifically liquidated in installments over the duration of a human life.

Despite the difference in function, annuities are simply another type of insurance, and both life insurance and annuities are based on the same fundamental principles. Both employ the pooling technique, and premiums in each case are computed on the basis of probabilities of death and survival as reflected by a mortality table.

*Classification of Annuities.* Annuities may be classified as to the (1) number of lives covered, (2) method of premium payment, (3) time when income begins, (4) method of disposing of proceeds, and (5) denomination in which benefits are expressed. Figure 7-3 shows this classification schematically.

*1. Number of Lives Covered.* This classification involves the question of whether annuity payments are made with reference to a single life or more than one life. The **joint and last-survivor annuity** provides that income payments continue for as long as *either* of two or more persons lives. It is most commonly used in husband/wife or other family relationships.

Since this annuity provides for payment until the last death, it will pay to a later date, on the average, than a single life annuity and, therefore, is more expensive than single life annuity forms. Stated differently, a given principal sum

**FIGURE 7-3**

**BASIS FOR ANNUITY CLASSIFICATION**

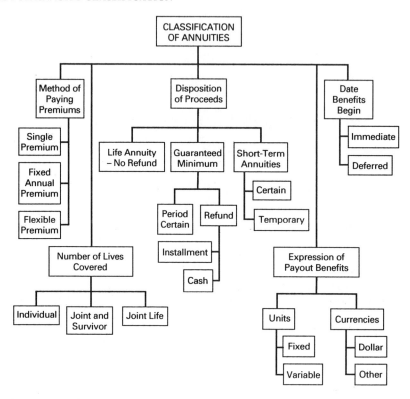

provides less income under a joint and last-survivor form than under a single-life annuity form at either of the two ages. In its usual form, the joint and last-survivor annuity continues the same income until the death of the last survivor. A modified form provides (assuming two covered lives) that the income will be reduced following the death of the first annuitant to two-thirds or one-half of the original income. This contract (or option) is known as a **joint and two-thirds** (or **joint and one-half**) **annuity**. Naturally, for a given principal, the modified form provides more income initially because of the later reduction.[1]

Another type of multilife annuity, known as a **joint-life annuity**, provides a specified income for two or more named persons, with the income ceasing upon the first death among the covered lives. Such contracts, although relatively inexpensive, have limited markets.

*2. Method of Premium Payment.* Annuities may be purchased with single or periodic premiums. Thus a single-life annuity could be purchased with a lump sum accumulated through savings, inheritance, or other media, or an individual may choose to spread the payment over a specified period by paying periodic premiums.

---

[1] The joint and last-survivor form found in private pension plans commonly provides that the income is reduced only when the employee dies first.

*3. Time When Income Payments Commence.* Annuities may also be classified as to whether income payments are deferred or immediate. An **immediate annuity** is purchased with a single premium and the first benefit payment is due one payment interval (e.g., a month or a year) from the date of purchase.

A **deferred annuity**, on the other hand, may be purchased with either a single premium or a periodic premium. Under a deferred life annuity, there must be more than one benefit payment interval before benefit payments begin. The longer the deferred period, the more flexibility permitted in premium payments. Normally, many years elapse before benefit payments commence.

*4. Disposition of Proceeds.* There are a great variety of options as to how annuity proceeds are distributed, including whether a refund feature exists and the duration of the benefit payout period. This subject is discussed in the following section, which deals with the nature of the insurer's obligation before and after income payments commence.

*5. Denomination of Benefits.* Traditionally in the United States, annuity benefits have been expressed in fixed dollars. With the advent of the variable annuity (see below), the units in which payout benefits are expressed forms another basis of classification. Similarly, annuity benefits may be denominated in non-U.S. currencies.

***Nature of Insurance Company's Obligation.*** An annuity can be considered as having an accumulation and a liquidation period. The **accumulation period** is that time during which annuity fund values accumulate, commonly prior to age 65. The **liquidation period** is that time during which annuity fund values are paid to the annuitant(s). The insurer's obligation upon the death of the annuitant ordinarily differs depending on whether death occurs during the accumulation or liquidation period.

*1. Accumulation Period.* During the accumulation period of an annuity, the insurer is obligated to return all or a portion of the annuity cash value if the purchaser dies. Minimum required cash values are established by law in most states to be equal to the contributions to date, less withdrawals and expenses, plus interest earnings. Many insurers also provide for a separate surrender charge, as discussed below.

*2. Liquidation Period.* The amount of money necessary to provide a given amount and form of income starting at a set age is the same, other things equal, regardless of the manner in which funds are accumulated. Consequently, the following discussion of the nature of the insurer's obligation during the liquidation period is applicable to both immediate and deferred annuities, as well as to settlement options (discussed in Chapter 9).

Broadly, the two classes of life annuity payouts are pure and refund. This discussion does not apply to annuities certain, whose income payments have no reference to life contingencies. The **pure life annuity**, also referred to as a **straight life annuity**, provides income payments that continue for as long as the annuitant lives but terminate on the annuitant's death. On the death of the annuitant, no matter how soon that may occur after the commencement of income, no refund is payable to the annuitant's estate or to any beneficiary. Under this form of income, the entire purchase price is applied to provide income to the annuitant, no part of it paying for any refund benefit. Thus the pure life annuity provides the maximum income per dollar of outlay. Because of the high probability of survival at the younger ages, the difference in income between a pure life annuity and one with a refund feature is small.

Regardless of questions of equity and technical soundness, most persons seem to oppose placing a substantial sum of money into a contract that promises little or no refund if they should die shortly after income payments commence. Therefore companies permit annuitants various refund options if death occurs shortly after annuity payments have begun. In contrast to the situation with the pure life annuity, not all of the purchase price of refund annuities is used to provide income payments. Part of the purchase price is applied to meet the cost of guaranteeing a minimum amount of benefits, irrespective of whether the annuitant lives to receive them. Thus for a given premium outlay, a smaller periodic income payment will be available under a refund life annuity than would be available under the pure life annuity. The minimum benefit guarantee or refund feature may be stated either in terms of a guaranteed minimum number of payments or a refund of the purchase price (or some portion thereof) in the event of the annuitant's early death.

One class of life annuities with refund features, often named **life annuity certain and continuous** or **life annuity with installments certain**, calls for a guaranteed number of monthly (or annual) payments to be made whether the annuitant lives or dies, with payments to continue for the whole of the annuitant's life if he or she should live beyond the guarantee period. Contracts are usually written with payments guaranteed for 5, 10, 15, or 20 years. Of course, the longer the guarantee period, the smaller the income payments, *ceteris paribus*.

Two important forms of annuity income promise to return all or a portion of the purchase price. The first form, the **installment refund annuity**, promises that if the annuitant dies before receiving income installments equal to the purchase price, the payments will be continued to a beneficiary until this amount has been paid. The second form, the **cash refund annuity**, promises to pay in a lump sum to the beneficiary the difference, if any, between the purchase price of the annuity and the simple sum of the installment payments made prior to the annuitant's death. For a given purchase price, the cash refund annuity provides a somewhat smaller income than the installment refund annuity, since the insurance company loses the interest it would have earned had the balance been liquidated in installments. In either case, the payments to the annuitant continue for long as he or she lives, even after recovery of the guaranteed minimum benefits.

Table 7-1 provides a comparison of the income provided under some of the important forms of annuities for a given principal. The figures are shown on a guaranteed rather than a current basis and utilize the same rate basis. Variations

TABLE 7-1    **IMMEDIATE LIFE ANNUITY MONTHLY INCOMES PER $1,000 (GUARANTEED BASIS)**

| Age Last Birthday | Pure | | 10 Years Certain and Continuous | | Cash Refund | |
|---|---|---|---|---|---|---|
| | M | F | M | F | M | F |
| 50 | $5.00 | $4.54 | $4.91 | $4.51 | $4.68 | $4.40 |
| 55 | 5.54 | 4.97 | 5.37 | 4.90 | 5.09 | 4.75 |
| 60 | 6.26 | 5.54 | 5.95 | 5.41 | 5.58 | 5.18 |
| 65 | 7.22 | 6.34 | 6.64 | 6.06 | 6.19 | 5.73 |
| 70 | 8.57 | 7.46 | 7.40 | 6.83 | 6.93 | 6.42 |
| 75 | 10.47 | 9.06 | 8.15 | 7.68 | 7.85 | 7.28 |
| 80 | 13.05 | 11.35 | 8.77 | 8.46 | 8.96 | 8.37 |

are intended to show the impact that the form of annuity income, the age of the annuitant at the date of commencement of income, and (where permitted) the sex of the annuitant have on the monthly payment available from a $1,000 principal sum.

It should be apparent from Table 7-1 that the cost of the refund feature is low at the younger ages, but becomes quite expensive at the higher ages. Not until about age 60 or 65 is any appreciable difference in income given up to add a refund feature. Consequently, the purchase of a pure life annuity when one is below age 60 or perhaps age 65 is often considered economically unsound for many persons.

## TYPES OF ANNUITY CONTRACTS

Only a limited number of different annuity contracts actually exists, although individual insurer variations can be great. Four categories of annuities are discussed below:

1. Flexible-Premium Deferred Annuity

2. Single-Premium Deferred Annuity

3. Single-Premium Immediate Annuity

4. Variable Annuity

*Flexible-Premium Deferred Annuity.* The **flexible-premium deferred annuity** (FPDA), one of the most popular individual annuity contracts in the United States, provides for the accumulation of funds to be applied at some future time designated by the contract owner to supply an income, if elected, for the annuitant. The interest credited on the cash values of personally owned annuities is not taxable to the contract owner as long as it remains on deposit with the life insurance company.[2] On liquidation, non-tax-qualified annuity payments are taxable as ordinary income to the extent that each payment

---

[2] Interest credited on non-tax-qualified, corporate-owned annuities is taxable. See Chap. 13.

represents previously untaxed income. Obviously, the tax-deferred nature of cash accumulations under such annuities represents a significant privilege that is justified as an instrument for encouraging individuals to provide for their retirement needs. Tax laws, by imposing certain restrictions on withdrawals from annuities prior to retirement, are intended to ensure that this privilege is not abused.[3]

FPDA contracts permit flexible contributions to be made as and when the owner desires, either monthly, yearly, or, with most companies, as often or as infrequently as the owner desires. There is no set contribution amount or required payment frequency. Although a premium payment is not generally required each year for FPDA contracts, companies usually establish a minimum acceptable payment level (e.g., $25 to $50) if a payment is to be made, and also encourage owners to establish target payment plans.

FPDA contracts have effectively supplanted an earlier product known as the **retirement annuity contract**. This contract provided for a fixed schedule of periodic premiums and had high loadings by today's standards. The product was not unbundled, so that its internal functioning was not transparent. Few of these contracts are sold today.

Keen competition for consumers' savings dollars among life insurers and between life insurers and other financial institutions continues to result in better-value FPDA contracts. The trend today is toward FPDA contracts with little or no front-end loads. Rather, most insurers use a back-end load, known as a **surrender charge**. The surrender charge is assessed in the event of a total surrender. Most contracts permit a free **withdrawal corridor** of 10 percent of the fund value.

The surrender charge is usually stated as a percentage of the total accumulation value and commonly decreases with duration. Thus an insurer may assess a surrender charge of 7 percent on all withdrawals during the first contract year, in excess of 10 percent of the fund balance, with this rate decreasing 1 percent per year, thus grading to zero in the eighth contract year, and with no surrender charge thereafter. Surrender charge percentages and durations vary considerably; some first-year charges are as high as 20 percent, but most are within the 5 to 10 percent range. A few policies do not have either identifiable back-end or front-end loads.

FPDA contracts guarantee the crediting of interest at no lower than the contract guaranteed rate, which is usually within the 3 1/2 to 4 1/2 percent range. While this rate may seem low, it must be recognized that the guarantee could easily span three or four decades or more and, therefore, could prove to be exceedingly valuable. For its part, the insurer would be foolish to guarantee high rates of such long durations. In any event, this type of long-term guarantee is not found in any other comparable savings media such as those offered by banks, savings associations, or money management accounts.

---

[3] See Chap. 13 for details. Note that payments under tax-qualified annuities are fully taxable.

The actual rate of interest credited at any time to the FPDA fund balance will be a function of the earnings rate of the insurer and its desired competitive position within the financial services marketplace. Some insurers utilize a **bonus rate** approach wherein the first year's considerations receive an extra 1 percent or so over their expected renewal interest rate. All rates are subject to change by the insurer, although most companies guarantee the current rate for at least the first contract year.

Table 7-2 illustrates the operation of a hypothetical FPDA during the accumulation phase. This annuity credits 8 percent on the full premium payment — that is, it has no front-end load. It provides for a graded surrender charge of 7 percent in the first year, with a 1 percent per year decrease thereafter. The illustration shows both guaranteed (at 4 percent) and nonguaranteed projected values and the difference between the net surrender value and the accumulated fund value. A variable premium pattern is assumed. Note that the fund values and cash surrender values are the same as from the eighth contract year.

The retirement income amount provided by a FPDA is a function of the accumulated fund balance, the annuitant's sex (where permitted), and the age at which the contract owner elects to have payments commence. At that time, the

**TABLE 7-2    HYPOTHETICAL FLEXIBLE-PREMIUM DEFERRED ANNUITY ACCUMULATIONS**

| Contract Year | Premium Payment | Year-End Cash Values Based on: | | Year-End Cash Surrender Values Based on: | |
|---|---|---|---|---|---|
| | | Guar. Rate (4%) | Current Rate (8%) | Guar. Rate (4%) | Current Rate (8%) |
| 1 | $2,000 | $2,080 | $2,160 | $1,934 | $2,009 |
| 2 | 2,000 | 3,923 | 4,423 | 3,688 | 4,223 |
| 3 | 1,000 | 5,120 | 5,859 | 4,864 | 5,564 |
| 4 | 1,000 | 6,365 | 7,408 | 6,110 | 7,111 |
| 5 | 500 | 7,139 | 8,541 | 6,925 | 8,284 |
| 6 | 0 | 7,425 | 8,540 | 7,277 | 8,369 |
| 7 | 0 | 7,722 | 9,223 | 7,645 | 9,131 |
| 8 | 0 | 8,031 | 9,961 | 8,031 | 9,961 |
| 9 | 10,000 | 18,752 | 21,558 | 18,752 | 21,558 |
| 10 | 5,000 | 24,702 | 28,682 | 24,702 | 28,682 |
| 11 | 0 | 25,690 | 30,977 | 25,690 | 30,977 |
| 12 | 0 | 26,718 | 33,455 | 26,718 | 33,455 |
| 13 | 300 | 28,099 | 36,455 | 28,099 | 36,455 |
| 14 | 493 | 29,735 | 39,904 | 29,735 | 39,904 |
| 15 | 0 | 30,925 | 43,097 | 30,925 | 43,097 |
| 16 | 2,000 | 34,242 | 48,704 | 34,242 | 48,704 |
| 17 | 0 | 35,611 | 52,601 | 35,611 | 52,601 |
| 18 | 5,000 | 42,236 | 62,209 | 42,236 | 62,209 |
| 19 | 8,000 | 52,245 | 75,825 | 52,245 | 75,825 |
| 20 | 15,000 | 69,935 | 98,091 | 69,935 | 98,091 |

usual range of benefit payout options is available, with each providing for both a guaranteed minimum interest rate and a current rate.

The purchaser of a FPDA can place undue emphasis on the stated current interest rate. The loading charges can be important. Thus a FPDA crediting 8.5 percent may not develop values as high as one crediting 8.0 percent because of the loading factor. In any event, prudence should be exercised in interpreting results that show high interest rates (by historical standards) projected for many years or even decades into the future. The wise course of action would suggest examining the insurer's past product performance record in an effort to develop a degree of confidence in the illustrated future values.

In some instances, an annuity that performs well during the accumulation phase may not offer equally attractive performance during the liquidation phase, and vice versa. Clearly, the buyer strives to have the best of both situations. Yet the rates used to convert accumulated fund values to monthly (or other) payments can vary substantially. For example, one study found that monthly annuity lifetime payments varied between $1,080 and $781 for a male, aged 65, whose accumulated fund value was $100,000.

*Single-Premium Deferred Annuity*. The name of the **single-premium deferred annuity** (SPDA) is truly descriptive, since it is a deferred annuity contract purchased with a single premium. As with the FPDA, a minimum stated rate of interest is guaranteed by contract to be paid throughout the duration of the contract, but most insurers pay competitive market rates. The rate actually credited is a function of the insurer's current investment earnings rate and its desired competitive posture in the market, and it is subject to change by the insurer. The current rate may be guaranteed for a single year or for as many as three or more years. Generally, the longer the guarantee period, the lower the rate. Many insurers follow a tiered rate approach wherein the first tier of funds received (e.g., $25,000) is credited with one interest rate and funds received in excess of this tier are credited with a somewhat higher rate (e.g., 0.25 percent higher). Some companies have as many as four tiers, each of which credits a higher rate.

The single premium is often unreduced by identifiable front-end loads. Provision is usually made for graded surrender charges, similar to those for the FPDA, and for withdrawal corridors with no surrender charges. SPDA contracts often have **bailout provisions**. These provisions stipulate that if the interest rate actually credited to the SPDA fund falls below a set rate (often set at 1 to 3 percent below the current rate being credited), the contract owner may withdraw all funds without any surrender charge. This provision is valuable, but any such withdrawal could result in a tax surcharge.[4] Also, if the insurer felt compelled to

---

[4] See Chap. 13.

so reduce its credited interest rate, this probably would occur because overall market interest rates had fallen significantly, and, therefore, it might prove difficult for the contract owner to find comparable financial instruments crediting a higher rate.

The **market-value annuity** (MVA) (also referred to as a **market-value adjusted annuity**) is a type of SPDA that permits contract owners to lock in a guaranteed interest rate over a specified maturity period, typically from three to ten years. If kept until maturity, the tax-deferred value reaches the amount guaranteed at issue. However, unlike the situation with other fixed-dollar annuities, if withdrawals occur, the cash value will be subject not only to possible surrender charges but also to a market-value adjustment. First introduced in the United States in 1984, the MVA is also included as an option with some insurers' variable annuities.

The adjustment may be positive or negative, depending on the interest rate environment at surrender. If interest rates at surrender were higher than those at time of issue, the adjustment would be negative. Conversely, if rates were lower, the adjustment would add to the cash surrender value.

The adjustment is intended to reflect the changes in market values of the assets—typically bonds—backing the annuities. Thus as interest rates rise, the market values of previously purchased bonds will decline, and vice versa, *ceteris paribus*. The theory for MVAs is that if the actual available cash surrender value reflects this market value, the insurer, in effect, shifts much of the risk of market-value changes of assets to the contract owner. Insurers can limit their disintermediation risk (i.e., the tendency to surrender during an increasing interest rate environment) and better match the maturity of assets backing the MVA with its corresponding liabilities.

The MVA is less flexible than many other annuities, but it can offer advantages to buyers. For one thing, there is the possibility of a positive adjustment. For another, the typically longer-duration guarantee can afford a greater sense of security. Also, in theory, the MVA should be able to offer higher interest credits than an equivalent-duration SPDA, since the buyer bears more risk.

Another SPDA variation is the **certificate of annuity** (COA), first offered in the United States in 1983. It provides for a fixed, guaranteed interest rate for a fixed period of time, typically three to ten years. It is similar to a bank-issued certificate of deposit, except that as an annuity, interest earnings are tax deferred. The COA differs from other annuities in that no unscheduled withdrawals are ordinarily permitted during the guarantee period. The full cash value is available on death and annuitization.

At the end of the selected guaranteed period, the owner can renew the COA for another period or select any of the standard annuity options. Many insurers' products carry no identifiable front-end or rear-end charges.

Since the contract does not permit early, unscheduled withdrawals, the interest rate credited to the cash value should be quite competitive, other things being the same. Individuals near retirement, who are interested in locking in an interest rate and who have few, if any, prospects of needing the funds during the guarantee period often purchase COAs.

The SPDA can be an important element in a retirement program. As with all insurance contracts, the contract should suit the needs of the client, and the insurer offering the product should be reliable. The comments regarding the need to exercise care with respect to FPDA interest rates apply here also.

*Single-Premium Immediate Annuity.* A **single-premium immediate annuity** (SPIA) provides that payments to the annuitant commence immediately after the insurer has received a single (typically large) premium payment. SPIAs are steadily growing in importance in the marketplace as consumers seek ways of enhancing the security of their economic future.

SPIAs are often used by those who have large sums of money and desire to have the fund liquidated for retirement income purposes. These funds may have been accumulated through personal investments, through savings, or from a lump-sum distribution under a pension or other employer-sponsored retirement plan.

Life insurance death proceeds are often paid out in installments via a SPIA. Commonly, one envisions such installments as being paid under a life insurance policy settlement option provision that itself is often an earmarked SPIA. The beneficiary's financial interest, however, may be better served by the beneficiary receiving the death proceeds as a lump sum, then shopping carefully for a SPIA.

A contemporary use of SPIAs has evolved from liability insurers' efforts to minimize their loss payouts. A **structured settlement annuity** (SSA) is a SPIA contract issued by a life insurer whereby the plaintiff (the injured party) receives (typically) monthly payments from the defendant in a personal injury lawsuit. Typically, the defendant and the plaintiff, together with their attorneys and a structured settlement specialist, negotiate a settlement package intended to compensate the plaintiff for his or her losses, including future earnings. Although most personal injury settlements consist of a lump-sum payment, a structured settlement involves periodic payments to the plaintiff. The periodic payments are funded through a SSA purchased by the defendant or the liability insurer from a life insurer that guarantees to make the agreed-upon payments usually for the life of the injured person (or a designated beneficiary).

In pricing the SSA, the life insurer faces both an investment risk and a mortality risk, as with all annuities. Unlike the situation with other annuities, however, the underwriters must assist in the pricing of the SSA. Where the SSA is concerned, most annuitants can be expected to exhibit substandard mortality experience, since most will have suffered some injury. To be competitive, the insurer must offer the lowest possible price to the liability insurer to win the sale.

The greater the assessed likelihood of an early death, the lower can be the insurer's offered price (or stated differently, the higher can be the benefits).[5]

*Variable Annuity.*[6] The **variable annuity** provides benefits that vary directly with the investment experience of assets that back the contract. Assets backing variable annuities, as with those backing variable life policies, are maintained in a separate account, and the variable annuity values directly reflect the account's investment results. By contrast, the life insurer's general account assets back the earlier-discussed products.

*1. Nature of the Variable Annuity.* The rationale for the creation of variable annuities was that they should offer, over the long run, protection against the debilitating effects of inflation on fixed incomes—the kind of income provided by fixed annuities. The hope was and is that long-run returns on common stocks and other investments will keep pace with inflation. (This is admittedly a hypothesis that remains to be proven.)

Under a FPDA, SPDA, or other fixed (nonvariable) annuities, the insurance company guarantees a minimum interest rate to be credited to the account during the accumulation period. In addition, a minimum annuity payout per dollar accumulated is guaranteed. A variable annuity does not have these interest guarantees. The contract owner bears the investment risk and receives the return actually earned on invested assets, less charges assessed by the insurance company.

The general account of an insurance company is restricted by state laws as to the kind and quality of investments it may hold. Since these investments support liabilities for products with interest guarantees, they should offer safety of principal and a predictable income stream. Few, if any, investment restrictions apply in establishing a separate account. Income, gains, and losses on separate account assets are credited to or charged against the separate account. Income, gains, and losses on the company's other business are kept apart from the separate account. Funds of variable annuity contract owners are held in the separate account, and the contract owners participate fully in the investment results.

Variable annuity premiums paid to the insurance company are placed in a special variable annuity account. Each year the premiums, after deduction for expenses, are applied to purchase accumulation units in the account, the number of units depending upon the current unit value. Thus if each unit, based on

---

[5] Life insurance is more expensive for persons in poor health than for those in good health because of the greater probability of an earlier death claim. Conversely, annuities for persons in poor health should be less expensive than for those in good health, because the insurer, on average, will have to make fewer payments for those with impaired health. SSAs are, at present, the only annuities sold at a reduced price to persons in poor health. Professors Murray and Klugman have argued that a market for such annuities should be developed. See Michael L. Murray and Stuart Klugman, "Impaired Health Life Annuities," *Journal of the American Society of CLU and ChFC,* Vol. 44 (Sept. 1990).

[6] The discussion of this area draws, in part, on Mary Jo Napoli, "Variable Annuities," *SOA Part 10 Study Note* (Itasca, IL: Society of Actuaries, 1985).

current investment results, is valued at $10, a premium of $100 after expenses will purchase 10 units the following year. If the unit value is changed, the $100 premium would purchase more or less than 10 units. This procedure would continue until annuity payouts were to begin. At that time, the accumulated total number of units credited may be applied, according to actuarial principles and based on current valuation of a unit, to convert accumulation units to annuity units to be valued annually for the annuitant's lifetime.

Instead of providing for the payment each month of a fixed number of dollars, the variable annuity provides for the payment each month or year of the current value of a fixed number of annuity units. Thus the amount of each payment depends on the dollar value of the annuity unit when the payment is made. The valuation assigned to a unit depends upon the investment results of the separate account. For example, if an annuitant were entitled to a payment of 100 annuity units each month, and the dollar values of annuity units for three consecutive months were $10.20, $9.90, and $10.10, the annuitant would receive an income for these months of $1,020, $990, and $1,010.

Variable annuities may be purchased on an FPDA, SPDA, or SPIA basis. In all cases, the usual range of payout options is available, and product expenses and charges are identified.

*2. Regulation of the Variable Annuity.* As a security, variable annuities are subject to the same federal laws as variable life (see Chapter 5). Thus requirements similar to or identical with those imposed on variable life insurance apply to variable annuities with respect to disclosure, sales loads, registration and financial standards, agent licensing, as well as other regulations.

State laws and regulations on variable annuities are not uniform, although many states have followed the procedures included in the **Model Variable Annuity Regulation** of the National Association of Insurance Commissioners. This regulation provides guidelines for separate account investments and requires that variable-annuity contracts state clearly the essential elements of the procedure for determining the amount of the variable benefits. Other policy standards are laid down, including a requirement that annual status reports be mailed to the contract owner.

*3. Suitability of Variable Annuities.* Purchasers of variable annuities might consider that they are undertaking a mutual fund-type investment within an annuity contract. Insurer separate accounts are like mutual funds and carry similar risk/reward characteristics. The buyer should appreciate this fact. Insurers today typically offer a range of investment options—sometimes from a menu of a dozen or more funds (separate accounts) and often with different investment managers. The investment manager's performance record can be a useful guide to possible future performance, although it offers no guarantee of success.

Ideally, the variable annuity will permit the owner to make several low-cost or free asset transfers among the various funds backing the annuity. This affords the buyer flexibility.

Finally, it might be useful to view variable annuities as being primarily an investment and fixed-value annuities as being primarily for savings; such are the risk/return differences.

## Uses and Limitations of Annuities

Annuities can be useful in both the tax-qualified and nonqualified markets. The annuitant has the benefit of the investment management offered by insurers. This can be important for older persons who may desire to be freed of investment cares and management.

Annuitants would enjoy monthly incomes at retirement age that are equal to or higher than those obtainable through the customary channels of conservative investment, if they are willing to have the principal liquidated. Each year, the insurer would pay to the annuitant the current income on his or her investment plus a portion of the investment itself. If the buyer exercised care in the purchase decision, the net return on his or her annuity should prove competitive with investments of comparable quality. When tax benefits are considered, the net return often will exceed those of comparable savings media. Of course, with fixed-dollar annuities, inflation can erode the purchasing power of the annuity payments.

The income is certain; the annuitant may spend it without fear of outliving it. In the absence of an annuity, the danger exists of spending too much or too little. With the annuity, the scale of spending is not only increased but is definite in amount.

*Uses in Tax-Qualified Markets.* Annuities are used as funding vehicles for retirement plans established under various sections of the U.S. Internal Revenue Code (IRC) that allow contributions to be excluded from the taxable income of the employee, the employer, or both. These plans differ greatly, and it is beyond the scope of this section to analyze comprehensively all of these features. Below are brief descriptions of the most common plan types. (A more complete description appears in Chapter 28.)

Annuities fund pension and profit-sharing plans qualified under IRC Section 401 for corporations and self-employed individuals. Annuities are also used with plans that are qualified under IRC Section 403(b). These plans, commonly referred to as **tax-sheltered annuity** (TSA) plans, are available to employees of public educational institutions and certain tax-exempt organizations. To a specified limit, plan contributions either by the employer or by the employee, through a voluntary salary reduction agreement, are excludable from the employee's taxable income. Employees' rights under such plans are nonforfeitable and must be nontransferrable. Withdrawals prior to retirement typically are subject to a 10 percent surcharge tax, in addition to full income taxation.

Annuities are also used to fund **public employee deferred compensation** plans. These plans are qualified under IRC Section 457 and may be established for persons who perform services for states, political subdivisions of states, agencies or instrumentalities of states or their political subdivisions, and certain rural electric cooperatives.

For tax years after 1986, individuals not participating in employer-sponsored retirement plans and those who do participate but whose annual incomes are below certain minimum levels have been able to contribute up to $2,000 of earned compensation to an **individual retirement account** (IRA). Contributions are tax deductible, and interest credited to IRAs accumulates on a tax-deferred basis. The contributions to an IRA by individuals who do not meet the qualification requirements are not tax deductible, but the earnings are tax deferred. Annuities can be used to fund IRAs.

A **401(k) plan** is a profit-sharing plan established by an employer under which up to three types of contributions are permitted: employer contributions, employee contributions from after-tax income, and employee salary reduction (elective) contributions. Neither employer nor elective contributions are included in the employee's taxable income. Furthermore, the employer may deduct both of these contributions from taxable income, up to a limit. Annuities can be used as 401(k) funding vehicles.

*Uses in Nonqualified Markets*. Both annuities and life insurance policies are used to fund "unfunded" **deferred compensation plans**—agreements with private employers under which an employee agrees to defer the receipt of current compensation until a later date.[7] Employees may defer up to 100 percent of compensation, or the plans may be limited to providing benefits in excess of those permitted under tax-qualified plans. These plans generally are limited to a select group of highly compensated employees. They are not explicitly provided for in the code, but they are supported by case law and revenue rulings. Relatively few annuities are used as informal funding vehicles for such plans now than in the past, since non-tax-qualified, corporate-owned annuities no longer enjoy income tax deferral on interest earnings.

Each year individuals purchase thousands of annuities unrelated to employment and not qualified under any plan for deductibility of contributions. Such annuities have the important advantage of deferring tax on investment earnings while providing contemporary investment returns. Figure 7-4 illustrates this concept.

A $1,000 per year contribution is assumed to be made to an annuity crediting 8 percent on the gross contribution (on a tax-deferred basis) and to another savings instrument earning 8 percent, but on a taxable basis. A combined federal and state marginal tax rate of 31 percent is assumed. The annuity fund

---

[7] See Chap. 15.

**FIGURE 7-4**

**THE BENEFITS OF TAX DEFERRAL: AN ILLUSTRATION**

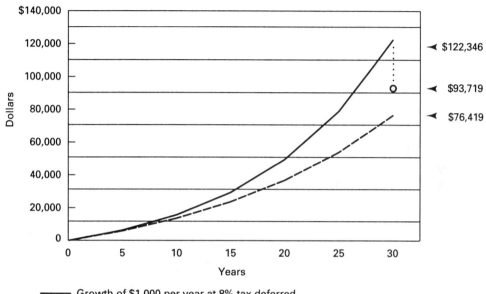

Growth of $1,000 per year at 8% tax deferred
Growth of $1,000 per year at 8% taxable return
Tax due ($28,627) after 30 years assuming lump sum distribution

Note: Assumes 31% marginal tax rate.

builds to over $122,000 in 30 years whereas the taxable fund grows to about $77,000. For a fair comparison, however, the assumption is made that the annuity value is taken as a single-sum distribution at that time, with the result that all deferred interest earnings would be subject to the 31 percent tax.[8] Even after paying almost $29,000 in taxes, the annuity purchaser would still be $17,000 ahead of the taxable investment.[9]

Even though annuity benefits do not escape taxation wholly, the fact that tax is deferred for several years means that the contract owner—not the government—has use of the money. The effect is that the power of compounding at before-tax rates yields a significantly larger sum than would otherwise be the case. Moreover, even if that sum were subject to immediate and full taxation later, the net result remains strongly in favor of the tax-deferred instrument.

[8] Amounts paid out on a periodic basis would receive more favorable tax treatment. See Chap. 15.

[9] This illustration assumes that the alternative savings instrument's earnings would be subject to yearly income tax at the 31 percent rate. Obviously, if a tax-favored instrument were used, results would differ. However, tax-favored investments—such as municipal bonds—ordinarily carry lower yields than taxable instruments.

## SPECIAL-PURPOSE LIFE INSURANCE POLICIES

In addition to the life insurance and annuity contracts already discussed, life insurance companies issue a wide variety of special policies and policy combinations. These special forms, based on the same principles that underpin all life insurance, differ only in that they are packaged to serve a particular market. The contracts typically were developed for specialized purposes and may not offer the same flexibility as do the more common forms of contracts. The amount of insurance sold under these contracts is small in proportion to the total sold each year in the United States.

### SURVIVORSHIP LIFE INSURANCE

The vast majority of life insurance sold in the United States is written on the life of one person. It is theoretically possible to write a life insurance policy on any number of lives and to construct it to pay on the death of the first, second, third, etc., or last of the group to die. In practice, two important plans have evolved: (1) the survivorship life policy and (2) the joint life policy.

**Survivorship life**—also referred to as **second-to-die** insurance—insures two (or more) lives and pays the death proceeds only on the death of the second or last insured to die. Most survivorship policies are whole life, but term and universal life survivorship policies exist.

Since the policy promises to pay only on the death of the second of two insureds, the policy's premiums are quite low relative to those which would be charged for a separate policy on each insured. If this year's probability of death is, say, 0.001 for one insured and 0.002 for the other insured, the probability of both insureds dying and, therefore, the policy face amount having to be paid is only 0.00002 (i.e., 0.001 times 0.002). Premiums are based on such joint probabilities under survivorship policies and are correspondingly low.

Premiums normally are due after the first death, although some policies provide that premiums cease at the first death. When payment of the face amount is contingent upon two deaths rather than one, required reserves are quite low. However, after the first insured dies, the probability of the insurer paying the death benefit no longer rests on the low joint-death probability, but then reverts to the single-life death probability. This fact necessitates that reserves increase substantially after the first death. With some insurers, cash values also increase.

Under U.S. estate tax law, assets bequeathed (in a qualifying manner) to a survivor spouse escape all federal estate taxation on the death of the first spouse. At the death of the survivor spouse (and assuming no remarriage), any remaining assets are fully subject to estate taxation at marginal rates ranging up to 50 percent and higher.

The survivorship life policy is particularly well-situated to meet the need for cash to cover estate taxes and related expenses on the second death. These policies are also commonly used to provide financial security for a disabled child or dependent relative in situations where one death would not necessarily result in financial disaster for survivors, but the deaths of both husband and wife (or other breadwinners) would. It is worth noting that some companies tend to offer more flexible underwriting with survivorship life in instances where one of the proposed insureds has a health problem.

The face amount of the typical second-to-die policy issued in the United States is high, usually exceeding $1,000,000, with premiums being comparatively low—perhaps $20,000 per year. The market for such high-value policies has become exceedingly competitive. As a result, prospective purchasers can find good value, since many insurers offer special-policy benefits in an effort to differentiate their policies from those of their competitors.

## JOINT LIFE INSURANCE

In contrast to the survivorship life insurance, **joint life insurance** promises to pay the face amount of the policy on the *first* death of one of two (or more) insureds covered by the contract. The policy is often used to insure both the husband and wife, with each being the beneficiary for the other, and in business buy-out situations involving two partners or two major stockholders. The policy pays only on the death of the *first* to die and is terminated at that time.

The survivor is without life insurance coverage under this policy. Contracts usually provide, however, that the survivor has the right to purchase a whole life policy on his or her life without providing evidence of insurability. Some contracts continue insurance temporarily, and most provide that if both insureds die in a common disaster, the insurer will pay the face amount on each death. The importance of having a contingent beneficiary is clear.[10]

The premium for a given face amount would be smaller than the total premiums that would be paid for two individual ordinary life policies covering each individual. Joint life coverage is also available under term and universal life plans. The market has recently witnessed some sales resurgence of these policies under the name of **first-to-die insurance**. Such contemporary policies seem to offer greater flexibility and value than earlier joint life policies.

## DEBIT LIFE INSURANCE

Dating from the 1800s in the United States and with roots in seventeenth-century England, the debit insurance business was the backbone of the U.S. life insurance industry until early in the twentieth century. Originally, **debit life insurance** was synonymous with **industrial insurance**—policies issued for small amounts, usually less than $1,000, with premiums payable weekly or monthly to an agent who called at the policyowner's home or place of employment. It was originally designed for low-income families who could not

[10] See Chap. 9.

afford the amounts of protection and premium payments associated with ordinary life and individual health insurance. The agent's assigned territory was referred to as the **debit** (derived from the agent's "debiting" the client's records for each premium payment) and gave the name to both a class of insurance and a means of marketing. Today, the term debit insurance encompasses any type of insurance sold through the debit (home collection of premium) system of marketing.

Industrial insurance today represents less than 0.3 percent of all life insurance in force, compared with 14.1 percent in 1950. Moreover, the vast majority of insurance is paid up. The decline in industrial insurance was due to industrial life insurance being narrowly defined legislatively and to the fact that life insurance amounts of under $1,000 provide little economic security while being quite costly per unit of coverage. Other important factors have been the rapid expansion of group insurance, the significant growth in the survivorship benefits under Social Security, and the adverse publicity given industrial insurance.[11]

Debit life insurance today encompasses **monthly debit ordinary** (MDO) insurance—ordinary policies typically written in the $5,000 to $25,000 range with premiums collected monthly at the policyowner's home. MDO contracts are based on ordinary (as opposed to the more conservative industrial) mortality tables and offer more flexibility. Since MDO is sold in larger face amounts, more underwriting is involved than with industrial insurance.

In recent years, industrial life insurance and MDO have come to be known as **home service life insurance**. While the debit (home service) life insurance in force has been relatively stable over the past several years, as a percentage of total life insurance in force in the United States, it continues to decline. Today it represents less than 2.0 percent of life insurance.

Whether a low-income person should purchase a debit life insurance policy is becoming a moot point as sales continue to stagnate and insurers emphasize premium-notice ordinary products.[12] The continuing decline of industrial life insurance, in particular, seems assured in view of inflation, the legislative definition of industrial life insurance, and numerous other factors.

Those who consider purchasing weekly-premium industrial insurance would be better off financially in purchasing an MDO or a regular ordinary policy. All other provisions of an MDO policy are the same as those of a premium-notice ordinary policy.

Debit life insurance was the focus of much public concern and debate in the late 1970s.[13] Problems alleged to exist with this type of insurance in general and

[11] For a discussion of these and other aspects of industrial insurance, including its unique contractual provisions, see Robert A. Marshall and Eli A. Zubay, *The Debit System of Marketing Life and Health Insurance* (Englewood Cliffs, NJ:Prentice-Hall, 1975).

[12] **Premium notice ordinary** (PNO) life insurance, sold by most if not all life insurers that sell debit insurance, is the term used in the debit business for the individual products discussed in Chaps. 4 to 6.

[13] See, for example, Elizabeth D. Laporte, *Life Insurance Sold to the Poor: Industrial and Other Debit Products* (Washington, DC: Office of Policy Planning, Federal Trade Commission, Jan. 1979). See also Life Insurers Conference, *Life Insurers Conference Response to the Elizabeth Laporte Report* (Richmond, VA:LIC, Mar. 1979).

industrial insurance in particular have included the high cost of benefits compared to other forms of insurance, high lapse rates, unfair contract provisions, overloading (the practice of selling a person more policies than he or she can afford), churning of policies (the practice of repeatedly selling a person new policies to replace old policies), misleading and high pressure sales tactics, and exorbitant profits. While acknowledging that some problems exist, particularly with the industrial product, industry spokespersons nonetheless have forcefully defended the home service system of marketing.

## FAMILY POLICY OR RIDER

Many companies issue a policy or, more commonly, a rider (a benefit supplement to a base policy) that insures all or selected members of the family in one contract, commonly called a **family policy** or **family rider**.[14] When issued as a policy, it provides whole life insurance on the father or the mother, designated as the principal insured, with a premium based on his or her age. Term insurance is generally provided on the wife and children, or on the father and children when the wife is the insured. When coverage is issued as a rider, no underlying insurance is provided through the rider on the principal insured's life. The policy to which the rider is attached provides the basic coverage, and the net result is possibly the same as it is with the family policy.

Coverage on the spouse (usually term insurance) may be a stated amount or may vary in amount with age. Insurance on the children is term for a fixed amount. All children living with the family are covered, even if they were adopted or born *after* the policy is issued. Coverage is afforded to children over a few days old (e.g., 15 days) and under a stated age, such as 18, 21, or 25, and it is usually convertible to any whole life plan of insurance, without evidence of insurability (and often for up to five times the amount of expiring term insurance). If the principal insured dies, the insurance on the spouse and children usually becomes paid up.

A unit of coverage under the policy may consist of $5,000 whole life on the principal insured, $1,000 or $1,500 whole life or term on the spouse, and $1,000 term on each child. When the insurance is issued as a rider, a certain number of units of coverage on the spouse's life is purchased whereby a unit might provide $5,000 term-to-age-65 coverage on the spouse and $1,000 of term insurance on each child.

The premium does not change on the inclusion of additional children (i.e., via birth or adoption). The premium for the children's coverage is based on an average number of children. In the event of the spouse's death prior to the insured's death, the insurance is paid to his or her named beneficiary.

An optional benefit closely related to the family rider provides life insurance coverage on additional insureds. This **other insureds** rider is most

[14] A similar policy, the **family maintenance policy**, provides a 20-year term insurance rider on the insured's life, with the amount payable in installments.

frequently used to insure other family members, usually the spouse or children. If the rider insures only the children, it is often referred to as a **children's rider**; otherwise it is the same as the family rider.

## SURVIVORSHIP ANNUITY

The **survivorship annuity**, also referred to as **reversionary annuity**, provides that if the beneficiary should outlive the insured, the beneficiary will receive a predetermined income for life, regardless of his or her age at the insured's death. If the beneficiary predeceases the insured, however, the contract terminates and no further premiums or benefits are payable. Although this product is sold by very few insurers today, its novel approach continues to provide insight into product design possibilities.

The size of a life income is normally a function of the beneficiary's age at the insured's death and cannot be known beforehand. The survivorship annuity, on the other hand, establishes a set amount prior to the insured's death. The policy premium, based on the joint probability of death of the insured and the beneficiary, would be relatively low if the policy were taken out when the insured were young and the beneficiary were old. For this reason, the policy can be attractive when a child desires to protect an aged parent or another aged relative.

A modified form of the survivorship annuity, the **life income policy**, differs only in that a minimum number of payments is guaranteed following the insured's death, irrespective of whether the beneficiary is alive to receive them. For the guaranteed benefits, the beneficiary may be changed, or a cash surrender value will be payable if the contract is discontinued.

## JUVENILE INSURANCE

Juvenile insurance is insurance written on the lives of children from the age of 1 day to 14 or 15 years of age and issued on the application of a parent or other person responsible for the support of the child. In the past, most companies and some states limited the amount of insurance that could be written on the lives of young children. This limitation is less common today.

Most companies permit the purchase of any reasonable amount of life insurance on a child's life, subject to underwriting requirements as to perceived need and adequacy of coverage on parents' and children's lives. Some companies will insure a child from the age of one day, but many require that the child be at least one month old. Because the insured under a juvenile policy is a minor, control of the policy is typically vested in the applicant (usually a parent) until the child attains age 18 or until the prior death of the applicant. Many companies will issue regular policies to minors on their own application, provided they are above the juvenile age limit set by the particular state involved.

Provision can be made in all forms of juvenile insurance for the waiver of premium payments in the event of the death or total disability of the person responsible for the payment of the premiums (usually the parent). This **payor benefit**, when added to the juvenile policy, provides that premiums will be waived until the insured (the child) attains a specified age, usually 25, or the paid-up date of the contract, whichever is earlier, in the event the premium payor dies or becomes disabled. Evidence of insurability must be furnished by the premium payor before the clause can be attached to a contract.

Juvenile insurance is sold to provide funds (1) for last-illness and funeral expenses, (2) for college education, (3) to start an insurance program for a child at a low premium rate, and (4) to assure that a child will have some life insurance even if he or she later becomes uninsurable. Whether any of these reasons is convincing to a parent or grandparent is a matter of judgment. It can be observed, however, that there often is inadequate insurance coverage on the parents' lives, and that the primary objective should be to insure fully against loss of income brought about by the death of the breadwinners. The death of a child, as sad as it is, rarely causes major financial loss to the family, and therefore life insurance on a child's life is of questionable need.

## Pre-Need Funeral Insurance

Life insurance benefits earmarked to pre-fund future funeral expenses are said to have first appeared in the United States in 1930. From a business that once evoked concerns about fairness and cost, it has evolved to what today is referred to as **pre-need funeral insurance**—life insurance intended to fund a prearranged funeral. With this type of insurance, a funeral provider and a (typically older) person enter into an agreement whereby the details of the goods and services to be delivered by the funeral provider are set out. The funeral provider agrees to provide the service whenever death occurs for the proceeds of the life insurance policy. The typical buyer is 65 to 70 years old and purchases a $2,500 to $5,000 single-premium whole life policy. Higher-issue age limits, lenient underwriting (and accompanying higher mortality), and a small policy size produce premium levels that reflect the realities of pricing. The market for these products is small but expanding.

Concern was expressed during the mid-1980s that consumers (1) did not understand that life insurance was being used to fund the funeral, (2) were unaware of certain restrictions on delivery of the goods and services, and (3) were unaware that they were dealing with a life insurance agent. As a result, the NAIC amended its life insurance advertising and disclosure model regulations to encompass funeral insurance and to require that these and certain other factors be made clear to purchasers.

## OPTIONAL BENEFITS AND RIDERS

The practice of adding supplemental policy benefits by endorsements (**riders**) to the contract permits flexibility in adapting basic plans to individual needs. Several such common riders are discussed below.

### DISABILITY BENEFITS

A common practice is to attach insurance contract riders that provide certain benefits in the event of total and permanent disability. The two most common disability benefits are (1) waiver of premium and (2) disability income. The definition of disability, a critically important aspect, usually is the same for both waiver of premium and disability income benefits.

*Definition of Disability*. Under the disability clauses in life insurance policies and annuity contracts, the risk covered pertains to total and permanent disability. Although phraseology varies greatly, the customary wording of the clause declares the policyowner to be entitled to the benefits promised when the insured's illness or injury results in his or her *total and permanent* disability.

As explained in more detail in Chapter 17, the word *total* proved difficult to interpret legally. Regardless of the exact language used, the interpretation given the clause by most insurers today contemplates all cases in which, because of illness or injury, the insured is unable to pursue his or her own occupation or any job for which he or she is reasonably suited by education, training, or experience.

Similarly, there has been doubt as to the meaning of the word *permanent*. The problem, however, is usually settled by the companies themselves, in that the clause specifies that total disability lasting continuously for a stated waiting period shall be presumed to be permanent until recovery.

*Waiver of Premium*. The **waiver of premium** benefit, offered by almost all companies, provides that in the event the insured becomes totally and permanently disabled before a certain age, typically 65, premiums (or mortality and expense charges) on the contract will be waived during the continuance of disability beyond a specified waiting period, customarily six months. The contract continues just as if the policyowner were paying the premiums. Thus dividends continue to be paid on participating policies, cash values continue to increase, and loans may be secured.[15] Sometimes the price for the benefit is included in the regular premium, but more often the waiver-of-premium provision is added to the life insurance or annuity contract for a small extra premium.

All premiums are waived during disability—not just those falling due after the waiting period. This differs from the case in disability income insurance and

---

[15] If the benefit is limited to a waiver of mortality and expense charges—as with some universal life policies—cash values may not increase.

in most waiver-of-premium provisions in individual health insurance policies. Most companies require six months of continuous disability before the waiver-of-premium benefit takes effect. As long as disability commences during the period of coverage, all premiums or charges are waived while it continues, or as otherwise specified in the contract. Many companies provide that for disability beginning after age 60 but before age 65, premiums are waived only to age 65. A disability is covered only if it starts prior to a stated age, frequently 65.

*Disability Income*. Companies providing a **disability income** benefit by rider often pay monthly 1 percent of the face of the life policy ($10 per month per $1,000). Many companies limit the maximum monthly income that they will issue to some stated figure, such as $1,000, with a further limit set on the amount the company will participate in within all companies. This latter limit may range up to $3,000 or more, with an additional limit frequently imposed, based on a percentage of net earned income. The majority of insurers consider six months' total disability as permanent and commence payments at the end of the sixth month. This is really the equivalent of a six-month elimination period with a one-month retroactive payment. Some companies impose a four-month waiting period.

Premiums on both the base policy and the disability income rider are waived during a period of covered disability. Dividends are paid as usual, the policy's death benefit is unaffected, and in other respects the basic life contract continues as though no disability had occurred. Should the insured recover, income payments cease and premiums are again due.

## ACCELERATED DEATH BENEFITS

Advances in medical technology have greatly increased the expected life span, so that previously terminal conditions are now survivable. Yet medical care and long-term-care costs can be financially catastrophic for a family. Accelerated benefit products evolved in response to this growing need for funds to ease such financial burdens.

**Accelerated death benefit** provisions (or riders) involve the payment of all or a portion of a life insurance policy's face amount prior to the insured's death because of some specified, adverse medical condition of the insured. Such coverage, also referred to as **living insurance**, may take one of three forms, as discussed below.

*Terminal Illness Coverage*. Several insurers offer some type of **terminal illness coverage** that provides that a specified maximum percentage (typically 25 to 50 percent) of the life policy's death benefit can be paid if the insured has been diagnosed as having a terminal illness. Most provisions require that the insured have a maximum of either six months or one year to live. Many companies make no explicit charge for the coverage, because they believe that they can absorb the costs of prepaying a portion of what would be a certain, soon death claim anyway. The benefit may be included in any kind of policy.

Companies typically provide for a maximum total living benefit payout (e.g., $250,000), irrespective of how large the base policy may be. A concern of many companies is that an unlimited benefit amount may lead to more fraudulent claims. It is not unusual for the insurer to secure a release from all interested parties (e.g., beneficiary and assignee), not just the policyowner, to avoid any future misunderstanding.

*Catastrophic Illness Coverage*. **Catastrophic illness coverage** provides for accelerated death benefit payments on approximately the same terms and conditions as terminal illness coverage, except that in this case the insured must have been diagnosed as having one of several listed catastrophic illnesses. Also referred to as **dread disease coverage**, the provision covers illnesses that typically include stroke, heart attack, cancer, coronary artery surgery, renal failure, and similar catastrophic diseases.

A forerunner of terminal illness coverage originated in 1983 with a South African insurer and migrated to the United Kingdom in 1985 via international reinsurers. Its U.S. debut was in 1988 by Jackson National Life Insurance Company.

Both terminal illness and catastrophic illness coverages provide that policy death benefits are reduced on a dollar-for-dollar payout basis. Cash values are reduced on either a dollar-for-dollar basis or in proportion to the death benefit reduction. According to the NAIC **Accelerated Benefits Guideline for Life Insurance**, prospective buyers of these coverages must be given numerical illustrations that reflect the effects of an accelerated payout on the policy's death benefit, cash value, premium, and policy loans. Additionally, consumers must receive a brief description of the accelerated benefits and definitions of the conditions or occurrences triggering payment. Any separate, identifiable premium charge must be disclosed.

The NAIC and other organizations were concerned that such benefits, especially the catastrophic illness coverage, could be "oversold." In the 1960s and before, certain dread disease policies with limited coverage fell into regulatory disfavor because of fear-based selling tactics and numerous claim disputes. Clearly, a weakness of these earlier policies and of this latest variation is that other illnesses can be equally devastating, yet no benefit would be provided for them. An adequate health insurance program should largely militate against the need for either of these coverages.

*Long-Term-Care Coverage (LTC)*. A third type of accelerated death benefit—**long-term-care coverage**—provides that monthly benefits can be paid if the insured is confined because of a medical condition. LTC coverage can be purchased as a stand-alone policy or as a rider to any type of life insurance policy.[16] To qualify for payments, the confinement must be covered, any preconfinement conditions and elimination periods met, and any minimum in-force requirements satisfied. To be covered, the confinement must be medically necessary and in a qualified facility. Although provisions vary, the rider may cover state-licensed skilled nursing facilities (SNF), intermediate care facilities, and custodial care facilities. Some cover home convalescent care.

Many riders carry some type of **prior confinement requirement** in a hospital or other high-care facility (e.g., an SNF) for a person to qualify for LTC benefits. Typically, the LTC confinement must have occurred within 30 days after discharge from the hospital (or other facility). Some riders have no prior-confinement requirement.

Riders routinely provide for an **elimination period**—the time between commencement of a covered confinement and the first benefit payment. This period may be from two to six months, depending on the policy terms.

Many insurers also require that the contract be in force for a minimum number of years—a so-called **in-force requirement**—before the insured is eligible to collect benefits. This period may range from three to ten years and may vary with issue age. Some contracts have no such requirements.

The monthly benefit typically equals 2 percent of the policy's face amount, subject to some monthly maximum payout and to a total maximum payout (e.g., 50 percent of the policy face amount). Some companies provide a tiered payout of, say, 20 percent of the first $150,000 and 0.5 percent of the excess face amount up to $1 million. Thus a $100,000 policy produces a monthly payment of $2,000. A $500,000 policy yields a $4,750 monthly benefit.

Amounts paid as benefits reduce the total death benefit dollar for dollar. While contract wording varies, the reduction typically will affect both the net amount at risk and the cash value proportionately.

Accelerated death benefit coverages are still fairly new to the North American market, and, therefore, it is difficult to discern trends. Certain tax and regulatory issues remain to be sorted out fully. Clearly, however, with the increasing emphasis that has been observed on insurance for its living benefits, the popularity of this class of coverage can be expected to grow.

## ACCIDENTAL DEATH BENEFIT

An **accidental death benefit** clause or rider (sometimes called **double indemnity**) may be added to most life insurance contracts. It provides that double or triple the face amount of insurance is payable if the death of the insured is caused by an accident.

From an economic standpoint, there is no reason why double or triple the policy face amount should be paid for an accidental death, as compared with

[16] See Chap. 16.

death from other causes. The financial loss to the family is equally great irrespective of the cause of death. Moreover, with respect to most persons, there is much less of a likelihood of accidental death than of death from other causes. The clause has value, of course, and its price is comparatively low, because of the relatively low probability of loss. The small premium, coupled with the belief (erroneous for the most part) by most persons that if they die, the cause of death will be an accident, are probably the main reasons for its appeal.

*Definition of Accidental Death.* A typical clause includes the following definition of accidental death: "Death resulting from bodily injury effected solely through external, violent, and accidental means independently and exclusively of all other causes, with death occurring within 90 days after such injury." The expression *accidental means* insists that both the *cause* and *result* of the death must be accidental. For example, if death occurs as a result of the insured's intentionally jumping from a moving vehicle, the results may be accidental, but the means are not accidental. Death caused by others, such as muggers and robbers, although intentional as to such other person, would be interpreted as accidental means under the clause. The original intention of the provisions was to limit the coverage to deaths that were purely and entirely accidental.

*Exclusions.* Certain causes of death (even when the causes and results are accidental) are excluded by the accidental death benefit provision. These exclusions fall into five classes: (1) deaths resulting from certain illegal activities; (2) deaths in which an accident was involved but in which illness, disease, or mental infirmity was also involved; (3) deaths from certain specified causes in which considerable doubt may exist about the accidental character of the death; (4) deaths resulting from war; and (5) deaths resulting from aviation, except for passenger travel on scheduled airlines. The rather numerous exclusions in the accidental death benefit clause indicate the practical difficulties inherent in this form of coverage.

*Time and Age Limits.* To be covered, death typically must occur within 90 days of an accident. The purpose of this restriction is to assure, reasonably, that the accident is the sole cause of death. In general, the time limitations are enforced, although some serious problems can be created, with some courts holding that the 90-day requirement need not be strictly applied.

Accidental death coverage usually expires at age 65 or 70. The majority of companies grade their premium charges by age at issue, and a number of companies now offer multiple indemnity (two, three, or more times the face amount) coverage.

## GUARANTEED INSURABILITY OPTION

One of the problems faced by young people just starting their careers is a combination of limited income and a growing future need for life insurance protection as their life cycle evolves. (This problem is highlighted in Chapter 12.) The **guaranteed insurability option** (GIO) was developed to permit young individuals to be certain that they would be able to purchase additional insurance as they grew older, regardless of their insurability. This rider, also known as the **additional purchase option**, permits an insured to purchase additional amounts of insurance at stated intervals without providing evidence of insurability. The usual rider gives the insured the option of purchasing additional insurance (in finance terms, a **put**) at three-year intervals, provided the insured has not attained a specified age, the most common being age 40. Special option dates may be provided for such life events as birth or adoption of a child and marriage.

In most cases, the amount of the additional insurance is limited to a multiple of the basic policy face amount or an amount stipulated in the policy for the additional purchase option, whichever is the smaller. Although the maximum amount of each option was originally $10,000, a number of companies now offer up to $50,000 or more per option date. The option requires an extra premium that is based on the company's estimate of the extra mortality that will be experienced on policies issued without evidence of insurability. The premium is payable to the last option date and, for the insured, is the cost of insuring his or her insurability.

For purposes of illustration, assume that the owner/insured purchases a $25,000 ordinary life policy at age 21 and that the guaranteed insurability option is included. Under this option, the company agrees to issue, without evidence of insurability, and on the owner/insured's request, an additional policy on his or her life at each option date. To minimize adverse selection, option dates customarily occur at set ages, such as 25, 28, 31, 34, 37, and 40. Thus if the insured desires, he or she could add as much as $150,000 coverage in addition to the original policy of $25,000. Separate policies need not be issued when the option is included within a universal life or other flexible policy.

Although potentially beneficial, the GIO is not as flexible as one might prefer. It permits the exercise of the option at specified dates only, provides additional protection of relatively low amounts (for most companies), and requires the purchase of an additional insurance policy, with attendant policy fees and front-end loads (although many companies now permit internal policy increases in face amounts via the GIO, such as with universal life policies). Although it would admittedly be complex to devise, price, and administer, insurers could provide a useful service by devising a pure guaranteed insurability rider *and* policy with greater flexibility. Even so, the rider can prove of value, especially to those whose family health history suggests that potentially significant medical problems may develop.

## COST OF LIVING RIDER

The **cost-of-living-adjustment** (COLA) rider has already been discussed in connection with increasing term life insurance (see Chapter 4) and flexible premium life insurance. It is, therefore, sufficient merely to recall that this feature can usually be added as a supplemental benefit to most forms of life insurance. It can be useful when one's needs for life insurance are expected to change over time in approximately the same proportion as changes in the cost of living. Although for many persons the need for life insurance protection may increase, it will not normally increase in proportion to COLA increases. Consequently, this aspect of the rider should be examined carefully.

## ADDITIONAL INSURANCE COVERAGE

Insurers have for decades permitted policyowners to attach (typically) term riders to basic policies to enhance the total death benefit. Within the past few years a modified approach of this practice has evolved.

Applicants who today request that insurance riders be added to their base policies may purchase a high-value term life rider or a rider that permits them to make additional premium payments to accelerate cash-value buildup. This buildup may involve no increase in death benefit (as with dump-in premiums under universal life policies) or it may involve the purchase of units of paid-up additional insurance (as with the paid-up additions dividend option).

These riders enhance policy flexibility. Usually, the expenses and commissions associated with the premium for the additional insurance are lower than those for the base policy. Most insurers pass these lower expenses on to policyowners so that the riders can be the means of acquiring additional protection at or close to net rates.

# *Chapter 8*

# *THE LIFE INSURANCE CONTRACT: I*

**INTRODUCTION**

This and the following chapter provide an overview of the life insurance contract as a legal document. As will be seen, life insurance policies are sound, flexible legal instruments.

## DUAL NATURE OF CASH-VALUE CONTRACTS

All cash-value life insurance policies can be viewed as being composed of a savings element and a complementary amount of pure life insurance, such that the total equals the policy face amount. Although the central purpose of the contract is insurance protection, the contract also provides auxiliary rights to the policyowner if he or she wishes to alter the original arrangement. Many of these rights stem from the level-premium payment plan, wherein the policyowner pays more than the pure cost of current insurance protection, to permit accumulation of a fund against the rising cost of mortality in later years, when the actual premium paid alone would be insufficient.

Within fixed-premium life insurance contracts, the so-called savings element typically flows not from a desire to set aside savings as in a bank, but rather is a means of avoiding the loss of protection that would result if annual premiums reached impossibly high levels in later years. Notwithstanding this intent, the presence of a

177

savings element naturally led to increasing emphasis on the lifetime features of these policies.[1] The values built up have actually been saved by the policyowner. With the introduction of a nonforfeiture provision, the dual nature of the cash-value life insurance contract emerged, and the so-called prematurity rights have continued to be enlarged and emphasized. Universal life policies, with their clearly separate cash-value element, have simply heightened this awareness.

The contract provisions relating to nonforfeiture, assignment, and policy loans arise essentially because of the savings aspect of life insurance contracts. In addition, the savings element may be applied under the settlement options to provide a retirement income. The savings element in cash-value life insurance permits individuals to save, within the limits of the premium payments provision, through their policies and utilize the investment services of the life insurance company. The point here is that although the basic purpose of the life insurance contract is to provide a fund at the insured's death, the prematurity rights of the policy have become increasingly important.

## STATUTORY CONTROL OVER POLICY PROVISIONS

Although no statutorily standard policy exists in the United States, life insurance contract provisions are subject to considerable governmental control and regulation in all U.S. jurisdictions and virtually all countries internationally. In the United States, this control typically involves the requirements that (1) no policy form may be used until it is approved by the state insurance department and (2) policies must contain certain standard provisions, as specified in the insurance law.[2] In general, the statutes do not prescribe the exact wording to be used for these standard provisions; rather, they stipulate that actual policy wording must be at least as favorable as that of the statute. Provisions more favorable to the insured may be and are used.

The standard provisions generally required by the various states include those relative to (1) the entire contract clause, (2) the incontestable clause, (3) the grace period, (4) reinstatement, (5) nonforfeiture provision, (6) policy loans, (7) annual dividends, (8) misstatement of age, (9) settlement options, and (10) deferment of loan and cash-value payments.[3] These and other provisions are discussed below.

Individual states have other regulations that relate to the policy contract or its terms. New York, for example, expressly prohibits any exclusion from liability

---

[1] But see Institute of Life Insurance, *The Nature of the Whole Life Contract* (New York: ILI, June 1974). This concept of the dual nature of the whole life contract has led to consumer confusion.

[2] Not every state requires standard provisions as a matter of law. For example, Missouri and Connecticut have no statutorily required provisions, although Connecticut has adopted some standard provisions by regulation.

[3] For results of a survey of U.S. life insurance company practices regarding policy provisions, see John H. Thornton and Kennes C. Huntley, "A Survey of Life Insurance Policy Provisions, *Journal of the American Society of CLU and ChFC,* Vol. 4 (May 1990).

for death except for those set forth in its law.[4] Many states require that each policy form be identified by a code number and that a brief description of the policy be placed at the bottom of the first page (e.g., "whole life with premiums payable for life").

Life and health insurance policies are required to be written in simplified language in most states, including New York. Most of these laws and regulations are based on the **Life and Health Insurance Policy Language Simplification Model Act** of the National Association of Insurance Commissioners (NAIC). The laws and regulations require that policy language meet a readability ease test,[5] and that policies be printed in a minimum type size, with an accompanying table of contents (or index).

Because of the expense of maintaining a different policy form for use in each state, companies attempt to produce contracts that meet the requirements of all or substantially all states in which they do business. Occasionally, conflicting state requirements or company preferences will necessitate the use of special policy forms or modification through endorsements (supplementing policy terms) of the regular forms in particular states.

A host of provisions makes up life insurance contracts. Some are included to protect the policyowner (e.g., grace period to prevent inadvertent lapse); some are included to make the policy more flexible from the standpoint of the policyowner (e.g., clauses permitting a change of beneficiary); and some are included to protect the company (e.g., clauses excluding payment if the insured commits suicide within a certain time period).

While some provisions can be viewed as protecting both the company and the policyowner, the discussion of contract provisions in this and the following chapter is based on the above organizational pattern. It will also include a brief review of the law as it pertains to the agent.

## THE POLICY AS A CONTRACT

A life insurance policy is a contract, and it must, therefore, conform to the rules of general contract law. Before examining these basic rules as they apply to life insurance contracts, a summary of the characteristics that distinguish insurance contracts from many other contracts is presented. These characteristics underlie the distinctive judicial interpretations accorded life insurance contracts.

---

[4] Permissive exclusions: (1) war; (2) suicide, limited to two years; (3) aviation, unlimited; and (4) occupation or residence, limited to two years. New York Law, § 155(2).

[5] The Flesch readability test is usually used in these laws. The laws require that policies attain a certain minimum readability score. See Rudolph Franz Flesch, *The Art of Readable Writing with the Flesch Readability Formula*, 25th ed. (New York: Harper & Row, 1974).

## DISTINGUISHING CHARACTERISTICS OF LIFE INSURANCE CONTRACTS

First, the insurance contract is one of the **utmost good faith**—that is, each party is entitled to rely in good faith upon the representations of the other, and each is under an obligation not to attempt to deceive or withhold material information from the other. The rule of **caveat emptor**[6] does not generally apply. The company must depend to a great extent on the statements of prospective owners/insureds in assessing their acceptability for insurance, and the buyer must rely upon the insurer's good faith because the insurance contract is intricate and highly technical.

The life insurance contract is characterized as being a document  of **adhesion**, meaning that its terms and provisions are fixed by one party (the insurer) and, with minor exceptions, must be accepted or rejected *en totale* by the other party (the prospective policyowner). The fact that the contract is highly specialized and technical in nature also prevents it from being a bargaining contract. As a result, the courts have held that any ambiguities or unclear elements in the contract will be construed in favor of the party not participating in the construction of the contract wording—the policyowner..

The life insurance contract is a **valued policy**, meaning that the insurer agrees to pay a stated sum of money irrespective of the actual economic loss. Most property and liability and medical expense policies, by contrast, are contracts of indemnity. Under a contract of **indemnity**, insureds are never entitled to recover more than their economic loss. The insurer, at most, returns the insured to the same financial position in which he or she would have been had no loss occurred. Under a life insurance contract, the insurer promises to pay a definite sum of money, which does not purport necessarily to represent a measure of the actual loss. The rules relating to insurable interest discussed below reflect this characteristic.[7]

The contract is **conditional** in that the insurer's obligation to pay a claim depends upon the performance of certain acts, such as the payment of premiums and the furnishing of proof of death. In addition, the life insurance contract is **unilateral** in nature, meaning that only one party, the insurer, gives a legally enforceable promise. The owner of the contract makes no promise to make premium payments, but if he or she chooses to make them in a timely manner, the insurer is bound to accept them and meet its obligations under the contract.

Finally, the life insurance contract is classified as **aleatory**, as opposed to commutative. In a **commutative** contract, an exchange involving approximately equivalent values exists, whereas an aleatory contract involves the element of chance, and one party may receive more in value than the other. This important distinction is discussed further below.

---

[6] "Let the buyer beware."

[7] In cases where an individual is insured for business purposes, the extent of the applicant's possible loss in the event of the insured's death is an important factor in determining the amount of insurance to be issued.

## FORMATION OF THE LIFE INSURANCE CONTRACT

The agreement between a life insurance company and a person seeking insurance must meet all the requirements prescribed by law for the formation of a valid contract. For any contract to be valid, four requirements must be met: (1) the parties to the contract must be legally capable of making a contract; (2) an agreement must exist based on an offer made by one of the parties to the contract and an acceptance of that offer by the other party on the same terms; (3) there must be a valid consideration; and (4) the purpose of the agreement must be lawful.[8] A life insurance policy is a contract and it must, therefore, conform to these requirements.

***Capacity of the Parties.*** The parties to a contract must have the legal capacity to contract. If the insurance company is licensed to transact business in the state under consideration, and otherwise complies with the state insurance code, its capacity to contract is clear. Where the insurer is incompetent by reason of noncompliance or incomplete compliance with the requirements of the state in which the contract is executed, the question of the validity of the contract and the respective rights of the parties has not been uniformly decided. In some states, the contract may be void entirely. In others it may be voidable. A **void** agreement has no legal force or effect, whereas a **voidable** agreement is one that can be made void at the option of the innocent party. In the majority of states, however, the execution of the contract is penalized rather than prohibited and remains binding on both parties. The policyowner is even able to sue a nonadmitted insurer in the state courts where the policyowner resides, under the state's Long Arm Statute.[9]

In connection with the legal capacity of the applicant (proposed owner) to contract, no problem ordinarily arises unless the applicant is: (1) a minor, (2) intoxicated or under the influence of other drugs, (3) mentally incompetent, or (4) an enemy alien.

*1. Minors.* With few exceptions, the minimum age at which a person can enter into contracts (the **age of majority**) is 18. However, laws are not uniform and special age limitations may exist in a particular jurisdiction. In some states, minors have the legal capacity to enter into contracts if they are married. In the absence of contrary state law, contracts made by minors are voidable at the option of the minor, except for the reasonable value of necessaries.[10]

---

[8] Some contracts must be in a particular *form* to be binding upon the parties. New York, Georgia, and many other states require life insurance contracts to be in writing. The states also generally require the filing of policy forms with insurance departments for approval, so that, for all practical purposes, policies have to be in writing in every state.

[9] *McGee v. International Life Insurance Company,* 355 U.S. 220, 78 S. Ct. 199. 2 LEd.2d 233 (1957); *Vencedor Mfg. Co. v. Gougler Industries, Inc., et al.,* 557 F 2d 886 (1977).

[10] The term **necessaries** refers not only to basic needs such as food, clothing, and shelter but also can include other items judged by a court as appropriate for the person's circumstances.

Meanwhile, the other party, such as an insurance company, remains obligated to perform the contract. If the minor decides to void or repudiate the contract, the other party must return all of the premiums that have been paid. Of course, where the application for insurance on a minor's life is made by a competent adult, no question of capacity arises.

Although life insurance is not a necessary, it has important values to the insured and his or her family. To encourage insurance companies to provide insurance for older minors but without danger of later repudiation by them, many states have enacted statutes that give minors who are older than a specified age the legal capacity to contract for insurance. The specified ages range from 14 to 18, with 15 being the most frequent age. Some of these statutes additionally limit the parties eligible to be named beneficiaries under life insurance policies issued to such minors to spouses or parents.

*2. Intoxicated Persons.* To the extent that he or she is unable to understand the nature of the transaction in which he or she is engaged, a person under the influence of intoxicating liquor or drugs lacks legal capacity. The effect is to make such contracts voidable, and the individual, with some exceptions, may be able to repudiate the contract within a reasonable length of time after he or she recovers sufficiently to understand the consequences of his or her actions.

*3. Mental Incompetents.* Contracts made by an insane person are voidable and are treated in the same manner as are the contracts made by minors, provided no guardian has been appointed. If a person has been declared legally insane and a guardian has been appointed, all agreements made by the ward are void. As in the case of minors, an insane person may be held liable for the reasonable value of necessaries.

*4. Enemy Aliens.* Trading with enemy aliens in time of war is illegal, and no valid contract can be entered into during such a period. Contracts already in force between domestic citizens and enemy aliens are either suspended or terminated by declaration of war. Court decisions in regard to life insurance contracts under such conditions are not uniform.

***Mutual Assent.*** As in the case of other contracts, an offer and an acceptance must exist before the life insurance contract is created. However, the process by which an insurance contract comes into being is somewhat different from that for other contracts. An applicant for life insurance rarely comes to an insurance company seeking insurance. Instead, the applicant is usually first contacted by an insurance agent, who solicits an application that is submitted to the insurance company.

The life insurance contract can be created either by payment of the first premium with the application or by submitting the application without payment of a premium. The latter situation is merely an invitation to the insurance company to make an offer to insure. The insurer can make the offer by issuing the policy. The applicant can then accept the insurer's offer by paying the premium at the time the policy is delivered.

*1. Premium Receipts.* When the premium is paid with the application, three general categories of premium receipts provide some form of temporary coverage. The **approval conditional premium receipt** provides that insurance will be effective only after the application has been approved by the company. Thus the period of protection—from the date of approval until the date the policy is issued or delivered—is typically minimal. The approval premium receipt is of interest primarily from a historical standpoint, since it has largely been replaced by the insurability premium receipt.

The **insurability conditional premium receipt** provides that the insurer is considered to have made an offer conditional upon the proposed insured's insurability, and the applicant accepts the conditional offer by payment of the premium. The insurance becomes effective as of the date of the conditional receipt or, if later, the time of the physical examination, provided that the proposed insured is found insurable. The delivery of the policy itself is not essential. Under this arrangement, if the proposed insured were to die before the application and other information reached the company's home office and the proposed insured otherwise would have been insurable according to the company's usual standards, the claim would be paid. Insurers have paid many such claims. The purpose of this type of receipt is, of course, to provide protection, assuming that the proposed insured is insurable, between the date of the conditional receipt (or physical examination, if later) and the time of policy delivery.

The **binding premium receipt** provides insurance that is effective from the date the receipt is given. Usually, both the conditional and binding receipts stipulate a maximum amount that would be payable if death occurred during the period of coverage under the receipt. The coverage is provided for a stipulated, fixed time period or until the insurance company renders an underwriting decision on the application—whichever is less.

Infrequently, the premium is paid with the application, but no receipt is issued. In such cases, no contract is in force until the policy is issued and delivered. Here the applicant is considered to have made an offer that he or she may withdraw at any time before acceptance by the company.

*2. Policy Effective Date.* In the absence of complications, the **effective date** of a policy is one that is mutually agreed upon by the company and the applicant. However, complications can arise, the consequences of which can bring the true policy effective date into dispute.

In some cases, a policy may be backdated to "save age." **Backdating** is the practice by which an insurer calculates premiums under the policy based on an earlier age for the proposed insured. Premiums are thereby lower than they otherwise would be. Backdating beyond six months is typically prohibited by state law. Although backdating does not alter the effective date of the protection, it does raise two important questions. First, when is the next premium due? Second, from what date do the incontestable and suicide periods run?[11] A few courts have held that a full year's coverage must be provided for the annual premium. However, the majority of the decisions have held that the **policy date** (i.e., the date appearing on the contract) determines the date on which subsequent premiums are due, even though this means that less than one full year's protection is granted during the first year.[12]

With regard to the suicide and incontestable clauses, the general rule is that the earlier of either the effective date or the policy date establishes the point of measurement. Thus with a backdated policy, the clauses generally run from the policy date. When the policy date is later than the effective date, the clauses are held to run from the effective date. When the clauses themselves specify a certain date, this date is usually recognized.

*Consideration*. In the life insurance contract, the consideration given by the applicant for the promises of the company consists of the statements in the application and the payment of the first premium. Premium payments subsequent to the first are not part of the legal consideration, but are simply conditions precedent that must be performed to keep the contract in existence.

The insurer may agree to accept a check, note, or, in the absence of a prohibitive statute, services in payment of the first premium. Although a check is customarily considered cash, payment by check is usually accepted only as a conditional payment. This means that if a check is not paid when presented, no payment is considered to have been made, and the insurer's promise is no longer binding, regardless of the policyowner's good faith.

If an agent has company authority to deal in promissory premium notes, the note is adequate consideration. Thus unless the note has a provision that the policy will be repudiated if the note is not honored at maturity, the premium is considered paid and constitutes adequate consideration for the contract. In such cases, the note is a separate transaction, and the company's action is limited to its rights under the note if the latter is not honored at maturity.[13]

*Legal Purpose*. To be valid, a contract must be for a legal purpose and not contrary to public policy. For example, in most jurisdictions, gambling transactions are illegal and, therefore, unenforceable at law. Gambling transactions and life insurance contracts are both aleatory, as opposed to commutative, in character.

---

[11] See *Lentin v. Continental Assurance Co.*, 412 Ill. 158, 105 N.E.2d 735, A.L.R.2d 463 (1952).

[12] See Robert E. Keeton, *Insurance Law, Basic Text* (St. Paul, Minn.: West Publishing Co., 1971), p. 331, and John Appleman, *Insurance Law and Practice* (St. Paul, Minn.: West Publishing Co., 1980), §7953.

[13] There are conflicting decisions as to the effect of a forfeiture provision when it is included only in the policy or the note. When the forfeiture provision is contained in both the policy and note, the provisions have uniformly been held valid and enforceable. See ibid., §3281.

In a commutative agreement, an exchange of approximate equal values is intended. For example, in a real estate sale, the seller relinquishes ownership of property whose value is established mutually by the parties. In return, the buyer pays an amount equal to the agreed value. In contrast to the commutative agreement is the aleatory agreement. Each party to such an agreement recognizes that one of them may obtain more than the other, but each also recognizes that the outcome is governed by chance. Gambling and wagering arrangements are aleatory. The distinction between a contract of insurance and a wagering contract is vitally important. One's purpose in entering a wager is the hope, through chance, of gaining at the expense of others. One's purpose in entering an insurance contract is the avoidance of loss and the transforming of uncertainty into certainty.[14] The requirement that there be an insurable interest in insurance takes the agreement out of the gambling category. This subject, so vital to insurance, is discussed in detail in a separate section below.

In addition to the fact that a life insurance contract will fail when there is no insurable interest on the part of the applicant in the insured, a contract may be illegal and against public policy for other reasons. As was mentioned earlier, a contract with an enemy alien is held to be against public policy and void. Also, a contract is illegal and void (and the insurer is relieved from paying the death claim) when it is negotiated with intent to murder.

## INSURABLE INTEREST

A contract of life insurance must, according to law, be based on an insurable interest. While this phrase is not subject to precise definition, a person has an **insurable interest** in another's life if he or she can reasonably expect to benefit from that person's continued life, and, conversely, if he or she would suffer financial loss on the person's death. An insurable interest cannot be supported on mere personal interest or affection, but it does arise in numerous relationships.

In the absence of a valid insurable interest, life insurance policies are unenforceable at law.[15] In the first place, unless they are based on a valid insurable interest, they are wagers and thus void because they are against public policy or contrary to statutes prohibiting gambling. More important, such contracts would be an incentive to crime in that they could encourage the taking of human life. Most states incorporate this interpretation into statutory law and provide that such contracts are "void unless the benefits are payable to the individual insured or his personal representative or to a person having, at the

---

[14] The combination of a large number of risks and the law of large numbers removes, to a great extent, the speculation on the part of insurance companies. They are not gambling either. Also, when all policyowners are viewed as a group, there is an exchange of approximately equal value between the policyowners and the company.

[15] *Warnock v. Davis* 104 U.S. 775, 779 (1881); *Peoples Life Insurance Co. v. Whiteside* 94 F.2d 409 (1938).

time of such contract, an insurable interest in the individual insured."[16] This doctrine evolved out of regard for public welfare rather than for the protection of insurance companies. The presence of an insurable interest removes the insurance policy from the wagering category. Conversely, the absence of an insurable interest renders the policy a mere wager.

An insurer has both a strong financial motivation and a legal duty to ascertain that an insurable interest exists. Although the insurer may be relieved from paying the death proceeds under a policy issued with no insurable interest, it nonetheless incurs substantial expenses in such an arrangement and runs the great risk of encouraging early death. The latter problem gives rise to additional mortality costs to the company, since not all insurable interest deficiencies will be discovered. It is perhaps of greater importance that the insurer becomes exposed in tort for a breach of its duty to use reasonable care to avoid creating an incentive for the beneficiary to murder the insured. Thus in one well-known case, three life insurers issued policies in the amounts of $500, $1,000, and $5,000 on a child's life, with the child's aunt-in-law as applicant and beneficiary. The jury held that the insurer's failure to ascertain whether, in fact, an insurable interest existed supplied the motive for the aunt-in-law's act of murdering the child. The $100,000 wrongful death judgment in favor of the child's father against the insurers was substantially greater than the life policies' face amounts.[17]

In discussing insurable interest in life insurance, three roles usually are involved: (1) applicant, (2) insured, and (3) beneficiary. In many cases, the insured persons are also the applicants/owners, and many even designate themselves (i.e., their estate) as beneficiaries. In this text, the word **applicant** is used to denote the person who makes the application for insurance and who is proposed to be the policyowner. In analyzing the question of what constitutes a valid insurable interest, the question is examined from the standpoint of whether the policy is applied for by the insured on his or her own life or by someone else.

***Insurable Interest in One's Own Life.*** A fundamental principle of law is that every person possesses an insurable interest to an unlimited extent in his or her own life, and that he or she may make the insurance payable to whomever he or she wishes.[18] An alternative, yet functionally equivalent, view is that questions of insurable interest do not arise in such circumstances. With either view, where the applicant is also the person whose life is to be insured, courts have refused to require any specific relationship to exist between the amount of insurance and the value of the life on which it is taken. When the contract is taken without collusion and without intent to violate the laws prohibiting wagers, the natural love of life is held to constitute a sufficient insurable interest and to support a policy for any

---

[16] Georgia Statutes, 1969, §56–2404.

[17] *Liberty National Life Insurance Co. v. Weldon* 267 Ala. 171, 100 So 2d (1957).

[18] 44 Am. Jur. 2e, Insurance, §1729, *Bell v. Phillips et al.*, Tex., 152 F.2d 188 (1946).

amount.[19] Although legally there is no limit to the amount of insurance that may be taken out by an individual on his or her own life, in practice life insurance companies limit the amount issued to a sum that is not unreasonably large relative to the insured's financial status and earning capacity.

*Insurable Interest in Another Person's Life.* Court decisions are not uniform with respect to circumstances where the applicant is not also the proposed insured. The majority rule is that the applicant must have an insurable interest in the proposed insured's life. The minority rule is that the beneficiary must have such an interest or be related to the proposed insured by a stated degree of kinship. States following this rule generally provide that death proceeds are to be payable to the insured's estate if the required relationship does not exist on the insured's death. Even in cases where the interest exists, a policy obtained without the knowledge and consent of the insured is contrary to public policy and void.[20] Insurable interest may arise out of one or more of the following three classes of relationships.

*1. Insurable Interest in Family and Marriage Relationships.* U.S. courts have generally held that certain close relationships create an insurable interest, even though the element of financial dependence is not necessarily present. Thus the relationship of husband and wife is presumed to establish an insurable interest on behalf of either party in the other's life. Most courts have added the relationship of parent and child, grandparent and grandchild, and siblings, but have generally refused to extend it further. As regards other relationships, the courts have taken the position that the interest should be based upon a reasonable expectation of deriving pecuniary benefit from the continuance of the insured's life.

*2. Insurable Interest in Creditor–Debtor Relationships.* The rule is well settled that a creditor has an insurable interest in the life of his or her debtor, although the important question of an acceptable amount of insurance, as compared with the amount of debt, is not well settled. Where a creditor has paid the premiums for a policy insuring the debtor's life, the creditor's insurable interest, arguably, should not be limited solely to the face of the indebtedness. The creditor should be reimbursed for an amount equal to the debt, the premiums paid, and interest on both. The courts are not uniform concerning the validity of a policy in which the amount of insurance greatly exceeds the debt.

The rule adopted by the U.S. Supreme Court places an indefinite restriction upon the creditor's insurable interest by providing that the relationship between

[19] This rule does not apply, therefore, when the proposed insured is the applicant in name only and, in reality, the parties have agreed that the beneficiary is to be the policyowner. In *Dresen v. Metropolitan Life Ins. Co.*, 195 Ill. App. 292 (1915), the proposed insured applied for and had issued a policy on her life, with her paramour named as beneficiary. After she paid the first three premiums, her paramour paid all those remaining. The policy was declared void for lack of insurable interest.

[20] Am. Jur. 2d, Insurance, §1741. Some states (e.g., Louisiana) permit either spouse to take insurance on the life of the other without the consent of the insured. But see consequences where the husband took out over $1 million of term insurance on his wife in *State v. Thompson* (Minn.), 139 N.W. 2d 490 (1966).

the amount of insurance and the amount of the debt must not be so disproportionate as to make the policy take on the appearance of a wagering contract as distinguished from its legitimate purpose—security for the indebtedness. In *Cammak v. Lewis*, for example, the court declared a policy of $3,000 taken out by a creditor to secure a debt of $70 to be "a sheer wagering policy, without any claim to be considered as one meant to secure a debt."[21] The U.S. Supreme Court has made the relationship between the debt amount and the insurance amount an important factor to be considered, but it has never defined this relationship precisely. Various theories were used by courts to make the insurance proceeds in excess of the debt payable to the estate of the debtor or other beneficiary designated by the debtor. Where the law was not explicit and the terms of the transaction not clear, the most popular theory for making such payments is that the creditor is the trustee for the benefit of the debtor's estate.[22]

**Credit life insurance**, a special class of insurance for use in credit transactions, has become commonplace. In the majority of jurisdictions, these policies must be in the form of decreasing term (expiring when the loan is fully paid). If the loan is paid earlier, most of the statutes require a refund of unearned premium.

There is a basic conceptual difference between ordinary insurance and credit life insurance. In credit life insurance, the debtor pays the premiums directly or indirectly and purchases the policy as part of the credit transaction. Normally, the policy has no property value unless the insured dies. Although ostensibly for the benefit of the creditor, the policy is a form of special collateral and provides protection to the debtor/insured's estate. In the event of debt prepayment, any unearned premiums should be the property of the debtor.

All states have adopted some variation of the NAIC's **Model Bill to Provide for the Regulation of Credit Life Insurance** or the **Uniform Commercial Credit Code** (UCCC) provisions relating to credit insurance, which are patterned on the NAIC Model Bill. These laws require certain disclosures to be made to a debtor in connection with credit life insurance and that there be a refund of unearned premiums. The courts are empowered and instructed to refuse to enforce contracts that are unconscionable.[23] The enforcement of these laws is generally left to state insurance departments.

Under current credit practices, premiums included in charges for loans must be disclosed to the debtor. The UCCC provides that credit life insurance cannot exceed the loan amount and also requires uniformity in premiums.[24] In most states, the amount of insurance in excess of the unpaid indebtedness is payable to a beneficiary other than the creditor, named by the debtor, or to the debtor's estate.[25]

[21] 15 Wall. 244, 82 U.S. 647.
[22] See Appleman, *Insurance Law and Practice*, §§20 and 1311–1352, for current literature in this area.
[23] *UCCC*, §2–302; §4–202.
[24] *UCCC*, §4–202.
[25] Georgia Statues, 1969, §56–3306(2).

*3. Insurable Interest in Other Business Relationships.* Numerous business relationships, other than that of creditor and debtor, can justify the purchase of insurance by one person on the life of another. In each instance, however, the insurable interest must be based on a substantial pecuniary interest existing between the parties. Thus an employer may insure the life of an employee and the employee the life of an employer; a partner the life of a copartner and the partnership the life of each partner; and a corporation the life of an officer. Similarly, a surety on a bond, although no default on the bond has occurred, has an insurable interest in the life of the principal. A corporation holding a property interest contingent upon another person reaching a certain age may protect itself against the loss of the contingent right through the death of that person before he or she has attained the prescribed age. The courts have even held that those who furnish funds for corporate enterprises have an insurable interest in the lives of the managers and promoters of the corporations. Certain stockholders have purchased life insurance on the lives of prominent financiers who were instrumental in financing and promoting the corporations whose stock they held. In all cases, however, the person being insured must give his or her consent to the transaction.

*The Time and Continuity of Insurable Interest.* In property insurance, the general rule is that insurable interest must exist at some time during the period of coverage and at the time of the loss. In other words, an insurable interest is not necessary at the time the property insurance contract is made. In life insurance, by contrast, insurable interest must exist at the inception of the contract. The contract will not thereafter be voided if the interest ceases, unless the provisions of the policy are such as to bring about that result. The fact that insurable interest need exist only at the inception of the contract is a corollary to the view that life insurance policies are not contracts of indemnity. This view is also reflected in the fact that when an insured is executed for a crime, the proceeds are payable to the appropriate beneficiary. Similarly, when a beneficiary murders the insured, the proceeds still must be paid, but, of course, to an innocent beneficiary.[26]

## GOVERNING LAW

Generally speaking, contract validity will be governed by the law and usages of the place where the contract is made. This is held to be where the last and essential acts necessary to formation of a contract took place. Several jurisdictions' laws, including those of another country, may appear to apply, but in a conflicting manner (conflict of laws), and the general rule becomes subject to special interpretation. Thus in a case where an insured was a citizen of Missouri and made application for insurance in Oklahoma to a Tennessee insurer, the state of domicile was held to have had a more significant relationship

---

[26] This assumes that the beneficiary did not procure the policy with the intent of murdering the insured, which would make the contract **void ab initio**.

to the parties, and, therefore, Missouri law applied.[27] Similarly, assignments and other matters relating to contract performance are governed by the law of the place of performance, regardless of the place where the original contract was made.

## THE APPLICATION AND ITS INTERPRETATION

An application for life insurance may be defined as the applicant's proposal to the insurer for protection and may be considered as the beginning of the policy contract. In this document, the proposed insured is required to give true answers to questions relating principally to his or her personal and family history, habits, total insurance already in force, and other applications for insurance that either are pending or have been postponed or refused. The policy usually stipulates that insurance is granted in consideration of the application, which is declared to be a part of it, and generally contains a clause to the effect that the policy and the application (a copy of which is attached to the policy when it is issued) "constitute the entire contract between the parties." Most state laws require the annexation of applications to policies, on penalty of the company's being **estopped** (i.e., prevented) from denying the correctness or truth of information in the application.

In deciding whether to assume a given risk, the insurer relies in part on information furnished by the proposed insured. Consequently, the company is entitled to have all information that may have an influence on its decision whether to assume a given risk, especially given the aleatory nature of the life insurance contract. As a result, the applicant should act in good faith, and if the information given is false or incomplete, the insurer may be in a position to rescind or cancel the contract, although the incontestable clause may bar any such action (see below). Thus either the failure of the proposed insured to disclose fully all pertinent information (doctrine of concealment) or the falsity of positive statements made by the proposed insured may be grounds for rescinding the contract (doctrines of warranties and representations).

*Concealment.* Courts have repeatedly stated that insurance policies are contracts involving the utmost good faith. In early cases, it was held that they were based upon chance and that the withholding of any essential facts by either party rendered the risk actually insured different from that intended. The validity of the policy therefore depended upon the full disclosure of all material information. The **test of the materiality** of a fact concealed (or misrepresented as discussed below) is whether its knowledge by the company would have caused it

---

[27] V.A.M.S. 375, 420, 376, 620; 36 O.S. 1971, §4024; *Moss v. National Life & Acc. Ins. Co.* (D.C. Mo. 1974), 385 F. Supp. (1921); *Mutual of Omaha Ins. Co. v. Russell*( C.A. Kan.) 402 F. 2d 339, 29 A.L.R. 3d 753, certiorari denied 80 S.Ct. 1465, 394 U.S. 973, 22 L.Ed.2d 753 (1968) (flight policy issued to a Kansas citizen in Missouri and court applied Kansas law).

to have issued the insurance on less favorable terms or conditions or at a higher premium. Whether a fact is material and should have been revealed is generally a question for a jury.

The doctrine of concealment, which was developed in connection with marine insurance, was primarily for the protection of the underwriter and at one time was applied to all branches of insurance, but as the business developed, the courts concluded that some relaxation of the rule should be made. With respect to life insurance, the question was thoroughly reviewed in the case of *Penn Mutual Life Insurance v. Mechanics' Savings Bank and Trust Company.*[28] In this case the court held that "no failure to disclose a fact material to the risk, not inquired about, will void the policy, unless such nondisclosure was with intent to conceal from the insurer a fact believed to be material; that is, unless the nondisclosure was fraudulent."[29]

*Warranties.* Closely associated with the common-law doctrine of concealment and representations is the doctrine that a **warranty** must be absolutely and literally true. A forfeiture will result if the falsehood of merely the statement can be shown, irrespective of its materiality. A company need prove only that a warranted statement is incorrect. The courts assume that the materiality of the thing warranted has been established and that all inquiry on the subject is precluded.

Because of the hardship and injustice that the technical enforcement of the common-law rule pertaining to warranties sometimes caused, and also because certain insurance companies took undue advantage of warranties in their policies, the states passed statutes protecting insureds against technical avoidance of life insurance contracts because of breech of warranties. These statutes differ widely, but, in effect, they provide that all statements purporting to be made by the insured shall be deemed representations and not warranties.

*Representations.* In general, a **representation** is a statement made to an insurer for the purpose of giving information or inducing it to accept a risk. A **misrepresentation** occurs when the information given is incorrect.

As a general rule, representations are construed liberally in favor of the insured and need be only substantially correct. The tendency of court decisions has been in the direction of protecting the insured by giving him or her the benefit of the doubt wherever possible. The rule formerly was that a material false representation rendered a policy voidable at the option of the company, even though there was no fraudulent intent on the part of the insured. This rule has been modified in certain states either by court decision or by statute.[30] Thus one court has stated that "a forfeiture does not follow where there has been no

[28] 72 Fed. 413 (C.C.A.), 1986; *Blair v. National Security Insurance Co.,* 126 F.2d 955 (1942).

[29] Ibid., 434, 441; *Haubner v. Aetna Life Ins. Co.,* 256 A.2d 414 (D.C. App. 1969)(insured has affirmative duty to disclose material information).

[30] In France and Japan, insurers can rescind contracts only if they can prove fraudulent intent.

deliberate intent to deceive, and the known falsity of the answer is not affirmatively shown."[31] Intent is a state of mind, and, in effect, some courts require that the insurer show not only that the representations in the application were false, but also that they were fraudulently made.[32] However, in those jurisdictions that provide that the misrepresentations only have to be material, a rescission is permitted without regard to intent or even knowledge.[33] Some state statutes provide that the policy will not be invalidated unless the misrepresentation is made with intent to deceive; others, that the misrepresentation must have contributed to the loss. The general purpose of such laws is to prevent a forfeiture of the policy unless the company has been deceived to its detriment.

The application of the law regarding representations varies widely. Thus in many jurisdictions today, to void a policy the insurer must show that (1) the misrepresentation is material; (2) it was false; (3) the insured knew that it was false when he or she made it or made it recklessly without any knowledge of the truth; (4) the insured made the representation with the intention that the insurer would act upon it; and (5) the insurer did act upon it.[34]

## PRESUMPTION OF DEATH—DISAPPEARANCE

A well-settled rule in U.S. law is that when a person leaves his or her usual place of residence and is neither heard of nor known to be living for a term of seven years, the presumption of life ceases and that of death arises. Therefore if an insured disappears for a period of seven years and the absence is unexplained, he or she is presumed to be dead, and the insurance company is required to pay the policy death proceeds. The only presumption, however, is that of the fact of death; there is none as to the time of death. However, if evidence is presented that the absent person, within the seven years, encountered some specific peril, or within that period came within the range of some impending or immediate danger that might reasonably be expected to destroy life, the court or jury may infer that life ceased before the expiration of the seven years. In such cases, the insurer must pay the face of the policy plus interest thereon from the date of *proof* of death.

The insured is presumed to be alive until the end of the seven-year period. Therefore the policy must be maintained in force or the beneficiary is not entitled to the proceeds, unless it can be proven that death occurred before the policy terminated or unless a death benefit has remained in force under one of the policy's nonforfeiture options. The time of death may become important in case a primary beneficiary dies during the seven-year period and there is a contingent

[31] *Kuhns v. N.Y. Life Ins Co., Appellant,* 297 Pa. 418, 423, 147 A.76 (1929); *Travellers Ins. Co. v. Heppenstall Co.,* 61 A. 2d 809, 812 (Pa. 1948).

[32] *Russ v. Metropolitan Life Ins. Co.,* 270 A.2d 759, 112 N.J. Super. 265 (1970); *Kizirian v. United Benefit Life Ins. Co.,* 1191, A.2d 47 (1956); *Evans v. Penn Mutual Life Ins. Co. of Philadelphia,* 322 Pa. 547, 186 A. 133 (1946).

[33] West's F.S.A., §617.409; *Garwood v. Equitable Life Ass. Soc.,* Fla, 299 So.2d 163 (1974).

[34] *West v. Farm Bureau Mut. Ins. Co. of Michigan,* 234 N.W.2d 485, 63 Mich App. 279 (1975).

beneficiary. In the absence of an agreement between the parties, a court may have to decide on the distribution of policy proceeds.

Although rare, situations arise wherein the insurer has paid the death proceeds to the beneficiary on the presumption that the insured died, and the insured reappears. What rights, if any, does the insurer have to recover proceeds in such instances?

The general rule is that if the insurer paid the full death proceeds in good faith, the insurer has the right to recover the amount paid on the basis that it was paid under a mistake of fact. If, however, payment by the insurer was less than the full policy amount, as in a compromise settlement, it cannot be recovered.

## INSURING AGREEMENT

In the insuring agreement, the company agrees to pay the policy face amount immediately to the beneficiary upon receipt of written proof of the insured's death, subject to the provisions of the policy. An illustrative clause contains the insurer's promise:

> If the insured dies while this policy is in force, we will pay the sum insured to the beneficiary, when we receive at our home office due proof of the insured's death, subject to the provisions of this policy.

The owner's consideration for this promise is, of course, the application and payment of the initial premium. The promise will continue in effect in accordance with the policy provisions as long as the required condition—payment of renewal premiums—is met.

## DUTY OF GOOD FAITH AND FAIR DEALING

Courts have held that insurance contracts carry an implied covenant of **good faith and fair dealing** that requires each party to the contract to avoid impairing the rights of the other. While the doctrine has not developed consistently across the states, perhaps it is most commonly applied when an insured has not been dealt with fairly by his or her insurer.

Thus in one well-known case involving a time limitation on the right to sue under a disability contract, the court concluded:

> In situations where a layman might give the controlling language of the policy a more restrictive interpretation than the insurer knows the courts have given it and as a result the uninformed insured might be inclined to be quiescent about the disregard or nonpayment of his claim and not to press it in a timely fashion, the company cannot ignore its obligation. It cannot hide behind the insured's ignorance of the law; it cannot conceal its liability. In these circumstances it has the duty to speak and disclose, and to act in accordance with its contractual undertaking.[35]

---

[35] *Bowler v. Fidelity and Casualty Company of New York*, 53 N.J. 313, 250 A.2d 580 (1969).

## THE LAW AS IT PERTAINS TO THE AGENT

Since life insurance is written almost exclusively by corporations, in most instances transacting business in many states, the agent is a factor that is necessary to the business's success. If the agent is to perform properly the duties connected with the solicitation of business, he or she must be given certain authority.

## OVERVIEW

Agency is a relationship between two parties against all others. The entity that creates the agency relationship is the **principal**. An **agent** is the principal's representative. Agency law classifies agents in accordance with the type of authority granted by the principal:

1) Actual or express

2) Implied

3) Apparent or perceived

**Actual** or **express authority** is that granted to an agent by the principal in specific language or terms. It may involve wide or general authority, or it may be limited to a narrow field or even to a specific act. **Implied authority** is that associated with certain duties, such as the cashier's authority to take payment for merchandise at a checkout counter. **Apparent** or **perceived authority** is that which a third person believes the agent possesses because of circumstances made possible by the principal and upon which the third party is justified in relying. Apparent authority is based on the principle of estoppel. That is, if the principal clothes another with certain vestiges of authority, such as receipt books, application forms, specimen policies, sales literature, and similar items that lead a third party to reasonably believe that an agency relationship exists, the principal will not be allowed to declare later that no agency existed.

State laws require that insurance agents possess certain minimum levels of knowledge about life insurance and, in some cases, a certain amount of training before a license will be granted. Agents are further required by state regulations to observe certain rules of conduct. The insurance company, in turn, may provide additional rules. However, unless such rules are known to the applicant, they may not be binding upon him or her. Insurers are well aware of the powers granted to their agents and of the potential for abuse. Accordingly, they take measures to place third parties on notice of the limitations of the powers granted their agents. These limitations may appear in special notices or lettering in receipt books, applications, or other documents given to the applicant and which the applicant should read.

## POWERS OF THE AGENT

Two classes of agents exist in law: (1) **general agents** and (2) **special agents**. A general agent's powers are coextensive with those of his or her principal within the limit of the particular business or territory in which the agent operates. A special agent's powers usually are far more limited, extending only to acts necessary to accomplish a particular transaction he or she is engaged to perform. However, the terms *general agent* and *special agent* have other meanings in the insurance industry and vary depending on whether they apply to non-life insurance (fire, marine, and casualty insurance) or life insurance. In the former, a general agent has wide authority to enter into insurance contracts, whereas in the life insurance field, a general agent almost always has limited authority. Thus the person who may be designated as a general agent for life insurance solicitation purposes is really a special agent in the eyes of the law. This designation can be even more confusing because the term special agent is also used to identify a person who acts as a soliciting agent and who works for a general agent. Such a special agent has even less authority than his or her general agent but, as with the general agent, he or she is considered to be a special agent in the eyes of the law.

Agents acting within the actual or apparent scope of their authority make their principal (the insurance company) liable for their wrongful or fraudulent acts, omissions, and misrepresentations. Provided that the policy or application contains no restrictions on the agent's authority, the acts and knowledge of the agent in relation to anything pertaining to the application or policy generally are held by the courts to be the acts and knowledge of the company. This estops it from taking advantage of any forfeiture occasioned by the agent's errors or fraudulent acts.

Much litigation has arisen from what may be termed agents' over-enthusiasm. It takes time to complete an application, take premium payments, and give receipts. Meanwhile, the agent usually engages in general conversation with remarks such as "You have a good deal," "You're covered," and other comments. The remarks may be unrelated to any questions posed by the applicant. If problems develop later, it becomes extremely difficult to determine what was said, as well as what conversation was related to the subject. To guard against this, most insurers try to call attention to the limitations of the agent's authority by the use of larger type size or color in receipts or other documents or literature provided to the applicant. If the applicants fail to read such warnings, they may have difficulty claiming that they were misled.

Although there is no unanimous decision on the subject, the weight of authority has rested on the idea that, in the absence of restrictions, the company is liable not only for the acts of its agents, but also for the acts and knowledge of subagents and employees to whom the agent has delegated authority. In insurance, it is a common practice and one frequently found necessary for agents to employ others to assist them in their work. Since authority has been delegated to them, the courts have regarded it as "just and reasonable that insurance companies should be held responsible not only for acts of their agents, but also for the acts of the subagents employed within the scope of their agents' authority." Although it may be argued that the company has not authorized its agents to delegate their authority to others and that it would therefore be an unreasonable extension of the company's liability, it must be remembered that agents are employed by the companies in accordance with the usages and necessities of the business.

## POLICY LIMITATIONS

As a general practice, life insurance companies insert a provision in their policies or application forms prohibiting their agents from altering the contract in any way. Although the wording of such clauses is not uniform, the following may be regarded as representative of the usual provision:

> A change in this policy is valid only if it is approved by an officer of the Company. The Company may require that the policy be sent to it for endorsement to show a change. No agent has the authority to change the policy or to waive any of its terms.

Despite the apparent reasonableness of these policy provisions, court decisions dealing with the matter are by no means in harmony, and, as a result, various rules have been formulated.[36] One such rule provides that policy limitations upon any agent's authority operate as notice to the proposed insured of the limited extent of the agent's powers and thus protect the company.[37] In another group of cases, the courts have adopted an attitude that is more favorable to the policyowner/insured by holding that such policy restrictions upon an agent's authority are not conclusive as to those matters involved before the contract is completed, but relate only "to the exercise of the agent's authority in matters concerning the policy after its delivery and acceptance, the theory in the main being that no presumption can reasonably attach that the insured was cognizant of such provisions or could anticipate that they would be incorporated into the policy."[38] Still another rule holds, in effect, that restrictions in the policy relate only to acts before a loss has occurred.[39]

Perhaps the rule having the most support at present is one prohibiting the company from rescinding the insurance in case of policy violation (1) wherein the company or any agent clothed with actual or apparent authority has waived,

[36] George James Couch, *Couch Cyclopedia of Insurance Law,* 2nd ed. (Rochester, N.Y.: Lawyers Co-operative Publishing Co., 1959–1968), §26:82.

[37] Ibid., §26:83.

[38] Ibid., §26:86.

[39] Ibid., §26:88.

either orally or in writing, any provision of the policy, or (2) wherein the company, because of some knowledge or acts on its part or on the part of its agent, is estopped from setting up as a defense the violation of the terms of the contract.[40] Courts generally are reluctant to allow parol (oral) evidence to alter the interpretation of a written document. However, whether the courts rely on an oral waiver of policy provisions or upon the doctrine of estoppel, the company is held bound.[41] This holds even though some provision of the contract has been violated and the policy contains a provision limiting the agent's power to make policy changes.

## DOCTRINE OF REASONABLE EXPECTATIONS

When one makes a payment, the normal expectation is that one has purchased something for value given. To suggest that this is not true strikes a discordant note. Courts have used strong language to condemn restrictive language in policies, receipts, and other literature given to the applicant as well as aggressive sales promotions to acquire new customers. One court pointed out that in such a situation the confusion that existed was the creation of the insurer and that the **reasonable expectations** of the policyowner would not be frustrated.[42] In another case, one dealing with conditional receipts, Judge Learned Hand, said: "An underwriter might so understand the phrase, when read in its context, but the application was not to be submitted to underwriters: it was to go to persons utterly unacquainted with the niceties of life insurance, who would read it colloquially. It is the understanding of such persons which counts. . . . To demand that persons wholly unfamiliar with insurance shall spell all this out in the very teeth of the language used is unpardonable."[43] Still other courts, while not specifically overruling the prohibitions against oral contracts as stated by the Supreme Court, utilize the doctrines of waiver, estoppel, or election to prevent forfeiture of coverage.[44]

In the course of their daily business, agents are frequently asked to express opinions on the meaning of policy provisions. It is of the utmost importance that a clear understanding exist between the company and its agents as regards the expression of such opinions. What *is* the legal effect of the agent's opinion? Early U.S. law was extremely legalistic. A person was required to read and know what he or she had signed. Thus the *mere opinion* of an *agent* could not change

[40]Ibid., §26:90.

[41] For a discussion of this point, see W. R. Vance and B. M. Anderson, *Handbook of the Law of Insurance*, 3rd ed. (St. Paul, Minn: West Publishing Co., 1951), chaps. 8 and 9; and Keeton, *Insurance Law, Basic Text*, pp. 341–347.

[42] *Allen v. Metropolitan Life Ins. Co.*, 208 A. 2d 638, 44 N.J. 294 (1965).

[43] *Garnet v. John Hancock Mutual Life Insurance Co.*, Conn.,, 160 F 2nd 599 at 601 (1947), quoted by dissent in *Morgan v. State Farm Life Insurance Co.*, 400 P 2nd 223, 240, One. 113 (1965).

[44] *McGowan v. Prudential Ins. Co. of America*, D.C. Pa., 253 F. Supp. 415, reversed 372 F. 2d 39 (1966); *Fesmire v. MFA Mut. Ins. Co.*, D.C. Tenn., 293 F. Supp. 1214 (1968).

the clear meaning of a written contract. To suggest such action was to strike at the very heart of contract law, particularly when the actual authority of the agent was limited. This response ignored the realities of insurance practices.

The insurance industry has worked hard over the past 50 years to improve the image of the insurance agent. Advertisements proclaim the expertise and professionalism of the insurance agent. Prospective applicants are told of the reliability and dependability of the insurer, if only they will submit to the tender ministration of the insurance agent. State insurance departments insist on minimum educational qualifications, and insurers spend enormous sums of money in agent training to support professionalism. Therefore it should not come as a surprise that the courts have taken the insurers at their advertised word.

In the field of automobile sales, courts have decided that automobile manufacturers should not be permitted to advertise the virtues of their product and at the same time insist on standing on the terms of the sales contract disclaiming warranties. For the same reason, neither should an insurer be allowed to advertise the expertise of its agency force and then deny these very qualities after the product has been purchased. The concern is that to ignore the disparity of the bargaining positions between the average insurance purchaser and the relatively well educated insurance agent is to invite overreaching on the part of insurers. Accordingly, when an insurance agent renders an opinion that is contrary to the written contract and the proposed policyowner relies on such an opinion, the insurer may be bound.[45] The courts will, in effect, apply the principles of estoppel, at least implicitly if not explicitly.

## AGENT'S LIABILITY TO PRINCIPAL FOR MISCONDUCT

The relation of the agent to his or her principal is such that the agent should never further his or her own personal interests by disobeying or exceeding the principal's instructions. Any misconduct of the agent makes him or her personally liable to the principal for resultant damage. This responsibility is based on the law of agency. Any loss or damage to the principal must be indemnified by the agent. Examples of agents' misconduct are exceeding specific authority, binding unacceptable risks, failure to transmit information concerning risks, collusion with the applicant, incorrect statements concerning the proposed insured, failure to transmit funds collected on behalf of the principal, and failure to follow explicit instructions issued by the principal. In practice, however, most cases involving serious violation of agency agreements are resolved by the agents' discharge and a revocation of license.

---

[45] *Farly v. United Pac. Ins. Co.*, 525 P. 2d 1003, 269 Ore. 549 (1974); *Harr v. Allstate Ins. Co.*, 255 A. 2d 208, 54 N.J. 287 (1969); Keeton, *Insurance, Basic Text*, Chap. 6; Appleman, *Insurance Law and Practice*, §7307.

## INSURER'S LIABILITY FOR DELAY, IMPROPER REJECTION, OR FAILURE TO ACT

Many courts have held that when an insurer retains an applicant's premium but has not issued the insurance policy, elementary justice dictates that a contract of insurance is in existence or else the company is liable for damages caused because of its delay or failure to insure. The insurer's liability may derive from the contract because of a receipt or otherwise, or it may be in tort for damages generally. In most cases, these damages will be the face amount of the proposed policy.

The tort (negligence) action is the majority view, but other conduct by the insurer may justify coverage. For example, the failure to return the premium promptly with the rejection has been held to be unconscionable and thus provides interim coverage.[46] In other cases, the courts have not been concerned with the relationship between the insurance company and its agents. Instead, they have viewed the company and its agent from the standpoint of the applicant. This has given rise to the concept of reasonable expectations discussed earlier. The conduct of some insurers has been judged to be in bad faith and coverage reinstated.[47] The amount of delay that may be involved varies with the circumstances. Often, either the agent or the company, or both, may be aware of circumstances that require an acceptance or rejection within a definite time limit. One example of this involved a case wherein an individual made an application for insurance with the intention of replacing existing insurance. It was clear to the court that the insurer should have recognized the need for a decision before the existing policy lapsed. This was particularly true in the court's view in cases in which the individual insured was no longer insurable.[48]

## PROVISIONS PROTECTING THE POLICYOWNER

A life insurance policy is a piece of property.[49] The owner of the policy may be the individual on whose life the policy is written, it may be the beneficiary, or it may be someone else. In most cases, the insured is the owner of the policy. The

[46] *Smith v. Westland Life Ins. Co.*, 115 Cal. Rptr. 750 (1974).

[47] *Life Ins. Co. of Southwest v. Nims*, 512 S.W. 2d 712, Tex. Civ. App. (1974).

[48] *Prince v. Western Empire Life Ins. Co.*, 428 P. 2d 163, 19 Utah 174 (1967) (application to replace $80,000 of existing insurance that the insured applicant allowed to lapse; insured killed in the meantime).

[49] Legally, the term **property** refers not to the object itself, but to the ownership rights associated with the property—i.e., rights of possession, control, and disposition. If the ownership rights are associated with land and objects permanently attached to land, such as buildings, the property is referred to as **real property**. If the ownership rights concern movable property, such as automobiles, furniture, stocks, and insurance policies, the property is classified as **personal property.**

There are two types of personal property: (1) choses in possession and (2) choses in action. **Choses in possession** are tangible objects (e.g., jewels). **Choses in action**, by contrast, refer to ownership rights evidenced by something tangible, but something that does not have value in itself. Thus an insurance policy is a chose in action since the contract itself has no value; it evidences an intangible of value. To recover value from a chose in action, legal action may be necessary.

person designated as the owner has vested privileges of ownership, including the right to assign the policy as collateral, receive cash values and dividends, borrow against the policy, designate a new owner, and change the beneficiary (unless this action is subject to restrictions, as discussed below). At the death of the insured, the beneficiary becomes the owner of the proceeds and other rights under the policy. A number of policy provisions are intended to protect the owner of the policy.

## ENTIRE CONTRACT CLAUSE

The **entire contract clause** provides that the policy itself and the application, if a copy is attached to the policy, legally constitute the entire contract between the parties. The clause protects the policyowner in that the company cannot, merely by reference, include within the policy its procedural rules or, unless a copy is attached, the application or the statements made to the medical examiner. This clause also protects the company in that the application, if made part of the contract (which it ordinarily is), becomes part of the consideration for the contract, and material misrepresentations made by the applicant can be used by the company in denying liability (but see following section on the incontestable clause) or seeking reformation or rescission of the contract.[50]

## INCONTESTABLE CLAUSE

The **incontestable clause** was introduced by life insurance companies on a voluntary basis to provide greater assurance to the public that relatively innocent misstatements by applicants would not be the cause of a claim being denied. Its roots date back to mid–nineteenth century England when insurers sought to allay public concern through the inclusion of an **indisputable clause**; this clause was intended to address the then ultratechnical application of the doctrine of warranties by many insurers.[51] Since many English insurers sold life insurance in the United States, this innovation and the resulting competition by the British soon forced U.S. life insurers to adopt the same practice. The Manhattan Life, using a five-year time limit, is said to be the first U.S. insurer to have incorporated the clause in its contracts.[52]

---

[50]A **reformation** is an equitable remedy wherein a contract is reformed—redrafted—to conform to the original intention of the parties. This remedy is often used when a mistake has been made by one or both of the parties in drafting a contract (e.g., misspelled name).

A **rescission**, which is also an equitable remedy, typically involves more serious contentiousness and a cancellation or avoidance of a contract. This remedy is frequently used when fraud or other material misrepresentation is involved.

[51] See Luis M. Villaronga, *The Incontestable Clause: An Historical Analysis*, S. S. Huebner Foundation Monograph Series No. 5 (University of Pennsylvania, 1976).

[52] Ibid., p. 7.

The clause's use spread widely, because it was perceived as a means of addressing the public's concern about the quality and trustworthiness of U.S. life insurers following a severe post-Civil War depression that resulted in numerous insolvencies. The depressed economic conditions of the 1870s saw insurers seeking new ways of gaining a competitive advantage through contract liberalization. The 1879 adoption of the clause by the Equitable Life Assurance Society gave the clause its greatest impetus.[53]

A typical policy provision reads as follows:

> Except for accidental death and disability premium payment benefits, we cannot contest this policy after it has been in force for two years while the insured is alive.

The clause, which can have a maximum limit of two years, has been given a broad interpretation in the United States.[54] It prevents a life insurance company from voiding a life insurance contract after the passage of the specified time even on grounds of material misrepresentation or fraud in the application for the contract. The rationale for this broad interpretation is the protection of beneficiaries. From the standpoint of the owner and the beneficiary, the incontestable clause removes the fear of lawsuits, especially at a time—namely, after the death of the insured—when it may be difficult for the beneficiary successfully to combat with competent testimony a company's charge of misrepresentation. The lawsuit could be particularly difficult to contest in view of the fact that the insured individual who made the representations that form the basis of the contract is no longer alive to present his or her side of the case.

From the standpoint of public policy, it is undesirable to have dependents subject to a forfeiture for violations that might remain unknown for many years and, at the death of the insured, leave the dependents without protection (which was the basic purpose of the life insurance contract). Moreover, if a policy is contested, the issue is typically resolved in the courts. This involves delay in claim settlement at the very time when the need for speedy payment is greatest. The law grants insurers only the first two policy years in which to initiate this process. Thereafter they are barred from contesting the validity of the contract, unless the insured dies before the two years have expired; then there is generally no time limit on such a challenge.

The incontestable clause is similar to a short statute of limitations. By inserting the policy provision, the company undertakes to make all necessary investigations concerning the good faith and all other circumstances surrounding the application within the time limit stipulated in the clause. It limits the period of time the insurer can use the defense of fraud, concealment, or material misrepresentation to defeat the contract. The company agrees not to resist claim

---

[53] Ibid., p. 8.

[54] Other countries also use an incontestable clause, although the time limit differs. For example, in Germany the time limit is ten years and in Spain it is one year. Japan's limit is two years.

payment if premiums have been paid, if no violation of the contract has come to light during the stipulated time limit following the issuance of the policy, and if, during the time, the company has taken no action to rescind the contract.[55]

## GRACE PERIOD

The usual **grace period** provision permits premiums to be paid for up to 31 days after the due date, and it is important to note, during this period, the policy remains in effect. Some companies now include 60- or 61-day grace periods. If the insured dies during the grace period, the company is permitted to deduct the overdue premium plus interest from the settlement with the beneficiary. The provision's purpose is to protect the policyowner against unintentional lapse. If it were not for this provision and the payment were even one day late, insurers could require evidence of insurability to reinstate the policy.

Although companies are permitted under the law to charge interest, they rarely do so because of the small amounts involved and the expense of collection. Since the company collects a premium only in the event of death within the grace period, most of those who lapse pay no share of the cost of insurance for that period; in essence they receive a month's free protection.

## NONFORFEITURE PROVISION

In the early days, life insurance policies had no cash values. If a policy lapsed, the policyowner "forfeited" any "excess" contributions. Laws now prohibit such forfeitures.

Under **Standard Nonforfeiture Laws**, policies must contain a statement about the mortality table and rate of interest used in calculating the nonforfeiture values provided by the policy, as well as a description of the method used in calculating the values. In addition, a table is required showing the cash surrender and other nonforfeiture options for each of the first 20 years. (These options are discussed in the next chapter.) Nonforfeiture values must be equal to or greater than those required by the law.

Much misunderstanding surrounds cash-value calculations for traditional policies and the stated interest rate. The rate is sometimes mistakenly thought to be a policy's rate of return. This misunderstanding does not apply to the same extent with policies such as universal life (UL) and current assumption whole life (CAWL), wherein cash values are derived by using the so-called retrospective approach (see Chapter 20 for details). Traditional policies use the prospective approach.

---

[55] There have been a few cases in which the fraud associated with the issuance of the policies has been so outrageous that policies were allowed to be voided from their inception, even though the period of contestability had expired. See Joseph M Belth, ed., *The Insurance Forum*, Vol. XII, No. 9 (Sept. 1985), p. 84.

The prospective method utilizes a discount approach and derives a present value figure as the cash value. Thus the *higher* the interest rate stated in a prospective-based cash-value (i.e., traditional) policy, the *lower* will be the cash value, other things being the same. Conversely, the *lower* the interest rate used, the *higher* will be the policy's cash values, other things remaining equal. Hence if two traditional whole life policies were identical in every way except that one carried a cash-value interest rate of 3 percent and the other a rate of 5 percent, the policy with the 3 percent rate would have the higher cash values. As a practical matter, of course, things are rarely "identical." Usually—but not always—a policy with a higher cash value has a higher premium, lower dividends, or both. Even if the "identical" assumption is relaxed, one cannot judge the effective rate of return on cash-value policies by reference to this nonforfeiture policy interest provision.

Some persons who do not understand life insurance fundamentals often seize on this low-stated cash-value interest rate and assert that this is the policy's rate of return. This is incorrect. It is merely a conservative discount rate used to derive cash values on a prospective basis.

In contrast to the situation that exists with traditional policies, UL and CAWL policies' stated interest rates—either guaranteed or current rates—are not used to derive cash values on a discount basis. They are simply applied to add amounts to an already (usually) existing cash value—that is, they are used in interest compounding, not discounting. Thus the *higher* the interest rate used, the *higher* are the resultant cash values and vice versa, other things being equal. Again, other things rarely are equal. As illustrated in preceding chapters, one policy may credit a higher interest rate than another, yet have higher loading charges assessed against the cash values, with the result that the total value is less on the higher interest contract.

## REINSTATEMENT PROVISION

Another standard provision relates to reinstatement. This is the situation wherein (1) the premium has not been paid within the grace period or, with respect to UL and CAWL policies, the policy has insufficient cash value to pay the monthly mortality and expense charges; (2) the policy, therefore, has lapsed; and (3) the policyowner desires to reactivate the policy.

*Nature of Provision.* A key condition for reinstatement is that the insured must furnish evidence of insurability that is satisfactory to the company. Otherwise, insureds in poor health would routinely apply for reinstatement; in other words, the insurer would be subject to adverse selection. Experience shows that the impaired are more apt than the unimpaired to seek reinstatement.

Most unintentional lapses are followed within a short period of time (two to four weeks) by a reinstatement application. The insurer usually takes a liberal view in such cases, since the chance of adverse selection is minimal. Companies have the contractual right to require a medical examination and other evidence of insurability, but, in practice, only limited evidence typically is required for recent lapses. The longer the period since lapse, the more closely requirements coincide with those for new applications.

The term *evidence of insurability* is broader than the term *good health*. Insurability connotes meeting standards with regard to occupation, travel, other insurance, and financial condition, as well as the physical characteristics and health status of the insured. The classic example of the distinction between good health and insurability is the case of a criminal condemned to death—such a person may be in perfect health, but he or she is hardly insurable.[56]

The term *satisfactory to the company* has generally been held to allow the insurer to require evidence that would be satisfactory to a reasonable insurer.[57] An insurer is in business to accept, not to decline applications, and if the person is insurable, the presumption must be that he or she will be accepted.

A second condition of reinstatement is the payment of past-due premiums or, with respect to some UL policies, past-due monthly deductions, with interest thereon. The usual terms require payment of the overdue amounts, less any dividends that would have been paid, usually with interest at 6 or 8 percent. Any outstanding policy loan also must be either repaid or reinstated through payment of past-due interest. Theoretically, nothing should be levied for past due mortality charges, since no coverage was provided during the period of lapse. As a result, some states limit the maximum past-due amount that insurers may collect to any increase in reserve between the time of lapse and reinstatement.

The reinstatement provision was originally included voluntarily by companies to safeguard accumulated policy values. Under these older contracts, if the premium was not paid when due, not only did the policy lapse, but accumulated policy values were forfeited.

The standard reinstatement provision does not require that reinstatement be permitted if the policy has been either surrendered or continued as extended term insurance and the full period of coverage has expired. Many companies include this restriction in their contracts. If the extended term period has not expired and has several years to run, insurers often will reinstate the policy without evidence of insurability.

***Considerations in Reinstatement.*** Although company practice is liberal, reinstatement is seldom permitted by companies or required by law more than five years after lapse, due to the high costs involved. The reasons that reinstatement of a recently lapsed policy may be to the policyowner's advantage compared to purchasing a new policy include:

1) The lapsed policy may have a lower premium rate per $1,000, since it may have been issued at a younger age.

[56] *Kallman v. Equitable Life Assurance Society*, 248 App. Div. 146, 288 N.Y. Supp. 1032 (1st Depart. 1936): affirmed, 272 N.Y. 648, 5 N.E.2d 375 (1936).

[57] 18 Cal. 2d 635, 117 P.2d at 7 (1941).

2) The incontestable and suicide periods of the lapsed policy may have expired or be closer to expiration.[58]

3) The owner usually will incur front-end loads again on the purchase of a new policy, whereas these amounts may have already been paid under the lapsed policy.

4) Initial cash-value increases under new policies usually are less than those found with older policies, other things being equal.

5) The older policy may contain provisions that are more liberal (e.g., lower policy loan rate or more attractive settlement option rates) than those found in new policies.

6) The insurer for the lapsed policy may be more disposed to reactivate the policy (by imposing a lower standard of insurability) than the issuer of a new policy.

On the other hand, the preceding arguments could prove to be unpersuasive for one or more of the following reasons:

1) The new policy may, in fact, have a lower premium rate per $1,000 even at the higher issue age, since competition has driven rates to new lows and, with respect to term policies, payment of back premiums rarely makes sound economic sense.

2) In the absence of an insured who intends to misrepresent information, the fact that a new period of contestability may be incurred can be of little importance.

3) In the absence of an insured who intends to commit or has tendencies toward committing suicide, the fact that a new suicide period may be incurred can be of little importance.

4) Some policies today have little or no front-end load, and, even with the payment of a new front-end load, a new policy may be superior, from a cost standpoint to the older one.

5) Similarly, initial cash-value increases on a new policy could be equal to or greater than those of an older policy.

6) The newer policy may contain more liberal provisions (e.g., premium payment flexibility, greater participation in the insurer's investment experience) than those in the old policy.

---

[58] The law is not entirely clear, but the majority view is that the incontestable clause is reinstated, making the policy contestable again, but only with respect to statements made in connection with the reinstatement application. A second view is that the original contestable period is effective, while a third and very much a minority view holds that the original contestable period is effective with respect to the policy as a whole, but that the reinstatement itself is a separate agreement that has no incontestable period and can be contested for fraud at any time. See William F. Myer, *Life and Health Insurance Law* (Rochester, N.Y.: The Lawyers Co-Operative Publishing Co., 1972), §8:17. In contrast, the courts have been virtually unanimous in holding that the suicide clause does not run again. Ibid., §10:1.

7) The money paid in interest and back charges may be more profitably used to fund the purchase of additional insurance or to lower the effective cost of the new policy.[59]

Therefore, as is often the case in life insurance, no clear-cut answer exists as to whether policyowners are better off financially by reinstating an older policy or purchasing a new one. If the old policy is a guaranteed-cost, nonparticipating contract that was issued some years ago, it frequently is advantageous to purchase a new contract rather than seek reinstatement.

## MISSTATEMENT OF AGE OR SEX

Most states' laws require that policies include a provision that if the insured's age is found to have been misstated, the amount of insurance shall be adjusted to be that which would have been purchased by the premium had the correct age been known.[60] For example, consider a $50,000 ordinary life policy issued at age 35 at a $900 annual premium. Assume that when the death claim was filed, the true issue age was found to be 36 and $50,000 of coverage at this age would have required a premium of $960. The amount payable by the company would then be 900/960 of $50,000, or $46,875. Although this is not a standard provision, the amount payable would be adjusted in a similar manner if a misstatement of sex had been made on the application.[61]

If the error in age is discovered while the policy is still in force, the procedure followed depends upon whether the age has been under- or overstated. If the age has been understated, the insured is usually given the option of paying the difference in premiums with interest or of having the policy reissued for the reduced amount. With an overstatement of age, a refund is usually made by paying the difference in reserves. This provision, originally included in policies voluntarily by many insurers, is intended to deal contractually with the potential problem of having a misstatement of age being considered a material misrepresentation, and thus being the basis for policy avoidance. By insurers addressing this issue by policy provision, they make certain that the incontestable clause does not apply to age misstatements.

---

[59] Some companies by practice (rarely by contract) permit a lapsed policy to be reinstated through a procedure that does not involve payment of all back premiums. This **reinstatement by redating** procedure involves a redating and reissuance of the policy.

[60] The question arises as to how one measures age. Some U.S. companies define age as that for the last birthday. Most companies, however, use the age to the nearest birth-date anniversary. Thus if a 45-year-old woman is less than six months from her next birth-date anniversary, she will be considered to be age 46.

[61] Proposals are under consideration in Congress and several state legislatures to eliminate sex as a rating factor in all lines of insurance (see Chap. 24). Misstatements of sex are not common and usually occur because of a transcribing error, not because the proposed insured was unsure of his or her gender!

## PROVISIONS PROTECTING THE COMPANY

Several life insurance contract provisions primarily protect the life insurance company against adverse selection. These include the suicide clause, the delay clause, and certain hazard restriction clauses.

### SUICIDE CLAUSE

At one time, life insurance contracts excluded the risk of suicide entirely. This was unfortunate since the very purpose for which the policy was purchased—to protect dependents—could thus be defeated. In addition, it was not necessary to exclude suicide completely to protect the company. Suicide is one of the causes of death that make up the total mortality rate, and such deaths are included in the mortality tables upon which premiums are based. However, the company must protect itself against cases when insurance is purchased in contemplation of suicide. Adequate protection against this adverse selection possibility can be obtained by excluding the suicide risk for the first one or two policy years. This provision also protects the policyowner in that it helps assure other policyowners that they will not pay more than their equitable share of insurance costs.

The clause is intended to protect against adverse selection— not to exclude the risk of suicide as such. Its inclusion is optional, but since the insurer would not be able to exclude suicide-based death claims were it omitted, virtually every insurer includes it. Most state laws permit an exclusion of up to two years, and this is the usual practice. A number of companies, however, use a one-year exclusion. A typical suicide clause reads as follows:

> For the first two full years from the original application date, we will not pay if
> the insured commits suicide (while sane or insane). We will terminate the policy
> and give back the premiums paid to us less any loan.

The question of whether a death is suicide or due to other causes is almost always left to a jury. The legal presumption is that a person will not take his or her own life, so the burden of proof of suicide rests with the insurer. This fact, plus the tendency of courts to seek ways of ruling for dependents, often makes it exceedingly difficult to prove suicide. For example, some courts have held that an "insane" person, by definition, cannot commit "suicide," since suicide requires a knowledge of right and wrong. This result has emerged even in the face of the "while sane or insane" policy language. Thus, under this interpretation, an insane person who takes his or her own life has not committed suicide, and the company would be required to honor the death claim. Where death is in fact determined to be by suicide and within the period of exclusion, the company will refund the premiums paid, with or without interest, depending on the contract.

## DELAY CLAUSE

Life insurance policies must contain a provision granting the company the right to defer cash-value payment or the making of a policy loan (except for purposes of paying premiums) for up to six months after its request. This provision is intended to protect the company against "runs," wherein investments might have to be liquidated under adverse circumstances. The clause had been primarily of historical interest until the recent adverse times for some insurers. As the experience of at least one recent financially troubled insurer revealed, the clause does not always help.

## HAZARD RESTRICTION CLAUSES

The life insurance policy is an "all risk" contract, with the law permitting only limited exclusions. One of these, the **aviation exclusion**, denies coverage in case of death from aviation. It is included in U.S. life insurance contracts today only under certain exceptional circumstances. All companies cover fare-paying passengers on regularly scheduled airlines. Similarly, anticipated flights on unscheduled airlines usually do not result in any policy restrictions or an increased rate. Even private pilots and the pilots and crews of commercial airlines are insured with standard or with only slightly extra rates. Aviation restrictions are still strictly applied in the case of military pilots. Virtually all coverage restrictions can be eliminated, however, if the insured is willing to pay an extra premium.

    **War exclusion** clauses normally provide for a return of all premiums paid with interest or a refund equal to the policy's reserve if death occurs under the military conditions excluded in the policy. Companies usually insert war clauses in their contracts during periods of impending or actual war, particularly for policies issued to persons of draft age. War clauses are typically canceled at the end of the war period.

    The major purpose of war exclusion clauses is to control adverse selection by insurance buyers. Persons entering military service would be a larger than normal proportion of individuals buying insurance, and also they would be inclined to buy larger policies than otherwise. Such clauses can benefit proposed insureds in that they might be refused coverage altogether if the insurer could not protect itself from an extra military hazard. The experience of many companies after both World War I and World War II showed that they could have covered the war risk without imposing extra premiums. Without such clauses, however, the potential adverse selection involved could have significantly impacted the overall mortality experience.

    In general, there are two types of war clauses: (1) the status type and (2) the results type. Under the **status** type of clause, the insurer will not pay for the insured's death while he or she is in the military service, regardless of the cause of death. Some companies liberalize this clause by excluding only death outside the "home area." Usually, this home area is defined as the United States and Canada, but other definitions are not rare. Under the **results** type of clause, there is no coverage if the death is a result of war. The basic distinction between the clauses resides in the significance of the cause of death: under the status clause, if the insured is in military service, the cause of death is immaterial, so that even if a person slipped on a bar of soap while taking a bath at home and death resulted, there would be no coverage. Under the results clause, the cause of death would have to be related to military activity.[62]

The validity of war clauses has not been the subject of much litigation, but the clause's interpretation has given rise to a large volume of cases. Much litigation has revolved around the question of whether a particular clause is a status clause or a results clause. Other litigation has related to the nature of death and the existence of war itself.[63]

[62] *Hazle v. Liberty Life Ins. Co.,* 186 S.E. 2d 245, 257 S. C. 456 (1972).

[63] See *Berley v. Pennsylvania Mutual Life Insurance Company,* 373 Pa. 231, 95 A.2d 202 (Pa. 1953), and *Stucker v. College Life Insurance Co. of America,* 208 N.E. 2d 731 (Ind. 1965).

# Chapter 9

# THE LIFE INSURANCE CONTRACT: II

## PROVISIONS PROVIDING POLICYOWNER FLEXIBILITY

Life insurance policies have always been flexible financial instruments and are becoming even more so. This chapter covers policy provisions that supply this flexibility and presents an overview of creditors' rights in life insurance.

### THE BENEFICIARY CLAUSE

The beneficiary clause in a life insurance contract permits the policyowner to have policy death proceeds distributed to whomever and in whatever form he or she wishes. The policyowner can prepare a plan of distribution in advance that accomplishes his or her personal objectives by allowing appropriately for future contingencies.

*Nature of Designation.* The rights of the policyowner and the beneficiary depend upon whether a beneficiary designation is revocable or irrevocable. A **revocable designation** is one that may be changed by the policyowner without the beneficiary's consent. By contrast, an **irrevocable designation** is one that can be changed only with the beneficiary's express consent. Irrevocable designations are used in situations in which a policyowner does not want to or cannot retain the right to change beneficiaries, such as with divorce settlements. Irrevocably named beneficiaries have a vested right in the policy that is so complete that neither the policyowner nor his or her creditors can impair it without the beneficiary's consent.[1]

[1] *Condon v. New York Life*, Iowa 658, 166 N.W. 452 (1983).

210

Thus with an irrevocable beneficiary designation, unless some specific policy provision authorizes the policyowner to make policy loans, surrender the policy, or exercise other specific prematurity rights or privileges, he or she may not take any action that will in any way diminish or affect the beneficiary's right to receive the full amount of insurance at the insured's death. In the usual case, it is as if the beneficiary and the policyowner were joint owners of the policy—that is the practical effect of an irrevocable designation. The policyowner cannot act without the consent of the irrevocable beneficiary (and, of course, the beneficiary has no rights to effect any policy changes).

Today virtually all policies contain a provision reserving to the policyowner the power to change the beneficiary or beneficiaries while the policy is in force. When this right is reserved, as it is with revocable designations, the named beneficiary obtains no vested rights in the policy or in its proceeds, but possesses only a "mere expectancy until after the maturity of the contract." Thus when the policyowner reserves the right to change the beneficiary, he or she is regarded, in the absence of any other assignment of policy rights, as the complete owner of the policy.

***Designating the Beneficiary*** The importance of exercising care in the beneficiary designation cannot be overemphasized. If the policyowner's intentions are to be carried out effectively, the language must be precise and unambiguous.

Numerous examples may be cited to illustrate the need for care in describing beneficiaries. Consider some class designations. "To my children" is a designation that invites misunderstanding and possibly litigation. The policyowner who designates "my minor children" may not be thinking about the fact that eventually children will reach adulthood. When a husband's policy was payable to "the insured's children," the term was judged to include those from a former wife but not his wife's children by a former husband.

Adopted children are included in the term *children*, whereas stepchildren may not be included. The term *dependents* is limited to those actually dependent upon the policyowner for support. Illegitimate children, if they are acknowledged by the policyowner, are generally included in the designation children. However, if the policyowner fails to legitimize them, generally they will not be considered.

The term *relative* has been held to include "those by marriage as well as by blood, but not an illegitimate child"; the term *heirs* refers to "those who take under the status of descent and distribution."[2] Even if the intended persons finally receive the policy proceeds, litigation and delay can erode proceeds, and the sheer human aggravation can foster ill will and invites family discord. Too often, the construction of the beneficiary designation receives far too little care and attention.

[2] For the manner in which the courts have interpreted the various terms that are commonly used in designating beneficiaries in life insurance policies, see 44 Am. Jur. 2d, Insurance §§1727–1790.

*Contingent Beneficiary.* The time between when the beneficiary is designated and the insured dies may be many years. If the **primary beneficiary** predeceases the insured, proceeds ordinarily would be payable to the insured's estate in the absence of any further designation. This result may not be the most desirable one. A **contingent beneficiary** designation, whereby one or more persons are named to receive death proceeds if the primary beneficiary is not alive at the insured's death, can solve this problem. Also, a contingent beneficiary could be named to receive any payments still to be made under a settlement option (see later) after the death of a primary beneficiary who had outlived the insured. Any contingent or later (called **tiertiary**) designation typically is made at the same time that the primary beneficiary is designated. A beneficiary designation with both primary and contingent (also called **secondary**) beneficiaries might read: "Proceeds to be paid to Thomas S. Nina, husband of the insured, if living; otherwise to Bart Simpson, nephew of the insured."

*A Minor as Beneficiary.* The designation of a minor as beneficiary presents unique problems. For example, if a minor beneficiary is named irrevocably, the policyowner is prevented from exercising any rights under the policy, since the minor must consent to any action, yet he or she lacks the capability to do so. A guardian must be appointed, and even then the guardian would most likely not have the authority to provide the necessary consent to a change, since the change would, in all likelihood, tend to diminish the minor's estate without resulting in any offsetting advantage. A guardian is committed to conserving the minor's estate.

Minor beneficiaries also raise the question of how payment of the proceeds is to be accomplished if the policy matures and becomes payable before the beneficiary has reached the age of majority. A minor is not legally competent to receive payment and cannot give a valid release for it. To avoid the possibility of having to pay a second time, insurers generally will not make payment of any substantial amount directly to minor beneficiaries, but will instead require the appointment of a guardian. This process is time-consuming and can be expensive.

*Change of Beneficiary.* In the absence of an irrevocable beneficiary designation, the policyowner may change the designation at will. The policy provides the method for accomplishing this, and although companies usually require it be followed carefully, in the majority of cases a beneficiary change is a routine matter.

If the policyowner has done all that he or she can to effect a beneficiary change, but did not follow the procedure because of factors beyond his or her control, a beneficiary change will be deemed to have been accomplished, notwithstanding the failure to comply fully with the policy requirements. The courts reached this result by using the **doctrine of substantial compliance**.[3]

---

[3] Vernon's A.T.C. Insurance Code, §3.48, and *Pena v. Salinas*, 536 S.W. 2d 671, Tex. Civ. App. (1976).

Thus, for example, when a policyowner signed the change of beneficiary form and sent it to his wife to deliver to the company agent but was killed before the delivery to the agent, the change of beneficiary was held effective.[4] In another case, the policyowner/insured requested change of beneficiary forms, signed them, but delayed forwarding them to the company, although there was ample time and opportunity. The forms were mailed after the death of the insured, but this was held to be an ineffective change of beneficiary.[5]

*Common Disaster*. The beneficiary's right to receive life insurance policy proceeds is usually conditioned on his or her surviving the insured. Usually, survivorship poses no problem, but if the insured and the beneficiary die in the same accident and no evidence shows who died first, the question arises as to whom the proceeds are payable. No common-law presumption based on age or sex exists as to who died first. With much diversity in the decisions, courts in states that have not adopted the Uniform Simultaneous Death Act (see below) have awarded the proceeds to the insured's estate, in the absence of a contingent beneficiary, particularly where the insured had reserved the right to change the beneficiary.

Most states, however, have enacted the **Uniform Simultaneous Death Act**. This act, which is not confined to insurance, provides in a section on insurance that "where the insured and beneficiary in a policy of life or accident insurance have died and there is not sufficient evidence that they have died otherwise than simultaneously, the proceeds of the policy shall be distributed as if the insured had survived the beneficiary." This, of course, resolves the question of survival in those states in which the act is effective, but it fails to solve the main problems facing policyowners and insurance companies. Specifically, if the proceeds are payable in a lump sum and no contingent beneficiary is named, no matter who is determined to have survived, the proceeds will be paid into the probate estate of the insured or the beneficiary. This possibly will subject the proceeds to depletion through potentially unnecessary probate and related costs, additional taxes, and the claims of creditors.

Related to this issue are the much more frequent short-term survivorship situations, in which the beneficiary survives the insured by a short period of time. Here survivorship is not questioned, but similar problems exist. In addition, shrinkage in the proceeds is a possibility because of prior election of a life income settlement option, under which the entire proceeds are considered fully earned even though the beneficiary lived to receive only one or a few installments.[6]

In approaching this problem, many companies use a **survivorship clause** (also called a **time clause**) which provides that the beneficiary must survive the

[4] *Pabst v. Hesse*, 173 N.W. 2d 925, 286 Minn. 33 (1970).

[5] *Magruder v. Northwestern Mut. Life Ins. Co.*, 512 F.2d 507, C.A. Tenn. (1975).

[6] If a minimum number of installments was guaranteed, installments equal to the guaranteed number would be paid.

insured by a fixed period after the insured's death to be entitled to the proceeds. This clause, in conjunction with the naming of contingent beneficiaries, can prevent the proceeds from falling into the probate estate of either an owner/insured or the original beneficiary. Another provision sometimes utilized is a direction that the proceeds are payable to the beneficiary only if he or she is alive at the time of payment. The latter provision, with the proper use of the income settlement options, will also avoid most of the problems mentioned above.[7]

## SETTLEMENT OPTIONS

The value of life insurance is never more evident, and financial decisions are never more difficult, than at the time of a death. Thus policyowners should carefully consider the manner in which death proceeds will be paid. Failure to arrange for the proper payment of proceeds may defeat the very purpose for which the insurance was intended.

Some 90 percent of all life insurance policy death proceeds are paid to beneficiaries by life insurers as a single sum of money shortly after the insured's death. Often the beneficiary is ill prepared emotionally and otherwise to make decisions concerning the disposition of what are often large sums. Poor investment and purchase decisions are too easily made during periods of distress. Would it often not be wiser to permit the insurer to retain the proceeds for a while before decisions are made?

The following section discusses the policy provisions—the **settlement options**—that permit the policyowner (or beneficiary) flexibility in deciding how death proceeds will be paid. Most insurers also permit cash values to be paid out under one or more settlement options. This can be particularly valuable at retirement, when the policyowner may no longer need the insurance protection and desires to annuitize the policy's cash value as a retirement benefit.

*Legal Nature.* Following the insured's death, a contractual relationship exists between the insurance company and the beneficiary, whether the proceeds are payable in a lump sum or under a settlement option. If the policyowner, during the insured's lifetime, sets up the settlement arrangement, performance of that agreement after the insured's death is regarded merely as a continuation of the third-party beneficiary arrangement. If, on the other hand, a beneficiary elects to receive the proceeds under one of the settlement options, some courts have held that a new direct contractual relationship is established between the company and the beneficiary. In either case, however, as a party to a direct contractual relationship or as a third-party beneficiary, the beneficiary may enforce his or her rights under the life insurance contract or subsequent settlement agreement.

---

[7] Also, some insurers include a **turnaround provision** within their contracts. This provision, used primarily for policies purchased for business purposes, permits the policyowner, if he or she is other than the insured, to change the beneficiary for up to 60 days following the insured's death.

*Types of Options.* Settlement options are usually designated in the contract, and most contracts provide a choice from among the options discussed below. Although most companies permit arrangements not specifically granted by contract, virtually all companies are more liberal respecting income settlement plans adopted by the policyowner before death than in regard to those requested by the beneficiary. The policyowner may give the beneficiary as much or as little flexibility in designating the settlement option as the policyowner desires. Thus a policyowner could totally "lock in" the manner in which proceeds would be paid to the beneficiary, with neither the insurer nor the beneficiary having any right to alter the arrangement at the insured's death. Alternatively, the policyowner could design a settlement agreement that, on the death of the insured, gave the beneficiary total freedom to alter its terms, but, in the absence of a change by the beneficiary, the policyowner's wishes would be followed by the company. Of course, a "flexibility" continuum exists between these two extremes. Insurers will work closely with the policyowner to provide for the desired degree of flexibility.

*1. Cash.* In a strict sense, a **cash** or **lump sum** settlement is not an "option," because life insurance contracts usually provide for lump sum settlement in the absence of any other direction by the policyowner or beneficiary. Proceeds paid to the beneficiary in a lump sum are usually afforded no protection against the beneficiary's creditors. Such protection usually can be arranged in connection with the income options, but, as discussed later in this chapter, only if they are elected before the insured's death.

Many policies provide for interest to be paid from the date of death, even if a settlement option had not been elected. Indeed, several states require the payment of such interest. Although lump sum settlements may be indicated, the interest option (discussed next) is very flexible and permits adjustments to be made in light of changing economic, health, and other circumstances.

*2. Interest Option.* Under the **interest option**, the proceeds remain with the company and only the interest earned thereon is paid to the beneficiary. A minimum interest rate is guaranteed in the contract, although companies routinely credit a higher rate. In most companies, the interest cannot be left to accumulate and compound, but must be paid out monthly, quarterly, semiannually, or annually. Since there are legal limits as to the length of time a principal sum may be kept intact (see below), companies frequently limit the time that they will hold a principal sum under this option to the lifetime of the primary beneficiary or 30 years, whichever is longer.

The interest option is one of the most widely used options. Its main advantage is that it assures the beneficiary freedom from investment worries, while guaranteeing both principal and a minimum rate of return. The right of withdrawal and the right to change to another option are the sources of flexibility in the interest option, and this option is usually the foundation upon which most comprehensive settlement agreements are formulated. Depending upon individual company rules and state laws, the primary beneficiary may be given:

1. The right to name who is to receive any balance at his or her death, or the right to change the contingent beneficiaries previously designated by the policyowner.

2. The right to make withdrawals of all or part of the principal, subject to any limitations prescribed by the policyowner in the settlement agreement Most companies permit any reasonable combination of limiting factors (so much money per year, distribution at certain ages, and so forth), or the proceeds may be held without any withdrawal privileges.

3. The right to change to another settlement option at a later time when circumstances may have changed. For example, the proceeds may be left under the interest option, with the right of the primary beneficiary to change to any other option, including the life income option (see below), at a later date.

4. Protection from most creditors, if a spendthrift clause is included in the policy.

*3. Fixed-Period Option.* This is one of the two options based on the concept of systematically liquidating principal and interest over a period of years, *without reference to life contingencies.* The other is the fixed-amount option (discussed below).

The **fixed-period option,** as its name indicates, provides for the payment of the proceeds in installments over a definite period of months or years, usually not longer than 25 or 30 years. If the primary beneficiary dies during the fixed period, the remaining installments (or their commuted value) are paid to the contingent beneficiary. The amount of proceeds, the period of time, the guaranteed minimum rate of interest, and the frequency of payments determine the amount of each installment. Any interest in excess of the guaranteed rate is usually paid at the end of each year.

The fixed-period option is valuable when the most important consideration is to provide income for a definite period, as in the case of a readjustment period following the insured's death or while children are in school. Most companies permit policyowners to give the beneficiary the right to receive the present value of all remaining installments in a lump sum; this is referred to as the **right to commute.** Some companies permit the beneficiary to select the date when payments are to begin. However, aside from these options, the fixed-period option is not very flexible.

Since the basic characteristic of this option is the period of time selected, outstanding policy loans at the insured's death reduce the amount of each installment but do not affect the number of installments. For the same reason, any dividend accumulations or paid-up additions payable with the proceeds will increase the beneficiary's income while the number of installments remains the same.

4. *Fixed-Amount Option.* Under the **fixed-amount option**, the income amount is the primary consideration rather than the time period over which the proceeds and interest are to be liquidated. A specified amount of income is designated, such as $2,000 per month, and payments continue until the principal and interest thereon are exhausted.

Fixed-amount options can be more advantageous than fixed-period options, because they are more flexible. Most companies permit the policyowner to specify varying amounts of income at different times, and the beneficiary may be given the right of withdrawal in whole or in part, or the right to withdraw up to a certain sum in any one year on a cumulative or noncumulative basis. In the case of both the fixed-period and fixed-amount options, the commencement of installments can be deferred to a particular time by holding the proceeds under the interest option until that time.

Since the amount of each installment is the controlling factor under this option, dividend accumulations or additions payable with the proceeds, together with any excess interest earned while installments are being paid, increase the number of installments but do not affect the installment amount. Conversely, loans outstanding at the insured's death or withdrawals of principal by the beneficiary decrease the number of installments.

A special rule often governs minimum installments under the fixed-amount option. Usually, at least $50 per year or a minimum of a stated amount per month is required to be paid out for each $1,000 of proceeds. The rule is in keeping with the purpose of the option—that is, to exhaust the principal and interest within some reasonable length of time.

The fixed-amount and fixed-period options represent the same idea expressed in different ways. Both systematically liquidate principal and interest over a period of years, without reference to a life contingency. For this reason, the guaranteed interest factor is usually the same for both options in a given contract.

5. *Single Life Income Options.* The several forms of single life income options represent the other broad class of settlement options—those that liquidate principal and interest *with reference to life contingencies*. These options are unique to life insurance companies. No other financial institution can make such an arrangement with its clients. Single life income options are life annuities and thus serve the same economic functions.

The amount of each installment depends on the type of life income (annuity) selected, the amount of the proceeds, the rate of interest being credited, the age of the beneficiary when the income commences, and the sex of the beneficiary (where permitted). The most common forms of life income options are (1) the pure life income option, (2) the refund life income option, and (3) the life income option with period certain.

With the **pure life income option**, installments are payable only for as long as the primary beneficiary (the income recipient) lives. In other words, no further payments are due to anyone when the primary beneficiary dies. Since no refunds or further payments are made at the beneficiary's death, the pure life income option provides the largest life income per $1,000 of proceeds for a given beneficiary. However, most persons hesitate to risk forfeiting a large part of the principal on early death, particularly if there are relatives to whom they wish to leave funds. For example, this form probably is inappropriate for many widows or widowers with young children, since it affords no protection to the children in the case of early death.

The refund life income option may take the form of a **cash refund annuity** or an **installment refund annuity**. Both annuities guarantee the return of an amount equal to the principal sum, less the total payments already made. The difference in the two forms is that, under the cash refund option, a lump-sum settlement is made following the primary beneficiary's death instead of the installment payments being continued.

Under the **life income option with period certain**, the most widely used life income option, installments are payable for as long as the primary beneficiary lives, but should this beneficiary die before a predetermined number of years, the company continues the installments to a second beneficiary until the end of the designated period. The usual contract contains two or three alternative periods, the most popular ones being 10 and 20 years, but others may be obtained on request. This option is frequently useful where a widow or widower and minor children are concerned, since it assures the desired income for life while still guaranteeing that the income will last until the children are grown, regardless of the parent's date of death.

Table 7-1 in Chapter 7 shows three forms of single life income options. Observe that the longer the guarantee period, the less the monthly proceeds. Moreover, as expected, the older the beneficiary, the greater the life income. A drawback of the life income option is that the income amount to be received by the beneficiary cannot be ascertained prior to the death of the insured, since it depends on the beneficiary's age. The amounts shown in Table 7-1 are calculated on the basis of the insurer's guaranteed minimum rate of interest. Normally, the actual amounts paid are higher than the minimums guaranteed.

6. *Joint and Survivorship Life Income Option.* Under the **joint and survivorship life income option**, if the second beneficiary is still living at the death of the first beneficiary, installments are continued during the secondary beneficiary's lifetime. As is the case with joint and survivorship annuities, this option may continue payment of the same income to the surviving beneficiary or reduce the installments to two-thirds ("joint and two-thirds"), three-fourths ("joint and three-fourths"), or one-half ("joint and one-half") of the original amount and continue the payment of this reduced amount for the surviving beneficiary's lifetime. Some companies grant joint and survivorship options with a period certain of 10 to 20 years.

The joint and survivorship option can be particularly useful in providing retirement income for a husband and wife. In such cases, the proceeds of a matured endowment or annuity or the cash values of any policy are applied under this option.

7. *Other Settlement Arrangements.* Virtually any desired income pattern may be obtained by using the various options described above, either singly or in some combination. In many instances, the policyowner may find that he or she can best provide for beneficiaries by selecting a combination of settlement options. Furthermore, he or she may elect that options operate concurrently, successively, or both ways.

Some companies provide options designed to meet a specific need or serve a particular purpose. These special options are usually a combination of the basic options to fit a particular situation, with an attractive sales title applied to them. For example, a so-called **educational plan** option provides a fixed-dollar income during nine or ten months of each college year, with a modest "graduation present" in cash after the final installment. This is really a combination of the fixed-amount and interest options, with appropriate limitations placed on them to produce the desired effect.

In an effort to provide better service to beneficiaries and to retain more of the policy proceeds within the insurer corporate family, many insurers provide beneficiaries the option of having proceeds paid into an insurer-sponsored **flexible spending account**. Some insurers automatically establish such an account for beneficiaries, subject to a minimum death benefit (e.g., $10,000). Instead of receiving a lump sum check, the beneficiary is free to leave proceeds in this interest-bearing account or to write checks to withdraw any portion or all of the proceeds. This option meets the objective of providing the beneficiary with time to decide about the disposition to be made of the funds.

Notwithstanding the wide variety of settlement plans offered by the various options or combinations of options, situations do arise when the standard options do not fit exactly. Upon submission of the facts, the company usually is willing to develop a special settlement plan, within reasonable limits.

In those cases where an individual desires greater flexibility than the insurance company will permit, consideration should be given to the use of an individual trustee or the services of a trust company. This is particularly to be considered if discretionary powers are indicated. A life insurance company normally will not accept any arrangement whereby it must exercise discretion in carrying out the terms of the agreement.

*Rule against Perpetuities*. It is in the public interest that property stays in circulation. To this end, rules limit the length of time during which property owners can reserve to themselves enjoyment of property. The common law **rule**

**against perpetuities** provides that the vesting of the ownership of property cannot be deferred for longer than a life or lives in being and 21 years (plus the period of gestation) thereafter. Simply put, this time limit is 21 years after the death of persons living and identified with a given transaction, measured from the date the property is transferred or the interest in the property is created.

The common-law rule has been modified by statute in a few states. Thus in New York the law provides that absolute ownership of personal property shall not be suspended by any limitation or condition that could extend beyond two individual lives in being at the date of the instrument creating the limitation or condition.[8]

Although little litigation exists on this point,[9] the rule against perpetuities is generally believed not to be applicable to settlement agreements, because the latter life insurance agreements merely create a debtor-creditor relationship. From a practical point of view, family needs usually can be met within these limitations. Consequently, companies usually avoid any possible application of the rule against perpetuities by prohibiting agreements that would violate these rules.

*Rule against Accumulations.* The **rule against accumulations** prohibits the accumulation of income for any unreasonable period. In this connection, all state laws permit such accumulations during a beneficiary's minority, but many prohibit them for an adult. The laws of a few states, however, permit the accumulation of income during some specified period, such as 10 years, even though the beneficiary is an adult.

In general, since the laws restricting the accumulation of income are believed to apply to life insurance settlement options, insurers usually permit accumulations of interest under settlement options *only* during the minority of beneficiaries, regardless of whether the law in a given state specifically refers to settlement options. In fact, some companies will not permit any accumulations.

## ASSIGNMENT PROVISION

Ownership rights in life insurance policies, like other types of property, can be transferred by the current owner to another person. Such transfers are referred to as **assignments**. Assignments are of two types: absolute and collateral.

*Absolute Assignments.* An **absolute assignment** is the irrevocable transfer to another person by the existing policyowner of *all* of his or her rights in the policy. In other words, it is a change of ownership. In the case of a gift, the assignment is a voluntary property transfer involving no monetary consideration. Gifts of life insurance policies are frequently made among family members for both personal and tax reasons.[10]

[8] Section 11, New York Personal Property Law.

[9] In *Holmes v. John Hancock Mutual Life Insurance Company*, 228 N.Y. 106, 41 N.E. 2d 909 (1942), the court held that the New York statute regarding perpetuities did not apply to a settlement agreement.

[10] See Chap. 14.

From time to time, a life insurance policy is sold for a valuable consideration. For example, a policy owned by a corporation on the life of a key employee may be sold for an amount equal to its cash value to the employee upon employment termination. As with a gift, these transactions are accomplished through an absolute assignment of policy rights, typically by using an absolute assignment form furnished by the insurer.

As pointed out earlier, an irrevocable beneficiary must consent to an assignment of the policy, since he or she is, in effect, a joint owner. In the case of a revocable beneficiary, many courts have held that an absolute assignment, by itself, does not change the beneficiary.[11] Other courts have held the opposite. The new owner, of course, can change the beneficiary by following the customary procedures.

*Collateral Assignments.* A **collateral assignment** is a partial, temporary transfer of policy ownership rights to another person. Collateral assignments are ordinarily used as collateral security for loans from banks or other lending institutions (or persons). Such assignments are partial in that only *some* (not *all* as in an absolute assignment) policy rights are transferred. They are temporary in that the transferred partial rights revert to the policyowner upon debt repayment.

The vast majority of life insurance policy collateral assignments use the American Bankers Association (ABA) Collateral Assignment Form No. 10. The form was developed jointly by the American Bankers Association and the Association of Life Insurance Counsel. The ABA Form 10 attempts to provide adequate protection to the lender and, at the same time, permits the policyowner to retain certain rights under the policy. Thus the assignee (e.g., the lending institution) obtains the right to (1) collect the proceeds at maturity, (2) surrender the policy pursuant to its terms, (3) obtain policy loans, (4) receive dividends, and (5) exercise and receive benefits of nonforfeiture rights. On the other hand, the policyowner retains the right to (1) collect any disability benefits, (2) change the beneficiary (subject to the assignment), and (3) elect optional modes of settlement (subject to the assignment). Under the form, the assignee also agrees (1) to pay to the beneficiary any proceeds in excess of the policyowner's debt; (2) not to surrender or obtain a loan from the insurance company (except for paying premiums) unless there is default on the debt or premium payments, and then not until 20 days after notification to the policyowner; and (3) to forward the policy to the insurer for endorsement of any change of beneficiary or election of settlement option.

*Policy Assignment Provision.* Although policies are assignable in the absence of policy assignment provisions, life insurance companies include in their policies an assignment clause of some kind. Although much variation exists in the wording, one company's provision reads:

---

11 *Continental Assur. Co. v. Connoy,* 209 F.26 539 (3rd Cir. 1954), and *Rountree v. Frazee,* 282 Ala. 142, 209 So.2d 424 (1968).

You can assign this policy. We will not be responsible for the validity of an assignment. We will not be liable for any payments we make or actions we take before notice to us of an assignment.

Assignment provisions of life insurance policies do not prohibit an assignment without the company's consent, but simply provide that the company need not recognize the assignment until it has received written notice of it, and that it assumes no responsibility as to its validity. The company's major concern is to avoid paying the claim twice.

## CHANGE OF PLAN PROVISION

Many policies contain a provision granting the policyowner the right to change the policy form. The conversion feature discussed in Chapter 4 on term insurance is an example of a change of plan provision. Most companies limit the change to plans of insurance involving a higher premium rate, although some permit a change to a lower premium rate plan, but only with satisfactory evidence of insurability. Flexible premium policies, in essence, contain a very broad change of plan provision.

In connection with a change to a higher premium rate plan of fixed-premium life insurance, the policyowner usually must pay the difference between the policy reserve on the new form and the policy reserve under the original policy. Changes to plans with higher premium rates do not necessitate evidence of insurability.[12] Companies that do not grant changes to lower-premium plans as a matter of contract right usually will do so as a matter of practice. Since evidence of insurability is required, the incontestability clause is reinstated in the same manner as for a reinstatement. If a change to a lower-premium form is requested, any decrease in reserve or cash value occasioned by the change would be paid by the company to the policyowner.

## CHANGE OF INSURED PROVISION

Some companies include a policy provision permitting a change of insureds. This provision can be particularly useful for corporate-owned life insurance. In the past, when an employee whose life was insured for the benefit of the corporation either retired or otherwise terminated employment, the life insurance would have to be surrendered (or sold) and new insurance purchased on the life of the replacement employee. The change of insured provision, which is subject to insurability requirements, eliminates this necessity and, in effect, also eliminates the front-end load that otherwise would be payable on a newly purchased contract.

---

[12] As a general rule, an insurer will attempt to reserve the right to underwrite any policy change involving an increase in a policy's net amount at risk or other policy benefit. Conversely, changes involving a decrease in a policy's net amount at risk or other policy benefit do not require evidence of insurability. Thus a change from a lower-premium policy form to a higher-premium form—being a change to a higher-reserved policy (and, therefore, to a lower net amount at risk), *ceteris paribus*—requires no evidence of insurability.

## NONFORFEITURE OPTIONS

Another provision of cash-value life insurance policies affords the policyowner, who chooses to terminate his or her life insurance, the option of utilizing the cash surrender value in several ways. Cash-value policies typically stipulate that the surrender value may be taken in one of three forms: (1) cash, (2) a reduced amount of paid-up insurance of the same kind as the original policy, or (3) extended term insurance for the full face amount.

*Cash*. The policy may be surrendered for its net cash surrender value as of the surrender date. Of course, when this option is elected, the protection ceases and the company has no further obligation under the policy. Consequently, even though this option can provide a ready source of cash for emergencies and other needs, it should be elected only after careful consideration. Almost the same amount of cash may be obtained through a policy loan (see below), and this may be a better alternative than surrendering the policy.

The available net cash surrender value is the gross cash value shown in the policy, decreased by any surrender charges (which are common in universal life policies) and the amount of any policy loans outstanding, and increased by the cash value of any paid-up additions, any dividends accumulated at interest, and any prepaid premiums.

Besides a complete policy surrender, some policies provide for partial surrenders. As noted in Chapter 6, this is a common feature in universal life (UL) policies. Additionally, many policies provide living benefits riders that can prove useful in certain family emergencies (see Chapter 7). Traditional participating whole life and endowment policies as well as policies with paid-up additions riders provide that paid-up additions (see "Dividend Options" below) may be surrendered, in whole or in part. Furthermore, as a matter of practice (not by contract guarantee), many companies permit a partial surrender of traditional cash-value policies. However, unlike the situation with a UL policy, the face amount is typically reduced by an amount equal to the proportion by which the cash value is reduced. For example, if $6,000 of a $10,000 cash value is surrendered on a $50,000 ordinary life policy, the face amount may be reduced by 60 percent. This reduction is intended to minimize adverse selection.

*Reduced Paid-Up Insurance.* A second option permits the policyowner to use the net cash surrender value as a net single premium to purchase a reduced amount of paid-up insurance of the same type as the original basic policy, exclusive of any term or other riders. All riders and supplementary benefits, such as for disability and accidental death, are terminated, and no further premiums are payable. The exchange is made at net rates, so it is based on mortality and interest only, not on expenses.

Table 9-1 shows that after 10 years, each $56 of cash value could be exchanged for $344 of paid-up whole life insurance. This option would be appropriate when a smaller amount of whole life insurance would be satisfactory

**TABLE 9-1     MINIMUM NONFORFEITURE VALUES,
PER $1,000 (*1980 CSO MORTALITY TABLE*,
7 1/2% INTEREST, ORDINARY LIFE,
MALE, AGE 35)**

| End of Year | Cash Value | Paid-Up Insurance | Extended Term Insurance[a] | |
|---|---|---|---|---|
| | | | Year | Days |
| 1 | $ 0 | $ 0 | — | — |
| 5 | 14 | 112 | 3 | 295 |
| 10 | 56 | 344 | 10 | 64 |
| 15 | 108 | 517 | 13 | 28 |
| 20 | 171 | 646 | 13 | 343 |

[a] Based on the 1980 *Commissioners Extended Term Table*.

and it was desirable to discontinue premium payments. It could be attractive, for example, to the policyowner/insured who is approaching retirement, when typically an individual's income and need for life insurance are reduced.

The paid-up option may not be available, as such, under UL policies. The same result can be achieved, however, by decreasing the UL face amount to a level that the existing cash value will support indefinitely with no further premium payments.

***Extended Term Insurance.*** The third nonforfeiture option permits the policyowner to exchange the net cash surrender value for paid-up term insurance for the full face amount.[13] The length of the extended term insurance (ETI) period is determined by applying the net surrender value as a single term insurance premium, to provide level term insurance for whatever duration the funds will carry the policy.

Referring again to Table 9-1, it should be noted that the tenth-year cash value of $56 per $1,000 face amount may be used to purchase $1,000 term insurance coverage (the full face amount), to remain in effect for 10 years and 64 days. If the policyowner fails to make a specific election to the contrary, this option is usually the automatic one. The ETI option would be appropriate if the need for the full amount of insurance protection continued but the financial capacity or desire to meet premium payments had diminished.

The ETI option does not exist as such under UL policies, although the same effect can be accomplished. If the UL policyowner ceases to pay premiums, the policy's face amount is maintained in force for as long as the cash value is sufficient to pay monthly mortality and expense charges. This constitutes the normal operation of the UL policy and, therefore, need not be viewed as a nonforfeiture option. The end result of this "runoff," however, is similar to that found under the conventional ETI option. Therefore, in effect, ETI is the automatic UL option.

[13] If policy loans or paid-up dividend additions are outstanding, both the face amount and cash value are decreased or increased accordingly.

## Policy Loan Clause

All states require inclusion of policy loan provisions in cash-value policies. The provision usually states, in effect, that (1) the company will lend to the policyowner an amount not to exceed the policy cash value less interest to the next policy anniversary; (2) interest is payable annually at a rate specified in the policy; (3) unpaid interest will be paid automatically by a further loan against the policy's cash value; (4) if the total indebtedness equals or exceeds the cash value, the policy will terminate, subject to 31 days' notice to the policyowner; and (5) the policyowner may repay the loan either in whole or in part at any time. Policy loans can be a source of flexibility for the policyowner. No one need approve the loan and it is confidential.

The amount available for loan usually is predicated on the policy's cash value, including the cash value of any paid-up additions. A policy loan is not actually due and repayable until either the policy itself matures or the total indebtedness, including unpaid interest, equals or exceeds the cash value. The automatic continuation of the loan is one of the unique features of policy loans.

*Policy Loan Interest Rate.* The policy loan interest rate or the procedure for determining it is required to be specified in the policy. In the past, state law limited the maximum interest rate that insurers could assess on policy loans to below-market rates. When market rates are above the contractual policy loan rate, a natural economic incentive is created to borrow at the favorable policy loan interest rate and to invest the proceeds at the higher market interest rate. The practice, known as **disintermediation**, occurs periodically, especially on older policies that carry fixed policy loan rates of 5 or 6 percent. To rectify the imbalance, the NAIC adopted a new **Model Policy Loan Interest Rate Bill** that permits variable interest rate policy loans. All states have enacted this bill or a comparable one.

Under the Model Bill, insurers can change the policy loan interest rate up to four times a year. Companies are required to evaluate the need for a policy loan interest rate change at least once each year. The rate is not permitted to exceed the greater of Moody's Composite Yield on seasoned corporate bonds two months prior to the determination date or the interest rate credited on cash values plus 1 percent. The insurance company is not permitted to increase the applicable policy loan interest rate unless the defined ceiling permits a change of at least one-half of 1 percent upward. The bill does not require the insurance company to increase the policy loan rate whenever it would be permissible, nor does it prohibit insurers from using fixed rates. On the other hand, when interest rates are declining, the legislation requires that the insurance company reduce the variable loan interest rate whenever the ceiling rate has declined to at least one-half of 1 percent below the rate currently being charged on policy loans. This requirement generally assures that the applicable interest rate will decline as market interest rates decline.

Some jurisdictions also have provisions requiring that certain representations be given to the state insurance department for interest rates in excess of 6 percent. Most of them concern a showing that policyowners will benefit through higher dividends, lower premiums, or both.

Enactment of the NAIC Model Bill does not make variable interest rates applicable to policy loans on existing policies. It is applicable only to new policies issued with the variable interest rate provision. As discussed in Chapter 5, several companies have offered their policyowners the variable loan interest rate provision in exchange for more liberal dividends.

*Automatic Premium Loan.* Although it is not usually required, many companies include the **automatic premium loan** (APL) provision that provides that if a premium is unpaid at the end of the grace period, and if the policy has a sufficient cash value, the amount of the premium due will be advanced automatically as a loan against the policy.[14] UL policies, because of their nature, do not have APL provisions.

In some states, the policyowner must specifically elect to make the provision operative. The purpose of the APL provision is to protect against unintentional lapse, as when a premium payment is overlooked. If the policy were allowed to lapse, the nonforfeiture options would be effective, but if the policyowner wanted to reinstate the policy, he or she might have to furnish evidence of insurability satisfactory to the insurer. With the APL, the policyowner need only repay the loan and the original policy death benefit continues. A disadvantage of the APL is that it may tend to encourage laxity in payment of premiums and can result in indebtedness exceeding the cash value. This problem will be recognized as the same type of concern as that existing with UL policies, wherein mortality and expense charges are deducted from the cash value.

*Borrowing Your Own Money?* The policy loan feature of cash-value insurance policies has been the subject of considerable misunderstanding and misinformation. Some persons contend that the insurance company should not charge interest on policy loans, since "you're borrowing your own money." This view is incorrect and demonstrates a lack of understanding of life insurance fundamentals.

Policy loan interest should be charged for two reasons. First, in calculating the premiums to charge the public, life insurers assume in their computations that the assets generated by the total net cash inflows from the policies will be invested and will earn interest. The company discounts (lowers) premiums in advance in anticipation of these interest earnings. If the policyowner removes

---

[14] Rhode Island requires that all new policies issued in that state contain an automatic premium loan provision, unless the policyowner elects otherwise. Maryland requires it to be offered. It is not a statutory requirement in other states.

(via a policy loan) his or her proportionate share of these assets, and if the insurer charged no interest on this loan, then the company's assumptions regarding future earnings on these assets would not be realized. If the insurer did not charge interest for loans, it logically also should not discount premiums in anticipation of future investment earnings. The net result would be that premiums would be significantly higher, but policyowners would not have to pay interest "to borrow their own money."

The second reason for charging policy loan interest is that this policy benefit advance—or loan—should carry an interest charge for the same reason that other loans carry such charges. Although many persons (and even insurance laws and regulations) refer to a policyowner's right to "borrow the policy's cash value," this phraseology is both misleading and wrong. Policyowners cannot borrow their cash values. Rather, they have a contractual right to borrow money from their life insurance company by using their policy's cash values as security for the loan. The transaction is analogous to the holder of a bank certificate of deposit (CD) borrowing the face amount of the CD from the bank on the security of the CD.

## PROVISIONS REGARDING SURPLUS DISTRIBUTION

Virtually all states require that divisible surplus accumulated on behalf of a given block of participating policies be distributed annually to the policyowners. States increasingly are requiring somewhat similar treatment with respect to excess interest and other earnings on UL and the interest-sensitive types of policies. Both participating and interest-sensitive policies are required to have policy provisions relative to distribution of these excess amounts. The functioning of these provisions, as applied to the interest-sensitive types of policies was discussed in Chapter 6, so their treatment here will be brief, focusing chiefly on fixed-premium participating policies. Before discussing the specific options under which surplus is distributed, it is important to understand further details regarding the nature of the surplus distribution process itself.

*Nature of Surplus Distribution.* As pointed out in Chapter 2, surplus under participating policies is derived from any of three possible sources: (1) mortality experience being more favorable than that assumed; (2) expenses being lower than those assumed; and (3) investment earnings being greater than those assumed.

In determining how to apportion divisible surplus (see below), the **contribution principle** should ideally be followed by the company. The principle holds that aggregate divisible surplus should be distributed among policies in the same proportion as the policies are considered to have contributed to surplus.

How the contribution principle is applied to derive individual policy dividends need not be discussed here. While not an exact science, actuarial techniques have been developed that capture the principle's intent,[15] although life insurance policies themselves are silent on this point. Some insurers do not follow the principle. This leads to inequitable treatment of various classes of policies and can be detrimental to particular policyowners.

An insurance company's board of directors determines, in the aggregate, the amount of surplus to be distributed each year to policyowners. This decision is made in light of the company's financial position, profitability objectives, and other factors. Actuarial advice is provided to management and the board to assist in making this decision. Management, with board approval, decides how to apportion the divisible surplus among the various blocks of policies. Insurance policies are silent as to the proportion of total surplus that is to be distributed among policies.

Some states limit the aggregate amount of surplus a mutual life insurer can accumulate to a stated percentage of policy reserves (e.g., 10 percent in New York). Some place similar limitations on stock insurers selling participating life insurance, wherein no more than a stated percentage (e.g., 5 percent) of profits flowing from participating insurance can flow to stockholders. However, most insurance codes are silent on these matters.

Even if divisible surplus or excess interest income is reasonable in amount and if the contribution principle is followed, different methods of allocating mortality charges, expenses, and investment income can produce differing results. Perhaps the most important element in this respect applies to investment income allocation.

As mentioned in Chapter 6, some insurers follow the so-called **portfolio average method** (PAM) of investment income allocation and others follow the **investment generation method** (IGM). The IGM itself has variations, with some insurers including an element of projected earnings while others do not.

The portfolio method develops a more stable dividend pattern than the IGM. In periods of generally rising investment returns, the IGM allows an insurance company to illustrate and pay out higher amounts, other things being equal, than can a company that utilizes the PAM. In periods of declining investment returns, the opposite occurs. If investment returns remain stable over several years, results under the two methods converge. State regulation of these practices is inconsistent. Thus a company could—in theory—change from one method to the other and back again, to take advantage of trends in current interest earnings for purposes of having new policy illustration, appear favorable. The problem, of course, is that older policyowners could suffer from such changes, and new policies become old ones after some years. The NAIC Model Cost Disclosure Regulation attempts to address this potential problem.[16]

[15] See Chap. 21.
[16] See Chap. 10.

*Direct Recognition.* As discussed in Chapter 6, many companies' insurance policies include a **direct recognition provision** that permits the company to recognize directly in its excess interest or dividend formula the extent of policy loan activity within the policy. These provisions increase the effective cost of policy loans and result in higher dividends or excess interest paid under nonborrowing policies. Such provisions link the policy loan and surplus distribution or excess interest provisions, whereas without the provisions they are not *directly* related. This linkage makes loan decisions more complex. Traditional planning techniques must be modified to properly evaluate policy loan economics.[17]

*Dividend Options.* The various options available to policyowners in receiving their policies' share of distributable surplus—the **dividends**—provide policyowners with another potentially important source of flexibility. The five most common dividend options are: (1) pay in cash, (2) offset part (or all) of the premium payment, (3) purchase paid-up additional insurance, (4) accumulate at interest, and (5) purchase one-year term insurance. These options can be changed at any time under most policies. With interest-sensitive policies, excess interest earnings are earmarked to increase the policy's cash value or to reduce the level of future premiums, or both.

*1. Cash.* Most states require that the dividend be made available in cash. Under this option, the insurer mails a check for the dividend to the policyowner each year. Policyowners usually find one of the other options more attractive. This option is more costly for the company to administer.

*2. Apply Toward Premium Payment.* Although applying the dividend toward payment of the next premium under the policy is the economic equivalent of cash, a substantial number of policyowners elect this option to reduce their current outlay of funds. They could, of course, take the dividend in cash and remit the full premium, obtaining the same net effect.

*3. Purchase Paid-Up Additions.* The policyowner may have the dividend applied to the purchase of paid-up additional insurance under the policy. With this option, the dividend is applied as a net single premium at the insured's attained age to purchase as much paid-up insurance as it will provide of the same type as the basic policy.[18]

The right to purchase a series of paid-up additions at net rates can be attractive. This option can be especially attractive for an insured whose health has become impaired. No evidence of insurability is required at the purchase of each additional insurance amount. Paid-up additions themselves may be

---

[17] For one approach to making this evaluation, see Steven Gardiner and Thomas Mahoney, "Policy Loan Planning in the 1980s," *Journal of the American Society of Chartered Life Underwriters,* Vol. XXXIX (Sept. 1985).

[18] In operation, this option resembles the reduced paid-up insurance option that is available in connection with surrender values.

participating or nonparticipating. If they are participating, the annual dividends on the paid-up additions would further enhance the policy's total cash value and death benefit. Most companies permit changes to this option after issue, often without evidence of insurability.

Some individuals do not wish to purchase single-premium life insurance, and paid-up additions, although small in amount, are a type of single-premium life insurance. Some consider it wiser to use dividends to reduce current premiums to permit the purchase of additional annual-premium insurance. Even so, purchasing paid-up additions can be a worthwhile approach to increasing insurance protection. The additions offer further flexibility because of their cash value. This cash value can be obtained, in whole or in part, by selective surrender of the paid-up additions, without disturbing the basic policy.

*4. Accumulate at Interest.* Dividends may be allowed to accumulate at interest under the contract. The insurer guarantees to pay a minimum rate of interest, although companies typically credit higher rates than the guaranteed minimum. These accumulations can be withdrawn at will by the policyowner. If death occurs, the policy's face amount plus dividend accumulations is paid, and, in the event of surrender, the cash value plus dividend accumulations will be paid.

*5. Purchase One-Year Term.* Some companies make available an option to apply the dividend to purchase one-year term insurance. The option takes one of two forms. One form applies the dividend as a net single premium to purchase as much one-year term insurance protection as it will buy. The other form purchases one-year term insurance equal to the policy's cash value, with the excess dividend portion applied under one of the other dividend options. The latter form is often used in connection with sales presentations involving split-dollar insurance (see Chapter 15). The object is to assure the beneficiary payment of an amount equal to the policy face amount if the insured dies, even though the cash value may be fully pledged.

*6. Other Options.* Companies often permit dividends to be used in other ways. One way is to "pay up" the policy earlier than otherwise. This **vanishing premium option** can be elected to pay up the policy when the cash value of the policy (and of any dividend additions) plus any existing dividend accumulations at the end of a policy year equals or exceeds the net single premium for the attained age of the insured (according to a given mortality table and a stipulated rate of interest) for an amount of insurance equal to the policy's face amount.

Another dividend option, the **add-to-cash-value option**, is similar to the paid-up additions option in that it permits the dividend to accumulate additional cash value but, unlike the additions option, involves no additional pure insurance protection. In other words, the option generates only a dollar of additional death benefit for each dollar of additional cash value. This option permits companies selling whole life insurance to match the UL cash value and death benefit growth.

## CREDITOR RIGHTS IN LIFE INSURANCE

The rights of creditors in claiming life insurance funds are determined by (1) the nature of the beneficiary designation, (2) federal bankruptcy laws, and (3) state exemption statutes. The nature of the beneficiary designation and the change-of-beneficiary clause is critically important as viewed from the standpoint of creditors.

### RIGHTS OF THE POLICYOWNER'S CREDITORS

Treatment of debtors in early times was often harsh. The framers of the U.S. Constitution recognized the need for rehabilitation of debtors. Thus bankruptcy laws were designed to provide an equitable distribution of the assets of debtors, while giving them an opportunity for rehabilitation. A revised **Bankruptcy Reform Act**, effective in 1979, codified all previous laws related to bankruptcy under Title 11 of the U.S. code.

The Act permitted states to "opt out" of the code's application, thus limiting bankrupts to the state protection. Most states, in fact, opted out, so that only in about a dozen states does the bankrupt have a choice of electing the state exemption or the Bankruptcy Act's exemption.

*The Federal Bankruptcy Law.* Insolvency is not the same as bankruptcy. Insolvency is the inability to pay one's debts. Bankruptcy is the application of bankruptcy laws to a debtor, who may or may not be insolvent. One becomes bankrupt when one comes under the protection of the bankruptcy laws.

Title to a bankrupt person's property vests in the trustee, the person appointed by the bankruptcy court to take over the bankrupt's estate. The estate may include so-called exempt property at the beginning of the proceedings. Exempt property is excluded from the bankrupt creditor's claims. Section 522 provides the debtor with a choice of either state or federal exemptions. The act provides for, among other provisions, a modest homestead exemption. To avoid discrimination against nonhomeowners, the act provides an equivalent exemption of other property if the homestead exemption and certain other exemptions are not used.

If the insured/policyowner has named a beneficiary other than himself or herself, his or her estate, or his or her legal representatives, and has not reserved the right to change the beneficiary, the beneficiary has a vested interest in the policy, and the creditors of the insured/policyowner have no interest in the insurance proceeds.[19] If the policy is made payable to the insured/policyowner, his or her estate, or legal representatives, it is subject to the claims of creditors in case of bankruptcy, except for any other exemptions. If the insured/policyowner

[19] *Central National Bank of Washington v. Hume*, 128 U.S. 195 (1888); *Morse v. Commissioner of Internal Revenue*, 100 F.2d 593 (1939).

names a beneficiary not in the classes listed above, but reserves the unqualified right to change the beneficiary, the policy will pass to the trustee in bankruptcy if it has a cash surrender value, and to the extent of such value. Except for the application of either federal or state exemption statutes, the courts can be expected to interpret a revocable beneficiary designation as giving the trustee in bankruptcy the power to distribute a policy's cash value among creditors.

When the policy has no cash surrender value, the courts have held that the trustee has no interest in it. In *Morris v. Dobb, trustee*, a husband took out a policy payable to his legal representatives and subsequently transferred it to his wife four months prior to filing a bankruptcy petition. The policy had no cash value, and the court ruled that the trustee had no interest in the policy.[20]

Cases often arise wherein, shortly following the filing of the petition in bankruptcy, a policy payable to the insured/policyowner or his or her representatives matures through the death of the bankrupt. In this instance, are the creditors entitled to the policy proceeds? The question was decided by the Supreme Court and incorporated into the Bankruptcy Reform Act.[21] According to current law, the trustee in bankruptcy obtains title only to the net cash surrender value of the policy at the time of the filing of the bankruptcy petition. The trustee's interest does not extend to any other policy values, such as the protection afforded on the insured's life.

The Bankruptcy Reform Act also reserves to the bankrupt an aggregate interest (originally $4,000) in life insurance policies on his or her life. Amounts in excess of this are payable to creditors unless they are exempted by state laws.

From the standpoint of protection from creditors, whether one should retain the right to change beneficiaries will largely depend on the exemption laws of the state as well as those of the federal bankruptcy law. Although failure to retain the right to change the beneficiary puts the proceeds and cash values of life insurance policies beyond the reach of creditors, it greatly limits the insurance policy's usefulness. The free use of an insurance policy may outweigh the benefit of it being secured from protection from creditors. When life insurance is only a modest part of a developing estate, the right to change beneficiaries often should be reserved, so that the policy can be available as an asset with free assignability. As the insured/policyowner begins to expand his or her business activity, the desirability of retaining this feature of the policies can be reviewed. In any event, a change of ownership may be preferred to an irrevocable beneficiary designation.

***State Exemption Statutes.*** From earliest times, Congress has deferred to state exemption statutes. The National Bankruptcy Act of 1898 had a provision to this effect, which has been retained in the latest Bankruptcy Reform Act.[22]

---

[20] 110 Ga. 606, quoted *In Re Buelow*, 98 Fed. 86 (1900); *Burlingham v. Crouse*, 228 U.S. 459 (1913).

[21] See, e.g., *Burlingham v. Crouse*, 228 U.S. 459 (1913); *United States v. Binham*, 76 F. 2d 573 (1935).

[22] 198 U.S. 202 (1905); *Meyer v. U.S.*, 375 U.S. 233, 239 (1963); *In the matter of Marvin M. Summers, Bankrupt*, 253 F.Supp. 113 (1966).

State exemption statutes protect policy values from the claims of the policyowner's creditors even if the policyowner is not bankrupt, although the bulk of litigation has involved bankruptcy. Such statutes vary substantially from state to state, so generalizations are limited.

Almost all states provide protection for a policy's cash values, with many of the statutes modeled after that of New York. Previously, many statutes limited protection to the spouse and children, but most states no longer follow this practice.

Most state laws do not require that the policyowner must have relinquished the right to change the beneficiary for the policy values to be exempt. However, they often do require that the beneficiary be a member of a specified class entitled to protection under the statute.

The right to procure a policy's cash surrender value has been held to be a right that is purely personal to the policyowner. It is a condition precedent in the insurance contract whereby the insurance company does not develop any obligations until certain procedures are observed. Accordingly, no debt is due the policyowner from the insurance company until the policyowner has created the debt by the exercise of the option.[23] Similarly, the cash surrender value of an endowment insurance policy is not a vested interest and thus not an asset of the bankrupt debtor.[24] Any payments, however, made to the policyowner, such as cash surrender values or dividends that have been deposited to the debtor's account, typically are not exempt.

Many statutes are quite brief. For example, Nebraska provides that "all and every benefit accruing under any annuity contract or any other policy . . . shall be exempt from attachment . . . and all claims of creditors and of beneficiary if related by blood or marriage."[25]

Under the laws of California, Indiana, Ohio, Maine, New York, Washington, Wisconsin, and other states, endowment policies are included in the exemptions granted to the debtor.[26] However, the cash values of annuities, generally, are not protected unless expressly provided for by statute.

Some of the laws providing exemption are applicable only if the named beneficiary is of a certain class, such as the individual's spouse or children or a dependent relative. Others are broader in scope. A few enactments limit the amount of the annual premiums payable for exempt insurance. Under other statutes, the limitation is based on the total amount of insurance proceeds instead of on the amount of annual premiums paid, although such policy amount limitations are becoming less common.

---

[23] R.C.W.A. 48.18.410. *In re Elliott*, 446 P.2d 347, 72 Wash.2d 600 (1968).

[24] *In re Privett*, C.A. Okla., 435 F.2d 261 (1970).

[25] Law of 1933, amended 1941, Sec. 44–37.

[26] 30 A.L.R.2d 751 (1952); Am. Jur.2d, Bankruptcy §666.

## RIGHTS OF THE BENEFICIARY'S CREDITORS

*Prior to Maturity*. In the absence of a statute exempting the proceeds or cash values of life insurance from the claims of the beneficiary's creditors, the question of whether such creditors can reach the cash value depends upon whether the beneficiary possesses a property right in the policy. If the beneficiary does not possess such a right in the policy, his or her creditors cannot reach the cash values. Remember that a revocable beneficiary has a mere expectancy, and consequently no property right exists to be attached. Even in the case of an irrevocably named beneficiary, creditors of such a beneficiary cannot reach the cash value of the policy, since the beneficiary does not possess the right to obtain the cash value without the consent of the owner.

*At Maturity.* The rights of a beneficiary, whether designated revocably or irrevocably, vest absolutely at the insured's death. In the absence of an exempting statutory provision, the beneficiary's creditors are entitled to the insurance proceeds as soon as that right vests in the beneficiary.[27]

Some of the state laws exempting life insurance proceeds and avails from claims of creditors expressly refer only to creditors of the policyowner/insured. However, many states have broad statutes that exempt the proceeds of life insurance against the creditors of both the insured and the beneficiary. Most such statutes limit the exempt insurance to a stated amount, and some apply the beneficiary's exemption only to group life insurance proceeds. State statutes frequently provide that proceeds payable to beneficiaries under fraternal benefit policies are exempt from claims of creditors.

## SPECIAL PRIORITIES AND CONSTRAINTS

The general rules applying to creditors' rights in life insurance cash values and proceeds do not apply to federal tax liens and situations involving misappropriated funds. Also, most states will permit the use of spendthrift trust clauses to protect life insurance proceeds from creditors of the beneficiary.

*Tax Liens.* The tax collector takes a dim view of anyone, dead or alive, who fails to pay taxes due. Under a federal government tax lien, the government need not prove that the debtor or taxpayer is insolvent when it places levies on the taxpayer's assets. If the policyowner/insured retains certain rights under a policy of insurance, these rights can be reached by the government,[28] even in the face of

---

[27] *Murray v. Wells*, 53 Iowa 256 (1880); §640; 57 A.L.R. 692. In the case of *Holmes, appellant v. Marshall*, 145 Cal. 777 (1905), the court held that under certain conditions, the exemption extends "not only against the debts of the person whose life was insured, and who paid the premiums, but also to the debts of the beneficiary to whom it is payable after the death of the insured." See also S. Dak. L. Ch. 58–12–4 (1966).

[28] 26 U.S.C.A. (I.R.C. 1954), §7403; *U.S. v. Sterkowica*, 266 F. Supp. 703 (1967); Appleman, *Insurance Law and Practice*, §10905.

state exemption statutes. Under federal tax lien law, life insurance companies are required to pay to the federal government the net cash surrender values of policies as of the time of judgment.

*Misappropriation of Funds.* While beneficiaries' rights in life insurance proceeds have been greatly enlarged by legislation, it is contrary to public policy to permit life insurance to shelter assets that equitably belong to another. Thus when premiums are paid from misappropriated funds, the right to follow the embezzled funds is not lost merely because the money was used to buy life insurance.

In general, the aggrieved party can follow the wrongfully acquired funds and enforce its rights against the proceeds under the constructive or resulting trust theory. Under this theory, the person holding the funds does so as a trustee for the other party.

Little uniformity exists as to the amount of recovery. In some cases, the premiums paid by the policyowner following his or her insolvency were obtainable by the aggrieved party, and in others, the aggrieved obtained proceeds in the proportion that the premiums paid subsequent to the insolvency bore to the sum total of the premiums paid on the policy. Thus when a policyowner's clear intention is to defraud his or her creditors by taking out insurance or by assigning it, the beneficiary is not protected against claims of the policyowner's creditors.

*Spendthrift Trust Clause.* In addition to the broad statutes that exempt life insurance proceeds from the claims of the creditors of both the insured and the beneficiary, a majority of states permit policyowners to include in the policy installment settlement provisions a so-called **spendthrift trust clause**, which will protect the proceeds from claims of the beneficiary's creditors.

The clause can be attached to a policy in the form of an endorsement or rider and becomes a part of the policy. Under the clause, the beneficiary has no power to assign, transfer, or otherwise encumber the payments. The payments are not subject to any legal process, execution, garnishment, or attachment proceedings. In a majority of states, the provisions extend only to beneficiaries other than the policyowner. Otherwise, such a device could be used by a policyowner to defraud creditors.

If the mode of settlement is selected by the beneficiary, the payments received are not secure from the claims of the beneficiary's creditors, as is the case of the spendthrift trust arrangement. The spendthrift clause protects only the money being held by the insurance company. Once money is paid to the beneficiary, it loses its distinction as unpaid life insurance proceeds.

The outstanding characteristic of spendthrift statutes is the permissive nature of the exemption. The company and the policyowner must agree on the exemption before it can become operative. Practically, this means that the policyowner must insert the clause in the policy's installment settlement provisions. Such clauses severely restrict the beneficiary's prerogatives under the settlement payout. The spendthrift trust clause should be used only after appropriate consideration of other planning objectives.

In the majority of states in which no statute exists, the courts have upheld the use of spendthrift clauses. In only a few states are the clauses not valid, and even in these a discretionary trust may be used to accomplish the same thing.

# Chapter 10

# LIFE INSURANCE AND ANNUITY COST ANALYSIS AND DISCLOSURE

The preceding two chapters presented the legal and operational aspects of life insurance contracts, an understanding of which is essential to sound policy evaluation. This chapter continues the policy evaluation theme, but considers life insurance policies from a cost standpoint.

## THE LIFE INSURANCE PURCHASE DECISION

Many individuals shop carefully before deciding on the type and amount of life insurance to buy and from whom to buy it. However, the majority of buyers do little or no comparison shopping and may make unsound decisions regarding the particular type and amount of life insurance to buy or the insurance company from which to buy it. A little knowledge often can result in substantial savings.

Making a wise life insurance purchase decision is not easy. One must first decide whether any life insurance is needed. If some life insurance is appropriate, the *amount* must be decided upon next. (These two issues are analyzed in Chapter 12.)

Questions must also be answered as to the *type* of insurance to buy and *from whom* to buy it. These decisions typically involve discussions with one or more life insurance agents and a determination as to how much to spend for life insurance, as well as an assessment of the possible cost of the life insurance being considered.

The buyer should not necessarily seek that mirage called "the best buy." Rather, the buyer should seek a policy that seems reasonably priced in relation to other policies available from other sound life insurance companies.

**LIFE INSURANCE POLICY COST ANALYSIS**

### THE NEED FOR COST COMPARISONS

Life insurance policy costs can vary greatly. Cost variations can result from differences in company operational efficiency, investment performance, underwriting policy, profit objectives, the costs associated with marketing, and a host of other variables. A higher-cost policy may reflect either better value or simply an expensive policy with little or no justifiably offsetting benefits.

Many life insurance purchasers do not procure relatively low-cost, high-quality policies because:

1. They are unaware of cost and quality differences,

2. They engage in little or no comparison shopping, or

3. They have difficulty estimating costs and product quality.

Although awareness is rising, many consumers remain unaware of the quality and cost differences among life insurance policies. Product quality includes the solidity, service, and performance characteristics of the company backing the policy, plus the policy's terms, conditions, and benefits. Consumers often erroneously equate a policy's premium with its cost, thereby indicating a basic ignorance concerning the other factors entering into cost determination. The premium is a measure of the annual outlay for a policy, not its cost. Cost includes all elements of a policy (premiums, death benefits, cash values, and dividends), not just premiums.

Because many consumers are unaware of cost and quality differences, they engage in little or no comparison shopping. This failure to shop carefully for life insurance often results ultimately in a dissatisfied customer who lapses or replaces his or her insurance.

Consumers are far from alone in encountering difficulty in estimating policy costs and quality. Policy cost and quality are inextricably bound with insurer quality. The discussion in Chapter 11 on insurance company evaluation is, therefore, critical to any policy evaluation. With this fact in mind, an evaluation of estimated policy cost is nonetheless important.

### COMMON METHODS FOR COMPARING POLICY COSTS

The objective of any method used to compare the cost of one life insurance policy with that of another is to guide a prospective policyowner to a competitively priced policy or group of policies. The cost of life insurance to any individual is dependent on that particular individual's unique circumstances and the actual cash flows experienced under the policy. This can be determined only after the contract terminates by death, maturity, or surrender. For this reason, many experts contend that the best means of estimating future policy performance should include an evaluation of the past performance of the insurer's policies.

Past performance is often a useful indication of likely future performance, and any evaluation of a potential policy ideally should include an examination of the insurer's historical record with respect to older policies. This information sometimes can be obtained from various publications, especially those of the A.M. Best Company. Unfortunately, relevant historical policy information often is unavailable for a variety of reasons: the particular policy under review may have been sold for only a short time period; the insurer itself may be relatively new; or the data are not published. Even if available, the data may be irrelevant since the insurer's philosophy or performance characteristics may have changed.

No method of comparing life insurance costs takes into consideration all possible purchase decision factors. Cost information should be supplemented with benefit and other information. However, the reader should start with an appreciation of some of the more common cost comparison methods. Eight methods are discussed in this chapter. Other cost comparison methods exist, but they are not covered here.[1] With one exception, the methods can be useful in appropriate circumstances as an aid in life insurance policy cost evaluation. A summary table at the end of this section highlights the main characteristics of each method.

*Traditional Net Cost Method*. The **traditional net cost** (TNC) method, in use for years, is the easiest cost comparison method to understand and calculate, but it also can be the most misleading. To derive cost estimates under the TNC method, one adds the illustrated premiums over a stated time period (usually 10 or 20 years) and subtracts from this figure the sum of the policy's illustrated dividends, if any, taken to the end of the period. From this result is subtracted the policy's illustrated cash value (and terminal dividends, if any) at the end of the chosen period. Dividing by the face amount (in thousands) and the number of years in the time period yields the TNC per thousand per year.[2]

The TNC method is sometimes used to compare the costs of two or more life insurance policies. Although the traditional method can be helpful for determining income tax liabilities[3] under a single life insurance policy, its results are misleading when used to estimate policy costs. By ignoring the time value of money, it fails to weight fairly life insurance policy fund flows. Moreover, the TNC can be manipulated easily by lowering dividends or cash values on policies in their early years and increasing them in later years, thus appearing to lower policy costs. Use of this method for comparing policy costs is illegal in most states.

[1] See, for example, Society of Actuaries, *Analysis of Life Insurance Cost Comparison Index Methods* (1974).

[2] See formula 1 in the chapter appendix for the TNC formula.

[3] See Chap. 13.

A variation of the TNC method is often used in policy illustrations. Many insurance companies and agents include in their illustrations a column that shows the policy's annual increase in cash value netted against that particular year's net premium (i.e., gross premium less illustrated dividend). The buyer may infer or the agent may imply that the year's increase in cash value is due solely or chiefly to that year's premium payment. This usually is untrue since the increase may be due chiefly to interest credited to the cash value, not the premium payment.

*Interest-Adjusted Net Cost Method.* The **interest adjusted net cost** (IANC) method was developed to correct for the omission within the TNC method of the time value of money. The IANC analysis, like the TNC analysis, is conducted over set time periods (typically, 10 and 20 years) and considers a policy's estimated premiums, death benefits, cash values, and dividends in much the same manner as the TNC method, except that interest is recognized.

To calculate a policy's IANC (also called the **surrender cost index**), the premiums and illustrated dividends are accumulated at some assumed interest rate over the selected time period. The accumulated dividends are subtracted from the accumulated premiums. From this figure is subtracted the cash value (and illustrated terminal dividend, if any) at the end of the time period. The result of this calculation is then divided by the value of one accumulated per year for the time period at the assumed interest rate and by the face amount in thousands.[4] If the interest rate assumed in the IANC analysis were zero, the policy's TNC would be obtained.

The NAIC **Life Insurance Disclosure Model Regulation** (see below) requires that there be two interest-adjusted cost indices for a policy: a surrender cost index and **net payment cost index**. The payment index is an estimate of the average annual net premium outlay (premium less illustrated annual dividend), adjusted by interest to reflect the time when premiums and dividends are paid during a 10- or 20-year period. The surrender cost index is the payment index less the annualized equivalent of the cash value available to the policyowner at the end of the 10- or 20-year period, adjusted for interest. Interest-adjusted indices can be of value in showing the relative estimated costs of two or more similar policies.

The IANC method can be used to compare similar policies only, since a fair comparison requires approximately equal outlays.[5] The IANC method has other limitations. The method is subject to manipulation in much the same way as, although to a lesser extent than, the TNC method. As with other methods, it provides a valid measure of cost only over the time period chosen and then only if all assumptions proved to be fact, which is highly unlikely.

---

[4] See formula 2 in the chapter appendix for the IANC formula.

[5] If outlays were held approximately equal for two policies, one of which had a significantly lower premium than the other (i.e., they were dissimilar), some form of "side fund" arrangement would be necessary under the lower premium policy. If a fair comparison were to be made, this, in turn, would necessitate an adjustment downward in the lower-premium policy's face amount to maintain approximately equal total death benefits under each plan. For further details, see the discussion later in this chapter on the cash accumulation method.

IANC indices (both surrender and net payment) are often shown on both a guaranteed and an illustrated (or projected) basis. As mentioned below, this is required under the latest NAIC model disclosure regulation. The previous NAIC model regulation effectively required the same thing. It mandates that an **equivalent level annual dividend** (ELAD) be shown. The ELAD is interpreted as that portion of the pricing of a participating policy that is not guaranteed. It represents the average annual illustrated dividend, weighted for the time value of money. It is calculated by accumulating the annual illustrated dividends at interest and dividing the result by the appropriate interest factor to obtain a level annual equivalent to the (nonlevel) illustrated dividends.[6]

Table 10-1 shows IANC figures at 5 percent for policies whose gross premiums per $1,000 appeared in Table 5-2. Observe that (1) little relationship exists between premiums charged and projected net costs, and (2) net costs vary greatly among these similar policies.

Policy A's gross premium is $11.83 per $1,000 of insurance, and its projected 20-year IANC is $1.36 per $1,000. This 1.36 index can be interpreted as follows. If a 35-year-old male bought this ordinary life policy and paid the stipulated premium for 20 years and, at that time, surrendered the policy, the policyowner's average annual cost per $1,000 of insurance would have been $1.36, *assuming* that dividends were paid exactly as illustrated and, furthermore, that the policyowner valued money at 5 percent per year (the interest rate specified by most states' life insurance cost disclosure regulations). *Cost* here means the average annual amount estimated to be retained by the insurer for its benefit payments, expenses, and profit.

**TABLE 10-1**    **INTEREST-ADJUSTED NET COST FIGURES FOR SELECTED ORDINARY LIFE POLICIES (FROM TABLE 5-2, AGE 35, MALE, $25,000)**

| Type of Policy | Company | Gross Premium per $1,000 | 20-Year IANC per $1,000 |
|---|---|---|---|
| Participating | A | $ 11.83 | $ 1.36 |
| | B | 13.95 | 1.28 |
| | C | 14.20 | 0.34 |
| | D | 15.66 | 1.20 |
| | E | 16.01 | 2.76 |
| | F | 21.68 | 5.49 |
| Nonparticipating | G | 10.70 | 3.99 |
| | H | 11.37 | 1.47 |
| | I | 12.22 | 6.63 |
| | J | 14.04 | 6.06 |
| | K | 17.00 | 9.45 |
| | L | 18.60 | 8.98 |

*Source*: A. M. Best Co.

[6] See formula 4 in the chapter appendix.

An understanding of the interest-adjusted method is important because its indices are required to be provided to prospective life insurance purchasers in the majority of states in the United States, and, even in those states without such a requirement, many insurers routinely provide the indices on their policy illustrations. The method is not commonly used by agents and financial consultants when they prepare their own cost comparisons between two or more policies. Other methods, some of which are discussed below, are usually more suitable, especially when dissimilar policies are being compared.

*Equal Outlay Method.*[7] One method used by some planners to compare the costs of two or more policies is the **equal outlay method** (EOM). This method assumes that equal amounts of money are expended under each of two or more proposed insurance arrangements. It can be used to compare both similar and dissimilar policies, although not without some problems. When both policies have flexible-premium payments, both premiums and face amounts can be set at the same levels, thereby permitting the comparison to focus on the competing policies' surrender values at specific future points. Other things being the same, the policy with the larger illustrated future values is preferred.

Table 10-2 illustrates this approach. Cash surrender values on two universal life (UL) policies are shown on two bases: guaranteed and current. The planned annual outlay for both policies is illustrated as $1,000 per year and death benefits are set at $100,000 per year. Both policies guarantee a minimum interest rate of 4.0 percent and currently credit 9.0 percent. On both bases, policy B illustrates greater values at every duration. Thus, other things being the same (e.g., credibility of illustrations, contract provisions, agent service, company quality, etc.), policy B would be preferred to policy A.

The EOM is also used to compare the illustrated values of two or more policies when one policy is a fixed-premium contract. The premiums for the flexible-premium policy are set to be equal to those for the fixed policy. The flexible premium pattern could be assumed to track exactly either the fixed-premium policy gross premium or net premium (yearly premium less illustrated dividend) pattern. Future cash values then can be compared as they were under the previous example.

As a practical matter, such comparisons are only rarely made on the basis that both future premium and death benefit patterns are equalized. The usual way is to hold outlays constant and set only *initial* policy death benefits approximately equal. One would normally attempt to obtain only a close match of subsequent death benefit amounts.

With the use of this method, for example, the ordinary life policy illustrated in Table 5-3 could be compared with the Table 10-2 UL policy. If future results followed exactly those illustrated for both policies, the UL policy would afford higher values than would the ordinary life policy. Of course, the likelihood of

---

[7] This term is that of the authors and is not necessarily used generally.

**TABLE 10-2     EQUAL OUTLAY METHOD: TWO UNIVERSAL LIFE POLICIES**
**(FOR 35-YEAR-OLD NONSMOKING MALE)**

| Year | Policies A and B | | Cash Surrender Values | | | |
|---|---|---|---|---|---|---|
| | Planned Annual Premium | Annual Death Benefits | Guaranteed Basis | | Current Basis | |
| | | | Policy A (4%) | Policy B (4%) | Policy A (9%) | Policy B (9%) |
| 1 | $1,000 | $100,000 | $ 123 | $ 718 | $ 125 | $ 789 |
| 2 | 1,000 | 100,000 | 798 | 1,493 | 950 | 1,714 |
| 3 | 1,000 | 100,000 | 1,485 | 2,249 | 1,844 | 2,720 |
| 4 | 1,000 | 100,000 | 2,181 | 3,018 | 2,813 | 3,807 |
| 5 | 1,000 | 100,000 | 2,888 | 3,796 | 3,862 | 4,988 |
| 6 | 1,000 | 100,000 | 3,588 | 4,581 | 4,996 | 6,253 |
| 7 | 1,000 | 100,000 | 4,294 | 5,367 | 6,221 | 7,686 |
| 8 | 1,000 | 100,000 | 4,999 | 6,157 | 7,543 | 9,116 |
| 9 | 1,000 | 100,000 | 5,700 | 6,944 | 8,971 | 10,788 |
| 10 | 1,000 | 100,000 | 6,396 | 7,739 | 10,513 | 12,479 |
| 11 | 1,000 | 100,000 | 7,098 | 8,510 | 12,179 | 14,359 |
| 12 | 1,000 | 100,000 | 7,755 | 9,882 | 13,982 | 16,394 |
| 13 | 1,000 | 100,000 | 8,409 | 10,038 | 15,936 | 18,595 |
| 14 | 1,000 | 100,000 | 9,039 | 10,778 | 18,058 | 20,979 |
| 15 | 1,000 | 100,000 | 9,638 | 11,488 | 20,349 | 23,548 |
| 16 | 1,000 | 100,000 | 10,201 | 12,159 | 22,839 | 26,338 |
| 17 | 1,000 | 100,000 | 10,719 | 12,795 | 25,542 | 29,361 |
| 18 | 1,000 | 100,000 | 11,185 | 13,385 | 28,479 | 32,644 |
| 19 | 1,000 | 100,000 | 11,590 | 13,922 | 31,671 | 36,807 |
| 20 | 1,000 | 100,000 | 11,926 | 14,396 | 35,141 | 40,079 |

actual future values tracking the illustrated values is slight. The UL policy's projected values are based on new money interest assumptions, while the ordinary life policy's illustrated future values are based on the insurer's current portfolio rate of return. Thus, if one believed that new money rates were likely to remain at the UL level, the UL projections could roughly be realized. However, if this occurred, dividends actually paid under the ordinary life policy presumably would be higher than those illustrated. No cost comparison method can adequately address this problem of incompatability, which really relates to the assumptions that underlie illustrative pricing rather than to the specific comparison method chosen.

The equal outlay method also can be used to compare two or more fixed-premium policies or a flexible-premium and a fixed-premium contract wherein the fixed contract's premium is below the minimum required for the flexible contract. The procedure is often used in making "term versus whole life" comparisons and "term versus universal life" comparisons. The method can be used for any two policies in which one has a higher premium than the other. It can be simpler than techniques discussed below, but it also can result in unfair comparisons, as will be explained.

To illustrate, assume that our trusty 35-year-old male nonsmoker is interested in comparing a yearly renewable term (YRT) policy with an ordinary life policy. The aggregate YRT premiums shown in Table 4-2 and the ordinary life premiums and values from Table 5-3 are used. The equal outlay procedure requires that the outlays for the two plans be equal. This is accomplished by assuming that annual differences between the higher-premium policy and the lower-premium policy are accumulated each year at some reasonable after-tax rate of return. The outlays for the two arrangements are thus held equal.

Table 10-3 illustrates this procedure by assuming that dividends on the ordinary life policy are used to purchase paid-up additional insurance. The ordinary life's annual premium is $1,533, and the initial premium for the YRT policy is $145. The difference is $1,388. The difference in the second year's premiums is $1,385. This difference is added to that of the previous year's fund balance ($1,388 plus interest of $83) to yield a beginning fund balance for policy year 2 of $2,856 (not shown). This procedure is continued for several more years.

Table 10-3 shows that side fund values are projected to be greater than those of the whole life policy through policy year 12. From policy year 13 onward, the whole life's illustrated cash values are greater than the side fund's projected balance.

The analysis is not unbiased, since the YRT arrangement provides a higher death benefit in the early years for the same outlay. To have a fair comparison, total death benefits should be held equal. One could then simply compare the future estimated values, as in the case of the two UL policies. If this were done, either the face amount of the higher-premium policy should be increased to that of the term-plus-side-fund death benefit or the term policy face amount should be decreased. Either approach would result in slightly more money being credited to the side fund.[8]

An attempt, however, is made to maintain only approximate equality of death benefits. This is usually accomplished by using dividends under participating policies to purchase paid-up additions or one-year insurance equal to the policy's cash value. This also could be handled by attaching a cost-of-living feature to the policy.

The term arrangement's total projected death benefits exceed those of the ordinary life policy through policy year 10 and, as with the side fund balance, exceeds the ordinary life figures by substantial amounts in the early policy years. The ordinary life's illustrated death benefits become substantially greater than those under the YRT arrangement in later years.

Where does this analysis leave us? First, if the need for insurance is, say, for 11 years or less, the YRT arrangement seems superior based on illustrated

---

[8]In the first instance, the whole life premium would need to be raised to support the higher face amount, which would mean more money for the side fund. In the second instance, the term premium would be lowered to support the lower face amount, thus resulting in the premium savings being available for the side fund.

**TABLE 10-3  EQUAL OUTLAY METHOD: ORDINARY LIFE AND YRT (FROM TABLES 4-2 AND 5-3)**

| (1) | (2) | (3) | (4) | (5) | (6) | (7) | (8) |
|---|---|---|---|---|---|---|---|
| | | | | Plan Values | | Death Benefits | |
| Year | Ordinary Life Premium | YRT Premium | Difference Between Premiums | Difference Compounded at 6 percent | Ordinary Life Cash Surrender Value[a] | YRT Plus Side-Fund[b] | Ordinary Life with Paid-Up Additions |
| 1 | $1,533 | $145 | $1,388 | $1,471 | $ 15 | $101,471 | $100,078 |
| 2 | 1,533 | 148 | 1,385 | 3,028 | 1,195 | 103,028 | 100,550 |
| 3 | 1,533 | 154 | 1,379 | 4,671 | 2,515 | 104,671 | 101,410 |
| 4 | 1,533 | 162 | 1,371 | 6,405 | 3,991 | 106,405 | 102,655 |
| 5 | 1,533 | 172 | 1,361 | 8,232 | 5,634 | 108,232 | 104,285 |
| 6 | 1,533 | 185 | 1,348 | 10,154 | 7,456 | 110,154 | 106,286 |
| 7 | 1,533 | 200 | 1,333 | 12,177 | 9,476 | 112,177 | 108,661 |
| 8 | 1,533 | 219 | 1,314 | 14,300 | 11,704 | 114,300 | 111,393 |
| 9 | 1,533 | 242 | 1,291 | 16,526 | 14,163 | 116,526 | 114,491 |
| 10 | 1,533 | 268 | 1,265 | 18,859 | 16,870 | 118,859 | 117,938 |
| 11 | 1,533 | 288 | 1,245 | 21,310 | 19,843 | 121,310 | 121,743 |
| 12 | 1,533 | 333 | 1,200 | 23,861 | 23,100 | 123,861 | 125,869 |
| 13 | 1,533 | 373 | 1,160 | 26,522 | 26,664 | 126,522 | 130,325 |
| 14 | 1,533 | 417 | 1,116 | 29,296 | 30,534 | 129,296 | 135,033 |
| 15 | 1,533 | 466 | 1,067 | 32,185 | 34,733 | 132,185 | 139,997 |
| 16 | 1,533 | 521 | 1,012 | 35,189 | 39,287 | 135,189 | 145,215 |
| 17 | 1,533 | 581 | 952 | 38,309 | 44,224 | 138,309 | 150,700 |
| 18 | 1,533 | 646 | 887 | 41,509 | 49,571 | 141,548 | 156,454 |
| 19 | 1,533 | 716 | 817 | 44,907 | 55,359 | 144,907 | 162,486 |
| 20 | 1,533 | 791 | 742 | 48,388 | 61,621 | 148,388 | 168,807 |

[a] Guaranteed cash surrender value plus illustrated cash surrender value of paid-up additional insurance.

[b] $100,000 YRT face amount plus column 5.

values and the stated assumptions. This result is expected and would be found with most forms of whole life versus term comparisons. Whole life and universal life policies usually have low early cash surrender values because of high acquisition and other first-year expenses.

On the other hand, this ordinary life policy's relative position appears to improve continuously from a cost standpoint (based on these assumptions) as time passes. However, an unequivocal endorsement of the ordinary life policy could not be made, even if future values were fixed and the planning horizon were longer than 10 or 12 years, because the equal outlay method is incapable of rendering totally fair comparisons if total death benefits cross at any point in the analysis. It is possible that the additional amounts available to a side fund, brought about by causing the early death benefits to be equal, would more than make up for the later inferior position of the YRT arrangement.

In such ambiguous cases, the analyst may be compelled to use the cash accumulation or other methods that adjust for unequal death benefits (see below). However, the other methods require a computer. This method does not.

As with all cost comparison methods, the EOM is no better than the assumptions that underlie the calculations. The assumptions used here will seem reasonable for some persons and during certain economic times, but not for others. Since this method relies on illustrated future values, great care should be taken to avoid ascribing unwarranted precision to the analysis. Furthermore, this method, like others, is only one of the tools available in making the purchase decision. Other important quantitative and qualitative factors also should be considered, such as the professionalism of the agent, the quality of the company, and contractual provisions.

The analyses above and elsewhere do not actually require an individual to save the difference in premiums. Whether a given individual chooses actually to create a side fund is a human rather than costing decision.

*Cash Accumulation Method.* The **cash accumulation method** (CAM) is a more sophisticated cost comparison method than the equal outlay method.[9] The CAM functions in the same way as the EOM in that (1) outlays for two (or more) plans being compared are set at equal levels, (2) annual premium differences are accumulated at some assumed interest rate, and (3) one simply observes the cash value/side-fund differences over time in an effort to draw meaningful cost-based conclusions. The CAM corrects, however, for the unequal death benefit bias of the equal outlay method. The face amount of the lower-premium policy (e.g., term) is hypothetically adjusted each year so that the sum of the side fund and the new face amount of the term policy exactly equals the face amount of the higher-premium (e.g., whole life) policy. In the early policy years, this often means that the lower premium policy's face amount will be declining.[10]

---

[9] See Michael L. Murray, "Analyzing the Investment Value of Cash Value Life Insurance," *The Journal of Risk and Insurance*, Vol. XLIII (Mar. 1976), pp. 121-128.

[10] This decline sometimes is reversed. The direction and magnitude of the face amount change is a function of the relative costliness of the policies being compared.

Table 10-4 illustrates the CAM applied to the same two policies as in Table 10-3. The 6 percent after-tax interest assumption is maintained. The outlays are held at the same level by accumulating the annual differences at interest, as are the total illustrated death benefits (columns 8 and 9). This eliminates the bias in Table 10-3 against the YRT plan that existed in the early policy years.[11] As a result of a lower YRT face amount and, thereby, a lower YRT premium in early years, the accumulated differences are larger than with the EOM comparison.

Under this CAM comparison, one observes that the illustrated cash surrender value of the ordinary life policy first exceeds the projected side fund balance in policy year 13, and that by policy year 20 the projected difference between the two values has widened, reaching $13,826 ($61,621 less $47,795). Although not shown here, differences past year 20 track a similar pattern.

In the early policy years, there appears to be a clear cost advantage for the term arrangement, and, as expected, the advantage is even greater than that which existed under the equal outlay method. Since the death benefits under each plan are held equal, one can focus on the fund versus cash value differences.

Which plan is the better buy? The best answer is: "It depends." If the prospective purchaser is more interested in short- to medium-term results, the term arrangement appears superior, *based on the stated assumptions and with other things being the same.* If a longer-term view is taken, the ordinary life plan may be the preferred approach, *based on the stated assumptions and with other things being equal.* It should be remembered that in all cost analyses, the benefits surrounding the policies being compared are assumed to be the same. This is rarely the case.

The interest rate assumed in the analysis can be of crucial importance. Table 10-5 shows 10- and 20-year figures for the column 5 (accumulated differences) and column 6 (ordinary life cash surrender) values in Table 10-4 at various interest rates. The variations in values can be great. At an after-tax interest rate between 7 and 8 percent over the 20-year period, the benefit swings in favor of the term arrangement.

A comment should be made about the process of equalizing death benefits. In effect, few purchasers of term insurance actually would cancel (or add) portions of term coverage each year to match exactly the side fund change. This would not only be inconvenient, but it could result in the policy face amount falling below the required company minimum amount. The CAM does not actually *require* that the term policy's face amount be changed each year, or any year. Neither the CAM nor any other cost comparison method is intended to dictate how an insurance program should be structured; this is a separate

---

[11] Although not a problem with this analysis (since dividends are earmarked to purchase paid-up additional insurance), any dividends paid in cash or accumulated at interest should be included as a part of the total death benefit if the insurer pays such dividends on death. Similarly, terminal dividends paid on death should be included. Any regular or terminal dividends paid on policy surrender should also be included as a part of the surrender value.

TABLE 10-4 CASH ACCUMULATION METHOD: ORDINARY LIFE AND YRT (FROM TABLES 4-2 AND 5-3)

| (1) | (2) | (3) | (4) | (5) | (6) | (7) | (8) | (9) |
|---|---|---|---|---|---|---|---|---|
| | | | | Plan Values | | | Death Benefits | |
| Year | Ordinary Life Premium | YRT Premium | Difference Between Premiums | Difference Compounded at 6 percent[a] | Ordinary Life Cash Surrender Value[b] | YRT Face Amount | YRT Face Amount Plus Side Fund[c] | Ordinary Life and Paid-up Additions Face Amounts |
| 1 | $1,533 | $143 | $1,390 | $1,473 | $ 15 | $98,605 | $100,078 | $100,078 |
| 2 | 1,533 | 144 | 1,389 | 3,034 | 1,195 | 97,516 | 100,550 | 100,550 |
| 3 | 1,533 | 149 | 1,384 | 4,683 | 2,515 | 96,727 | 101,410 | 101,410 |
| 4 | 1,533 | 156 | 1,377 | 6,424 | 3,991 | 96,231 | 102,655 | 102,655 |
| 5 | 1,533 | 165 | 1,368 | 8,259 | 5,634 | 96,026 | 104,285 | 104,285 |
| 6 | 1,533 | 178 | 1,355 | 10,191 | 7,456 | 96,095 | 106,286 | 106,286 |
| 7 | 1,533 | 193 | 1,340 | 12,223 | 9,476 | 96,438 | 108,661 | 108,661 |
| 8 | 1,533 | 213 | 1,320 | 14,356 | 11,704 | 97,037 | 111,393 | 111,393 |
| 9 | 1,533 | 237 | 1,296 | 16,591 | 14,163 | 97,900 | 114,491 | 114,491 |
| 10 | 1,533 | 265 | 1,268 | 18,931 | 16,870 | 99,007 | 117,938 | 117,938 |
| 11 | 1,533 | 289 | 1,244 | 21,385 | 19,843 | 100,358 | 121,743 | 121,743 |
| 12 | 1,533 | 339 | 1,194 | 23,933 | 23,100 | 101,936 | 125,869 | 125,869 |
| 13 | 1,533 | 387 | 1,146 | 26,584 | 26,664 | 103,741 | 130,325 | 130,325 |
| 14 | 1,533 | 441 | 1,092 | 29,337 | 30,534 | 105,696 | 135,033 | 135,033 |
| 15 | 1,533 | 502 | 1,031 | 32,190 | 34,733 | 107,807 | 139,997 | 139,997 |
| 16 | 1,533 | 574 | 959 | 35,138 | 39,287 | 110,077 | 145,215 | 145,215 |
| 17 | 1,533 | 654 | 879 | 38,178 | 44,224 | 112,522 | 150,700 | 150,700 |
| 18 | 1,533 | 744 | 789 | 41,305 | 49,571 | 115,149 | 156,454 | 156,454 |
| 19 | 1,533 | 845 | 688 | 44,513 | 55,359 | 117,973 | 162,486 | 162,486 |
| 20 | 1,533 | 957 | 576 | 47,795 | 61,621 | 121,012 | 168,807 | 168,807 |

[a](Column 4 plus column 5 for the previous year) x 1.06.

[b]Guaranteed cash surrender value plus illustrated cash surrender value of paid-up additional insurance.

[c]Column 5 plus column 7.

TABLE 10-5     CASH ACCUMULATION METHOD: EFFECT OF
CHANGING INTEREST ASSUMPTIONS
(TABLE 10-4 POLICY VALUES)

| (1) | (2) | (3) | (4) | (5) |
|---|---|---|---|---|
| Duration (Years) | After-tax Interest Rate Assumed (%) | Accumulated Premium Differences | Ordinary Life Surrender Value | Excess of (3) over (4) |
| 10 | 3 | $15,936 | $16,870 | -$934 |
| | 4 | 16,874 | 16,870 | 4 |
| | 5 | 17,871 | 16,870 | 1,001 |
| | 6 | 18,931 | 16,870 | 2,061 |
| | 7 | 20,056 | 16,870 | 3,186 |
| | 8 | 21,252 | 16,870 | 4,382 |
| | 9 | 22,522 | 16,870 | 5,652 |
| | 10 | 23,871 | 16,870 | 7,001 |
| 20 | 3 | 32,392 | 61,621 | -29,229 |
| | 4 | 36,841 | 61,621 | -24,780 |
| | 5 | 41,943 | 61,621 | -19,678 |
| | 6 | 47,795 | 61,621 | -13,826 |
| | 7 | 54,507 | 61,621 | -7,114 |
| | 8 | 62,207 | 61,621 | 586 |
| | 9 | 71,041 | 61,621 | 9,420 |
| | 10 | 81,174 | 61,621 | 19,553 |

decision. Its utility is in showing how relative costs and values vary by imposing a hypothetical equality requirement over outlays and death benefits.[12]

*Comparative Interest Rate Method.* Another popular method used to compare the relative costs of two policies is the **comparative interest rate** (CIR) method.[13] The CIR method is a special case of the CAM. It differs only in that it solves for the interest rate that causes the accumulated value of the annual differences in policy premiums (the side fund) to be equal to the higher-premium policy's cash surrender value at the end of the period of analysis. Stated differently, the CIR is the rate of return that must be earned on a hypothetical (or real) side fund in a "buy term, invest the difference" plan so that the value of the side fund will exactly equal the cash surrender value of the higher-premium policy at a designated point in time. The higher the CIR, the less expensive the higher-premium (e.g., whole life) policy relative to the alternative plan (e.g., term plus side fund). As with the CAM, outlays and death benefits are held equal. The CIR method requires a computer, since the solution interest rate is found by an iterative trial and error process.

Table 10-5 showed that at some interest rate between 7 and 8 percent, the 20-year figures switched from favoring the ordinary life plan to favoring the YRT arrangement.

[12] The CAM used here equalizes end-of-year death benefits. Beginning-of-year death benefits could have been used. Ideally, midyear figures should be used, but this adjustment complicates the analysis and adds little to precision.

[13] The CIR method is more commonly known in the life insurance industry as the **Linton Yield** method, named for the distinguished actuary, M. A. Linton of the Provident Mutual Life Insurance Company, who devised and used the method. See Joseph M. Belth, "The Rate of Return on the Savings Element in Cash-Value Life Insurance," *The Journal of Risk and Insurance*, Vol. XXXV (Dec. 1968), pp. 569-581, and Stuart Schwarzschild, "Rates of Return on the Investment Differentials between Life Insurance Policies," *The Journal of Risk and Insurance*, Vol. XXXV (Dec. 1968), pp. 583-595.

In fact, at 7.93 percent, the 20-year accumulated differences exactly equal the 20-year illustrated surrender value. Thus 7.93 percent is the 20-year comparative interest rate for the illustrated ordinary life policy, compared to the YRT policy and based on the stated assumptions.

The 7.93 percent CIR is calculated by assuming that dividends under the ordinary life policy are used to purchase paid-up additional insurance. The 20-year CIR for this policy reduces to 7.15 percent if dividends are assumed to be paid in cash (or netted against the premium). This difference implies that the use of the paid-up additions dividend option over this time period seems to be financially wise. This result occurs because this insurer's paid-up additions are purchased at net rates.

CIR results for this ordinary-life-policy/YRT combination are uniformly lower for durations of under 20 years. For example, the five-year CIR is -6.65 percent; this suggests that the consumer would have to *lose* 6.65 percent per year for five years for the YRT/side-fund arrangement to equal the ordinary life performance. The 10-year CIR is 4.00 percent. These low, early CIRs are consistent with the view that most whole life policies do not perform well if kept for periods of less than 10 or so years. Figure 10-1 shows the progression of the CIRs by duration in this policy.

The CIR method can be used to compare any two dissimilar policies, and if a standard set of term rates is used, CIRs of similar policies can be compared

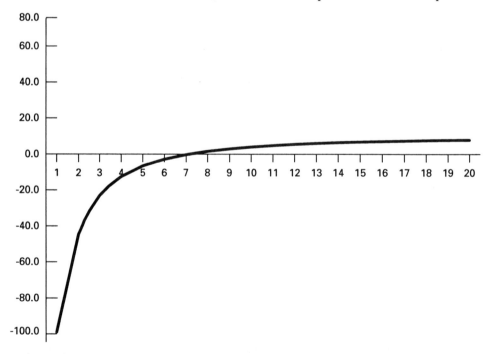

**FIGURE 10-1**

**COMPARATIVE INTEREST RATES BY DURATION: ORDINARY LIFE VERSUS YEARLY RENEWABLE TERM, USING TABLE 5-3 AND TABLE 4-2 VALUES.**

easily. Rankings of similar policies based on the IANC method are highly correlated with rankings based on the CIR method.

The CIR figure is sensitive to the level of the rates used for the lower-premium policy, just as the IANC method is sensitive to the interest rate used.[14] If one wanted to make a cash-value policy appear more attractive relative to a term policy, one would only need to select a high-cost term policy to use in the analysis to develop an attractive CIR. The opposite result could be obtained by reversing the bias.

A comparative interest rate has meaning as an interest rate that can be imputed to a policy. The CIR can be contrasted with the rate earned on other financial instruments, although the shortcomings in doing so should be understood. Cash values and other savings are not the same. For example, cash-value life insurance policies may enjoy certain advantages (e.g., favorable tax treatment, premium waiver features, etc.) that are not found in other financial instruments. Rarely is an evaluation of two financial instruments made solely on the basis of interest rates. For example, the interest rate credited to passbook savings is not compared without qualification to the yields on stock. These advantages are not considered in the CIR calculation. Moreover, the CIR is an imputed rate of return and, while analogous to an internal rate of return as that concept is understood in finance, it is not identical to it. It does not represent the actual rate of return that the company is crediting to the policy.

*Internal Rate of Return*. The **internal rate of return** (IRR) method is similar to the CIR method in that it involves solving for a rate of return, but it differs in that it makes no allowance for the policy's price of insurance protection. Two internal rates of return are typically shown with this method: a surrender-based IRR and a death-based IRR.

The surrender-based IRR is derived by solving for the interest rate that causes the accumulated premiums (net of dividends, if appropriate) at selected durations to equal that duration's *cash surrender value*. As already mentioned, no allowance is made in the calculation for the value to the policyowner (the price) of the insurance protection. In the early policy years, a policy's surrender-based IRR typically is negative. For policies without cash values, the IRR will be equal to negative 100 percent for all durations; this suggests, erroneously, that the premium payment has purchased nothing. With cash-value policies, this IRR typically increases yearly.

The death-based IRR is derived by solving for the interest rate that causes the accumulated premiums (net of dividends, if appropriate) at selected durations to equal the duration's *death benefit*. In the early policy years, a policy's death-based IRR typically is quite large, but it declines steadily with time.

The IRR figures can be interpreted as representing the yield that the policyowner, with the surrender-based IRR, or the beneficiary, with the death-

---

[14] The careful reader will have observed that most cost comparison methods either drive out a cost of insurance by assuming an interest rate (IANC) or drive out an interest rate by assuming a cost of insurance (CIR method).

based IRR, will have received if the policy is terminated by surrender or death. The implication of the method is that all premiums paid are properly allocated toward building the cash value, with the surrender-based IRR, or toward the death benefit, with the death-based IRR; neither of these is actuarially correct.

Table 10-6 illustrates both IRR calculations for the Table 5-3 ordinary life policy. Thus if the policy is surrendered at policy year five, the surrender-based IRR is projected to be -10.09 percent. If the policy death benefit were paid in policy year five, the death-based IRR would be projected to be 104.49 percent.

The two-pronged IRR method, as suggested, has shortcomings, yet, no more so than the combination of the surrender cost index and the net payment index which also are intended to reflect a measure of policy value on surrender and on death. The IRR method is commonly used in evaluation of life insurance policies purchased for business purposes. Other things being equal, the policy with the higher IRR figures is preferred.

***Yearly Rate of Return Method.*** The **yearly rate of return** (YROR) method[15] can be especially useful in analyzing cash-value policies. It involves

**TABLE 10-6     INTERNAL RATE OF RETURN METHOD: ORDINARY LIFE (FROM TABLE 5-3: DIVIDENDS PURCHASE PAID-UP ADDITIONAL INSURANCE)**

| (1) | (2) | (3) | (4) | (5) | (6) |
|---|---|---|---|---|---|
| Year | Ordinary Life Premium | Ordinary Life Surrender Value[a] | IRR on Surrender Value (%) | Ordinary Life Total Death Benefits[b] | IRR on Death Benefits (%) |
| 1 | $1,533 | $ 15 | -99.02 | $100,078 | 6,428.22 |
| 2 | $1,533 | 1,195 | -48.54 | 100,550 | 661.42 |
| 3 | $1,533 | 2,515 | -27.29 | 101,410 | 266.14 |
| 4 | $1,533 | 3,991 | -16.46 | 102,655 | 153.96 |
| 5 | $1,533 | 5,634 | -10.09 | 104,285 | 104.49 |
| 6 | $1,533 | 7,456 | -5.97 | 106,286 | 77.50 |
| 7 | $1,533 | 9,476 | -3.11 | 108,661 | 60.80 |
| 8 | $1,533 | 11,704 | -1.04 | 111,393 | 49.60 |
| 9 | $1,533 | 14,163 | 0.52 | 114,491 | 41.65 |
| 10 | $1,533 | 16,870 | 1.73 | 117,938 | 35.76 |
| 11 | $1,533 | 19,843 | 2.69 | 121,743 | 31.25 |
| 12 | $1,533 | 23,100 | 3.46 | 125,869 | 27.70 |
| 13 | $1,533 | 26,664 | 4.08 | 130,325 | 24.86 |
| 14 | $1,533 | 30,534 | 4.59 | 135,033 | 22.53 |
| 15 | $1,533 | 34,733 | 5.00 | 139,997 | 20.60 |
| 16 | $1,533 | 39,287 | 5.34 | 145,215 | 18.97 |
| 17 | $1,533 | 44,224 | 5.63 | 150,700 | 17.58 |
| 18 | $1,533 | 49,571 | 5.87 | 156,454 | 16.40 |
| 19 | $1,533 | 55,359 | 6.08 | 162,486 | 15.37 |
| 20 | $1,533 | 61,621 | 6.26 | 168,807 | 14.47 |

[a] Guaranteed cash surrender value plus cash value of paid-up additions.

[b] $100,000 face amount plus face amount of paid-up additions.

[15] See Joseph M. Belth, *Life Insurance: A Consumer's Handbook*, 2nd ed. (Bloomington, Ind.: Indiana University Press, 1985), pp. 89–91.

solving for the rate of return to make benefits available for a particular policy year equal to the investment in the policy for that year. The benefits under a cash-value life insurance policy are the cash value and dividend (if any) at the end of the policy year being analyzed, plus the expected value of the net death benefit for that year. The investment for a particular policy year is made up of the premiums paid that year plus the cash value at the beginning of the year. The YROR is derived by dividing the annual policy benefits by the corresponding year's investment and subtracting 1 from the quotient.

Because of this method's potential usefulness in policy analysis, the reader should be familiar with its details. The formula is:

$$YROR = \frac{\text{Policy Benefits}}{\text{Policy Investment}} \text{ minus } 1$$

An analogy might prove helpful. Assume that $1,000 was invested in a no-load mutual fund that developed a value (benefit) of $1,080 at the end of the first year. Assume that another $1,000 was invested at the beginning of the second year and that the total fund value at the end of the second year was $2,330. The first year's rate of return would be calculated as follows:

$$YROR_1 = \frac{\text{Benefits}}{\text{Investment}} - 1$$
$$= \frac{\$1,080}{\$1,000} - 1$$
$$= 0.08$$

The second year's return would be:

$$YROR_2 = \frac{\$2,330}{\$1,000 + \$1,080} - 1$$
$$= 0.12$$

In other words, the effective first-year return on the fund was 8 percent. The second year's return was 12 percent. Note that the second year's investment includes the $1,080 together with the additional payment of $1,000, since leaving the $1,080 value intact is, for purposes of analysis, equivalent to investing $1,080.

A similar procedure is followed for life insurance YROR computations. A key difference is that cash-value life insurance policies provide savings *and* death protection. The value of this death protection benefit should be included in the calculations. The YROR formula for a cash value life insurance policy is:

$$YROR_t = \frac{CV_t + D_t + (YP_t)(F_t - CV_t)(0.001)}{P_t + CV_{t-1}} - 1$$

where:

$CV_t$ = illustrated cash surrender value at the end of policy year $t$

$D_t$ = illustrated dividend at end of policy year $t$ (if not already included in the premium, $P_t$)

$YP_t$ = assumed yearly price of insurance per $1,000 of protection in policy year $t$

$F_t$ = illustrated death benefit at end of policy year $t$

$P_t$ = illustrated premium at beginning of policy year $t$

Table 10-7 illustrates a YROR calculation using the YRT premiums of Table 4-2 and the lower-cost UL policy of Table 10-2. Values shown are based on current assumptions only.

To illustrate, the ninth year's YROR calculation will be followed through in detail. The ninth year's benefits are:

| | |
|---|---|
| Ninth-year illustrated surrender value | $10,788 |
| Ninth-year price of insurance | 216 |
| Total value of ninth year's benefits | $11,004 |

**TABLE 10-7     YEARLY RATE OF RETURN METHOD: UNIVERSAL LIFE $100,000 FACE AMOUNT (USING TABLE 4-2 YRT RATES AS PRICE OF PROTECTION)**

| (1) Policy Year | (2) Planned Premium | (3) Beginning of Year Investment [(2)+(4) previous] | (4) Year-End Surrender Value | (5) Price of Protection per $1,000 | (6) Total Price of Protection[a] | (7) Yearly Rate of Return (%) |
|---|---|---|---|---|---|---|
| 1 | $1,000 | $ 1,000 | $ 789 | $1.45 | $144 | -6.71 |
| 2 | 1,000 | 1,789 | 1,714 | 1.48 | 145 | 3.94 |
| 3 | 1,000 | 2,714 | 2,720 | 1.54 | 150 | 5.74 |
| 4 | 1,000 | 3,720 | 3,807 | 1.62 | 156 | 6.53 |
| 5 | 1,000 | 4,807 | 4,988 | 1.72 | 163 | 7.16 |
| 6 | 1,000 | 5,988 | 6,253 | 1.85 | 173 | 7.32 |
| 7 | 1,000 | 7,253 | 7,686 | 2.00 | 185 | 8.52 |
| 8 | 1,000 | 8,686 | 9,116 | 2.19 | 199 | 7.24 |
| 9 | 1,000 | 10,116 | 10,788 | 2.42 | 216 | 8.78 |
| 10 | 1,000 | 11,788 | 12,479 | 2.68 | 235 | 7.85 |
| 11 | 1,000 | 13,479 | 14,359 | 2.88 | 247 | 8.36 |
| 12 | 1,000 | 15,359 | 16,394 | 3.33 | 278 | 8.55 |
| 13 | 1,000 | 17,394 | 18,595 | 3.73 | 304 | 8.65 |
| 14 | 1,000 | 19,595 | 20,979 | 4.17 | 330 | 8.74 |
| 15 | 1,000 | 21,979 | 23,548 | 4.66 | 356 | 8.76 |
| 16 | 1,000 | 24,548 | 26,338 | 5.21 | 384 | 8.86 |
| 17 | 1,000 | 27,338 | 29,361 | 5.81 | 410 | 8.90 |
| 18 | 1,000 | 30,361 | 32,644 | 6.46 | 435 | 8.95 |
| 19 | 1,000 | 33,644 | 36,807 | 7.16 | 452 | 10.75 |
| 20 | 1,000 | 37,807 | 40,079 | 7.91 | 474 | 7.26 |

[a] ($100,000 - col. 4) x (col. 5) x (0.001).

The $216 price of insurance is based on the policy's net amount at risk and is calculated as follows:

$$\text{Cost of insurance} = (YP9)(F9\text{-}CV9)(0.001)$$
$$= (2.42)(100,000 - 10,788)(0.001)$$
$$= \$216$$

The ninth year's investment is:

| | |
|---|---|
| Ninth-year premium payment | $1,000 |
| Eighth-year (beginning of ninth year) surrender value | 9,116 |
| Total ninth-year investment | $10,116 |

Thus

$$\text{YROR}_9 = \frac{\text{Benefits}}{\text{Investment}} - 1 = \frac{\$11,004}{\$10,116} = 8.78\%$$

This may be compared to the ninth-year figure shown in column 7 of Table 10-7. Other years' computations are similarly calculated.

The YROR gives a *year-by-year* rate of return for a cash-value policy while the CIR (and the IRR) gives an *average* rate of return. The YROR calculations can be made without a computer, but can be time-consuming if many years' figures are desired. Yearly prices of protection are needed for both methods.

The YROR can be helpful in situations in which a person is deciding whether to retain a policy for another year or in which a policy's year-to-year performance is of interest. This method should be used only for policies with cash values, and the results should be interpreted cautiously when cash values are small.

*Yearly Price of Protection Method.* Whereas the YROR method assumes a mortality cost (or price of protection) and derives a rate of return figure, the **yearly price of protection** (YPP) method assumes a rate of return and derives a yearly price of protection figure. The resultant figure represents an estimate of the internal price, in a given year, of the net protection (death benefit less cash value) provided under a policy. The beginning-of-year policy investment (i.e., the end-of-previous year's cash value plus current premium) is first accumulated at interest to the end of the year. From this result is subtracted the end-of-year policy cash surrender value (i.e., cash value plus dividend). The resultant figure is then divided by the year's net amount at risk in thousands to derive a measure of the policy's yearly price.[16]

The YPP gives *year-by-year* costs for a life insurance policy while the IANC method gives an *average* cost. A computer is not necessary to derive YPP figures, although if several years' figures are desired, the calculation can be

---

[16] See formula 6 in the chapter appendix.

tedious. Advantages of the YPP method are the same as those of the YROR method, although the resulting YPP figures have no intrinsic meaning by themselves.[17] When one compares them to a set of yearly renewable term premiums, however, one can obtain an idea of the costliness of the policy's protection element.[18]

Although the YROR method is to be used only with policies that have cash values, the YPP method may be used fairly with both term and cash-value policies. However, the YPP method should not be used with policies whose cash values approach or exceed their face amounts, since the small net amount at risk can cause wide (and not very meaningful) fluctuations.

## COST ANALYSES OF EXISTING POLICIES

The preceding cost comparison methods, when adjusted, can be used to compare an existing older policy with a new one. Such comparisons are often necessary to help determine whether an existing policy should be replaced with a new one.

The *interest-adjusted method* can be used to compare an existing policy with a proposed one, provided they are of the same type. Adjustments, however, are necessary in the calculation and they can cause more confusion than clarity. In any event, the method is rarely used in replacement evaluations.[19]

The *equal outlay method* is often used in comparing an existing to a proposed policy. If the proposed policy is a flexible-premium contract, the analysis is simple. The only change that must be made is to assume some appropriate disposition of the existing policy's cash value. This potential surrender value could be paid into the proposed policy or it could be maintained outside the insurance program.[20] If the cash value is assumed to be paid into the new policy, no other special adjustments are necessary for a reasonably fair analysis, assuming the death benefits of the two policies are held roughly equal. One simply illustrates future values of the two policies and compares results. If, however, the released cash value is not paid into the new policy and if the amount involved is not inconsequential, two adjustments should be made for a reasonably fair analysis. First, the death benefits should be made approximately equal, and second, the time value of money associated with the released cash value should be recognized.

---

[17] One authority believes this method to be of great importance in the life insurance purchase decision. His book on buying life insurance provides benchmark yearly prices as guidelines. See Belth, *Life Insurance: A Consumer's Handbook.*

[18] A technical adjustment to the YRT term premiums would be required to permit a fair, direct comparison. Because the formula develops end-of-year figures and YRT premiums are for the beginning of the year, one year's interest should be added to each YRT premium.

[19] The necessary formulas can be found in Harold Skipper, Jr., "Cost Disclosure in Life Insurance Replacement," *The Journal of the American Society of Chartered Life Underwriters*, Vol. XXXIV (Oct. 1980), pp. 48-49.

[20] The potential income tax implications of maintaining the values outside the program should be considered (see Chap. 13).

A comparison between two *fixed-premium policies* can be made using the equal outlay method if adjustments are made to minimize bias. Results, however, are still frequently ambiguous. A cost-based decision can be made using these results *if* the policy against which the method is biased proves superior.

In exploring the replacement alternative under this approach, the cash surrender value realized under the existing insurance must be recognized. This can be done in either of two ways. First, it can be assumed that the released surrender value is invested. Thus the total death benefit of the proposed arrangement would be the proposed policy's face amount plus a side fund composed of the released surrender value. To compare similar death benefits, therefore, one should use a face amount for the proposed policy that is equal to the net amount of risk of the existing policy. The released cash value should also be shown, at interest, as being available to augment the total value available on surrender under the proposed arrangment. One then equalizes outlays by accumulating the differences, as before.

As an alternative, the analysis under the equal outlay method can be made by assuming that a maximum policy loan is obtained from the existing policy. In essense, this enables the analysis to ignore the cash surrender value of the existing policy, since it would be available for outside investment under either the existing or the proposed arrangement. Also, it results in an automatic adjustment within the existing policy to permit a fairer comparison. The net death benefit of the existing arrangement would be the face amount less the loan. The death benefit of the proposed plan should be set at this same level. This, of course, results in a lower outlay for the proposed policy than would otherwise be the case. Also, the existing policy's future surrender values should be lowered by the loan amount, *and* the policy loan interest payment should be included as a part of the existing policy's yearly outlay.

The latter is, in many ways, easier to follow and implicitly takes into consideration the possible advantage accruing to the existing policy from a low policy loan interest rate. After making the necessary adjustments, one then proceeds as before, equalizing outlays under the two arrangements by accumulating the differences.

Under this method, an older term policy could be similarly compared to a new term or cash-value policy, and an older cash-value policy could be compared to a new term or other cash-value policy. The procedure is essentially the same. However, whenever fixed-premium contracts are involved, results often are not as clear as desired. An accepted premise with respect to possible policy replacement is: *If in doubt, do not replace.*

The ambiguous results of the equal outlay method, as a technique for comparing existing and proposed policies, can usually be avoided through use of the *cash accumulation* or *comparative interest rate* methods. An essential adjustment in using both of these two methods, however, is to treat the present cash surrender value of the existing policy as an additional first-year payment under that policy or to recalculate its outlays and values, assuming a maximum policy loan. This permits a fair analysis. Aside from this adjustment, however, the analysis is conducted as before and interpreted accordingly.

The *internal rate of return* method is not commonly used in replacement evaluations. IRR figures for an existing and a proposed policy often yield ambiguous results.

The *YROR* method can be particularly instructive in replacement evaluation if the existing policy has cash values and is proposed to be replaced by a term policy. YROR figures are derived directly, using the term rates as the yearly prices of protection. If the YROR figures are low, a replacement may be in order.

Similarly, the YPP method can be used to compare an existing term policy to a proposed cash-value policy. The YPP figures for the cash-value policy only need be compared directly to the term rates.[21] At times, however, the results can be ambiguous under this method.

## COST COMPARISON LIMITATIONS

Cost comparison methods yield precise figures. This precision can lend an unwarranted aura of authenticity and credibility to results. All cost comparison methods have limitations, many of which were discussed above. One particularly important limitation is that *all methods rely on policy dividend illustrations or projections of nonguaranteed policy values.*

When cost comparison methodologies were originally developed, they were arguably more useful than they are today. Policies issued at that time had fixed-premium patterns with fairly consistent design features and profit margins. For all practical purposes, the only nonguaranteed policy elements with which one had to contend were dividends, and they were typically illustrated conservatively. In other words, the likely variation of actual values from illustrated policy values was less then than now. Correspondingly, cost comparisons based on illustrated values usually more closely reflected actual policy results then than they do now.

The wide potential variation of actual values from illustrated values has led many persons to conclude that cost comparisons of many contemporary products may be fundamentally inappropriate. A Society of Actuaries' committee, in recommending against use of certain comparisons, said that prospective comparative performance measures for many of today's nonguaranteed products were analogous to a stockbroker advising a consumer whether to buy a particular stock by using a 30-year projection of the stock's last quarterly dividend and price movement.[22]

Whether variations inherent in policy illustrations today are so great as to warrant the abandonment of comparative performance measures remains an

---

[21] But see footnote 18.

[22] *Final Report of the Task Force for Research on Life Insurance Sales Illustrations* (Society of Actuaries, 1992).

unsettled issue. In fact, comparisons are being made, and with the implicit endorsement of the U.S. insurance regulators. In view of this reality, perhaps greater discipline is needed in product design, especially as it relates to nonguaranteed policy elements. Certainly, a meaningful understanding of the assumptions underpinning illustrated values is a necessary prerequisite for cost comparisons.

Since values illustrated for many years into the future are highly uncertain, the use of shorter planning horizons is probably more appropriate today. On the other hand, the long range should not be ignored, particularly when major differences exist.

As discussed in Chapter 13, life policy benefits and those from other sources might not be taxed the same. The cost analyses shown here do not explicitly consider any income, estate, or other taxes that might be due on policy benefits.[23] For example, many states exempt life insurance death proceeds paid to certain specified beneficiaries (e.g., family members) from inheritance taxes. The tax, however, is imposed on other assets that pass at death. Thus this (usually) 6 percent tax would mean that a $94,000 life insurance policy would be equivalent to $100,000 of other assets.

Also, life insurance death proceeds may enjoy certain protection from creditors' claims (see Chapter 9), which in some cases is an advantage that should be considered. These and other considerations should enter into any analysis when insurance is being compared with noninsurance financial instruments.

Another limitation of cost comparison methods is that they usually are predicated on annual premiums. However, only about 20 percent of policyowners pay premiums annually. Insurers incur extra expenses on policies for which premiums are paid monthly, quarterly, or semiannually and they also lose the use of the funds. Since expenses and lost interest can vary considerably, a consumer could be misled into purchasing a policy whose cost is relatively low when it is illustrated using annual premiums but whose cost is uncompetitive when the actual mode of premium payment is other than annual.[24]

Implicit carrying charges associated with nonannual premiums can be determined, and the results factored into the purchase decision. These formulas may be used to calculate the implicit carrying charges in life insurance premiums:

---

[23] Thus the cash surrender values shown throughout this chapter are on a before-income-tax basis. The assumption implicit in this approach is that the relevant policies are held until death, in which case any gain is exempt from income tax, or that taxation of gains is avoided via a qualified policy exchange. If one were interested in the surrender of policies and the possibility of incurring income taxes on any gain, after-tax cash surrender values should be used. These values are found by subtracting any expected taxes due on surrender from the policy's cash surrender value (see Chap. 13 for a discussion of the circumstances under which surrenders result in taxable income and the method of calculating the taxable income).

[24] See Harold Skipper, Jr., "The Effect of Premium Payment Frequency on Life Insurance Cost Rankings," *The Journal of Risk and Insurance*, Vol XLVII (June 1980).

| Mode | Formula |
|---|---|

Monthly

$$\frac{36(12M - A)}{13A + 42M}$$

Quarterly

$$\frac{12(4Q - A)}{5A - 2Q}$$

Semiannually

$$\frac{2(2S - A)}{A - S}$$

M is the monthly premium, Q is the quarterly premium, S is the semiannual premium, and A is the annual premium.[25] As a simple example, assume that a $1,000 annual-premium policy has a monthly premium of $90. The implicit carrying charge, using the first formula above, is:

$$\frac{36(12 \times 90 - 1,000)}{13(1,000) + 42(90)} = \frac{36(80)}{16,780} = 17.2\%$$

Another potential shortcoming of cost comparisons is that they often exclude supplementary benefits that may be purchased, such as waiver of premium or family coverage. This omission is appropriate if the benefit is not included in both policies. Otherwise, the policy comparisons should be based on the entire package. An insurer may have a reasonably attractive basic life policy but may charge excessively for the options (not unlike the situation one may encounter when purchasing an automobile).

Other potential limitations include the fact that some cost comparison methods can be used fairly to compare similar policies only. Furthermore, some methods focus on one or two policy years only, possibly ignoring other equally important years. All methods must make some arbitrary assumptions to derive costs. The appropriateness of these assumptions for the buyer should be explored. Finally, it is very important to note that no method is capable of factoring into the cost formula the quality and integrity of the advisor and insurer.

Table 10-8 provides a summary of the key characteristics of the cost comparison methods discussed in this chapter. The table is intended only to highlight points, and, as with all such summaries, it is subject to numerous qualifications.

---

[25] Joseph M. Belth, "A Note on the Cost of Fractional Premiums," *The Journal of Risk and Insurance*, Vol. XLV (Dec. 1978).

**TABLE 10-8    SUMMARY OF KEY POINTS OF COMMON COST COMPARISON METHODS**

| | Traditional Net Cost | Interest Adjusted Net Cost | Equal Outlay | Cash Accumulation | Comparative Interest Rate | Internal Rate of Return | Yearly Rate of Return | Yearly Price |
|---|---|---|---|---|---|---|---|---|
| Technique: | Sum prems less CV and dividends; ignores interest | Sum prems at interest less sum dividends at interest and CV | Accumulate premium differences at interest | Accumulate premium differences at interest while holding death benefits constant | Accumulate premium differences at interest rate that causes equal future values and equal death benefits | Accumulate premiums at interest rate that causes premiums to equal surrender value and to equal death benefit | Ratio of policy "benefits" to "investment" | Policy "investment" less "benefits" |
| Solves for: | "Net cost" | Average net cost | Surrender value and death benefit differences | Surrender value differences | Average rate of return that causes equality | Internal rate of return on surrender and on death | Yearly rate of return | Yearly price of protection |
| Assumptions Needed: | Money has no time value | Rate of return | 1. Rate of return  2. Equal outlay | 1. Rate of return  2. Equal outlay  3. Equal death benefits | 1. YRT rates  2. Equal outlay  3. Equal death benefits | Full premium needed to develop CV and to develop death benefit | YRT rates | Rate of return |
| Compares Similar Policies? | No | Yes | Yes, but results often ambiguous | Yes | Yes, if common YRT rates used | Yes | Yes, if common YRT rates used | Yes |
| Compares Dissimilar Policies? | No | No | Yes, but results often ambiguous | Yes, with care | Yes, with care | No | Yes | Yes |
| Requires Computer? | No | No, but time-consuming | No, but time-consuming | Yes | Yes | Yes | No | No |
| Useful for Replacement Evaluation? | No | No | Yes, with modification | Yes, with modification | Yes, with modification | No | Yes, but results often ambiguous | Yes, but results often ambiguous |

CV denotes cash value and YRT denotes yearly renewable term.

## ANNUITY CONTRACT COST ANALYSIS

As discussed in Chapter 7, annuities can offer exceptional value. During their accumulation phases, annuities have little or no element of pure life insurance protection. Annuity cost comparisons are, therefore, simpler than life insurance cost comparisons.

Although less complex, annuity cost comparisons are no less essential. If an annuity provides for a front-end load, a back-end load, or both, one should not attempt to assess its competitiveness by using the advertised rate of return. Rather, an effective yield based on gross contributions should be calculated.

Table 10-9 provides an illustration of the importance of this concept. The purchaser is assumed to contribute $1,000 per year to a flexible-premium deferred annuity. The insurer currently credits 8.25 percent to the net cash value. Projected cash surrender values for selected future years are shown in the third column. The purchaser might be shown these values and advised that the current accumulation rate was 8.25 percent. This rate is based on contributions net of expenses and is not representative of the annuity's effective yield.

The final column gives the effective average yields for selected time periods. The impact of the loads is obvious. If the insurer credited 8.25 percent to the net contribution, and if the annuity were terminated at the end of the tenth year, the effective yield would be 5.78 percent, not 8.25 percent.

The calculation to derive the effective yield is the same as that of the internal rate of return (IRR) method presented earlier. It is the interest rate that causes a stream of payments to equal a stipulated future value. It should be based on *gross contributions* and on the contract cash surrender value, free of all surrender charges.

An easy way to estimate an annuity's IRR (if it provides for level premium payments) is first to divide the gross premium into the accrued net surrender

**TABLE 10-9    ILLUSTRATIVE ANNUITY YIELDS**

| (1) Year | (2) Annual Contribution | (3) Cash Surrender Value | (4) Advertised Yield (%) (Based on Net Contribution) | (5) Effective Yield[a] (%) (Based on Gross Contribution) |
|---|---|---|---|---|
| 1 | $1,000 | $ 866 | 8.25 | -13.48 |
| 2 | 1,000 | 1,717 | 8.25 | -9.76 |
| 3 | 1,000 | 2,647 | 8.25 | -6.12 |
| 4 | 1,000 | 3,750 | 8.25 | -2.57 |
| 5 | 1,000 | 4,988 | 8.25 | -0.08 |
| 10 | 1,000 | 13,796 | 8.25 | 5.78 |
| 15 | 1,000 | 26,889 | 8.25 | 7.00 |
| 20 | 1,000 | 46,350 | 8.25 | 7.46 |
| 25 | 1,000 | 75,278 | 8.25 | 7.69 |
| 30 | 1,000 | 118,277 | 8.25 | 7.82 |

[a] From date of issue to year indicated.

value for the points of analysis. This gives an annuity factor for which a corresponding interest rate can be found. A compound interest table (that shows the accumulated value of 1 per year paid at the beginning of each year) is entered at the selected number of years and the annuity factor closest to the calculated factor is located. One has then but to observe the interest rate applicable to that factor. The same approach can be followed for a single-premium deferred annuity by using a compound interest table showing accumulations of a single principal payment of 1.

For nonlevel contributions, a computer is usually necessary. Annuity projections may be based on portfolio rates or new-money rates. This difference should be recognized.

## COST AND BENEFIT DISCLOSURE

Most states require that certain information be provided to a prospective policyowner about the policy he or she is considering purchasing. Special disclosure requirements apply to existing policies when a replacement is being proposed, and also to flexible-premium policies. Additionally, disclosure is provided for through annual statement filings and via certain voluntary guidelines of *The American Society of CLU & ChFC.*

### BACKGROUND OF DISCLOSURE ISSUE

Although recommendations for improving life insurance disclosure were made as early as 1906 via the Armstrong Investigation in New York and in 1908 by the Wisconsin insurance commissioner, significant activity on the issue did not occur until the 1960s, beginning with the actions of the late Senator Philip A. Hart. Following Hart's threat of federal legislation, an industry study committee concluded in 1970 that the most suitable cost comparison method to be used in state-supported disclosure regulation was the interest-adjusted cost method.[26]

The NAIC adopted an interim model life insurance disclosure regulation in 1973 and a final version in 1976.[27] The final version, the NAIC **Life Insurance Solicitation Model Regulation**, incorporated the interest-adjusted method for cost comparisons. (Its details are discussed later.)

Important U.S. congressional subcommittee hearings on life insurance marketing and cost disclosure were held in 1973 and 1978,[28] both of which

---

[26] *Report of the Joint Special Committee on Life Insurance Costs* (1970).

[27] The NAIC, as explained in Chap. 33, has no regulatory power. As a voluntary association of all states' chief insurance regulatory officials, the NAIC adopts so-called model laws and regulations that have no legal effect by themselves, but are intended to serve as guides for the states that choose to enact legislation or regulations on the topic.

[28] *The Life Insurance Industry—Parts 1, 2, and 3* (Washington, D.C.: U.S. Government Printing Office, 1973) and *Part 4* (1974) and *Life Insurance Marketing and Cost Disclosure* (Washington, D.C.: U.S. Government Printing Office, 1978).

raised questions about existing disclosure and marketing practices. The Federal Trade Commission (FTC) staff was also investigating marketing problems in the life insurance business and released its report in 1979.[29] The report identified several consumer problems in life insurance marketing and cited several reasons for these problems. It presented detailed recommendations by FTC staff members as to how they believed the problems could be remedied. The FTC staff believed significant changes should be made in the NAIC approach to cost disclosure, and its report caused much turmoil within the U.S. life insurance industry. The industry testified vigorously against the report.

The NAIC had been mindful of the criticisms of its solicitation regulation. As a result, it formed a Cost Disclosure Task Force in 1979 to solicit comments on the issues involved and to evaluate the regulation. The task force's 1980 report encountered strong opposition and was shelved.

The Virginia Bureau of Insurance released a report in 1981 on some problems and issues associated with life insurance and annuity products and their marketing.[30] An alternative approach to disclosure was recommended, one that relied on the comparative interest rate method for cash-value policies and on a disclosure system that permits the individual to control the quantity of data he or she receives. The Virginia report also recommended the substitution of a single, comprehensive life insurance and annuity disclosure regulation for the several separate NAIC regulations.

## NAIC DISCLOSURE REQUIREMENTS

Over 40 states require that cost and benefit disclosures be made to prospective life insurance purchasers as recommended in the NAIC **Life Insurance Disclosure Model Regulation** or its predecessor. The regulations require that a prospective purchaser be supplied with (1) a **Buyer's Guide** that contains an explanation of life insurance products and how to shop for them, and (2) a **Policy Summary** containing pertinent data about the particular policy the prospect is considering. The regulation does not apply to annuities, credit life insurance, group life insurance, variable life insurance, and life insurance policies issued in connection with pension and welfare plans.

*Disclosure Requirements*. In general, the insurance company is required to provide to all prospective purchasers a Buyer's Guide and a Policy Summary prior to accepting the applicant's initial premium or premium deposit. There are two exceptions: if the policy for which application is being made contains an unconditional refund provision of at least ten days' duration or if the Policy Summary contains such an unconditional refund offer. In these cases, the Buyer's

---

[29] *Life Insurance Cost Disclosure* (Washington, D.C.: 1979).

[30] *Life Insurance Products, Disclosure and Marketing Practices* (Richmond, Va.: Virginia Bureau of Insurance, 1981).

Guide and Policy Summary may be delivered with or prior to delivery of the policy. Most states mandate a 10-day "free look" requirement, and many insurers allow a 30-day look. The insurer is also required to provide a Buyer's Guide and a Policy Summary to any prospective purchaser who requests it.[31]

The Disclosure Regulation requires that an agent inform any prospective purchaser of the full name of the company for which he or she is acting as a life insurance agent. The sales person is prohibited from using terms like financial planner, investment advisor, financial consultant, or financial counseling in such a way as to imply that the agent is generally engaged in a fee-for-service advisory business, unless that is actually the case. The use of the TNC method of cost comparison is prohibited except to show a policy's cash flow pattern.

The latest version of the NAIC Disclosure Model Regulation is in effect in very few states. It eliminates the use of the ELAD and substitutes for it a requirement that two sets of surrender and payment indexes be calculated—one on a guaranteed basis alone and the other on an illustrated- or projected-value basis. It also provides that existing policyowners have the right to obtain certain policy data. The earlier regulations do not require this, although Alabama and Georgia have such provisions in their regulations.

The latest model regulation requires the method of investment income allocation (i.e., new-money or portfolio average) be shown on the Policy Summary issued, and that if an insurer fails to follow the contribution principle, a statement to that effect must also be included. Any change from one investment income allocation method to the other requires that affected policyowners of the company be notified.

Other items contained in the latest model regulation but not in most states' actual regulation include the use of a discontinuity index to be calculated (but not provided to the consumer) in an effort to detect policies with manipulated values. Additionally, the latest model provides for modified disclosure requirements for certain special life insurance plans, such as universal life and enhanced ordinary life as well as pre-need funeral contracts.

A further modification of the disclosure regulation, which has not been adopted by any state yet, would, in effect, substitute a **Life Insurance Yield Comparison Index** for the surrender cost comparison index. This yield index is calculated by using a standard, prescribed set of term (mortality) rates, which are applied to the policy's net amount at risk (rather than to the difference between the policy's death benefit and a hypothetical side fund, as in the CIR method).

*The Buyer's Guide.* The Buyer's Guide is intended to help prospective purchasers (1) decide how much life insurance to buy, (2) decide what kind of policy to buy, and (3) compare the costs of similar life insurance policies. The language of the guide is mandated by the regulation.

---

[31] For purchasers of policies whose equivalent-level death benefit does not exceed $5,000, a modified Policy Summary may be provided.

The suggestion in the Buyer's Guide for choosing an appropriate amount of life insurance to buy is general; it advises the consumer to figure out how much cash and income would be needed if the insured died. The guide explains briefly the principal types of life insurance—term, whole life, and variations —and points out positive and negative aspects of each. The consumer is advised that "cost comparison index numbers . . . can point the way to better buys" and is admonished that: "a policy with smaller index numbers is generally a better buy than a similar policy with larger index numbers. . . ." These index numbers are contained in the Policy Summary.

The Buyer's Guide used in most states explains the distinction between participating and nonparticipating life insurance, although the newer Buyer's Guide in the latest model regulation focuses more on guaranteed and nonguaranteed values. The Buyer's Guide includes a general description of the Surrender Cost Comparison Index (the name used by the NAIC for the IANC ) and the Net Payment Cost Comparison Index, and advice on how to use them. These indices are to be computed on both guaranteed and illustrative bases.

*The Policy Summary*. The Policy Summary is a document containing information and data on the specific policy being considered by the consumer. The name and address of the insurance agent (if any) and the insurance company must appear in the summary, along with the generic name of the insurance policy (e.g., whole life insurance).

The Policy Summary must contain certain policy data (premiums, death benefits, cash values, and dividends) for the first five policy years, and for representative policy years thereafter, in sufficient number to illustrate clearly the pattern of premiums and benefits. These years must include the tenth and twentieth years, and there must be data for "at least one age from 60 through 65 and policy maturity."

In addition to the above policy data, the effective policy loan interest rate must be stated and 10- and 20-year surrender cost and net payment cost indices must be provided. The procedure with which to calculate the indices is mandated by the regulation—a 5 percent interest assumption is to be used. In most states, if the policy is participating, the equivalent level annual dividend (ELAD) must be disclosed. (Each of these figures was discussed earlier in this chapter.)

## UNIVERSAL LIFE DISCLOSURE REGULATION

The NAIC also adopted a **Universal Life Insurance Model Regulation**. This regulation establishes minimum valuation and nonforfeiture standards for UL and CAWL policies, and mandates certain policy provisions. It also supplements, to an extent, disclosure requirements of the above disclosure regulation. For example, it requires that a policyowner must receive, at least annually, a report that summarizes the recent activity in the policy, including full policy values.

About one-quarter of the states have adopted this regulation or some variation of it, and other states impose some of the regulation's requirements. As a practical matter, most companies voluntarily comply with the regulation anyway.

## ANNUITY DISCLOSURE REGULATION

The NAIC **Model Annuity and Deposit Fund Disclosure Regulation** applies to individual deferred annuities, selected group annuities, and deposit funds accepted in connection with life insurance and annuity contracts. The regulation's purpose is to help the prospect select an appropriate annuity and to understand its features. Only a handful of states have adopted the regulation.

The regulation requires that prospective purchasers be provided a prescribed **Buyer's Guide to Annuities** and a **Contract Summary**. The Buyer's Guide explains what an annuity is and the types of annuity contracts. General annuity features, typical charges, and benefits are summarized. The guide points out that a yield on gross premiums at the end of ten years and at the time income payments are scheduled to begin is provided in the Contract Summary. This yield figure, according to the guide, should be used to compare annuity contracts, since it takes into account both illustrated interest credits and all charges.

The Contract Summary provides the same generic type of information for an annuity that the Policy Summary does for life insurance policies, although the information is adjusted to accord with the nature of the contract. In addition to the two yield figures, the summary should provide relevant data on all policy elements for each of the first ten years and for sufficient representative contract years thereafter to illustrate clearly the pattern of considerations and benefits.

## ANNUAL STATEMENT DISCLOSURE

Insurers are required to file detailed financial statements annually in each state in which they are licensed. These statements, as explained in Chapter 32, contain the insurer's balance sheet, income statement, and a host of schedules and exhibits that relate to the insurer's investments and operations.

Two aspects of these annual statements provide information that can be helpful in evaluating life insurance policy performance. First, Schedule M requires that the insurer describe in detail the precise methods and assumptions used to calculate policy dividends. Although insurer compliance with this requirement is uneven, the interested person nonetheless could use this information to learn more about the assumptions underpinning an insurer's dividend illustrations.

Second, Exhibit 8 of the annual statement can be a particularly fruitful source of information about the insurer's practices with respect to the policies it offers that contain nonguaranteed elements, including the perceived ability of the insurer to support its nonguaranteed policy elements. This interrogatory has the insurer first identify whether it issues policies that contain any nonguaranteed elements, whether via surplus participation or other means, and then the nature of the nonguaranteed elements. Insurers who issue participating insurance must disclose whether they follow the contribution principle in surplus distribution, and, if not, they are required to explain how their practices differ.

For nonparticipating contracts containing nonguaranteed elements, the insurer is to state the policy it intends to follow with respect to the determination and redetermination of the contracts' nonguaranteed elements. Finally, and of particular potential importance, the insurer is to state whether any of the experience factors (mortality, interest, expenses, or other) included in its nonguaranteed policies differ from its actual current experience, and if so, how. If a substantial probability exists that current policy illustrations cannot be supported by the insurer's current or anticipated experience, this fact is to be disclosed. Clearly, a prospective purchaser would be keenly interested in knowing whether an insurer's current policy illustrations were not supportable by the insurer's actual operational results. Other things being equal, one would be justifiably skeptical about the likelihood of realizing such a policy's illustrated values.

## LIFE INSURANCE ILLUSTRATION QUESTIONNAIRE

The *American Society of CLU and ChFC* created a Life Insurance Illustration Questionnaire that is available for agents and others seeking information about the various non-guaranteed performance assumptions that back insurers' policy illustrations. The questionnaire is designed for all policies with non-guaranteed pricing elements and is provided to relevant insurers with the hope that they will answer it fully, thus providing the advisor and his or her customers insight into the insurer's pricing practices.

For participating policies, the insurer is to specify whether the contribution principle (see Chap. 9) is followed and, if not, to explain how its surplus distribution practice differs from the contribution principle. Insurers also are requested to disclose whether the underlying experience factors for any nonguaranteed policy element differ from current experience and, if so, to describe the differences. This information is useful in assessing the extent to which the insurer's illustration practices appear reasonable and fair.

The insurer is asked to indicate whether there is a substantial probability that currently illustrated values will change if current experience continues unchanged. These queries are similar to those in the NAIC Exhibit 8 interrogatory.

There follows a series of questions that deals with underlying mortality assumptions. Thus the insurer is asked to indicate whether mortality charges are lower than actual company experience would justify and whether some element of future mortality improvement is included in the illustrated charges.

Another section of the questionnaire deals with interest rate assumptions. Here the insurer is to describe the basis (new money, investment generation, portfolio average) of the interest rate used in any nonguaranteed pricing elements, including whether the company's actual investment earning rates on the assets backing the policy's liabilities exceed the rates being credited to the policy.

The final two sections of the questionnaire seek information about expense charges and company persistency, similar to that mentioned above. One important question is whether policy values would be negatively affected if actual persistency was better than that assumed—in other words, do policy values rely on excessive lapses and thus might not be realized if persistency was better than anticipated.

The intent of these and the other questions is to develop information useful in assessing (1) whether the insurer's policy illustration is predicated on realistic, current company experience or on a less sound basis and (2) the extent to which actual policy values may be subject to fluctuations.

Neither this questionnaire nor any professional practice standard or regulation requires disclosure to prospective purchasers of the fact and extent of agents' commissions. Many persons outside the life insurance industry believe that consumer disclosure should include information on commission payments, to alert the prospective buyer as to the nature and extent of the agent's interest in the sales transactions.

## LIFE INSURANCE POLICY REPLACEMENT REGULATION

The very mention of the word *replacement* evokes strong opinions and emotions from many within the U.S. life insurance business. Replacement activity has been and remains at a high level. Some insurance executives and agents express alarm over this fact, arguing that life insurance consumers are losing millions of dollars by switching policies. Others argue that replacement is usually in the consumer's interest, that an existing life insurance policy should not be any more sacred or immune to replacement than any other consumer purchase, and that today's products are superior to older policies. Some agents and insurers have a marketing strategy that is based on replacement of existing insurance.

## THE 1970 AND 1979 NAIC MODEL REPLACEMENT REGULATIONS

In 1970, the NAIC adopted its first **Model Life Insurance Replacement Regulation**. This regulation had a clear antireplacement bias. The notice that was required to be provided to the consumer contemplating replacement pointed out that "as a general rule, it is not advantageous to drop or change existing life insurance in favor of a new policy."

The NAIC adopted a revised replacement regulation in 1978 that represented an improvement over the previous regulation. Several states' replacement regulations are patterned after this version.

Under this regulation, the agent who proposes a replacement must provide the policyowner with a **Replacement Notice** and a completed **Comparative Information Form**. The agent is to leave copies of all sales materials used with the applicant and to send to the replacing insurer signed copies of the notice and the Comparative Information Form, plus copies of all sales proposals. An agent who attempts a conservation effort must leave with the consumer a copy of all materials used in connection with that effort, and must submit to his or her own insurer a copy of the same material.

The replacing insurer is to send to the existing insurer a verified copy of the Comparative Information Form within three days of receipt of the insurance application. Furthermore, the replacing insurer must either delay issuance of the new policy for 20 days or provide a 20-day unconditional refund offer with the replacing policy.

If the existing insurer undertakes a conservation effort, it must either complete, correct, and send to the consumer the Comparative Information Form it received from the replacing insurer or send the consumer a Policy Summary completed in compliance with the disclosure regulation. Cost comparison information need not be included in the Policy Summary. The existing insurer is, in turn, to provide the replacing insurer with a copy of the materials it sent to the consumer in its efforts to conserve the policy.[32]

Both the older and newer versions of the regulations have shortcomings. Critics claimed that the regulations constituted a road map as to how to replace. On the other hand, claims were made that the regulations discouraged many justifiable replacements, because of the time-consuming task of compliance. Others pointed out that the disclosure form provided much policy data, the usefulness of which was at best questionable and at worst counterproductive.[33]

## THE 1984 NAIC MODEL REPLACEMENT REGULATION

In 1984 the NAIC adopted its latest replacement regulation. This model is patterned, in key parts, after the replacement regulation adopted by Virginia in 1982. The Virginia regulation which resulted from the criticisms contained in the report cited earlier, itself benefited from some pioneering work in this respect by Alabama. Several states' regulations are similar to this latest model.

---

[32] Contrary to the stated belief of some of the authors' students, the U.S. postal service did not draft this regulation in an effort to promote use of the U.S. mails, appearances aside!

[33] The regulations were criticized for other reasons as well. See *Life Insurance Products, Disclosure and Marketing Practices*, pp. 85-93, and James W. Newman and Harold Skipper, Jr., "Regulating Life Insurance Replacement Activity," *Journal of Insurance Regulation*, Vol. I (Sep. 1982).

The new regulation retains much from its predecessors, but it eliminates the requirement that a comparison form be used. The applicant is to be provided with a notice, but it is far simpler than earlier notices and puts more of the burden on the consumer to protect his or her own interest. Other differences in procedure are required. Although acknowledged to be an improvement over earlier model regulations, the 1984 model is still considered by some to be less than what had been desired.

## THE REPLACEMENT DEBATE

Arguments as to whether replacements are "good" or "bad" provide the individual buyer little guidance. The question is whether a *particular* proposed replacement is in the policyowner's best interest. Generalizations are of no help in attempting to answer this question.

Many replacements are, no doubt, contrary to the policyowner's best interests. No less doubtful is it that many other replacements are justified. The policyowner considering replacement should weigh several factors. For example, most cash-value life insurance policies have their initial costs charged, one way or another, against early cash values. These initial high costs would have already been met under an older policy. However, a cost analysis can help determine whether this argument is persuasive, just as a cost analysis can help reveal whether a higher premium rate for a new policy seems justified financially.

Most persons who replace life insurance believe that they benefit financially by the move. Figure 10-2 shows results of a survey that asked why policyowners replaced their policies. In many cases, the replacement was related to changing individual needs, not to perceived cost advantages.

It should always be considered that incontestable and suicide clauses begin anew under new policies, but this fact is rarely persuasive enough by itself to forestall a replacement. Moreover, some companies will waive these clauses on new policies to the extent that they had elapsed under the older policy.

It is often said that existing policies may have more favorable provisions than new policies and that cost analyses alone do not reveal this. This can be correct; however, the opposite can also be true. In any event, the importance of evaluating policy contractual provisions should again be mentioned as a key element in policy evaluation.

If an older policy is not perceived as serving the consumer's needs, the existing insurer may be willing to make an internal exchange on more beneficial terms than those that a new insurer may be willing to offer. Also, older policies sometimes can be adjusted to meet new circumstances through changes in dividend options or through policy loads and other alterations.

A proposed policy replacement should be approached with no prejudices either for or against replacement. Replacement is neither good nor evil. It is a

**FIGURE 10-2**

**REASONS FOR REPLACING***
*Source*: LIMRA, Replacement Now (I/R Code 81.00), April 17, 1985, p. 5

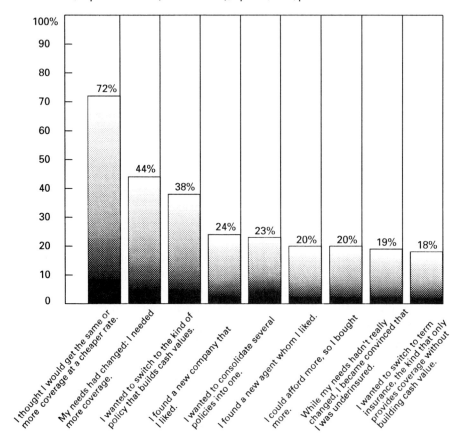

*Multiple responses permitted.

neutral activity and a sound, fair analysis will help determine whether, in a given situation, it should be undertaken. As a general rule, if results of the analysis do not provide a reasonably clear decision in favor of replacement, the policyowner probably should not replace. In any event, a policyowner should never discontinue existing coverage before the new coverage is approved for issuance by the replacing company and is in effect.

# *Appendix*

## FORMULAS FOR SELECTED COST COMPARISON METHODS

Symbols used in the formulas below are:

| | | |
|---|---|---|
| $n$ | $=$ | number of years |
| $P_t$ | $=$ | illustrated premium at beginning of policy year $t$ |
| $D_t$ | $=$ | illustrated dividend at the end of policy year $t$ |
| $CV_n$ | $=$ | illustrated cash value plus terminal dividend at the end of policy year $n$ |
| $F_t$ | $=$ | illustrated death benefit at end of policy year $t$ |
| $i$ | $=$ | assumed interest rate |
| $YP_t$ | $=$ | assumed yearly price of insurance per \$1,000 in policy year $t$ |
| $DB_t$ | $=$ | illustrated death benefit at the beginning of policy year $t$ |

### TRADITIONAL NET COST METHOD

The formula for the traditional net cost for a period of $n$ years is

$$TNC_n = \frac{\sum_{t=1}^{n} P_t - \sum_{t=1}^{n} D_t - CVn}{(F_n)(0.001)(n)} \tag{1}$$

### INTEREST-ADJUSTED NET COST METHOD

The formula for the interest-adjusted net cost for a period of $n$ years is

$$IANC_n = \frac{\sum_{t=1}^{n} P_t(1+i)^{n-1+t} - \sum_{t=1}^{n} D_t(1+i)^{n-t} - CVn}{(F_n)(0.001)\left[\sum_{t=1}^{n}(1+i)^t\right]} \tag{2}$$

If the policy death benefit is not level over the period of evaluation, an **equivalent level death benefit** may be calculated as follows and substituted for $F_n$ above:

$$ELDB_n = \frac{\sum_{t=1}^{n} DB_t (1+i)^{n-t+1}}{\sum_{t=1}^{n} (1+i)^t} \tag{3}$$

The net payment index formula is identical to (2) above except the cash value $(CV_n)$ term is omitted.

## EQUIVALENT LEVEL ANNUAL DIVIDEND

The formula for the equivalent-level annual dividend (ELAD) for a period of $n$ years is

$$ELAD_n = \frac{\sum_{t=1}^{n} D_t (1+i)^{n-t}}{(F_n)(0.001)\left[\sum_{t=1}^{n} (1+i)^t\right]} \tag{4}$$

## YEARLY RATE OF RETURN METHOD

The formula for the yearly rate of return method for policy year $t$ is

$$YROR_t = \frac{CV_t + D_t + (YP_t)(F_t - CV_t)(0.001)}{P_t + CV_{t-1}} - 1 \tag{5}$$

## YEARLY PRICE OF PROTECTION METHOD

The formula for the yearly price of protection method for policy year $t$ is

$$YPP_t = \frac{(1+i)(P_t + CV_{t-1}) - (CV_t + D_t)}{(F_t - CV_t)(0.001)} \tag{6}$$

# Chapter 11

# *Insurance Advisor and Company Evaluation*

Insurance purchasers want high-quality insurance that offers good value; stated differently, they want well-suited, low-cost insurance with favorable contractual terms, from a financially secure, well-managed insurer. The three preceding chapters covered various contractual and cost aspects of life insurance evaluation. This chapter continues the evaluation theme with an examination of insurance suppliers and advisors. All of these elements together define high quality and good value.

## INSURANCE ADVISOR EVALUATION

### IMPORTANCE OF AN ADVISOR

Although some insurance purchasers do not need the services of an insurance agent or other advisor, most probably do. Life insurance products are complex financial instruments, and most persons are not well enough informed about the intricacies of policy suitability, availability, and cost to make wise purchase decisions without some advice.

Many individuals offer this advice—some for a fee and most for a commission. A competent, informed, trustworthy insurance advisor is perhaps a consumer's best assurance against making an unwise purchase decision.

Regrettably, some agents and other insurance advisors, although well intentioned, simply are not well informed. Too often, the state agent's licensing examination is not sufficiently rigorous to disqualify those with inadequate knowledge. Additionally, in most states, many persons who give advice about life insurance are not required by the state to demonstrate any level of professional competence in life insurance matters.

The use of an unqualified advisor can result in an inadequate, poorly designed, or unnecessarily costly insurance program. The risk is not only that the insurance will cost more than is necessary, but, what is potentially more important, that the insurance will not deliver in the manner or at the time most needed.

## PERSONS PROVIDING LIFE INSURANCE ADVICE

For most individuals, a licensed life insurance agent is the source of both advice and the policy. To become an agent, states require applicants to pass a qualifying examination and, in many jurisdictions, to undertake certain minimum continuing education activities to renew the license.[1]

Personal financial planners also offer advice on insurance. Most planners also sell insurance for a commission—that is, they are licensed agents. Some planners do not sell insurance, instead they offer advice on a fee-only basis.

Many accountants offer insurance advice, most of them for a fee and some of them on a commission basis—that is, they are licensed agents. Attorneys often are involved in more complex insurance cases and offer their services as insurance advisors from a legal and tax viewpoint.

## EVALUATING ADVISORS

From the buyer's standpoint, a good agent or other advisor is one who does the following:

1.   Places the interest of the client first

2.   Has up-to-date knowledge of the business

3.   Gives clients continuing service

How does one find such an advisor? It is not easy. Helpful sources of information can include local business and professional persons, current clients of the prospective advisor, and insurance advisors themselves, although this word-of-mouth approach is far from foolproof. The value of the opinions of business and professional persons depends on their knowledge of life insurance and their experience with a prospective advisor. The advisor's clients may be limited in their perspective by lack of experience with other advisors; they may not know what services to expect. On the other hand, if an individual is pleased with an advisor and his or her service, this can be an important sign.

A potential proxy for client satisfaction with agents is whether the agent has qualified for the National Quality Award (NQA). Preferably, the agent would

---

[1] See Chap. 33 for a discussion of the types of agents, and Chap. 34 for a discussion on their regulation.

have qualified for the NQA for many consecutive years. The NQA is awarded each year only to those agents who experience low lapse (voluntary policy termination) rates on the business they wrote in the previous year. This fact suggests that their clients are pleased with their insurance purchases.

Most individuals do not have the opportunity or inclination to investigate a prospective advisor carefully. There are, however, several additional inquiries that can be made with relatively little effort.

*First,* what is the advisor's level of education and training? The greater the education and professional training, the better. Of course, lack of a college degree or specialized professional training should not be a determinative criterion.

In this connection, one might prefer to deal with advisors who hold recognized professional designations. There are dozens of insurance and financial planning-related professional designations that can be appended to the advisor's name. Many are highly specialized and may not be relevant to life insurance. Other professional certifications have not yet proven themselves as to durability or professional substance. Three designations worthy of consideration by the buyer are: (1) Chartered Life Underwriter (CLU), (2) Chartered Financial Consultant (ChFC), and (3) Certified Financial Planner (CFP).

The CLU program is the oldest and best known of the three. To obtain and use the CLU designation, the student must pass ten examinations and meet certain character and experience requirements. The examinations relate to economics, finance, and accounting, as well as to insurance law, employee benefit planning, understanding of life products and markets, business, estate, and personal uses of life and health insurance, and investments. A specialized study track permits candidates to focus more on multiline insurance applications.

The ChFC and CFP professional designations are broader in scope than the CLU designation. The CFP program, which predates the ChFC program, requires candidates to pass six comprehensive examinations. The ChFC program requires the student to pass ten examinations, some of which are waived if the student is already a CLU. Both CFP and ChFC examinations test students' understanding of the broad concepts and applications of personal financial planning. The successful candidate in each program must meet certain character and experience requirements.

Although only the CLU designation is oriented specifically toward life insurance and its uses, both the CFP and ChFC programs are designed to help ensure that the individual is well versed in life insurance fundamentals and their application. Individuals who hold one or more of these professional designations should be presumed to be knowledgeable professionals. Of course, there are also capable advisors who do not hold a professional designation. Furthermore, no professional designation is a guarantee of competence or trustworthiness.

*Second,* the advisor should have been involved in the life insurance business long enough to acquire the knowledge and skills needed to provide quality advice and service. Some writers recommend a minimum experience of five years as necessary to assure professional qualifications. Even a relatively new advisor, however, may have support services that provide reasonable assurance that his or her relative lack of experience will not be detrimental to the client. Also, not every individual situation requires the most highly trained advisor, such as one who might, for example, specialize in intricate estate planning or tax work. Relatively new, younger advisors frequently relate well to young men and women who are just beginning their families and careers. Moreover, there is something to be said for having an advisor of approximately the same age as the client so that their working lifespans closely coincide.

*Third*, it would be helpful to know how the agent or advisor maintains. current knowledge in his or her field. When was the last time he or she attended an advanced education or training program or seminar? Is the person working toward a professional designation? What professional certification exams have been passed?

*Fourth*, if the advisor is an agent, the extent to which business can be placed with more than one insurer and whether all types of insurance are sold can be important. An agent who does not hold a securities license cannot offer variable life and annuity products. Some agents represent only one insurer and cannot place business with other companies. In some markets, this limitation may not be a problem, depending on the quality of the company represented and its products. For more specialized needs, this could pose difficulty for the client, since no one company is best in everything.

*Fifth*, irrespective of the advisor's competence, professional designations, and the like, does he or she seem to be the type of person in whom one can place complete trust? The buyer can disclose much confidential information and can render himself or herself vulnerable in both a practical and emotional sense. Intuition plays an important and worthy role here.

## ADVISOR RESPONSIBILITIES

*Ethical, Professional, and Legal.* Insurance advisors have ethical, professional, and legal responsibilities to their clients. Ethical responsibilities are the ones that flow from society's unwritten standards of moral conduct. One test is whether the advisor's peers would find his or her conduct above reproach if they were fully aware of all aspects of that conduct.

Advisors may also have professional responsibilities. Many advisors are members of professional societies, such as the Society of Certified Public Accountants, the American Bar Association, the International Board of Certified Financial Planners, the American Society of CLU & ChFC, and others. These societies' rules attempt to establish minimum levels of acceptable professional conduct, and continuing society membership is conditioned on compliance with those rules. The common theme running through these and other such professional societies is that members pledge themselves to consider the client's interest above all others, especially their own.

Finally, responsibilities are imposed on advisors by the law. Thus, for example, state laws prohibit agents from replacing an existing life insurance policy through misrepresentation (twisting), from commingling of customer funds with their own, and from making any false or misleading statements to consumers. Additionally, certain disclosure requirements must be followed (see Chapter 10).

An increasingly important aspect of an advisor's legal responsibilities stems from common-law standards of conduct. Generally, advisors must exercise at least the degree of care as that exhibited by a reasonably prudent person of their peer group. Thus the conduct of an attorney expert in tax law will be judged against that of other tax attorneys in this area. Similarly, a life insurance agent's conduct will be judged against that of other, reasonably prudent insurance agents.

The situation, however, can become complex. An agent professing no particular expertise other than that required of a licensed agent will not ordinarily be held to as high a standard of conduct as agents who hold themselves out as experts.[2] The courts have been quite willing to judge agents' responsibilities and conduct on the degree of expertise that they themselves profess to have. Thus, in one case, an agent was found negligent in failing to arrange properly the ownership of a life insurance policy to fund a business continuation agreement, the consequence of which was unanticipated state and federal estate taxation.[3] In another case, a life insurance agent was held liable for selling a policy unsuitable to the insured's needs.[4] A particularly important contemporary concern of U.S. life insurance agents and advisors is the potential for liability resulting from an insurer's insolvency, and this is the focus of the next section.

***Due Care and Due Diligence***. U.S. courts have established a general rule that life insurance agents are not liable for an insured's loss due to an insurer's insolvency if the insurer was solvent at the time the policy was procured.[5] This rule seems to require, therefore, that agents inquire into the insurer's solvency at the time the insurer is recommended and ensure that the insurer is licensed to do business in the jurisdiction where the policy is sold.

A recent Texas case, however, suggested that agents retain a continuing responsibility to monitor insurer solvency.[6] Although the agent was released

---

[2] See, generally, Burke A. Christensen, "Insurance Agent or Broker Liability to the Insured," *Journal of Insurance Regulation*, Vol. 10 (Spring 1992), pp. 313-341.

[3] *State Farm Life v. Fort Wayne National Bank*, 474 N.E. 2d 524 (Ind. 1985). See Chap. 15 for business continuation agreements and their taxation.

[4] *Knox v. Anderson*, 159 F. Supp. 795, 162 F. Supp. 338 (D. Haw. 1958), 297 F.2d 702 (9th Cir. 1961) *cert. denied*, 370 U.S. 915 (1962).

[5] See Christensen, p. 339.

[6] *Higginbotham & Associates, Inc., v. Greer*, 738 S.W. 2d 45 (Tex. App. 1987).

from liability to the insured as a result of an insurer's insolvency, the court further held that agents were obligated to use all of the tools available to them to monitor insurer solvency and to stay abreast of industry developments. Irrespective of any particular court's general interpretation of an agent's responsibilities in this area, it seems clear that agents who represent themselves as being knowledgeable about insurer financial condition are likely to be held accountable for that representation.

The terms **due care** and **due diligence** have come to mean the process through which an insurance advisor investigates the quality and value of the insurance program that he or she is recommending to a client. The term *due diligence* historically has applied exclusively to the securities business. It is the process by which a broker/dealer ensures that an investment is as represented.

Increasingly, however, the term has been adopted by life insurance advisors, much to the chagrin of legal authorities, who see vast legal differences in the application of the concept to insurance and securities. The term *due care* has been recommended as a more accurate substitute. Whatever the correct term, the objective is the same. To many insurance advisors, it involves investigation into the four areas illustrated in Figure 11-1. The balance of this chapter focuses on the insurer financial strength and performance portion of the figure.

## ORGANIZATIONS PROVIDING LIFE INSURANCE

Several types of organizations offer life insurance, five of which are presented here. (Government-provided life insurance coverage under social insurance programs is discussed in Chapter 25.)

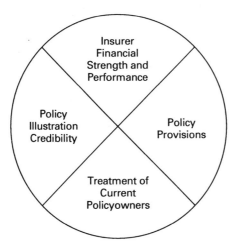

**FIGURE 11–1**

**ELEMENTS OF ADVISORS' PROFESSIONAL RESPONSIBILITIES**

## COMMERCIAL LIFE INSURANCE COMPANIES

Commercial life insurers are organized as either stocks or mutuals.[7] A **stock life insurance company** is owned by its stockholders and is organized and incorporated under a state's laws for the purpose of making a profit for its stockholders. Policyowners have no ownership interest in stock companies.

A **mutual life insurance company** is owned by its policyowners. It is also organized and incorporated under a state's laws, but it has no stockholders. Policyowners share in corporate profits through dividends paid on their policies.

Over 2,000 commercial life insurance companies are domiciled in the United States, although the actual number of active insurers competing in the market is substantially less. At least 30 of these insurers have been in business for more than a century.

Stock insurers comprise 95 percent of the total, with mutuals accounting for the balance. Mutual companies, which are generally older and larger than the stock companies, had 43.8 percent of the assets of all U.S. commercial life companies and accounted for 39.4 percent of life insurance in force. Since the late 1960s, several companies have converted from the status of a mutual company to a stock company, and two stock companies have converted to mutuals. Figure 11-2 compares mutual and stock life insurance companies in the United States by number, assets, and life insurance in force.

Comparisons are often made between stock and mutual insurers. A few of the arguments for each are examined here.

*Control.* Since a stock insurer is owned by shareholders, the directors and officers answer to them and not directly to the policyowners. Control legally lies with the holders of the majority of the stock. Just as with other large

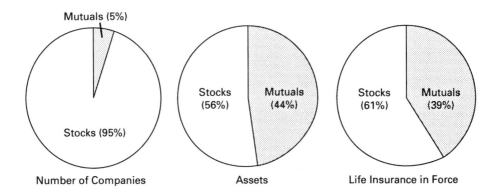

Number of Companies            Assets            Life Insurance in Force

**FIGURE 11-2**

**SELECTED STOCK AND MUTUAL LIFE INSURER COMPARISONS**

[7] For a more detailed treatment of commercial life insurers, see Chap. 29.

corporations, however, a stock insurance company with a large number of widely scattered stockholders typically is controlled by its management group through proxy arrangements. The likelihood that management of a substantial and well-established stock life company will ignore the interests of policyowners is, however, slim because of competition and insurance regulatory oversight. In some cases, limited management participation by policyowners is permitted.[8] For example, policyowners may be given the right to elect several directors, although usually only a minority of them.

In a mutual insurer, policyowners theoretically own the company and control management. In practice, this is true only to a limited extent. The limited effectiveness of policyowners' control of a mutual company is due to (1) policyowners generally not perceiving themselves as owners of the company but rather as customers, (2) policyowners being numerous and widely scattered geographically, (3) policyowners having little capacity or inclination for intercommunication, (4) the stake of each policyowner in the insurer being proportionally small, and (5) many policyowners not understanding the nature of a mutual company nor knowing or caring that they have a right to vote in elections of directors. As a practical matter, mutual companies typically are controlled more by their management group through proxy arrangements than by policyowners.

*Security*. Another long-debated aspect of the stock versus mutual issue relates to which is the more secure financially. Proponents of the stock form sometimes argue that in a stock company's initial development period, its capital and surplus can be larger than the initial surplus of a mutual insurer and that, therefore, the stock insurer could be considered more secure. Even in states where this may be true, the element of security becomes much less important with time. Proponents of the mutual form often note that an additional margin of security is available to policyowners through the conservatism built into participating policy premiums. If necessary, mutual insurers could absorb adverse experience through reduced dividend payouts. Increasingly, however, stock insurers are afforded the equivalent option through the nonguaranteed elements of their nonparticipating policies.

The relative security of stock and mutual companies is largely an academic question. The basic issues underlying financial security are sound and efficient management and adequate supervision and control by government authorities.

*Cost*. Another dimension of the stock versus mutual debate has been the question of relative product cost. Proponents of mutual companies have argued that since profits flow to policyowners, their policies will be less costly than those sold by stock companies, since stockholders benefit from favored financial results.

[8] In some countries, it is required.

Generalizations on the question of cost are dangerous. Some mutual companies are more efficiently run than some stock companies, and vice versa. Even if a given insurer is efficiently operated, there remains no guarantee that policyowners—either in a mutual or stock company—will receive the benefit. Stock companies may pay out substantial dividends to stockholders. Mutual companies may elect to restrict policyowner dividend payments in order to build surplus.

Whether a particular policy is low cost usually is not a function of organizational form, but rather of insurer efficiency and the extent to which the insurer passes on to policyowners resulting efficiency gains. As was clear from earlier chapters, the variations are great.

## FRATERNAL BENEFIT SOCIETIES

Fraternal benefit societies have several features that distinguish them from commercial insurance companies. Since fraternals are not covered elsewhere in this volume, their operations will be covered here in some detail.

*Background*. Fraternal benefit societies had their genesis during the latter decades of the 1800s and in the early 1900s, at the time of the immigration influx into the United States and Canada. Many ethnic and nationality groups saw the need to preserve their cultural heritages and to provide a modicum of life insurance protection for their families as they struggled to gain economic freedom in their new country. The fraternal benefit system was born in that environment, and many societies now operating trace their origins to that time.

Over 150 fraternal benefit societies operate in the United States and Canada. Nearly one-half of them are small societies operating in a single jurisdiction only. Other small or medium-sized societies are licensed in several states. A few societies are licensed in all states, and some do business in Canada.

Fraternal benefit societies in the United States and Canada had over $190 billion of life insurance in force at year-end 1991, with more than nine million life insurance certificates outstanding. Societies writing accident and health insurance had over 800,000 certificates outstanding. Life insurance premiums totaled over $3.0 billion, and accident and health insurance premiums totaled nearly $200 million. Although that amount of business seems large, it is less than 2 percent of the total business of commercial life, accident, and health insurers.

*Structure*. Fraternal benefit societies are organized and regulated under an entirely different set of laws than are commercial insurers in both the United States and Canada. To be called a fraternal benefit society, the organization must have a representative form of government, operate under a lodge system, and provide fraternal and insurance benefits to members and family dependents. Societies must be organized and must operate for one or more social, intellectual, educational, charitable, benevolent, moral, fraternal, patriotic, or religious purposes for the benefit of their members.

Membership in many societies is based on the particular background of the individual society and the purpose for which it was formed. A society may serve persons of a particular ethnic or nationality group, a particular religious denomination or sect, or a particular occupational background.

A society must have a representative form of government. This means that the supreme governing body of a society must be elected either directly by the members or by delegates from the local lodges or intermediate bodies chosen in accordance with a society's constitution and bylaws. Proxy voting is prohibited, thus precluding the use of this device as a means of perpetuating a management group. The supreme governing body of a society must be elected and meet at least once every four years and elect a board of directors to conduct the business of the society between such meetings.

Operating under the lodge system requirement means that a society must organize local lodges into which members are admitted in accordance with a society's bylaws, rules, and ritual. Lodges are generally required by state law to have monthly or, in a few states, at least quarterly, meetings. Licensed fraternal benefit societies have more than 40,000 lodges.

In addition to the requirement of providing insurance benefits to their members, fraternal benefit societies provide numerous and varied volunteer, charitable, institutional, recreational, health, educational, religious and membership activities and benefits through local lodges. Society members perform countless fraternal service acts annually for the benefit of their fellow members and the general public.

*Tax-Exempt Status.* Because of their lodge system of operation and performance of fraternal benevolent, charitable, and volunteer activities for members and the general public, fraternal benefit societies are exempt from income taxation under the U.S. Internal Revenue Code (IRC).[9] The laws of every state declare fraternal benefit societies to be "charitable and benevolent" institutions, and exempt them from premium taxation. While acknowledging the charitable and benevolent work of many fraternals, critics of their tax-exempt status note that (1) the extent of this type of work varies among fraternals, and (2) more important, tax neutrality principles would argue that government should not show tax favoritism among competitors.[10]

*The Fraternal Insurance Contract.* Fraternal benefit societies provide insurance benefits through what is called a fraternal certificate, to differentiate it from a commercial insurance policy. The fraternal insurance product may contain the same or similar provisions as those found in a commercial insurance policy,

---

[9] IRS § 501 (c) (8).
[10] See tax discussion in Chap. 34.

because the laws of most states either prescribe standard and prohibited provisions akin to those required for commercial policies or require that the fraternal certificates meet the standard contract provisions required for commercial life, accident, and health policies.

A fraternal insurance certificate must, nevertheless, contain two significant, unique provisions. One is the so-called **open contract** provision that requires the certificate to state that the society's constitution and bylaws, and any future changes therein, are a part of the contract with the member. Furthermore, any such changes shall bind the insured member and his or her beneficiaries, as though such changes had been made prior to the time of the application for insurance. No change may destroy or diminish the insurance benefits provided by the certificate. Under the *closed* contracts of commercial insurers, the terms of the contract and the application therefore constitute the entire agreement between the insurer and the policyowner.[11]

The other unique provision is the **maintenance of solvency** provision. The statutes in every state require that a society provide in its bylaws that if the reserves for any or all classes of insurance become impaired, the board of directors may require insured members to pay an amount equal to an equitable portion of the deficiency. If such payment is not made, it either (1) must stand as an indebtedness against the certificate, with interest, or (2) the insured member may accept a proportionate reduction in benefit under the certificate. It is because of this feature that fraternal benefit societies are exempt from state guaranty fund laws.

*Reserve Requirements*. The laws of all states and Canada require fraternal insurance certificates to be valued annually on specified tables of mortality. Some jurisdictions permit societies to value their newly issued certificates on any modern table authorized for commercial life insurers. Most societies value their current certificates on the *1980 CSO Table*.

In the early days of fraternal benefit societies, many operated on a **pure assessment system**. Later they moved to a graded-assessment system. These systems were abandoned long ago. All societies now operate on a sound actuarial basis by establishing proper certificate reserves in accordance with modern mortality tables.

The pure assessment system is nevertheless of historical interest, since it provides insight into the need for risk-based pricing. The system required premium payments from members only when one died. These payments were used to provide the death benefits promised to the insured. No advance premium payments were collected and no advance funding was involved. Fundamental to the assessment system was the assumption that an annual influx of new, younger members would tend to maintain the same age distribution (and, therefore, mortality risk) for the whole group, which would prevent the cost of insurance

[11] See Chap. 8.

from increasing. The inequity of equal assessments, irrespective of members' ages, eventually became apparent and adversely affected the ability to secure and retain new members at the younger ages.

The defects of the pure-assessment system led to the adoption of the **graded-assessment system**, under which assessments were graded upward by age at entry. This modification still failed to recognize the basic fact that the cost of insurance on a year-to-year basis depends on the current age. A few of the societies, realizing this fact, followed the yearly renewable term (YRT) plan for assessments. This was a financially sound plan, but as commercial companies had discovered, prohibitive costs developed at the older ages.

Gradually, the societies realized that life insurance pricing should be based either on the YRT plan or, if whole life insurance was to be provided, on the level-premium plan with attendant reserves. The ultimate transition to a sound actuarial basis, which has been accomplished by all fraternal societies of consequence, was aided by state legislation initiated by the fraternals themselves through the National Fraternal Congress of America and the Associated Fraternities of America.

*Products*. Fraternal benefit societies in most states and Canada are permitted to issue death, endowment, annuity, temporary or permanent disability, hospital, medical, and nursing coverage. Some societies have chosen to limit their insurance operations to life, endowment, and annuity benefits, while others confine their insurance operations to accident and health, or accident only, benefits.

*Model Fraternal Code*. The National Fraternal Congress of America, in conjunction with the National Association of Insurance Commissioners, adopted a Uniform Fraternal Code model bill in 1962 that has been enacted in more than one-half of the states. Portions of it were enacted in other states.

In 1983 the National Fraternal Congress of America drafted and adopted a Model Fraternal Code for the organization and supervision of fraternal benefit societies. That code, enacted in more than 20 states, modernizes the law relating to fraternal benefit societies. It authorizes societies to issue such benefits as are now authorized, or may in the future be authorized by statute or administrative regulation for life insurers, but that are not inconsistent with the membership and other requirements of the laws governing fraternal benefit societies. The Model Fraternal Code also permits fraternal benefit societies to establish separate accounts for writing variable products and to carry out their stated purposes indirectly through subsidiary corporations or affiliated organizations.

## SAVINGS BANKS AS INSURERS

Three states—Connecticut, Massachusetts, and New York—permit savings banks to sell life insurance. Although the business and assets of mutual savings bank life insurance are substantial, they are relatively insignificant when compared with the aggregate figures for commercial life insurance companies. Just as with fraternal life insurance, a somewhat detailed discussion is presented here on mutual savings bank life insurance, since it is not covered elsewhere in this volume.

*Background*. Massachusetts, in 1907, became the first state to empower its mutual savings banks to establish life insurance departments for the purpose of providing life insurance and annuity benefits to residents and those working in the state. Similar laws were enacted in New York in 1938 and in Connecticut in 1941.

The Massachusetts law was the result of proposals made by Louis D. Brandeis following the Armstrong investigation in New York.[12] The testimony taken in the investigation had emphasized the excessive amounts spent by some insurers at that time for commissions on new business and also had brought out the comparatively high cost of weekly premium industrial insurance and its high rates of lapse.

The purpose of the Massachusetts law was to provide low-cost, over-the-counter insurance to all residents of the commonwealth who wanted it. The reduction in cost under the savings-bank system depended primarily on the elimination of the sales costs incurred by commercial companies, chiefly through eliminating commissions to soliciting agents, and the benefit of a lower rate of lapse.

Bills for the establishment of savings bank life insurance have been introduced in a number of other states where savings banks are not as strong and numerous, but since the Connecticut bill in 1941, no new enabling legislation has passed. The most active opposition to savings bank life insurance has come from life insurance agents who consider savings bank life insurance an unfair threat to their means of livelihood. In the past, commercial life insurance companies opposed such bills mainly on the ground that they were discriminatory, in that the insurance departments of the banks were not made subject to the same conditions and requirements as those to which the commercial insurance companies were subject. Recent legislation has generally provided for the same requirements and conditions as those that apply to commercial companies.

*Nature*. Savings bank life insurance is transacted on an over-the-counter basis or by mail and without the use of soliciting agents. This is a type of **direct response** marketing.[13] This approach can result in considerable savings in expenses, fewer lapses, and a low cost to policyowners.

Since a savings bank is not equipped to handle many of the technical details of life insurance administration, each state has a central organization that

[12] This was an investigation by the state of New York, in 1905, into many phases of life insurance company operations. Louis D. Brandeis acted as counsel for the Policyholders Protective Committee, which had been formed as a result of the investigation (see Chap. 3).

[13] See Chap. 33.

furnishes actuarial, medical, and certain other services for the banks. The central organization computes the premium rates that are the same for all issuing banks in a given state, and also prepares policy forms, application blanks, and so on. Thus in some ways, the savings bank life insurance system is similar to a single life insurance company, with the central organization serving as the home office and the individual banks as branches. Each issuing bank, however, is an independent unit, issues its own contracts, maintains records, and retains and invests the assets of its own insurance department.

The surplus funds belonging to the insurance department of a bank are available only to the policyowners of that bank. In addition, the assets and liabilities of the banking and insurance departments of a given issuing bank are segregated. Furthermore, an equitable allocation of expenses between the banking department and life insurance department is required. The central organization, however, maintains a contingency or guaranty fund (established by the contributions of the insurance banks) that is available to protect policyowners of all participating banks in the event of financial difficulty.

An important feature of savings bank life insurance, which lends stability to the system, is the so-called **unification of mortality**. Because relatively small amounts of insurance are issued and in force in many of the banks, the mortality experience of individual banks is subject to relatively large yearly fluctuations. To increase the financial stability of the individual banks, mortality costs for all participating banks in a given state are pooled. Each bank then shares proportionately in the pooled mortality cost.

The banks have authority to sell the usual types of ordinary policies, annuities, and group insurance. Sales of term insurance—especially decreasing term insurance to cover the unpaid balance of a mortgage—have been proportionately higher than in commercial companies. Waiver of premium benefits are available in all three states. Disability income benefits are not available under the ordinary forms of policies issued, and only New York permits accidental death benefits to be issued on ordinary policies.

The terms of the contracts are similar to those of commercial insurers, and all contracts are participating. Cash and loan values and nonforfeiture options are available after one year[14] and, in the early years, are more liberal than in the usual commercial-company contracts. These favorable values reflect the lower first-year expense, due to the absence of agents' commissions and other agency expenses and low overhead costs.

The amount of insurance obtainable by any one applicant is limited by law in each state. The limit in Massachusetts is $500,000. The New York limit is $50,000 for individual coverage and $250,000 for group coverage. In Connecticut the limit of insurance obtainable by one applicant is $100,000 for individual coverage and $200,000 for group coverage. Effective January 1, 1986,

---

[14] In Connecticut, the cash value is available after six months' premiums have been paid.

the individual and group limits were tied to the consumer price index. The minimum policy in Connecticut is $1,000; in Massachusetts it is $2,500 and in New York, $2,000. Savings bank life insurance is available only to residents of or workers in the state, but of course, it remains in force if the policyowner leaves the state.

## WISCONSIN STATE FUND

Wisconsin is the only U.S. state wherein the government is authorized to sell life insurance. The Wisconsin State (Life) Fund, established in 1911, permits certain designated government officials and state banks to sell life insurance coverage through the state fund, but only within the state. All applications are processed and supervised through the insurance commissioner's office and administered by the state treasury department.

The fund engages in no advertising and employs no agents, so the insurance costs are low. The total amount of insurance in force is small.

## THE U.S. GOVERNMENT

The U.S. federal government is a major seller of individual life insurance coverage. Again, because these programs are not covered elsewhere in this volume, they will be discussed here in some detail. Four major programs are discussed.

*United States Government Life Insurance*. The oldest of the government life insurance programs, **United States Government Life Insurance** (USGLI), was established by Congress in 1919. It granted renewable term insurance, up to a maximum of $10,000, to those in the military and naval services, for the benefit of selected beneficiaries only. Later, the right of conversion to cash-value policy plans was accorded. By the time the War Veterans' Act was passed in 1924, USGLI was extended to all members of the armed forces, and in 1928 a special disability income rider was made available. Sales of USGLI were terminated in 1951, and today the total amount in force under this program is small. All USGLI policies were declared paid up as of January 1983.

*National Service Life Insurance*. The second of these programs, **National Service Life Insurance** (NSLI), was established by the National Service Life Insurance Act of 1940. After passage of this act, USGLI could only be obtained by individuals entering service between 1921 and 1940 or upon their reenlistment. During World War II, the NSLI program became the largest single life insurance operation in history, with a peak of over $121 billion of life insurance in force. Following World War II, only a small percentage of insureds renewed their term insurance or converted to cash-value forms of life insurance made available to them.

Under NSLI, the face amount of the insurance issued ranged from a minimum of $1,000 to a maximum of $10,000, in multiples of $500. Even though some individuals may have both NSLI and USGLI in force, the maximum government life insurance permitted under all plans combined is $10,000. In addition to a five-year term policy, NSLI made available five whole life policy forms and three endowment forms.

NSLI is participating, and dividends declared by the Administrator of Veterans Affairs may be used in the traditional ways. NSLI dividends have been liberal, and the net cost of these policies has been exceedingly favorable. The U.S. government absorbs all administrative expenses and reimburses the NSLI Trust Fund for certain service-connected deaths.

In view of the far-reaching extent of this government insurance program, many feared that NSLI would seriously interfere with commercial insurance. These fears proved largely unfounded. The government's system seems to have made the younger generation more life insurance-minded. Moreover, a maximum of only $10,000 insurance was available, and only a small proportion of service personnel retained their government insurance after discharge.

*Gratuitous-Indemnity Program*. The Servicemen's Indemnity Act of 1950, passed after a long series of investigations into the operation, cost, and justification of the entire government life insurance program, essentially ended the sale of new NSLI to those in the service. It automatically insured persons on active duty between 1950 and 1956 for $10,000, less the amount of any NSLI and USGLI maintained in force.

The **gratuitous-indemnity benefit** was payable only in monthly installments for ten years, and only to a restricted group of beneficiaries. Following discharge from service, the veteran had the right to apply for NSLI if he or she applied within the stipulated time period. Owners of regular NSLI and USGLI in active service were permitted either to cancel their old policies and come under the gratuitous-indemnity plan (reacquiring them after discharge) or to continue NSLI or USGLI in force, with the pure insurance risk part of the premium waived by the government. The law also provided two new types of insurance for veterans: **Veterans Special Term Insurance**, available through 1956, and **Service Disabled Veterans Insurance**, the latter being the only government life insurance program still open to new business.

The Servicemen's and Veterans' Survivor Benefit Act of 1956 made sweeping changes in the entire program. Among other things, the act terminated the gratuitous-indemnity program as of January 1, 1957. Social Security benefits were extended to service members and dependents on a full contributory basis. With this action, the extension of government life insurance benefits to new personnel was terminated. A considerable amount of government life insurance remains in force, particularly under the NSLI program.

*Servicemen's Group Life Insurance.* Established in 1956, **servicemen's group life insurance** (SGLI) provides members of the uniformed services on active duty with group insurance written by commercial life insurance companies. Similar in concept to the federal employees group life insurance plan, the program is administered through a primary insurer licensed in all states. Other insurers may participate as reinsurers even though they are not so widely licensed, subject to Veterans Administration approval of the criteria for selecting such companies. Approved companies may elect to participate in converting SGLI to individual policies, irrespective of whether they act as reinsurers of the group plan.

Premiums paid by service personnel cover normal peacetime mortality costs and administration expenses. All costs attributable to the extra hazards of military service are paid by the federal government.

Insurance is provided automatically to full-time active-duty persons in the uniformed services. The insurance remains in effect during active duty and for 120 days after separation from service, unless it is terminated earlier at the insured's request, and unless the insured is totally disabled at the time of separation or release from active duty.

Each eligible person is covered automatically for $35,000 of group term insurance without evidence of insurability, unless he or she takes affirmative action in writing to elect either (1) to have no insurance at all under the program or (2) to be covered for $5,000, $10,000, $15,000, $20,000, $25,000, or $30,000. There are no other choices.

The Veterans Insurance Act of 1974, amended as of October 17, 1981, established a postseparation insurance program that provides for conversion of SGLI, at reasonable rates, to a five-year, nonrenewable term policy known as **Veterans Group Life Insurance** (VGLI). At the end of the term period, the insured has the right to convert the insurance to an individual cash-value policy with any of the participating insurers. A list of eligible companies is furnished by the office of SGLI. The new policy is issued at standard rates regardless of the insured's health and for not more than the amount of VGLI. The conversion privilege is identical to that which existed under the prior law and applies to all VGLI coverage.

## LIFE INSURANCE COMPANY EVALUATION

Many organizations provide life insurance, although, for practical purposes, stock and mutual insurance companies and, to a lesser extent, fraternal benefit societies are the only suppliers of individual life insurance to the general population. Further discussion will, therefore, focus on these insurers.

### IMPORTANCE OF INSURER SELECTION

Life insurance involves a long-term financial guarantee. The life insurance guarantee differs from guarantees on other consumer products in at least two important respects. First, in life insurance, the guarantee is the product. There is no inherent value in the pieces of paper called a life insurance policy. Only the guarantee embodied in the policy has value. Second, the duration of the life insurance guarantee is potentially much longer than most others. The insurer states, essentially, that it intends to fulfill all of its obligations under an insurance policy whenever it is called upon to do so—tomorrow or 50 years hence. For these two basic reasons, the financial strength and integrity of a life insurance company are more vital to its customers than would be true of most other enterprises.

With the recent increase in insurer insolvencies, the issue of financial strength has become far more important than in past times, when life insurer financial difficulty was comparatively rare. Today, it is more important than ever that insurer selection be made on the basis of an informed, unbiased evaluation.

In addition to the issue of financial strength, life insurance purchasers are interested in product value. Efficiently operated insurers are in a better position to continue to offer their customers good product value.

## CRITERIA FOR INSURER EVALUATION

Insurer evaluation should be formed around at least four general criteria: (1) financial soundness and performance, (2) product availability, (3) service quality, and (4) fair dealing. Each is discussed below.

***Financial Soundness and Performance***. The most important element of insurer evaluation is its financial soundness. If an insurer is of questionable financial strength, all other evaluation aspects can be meaningless.

It is difficult to establish general rules as to what makes a company safe. Many insurers point to their large amounts of insurance in force, implying that this connotes safety. Others similarly might focus on their total assets or policy reserves; they may suggest that high levels mean correspondingly high security.

Yet an insurer's size in terms of assets has little to do with safety, even though the relative conservatism of the valuation basis often has a direct relationship to security. Assets are accumulated from premiums and investment income and stand behind the policy liabilities that represent the insurer's present estimate of the amount necessary, with future premiums and earnings, to meet its contractual obligations as they fall due. Minimum reserves are established by state law, but most well-established insurers maintain reserves in excess of these minimums. The extent to which an insurer maintains reserve liabilities in excess of the minimum is a function of management philosophy and can be influenced by federal income tax laws.[15]

Although the entire financial picture, as measured by assets, liabilities, insurance in force, level of premiums, mortality experience, and so on, can be

[15] See Chaps. 13 and 34.

informative in appraising a life insurance company, much more information is needed to conduct an adequate appraisal. Even then, because of the complexities involved, it is exceedingly difficult for someone working only with published data and information to make an informed assessment of insurer strength, although obvious problems sometimes can be identified through a financial analysis based on published data. Greater reliance, however, is placed on the evaluation of specialty rating services. Later sections of this chapter delve more deeply into these matters.

*Product Availability*. The range and quality of products offered by insurers have obvious relevance to insurer evaluation. Most insurers do not attempt to serve all markets; many specialize in one or a few areas only. Organizational structure, service facilities, and cost of operation differ widely, depending on the insurer's target markets, and one type of operation may have an impact on the cost of another.[16]

Individual insurers vary considerably in the quality and types of policies made available. For example, some high-quality companies choose not to offer a full range of individual life and health insurance products to all markets. Thus even if a given company were judged to be otherwise acceptable, its product offerings might eliminate it from consideration.

Another significant factor relates to the insurer's underwriting practices. Many insurers issue substandard business, and companies differ as to what constitutes a standard risk. Some insurers are more liberal than others in the flexibility permitted in utilizing settlement options. Agents and other financial advisors typically are well informed about individual insurer product availability. In some instances, access to specialty brokers may prove necessary.

*Service Quality*. *Service* is a term that has a variety of meanings. Variations of service are more a matter of management efficiency and philosophy than of insurer type. Some insurers handle a request for information, a policy loan, the processing of a claim for benefits, and other aspects of life insurance service much more efficiently and courteously than do other companies. The service aspect of life insurance has become much more important with the advent of more flexible policies and the greater emphasis nationally and worldwide on improving service.

There is great variation in the level of service rendered by agents and other financial advisors. Some insurers place great emphasis on agent training and spend large sums to keep agents informed about legal and tax changes, as well as other changes that vitally impinge on the service an agent renders. The agent's *willingness* and *desire* to provide quality service often is a separate issue altogether and may be influenced by service incentives built into the agent compensation package.

---

[16] In other words, **economies of scope** can affect operational performance.

The quality of service rendered by an insurer depends totally on the quality of its employees. An insurer that invests heavily in its human capital (see Chapter 12) and hires highly qualified employees has an edge over insurers that do not. This dimension of insurer evaluation is difficult to assess, but consumer instinct often is a good guide. As discussed later, an insurer's lapse rates probably reflect service quality differences among otherwise similar insurers.

*Fair Dealing*. A buyer will want to purchase insurance from, and the conscientious agent will want to sell insurance for, only those insurers that treat policyowners fairly. Fairness extends to all aspects of insurance company operations, from underwriting and pricing, to service and claims.

A key element of fairness deals with an insurer's actual or implicit promise to permit owners of participating policies or current assumption nonparticipating policies to share equitably in the insurer's favorable experience. As illustrated in Chapter 4 and elsewhere, this does not always happen, although the majority of life insurers probably strive for fairness.

Determining whether a particular insurer will deal fairly with its policyowners is not easy. To an extent, regulatory oversight can ensure some degree of fairness, but the latitude enjoyed by company management in terms of reasonable surplus and other allocations among policyowners is great.

With regard to insurers selling participating insurance, a hint of an insurer's past philosophy can be gleaned by comparing its past dividend illustrations to dividends actually paid.[17] Frozen or below-illustrated actual dividend payments should be viewed with suspicion, although, because of current pricing techniques and the current economic environment, one cannot be at all certain that future payments will equal past illustrations.

One particularly intransigent fairness problem relates to the practice of some insurers and agents in showing unrealistic policy illustrations. As discussed in the preceding chapter, the use of certain regulatory information can be helpful in determining whether illustrations are supportable by current and anticipated operating experience. A knowledge of insurers' methods of investment income allocation is important. A knowledge of insurers' overall operating performance can provide a "reality check" for evalutating policy illustrations.

Fair dealing is nothing more than ethical behavior. Any unethical insurer behavior revealed through the consumer's or advisor's experience or through the news media should cause one to question an insurer's commitment to treating policyowners fairly.

## SOURCES OF INFORMATION ABOUT LIFE INSURERS

Sources of information about particular life insurers include (1) rating agencies, (2) governmental associations and agencies, (3) insurance companies and their

---

17 Information on this is available in publications such as Best's *Flitcraft Compend* (Oldwick, N.J.: A. M. Best Co., annually) and selected issues of *Best's Review*.

trade associations, (4) agents and other insurance advisors, and (5) publications and other public sources. Each is discussed below.

*Rating Agencies.*[18] As alluded to earlier, it is virtually impossible for the average person, on his or her own, to assess an insurer's financial position. Yet insurance buyers need this type of information if they are to make informed purchase decisions.

Several rating agencies specialize in financial evaluations of insurers. Their activities have become increasingly prominent since the recent financial difficulties experienced by some insurers. The ratings issued by these agencies represent their opinions of the insurers' financial condition and their ability to meet their obligations to policyowners. Rating downgrades are watched closely.

Since rating agencies provide a worthwhile service to those interested in insurer financial condition, the four leading agencies are discussed below. There are other services and these are mentioned briefly. The ratings provide a means by which consumers can differentiate among various companies. Stockbrokers and other financial analysts may also use rating agency evaluations as a means of understanding more about a stock insurance company. Rating agency evaluations are subjective and are not a guarantee as to future performance by the insurer. Nonetheless, they do provide important information that enhances the public's knowledge about and perspective on insurers.

By necessity, insurance company ratings involve a considerable number of qualitative judgments by the raters that reflect their background, experience, and knowledge. Because the definition and understanding of the risks in the insurance business and the risks faced by a particular company are to a large degree subjective, the rating process involves a great deal of discretion.

Not all insurers receive a rating from each rating agency. Some agencies rate most insurers whereas others rate only selected companies. Not having a rating from a specific rating agency does not necessarily imply that something is wrong with a company. It may mean that the management of the company believes that the expenditure of time, money, and other resources involved in obtaining a rating is not warranted, that it is not necessary to have a rating from a particular agency, or that the company's lines of business are outside the scope of what an agency evaluates.

Given the subjective elements that enter into the rating process, a rating for a given insurer is, at best, only an indicator of relative financial strength. Different agencies have different portrayals of the financial and other operations of the same company. Thus subjectivity of ratings is reflected in the different ratings that are assigned an insurer by different rating agencies. An individual who uses insurance company ratings should be aware of the differences in the

[18] This section draws on *Insurance Company Rating Agencies: A Description of Their Methods and Procedures* (Kansas City, Mo.: NAIC, 1992) and *Life Insurance Industry Rating Agencies.* Copyright 1992, LOMA (Life Office Management Association Inc.). Adapted with the permission of the publisher.

rating processes of the agencies and in the types of information they use to arrive at an opinion regarding a given company.

Agencies use a wide variety of information in developing their ratings. Sources of information include publicly filed forms with the states (NAIC annual statements and supplementary data), special requests to insurers for information, visits to the company, visits of the company's management to the rating agencies, written and verbal communication between the two, and combinations of some or all of these methods. Types of information used in the rating process may include a review of historical information and trends, an assessment of the quality of the insurer's management, a review of current operations, an analysis of different types of financial information, and a review of management's future plans and aspirations.

*1. Risks of an Insurer.* All ratings involve a subjective evaluation of the risks associated with a life insurance company. The evaluation by the rating agency is an attempt to categorize the relative risk (contingencies) of an insurer in relation to other insurers. Each agency publishes a rating scale in order to facilitate this comparison.

Well before the recent concern over ratings (and the resultant proliferation of rating agencies), the Society of Actuaries had identified four types of risks faced by life insurers. Today an examination of these risks is a key part of evaluating the overall risk profile of a life insurance company.[19]

The **asset depreciation (C-1) risk** is the risk of losses in bonds, mortgages, stocks, real estate, and other investments through either default on payment of interest or principal or through loss of market value. **Pricing inadequacy (C-2) risk** is the risk that premium rates will be unable to cover unfavorable changes in mortality, morbidity, health care inflation, and so on.

**Interest rate change (C-3) risk** is the risk of unexpected cash outflows or cash inflows during periods of rising or falling interest rates, with negative disinvestment or investment implications for the life insurer. **General business (C-4) risk** derives from such factors as expansion into new geographic areas or lines of business, changes in the tax law, fraud, lawsuits, contingent liabilities, and other environmental sources of risk that do not fit into the C-1 through C-3 categories. Runs on life insurer assets by policyowners would also fit into this category of risk. Many life insurer insolvencies derive primarily from C-4 risks that involve management fraud or a misallocation of assets.

*2. Differences in Ratings and Rating Scales.* Table 11-1 demonstrates the variations in the rating scales used by different agencies. The rating systems in the table cannot be compared absolutely because of differences in the meanings of different rating categories among the agencies. For example, an A- rating from A.M. Best may not mean the same thing as an AA- rating from Duff & Phelps. Descriptions of the rating scales as provided by the agencies are included in this chapter's Appendix A.

19 See Chap. 30.

*3. Factors in the Rating Process.* The most important piece of information in the rating process is probably the life insurer's level of surplus. Here the primary question involves whether the insurer's surplus is adequate to cover its financial obligations under adverse economic conditions and other circumstances.

Besides the perceived required surplus, other quantitative factors may be reviewed and may guide the agency in determining its ultimate rating. These factors may be revealed in reports on individual companies published by an agency. Some agencies also provide a generic discussion of these factors, listing and describing them in a general report to interested audiences.

A critical aspect in a rating agency evaluation is an analysis of the composition of the insurer's investment portfolio. There are many levels of investment quality within the categories of corporate securities, mortgages, and real estate. In this regard, mortgage loans and direct real estate investments have caused special problems for the U.S. life insurance industry in recent years, as a result of declining real estate values and increases in mortgage loan defaults.

An important aspect of the rating process for many agencies is a review of the insurer's asset-liability management process. This review may identify a potential mismatching of asset and liability cash flows and the resulting potential investment risk. The rating agency wants to understand the insurer's risk with regard to its asset-liability management practices.

Rating agencies use many qualitative factors in analyzing an insurer. These factors provide the evaluator with an intuitive feeling about the company's strategic direction, the competence of its management, and related factors. Four leading rating agencies—A.M. Best, Standard and Poor's, Moody's, and Duff & Phelps—are discussed below. A brief overview of other rating services follows.

*4. A. M. Best Company.* Incorporated in 1899, A.M. Best Company has published *Best's Insurance Reports* since 1906; in these reports, the company assesses the financial condition of life and health insurers operating within the United States. Best is privately held and derives almost all of its income from the sale of its reports and more than 45 publications and services. Customers who purchase the company's publications include consumers, agents, brokers, banks, municipalities, and insurers.

The objective of Best's rating system is to evaluate the factors that affect the overall performance of an insurer, in order to provide an opinion as to its relative financial strength and its ability to meet its contractual obligations. All life insurance companies are eligible to be considered for a Best's rating; however, approximately 43 percent of the companies reported on in the Life-Health edition of *Best's Insurance Reports* are not assigned a Best's rating. (See the discussion of Best's ratings in Appendix A.)

A rating is established annually and the review of the rating is based upon the insurer's six- and nine-month quarterly financial reports, or on more frequent reports, if necessary. The insurer is notified of any proposed change in its rating.

**TABLE 11-1    RANGE OF RATING AGENCY SCALES FOR LIFE INSURANCE COMPANIES**
**(THIS TABLE SHOULD NOT BE USED TO INFER COMPARABILITY OF SCALES.)**

| A.M.Best | Standard & Poor's | | Moody's Investors |
|---|---|---|---|
| | Financial Strength | Solvency | |
| A++ (Superior) | AAA (Superior) | BBBq(Adequate | Aaa (Exceptional) |
| A+ | AA+ (Excellent) | or better) | Aa1 (Excellent) |
| A (Excellent) | AA | BBq (May be adequate) | Aa2 |
| A- | AA- | Bq (Vulnerable) | Aa3 |
| B++ (Very good) | A+ (Strong) | | A1 (Good) |
| B+ | A | | A2 |
| B (Good) | A- | | A3 |
| B- | BBB+ (Adequate) | | Baa1 (adequate) |
| C++ (Fair) | BBB | | Baa2 |
| C+ | BBB- | | Baa3 |
| C (Marginal) | BB+ | | Ba1 (Questionable) |
| C- | BB | | Ba2 |
| D (Below | BB- | | Ba3 |
| minimum | B+ | | B1 (Poor) |
| standards) | B | | B2 |
| E (Under state | B- | | B3 |
| supervision) | CCC+ | | Caa |
| F (In liquidation) | CCC | | Ca |
| | CCC- | | C |
| | CC | | |
| | C | | |
| | D (Liquidation) | | |

The rating is also communicated to subscribers of *Best's* Rating Monitor and *Best's Link* and *Best Line*. Many libraries carry *Best's Insurance Reports*.

The determination of Best's rating is based on the information in the NAIC annual statements, supplemental information from each insurer, and computer analysis of the data. Best also uses quarterly NAIC statement filings, state insurance department examination reports, audit reports prepared by certified public accountants, asset-liability reports, annual reports to stockholders and policyowners, and reports filed with the SEC. No visit with management is required, although many insurers request meetings with Best's analysts.

Best's quantitative evaluation of an insurer's financial condition and operating performance is based on an analysis of five years of reported financial experience that utilizes key financial tests and other supporting data. These tests analyze profitability and the quality of assets and reserves, measure leverage, and determine liquidity.

**TABLE 11-1    (CONTINUED)**

| Duff & Phelps | Fitch Investors | Thomson BankWatch | Townsend & Schupp | Weiss Research |
|---|---|---|---|---|
| AAA (Highest) | AAA | A | AAA | A+ (Excellent) |
| AA+ (Very High) | AA+ | A/B | AA+ | A |
| AA | AA | B | AA | A- |
| AA- | AA- | B/C | AA- | B+ (Good) |
| A+ (High) | A+ | C | A+ | B |
| A | A | C/D | A | B- |
| A- | A- | C | A- | C+ (Fair) |
| BBB+ (Below avg.) | BBB+ | D/E | * | C |
| BBB | BBB | E | | C- |
| BBB- | BBB- | | | D+ (Weak) |
| BB+ | BB+ | | | D |
| BB | BB | | | D- |
| BB- | BB- | | | E+ (Very |
| B+ | B+ | | | weak) |
| B | B | | | E |
| B- | B- | | | E- |
| CCC+ | CCC+ | | | F(Failed) |
| CCC | CCC | | | U (Unrated) |
| CCC- | CCC- | | | |
| | CC+ | | | |
| | CC | | | |
| | CC- | | | |
| | C+ | | | |
| | C | | | |
| | C- | | | |
| | D | | | |

*Anyone worse than A- is not given a rating.

Best's review of an insurer includes a qualitative evaluation of its performance, such as the composition of its book of business; the amount, appropriateness, and soundless of its reinsurance; the quality, estimated market value, and diversification of investments; the adequacy and valuation basis of its policy reserves; and the experience and competency of its management.[20]

*5. Standard & Poor's.* For over 50 years, Standard & Poor's (S&P) has assigned ratings on long-term debt, commercial paper, and preferred stock for thousands of companies, including life insurance companies. In 1971 it began rating the claims-paying abilities of property-casualty companies, and in 1983 it began making public claims-paying ability ratings for some life insurers. In 1991, S&P introduced its system of qualified solvency ratings for life insurers and property-casualty insurers.

[20] Best's ratings procedures have been criticized as being too liberal, and as resulting in higher-than-justified ratings and a reluctance to downgrade. See "The Dilemma of the A.M. Best Company," *The Insurance Forum* (Dec. 1990).

S&P's primary customer is the insurer being rated, which must request a rating. The annual fees paid by rated companies constitute its primary source of revenue. Of less importance as revenue sources are the periodic reports to subscribers, including a monthly listing of claims-paying-ability ratings; a quarterly digest of claims-paying-ability ratings and reports; and a quarterly loose-leaf service containing comprehensive reports on all insurance companies rated. Individual insurer reports are also available.

Standard & Poor's has two types of ratings for life insurance companies (exclusive of debt ratings): a claims-paying-ability rating and a qualified solvency rating. The qualified solvency rating is for insurers who have no claims-paying-ability ratings. Over 200 life insurance companies have received claims-paying-ability ratings; more than 700 have received qualified solvency ratings. The ratings are shown in Appendix B.

S&P follows its rated insurers on a continuous basis, monitoring quarterly earnings reports, market developments, and other pertinent information. A formal review, including a meeting with management, takes place at least once a year. An insurer's claims-paying ability rating is reviewed whenever new information indicates that there is a potentially significant change in financial strength.

Claims-paying-ability ratings and company reports are available to the public for a fee and may also be available in libraries. Several insurer ratings without accompanying reports can also be obtained free of charge by telephone.

For the claims-paying-ability rating, the insurer to be rated requests the rating from S&P's Insurance Rating Service. The insurer then provides S&P with both statutory and GAAP financial statements for five years, along with other financial information requested by S&P, including earnings projections for three to five years. S&P analysts conduct the quantitative part of the rating by reviewing these data and calculating a multitude of ratios and other statistics. The focus is on growth rates, revenue mix, market share, underwriting performance ratios, investment performance ratios, financial leverage ratios, liquidity ratios, profitability ratios, and earnings projections.

The ultimate rating depends in large part on risk-adjusted capital, operating cash flow, and earnings, although judgment can have a significant impact on the rating. S&P analysts then meet with the insurer's senior management to review key issues. The insurer may appeal the S&P rating, and S&P will reconsider it if information is shown to have been inaccurate or misinterpreted. If the insurer is still not satisfied, it may decline the rating, in which case S&P will not publish it.

For the qualified solvency rating, S&P calculates dozens of statistics from NAIC data, although only a small number of these are considered most predictive. From these statistics S&P determines the rating. The insurer is not consulted about the rating and may not decline it.[21]

---

[21] S&P's qualified solvency rating has been criticized for putting undue pressure on insurers to pay S&P's fee to obtain a claim-paying-ability rating.

*6. Moody's Investors Service.* Moody's Investors Service was founded in 1900, but Moody's has been rating insurance companies' financial strengths since 1986. Moody's life insurance company ratings are called financial strength ratings and measure a company's ability to pay claims and other policyowner obligations. The ratings, shown in Appendix C, are the same as are used for Moody's bond ratings. Several dozen insurers have a financial strength rating. Once an insurer is rated, the rating is continuously under review.

U.S. life insurers no longer have the right to refuse a rating. Moody's rates some insurers on its own initiative if it believes such a rating is of significant interest. All results are published in Moody's *Life Insurance Credit Research Service.*

Moody's describes its rating process as a teaching process whereby an insurer's management has the opportunity to communicate its understanding of its insurance operations and its plans and strategies for addressing the opportunities and potential problems it sees, as well as, in general, to demonstrate its experience and competence. This qualitative review of management is a key part of Moody's overall rating process. Other subjective criteria that Moody's considers include product distribution, value creation, franchise strength, economic and regulatory environments, competitive position, and relationships to a parent, subsidiaries, or affiliates. The quantitative part of Moody's rating process reviews capital adequacy, investment risk, profitability, asset/liability management, liquidity, and holding company financial leverage. Moody's data sources are publicly available statutory and GAAP information, as well as internal financial reporting such as modified GAAP, value-added, and other information used to manage the insurer. At least five years of historical performance—and, if available, a three-year forecast—are reviewed.

*7. Duff & Phelps.* Duff & Phelps Credit Rating Company has been providing investment research to institutional clients since 1932. The firm began offering public credit rating services in 1980 and insurance claims-paying-ability ratings in 1986.

Duff & Phelps rates several dozen leading insurance companies and groups, including life insurers, property and casualty insurers, and specialty underwriters. Its ratings, summarized in Appendix D, reflect the relative ability of the insurer to pay its policy and contract obligations. Its rating services also provide analytical and statistical information on the insurer's solvency and liquidity. Unless otherwise indicated, its rating is of a single legal entity; however, the rating reflects its judgment concerning the financial strengths and weaknesses implied in the relationship between the entity being rated and its parent, affiliates, or subsidiaries.

Each rating is reviewed on a formal basis at least once per quarter and may be upgraded, downgraded, or put on the Duff & Phelps Watch List (indicating either a potential upgrade or downgrade). A full-scale review of each claims-paying-ability rating is conducted on an annual basis. Insurer management meets with the Duff & Phelps Credit Rating Committee on an annual basis and more often if necessary.

As with the other three major rating services, Duff & Phelps's ratings involve quantitative and qualitative analyses. Quantitative factors are based on ratios and historical growth measures developed from statutory financial reports. The trends in key quantitative factors influence conclusions.

Qualitative analysis focuses on the economic fundamentals of the insurer's principal lines of business; its competitive position and management capability; the relationship of the insurer to its parent, affiliates, or subsidiaries; and asset/liability management practices.

In general, the absolute level of a insurer's leverage is usually weighted heavily in the rating, but trend and volatility of absolute measures or demonstrated significant parent support can make a meaningful difference. Client companies can elect to have a claims-paying-ability rating done on a private, confidential basis. Duff & Phelps may, however, determine and publish a rating that is based wholly on publicly available information if requested to do so, providing it has no rating contract with the insurer.

*8. Other Rating Services.* There are several other insurance rating agencies and they are briefly discussed here. Conning & Company, formed in 1912 as a retail brokerage firm, expanded its focus during the 1960s and 1970s to become an investment bank specializing in the insurance industry and related businesses. Conning provides a wide range of research and corporate finance services. Its life insurer rating service began in 1980 at the request of a pension fund administrator who needed assistance in evaluating a number of guaranteed investment contract (GIC) writers. Conning provides qualitative letter ratings, presented as actual-to-target surplus ratings, to its clients.

Fitch Investors Service, founded in 1913, was the first rating organization to provide a complete list of bonds for investors. In 1989 it began rating insurers. Fitch's claims-paying rating is a measure of an insurer's financial strength. Ratings are monitored continuously and reviewed annually.

Thomson BankWatch began rating U.S. banks in 1974, international banks in 1979, U.S. thrifts in 1984, securities brokers in 1990, and insurance organizations—including life insurance companies—in 1991. Thomson BankWatch's ratings are intended to convey the relative credit risk of an obligation of the company over the ensuing 6 to 18 months. Only a few insurance companies have been rated.

The Townsend & Schupp Company produces two different types of ratings. One is called LIBRA (Life Insurance Business Risk Analysis), and the other is called LIBRA Plus. LIBRA produces a quantitative measure of the risk exposure of the insurers evaluated. The LIBRA universe includes the 100 largest life insurance companies (by assets), plus 30 GIC and structured settlement writers.

LIBRA Plus encompasses a larger universe of insurers that are given a qualitative letter rating. The main subscribers to this service include corporate treasurers buying GICs, large life insurance independent agencies, trust fund fiduciaries, and life insurance companies interested in the competition. Insurers do not pay to be rated.

Weiss Research, founded in 1971, has been rating insurance companies since 1989. Weiss's rating is called a safety rating and is on a scale of A to F. Insurance companies do not pay to be rated and they cannot decline to have their ratings published. Weiss's target customer is the average consumer of insurance products. The ratings are available in some libraries. Weiss's primary source of information for rating companies is publicly available data purchased from the NAIC. Weiss does not visit the companies it rates.[22]

***Governmental Agencies***. State insurance departments are a potential source of insurer information. Each department can advise whether a given insurer is licensed and in good standing within the state. Additionally, insurers must file detailed annual financial statements with each state in which they are licensed. These financial statements, prepared in accordance with statutory accounting principles (SAP), contain the insurer's balance sheet, income statement, and numerous supporting exhibits and schedules.[23] These publicly available annual statements contain a wealth of information on insurers. Many states require that insurers file abbreviated financial statements on a quarterly basis.

Each state's insurance supervisor is charged with conducting periodic (e.g., every three years) on-site financial examinations of its domestic insurers.[24] Examinations also may be conducted whenever the insurance regulator deems necessary. Examination reports contain the opinion of the examiner team as to whether the insurer is fully in compliance with state law, and any variances are noted. Many insurer operational aspects are noted, along with verification of the financial statement information. Insurer examination reports, available for public review, can be a source of useful information. Regrettably, many of these reports are outdated by the time they become available.

State insurance departments receive and dispose of complaints about insurers. The nature of the complaints against specific insurers may be available. Insurers against whom many complaints are lodged relative to their total business within the state, often are found to be in financial difficulty.

---

[22] Weiss's rating approach has been controversial. See "The Weiss Ratings of Life Insurance Companies," *The Insurance Forum* (Dec. 1990). In this issue, the editor concludes: "For a rating system to be widely accepted, I believe that the system must achieve respectability not only from among members of the public but also among the rated companies. In my opinion, the Weiss system in its present form will not achieve respectability in the insurance industry."

[23] See Chap. 32.

[24] See Chap. 34.

Either state insurance departments or the NAIC may be a source of information from the NAIC's Insurance Regulatory Information System (IRIS). IRIS assists state insurance departments in overseeing the financial condition of insurers.[25] IRIS has two phases: a statistical phase and an analytical phase.

The **statistical phase** involves the calculation of 12 financial ratios based on data extracted from each insurer's annual statement that is required to be filed with the NAIC. Insurers with four or more ratios outside of a prescribed "usual range" are earmarked for further review—and this becomes the so-called **analytical phase**. Typically, about one-fifth of all U.S. life insurers have four or more ratios outside the usual range. Chapter Appendix E describes the 12 IRIS life/health ratios and gives their usual ranges.

During the analytical phase, a team of examiners from various state insurance departments meets to review the outlier insurers' and selected other insurers' annual statements. The team assigns a first, second, third, or no priority to each insurer. These designations are meant to establish the order in which the insurers should be reviewed by their domiciliary state. Insurers within the no-priority designation can be put into the state's normal review process.

The information from the statistical phase of IRIS is available to the public. Information from the analytical phase is not available.

The fact that an insurer has four or more ratios outside the usual range does not necessarily indicate that it is facing financial adversity, but the information can be significant. Explanations for this fact ideally should be sought from the state insurance commissioner's office or from the insurer itself, although the insurer may not provide an unbiased assessment.

Besides obtaining information from the state governments, information about stock insurers may be available through the filings required of the Securities and Exchange Commission (SEC). So-called 10-K forms contain insurer financial information prepared in accordance with generally accepted accounting principles (GAAP).[26] This information and related disclosure information can provide more insight into insurer operations.

*Insurance Companies and Trade Associations*. The insurance companies from which one considers purchasing a product are themselves obvious sources of information. Certainly they can give information of the type they provide to state regulators and the SEC. They also can reveal their ratings and provide their explanation for them.

Insurers can be asked for any information that would permit one to assess the company's level and quality of service and how they treat existing policyowners in relation to matters of equity and fairness. Insurers can be asked

---

[25] See Chap. 32.
[26] See Chap. 34.

whether they have been identified as a priority company through the NAIC's IRIS evaluation. If unusual IRIS ratios are exhibited or if any other aspect of company operation or management raises questions, the insurer itself can be asked to provide explanations. Of course, one must be aware that insurer responses may not be free of bias.

Insurer trade associations sometimes are asked to provide limited information on their members, especially if a member insurer has received adverse publicity. The major U.S. life and health insurance trade associations include the American Council of Life Insurance (ACLI) in Washington, D.C. (whose members account for over 90 percent of U.S. life insurance in force), the National Fraternal Congress of America in Naperville, Illinois (whose members are fraternal insurers), the Life Insurers' Conference (LIC) in Atlanta (whose members are primarily small to medium-size home service life insurers), the Health Insurance Association of America (HIAA) in Washington, D.C. (whose members account for the great majority of health insurance written by commercial life insurers), and the Blue Cross/Blue Shield Association of America in Chicago (whose members are Blue Cross/Blue Shield organizations).

*Publications and Services*. For most consumers and advisors, insurance publications and related publications as well as the general business press usually are the first sources of adverse information on insurers. Reporters who delve into details of insurer operation and management often have provided early warnings of impending insurer difficulty. (On the other hand, news reports also have been the cause of "runs" on life insurers that were apparently otherwise in reasonable financial condition.) Another publication of potential value is *Best's Key Rating Guide*. Published annually by A.M. Best Company, this volume gives five-year financial summaries in the form of financial ratios and related information. Increasingly, information about life insurers is available through on-line or diskette services. These services, often available through libraries and vendors, can provide up-to-date, detailed financial information and other information about many insurers, extracted from news articles and magazines as well as from insurer annual reports.

*Insurance Advisors*. It is important for agents and other financial advisors to keep abreast of developments within the financial services community. Agents and other financial advisors can be important sources of information on insurers. Indeed, insurance advisors are the sole source of insurer information for the majority of insurance purchasers.

Of course, advisors obtain their information from the sources discussed above, but also from an informal network of "street talk." For example, many agents and other advisors, because of their own solvency concerns, were not recommending that their clients purchase insurance from Executive Life, even when major rating services gave the now-failed insurer their highest ratings.

If two or more agents are competing for a customer's business, each may have an additional incentive to secure information on the financial condition of its competitor insurers. The client can thereby become better informed, but must exercise care in evaluating the competitors' claims.

For most life and health insurance buyers, the agent is the most important source of insurer information. For this reason, the care with which the advisor is selected is even more critical.

## Elements of a Life Insurer Evaluation

With the preceding discussion in mind, the elements of one possible approach to insurer evaluation may be laid out. The approach suggested here is but one of many. Whatever approach is followed, the objective should be to maximize the chances of a consumer doing business with a financially strong insurer with impressive performance characteristics.

*Overview of Insurer.* Any evaluation should begin with a complete identification of the insurer, including its full name and address. The insurer's history, including its age and its management, can provide insight. Whether the insurer is organized as a stock, mutual, or fraternal ordinarily is noted, and there should be a review of any affiliation, especially via holding company or other upstream ownership arrangements.[27]

A committed, strong parent company can be a source of additional financial strength for the insurer. A less-than-committed parent company can view the insurer as a ready source of cash.[28]

The size of the insurer as measured by assets, premium income, life insurance in force, surplus, or all four of these usually is noted, although size is no guarantee of solidity. Larger insurers can have a naturally greater spread of risk via number and diversification of policyowners and assets. On the other hand, smaller insurers often focus on particular market segments and can obtain risk spread through reinsurance and appropriate investment management. The insurer's mix of business by major line (individual, group and credit life, health, and annuity) and mix of assets often are noted.

*Licenses.* An insurer should be licensed and in good standing to sell insurance in the prospective policyowner's jurisdiction. Large insurers usually are licensed in more states than are smaller insurers, thus permitting a better geographical risk spread, although, again, reinsurance can achieve the same effective result for smaller insurers. Also, some insurers believe that they can operate more efficiently and effectively by avoiding some jurisdictions.

The state of New York has long been recognized as a leader in insurance regulatory vigilance. Unlike the situation in other states, life insurers licensed to

---

[27] See Chap. 29.

[28] State laws are designed to minimize abuses, but they can never be wholly effective (see Chap. 34).

conduct business in New York are subject to key portions of New York law in all states in which they do business. This extraterritorial aspect of New York law makes its regulation all the more important. Many authorities believe, therefore, that the fact of being licensed in New York can itself be considered as positive for an insurer.

*Rating Agency Evaluations.* The ratings and accompanying commentary by the major rating services should, of course, be included as a key element of life insurer evaluation. Obviously, the higher the ratings, the better.

Rating agencies issue *opinions* as to insurers' financial condition and operating results. As Joseph M. Belth, a well-know insurance authority, noted:

> A high rating of a company is not a guarantee that the company will survive, nor is it a forecast that the company will survive. A low rating . . . is not a suggestion that the company will fail, nor is it a forecast that the company will fail. A rating . . . is nothing more than a rating firm's expression of opinion about the financial condition of the company at the time the rating is announced.[29]

Even so, one is well advised to select among insurers that are highly rated by the major rating services. The rating services provide a reasoned, independent financial evaluation. How the ratings are used is an individual decision. Belth has suggested that, as a conservative approach to selection, an insurer should meet two criteria:

(1) It should be in the top two rating categories of at least two of the four major rating firms.

(2) It should not fall below the fourth category of any of the four major rating firms.[30]

*Financial Analysis.* Even with the complexities involved in evaluating insurers' financial condition, many individuals—advisors, consumers, and others—will, nonetheless, wish to conduct their own evaluations, ordinarily as a supplement to rating agency evaluations. Regrettably, such evaluations typically must rely on publicly available financial and other information. Publicly available financial data are, for the most part, based on statutory accounting principles. Limited financial data based on generally accepted accounting principles might also be available.

As discussed in Chapter 32, both SAP and GAAP provide static, historical insurer data. Neither reflects the risks inherent in company operations, and neither captures the embedded value inherent in a going concern. Use of SAP, in particular, can mislead. For example, a growing, vibrant insurer might show low

---

[29] Joseph M. Belth, "The Quandary of the Life Insurance Agent in a Time of Uncertainty," *Journal of the American Society of CLU & ChFC*, Vol. 46 (May 1992), p. 75.

[30] Belth, "The Quandary of the Life Insurance Agent in a Time of Uncertainty," p. 76.

profitability because SAP requires that expenses be written off in the year they are incurred (whereas GAAP seeks to match the incurred expenses with the expected revenue flows). By contrast, a struggling insurer in decline might show high profitability under SAP because its low new business writings did not produce a high first-year expense drain (whereas GAAP would reveal a more accurate trend).

Even with these and other deficiencies, the analyst typically has no choice but to rely heavily on SAP-based data. In doing so, care should be exercised, however. No ratio should be viewed by itself as necessarily determinative. Rather, the collection of ratios should be used to form an overall impression.

Five categories of investigation are set out below. They are: (1) surplus adequacy, (2) asset quality, (3) profitability, (4) liquidity, and (5) leverage. These categories cover the traditional elements of a financial analysis. Ratio analysis is used exclusively. Of course, the problem with ratio analysis is that it does not reveal interrelationships among the variables, and it thus possibly omits important information. Until workable, easy-to-use multivariate approaches to financial analysis are available, however, univariate ratio analyses must suffice.

No attempt is made here to suggest acceptable values for the ratios. Each must be considered in light of prevailing industry values at the time of evaluation. The NAIC and A.M. Best provide this information.

*1. Surplus Adequacy.* In evaluating the adequacy of an insurer's surplus, it is necessary to recognize that the asset valuation reserve (AVR) and the interest maintenance reserve (IMR) are not, in fact, true liabilities. As discussed in Chapter 32, they are earmarked surplus designed to minimize fluctuations in free surplus. Thus since neither the AVR nor the IMR represents amounts that are actually owed to anyone, they should be excluded from all SAP liability values and added to SAP capital and surplus figures.

The relative level of an insurer's surplus is perhaps the most useful item in assessing financial condition. Surplus is the excess of assets over (adjusted for the AVR and IMR) liabilities. Insurers need surplus to absorb unanticipated fluctuations in asset values and in operational results—that is, to cover C-1 to C-4 risks. The greater the surplus relative to an insurer's obligations, the more secure it is, other things being the same.

As an absolute figure, the amount of surplus has relatively little meaning. Two surplus ratios, however—**surplus adequacy** and **rate of surplus formation**—can prove instructive. The first ratio is:

$$\text{Surplus adequacy} = \frac{\text{Adjusted surplus}}{\text{Adjusted liabilities}} \quad (1)$$

Adjusted surplus is statutory surplus plus the AVR and IMR. Adjusted liabilities are statutory liabilities less the AVR and IMR.[31] The higher the ratio, the greater the indication of financial strength, although surplus and reserve

---

[31] Other refinements of SAP values are sometimes made—for example, to account for any voluntary reserves, redundancy in policy reserves, any surplus notes, and separate account business.

levels can vary substantially, depending on an insurer's mix and age of business. The ratio ignores the degree of conservatism inherent in one insurer's reserves versus that of another.[32] For this reason, it should be interpreted with care, and preferably only with similarly situated insurers.

A second useful measure of surplus adequacy is the rate of surplus formation:

$$\text{Rate of surplus formation} = \frac{\text{Growth rate of adjusted surplus}}{\text{Growth rate of adjusted liabilities}} \qquad (2)$$

Calculated over a reasonable time period, such as five years, this ratio ideally should be positive. A consistent, substantial increase in surplus relative to liabilities suggests that the insurer's financial security is likewise increasing. The higher the ratio, the better, *ceteris paribus*. Other measures of surplus adequacy are sometimes used.[33] Most are variations or refinements on the above two ratios.

*2. Asset Quality.* The lower the quality of an insurer's assets, the greater the surplus needed to absorb adverse fluctuations, *ceteris paribus*. Indeed, an insurer can appear to be in a strong surplus position yet, because of the riskiness of its assets, it actually may be vulnerable.

Assets back an insurer's liabilities. **Admitted assets** are those that may be included in determining an insurer's statutory solvency (those counted in measuring the excess of assets over liabilities). **Nonadmitted assets** are not recognized by regulatory authorities in assessing solvency and include items such as furniture, certain equipment, and agents' balances.

Invested assets are the income-producing assets of an insurer. There are variations from company to company with respect to the make-up of assets. This diversification offsets risk of adverse investment performance in a particular category.

A bond is a debt instrument that promises to pay a set amount after a fixed period of time. It may also generate annual interest income. Because a life insurance company guarantees the payment of certain amounts to policyowners in the future, bonds are a popular investment medium. Performance in this area may have a substantial impact on product performance.

---

[32] See Chap. 20.

[33] Another measure of an insurer's surplus position is surplus per $1,000 of insurance in force, but this ratio is not very meaningful. It gives too much weight to group insurance and no weight to annuities, supplementary contracts, health insurance, and the minor types of liabilities, all of which need surplus held for them.

Two other ratios used at times as measures of company strength involve the substitution of assets for surplus. These ratios are: (1) assets as a percentage of liabilities and (2) assets per $1,000 of insurance in force. Since assets equal liabilities plus surplus, the ratio for assets as a percentage of liabilities is simply 100 percent plus the figure for the surplus as a percentage of liabilities. Therefore a comparison of insurers on the ratio of surplus to liabliities or the ratio of assets to liabilities will produce identical results.

By contrast, the amount of assets per $1,000 of insurance in force is almost completely meaningless as a measure of insurer strength. Rather than measuring financial strength, this figure reflects the age and composition of the insurer's business. A company with large reserves for annuities and supplementary contracts could conceivably have assets of over $1,000 per $1,000 insurance in force and yet be in serious financial difficulty.

Bonds of average or below-average quality (non-investment grade) can yield higher returns, but the principal and payment of interest may also be at risk. Some portion of the insurer's bond portfolio can also be in or near default, thus risking loss of both principal and interest. Investment prudence is the key. Limited investment in bonds of average or below-average quality should not be considered imprudent.

The ratio of non-investment grade bonds to adjusted surplus reveals the extent to which the insurer's surplus could cover those bonds in the event that a severe economic downturn affected their performance. Therefore, the first asset quality ratio is:

$$\text{Investment in junk bonds} = \frac{\text{Non} - \text{investment grade bonds}}{\text{Adjusted surplus}} \tag{3}$$

**Non-investment grade bonds** is taken here to mean the sum of an insurer's investments in below-investment grade (junk) bonds and bonds in or near default. Obviously, the lower the investment in junk bonds the better, *ceteris paribus*.

Next to bonds, mortgages often are an insurer's most popular investment category. The trend in recent years has been to commercial mortgages. In adverse economic times, insurers may experience adverse mortgage performance. The ratio of mortgages in default to adjusted surplus indicates the extent to which an insurer's surplus can cover mortgage defaults. Thus:

$$\text{Mortgage default ratio} = \frac{\text{Mortgages in default}}{\text{Adjusted surplus}} \tag{4}$$

**Mortgages in default** is taken here to be the sum of an insurer's mortgages on which interest is overdue by more than three months, mortgages in the process of foreclosure, and properties acquired in satisfaction of debt. The lower the mortgage default ratio, the better.

Another potentially important asset quality ratio is:

$$\text{Investment in common stock} = \frac{\text{Investment in common stock}}{\text{Adjusted surplus}} \tag{5}$$

Common stock value can fluctuate greatly from year to year. The **investment in common stock ratio** is an indication of the extent to which an insurer's surplus could be affected by these fluctuations.

*3. Profitability.* Profit is essential for an enduring, strong insurer. It reflects the ability and competence of management. Insurers with comparable product mixes provide a more relevant basis for comparison. Results of insurers with substantially dissimilar life product mixes are subject to misinterpretation; for example, an insurer specializing in individual term life insurance would most likely show a higher expense ratio than one specializing in group term life insurance.

More than a single year should be examined to detect unusual trends and variations, since many factors may distort results. In particular, reinsurance can cause great fluctuations in premiums and reserves. Also, ratios based on SAP data, over a longer time period, are more meaningful.

Four profitability ratios are potentially important:

$$\text{Return on equity} = \frac{\text{Net gain from operations}}{\text{Adjusted surplus}} \qquad (6)$$

This ratio reflects the return on an insurer's capital and surplus from insurance operations and investments. **Net gain from operations** is the approximate SAP equivalent of net income under GAAP. The higher an insurer's return on equity, the more effectively an insurer uses its owner's funds.

As discussed more fully below, an insurer's investment yield is a potentially important factor in product performance evaluation. The ratio is:

$$\text{Yield on investments} = \frac{\text{Net investment income}}{\text{Invested assets}} \qquad (7)$$

This ratio reflects how well investments are being managed. The higher the yield, the better, other things being the same. Unfortunately, other things rarely are the same. A higher yield may reflect higher risk. This is another reason why the asset quality evaluation is important.

The rough insurer counterpart to return on sales is measured by the ratio of net operating gain to total income. That is:

$$\text{Net operating gain to income} = \frac{\text{Net gain from operations}}{\text{Total operating income}} \qquad (8)$$

**Total operating income** basically is the sum of premium and investment income. This ratio is a measure of the average profitability within each dollar of revenue. Clearly, the higher the ratio the better. Again, however, results should be interpreted with caution and only over time because of the use of SAP-based data.

*4. Liquidity.* Adequate liquidity should be maintained to meet an insurer's expected and unexpected cash needs. Otherwise, assets may have to be sold at disadvantageous prices. One useful measure of liquidity is:

$$\text{Current liquidity} = \frac{\text{Unaffiliated investments}}{\text{Adjusted liabilities}} \qquad (9)$$

**Unaffiliated investments** refers to the assets of an insurer made up of investments other than bonds, stock, and other investments held in affiliated enterprises, less property occupied by the insurer, typically its home office. The current liquidity ratio, therefore, measures the proportion of net liabilities covered by cash and unaffiliated investments. The lower the ratio, the more vulnerable the insurer to the collectibility of premium balances or the marketability of affiliates.

Three other liquidity ratios of importance are:

$$\text{Investment in real estate} = \frac{\text{Investment in real estate}}{\text{Adjusted surplus}} \qquad (10)$$

$$\text{Investment in affiliates} = \frac{\text{Investment in affiliates}}{\text{Adjusted surplus}} \qquad (11)$$

$$\text{Nonadmitted asset proportion} = \frac{\text{Nonadmitted assets}}{\text{Adjusted surplus}} \qquad (12)$$

The ratios of investments in real estate,[34] in subsidiaries,[35] and in nonadmitted assets[36] to surplus each measure the extent to which an insurer's investment portfolio may be illiquid. Also, these asset classes often are nonincome producing, and excessive investment in them may result in financial difficulty. The lower these ratios, the better, *ceteris paribus*.

*5. Leverage.* Leverage is a measure of how intensively a company uses its equity. Leverage increases return on equity, but it also increases risk. In the context of insurance, three measures of leverage are commonly used. The first is the ratio of adjusted liabilities to adjusted surplus. This ratio is the reciprocal of the surplus adequacy test discussed above, and, therefore, it is simply another way of viewing the same thing. Either ratio may be used in a financial evaluation.

The second ratio measures the intensity of surplus use in premium writings:

$$\text{Net premiums to surplus} = \frac{\text{Net premiums written}}{\text{Adjusted surplus}} \qquad (13)$$

The ratio measures the insurer's exposure to pricing errors. The higher the ratio, the greater the exposure, *ceteris paribus*. Ideally, this ratio should be used to compare insurers of comparable product mixes.

A final leverage measure reveals the extent to which an insurer relies on reinsurance. All insurers purchase reinsurance to reduce claims fluctuations. Some insurers rely on reinsurance, not for claim fluctuation purposes, but to reduce the strain on their surplus caused by the insufficiency of funds collected to cover liabilities established under SAP. Financial problems can arise from undue reliance on such reinsurance.

If the surplus strain were to continue for many years, the insurer's solvency could be in jeopardy. If the insurer continued to rely heavily on reinsurance to relieve the strain, its profitability could be expected to suffer. After all, reinsurers themselves intend to make a profit from their sales.

[34] This is IRIS ratio 6.
[35] This is IRIS ratio 7.
[36] This is IRIS ratio 5.

Finally, excessive reliance on reinsurance may introduce an additional solvency risk for the direct writing insurer. If the reinsurer were to default on its obligations, the direct writing insurer's solvency could be undermined.

A commonly used measure of the extent to which the insurer relies on surplus relief reinsurance is:

$$\text{Surplus relief} = \frac{\text{Reinsurance commissions and expense allowances}}{\text{Adjusted surplus}} \quad (14)$$

**Reinsurance commissions and expense allowances** include all commissions and expense allowances paid to the direct writing insurer by its reinsurers, less reinsurance commissions and expense allowances that the direct writing insurer may have paid on any reinsurance business that it assumed. The ratio reflects the extent to which an insurer's surplus is dependent on payments from reinsurers. The lower the ratio, the better, other things being the same.

*Product Performance Indicators.* Most of the preceding ratios reflect an insurer's financial condition. Emphasis was placed on solvency, with insurer performance being relevant to the extent that it might affect solvency.

Although insurance purchasers report that they are primarily concerned with the solvency of their insurer, they also value product performance. Regrettably, as discussed in Chapter 10, there is no foolproof means of prospectively evaluating insurer product performance. Some insurer performance measures, however, can be helpful in gaining insight into the product performance *potential* of an insurer. The four major components comprising insurance product cost are discussed below.

*1. Lapse Rates.* Lapse rates measure the proportion of policyowners who voluntarily terminate their insurance during a year. Lapse rates are generally higher in the first policy year than they are in subsequent years. Lapse rates vary by the socioeconomic and demographic characteristics of an insurer's policyowners. High lapse rates are expected for some target markets and product types.

The lapse rate can be viewed as a proxy for policyowner satisfaction. Insurers with low lapse rates must be providing their customers with the quality of products and services they desire. High lapse rates may be inherent in an insurer's selected market, or they may reflect policyowner dissatisfaction.

Excessive lapses can have a negative impact on:

- Expenses—the insurer will be unable fully to recover initial expenses; thus they must be passed on to persisting policyowners, raising their costs.

- Investments—the insurer may lose planned investment cash flows; this may result in forced sales of investments at a loss in order to meet surrender demands.

- Mortality antiselection—in general, uninsurables tend not to lapse, causing the insurer to experience a greater proportion of death claims than expected if the lapse rate is high.

Thus, lapses can negatively affect each of the three major factors affecting life insurance cost. Because of this fact and because it is a proxy measure for policyowner satisfaction, if one had to select only one proxy product performance indicator, it probably would be the lapse rate.

Comparable product sale mixes produce more comparable and relevant bases for comparison. Comparisons between insurers with substantially dissimilar life product mixes should be avoided.

*2. Investment Yield.* As noted above, the yield on an insurer's investments can be an important factor in assessing insurer profitability. Investment yield is also important to customers because an insurer earning a strong investment return is in a position to pass that superior return on to policyowners.

The net rate of investment return before federal income taxes is a sound basis on which to compare insurers, provided differences in asset risk are considered. Although it is also useful for measuring product performance, it is arguably less important today than in past times. The spread between the actual return and the interest credited on a particular product line is the more critical performance measure.[37]

*3. Expenses.* The insurance customer desires quality service, but at the lowest possible cost. The ratio of ordinary life general expenses to premiums provides a measure of how much of each premium dollar received is needed to cover an insurer's expenses. The lower the ratio, the better, *ceteris paribus.*

Comparisons between insurers with substantially dissimilar life product mixes probably should be avoided, since expenses naturally vary by product type. Moreover, insurers with large blocks of new business relative to renewal business can be expected to exhibit a higher ordinary expense ratio because of the higher first-year expenses of new business.

*4. Mortality.* A low ratio of actual mortality to expected mortality is a measure of favorable mortality experience. This is important because mortality savings can be passed on to participating policyowners in the dividend or, in the case of nonparticipating current assumption products, in a product's mortality charge. Although many factors can distort this ratio, it is the only available measure for comparing mortality experience between companies. The A.M. Best Co. uses this ratio when reviewing company mortality experience, and it renders a comment about the extent to which the insurer's ratio is favorable. When using this ratio to determine its comments, Best takes into consideration the age of the company's business and types of business.

*Conclusion.* It is clear, therefore, that there are no completely satisfactory means for comparing the financial condition and operational performance of insurers. As a consequence, substantial reliance continues to be placed on rating

[37] See Chap. 30.

agencies' evaluations of insurers. Also, one might be able to glean much from comparing a few, simple financial ratios with national norms and those of competing insurers. With all of this done, however, the fact remains that insurance customers still must rely in good faith on the integrity and trustworthiness of insurance company management.

# *Appendix A*

## EXPLANATIONS OF BEST'S RATINGS

### *A++ and A+ (Superior)*

Assigned to companies which, in our opinion, have achieved superior overall performance when compared to the standards established by the A.M. Best Company. A++ and A+ (Superior) companies have a very strong ability to meet their policyholder and other contractual obligations over a long period of time.

### *A and A- (Excellent)*

Assigned to companies which, in our opinion, have achieved excellent overall performance when compared to the standards established by the A.M. Best Company. A and A- (Excellent) companies have a strong ability to meet their policyholder and other contractual obligations over a long period of time.

### *B++ and B+ (Very Good)*

Assigned to companies which, in our opinion, have achieved very good overall performance when compared to the standards established by the A.M. Best Company. B++ and B+ (Very Good) companies have a strong ability to meet their policyholder and other contractual obligations, but their financial strength may be susceptible to unfavorable changes in underwriting or economic conditions.

### *B and B- (Good)*

Assigned to companies which, in our opinion, have achieved good overall performance when compared to the standards established by the A.M. Best Company. B and B- (Good) companies generally have an adequate ability to meet their policyholder and other contractual obligations, but their financial strength is susceptible to unfavorable changes in underwriting or economic conditions.

### *C++ and C+ (Fair)*

Assigned to companies which, in our opinion, have achieved fair overall performance when compared to the standards established by the A.M. Best Company. C++ and C+ (Fair) companies generally have a reasonable ability to meet their policyholder and other contractual obligations, but their financial strength is vulnerable to unfavorable changes in underwriting or economic conditions.

### *C and C- (Marginal)*

Assigned to companies which, in our opinion, have achieved marginal overall performance when compared to the standards established by the A.M. Best

Company. C and C- (Marginal) companies have a current ability to meet their policyholder and other contractual obligations, but their financial strength is very vulnerable to unfavorable changes in underwriting or economic conditions.

## D (Below Minimum Standards)

Assigned to companies which meet our minimum size and experience requirements, but do not meet the minimum standards established by the A.M. Best Company for a Best's Rating of "C-."

## E (Under State Supervision)

Assigned to companies which are placed under any form of supervision, control, or restraint by a state insurance regulatory authority such as conservatorship or rehabilitation, but does not include liquidation. May be assigned to a company under a cease and desist order issued by a regulator from a state other than its state of domicile.

## F (In Liquidation)

Assigned to companies which have been placed under an order of liquidation or have voluntarily agreed to liquidate.

## Ratings Not Assigned by Category

•**NA-1 Special Data Filing**: Assigned primarily to small mutual and stock companies that are exempt from the requirement to file the standard NAIC annual statement. These company reports are based on selected financial information obtained by the A.M. Best Company.

•**NA-2 Less than Minimum Size:** Assigned to companies that file the standard NAIC annual statement but do not meet our minimum size requirement. To assure reasonable financial stability, we require a company to have a minimum policyholders' surplus of $1.5 million. This rating classification is also assigned to a company that is effectively dormant, has no significant premium volume, or has no net insurance business in force. Exceptions are: the company is 100% reinsured by a Best's Rated company; or is a member of a group participating in a business pooling arrangement; and a company writing stable lines of business that has demonstrated a long history of above average performance when compared to Best's Rating standards. Companies assigned the NA-2 Rating classification are eligible for the assignment of Best's Financial Performance Index (FPI).

•**NA-3 Insufficient Operating Experience:** Assigned to a company which meets, or we anticipate will meet, our minimum size requirement, but has not accumulated five consecutive years of representative operating experience. This requirement pertains only to the age of the company's financial performance and does not relate to the actual experience of its management. Our operating experience requirement requires consistency in both the types of coverages written and the relative volume of gross and net premium writings. Additional years of operating experience may be required if a company exhibits substantial growth in new business or change(s) in product mix whereby the development of the company's business or reserves may not be sufficiently mature at the end of five years to permit a satisfactory evaluation. Companies assigned to the NA-3 category are eligible for assignment of Best's Financial Performance Index (FPI).

•**NA-4 Rating Procedure Inapplicable:** Assigned to a company when the nature of its business and/or operations is such that our normal rating procedure does not properly apply. Examples are: companies writing lines of business not common to the property-casualty or life/health fields; companies writing financial guaranty insurance; companies retaining only a small portion of their gross premiums written; companies which have discontinued writing new and renewal business and have a defined plan to run-off existing contractual obligations; companies that discount loss reserves to the extent that the anticipated future investment income represents a significant part of their current policyholders' surplus; and companies not soliciting business in the United States. This rating is also assigned to life/health companies whose sole operation is the acceptance of business written directly by a parent, subsidiary, or affiliated insurance company; or those writing predominantly property/casualty insurance under a dual charter.

•**NA-5 Significant Change:** Generally assigned to a previously rated company which experiences a significant change in ownership, management, or book of business whereby its operating experience may be interrupted or subject to change; or any other relevant event that has or may affect the general trend of a company's operations. This may include pending mergers, sale to a new owner, substantial growth in premium writings or a significant redirection of marketing emphasis. Depending on the nature of the change, our rating procedure may require a period of one to five years before the company is again eligible for a rating.

•**NA-6 Reinsured by Unrated Reinsurer:** Assigned to a company that has a substantial portion of its book of business reinsured by/or has reinsurance recoverables from non-Best's Rated reinsurers that represent a substantial portion of its policyholders' surplus. Exceptions are non-Best's Rated foreign reinsurers that comply with our reporting rquirements and satisfy our financial performance standards.

•**NA-7 Below Minimum Standards:** Discontinued in 1992 and replaced by the Best's Rating of D.

•**NA-8 Incomplete Financial Information:** Assigned to a company that is eligible for a rating, but fails to submit complete financial information for the current five-year period under review. This requirement includes all domestic insurance subsidiaries in which the company's ownership exceeds 50%.

•**NA-9 Company Request:** Assigned to a company that is eligible for a Best's Rating, but requests that the rating not be published. The majority of these companies, such as captives, operate in markets that do not require a rating, but cooperate with our request for financial information in order that a report can be prepared and published on their company. The classification is also assigned to a company that requests its rating not be published because it disagrees with either our rating assignment or our rating fee. In this situation, our policy normally requires a minimum of two years to elapse before the company is again eligible for the assignment of a rating.

•**NA-10 Under State Supervision:** Discontinued in 1992 and replaced by the Best's Rating of either E or F.

•**NA-11 Rating Suspended:** Assigned to a previously rated company that has experienced a sudden and significant event affecting the company's financial position and/or operating performance, of which the impact cannot be evaluated due to lack of timely or appropriate information.

# *APPENDIX B*

## EXPLANATIONS OF STANDARD & POOR'S RATINGS

### *Secure Claims-Paying-Ability Ratings:*

| | |
|---|---|
| AAA | Insurers rated "AAA" offer *superior* financial security on both an absolute and relative basis. They possess the highest safety and have an overwhelming capacity to meet policyholder obligations. |
| AA+ AA AA- | Insurers rated "AA" offer *excellent* financial security, and their capacity to meet policyholder obligations differs only in a small degree from insurers rated "AAA." |
| A+ A A- | Insurers rated "A" offer *good* financial security, but their capacity to meet policyholder obligations is somewhat more susceptible to adverse changes in economic or underwriting conditions than more highly rated insurers. |
| BBB+ BBB BBB- | Insurers rated "BBB" offer *adequate* financial security, but their capacity to meet policyholder obligations is considered more vulnerable to adverse economic or underwriting conditions than that of more highly rated insurers. |

### *Vulnerable Claims-Paying-Ability Ratings:*

| | |
|---|---|
| BB+- BB BB- | Insurers rated "BB" offer financial security that may be adequate, but caution is indicated since their capacity to meet policyholder obligations is considered vulnerable to adverse economic or underwriting conditions and may not be adequate for "long-tail" or long-term policies. |
| B+ B B- | Insurers rated "B" are currently able to meet policyholder obligations, but their vulnerability to adverse economic or underwriting conditions is considered high. |
| CCC+ CCC CCC- | Insurers rated "CCC" are vulnerable to adverse economic or underwriting conditions to the extent that their continued capacity to meet policyholder obligations is highly questionable unless a favorable environment prevails. |
| CC C | Insurers rated "CC" or "C" may not be meeting all policyholder obligations, may be operating under the jurisdiction of insurance regulators, and are vulnerable to liquidation. |
| D | Insurers rated "D" have been placed under an order of liquidation. |

*Qualified Solvency Ratings:*

BBBq    Results of our quantitative tests on the insurer's past performance as disclosed in statutory financial statements are consistent with those of insurers offering *above average* security.

BBq     Results of our quantitative tests on the insurer's past performance as disclosed in statutory financial statements are consistent with those of insurers offering *average* security.

Bq      Results of our quantitative tests on the insurer's past performance as disclosed in statutory financial statements are consistent with those of insurers offering *below average* security.

# *APPENDIX C*

## EXPLANATIONS OF MOODY'S RATINGS

### *Financial Strength Ratings:*

Aaa
*Exceptional.* Insurance companies that are rated Aaa are judged to be of the best quality. Their policy obligations carry the smallest degree of credit risk. While the financial strength of these companies is likely to change, such changes as can be visualized are most unlikely to impair their fundamentally strong position.

Aa1
Aa2
Aa3
*Excellent.* Insurance companies that are rated Aa are judged to be of high quality by all standards. Together with the Aaa group they comprise what are generally known as high-grade companies. They are rated lower than the best companies because long-term risks appear somewhat larger.

A1
A2
A3
*Good.* Insurance companies that are rated A possess many favorable attributes and are to be considered upper-medium grade. Factors giving security to punctual payment of policyholder obligations are considered adequate but elements may be present that suggest a susceptibility to impairment sometime in the future.

Baa1
Baa2
Baa3
*Adequate.* Insurance companies that are rated Baa are considered as medium grade, i.e., their policyholder obligations are neither highly protected nor poorly secured. Factors giving security to punctual payment of policyholder obligations are considered adequate for the present, but certain protective elements may be lacking or may be characteristically unreliable over any great length of time. These companies' policy obligations lack outstanding investment characteristics and in fact have speculative elements as well.

Ba1
Ba2
Ba3
*Questionable.* Insurance companies that are rated Ba are judged to have speculative elements; their future cannot be considered as well assured. Often the ability of these companies to discharge policyholder obligations may be very moderate and thereby not well safeguarded during other good and bad times in the future. Uncertainty of position characterizes policyholder obligations of insurance companies in this class.

B1
B2
B3
*Poor.* Policyholder obligations of insurance companies that are rated B generally lack characteristics of the desirable insurance policy. Assurance of punctual payments of policyholder obligations over any long period of time is small.

Caa     *Very poor.* Insurance companies that are rated Caa are of poor standing. They may be in default on their policyholder obligations or there may be present elements of danger with respect to punctual payment of policyholder obligations and claims.

Ca      *Extremely poor.* Insurance companies that are rated Ca are speculative in a high degree. Such companies are often in default on their policyholder obligations or have other marked shortcomings.

C       *Lowest.* Insurance companies that are rated C are the lowest-rated class of insurance companies and can be regarded as having extremely poor prospects of ever attaining real investment standing.

# *APPENDIX D*

## EXPLANATIONS OF DUFF & PHELPS'S RATINGS

### *Claims-Paying Ability Ratings:*

| | |
|---|---|
| AAA | Highest claims paying ability. Risk factors are negligible. |
| AA+<br>AA<br>AA- | Very high claims paying ability. Protection factors are strong. Risk is modest, but may vary slightly over time because of economic and/or underwriting conditions. |
| A+<br>A<br>A- | High claims paying ability. Protection factors are average and there is an expectation of variability in risk over time because of economic and/or underwriting conditions. |
| BBB+<br>BBB<br>BBB- | Below average claims paying ability. Protection factors are average. However, there is considerable variability in risk over time because of economic and/or underwriting conditions. |
| BB+<br>BB<br>BB- | Uncertain claims paying ability and less than investment grade quality. However, the company is deemed likely to meet these obligations when they are due. Protection factors will vary widely with changes in economic and/or underwriting conditions. |
| B+<br>B<br>B- | Possessing risk that policyholder and contractholder obligations will not be paid when due. Protection factors will vary widely with changes in economic and underwriting conditions or company fortunes. |
| CCC+<br>CCC<br>CCC- | There is substantial risk that policyholder and contractholder obligations will not be paid when due. Company has been or is likely to be placed under state insurance department supervision. |

# APPENDIX E

## THE NAIC'S IRIS RATIOS AND THE RANGES OF USUAL VALUES

Ratio 1:  Net Change in Capital and Surplus
*Greater than -10 percent and less than 50 percent*

Ratio 1A:  Gross Change in Capital and Surplus
*Greater than -10 percent and less than 50 percent*

Ratio 2:  Net Gain to Total Income
*Greater than 0 percent*

Ratio 3:  Commissions and Expenses to Premiums and Deposits
*Less than 60 percent*

Ratio 4:  Adequacy of Investment Income
*Greater than 125 percent and less than 900 percent*

Ratio 5:  Nonadmitted to Admitted Assets
*Less than 10 percent*

Ratio 6:  Real Estate to Capital and Surplus
*Less than 200 percent for companies with capital and surplus greater than $5 million; less than 100 percent for companies with capital and surplus equal to or less than $5 million*

Ratio 7:  Investments in Affiliates to Capital and Surplus
*Less than 100 percent*

Ratio 8:  Surplus Relief
*Greater than -99 percent and less than 30 percent for companies with capital and surplus greater than $5 million; greater than -10 percent and less than 10 percent for companies with capital and surplus equal to or less than $5 million*

Ratio 9:  Change in Premium
*Greater than -10 percent and less than 50 percent*

Ratio 10:  Change in Product Mix
*Less than 5.0 percent*

Ratio 11:  Change in Asset Mix
*Less than 5.0%*

# Chapter 12

# LIFE INSURANCE PLANNING

## INTRODUCTION

Chapter 1 presented an overview of the personal financial planning process and the elements that are common to such plans. It suggested, generally, how life and health insurance can be useful in financial planning. Subsequent chapters were intended to help the reader develop an understanding of (1) life insurance fundamentals, (2) the various types of life insurance products, and (3) aspects of sound evaluation of life insurance and annuity products and insurers. This chapter begins a process of examining, in more detail, some of the ways that life insurance products can fit into individual financial plans.

The main purpose served by life insurance—protection against the financial consequences of death—is covered in this chapter. Chapter 13 examines the income, estate and gift taxation of life insurance products, and some of the ways that they can be used to optimum tax advantage. Chapter 14 introduces the reader to estate planning and suggests how life insurance can be useful in this area. It also covers the use of life insurance products in retirement planning. The business uses of life insurance are discussed in Chapter 15. The nature and role of health insurance in financial planning are discussed in Chapters 16 and 17.

## THE INDIVIDUAL AND ECONOMIC SECURITY

Humanity's quest for security is universal. Although security means different things to different individuals, there appears to be one common frame of reference. All views of security relate to needs or wants.

326

Economic security can be evaluated only for a particular individual, family, business, or country at a given point in time. Security in general can be thought of as peace of mind and freedom from uncertainty; insecurity implies feelings of doubt, fear, and apprehension.

Insecurity relates to the lack of confidence or the uncertainty of individuals regarding one or more of their needs. Social scientists agree that needs are almost unlimited and change over time. As soon as one need is satisfied, another appears. They also suggest, however, that a *priority* of need levels exists.

As the more basic needs are encountered, they claim priority, and efforts to satisfy higher needs must be postponed. A. H. Maslow, a pioneer researcher in this area, developed a need priority of five levels:

1. Basic physiological needs
2. Safety from external danger
3. Love, affection, and social activity
4. Esteem and self-respect
5. Self-realization and accomplishment[1]

The significant point for the purpose of this discussion is that need levels have a sequence of domination. When physiological needs are satisfied, the safety needs tend to dominate. For the majority of individuals in the United States and other developed countries today, basic physiological needs are reasonably well satisfied. In parts of the world with low productivity or famine or disaster, however, the priority of physiological needs is clear, because the first level of survival is the issue.

Although physiological needs are essentially finite (one can benefit from only so much food, clothing, and shelter), needs at the third, fourth, and fifth levels are potentially infinite. Accordingly, higher-order needs are likely to be the dominant ones in more advanced economies. Lower-order needs are satisfied primarily through a person's labors, wages, and accumulated wealth. One must have money to fulfill physiological and economic security needs. One's higher-order needs, on the other hand, are satisfied primarily through symbolic behavior of psychic and social content. One senses meaning in experiences and derives satisfaction from them—a behavior of a totally different order from economic behavior. Thus individuals strive to satisfy their needs as they perceive them from a frame of reference that has been built over a lifetime of individual, family, and other environmental influences. Each individual is dominated by a need level that is reflective of his or her economic, psychological, and social circumstances.

How much security is good? How much is bad? How do risk and uncertainty, qualitatively and quantitatively, relate to economic security—to the family's life cycle and the human life cycle? As mentioned earlier, the response to risk and uncertainty varies widely, depending on factors such as educational experience, sex, maturity, relationships of love and friendship, and age.

---

[1] A. H. Maslow, "A Theory of Human Motivation," *Psychological Review*, Vol. 1 (1943), pp. 370–396, and Maslow, *Motivation and Personality* (New York: Harper & Row, 1954).

Paul Tillich has stated that man is most human at the point of choice—when engaged in decision-making. This capacity permits one to maintain his or her individual identity, to develop a self-image based on a matrix of values—one's individual value system. An individual's reaction to various degrees of uncertainty in life influences decisions and provides an individualistic identity.

It is only with reasonable economic security (i.e., physiological and safety needs reasonably satisfied) that one is motivated by, and makes decisions based on, the higher-order needs, such as self-realization and accomplishment. Therefore a reasonable level of economic security can provide one with the opportunity to become more attuned to oneself, to find greater meaning in life, and to ponder interrelationships with other humans.

Social insurance and group insurance often provide a foundation upon which a responsible person can design an individualized security program that provides an environment for creative life and living. Individual life insurance and health insurance represent the opportunity to bring an appropriate level of economic security to the individual and his or her family, which can permit family members the freedom to decide where to live, where to work, where and when to retire, if and when to marry, and how to live. Regardless of death or disability, life and health insurance can permit members of a family to continue to live in accordance with *their* life plan. In short, economic need will not force them into an unwanted life-style. The self-respect and confidence that arise from the conscious, individualized decisions involved in building a security program can contribute in some small way to the creative risk-taking that is essential to individual fulfillment.

If there is truth to the view that human growth involves intelligent decision-making and that individual identity is critically important to human growth and fulfillment, careful attention should be given to maintaining an environment wherein we retain a sense of personal responsibility for our welfare and that of our family. The opportunity to identify one's goals and needs, to develop an individual matrix of values, and to implement these through individual decisions regarding one's tailor-made economic security program are important elements in maintaining a virile, creative society.

Contemporary capitalism is a political, economic, and social system under which the individual and individual responsibility are paramount. It assumes that financial compensation is geared generally to contribution. It further assumes that free individuals with reasonable economic security can control their own destinies through risk-taking, while protecting their loved ones by consciously arranging a tailor-made security program that is consistent with their individual goals and objectives.

The institution of life insurance provides a vehicle through which individuals can secure their human life values (their potential estates) while seeking their goals (risk-taking), with the assurance that their families will not suffer if their skills and talents are eliminated by premature death or disability.

## THE ECONOMIC BASIS FOR LIFE AND HEALTH INSURANCE

### THE CONCEPT OF HUMAN CAPITAL

Economists since Adam Smith have recognized that people are important elements of a nation's wealth. Economic research related to *investment* in human capital has recently gained substantial recognition.[2] Investment in human capital (e.g., education) has become one of the most cogent explanations for the differences in countries' rates of economic growth as well as differences in wage rates between countries and within countries.

The most distinctive feature of economic systems is the growth in human capital. The increased productivity arising from investments in human capital is so significant that human resource management has come to the fore as a major management responsibility in every type of institution in virtually every major society. It would be useful, therefore, if we could establish a conceptual framework for estimating the value of assets in the form of human capital.

Human resources obviously have both quantitative and qualitative dimensions. How can the magnitude of investment in human capital formation be estimated? In the case of physical capital goods, the practice is to estimate the magnitude of *physical* capital formation by *expenditures* made to produce the capital goods. Estimating human capital formation is complicated by the necessity to distinguish between expenditures for *consumption* and for *savings* (or *investment*). Much of what is called consumption constitutes investment in human capital. Thus direct expenditures on education, health, and migration to take advantage of better job opportunities are clear examples, as are earnings forgone by attending school and by workers acquiring on-the-job training. In these and other ways, the quality of human effort can be greatly improved and its productivity enhanced.

One method for estimating human capital relies on its yield rather than its cost. The marketplace tends to reflect investment in personal development through the wages and salaries that a human agent earns. The resulting increase in earnings can be viewed as the yield on the investment. (In principle, the value of the investment can be determined by taking the present value of the potential future earnings, just as the value of physical capital goods can be determined by discounting its income stream.) Thus those with college degrees typically earn more than those without them. This earnings differential can be thought of as the return on an investment in education, net of opportunity costs.

---

[2]The 1992 Nobel Memorial Prize for Economics was awarded to Professor Gary S. Becker for his pioneering research on human capital. See Gary S. Becker, "*Investment in Human Capital: A Theoretical Analysis,*" The Journal of Political Economy, Vol. 70 (Oct 1962), pp. 9–49; and Gary S. Becker, *Human Capital,* 2nd ed. (New York: National Bureau of Economic Research, 1975).

## THE HUMAN LIFE VALUE CONCEPT

The human life value concept is one segment of the general theory of human capital. Although this general area of inquiry has been under discussion for over four centuries, only recently has the interrelationship between human capital and life insurance been acknowledged.[3] There was some semblance of the idea expressed in the Bible, in the Code of Hammurabi, and in early Anglo-Saxon law, where it was used to determine the compensation to be allowed to the relatives of an individual killed by a third party. In recent years, the valuation of a human life in connection with legal actions seeking recovery for wrongful death has gained considerable prominence. A considerable body of literature has developed in this area, contributing to a more scientific approach to the calculation of damages (including human life values) in wrongful-death cases.[4]

Apparently, the concept was first applied to life insurance in the 1880s through the efforts of Jacob L. Green, then president of the Connecticut Mutual Life Insurance Company. It was not, however, until the 1920s that the human life value concept became established as an economic basis for life insurance.

***Human Life Value Defined.*** In contrast to human capital, which is the production potential of an individual, human life value is a measure of the actual future earnings or service of an individual—that is, the capitalized value of an individual's net future earnings after subtracting self-maintenance costs.[5] From the standpoint of dependents, an individual's human life value is the measure of the value of benefits that the dependents can expect from their breadwinner or supporter. Similarly, from the viewpoint of an organization, the human life value of a key employee is a measure of the value of his or her services to the firm. Thus there is not necessarily only a single human life value. A given human life value is a function of its purpose and value to others.

***Significance of the Human Life Value Concept.*** In 1924 S. S. Huebner proposed the human life value concept as a philosophical framework for the analysis of basic economic risks faced by individuals. This concept has been widely accepted by those associated with the institution of life insurance. In Huebner's view, the concept meant more than just a statement that a human life has an economic value. Rather, it involved the following five important concepts:

[3] Sir William Petty (1623–1687) was the first economist credited with using the concept of the economic value of a man. Fifty years passed before another economist, Richard Cantillon (1680–1734), made another contribution to the concept of human capital. Then followed Adam Smith (1723–1790), Johann H. von Thünen (1783–1850), John Stuart Mill (1806–1873), and others. In 1853 Sir William Farr, an economist and statistician, derived the first set of equations used to describe the human life value. In so doing, he laid the basic foundation of the theory as we know it today. See Alfred E. Hofflander, "The Human Life Value: An Historical Perspective," *The Journal of Risk and Insurance*, Vol. 33 (Sept. 1966), pp. 381–391.

[4] See, for example, Stuart M. Speiser, *Recovery for Wrongful Death—Economic Handbook* (Rochester, N. Y.: Lawyers Co-operative Publishing Co., 1970); see also Philip Eden, *Existing Human Life Values*, 2nd ed. (Berkeley, Calif.: Techpress International, 1985).

[5] The human life can be viewed as having two components: economic and hedonic. The hedonic approach places value on the enjoyment one derives from living.

*1. The human life value should be carefully appraised and capitalized.* The human life value is based on the fact that persons who earn more than is necessary for their self-maintenance have a monetary value to those who are dependent upon them. Thus it may be defined as the capitalized value of that part of the earnings of individuals devoted to the support of family dependents, business associates, and others who benefit from their economic earning capacity.

The primary purpose of life and health insurance is the protection of the family. Every family is dependent for subsistence upon an income that necessarily varies in amount with circumstances. In some instances, this income is obtained from the return on invested funds that have been accumulated or inherited, but in the overwhelming majority of cases, the subsistence of the family depends upon the current earnings of the breadwinner. He or she has assumed responsibility for the support of dependents, and dependent family members look to the breadwinner for adequate maintenance. His or her life has an economic value (and the same is also often true of other family members) to the dependent members of the family, and it is this value of one life in relation to another that justifies the existence of life and health insurance. Such a relationship may also exist with business associates whenever they pool their capital and skills in an enterprise. In fact, whenever continuance of a life is financially valuable to others, an economic basis for life and health insurance exists.

*2. The human life value should be recognized as the creator of substantially all property values.* The human life value is key to turning property into a productive force.[6] In other words, the human life value is the cause and property values are the effect.

*3. The family is an economic unit, organized around the human life values of its members.* The family needs to be organized and managed, and its economic values finally liquidated in the same manner that other enterprises are organized, operated, and liquidated.

*4. The human life value and its protection should be regarded as constituting the principal economic link between the present and succeeding generations.* The realization of the potential net earnings of the breadwinner constitutes the economic foundation for the proper education and development of the children in the event of the breadwinner's premature death or disability, and the protection of the children against the burden of parent financial support.

*5. In view of the significance of human life values relative to property values, the scientific principles of business management utilized in connection*

---

[6] Income of the United States and many other countries has been increasing at a higher rate than the rate of increase of combined amount of land, hours worked, and stock of reproducible capital used to produce the income. This would appear to represent a return on the investment made in human capital, and it is additional evidence of the critical role of human capital in economic systems.

*with property values should be applied to life values.* Principles such as appraisal, conservation, indemnity, and depreciation should be applied to the organization, management, and liquidation of human life values. These principles have been applied to property values for decades.

***The Qualitative Characteristics of the Life Value.*** A person possesses two estates—an "acquired" estate and a "potential" estate. The former refers to what one has acquired—one's property estate. The latter refers to one's monetary worth as an economic force—that is, one's capability of earning for others beyond the limits of one's own self-maintenance, and, if given time, the ability to accumulate surplus earnings into an acquired estate. The insurable value of an individual's economic possibilities may be defined as the monetary worth of the following economic forces that are incorporated within one's being: (1) ethical behavior; (2) good health; (3) the willingness to work; (4) willingness to make an investment in the mind; and (5) creative ability and judgment.

***The Quantitative Characteristics of the Human Life Value.*** The human life value may be defined, quantitatively, as the capitalized value of the expected net earnings of an individual. The same economic and statistical principles are applicable whether one is concerned with the appraisal of the value of property or the earning capacity of human beings.[7] The general elements of appraising potential earnings for an individual require a projection, over his or her expected work life, of such items as basic earnings, incentive earnings, and fringe benefits. These elements may generally be expected to vary with such criteria as occupation and industry, age, residence, education, and mobility. The process is still further complicated by the necessity of projecting change in each of these considerations.

***Human Life Value Subject to Loss.*** The human life value is subject to loss through (1) premature death, (2) disability, (3) retirement, and (4) unemployment. It should be clear that any event affecting an individual's earning capacity has a corresponding impact on his or her human life value (potential estate).

The probability of loss from death and disability is significantly greater than from the other commonly insured perils. Less than 1 building in every 100 ever experiences a significant fire or other loss throughout its entire history, whereas 1 of every 5 workers dies before age 65, and all remaining workers die thereafter. Moreover, the average property loss in well-protected cities does not exceed 10 to 15 percent of the property value involved; that is, it is a partial loss. Perhaps only 1 of every 30 fires results in what is substantially a total loss. The death peril, on

---

[7] Some persons and cultures are uneasy about human life valuation. The market for property is well developed, and it is relatively easy to determine the price of goods and commodities, especially if they are homogeneous. Each human life, however, is unique. Placing a value on human life is, therefore, difficult since society does not condone the sale of persons. Society does, however, permit sale of a person's services. It is the value of a person's services that the human life value concept actually is measuring. Placing an economic value on a person's life (services) is not immoral; it is the concept of ownership of another person that society finds immoral.

the contrary, always results in a total loss to the potential estate. The same is true of many total-disability claims. Reasoning from this standpoint, it does seem that the death peril to the potential estate is much more serious than are fire and other perils to the acquired estate. The same can be said for disability. Yet property insurance is almost universally taken as a matter of course, whereas death and disability insurance protection often are avoided or purchased in amounts far less than the individual's human life value.[8]

Life insurance and health insurance, thus, make possible the preservation of an individual's human capital in the face of an uncertain lifetime. The human life value concept provides the philosophical basis for operationalizing the insurance purchase decision.

## ECONOMIC THEORIES OF CONSUMPTION AND LIFE INSURANCE

Individuals occupy their time either in activities that produce income (or its equivalent) or in those that do not. For the sake of simplicity, economists label these two states of nature as work and leisure. One's investment in self—in human capital—plus one's preferences, time, wealth, income, and a host of other factors, influence how a given individual will allocate his or her time between work and leisure. As Figure 12-1 illustrates, work gives rise to income, which in turn is spent on consumption or is saved. Economic theories of consumption seek to explain consumer consumption (and savings) behavior over one's lifetime.

Economics is concerned with both positive and normative issues. **Positive issues** involve explanations of observed economic behavior; the concern is with "what is" questions. By contrast, **normative issues** are involved in questions relating to "what ought to be."

The human life value (HLV) concept, therefore, provides a *normative* economic approach to life and health insurance planning. It suggests how one

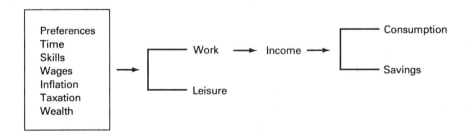

**FIGURE 12-1**

**CONSUMPTION SCHEMATIC**

[8] The economist would immediately want to know why this postulate may be true. Is it that individuals underestimate the likelihood of their own death or loss of health or perhaps their own economic value? Are their incomes too low? Are life insurance and disability insurance perceived as offering poor value? Although the following sections explore some of these issues, the fact remains that our knowledge is sketchy.

"ought" to behave. Stated differently, it provides an economic rationale for life (and health) insurance purchase from a replacement cost perspective. By this, it is meant that individuals interested in complete *replacement* of themselves as wage earners (net of self-maintenance costs) would be drawn to its logic and simplicity. As a *positive* economic concept, however, it can lead to results that are inconsistent with actual consumer behavior. The HLV concept provides an economic *rationale* for the purchase of life insurance, but not an economic *explanation* for its purchase.

With this in mind, it will prove insightful to examine briefly economic theories that provide an economic explanation for the purchase of life insurance—that is, to focus on the positive economics of life insurance. To do so, it is necessary to examine economic theories of consumption, since life insurance purchases reduce current consumption (by virtue of the premium payment) in order to protect the consumption ability of dependents.

***Economic Theories of Consumption.*** This section reviews three consumption theories. Each theory begins with the common assumption that observed consumer behavior is an attempt by rational consumers to maximize their **lifetime utility**. The British philosopher Jeremy Bentham is generally credited with the introduction of the concept of utility. He declared in 1823:

> By the principle of utility is meant that principle which approves or disapproves of every action whatsoever, according to the tendency which it appears to have to augment or diminish the happiness of the party whose interest is in question.[9]

Individuals, therefore, prefer more of a "good" than less of it and less of a "bad" than more of it. In other words, they seek to maximize their utility (or minimize their disutility). Individuals can be expected, furthermore, to maximize their utility over their lifetimes—that is, to arrange their affairs as best as they can to derive maximum enjoyment (and minimum discomfort) throughout their lives.

The maximization of lifetime utility, therefore, involves attempts by consumers to allocate their lifetime incomes in such a way as to achieve an optimum lifetime pattern of consumption. This means planning for the future and not necessarily "living only for today." Several elements of utility theory warrant a brief explanation.

First, consumers are presumed to behave in a certain, consistent manner. Thus if Joe says that he prefers an Audi to a Buick and a Buick to a Chevrolet, utility theory assumes that Joe prefers an Audi to a Chevrolet. Implicit within this scheme is the idea that Joe can, in fact, make comparisons of the competing items. A further presumption is that individual preferences can be rank-ordered through utility theory.

Individuals, of course, do not always act rationally; they are sometimes inconsistent. Nonetheless, the concept of utility—the economic theory of

---

[9] Jeremy Bentham, *An Introduction to the Principles of Morals and Legislation*, 1823 ed., Chap. 1.

consumer choice—is considered by most economists to provide a useful investigative tool that can reasonably reflect reality for individual consumers.[10]

*1. The Absolute Income Hypothesis.* Theories of consumption largely date from the era of the noted economist John Maynard Keynes. In 1935 he observed that, on average, the larger a person's income, the smaller the proportion devoted to consumption (and the larger the proportion devoted to savings).[11] His theory (sometimes referred to as the **absolute income hypothesis**) suggests, in effect, that as average household income increases, the proportion consumed (saved) should decrease (increase) to that observed for other households within the new, higher-income bracket. The theory has strong intuitive appeal and formerly was widely accepted. With the passage of time, other theories have come to enjoy broader support.

*2. The Relative Income Hypothesis.* A variation of the Keynes view by James S. Duesenberry argues that consumption depends on the household's income *relative* to the income of neighboring households and households with which it identifies, rather than the *absolute* level of income.[12] Thus this theory holds that if a household's income were to rise but its relative income position remained unchanged, its division between consumption and savings would remain unchanged. Similarly, if a household's income were to remain unchanged but the income of others with whom it identified rose, this **relative income hypotheses** would hold that a greater proportion of household income then would be allocated to consumption—in an effort to "keep up with the Joneses."

An interesting recent extension of Duesenberry's work argues that certain consumption items typically cannot be observed (e.g., the amount spent on insurance) and that consumption expenditures thereby vary, depending on the observability of goods and services.[13]

*3. The Life-Cycle/Permanent Income Hypothesis.* Both the absolute and relative income hypotheses suggest that current consumption is some function of a household's current level of income. Consumption theories posed by Ando and Modigliani[14] and by Friedman[15] take a different view of income. According to

---

[10] See Jack Hirshleifer, *Price Theory and Applications*, 4th ed. (Englewood Cliffs, N.J.: Prentice Hall Inc., 1988), Chap. 3.

[11] In economic terms, the smaller the marginal propensity of a person to consume, the larger is his or her marginal propensity to save. See John Maynard Keynes, *The General Theory of Employment, Interest, and Money* (New York: Harcourt, Brace & World, Inc., 1935), Chap. 8.

[12] James S. Duesenberry, *Income, Savings, and the Theory of Consumer Behavior* (Cambridge, Mass.: Harvard University Press, 1949).

[13] Robert H. Frank, "The Demand for Unobservable and Other Nonpositional Goods," *American Economic Review* (Mar. 1985), pp. 101–115.

[14] Albert Ando and Franco Modigliani, "The 'Life Cycle' Hypothesis of Savings: Aggregate Implications and Tests," *American Economic Review* (Mar. 1963).

[15] Milton Friedman, *A Theory of the Consumption Function* (Princeton, N.J.: Princeton University Press, 1957).

the Ando-Modigliani **life cycle hypothesis** of consumption, an individual's income can be expected to be low in the beginning and end stages of life and high during the middle of life.

In spite of these life cycle changes in income, however, the individual can be expected to maintain a roughly constant or modestly increasing level of consumption. Figure 12-2 is a stylized presentation of a life cycle of income ($y$) and consumption ($c$). The shaded areas in early life and in later life represent periods when consumption exceeds income—that is, periods of dissavings. In early life, the family typically makes good the deficit; in later life, personal savings are ordinarily drawn down. The area above enclosed by $y$ represents savings—the period during which any earlier debts are repaid and amounts accumulated for retirement.

Friedman's **permanent income hypothesis** for consumption, like the life cycle hypothesis, assumes that the individual wishes to smooth out his or her level of lifetime consumption but does so through an individual assessment as to his or her *permanent* level of income.

Permanent income is stable, reflecting some type of weighted (for the time value of money) average of the consumer's expected future income. It is an annualized measure of the individual's human capital (as with the HLV concept, but with no diminution for self-maintenance expenses). Variations of actual from permanent income (so-called transitory income) reflect factors of a chance or accidental nature and do not affect consumption—at least not unless they cease to be chance fluctuations.

Consumption also has its permanent and transitory components. The yearly difference between total income and total consumption is savings, which can

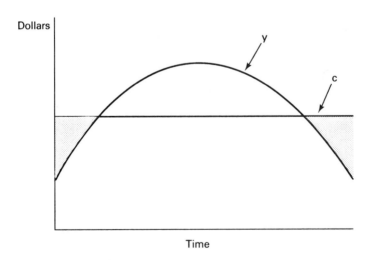

**FIGURE 12-2**

**AN ILLUSTRATION OF THE LIFE CYCLE OF INCOME AND CONSUMPTION**

fluctuate greatly from year to year under this hypothesis since the transitory income and consumption components fluctuate annually independently of each other.

The life cycle and permanent income models are closely related. Households with large, positive transitory incomes in Friedman's model could be in the middle years of the Ando-Modigliani life cycle, and households with large, negative transitory incomes could be in the early or later life cycle states. As a result, the hypotheses are often viewed together or even as different conceptualizations of the same issue. In any event, today they are widely accepted reasonable explanations of the consumer problem of dividing consumption (and, therefore, savings) between the present and the future.

***Consumption Theories and Life Insurance.*** In their earliest forms, none of the consumption theories appropriately allowed for the possibility of bequests or for an uncertain time of death. Obviously, these two extensions are of direct relevance to an economic theory of life insurance consumption.

In his seminal paper, Yaari examined the role of life insurance within the context of the life cycle model by including the risk of dying. He showed *conceptually* that an individual increases expected lifetime utility (enjoyment) by purchasing life insurance and annuities.[16]

Pissarides extended Yaari's work by examining the combination of the motivation of savings for retirement and for bequests via life insurance.[17] He proved that life insurance was theoretically capable of absorbing all fluctuations in lifetime income and, thereby, could enable consumption and bequests to be independent of the timing of income. As a result, the same effective consumption pattern could be achieved through the appropriate use of life insurance as could be achieved if the time of death were known with certainty.[18] Without life insurance, the lifetime consumption pattern would be different and involve less enjoyment (utility).

The preceding conceptual economic findings probably come as no particular surprise to thoughtful students of insurance. This observation, however, in no way diminishes the importance of the research. Practical, real-world problems and consumer decision-making can appear bewildering and confusing in the absence of a systematic theory to put them into some intellectual order. Theories lead to tests that confirm, refute, or cause

---

[16] Menahem Yaari, "Uncertain Lifetime, Life Insurance, and the Theory of the Consumer," *Review of Economic Studies* (Apr. 1965), pp. 137-150. This finding was confirmed by Stanley Fischer, "A Life Cycle Model of Life Insurance Purchases," *International Economic Review* (Feb. 1973), pp. 132-152.

[17] C. A. Pissarides, "The Wealth-Age Relation with Life Insurance," *Economica* (Nov. 1980), pp. 451-457.

[18] Ibid., p. 455. Pissarides introduces the concept of perfect life insurance, by which he means that the insurance is actuarially fair, and is instantaneously adjustable to meet changing consumer desires and the transferability of budget constraints. In a more practical world, consumption would be affected.

In each of the papers discussed here, the concept of actuarially fair life insurance (and annuities) is used by the researchers. **Actuarially fair** to economists translates as roughly net premiums to actuaries (see Chap. 19)—that is, premiums are not loaded for expenses or profits.

modification of the theory.[19] In so doing, we learn more about consumer preferences and choice. Better-suited products and services offering good value often result.

## LIFE INSURANCE AND PSYCHOLOGY[20]

The preceding discussion should have made clear the role of life products in ensuring that a family will be able, at a minimum, to meet the lower-order physiological and safety needs were the principal family breadwinner to die or become disabled. The discussion further highlighted the role of economic security—and therefore life and health insurance—in higher-order development.

This section focuses on the psychological aspects of economic uncertainty, attempting to draw inferences that may promote further understanding of the life insurance purchase decision. The treatment here is unavoidably incomplete, for the subject matter touches on the most complex of human motivations and emotions. It is intimately tied with perhaps the most unpleasant of subjects— death—and the fears that accompany it.

Of course, the way a society and a family view death—whether it is, in effect, celebrated, dreaded, or somewhere between the two extremes—influences why an individual would consider purchasing life insurance. In many instances, individuals act as if they consider themselves immortal; they are psychologically unwilling or unable to face their own mortality.

The subject of death can be intertwined with one's religious beliefs and convictions. Indeed, the sometimes intimate relationship between religious commitment and security reinforces the view that we are not dealing with a logical, economic problem alone, but also with a psychological one. As such, until psychology can provide a complete explanation for human decision-making (which most likely is never), any presentation on the psychological aspects of life insurance purchases will itself remain incomplete.

*Anxiety.* Implicit within and running through Maslow's hierarchy of needs is the desire to reduce psychological uncertainty. Such uncertainty gives rise to anxiety. **Anxiety** may be defined as a collection of fears resulting in an unpleasant uneasiness, stress, generalized pessimism, or various risk-aversion attitudes. Psychologists consider that an individual's capacity to tolerate and manage anxiety is a sensitive measure of the healthy integration of his or her personality.

[19] See, for example, John J. Burnett and Bruce A. Palmer, "Examining Life Insurance Ownership Through Demographic and Psychographic Characteristics," *The Journal of Risk and Insurance,*" Vol. 52 (Sept. 1985), pp. 453-467 and Robert Ferber and Lucy Chao Lee, "Acquisition and Accumulation of Life Insurance in Early Married Life," *The Journal of Risk and Insurance,* Vol . 47 (Dec. 1980), pp. 713-734.

[20] This section draws on Irving Pfeffer and David R. Klock, *Perspectives on Insurance* (Englewood Cliffs, N.J.: Prentice Hall, Inc., 1974), Chap. 14.

Anxiety is not an absolute condition. It ranges from extreme neurotic anxiety with an overreaction to a perceived threat to a range of normal anxiety with a reaction that is proportionate to the threat. Normal anxiety can be dealt with constructively at the level of conscious awareness or it can be relieved by various risk-management techniques.

Insurance is a device that can be used to reduce psychological uncertainty. In this respect, it can be akin in its effect to psychiatry, education, religion, and other anxiety-reducing mechanisms. Insurance enhances peace of mind and financial security, and it can provide a partial relief from anxiety.

Anxiety is often fostered, sometimes inadvertently, through the financial planning process. In establishing objectives for the family, consideration is given to events that are among life's most stressful:  death, loss of health, retirement, and divorce.

A scale to measure the relative degrees of life change inherent in various life events has been developed. Table 12-1 lists several life event changes commonly associated with financial planning and shows their relative ranking and their so-called life change unit (LCU) value (with 100 being the greatest value). Life changes induce stress. Note that the death of a spouse is potentially the most stressful of life's events.

Financial planners and insurance salespersons sometimes use the possibility of these life events to arouse anxiety within their clients—to motivate them to reflect on the possible financial consequences of the occurrence of the events. The advisor can then paint a picture of freedom from or at least reduction in anxiety. If this is done properly and with sensitivity by the advisor, the individual may be motivated to act. If it is done crudely, the reaction may be one of distaste and, therefore, may lead to inaction or even hostility. The prospect's willingness to buy or follow advice usually is a function of his or her informational set, emotional condition, trust, and the manner in which the subject matter has been presented by the advisor.

**TABLE 12-1     RANKINGS AND RELATIVE DEGREES OF LIFE CHANGE IN SELECTED LIFE EVENTS**

| Rank | Life Event | LCU Score |
|---|---|---|
| 1 | Death of spouse | 100 |
| 2 | Divorce | 73 |
| 4 | Death of a close family member | 63 |
| 6 | Personal injury or illness | 53 |
| 9 | Retirement | 45 |
| 11 | Major change in health of a family member | 44 |
| 16 | Major change in financial state | 38 |
| 17 | Death of a close friend | 37 |

*Source:* Richard H. Rahe, "Life Change and Subsequent Illness Reports," in *Life Stress and Illness*, E.K. Eric Gunderson and Richard H. Rahe, eds. (Springfield, Ill.: Charles C. Thomas, 1974), pp. 60-61.

We learn from psychology that anxiety is an inhibitor and that the healthy or normal response is to deal with it constructively. This can be done in some instances through mechanisms such as insurance that, instead of repressing the fears, threats, or conflicts, transfers the source of insecurity and permits the individual to make a better adjustment to his or her environment.[21]

*Emotions.* Although most persons believe that they act in a rational manner and, as discussed earlier, utility theory presumes rationality, emotions are a primary determinant of behavior. This is particularly true of the life insurance purchase decision. **Emotions** are learned reactions to a set of experiences or perceptions that have either been very favorable or very distressing. Contact with events or thoughts that recall these experiences can stimulate a desire to remove or satisfy the resulting emotions. For example, individuals who have experienced severe financial difficulty as children or because of the death of a parent or other supporter might be strongly motivated to avoid recurrence of that status for their families through the purchase of insurance.

Emotions can be learned from the experiences of others. Because emotions can be generalized from one set of circumstances to another, many insurance salespersons are successful in communicating to a client the emotional consequences of failing to obtain insurance protection. The purchase of insurance can provide the individual with an overt and constructive outlet for his or her emotional concern.

Stuart Schwarzschild made this most fundamental point in an article titled simply "The Love Theory."[22] He noted, in effect, that irrespective of the economic bases upon which life insurance should be purchased, the underlying motivation for the vast majority of life insurance purchasers revolves around the emotions of love and affection that the insured holds for those in some way dependent upon him or her.

## THE ENVIRONMENT FOR LIFE INSURANCE PLANNING

Individuals, in their life (and health) insurance purchase decisions, are both affected by and affect the environment in which life insurance planning takes place. A general appreciation of the broad environmental factors influencing life

---

[21] This explanation does not account for the phenomenon of gambling, also indulged in by insurance-minded individuals. The rational economic person might engage in betting activity for its thrill and excitement but would never engage in systematic gambling in practice, since the expected value (average payoff) would be less than the cost of playing the game. See Paul A. Samuelson, *Economics*, 9th ed. (New York: McGraw-Hill Book Company, 1973), pp. 424–426. Samuelson sets out the standard economic argument that on the basis of diminishing marginal utility, gambling is economically disadvantageous while insurance is advantageous.

Recent research in economic behavior has described theoretical reasons based on psychology and economics for why an individual might both gamble and purchase insurance. See D. Kahnemon and A. Tversky, "Prospect Theory: An Analysis of Decisions under Risk," *Econometrica*, Vol 47 (Mar. 1979), pp. 263–291; and Mach Maching, "Choices under Uncertainty: Problems Solved and Unsolved," *Journal of Economic Perspective*, Vol. 1 (1987), pp. 121–154.

[22] Stuart Schwarzschild, "The Love Theory—New Rationale for the Purchase of Life Insurance," *Best's Review*, Life/Health ed., Vol. 73 (Sept. 1972), pp. 46–48.

insurance planning is desirable as a prelude to an examination of the life insurance planning process itself.

This section explores four classes of environmental influences: (1) the demographic environment, (2) the economic environment, (3) the political environment, and (4) the cultural environment.

## THE DEMOGRAPHIC ENVIRONMENT

That much of the world's population, including that of the United States, is aging is well recognized. This aging has resulted from changes in fertility rates and in mortality rates. Specifically, many countries, especially the United States, experienced atypically high birth rates following World War II, followed by a gradual but substantial decline in these rates. Figure 12-3 illustrates this phenomenon for the United States. Other developed countries—especially in Europe—have witnessed even lower fertility rates, to the point below that of the replacement rate.[23]

As a consequence of the high post-World War II birth rate, many countries have experienced a so-called baby boom generation, which, for the United States, is often defined as the persons born between 1946 and 1964. These baby boomers represent a substantial bulge in the U.S. population, as illustrated in Figure 12-4.

A companion phenomenon of the past few decades has been the increase in life expectancy. Figure 12-5 shows how U.S. life expectancy has increased

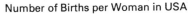

Number of Births per Woman in USA

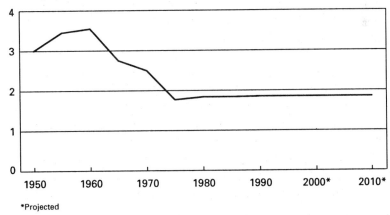

*Projected

**FIGURE 12-3**

**U.S. FERTILITY RATES: 1950 TO 2010**

*Source:* U.S. Bureau of the Census

[23] In other words, the country's population will begin to decline after some time if the fertility rate continues at the low level, in the absence of substantial net immigration.

**FIGURE 24-4**

**THE MIDDLE AGING OF THE UNITED STATES**
*Source:* The Boettner Institute of Financial Gerontology

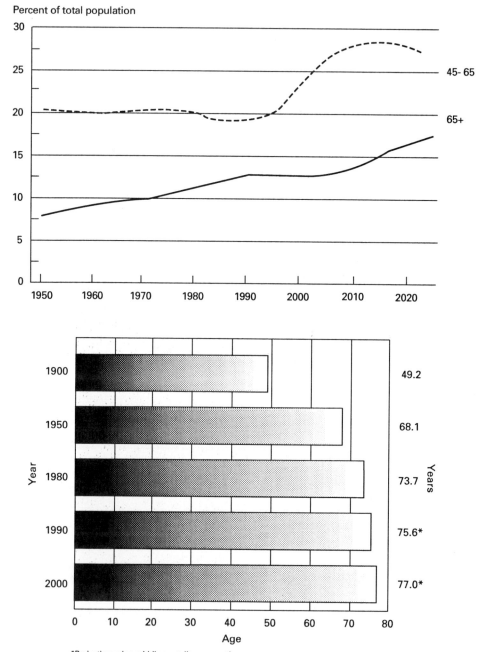

**FIGURE 12-5**

**EXPECTATION OF LIFE AT BIRTH IN THE UNITED STATES**
*Source:* Metropolitan Life Statistical Bulletin, July–Sept. 1985, and U.S. Bureau of the Census

during the twentieth century. Figure 12-6 shows life expectancy for selected countries for 1980 and 2000. An increasing live expectancy has resulted in an increasing proportion of older persons in many societies. As discussed more fully in Chapter 14, this growth can be expected to put new burdens on retirement systems worldwide.

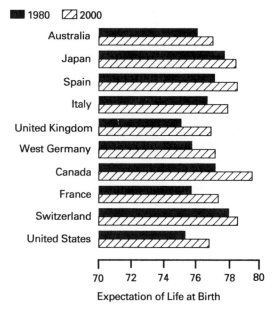

**FIGURE 12-6**

**LIFE EXPECTANCY RATES FOR SELECTED COUNTRIES**
*Source:* U.S. Census Bureau, unpublished data

The existence of baby boom generations in the United States and elsewhere continues to enhance demand for the products sold by life insurance companies. These individuals, for the most part, are in their prime child-rearing years, and, as discussed earlier, the demand for life insurance can be expected to reflect this fact.

The changing nature of U.S. households is altering the character of the demand for life products. The average size of the U.S. household continues to diminish, as Figure 12-7 illustrates. Much of this decline is attributable to the fact that the proportion of one-person households continues to grow, accounting for one in four U.S. households. These one-person households often have the need, at best, for only modest amounts of life insurance. On the other hand, their very singleness puts them at even greater financial risk from a disability and heightens the need for adequate retirement planning.

Figure 12-8 provides some idea of how the composition of U.S. households has been changing. Married couples are expected to continue to

**FIGURE 12-7**

**AVERAGE SIZE HOUSEHOLD IN THE UNITED STATES**
*Source:* Statistical Abstract of the U.S.

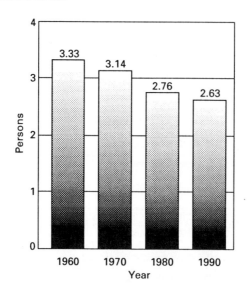

account for a declining majority of households, with roughly one-half of them having no children under the age of 18 present in the home. Double-income families are the rule rather than the exception in the United States and in many other (especially European) countries. In such situations, the death of either spouse could severely disrupt the family's standard of living.

Single-parent householders are becoming more common because of divorce and, to a lesser extent, because of the spouse's death. Dependent children in such situations often give rise to substantial life insurance needs.

Because of lower mortality rates, there are fewer orphans today than in past times, more children who have living grandparents, and more adult children with elderly living parents.[24] Thus the likelihood of a middle-aged U.S. couple having two or more parents alive had risen from only 20 percent in 1940 to almost 50 percent by 1976.[25] Today the probability likely exceeds 50 percent. Because these parents are themselves older today than was the case several decades ago, the nature of any care-giving responsibility is likely to be greater, more complex, and more expensive.[26] Usually, the responsibility for care of elder parents falls on their children, more particularly on the daughter (or daughter-in-law).[27] As one commentator observed:

---

[24] Neal E. Cutler, "International Demographic Trends in Aging, Retirement, and Personal Health Care: Implications for Insurance and Financial Services," *Proceedings of the International Insurance Society* (1991).

[25] P. Uhlemberg, "Death and the Family," *Journal of Family History*, Vol. 5 (1980), pp. 313–320.

[26] Cutler, "International Demographic Trends."

[27] Ibid.

**FIGURE 12-8**

**DISTRIBUTION OF U.S. HOUSEHOLDS BY TYPE 1970–2000**

*Source:* Statistical Abstract of the United States

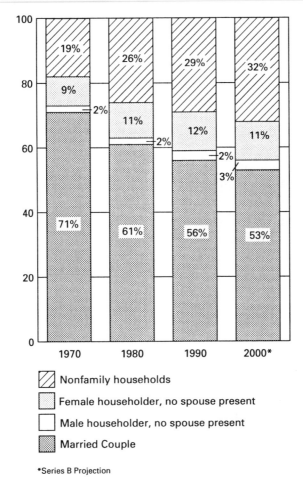

Nonfamily households

Female householder, no spouse present

Male householder, no spouse present

Married Couple

*Series B Projection

More and more women are on the Daughter Track, working, raising kids and helping aging parents....Most [elderly U.S. citizens] are cared for by family members, at home, for free—and most families wouldn't have it any other way....The average American woman will spend 17 years raising children and 18 years helping aged parents.[28]

Gerontologists refer to the phenomenon of middle-aged daughters caring for both teenage children and elderly parents as a "generation in the middle" or "the sandwich generation."[29] Were the care giver to die, the likelihood increases substantially that the elder parent(s) would then need more intensive (and

[28] M. Beck, "Trading Places," *Newsweek* (July 16, 1990), pp. 48–54.

[29] Cutler, "International Demographic Trends."

expensive) professional care and possibly institutionalization. In the absence of substantial personal resources, life insurance coverage on the care giver's life often is a logical financial decision.

## THE ECONOMIC ENVIRONMENT

As stated in Chapter 3, demand for life insurance products and the level of a country's economic development are directly related. The greater the per capita income, the greater both the absolute and relative amounts that are spent with life insurers.

Other aspects of the economic environment affect one's need for life insurance. For example, high inflation is generally considered detrimental to life insurance demand. Although there are life products in the United States and elsewhere that have built-in inflation hedges, individuals nonetheless seem to view life insurance less favorably in an inflationary environment.

Inflation within the United States has varied substantially over the past several decades, as shown by Figure 12-9. As discussed more fully later in this chapter, inflation renders life insurance planning more complex and its results less certain.

Prevailing investment returns and interest rates within an economy also influence life insurance demand. As Figure 12-10 shows, prevailing rates within the United States have varied in line with inflation variations. Interest rates can

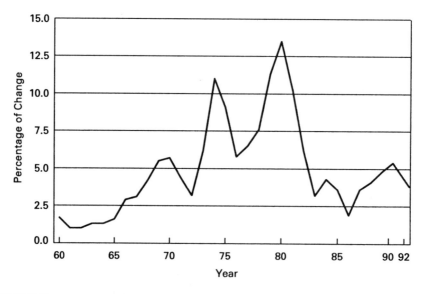

**FIGURE 12-9**

**PERCENTAGE CHANGE IN U.S. CONSUMER PRICE INDEXES**
*Source:* U.S. Bureau of Labor Statistics

**FIGURE 12-10**

**U.S. TREASURY BILL RATES**
*Source:* Federal Reserve Bulletin

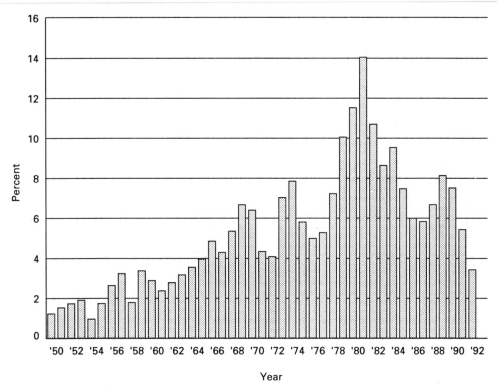

influence the life insurance purchase decision in at least two ways. First, if the effective return within a cash-value policy compares favorably with savings media of comparable security, one would expect to find the prospective saver drawn to life insurance, given its other positive features.[30] Conversely, if the policy's effective yield is low in comparison with alternatives, the individual can be expected to consider alternatives seriously.

The second impact that interest rates can be expected to have on life insurance purchases occurs within the planning process itself. As explained in principle earlier in this chapter and in practice later in this chapter, the life insurance planning process typically requires the use of a discount rate. The selected rate can have an important bearing on the calculation of the amount of life insurance needed.

Finally, the employment status of an individual influences the purchase decision. Unemployed and underemployed persons rarely feel as though they can afford to purchase life insurance, even though their very status may suggest an even greater need (because they probably have less or no employer-provided life insurance coverage).

[30] See Chap. 3.

## THE POLITICAL ENVIRONMENT

The decisions made by public policymakers—insurance regulators, the courts, legislatures, and others—can have a profound impact on the desirability of life insurance purchases. Their decisions determine *what* life products can be sold, *who* can sell them, and *how* they can be sold.

Thus in the United States, state statutory requirements coupled with the policy approval process (see Chapter 34) determine whether a given insurance product can be legally sold within a state. Most countries have such requirements. Similarly, tax laws and other laws greatly influence product design and value. For example, the repeal of the U.S. federal law providing for the tax-deferred accumulation of interest on life product cash values would undoubtedly decrease the attractiveness of cash-value policies.

Governments also determine who can supply (sell) life products. Minimum capital and surplus or solvency margin standards plus other requirements for insurer licensing serve as marketplace gatekeepers (see Chapter 34). Too lax a standard can result in financially unsound insurers operating within a market, thereby undermining consumer confidence in the industry. Too strict a standard can result in less consumer choice and value. A balance is needed.

Governments determine whether and under what circumstances nonnational insurers and nonnationally owned domestic insurers can enter and compete within their markets. The various U.S. state markets generally make few, if any, fundamental distinctions between U.S. and non-U.S. firms or ownership, but many other countries impose various barriers to nonnational firms or ownership.[31]

Besides determining which among several possible private insurers can operate within a market, policymakers also must decide the appropriate role of the government itself within the economic security market, as alluded to earlier. Extensive Social Security benefits can virtually usurp the need for privately purchased life insurance. Within the United States, the Life Insurance Marketing and Research Association estimates that the amounts spent for life insurance protection over the past several years have been split roughly 50/50 between private life insurers and the public sectors (primarily in the form of Social Security survivor benefits). In many other countries, especially in Europe, the public sector portion greatly exceeds that of the private sector.

In a few states in the United States and in many other countries, banks are permitted to provide life products. Consumer choice, perhaps convenience, and possibly value could be enhanced through this practice, although there is concern on the part of many as to the appropriateness of such a practice (see Chapter 34).

Public policymakers also determine how life products may be sold. Again, in some states in the United States and in most developed countries, banks are permitted to market insurance. Insurance laws and regulations in the United States and elsewhere determine and the insurance supervisor enforces the

---

[31] See, for example, Harold D. Skipper, Jr., "Protectionism in the Provision of International Insurance Services," *Journal of Risk and Insurance*, Vol. 54 (Mar. 1987).

minimum qualifications for persons to be licensed as agents or brokers. Variations in the quality of this intermediary licensure result in differences in the quality and quantity of agent/broker advice and service by market. Governments also often regulate the direct selling of life products to consumers by insurers.

## THE CULTURAL ENVIRONMENT[32]

As alluded to earlier, the cultural environment can have an important effect on the life insurance purchase decision. **Culture** is a pattern of traditional ideas and values that continually evolve and accumulate as basic values and beliefs. Cultures are constructed from subcultures that continually shift within the central entity. With the U.S. culture, the following basic values are believed to influence the insurance purchase decision: dignity of the individual, personal freedom, self-reliance, and concern for material success. Many other cultures share these values to greater or lesser degrees and have other values as well. The primary function of insurance is to reduce uncertainty and thus to allow individuals to pursue their other activities with less anxiety. This adds to personal freedom and dignity. Furthermore, insurance permits individuals to be more self-reliant in the face of uncontrollable risks. In addition, as noted earlier, life insurance hedges one's human life value and can itself be a financial asset.

Although many persons recognize social goals and adhere to a pattern of behavior that is consistent with their attainment, others require a stimulus. Insurance agents are often successful in persuading individuals to purchase insurance by stressing the social role of insurance. For example, society expects the family breadwinner to provide a flow of income for his or her family. Failure to have a supplementary income in the event of death or disability would be in conflict with this expected social role. The purchase of insurance guarantees that the breadwinner/insured will fulfill this imputed family responsibility.

The emphasis on the expected role within a culture is frequently employed when an individual is about to enter a different subculture. For example, individuals about to marry, or a college student about to graduate, or a woman about to have a child may be assured that life insurance should be a part of their new way of life. The policy is bought to demonstrate membership in the new group (although, obviously, its coverage may be justified on sound economic grounds).

In some cultures and with certain relationships (as between close friends, for example), it might be socially unacceptable to refuse the offer to purchase insurance, because saying no is considered impolite. Too often, in such circumstances, the policy is purchased, but it lapses shortly thereafter.

Cultural perceptions of the role of life products can vary substantially. In many countries, especially in Asia, life products are sought primarily as savings instruments, and this is consistent with a high cultural propensity to save. In

---

[32] This sector draws on Pfeffer and Klock, *Perspectives on Insurance.*

other countries, especially in the Middle East, life insurance is sometimes viewed as inappropriate because of religious beliefs (although life products and insurer operations can be made to comport fully with these beliefs). Within the United States, consumers by substantial margins view life insurance first and foremost as protection against premature death.

## THE LIFE INSURANCE PLANNING PROCESS

The financial consequences of premature death constitute one of the personal loss exposures faced by all individuals (see Chapter 1). As such, the risk-management (or financial planning) process can provide an excellent framework for its evaluation and treatment.

Other approaches are sometimes followed to estimate the financial impact of death on others and, thereby, the need for life insurance. Unless the approach incorporates all steps of the risk-management process, any resulting plan may be faulty. For example, life insurance equal to five, six, or seven times the breadwinner's annual salary is sometimes suggested as appropriate for the average family. This and other such simple approaches ignore potentially vital aspects of sound risk management.

The term **life insurance programming** has been used for decades to describe the risk-management process applied to life insurance planning. Following the risk-management approach provides an analysis matrix and minimizes the chance that one or more important elements might be overlooked.

The reader may recall the six-step risk-management process:

1.   Gather information
2.   Establish objectives
3.   Analyze information
4.   Develop the plan
5.   Implement the plan
6.   Monitor and revise the plan periodically

The process helps determine whether any life insurance is needed and, if some is needed, the amount. A judgment as to the most suitable type of life insurance and as to the insurer from which to purchase it also should result from the process. The process, ideally, should not take a static view of an individual's needs, but rather should be capable of factoring into the analysis the possibility of changing financial requirements over time.

### GATHER INFORMATION

The first step is the gathering of the relevant quantitative and qualitative information on an individual to permit a sound identification of financial loss exposures arising from his or her death. As mentioned in Chapter 1, this involves identification and valuation of the individual's assets and liabilities, as well as information on the person's income and expenditures. The information is often gathered through a fact-finding questionnaire.

*Assets.* Assets normally are divided into two categories: liquid and nonliquid. **Liquid assets** are available to be liquidated with reasonable price certainty on the individual's death. They normally include stocks, bonds, money market and savings accounts, mutual funds, amounts available on death in pension, profit-sharing, or individual retirement accounts and any other such assets. All assets should be assessed at current market value. If real estate is to be sold, its value should be included, as would any interest to be sold in a closely held business. The latter assets, however, may be difficult to sell quickly at their market value under the circumstances following the owner's death.

**Nonliquid assets** might include the family's house, automobiles, personal effects such as clothing and jewelry, and household goods. These assets are usually passed to heirs intact. The realizable value of any of these items to be sold on death should, however, be included as a liquid asset.

The net death benefit of any life insurance (gross death benefit less policy loans) payable to or for the benefit of the family should be included as a liquid asset for life insurance planning purposes. This is appropriate since one is attempting to estimate the resources and liabilities of an individual assuming he or she dies today.

Life insurance cash values are not normally shown as separate assets for death planning purposes. They are subsumed in life insurance death proceeds. If an important part of one's savings program is funded via insurance cash values, it can be more revealing and helpful to list net cash values as assets available on death. An advantage of this approach is that the personal balance sheet can be used for death, retirement, and other savings and investment planning programs. If this is done, life insurance death proceeds should be shown on a protection element basis.

*Liabilities.* A review of the individual's liabilities will show which ones are to be paid at death and which ones are to be transferred to heirs. Most liabilities must be paid at death. Some liabilities may be assumable by others (e.g., some mortgage loans) or they may be in more than one person's name.

Typical liabilities to be paid on death include outstanding balances on credit and charge cards, tax obligations, personal loans and notes, and auto loans. If the home mortgage loan is to be paid off, its outstanding balance would be included. If it is not to be paid off, it should be excluded but its monthly payment recognized as a possible income need (see below).

*Income.* The information-gathering process will show total family income. For a *single-parent family*, this income usually is derived primarily or solely from the parent's salary. A single-parent family unit is more likely than a two-parent family to have income from outside the unit. Thus a divorced individual may be receiving alimony or child support payments. A divorced person sometimes receives financial support from parents or grandparents, and a widowed spouse may be receiving income from the deceased spouse's employer, insurance, or government sources.

Since the single parent's salary is usually the most important income source, the parent's death could have a financially devastating impact on the children. This potential income loss should be clearly recognized and dealt with.

The divorced single parent also could have his or her income disrupted by the death or disability of the former spouse who provides child support or other financial assistance. Similarly, a parent or relative's voluntary financial support to a single-parent family could cease on the donor's death. Both situations should be identified as potential loss exposures and addressed.

The income of a *two-parent, dual-wage-earner family* could be materially affected by the death of either wage earner. This should be factored into the analysis (see below) just as one would consider the impact on a *two-parent, single-wage-earner family*. In this instance, a family member may earn little or no income, yet his or her death may still have an adverse financial effect on the family. Consider the spouse who earns little or no outside income, but maintains the household. The death of such a nonwage earner can result in major increases in family expense. If the surviving spouse and children cannot or will not perform the necessary household functions formerly performed by the deceased spouse, the family may be forced to secure outside household services (e.g., a housekeeper) and rely increasingly on service businesses (e.g., dry cleaners, restaurants, auto service firms, and child-care providers). Total household expenses could rise significantly. Also, postmortem expenses (see below) can be significant. These potential loss exposures often are overlooked.

***Savings and Investment Programs.*** The death of a parent causes a disruption in savings. Perhaps the most common concern in this respect is disruption of saving to fund college education for children. An otherwise soundly conceived plan to accumulate funds to finance education can be completely disrupted by the death of a parent. As a result, most parents consider the contingency of disruption of planned savings and investment programs as falling properly in the loss exposure category.

***Postmortem Expenses.*** Death itself creates expenses and taxes—so-called **postmortem expenses**. For example, probate costs will be incurred. **Probate** is the process of filing, validating, and executing a will by a court.[33] Probate costs vary significantly from state to state and as a function of the estate size. Costs commonly range from 2 to 5 percent of the gross estate, but they can be higher. Executor fees also may be incurred.

Postmortem expenses include estimated final illness expenses. Of course, a well-designed and implemented financial plan should provide for health

[33] See Chap. 14.

insurance or other means for meeting these expenses. Also, funeral expenses, which today average around $5,000, should be recognized in the financial plan.

Estate and inheritance taxes can constitute a major postmortem expense for those whose net worth is large (see Chapter 13). Inheritance taxes vary from state to state and in the manner of their application. They often range from 1 to 14 percent of the value of the property inherited, with exemptions for the surviving spouse and children. Inheritance taxes and federal estate taxes should be estimated and included as a postmortem expense to be met on death.

*The Spouse.* The preceding discussion has generally assumed that information gathering and loss exposure identification have been on one spouse only—the chief family income earner. However, the same information-gathering/loss identification process should be followed for the other spouse as well. Good risk-management principles consider the financial consequences of all possible loss combinations. A dual-wage-earner family often requires the income from both persons. The death of either earner or both earners could be devastating financially for the family unit. As suggested above, even if one spouse is not a wage earner, his or her death could create financial hardships. The fact remains, however, that priority should be placed on the principal wage earner.

## ESTABLISH OBJECTIVES

As discussed in Chapter 1, a family should establish not only overall financial objectives but specific subobjectives as well. For life insurance planning purposes, this usually means that the individual must—often along with his or her spouse—determine the income levels desired for the survivor on the death of either spouse. This can be difficult, and there is no correct answer.

A commonly stated objective is for the survivor to be able to maintain his or her current living standard after the death of his or her spouse. This may translate into a survivor income need of at least 60 percent of the pre-death family income. The amount would be less than the current total family income, since the deceased spouse's self-maintenance expenses would end. For a family with children, self-maintenance expenses normally are considerably less than one-half of the total family income.

Postdeath income objectives are often predicated on the human life value concept. The idea is to estimate the financial impact on income recipients of the death of the main income earner and to replace that amount of lost income—in other words, to replace (financially) the deceased person as a source of earnings. This is the same as maintaining the current living standard.

One must also establish objectives regarding such things as:

- Liabilities to be paid off on death
- The amount of money to be provided to cover postmortem expenses

- The amount of money (if any) to be established as a family emergency fund
- The amount of money (if any) to be established as a fund to finance education
- The amount of money (if any) to be left to friends and relatives and to charitable institutions or other institutions

Merely to conclude that a certain amount of money would be desirable for a particular purpose is not sufficient. One must also decide how to provide the money and over what time period. For example, if an education fund is to be established, this goal-setting exercise should address the issue of how the money will be paid (e.g., as a lump sum, annually, or monthly).

The objective-setting process usually takes place as part of information gathering. The advisor leads the client through a loss exposure identification/ objective-setting exercise, providing guidance yet being careful not to impose his or her own values.

Objectives often are changed or adjusted as the costs of their implementation become clearer. These costs emerge from the next two steps in the process.

## ANALYZE INFORMATION

The third step in the process is to analyze the relevant data and loss exposures in light of the individual's stated objectives. In risk-management terms, this step involves an attempt to measure the financial consequences of the losses.

The discussion in Chapter 1 mentioned that loss analysis has two dimensions: frequency and severity. For life insurance planning purposes, loss frequency (i.e., probabilities of death) information has little or no utility to the individual. The individual will either live or die. Sound risk-management analysis presumes that the potential loss will occur and attempts to measure its likely financial consequences. A plan of action is then developed (see next step) to deal with the potential loss in case it does, in fact, occur.

Applied to life insurance planning for an individual, this means that the analysis of the financial consequences of death should *assume death is about to occur*. The analysis yields a measure of the potential loss severity (i.e., the consequences of death) from a financial point of view. Thus this step's function really is to estimate loss severity only.

The needed analysis usually is neither simple nor precise. This is because the analysis necessarily involves assumptions concerning the future, and actual results will invariably differ from assumptions. Even so, the exercise has merit. If done properly, it provides an idea of the possible range of the family's financial loss that will be caused by an individual's death, as well as the extent of disruption to present plans that would occur. Although this and the next step (plan development) are presented here separately, they often are accomplished together.

Several approaches can be followed in measuring the financial consequences to a family (or a business or others) of the death of one of its members. In all cases, however, the basic approach is the same. The family (or others) will have certain resources from which to meet its objectives (in whole or in part). To the extent that existing resources do not meet the objectives fully or fail to provide a good match, the individual will be faced with three choices: (1) revise the financial objectives downward or otherwise acknowledge that a gap exists between resources and objectives, (2) ensure that additional resources will be available on death, or (3) a combination of (1) and (2).

The postdeath financial objectives established by individuals usually fall into two categories: (1) cash and (2) income.

*Cash Objectives*. Cash objectives (or needs) require a single-sum cash amount to fulfill. They are the easiest to estimate. Typical cash needs arise from the need or desire to pay outstanding liabilities such as auto and personal loans, charge card balances, and incurred income tax liabilities. If an objective is to pay an outstanding mortgage loan balance, this too would be included.

Cash needs also might arise from a desire to establish or augment an educational fund. Postmortem expenses, for the most part, also fall into this category. Each of these cash needs will have been identified in the information-gathering/objective-setting stages.

*Income Objectives*. Quantifying income objectives (needs) requires assumptions that render approximations only. Deriving a measure of a family's (or other's) postdeath income needs involves, first, a determination of the annual net amount needed, taking into consideration all important variables such as likely income resources (e.g., Social Security), changing family responsibilities, and inflation. Second, these annual net income amounts are converted to a single-sum (present value) equivalent. This involves assumptions as to future interest rates.

The process appears simple and is simple in concept. Needed assumptions, however, as to future inflation and interest rates render the analysis more complex. In addition, several methods can be used to derive the needed figure. Some aspects of these important elements are reviewed below.

*1. Available Methods*. There are several methods that can be used to analyze income needs. The two most common ones are (1) the capital liquidation and (2) the capital retention approaches. The **capital liquidation** approach assumes that both principal (capital) and interest are liquidated over the relevant time period to provide the desired income. The **capital retention** approach assumes that the desired income is provided only from the investment earnings of the principal and that no part of the desired income is from capital. In other words, the capital is retained undiminished, even after death.

Each method has advantages and drawbacks. The liquidation approach requires a smaller capital sum to provide a given income level than does the retention approach. The retention approach permits a capital sum to be passed on to the family's next generation (or to whomever is designated). It is considered more conservative, since in an emergency capital could be invaded.

When the need for income is for the whole of life, the capital liquidation method can be approached in one of two ways. *First*, the future desired lifetime income can be funded through the purchase of a life annuity from a life insurance company. The annuitant cannot outlive the income, but, for reasons examined in Chapter 7, the purchase probably should not be made before age 60, 65, or 70. Income needed prior to this time could be provided from life insurance through the fixed period settlement option or from other sources.

The *second* way of funding lifetime income is to assume a maximum age beyond which the income recipient is unlikely to live and to provide for the complete liquidation of principal and interest between the present and that age. Some analysts use age 80 as the terminal age. This approach to funding "lifetime" income can be achieved through the fixed-period settlement option or through other means.

Each of these capital liquidation approaches has advantages and drawbacks. The critical decision variable in the second approach is the maximum age. If the terminal age is set too low, the income recipient may outlive the income—a result that could be disastrous. The higher the age, the higher the principal sum required to fund the income.

Other things being the same, the life annuity will generate a higher income than the other liquidation approach (assuming a high terminal age), since each payment contains an element of survivorship benefit. Moreover, with the life annuity, the income recipient cannot outlive the income.

Most annuities purchased today—both as individual products and as policy settlement options—permit only level payouts or have the payout vary with current investment performance (which may not track inflation). The approach of establishing a fixed maximum age, if it is properly funded, permits an income stream that can be increased with inflation but simultaneously will reduce the age to which income will be payable.

The decision to follow the capital retention or one of the capital liquidation methods is not an all-or-nothing proposition. One need not either pay out *all* capital or retain *all* capital. There is a continuum between the two extremes.

*2. Inflation Assumptions.* The effects of inflation on anticipated future income needs and resources and other relevant areas should be factored into the analysis. Future inflation rates are difficult to predict. As shown in Figure 12-9, U.S. consumer price changes since the 1960s have ranged from 1 to 14 percent.

The best approach to factoring inflation into any analysis often is to select a range of inflation rates and determine the sensitivity of results to changing inflation assumptions. Unless presented in a clear, simple manner, however, this type of sensitivity analysis can obscure the broader purpose of the analysis. Care must be taken to avoid this result.

*3. Interest Assumptions.* The interest rate selected for discounting can greatly influence results, especially when sums are discounted over many years. The interest rate chosen affects both needs and resources, since each is subject to discount.

The selected interest rate ordinarily is that which can be earned after taxes in the present economic environment on secure, fairly liquid investments—that is, a conservative rate. Speculative investments are not generally advised for this family financial planning.

Figure 12-10 showed interest rates credited on three-month U.S. Treasury bills in the past. These prevailing rates are referred to as **nominal interest rates**. Nominal interest rates are influenced by consumer inflation expectations. The difference between the nominal interest rate and the inflation rate is referred to as the **real interest rate**. The real interest rate typically will be positive in a healthy economy, and most economists anticipate that the real rate will be around 2 or 3 percent in the United States. Viewed historically, the U.S. real interest rate has actually varied from a low of -6 percent to as much as +6 percent. Such extremes have always been considered to be and are anticipated to remain temporary anomalies. The real rate of interest can be expected to average in the 1 to 3 percent range over the long term.

As with inflation, a range of interest rates ideally should be applied to the analysis, to determine results under changing assumptions. To simplify tax considerations, the interest rate selected should be an after-tax rate. This requires an estimation of the income recipient's marginal income tax bracket. Thus if a gross taxable investment return of 9 percent is expected, and if the income recipient is expected to be in the 30 percent marginal tax bracket, the effective after-tax return is 6.3   percent.[34] If investment returns are expected to be tax exempt, the gross return will be the same as the after-tax return.

*4. The Interaction of Inflation and Interest.* The interaction between the assumed inflation rate and the assumed discount (interest) rate should be understood. Consider, for example, that a $10,000 per-year income is desired for five years and that an after-tax discount rate of 8 percent is judged reasonable. If inflation is ignored, the present value of five $10,000 per-year payments at 8 percent interest, with the first payment made now, is $43,120.[35]

---

[34] The formula is (gross rate of return) x (1.0 - tax rate). Thus (0.09) x (1.0 - 0.30) = 0.063.

[35]
$$(\$10,000) \times \left[ \sum_{t=1}^{5} \left[ \frac{1}{1+i} \right]^{t-1} \right] = (\$10,000) \times (4.312) = \$43,120$$

A nonlevel payment stream (such as that developed if inflation is considered) requires a different approach.[36] Assume the same five $10,000 per-year payments and 8 percent after-tax interest rate as before. Assume also that inflation is estimated to be 5 percent annually over the payout period and that it is desired to provide the equivalent purchasing power of today's $10,000 for each payment.

Table 12-2 illustrates the calculation for this inflation-adjusted income stream. It shows that $47,298 invested to earn 8 percent after taxes will just be sufficient to provide a yearly income whose purchasing power remains constant in the face of a 5 percent inflation rate. As expected, this sum is greater than that needed if one ignores inflation.

Sometimes a reasonable approximation for the present value of an inflated income series can be obtained by discounting at the real interest rate; that is, the difference between the nominal interest rate and the assumed inflation rate. For example, the present value of the five $10,000 annual payments at 3 percent (8 percent -5 percent) is $47,171 rather than $47,298. The difference is not significant. If the time period involved is not great and if only a good approximation is sought—which is usually the case in such planning—this approach can suffice. The true present value, however, will always be understated where both the nominal and real rates are positive—the usual situation.

The preceding example assumed capital liquidation over a fixed period. What if a lifetime income is needed? To derive the needed present value, one can calculate the present value of income payments to a certain advanced age then add to that figure the present value of the purchase price at that time of a life annuity.

An example will illustrate the concepts involved. Assume that a $10,000 after-tax annual income is desired for the full lifetime of a 35-year-old. Assume 8 percent to be a reasonable after-tax return and inflation to be at 5 percent.

**TABLE 12-2     PRESENT VALUE OF $10,000 PER YEAR WITH INFLATION OF 5 PERCENT (FIRST PAYMENT NOW)**

| (1) | (2) | (3) | (4) | (5) |
|---|---|---|---|---|
| Year | Annual Payment in Today's Dollars | Annual Payment in Inflated (5%) Dollars $[(2) \times (1.05)^t]$ | Present Value Factor at 8% | Present Value at 8% of Inflated Payments |
| 0 (Now) | $10,000 | $10,000 | 1.0000 | $10,000 |
| 1 | 10,000 | 10,500 | 0.9259 | 9,722 |
| 2 | 10,000 | 11,025 | 0.8573 | 9,452 |
| 3 | 10,000 | 11,576 | 0.7938 | 9,190 |
| 4 | 10,000 | 12,155 | 0.7350 | 8,934 |
| | | | | $47,298 |

[36] Any plan that provides for a level income stream in an inflationary environment in reality provides a steadily decreasing real income.

The problem can be approached in stages. First, assume that a life annuity will be purchased at some advanced age (e.g., age 70) to fund the post-70 lifetime income need, and that income prior to then will be provided from a fund established for that purpose, such as the fixed period annuity option. The amount of money needed to fund the inflated payments from age 35 to age 70 is $225,510, derived using the procedure illustrated in Table 12-2. To determine the value today of the purchase price of the annuity that begins at age 70, the amount of the (inflated) annual income at age 70 must be known. While the purchasing power is to be $10,000, the nominal value would be $55,160.[37] In other words, at 5 percent inflation, $55,160 in 35 years would have the same purchasing power as $10,000 today.

At age 70, a decision would be required as to the best type of annuity to be purchased. An analysis of the pros and cons of variable annuities, indexed annuities, and flexible-premium deferred annuities could be conducted at present under various payout assumptions designed to hedge the inflation risk. Realistically, however, the annuity (and other investment) products available many years from now may bear little resemblance to products that exist today. Thus unless the income recipient were now within a short time period of purchasing a life annuity, any detailed analysis as to the most appropriate annuity type and how best to structure the annuity payout might be largely wasted effort.

Hence, for long-term income planning, one probably should merely estimate an annuity purchase price for the projected (inflated) income. This price should be based on current guaranteed purchase rates. These long-term guaranteed rates typically will be based on a 2 1/2 to 4 percent interest assumption, with the insurer actually crediting contemporary rates of return. By using the guaranteed rates, however, implicit allowance is made for inflation.

An insurance company would charge a 70-year-old between $600 and $900 for each $100 of annual income desired, with the income starting at age 70. Thus, for an income of over $55,000, the purchase price at age 70 might be (with rounding) between $330,000 and $500,000. Using the lower figure, one has but to calculate the value at age 35 of the $330,000 sum needed at age 70. Discounting at 8 percent yields a present value of $22,308.[38] Stated differently, $22,308 today will grow to $330,000 in 35 years at an after-tax earnings rate of 8 percent.

Therefore the total amount of money estimated to be needed now (at the income recipient's age 35) to provide $10,000 annually for life in constant purchasing power is $247,818, the sum of the two present value figures ($225,510 + $22,308 = $247,818).

This precise-appearing number should be recognized for what it is: our best guess. It is based on numerous assumptions, a change in any one of which could affect results significantly. For example, if all other assumptions remained the same but the actual after-tax return were 7 instead of 8 percent, the sum needed

[37] ($10,000) x $(1.05)^{35}$ = ($10,000) x (5.516) = $55,160
[38] ($330,000) x $[1/1.08]^{35}$ = ($330,000) x (0.0676) = $22,308

today to fund the $10,000 income stream would be increased to $289,527. In cases such as those investigated here, liberal rounding should be normal practice. Thus the $247,818 figure might become $250,000 (a typical premium banding amount) and $289,527 might become $300,000.

If a lifetime income is desired, but without using a life annuity, one can utilize either (1) the capital liquidation approach that requires the establishment of a maximum age beyond which the income recipient would be highly unlikely to live or (2) the capital retention approach.

Under the capital liquidation approach *not* involving a life annuity, a calculation is performed for an income stream that is to cease only at an advanced age, such that the income recipient is highly unlikely to outlive it. This procedure follows that used to derive present values in Table 12-2. Continuing the same example, assume that income was desired to age 85; that is, $10,000 of *real* income would be needed for 50 years. The present value of this stream is $242,112.[39]

Under the capital retention approach and using the same interest and other assumptions as before, but ignoring inflation for now, one would ask the question: What amount of money must be available now, the income alone from which would provide $10,000 per year? The answer is obtained by dividing the interest rate into the desired annual income. The result, $125,000, is easily verified by multiplying $125,000 by the 8 percent earnings assumption, to show that it produces the needed $10,000.[40]

To ignore inflation in the capital retention approach can be as foolish as doing so under the capital liquidation approaches. The hypothetical income recipient would want to receive $10,000 this year, $10,500 next year, and so on. The capital sum necessary to provide these inflated income payments is $360,000.[41] In

---

[39] This figure can be found by the use of a shortcut formula for the present value of a series of steadily increasing (or decreasing) payments:

$$A = P\left[\frac{1-e^n}{1-e}\right]$$

where

$A$ = the present value figure sought

$P$ = the initial payment

$e = \dfrac{1+r}{1+i}$

$r$ = the assumed inflation rate

$i$ = the assumed discount rate

[40] Note, however, that the $125,000 would generate the $10,000 at the *end* of the year. If it were desired to have the first payment made now, $10,000 should be added to the $125,000 principal, to yield a needed amount of $135,000.

[41] A shortcut formula for deriving the capital sum ($C$) needed to provide a steadily increasing income stream in perpetuity is:

$$C = \frac{P}{1-e}$$

where $e$ and $P$ are as defined in footnote 39 and $e$ is between 0 and 1. If $e$ is greater than 1, there is no shortcut formula. If $e$ is 1 (i.e., $i = r$), the value is undefined.

deriving a measure of the financial consequences of death, it often proves more convenient to net expected future income resources against future expected income needs, and then to derive a present value for the annual differences.

*Difference between Resources and Objectives*. The final step in the analysis process is to net the resources available against the established needs for cash and net income to derive a figure for the shortfall (or overage) of resources to meet needs. This figure represents a measure of the net financial consequences of death (the loss) to the family, based on the objectives identified earlier. Ideally, a range of figures would be developed based on various interest, inflation, and other relevant assumptions to provide an idea as to the sensitivity of the results to the assumptions.

*Static versus Dynamic Analysis*. The range of values developed above for the financial consequences of death is valid for the year of analysis only. That is, the measure represents the financial consequences of death assuming death occurs at the present. The financial analysis is incomplete, however, unless some idea can be obtained as to probable future figures. The financial consequences of death can be expected to vary with time. It may either increase or decrease.

If net needs are estimated to decrease over time, the death benefit of any policy purchased to fill the gap should also decrease. If needs are expected to increase, the policy purchased to help meet the needs should be flexible enough to track future anticipated increases.

The traditional static approach to planning answers the questions: "What if the individual were to die today?" The purpose of the question is to derive a quantitative measure for the adverse financial consequences of death. The procedure to convert from the traditional static planning approach to a dynamic approach is conceptually simple. The dynamic approach asks the same question as does the static approach, but it is repeated for each succeeding year; thus:

- What if the individual were to die today?
- What if the individual were to die next year?
- What if the individual were to die two years from now?
- What if the individual were to die three years from now?
- And so on.

To answer each question, future resources must be estimated. The future needs already would have been estimated, but a revised present value calculation would be necessary. The estimation of future resources and needs is not easy. It requires assumptions as to future savings and investment habits, future earnings, as well as a host of other items.[42] The process can be exceedingly complex. The objective is to obtain some idea of the likely *pattern* of future resources and needs, while avoiding becoming bogged down in details.

[42] See Joseph M. Belth, "Dynamic Life Insurance Programming," *The Journal of Risk and Insurance*, Vol. 31 (Dec. 1964) and Terry Rose and Robert I. Mehr, "Flexible Income Programming," *The Journal of Risk and Insurance*, Vol. 47 (Mar. 1980).

If a broad, integrated financial plan of the type discussed in Chapter 1 has been developed, it will contain projections as to future savings, investments, earnings, and other aspects of resources. If they are reasonable, these figures can be used to estimate the financial consequences of death occurring in future years. If there is no overall financial plan from which to draw these projections/ estimates, these figures should be developed.

Because of the highly subjective nature of the needed assumptions, one should not be too concerned with precision. Since future investment, savings, or other goals sometimes are not met, the projections should be conservative.

## PLAN DEVELOPMENT

The next step in the personal financial planning/risk-management process is to develop a plan to accomplish the stated objectives, based on the analysis of the financial consequences of death. This plan should evolve only after the various alternative means of treating the loss exposure have been explored. The plan usually emerges as the relevant information is being analyzed in light of objectives.

In considering alternatives, the planning time frame can be separated into short-run and long-run periods. The viable alternatives available to the individual over the short run usually are exceedingly limited, with more emerging over the long run.

Viable short-run alternatives are those that can be adopted now and in the near future to fill the financial gap created by the client's death. In the short run, there is insufficient time to increase savings or investments meaningfully, and the client has little or no control over the level of other resources (e.g., Social Security).

The longer term affords more alternatives. Sufficient time exists to implement an enhanced savings/investment program to fill a financial void. One may choose to enhance savings through life insurance policy cash values, through an annuity, or through savings outside the insurance mechanism. As discussed below, an insurance-funded savings program can offer several important advantages over other savings media, although the benefits of diversification should be kept in mind.

The dynamic analysis results should suggest a pattern of future needs. An increasing, decreasing, constant, or fluctuating future need pattern may be revealed. Ideally, the insurance purchased to fill this need should be capable of tracking the estimated future pattern. Also, since actual results rarely follow estimations exactly, the plan (insurance) should be sufficiently flexible to adapt to unanticipated changes.

The prior information-analysis step should include a review of existing life insurance policies and annuities from a cost as well as a structure viewpoint. If existing policies are not well suited to current needs or not competitively priced, replacement should be considered. If replacement is justified, an alternative to the existing policy should emerge at this stage. If the existing policy is judged suitable and cost-effective, any recommended change in the beneficiary designation, ownership, settlement option, or other area is a part of plan development.

In developing a plan, one or more low-cost life insurance policies from high-quality companies that are suitable in light of the client's characteristics, objectives, and current financial condition should be identified. How the policy is to be structured (premium payment, settlement options, beneficiary designations, dividend options) should be included in the plan.

The plan should not evolve in isolation from other death-planning needs, such as establishment or revision of wills and trusts.[43] A comprehensive plan includes more than taking care of legal necessities. A clearly established pre-death plan should guide the survivors (and the executor) through this most traumatic of life's events. Most agents and financial planners are not qualified to develop and implement all aspects of a plan. A team approach is needed.

## PLAN IMPLEMENTATION

Once a plan has been developed and agreed to by the individual, the program must be implemented. Plan implementation usually means, among other things, completing the necessary life insurance application and providing funds to pay the first premium. If changes are needed in existing policies or if the policies are to be replaced, the necessary forms must be secured, completed, and furnished to the appropriate insurers.

The life insurance dimension of the plan is not fully implemented until the policy sought is issued on an acceptable basis and structured in line with earlier established goals. (The necessity for clarity in all areas of the contract, especially the beneficiary designation, was made clear earlier.)

## PLAN MONITORING AND REVISION

*If* the individual's future were to evolve exactly as had been estimated, *if* assumptions as to future inflation rates, interest rates, and other areas proved to be fact, *if* no important tax law or other changes were made, and *if* no better life insurance or other financial products became available in the future marketplace, plan revision would be unnecessary. Clearly, this will not happen. Deviations of actual from estimated results should be expected.

Important life events such as marriage, divorce, important business undertakings, home buying, birth of children, children attaining financial independence, and the like, should trigger an automatic reevaluation of the

[43] See Chap. 14 on estate planning.

program. In general, program evaluation should take place every one to three years, irrespective of the happening of important life events.

Any significant changes in environmental factors should also trigger reevaluation. New insurance and other financial products can render older products obsolete. Changes in Social Security, inflation rates, interest rates, employee benefit programs, tax laws, and a host of other variables can cause a program to go off its mark.

Both the individual and the advisor should be attuned to environmental and personal changes that can have an impact on the implemented program. Ideally, the insurance products selected to implement the program would be sufficiently flexible to adapt to changes. A policy that provides for experience participation contains an automatic mechanism for at least partially adapting to changing economic conditions. The guaranteed right to purchase additional insurance without evidence of insurability, either by increasing the existing policy's face amount or by purchase of a new policy, can be another mechanism permitting flexibility. Universal life and other policies that permit premium payment flexibility and policy death benefit adjustability can be particularly well adapted to changing life cycle needs.

## ILLUSTRATION

An illustration should be helpful in bringing together the concepts discussed above. For reasons of space, the presentation focuses on the analysis and plan design steps.

*Relevant Information/Objectives.* Steve and Debbie Williams, both age 35, have two children, Philip, age 7, and Gwen, age 2. Steve is the manager of a clothing store and Debbie is a grammar school teacher. The total annual before-tax family income is $100,000, which translates to $70,000 after taxes. Steve earns $63,000 ($45,000 after taxes); Debbie earns $37,000 ($25,000 after taxes).[44] Other relevant financial information is summarized below:

|  | If Steve Dies First | If Debbie Dies First |
|---|---|---|
| Nonliquid Assets |  |  |
| Home | $130,000 | $130,000 |
| Autos | 13,000 | 13,000 |
| Household/personal effects | 37,000 | 37,000 |
|  | $180,000 | $180,000 |
| Liquid Assets Available on Death |  |  |
| Individual life insurance | $50,000 | $     0 |
| Group life insurance | 25,000 | 50,000 |
| Pension plan death benefit | 10,000 | 0 |
| Savings/investment | 20,000 | 20,000 |
| Checking account balance | 2,000 | 2,000 |
|  | $107,000 | $ 72,000 |

[44] The analysis could have assumed that Steve earned $37,000 and Debbie earned $63,000. Since earnings of the average female worker are still lower than the earnings of the average male worker, Steve is shown with the higher figure. This is no way should be interpreted as suggesting that average earnings for females should be lower.

Cash Needs on Death Based on Objectives

| | | |
|---|---|---|
| Mortgage loan balance | $110,000 | $110,000 |
| Auto loan balance | 10,000 | 10,000 |
| Establish emergency fund | 20,000 | 20,000 |
| Establish educational fund | 50,000 | 50,000 |
| Charge card balances | 3,000 | 3,000 |
| Funeral expenses | 5,000 | 5,000 |
| Probate/administration expenses | 3,000 | 3,000 |
| | $201,000 | $201,000 |

Annual Income Objectives/Resources
Desired after-tax family income on death

| | | |
|---|---|---|
| • with both children at home/in college | $ 45,000 | $ 45,000 |
| • with one child at home/in college | 43,000 | 43,000 |
| • with no child at home/in college | 40,000 | 40,000 |

Social Security survivor benefits[45]

| | | |
|---|---|---|
| • both children under 18 | | |
| or, if in college, under 22 | $13,050 | $9,360 |
| • one child under 18 | | |
| or, if in college, under 22 | 6,525 | 4,680 |
| • at survivor's age 65 | 8,700 | 6,420 |

Steve and Debbie, with the counsel of their agent, have determined that their overall objective is for each to be able to maintain his or her standard of living if the other died. As shown above, they estimate that $45,000 per year after taxes would be needed by the survivor while both children are at home, that $43,000 would be needed while only Gwen was at home, with $40,000 needed thereafter. These income objectives assume that the mortgage loan and other debts are paid off (a desired objective). They also desire to establish an educational fund of $50,000 for the children's education and to have an emergency fund of $20,000.

*Static Analysis.* In conducting a static analysis, several assumptions are necessary. The key ones here are:

| | |
|---|---|
| Reasonable after-tax earnings (discount) rate | 7 percent |
| Average annual inflation rate | 4 percent |
| Average annual wage increase rate | 5 percent |

Moreover, it is assumed that a life annuity will be purchased at age 70 to fund needed lifetime income from that age, and that the annual income objective as well as Social Security benefits increase each year with the inflation rate.

Table 12-3 illustrates the derivation of the present value of net income needs, assuming Steve dies first. Column 2 shows the annual income objective in today's dollars and column 3 shows the equivalent in inflated dollars. Column 4 shows the estimated annual Social Security survivor (children's) benefit (inflated at 4 percent) that would be payable. Debbie's annual income is shown in column 5. These figures are increased by 5 percent per year. The column 6 figures are

---

[45] Social Security survivor benefits are based on the insured status and past earnings record of the worker (see Chap. 25).

**TABLE 12-3    PRESENT VALUE OF NET INCOME NEEDS**

| | (1) | (2) | (3) | (4) | (5) | (6) | (7) |
|---|---|---|---|---|---|---|---|
| Year | Debbie's Age | Annual Income Objective | Annual Income Objective (at 4%) | Annual Social Security Benefit (at 4%) | Debbie's Annual Earnings (at 5%) | Annual Income Shortage | Value Today of Inflated Income Shortages |
| | | | | - | -   = | | |
| 1 | 35 | $45,000 | $45,000 | $13,050 | $25,000 | $6,950 | $6,950 |
| 2 | 36 | 45,000 | 46,800 | 13,572 | 26,250 | 6,978 | 6,521 |
| 3 | 37 | 45,000 | 48,672 | 14,115 | 27,562 | 6,995 | 6,109 |
| 4 | 38 | 45,000 | 50,619 | 14,679 | 28,941 | 6,999 | 5,713 |
| 5 | 39 | 45,000 | 52,644 | 15,267 | 30,388 | 6,989 | 5,332 |
| 6 | 40 | 45,000 | 54,749 | 15,877 | 31,907 | 6,965 | 4,966 |
| 7 | 41 | 45,000 | 56,939 | 16,512 | 33,502 | 6,925 | 4,614 |
| 8 | 42 | 45,000 | 59,217 | 17,173 | 35,177 | 6,867 | 4,276 |
| 9 | 43 | 45,000 | 61,586 | 17,860 | 36,936 | 6,789 | 3,951 |
| 10 | 44 | 45,000 | 64,049 | 18,574 | 38,783 | 6,692 | 3,640 |
| 11 | 45 | 45,000 | 66,611 | 19,317 | 40,722 | 6,571 | 3,341 |
| 12 | 46 | 45,000 | 69,275 | 20,090 | 42,758 | 6,427 | 3,053 |
| 13 | 47 | 45,000 | 72,046 | 20,893 | 44,896 | 6,257 | 2,778 |
| 14 | 48 | 45,000 | 74,928 | 21,729 | 47,141 | 6,058 | 2,514 |
| 15 | 49 | 45,000 | 77,925 | 22,598 | 49,498 | 5,829 | 2,261 |
| 16 | 50 | 43,000 | 77,441 | 11,751 | 51,973 | 13,716 | 4,971 |
| 17 | 51 | 43,000 | 80,538 | 12,221 | 54,572 | 13,745 | 4,656 |
| 18 | 52 | 43,000 | 83,760 | 12,710 | 57,300 | 13,749 | 4,353 |
| 19 | 53 | 43,000 | 87,110 | 13,218 | 60,165 | 13,726 | 4,061 |
| 20 | 54 | 43,000 | 90,594 | 13,747 | 63,174 | 13,674 | 3,781 |
| 21 | 55 | 40,000 | 87,645 | 0 | 66,332 | 21,313 | 5,508 |
| 22 | 56 | 40,000 | 91,151 | 0 | 69,649 | 21,502 | 5,193 |
| 23 | 57 | 40,000 | 94,797 | 0 | 73,131 | 21,665 | 4,890 |
| 24 | 58 | 40,000 | 98,589 | 0 | 76,788 | 21,801 | 4,599 |
| 25 | 59 | 40,000 | 102,532 | 0 | 80,627 | 21,905 | 4,318 |
| 26 | 60 | 40,000 | 106,633 | 0 | 84,659 | 21,975 | 4,049 |
| 27 | 61 | 40,000 | 110,899 | 0 | 88,892 | 22,007 | 3,790 |
| 28 | 62 | 40,000 | 115,335 | 0 | 93,336 | 21,998 | 3,540 |
| 29 | 63 | 40,000 | 119,948 | 0 | 98,003 | 21,945 | 3,301 |
| 30 | 64 | 40,000 | 124,746 | 0 | 102,903 | 21,843 | 3,070 |
| 31 | 65 | 40,000 | 129,736 | 28,218 | 0 | 101,518 | 13,336 |
| 32 | 66 | 40,000 | 134,925 | 29,346 | 0 | 105,579 | 12,962 |
| 33 | 67 | 40,000 | 140,322 | 30,520 | 0 | 109,802 | 12,599 |
| 34 | 68 | 40,000 | 145,935 | 31,741 | 0 | 114,194 | 12,246 |
| 35 | 69 | 40,000 | 151,773 | 33,011 | 0 | 118,762 | 11,902 |

Present value of column 7    $193,144

the amounts by which Social Security and Debbie's income fall short of the desired objective.

The amounts become significant, but the purchasing power is the relevant concern, not the absolute size of the numbers. Thus if inflation averaged 4 percent, a $101,518 income at age 65 would have the same purchasing power as $31,300 today [the $31,300 being the difference between the income objective ($40,000) and the noninflated Social Security benefit ($8,700)].

The present value of each column 6 figure is shown in column 7. The discount rate used is 7 percent. Summing the column 7 figures yields $193,144, the present value of the entire income stream to age 70. In other words, if all assumptions actually materialized as fact in the future, $193,144 would be exactly sufficient to provide an annual (inflated) income to precisely fill the income gap revealed in column 6.

The preceding calculation allows for income only through age 69. If a lifetime income is desired, provision should be made for income beyond this period. At age 70, the needed (real) income of $40,000 would require a nominal income then of $157,840. Social Security benefits are estimated to be $34,330, thus leaving a shortfall at age 70 of $123,510. If the capital liquidation approach is used wherein an annuity would be purchased at age 70 to fund this and future income shortfalls, its estimated purchase price at age 70 would be $741,060.[46] The value today of this needed amount is about $70,000.[47]

The following is a summary of the net life insurance needed:

|   |   |   |
|---|---|---|
| | Present value of income stream to age 70 | $193,144 |
| + | Present value of annuity for age 70 and later | 70,000 |
| + | Cash needs objectives | 201,000 |
| = | Total needed to fulfill objectives | $464,114 |
| - | Existing resources | 107,000 |
| = | Shortage of resources over needs | $357,144 |

The analysis reveals that if the stated objectives are not modified and are to be met, an additional $357,000 of life insurance is needed on Steve's life.

The result is influenced by the interest and inflation assumptions. Table 12-4 shows how the net result varies at different inflation and interest rate assumptions. The level of these assumptions greatly influences results. Since results are so sensitive to the assumptions resulting net figures over such long time periods are, at best, educated guesses. The appearance of scientific precision should not obscure this simple truth.

The same analysis should be conducted assuming Debbie dies first. Recall that the family's income and other objectives apply irrespective of who dies first and that the same financial and income formation applies as before. The only exceptions are that Steve's life insurance (total of $75,000) and pension death benefit ($10,000) must be excluded as liquid resources and the Social Security survivor benefit, based on Debbie's lower earnings, would be lower. Also, Debbie's employer provides $50,000 of group term coverage.

The cash needs are the same as for the analysis with Steve—that is, $201,000. Existing resources are $72,000, showing a net deficit of $129,000.

[46] Using a purchase price of $600 per $100 of annual income.

[47]
$$(\$741,060)x\left[\frac{1}{1.07}\right]^{35} = \$69,437$$

**TABLE 12-4    VARIABILITY OF RESULTS WITH CHANGING INFLATION
AND INTEREST ASSUMPTIONS
(ASSUMES STEVE DIES FIRST—STATIC ANALYSIS)**

| Interest Assumption % | Inflation Assumption (%) | | | | |
|---|---|---|---|---|---|
| | 0 | 2 | 4 | 6 | 8 |
| 0 | $1,184,000 | $1,399,000 | $1,772,000 | $2,414,000 | $3,522,000 |
| 1 | 896,000 | 1,059,000 | 1,339,000 | 1,819,000 | 2,643,000 |
| 3 | 543,000 | 639,000 | 800,000 | 1,073,000 | 1,536,000 |
| 5 | 360,000 | 418,000 | 513,000 | 672,000 | 938,000 |
| 7 | 261,000 | 298,000 | 357,000 | 451,000 | 608,000 |
| 9 | 207,000 | 231,000 | 268,000 | 327,000 | 421,000 |
| 11 | 176,000 | 192,000 | 216,000 | 254,000 | 313,000 |

Steve earns more than the desired income objective. The present value of the excess of his after-tax income plus Social Security over the desired income is more than the $129,000 deficit. If, therefore, it were decided not to pay off the mortgage and other debts, but rather to continue to make payments from current income, there probably would be no need for additional life insurance on Debbie's life. If it is desired to pay the mortgage loan in full, the amount of life insurance needed would be around $129,000.

*Dynamic Analysis.* The preceding analysis developed a life insurance figure assuming death occurred at present; however, would $357,000 be the amount needed assuming death occurred next year? What about in two years? Three years? The answers to this series of questions can be exceedingly important. At $357,000, Steve could be either grossly overinsured or underinsured in later years.

The dynamic approach requires assumptions as to future liquid assets and cash needs. Thus the declining outstanding mortgage will lessen future cash needs. Inflation, however, most likely will drive up credit card balances and probable funeral and probate costs. If the emergency fund is to maintain its purchasing power, it also must increase with inflation. The value of savings and investments might be expected to rise, as would employer-provided pension plan death benefits. Indeed, *all* elements of Steve and Debbie's pro forma financial situation are dynamic, over time. Accumulated resources, income sources, and cash and income needs all change as Steve and Debbie move through their family life cycle.

To illustrate this process, assume that the pension plan death benefit increases 15 percent annually and that the value of savings and investments increases 10 percent annually. These rates of increase are assumed to include both reinvestment of earnings and additional contributions. Checking account balances, charge card balances, postmortem expenses, and desired emergency fund balances are assumed to increase with the inflation rate.

Tables 12-5 and 12-6 summarize these figures, over time, based on the same assumptions and information used in the static analysis plus the additional stated

**TABLE 12-5     ESTIMATED ANNUAL VALUES OF FUTURE LIQUID ASSETS**

| Assuming Death Occurred In Year | Pension Plan Death Benefits (at 15%) | + Savings and Investment Balances (at 10%) | + Checking Account Balances (at 4%) | + Total Life Insurance Assuming No Change | = Annual Projected Liquid Asset Values |
|---|---|---|---|---|---|
| 1 | $10,000 | $20,000 | $2,000 | $75,000 | $107,000 |
| 2 | 11,500 | 22,000 | 2,080 | 75,000 | 110,580 |
| 3 | 13,225 | 24,200 | 2,163 | 75,000 | 114,588 |
| 4 | 15,209 | 26,620 | 2,250 | 75,000 | 119,078 |
| 5 | 17,490 | 29,282 | 2,340 | 75,000 | 124,112 |
| 6 | 20,114 | 32,210 | 2,433 | 75,000 | 129,757 |
| 7 | 23,131 | 35,431 | 2,531 | 75,000 | 136,092 |
| 8 | 26,600 | 38,974 | 2,632 | 75,000 | 143,206 |
| 9 | 30,590 | 42,872 | 2,737 | 75,000 | 151,199 |
| 10 | 35,179 | 47,159 | 2,847 | 75,000 | 160,184 |
| 11 | 40,456 | 51,875 | 2,960 | 75,000 | 170,291 |
| 12 | 46,524 | 57,062 | 3,079 | 75,000 | 181,665 |
| 13 | 53,503 | 62,769 | 3,202 | 75,000 | 194,473 |
| 14 | 61,528 | 69,045 | 3,330 | 75,000 | 208,903 |
| 15 | 70,757 | 75,950 | 3,463 | 75,000 | 225,170 |
| 16 | 81,371 | 83,545 | 3,602 | 75,000 | 243,517 |
| 17 | 93,576 | 91,899 | 3,746 | 75,000 | 264,222 |
| 18 | 107,613 | 101,089 | 3,896 | 75,000 | 287,598 |
| 19 | 123,755 | 111,198 | 4,052 | 75,000 | 314,005 |
| 20 | 143,318 | 122,318 | 4,214 | 75,000 | 343,850 |
| 21 | 163,665 | 134,550 | 4,382 | 75,000 | 377,598 |
| 22 | 188,215 | 148,005 | 4,558 | 75,000 | 415,778 |
| 23 | 216,447 | 162,806 | 4,740 | 75,000 | 458,993 |
| 24 | 248,915 | 179,086 | 4,929 | 75,000 | 507,930 |
| 25 | 286,252 | 196,995 | 5,127 | 75,000 | 563,373 |
| 26 | 329,190 | 216,694 | 5,332 | 75,000 | 626,215 |
| 27 | 378,568 | 238,364 | 5,545 | 75,000 | 697,477 |
| 28 | 435,353 | 262,200 | 5,767 | 75,000 | 778,320 |
| 29 | 500,656 | 288,420 | 5,997 | 75,000 | 870,074 |
| 30 | 575,755 | 317,262 | 6,237 | 75,000 | 974,254 |
| 31 | 662,118 | 248,988 | 6,487 | 75,000 | 1,092,593 |
| 32 | 761,436 | 383,887 | 6,746 | 75,000 | 1,227,069 |
| 33 | 876,651 | 422,276 | 7,016 | 75,000 | 1,379,943 |
| 34 | 1,006,998 | 464,503 | 7,297 | 75,000 | 1,553,798 |
| 35 | 1,158,048 | 510,954 | 7,589 | 75,000 | 1,751,590 |

assumptions. Estimated future liquid asset values available if Steve were to die in each year are shown in Table 12-5. For example, the total liquid asset value, if Steve were to die in year 7, is estimated at about $136,092, composed of a $23,131 pension plan death benefit, $35,431 in then current investments and savings, a $2,531 checking account balance, and the $75,000 of life insurance. No change is assumed in the life insurance since this is the value sought.

Table 12-6 follows the same approach, but it is based on liabilities and objectives. Thus if Steve were to die six years from the present (year 7), the then outstanding mortgage balance would be $104,764. Charge card and personal loan balances, estimated to grow at the inflation rate, might be around $16,449

**TABLE 12-6    AN ILLUSTRATION OF DYNAMIC NEEDS ANALYSIS**

| (1) | (2) | (3) | (4) | (5) | (6) |
|---|---|---|---|---|---|
| Assuming Death Occurs In Year | Annual Mortgage Loan Balance | + Annual Balances on Other Debts (at 4%) | + Annual Emergency Fund (at 4%) | + Annual Educational Fund Balances (at 7%) | + Annual Post-mortem Expenses (at 4%) |
| 1 | $110,000 | $13,000 | $20,000 | $50,000 | $8,000 |
| 2 | 109,366 | 13,520 | 20,800 | 53,500 | 8,320 |
| 3 | 108,651 | 14,061 | 21,632 | 57,245 | 8,653 |
| 4 | 107,846 | 14,623 | 22,497 | 61,252 | 8,999 |
| 5 | 106,939 | 15,208 | 23,397 | 65,540 | 9,359 |
| 6 | 105,916 | 15,816 | 24,333 | 70,128 | 9,733 |
| 7 | 104,764 | 16,449 | 25,306 | 75,037 | 10,123 |
| 8 | 103,466 | 17,107 | 26,319 | 80,289 | 10,527 |
| 9 | 102,003 | 17,791 | 27,371 | 85,909 | 10,949 |
| 10 | 100,355 | 18,503 | 28,466 | 91,923 | 11,386 |
| 11 | 98,498 | 19,243 | 29,605 | 98,358 | 11,842 |
| 12 | 96,405 | 20,013 | 30,789 | 52,621 | 12,316 |
| 13 | 94,047 | 20,813 | 32,021 | 56,305 | 12,808 |
| 14 | 91,389 | 21,646 | 33,301 | 60,246 | 13,321 |
| 15 | 88,395 | 22,512 | 34,634 | 64,463 | 13,853 |
| 16 | 85,020 | 23,412 | 36,019 | 68,976 | 14,408 |
| 17 | 81,218 | 24,349 | 37,460 | 0 | 14,984 |
| 18 | 76,934 | 25,323 | 38,958 | 0 | 15,583 |
| 19 | 72,106 | 26,336 | 40,516 | 0 | 16,207 |
| 20 | 66,666 | 27,389 | 42,137 | 0 | 16,855 |
| 21 | 60,536 | 28,485 | 43,822 | 0 | 17,529 |
| 22 | 53,629 | 29,624 | 45,575 | 0 | 18,230 |
| 23 | 45,845 | 30,809 | 47,398 | 0 | 18,959 |
| 24 | 37,075 | 32,041 | 49,294 | 0 | 19,718 |
| 25 | 27,192 | 33,323 | 51,266 | 0 | 20,506 |
| 26 | 16,056 | 34,656 | 53,317 | 0 | 21,327 |
| 27 | 3,507 | 36,042 | 55,449 | 0 | 22,180 |
| 28 | 0 | 37,484 | 57,667 | 0 | 23,067 |
| 29 | 0 | 38,983 | 59,974 | 0 | 23,990 |
| 30 | 0 | 40,542 | 62,373 | 0 | 24,949 |
| 31 | 0 | 42,164 | 64,868 | 0 | 25,947 |
| 32 | 0 | 43,851 | 67,463 | 0 | 26,985 |
| 33 | 0 | 45,605 | 70,161 | 0 | 28,064 |
| 34 | 0 | 47,429 | 72,968 | 0 | 29,187 |
| 35 | 0 | 49,326 | 75,886 | 0 | 30,355 |

six years from now. At that time, $25,306 would be required to maintain the same $20,000 emergency-fund-purchasing power, based on the inflation assumption of 4 percent.

The next column of the table shows that the value needed to fund the college education then would be $75,037. This deserves comment. Steve and Debbie desire a $50,000 educational fund established if either Steve or Debbie died at present. At a 7 percent assumed earnings rate, this means that they believe they will need $98,358 by year 11 (when Philip's age is 17). Thus the

**TABLE 12-6    CONTINUED**

| (7) | (8) | (9) | (10) | (11) |
|---|---|---|---|---|
| Cash Needed in Year of Death to Purchase Annuity = at Age 70 | Annual Total Cash Needs | + Present Value in Year of Death of Income Shortage to Age 70 | - Total Estimated Resources | = Additional Life Insurance Needed in Year of Death |
| $70,000 | $271,000 | $193,144 | $107,000 | $357,144 |
| 74,900 | 280,406 | 199,228 | 110,580 | 369,054 |
| 80,143 | 290,385 | 205,707 | 114,588 | 381,504 |
| 85,753 | 300,971 | 212,622 | 119,078 | 394,515 |
| 91,756 | 312,199 | 220,017 | 124,112 | 408,104 |
| 98,179 | 324,105 | 227,940 | 129,757 | 422,288 |
| 105,051 | 336,730 | 236,443 | 136,092 | 437,081 |
| 112,405 | 350,113 | 245,585 | 143,206 | 452,482 |
| 120,273 | 364,297 | 255,429 | 151,199 | 468,527 |
| 128,692 | 379,326 | 266,044 | 160,184 | 485,186 |
| 137,701 | 395,246 | 277,507 | 170,291 | 502,462 |
| 147,340 | 359,484 | 289,901 | 181,665 | 467,720 |
| 157,654 | 373,647 | 303,317 | 194,473 | 482,492 |
| 168,689 | 388,592 | 317,855 | 208,903 | 497,544 |
| 180,498 | 404,354 | 333,623 | 225,170 | 512,807 |
| 193,132 | 420,967 | 350,740 | 243,517 | 528,190 |
| 206,652 | 364,662 | 360,615 | 264,222 | 461,056 |
| 221,117 | 377,915 | 371,151 | 287,598 | 461,468 |
| 236,595 | 391,760 | 382,420 | 314,005 | 460,175 |
| 253,157 | 406,204 | 394,502 | 343,850 | 456,857 |
| 270,878 | 421,250 | 407,487 | 377,598 | 451,139 |
| 289,840 | 436,898 | 413,206 | 415,778 | 434,326 |
| 310,128 | 453,140 | 419,124 | 458,993 | 413,272 |
| 331,837 | 469,966 | 425,281 | 507,930 | 387,316 |
| 355,066 | 487,353 | 431,724 | 563,373 | 355,704 |
| 379,921 | 505,276 | 438,507 | 626,215 | 317,567 |
| 406,515 | 523,693 | 445,689 | 697,477 | 271,906 |
| 434,971 | 553,189 | 453,340 | 778,320 | 228,209 |
| 465,419 | 588,366 | 461,535 | 870,074 | 179,828 |
| 497,999 | 625,863 | 470,362 | 974,254 | 121,971 |
| 532,859 | 665,838 | 479,915 | 1,092,593 | 53,160 |
| 570,159 | 708,457 | 404,885 | 1,227,069 | -113,727 |
| 610,070 | 753,900 | 320,257 | 1,379,943 | -305,785 |
| 652,775 | 802,358 | 225,187 | 1,553,798 | -526,253 |
| 698,469 | 854,036 | 118,762 | 1,751,590 | -778,792 |

amounts necessary in the intervening years must be such as to grow to $98,358 by year 11.

The simplifying assumption is made that one-half the fund balance is paid to Philip at his age 18, and the balance, accumulated at interest, is paid five years later when Gwen enters college at her age 18. Thus no educational fund is shown as needed beyond her age 18. If, in fact, both Steve and Debbie survived to this point, they presumably would have already made provision for their children's education.

Continuing across the table at year 7, it is seen that an estimated $10,123 would be needed at that time to cover postmortem expenses. Column 7 shows the estimated cash amount needed, $105,051 in year 7, to fund the purchase, at age 70, of the life annuity referred to earlier.

Column 8 is the simple sum of columns 2 through 7. It shows the amount required to fund all cash needs each year, if death were to occur in that year. Hence if death were to occur in year 7, an estimated $336,730 would be required to fund fully all of the columns 2 through 7 needs.

The present value of the income stream necessary to fill the income gap to age 70 appears in column 9. The yearly shortage figures were shown in Table 12-3. Their present value was $193,144—the figure shown for the first year in column 9. If death occurs in year 2, not in year 1, the amount needed to fund the income shortages as of year 2 is estimated to be $199,228; as of year 3, $205,707, and so on. Thus if death were to occur in year 7, an estimated $236,443 would be required *at that time* to fund the Table 12-3 income shortages from the seventh year to age 70.

Total projected annual resources (column 10) are then netted against the sum of yearly cash and income needs to derive yearly figures that represent the total projected annual shortages of resources to meet needs (column 11). If the assumptions used to derive these figures actually materialized as fact in the future, the column 11 figures would represent the amounts of life insurance that Steve should have in force on his life in each year.

As shown in Figure 12-11, the estimated needed amounts increase through year 11. The needed amount then decreases because one child (Philip) is considered "out of the nest." Projected needs begin to increase again but then decline in year 17, when Gwen has left the nest. Amounts thereafter remain around $400,000 for several years then drop precipitously as total estimated resources reach high levels. If all assumptions are realized, the need for life insurance protection is estimated to cease at about age 65. This assumes a constant savings pattern as well as large employer-provided funding. Whether these will be realized in fact is always questionable, and therefore a financial plan should be flexible enough to adapt to unrealized hopes.

A note of caution is in order. The precise-appearing numbers can lend an unwarranted aura of authenticity to these types of analyses. In Table 12-6, column 11 figures shown for many years into the future should be regarded more as educated guesses than as established needs. Credence should be given to the general level of the first five or perhaps ten years' values, but, beyond that, one would be well advised to seek general trends only. The intent of this exercise is to show how future death patterns can be estimated and to highlight the great importance of selecting a policy that can adjust to the future pattern.

**FIGURE 12-11**

**PROJECTION OF LIFE INSURANCE NEEDS (i = 4%, r = 7%)**

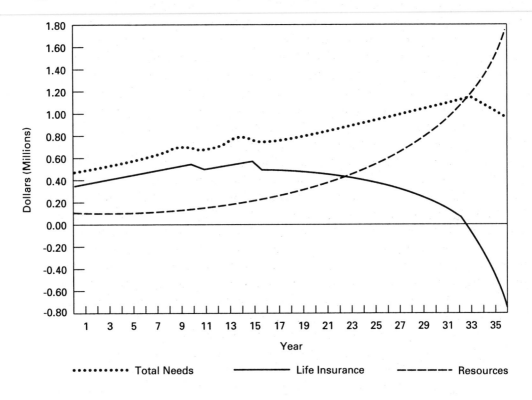

# *Chapter 13*

# *L*IFE *I*NSURANCE *AND ANNUITY TAXATION IN THE UNITED STATES*

Because of their socially worthwhile role, life insurance and annuity contracts are accorded certain favorable tax treatment in the vast majority of countries, including the United States. This chapter introduces the U.S. federal income, estate, and gift tax treatment of life insurance and annuities as contained in the Internal Revenue Code (IRC), and suggests ways of avoiding adverse tax consequences.

## INCOME TAX TREATMENT OF LIFE INSURANCE

In examining the income taxation of life insurance, it will prove convenient to examine the tax treatment by component of the life insurance policy.

### PREMIUMS

Premiums paid in the United States for individual life insurance policies are considered a personal expense and are not deductible for income tax purposes.[1] This treatment applies to government life insurance as well as to life insurance issued by commercial insurers and fraternal benefit societies.

Of course, premiums paid to fund life insurance payable to a charity may be deductible as charitable contributions, and premiums paid for life insurance under an alimony agreement may be deductible as alimony payments. Moreover, premiums paid by employers for life insurance protection that benefits employees are deductible as a business expense.

[1] In the majority of countries, premiums paid for life insurance policies are tax deductible.

374

## DEATH PROCEEDS

*Section 101(a)(1) Treatment.* The general rule is that life insurance death proceeds are exempt from federal income tax.[2] Thus if an insured under a $100,000 life insurance policy died after premiums of $3,000 had been paid, the general rule holds that the entire $100,000 would be received income-tax-free by the beneficiary, irrespective of the cash-value amount or of past premiums paid, and irrespective of who was the policyowner, insured, beneficiary, or premium payor. **Death proceeds** include not only the policy face amount, but any additional insurance amounts paid by reason of the insured's death, such as accidental death benefits and the face amount of any paid-up additional insurance or any term rider. Death proceeds paid under an annuity contract are not considered life insurance death proceeds and are not exempted under this section.

*Exceptions to Section 101(a)(1) Treatment.* The general rule is simple, but, regrettably, it has complicating exceptions. These exceptions are discussed below briefly.

1. *Transfer for Value Rule.* If a life insurance policy or any interest in a policy is transferred to another person for a valuable consideration, the death proceeds lose their income tax exempt status, in whole or in part.[3] The amount of the consideration paid plus all net premiums paid by the transferee (the person to whom the policy or interest was transferred) may be recovered income-tax-free on death. The excess of the gross death proceeds over the consideration paid plus net premiums paid would be taxable to the beneficiary as ordinary income. Thus if Barbara sold her $100,000 policy to Heather (i.e., changed ownership) for $3,000 and if Barbara died ten years later with Heather having paid $12,000 in premiums (net of dividends), the beneficiary would receive $15,000 tax free ($3,000 consideration plus $12,000 premiums paid), but the $85,000 balance would be ordinary income for tax purposes.

The **transfer for value rule** applies to any transfer for a valuable consideration of a right to receive all or a part of the death proceeds of a life insurance policy. The most common situation in which the rule is invoked involves sales of policies, but the rule is not limited to sales; it applies to any transfer involving a valuable consideration.

Certain transactions are exempt from the transfer for value rule:

1. When the transfer (by sale or otherwise) is to the insured. (For example, a corporation sells a key person policy it owns to the insured/key employee when the employee resigns.)

2. When the transfer (by sale or otherwise) is to
   (a)    a partner of the insured;

[2] Internal Revenue Code (IRC), §101(a)(1).
[3] IRC §101(a)(2).

    (b)    a partnership in which the insured is a partner; or
    (c)    a corporation in which the insured is an officer or shareholder.

3.    Transfers that do not involve a tax basis change, including:
    (a)    a tax-free corporate organization or reorganization; or
    (b)    a bona fide gift.

Thus, irrespective of any earlier transfers for value, if ownership of the policy is acquired by the insured, death proceeds are income-tax-exempt (item 1 above). Similarly, any transfer in connection with the business applications noted in items 2 or 3(a) results in death proceeds being accorded IRC Section 101(a)(1) treatment (i.e., income tax exempt). Finally, when a policy is transferred, *not* for a valuable consideration, but as a gift, death proceeds remain income-tax-exempt. Thus a gift of a policy on one spouse's life to the other spouse through an absolute assignment (i.e., change of ownership) ordinarily falls outside the transfer for value rule.

*2. Failure to Meet IRC Definition of Life Insurance.* IRC Section 7702 contains a definition of life insurance for purposes of determining whether a policy qualifies for favorable tax treatment. This definition is important for many reasons and is discussed in detail below.

In general, however, the definition attempts to limit the code's favorable life insurance tax treatment to policies whose savings elements (cash values) do not predominate over the protection element. Two tests are prescribed to make this determination (see below). If the policy fails to meet both of these two tests, the policy is treated, for tax purposes, as if it were a combination of (1) pure term life insurance equal to the policy's net amount at risk and (2) a taxable fund equal to the policy cash value. The pure term portion is subject to Section 101(a)(1) treatment (i.e., income-tax-exempt). The cash value portion does not receive Section 101 treatment (i.e., any gain over its basis would be subject to ordinary income taxation). Its basis would be measured as discussed below and would include any amounts on which income taxes had already been paid.

*3. Other.* Other highly specific reasons can cause life insurance death proceeds to be taxed, wholly or partly. It appears that a lack of insurable interest at the time of a life insurance policy's issuance will cause the contract to be considered a wager, and, therefore, death proceeds received in excess of premiums paid (net of dividend credits) would be taxable as ordinary income.[4] Whether an insurable interest existed would be determined under the applicable state law. Also the state law would determine whether *any* proceeds would be paid. Recall that to have a valid contract, an insurable interest need exist at policy inception only, not at time of claim.[5]

---

[4] See, for example, *Atlantic Oil Co. v. Patterson*, 331F. 2d 516 (5th Cir. 1964).
[5] See Chap. 8.

Other situations that can invite income tax treatment include:

- Proceeds received under a qualified pension or profit-sharing plan

- Proceeds received by a creditor from life insurance on the debtor/insured's life

- Proceeds received as corporate dividends or compensation

- Proceeds received as alimony

- Proceeds received as restitution of embezzled funds

Finally, death proceeds payable to a corporation may attract ordinary income tax treatment via the corporate **alternate minimum tax** (AMT). This tax is intended to ensure that no taxpayer with substantial economic income avoids significant tax liability. The details of the AMT are beyond the scope of this text, but, in effect, certain tax preference and other items that may escape inclusion in a taxpayer's regular taxable income are added to that regular income and a tax rate and exemption applied to this new **alternative minimum taxable income** (AMTI). Any positive difference between the AMT and the tax due on the regular taxable income must be paid in addition to the normal tax.

Life insurance death proceeds received by a corporation (and increases in policy cash values) are tax preference items and, thus, could give rise to an AMT situation. In such instances, good planning may call for the insurance to be purchased outside the corporation.[6]

***Tax Treatment of Settlement Options.*** Life insurance death proceeds can be paid out under one or more of the settlement options.[7] The favorable income tax treatment of the policy (lump sum) death proceeds is unaffected by election of a settlement option, although income taxes may be due on any interest paid on the death proceeds.

Under the **interest option**, interest received by the beneficiary is taxable as ordinary income. Interest retained by the insurer also is taxable unless the beneficiary cannot withdraw either principal or interest for a stated time period. At the end of the time period, all previously accrued untaxed interest would be taxable.

Under the **installment settlement option** and **life income settlement option**, each payment is deemed to be composed of part principal and part interest. The portion deemed to be a return of principal is not taxed. The procedure for deriving this portion is to calculate an **amount held by the insurer** (usually, the single-sum amount payable at the insured's death) and prorate this amount over the actual or expected payment period. Amounts in excess of the annual prorated principal are treated as interest and are taxable income to the recipient.[8]

---

[6] See Chap. 15.

[7] See Chap. 9.

[8] Spouses of insureds who died before October 23, 1986, may exclude up to $1,000 of interest annually in addition to the prorated tax-free return of principal.

To derive the prorated amount excludable as a return of principal under the **fixed period option**, the amount held by the insurer is divided by the number of installments within the fixed period. The excess of each payment over this amount is deemed interest income. Thus if $100,000 of death proceeds is to be paid over a ten-year fixed period and the payments are $15,000 per year, $10,000 ($100,000 divided by ten years) is excluded from yearly taxable income as being a return of principal.

The procedure to derive the excludable amount of each payment under the **fixed-amount option** entails dividing the amount held by the insurer by the number of payments required to exhaust the principal at the *guaranteed* interest rate. The amount of each payment in excess of this figure is deemed to be interest. Payments made beyond the guaranteed period are considered to be interest only and, therefore, fully taxable.

The amount to be excluded from taxable income of each payment under one of the **life income settlement options** is determined by reference to the recipient's life expectancy. The amount held by the insurer is divided by the recipient's life expectancy, as determined by IRS-prescribed mortality tables, to derive the excludable portion of each payment. If the life income option contains a refund feature or guaranteed minimum number of installments, the amount held by the insurer is reduced by a factor intended to represent the actuarial value of the refund or guarantee feature. The insurer furnishes this figure.

For example, assume $100,000 of death proceeds are to be paid under the life income option with a ten-year period certain. The beneficiary is a 60-year-old male with a life expectancy, according to the IRS's mortality table, of 24.2 years. The insurer advises that the actuarial value of the ten-year period certain feature is 8 percent of the amount held by the insurer. Stated differently, the contingent beneficiary's interest in the payouts is valued at 8 percent of the total, since there is a chance that the primary beneficiary might die during the ten-year period. Thus the $100,000 proceeds would be reduced by 8 percent to $92,000, which, when divided by the 24.2-year life expectancy yields $3,802, the amount excludable annually as return of principal. The same exclusion amounts apply for as long as the payments are made to the primary beneficiary, even beyond the individual's life expectancy.

## LIVING PROCEEDS

IRC Section 72 governs the income taxation of proceeds received under a life insurance policy during the insured's lifetime—so-called living proceeds.[9] Living proceeds can include policy dividends, cash values, matured endowments, policy loans, and accelerated death benefits.

An understanding of certain 1988 changes to the IRC is an important prelude to the discussion. These changes were occasioned by the practice of

---

[9] Income taxation of annuities is also addressed under this code section (see later in this chapter).

many insurers selling single-premium whole life policies more as tax-preferred savings instruments than as policies providing protection against the financial consequences of premature death.

With these changes, a new class of life insurance policies—modified endowment contracts—was created for tax purposes. A **modified endowment contract** (MEC) is a life insurance policy entered into on or after June 21, 1988, that meets the IRC Section 7702 definition of life insurance (see later in this chapter), but that fails to meet the so-called seven-pay test. A MEC is subject to tax rules that differ from non-MEC life insurance policies.

A life insurance policy fails to satisfy the **seven-pay test** if the cumulative amount paid under the contract at any time during the first seven contract years exceeds the amount that would have been paid on or before such time had the policy's annual premiums been equal to the net level premium for a seven-pay life policy. The seven level premiums are determined at policy issuance, and the policy death benefit is taken to be that of the first contract year, irrespective of any scheduled benefit decreases.

If a policy is materially changed after issuance, the seven-pay test must be applied taking into account the cash value prior to the change. A **material change** is any increase in benefits or any exchange for another policy. Three exceptions include benefit changes due to (1) premium amounts necessary to fund the lowest death benefit during the first ten years, (2) dividends or interest, and (3) certain cost-of-living increases.

Certain living benefits payable under a MEC are taxed more as an annuity than as otherwise qualifying life insurance. The tax treatment of death benefits is unaffected by whether a policy is a MEC.

*Policy Dividends*. Unless a policy is a MEC, dividends are considered a nontaxable return of excess premiums. This result is unaffected by the dividend option selected. If dividends are left to accumulate at interest, the interest credited on the accumulation is, of course, taxable.

Two exceptions exist to this general rule. First, if the policy is a MEC or fails to meet the IRC definition of life insurance (see later in this chapter), dividends are taxable, unless they are used to purchase paid-up additional insurance. Additionally, dividends payable under a MEC may be subject to a 10 percent penalty tax. Second, if the total of the *dividends received* under a non-MEC policy exceeds the total of the premiums paid, all dividend amounts received in excess of the sum of premiums paid constitute ordinary income.

*Cash Values*. Tax consequences can arise from a policy's cash value.

1. *Interest on Cash Value*. The interest credited on a life insurance policy's cash value is not included in current taxable income if the policy meets the IRC definition of life insurance. This favorable tax treatment applies also to MECs. Whether this so-called inside interest buildup is ever taxed is a function of whether the policy matures as a death claim or is surrendered for its cash value.

If the policy matures as a death claim, taxes on the interest are avoided altogether since the cash value is, in effect, merged into the death claim payment, which itself ordinarily is received income-tax-free. If the policy is surrendered for its cash value, taxes may be due on any gain (as discussed below).

Debate continues over whether sound public policy should permit the tax-advantaged inside interest buildup within life insurance policies. Critics claim that this favorable tax treatment is unjustified since it distorts the savings market, making life insurance products artificially more attractive that many other savings instruments. They also note that the government loses tax revenues because of this tax favoritism.

Proponents of the status quo point to the socially worthwhile benefits of life insurance, arguing that the current tax treatment provides reasonable safeguards against abuse while encouraging families to make provisions for their financial security. They also note that the income may not actually be received by the policyowner unless the policy is surrendered, much as the homeowner does not actually receive his or her home's appreciated value without selling the home.

The U.S. General Accounting Office (GAO), in a study of the issue for the U.S. Congress, concluded that the tax preference may encourage savings and long-term capital formation via life insurance companies but not for the entire economy.[10] The GAO furthermore found that only one argument for maintaining the current tax preference had potential merit—that of providing for one's dependents.[11] Until such time, if ever, as Congress changes current law, however, life policies will continue to accrue inside interest on a tax-favored basis.

2. *Cash Surrender Payments.* The general rule for taxation of lump-sum cash surrender value payments on life insurance policies is the cost recovery rule. Under the **cost recovery rule**, the amount included in the policyowner's gross income upon policy surrender is the excess of the gross proceeds received over the cost basis. The **cost basis** of a life insurance contract normally is the sum of the premiums paid less the sum of any dividends received in cash or credited against the premiums. When dividends purchase paid-up additional insurance or are left to accumulate at interest, the cash value of the additions and the value of the accumulations are includable in the gross proceeds.

For example, assume that the owner of a $100,000 ordinary life policy with an annual premium of $1,300 surrendered the policy for its cash value of $30,000 at the end of 20 years and that the sum of all dividends over the 20-year period was $19,000. The amount subject to ordinary income tax treatment is calculated as follows:

---

[10] *Tax Treatment of Life Insurance and Annuity Accrued Interest* (Washington, D.C.: G.A.O., 1990), pp. 38-41.

[11] Ibid., pp. 41–43.

|        |                          |          |                        |
|--------|--------------------------|----------|------------------------|
|        | Sum of premiums paid     | $ 26,000 |                        |
| Less:  | Sum of dividends received| -19,000  |                        |
| Equals:| Cost basis               | $ 7,000  |                        |
|        | Gross proceeds           | $ 30,000 | (cash surrender value) |
| Less:  | Cost basis               | -7,000   |                        |
| Equals:| Taxable gain             | $ 23,000 |                        |

Premiums paid for supplementary benefits such as the waiver of premium and accidental death benefit features are not a part of the basis. Premiums waived under the waiver of premium feature, logically, should be included in the basis.[12] If policy loans are outstanding on surrender, the net surrender value (cash surrender value less loan) constitutes the gross proceeds, but the loan amounts previously received lower the basis.

The cost basis of a life insurance policy includes the pure cost of insurance. Theoretically, yearly mortality charges should be excluded from the basis as representing current expenditure and not as an investment. Thus, to the extent that these mortality charges are included in the basis, taxable income to the policyowner technically is understated by that amount.

Losses on surrender of a life insurance policy normally cannot be recognized for income tax purposes. The rationale for not allowing a deductible loss is that the method for computing taxable gain (and loss) makes no allowance for the cost of pure insurance protection, and, therefore, any loss is assumed to be composed, in whole or in part, of such mortality costs.

This cost recovery rule generally applies to life insurance cash-value withdrawals and partial surrenders. Exceptions occur for cash distributions received under MECs and as a result of certain policyowner-initiated reductions in policy benefits or withdrawals. In these latter situations, the distribution will be taxed as ordinary income to the extent untaxed income exists in the contract and subject to certain ceiling amounts.[13] Distributions from modified endowment contracts are subject to the so-called **interest first rule**, wherein distributions are taxable as income to the extent that the cash value of the contract immediately before the payment exceeds the contract's cost basis. Additionally, a 10 percent penalty tax may apply to distributions prior to age 59 1/2.

3. *Policy Exchanges.* If one or more insurance policies are being surrendered and, in the process, being replaced by new insurance, any otherwise taxable gain may be avoided if the transaction qualifies as an IRC Section 1035 (nontaxable) exchange. To qualify as a nontaxable exchange, the exchange must be of (1) a life insurance policy for another life insurance policy or endowment or annuity contract; (2) an endowment for an annuity contract or another endowment of no greater maturity date than the replaced endowment; or (3) an

[12] However, in *Estate of Wong Wing Non,* 18 TC 204 (1952), the tax court did not follow this logic.
[13] IRC §7701(7)(B).

annuity for another annuity. In such situations, no gain need be recognized on exchange (replacement). The adjusted basis of the old policy is carried over to the new contract.

The distinction between an exchange and a surrender and purchase is not always clear. Several IRS private letter rulings suggest that, in general, the contracts to be replaced should be assigned to the replacing insurance company, without the policyowner actually receiving any surrender value proceeds. Other approaches have also been suggested.[14]

*Matured Endowments*. Living proceeds received from a matured endowment are taxed in the same manner as proceeds received on policy surrender. The basis is subtracted from the gross proceeds to derive taxable income.

*Policy Loans*. Policyowners can secure loans under their cash-value policies up to the amount of and on the security of the policy's cash value. The interest rate charged or the method used to derive the interest rate to be charged on such loans is stated in the contract.

*1. Interest Payments*. Until tax year 1990, individual policyowners could, with exceptions, deduct from taxable income at least some of the interest paid on policy loans. For tax years beginning after 1990, no deduction for such personal interest is allowed.

Policy loan interest paid on policies owned by a business and covering the lives of officers, employees, or other persons financially interested in the policyowner's business is deductible, subject to certain constraints. Interest deductions on policies purchased after June 20, 1986, are allowed only on policy loans of less than $50,000 per individual insured. The $50,000 limitation does not apply to policies purchased prior to June 21, 1986.

To obtain the deduction, the interest actually must be paid. If added to the existing loan or deducted by the insurer from the proceeds of a new loan, it is not deductible. In these two latter cases, a deduction will be allowed if and when the interest is actually paid, including paid by deduction on policy surrender or maturity.

The preceding business-related deduction does not hold when policy loans are used to finance life insurance under a systematic plan of borrowing. Thus interest due on loans to finance the purchase of single-premium life insurance policies (after March 1, 1954) is not tax deductible.[15] A single-premium policy is defined as one under which substantially all of the premiums due on the policy are paid within the first four policy years, or a substantial number of future premiums are deposited with the insurer in the first year.[16]

---

[14] See T. P. Manno and R. T. Nolan, "Internal Revenue Code §1035 and the Other Side of Exchange Programs," *The Journal of the American Society of CLU*, Vol. 39 (Nov. 1985); and J. Timothy Lynch, "Exchanges of Insurance Policies under Internal Revenue Code§1035: The Myths and the Realities," *CLU Journal*, Vol. 37 (Oct. 1983).

[15] IRC §264(a)(2). See Rev. Rul. 79-41.

[16] IRC §264(b).

IRC Section 264(a)(3) further provides that a deduction is denied for interest paid on an indebtedness "incurred or continued to purchase or carry a life insurance, endowment, or annuity contract . . . pursuant to a plan of purchase which contemplates the systematic direct or indirect borrowing of [sic] part or all of the increases in the cash value of such contract (either from the insurer or otherwise)." This rule applies only to contracts purchased after August 6, 1963, and contains four exceptions.[17] If a financing plan meets at least one of these exceptions, business interest is deductible.

The first exception is the **four-in-seven exception**, under which a deduction is allowed if no part of (at least) four of the first seven annual premiums due on a policy is paid through borrowing, either from the policy or elsewhere. A new seven-year period begins if a substantial increase in premiums occurs.

If borrowing in any year exceeds the premium for that year, the excess is considered to be borrowings used to finance the previous year's premium. Thus the four-in-seven test is violated if policyowner borrowings during the seven-year period exceed an amount equal to three years' premiums, irrespective of when the borrowing takes place during the period. The four premiums can be paid in any order. Also, it appears that once the seven-year requirement has been satisfied, borrowings beyond that period can be at any level.

The second of the four exceptions holds that, irrespective of whether a systematic plan of borrowing exists, if the interest paid on borrowings to pay premiums does not exceed $100 during a taxable year, the interest is deductible subject to the constraints mentioned earlier.

The third exception is that a business interest deduction will not be denied if indebtedness is "incurred because of an unforeseen substantial loss of income or unforeseen substantial increase in . . . financial obligations."[18]

The final exception states simply than an interest deduction on indebtedness will not be denied "if such indebtedness was incurred with [a] . . . trade or business."[19] This exception is not as broad as it may appear. It is intended to be used when loan proceeds are applied to finance usual business or commercial activities, such as business expansion. It does not provide an exception for life insurance financed to fund key person, split-dollar, deferred compensation, and employee retirement benefits.[20] The four-in-seven exception normally is used in these business situations.

2. *The Loan Payment.* The general rule is that the taking out of a loan under a life insurance policy does not, in itself, constitute a taxable distribution. If the policy is a MEC, however, policy loans are themselves taxable as income to the extent that the cash value of the contract immediately before the payment

---

[17] IRC §264(c).
[18] IRC §264(c)(3).
[19] IRC §264(c)(4).
[20] See Chap. 14.

exceeds the contract's costs basis. The 10 percent penalty tax may also apply if the loan is taken out before the insured reaches age 59 1/2.

3. *A Potential Tax Trap.* A non-MEC life insurance policy under which substantial loans are outstanding can constitute a tax trap for the ill-informed. Recall that policy loans reduce a policy's costs basis. Cumulative loans can exceed the premiums paid by a substantial amount. The net cash value (cash surrender value less loan) of such policies typically is small. Upon surrender of such a policy, the owner would receive a check for the small net cash value, but, at the same time, would have caused the cost recovery rule to be invoked. As a result of a negative cost basis, the owner potentially could face a monumental tax bill for surrendering a policy that contained virtually no net cash value. This pitfall can be especially cruel if the surrender occurs because of financial reverses.

*Accelerated Death Benefits.* As discussed in Chapter 7, some life insurance policies provide that the death benefit can be paid (accelerated) if the insured has one of several dread diseases or illnesses, or is permanently confined to a nursing home. The income tax treatment of these payments was unsettled as this book was going to press.

IRS-proposed regulations would make it clear that insureds who become terminally ill and whose policies contain a qualified accelerated death benefit (ADB) clause would receive such benefits income-tax free if death is expected to occur within 12 months. The regulations define a qualified ADB clause and the requirements for a terminal illness. The proposed regulations also would clarify the tax treatment of other living benefits by, in effect, permitting some or all of the payment to be taxed as a health insurance benefit rather than as a life insurance policy benefit. Thus, the cost recovery rule could be avoided with respect to that portion of the benefit that was deemed to be a health insurance payment—a decided tax concession to the insured.

## IRC DEFINITION OF LIFE INSURANCE [21]

*Background.* During the mid-1970s, the design of life insurance products, which had been relatively stable for several decades, began to change. Some of the new insurance products functioned more as short-term investments than as vehicles for protection against premature death or accumulation of long-term retirement funds. Consequently, these new products raised significant questions as to the appropriateness of certain tax benefits that had been provided for traditional types of life insurance policies.

---

[21] This section draws from Arthur Anderson & Co., *The 1984 Tax Reform Act: Impact on the Insurance Industry* (1985), pp. 39-41, and Ernst & Whinney, "Qualification as a Life Insurance Contract," No. K 58236, Dec. 21, 1984.

In response to the issues raised by the new products, the Tax Equity and Fiscal Responsibility Act of 1982 (TEFRA) provided a definition of life insurance for flexible-premium (universal life) products. Moreover, the taxation of annuities was modified to reduce incentives for their use as short-term investment vehicles.

The Deficit Reduction Act of 1984 greatly expanded and refined the provisions enacted by TEFRA. Specifically, the new law added Section 7702 to the IRC, which provided, for the first time, a federal, statutory definition of life insurance. It also modified the annuity taxation rules enacted by TEFRA to inhibit further the use of annuities as short-term investment vehicles. Failure of a policy to meet the definition results in the policy being treated as a combination of term insurance and a taxable side fund.

Traditional whole life policies generally contain an established actuarial relationship among premiums, reserves, cash values, and death benefits. The policy reserve is defined as the amount that, when added to the present value of future premiums payable under the policy, will equal the net single premium at the policyowner's attained age. Policy cash values generally are either slightly less than or equal to the policy reserve.

With the development of flexible-premium policies, these relationships became more complex. Most early universal life policies were designed simply with a corridor of pure life insurance protection between the policy's cash value and the face amount, rather than incorporating a specific actuarial relationship. The corridor was established to ensure that the policy contained at least some element of pure life insurance protection. As a result, some universal life policies were established with cash values substantially in excess of the amount actuarially required to prefund future mortality charges. Congress was concerned that the excess premiums paid into these types of policies were more in the nature of an investment than a premium required to support an insurance benefit.

To address this situation, Congress mandated that life insurance policies must meet one of two tests specified in the new IRC Section 7702. Whichever test is chosen, that test must be met for the entire life of the contract.

***Description of Alternative Tests.*** To qualify as a life insurance contract, the contract must meet the criteria of *either* of the following tests.

The first test applies mainly to traditional cash-value policies. This **cash-value accumulation test** requires that, by the terms of contract, the cash surrender value cannot at any time exceed the net single premium required to fund future contract benefits. The net single premium is calculated by assuming an interest rate equal to the greater of 4 percent or the rate guaranteed in the contract. The mortality charges are based on those specified in the contract, or, if not specified, the mortality charges used in determining statutory reserves for that contract. For contracts issued after October 20, 1988, the mortality charges must be reasonable and cannot exceed those of the prevailing mortality table required by the state insurance regulators (currently, the *Commissioners 1980 Standard Ordinary Mortality Table*).

The second test intended for universal life and related policies requires that both a guideline premium and a death benefit requirement be met.

- The **guideline premium requirement** is met if the cumulative premiums paid under the contract do not exceed, at any time, the greater of the "guideline single premiums" or the sum of the "guideline level premiums" at that time. The guideline single premium is computed using interest at the greater rate of 6 percent or the rate guaranteed in the contract. Mortality charges are based on the same standard as applies to the cash-value accumulation test. The guideline level premium is computed in a manner similar to the computing of the guideline single premium, except that the minimum interest rate is 4 percent rather than 6 percent.

- The **death benefit requirement** is met if death benefits exceed 250 percent of the cash value for an insured of attained age up to age 40, grading down to 100 percent of the cash value at attained age 95. Table 13-1 shows applicable percentages for various ages. Thus if a 35-year-old owns a cash-value policy whose cash value is $10,000, the policy death benefit must be at least $25,000 ($10,000 x 250 percent) for the policy to meet the death benefit requirement.

*Computational Rules*. The law provides several significant rules for calculations related to the above qualification tests. For one, any future net amount at risk cannot exceed the net amount at risk existing when the policy was issued. In addition, when future policy benefits are changed (e.g., a scheduled change in death benefits or the purchase of paid-up additions), a new calculation must be made to determine whether the policy continues to qualify as life insurance.

**TABLE 13-1    IRC SECTION 7702 CORRIDOR REQUIREMENTS AT SELECTED AGES**

| Insured's Attained Age at Beginning of Contract Year | | Percentage Decreases Ratably | |
|---|---|---|---|
| Greater Than | Not More Than | From | To |
| 0 | 40 | 250 | 250 |
| 40 | 45 | 250 | 215 |
| 45 | 50 | 215 | 185 |
| 50 | 55 | 185 | 150 |
| 55 | 60 | 150 | 130 |
| 60 | 65 | 130 | 120 |
| 65 | 70 | 120 | 115 |
| 70 | 75 | 115 | 105 |
| 75 | 90 | 105 | 105 |
| 90 | 95 | 105 | 100 |

The law requires that, for purposes of the definitional tests, the policy maturity age must be assumed to be between ages 95 and 100. This rule generally prevents policies endowing before age 95 from qualifying as life insurance. The definition of life insurance generally applies to policies issued after December 31, 1984.

If the policy fails to meet the definitional tests, a part of the increase in the cash surrender value during a year can be subjected to ordinary income taxation. A taxable amount will result if the benefits received under a life insurance policy exceed the premiums paid during the year. "Benefits" are the sum of (1) the increase in net surrender value, (2) the cost of pure life insurance protection, and (3) dividends received. The cost of the pure insurance protection is the lesser of the cost determined by multiplying the net amount at risk by (1) the applicable IRS uniform premium rate or (2) the mortality charge, if any, stated in the contract.

If a life insurance policy meets the definitional requirements originally but later fails to do so, all prior years' deferred income is to be included in the taxpayer's/policyowner's gross income in the year when the policy first fails to meet the test. The policyowner must rely on the life insurance company to ensure that the policy does not inadvertently fail to meet the IRC definition. Insurers are and should be capable of providing this guidance.

Failure to meet the IRC definition also excludes the cash-value portion of any life insurance policy from the favorable IRC Section 101(a)(1) treatment— that is, the cash value portion is not treated as death proceeds. The net amount at risk in such policies does, however, qualify for Section 101(a)(1) treatment.

## INCOME TAX TREATMENT OF ANNUITIES

Tax rules on annuities have changed over the past few years because of an attempt to discourage the use of annuities as short-term tax-deferred investments rather than as long-term retirement funding vehicles.

## TAX TREATMENT DURING ACCUMULATION PERIOD

In general, interest credited to the cash values of personally owned annuities accumulates tax deferred. This means that, with the exceptions noted below, the contract owner need not include this interest income in his or her gross income until such time as annuity liquidation begins.

Any dividends paid, cash-value withdrawals, loans, and amounts received on partial surrender of an annuity, however, will be taxable as ordinary income to the extent that the contract cash value exceeds the cost basis (usually the premiums paid). The balance is received as a recovery of investment and is tax free.

Not only must post-1982 annuities and contributions follow this interest first rule, but a further 10 percent penalty tax may be imposed on taxable payments received after December 31, 1986, under an annuity. The penalty does not apply to (1) a series of substantially equal lifetime periodic payments, (2) any payments made to the contract owner (or annuitant) who is at least 59 1/2 years old, or (3) any payments under a tax-qualified retirement plan. Also, withdrawals because of death or disability do not incur the penalty.

Amounts received on contracts effective before August 14, 1982, are taxed under the cost recovery rule, whereby the owner/taxpayer can recover tax free an amount equal to his or her investment in the contract. Only after full recovery of the basis are further withdrawals taxable. Much of the former tax abuse through annuities centered around this favorable rule.

## Tax Treatment during Liquidation Period

The income tax rules for taxation of annuity payouts are identical in principle to those discussed earlier with respect to life insurance settlement options. Therefore emphasis will be placed here only on the differences in treatment. Some of the differences are as follows.

An exclusion ratio must be derived. The resulting ratio, when multiplied by the amount of each guaranteed payment, represents the amount of each annuity payment that can be excluded from gross income. The **exclusion ratio** is the ratio of the investment in the contract to the expected return under the contract. The tax effect of recovering the cost basis over the life expectancy of the annuitant is the same as that followed for settlement options. Once an amount equal to the investment in the contract has been received by the annuitant, further payments are fully taxable.

The **investment in the contract** normally is the premium cost, net of dividends *received* and not previously taxed. Under settlement options, the death proceeds constitute the contract investment. The **expected return** of the contract is, in general, the total amount the annuitant can expect to receive under the contract.

The tax treatment of the fixed period and fixed amount annuity payout options is the same as that of the equivalent settlement option. The tax treatment of the life income options is the equivalent of that of the life income settlement options.

## FEDERAL ESTATE TAX TREATMENT OF LIFE INSURANCE AND ANNUITIES

Life insurance and annuity death proceeds often are subject to federal estate taxation. To understand how estate taxation applies to these death proceeds, an understanding of the federal estate tax law is necessary. This section introduces the reader to the details of federal estate taxation. State death taxes also should be considered in the planning process. The following chapter examines estate planning and some uses of life insurance in estate planning.

## OVERVIEW OF FEDERAL ESTATE TAX

The federal estate tax is a tax on a person's right to transfer property on his or her death. Although not a tax on the property itself, it is calculated on the value of such property. The tax, introduced at a modest level in 1916, can be of great importance in large estates. Generally, anyone who dies in 1987 or later leaving a gross estate of more than $600,000 must file a federal estate tax return (Form 706).

The federal estate tax is a graduated tax, starting at 18 percent and building to a 50 percent marginal rate for taxable amounts over $2.5 million. An additional 5 percent marginal tax rate is applied to estates in the $10,000,000-to-$18,340,000 range as representing a phaseout of the graduated rates and the unified credit.

The first step in calculating the federal estate tax owed is to measure the value of the decedent's gross estate. The **gross estate** is, roughly, the value of all property or interests in property owned or controlled by the deceased person.

Next, allowable deductions are subtracted from the gross estate. The result is the **taxable estate**. **Allowable deductions** include funeral and administration expenses, debts of the decedent, as well as bequests to charities and the surviving spouse. The gross estate less all allowable deductions *except* bequests to the surviving spouse and to charities is referred to as the **adjusted gross estate**.

To the taxable estate is added **adjusted taxable gifts**, which are taxable gifts made after 1976. The sum is referred to here as the **tentative tax base**. The reason for this addition is that the current estate tax law is part of a so-called unified transfer tax law that applies to both transfers made at death and transfers made during life. It is necessary to add the value of lifetime taxable transfers (gifts) back to the tax base to derive the appropriate marginal tax bracket. As will be seen, however, a credit can be taken for gift taxes paid after 1976.

The appropriate **tax rate** is then applied to the tentative tax base to derive the tentative federal estate tax. This figure is only tentative, since from it may be subtracted certain credits for gift and other taxes paid as well as the so-called **unified credit**. The unified credit is available to everyone, and, as of 1987 and later, it can offset up to $192,800 of transfer (both estate and gift) taxes. The practical effect of this unified credit is to eliminate transfer taxes on total lifetime and testamentary transfers of $600,000 or less.

After applying all applicable credits against the tentative federal estate tax, one arrives at the amount of **federal estate taxes owed**. The federal government expects to receive this amount of money within nine months of the decedent's death. An extension of up to 12 additional months can be granted by the IRS in certain circumstances.

Table 13-2 summarizes the preceding steps. Under each major category are found the relevant items that compose the category, along with the applicable IRC section. The balance of this section presents somewhat more detailed information regarding the federal estate tax, beginning with an elaboration of the gross estate.

## GROSS ESTATE

The gross estate, the starting point for estate tax computation, is composed of the value of the decedent's interest in all property. Outright ownership of property is not required for its value to be includable in the gross estate.

The value for estate tax purposes is the **fair market value** of the property at the date of death or, if a lower estate value would result (e.g., because of investment losses), six months after death—the so-called **alternate valuation date**. A penalty of from 10 to 30 percent of the amount of tax owed can be imposed by the IRS for undervaluation. Special valuation rules are available for real property used for farming and other business purposes.[22]

The gross estate is derived by summing the values of each of the categories shown under the heading Gross Estate in Table 13-2. Some are reviewed briefly below.

*Property Owned by the Decedent (Section 2033)*. This category includes all property of the decedent passing by will or by the state's intestacy laws if the decedent died without a valid will. Thus the value of all personal property, such as personal effects, automobiles, and jewelry, and of real property, such as one's home, vacant land, and business, are included within this category. For most persons, this is the largest single category of the gross estate. If the decedent had been the owner of a life insurance policy *on someone else's life* (i.e., the decedent was not insured), the interpolated terminal reserve plus any unearned premiums for the policy would be included in the decedent's gross estate.

*Certain Gifts*. The IRC provides that the value of certain classes of gifts also must be included in the gross estate. They fall into four categories.

First, certain gifts (Section 2035) made by the decedent within three years of his or her death are to be brought back into the gross estate. These include transfers in which the donor/decedent had retained certain interest in or power over the gifted property and gifts of life insurance policies. Gift taxation is discussed below.

Second, gifts with a life interest retained (Section 2036) are brought back into the gross estate. Such gifts are those where the decedent gifted property to someone but retained for life the right to receive income from the property, the right to use the property, or the right to designate who ultimately receives the property or income. For example, assume that Chris gave her house to her son but had retained the right to live in the house for the rest of her life. Section 2036 of the IRC requires that the value of the house be included in Chris's gross estate.

[22] IRC §2032A.

**TABLE 13-2**    **FEDERAL ESTATE TAX COMPUTATION**

| Gross Estate | - | Allowable Deductions | = | Taxable Estate | + | Adjusted Taxable Gifts | = | Tentative Tax Base | x | Tax Rate | = | Tentative FET | - | Credits | = | Federal Estate Tax |
|---|---|---|---|---|---|---|---|---|---|---|---|---|---|---|---|---|
| Owned property (Sec. 2033) | | Funeral expenses (Sec. 2053(a)(1)) | | | | Gifts made after 1976 that are not otherwise includable in the gross estate, net of annual exclusions taken (Sec. 2001(b)) | | | | See Table 13-3 (Sec. 2001(c)) | | | | Unified credit (Sec. 2010) | | |
| Dower and curtesy interests (Sec. 2034) | | Administration Expenses (Sec. 2053(a)(2)) | | | | | | | | | | | | State death taxes paid (Sec. 2011) See Table 13-4 | | |
| Gifts within 3 years of death (Sec. 2035) | | Claims against estate (Sec. 2053(a)(3)) | | | | | | | | | | | | Gift taxes paid (Sec. 2012) | | |
| Gifts with life interest retained (Sec. 2036) | | Mortgages and other debts (Sec. 2053(a)(4)) | | | | | | | | | | | | Federal estate taxes on previous transfers (Sec. 2013) | | |
| Gifts taking effect at death (Sec. 2037) | | Unreimbursed casualty and theft losses (Sec. 2054) | | | | | | | | | | | | Foreign death taxes paid (Sec. 2014) | | |
| Revocable gifts (Sec. 2038) | | Charitable, public and religious bequests (Sec. 2055) | | | | | | | | | | | | | | |
| Annuities (Sec. 2039) | | Bequests to surviving spouse (Sec. 2056) | | | | | | | | | | | | | | |
| Joint interests (Sec. 2040) | | | | | | | | | | | | | | | | |
| Powers of appointment (Sec. 2041) | | | | | | | | | | | | | | | | |
| Life insurance death proceeds (Sec. 2042) | | | | | | | | | | | | | | | | |
| Transfers for insufficient consideration (Sec. 2043) | | | | | | | | | | | | | | | | |
| Certain marital deduction property (Sec. 2044) | | | | | | | | | | | | | | | | |

Third, gifts taking effect at death (Section 2037) may be includable in the gross estate. A gift taking effect at death occurs when property is given to someone (in trust or otherwise) but with the stipulation that he or she may take possession or enjoyment of it only upon the donor's death. If the likelihood of the gift reverting to the donor immediately before death is greater than 5 percent, the entire value is includable in the gross estate. For example, assume that John established a trust for his granddaughter, with the trust corpus (assets) to be paid to her on his death, but if she predeceased him, the corpus is to revert to him. If the chance that he would survive his granddaughter was greater than 5 percent, the value of the entire gift would be includable in his gross estate.

Fourth, gifts made by the decedent wherein he or she retained the power to alter, amend, revoke, or terminate the gift are revocable gifts (Section 203) and are includable in the gross estate.

*Annuities (Section 2039).* If a decedent was receiving annuity payments at his or her death—either from purchase of an annuity or under a life insurance policy settlement option—and if those payments ceased at the annuitant's death, there is no property interest to include in the gross estate. Annuity and settlement option payouts often provide for a refund or guaranteed income feature, and many are of the joint and survivor type.[23] If income (or other) payments are to be made to another person on the annuitant's death, the present value of those survivor benefits might be includable in the estate.

A **premium payment test** is applied to determine the extent to which these survivor benefits are included in the decedent's gross estate. If the decedent paid no part of the contract purchase price, the entire value of the survivor benefits is excluded from the gross estate. If the decedent paid the full contract purchase price, the opposite result occurs. If the decedent paid only a part of the purchase price, that proportionate share of the survivor benefit is included in the gross estate.

For example, if Martin contributed the full $50,000 toward the purchase of a joint and last survivor annuity and the value of the survivor benefit on his death was determined to be $40,000,[24] the entire $40,000 would be includable in his estate. If Martin had paid one-fourth of the purchase price, $10,000 would be includable, and if the full purchase price had been contributed by the survivor, no part of the survivor benefit would be included in his gross estate.

The cash value of an annuity *during its accumulation period* would be includable in the decedent's estate under this code section if, and to the extent that, the decedent had made contributions toward its purchase.

*Joint Interest Property (Section 2040).* Property owned jointly during lifetime by the deceased person and someone else, referred to as **joint interest property** under the IRC, is includable, in whole or in part, in the decedent's gross

[23] See chaps. 7 and 9.

[24] Measured by determining the amount that the same insurance company would charge the survivor, based on his or her attained age, for a single life annuity.

estate. The extent to which this property is includable is a function of the nature of the ownership interest. Although state variations exist, in general, four types of joint ownership are found.

Property is held in **joint tenancy** with **right of survivorship** when it is owned by two or more persons and, on the death of any of the owners, his or her ownership interest passes automatically to the survivors. Ownership is not considered as vested in the individuals but as vested in the owners as a group. As such, 100 percent of the property's value is includable in the decedent's gross estate, *except* to the extent to which the survivors contributed to the property's purchase. Thus if Inbum's estate, on whom the burden rests, can prove survivors contributed $80,000 toward a $100,000 property purchase price, only 20 percent of the property's current value would be includable in his estate. Under a joint tenancy, the decedent's heirs have no claims against the property; the surviving owners continue to be the sole owners, but as a group. Ownership interest arising from a joint tenancy is not and cannot be passed by will.

A **tenancy by the entirety** is a joint ownership of property created only between spouses. As with the joint tenancy, it provides a right of survivorship. Unlike the joint tenancy, however, the property is deemed to be owned 50 percent by each spouse, irrespective of who contributed the purchase price. Thus 50 percent of the then property value is includable in the gross estate of the first spouse to die. Ownership interest does not pass by will, but rather by the nature of the ownership.

A **tenancy in common** is a joint-ownership arrangement wherein each member owns his or her share outright (not as a member of the group) and wherein his or her ownership interest can be passed to heirs by will. On the death of a member of a tenancy in common, his or her proportionate share is includable in the gross estate.

Eight states in the United States have **community property** laws.[25] In addition, Wisconsin adopted a marital property system in 1986 that is similar to community property in many respects. These laws establish that property acquired during marriage is the property of the marriage community, and, as such, on the death of one spouse, one-half of the value is includable automatically in the decedent's estate, irrespective of the proportions of the purchase price paid by the decedent. Rules pertaining to community property law vary greatly from state to state.

*Power of Appointments (Section 2041)*. If a decedent held a general power of appointment over property on his or her death, the value of the property is includable in the gross estate. A **general power of appointment** exists when the individual has the right to dispose of property that he or she does not own and could make the disposition in favor of the holder or the holder's creditors or

---

[25] The community property states are Arizona, California, Idaho, Louisiana, Nevada, New Mexico, Texas, and Washington.

estate. For example, Daniel may be receiving a lifetime income under a trust and have the power to withdraw all or a portion of the trust corpus during his lifetime. This right to invade the trust corpus is a general power of appointment and will cause the entire value of the trust to be includable in Daniel's gross estate on death, even though he may never have actually exercised the withdrawal right. Property over which an individual has  general power of appointment will not be includable in the gross estate if the holder's right to consume or invade the property is limited by defined standards, such as those relating to maintenance of his or her health, maintenance, education, or support. A **special power of appointment**, wherein the individual has the power to appoint anyone *other than* himself or herself or his or her estate or creditors to receive property, does not cause property to be includable in the gross estate.

*Life Insurance (Section 2042).* IRC Section 2042 provides that life insurance death proceeds are includable in a decedent's/insured's gross estate for federal estate tax purposes if (1) the proceeds are payable to or for the benefit of the decedent's estate or (2) the insured possessed, at death, any incidents of ownership in the policy.[26]

Thus even if the insured did not own the policy, the death proceeds would be includable in his or her gross estate if it received the proceeds, either because it was named beneficiary or because no named beneficiary was eligible (e.g., all named beneficiaries predeceased the insured). Also, proceeds payable, not "to," but "for" the benefit of the decedent's estate are includable in the gross estate. For example, assume that Glen is the owner and beneficiary of a $250,000 policy on Thelma's (his wife's) life and that he collaterally assigns the policy to a bank to cover her loan of $100,000. If she dies, the $100,000 debt—which would be includable as an estate liability—would be paid off. The $100,000 death proceeds utilized to extinguish the estate's debt is, therefore, includable in Thelma's estate even though Glen was both owner and beneficiary of the policy.

If the deceased insured possessed no incidents of ownership in the policy and if proceeds are not payable to or for the benefit of the estate, proceeds escape inclusion in the gross estate. Incidents of ownership include the right to change the beneficiary, the right to surrender or otherwise terminate the policy, the right to assign the policy, the right to obtain a policy loan, or, in general, the ability to exercise any important right of the policy. Complete policy ownership certainly will cause death proceeds to be includable in the estate, but possession of only one important policy right—even without total ownership—normally causes the entire proceeds to be includable in the gross estate.

A policy can be removed from the gross estate even though the insured was the owner if it is given to someone else via absolute assignment (and provided proceeds are not payable to or for the benefit of the estate). If the ownership

---

[26] The reader is reminded that IRC §101(a)(1) exempts life insurance death proceeds from *income* taxation. IRC §2042 concerns *estate* taxation..

transfer occurs within three years of the date of death, however, the policy proceeds will be includable in the gross estate as a gift made within three years of death (IRC Section 2035).[27]

*Miscellaneous*. Certain other interests are includable in the gross estate: (1) dower and curtesy interests (Section 2034) and (2) certain marital deduction property (Section 2044). A dower (for the wife) or a curtesy (for the husband) is a statutory requirement directing that a surviving spouse must receive at least a certain minimum proportion of the estate of the deceased spouse.

Transfers for insufficient considerations (Section 2043) are those wherein the amount paid for property was below fair market value (e.g., Bettie sold her business to deAnn, her daughter, for below fair market value). The excess of the fair market value over the consideration received is includable in the gross estate.

## THE TAXABLE ESTATE

After deriving the gross estate value, the next step is to derive the taxable estate. The **taxable estate** is the gross estate less allowable deductions. IRC Sections 2053 to 2056 define these deductions. Each of these four sections is discussed below.

*Expenses, Debts, and Claims (Section 2053)*. Deductions are permitted for the cost of the decedent's funeral and for the expenses associated with the administration of the estate. These latter expenses include items such as appraisal fees, attorney's fees, and executor's commissions.

Claims against the estate—such as those arising from unpaid property, income and other taxes owed prior to death—are deductible. Indebtedness of the decedent can be deducted provided the asset (if any) to which the indebtedness applies is included in the estate. Thus mortgage and auto loan balances at the time of death are deductible. Other debts such as those arising from consumer loans and charge card balances are also deductible provided the decedent is legally responsible for their payment.

*Unreimbursed Losses (Section 2054)*. Casualty and theft losses incurred during estate settlement are deductible from the gross estate. If the loss is indemnified by insurance or otherwise, only the net loss is deductible.

*Charitable and Related Transfers (Section 2055)*. Property left to qualified religious, charitable, scientific, literary, and educational organizations as well as property left to foster amateur sports competition and the prevention of cruelty to children or animals is deductible. Additionally, bequests to qualified veterans' organizations are deductible.

---

[27] This area can become complex. Also, policy proceeds can be includable in the gross estate if the transfer falls within one of the rules of IRC §2035, 2038, or 2041.

*Transfers to Surviving Spouse (Section 2056)*. For most families, the deduction permitted for property left to a surviving spouse is the most important deduction. This **marital deduction** permits a deduction from the gross estate of any property passing to the surviving spouse. Thus if all net assets are left to the surviving spouse, the taxable estate is zero.

Certain property may not qualify for the marital deduction even though it is left for the spouse's benefit. For example, if Monique's will provides that her surviving husband will receive income from her business for as long as he lives but that, upon his death, the entire business passes to her daughter, the property is considered **terminable interest property** and, as such, does not qualify for the marital deduction. In general, a property interest that passes to a surviving spouse but that would not be includable in the spouse's estate is terminable interest property and fails to qualify for the marital deduction.

Certain qualified terminable interest property does, however, qualify. In general, such property is that which passes to the surviving spouse and is characterized by (1) the surviving spouse being entitled to a lifetime income payable at least annually from the property and (2) no one (including the spouse) having the power to appoint any part of the property to anyone other than the spouse during the spouse's lifetime.

## TENTATIVE TAX BASE

To the taxable estate is then added the value of adjusted taxable gifts to derive a tentative tax base. Adjusted taxable gifts are those made after 1976 for which a gift tax return was filed, which are not otherwise includable in the decedent's gross estate, and which are net of permitted annual gift exclusions.

The current estate tax law is part of a transfer tax law that applies to both living and testamentary (i.e., death) transfers. This unified approach means that it is necessary to add back for estate tax purposes the value of property gifted during life, which did not qualify for the annual exclusion. This permits the calculation of a transfer tax based on all taxable transfers, both living and testamentary. A credit is permitted (as discussed below) for previous gift taxes paid, but since the unified transfer tax is a progressive tax, a recalculation is necessary.

Individuals are permitted to give away annually up to $10,000 per donee (gift recipient) and not pay any gift tax or even file a return. If a spouse joins in the gift, up to $20,000 per donee annually may be given without incurring any gift tax. Moreover, one spouse may give the other any amount and incur no transfer tax liability, since the unlimited marital deduction is available for such gifts.

The value of adjusted taxable gifts is the sum of all post-1976 gifts, net of exclusions and deductions. Also, unlike the taxes on incomplete gifts includable in the gross estate, gift taxes paid on these adjusted gifts may be excluded from the gross estate. The value included in the tentative tax base is the property value at the time of the gift, not its fair market value at date of death.

## TENTATIVE FEDERAL ESTATE TAX

To the tentative tax base is applied the appropriate federal estate tax rate to derive the tentative federal estate tax. Table 13-3 gives these transfer tax rates by bracket for the year 1993 and later. If the tentative tax base is over $10,000,000, an additional 5 percent marginal tax rate is applied to the value between $10,000,000 and $18,340,000. This additional tax is intended to phase out the benefits of a graduated tax rate and of the unified credit. Otherwise, the tax brackets and rates are as shown in Table 13-3, except for the $10,000,000 bracket.

## FEDERAL ESTATE TAX OWED

The actual federal estate tax owed is obtained by netting certain permissible credits against the tentative federal estate tax.

*Unified Transfer Tax Credit (Section 2010).* Tax law permits a substantial unified credit to be applied against estate (and gift) taxes otherwise due. This unified credit ($192,800) is applied on a cumulative basis to all lifetime and testamentary transfers. It applies as a dollar-for-dollar offset against the tax. The credit is sufficient to avoid all estate taxes on a computational tax base of $600,000.

**TABLE 13-3    ESTATE AND GIFT TAX RATE SCHEDULE, EFFECTIVE 1993**

If Tentative Tax Base:

| Is More Than | But Does Not Exceed | The Tentative Tax is | |
|---|---|---|---|
| $0 | $10,000 | 18% | |
| 10,000 | 20,000 | $1,800 plus 20% of the excess over | $10,000 |
| 20,000 | 40,000 | $3,800 plus 22% of the excess over | $20,000 |
| 40,000 | 60,000 | $8,200 plus 24% of the excess over | $40,000 |
| 60,000 | 80,000 | $13,000 plus 26% of the excess over | $60,000 |
| 80,000 | 100,000 | $18,200 plus 28% of the excess over | $80,000 |
| 100,000 | 150,000 | $23,800 plus 30% of the excess over | $100,000 |
| 150,000 | 250,000 | $38,800 plus 32% of the excess over | $150,000 |
| 250,000 | 500,000 | $70,800 plus 34% of the excess over | $250,000 |
| 500,000 | 750,000 | $155,800 plus 37% of the excess over | $500,000 |
| 750,000 | 1,000,000 | $248,300 plus 39% of the excess over | $750,000 |
| 1,000,000 | 1,250,000 | $345,800 plus 41% of the excess over | $1,000,000 |
| 1,250,000 | 1,500,000 | $448,300 plus 43% of the excess over | $1,250,000 |
| 1,500,000 | 2,000,000 | $555,800 plus 45% of the excess over | $1,500,000 |
| 2,000,000 | 2,500,000 | $780,800 plus 49% of the excess over | $2,000,000 |
| 2,500,000 | No limit | $1,025,800 plus 50% of the excess over | $2,500,000 |

*Credit for State Death Taxes Paid (Section 2011).* States levy their own forms of death taxes. The state tax may be on an heir's right to receive property (an **inheritance tax**) or on a decedent's right to transfer property (an **estate tax**). Whatever form the tax takes, federal law permits a credit against the federal estate tax for death taxes paid to states, subject to a maximum.

Table 13-4 shows maximum permissible credits.[28] The states whose laws would not otherwise develop a tax as high as the permissible federal credit often utilize a **credit estate tax**. These laws stipulate that the state death tax will be the greater of (1) the tax developed by applying the state's computational tax rules or (2) the maximum credit permitted for state death taxes in federal law.

*Credit for Gift Taxes Paid (Section 2012).* Previous gift taxes paid can be taken as a credit against the estate tax. This treatment is appropriate since the value of previous gifts is added back into the estate.

**TABLE 13-4     MAXIMUM CREDITS FOR STATE DEATH TAXES**

| If Tentative Tax Base: | | |
|---|---|---|
| Is More Than | But Does Not Exceed | The Maximum Credit is |
| $0 | $100,000 | $0 |
| 100,000 | 150,000 | $0 plus 0.8% of the excess over $100,000 |
| 150,000 | 200,000 | $400 plus 1.6% of the excess over $150,000 |
| 200,000 | 300,000 | $1,200 plus 2.4% of the excess over $200,000 |
| 300,000 | 500,000 | $3,600 plus 3.2% of the excess over $300,000 |
| 500,000 | 700,000 | $10,000 plus 4% of the excess over $500,000 |
| 700,000 | 900,000 | $18,000 plus 4.8% of the excess over $700,000 |
| 900,000 | 1,100,000 | $27,600 plus 5.6% of the excess over $900,000 |
| 1,100,000 | 1,600,000 | $38,800 plus 6.4% of the excess over $1,100,000 |
| 1,600,000 | 2,100,000 | $70,800 plus 7.2% of the excess over $1,600,000 |
| 2,100,000 | 2,600,000 | $106,800 plus 8% of the excess over $2,100,000 |
| 2,600,000 | 3,100,000 | $146,800 plus 8.8% of the excess over $2,600,000 |
| 3,100,000 | 3,600,000 | $190,800 plus 9.6% of the excess over $3,100,000 |
| 3,600,000 | 4,100,000 | $238,800 plus 10.4% of the excess over $3,600,000 |
| 4,100,000 | 5,100,000 | $290,800 plus 11.2% of the excess over $4,100,000 |
| 5,100,000 | 6,100,000 | $402,800 plus 12% of the excess over $5,100,000 |
| 6,100,000 | 7,100,000 | $522,800 plus 12.8% of the excess over $6,100,000 |
| 7,100,000 | 8,100,000 | $650,800 plus 13.6% of the excess over $7,100,000 |
| 8,100,000 | 9,100,000 | $786,800 plus 14.4% of the excess over $8,100,000 |
| 9,100,000 | 10,100,000 | $930,800 plus 15.2% of the excess over $9,100,000 |
| 10,100,000 | No limit | $1,082,800 plus 16% of the excess over $10,100,000 |

[28] The actual IRC table shows figures based on the *adjusted* taxable estate rather than the taxable estate, as shown in Table 13-4. The adjusted taxable estate is the taxable estate reduced by $60,000. This $60,000 adjustment has been included in Table 13-4 to simplify the presentation. Results are unaffected.

***Other Credits***. Two final credits are permitted. First, to prevent double taxation, a credit is allowable for death taxes paid to another country or U.S. possession if (1) the value of the property is includable in the gross estate and (2) the property is situated in that other country or possession.

Second, it sometimes happens that one person leaves property to another and the second dies within a short time of the first person's death. If estate tax was paid by the first decedent on the property left to the second decedent, part or all of that tax may be available as a credit against the estate tax bill of the second decedent. The permissible credit, a function of the time elapsed between the deaths, is a decreasing percentage of the estate tax paid on the first death transfer:

- 100 percent if deaths occur within two years

- 80 percent if deaths occur within three or four years

- 60 percent if deaths occur within five or six years

- 40 percent if deaths occur within seven or eight years

- 20 percent if deaths occur within nine or ten years

- 0 percent if deaths occur ten or more years apart

## ILLUSTRATION

An illustration will be used to try to "unify" the preceding points. Assume that Mike Magnus, aged 48 and a resident of Georgia, dies, leaving behind his wife, Dawn, and their two children, Yoko and Cary, both adults.

Table 13-5 shows the personal balance sheet for Mike and Dawn just before Mike's death. The current market values and the nature of the ownership interests are given. Dawn is beneficiary under the annuity.

In addition to the assets shown in Table 13-5, Mike was the insured and owner of $100,000 of group life insurance. Dawn is beneficiary. Only two years earlier, Mike had transferred ownership of a $500,000 term life policy to his daughter, Yoko, and she promptly named herself as beneficiary. Mike continued to pay premiums of the policy. Four years ago, Mike and Dawn had given their son, Cary, $200,000 to help him start a landscaping business.

Mike's will provides that Dawn should receive the $300,000 in common stock, the autos, and Mike's personal effects. It also provides (perhaps unwisely) that the entire mortgage loan is to be paid off. The real estate investment (a $1,000,000 office complex) is to be held in trust for the children, with Dawn receiving the income from the investment for her lifetime. She is given no rights to alter this trust arrangement. Mike stipulated that Georgia State University was to receive $10,000 for its music program. The balance of the estate is to be divided equally between his two children.

**TABLE 13-5    ILLUSTRATION: PERSONAL BALANCE SHEET
OF MIKE AND DAWN MAGNUS**

|  | Market Value | Nature of Ownership/Liability |
|---|---|---|
| **Assets** | | |
| Residence | $200,000 | Tenants by the entirety |
| Common stock | 300,000 | Mike |
| Corporate bonds | 200,000 | Mike |
| Vacant land | 300,000 | Dawn |
| Real estate investments | 1,000,000 | Mike |
| Annuity cash values | 300,000 | Mike |
| Personal effects | 50,000 | Dawn |
| Personal effects | 50,000 | Mike |
| Checking and savings account | 40,000 | Tenants by the entirety |
| Autos | 40,000 | Mike |
| Total assets | $2,480,000 | |
| **Liabilities** | | |
| Home mortgage | $100,000 | Tenants by the entirety |
| Charge-card balance | 5,000 | Dawn |
| Charge-card balance | 5,000 | Mike |
| Auto loans | 20,000 | Mike |
| Total liabilities | 130,000 | |
| Net worth (assets less liabilities) | $2,350,000 | |

The value of items included in Mike's gross estate are summarized as follows:

| Item | Value | Justification |
|---|---|---|
| Residence | $100,000 | Dawn considered as owning 50% of value (Section 2040) |
| Common stock | 300,000 | Ownership (Section 2033) |
| Corporate bonds | 200,000 | Ownership (Section 2033) |
| Real estate investment | 1,000,000 | Ownership (Section 2033) |
| Annuity cash value | 300,000 | Annuity (Section 2039) |
| Personal effects | 50,000 | Ownership (Section 2033) |
| Checking/savings account | 20,000 | Dawn considered as owning 50% of value (Section 2040) |
| Autos | 40,000 | Ownership (Section 2033) |
| Group life insurance | 100,000 | Life insurance with incidents of ownership by insured (Section 2042) |
| Personal life insurance | 500,000 | Gift made within three years of death (Section 2035) |
| TOTAL | $2,610,000 | |

Allowable deductions would be:

| Item | Amount | Justification |
|---|---|---|
| Funeral expenses | $5,000 | IRC Section 2053(a)(1) |
| Administration expenses | 90,000 | IRC Section 2053(a)(2) |
| Claims against estate | 10,000 | Income and property taxes IRC Section 2053(a)(3) |
| Debts | 75,000 | One-half of the mortgage plus $5,000 charge balance and $20,000 auto loan. IRC Section 2053(a)(4) |
| Charitable bequests | 10,000 | IRC Section 2055 |

| Marital deduction | $300,000 | Common stock |
| | 40,000 | Autos |
| | 50,000 | Personal effects |
| | 100,000 | His share of residence |
| | 20,000 | His share of checking/savings |
| | 100,000 | Group life insurance |
| | 610,000 | Total: IRC Section 2056 |
| TOTAL | $800,000 | |

To the taxable estate of $1,810,000 would be added the value of adjusted taxable gifts. The $500,000 term policy given to the daughter does not fall within this category. The $200,000 given jointly by Mike and Dawn to Cary is includable as an adjusted taxable gift, but only to the extent of one-half of the value of the gift (because it was a joint gift) and only after taking the $10,000 annual gift exclusion.

Thus the computational tax base is:

| | Taxable estate | $1,810,000 |
| Plus: | Adjusted taxable gifts | 90,000 |
| | Computational tax base | $1,900,000 |

By referring to the $1.5 to 2.0 million bracket of Table 13-3, it can be seen that the tentative federal estate tax is (1) $555,800 plus (2) 45 percent of the excess of $1,500,000 (the $400,000) or $180,000, for a total of $735,800.

Credits available to offset the tentative tax are (1) the unified transfer credit and (2) the state death tax credit. The gift tax credit is not available, since no gift taxes actually were paid on the earlier gifts.

The unified credit is $192,800. Note that the maximum state death tax credit given in Table 13-4 is $70,800 (for the first $1.6 million) plus 7.2 percent of the excess of the taxable estate, or $15,120 ($219,000 x 7.2 percent) for a total of $85,920.

Thus the federal estate tax actually owed would be calculated as follows:

| | Tentative federal estate tax | $735,800 |
| Less: | Unified credit | -192,800 |
| Less: | State death tax credit | -85,920 |
| | Federal estate tax owed | $457,080 |

It is instructive, at this point, to summarize the cash needs of Mike's estate. They derive from amounts needed to:

| | |
|---|---|
| Pay mortgage | $100,000 |
| Pay Mike's credit charge card balance | 5,000 |
| Pay auto loans | 20,000 |
| Pay funeral expenses | 5,000 |
| Pay administration expenses | 90,000 |
| Settle estate claims | 10,000 |
| Make charitable bequests | 10,000 |
| Pay state death taxes | 85,920 |
| Pay federal estate taxes | 457,080 |
| Total liquid needs | $783,000 |

This amount must be paid by Mike's executor from estate resources. Even though the estate net worth is considerable, the estate's liquidity is not great. Assuming that the property distribution directed by Mike's will is to be followed, the only remaining liquid assets in the estate are the corporate bonds of $200,000—clearly insufficient to cover the $783,000 cash needs. This means that other assets must be liquidated to settle the estate's obligations, and the estate's obligations must be met *before* distribution of property to the heirs. Note that the *entire* estate tax obligation could have been eliminated had Mike's will directed that optimum advantage be taken of the marital deduction. This oversight plus the lack of consideration relative to other planning techniques is an example of poor planning. This and other problems are discussed more fully in Chapter 14.

## GIFT TAX TREATMENT OF LIFE INSURANCE AND ANNUITIES

As with the federal estate tax, the federal gift tax is imposed upon the right of transferring property to another. The estate tax reaches those transfers that take place when a property owner dies, whereas the gift tax reaches those transfers that take place during the property owner's lifetime.

Despite the imposition of this tax, there can be certain advantages to making gifts. To understand these, an overview of the general provisions of the gift tax law is presented below. There follows an examination of the gift tax treatment of life insurance in particular. Chapter 14 examines the planning aspects of gifts in more detail.

### OVERVIEW OF FEDERAL GIFT TAX LAW

A lifetime gift to an individual incurs a federal gift tax generally at the same rate as does the federal estate tax. The unified rate schedule in Table 13-3 shows the tentative tax relating both to taxable estate transfers and to taxable gifts. As in the estate tax situation just covered, the unified credit is applied directly to reduce the tentative gift tax.

The amount of gift tax payable in a specific taxable period is determined by a three-step process:

1. Add all of the donor's lifetime taxable gifts, including prior gifts and current gifts. Taxable gifts do not include the $10,000 per year per donee exclusion for present interest gifts.

2. Apply the unified rate schedule to the total taxable gifts to derive the tentative tax.

3. Subtract the unified estate and gift tax credit. The result is the gift tax payable in the current period.

*Gift Tax Exclusion*. The federal gift tax law is not aimed at the usual exchange of gifts associated with birthdays, holidays, and similar occasions. Therefore, beginning in 1982, the law permitted the donor to make this type of gift without tax by excluding the first $10,000 of outright gifts in any one year to any one recipient.

This annual $10,000 exclusion applies to gifts made to each recipient, irrespective of how many are included in the donor's plans each year. Moreover, it is available year after year. This means that an individual could give $10,000 to a large number of recipients each year without incurring any gift tax liability.

The exclusion is applied to each donee individually, and if a donee receives less than $10,000, the exclusion is limited to the actual amount of the gift. If Bill gives $9,000 to Deborah and $11,000 to Nancy, Bill can exclude only $19,000 ($9,000 for Deborah and $10,000 for Nancy) and he would have $1,000 in taxable gifts for the year.

The annual exclusion is available only when the gift is one of a present interest. A **present interest** is one wherein the donee must have possession or enjoyment of the property immediately rather than at some future date. The exclusion is not available in connection with gifts of **future interest** in property—that is, any interest in property that does not pass into the donee's possession or enjoyment until some future date.

*The Gift-Splitting Privilege*. When married residents of community property states make a gift, the gift is usually considered as being one-half from each spouse. This is, of course, because each usually is considered the owner of a one-half interest in the community property. In accord with the general plan of equalizing the tax treatment in community and noncommunity property states, the gift tax law contains a provision allowing married couples to split their gifts. Thus when a married individual makes a gift of personal property to someone other than a spouse, it may be regarded as made one-half by each spouse. This privilege of splitting a gift when made to a third party is extended only to property given away by a husband or wife. The taxpayer is given the advantage of doubling the annual exclusion. Therefore a married individual can make gifts of $20,000 per year to any one beneficiary without incurring any gift tax liability if the spouse consents to splitting the gift.

*Deductions*. As with the federal estate tax marital deduction, the **gift tax marital deduction** permits tax-free transfers between spouses. This deduction is available without limit.

Just as with the federal estate tax, the gift tax law also permits full deduction for gifts to qualified charities. These charitable organizations generally are of the same type as the ones mentioned previously in the discussion of the estate tax charitable deduction. Gifts to private individuals can never qualify for the charitable deduction, no matter how needy or deserving the beneficiaries may be.

## GIFTS OF LIFE INSURANCE

Life insurance is often the subject of gifts. In fact, a life insurance policy is especially well suited for gifts. Gifts of life insurance include gifts of the policy itself, gifts of premium payments, and gifts of policy proceeds. Each of these is dealt with individually, since the valuation of each differs.

*Gifts of Life Insurance Contracts*. If an insured irrevocably assigns all of his or her rights in an existing policy, he or she has made a gift of the policy. Of course, if the insured/owner receives an adequate consideration for the transfer, it is not a gift. If the policy applicant (proposed policyowner) is someone other than the insured, no gift of the policy ordinarily would have been made. If the insured pays the premium, the premium amount is a gift. If the policy is an annual premium contract and the donor continues to make premium payments, each premium the donor pays thereafter is a gift in that amount.

If a donor gives the donee a single-premium or paid-up life insurance policy issued in a prior year, the value of the gift equals the **replacement cost** of the policy. The replacement cost of a policy equals the single premium that an insurance company would charge for a comparable contract issued at the insured's attained age.

If a donor gives a donee a life insurance policy that was issued in some previous year, and upon which premiums remain to be paid, the value of the gift is the policy's **fair market value**. This value is the policy's replacement cost. If a comparable contract is not ascertainable, the fair market value equals the **interpolated terminal reserve** (an amount equal to the policy reserve interpolated to the date of the gift) plus the value of unearned premiums and any accumulated dividends, and less any indebtedness against the policy. The reserve value, not the cash surrender value, is considered, although the difference often is negligible except in the early policy years. The following example illustrates the computation of a policy's interpolated terminal reserve.

Assume that a gift is made today of a policy whose issue date was ten years, eight months ago. This year's annual premium of $1,800 was paid on its due date, eight months ago. The tenth and eleventh year's terminal reserves are shown below, along with the computation:

|        | 11th year terminal reserve | $16,000 |
|--------|----------------------------|---------|
| Less:  | 10th year terminal reserve | -13,900 |
| Equals:| Increase in reserve        | $2,100  |

Thus the value of the gift will be composed of three parts:

1.   Pro-rata reserve increase         $1,400
     (8/12 of increase of $2,100)

2.  Pro-rata annual premium paid     600
    (4/12 of premium of $1,800)

3.  Beginning year reserve     13,900
    Total gift value     $15,900

*Gifts of Premiums*. When an individual makes the premium payments on a life insurance policy that he or she neither owns nor is the insured, the individual has made a taxable gift to the policyowner in an amount equal to the premium paid, subject to the $10,000 annual exclusion. Thus if Larry makes a premium payment on a policy owned by Debbie on her own life and under which Jay is the beneficiary, Larry has made a gift to Debbie in the amount of the premium payment.

Similarly, premiums paid by an insured are gifts if the insured has no incidents of ownership in the policy and proceeds of the policy are payable to a beneficiary other than his or her estate. Premiums paid by a beneficiary on a policy that he or she also owns are not gifts.

*Gifts of Insurance Proceeds*. Under ordinary circumstances there is no gift when life insurance proceeds are paid to a beneficiary. In some extraordinary instances, however, there may be a taxable gift.

When one person owns a policy, a second is the insured, and a third is the beneficiary, a gift can be considered as occurring from the policyowner to the beneficiary. The amount of the gift equals the full amount of the insurance proceeds.

Thus if Nan owns a policy of life insurance on her husband's life, with their children named as revocable beneficiaries, Nan will be deemed to have made a gift to the children in the full amount of the proceeds when they are paid at her husband's death. There is no real intent to make a gift in the literal sense, but a taxable gift has been made nevertheless.

A gift of endowment insurance proceeds likewise occurs when, upon the maturity of an endowment insurance policy, the proceeds are paid to a revocable beneficiary of the policy who is someone other than the owner.

## GENERATION-SKIPPING TRANSFER TAX

The IRC provides for a **generation-skipping transfer** (GST) **tax** to be levied when a property interest is transferred to persons who are two or more generations younger than the transferor.[29] The transferor in the case of property subject to the federal estate tax is the decedent, and for property subject to the gift tax, the transferor is the donor. This special tax is intended to ensure that transfer taxes are paid by wealthy persons who might otherwise seek to avoid a

[29] IRC §2611(a) and 2613.

generation of transfer taxes by passing their property to heirs (so-called **skip persons**) beyond those of the immediately following generation. The tax is in addition to any federal estate or gift taxes owed because of the transfer. For example, a grandmother could gift property directly to her granddaughter rather than to her son, thereby possibly skipping a generation of transfer taxes that otherwise might have been incurred because of a transfer to the son, and then by the son to the granddaughter.

A GST may occur from a direct transfer of property or from a distribution of property from a trust to a skip person or, in certain instances, when a skip person's interest in a trust terminates.

The amount of the GST tax is a function of the property value transferred and the applicable tax rate. Each person may transfer up to $1.0 million during his or her lifetime and avoid the GST tax. If the spouse joins in the transfer, a $2.0 million lifetime exemption applies. The applicable tax rate recognizes this exemption but, above the exemption, subjects the transferred property to the maximum transfer tax rate (50 percent for 1993 and later). As can be seen, therefore, the GST tax will be of little importance to persons of modest wealth, but those with greater wealth could incur substantial taxes under this provision.

Life insurance death proceeds, irrespective of the manner in which they are paid, can attract the GST tax, if they are paid to a skip person. This unpleasant result can be avoided by avoiding inclusion of the death proceeds in the insured's estate and through appropriate use of life insurance trusts, as discussed in Chapter 14.

# Chapter 14

# LIFE INSURANCE
# IN ESTATE
# AND RETIREMENT PLANNING

Previous chapters suggested some ways in which life insurance can be useful as a savings instrument and in estate planning. This chapter expands these discussions. Estate planning is discussed first, specifically the nature of the estate planning team and the various tools used in estate planning, including life insurance. Retirement planning and uses of life insurance as a savings instrument are discussed next.

## ESTATE PLANNING

A common misconception is that an estate is only the property that one leaves at death. The term *estate planning* in its broadest sense encompasses the accumulation, conservation, and distribution of an estate. The purpose of the estate planning process is to develop a plan that will enhance and maintain the financial security of individuals and their families. Estate planning has come to include lifetime financial planning that may lead to increases in the individual's estate as well as the conservation of existing assets.

### IMPEDIMENTS TO A WELL-PLANNED ESTATE[1]

Most individuals do not realize that even if they have not created an estate plan and executed the appropriate documents to implement their plans, a plan has been created for

---

[1] This and the next two sections draw heavily on Susan M. Harmon and Gwenda L. Cannon, "Estate Planning: An Overview," in Susan M. Harmon, ed., *Readings in Estate and Gift Tax Planning*, 2nd ed. (Bryn Mawr, Pa.: The American College, 1983). Used with permission.

them. The plan will be imposed on them by the state in which they reside. Each state has its own statutory scheme for the disposition of its citizens' property at death if the resident dies either without a valid will or having made an incomplete disposition of property.

These **intestate succession statutes** are based on degrees of consanguinity (blood relationship) to the decedent rather than on the distribution of property according to the intentions and desires of the deceased individual. Without a will, one may not leave property to charity. Neither may an unrelated friend inherit property from the deceased. If no relatives exist, the property will be distributed to the state. The property is said to have **escheated** to the state. Intestate succession statutes and wills apply only to property of the probate estate and not to property that passes by contract (such as life insurance death proceeds).

A current valid will is essential to having an updated estate plan, and the will should be reviewed periodically to assure that a property owner's most recent intentions will be honored at death. If family circumstances or laws have changed dramatically since the will was written, the will's provisions may be seriously out of touch with the property owner's current wishes, but the existing will is the one that will be followed until and unless it is replaced with a later valid will. This situation can produce disturbing results.

The potential estate and gift tax relief that the current federal estate and gift tax laws appear to provide may make many individuals believe that they no longer have a need for a carefully planned estate. The truth is in direct contradiction to this viewpoint, since only by utilizing the tax laws to maximum advantage can property owners carry out their postdeath intentions and prevent the unnecessary erosion of their estates due to taxes. For example, the unlimited marital deduction that allows an individual to pass an entire estate to a surviving spouse free of federal gift and estate taxes appears to offer relief from taxation. In reality, use of the unlimited marital deduction may be enormously expensive, since property will pass to others unprotected by the marital deduction at the death of the second spouse.

Tax relief should not be the primary objective of estate planning. The best estate plan is one that accurately reflects the individual's wishes, needs, and objectives in a manner that reduces the potential tax liability to the lowest level consistent with the individual's aims. This means that various tax options as well as their cost in terms of rigidity, loss of control over assets, and tax liability should be clearly understood. An estate plan that reduces the estate tax liability to zero is a poor plan if the cost is the perversion of the individual's wishes.

Estate tax liability often is predetermined by the form of ownership in which the asset is held prior to the owner's death. An example of an asset that frequently is owned or positioned improperly is life insurance. If the insured retains any incidents of ownership in the life insurance, the proceeds are includable in his or her gross estate. This could subject proceeds to unnecessary taxation, although use of the unlimited marital deduction could postpone estate taxation of proceeds. Proper ownership of assets, including life insurance, must be analyzed on a case-by-case basis. Also, there is a danger in ownership transfer to the spouse if the marriage is less than solid.

Another form of property ownership that can be problematic in estate planning is joint tenancy with right of survivorship. If insufficient thought is given to the way in which assets are titled, all or most property may be owned in this form. This could mean that the surviving spouse would inherit too much of the property relative to the children, possibly resulting in excessive estate tax liabilities at the second death.

Another impediment to effective planning relates to inadequate health insurance. The cost of a protracted period of disability may so erode an otherwise adequate estate that the estate owner leaves nothing to the beneficiaries at death. Adequate health insurance protection is an important consideration in planning any estate. Disability protection, in particular, often is ignored or misunderstood despite the fact that there is a greater likelihood of a significant period of disability before retirement age than there is of an early death.

Still another impediment that should not be underestimated is inflation. At the very least, continuing inflation necessitates periodic reviews of existing estate plans to keep abreast of projected estate tax liabilities, since these can be affected by inflation through "bracket creep" even though the real value of assets has not increased materially. It also is necessary to review asset valuations, projected income from assets held, and amounts of life insurance in terms of constant dollars to assure that the estate owner's family would continue to be adequately protected.

Inadequate liquidity may be a major problem in an otherwise well-planned estate. Three factors are particularly important in assessing liquidity needs in estate planning: (1) the amount and terms of debt of the estate owner, (2) the projected estate tax liability, and (3) the type of assets that comprise the estate.

At the time of an estate owner's death, the amount and terms of debt for which a decedent is personally responsible may dramatically reduce either the actual assets or the net income stream that would be available to the beneficiaries. The same is true of estate tax liabilities.

The type of assets owned at the time of death also will affect the estate's ability to meet its liquidity needs. For example, when a closely held business is the primary estate asset and has been the principal source of income to the decedent and the family through the decedent's salary and bonuses, there is frequently an immediate family cash shortage following a businessowner's death. Financial stress compounds problems at the time when the family is trying to deal with death. Furthermore, if no advance planning is done, assets, including the family business, may have to be sold under disadvantageous market conditions at greatly reduced prices to pay estate bills or taxes. Such situations should be anticipated and appropriate plans implemented to avoid these problems. If the business is to be sold, the arrangements for the sale should be reduced to legally enforceable agreements. Liquidity may be available from retirement plans or life insurance proceeds. Also, salary continuation plans are a possible way to soften the financial shock of a breadwinner's death.

## THE ESTATE PLANNING PROCESS

The estate planning process is identical in principle to the overall financial planning process. First, data must be obtained and objectives established. This would normally be done as a part of the fact finding for the overall personal financial plan. The existing estate plan must be evaluated for potential inadequacies. A plan is then designed for, presented to, and approved by the individual. After review and approval, the plan must be implemented, including the execution of any necessary legal documents and transfers of property. Finally, the individual should be made aware that a periodic review of the plan is desirable, to determine if changes in financial positions, family relationships, goals, tax laws, or other circumstances necessitate changes in the plan.

The creation of a comprehensive and creative estate plan is a highly rewarding experience for the estate planning practitioner. Although the emphasis placed on certain aspects of estate plans varies depending on the knowledge and background of the practitioner, the primary objective of a good planner should be to effectuate and implement the desires and objectives of the individual for whom the plan is created, in an efficient and effective manner. The individual is the director of the plan. The professionals are the producers. An estate plan reflects the values of the individual. It may evidence his or her cares and concerns for other human beings as well as for himself or herself. The plan may also reflect his or her own self-interest, grievances, and grudges. Much will be revealed about the individual's character, philosophy of life, and attitudes by the types of planning options selected and the reasons for which he or she selects them.

## THE ESTATE PLANNING TEAM

Individuals from more than one professional discipline are qualified to assist clients in estate planning. The greatest benefit and the best results for an individual can be obtained from an approach that enlists a variety of advisors to assist in total financial planning, including estate planning. If, however, the individual is interested only in estate planning or only in death planning, the estate planner should perform these tasks. Perhaps the individual will become interested in more complete planning through a successful relationship.

The estate planning team has traditionally consisted of an attorney, an insurance specialist, a bank trust officer, an accountant, and an investment counselor. A newer member of the team, who also may be one of the preceding specialists, is the financial planner. It is frequently the financial planner or the insurance specialist who made the first contact with the client, sensitized him or her to the need for estate planning, and motivated him or her to become involved in the process. This person often acts as coordinator for the entire plan, although any other capable member of the team might fill this role.

The accountant is the advisor most likely to have annual contact with the client through preparation of the client's tax returns. This gives him or her the opportunity to be familiar with the size, amount, and nature of the individual's estate. The accountant may be the person who can most easily provide a valuation for any asset in the estate when it is not easily ascertainable. Valuation is particularly crucial if one recommendation in the estate plan is a buy-sell agreement to provide for a transfer of a business interest upon death or disability.[2] The accountant also may be of help in preparing a final estate tax return.

The trust officer may be the person to whom the individual initially turned for information and for estate planning services if professional management was desired in the administration of trusts. A good trust officer will be familiar with estate planning and the various estate planning tools. The long-term nature of the relationship between the trustee and the beneficiaries argues for great care to be exercised in trustee selection. As executors or trustees, trust officers have primary responsibility for gathering and safeguarding the assets, settling the estate, investing estate assets during the administration period, and making distribution, as necessary, to the estate or trust beneficiaries. The bank trust department also may be responsible for filing estate and other fiduciary tax returns.

The life insurance specialist plays an important role on the estate planning team, because he or she can provide products that will supply the estate with the necessary cash to pay the estate tax and other liabilities as well as to fund the income needs of the surviving family members. Life insurance is the primary asset of many estates, and, consequently, the major source of family income after an estate owner dies.

The attorney is a crucial member because plans usually cannot be executed properly without knowledge of the law. Furthermore, only the attorney is licensed to practice law. The attorney is responsible for legal advice and for preparing documents assuring that the individual's intentions are expressed in legally enforceable documents that will serve as the basis for carrying out the plan. These documents virtually always include wills and many include trusts, buy-sell agreements, and other documents if a sophisticated estate plan has been elected.

Estate planning has become vastly more complicated and challenging as a field of practice. The effective estate planner is familiar with applicable local and federal law and has a good working knowledge of subject matter pertaining to property, probate, wills and trusts, federal and state taxation, corporations, partnerships, business, insurance, and divorce. An estate planner must be able to explain relevant portions of these subjects in plain language.

[2] See Chap. 15.

## ESTATE PLANNING TOOLS[3]

Tools available for estate planning should be used to ensure that (1) assets are sufficient to meet objectives, (2) beneficiaries receive assets in the proportion and manner desired, (3) the minimum in income, estate, gift, and state death taxes and other transfer costs is paid, subject to accomplishing the desired objectives, and (4) sufficient liquidity exists to cover transfer costs. Several estate planning tools are examined below with the above objectives in mind.

*Wills.* A **will** is a legal declaration of an individual's wishes as to the disposition to be made of his or her property on death. It is the principal means by which most estate plans are implemented. A will affords the opportunity not only to declare beneficiaries, but also permits the implementation of plans to save income, estate and gift taxes; name an executor; arrange for the payment of obligations; and establish trusts, among other things. As with the estate plan, it should be reviewed frequently and kept up to date so that objectives are met.

A will is an **ambulatory instrument**, meaning that it does not take effect until the death of the **testator**, the person making the will. Therefore it can be changed at any time during life. A new will can expressly revoke any prior wills. A **codicil** changes the part of the will with which it is inconsistent. A will can be revoked by physically destroying or mutilating it. Individual state law must be carefully followed in revoking a will and in crafting a new one to ensure its validity.

Wills also may be modified by state law. For example, a bequest to a former spouse that is executed prior to divorce typically is invalid. Some states even declare the entire will invalid upon divorce. Generally, a beneficiary is prohibited from obtaining a share under the will if the beneficiary murdered the testator.

Children born or adopted after a will is executed might be permitted to share in the estate, even though they were not mentioned in the will. In at least one state, however, the failure to contemplate after-born children renders the entire will invalid.

Since only the original will is valid, it is important that it be kept in a safe place and that others know its location. Generally, a safe-deposit box is not a good place to keep a will. Invariably, so it seems, when a safebox is used, the testator dies on Friday night, and it may be impossible to obtain the will until Monday. There might be a need to read the will immediately, to be certain that all the testator's instructions are carried out.

It generally is not a good idea to distribute a large number of copies of a will. The estate planner, the attorney, or perhaps the executor could keep the original and probably should have copies, but too many additional copies would be hard to collect and destroy should a change be made in the will. If copies of old wills are left in the hands of others, it is possible that someone with a copy will not know that changes have been made and may attempt, in good faith, to begin carrying out instructions that are no longer valid.

---

[3] This section draws on Fred A. Tillman and Jack Rice, *Who's Next Please?* (Indianapolis, Ind.: Russell R. Muller Retail Hardware Research Foundation, 1982), Chap. 9.

A will must meet technical and legal requirements. First, the testator must be of proper age. In most states this is the age of majority; some states allow a younger person to make a will, although such wills invite legal challenges. The testator must be competent to make a valid will. Competency means that the testator understands that he or she is making a will, knows the extent and nature of the property being disposed of, and knows the natural objects of his or her bounty. The will must be free from fraud, duress, and undue influence.

The will also must be in writing and properly executed, according to applicable state law. Oral wills generally are not valid, with some exceptions. The will must be signed, indicating intent to make a will, and generally attested to by the appropriate number of witnesses (which varies from state to state).

In many states, a surviving spouse is entitled to what is called a statutory or forced-heir share of the deceased spouse's property—usually a one-third share. If the decedent's will leaves a lesser amount to the surviving spouse, the survivor can elect against the will and receive the same amount that would have been received had the testator died without a will. In some states, the right to elect against the will extends to children as well.

*Living Wills*. An estate's value can be substantially reduced because of extraordinary, end-of-life medical measures intended to extend life. Indeed, an average of about 15 percent of lifetime medical expenses is incurred in the last six months of life. In response to this potential situation, individuals in increasing numbers are executing living wills. A **living will** is a legal instrument setting forth the individual's wishes as to the use of life-sustaining measures in case of terminal illness, prolonged coma, or serious incapacitation.

State requirements for living wills vary but most statutes require the inclusion of an express statement that the individual is "of sound mind," is voluntarily making the declaration, and desires no artificial prolongation of the dying process. State laws typically define key terms, such as "life-sustaining procedure" and "terminal illness," and require that the living will be signed, dated, and witnessed, in the manner of a testamentary will. No witness may have any interest in the individual's estate.

Living wills offer some clear advantages in this age of impressive life-prolonging technology, which may, unfortunately, not translate into improving quality of life. A living will ensures that the individual's (as opposed to some well-intentioned family member's) wishes are being carried out. A living will also can ease the anguish a family member may suffer in making what probably could be an excruciating life-or-death decision.[4]

*Gifts*. A **gift** is the transfer of property ownership for less than an adequate price. The difference between fair market value and the sales price defines a gift.

---

[4]A related, companion financial planning tool is the **durable power of attorney**. This legal instrument allows individuals to protect themselves when they have become incapacitated or have been declared incompetent to conduct their own affairs. The individual names a representative to act for him or her, rather than having a court appoint a conservator or guardian.

Obviously, the person named to hold the power should be one in whom the individual has the utmost trust. Upon recovery, the individual regains full control of his or her affairs. Upon death, the power is terminated.

For a gift to be complete, the **donor** (gift giver) and **donee** (gift recipient) both must be competent, and the donor must have a clear intent to make a gift. Furthermore, the donor must give up ownership and control, and the gift must be delivered and accepted by the donee. A gift is not considered complete for tax purposes if it is delivered and then borrowed back for an indefinite period of time.

As mentioned in Chapter 13, $10,000 can be given away in property or cash each year to any one person, regardless of relationship, without incurring gift tax liability. A gift can be split between husband and wife, irrespective of which one owns the property. With a split gift, up to $20,000 per year per donee can be given without gift tax consequences.

By making gifts (in property or cash) within the annual exclusion, the value effectively is removed from the estate for tax purposes. In other words, $10,000 ($20,000 if it is a split gift) per year can be given to any one person, with no gift tax liability incurred, and the gifted property will be removed from the estate. If a gifting program is started early and continued, a series of annual exclusion gifts can substantially reduce estate taxes.

If a gift of more than $10,000 ($20,000 if it is a split gift) is made to any one person during the calendar year, a taxable gift has been made. A federal gift tax return should be filed, and gift tax will be assessed according to the tax rate schedule. It is not necessary actually to pay tax to the federal government until the unified tax credit amounts have been exhausted.

What are the advantages of making taxable gifts, particularly since these gifts are added back to the estate for estate tax purposes under current law?

1. Individual gifts, up to the amount of the annual exclusion, are not added back to the estate for purposes of calculating federal estate tax. Thus the estate is reduced by the amount of the annual exclusion.

2. A credit is allowed against any federal estate tax due, equal to the amount of any gift tax paid during lifetime. That is, taxes are not paid twice on the same transfer.

3. The gift tax is tax exclusive whereas the estate tax is tax inclusive. In other words, the assets used to pay gift taxes are not themselves subject to tax, yet assets used to pay estate taxes are included in calculating the tax.

4. No federal estate tax is due on the appreciation of the value of the gift from the date of gift to the date of death. For example, suppose Judy gave her daughter, Kerrie, property valued at $100,000. Five years later, the year of Judy's death, the property has increased in value to $200,000. The market value at the date of gift less the annual exclusion is $90,000 ($100,000 minus $10,000). This amount will be added back to Judy's estate. Thus the appreciation from the date of gift to the date of death ($100,000) will be excluded from the estate for federal estate tax purposes.

5. If a gift is made to someone other than the spouse, federal income tax can be saved if the property transferred would have otherwise produced taxable

income to the donor. For example, should Ginny give her adult son
income producing property, he, rather than she, will pay the income tax on
amounts earned. If the son is in a lower tax bracket, total federal
income taxes due will be lower than otherwise.

There are other reasons for making gifts besides just to save taxes. The
principal reasons are:

1. Individuals derive satisfaction from giving to others.

2. The expense of administration and other costs associated with processing
   the estate can be minimized or avoided by giving the property away during
   lifetime. (Avoiding this expense, however, may negate primary planning
   objectives.)

3. Anyone can review the public records of a probate court. By making a
   gift, the property is removed from probate and privacy is retained.

4. By giving the property away, management responsibilities are shifted to
   other persons—the new owners.

5. Should a person believe that he or she is no longer able to manage assets
   properly, the assets might be given away to protect their value.
   Unfortunately, most persons are unable to recognize when they are no
   longer competent to make the appropriate decisions.

6. Making gifts to children can provide them the opportunity to learn how to
   manage money or property.

7. If an individual has assets that he or she wishes to go to a particular
   individual and anticipates the possibility of family disharmony, making a
   gift during lifetime can be extremely important to meet the objective. If a
   will does not exist or is declared invalid because of a will contest, property
   that passes through the estate could ultimately be passed to unintended
   individuals. By giving the property away, this risk is eliminated.

A life insurance policy typically is an excellent type of property to use for a
gift. The value of the gift is the sum of the unearned premium and the
interpolated terminal reserves, as discussed earlier.[5] Were the policy included in
the estate at the time of death, the estate tax value would be the amount of the
death proceeds. If the face amount of the policy were $100,000 and the value for
gift purposes were no more than $10,000, the policy could be transferred by gift
within the annual exclusion, and there would be no gift tax consequences. Of
course, the donor must live for more than three years from the date of the gift to
avoid inclusion of the policy proceeds in his or her estate under IRC Section
2035.

Greatly appreciated property may make an appropriate gift. If sale of the
property is anticipated, a gift to a person who is in a lower income tax bracket

[5] See Chap. 13.

can make good financial sense. The donee would then sell the property and pay less taxes on the gain. The gift tax consequences should be compared with the income tax consequences to determine whether taxes in the overall transactions are lessened.

If the property will be sold after death, it often should be retained rather than given away. This is because of the stepped-up basis assigned to appreciated assets included in the estate versus the carry-over basis of assets transferred by gift. If property is given away and the donee sells it, income tax must be paid on the gain. If the property is retained and its value included in the estate, an estate tax must be paid on the fair market value of the property. The value of the property included in the gross estate, however, becomes the new basis to be used by the beneficiaries or the estate for income tax purposes.

Suppose Larry owns only one piece of property. He paid $10,000 for it and it is now worth $200,000. If he gives the property away and the donee sells it, income tax must be paid by the donee on the $190,000 gain. If he does not give away the property but retains it until his death, naming the person to whom he would have given it during lifetime as the beneficiary, the value of the property ($200,000) will be included in his estate for estate tax purposes. The $200,000 value becomes the new income tax basis for the beneficiary. If the property is then sold for the $200,000 fair market value, there is no gain and no income tax has to be paid by the beneficiary. Thus income tax is avoided.

As can be seen, it might be better for tax purposes to keep property rather than to give it away. Of course, one must determine in each case whether a tax savings would likely take place. The additional costs associated with probate should not be overlooked. These costs might be sufficient to offset any tax savings.

There are other potential disadvantages to making taxable gifts in excess of the equivalent exemption amount. One disadvantage, of course, is the loss of control. Moreover, the transfer tax is paid earlier than would otherwise be the case if the assets were held until death.

*Joint Ownership of Property.* The various types of joint ownerships, presented earlier, need not be discussed again except to point out that joint ownership can be a means of bypassing the probate estate and, thus, avoiding probate costs. This can be helpful in some situations.

A potential disadvantage of joint ownership should be noted. Under a tenancy by the entirety (right of survivorship between husband and wife), the tax law requires that 50 percent of the fair market value of the property be included in the gross estate of the first joint tenant to die. Although this form of ownership avoids estate tax on one-half of the total property value in the first estate, 100 percent of the fair market value at the time of the death of the surviving spouse would be included in his or her estate. This is true because he or she would receive the first decedent's interest through survivor's rights. (This, of course, assumes that the surviving spouse does not sell or give away the property during his or her lifetime.)

Since only 50 percent of the value of the property was included in the first spouse's estate, the stepped-up basis for income tax purposes would apply only to that part of the total value. The excluded 50 percent would not benefit from the stepped-up basis. If the property might be sold during the surviving spouse's lifetime, this area should be examined carefully. It might be better if the entire property value were includable in the gross estate to obtain a stepped-up basis on the total value of the property.

*Trusts*. A **trust** is a legal arrangement whereby one party transfers property to someone else who holds the legal title and manages the trust property for the benefit of others. The person who establishes the trust is the **grantor** (or settlor). The person who receives the legal title and manages the property is the **trustee**, and the person for whose benefit the property is held is the **beneficiary**. As the word *trust* implies, faith and confidence are placed in the trustee to act solely on the beneficiary's behalf. Legally, the trustee has a fiduciary responsibility to act in accordance with the law and the provisions of the trust instrument.

Trusts are most effective estate planning tools. They often supply elements that are impossible to obtain through a direct gift. Income, estate, and gift tax savings also can be effected through the use of trusts. Trusts can eliminate the need for guardianship of property. One can provide a life income for family members, with the principal of the trust distributed to charity. Assets can be protected from creditors through the use of a trust.

Many types of trusts exist, each designed to meet specific objectives. Trusts can be created during lifetime (an **inter vivos** or **living trust**) or through one's will (a **testamentary trust**). Thus one can transfer property to a living trust or retain ownership until death and then pass the property to a trust by will. A living trust can be revocable or irrevocable. With a **revocable trust**, the grantor can retain the power to terminate the trust at will and regain ownership of the property. With an **irrevocable trust**, he or she permanently relinquishes ownership and control.

A revocable trust might be desirable as a device for transferring assets directly to beneficiaries outside of the probate estate. This avoids probate costs in estate settlement. Because the property is outside of probate, the business of the trust can continue on an uninterrupted, confidential basis, or the trust can be terminated and assets distributed to the beneficiaries confidentially and without administrative delay.

A revocable trust is not without disadvantages. No income, estate, or gift tax savings exist under a revocable trust. The transfer into the trust does not constitute a completed gift; therefore, no gift tax is assessed. Since a complete gift is not made, effective ownership of the property is retained by the grantor for tax purposes. Thus the trust property will be included in the taxable estate, and trust income is taxable to the grantor. Administration and management charges in many cases must be paid under a trust arrangement. These charges offset savings in probate generated from the use of a trust.

Control and ownership are relinquished over property placed in an irrevocable trust. This loss of flexibility could be a high price to pay should conditions change.

When property is placed in an irrevocable trust, generally a complete gift has been made that may have gift tax consequences. Of course, income and estate tax savings applicable to any gift of property or cash may result.

*1. Marital Deduction and Residuary Trusts.* The marital deduction can be an important estate planning device. The marital deduction provisions of the IRC provide for an unlimited deduction for property left to the surviving spouse. It is, therefore, possible to leave everything to the surviving spouse and incur no federal estate tax. To do so, however, might actually result in a higher total estate tax liability when the taxes on the estates of both spouses are taken into consideration.

Suppose that, after deductions for expenses, debts, and losses, Len's estate has a value of $2,000,000. If the entire value were left to his surviving spouse, Becky, and not dissipated or given away under the annual exclusion during her lifetime, an estate tax of $561,000 would be imposed upon Becky's subsequent death (provided death occurs in 1993 or later) and probate cost probably would be at least $60,000 (3 percent of probate estate). This would result in $1,379,000 being left ultimately to the children ($2,000,000 - $561,000 - $60,000).

There are better ways to provide for the surviving spouse. Assuming Len died in 1993 or later, he could have left Becky $1,400,000 under the marital deduction. This amount would not be taxed in Len's estate. The $600,000 balance, which could be left to the children or others, is equal to the exemption equivalent, and the unified credit would equal the amount of tentative tax based on the taxable estate. Thus no estate tax would be payable.

Assuming that Becky owns no other assets and does not dissipate or give away the $1,400,000 received from Len, her estate would pay estate taxes of $301,940, after application of the unified credit (and estimated postmortem costs of $42,000). The other $600,000 escapes all estate taxation on Becky's death.

Trust arrangements typically are used as a vehicle to effect the above plan through what is known as a **two-trust will**. Testamentary trusts are established to permit the surviving spouse to have substantial enjoyment of all of the estate owner's property during his or her lifetime, to bypass the surviving spouse's estate as to the property that will eventually go to others, and to qualify an optimal amount of the assets for the estate tax marital deduction.

First, a **marital trust** is established to receive property that qualifies for the marital deduction when the first spouse dies. When the surviving spouse dies, any amounts not consumed or given to others will be taxed in his or her estate.

Although it is not necessary to establish a trust for the marital deduction property, it may prove convenient to do so for investment management and administration purposes.

Generally, the marital trust must provide that the surviving spouse has the right to consume or give away the principal of the trust. This general power of appointment gives the spouse the right to invade principal whenever desired and permits it to qualify for the marital deduction. The trust must provide for the distribution of income to the spouse at least annually. If the trust remains intact and the surviving spouse does not exercise the power of appointment, either during lifetime or through his or her will, the property of the trust can be distributed to beneficiaries as designated in the will of the first spouse to die.

Generally, a property interest will not qualify for the marital deduction unless it is includable in the surviving spouse's gross estate. Certain terminable interest property passing to a surviving spouse does not qualify for the marital deduction. As discussed in Chapter 13, however, the law allows so-called **qualified terminable interest property** (QTIP) to qualify for the marital deduction. QTIP property must meet these tests:

• It passes to the spouse.

• The surviving spouse is entitled to all the income from the property, payable at least annually.

• No one (including the spouse) has the power to appoint any part of the property to anyone other than the spouse during the spouse's lifetime.

The QTIP election can be of great importance in estate planning. It permits a decedent to provide for his or her spouse during lifetime, yet can direct property to others—for example, the children—without loss of the marital deduction. A trust is commonly used. Thus a **QTIP trust** can offer the same tax advantages as other approaches while retaining assets under terms that have been established upon the first spouse's death.

The spouse may be given the power to invade the trust corpus for reasons of health, education, maintenance, and support. In addition, the spouse may be given the right to take the greater of $5,000 or 5 percent of the trust corpus per year (a so-called **5 by 5 power**).

The QTIP trust is commonly used to ensure that on the death of one spouse, the remarriage of the surviving spouse will not result in the children of the first marriage being left nothing. The executor of the deceased spouse must make an irrevocable election to classify property as QTIP.

Property that is not left to the surviving spouse outright, in the marital (or QTIP) trust, or not used to meet expenses, taxes, and other bequests is placed in a second trust known as the nonmarital or **residuary trust**. The surviving spouse has the right to the income for life from the residuary trust property. The income from the residuary trust would supplement the income provided by the marital trust and the principal could also be available, if needed, in accordance with the 5 by 5 power and the right to invade for health, education, and support reasons. On the death of the surviving spouse, all right to income from the residuary trust is terminated, and the trust property would not be taxed in his or her estate. This gives the surviving spouse the effective use of all the decedent's property during his or her lifetime, without having the residual trust included in that spouse's estate for federal estate tax purposes.

Figure 14-1 compares (1) the simple will approach, in which Len's $2,000,000 net estate is left outright to Becky, and (2) the two-trust arrangement in which the $2,000,000 estate is divided between the marital and residuary trusts.[6] The residuary trust receives property equivalent in value to that necessary to utilize fully the unified credit—that is, $600,000. Since it is a trust, no probate costs are assessed against its value on the beneficiary's death, and since the beneficiary does not own the trust, it is excludable from her estate. These two sources constitute the savings of $277,060 of the trust arrangement over the simple will arrangement. As a result of the use of the marital deduction and the two-trust will, the deceased couple's children and other beneficiaries would receive a significantly larger share of the estate than if it were necessary to pay estate tax.

2. *Trusts for Minor Children.* Many persons make gifts from time to time to their minor children, to accumulate a substantial fund for education or other use when they are old enough to handle the responsibility. A trust can be useful in such situations.

The tax code, however, will not allow an annual exclusion for a gift of a future interest. Unless the beneficiary has the right to the present possession and enjoyment of the property, the annual exclusion will not be allowed. Thus the annual exclusion would not be available for a gift to a minor in trust if the funds were not presently available to that minor.

One way to avoid this problem is to establish the trust for minors known as a **Section 2503(c) trust**. By meeting the requirements for this trust, a gift can be made to minors without the loss of the $10,000 annual gift tax exclusion. To qualify for the annual exclusion, the trust must contain these provisions: (1) the trustee has the discretion to distribute both principal and income; (2) the beneficiaries are entitled to receive the principal of the trust when they reach age 21; and (3) should any of the beneficiaries die before reaching maturity, his or her share of the assets would pass through his or her estate.

By meeting the requirements of the trust, income can be accumulated until the minor reaches age 21 and the $10,000 annual exclusion per beneficiary can be used. This type of trust for minors is a popular device. It is often used by grandparents who wish to establish an educational fund for their grandchildren. There could also be a provision that the trust could be continued beyond age 21,

---

[6] Modified from an illustration in *Advanced Sales Course*, Life Underwriter Training Council.

**FIGURE 14-1**

**SIMPLE WILL VERSUS TWO-TRUST ARRANGEMENT**
*Source:* Modified from an illustration from *Advanced Sales Course*, 8th ed. (Washington, DC: Life
Underwriter Training Council, 1985), Vol. 9, p. 170.

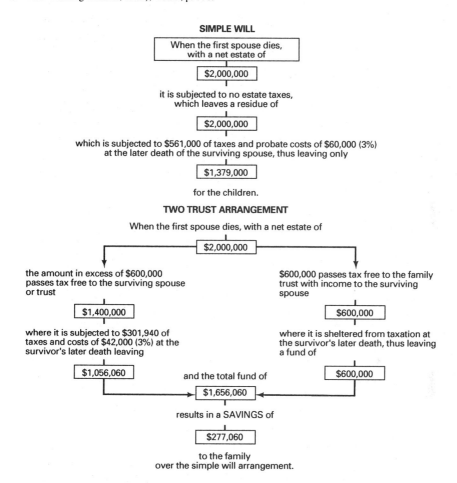

**SIMPLE WILL**

When the first spouse dies,
with a net estate of

$2,000,000

it is subjected to no estate taxes,
which leaves a residue of

$2,000,000

which is subjected to $561,000 of taxes and probate costs of $60,000 (3%)
at the later death of the surviving spouse, thus leaving only

$1,379,000

for the children.

**TWO TRUST ARRANGEMENT**

When the first spouse dies, with a net estate of

$2,000,000

the amount in excess of $600,000
passes tax free to the surviving spouse
or trust

$1,400,000

where it is subjected to $301,940 of
taxes and costs of $42,000 (3%) at the
survivor's later death leaving

$1,056,060

$600,000 passes tax free to the family
trust with income to the surviving
spouse

$600,000

where it is sheltered from taxation at
the survivor's later death, thus leaving
a fund of

$600,000

and the total fund of

$1,656,060

results in a SAVINGS of

$277,060

to the family
over the simple will arrangement.

provided the beneficiaries agree to this continuation. A generation-skipping
transfer tax could be imposed in such situations if the amounts involved were
substantial (see Chapter 13).

Thus with a Section 2503(c) trust, gifts of life insurance policies in trust for
minors should qualify as those of a present interest if (1) any policy value may
be used for their benefit, (2) policy ownership vests at age 21, and (3) the policy
proceeds or value would be includable in the child's gross estate were he or she
to die prior to age 21. Any premiums paid by the grantor should also qualify as
present interest gifts.

Gifts also can be made to minors under the **Uniform Gifts to Minors Act**
or under the more recent **Uniform Transfers to Minors Act**. Under these acts,

an adult is named custodian for the minor and manages the property through a custodian account. The property is distributed to the minor at age 18 or 21, depending on state law.

*3. Crummey Trusts.* A recent trust innovation is called the **Crummey trust**. In spite of its name (which came from the name of the litigant who fought and won the battle with the IRS), the Crummey trust is a useful device. The annual exclusion is available for gifts made to such an irrevocable trust, provided the beneficiaries have a reasonable opportunity to demand distribution of amounts contributed to the trust. If a reasonable time period for the demand expires without this request having been made, the trust instrument usually provides that gift amounts cannot be later taken down by the beneficiaries, yet remain eligible for the annual exclusion.

A Crummey provision ordinarily works as follows. The grantor makes a gift to an irrevocable, living trust. The trust beneficiaries often are the grantor's children, grandchildren, or both.[7] The beneficiaries are notified by the trustee that they have the power for a defined period (typically 30 or 60 days) after receiving notification to withdraw some portion of the transferred property. The simultaneous acts of the grantor transferring property to the trust and the beneficiaries being permitted to withdraw the same property from the trust is tantamount to the grantor giving the property to the beneficiaries outright, thus qualifying for the $10,000 annual exclusion.

Of course, it is not anticipated that the beneficiaries will, in fact, withdraw any property from the trust during the defined period. Each beneficiary is given a short-term general power of appointment. By not executing their powers, the beneficiaries permit their powers to lapse. The lapse of a general power is a gift taxable transfer, unless the property is subject to a 5 by 5 power. As a consequence, limiting each beneficiary's Crummey power to $5,000 guarantees that the lapse will not be treated as a taxable gift from each beneficiary to all other beneficiaries.

An irrevocable life insurance trust with a Crummey provision can be an effective estate planning tool. A gift to such a trust qualifies as a present interest gift and, therefore, for the $10,000 ($20,000 if it is a split gift) annual exclusion. The trustee can use such gifts to pay the premiums on a life insurance policy on the life of the donor, and the policy death proceeds should not be includable in the donor's gross estate on his or her death.

*4. Irrevocable Life Insurance Trusts.* As noted earlier, the value of a life insurance policy for gift tax purposes is the interpolated terminal reserve plus any unearned premium rather than the policy face amount. This makes the gift of a life insurance policy a popular tax-saving device. Many persons use a trust. Under an **irrevocable life insurance trust**, an insurance policy on the grantor's life is owned by an irrevocable trust, with the policy proceeds payable to the trust

---

[7] If the grandchildren are beneficiaries, a generation-skipping transfer tax may be incurred if substantial amounts are involved.

as beneficiary. Generally, should the grantor live more than three years from the date the trust is established, and if all incidents of ownership in the policy are relinquished, the proceeds will not be a part of the grantor's taxable estate. If the policy is applied for and owned by the trustee from its inception, the policy death proceeds should be excluded from the gross estate even if death occurs within the first three years, provided the purchase of the insurance was at the discretion of the trustee.

The trustee pays policy premiums from either the trust corpus or from annual gifts to the trust from the grantor. The latter is the more common case, although the gifts should not be designated as premium payments. The trustee will have been given the authority (at his or her discretion) to purchase insurance and, if desired, to use trust funds—including those gifted annually by the grantor—to pay premiums.

The funds gifted to the trust by the grantor/insured should qualify as gifts of a present interest if the trust contains a Crummey provision. To avoid the donor incurring gift taxation, the gifts should not exceed $10,000 ($20,000 if it is a split gift) per trust beneficiary. To avoid the beneficiaries incurring gift taxation from allowing their short-term general power of appointment to lapse, the donor's annual gifts should not exceed the product of the number of trust beneficiaries times $5,000 (or 5 percent of trust corpus, if this is the greater amount).[8]

Death proceeds can be invested or distributed to trust beneficiaries through arrangements that are not available under life insurance policy settlement options. Therefore, it generally is more desirable to have policy proceeds paid in a single sum to the trust rather than have the insurance company pay the proceeds on an installment basis with interest. Of course, there is no guarantee that the trustee will make wise investments, and there are no guarantees with the trust as there are under an insurance contract.

The need for an insurance trust rather than the outright gift of life insurance should be carefully considered. The $10,000 annual exclusion can be made available for the outright gift of a life insurance policy, as well as for the premiums paid on a policy by the donor. When a policy is assigned to such a trust or when premiums are paid on policies held in such a trust, the $10,000 annual exclusion may not be available unless a Crummey provision is included in the trust instrument. Therefore the gift of a policy in trust and the future premium payments can be fully taxable gifts that are later added back to the estate for estate tax purposes. Also, there are no income tax savings for an insurance trust if the policy insures either the donor or his or her spouse. If the trust were sufficiently funded so that the income to the trust were adequate to pay the premiums, the trust income would still be taxed to the grantor.

---

[8] Additional considerations can apply, including the use of a so-called **hanging-power** to avoid any constraint imposed by the 5 by 5 power. With a hanging power, amounts in excess of the 5 by 5 power limit are accumulated to the point in time when no additions are made to the trust. These amounts are then utilized under the continuing annual 5 by 5 safe harbor rule until they are exhausted. See Edward H. Stone, "Crummey Rules Have Changed," *Journal of the American Society of CLU & ChFC* (Sept. 1989).

## LIFE INSURANCE FOR ESTATE LIQUIDITY[9]

Life insurance is often the best way to provide the liquidity needed for estate clearance. Even so, several questions remain to be answered. In particular, what products should be purchased? Who should own the policy? How should the beneficiary designation be structured? How can the insurance be structured to have the funds available to the person who must pay estate costs?

Since the marital deduction coupled with the unified credit may eliminate or greatly reduce estate taxes at the death of the first spouse, the focus for liquidity to meet estate taxes often centers on the second spouse's death. Assuming that life insurance is the best means to provide this liquidity, several ways are available for providing the cash economically. One way would be to use individual policies that insure both lives in a sufficient amount to meet the projected need. A second approach would be to use a joint life policy that provides for payment of the face amount at the first death. A third approach would be to use a second-to-die policy that pays the face amount when the second insured dies, rather than the first.

Finally, only one spouse might be insured. If the insured is the first to die, the proceeds can be retained for ultimate liquidity needs. This may be the only solution if one spouse is uninsurable, and it may be reasonable even if both are insurable if the surviving spouse could invest the proceeds to supplement income.

Formerly, cross ownership of life insurance between spouses was not uncommon. The obvious reason was to avoid the inclusion of insurance proceeds in the estate of the insured. Now, with the unlimited marital deduction, less need exists for insurance to be owned by the spouse of the decedent insured.

In large estates and with large amounts of insurance, it may be appropriate to have the insurance owned by a party other than the insured or spouse. A trust is one alternative. A child may be another. Use of an irrevocable trust as owner may be especially wise if the insurance is not to be used at the first death, but instead retained for meeting estate liquidity needs on the second death. As noted earlier, gifts to the trust (which can be used by the trust to pay life insurance premiums) can qualify for the $10,000 annual gift tax exclusion if the trust contains a Crummey provision.

Special care should be taken in designating ownership of joint policies. If the surviving spouse/insured is owner of a second-to-die policy, the proceeds will be included in the estate of the second to die. With a first death policy, the survivor may be able to gift the proceeds before being subjected to tax, although if the survivor is elderly, this possibility may be remote.

It cannot be assumed that if insurance is payable to the surviving spouse or to the children of the estate owner, it will somehow help the executor pay estate clearance costs. Common alternatives include:

---

[9] This section draws on *Advanced Sales Course*, Life Underwriter Training Council.

1. Having the insurance payable to the estate.

2. Relying on the beneficiary to lend money to the estate.

3. Relying on the beneficiary to buy assets from the estate.

The first alternative has several disadvantages:

- Proceeds will be includable in the estate and subject to tax, although the marital deduction could negate this tax. (Note, however, that the marital deduction is not available for assets used to pay estate taxes.)

- In most states, administration costs will be increased, since they are a percentage of probate assets.

- Proceeds become subject to the claims of estate creditors.

- State death tax exemption for insurance proceeds may be lost.

The likelihood of the second or third alternative functioning as planned depends on who is named beneficiary. There is the greatest likelihood of the estate owner's plans being carried out when the insurance is payable to a trust, with the trustee authorized to either lend money to the estate or purchase assets from the estate. To be effective, trust provisions cannot require the trustee to loan money or purchase assets from the estate without jeopardizing the estate tax advantages of using a trust. As mentioned above, they merely give the trustee the power to do so at the trustee's discretion. In most instances, a trustee could be expected to loan money or purchase assets should the need arise and the trust instrument has authorized (but not required) such action.

It is common to have insurance purchased for estate liquidity owned by and payable to an irrevocable, inter vivos trust, with trust income payable to the spouse for life and corpus payable to the children at the spouse's death. This follows the two-trust arrangement discussed earlier. In fact, the will of the insured estate owner often pours the nonmarital share of the estate into the irrevocable insurance trust.

## LIFE INSURANCE AND THE GENERATION-SKIPPING TRANSFER TAX[10]

Life insurance can become involved in a generation-skipping transfer (GST) and, thereby, provoke a GST tax. As discussed in Chapter 13, a GST tax may be levied when property is transferred to a person who is two or more generations younger than the transferor. The transferee is referred to as the **skip person**. In general, a GST can evolve from (1) the payment of premiums, (2) the transfer of policies, and (3) the payment of death proceeds.

---

[10] This section draws on "Generation-Skipping Transfer Tax," *Advanced Sales Reference Service* (Cincinnati, Ohio: The National Underwriter Company, 1992).

*Transfers of Funds to Pay Premiums*. Generally, funds transferred to a skip person to pay premiums on a life insurance policy or an annuity are considered a GST. Additionally, transfer to a trust wherein a skip person is beneficiary may result in a GST when the property is transferred to the trust, such as amounts to pay premiums on a policy owned by an irrevocable life insurance trust. The $10,000 annual gift tax exclusion ($20,000 if it is a split gift) and the $1,000,000 lifetime GST exemption ($2,000,000 if a spouse joins in the transfer) may be available to reduce or eliminate any GST tax.

Thus present interest gifts of funds of $10,000 or less to cover premiums on life insurance—in trust or otherwise—would not ordinarily invoke any GST tax. Nontaxable gifts are not subject to the GST tax.

*Transfer of Policies*. A GST generally occurs when a life insurance or annuity contract is transferred to a skip person. Additionally, such an insurance contract transferred to a trust with a skip person as beneficiary may result in a GST. Again, the $10,000 annual exclusion and $1,000,000 lifetime exemption would be available.

*Policy Death Proceeds*. Regardless of the manner of payment of life insurance or annuity proceeds, a GST will have been made if policy benefits are transferred from an insured or annuitant to a skip person. Thus if a surviving grandparent is the insured and owner of a $3,000,000 life insurance policy and a grandchild is beneficiary, a GST will have occurred on the lone grandparent's death, and $1,000,000 of GST tax would be due on the transfer.[11]

*Leveraging the $1.0 Million Exemption*. As already noted, a transferor is allowed a $1.0 million lifetime exemption ($2.0 million if the spouse joins in the transfer). Thus an insured/transferor may transfer a policy or funds to pay premiums on a policy to a skip person and, through use of the lifetime exemption, possibly avoid any GST tax. Death proceeds received also would be GST tax-free. Thus leveraging of the $1.0 million GST lifetime exemption can be accomplished by allocating the exemption against the premium dollars (or against the value of the policy on policy transfer) versus the higher ultimate value of the death proceeds. Leveraging of the $1.0 million exemption can also be accomplished for premiums on policies in an irrevocable life insurance trust or for policy transfer to such a trust. Allocation of the $1.0 million exemption is, however, postponed.

For example, assume that Richard creates an irrevocable life insurance trust for the benefit of his children and grandchildren. Each year he transfers $50,000 to the trust, to be used (at the trustee's discretion) to make premium payments on a $2.0 million policy on his life. Each year he allocates $50,000 of his $1.0 million GST exemption to each transfer.

---

[11] Value of the property interest ($3,000,000) less lifetime exemption ($1,000,000) times maximum federal estate tax rate (50 percent).

Assuming Richard makes no other allocations of his $1.0 million exemption, the trust will not be subject to any GST tax during its first 20 years. At the end of 20 years, Richard will have used up his $1.0 million GST exemption, and additional amounts contributed to the trust will be subject to the GST tax.

If Richard died during the 20-year period, no GST tax would be due on the $2.0 million death proceeds. If he died after the first 20 years, a pro rata share of the death proceeds might be subject to the GST tax. Of course, to ensure that no GST tax would ever be payable, one ideally would use a policy that became paid up before the transfers to the trust exceeded the $1.0 million GST exemption.

## RETIREMENT PLANNING

A plan for the accumulation, conservation, and distribution of an estate should not evolve without equal consideration being given to retirement income objectives and the means by which assets are accumulated to meet these objectives. As noted by Gentaro Kawase, chairman of the Nippon Life Insurance Company, insurance needs increasingly are shifting from an emphasis on "for death" and "for others" to "for life" and "for myself."[12] This change in planning emphasis can be expected to continue as the over-65 segment of the U.S. population continues to grow, as illustrated in Figure 14-2. This section examines the environment in which one of the most important "for life" planning objectives (retirement) is conducted and presents the steps of the retirement planning process, with particular reference to private savings.

The U.S. retirement income system often is described as being like a three-legged stool. One leg is the Social Security system. Another is employer-sponsored retirement plans, and the third leg is the individual's private initiative. An individual's initiative may take the form of personal savings or postretirement employment. Obviously, reliance on employment is a dubious choice, since we cannot know whether one's health will permit it or whether the opportunity will present itself.

### THE ENVIRONMENT FOR RETIREMENT PLANNING

Retirement planning, as a subset of financial planning, can be rationally conducted only with an understanding of relevant environmental factors. An overview of some of these factors is presented below.

*Longevity*. Individuals live longer today than at any time in the past. In the 1880s, when life expectancy was 45 years, the German chancellor Otto von

[12] Gentaro Kawase, "The New Century Survival Strategies for the Japanese Life Insurance Industry," *International Insurance Society Proceedings* (1990), pp. 119–129.

**FIGURE 14-2**

**THE 65+ AGE GROUP, 1970–2030 (PERCENTAGE OF TOTAL U.S. POPULATION)**
*Source:* Organization for Economic Cooperation and Development

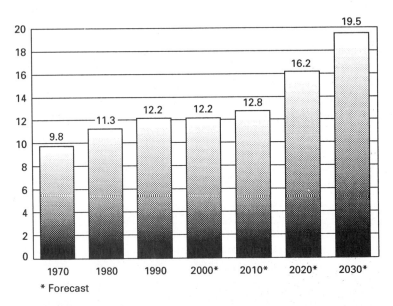

\* Forecast

Bismarck established age 65 as a national retirement age. It is perhaps surprising that over a century later, age 65 remains synonymous with retirement.

In the much less distant past, the average person retired at age 65 and died at age 72. Provision needed to be made for only seven years' retirement income on average. Today U.S. women who attain age 65 can expect to live roughly another 19 years, and men can expect to live to age 80. Because of this fact, substantially increased amounts of funds are needed to provide retirement income.

Moreover, despite longer life spans, better health, and changes in laws to encourage employment, individuals have actually been retiring earlier than they did formerly. This fact can lead to erroneous conclusions for today's workers who are years away from retirement. Their parents, with memories of the 1930s economic depression, often were determined savers, in contrast to many of today's baby boomers. Additionally, their timing was fortuitous: they worked during economically robust years when employers were generous with benefits. Investments in homes yielded returns substantially in excess of inflation and overall investments performed well. Social Security benefits were and remain relatively more generous for them than for following generations. Prospects that such favorable circumstances will be repeated in the next few decades seem remote, with the result that today's workers probably would be well advised not to count on an early retirement under such favorable conditions.

***Inflation.*** Inflation remains the archenemy of retirement planning. Although a 4 percent inflation rate may seem reasonable, the result is a doubling of prices in 18 years. Figure 14-3 illustrates the long-term debilitating effects of inflation on retirement income.

Table 14-1 is the counterpart of Figure 14-3: it shows the nominal amounts needed in the future to maintain $10,000 in real income in the face of various inflation rates. Thus if inflation were to average 6 percent, the retiree would need $32,071 in income in year 20 to have the same purchasing power as $10,000 today.

Thus if one wishes to establish a retirement income whose purchasing power does not diminish with inflation, provision must be made for a constantly rising nominal retirement income, unless one believes inflation will cease. This fact complicates the retirement planning process in the same way that it complicates the life insurance planning process, as discussed in Chapter 12.

***Retiree Health.*** Most retirees enjoy relatively good health, and prospects are bright that tomorrow's retirees will be even healthier still. Fully one-half of persons who are 75 to 84 years old are free of health problems that require special care or that curb activities. Even among those aged 85 and over, one-third report no limitations on their overall health.

Even so, the aging process takes its toll, and, in general, the older a person becomes, the greater will be his or her likely need for health care services. Often, the most financially debilitating health-related retiree expense relates to long-term-care costs.

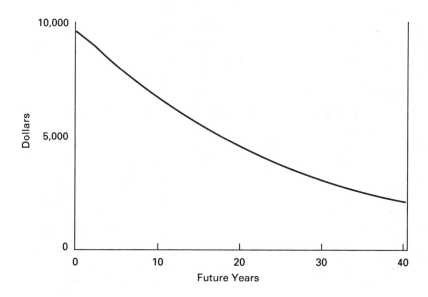

**FIGURE 14-3**

**INFLATION'S EFFECT ON RETIREMENT INCOME: PURCHASING POWER IN THE FUTURE OF $10,000 TODAY (ASSUMING 4 PERCENT INFLATION)**

TABLE 14-1     AMOUNTS NECESSARY TO MAINTAIN $10,000 PURCHASING POWER
               AT VARIOUS DURATIONS AND INFLATION RATES

| | Inflation Rates (%) | | | | |
| --- | --- | --- | --- | --- | --- |
| Years | 0 | 2.0 | 4.0 | 6.0 | 8.0 |
| 5 | $10,000 | $11,041 | $12,166 | $13,382 | $14,693 |
| 10 | 10,000 | 12,190 | 14,802 | 17,908 | 21,589 |
| 20 | 10,000 | 14,859 | 21,911 | 32,071 | 46,610 |
| 30 | 10,000 | 18,114 | 32,434 | 57,435 | 100,627 |
| 40 | 10,000 | 22,080 | 48,010 | 102,857 | 217,245 |

An estimated one in four U.S. citizens over age 65 will spend some time in a nursing home, at an annual cost of from $25,000 to $70,000. The Brookings Institution estimates that by the year 2020, costs could be $158,000 per year. Such unanticipated costs can quickly wreck an otherwise soundly conceived retirement plan.

Contrary to the views of most persons, the federally sponsored health plan for the aged—Medicare—covers only a minor portion of nursing home bills. On the other hand, Medicaid—the predominantly state-sponsored program for the indigent—pays a significant portion of nursing home costs, but only if the individual can qualify—that is, only if the person is poor.

As a result, some financial advisors urge retirees to give away their assets just prior to entering a nursing home. Timing can be problematic, however, and losing control of one's finances and becoming dependent on welfare are not attractive prospects for many retirees.

One alternative is to purchase long-term-care insurance, as discussed in Chapter 16. Another is to continue life insurance coverage into the retirement years that provides for an accelerated death benefit, as discussed in Chapter 7.

*Social Security*. As discussed in Chapter 25, Social Security benefits are heavily skewed in favor of lower-income workers. Those with moderate to high incomes, therefore, cannot depend on Social Security retirement benefits to provide a significant share of their retirement income.

This fact is illustrated in Figure 14-4. It shows the results of a Georgia State University study of retiree wage replacement ratios in the United States. Conventional wisdom has it that retirees need a retirement income of about 70 percent of their preretirement wages to maintain a standard of living in retirement that is equivalent to the one enjoyed before retirement. Obviously, individual circumstances could greatly influence this figure, but it is a useful point of departure.

As Figure 14-4 illustrates, all income groups, except those earning $80,000 and above, achieved at least the 70 percent figure. Note, however, that for the lower-income groups, the preponderance of retirement income is derived from Social Security retirement benefits. With increasing income, the relative importance of Social Security diminishes.

**FIGURE 14-4**

**INCOME REPLACEMENT RATIOS (BASED ON WORKER AGE 65 AND SPOUSE AGE 62)**
*Source:* Bruce A. Palmer, RETIRE Project, Center for Risk Management and Insurance, Georgia State
University (1991).

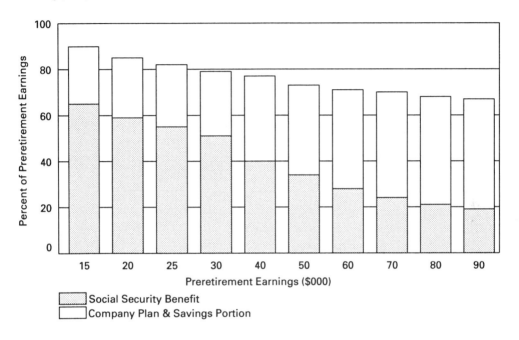

Social Security Benefit
Company Plan & Savings Portion

Thus if similar results can be projected for future retirees, middle- to upper-income persons can count on Social Security providing from about 50 to 25 percent and less of their retirement income. The balance must come from personal savings and employer-sponsored retirement plans.

Whether similar results can be realistically projected into the future is questionable. Already the U.S. Congress has begun taxing Social Security benefits for higher-earning retirees (see Chapter 25), in effect applying a modified means test. For couples earning more than $32,000 and single persons earning more than $25,000, one-half of these benefits is includable in taxable income. Moreover, in the year 2000, the lowest age at which the full retirement benefit can be collected will begin gradually increasing from the current age 65.

Further cost-reduction measures may be reasonably expected. Currently, the ratio of tax-paying workers to retirees is about 3.3 to 1. By the year 2029 (the year that the last of the baby boomers reaches age 65), the ratio will have dropped to less than 2 to 1. Although much of the current and future Social Security taxes is intended to be reserved to cover the projected shortfall of the then benefit payments over the then Social Security tax revenues, it is less than obvious that the system will function as hoped. For one thing, these current surpluses are being used to cover current U.S. federal budget deficits. The Social

Security Trust Fund is lending the surpluses for other federal uses; the Trust Fund, in effect, holds IOUs from other parts of the government.

If these surpluses continue to be "borrowed" for other uses, the question arises as to who will repay the loans at the time the baby boomers begin retiring in large numbers. The only groups with funds to meet these obligations are workers and retirees. Some estimate that, by 2040, workers could find Social Security taxes taking as much as 40 percent of their pay if benefits remain roughly at today's levels. Any result even close to such a figure could be expected to create substantial intergenerational conflict. The alternative is to provide retirees with relatively lower retirement benefits. Realistically, the most feasible scenario would seem to be some combination of higher worker taxes and lower retiree benefits. The net effect of all of the above would suggest that today's workers may be wise to place less reliance on the Social Security system providing as generous retirement benefits as those provided to past or current retirees.

Irrespective of the degree of faith one has in the level of the Social Security retirement benefits, it is wise periodically to request updated information on the likely benefit level that would be available on retirement. The Social Security office can provide the form for requesting this information.

***Employer-Provided Benefits***. About one-half of all employees are covered by an employer-sponsored retirement plan. The larger the employer, the greater the likelihood that a retirement plan is available. Employees without this coverage must rely exclusively on Social Security benefits, on their personal assets, and possibly on postretirement employment for retirement income.

Most employed individuals might be surprised to discover the relatively low levels of likely future employer-sponsored retirement benefits. Figure 14-5 shows the breakdown of income for those aged 65 and over by broad category. Note that, for the average person, only 15 percent of total income was provided by an occupational pension.

The current generation of workers changes jobs more frequently than did its parents—an average of five times during the working lifetime. The Congressional Research Service estimated that the effect of five job changes would leave a person with one-half the pension amount of the individual who did not change jobs.

Additionally, many employers are discontinuing their retirement plans altogether or shifting away from defined benefit plans to defined contribution plans. **Defined benefit plans** guarantee a monthly retirement benefit based on some combination of salary and length of service (see Chapter 28). The employer is responsible for ensuring that adequate funds exist to provide the promised benefit.

With **defined contribution plans**, which include profit-sharing and 401(k) plans, the employer contributes a certain amount annually to each participant's account. With 401(k) plans (see Chapter 28), the employer typically matches

**FIGURE 14-5**

**PERCENT OF AGGREGATE INCOME OF U.S. POPULATION AGE 65 AND OVER BY MAJOR INCOME SOURCE**
*Source:* Susan Grad, "Income of the Population 55 and Over, 1986," SSA Publication No. 13–11871 (June 1988), Table 47.

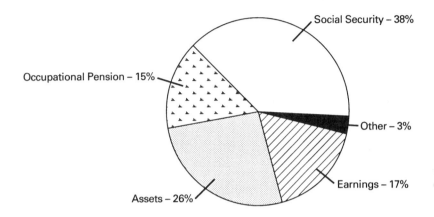

some portion or all of the amounts contributed by employees. The failure of many employees to participate plus a reasonable matching percentage mean that the typical 401(k) plan costs the employer perhaps only 1 to 2 percent of payroll. With profit-sharing plans, the employer need not make any contribution in unprofitable years. By contrast, employer contributions to defined benefit plans average some 7 percent of payroll. In effect, therefore, the trend in employer-sponsored plans is to shift the risk from the employer to the employee.

Even so, defined contribution plans offer advantages. The employee usually has some voice in his or her account investments and, with wise decisions, can accumulate substantial sums. Additionally, these plans are more portable than defined benefit plans, thus resulting in less or no loss with job changes.

In summary, therefore, the typical employee probably is well advised not to be overly optimistic about the proportion of retirement income that might be provided through occupational plans. Employer-sponsored plans are founded on what the employer perceives it can afford to provide, not on what the employee may need in the future.

The preceding discussion of the environment in which contemporary retirement planning takes place should serve to emphasize the growing importance and role of private initiative in the provision of retirement income. The earlier a retirement savings plan is established, the less painful it is financially. The "magic of compounding" truly is an important ally of the saver, as the figures in Table 14-2 figure confirm.

TABLE 14-2    THE BENEFIT OF STARTING
A SAVINGS PLAN EARLY IN LIFE:
ANNUAL AMOUNTS REQUIRED
FOR $100,000 AT AGE 65
(ASSUMES 7 PERCENT INVESTMENT YIELD)

| If Saving Starts At Age | Needed Annual Savings Is: |
|---|---|
| 25 | $468 |
| 35 | 989 |
| 45 | 2,280 |
| 55 | 6,764 |

## THE RETIREMENT PLANNING PROCESS

The retirement planning process is conceptually identical to and a subset of the personal financial planning process. The discussion of the process that follows is structured around the process steps.

*Gather Information*. Both death-related and retirement-related information typically would be gathered at the same time. The needed information includes existing liquid assets that could be used to provide retirement income and information concerning employer-sponsored retirement plans and other such sources of retirement income.

Information regarding probable retirement benefits provided under the Social Security program also should be obtained, as should eligibility for other government benefits. Estimates are necessary in most cases. If the time to retirement is long, estimates will, at best, be gross approximations only.

*Establish Objectives*. Retirement income objectives usually are couched in general terms, such as being able to maintain one's current standard of living during retirement. As mentioned earlier, many experts suggest a retirement income objective of 70 percent of preretirement wages. For low-wage earners, this figure may provide an unacceptably low standard of living; for high-wage earners, it may be too ambitious a goal. Irrespective of the ultimate target wage replacement ratio, consideration should be given to the fact that work-related expenses will cease and that Social Security, federal income, and state and local taxes will cease or greatly diminish on retirement. Additionally, the proportion of income devoted to preretirement savings will cease as the individual enters the "dissavings" period of life.

The complexities in quantifying the future desired amount are discussed below. Quantifying this general objective is desirable but not easy.

*Analyze Information*. With objectives established, the relevant information gathered earlier must be analyzed to measure the financial consequences of retirement. The present value of future income needs should be netted against the present value of future estimated resources. The result is a measure of the net present value of the shortage of resources to meet the desired income objective.

Interest rates used should be reasonable in light of historical and current trends, as should projected inflation rates. Utilizing the assumed inflation rate, one would determine the (inflated) level of income desired at retirement age, based on a projection of the current-day equivalent. Next, the expected annual income resources would be netted against the desired annual income needs. Three classes of common resources are: (1) employer-sponsored income, (2) government-provided income, and (3) income from individual resources.

The uncertainties associated with the Social Security system were presented earlier. The system's future benefits may be relatively less generous than those provided today or in the past. An estimate of future benefits can be obtained from the Social Security office, and those figures may then be either factored into the analysis as given or reduced by some amount and then factored into the analysis.

The same Social Security estimation quandary exists for retirement planning and pre-death planning, although it is more complex here. No resolution will be perfect. The additional complexity comes about because the Social Security *survivor* benefit is, for the present, a known, calculable product, and near-term projections probably are reasonable. For persons who are not near retirement, however, projecting Social Security *retirement* benefit levels several decades from the present is speculative. As a result, these calculations should be viewed as providing gross estimates only. In any event, Social Security retirement benefits should be netted against the retirement income need to derive annual deficit figures.

Employer-sponsored retirement benefits can be equally, if not more, troublesome to estimate. Individuals change employers. Even if one remained with the same employer until retirement, there is no guarantee that the benefit plan would remain the same. Plans are changed. Even if neither the employer nor the plan was changed, obtaining reliable estimates for future benefits can be difficult. As discussed in Chapter 28, retirement benefits provided under an employer-sponsored pension, profit-sharing, or other such plan are a function of the plan benefit formula and future employer funding levels.

Even so, an attempt should be made to establish a conservative estimate for retirement income from employer-sponsored sources. One approach is to determine from the employer the employee's projected benefit level, to determine what is believed to be the expected wage replacement ratio at retirement. The wage replacement ratio is the fraction found by dividing (1) the postretirement, employer-sponsored retirement income by (2) the preretirement annual wage.

Thus, if the employer-sponsored retirement income is expected to be 40 percent of the preretirement wage level, and if the retirement income need is 70 percent of the preretirement wage level, one need examine only a 30 percent net retirement income level from nonemployer sources. Projected personal savings and investments also should be netted against the retirement income need.

Using either the capital retention or one of the two capital liquidation approaches, one then derives an inflation- and interest-adjusted figure for the present value of the future income stream as of the planned retirement age.[13]

For example, assume that George, aged 45, earns $75,000 today and anticipates that his future raises will average at least 6 percent per year. He anticipates retiring at age 65 on an amount equal to 70 percent of his then preretirement income.

His anticipated income just before retirement is found by accumulating his current $75,000 salary at 6 percent for 20 years, to yield about $240,000.[14] In other words, George expects to be earning $240,000 per year just prior to retirement. (This amount seems large, but if inflation were to average 4 percent over the 20-year period, the actual purchasing power of the $240,000 in today's dollars would be about $110,000.[15])

Assume that George's Social Security benefit is estimated to provide an inflation-adjusted retirement income equal to 20 percent of his preretirement salary. Assume further that George estimates that his employer-sponsored plan will provide a retirement income equal to an additional 30 percent of his preretirement salary. Thus George—a fortunate fellow—believes that the combination of Social Security and his employer's retirement plan will meet 50 percent of his 70 percent retirement goal. He need only provide for the additional 20 percent, or $48,000, from his personal resources.[16]

If George wishes to maintain purchasing power throughout his retirement years, the $48,000 figure should increase yearly by the inflation rate.[17] Thus with a 4 percent inflation assumption, George will need $49,920 the following year, $51,917 the year after that, and so on, to maintain a real income of $48,000.

If George wanted to purchase an annuity to provide this amount, the probable cost at age 65 would be $700 to $1,100 for each $100 of annual income desired. Using the higher figure to implicitly account for inflation, George should aim to have accumulated about $528,000 by age 65.[18]

To accumulate this sum through level contributions to an annuity or other savings vehicle would require annual payments of about $12,000 if the savings

---

[13] See Chap. 12.

[14] $75,000 x $(1.06)^{20}$ = $75,000 x 3.2071 = $240,532.

[15] $$\$75,000 \times \left[\frac{1.06}{1.04}\right]^{20} = \$75,000 \times (1.01923)^{20} = \$109,775$$

[16] $240,000 x 0.20 = $48,000. Technically, if the $240,000 figure were his income at age 64, his first-year retirement income should be increased by one year's inflation rate, to maintain its purchasing power. Given the uncertainty inherent in the calculation, this degree of precision is ignored here.

[17] This analysis assumes that the Social Security retirement benefit and the employer-provided benefit will each also increase with the inflation rate. This assumption probably is reasonable for Social Security, but perhaps not as reasonable for the employer plan. If George wished to allow for a constant employer benefit in the calculation, needed future income should be increased by an additional amount equal to the employer-provided benefit ($240,000 x 0.40) times the compounded inflation rate.

[18] $48,000 x $1,100/$100 = $528,000

medium earns 7 percent.[19] If George would like his annual retirement savings to grow along with his expected 6 percent salary increases, he could begin saving about $5,500 and increase it by 6 percent per year.[20] This steadily increasing contribution would also grow to the needed $528,000 amount if all assumptions proved to be realized.

*Develop Plan*. Next, the alternative means of accumulating the needed sum should be explored. For example, one could establish a tax-qualified individual retirement account or annuity (IRA) and begin making level, increasing or some other pattern of annual contributions. Other means for accumulating the amount might include:

- Purchasing a non-tax-qualified flexible-premium deferred annuity.

- Establishing a non-tax-qualified savings or investment program.

- Establishing a non-qualified deferred compensation plan with the employer, if feasible.[21]

- Having the employer establish a 401(k) arrangement, if feasible.[22]

- Having the employer establish a tax-sheltered annuity plan, if feasible.[23]

- Utilizing cash values of needed life insurance protection.

- Finding a rich, generous friend or relative.

- Combinations of the above.

One or several of these arrangements usually proves feasible. Ideally, contributions would be income-tax-deductible, earnings would accumulate on a tax-deferred basis, and withdrawal incomes would be tax-free. The advantages and disadvantages of annuities and life insurance cash values in this regard were noted earlier.

One aspect of plan development that often emerges just prior to retirement revolves around decisions as to whether employer-sponsored (and other retirement) income amounts should be paid as a life annuity, and if so, whether the single-life or joint-and-last-survivor-life annuity seems more attractive. (The

---

[19]
$$\$528,000 \div \left[ \sum_{t=1}^{20}(1.07)^t \right] = \$528,000 \div 43.865 = \$12,037$$

[20] The first-year savings amount would be

$$\$528,000 \div \left[ \sum_{t=1}^{20}(1.07)^t (1.06)^t \right] = \$528,000 \div \sum_{t=1}^{20}(1.1342)^t$$
$$= \$528,000 \div 96.44 = \$5,475$$

[21] See Chap. 9.
[22] See Chap. 28.
[23] See Chap. 28.

potential advantages of annuities were noted in Chapter 7.) If a joint-life annuity payout seems desirable, the prospective retiree may find that a larger effective payout can be achieved by using a combination of the single-life option and life insurance on the annuitant's life. The decision as to which approach is superior would turn on whether the additional income realized from electing the single-life annuity over the joint-life annuity was sufficient to pay the premiums on a life insurance policy whose face amount would provide an income to the other person (e.g., a spouse) that is at least equal to that which would have been provided under the joint-and-last-survivor annuity.

*Implement Plan*. After the plan alternatives have been considered and a plan developed and agreed upon, the plan should be implemented. This may entail applying for an annuity, following through with the paperwork to establish an IRA or other tax-qualified plan, or making other commitments.

The key to sound plan implementation is less the paperwork mechanics and more a firm commitment by the individual to make the necessary contributions regularly. More individually crafted retirement plans fail from lack of commitment than for any other reason.

*Monitor and Revise Plan*. As with pre-death planning, actual results under one's retirement plan are highly unlikely to track precisely those assumed for the future. This necessitates periodic fine-tuning and, occasionally, a complete overhaul. Again, important life events and environmental changes can materially affect results.

# Chapter 15

# BUSINESS USES
## OF LIFE INSURANCE

Life insurance is most often purchased for family or other personal reasons. The preceding chapters emphasized this fact. However, life insurance can serve important business purposes as well. This chapter discusses these uses.

The business uses of life insurance are numerous. Most of these uses can be classified into one or more of the following categories:

- Key-employee indemnification

- Credit protection

- Business continuation arrangements

- Special employee compensation plans

### KEY-EMPLOYEE INDEMNIFICATION

The purpose of key-employee indemnification is to insure a business firm for the loss of earnings brought about by the death or disability of a key officer or other employee. Many business firms have been built around a single individual whose capital, energy, technical knowledge, experience, or power to plan and execute make him or her a most valuable asset of the organization and a necessity to its successful operation. Numerous examples illustrate the dependence of a successful business upon the personal equation. Thus a corporation may be vitally interested in one of its officers whose financial worth as an endorser, or ability as an executive, may be the basis of its general credit rating. A manufacturing or mining enterprise may be dependent upon someone who alone possesses the chemical or engineering knowledge necessary to the concern. A publishing house may have engaged someone who alone can be the author of a proposed work, and who may be obliged to incur considerable outlay before it is written. The sales manager of a large business establishment may have made herself indispensable through her ability to organize an efficient body of salespeople, to employ the most effective methods of selling, and to develop profitable markets.

These are only a few of the many examples that might be given to illustrate the importance of a human life (as an asset) to the successful operation of a business. This importance was recognized in a well-known 1951 tax court case. The court stated:

> What business purpose could be considered more essential than key man [or woman] insurance? The business that insures its buildings and machinery and automobiles from every possible hazard can hardly be expected to exercise less care in protecting itself against the loss of two of its most vital assets— managerial skill and experience.[1]

Economic losses due to death or disability may be guarded against by making the business itself the owner and beneficiary of appropriate policies on the lives of key officers or other employees. In the event of death or disability, the business will be indemnified promptly for the loss of the services of the deceased or disabled employee, and the proceeds received will aid in bridging the period necessary to secure the services of a worthy successor or substitute.

In any specific case, it is difficult to determine accurately the economic loss that would be suffered by the business concern in the event of the key person's death or disability. The problem of estimating the loss may be approached by estimating the present value of lost earnings or it may be measured by the additional compensation necessary to secure an experienced replacement. For example, assume that Younghee and her husband Doocheol are co-owners of a Korean restaurant that has achieved regional fame since it opened ten years ago, garnering many favorable reviews for the quality of its food and service. Both Younghee's talents as the restaurant's master chef and Doocheol's meticulous attention to the details of service are indispensable elements.

Assume further that the restaurant's annual gross revenue has grown to be $2,000,000, from which the family nets $200,000 before taxes. The book value of the restaurant is $300,000. Because of Younghee's widely established reputation, if she were to die or become disabled to the degree that she could no longer perform her duties as chef, the business would suffer a substantial decline. In fact, it is estimated that total revenues would immediately fall by 50 percent, with the result that total income to the family would decline by 75 percent, to $50,000—a $150,000 per-year decline.

---

[1] *The Emeloid Co. v. Comm.*, 189 F. 2d 230 (3rd Cir. 1951).

Were Doocheol to die or be unable to work because of disability, it is estimated that total revenues would suffer a more gradual, but progressively steeper decline, with the result that net family income would fall by one-fourth (i.e., $50,000) during the year following death or disability, with increasing declines thereafter, ultimately reaching 75 percent.

The likelihood of securing a replacement chef of the equivalent fame of Younghee is slim. The likelihood of engaging someone with Doocheol's managerial talents is high, but it would be necessary to pay a substantial wage.

Thus if Younghee were to die or become disabled and the intention was that the business maintain its approximate before-tax income level, life insurance and disability insurance on Younghee could be purchased that was equal to the present value of the projected lost earnings (i.e., $150,000 per year). If a ten-year time period and a 12 percent discount rate were judged reasonable, then about $850,000 of life and disability insurance on Younghee would meet the need.[2]

A competent replacement for Doocheol would require an estimated salary of $120,000 per year—some $70,000 per year more than the business currently pays Doocheol. If the same ten-year planning horizon and 12 percent interest is used, it is calculated that the business would need about $400,000 of life and disability insurance on Doocheol's life to meet the goal.[3]

Consideration should be given to the question of whether the loss is a temporary or permanent one. The degree of accuracy with which the value of the economic loss produced by the death or disability of a key person can be determined varies according to the type of business, particular function of the key person, and other circumstances.

Procedurally, the business entity (be it a corporation, partnership, or sole proprietorship) generally is the applicant, owner, beneficiary, and premium payor. The policy type should be selected based on the expected need duration and with respect to the possible desire to have cash values available for other purposes (e.g., as loan collateral or to informally fund a deferred compensation arrangement). Whole life and universal life policies are most often used for key employee indemnification. If the need is short term or if there is a desire to accumulate funds outside the life insurance policy, term life insurance policies may be preferable.

The income tax treatment of key employee life insurance is straightforward, being similar to that for personally owned insurance.[4] Unless the business would

---

[2] $150,000 x $(1/1.12)^{10}$ = $150,000 x 5.560 = $847,500. The 12 percent discount rate is the firm's internal cost of capital. The appropriate time period is a matter of personal and business judgment, based on factors such as age, and personal and business objectives.

On an after-tax basis, less insurance probably would be needed, since proceeds typically would be received income tax free. The firm's marginal tax bracket and whether any alternative minimum tax treatment would be invoked would determine whether the amount could be reduced.

[3] $70,000 x $(1/1.12)^{10}$ = $70,000 x 5.560 = $395,500. See remarks in footnote 2.

[4] See Chap. 13.

be subject to the alternative minimum tax (see below), no income tax is attributable to either cash-value increases or receipt of policy death or disability proceeds. Premiums paid are not deductible.[5]

Policy death proceeds will not be includable in the key employee/insured's gross estate for federal estate tax purposes if the insured possessed no incidents of ownership in the policy and if the proceeds are not payable to or for the benefit of the insured's estate. If the insured had an ownership interest in the business, however, the death proceeds payable to the business would be considered in deriving the value of the business for estate tax purposes. Presumably, the loss of the key person would be an offsetting factor in the evaluation.

## ENHANCEMENT OF CREDIT

Anything that stabilizes the financial position of a firm improves its general credit rating. Life insurance can serve to enhance the credit of a business organization by indemnifying for the loss of a key person or assuring the firm's continuation as a going concern in the event of the owner's death. Insuring the lives of key persons assures banks and other lending institutions as well as suppliers that the business will have a financial cushion if one or more key personnel dies or becomes disabled. In addition, if a cash-value form of life insurance is used, the firm's liquidity is enhanced through the accumulation of cash values that are available at all times. The cash values are balance sheet assets. Similarly, if prospective lenders or other creditors are assured of the firm's continuation as a going concern in the event of the death or disability of the owner(s), the firm will not only be able to obtain a larger line of credit, but usually will be able to obtain it on better terms.

In addition to its role in the general improvement of a firm's credit rating, a life insurance contract is useful because it may be pledged as collateral. The cash value of life insurance is pledged to a lender via a collateral assignment form. Under such an arrangement, the basic security for the loan lies in the contract's savings element, with the loan amount covered by the policy's cash value. If the borrower dies before the loan is repaid, the lender simply deducts the borrower's obligation from the proceeds, the excess being paid to the designated beneficiary. If the borrower is unwilling or unable to repay the loan at maturity, the lender can recover its funds either by surrendering the policy for cash or by exercising the policy loan privilege. In the normal course of events, the loan is repaid at maturity and the policy reverts to the borrower. Policyowners frequently borrow directly from the insurance company by utilizing the policy loan privilege. The concept of the loan is the same, however, with the policy being assigned to the

---

[5]An argument can be made that an economic value at least equal to the yearly price of protection (see Chap. 10) should be deductible by the business, in the same way that a business can deduct premiums paid for property and liability insurance protection.

insurance company instead of a bank or other lender. The rate of interest charged on policy loans often is more favorable than that charged by lending institutions, although limits apply.

A policy may also be pledged as collateral with a different purpose in mind. The purpose may be to protect the lender against loss arising only out of the death of a key person or the borrower. Thus life and health insurance may be used advantageously in the large number of instances when a businessperson, already established in business, may need more credit for its proper development, but the banker does not believe that the business warrants further loans. To the banker, the individual at the head of the business is an important asset. The bank may believe that although the business itself does not warrant another loan, the business plus the individual who manages it would justify the extension of further credit. The contingency of early death or disability, however, must be provided for. In other words, a life or health insurance policy in favor of the creditor is a hedge against the contingency of the loss of the value of the life upon which the repayment of the loan is primarily dependent.

In this case, the loan is not made against the cash value of the policy itself. In fact, it is new life insurance taken for credit purposes, and, therefore, it normally would not as yet have a cash value. The real security behind the loan is the demonstrated business ability of the borrower.

In addition to its use in short-term credit situations, life insurance may be used as collateral in connection with bond issues. For example, assume that a firm raises $500,000 in bonds that mature in 20 years, and that the nature and organization of the business are such as to make it chiefly dependent for its credit and successful operation upon Robert. Under these circumstances, Robert's unexpected death might impair the concern to such an extent that the liquidation of its assets might not prove sufficient for the full redemption of the bonds. Thus life insurance can be the means of assuring creditors that the bonds will be redeemed upon maturity, thereby helping to reduce the use of any severe restrictions and the interest rate charged.

## BUSINESS CONTINUATION ARRANGEMENTS

Privately held businesses are a major source of U.S. economic activity and employment. Fully 18 percent of financial assets held by U.S. households is invested in privately held, mostly family-run businesses—a larger proportion than that which households hold in shares of public corporations. Although the majority of privately held firms are small, at least 41,000 family-held businesses nationwide have annual sales of more than $25 million.[6]

Problems of business succession are, by definition, particularly acute for privately held firms, yet owner-managers more often than not fail to address

[6]Terence P. Paré, "Passing On the Family Business," *Fortune* ( May 7, 1990), p. 81.

them. In one survey, only 45 percent of family business owners had identified a successor, and only one in three had prepared a succession plan.[7]

Moreover, as noted in *The Wall Street Journal*, even business owners who plan for succession often overlook critically important issues.[8] The *Journal* notes that survivors often find themselves facing creditors who doubt their business abilities and therefore reduce credit lines and call loans. Many customers try to take advantage of successors, as do many employees.[9] Every ownership transfer involves some difficulty, with fewer than one-in-three family businesses reported as surviving without major difficulties into the second generation.[10] Clearly, the greater the degree of care and thought exercised in business continuation planning, the greater the likelihood of business survival for the benefit of all stakeholders. Yet, too often, those who built and control the business refuse to plan; to do so is to face one's own mortality.

In the case of a sole proprietorship, partnership, or close corporation,[11] the problems of business stability and continuation following the death or disability of one or more of its owners are, therefore, critically important to both the family of the deceased owner and the surviving owners and employees. To understand the vital role that life and health insurance can play in this regard, it will be necessary to review briefly the effects that the death or disability of an owner can have on the stability and continuation of each business form.

## SOLE PROPRIETORSHIPS

The sole proprietorship form of business enterprise is the simplest to establish and operate. In the absence of work in professions or trades that themselves require licensing or other documentation, the sole proprietor may establish himself or herself in business by the mere declaration that he or she is in business. The **proprietorship** is characterized by a unity of ownership and management in a single individual. No legal distinction exists between the proprietor's personal and business assets and liabilities.

A sole proprietorship is a fragile business enterprise because of its dependence on a single individual. Upon the death of the proprietor, the proprietor's personal representative generally is obligated to liquidate the business, thus possibly losing the business going concern value for the proprietor's heirs. A properly funded advance agreement whereby the sole

---

[7]Barbara Marsh, "When Owners of Family Businesses Die, Survivors Often Feel Unsuited to Fill Void," *The Wall Street Journal* (May 7, 1990), p. 81.

[8]Ibid.

[9]Ibid.

[10] Paré, "Passing on the Family Business," p. 81.

[11]A close or closely held corporation is characterized as one wherein a small number of persons are stockholders who, typically, control the company as directors and run its affairs as officers. Closely held stock usually is traded privately, if at all, and is not bought or sold on any organized stock market.

proprietor agrees to sell and another party agrees to purchase the business interest on the proprietor's death could preserve the firm's going concern value for the estate beneficiaries.

Prospective buyers might include a friendly competitor or one or more key employees. A binding buy-and-sell agreement between the proprietor and a friendly competitor could be negotiated and funded by life insurance purchased by the competitor or a trust on the proprietor's life. Premiums would be paid by the competitor.

Alternatively, one or more key employees, dependent perhaps on the business for their livelihood, might find the prospects of acquiring the business on the proprietor's death attractive. A buy-and-sell agreement funded by life insurance on the proprietor's life could guarantee their eventual ownership while acting as an inducement for the key employee(s) to remain with the business. The policy could be owned by and payable to the employee or owned by and payable to a trust that collects the proceeds and supervises execution of the agreement. Full funding of such agreements via life insurance has become even more attractive since personal interest is no longer tax deductible, so that the alternative of having employee-purchasers secure loans to effect the buyout is less unappealing.

Premiums for this life insurance are not tax deductible, but death proceeds ordinarily would be received income-tax-free. If the key employee(s) do not have sufficient funds to pay the required premiums, the proprietor could assist the employee(s) through a split-dollar arrangement (see later in this chapter).

## PARTNERSHIPS

*Potential Problems Flowing from the Partnership Form.* A **partnership** is a voluntary association of two or more persons for the purpose of conducting a business for profit as co-owners. The partnership form of business organization has a number of advantages, but it is subject to the general rule of law that any change in the membership of the partnership causes its dissolution. The law provides that upon the death of a general partner, the partnership is dissolved and the surviving partners become liquidating trustees, charged with the responsibility of immediately winding up the business and paying over to the estate of the deceased a fair share of the liquidated value of the business. Liquidation of a business, which involves the forced sale of assets, almost invariably results in severe asset shrinkage. Under these conditions, accounts receivable might bring only a fraction of their normal value; inventory and plant must be disposed of, often at sacrifice prices; and goodwill is completely lost. From the viewpoint of the survivors, liquidation not only produces losses to them by shrinkage in asset values but, more important, destroys their very means of earning a living.

The seriousness of the consequences often leads survivors to attempt to continue the business by buying out the interest of the deceased partner and reorganizing the partnership. This procedure usually is not practicable, however, for two reasons. First, in most cases, it is not possible to raise the necessary cash. Second, even if the surviving partners can raise the cash to purchase the interest of the deceased, they must prove that the price paid for the interest is fair. Their fiduciary status makes this impracticable. In fact, in some states, they are not permitted to purchase the interest, since it in effect involves a trustee purchasing trust property.

In the usual case, it also is impracticable for an heir who has not already been involved in the business to become a member of the reorganized partnership or to purchase the interests of the surviving partners. The record of litigation clearly indicates that in the absence of advance agreement among the partners, attempts to continue the business are fraught with legal and practical complications.[12]

*Partnership Buy-and-Sell Agreements.* As a means of avoiding the above difficulties, it is increasingly common for the members of a partnership to enter into a buy-and-sell agreement that binds the surviving partners to purchase the partnership interest of the first partner to die, at a prearranged price set by the agreement, and obligates the estate of the deceased partner to sell this interest to the surviving partners. The value of the various partnership interests is determined at the time the agreement is entered into and periodically revalued, or a formula for value determination is included in the agreement.

Partnership buy-and-sell agreements are of two types: entity and cross-purchase. Under the **entity** approach, the partnership itself is obligated to buy out the ownership interest of any deceased partner, with each partner having bound his or her estate to sell if he or she is the first to die.

Under a **cross-purchase** approach, the agreement is among the partners themselves, not between the partnership and the partners. Each partner binds his or her estate to sell his or her partnership interest to the surviving partners, and each surviving partner binds himself or herself via the agreement to buy the interest of the deceased partner.

*Use of Life Insurance.* Life insurance commonly is used to fund such agreements. Under the entity approach, the partnership itself applies for, owns, and is beneficiary of a life insurance policy on each partner's life. The face amount of each policy usually is equal to the value of the insured partner's partnership interest. Under the cross-purchase approach, each partner applies for, owns, and is beneficiary of a life insurance policy on each of the other partners' lives. The face amount of each policy usually is equal to the agreed-upon value of

[12]For a thorough treatment of the problems of business continuation and the use of life and health insurance in solving the problems, see Edwin H. White and Herbert Chasman, *Business Insurance*, 5th ed. (Englewood Cliffs, N.J.: Prentice-Hall, 1980).

the interest that the surviving partner/policyowner would purchase from the deceased partner's estate.

Upon the first death among the partners, the operation of the plan is simple. The life insurance proceeds are used by the partnership or surviving partners, as the case may be, to purchase the interest of the deceased from his or her estate. The partnership is reorganized by the surviving partners and continued in operation, and the heirs of the deceased receive in cash the going concern value of the involved partnership interest. All parties benefit by the arrangement, and the problems of liquidation are obviated. The surviving partners can enter into a new buy-and-sell agreement or amend the original agreement to account for changes in the value of their respective interests. Funding instruments, including life insurance, should be reviewed and updated.

*Special Considerations of Personal-Service Partnerships.* The business continuation arrangement of a personal-service partnership (e.g., for attorneys or physicians) usually differs from that discussed above. Provision usually is made for a continuation of income to the deceased partner's estate or heirs for a specified time period, with the income amount possibly based on a profit-sharing agreement. A separate agreement might provide for the purchase and sale of the deceased partner's tangible business assets.

When a partner is totally disabled, his or her special talents, knowledge, and ability may no longer be available to the partnership. Instead, the disabled partner becomes a drain on the business financially, and the nondisabled partner(s) must assume the disabled partner's responsibilities and duties with inadequate compensation. The nondisabled partners face the problem of earning sufficient money to provide for their usual shares of partnership profits as well as those of the disabled partner. If they hire a capable replacement for the disabled partner, it is even more difficult to maintain the disabled partner's salary. On the other hand, if a replacement is not hired, the burden on the nondisabled partners may become unbearable, particularly if the disability lasts a long time.

As in the case of death, the alternative of taking in family members who are not already active in the business is fraught with dangers and problems. Similarly, liquidation is not ordinarily a desirable solution. Over and above the possible losses brought about by the forced sale of the business, the nondisabled partners must start building their careers again. As in the case of the death of a partner, the ideal solution is a properly drawn buy-and-sell agreement that binds the nondisabled partners to purchase the partnership interest of the disabled partner at a price set by the agreement and that obligates the disabled partner to sell that interest to the nondisabled partners. The agreement can be funded by disability income insurance policies or disability buyout policies that provide a lump sum payment on total disability (see Chapter 16).

*The Tax Aspects of Partnership Buy-and-Sell Agreements.* The income tax treatment of partnership buy-and-sell life insurance is the same as that for personal insurance. That is, premiums are not deductible whether paid by the partnership or a partner. Death proceeds receive IRC section 101(a) treatment (i.e., normally income-tax-free). The cost basis of each surviving partner is increased by the proceeds received by the partnership in the case of the entity plan, and by the amount paid for the deceased partner's interest under the cross-purchase plan.

Life insurance death proceeds are excluded from the gross estate of the insured unless the insured possesses any incidents of ownership or the proceeds are payable to or for the benefit of the insured's estate. Any death proceeds payable to the partnership normally would increase the value of the partnership for estate tax purposes.

In the past, the purchase price established by a buy-and-sell agreement would fix the value of the business for estate tax valuation purposes if certain conditions were met, even if the fixed value were substantially less than the fair market value. For buy-and-sell agreements entered into or substantially modified after October 8, 1990, the value of a closely held business interest (both partnership and corporation) is to be determined without regard to any agreement exercisable at less than fair market value unless the agreement:

- is a bona fide business arrangement;

- is not a device to transfer property to members of the decedent's family for less than an adequate consideration; and

- has terms comparable to those entered into through an arm's-length transaction.[13]

## CLOSE CORPORATIONS

*Potential Problems Flowing from the Corporate Form.* Although the death of a stockholder does not legally dissolve a corporation, the nature of a close corporation leads to practical problems that often make retirement of the deceased's interest desirable. The practical difficulties encountered in attempting to continue the closely held business in operation following the death of a stockholder stem from the facts that (1) the stockholders of a close corporation typically are also its officers, (2) earnings are distributed primarily in the form of salaries, and (3) there is no ready market for the stock. Close corporations are so similar to partnerships in their basic operation that they have been described as "incorporated partnerships." Consequently, a prearranged plan to retire a stockholder's interest following death or total disability can be vital for the stockholders in a close corporation.

[13]IRC § 3703. In addition, case law has established the following four conditions: (1) the estate of the deceased must be obligated to sell the business interest on death, (2) the deceased owner must have been prohibited during life from selling his or her business interest without first offering to sell it to the other party or parties at no more than the contract price, (3) the sale price must have been fair and adequate at the time the agreement was made, and (4) the price must be fixed by the terms of the agreement or by a formula or method set out in the agreement.

Upon the death of a majority stockholder in a close corporation, the surviving stockholders have four alternatives: (1) to accept an adult heir of the deceased into management of the firm; (2) to pay dividends that are approximately equivalent to the salary of the deceased stockholder, to the heir or heirs; (3) to admit into active management of the firm outside interests to whom the stock of the deceased may have been sold; or (4) to purchase the stock from the estate of the deceased.

All of these measures may prove undesirable or impracticable. In the first case, an adult heir who has not had a previous meaningful involvement in the business normally would be able to contribute little to the management of the business, and might be a source of constant disruption in its operation. The second alternative probably would be unpalatable to the survivors, since they would be bearing all the burdens of management but would be sharing the fruits of their labor equally with someone who was contributing nothing but capital to the firm.

If the survivors chose to pay less in dividends than the approximate salary of their former associate, this could lead to dissatisfaction on the part of the heir and other complications. The entrance of outsiders into the management of the firm could prove highly unsatisfactory. Associates in a close corporation, as in a partnership, typically join forces because they work well together and each has a certain contribution that, taken together, produces a vigorous, profitable combination. In many cases, the outsiders may not be acceptable and they may lead to a disruption of the business or, in extreme cases, even to liquidation of the firm. More important, if the outsiders' stock constitutes a majority interest, the survivors would be at the mercy of the new owners, who would control such matters as compensation and dividend policy. The final alternative may not be practicable because the survivors may be unable to raise the cash, agreement may not be possible as to a fair price, or the heirs may simply refuse to sell.

The minority stockholder situation poses potential problems that are no less formidable. The minority stockholder's heirs, while they may not be able to exercise control, nonetheless may be able to render life miserable for the survivors. All stockholders have rights, such as being entitled to a proportionate share of dividends, to examine the corporate records (with legitimate reason), and generally to participate in all stockholder activities. Lawsuits by disgruntled minority stockholders are not uncommon.

The majority stockholder's beneficiaries can enforce their wills on the surviving stockholders; minority stockholder's beneficiaries generally cannot. This distinction, however, might be more apparent than real. In the first instance, the surviving minority stockholders may decide to abandon the business altogether and start out afresh on their own. The heirs of the deceased majority shareholder may be at the mercy of the minority stockholders, since the minority stockholders may be the ones who understand the business best and are most likely to continue it as a successful, going concern.

Clearly, however, the beneficiaries of a deceased minority stockholder are in an unenviable position. They own stock that was possibly subject to substantial federal and state death taxes yet may have little or no marketability. Who would rationally purchase a minority interest in a closely held corporation? Additionally, they receive no income from their investment, since closely held corporations rarely pay dividends.

The beneficiaries of a deceased majority stockholder face the possibility of trying to sell their stock either to the surviving stockholders or to outsiders, neither of whom would normally be predisposed to offer a reasonable price. Indeed, the surviving stockholder/officers most likely would not have the resources to buy out the majority interest, and, even if they did, they might prefer to take this amount of money and start a new business. Outsiders would purchase a majority interest only with the greatest of caution, since the principal value of the business often is in the remaining employees, who could resign. Alternatively, the beneficiaries could demand an active role in the business or demand cash dividends, and either course could lead to ruin.

*Corporate Buy-and-Sell Agreements.* These and other difficulties can be avoided by a properly drawn buy-and-sell agreement. Such agreements may be of the entity (usually called stock-redemption) or cross-purchase type. The agreement binds the surviving stockholders (**cross purchase**) or corporation (**stock redemption**) to purchase the stock of the deceased stockholder at a price set by the agreement, and it obligates the estate of the deceased stockholder to sell his or her stock to the surviving stockholders (cross purchase) or the corporation (stock redemption). As in the case of the partnership agreement, each stockholder's interest is valued at the time the agreement is drawn up, and it should be revalued periodically and the agreement amended to incorporate the new values. Funding instruments should be reviewed and changed when necessary.

*Use of Life Insurance.* These agreements are most commonly funded with life insurance policies. Each stockholder is insured for the value of the stock interest owned, the insurance being owned by either the corporation or the other stockholders. Upon the first death among the stockholders, the life insurance proceeds are used by the corporation or surviving stockholders, as the case may be, to purchase or retire the stock of the deceased from his or her estate. The business future of the survivors is assured, and the estate beneficiary receives cash instead of a speculative interest.

The stockholders of a close corporation who are active in the business are in a position similar to that of partners in a partnership. Consequently, the possibility of a working owner becoming disabled is a serious risk for the business. (The basic problems and available solutions are discussed in Chapter 16.) The best available solution lies in funding a properly drawn buy-and-sell agreement with appropriate amounts of disability insurance.

***The Tax Aspects of Corporate Buy-and-Sell Agreements.*** Premiums paid for life insurance to fund corporate buy-and-sell agreements are not income-tax-deductible under either the stock-redemption or cross-purchase approaches. Death proceeds and cash value increases do not ordinarily give rise to taxable income, in the absence of an alternative minimum-tax situation (see below).

It is possible to run afoul of the transfer for value rule with life insurance purchased to fund a stock-redemption buyout agreement.[14] If life insurance is owned by a corporation to fund an entity buyout agreement and it is decided later to change to a cross-purchase agreement, the corporate-owned policies could not be transferred directly to the relevant stockholder (i.e., to someone other than the insured) without activating the transfer for value rule (and its value possibly being treated as a dividend). The rule allows exceptions for transfers between partners and the partnership but not for transfers from corporations to stockholders.[15]

As with the partnership entity buy-and-sell agreement, life insurance policy death proceeds will not be includable in a deceased stockholder's estate unless the stockholder held one or more incidents of ownership or unless the proceeds were payable to or for the benefit of the stockholder's estate. Death proceeds payable to the corporation may, however, cause the deceased stockholder's stock value to rise.[16]

Another consideration in using corporate-owned life insurance to fund these agreements is whether life insurance cash value increases or policy death proceed payments would invoke the **alternative minimum tax** (AMT). Such a tax is imposed with respect to so-called "tax preference items."[17] Subject to various adjustments, the AMT rate is 20 percent and is invoked if application of the AMT procedure produces a greater tax than that produced by application of regular tax law. Tax preference items are, in general, amounts that accrue to the corporation but are not includable in its taxable income.[18] The AMT could apply when (1) a policy's yearly cash value increase exceeds that year's net premium or (2) death proceeds paid exceed the policy's cash value.

Under most cash-value life insurance contracts sold today, the yearly cash value increases, after the first few policy years, exceed the net annual premium. Also, death proceeds will exceed a policy's cash value with virtually all life insurance policies (i.e., policies will have a positive net amount at risk). Either or both instances could trigger the AMT, depending upon the details of the particular corporation, although for the majority of corporations the cash-value increase is unlikely to cause an AMT problem.

[14]Recall that a life insurance policy transferred to another person for a valuable consideration can cause a portion of the death proceeds to be treated as ordinary income to the beneficiary. (See Chap. 13.)

[15]Some authorities have suggested that this problem can be avoided if the stockholders are also partners in a bona fide partnership, since a transfer to partners is a transfer for value exception.

[16]See footnote 13.

[17]IRC §55–59.

[18]IRC § 57.

If corporate ownership of a life insurance policy would trigger the AMT, consideration should be given to the cross-purchase approach wherein the corporation is neither the owner nor the beneficiary of the policies. Note also that the AMT could be triggered by key person life insurance as well as other instances involving corporate-owned life insurance (see below).

*Factors to Consider When Choosing a Buy-and-Sell Agreement.*[19] Many factors—both financial and otherwise—should be considered when choosing the type of corporate buy-and-sell agreement. Several are summarized below.

*1. Tax Factor.* The relative tax brackets of the corporation and the shareholders may influence whether the cross-purchase or stock-redemption approach is preferred. If the corporation is in a lower tax bracket than the stockholders, a redemption plan may be preferred, as premium payments would take a smaller share of the corporation's after-tax income than that of the shareholders' after-tax income. Conversely, if the stockholders are in a lower bracket than the corporation, a cross-purchase plan may be preferable, as premium payments would take relatively less of shareholders' after-tax income relative to that of the corporation. Also, if the life insurance would cause the corporation to be in an AMT situation, a cross-purchase arrangement may be preferred.

If other factors suggest the use of a cross-purchase plan, even though the corporation is in a lower tax bracket than the stockholders, consideration can be given to funding the insurance through a split-dollar arrangement with the corporation (see below). This approach can utilize the corporation's lower bracket.

*2. Ease of Administration.* In any stock purchase plan, the creation of a sinking or insurance fund is desirable. With only two stockholders, there is little difference in the ease of administration with either a stock redemption or a cross-purchase plan. Each requires the purchase of only two insurance policies—either by the corporation for a redemption or the stockholders themselves for a cross purchase.

As the number of involved stockholders increases, the situation becomes more complicated. Under a stock-redemption plan, the corporation need purchase only one policy per stockholder. Under a cross-purchase plan, however, each stockholder generally would purchase a policy on each of the other stockholders' lives. The total number of policies needed for a cross-purchase arrangement is $n(n - 1)$, where $n$ is the number of stockholders. Thus, with five shareholders, 20 policies would be needed.

*3. Effect upon Stock Basis.* With a stock-redemption plan, the corporation purchases stock from the selling stockholder or estate. The purchased stock becomes treasury stock and is no longer considered to be outstanding. The other stockholders retain their original stock with no increase in cost basis, even though

[19]This area draws from *Advanced Sales Course*, Life Underwriter Training Council.

they will now own a larger percentage of the shares outstanding and thus a larger percentage of the corporation. Since their basis has remained the same while their control and ownership have increased, upon subsequent sale these two factors will increase their taxable gain. With a cross-purchase plan, the remaining stockholders purchase stock with their own funds, thereby acquiring an increase in basis that is equal to the purchase price of the new shares. Upon any subsequent sale, this new basis reduces the amount of any taxable gain realized by the selling stockholder.

To demonstrate the effect of both plans on an individual's cost basis, assume that the ABC Corporation has a fair market value of $1,500,000. Alain, Bruce, and Claude have an equal ownership interest based on each having invested $100,000 in the business. Thus the value of each owner's share is $500,000, and each owner would be insured for this amount. Each owner's cost basis is $100,000. Assume that Alain dies and subsequently Bruce retires and sells to Claude, as outlined below:

*Impact of Death and Later Sale Under a Stock-Redemption Plan*

- Assume Alain dies, whereupon the corporation collects $500,000 in death proceeds and redeems his stock.
- The business value remains $1,500,000, so

  Bruce's value  =  $750,000 and the cost basis remains $100,000

  Claude's value =  $750,000 and the cost basis remains $100,000

- When Bruce subsequently retires and sells to Claude (a living buyout), assuming no change in value, the result is a $650,000 capital gain for Bruce ($750,000 - 100,000).

*Impact of Death and Later Sale Under a Cross-Purchase Plan*

- Assume Alain dies, whereupon Bruce and Claude each collect $250,000 death proceeds and buy Alain's stock.
- The business value remains $1,500,000, so

  Bruce's value  =  $750,000 but the cost basis is

  $100,000 + $250,000 = $350,000

  Claude's value =  $750,000 but the cost basis is

  $100,000 + $250,000 = $350,000

- The result is:

  | | | |
  |---|---|---|
  | Sale Price | = | $750,000 |
  | Less: Cost Basis | = | -350,000 |
  | Equals: Capital Gain | = | $400,000 |

This outcome can be an important consideration if one or more stockholders is likely to sell his or her shares during life. If the shareholder is likely to retain the stock until death, the stock will obtain a step up in basis to its then current fair market value on the death of the stockholder. The result, therefore, would be the same, irrespective of whether the ownership interest had increased through a cross-purchase or entity agreement.

*4. Accumulated Earnings Problem.* The Internal Revenue Code (IRC) imposes an accumulated earnings penalty tax on corporations that accumulate earnings and profits beyond that needed for legitimate business purposes to prevent the amounts from being taxed to shareholders.[20] The tax is in addition to the corporation's regular tax liability and is applied at a 28 percent rate.[21] In general, however, an aggregate of $250,000 may be accumulated for any reason without danger of incurring the tax.

Several cases have recognized as a legitimate business purpose the accumulation of funds for the buyout of a minority shareholder to eliminate dissent or to promote management efficiency.[22] The courts disagree, however, as to whether an accumulation to redeem a majority interest serves a legitimate business purpose.[23]

A cross-purchase plan avoids the accumulated earnings concern altogether since the policies are not owned by the corporation. If other concerns suggest the need for a stock-redemption plan even in the face of an otherwise potential accumulated earnings problem, consideration can be given to not obligating the corporation to carry life insurance and use the proceeds to purchase the decedent's stock. Instead, the corporation's liquidity need can be met by carrying key-person life insurance on the shareholder. Life insurance purchased to indemnify the corporation for loss of a key person's service has been held to be a reasonable business need, and earnings used for such a purpose should avoid attracting the penalty tax.[24] Similarly, earnings accumulated to meet a corporation's obligations under a deferred compensation agreement (see below) should be considered a reasonable business need.[25]

*5. Corporate Creditors.* Under a stock-redemption plan, the corporation is the owner and beneficiary of the life insurance policies funding the arrangement. Any policy cash values and death proceeds are, therefore, subject to attachment by the creditors of the corporation, since the policy values are general corporate assets. This problem is not encountered under a cross-purchase plan.

---

[20]IRC § 537.

[21]IRC § 531.

[22]*Mountain State Steel Foundries, Inc. v. Comm.,* 284 F. 2d 737 (4th Cir. 1960); *Oman Construction Co. v. Comm.,* TC Memo 1965-325; *Dill Mfg. Co. v. Comm.,* 39 BTA 1023 (1939); *Gazette Publishing Co. v. Self,* 103 F Supp. 779 (E.D. Ark. 1952); and *Farmers Merchant Investment Co. v. Comm.,* 29 TC Memo (CCH) 705 (1970).

[23]*John B. Lambert & Asso. v. U.S.,* 76-1 USTC (CCH) 84, 271 (Ct. Cl. 1976) and *Cadillac Textiles, Inc. v. Comm.,* 34 TC Memo (CCH) 295 (1975).

[24]*Harry A. Koch Co. v. Vinal,* 228 F. Supp. 782 (D. Neb. 1964); *Vuono-Lione, Inc. v. Comm.,* TC Memo 1965-96; and *Emeloid Co. v. Comm.,* 189 F.2d 230 (3rd Cir. 1951).

[25]*John P. Scripps Newspapers v. Comm.,* 44 TC 453 (1965) and *Okla. Press Publ. Co. v. U.S.,* 437 F.2d 1275 (10th Cir. 1971) on remand, 28 AFTR 2d 71-5722 (E.D. Okla. 1971).

*6. State Law Restrictions.* The laws of most states provide that corporate redemptions can be made only from available corporate surplus. Thus no surplus—no redemption. Insurance proceeds and contributions to capital can help alleviate this problem under a stock-redemption plan. The problem is not faced under cross-purchase buyouts.

*7. Loan Limitations.* Many close corporations operate on credit. In the normal course of business, this fact presents no problems. The loan agreements used by most banks, however, contain a restriction prohibiting the payment of dividends or redemption of stock without the bank's prior consent. If credit is likely to be an important element in business operations, a stock redemption agreement could fail unless it were fully funded and the indebtedness satisfied, so that creditors would not object to a redemption. Again, this issue does not arise with a cross-purchase agreement.

*8. Attribution Rules.* As a general rule, a complete redemption of a shareholder's stock by a corporation will result in capital gains treatment.[26] A redemption of only a portion of a shareholder's stock, however, generally will invoke dividend treatment—an undesirable result. Hence, most stock redemption buyout plans involve the *complete* redemption of stock.

A problem can arise, however, in certain family-owned and other corporations because of the IRC's attribution rules, the effect of which can be to attribute the stock owned by family members or estate beneficiaries to a decedent.[27] Thus if Nancy owns 100 shares of stock in Nancy's Fancy Books and her husband, Carlos, also owns 100 shares, Carlos's ownership interest will be attributed to Nancy on her death. In this instance, a complete redemption of Nancy's 100 shares would be deemed only a partial redemption and, thereby, would invoke unfavorable dividend treatment. The family attribution rules can be waived provided the shareholder from whom the stock is redeemed:

- retains no interest in the corporation, except as a creditor, immediately after the redemption;

- does not acquire any interest in the corporation, except by bequest or inheritance, within 10 years of the redemption; and

- files an agreement to notify the IRS if he or she obtains a forbidden interest within the 10-year period.[28]

The waiver of family attribution is not allowed if certain interfamily transfers occurred within the ten-year period preceding the redemption. If a disallowed transfer did occur but income tax avoidance was not its principal purpose, the waiver will be permitted nonetheless.[29]

[26]IRC § 302(b)(3).
[27]IRC § 318.
[28]IRC § 302(c)(2)(A).
[29]IRC § 302(c)(2)(B).

*Section 303 Stock Redemptions.* Many estates are composed largely of stock in a closely held business. Such estates often have liquidity problems. These problems can cause a forced, disadvantageous sale of estate assets or even business liquidation. Congress enacted IRC Section 303 to help alleviate these problems.

Specifically, a tax-free stock redemption can be effected for an amount to cover federal and state death taxes, funeral expenses, and estate administration expenses, provided certain conditions are met. This redemption can be important since normally a partial redemption of stock is treated as a taxable dividend to the redeeming stockholder. To qualify for a Section 303 redemption, the value of the stock must be includable in the decedent's gross estate and must represent more than 35 percent of the decedent's adjusted gross estate. The redemption must be made within 3 years and 90 days of the filing of the estate tax return.[30]

This technique clearly can be useful when the stockholder's business ownership represents a major portion of the total estate assets. Life insurance is a natural funding vehicle for Section 303 redemptions. The corporation applies for, owns, and is the beneficiary of a policy whose face amount is sufficient to provide the corporate funds needed to effect the redemption. The income tax treatment of this insurance is essentially that of key-employee insurance, although the life insurance might be subject to any accumulated earnings taxation of the corporation.[31] Additionally, an AMT situation can exist.

## SPECIAL EMPLOYEE COMPENSATION PLANS

Individually issued life insurance policies often are used to provide supplementary benefits to selected employees. The employees typically are those whose skills, talents, and experience render them valuable assets to the business. Through these supplementary plans, the employer can provide benefits beyond those offered to rank-and-file employees. The objective, of course, is to attract and retain these talented employees by rewarding them in special ways.

These plans are typically **nonqualified**, meaning that the employer makes no effort to meet the qualification requirements of the IRC for tax-favored treatment of the plan costs or benefits. A qualified plan must meet certain nondiscrimination requirements and a host of other requirements.[32] In a qualified plan, the employer's contributions are immediately tax deductible, and the employee enjoys certain tax advantages as well. The very purpose of a special employee compensation plan, however, is to discriminate in favor of a select few

[30]See Chap. 13 for discussion of the gross estate and the adjusted gross estate.

[31]IRC § 537. Although the accumulation made to fund a Section 303 redemption in the year of the decedent's/stockholder's death and any year thereafter is explicitly exempted from any accumulated earnings tax [IRC § 537(b)(1)], there appears to be no substantial authority for concluding that life insurance purchased *before* the year of death would be similarly sheltered from any accumulated earnings tax.

[32]See Chap. 28 .

employees. Hence, such plans usually are nonqualified and premium payments are not deductible by the corporation for income tax purposes.

This section discusses two of the most common types of life-insurance-funded, nonqualified employee compensation plans: deferred compensation plans and split-dollar life insurance plans.

## NONQUALIFIED DEFERRED COMPENSATION PLANS

A **nonqualified deferred compensation plan** is a contractual arrangement under which compensation for services rendered is postponed, usually until retirement. If the plan is properly arranged, the employee will not pay tax on these deferred amounts until they are actually received (e.g., subsequent to retirement), when the individual may be in a lower marginal income tax bracket. The employer does not obtain an income tax deduction for these payments until such time as they actually are made available to the employee.

*Types of Plans.* The term *nonqualified deferred compensation* can take on a broad meaning. Here, three types of plans are considered. The first type, often referred to as a **traditional deferred compensation plan**, usually is employee-initiated. It provides for the employee to forgo some portion of present compensation or raises or bonuses, in return for which the employer agrees to pay a deferred income at some future time. The employee desires to avoid additional current income (which presumably is not presently needed) and current taxation on that income.

The second type of plan, often referred to as a **supplemental executive retirement plan**, typically is employer-initiated. Under this arrangement, the employer also agrees to pay a deferred income at some future time, but provides the plan as an additional incentive to attract or retain key employees. It involves no reduction in current income, serving instead as a benefit supplementary to that provided to rank-and-file employees. This and the preceding plan can include death and disability benefits as well as retirement payments. In regard to tax treatment and other respects, the two types of plans are the same. The difference between them involves motivations.

Finally, with **death benefit only** (DBO) **plans**, the employer promises to pay an income benefit to the employee's survivor upon the employee's death. No retirement benefit is involved in DBO plans, often because the employee will have an adequate retirement income from a qualified plan. DBO plans are less costly than other forms of deferred compensation plans and may help retain employees by providing them with a heightened sense of family security.

*Funded and Unfunded Plans.* Nonqualified deferred compensation plans may be funded or unfunded. A plan is **funded** if the employer establishes and maintains assets in an escrow account or trust fund as security for its promise to make future deferred compensation payments. The employee is said to have a beneficial interest in such plan assets.

An unfunded nonqualified deferred compensation plan exists when the employer has not formally earmarked assets to fund the plan, or, stated differently, when the employee must rely exclusively on the employer's unsecured promise to make deferred compensation payments. A plan is not considered funded merely because the employer establishes a reserve fund to meet future obligation under the plan, provided the fund is not formally linked to the obligation and remains a general asset of the business subject to attachment by its general creditors. The establishment of such reserve funds often is referred to as **informal funding**.

Employer contributions to a funded nonqualified plan are taxable to the employee, unless the employee's rights in the funds are subject to a "substantial risk of forfeiture." Whether a substantial risk of forfeiture exists is not easily determinable. Because of these and other tax uncertainties, nonqualified funded plans are used only in exceptional circumstances. Consequently, further discussion is limited to unfunded plans.

***Income Tax Treatment.*** Nonqualified deferred compensation plans have income tax implications both for employers and employees. Generally, the employer is not entitled to an income tax deduction until such time as amounts are actually or constructively received by the employee. Thus premium payments or other contributions to fund a deferred compensation plan informally are not deductible currently to the employer. When payments are made to the employee, upon retirement or to his or her heirs in the case of death, the employer may take a deduction for the payments, to the extent that they are deemed reasonable compensation.[33]

A properly drafted deferred compensation agreement should result in no income tax obligations to the employee during the deferral period. Payments will be treated as ordinary income to the employee when they are actually or constructively received by the employee. Income is considered **constructively received** if it is made available to the employee or if he or she could have taken it but chose not to. Income is not constructively received if it is subject to a substantial risk of forfeiture. Moreover, even if the employee's rights are *nonforfeitable*, there will be no constructive receipt provided (1) the agreement was entered into before the compensation was earned and (2) the employer's promise to pay is unsecured.

If the promise to pay is secured in any way, such as the employee being given an interest in assets or other media (e.g., life insurance) used to fund the agreement, the employee will be taxed on the **economic benefit** of the security interest. To minimize the chance of taxation under the economic benefits doctrine, deferred compensation agreements are made with provisions that rights to payments will be nonassignable and nontransferable.

---

[33] Generally, unreasonable compensation is not a problem. It can be a problem when the employee is also a substantial stockholder. In such cases, the IRS often argues that the compensation really is a disguised dividend and, therefore, not tax deductible to the corporation.

Contributions by an employer to an appropriately established irrevocable trust—a so-called **rabbi trust**—to hold assets from which deferred compensation payments will eventually be made are not taxable to the employees at the time the contributions are made. Rabbi trusts, named after the first such arrangement established for a rabbi, are intended to provide some psychological security to participating employees that they will receive benefits even when there has been a management change or a hostile takeover.

The trust terms provide that the trust's assets will remain subject to the claims of the employer's general creditors if the employer becomes insolvent. In the absence of such claims, the trust assets must be used solely to provide deferred compensation benefits.

Another type of trust, the so-called **secular trust**, provides employees with an even greater degree of security. Under this trust, trust assets are not subject to the claims of the employer's general creditors. Because trust contributions would, therefore, be taxable to the employees since a substantial forfeiture risk did not exist, as with the rabbi trust, these trusts are typically used when the employee is currently in a lower tax bracket or otherwise wants to recognize income currently.

Many deferred compensation agreements, beside DBO plans, provide survivor benefits. The IRC generally permits up to $5,000 to be paid income-tax-free as an employee death benefit to a deceased employee's beneficiary.[34] Thus deferred compensation survivor benefits ordinarily would be received income-tax-free to the extent of $5,000, if the employee's right to the benefit was forfeitable at the time of the employee's death. If the agreement provides for a substantial risk of forfeiture, the $5,000 exclusion should apply. Amounts in excess of $5,000 would be subject to ordinary income taxation in the hands of the beneficiary, but only as the amounts were received.

***Estate Tax Treatment.*** If an employee was receiving deferred compensation payments at his or her death, and if the agreement provided that these payments were to be continued after death, the present value of the remaining payments normally would be includable in the decedent's gross estate.[35] If payments were continued to the employee's spouse, they might qualify for the marital deduction. If payments ceased on death, there obviously would be nothing to include in the gross estate.

If death occurred during the deferral period, the present value of the future payments would be includable in the decedent's gross estate if the deceased employee had an enforceable right in the future to receive postemployment benefits. If the plan did not provide such postemployment benefits (such as with DBO plans), any payments made to the named beneficiary might not be included in the gross estate. Also, if the payment of survivor benefits is optional on the part of the employer, they escape inclusion in the gross estate.

[34]IRC § 101(b). Group life insurance is not considered to be an "employee death benefit" under this code section and group term life death proceeds are normally received income-tax-free. See Chap. 26.

[35]IRC § 2039(a).

*Uses of Life Insurance.*[36] Informal funding through life insurance is especially attractive when the plan provides for the payment of death benefits. When a reserve is established through investment in assets other than life insurance, and the employee dies shortly after the plan is begun, the size of the fund may be inadequate to meet the employer's obligation. When life insurance is used as an informal funding device, the premature death of the employee will not only give rise to the employer's obligation to pay death benefits, but also will create the funds with which to meet that obligation. The employer is the applicant, policyowner, premium payor, and beneficiary of the policy on the employee's life.

Another factor that enhances the attractiveness of life insurance as an informal funding device is the income-tax-deferred status of the cash-value buildup in the policy during the accumulation period. Earnings on most other forms of assets that might be used to accumulate a reserve would be currently taxable to the employer.[37]

Life insurance used to informally fund a nonqualified deferred compensation plan can involve an AMT situation for the corporation. This situation, however, should be less crucial than that with many other forms of corporate-owned life insurance. An additional offsetting item—deferred compensation expense—can be netted against cash-value increases and any death proceeds received. Although not tax deductible, deferred compensation expense is a valid expense for book purposes.

The employer may either use the policy's values to provide the promised benefits or retain the policy until the employee dies, recovering costs at that time. The first approach involves policy loans or surrender proceeds to make payments. Policy loans often are available at favorable interest rates and may be tax deductible.[38]

Benefits may also be met by surrendering portions (e.g., paid-up additions) or all of the policy. The disadvantage of this approach is that the employer forgoes tax-free death proceeds to secure surrender proceeds that are taxable to the extent that they exceed the employer's cost basis.

The **cost recovery method** may offer the best alternative for many employers. With this method, the employer purchases the life insurance with the clear intention of keeping it in force until the employee's death, whenever that may occur. The employer, therefore, is less concerned about the adequacy of the cash-value buildup than about purchasing an amount of life insurance that is adequate to allow it to recover the amount of employee benefit payments (either on an after-tax or a before-tax basis), the premiums paid, and the opportunity cost

---

[36]This section draws from White and Chasman, *Business Insurance*, pp. 553–555.

[37] In 1986 corporate-owned annuities lost much of their former attractiveness as an informal funding medium when the new tax law provided that interest credited on such annuity cash values was no longer tax deferred.

[38]See Chap. 13.

of the funds. Implicit in this approach is the assumption that the employer can meet employee payments from its cash flows.

Life insurance funding also makes available the waiver of premium benefit. This will relieve the employer of the obligation to pay premiums if the insured employee becomes permanently and totally disabled. The dollars that are no longer needed to pay premiums can be used either to provide disability income to the employee or to reduce the employer's costs under the plan.

The availability of settlement options, especially when the deferred compensation plan requires the employer to pay a life income to the employee, may be another reason for informal funding through life insurance. By electing a life income option, the employer can pass to the insurance company the risk of the employee living beyond his or her life expectancy. When a settlement option is used, care should be taken not to designate the employee or his or her beneficiary as the direct beneficiary under the terms of the life insurance policy. This is to avoid constructive receipt of the policy value by the employee or of the death proceeds by the employee's beneficiary. The employer should designate itself as beneficiary under the terms of the settlement option. The employer then receives the installment payments from the insurance company and in turn pays the employee from its funds.

## SPLIT-DOLLAR LIFE INSURANCE PLANS[39]

**Split-dollar life insurance** is an arrangement for providing funding for individually issued, cash-value life insurance. It is a funding method, not a type of policy. The arrangement divides or splits the death benefit, the living benefits, and possibly the premium between two parties—hence the name split-dollar insurance.

The objective of split-dollar plans is to join together the needs of one person with the premium-paying ability of another. Often this means cooperation between an employee and his or her employer but the concept can be applied to an infinite variety of other relationships: child-parent, stockholder-corporation, buyer-seller, and so on.

The split-dollar plan may provide employees with substantial amounts of life insurance protection, generally at a current outlay well below that which they would pay for the same policy purchased individually. The employer is free to discriminate among employees benefited by this plan. The employee also can be allowed to purchase the policy from the employer at termination or retirement, and this can provide the employee with a supplemental retirement benefit.

When used as a fringe benefit, split-dollar insurance proceeds are usually intended (1) as a death benefit to the employee's beneficiary and (2) as a reimbursement to the employer for its share of premiums paid. The same concept has gained added significance for the stockholder-employee in recent years.

[39]This section draws on White and Chasman, *Business Insurance*, pp. 560–585, and *Split Dollar Life Insurance* (Bryn Mawr, PA.; American Society of CLU, 1982).

*The Classical Split-Dollar Plan.* Although many variations of split-dollar plans exist, an understanding of the classical split-dollar plan will be helpful.[40] Under this arrangement, the employer and employee join in the purchase of a cash-value insurance contract on the employee's life. As shown in Table 15-1, the employer provides the funds to pay that part of each annual premium that is equal to the annual increase in the cash value. The employee pays the balance. The employer is entitled to receive death proceeds from the policy equal to the cash value, or at least a sufficient part thereof to equal its total premium payments. The employee names the beneficiary for the balance of any proceeds.

Although the employee's share of annual premiums may be substantial in the early years, it will decrease each year as the annual increases in cash value grow progressively larger. In many cases, the employee's share reaches zero after a relatively short time. As the employer takes over more of the obligation to pay premiums, its share of the death proceeds increases. Nevertheless, through the appropriate use of dividends or other options, the employee's share of the death benefit often can be maintained at an approximately constant amount.

*Split-Dollar Systems.* Two major systems have been developed for the establishment of a split-dollar life insurance plan: the endorsement system and the collateral assignment system.

*1. Endorsement System.* When a split-dollar plan is established under the **endorsement system,** insurance on the employee's life is applied for and owned by the employer. The employer is primarily responsible for premium payments. In the classical split-dollar arrangement, the employee agrees to reimburse the employer for the portion of each premium payment that exceeds the annual increase in the policy's cash value. The employer is named the beneficiary for that portion of the proceeds that is equal to the cash value—the exact amount of its cumulative premium payments. The employee designates a personal beneficiary to receive the remainder of the proceeds. The employee's rights are protected by an endorsement on the policy that modifies the employer's rights as policyowner. This endorsement provides that the designation of the employee's personal beneficiary to receive the proceeds in excess of the cash value cannot be changed without the insured employee's consent.

Some life insurers have adopted a slightly different approach to the split-dollar endorsement system. These companies permit the ownership of policy rights to be split, with the insured employee designated as owner of the portion of the death proceeds in excess of the cash value and the employer designated as owner of all the other rights and benefits under the policy.

If the split-dollar plan is terminated prior to the death of the insured employee, the employer recovers its premium outlay directly from the cash value that it controls as owner of the policy. This may be accomplished by surrendering

---

[40]Although the classical plan is much discussed and is the plan dealt with in the IRC, relatively few split-dollar plans are arranged in this manner. See "Variations of the Classical Split Dollar Plan" later in this section.

**TABLE 15-1     ILLUSTRATION OF CLASSICAL SPLIT-DOLLAR PLAN**
          **($250,000 ORDINARY LIFE)**

| | Corporation | | | | Insured/Employee | | | |
|---|---|---|---|---|---|---|---|---|
| | Male, Nonsmoker, Age 45 $4,660 Annual Premium | | | | Dividends Applied to Purchase One-Year Term For 20 Years Balance Applies to Paid-Up Additions | | | |
| Yr | Annual Before Tax Expend. | Annual After Tax Expend.* | Net Cash Value | Net Death Benefit | Annual Before Tax Expend. | Annual After Tax Expend.** | Net Cash Value | Net Death Benefit |
| 1 | $0 | $0 | $0 | $0 | $4660 | $4660 | $0 | $250000 |
| 2 | 125 | 125 | 125 | 125 | 4535 | 4535 | 0 | 250000 |
| 3 | 4660 | 4660 | 4785 | 4785 | 0 | 97 | 4039 | 254296 |
| 4 | 4660 | 4660 | 9445 | 9445 | 0 | 109 | 4466 | 255206 |
| 5 | 4660 | 4660 | 14105 | 14105 | 0 | 124 | 5347 | 257553 |
| 6 | 4660 | 4660 | 18765 | 18765 | 0 | 141 | 6846 | 261495 |
| 7 | 4660 | 4660 | 23425 | 23425 | 0 | 162 | 9087 | 266761 |
| 8 | 4660 | 4660 | 28085 | 28085 | 0 | 185 | 11957 | 273395 |
| 9 | 4660 | 4660 | 32745 | 32745 | 0 | 212 | 15486 | 281015 |
| 10 | 4660 | 4660 | 37405 | 37405 | 0 | 243 | 19451 | 289365 |
| 11 | 4660 | 4660 | 42065 | 42065 | 0 | 293 | 24118 | 298665 |
| 12 | 4660 | 4660 | 46725 | 46725 | 0 | 336 | 29613 | 309865 |
| 13 | 4660 | 4660 | 51385 | 51385 | 0 | 386 | 35711 | 321794 |
| 14 | 4660 | 4660 | 56045 | 56045 | 0 | 442 | 42405 | 334344 |
| 15 | 4660 | 4660 | 60750 | 60705 | 0 | 508 | 49696 | 347427 |
| 16 | 4660 | 4660 | 65365 | 65365 | 0 | 590 | 57587 | 360970 |
| 17 | 4660 | 4660 | 70025 | 70025 | 0 | 681 | 66090 | 374930 |
| 18 | 4660 | 4660 | 74685 | 74685 | 0 | 783 | 75473 | 389533 |
| 19 | 4660 | 4660 | 79345 | 79345 | 0 | 895 | 85498 | 404520 |
| 20 | 4660 | 4660 | 84005 | 84005 | 0 | 1053 | 95921 | 419639 |

*Assuming a corporate tax bracket of 25%.
**Assuming a 28% tax bracket for 20 years. Includes economic benefit value.

the policy or giving the insured employee the option to purchase it for an amount equal to its cash surrender value.

2. *Collateral Assignment System.* When a classical split-dollar insurance plan is established under the **collateral assignment system**, the insured employee applies for and owns the policy. He or she then designates his or her own personal beneficiary. The insured employee is primarily liable for premium payment. In a separate agreement, the employer obligates itself to lend the employee an amount equal to the annual increases in the cash value. Generally, this loan is made interest free. Thus the employee's out-of-pocket cost is limited to that portion of each annual premium that exceeds the annual increase in cash value. To protect the employer, the employee collaterally assigns the policy to the employer as security for the amount of the loan. At the insured employee's

death, the employer recovers the amount of its loan from the death proceeds, not as a beneficiary of the policy, but as a collateral assignee.[41]

*3. Factors Bearing on Choice of Split-Dollar Systems.* Several factors help suggest which split-dollar system should be used. One factor to consider is whether the employer wants the cash value available for use in its business during the term of the split-dollar plan. If it does, the endorsement system or split ownership variation is preferable. Under the collateral assignment system, the policy cash value generally is not available to the employer. Under the endorsement system, the employer as policyowner is free to borrow from the policy at any time and for any reason.

If the employee is not an officer or stockholder, the endorsement method may be preferable to the employer as a means of retaining key employees, since the policy and its protection would be lost in the event of employment termination.

When the parties intend to use the policy to fund a nonqualified deferred compensation arrangement, the endorsement method should be used. This is especially true when the insured employee is not a stockholder or officer of the corporation. Under the endorsement method, the employer owns the policy and the cash value. At the retirement of the insured employee, the employer can elect to take out a policy loan or to receive the cash value under a settlement option or continue to pay the premiums on the policy until the employee's death. In the latter case, the death proceeds could be used to offset the benefit paid under the deferred compensation agreement.

If the collateral assignment system is used, the insured employee is owner of the policy. If the policy is to be used to fund a deferred compensation plan, it will have to be transferred to the corporation. This would involve a transfer for value that would not come under the exceptions to the transfer for value rule for income tax purposes unless the insured employee was a stockholder or officer of the corporation,[42] in which case a portion of the death proceeds would be subject to ordinary income tax treatment.

If a policy already in force and personally owned by the insured employee is to be used to establish a split-dollar plan, it will be simpler to adopt the collateral assignment system. If the policy is a key-person policy owned by the employer, however, the simpler approach would be to utilize the endorsement system.

If it is desirable to have the employee accumulate some savings through the policy, the collateral assignment method ordinarily would be preferred. Under such **equity split-dollar plans**, the employer's interest in the cash value equals the sum of its premium contributions. With most single-life cash-value policies, the annual cash-value increases exceed the premium after a few years. Under an

[41]See Chap. 9 under "Assignment Provision."
[42]IRC § 101(a)(2). See Chap. 13 under "Transfer for Value Rule."

equity split-dollar plan, title to the excess of the gross policy cash value over that portion of the cash value due the employer because of its premium payments rests with the employee.

***Income Tax Consequences of Split-Dollar Plans.*** Split-dollar plans give rise to income tax consequences to both employees and employers.

*1. Income Tax Treatment of Employees.* Under a 1964 IRS ruling, the typical split-dollar plan is considered to result in a taxable **economic benefit** to the employee, represented by the amount of the annual premium cost that the employee should bear and of which he or she is relieved.[43] The value of the benefit, to be included annually in the employee's taxable income, is an amount equal to the one-year term cost of the life insurance protection to which the employee is entitled, less any portion of the premium provided by the employee. If the premium paid by the employee exceeds the economic benefit, there is no taxable income to the employee. However, no carryover is allowed of the excess premium. In deriving the annual economic benefit to the employee, the one-year term insurance rates contained in the government's so-called **PS 58 Rate Table** should be used. Table 15-2 gives these rates.[44]

**TABLE 15-2.     PS-58 RATES: ONE-YEAR TERM PREMIUMS, FOR $1,000 OF LIFE INSURANCE PROTECTION**

| Age | Premium | Age | Premium | Age | Premium |
|-----|---------|-----|---------|-----|---------|
| 15 | $1.27 | 37 | $3.63 | 59 | $19.08 |
| 16 | 1.38 | 38 | 3.87 | 60 | 20.73 |
| 17 | 1.48 | 39 | 4.14 | 61 | 22.53 |
| 18 | 1.52 | 40 | 4.42 | 62 | 24.50 |
| 19 | 1.56 | 41 | 4.73 | 63 | 26.63 |
| 20 | 1.61 | 42 | 5.07 | 64 | 28.98 |
| 21 | 1.67 | 43 | 5.44 | 65 | 31.51 |
| 22 | 1.73 | 44 | 5.85 | 66 | 34.28 |
| 23 | 1.79 | 45 | 6.30 | 67 | 37.31 |
| 24 | 1.86 | 46 | 6.78 | 68 | 40.59 |
| 25 | 1.93 | 47 | 7.32 | 69 | 44.17 |
| 26 | 2.02 | 48 | 7.89 | 70 | 48.06 |
| 27 | 2.11 | 49 | 8.53 | 71 | 52.29 |
| 28 | 2.20 | 50 | 9.22 | 72 | 56.89 |
| 29 | 2.31 | 51 | 9.97 | 73 | 61.89 |
| 30 | 2.43 | 52 | 10.79 | 74 | 67.33 |
| 31 | 2.57 | 53 | 11.69 | 75 | 73.23 |
| 32 | 2.70 | 54 | 12.67 | 76 | 79.63 |
| 33 | 2.86 | 55 | 13.74 | 77 | 86.57 |
| 34 | 3.02 | 56 | 14.91 | 78 | 94.09 |
| 35 | 3.21 | 57 | 16.18 | 79 | 102.23 |
| 36 | 3.41 | 58 | 17.56 | 80 | 111.04 |

[43]Rev. Rul. 64-328, 1964-2 CB 11.

[44]This table reflects one-year term costs based upon Table 38, U.S. Life & Actuarial Tables, and 2 1/2 percent interest. These rates are also used to determine the taxable economic benefit to an employee because of pension plan death benefits. See Chap. 28.

If the insurer of the insurance policy publishes rates for individual, initial issue, one-year term policies that are available to all standard risks, these rates may be used in place of the PS 58 rates.[45] Many insurers have term rates that are significantly lower than the PS 58 rates. Using the lower rates decreases the amount of taxable income imputed to the employee.

Many split-dollar plans today involve second-to-die policies. The economic benefit imputed to such policies is calculated by using the one-year term rates as given in U.S. Life Table 38 for joint and last survivor mortality.[46] These rates are substantially lower than the PS 58 rates—typically only 1 to 10 percent of the PS 58 rates, depending on age.

An example of how the economic benefit to the employee is determined should be helpful. (At this point, policy dividends will be ignored.) Assume that a $100,000 ordinary life policy with an annual premium of $2,000 is purchased under a classical split-dollar plan. In the year in question, the annual increase in cash value, and thus the employer's contribution toward the premium, is $1,800. The employee must, therefore, pay $200 ($2,000 - $1,800). Furthermore, assume that if the employee dies during the year, the portion of the death proceeds payable to the employer is $10,000 (the total of its premium contributions), with the remaining $90,000 of death proceeds payable to the insured employee's personal beneficiary.

To determine the amount of the taxable economic benefit to the employee, the first step is to calculate the term cost of the insurance protection provided to his or her personal beneficiary. Assume that the employee's attained age is 42. Based on the PS 58 Rate Table, the term cost of insurance protection is $5.07 per $1,000. Since $90,000 would be payable to the employee's personal beneficiary, the value of the insurance protection is $456 ($90,000 x $5.07/$1,000). The employee contributed $200 toward the premium payment. Hence the value of the net economic benefit and the amount included in his or her taxable income is $256 ($456 - $200). Each year the amount included in the employee's taxable income will vary because the term rate and protection amount will be different.[47]

The value of any policy dividends used to benefit the employee also is includable in his or her taxable income. As with the economic benefit treatment, the tax implications of any additional benefits received by the employee on account of policy dividends under a split-dollar plan will be the same whether the endorsement system or the collateral assignment system is used.[48]

Split-dollar plans are not designed to last forever. At some point, the economic benefit charges could become particularly burdensome, the employee will retire or resign, or business or personal reasons may necessitate the

---

[45]Rev. Rul. 66-110, 1966-1 CB 12.

[46]U.S. Tres. Reg. § 20.2931-7.

[47]Only policies purchased under split-dollar arrangements or utilized to establish such arrangements after November 13, 1964, give rise to a taxable economic benefit to the employee.

[48]Rev. Rul. 66-110, 1966-1 CB 12.

termination of the plan. Upon plan termination (other than by death), the policy often is made available to the employee.

Under an endorsement split-dollar plan, the employer may sell the policy to the insured or may execute a policy loan for its interest in the policy, then transfer ownership to the insured with the loan intact. In the first case, a sale to the insured should not give rise to a taxable event if the sales price equals the policy's fair market value. (It also will not invoke income taxation of the death proceeds since the transfer for value is to the insured—one of the exceptions.)

The transfer of the policy to the insured via the policy loan approach—a so-called **rollout**—can give rise to taxable income to the employee. The position of the IRS is that the transfer gives rise to taxable income to the extent that the net policy cash value (cash value less loan amount) exceeds the aggregate premiums paid by the employee.

This adverse tax effect can be avoided by a rollout when the cash value is about equal to or less than the cumulative premiums contributed by the employer. Alternatively, the collateral assignment method can be used, thereby presumably avoiding a policy transfer altogether and hence avoiding attendant taxable income.

*2. Income Tax Treatment of Employer.* Premiums paid by an employer on insurance covering the life of an employee when the employer is directly or indirectly a beneficiary under the policy are not deductible.[49] As a result, the employer is not allowed a tax deduction for its share of premiums under a split-dollar plan.

*3. Income Tax Treatment of Death Proceeds.* The income tax treatment of any death proceeds payable under a split-dollar plan will be governed by IRC Section 101(a).[50] Thus, in the absence of IRC Section 7702 (definition of life insurance) or transfer for value problems, both the employer and the personal beneficiary of the employee will receive their share of the proceeds income-tax-free.

***Estate Tax Treatment of Split-Dollar Plans.*** The IRC provides that death proceeds of insurance are includable in the gross estate of a decedent/insured if he or she possessed any incidents of policy ownership or if proceeds are payable to or for the benefit of the insured's estate.

Under the usual endorsement system, the employer is the sole owner of the life insurance policy. To protect the insured employee's rights under the agreement, the ownership rights of the employer are modified by endorsement that provides that the insured employee's personal beneficiary cannot be changed without the insured employee's consent. This is an incident of ownership. This ownership right might be avoided if the agreement provided that the beneficiary cannot be changed without the consent of the beneficiary, rather than of the insured. Even if the death

---

[49]IRC § 264(a)(1).
[50]Rev. Rul. 64-328, 1964-2 CB 11.

proceeds are includable in the insured's gross estate, they should qualify for the unlimited marital deduction if they are paid to the surviving spouse.

Under the collateral assignment system, the insured employee generally is the policyowner. As such, he or she can exercise all of the incidents of ownership, and the death proceeds should be includable in his or her gross estate for federal estate tax purposes.[51] The estate tax value of the proceeds should be the full proceeds, less the amount that must be paid to the employer in satisfaction of the debt owed to it under the split-dollar agreement.[52]

When the collateral assignment system is used and the insured employee wishes to avoid inclusion of the proceeds in his or her gross estate, the beneficiary for the insured employee's share of the proceeds should initially apply for and own the life insurance policy. The owner/beneficiary may be a trust, the insured's spouse, or any other third party. The policyowner should then enter into the collateral assignment split-dollar agreement with the insured's employer. Under this arrangement, the insured employee arguably has no incidents of ownership in the policy, and the proceeds should be excludable from his or her gross estate.

If a third party, such as an irrevocable trust, owns the policy, the insured employee is deemed to be making gifts of the economic benefit to the third party. Of course, any gift tax consequences can be offset by using the $10,000-per-donee annual exclusion for present interest gifts. It is advisable to have a Crummey withdrawal power with trusts. (See Chapter 14.)

When a split-dollar plan (regardless of the system) is instituted between a corporation and a majority stockholder-employee, the portion of the proceeds payable to a beneficiary other than the corporation may be includable in the gross estate of the insured majority stockholder-employee, even when the necessary steps have been taken to eliminate the possession of any incidents of ownership in the policy held directly by the insured. This result is based on an estate tax regulation that imputes the incidents of ownership possessed by a corporation in an insurance policy on the life of a majority stockholder to the stockholder to the extent that the proceeds are *not* payable to or for the benefit of the corporation.[53] Proceeds payable to the corporation are not includable in the stockholder's estate but are considered in establishing the value of the decedent's stock.

To avoid inclusion of these policy proceeds in the estate of a controlling shareholder, the corporation must be relegated to the status of a secured lender. To so qualify, the corporation must not have the right to terminate the policy in any way or to borrow against the policy.[54] An alternative is for an irrevocable trust to own the policy and to have the split-dollar agreement provide that the

[51]IRC § 2042(2).

[52]Reg. § 20.2053–7.

[53]Reg. § 20.2042-1(c)(6). See Rev. Rul. 82–145.

[54]Rev. Rul. 76-274 and 82-145. The technical soundness of the IRS position on policy loans has been questioned. See Louis S. Shuntich, "The Effect of Rev. Rul. 82-145 on Split Dollar Insurance Plans," *Journal of the American Society of CLU*, Vol XXXVII (Oct. 1983).

trustee will name the corporation as a revocable, creditor beneficiary without any ability to borrow or pledge. The corporation would have no rights in the policy under this approach.[55]

***Variations of the Classical Split-Dollar Plan.*** Under the classical split-dollar plan, the employer makes annual contributions of an amount equal to the increases in cash value, and the insured employee contributes the balance of the annual premium due, if any. In the first few years of the plan, the financial burden on the insured employee could be substantial. Also, when the employee's premium contribution exceeds the economic benefit, no carryover of the excess contribution to future years is allowed. As a result of these difficulties and other planning opportunities, several variations of the classical split-dollar approach have evolved, a few of which are discussed below.

*1. Reverse Split-Dollar.* If it is desirable for the employee, instead of the employer, to have rights to the cash value and for the employer, instead of the employee, to control the disposition of the death proceeds, a reverse split-dollar plan may be appropriate. Under **reverse-split dollar** (RSD), the traditional roles of employer and employee are reversed. Thus the pure death protection is made payable to the corporation, with the death proceeds equal to the cash value payable to the employee's beneficiary. The employee owns the policy (and the cash value) and endorses to the employer the right to name the beneficiary for a portion of the death proceeds.

The employee is responsible for the entire premium, with the employer paying the portion of the premium that reflects the value of its economic benefit. Since one of the goals of RSD in effect may be to transfer employer wealth to the employee, the economic benefit value paid by the corporation ordinarily would be the PS 58 rate rather than the insurer's lower term rate. By doing so, the corporation is subsidizing the purchase of the employee's life insurance. The employee will, thereby, pay less than the annual cash-value increase.

When the arrangement is terminated, the employer simply ceases to make further premium payments and relinquishes its right to a portion of the death benefits. The idea is that the employee obtains full policy control without tax consequences.

RSD has strong advocates and equally strong opponents. No IRS rulings on RSD have been made, so potentially important tax issues cannot be addressed with certainty.[56] RSD can be useful when the employer desires key-person protection or informal funding for a DBO plan or when death proceeds would be useful for a stock redemption. RSD can be of substantial value to the employee as a subsidized savings mechanism, and ultimately as meaningful death protection.

[55]Kenneth M. Cymbal, "Using Split Dollar Insurance to Transfer Wealth from a Closely Held Corporation," *Journal of the American Society of CLU & ChFC*, Vol. XLV (July 1991), p. 37.

[56]For a discussion of these and other RSD issues, see Cymbal, "Using Split Dollar Insurance," and Jeffrey W. Tegeler and Alfred O. Elder, "Reverse Split Dollar: A Reasoned Approach," *Journal of the American Society of CLU & ChFC*, Vol. XLV (July 1991).

Figure 15-1 illustrates how an RSD plan's initial $500,000 death benefit can be split between employer and employee. The illustration assumes that the corporation ceases its premium payments and policy involvement when the employee becomes 65.

*2. Equity Split-Dollar.* In a classic split-dollar plan, the employer's interest in the policy equals the greater of the policy's cash value or the aggregate of its premium payments. Under equity split-dollar, the employee obtains ownership of the excess of the cash value over any premium payments.

The IRS has ruled that certain equity split-dollar plans give rise to taxable employee income on the excess.[57] As mentioned earlier, the collateral assignment method conceptually should avoid this possibility, but the issue is not completely clear.[58]

*3. Alternative Premium Payment Arrangements.* Besides the premium payment approach of the classical, RSD, and equity split-dollar plans, several other alternative payment approaches are possible. For example, under the **averaging approach**, the employer pays a level amount each year that is equal to a specified fraction of the policy's cash value after a specified number of years. For example, each year the employer might pay one-twentieth of the twentieth-year cash value. The employee pays the balance of each premium. Thus the employee's contribution is leveled to ease his or her burden in the early policy years. Over the specified period (say 20 years), aggregate contributions by both the employer and the employee are the same as under the classical plan.

**FIGURE 15-1**

**REVERSE-SPLIT DOLLAR ILLUSTRATION**

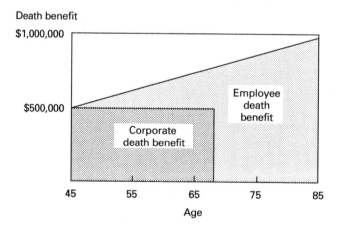

[57]Problems arose with plans in which the employee's rights in the plans were not forfeitable. See Rev. Rul. 66–110 and Private Letter Rulings 7916029 and 0310027.

[58]See Cymbal,"Using Split-Dollar Insurance."

Under the **PS-58 cost approach**, each year the employee pays an amount that is equal to that year's PS-58 cost. (Depending on the use of dividends, the death benefit may vary from year to year.) The employer pays the balance, if any, of each premium. A policy issued at a young age eventually may generate a PS-58 cost that is substantially greater than the gross annual premium.

Under the **employer-pay-all approach**, each year the employer pays the full premium. The employee makes no contribution to the premium and merely reports taxable income on the value of the economic benefit received each year.

The so-called **bonus plan** is a minor adaptation that combines aspects of the PS-58 and employer-pay-all approaches. The employer is willing to pay the entire cost of the plan. Cognizant of the fact that its expenditure on behalf of the employee's economic benefit is not deductible, the employer adopts a PS-58 cost plan and pays the employee a bonus that is sufficient to enable the employee to pay the PS-58 costs. The employer's expenditure is precisely the same as with the employer-pay-all approach, but a portion of it (equal to the PS-58 measured bonus) is presumably deductible as compensation. The employee now pays tax on the bonus, rather than on PS-58 costs.

The classical split-dollar plan allocates a death benefit to the employer that is equal to the greater of the sum of its aggregate contributions or the cash value. Another approach is to allocate to the employer a portion of the death proceeds that is equal to the employer's contributions accumulated at some specified rate of interest. This reflects the time value of money.

*Unsplitting the Policy.* Because of the insured's advancing age and hence increasing PS-58 costs, a time may come when the split-dollar arrangement is no longer attractive. (Of course, other considerations sometimes may lead to a similar conclusion.) Three alternatives for "unsplitting" split-dollar plans are: (1) conversion to key-person insurance; (2) a rollout; and (3) a spinout.

*1. Conversion to Key-Person Insurance.* Under this approach, the insured (or third-party owner) releases his or her interest in the policy to the corporation. This normally is an undesirable solution unless the insured is an officer or stockholder of the corporation, since it would appear to constitute a transfer for value. If the insured is a principal stockholder, he or she may prefer to have the corporation retain the policy death proceeds to be used in a Section 303 redemption or a postdeath total liquidation of the corporation.

*2. Rollouts.* A **rollout** occurs when the corporation makes a maximum policy loan or withdrawal or surrender of paid-up additions, followed by a transfer of its remaining ownership rights in the policy to the insured. The employer probably would sell the policy to the insured for the difference between the gross cash surrender value and the policy loan, if any.

The insured would have a continuing interest obligation on the policy loan. Since the corporation has recovered an amount equal to the cash value and no longer has any commitment under the split-dollar agreement, it can (if it wishes) give the insured employee annual bonuses that are equal to the gross interest payable.

*3. Spinouts.* Another approach is referred to as a **spinout.** Rather than taking a policy loan, the corporation merely transfers its interest in the policy as a bonus to the insured. Any transfer to a third-party owner should be a separate subsequent event, with the insured gifting the policy to the third-party owner to avoid a transfer for value.

Under a spinout, the insured is taxed on the value of the policy. If the insured chose to do so, he or she could borrow against the policy to pay the tax. This leaves the insured with a considerably smaller policy loan than he or she would have with the rollout. Again, the corporation may give the insured employee annual bonuses equal to the gross interest payable on this (smaller) loan.

*4. Caveat.* Each of the foregoing "unsplitting" techniques works nicely for a classical split-dollar plan. Under such a plan, the corporation's contributions are no more than the policy's cash value. However, with more ambitious plans (i.e., plans in which the corporate contributions have exceeded the increase in cash value), it is necessary to reckon with the excess of total corporate contributions over total cash value. This excess was, presumably, in the nature of a loan to the employee. A release or discharge of this indebtedness generates taxable income to the individual so enriched. The solution may be to undertake unsplitting only in a policy year when the cash value is as large as (or, at least, not much smaller than) the corporation's cumulative contributions. This approach will eliminate (or at least minimize) the problem of discharge of an indebtedness. (The potential tax problems of equity split-dollar plans were discussed earlier.)

***Other Uses of Split-Dollar Insurance Plans.*** In the typical employer-employee split-dollar plan, insurance is purchased on the life of the employee. An employee, however, may need insurance protection on the life of someone else. Split-dollar plans can be useful in these cases also.

*1. Sole Proprietor Buyout.* An individual who is the sole owner of a business may not have any family members to whom he or she wants to leave the business at death. It may be difficult to sell the business to an outsider at a fair price. In such a situation, it is not unusual for the business owner to seek out a key employee of the firm and offer to sell the business to him or her at the business owner's death. Although the employee may be eager to accept the offer, one major stumbling block often is the lack of funds with which to make the purchase. An obvious solution would be insurance owned by the employee on the life of the employer. To solve the problem of the employee not having sufficient funds, the employer may enter into a split-dollar insurance plan with the employee. In this case, the insurance is on the life of the employer rather than on the employee.

*2. Split-Dollar in a Cross-Purchase Buy-and-Sell Agreement.* One drawback to the use of a cross-purchase buy-and-sell agreement is that the stockholders are personally responsible for the payment of premiums on insurance used to fund the plan. The corporation can help finance the purchase of the needed insurance through the use of a split-dollar plan. When a split-dollar plan is entered into for this purpose, the collateral assignment system generally is used. Each stockholder applies for and owns a policy on the life of his or her co-stockholder(s). Each stockholder then collaterally assigns the policy he or she owns on his or her co-stockholder's life to the corporation as security for the corporation's premium payments.

If a split-dollar plan used to fund a cross-purchase buy-and-sell agreement is arranged under the endorsement system, it could result in a transfer-for-value problem. Under this system, normally the corporation applies for and owns the life insurance. It then transfers the right to receive a portion of the policy proceeds on the life of each stockholder to his or her co-stockholder. This is a transfer for value (the consideration being services rendered to the corporation) to a co-stockholder of the insured. Such a transfer does not come within any of the exceptions to the transfer-for-value rule and would thus subject the proceeds to income taxation. Some companies believe this potential problem can be avoided by setting up the ownership and beneficiary arrangement at policy inception, thereby avoiding any transfer.

When one of the parties to the cross-purchase buy-and-sell agreement is a majority stockholder-employee, the use of a split-dollar plan to help fund the agreement could create a serious estate tax trap. This is because the incidents of ownership in the life insurance policy on his or her life possessed by the corporation will be attributed to the majority stockholder-insured if the ownership incidents extend to the proceeds of the policy not payable to the corporation.[59] The result could be that the value of the stock in the corporation and the insurance proceeds received by the co-stockholder and used to purchase the stock will both be includable in his or her gross estate.[60]

*3. Split-Dollar in a Nonqualified Deferred Compensation Plan.* A split-dollar arrangement can provide the mechanism for informally funding a nonqualified deferred compensation plan. The employer's access to policy cash values provides the means from which payments are ultimately made.

*4. Family Split-Dollar Plan.* An employer–employee relationship is not necessary to take advantage of the benefits of a split-dollar insurance plan. For example, parents may be concerned about the lack of life insurance protection for their married child. They may be willing to assist the child's spouse financially in the purchase of insurance on his or her life, but they might not

[59]Reg. § 20.2042-1(c)(6).

[60]However, case law has held that no double inclusion will result if the buy-and-sell agreement is properly drafted, so as to bind the use of the insurance.

wish to do so at the expense of reducing the share of their estate to be passed on to others. In this circumstance, the parents can enter into a split-dollar plan with their child's spouse by the terms of which the parents will receive from the proceeds an amount equal to the premiums they paid. The child will then be protected by insurance on his or her spouse's life at a minimal outlay to them. Since this is not an employer–employee arrangement, there should be no taxable income. The value of the economic benefit received as a result of the arrangement, however, may be treated as a taxable gift from the parents. In most cases, however, a gift tax will not be payable since the economic benefit will not exceed the $10,000 annual exclusion.

## CORPORATE-OWNED LIFE INSURANCE FUNDING OF POSTRETIREMENT BENEFITS

Many employers desire to provide health insurance to a group of executives or to all their employees. With escalating health care costs and with changes in the accounting treatment of postretirement benefits of all types, many plans have been redesigned. **Corporate-owned life insurance** (COLI) has been used in many of these redesigned postretirement plans.

The Financial Accounting Standards Board (FASB) Statement 106 requires that employers accrue these benefits as a charge to earnings and as an on-balance-sheet liability as the benefits are earned, rather than as they are paid (which was the situation formerly). The existence of a balance sheet liability has prompted employers to provide either fully funded plans or other earmarked financing tools, such as life insurance.

Informal funding via COLI does not reduce the balance sheet liability. Rather, it creates a dedicated asset reserve from which benefits ultimately can be financed. The insurance, issued on the life of each covered employee, is owned by and payable to the corporation. The tax-free cash-value buildup can be used to pay the after-tax cost of retiree health insurance or the policy can be held until death (following the cost recovery philosophy mentioned earlier with split-dollar plans).

COLI cash values are assets that meet the accrued liability. Some have argued that a further asset that is equal to the present expected value of future death benefits should also be booked.

COLI proceeds should be received by the corporation free of income tax, provided there are no insurable interest problems—an uncertain situation according to many commentators.[61] Cash values should also accrue income-tax-

---

[61] See, however, Kenneth Black, Jr. and Kenneth Black III, "Insurable Interest and Key-Man Life Insurance Benefits, *CPA Journal*, Vol. 57 (Aug. 1987).

free unless the policies fail the IRC definition of life insurance. Premium payments cannot be deducted from taxable income, although payments to fund employee benefits (whether from policy values or elsewhere) are tax deductible.

Many employers purchase COLI with a view to financing the premiums through tax qualified policy loans.[62] Under these financed plans, interest on policy loans of up to $50,000 can be tax deductible, thus tax-leveraging the tax-deferred inside interest buildup. Some commentators have argued that these financial arrangements, although perhaps technically consistent with the letter of the law, are inconsistent with congressional intent and thereby invite changes in the law.

[62] See Chap. 13 for the requirements that make policy loan interest tax deductible.

# Chapter 16

# *INDIVIDUAL HEALTH INSURANCE: I*

## INTRODUCTION

Throughout the 1980s, U.S. health care costs were rising at a rate roughly three times that of general inflation. Government estimated that these costs represent some 15 percent of U.S. gross domestic product (GDP), with projections of 18 percent and higher by the year 2000. United States health-care spending is 25 percent higher than in other major countries, yet some 37 million citizens have no coverage.[1]

Spiraling health care costs have led to routine premium increases for employer-sponsored plans of 20 percent and more.[2] Because of these increases, the current concentration on cost containment and alternative health care delivery systems is not surprising.

In addition to the cost of health care due to illness and injury, millions of dollars of income are lost each year by employees unable to work because of disability. More than 374,000,000 workdays are lost each year in the United States because of illness or injuries.[3] Income replacement coverage (both individual and employer sponsored) is an important area of activity for insurers and other providers of health insurance protection.

Health insurance is also called accident and health insurance, accident and sickness insurance, and, in the laws of about a dozen states, simply disability insurance. These various terms broadly reference the two categories of health insurance known separately

---

[1] U.S. Health Care Financing Administration

[2] LIMRA, "The Invisible Boarder," *LIMRA's MarketFacts*, Jan./Feb. 1992, p. 38.

[3] Health Insurance Association of America, *Source Book of Health Insurance Data, 1992* (Washington, D.C.: HIAA), p. 104. Unless specifically noted otherwise, all statistical data presented in this chapter are from this source.

as medical expense insurance and disability income insurance. Each category in turn contains various distinctive plans of coverage to protect the insured against specific financial losses from injury or illness.

## HEALTH INSURANCE COVERAGES

Sometimes known as health care insurance, **medical expense insurance** provides a broad range of benefits that can cover virtually all expenses connected with hospital and medical care and related services for the insured and covered family members. Plans may be limited to basic benefits for specific kinds of medical services or may provide comprehensive benefits for all major medical expenses associated with severe injury or long-term illness. Benefits are usually paid as reimbursement of the actual expenses that an insured incurs. Some benefits, however, are paid as fixed amounts without regard to the actual costs of care.

**Disability income insurance**, often called loss of time or loss of income insurance, provides periodic payments when an insured is unable to work because of injury or sickness. Coverage is directly related, at least in part, to the insured's occupational duties and earnings. Benefits are usually paid monthly as fixed amounts while the insured is disabled, although certain business insurance plans may provide reimbursement-type coverage.

## INDIVIDUAL VERSUS GROUP COVERAGE

Both medical expense and disability income insurance are available on either a group or individual basis, although as pointed out below, most medical expense insurance, other than supplemental coverage, is now sold on a group basis, particularly among commercial insurance companies. The distinctions between group and individual insurance arise primarily in the ways in which they are marketed and the manner in which coverage is finally issued and administered.[4]

**Individual health insurance** is an arrangement in which coverage is provided to a specific individual under a policy that is issued solely to that individual. Except in mass marketing approaches, the insured must furnish evidence of insurability before a policy will be issued. Companies maintain separate records for each policy and conduct all transactions, including premium collection, on a direct basis with each insured.

**Group health insurance** refers to arrangements in which coverage is provided for groups of individuals under a single master contract issued to a group policyowner. The policyowner may be an employer, an association, a labor union, a trust, or any other legitimate entity not organized solely for the

---

[4]See chaps. 26 and 27. For a review of all aspects of health insurance, see Health Insurance Association of America, *Individual Health Insurance Part A and Part B* (Washington, DC: HIAA, 1992). See also *Group Life and Health Insurance Part A, Part B, and Part C* (Washington, DC: HIAA, 1992). HIAA course materials are available only to enrollees in HIAA courses, which lead to the Health Insurance Associate (HIA) designation. Contact HIAA Education, Suite 211, 1025 Connecticut Avenue, Washington, D.C., 20036.

purpose of obtaining insurance. Members of larger groups generally obtain coverage without having to furnish evidence of insurability, but evidence usually is required for groups of less than 10 lives, and short medical questionnaires may be required in some plans of up to 100 lives. Group medical expense plans generally cover the group member, his or her spouse, and dependent children.

Each member receives an employee benefit booklet that briefly describes the major provisions relating to medical expense and other employee benefits provided by the plan. The policyowner may pay the entire premium or require a partial contribution from each member, who remains covered while the master contract is in force and he or she maintains a valid relationship with the policyowner. Because of reduced marketing and administrative costs, group health insurance generally costs less than individual plans with comparable coverages.

This chapter provides an overview of individual medical expense insurance and the nature and provisions of the health insurance contract. Since 90 percent of all medical expense insurance coverage provided by life and health insurers is provided through the group mechanism,[5] a detailed treatment of medical expense insurance is deferred until the discussion of employee benefits.[6] By contrast, 38 percent of private-sector disability income insurance protection is provided by individual policies; hence, the specific discussion in the following chapter on disability income insurance and its uses is more comprehensive.

## INDIVIDUAL MEDICAL EXPENSE INSURANCE

### NEED FOR INDIVIDUAL MEDICAL EXPENSE INSURANCE

Individuals not covered by group or government health plans need protection through individual policies. Typical of this group are self-employed persons, students no longer covered by their parents' insurance, and persons under age 65 and not in the work force, such as early retirees and persons between jobs. For some the need is permanent; for others, it is temporary.

Individuals, whose basic need for health insurance is met through group or government plans, may still find that individual policies are useful because they supplement their other coverages. For example, Medicare does not pay for all the expenses of those who are covered by it.[7] Deductible and copayment features are built into the plan. Medicare does not cover some types of medical expenses at all. Furthermore, Medicare administrators set limits on the charges they will recognize as reasonable, so that the insured may end up paying a percentage of

---

[5]*Source Book of Health Insurance Data*, pp. 29–30.
[6]See Chap. 27.
[7]See Chap. 25.

some items covered by Medicare Part B. Many persons, therefore, want individual insurance policies to supplement Medicare and cover the medical expenses that they would otherwise have to pay themselves.

Similarly, many individuals, even though they are covered by a medical expense insurance plan—whether it be group or individual insurance—find that their existing insurance is inadequate for their needs. The plan may pay less than current hospital charges for daily room and board. In addition, there are limits on the amount existing insurance pays for various surgical procedures. Also, the maximum expense covered for a single illness may not be sufficient to cover the cost of some of the more advanced treatment techniques used today. Because of such limitations in their existing medical expense insurance coverage, many persons need some kind of supplemental individual policy. They may merely need a hospital indemnity policy that will pay an additional fixed amount for each day of hospital confinement, or they may want a policy to cover truly catastrophic expenses, with a deductible of several thousand dollars. Such a policy can provide coverage that extends beyond their existing coverage limits.

## Hospital-Surgical Coverage

**Hospital-surgical insurance** policies include specific benefit provisions covering (1) hospital room and board charges, (2) miscellaneous hospital expenses, (3) outpatient diagnostic x-ray and laboratory expenses, (4) maternity expenses, (5) surgical expenses, and (6) charges for physicians' nonsurgical services rendered in a hospital. Insurers market a wide variety of hospital-surgical insurance policies that vary considerably in the degree to which such expenses are covered. These policies are of relatively little significance in the marketplace today. Virtually all of the individual medical expense coverage sold today falls into either the major medical category or the supplementary and special policy category, aimed at specific target needs.

## Major Medical Coverage

**Major medical insurance** plans provide broad coverage and significant protection from large, unpredictable, and therefore unbudgetable medical care expenses. From the beginning, most such plans covered a wide range of medical care charges with few internal limits and a high overall maximum benefit.

*Supplemental Major Medical Expense Plans.* A supplemental major medical expense insurance plan is superimposed on a basic plan provided by the insurer or another company such as Blue Cross/Blue Shield. An insured individual is reimbursed for the charges covered under the reimbursement formulas in the basic plan as if the supplemental plan did not exist. Certain covered expenses are not reimbursed under the basic plan, either because of internal limits in the basic plan design, or because they are outside the scope of the basic plan. Covered expenses not reimbursed under the basic plan are subject to a deductible amount that must be paid by the insured before the supplemental major medical plan will begin reimbursement. This deductible is usually a fixed amount, typically in the range of $500 to $5,000. After this deductible amount has been satisfied, the supplemental major medical plan usually pays a percentage, such as 80 percent, of the remaining covered expenses. Thus, the claimant shares in the claim cost to the extent of the deductible plus the percentage of expenses not reimbursed as a result of the coinsurance provision under the major medical formula.

*Comprehensive Major Medical Plans*. Comprehensive major medical insurance covers virtually all types of medical care services and supplies. The reimbursement formula applies to the total covered expenses subject to a deductible. Thus a simple comprehensive plan could provide for the reimbursement of 80 percent of all combined covered expenses in a calendar year after a deductible of $100, up to a lifetime maximum of $1,000,000. The main advantages of comprehensive major medical plans are simple plan design and avoidance of duplicate coverage.

A variety of modified comprehensive designs were developed that provide some first-dollar coverage. In some plans, certain types of expenses, such as hospital expenses, are not subject to a deductible, and no coinsurance is applied on the initial hospital expenses, such as the first $2,000 or $5,000. Surgeons' fees may be treated similarly, subject to a usual and customary fee limitation. It is possible to waive or modify the deductible and coinsurance features for other services such as physicians' hospital visits and diagnostic tests, thus further matching the basic plus supplemental major medical concept. Most plans today provide a $1,000 or $2,000 maximum annual **out-of-pocket cap** on expenses paid by the insured individual (a stop-loss provision). The elements of a particular plan reflect both the desires of a policyowner and the underwriting practices of the insurer. Diagrams of a comprehensive plan both with and without first-dollar coverage are presented in Figure 16-1.

## SPECIAL INDIVIDUAL INSURANCE COVERAGES

In addition to hospital-surgical, major medical, and comprehensive major medical insurance policies, insurers offer a number of special individual policies to meet the needs of the insuring public. These include (1) hospital confinement indemnity, (2) temporary major medical, (3) Medicare supplement, and (4) specified-disease policies. In addition, in light of an ever-increasing elderly population, and the fact that Medicare does not provide long-term-care benefits, private long-term-care products are appearing on the market.

*Hospital Confinement Indemnity Policies*. In contrast with basic hospital expense insurance that is provided on a *reimbursement basis*, **hospital**

**FIGURE 16-1**
**COMPREHENSIVE MEDICAL POLICIES**

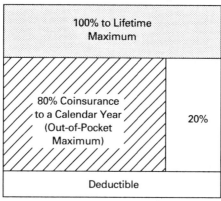

Comprehensive Medical Policy
(without first dollar coverage)

100% to Lifetime
Maximum

80% Coinsurance
to a Calendar Year
(Out-of-Pocket
Maximum)

20%

Deductible

Comprehensive Medical Policy
(with first dollar coverage)

100% to Lifetime
Maximum
(All Covered Expenses)

100%
To a Cap
on
Covered
Hospital
Expense

80% Coinsurance
on other
covered expenses

20%

Deductible

Plan Pays 100%
Plan Pays 80%
Insured Pays

**confinement indemnity** coverage pays a fixed sum for each day of hospital confinement. The benefit is most commonly sold as monthly amounts between $1,000 and $6,000 for continuous confinement of up to one year or more. The monthly amount shown in this way actually is an aggregate of potential daily payments in any 30-day period of hospitalization. Thus a policy that provides a $1,500 monthly payment would pay $50 for each day that the insured was hospitalized.

*Temporary Major Medical Policies.* A short-term version of major medical coverage, **temporary major medical,** is intended to cover an individual whose employment is temporarily interrupted and who does not have access to or does not elect group-priced **COBRA**.[8] Coverage usually continues for three or six months and cannot be renewed, or it is renewable for only one term if the coverage is on a three-month basis. This restriction is consistent with the coverage's purpose.

*Medicare Supplemental Policies*. As the name indicates, this health insurance product provides coverage that supplements the benefits provided by Medicare.[9] In all states, the term **Medicare supplement** may apply only to a policy that meets specific minimum standards set out in insurance law or regulation. Health insurers generally offer two basic types of policies: (1) the Medicare Wraparound policy and (2) the Comprehensive Medicare Supplement policy.

The **Medicare Wraparound** policy provides benefits that cover the deductibles and coinsurance amounts that individuals must pay personally under current Medicare provisions. Such policies may continue to pay benefits for hospital and nursing home confinement after Medicare benefits are exhausted. They may also pay more than the Medicare Part B copayment of 20 percent of "reasonable charges." Coverage, however, is limited through the application of maximum benefit limits.

The **Comprehensive Medicare Supplement** policy is similar to a Medicare Wraparound policy except that it generally has significantly higher maximum benefit limits or is unlimited with respect to the duration of confinement in a hospital or skilled nursing facility. Some comprehensive policies pay benefits toward Medicare Part B expenses that exceed the amount deemed reasonable by Medicare (when the insurer's claim payment exceeds the Medicare payment). They also may provide benefits for a variety of health care expenses that the Medicare program does not cover.

Federal standards contained in the Omnibus Budget Reconciliation Act (OBRA) require that there be a nationwide standardization of Medicare supplemental policies. The NAIC implemented the law in 1991 by designing 10 standard medicare supplemental plans to replace the thousands then on the market. States are required to adopt the standards, and any company selling so-called medigap policies that are not approved by the state or U.S. Department of Health and Human Services is subject to a fine.

*Specified Disease Policies*. So-called **dread disease** coverage refers to individual insurance that pays a variety of benefits up to substantial maximums solely for the treatment of a disease named in the policy, most typically cancer or heart disease. Benefits usually are paid as scheduled amounts of indemnity for designated events, such as hospital confinement, or for specific medical

---

[8]**The Consolidated Omnibus Budget Reconciliation Act of 1985** (COBRA) requires that employers who have more than 25 employees make health care plans available to former employees and qualifying family members for periods ranging from 18 to 36 months.

[9]See Chap. 25.

procedures, such as chemotherapy. Because insurance is limited to medical expenses associated with a single devastating disease, this coverage should be used only to supplement other health insurance.

## LONG-TERM-CARE INSURANCE

**Long-term-care** (LTC) **insurance** promises to pay expenses incurred if an individual needs to enter a nursing home or be cared for in his or her own home. Neither regular medical expense insurance policies nor Medicare covers such expenses.

More and more persons are becoming aware of the extraordinary costs of long-term care. It has been estimated that in 2030 the median age of the population in the United States will be 41.8 years, up from 33 years in 1990. In that year, more than 60 million individuals will be over 65 years of age, compared with about 35 million in 1990. Currently, the average cost of a nursing home stay in the United States is about $35,000 a year. When one considers that the typical confinement length is approximately two years, it is possible to calculate the total cost of nursing home confinement currently at about $70,000. In addition, the demand for nursing home care will have increased by about 80 percent between the years 1980 and 2000.[10]

Long-term-care insurance was first introduced more than 20 years ago. At that time, it was designed and marketed as nursing home insurance without providing coverage for alternative care such as home health care. Because long-term-care insurance was a new product, insurers neither knew how to define eligibility nor how to price it actuarially. Today, long-term-care insurance is into the fifth and sixth generation of policies. Long-term-care insurance products are still evolving to meet consumer needs. LTC benefits can be offered on either an individual or group basis. The LTC market developed initially through the individual product route, but group long-term-care insurance is playing an increasingly important role in this rapidly developing market. In 1987 only two employers offered employee-pay-all LTC insurance that met the industry standard. By mid-1990, however, more than 150 employers were involved. A recent survey indicated that 17 U.S. insurers were offering group long-term insurance policies.[11]

As is the case with any new product line, there is great variation in dollar benefits, definition of covered nursing facilities, length of time after which benefits are paid, limitations on coverage, and eligibility for benefits. The following overview of available current products should be read with this in mind.[12]

[10]Anthony J. Gajda, "Long Term Care Insurance," *Employee Benefits Journal*, June 1989, p. 11.

[11]*Life Insurance News*, May 1992, p. 126.

[12]This overview draws from *Long-Term Care*, 3rd ed. (Indianapolis, IN: Pictorial, Inc., 1992). For a detailed study of long-term care, see Anita Rosen and Valerie S. Wilbur, *Long-Term Care: Needs, Costs, and Financing* (Washington, DC: Health Insurance Association of America, 1992).

## COVERAGE

Most individual LTC policies are underwritten on the basis of the application and the attending physician's statements. Some insurers also interview the proposed insured by telephone, and some require a paramedical examination. Many companies that offer LTC policies utilize a single classification for all acceptable applicants. A few insurers have already refined the classification structure to create three or four categories of insurable classes.

There are three levels of care defined on the market: skilled nursing care, intermediate care, and custodial care. The trend among LTC policies is to provide coverage for all three levels. **Custodial care**, which means nursing home care of a nonmedical nature, is provided to persons who cannot perform basic living activities without assistance. The LTC policies include a list of **activities of daily living** (ADL), such as (1) eating, (2) bathing, (3) dressing, (4) toileting, and (5) transferring (moving about). The typical policy requires only that the insured be unable to perform two of the five ADLs. The NAIC model law requires that LTC policies provide the same level of benefits for all three levels of care. (See Table 16-1.)

Most LTC policies do not require a prior hospital stay before admission to a nursing home, nor do they require that an insured wait a specified number of days after a hospital discharge before he or she can be admitted to a nursing home. A significant number of contracts, however, do require a 30-day wait before admission.

The first LTC policies on the market did not cover senile dementia and Alzheimer's disease. Virtually all LTC policies now cover these two conditions and all other mental illnesses that can be demonstrated to be organically based.

Most LTC policies restrict coverage of **preexisting conditions**—undisclosed sickness that started or an injury that occurred prior to the issuance of the policy. The most common preexisting condition restriction is for six months (some policies use 12 or 24 months), although a few policies have no preexisting condition exclusions. Issue ages vary widely by company, such as 50–84, 55–79, 40–79, and 20–74. Some companies restrict LTC policies to the above-age-40 market, primarily because of concern over AIDS.

## BENEFITS

The benefit provisions in LTC policies set forth what will be payable by the insurer if an insured event occurs. These provisions relate to the types and levels of care for which benefits will be provided, any prerequisites for benefit eligibility, and the actual level of benefits payable.

The policies offered by many companies provide a choice of **elimination (waiting) periods** before benefits become payable. There is considerable variation in the waiting period options offered to consumers. Naturally, the longer the waiting period, the lower the premium, other things being the same.

The buyer is usually offered a choice from a schedule of maximum daily benefits and length of benefit periods. A typical LTC policy might offer the buyer

**TABLE 16-1**

**LEVELS OF NURSING CARE**

---

### Skilled Nursing Care

Skilled nursing care is the highest level of nursing care and demands the greatest expertise. Skilled nursing care is 24-hour care ordered by a physician, and provided by a registered nurse or licensed practical nurse. Often, hospitalization is the only alternative to such care, which can be provided less expensively in a skilled nursing facility.

Sometimes skilled nursing care is provided by a person other than a nurse. Examples include speech, physical, occupational and respiratory therapy provided by a licensed therapist.

### Intermediate Nursing Care

Intermediate nursing care is similar to skilled nursing care except that the patient does not receive or need 24-hour attention. Thus, intermediate nursing care is essentially skilled nursing care provided on a non-continuous basis.

### Custodial Care

Custodial care is the most basic level of nursing care. Custodial care is usually care of a nonmedical nature in which the patient receives assistance with the "activities of daily living." The persons providing custodial care need not be professionally trained nurses or other skilled medical personnel, and indeed, they usually are not. However, a physician must determine the need for custodial care, and a nurse must supervise the provision of such care.

### Home Care

When medical care or therapy is required for a patient living at home, such care is often provided by a visiting nurse or therapist. When personal services such as laundry, cooking and housecleaning are required, such services are usually provided by a visiting homemaker.

Other home care services include transportation to physicians, drugstores and supermarkets; "meals on wheel"--hot meals delivered to seniors living at home; and occasional home visits and telephone calls by volunteers, mostly to lift the spirits of patients.

---

*Source: Long-Term Care* (Indianapolis, Indiana: Pictorial, Inc., 1992), p. 50.

a **daily benefit** schedule of $20 per day, increasing in $10 increments to a maximum of $130 per day. The schedule of the **benefit periods** offered might be 1, 2, 3, or 5 years, or 2, 5, or 10 years. A lifetime benefit is included in only a few policies, but at this stage of development, such coverage is usually quite expensive.

An increasing number of LTC policies provide coverage for **home health care**. Home care is less expensive than nursing home care, and it is typically preferred by the elderly themselves. The maximum daily benefit is often 50 percent of the maximum daily benefit for nursing home care. The length of the benefit period is often the same for both coverages, but some policies require a different waiting period.

While the majority of LTC policies offer some kind of **inflation protection** for an additional premium, most LTC policies do not contain a **restoration of benefits** provision. Where it is included, this restoration of benefits provision states that after the insured has been out of a nursing home for a certain period of time (e.g., six months), full benefits under the policy are restored.

## PREMIUMS

LTC premiums are usually level, although a few companies utilize an increasing premium based on attained age, either annually or at periodic intervals. As would be expected, the annual premium fluctuates widely from one LTC policy to another, depending upon age at issue, waiting period, benefits, and other policy

**FIGURE 16-2**

**SCHEDULE OF ANNUAL PREMIUMS FOR SPECIFIC LTC POLICIES**

Policy #1
20-day waiting period
$80 daily for 6 years

| Age | Premium |
| --- | --- |
| 60 | $ 626 |
| 65 | 1,069 |
| 70 | 2,037 |
| 75 | 3,848 |
| 79 | 5,817 |
| 84 | 8,389 |

Policy #2
30-day waiting period
$80 daily for 5 years

| Age | Premium |
| --- | --- |
| 60 | $ 718 |
| 65 | 1,052 |
| 70 | 1,543 |
| 75 | 2,355 |

10% discount if nonsmoker

Policy #3
20-day waiting period
$80 daily for life

| Age | Premium |
| --- | --- |
| 60 | $ 902 |
| 65 | 1,393 |
| 70 | 2,174 |
| 75 | 3,517 |
| 79 | 5,836 |

Policy #4
No waiting period
$80 daily for life

| Age | Premium |
| --- | --- |
| 60-64 | $ 952 |
| 65-69 | 1,893 |
| 70 | 2,800 |
| 75 | 5,409 |
| 79 | 9,475 |

features. Figure 16-2 summarizes the annual premium schedule of four specific LTC policies at various ages.

Most policies do not require the payment of any fees, but nearly all LTC policies provide for a **waiver of premium**, usually after 60, 90 or 180 days of confinement or days of benefits paid. Some companies provide a discount if both spouses purchase a contract.

## RENEWABILITY

Virtually all LTC policies are issued on a **guaranteed-renewable** basis to some specified age, such as 79. Although the premium can be changed for all insureds of the same class of policies, the company cannot cancel the coverage. Some policies are guaranteed renewable for life. Very few are issued on a **noncancelable** basis (meaning the policy can neither be canceled nor the premium changed).

Figure 16-3 presents a summary of a sample of comprehensive LTC policies.

## REGULATION

As the long-term-care market developed, the NAIC wrote model legislation that has been adopted in a number of states. **The Long-Term-Care Insurance Model Act and Regulation** specifies minimum standards that products must meet to be considered long-term-care insurance. The model includes the following major provisions:

- Insurers must provide an outline of coverage and summarize the features of the policy.
- The individual policyowner must have a "free-look" period during which the policy can be canceled and the premiums returned for any reason.
- Waivers denying coverage for specific health conditions are prohibited.
- Insurers may not offer substantially greater benefits for skilled nursing care than for intermediate or custodial care.
- Policies must be guaranteed renewable, although state insurance commissioners may allow cancellation in limited circumstances.

The NAIC is considering amending the Long-Term-Care Model Act to require insurers to offer nonforfeiture benefits to LTC policyowners. Because of the recognition of the fact that product premiums would be significantly impacted, the approach appears to be taking the form of a mandated offer to consumers of an option to purchase products containing nonforfeiture benefits, without requiring that such benefits be included in all products offered.

The long-term-care insurance market is growing steadily. New products are being developed in an effort to meet the needs of the elderly. Of course, the need is not restricted to the United States. The projected aged 65 and above population

**FIGURE 16-3**

**SAMPLE LONG TERM CARE POLICIES**
*Source:Life Association News*, May 1992

| Policy | Premium at Age 55** | Premium at Age 65** | Age limit on purchase | Elimination period (days) | Maximum daily benefit | Benefit period (years) | Policy coordinates with Medicare | Prior hospital stay required |
|---|---|---|---|---|---|---|---|---|
| A | $320 | $680 | 18-84 | 0,30 & 100 | $100 | 2-5 | No | No |
| B | $358 | $901 | 55-85 | 0,30 & 90 | $120 | 2-10 & lifetime | Yes | No |
| C | $313 | $782 | 40-84 | 20,90, 180 & 365 | $120 | 2-6 | No | No |
| D | $480 | $920 | 50-84 | 0 & 100 | $150 | 1 to lifetime | Yes | No |
| E | $497 | $1,400 | 40-84 | 20 & 100 | $100 | 1-4 & lifetime | Yes | No |
| F | $538 | $947 | 20-79 | 30 & 90 | 100 % of expenses | Depends on policy | Yes | No |

among member countries of the Organization for Economic Cooperation and Development (OECD) shows a 91 percent increase between the years 1980 and 2050 and an increase in excess of 200 percent in the number of persons aged 80 and above during the same time period.[13]

The number of insurers world-wide that provide any type of long-term-care insurance has been growing rapidly, and, given the demand for health care of the elderly, many more are likely to enter this market in the future. Reinsurance facilities have been developed that provide support programs and guidelines that will make it possible for more small insurers to enter this market. The product development has been evolving quite rapidly. Continued interest on the part of federal and state government regulators and consumer advocate groups ensure that this high level of activity will continue. As additional data are generated regarding claims experience and individual policy provisions, the life insurance industry will be able to continue to refine its underwriting and classification structure.

## THE HEALTH INSURANCE CONTRACT

Health and life insurance policies share the common elements of general contract law and resemble each other in overall structure. However, individual health insurance contracts are more complex than those used in life insurance, since more than one loss may occur while the policy is in force, a more varied spectrum of losses is present, and the cause of loss is more often subjective. As a result, health insurance contracts require a much larger number of technical definitions and provide a greater range of optional coverages.

Of all insurance lines, disability income policies are the least amenable to generalized analysis and comparison. Such contracts are designed to permit flexible adaptation to the individual needs of the insured through a broad range of interrelated benefit patterns and optional coverages. Probably no other type of insurance relies as heavily on subtle distinctions in benefits and the language used to describe them.

Contract design and language differ from insurer to insurer and, often, from policy to policy within the same company. Intense competitive pressures force insurers to find that unique provision or that more precise definition that will distinguish their policies in the marketplace. Companies constantly change contracts as they restate old concepts in new ways and introduce innovative coverages for the disability risk. Nonetheless, there are basic criteria to be used for thoughtful analysis and evaluation of all individual health insurance contracts.

### REGULATORY CONSTRAINTS

The insurance laws of all states govern the form and content of the individual health insurance contract. Almost every form in use must be filed for approval of the insurance department in the state where it will be issued or delivered. In general, an insurance department can disapprove a form if it contains any

[13]Swiss Reinsurance Company, *Long Term Care Insurance* (Zurich, Switzerland: SRC, 1989), p. 5.

provision that is judged to be deceptive, inequitable, or misleading; or if the benefits provided are unreasonable in relation to the premiums charged.

All states have adopted some version of the NAIC **Model Uniform Policy Provisions Law** that covers matters as diverse as the size of type in which a form may be printed to the wording of certain provisions that must appear in the policy. Many states mandate specific benefits that must be included in individual health insurance policies. About two dozen states have regulations to standardize policy content, to prohibit uneconomic coverages, and to establish minimum standards for benefit amounts, definitions, and limitations in health insurance contracts.

Over one-half of the states have laws that require insurers to write insurance contracts in simplified language that is accessible to anyone with the equivalent of a tenth-grade education. At the time each form is filed with the insurance department, the insurer must certify that the form is readable on the basis of certain standard tests of written material.

As an adjunct to the state insurance laws, the decisions of various state and federal courts have an important effect on the way that health insurance contracts are written. These judicial opinions may give new interpretations to prevailing insurance principles or may restate existing insurance law. Also, the structure of the health insurance contract is influenced by federal laws on taxes, social insurance programs, human rights, and employment benefits.

## The Contractual Agreement

The health insurance contract is a financial agreement between the insured and the insurance company. It is a conditional promise of the insurer, made in exchange for the insured's premiums, to pay benefits at some future time if the insured suffers a covered loss. The policy describes in detail the rights and obligations of both the insured and the insurer.

For a loss to be paid, the insured must have kept the policy in force through the timely payment of premiums, and the insured must have suffered an economic or physical loss of the kind defined in the policy. Timely notice and satisfactory proof of loss must be furnished when there is a claim. If the insured meets all of these conditions, the insurer must renew the policy according to its terms, provide prompt service to help the insured file claims, and pay benefits when a valid loss occurs.

## Basic Elements

Six basic elements are common to all individual health insurance policies. These are: (1) the insuring clause, (2) the consideration clause, (3) the renewal provisions, (4) the exclusion provisions, (5) the general provisions, and (6) the benefit provisions.

All states require that the renewal provision, or a summary of it, be printed on the first page of the policy. In most states, the first page must also include a free-look provision that usually allows the insured a period of ten days from receipt of the policy in which to review it and, if desired, return it for a full refund of premiums paid.

With these two exceptions, companies are permitted to arrange the contract in whatever manner they choose, provided the overall appearance does not give undue prominence to any part of the text or create a misleading document. Most insurers draft a single policy to meet the requirements of the majority of states in which they operate and attach riders to modify the contract for use in states with special requirements.

## PROVISIONS IN HEALTH INSURANCE CONTRACTS

### THE INSURING CLAUSE

The insuring clause contains the company's promise to pay benefits. It also may describe the types of losses that the policy will cover, or it may simply tie the promise to all of the terms and limitations of the policy. The clause appears on the first page of the policy above the facsimile signatures of the secretary and president of the company.

Over the years, the insuring clause has evolved from a cumbersome provision, filled with complicated definitions and exclusions, to a reasonably simple and straightforward statement of the company's agreement to provide insurance. The following examples are taken from disability income contracts of four leading insurers and they display the various forms that the insuring clause may take.

In the first example, the insurer specifies the types of loss against which insurance is provided and defines the two causes from which loss must result:

> Subject to all the provisions of this policy, we insure you against disability or other loss resulting from:
> - *sickness*, which first makes itself known while this policy is in force; or
> - *injury*, which is accidental bodily injury that occurs while this policy is in force.

The second insurer includes the same elements as does the first, but it merely identifies the causes of loss, which are then defined elsewhere in the policy:

> We will pay for Total Disability or other covered loss resulting from Injuries or Sickness subject to the definitions, exclusions, and other provisions of this policy. Loss must begin while this policy is in force.

A third insurer uses only a simple sentence to promise insurance for loss that results from two specific causes:

> The company will pay the benefits provided in this Policy for loss due to Injury or Sickness.

In the final example, the insurer embraces the entire policy without otherwise identifying the kinds of loss or their causes:

The Company hereby furnishes insurance to the extent set out in this policy. All of the provisions on this and the pages which follow are part of this policy.

## THE CONSIDERATION CLAUSE

The consideration clause summarizes the factors that led the insurer to issue the policy and represents the insured's part of the insurance agreement. It generally is a simple statement that the insured has completed an application and paid a premium in exchange for the company's promise to provide insurance. The clause usually appears in or near the general provisions of the policy, although several major insurers omit it entirely from their contracts.

In the past, the consideration clause often was combined with the insuring clause or appeared in close conjunction with it. Regardless of where they are found in the policy, however, the two clauses together reflect the underlying principle of contract law that two parties have agreed in a "meeting of the minds."

Most companies use the consideration clause to make the application a part of the policy. Unless a copy of the application is included in the policy, the insurer cannot at a later time contest the insurance contract because of any misstatements or misrepresentations made by the insured in answer to questions in the application. The following example from a disability income policy is typical of the consideration clause:

> We have issued this policy in consideration of the representations in your application and payment of the first term premium. A copy of your application is attached and is a part of this policy.

## RENEWAL PROVISIONS

The renewal provision describes the renewal and premium arrangements of the policy. Individual health insurance contracts are classified according to their renewal rights, of which the most common are (1) noncancelable, (2) guaranteed renewable, or (3) conditionally renewable.

Renewal rights carry differing costs. Noncancelable policies have guaranteed premiums and are likely to be more expensive than those for which premiums can be changed. Policies that the company can refuse to renew under certain conditions and in which premiums can change generally are the least expensive forms of individual health insurance.

The various state insurance laws and regulations are not uniform in defining these renewal categories. Some states allow termination of guaranteed renewal rights in disability income policies at age 60, or earlier, or at the time the insured qualifies for retirement benefits under the Social Security Act. The definitions that follow are those in common use for each category in policies offered by the leading disability income companies.

*Noncancelable Contracts*.  A **noncancelable** policy gives the insured the right to renew the policy, typically to age 65, by timely payment of a stipulated premium. A guaranteed premium rate is set forth in the contract and may not be changed by the insurer. During that period, the company cannot cancel the policy or make any unilateral change in its benefits. This renewal category generally is limited to disability income insurance.

*Guaranteed Renewable Contracts*.  A **guaranteed renewable** policy also gives the insured the right to renew the policy, typically to age 65, by timely payment of the premium. During that period, however, the company has the right to change the premiums for all insureds of the same class at their original insuring ages, but it cannot cancel the policy or make any unilateral change in its benefits. This renewal category is used for both medical expense and disability income insurance.

*Conditionally Renewable Contracts*.  A **conditionally renewable** policy gives the insured a limited right to renew the policy to age 65, or some later age, by timely payment of the premium. The insurer has the right to refuse to renew coverage only for reasons stated in the policy by giving written notice to the insured 30 days in advance of the premium-due date. The insurer usually retains the right to change premiums and benefits for all insureds of the same class. This renewal category is used for both medical expense and disability income insurance.

The stated reasons for nonrenewal vary according to the type of insurance, but the insurer cannot refuse to renew coverage solely because of a change in the insured's health after the policy has been issued. The company may refuse to renew a specific class of insureds or may discontinue a policy series for all insureds in a single state. On an individual basis, the insurer may refuse to renew when the insured changes to a more hazardous occupation, when the economic need for the policy ends, or when the insured becomes overinsured through purchase of other insurance that will provide benefits in excess of the expected loss.

This provision is used in most specialized business disability income forms other than overhead expense insurance (see below). In such policies, the company retains the right not to renew on an individual basis when the covered business risk no longer exists or when other specified events occur. The insurer also may have the right to change benefits, but usually it guarantees that the premium rates will not change.

The conditional renewal provision appears uniformly in noncancelable and guaranteed renewable disability income policies to provide continuous coverage from age 65 to age 75 while the insured remains employed on a full-time basis. During this period, the insured pays a renewal premium at the rates then in effect for persons of the same attained age and class of risk. Monthly indemnity amounts are rarely reduced, but the benefit period usually is limited to two years during the conditional renewal period.

## EXCLUSION PROVISIONS

Most limitations in disability income contracts occur through operation of various definitions related to the benefit provisions. Also, sometimes it is deemed necessary to attach a rider or waiver to the policy of an individual insured, to exclude benefits for a specific health condition that was named in the application. All health insurance policies, however, contain a general exclusion provision to exclude loss for certain unpredictable or uncontrollable events.

The most common exclusion in disability income contracts provides that the policy will not cover loss that begins in the first two policy years from a preexisting condition. As a general concept, a **preexisting condition** is an undisclosed health condition that was present within a specified number of years before the policy was issued and required medical attention or caused symptoms for which a prudent person would have sought medical care.

The precise definition of a preexisting condition differs among the states. Some limit the period of treatment or symptoms to five years before the date of application. In others, it is held to one or two years, and three major states do not allow use of the prudent person test. The preexisting condition exclusion applies only to health conditions that the insured did not reveal in the application. Health conditions fully disclosed on the application are covered unless the insurer attaches a rider to exclude a condition by specific name or description.

Insurers may also exclude loss caused by war or act of war and by intentionally self-inflicted injury. Until recent years, all individual disability income contracts used an exclusion for normal uncomplicated pregnancy and childbirth. The major companies now omit the pregnancy exclusion in disability income policies intended for their most favorable occupational classes. Individual medical expense policies contain more numerous exclusions, similar to those of group insurance.[14]

A final important limitation, which is no longer part of the exclusion provision, appears in the general provisions of the policy and calls for the suspension of coverage while the insured is on active duty in the military service of any country or international authority. This **military suspense provision** allows the insured to place the policy back in force without evidence of good health when active duty ends.

## GENERAL PROVISIONS

The general provisions deal with premium matters, claims administration, and various legal rights of the insured and the insurer. Most of them are prescribed in the NAIC **Model Uniform Individual Accident and Sickness Policy Provisions Law**. Known as the Uniform Policy Provision Law (UPPL), it has been adopted in some version in all states. An insurer must use language at least

[14]See Chap. 27.

as favorable as the law's 12 required and 11 optional provisions, although provisions that are inconsistent with the coverage of the policy may be omitted.

*Required Provisions.* The three most significant of the required provisions allow a **grace period** of 31 days for payment of premiums, permit **reinstatement** under specific conditions if the policy has lapsed, and make the policy **incontestable** after two years so that the insurer cannot use misstatements in the application to void the policy or deny a claim. Several major insurers use the **time limit on certain defenses** to gain a fraudulent misstatement defense. The alternative incontestable provision does not permit a fraud defense after the contestable period whereas the time-limit-on-certain-defenses provision permits a challenge based on fraud.

The remaining mandatory provisions deal primarily with payment of claims and the periods of time within which the insured must give notice of claim and proof of loss. The required provisions are used uniformly among all insurers in both medical expense and disability income policies.

*Optional Provisions.* Most major insurers use only those optional provisions of the UPPL that allow for a benefit adjustment because of **misstatement of age** and that amend the contract to the minimum requirements of state law in **conformity with state statutes**. The remaining optional provisions generally are inappropriate for and not used with noncancelable or guaranteed renewable policies, since they deal with various benefit reductions or exclusions because of other insurance or changes in the insured's occupation or earnings after the date of policy issue.

## BENEFIT PROVISIONS

The benefit provisions are the central element of all health insurance contracts and describe in detail the conditions for benefit payment. Chapter 17 analyzes the various components of the benefit provisions in personal disability income policies. The comparable provisions of individual medical expense policies are in most respects identical to those for group medical expense insurance discussed later, and so they will not be duplicated here.[15]

[15]See Chap. 27.

# Chapter 17

# *INDIVIDUAL HEALTH INSURANCE: II*

## DISABILITY INCOME INSURANCE

Individual disability income policies are designed to provide monthly benefits to replace lost income when the insured is disabled as the result of sickness or injury. The primary policy benefits usually are clustered together in the contract under a prominent heading, and any supplemental or optional benefits appear in rider forms attached to the policy. Many companies' electronic systems integrate basic and optional coverages within a computer-printed policy that does away with the need for attachable riders.

The basic benefit arrangement in the policies of the major insurers consists of a monthly benefit for total disability and a waiver of premium benefit. The supplemental coverages most commonly include a monthly benefit for residual or partial disability; a monthly benefit paid when certain social insurance programs fail to provide benefits; a cost of living benefit; and a guarantee for purchase of additional insurance at a later date. These provisions are augmented by a policy schedule that summarizes the available benefits and by a series of technical definitions that control and limit the way in which benefits are administered.

The policy schedule is a computer-printed summary of the principal benefits of the insurance policy, including any supplemental coverages, and it usually appears immediately after the policy cover page. The schedule shows the effective date of insurance, identifies the insured and policyowner (if different), and displays the benefit amounts and the premiums charged for them.

## IMPORTANT DEFINITIONS

The technical definitions may be included in the benefit provisions, but more typically they form a separate part of the policy intended to define terms that are used to evaluate loss and control payment of benefits. Among the most important of these are the definitions of injury, sickness, preexisting conditions, and disability.

The major insurance companies uniformly define injury to mean **accidental bodily injury** that occurs while the policy is in force. This definition employs "results" language and has replaced an older provision that was known as an "accidental means" clause The distinction between the two definitions is important, since not all accidental bodily injuries result from accidental means.

Under the **accidental means** clause, a bodily injury must meet two tests to be a covered loss: both the *cause* of the injury and the *result* (the injury itself) must be unforeseen or unexpected. For example, a person who deliberately jumps from a wall and breaks a leg would not have a covered loss under the accidental means clause. Although the result—a broken leg—was unexpected, the cause—a voluntary leap—was not. On the other hand, loss would be covered under the accidental bodily injury definition, since the broken leg was an unexpected result even though the precipitating act was intentional. Most states now prohibit use of the accidental means clause in health insurance contracts.

Most leading insurers define sickness to mean sickness or disease that *first manifests* itself while the policy is in force. Some insurers use a modification of the "first manifest language" so that sickness means a sickness or disease that is *first diagnosed and treated* while the policy is in force. In either case, the intention is to cover only sickness that is first contracted after the policy takes effect.

Use of the **preexisting condition** limitation is customary in policies that contain a first-manifest or first-diagnosed definition of sickness. The limitation applies in the first two policy years, in order to exclude benefits for any loss that results from a medical condition that the insured misrepresented or failed to disclose in the insurance application. Although the limitation may vary from state to state, the following is typical of how a preexisting condition is defined:

> Preexisting condition means a medical condition which exists on the Effective Date and during the past five years either:
>
> 1. caused you to receive medical advice or treatment; or
> 2. caused symptoms for which an ordinarily prudent person would seek medical advice or treatment.

## DEFINING DISABILITY

Traditionally, individual disability income policies have been called "loss of time" insurance, because of the occupational definitions used to qualify the insured as disabled. A disabled person under these types of policies is presumed to have suffered a loss of income because he or she cannot be present in the workplace. The definitions of total disability and partial disability are premised on the inability of the insured to perform certain occupational tasks. In recent years, the concept of residual disability has largely replaced the partial disability provision as a means of paying proportionate benefits to an insured who will be working at reduced earnings as a result of sickness or injury. The residual concept differs from conventional indemnity plans, since it emphasizes protection of income rather than protection of occupational performance.

Essentially, insurance companies define **total disability** in two different ways. One is an **any gainful occupation** definition, which is popularly, if somewhat inaccurately, called "any occ." The other is an **own occupation** definition, which is usually referred to as "own occ."

Under an "any gainful occupation" clause, insureds are considered totally disabled when they cannot perform the major duties of any gainful occupation for which they are reasonably suited because of education, training, or experience.[1] Since the insured may be able to work at any of several suitable occupations even though he or she is incapable of working at his or her regular job, this clause is a more restrictive definition of disability than the "own occupation" definition. It can limit recovery of benefits under the policy.

On the other hand, an "own occupation" clause deems insureds to be totally disabled when they cannot perform the major duties of their regular occupations. A regular occupation is the one in which the insured was engaged at the time disability began. Under this definition, insureds can be at work in some other capacity and still be entitled to policy benefits if they cannot perform the important tasks of their own occupations in the usual way.

A number of insurers further define regular occupation as the recognized specialty (or recognized subspecialty) in which a medical, dental, legal, or accounting professional was engaged at the time disability began—for example, an orthopedic surgeon will be totally disabled, even while at work in a general medical practice, as long as he or she cannot perform the customary duties associated with orthopedic surgery.

The most common variation of the "own occupation" definition is the one that deems insureds to be totally disabled as long as they (1) cannot perform the major duties of their regular occupation and (2) are not at work in any other occupation. If insureds are disabled for their regular job, the insurance company can terminate disability benefits only if they voluntarily have chosen to work at some other job. If this provision is used, the company cannot insist that insureds resume work in some other suitable occupation.

---

[1] Although this is not commonly encountered today, except in limited benefit policies, some policies at one time provided that insureds were considered totally disabled only if they were unable to engage in *any* occupation. This exceedingly narrow definition generally has been supplanted by the newer "any occ" definition because of company practice and law.

Since several states require an "own occupation" definition for at least the first year of claim, the leading disability writers often combine both occupation clauses in the same policy form, to provide an "own occupation" definition for a specified period of time and an "any occupation" definition after that. The specified period will vary between two and ten years in the policies of the major insurers. Many insurers allow "own occupation" coverage to age 65 for their most favorable classes of insureds.

The following example is taken from a leading insurer's loss of time policy, which is available to its next-to-most-favorable rating class:

> Total Disability, before age 55 or before benefits have been paid for five years for a period of disability, whichever is later, means that due to Injuries or Sickness:
>
> 1. you are unable to perform the duties of your occupation; and
> 2. you are under the care and attendance of a physician.
>
> After you attain age 55 or after benefits have been paid for five years for a period of disability, whichever is later, Total Disability means that due to Injuries or Sickness:
>
> 1. you are unable to engage in any gainful occupation in which you might reasonably be expected to engage because of education, training, or experience, with due regard to your vocation and earnings at the start of disability; and
> 2. you are under the care and attendance of a physician.

Almost all insurers specify in the definition of disability or in a separate policy provision that an insured must be under the care and attendance of a physician to qualify for disability benefits. Most insurers do not interpret the medical care requirement literally, since common sense and various court decisions dictate that an insurer cannot deny benefits under this provision if medical care is not essential to the disabled insured's well-being or recovery. The insurer cannot insist that an insured maintain a physician-patient relationship for the sole purpose of certifying a disability.

It is common to include a definition of **presumptive disability** in policies that provide benefits for total disability. Under the presumptive clause, an insured is always considered totally disabled, even if he or she is at work, if sickness or injury results in the loss of the sight of both eyes, the hearing of both ears, the power of speech, or the use of any two limbs. Usually, the insurer begins benefits immediately upon the date of loss and waives the medical care requirement. The insured can work in any occupation and full benefits will be paid to the end of the policy's benefit period, while the loss continues.

## BASIC COMPONENTS OF THE BENEFIT PROVISION

Three basic components establish the premium and define the payment of benefits under disability income policies: (1) the elimination period, (2) the benefit period, and (3) the amount of monthly indemnity. All other parts of the policy relate to these common elements and are used to limit or expand their value in meeting the specific needs of the insureds at the time of loss. The strength of a particular disability income plan lies in how liberally the insurance company permits these elements to operate within the policy provisions and through its own administrative practices.

*The Elimination Period.* The **elimination period**, sometimes called the **waiting period**, refers to the number of days at the start of disability during which no benefits are paid. It is a limitation on benefits that is somewhat like the deductible used in medical expense insurance. It is meant to exclude the inconsequential illness or injury that disables the insured for only a few days and that is more economically met by using personal funds.

In general, insurers make available elimination periods of 30 days, 2 months, 3 months, 6 months, and 1 year. Since indemnities of the policy are paid at the end of each month of continuing disability, a 3-month elimination period usually means that a disabled insured will not receive benefits for at least 120 days from the time sickness began or injury occurred. Premiums are lower for policies with longer elimination periods. Most insurers require that the elimination period be the same for sickness and injury.

The major insurers allow for a temporary break in the elimination period so that the insured will not be penalized for any brief attempt to return to work before the elimination period has expired at the start of disability. The brief recovery generally is limited to six months or, if less, to the length of the elimination period. If the insured is then again disabled because of the same or a different cause after the interruption, the insurer combines the two periods of disability to satisfy the elimination period.

*The Benefit Period.* The **benefit period** is the longest period of time for which benefits will be paid under the disability policy. Usually the benefit period is the same for sickness and injury and is available for durations of two or five years, to age 65, and for life provided continuous, total disability begins before age 55, age 60, or (less commonly) age 65.

Most disabilities are of short duration. Roughly 98 percent of all disabled persons recover before one year has elapsed, and most disabled individuals recover within six months of the time disability began. On the other hand, if disability lasts beyond 12 months, chances of a return to productive work diminish markedly, particularly at older ages. The effect of extended disability can be financially devastating. Long benefit periods are more consistent with sound personal risk management principles.

All insurers include a provision that is related to the benefit period and that deals with consecutive or recurrent episodes of disability and identifies whether the company is dealing with a new or continuing claim. The typical provision states that the company will consider **recurrent periods of disability** from the same cause to be one continuous period of disability, unless each period is separated by a recovery of six months or more.

Among the major insurers, use of a 12-month recurrent provision is becoming common in policies with benefit periods to age 65 or longer. Oddly, a few state insurance departments prohibit this liberalized provision. The provision is to an insured's advantage, since a new elimination period will not be required for disability that recurs more than six months, but less than a year, after a brief recovery in a long-term claim.

This recurrence language protects the insured from multiple elimination periods, so that benefits for recurring loss due to the same cause become payable immediately for the unused portion of the original benefit period. Conversely, the provision allows for a new benefit period, and a new elimination period, if loss results from a different cause at any time after an earlier disability, or if loss recurs due to the same cause more than six months after recovery.

*The Benefit Amount.* The benefit of the personal disability income policy is almost always payable as a fixed amount of **monthly indemnity**. The indemnity for total disability generally is written on a **valued basis**, which means that the stated policy benefit is presumed to equal the actual monetary loss sustained by the disabled insured. This valued amount is not adjusted to the insured's earnings or other insurance payments at the time of claim for total or partial disability. During a period of residual disability, however, indemnity may be reduced in proportion to lost earnings of the insured. (See below.)

Insurers limit the amount of disability income coverage they sell to an applicant so that the total of all monthly indemnity does not exceed 85 percent of earned income for insureds with low annual incomes, and grading downward to about 65 percent or less for those in the highest income brackets. These limits take into account other compensation that may be available to the disabled insured (e.g., employer sick-pay plans, government programs, and other personal or group insurance). Insurers may also reduce these limits for individuals with significant unearned income or for those with net worths exceeding $3,000,000.

These limits are intended to avoid overinsurance, which occurs when benefits equal or exceed a disabled insured's pre-disability income. Insurers agree that overinsurance provides little incentive for a disabled insured to return to work, and, as a result, recovery often is delayed or does not occur at all. Existing insurance laws do not provide an effective mechanism for controlling overinsurance at point of claim, so companies must rely almost entirely on issue limits at the time of underwriting to avoid its effects.

Nevertheless, under the regular limits of the leading disability writers for personal insurance, an insured with adequate income in the more favorable risk classifications may acquire up to a maximum of $15,000 to $20,000 in monthly indemnity for total disability. This amount generally is separate from indemnity limits established for special business insurance policies, such as overhead expense insurance.

## BASIC BENEFIT ARRANGEMENTS

The basic benefit arrangement of a noncancelable disability income insurance policy consists of the benefit for total disability and a benefit for waiver of premium. These two components are common to all insurers, regardless of any additional coverages that may be included directly in the policy form. The benefit provision usually describes the circumstances of loss, the way in which the company will pay benefits, and at what point benefits may end.

*Total Disability Benefit.* The following is typical of the benefit provision for total disability:

> When you are totally disabled, we will pay the monthly indemnity as follows:
> * You must become totally disabled while this policy is in force.
> * You must remain so to the end of the elimination period. No indemnity is payable during that period.
> * After that, monthly indemnity will be payable at the end of each month while you are totally disabled.
> * Monthly indemnity will stop at the end of the benefit period or, if earlier, on the date you are no longer totally disabled.

*Waiver-of-Premium Benefit.* The waiver-of-premium benefit characteristically waives any premiums that fall due after the insured has been totally disabled for the shorter of 90 consecutive days or the elimination period, and it allows for refund of any premiums paid during this period. Further premiums are waived while the insured remains disabled, until age 65. Some insurers also may waive premiums that fall due within 90 days after recovery. The waiver-of-premium feature invariably terminates when the insured attains age 65.

*Other Benefits in the Basic Provision.* The basic provision often contains a number of minor but competitively necessary provisions that are not appropriate as optional benefit riders, since they do not carry a significant premium consideration. These supplemental benefit provisions include a transplant benefit, a rehabilitation benefit, a nondisabling injury benefit, and a principal (capital) sum benefit.

The **transplant benefit** provides that if the insured is totally disabled because of the transplant of an organ from his or her body to the body of another individual, the insurer will deem him or her to be disabled as a result of sickness. This provision also includes cosmetic surgery performed to correct appearance or a disfigurement.

The **rehabilitation benefit** generally allows a specific sum, often 12 times the sum of the monthly indemnity and any supplemental indemnities, to cover costs not paid by other insurance or public funding when the insured enrolls in a formal retraining program that will help him or her return to work.

The **nondisabling injury benefit** pays up to a specific sum, usually one-quarter of the monthly indemnity, to reimburse the insured for medical expenses incurred for treatment of an injury that did not result in total disability.

The **principal sum benefit** is a lump-sum amount payable if the insured dies accidentally. This provision requires that death be caused directly and independently by injury and that it occur within a specified number of days, usually 90 or 180, following the date of the accident.

The principal sum amount benefit also pays a lump sum, usually 12 times the sum of the monthly indemnity and any supplemental indemnities, if sickness or injury results in dismemberment or loss of sight and the insured survives the loss for 30 days. The lump sum is in addition to any other indemnity payable under the policy, and it is payable for two such losses in the insured's lifetime. The principal sum benefit usually is limited to the irrecoverable loss of the sight of one eye or the complete loss of a hand or foot through severance above the wrist or ankle.

## SUPPLEMENTAL OR OPTIONAL BENEFITS

Among the leading insurers, the most common optional or supplemental benefits are: (1) a residual disability benefit, (2) a partial disability benefit, (3) a social insurance supplement, (4) an inflation-protection benefit, and (5) provisions for increased future benefit amounts. Although some insurers may include one or more of these benefits in the basic benefit provision, they are more frequently available for an additional premium as optional benefit riders that are attached to the policy. The benefits and the premiums of each optional rider generally are shown on the schedule page.

*Residual Disability Benefit.* The **residual disability benefit** provides reduced monthly indemnity in proportion to the insured's loss of income when he or she has returned to work at reduced earnings. In policies that provide for a regular occupational definition of total disability, the residual benefit is payable only when the insured has returned to work in his or her own occupation. Most insurers allow the insured to be either totally or residually disabled to satisfy the elimination period of the policy and to qualify for waiver of premium.

The most common definition of residual disability employs a "time and duties" test that combines both occupational and income considerations, as follows:

Residual disability means that due to Injuries or Sickness:

1. you are not able to do one or more of your important daily business duties or you are not able to do your usual daily business duties for as much time as it would normally take for you to do them;

2.  your Loss of Monthly Income is at least 25 percent of your Prior Monthly Income; and

3.  you are under the care and attendance of a physician.

An alternative definition of residual disability is referred to as a pure income test and rests solely on loss of earnings:

> Residual disability means that you are engaged in your regular occupation and your Income is reduced due to Accident or Sickness by at least 20 percent of your Prior Income.

The specialty definition of total disability may also be used during residual disability, to avoid ambiguity in the event the insured is deemed totally disabled for his or her professional specialty but is at work and earning reduced income in a general practice. These definitions are commonly restricted to regular occupations, to avoid ambiguity when total disability is based on the "own occupation" provision.

Most insurers do not require that an insured sustain a prior period of total disability before claiming residual benefits. In effect, a residual claim can begin on the incurrence date, and reduced indemnity is payable at the end of the elimination period for the duration of the benefit period. From a practical standpoint, the vast majority of residual claims follow some period of total disability. Residual claims make up only a small portion of all disability claims, whether from incurrence date or as continuation following prior total disability.

The provisions for residual disability resemble those used for total disability, but they are accompanied by a series of technical definitions in order to define prior and current income and to describe the formula employed to compute the proportionate benefits. The customary formula is:

$$\text{residual indemnity} = \frac{\text{loss of income}}{\text{prior income}} \times \text{monthly indemnity amount}$$

In this formula, **loss of income** means the difference between the insured's prior income and current income. Usually, loss of income in excess of 75 to 80 percent of prior income is considered to be 100 percent loss. In all cases, income refers only to earned income and excludes unearned income from savings, investments, or real property.

**Prior income** is usually defined as the average monthly income for the tax year, with the highest earnings in the two or three years immediately before the date on which the insured became disabled. Most insurers index prior income at the end of each year of claim to adjust for increases in the cost of living.

**Current income** means the insured's earned income in each month while he or she is residually disabled. Insurers differ in their treatment of current income, but they calculate it either on the basis of cash actually received or on an accrual method, to exclude income that was earned but not collected before disability began.

For example, assume that Jerry, who is residually disabled, is receiving current income of $1,000 per month, but that he had a prior income of $3,000 per month. Assume also that the monthly indemnity is $2,000. Jerry could collect $1,333 under the residual benefit, which is calculated as follows:

$$\text{residual indemnity} = \frac{\$3,000 - \$1,000}{\$3,000} \text{ x } \$2,000 = \$1,333$$

Some insurers apply the residual benefit formula strictly throughout the benefit period. Several insurers use the exact rate of current income to compute benefits for the first six months of payment and then average current income at six-month intervals for the remainder of the claim. Other insurers guarantee a minimum benefit during the first six months of a residual claim by providing the greater of the residual indemnity from the formula or 50 percent of the monthly indemnity for total disability. The residual benefit is payable for the duration of the policy benefit period or until loss of income is less than 20 or 25 percent of prior income. Insurers usually do not renew residual disability provisions after the insured attains age 65.

*Partial Disability Benefit.* The residual concept generally has replaced the **partial disability benefit** for most professional and white-collar occupations. Many insurers, however, provide a partial disability provision as an optional benefit for their less favorable occupational risks. The typical partial indemnity is 50 percent of the monthly indemnity for total disability. It is payable for up to six months or, if less, for the remainder of the policy benefit period when the insured has returned to work on a limited basis after a period of compensable total disability. Partial disability customarily is defined in occupational terms with reference to time and duties. The following is typical of this definition:

Partial disability means that you are at work, but because of sickness or injury:

    1. you are unable to perform one or more, but not all of the major duties of your occupation; or,

    2. you are not able to be present at work for more than one-half of the time required in your usual work week.

*Social Insurance Supplement.* The **social insurance supplement** (SIS), or social insurance substitute, evolved as a response to the underwriting problem that is created by the existence of substantial benefits potentially available for disability under workers' compensation or for disability or retirement under the Social Security Act. Most insurance companies take these substantial benefits into account and, to avoid overinsurance at a later time, sharply limit the amount of conventional disability income insurance that will be issued to applicants with incomes below $35,000, particularly those in their less favorable occupational classes.

However, the insured may not always qualify for the anticipated benefits of the social insurance plans. He or she may suffer a loss that is not covered by workers' compensation or that does not meet the restrictive definitions of Social

Security for total and permanent disability. If the insurance company has limited the amount of personal insurance, the individual will be underinsured each month by several hundred dollars or more.

The SIS benefit, as it is popularly called, was developed to meet this potential coverage gap. The supplemental benefit provides an amount of monthly indemnity that approximates the amount the insured might reasonably expect to receive from Social Security for total disability. The SIS benefit is paid, under the conditions of the policy for total disability, when the insured is not receiving benefits from any social service plan. It is payable as a fixed amount of indemnity that ceases when the insured begins to receive any income from a social insurance plan or it may be reduced by a dollar-for-dollar offset of the benefit actually paid under the social insurance plan. If the offset method is used, the insurer usually specifies a floor amount below which the SIS benefit will not be reduced while total disability continues.

*Inflation Protection Benefits.* The **cost-of-living-adjustment** benefit, often referred to as COLA, provides for adjustments of benefits each year during a long-term claim so as to reflect changes in the cost of living from the time that the claim began. Adjustments are computed by the rate of change shown in the Consumer Price Index for All Urban Consumers (CPI-U) as published by the U.S. Department of Labor.

The method of adjustment is relatively complex, but generally it calls for a comparison of the CPI-U for the current claim year with the CPI-U for the year in which the claim began. If the CPI-U increased or decreased since the start of the claim, benefits for the next 12 months are adjusted by the percentage change in the CPI-U. The percentage change is limited to a specified rate of inflation, generally ranging between 5 and 10 percent compounded annually.

The adjusted policy benefits may increase or decrease each year as the CPI-U rises or falls, but the benefits cannot be reduced below the level specified in the policy on the date of issue. Some insurers apply a cap to limit increased benefits to a maximum of two or three times the original indemnities. Others place no limit on the maximum increase of adjusted benefits before the insured is age 65.

*Provisions for Increased Future Benefit Amounts.* Two kinds of optional benefits allow increases in future benefit amounts: the automatic increase benefit and the guarantee of future insurability. **Automatic increase benefit** provisions provide for scheduled increases in the monthly indemnity, typically in each of five consecutive years at a fixed rate of 5 or 6 percent, with annual premium increases at attained age rates for the portion of increased indemnity. The insured has the right to refuse one or more of the automatic increases during the five-year period and may, at the expiry of the schedule, apply to continue the automatic increases over another five-year period.

Some insurers make this provision available without a discernible premium charge as part of the policy on the date of issue, whereas others use a premium-bearing optional benefit rider.

When the insured recovers, the adjusted benefits generally are reduced to the level of those in force on the date of issue. A few insurers allow the recovered insured to retain permanently the adjusted benefits in the last year of claim upon payment of any required premium.

The **guarantee of future insurability**, or the future increase option, allows an insured to purchase additional disability income insurance in future years despite any changes in health. The total increase that the insured may obtain under this benefit varies among insurers, but most often it cannot exceed twice the monthly indemnity that the insured has in force in all insurers on the original policy's date of issue.

The insured may exercise purchase options once a year, typically until age 50 or 55. The amount of additional monthly indemnity that the insured can purchase each year is subject to the company's limits for insurance in relation to earned income, and, in some insurers, it may be further limited to a specific amount, typically $500. In other insurers, the insured can purchase all or part of the total increase option on any option date before age 45. After that, increases each year may not exceed one-third of the original total.

If the insured is disabled on an option date, he or she can purchase additional monthly indemnity, but the additional amounts at times will not apply to the current claim. Future increase options among the major insurers are now payable immediately for an existing claim, if the insured is disabled on the date he or she may otherwise have exercised the purchase option. Income requirements are based on the earned income at the start of the claim, and immediate benefit payments are subject to an elimination period that begins on the date of issue of the additional insurance coverage.

*Comparison of COLA, Automatic Increases, and Future Increase Guarantees.* COLA adjusts benefits while the insured is on claim to account for changes in the cost of living from the start of disability, when the claim lasts at least one year. Automatic increases are designed to keep insurance benefits current with changes in earned income or financial needs as a result of modest annual salary increases or the effects of inflation while the insured is not on claim. One insurer combines the automatic increase principle and COLA into a single benefit rider so that consistent adjustments occur annually whether the insured is healthy or disabled.

Future increase guarantees are designed to adjust insurance benefits for individuals who anticipate substantial annual income growth that is above the average national rate for salary changes or who expect periodic substantial changes in income as they mature in their professional or business roles.

## BUSINESS USES OF DISABILITY INCOME INSURANCE

Most major insurers have adapted the total disability benefit provisions of the personal disability income policy to meet specialized business needs. The following is an overview of the variety of coverages that are in use as individual disability insurance for business purposes. Except as otherwise noted, the policy provisions and the definitions of disability are identical to those of the personal contract.

The uses of health insurance to provide employee benefits for all employees, including key employees, are covered in the chapters on group insurance. In companies where little or no health insurance is provided to employees on a group basis, however, employers can use individual health plans to attract and retain key employees.

The basic need to offset the loss arising from the disability of a key employee or owner (sole proprietor, partner, or stockholder) of a business firm was explained in Chapter 15. Thus key employee indemnification and funding business continuation arrangements are important uses for individual disability income insurance. In addition, overhead expense insurance and a variety of special salary continuation plans constitute the other major business uses of individual disability income insurance products.

It is important to remember that the risk of a prolonged disability is often an even more serious threat than death at any age. The comparison of disability and death rates presented in Chapter 1 makes it clear that the chance of a serious disability is substantial.

### OVERHEAD EXPENSE INSURANCE

**Overhead expense insurance** covers the monthly business expenses of business owners and professionals in private practice when they are disabled. A reimbursement-type benefit is paid during total disability that is uniformly defined in occupational terms. The policies usually begin benefits at the end of 30 or 60 days of disability and pay up to a specified amount of benefit each month while disability continues until an aggregate benefit amount has been paid. The aggregate amount generally is a multiple of 12, 18, or 24 times the monthly benefit, rather than a specifically limited duration of months. The basic policy waives any premium due during disability. Most insurers allow insureds to purchase optional benefits that provide coverage during periods of partial or residual disability or that give the insured the right to purchase additional insurance at a future time without evidence of good health.

Covered expenses usually are those that the U.S. Internal Revenue Service accepts as deductible business expenses for federal income tax purposes. They include rent or mortgage payments for the business premises, employee salaries, installment payments for equipment (but usually not inventory), utility and laundry costs, business insurance premiums that are not waived during disability, and any other recurring expenses that the insured normally incurs in the conduct of his or her business or professional practice. The major insurers pay benefits on a cumulative basis, so that if the full monthly benefit has not been paid in a given month because of lower than expected covered expenses, any unpaid benefit is carried forward and is available to be paid in any month in which expenses exceed the designated monthly benefit. Benefits generally are available to insure up to $10,000 a month of covered expenses.

## DISABILITY BUY-OUT INSURANCE

Although offered by only a handful of major insurers, disability income insurance to fund business continuation arrangements (cross purchase or entity plans) is the second most common use of business disability income insurance. The policies provide cash funds to a business or professional partnership or small corporation to purchase the business interests of a totally disabled partner or stockholder. Policies are arranged so that benefits are not payable until after 12, 24, or 36 months of disability. The duration is chosen to correspond to a "trigger point," which is the date designated in the formal buy-sell agreement at which the healthy persons must buy out the totally disabled insured/owner.

Insureds generally are considered totally disabled if, because of sickness or injury, they are not able to perform the major duties of their regular occupations and are not actively at work on behalf of the business or practice with which they are associated. Benefits may be paid as monthly indemnity to a trustee, who then releases the total payment at the trigger point. More commonly, benefits are paid as a lump sum or under a periodic settlement arrangement in reimbursement for the actual amount paid by the buyers to purchase the disabled insured's interest.

The maximum benefits of buy-out policies are established at the time of underwriting and are based on the value of the business entity as determined by one or more generally accepted accounting methods. The maximum insurable percentage of an individual's worth in a business is about 80 percent for a lump-sum benefit. This insurable percentage reduces rapidly after age 60 (e.g., 50 percent at age 61 and 25 percent at age 62), since it is logical for business partners to begin planning for transition at the insured's retirement. Policies that provide monthly payments for three or five years in lieu of a lump sum also reduce the benefit substantially for ages near retirement. The maximum underwriting limit usually increases with the length of the elimination period.

Under **indemnity-type** disability policies, insurers must pay the maximum amount specified in the policy regardless of the actual value of the business at the time of the claim. Under **reimbursement** policies, on the other hand, insurers can reduce the benefit so that it does not exceed the actual value of the business at the time the buy-sell occurs. For this reason, indemnity policies rarely provide a maximum of more than $350,000 for any one insured, although reimbursement policies may be available with maximums of $1,000,000 on any one individual.

A **future buy-out expense** option is usually available. This provides the owner/insured the option of increasing the maximum buy-out expense benefit without evidence of insurability on specified option dates.

## KEY EMPLOYEE DISABILITY INCOME INSURANCE

**Key employee disability insurance** provides for payment of a monthly indemnity to a business entity during the total disability of an essential employee who is the named insured under the policy. Benefits begin after a specified period of disability—the elimination period—and they continue while the insured is disabled for up to 12 or 24 months.

The amount of indemnity is typically high, to reflect the value of the employee to the business, and generally it is and should be issued independently of any limits that the insurance company may have set for personal insurance. Although the payment of benefits depends on the disabled status of the insured, the policy itself is owned by the business entity and all benefits are paid directly to the business. The business firm may then use the indemnity to pay the salary of a temporary or permanent replacement. The funds may also be used to bolster credit, offset any loss of expected profit, or otherwise contribute to the solvency of the business until a replacement is recruited and trained. The maximum limits vary but can reach in excess of $15,000 a month.

It should be noted that key employee insurance is basically a specialty offering of companies that specialize in jumbo risks, such as Lloyds of London or the American International Group. Few, if any, standard commercial companies offer a policy with these characteristics.

## SALARY CONTINUATION PLAN

**Salary continuation plan** (SCP) is a generic term for a variety of marketing arrangements that provide disability income insurance on a personal basis for multiple employees of a single employer. The plan may be a formal or informal arrangement to replace salary or wages of a disabled employee. Ordinarily, the insurance company uses its regular personal disability income policy forms, but allows a premium discount because of multiple lives being covered and also guarantees a certain level of coverage to be issued to each employee without evidence of insurability.

At time of renewal, policies are list-billed to the common employer, who often is shown as owner of each employee's policy. The employees may contribute all or part of the premium, although many plans are employer-pay-all arrangements. When insureds leave employment, they have the right to continue the policies in force, but the premiums that they must pay personally on renewal will no longer be discounted.

SCPs are classed as business insurance since under certain circumstances the employer may deduct premiums for tax purposes, in which case benefits of the policy become ordinary taxable income for the covered employee. Because the plans are employment related, they are affected by a number of federal and state employment laws that prohibit discrimination because of sex or age and that protect employees' benefit rights.

## TAX TREATMENT OF INDIVIDUAL MEDICAL EXPENSE AND DISABILITY INCOME INSURANCE

Except in the case of long-term-care insurance, the income tax treatment of individual medical expense insurance generally is straightforward and simple. Premiums paid for personal individual health insurance coverage are deductible as unreimbursed medical expenses on an individual's federal income tax return, provided the individual itemizes deductions but only to the extent that all other unreimbursed medical expenses exceed 7.5 percent of the taxpayer's adjusted gross income. Premiums for personal individual disability income insurance protection are not deductible. Benefits received from personal health and disability income insurance policies are received free of income tax.

The income tax treatment of key employee disability income insurance and disability buy-out insurance is the same as that for personal coverage—that is, premiums are not deductible and benefits are received income tax free. Premiums paid for overhead expense insurance ordinarily are deductible by the business as a necessary business expense. Benefits received are all considered ordinary income, but they may be offset in whole or in part by the business expenses that the policy benefits are designed to cover.

The taxation of long-term-care insurance and accelerated benefit riders was not settled at the time this book was going to press. Internal Revenue Service proposed regulations would generally provide favorable tax treatment to such qualifying benefits.

[2]See Chap. 13.

# Chapter 18

# *FUNDAMENTALS OF LIFE INSURANCE MATHEMATICS*

The student cannot truly understand life and health insurance until he or she has developed a sound appreciation for the underlying mathematics. Chapter 2 provided an overview of the subject. This chapter begins a more detailed treatment. It presents a discussion of the raw materials—probability, mortality, and interest concepts—of life insurance mathematics and applicable principles. Chapter 19 applies these principles to develop net premiums. Assuming an understanding of net premiums, Chapter 20 examines the concepts and state regulations regarding life insurance reserves and surrender values. Chapter 21 then examines the computation of a gross premium rate structure and delves into nonguaranteed life insurance policy pricing and benefit elements. Finally, Chapter 22 presents various aspects of rate-making, reserving, and surplus distribution as they relate to health insurance.

## MEASUREMENT OF RISK IN LIFE INSURANCE

Some means of scientifically measuring risk is necessary if insurance is to be priced properly. This measurement of risk lies at the foundation of any system of insurance and is made possible through the application of the laws of probability.

## THE LAWS OF PROBABILITY

Three probability laws are used in life and health insurance: (1) the law of certainty, (2) the law of simple probability, and (3) the law of compound probability. The use of these principles facilitates the mathematical description of risk. The three laws may be stated as follows:

1. Certainty may be expressed by unity, or 1.

2. Simple probability, or the probability or chance that an event will occur, may be expressed by a fraction, which may take a value from 0 to 1.

3. Compound probability, or the chance that two independent events will occur, is the product of the separate probabilities that the events, taken separately, will occur.[1]

A general statement of the method for determining **simple probability** is: the *denominator* equals the total number of equally likely possible events or exposures (e.g., lives) and the *numerator* is composed of only those instances that satisfy some stipulated condition (e.g., deaths).

The corollary that *the sum of all the separate probabilities equals one* is based on the assumption that the events are mutually exclusive and exhaustive. Events are **mutually exclusive** if the occurrence of one of the events precludes the possibility of the occurrence of the other. For example, if a person dies at age 35, he or she clearly cannot die at age 36 or any other age. **Exhaustive** means the events under consideration cover all possibilities.

The **compound probability** that both of two independent events will occur equals the product of the simple probabilities that the events taken separately will happen. Suppose that two coins are tossed, and one wants to know the chance that both will fall heads up. Since the chance that each separate coin will fall heads up is one-half, the probability that *both* will falls head up is one-quarter (1/2 x 1/2).

According to the law of compound probabilities, only when two events are independent will the product of simple probabilities equal the probability that both events will occur. For two events to be **independent**, the happening of the one must have no effect upon the occurrence of the other.

## THE USE OF PROBABILITY TO FORECAST FUTURE EVENTS

These three laws of probability are useful in estimating the likelihood of future events. Future events can be estimated in one of two ways: (1) by **deductive reasoning** and (2) by **inductive reasoning**. The validity of the deductive reasoning depends on the completeness with which all the causes at work in the determination of any phenomenon are known. In the above coin-toss example, we knew by our powers of observation that the chance of a coin falling heads up was one-half. We *deduced* this. Deductive reasoning does not furnish a sound basis for insurance purposes. We cannot yet estimate loss probabilities (e.g., probabilities of death) deductively.

[1]Laws of compound probability in which the separate events are dependent do not enter into the present discussion.

We can, however, estimate such probabilities inductively. This logic flows from the assumption that what has occurred in the past will occur again in the future, if the same conditions are present. Reasoning inductively does not require an analysis of the causes of phenomena to be able to predict future events.

Inductive reasoning is applied in life insurance. From data showing ages at death in the past, probabilities of death and of survival in the future are estimated. This prediction is based on the assumption that a **law of mortality** exists. This law holds that certain causes are in operation that determine that out of a large group of persons a set proportion will die each year until all have died. It is assumed that the impact of the law of mortality would be subject to precise measurement if only the causes at work were known. It is not necessary, however, to know all the operating causes to predict fairly accurately the rate of mortality in a group of persons. By studying the rate of death within any group (if the group is sufficiently large) and noting all the circumstances that might, according to our best knowledge, affect that rate, it is possible to anticipate that any future group of persons with approximately the same set of circumstances can expect approximately the same rate of death. Thus a working basis is available for predicting future rates of death. Mortality statistics are necessary for developing a scientific plan of life insurance.

## The Law of Large Numbers

The accuracy with which the theoretical estimates approximate actual experience has important bearings on the success of any method of insuring lives. This accuracy depends on two factors: (1) the accuracy of the statistics underlying the estimates and (2) the number of units or trials taken.

With reference to the first factor, it should be obvious that accurate data are a fundamental requirement if an accurate measure of the law of mortality is to be obtained. Mortality statistics, from whatever source, should be scrutinized carefully to detect inaccuracies in the original data. Another dimension of accuracy is the presumption that future mortality experience can be reasonably approximated by past mortality experience—not always correct.

The second factor that determines accuracy of the estimates is the number of units or trials taken. As the number of trials is increased, the variation of actual from the true probable experience decreases, and if a very great number of trials is taken, actual and probable experience will coincide. This generalization is called the **law of large numbers**.[2] For example, if a coin were flipped 10 million times and there was exactly one-half chance that each flip would produce heads, the actual results would be so near 50 percent heads that the relative difference would be negligible. The law of large numbers is fundamental to insurance.

Premium rates are based on estimates of future probabilities of loss. These estimates are not valid representations of future experience unless a sufficiently

[2]See also the discussion in Chap. 2. In mathematical terminology, this statistical principle is known as **Bernoulli's theorem**.

large number of cases exists to guarantee that large fluctuations in results will be minimized. Prediction of future mortality rates in life insurance based on what has happened in the past can be made for a large group of persons. It cannot be made for a single individual or even a relatively small number of persons (such as 1,000). When a mortality table shows that persons of a certain age die at the rate of 7 per 1,000 per year, that does not mean that out of a group of 1,000 exactly 7 will die within a year, but, rather that out of a large group, containing many thousands, the deaths will most likely occur at approximately the rate of 7 per 1,000.

With reference to the predication of future mortality rates, the law of large numbers has a double application: (1) to the data base from which the statistics were drawn and (2) to the population to which the rates will be applied. Future mortality is estimated on the basis of past mortality data. The statistics used for this purpose, however, must include a sufficiently large group of representative individuals to ensure the operation of the law of large numbers. Assuming that the collected data are accurate and based on a large enough sample, they may be used to estimate future mortality. Then, in applying these mortality rates, a large enough number of individuals must be involved if the actual experience in the future is to be reasonably close to the anticipated experience.

## DISTRIBUTION OF LIFE INSURANCE CLAIMS

Suppose that a hypothetical life insurance company insures the lives of a certain number of persons in a single year and that the probability that any one of the insureds will die that year is 2 in 100. The insurer expects a certain number of claims (2 percent of all the insureds), but its actual claims may be more or less than the expected number. According to the law of large numbers, if the number of insureds is large enough, the actual claims will most likely show only a small relative deviation from the expected claims. Using probability theory, one can calculate the probabilities of various deviations from the expected claims, depending on the number of insureds.

Figure 18-1 shows the probability of various deviations when the number of lives insured is 1,000, 5,000, 25,000, and 50,000. In particular, the figure shows that the probability of actual claims being within 5 percent of expected claims is 18.2 percent if 1,000 lives are insured, 39.0 percent if 5,000 lives are insured, 74.2 percent if 25,000 lives are insured, and 89.0 percent if 50,000 lives are insured. Although not shown in the chart, the probability of actual claims being within 5 percent of expected claims is greater than 99.99 percent if 1,000,000 lives are insured.

## MORTALITY STATISTICS

The establishment of any plan of insuring against death requires some means of giving mathematical values to the probabilities of death. The preceding

**FIGURE 18-1**

**VARIATION OF ACTUAL CLAIMS FROM EXPECTED CLAIMS AS A PERCENTAGE OF EXPECTED CLAIMS (FOR SELECTED NUMBER OF LIVES INSURED FOR ONE YEAR WHERE THE PROBABILITY OF DEATH IN THAT YEAR IS 0.02)**

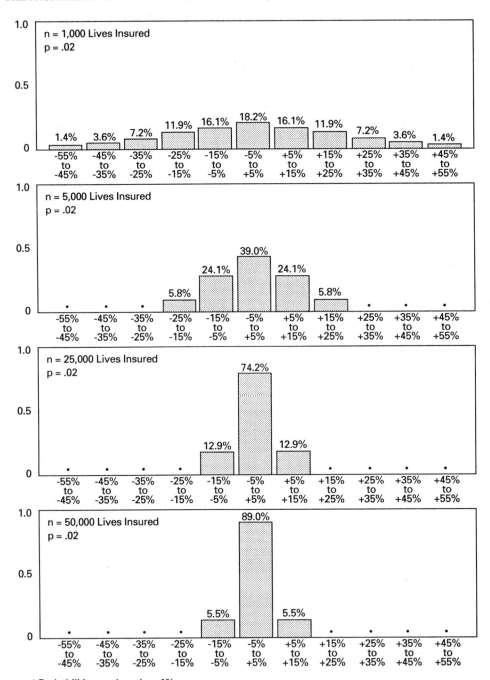

\* Probabilities are less than 1%.

discussion of the laws of probability demonstrated that this can be accomplished through the application of the laws of probability to mortality statistics. Mortality tables are presentations of these data organized in such a form as to be usable in estimating the course of future deaths.

The two basic sources of mortality statistics are:

1. Population statistics derived from census enumerations and death returns filed with registration offices

2. Statistics derived from insured lives

Both census enumerations and death registration records contain significant error. Census data, collected by a large number of individuals through personal interviews, are particularly susceptible to error. Frequently there is misclassification of information, inaccurate information is provided by the respondents either willfully or inadvertently, tabulation errors creep in, and, not infrequently, ages are reported as unknown. Records of death provided to the National Office of Vital Statistics are frequently incomplete and inaccurate.

On the other hand, the mortality statistics of insured lives tend to be quite accurate. The nature of the insurance process leads to a careful recording of the date of birth, the sex, and the date of death of insured individuals. This facilitates derivation of accurate death rates for the various age and sex classifications.

The mortality experience among insured lives is significantly different from that of the general population, because most insured lives have been subjected to an insurer's underwriting process. Virtually all mortality tables used today by life insurers are based on the experience of insured lives.

## MORTALITY TABLE CONSTRUCTION

The theory of probability is applied in life insurance through the use of a mathematical model known as a mortality table. A **mortality table** represents a record of mortality observed in the past and is arranged so as to show the probabilities of death and survival at each separate age. It shows a hypothetical group of individuals beginning with a certain age and traces the history of the entire group year by year until all have died. Since any description will best be understood by reference to an actual table, the *Commissioners 1980 Standard Ordinary Table of Mortality (1980 CSO Table)* for males is presented in Table 18-1.

*Overview.* The heart of the mortality table is the column "Yearly Probability of Dying," with the yearly probability of surviving being simply figured as 1 minus the probability of dying. The other essential features of a mortality table are the two columns of the "Number Living" and the "Number Dying" at designated ages.

**TABLE 18-1**    *COMMISSIONERS 1980 STANDARD ORDINARY (CSO) TABLE OF MORTALITY*

Male Lives

| Age (x) at Beginning of Year | Number Living at Beginning of Designated Year ($l_x$) | Number Dying during Designated Year ($d_x$) | Yearly Probability of Dying ($q_x$) | Yearly Probability of Surviving ($p_x$) |
|---|---|---|---|---|
| 0 | 10,000,000 | 41,800 | 0.004180 | 0.995820 |
| 1 | 9,958,200 | 10,655 | 0.001070 | 0.998930 |
| 2 | 9,947 545 | 9,848 | 0.000990 | 0.999010 |
| 3 | 9,937,697 | 9,739 | 0.000980 | 0.999020 |
| 4 | 9,927,958 | 9,432 | 0.000950 | 0.999050 |
| 5 | 9,918,526 | 8,927 | 0.000900 | 0.999100 |
| 6 | 9,909,599 | 8,522 | 0.000860 | 0.999140 |
| 7 | 9,901,077 | 7,921 | 0.000800 | 0.999200 |
| 8 | 9,893,156 | 7,519 | 0.000760 | 0.999240 |
| 9 | 9,885,637 | 7,315 | 0.000740 | 0.999260 |
| 10 | 9,878,322 | 7,211 | 0.000730 | 0.999270 |
| 11 | 9,871,111 | 7,601 | 0.000770 | 0.999230 |
| 12 | 9,863,510 | 8,384 | 0.000850 | 0.999150 |
| 13 | 9,855,126 | 9,757 | 0.000990 | 0.999010 |
| 14 | 9,845,369 | 11,322 | 0.001150 | 0.998850 |
| 15 | 9,834,047 | 13,079 | 0.001330 | 0.998670 |
| 16 | 9,820,968 | 14,830 | 0.001510 | 0.998490 |
| 17 | 9,806,138 | 16,376 | 0.001670 | 0.998330 |
| 18 | 9,789,762 | 17,426 | 0.001780 | 0.998220 |
| 19 | 9,772,336 | 18,177 | 0.001860 | 0.998140 |
| 20 | 9,754,159 | 18,533 | 0.001900 | 0.998100 |
| 21 | 9,735,626 | 18,595 | 0.001910 | 0.998090 |
| 22 | 9,717,031 | 18,365 | 0.001890 | 0.998110 |
| 23 | 9,698,666 | 18,040 | 0.001860 | 0.998140 |
| 24 | 9,680,626 | 17,619 | 0.001820 | 0.998180 |
| 25 | 9,663,007 | 17,104 | 0.001770 | 0.998230 |
| 26 | 9,645,903 | 16,687 | 0.001730 | 0.998270 |
| 27 | 9,629,216 | 16,466 | 0.001710 | 0.998290 |
| 28 | 9,612,750 | 16,342 | 0.001700 | 0.998300 |
| 29 | 9,596,408 | 16,410 | 0.001710 | 0.998290 |
| 30 | 9,579,998 | 16,573 | 0.001730 | 0.998270 |
| 31 | 9,563,425 | 17,023 | 0.001780 | 0.998220 |
| 32 | 9,546,402 | 17,470 | 0.001830 | 0.998170 |
| 33 | 9,328,932 | 18,200 | 0.001910 | 0.998090 |
| 34 | 9,510,732 | 19,021 | 0.002000 | 0.998000 |
| 35 | 9,491,711 | 20,028 | 0.002110 | 0.997890 |
| 36 | 9,471,683 | 21,217 | 0.002240 | 0.997760 |
| 37 | 9,450,466 | 22,681 | 0.002400 | 0.997600 |
| 38 | 9,427,785 | 24,324 | 0.002580 | 0.997420 |
| 39 | 9,403,461 | 26,236 | 0.002790 | 0.997210 |
| 40 | 9,377,225 | 28,319 | 0.003020 | 0.996980 |
| 41 | 9,348,906 | 30,758 | 0.003290 | 0.996710 |
| 42 | 9,318,148 | 33,173 | 0.003560 | 0.996440 |
| 43 | 9,284,975 | 35,933 | 0.003870 | 0.996130 |
| 44 | 9,249,042 | 38,753 | 0.004190 | 0.995810 |
| 45 | 9,210,289 | 41,907 | 0.004550 | 0.995450 |
| 46 | 9,168,382 | 45,108 | 0.004920 | 0.995080 |
| 47 | 9,123,274 | 48,536 | 0.005320 | 0.994680 |
| 48 | 9,074,738 | 52,089 | 0.005740 | 0.994260 |
| 49 | 9,022,649 | 56,031 | 0.006210 | 0.993790 |
| 50 | 8,966,618 | 60,166 | 0.006710 | 0.993290 |

**TABLE 18-1 (CONTINUED)**

| Age (x) at Beginning of Year | Number Living at Beginning of Designated Year ($l_x$) | Number Dying during Designated Year ($d_x$) | Yearly Probability of Dying ($q_x$) | Yearly Probability of Surviving ($p_x$) |
|---|---|---|---|---|
| 51 | 8,906,452 | 65,017 | 0.007300 | 0.992700 |
| 52 | 8,841,435 | 70,378 | 0.007960 | 0.992040 |
| 53 | 8,771,057 | 76,396 | 0.008710 | 0.991290 |
| 54 | 8,694,661 | 83,121 | 0.009560 | 0.990440 |
| 55 | 8,611,540 | 90,163 | 0.010470 | 0.989530 |
| 56 | 8,521,377 | 97,655 | 0.011460 | 0.988540 |
| 57 | 8,423,722 | 105,212 | 0.012490 | 0.987510 |
| 58 | 8,318,510 | 113,049 | 0.013590 | 0.986410 |
| 59 | 8,205,461 | 121,195 | 0.014770 | 0.985230 |
| 60 | 8,084,266 | 129,995 | 0.016080 | 0.983920 |
| 61 | 7,954,271 | 139,518 | 0.017540 | 0.982460 |
| 62 | 7,814,753 | 149,965 | 0.019190 | 0.980810 |
| 63 | 7,664,788 | 161,420 | 0.021060 | 0.978940 |
| 64 | 7,503,368 | 173,628 | 0.023140 | 0.976860 |
| 65 | 7,329,740 | 186,322 | 0.025420 | 0.974580 |
| 66 | 7,143,418 | 198,944 | 0.027850 | 0.972150 |
| 67 | 6,944,474 | 211,390 | 0.030440 | 0.969560 |
| 68 | 6,773,084 | 223,471 | 0.033190 | 0.966810 |
| 69 | 6,509,613 | 235,453 | 0.036170 | 0.963830 |
| 70 | 6,274,160 | 247,892 | 0.039510 | 0.960490 |
| 71 | 6,026,268 | 260,937 | 0.043300 | 0.956700 |
| 72 | 5,765,331 | 274,718 | 0.047650 | 0.952350 |
| 73 | 5,490,613 | 289,026 | 0.052640 | 0.947360 |
| 74 | 5,201,587 | 302,680 | 0.058190 | 0.941810 |
| 75 | 4,898,907 | 314,461 | 0.064190 | 0.935810 |
| 76 | 4,584,446 | 323,341 | 0.070530 | 0.929470 |
| 77 | 4,261,105 | 328,616 | 0.077120 | 0.922880 |
| 78 | 3,932,489 | 329,936 | 0.083900 | 0.916100 |
| 79 | 3,602,553 | 328,012 | 0.091050 | 0.908950 |
| 80 | 3,274,541 | 323,656 | 0.098840 | 0.901160 |
| 81 | 2,950,885 | 317,161 | 0.107480 | 0.892520 |
| 82 | 2,633,724 | 308,804 | 0.117250 | 0.882750 |
| 83 | 2,324,920 | 298,194 | 0.128260 | 0.871740 |
| 84 | 2,026,726 | 284,248 | 0.140250 | 0.859750 |
| 85 | 1,742,478 | 266,512 | 0.152950 | 0.847050 |
| 86 | 1,475,966 | 245,143 | 0.166090 | 0.833910 |
| 87 | 1,230,823 | 220,994 | 0.179550 | 0.820450 |
| 88 | 1,009,829 | 195,170 | 0.193270 | 0.806730 |
| 89 | 814,659 | 168,871 | 0.207290 | 0.792710 |
| 90 | 645,788 | 143,216 | 0.221770 | 0.778230 |
| 91 | 502,572 | 119,100 | 0.236980 | 0.763020 |
| 92 | 383,472 | 97,191 | 0.253450 | 0.746550 |
| 93 | 286,281 | 77,900 | 0.272110 | 0.727890 |
| 94 | 208,381 | 61,660 | 0.295900 | 0.704100 |
| 95 | 146,721 | 48,412 | 0.329960 | 0.670040 |
| 96 | 98,309 | 37,805 | 0.384550 | 0.615450 |
| 97 | 60,504 | 29,054 | 0.480200 | 0.519800 |
| 98 | 31,450 | 20,693 | 0.657980 | 0.342020 |
| 99 | 10,757 | 10,757 | 1.000000 | 0.000000 |

It will prove helpful to introduce some standard actuarial notation to simplify later discussion. These include:

$x$ = age

$l_x$ = number living at age $x$

$d_x$ = number dying during age $x$
  = $l_x \div l_{x-1}$

$q_x$ = probability of an individual dying during age $x$
  = $d_x \div l_x$

$p_x$ = probability of an individual age $x$ surviving one year
  = $l_{x+1} \div l_x$

A person of any age will either die or survive that year. Thus it can be seen that for any age,

$$q_x + p_x = 1 \qquad\qquad (1)$$

Moreover, it should be noted that each $d_x$ and $l_x$ is related as follows:

$$l_{x+1} = l_x - d_x \qquad\qquad (2)$$

In other words, the number of persons living at any age $x+1$ ($l_{x+1}$) can be found simply by subtracting the number dying ($d_x$) in the previous year from the number who were alive at the beginning of the previous year ($l_x$).

In the case of the *1980 CSO Table*, it is assumed that a group of 10,000,000 males ($l_0$) come under observation at exactly the same moment as they begin the first year of life (age 0).[3] Of this group, 41,800 die ($d_0$ = 10,000,000 x 0.00418) during the year, leaving 9,958,200 lives ($l_1$) to begin the second year.[4] The table proceeds in this manner to record the number dying each year of life and the number living at the beginning of each succeeding year, until only 10,757 of the original group are found to be alive by age 99, and these 10,757 die during that year.

***Derivation of Death Rates***. It is impossible for any insurance company to insure a group of several million persons of exactly the same age and sex and at exactly the same time. It would also be impossible to keep any such group under observation until all died since some persons would voluntarily terminate their policies. Insurance policies are written at all times of the year and on lives at various ages. It is possible, however, for one insurer or a group of insurers to keep a record of all insured lives, showing at each age the number of persons under observation and the number who die. If a sufficient volume of data is collected showing (1) the ages at which persons come under observation and (2) the number of each sex dying at each age, a mortality table may be constructed.

---

[3]The *1980 CSO Table* has separate tables for male and female lives. The illustrations throughout this mathematical discussion are based on male lives, but the reader should note that a distinction by sex is made in the actuarial processes employed by most companies.

[4]Applying formula 2, $l_0 - d_0 = l_1$, or 10,000,000 - 41,800 = 9,958,200.

Suppose, for illustration, that the following data have been collected for female lives:

| Age | Number of Life— Years Observed | Number Dying during Year |
|---|---|---|
| 0 to 1 | 10,000 | 80 |
| 1 to 2 | 30,000 | 90 |
| 2 to 3 | 150,000 | 600 |
| 3 to 4 | 80,000 | 360 |

From these figures, death rates may be computed for the respective ages in the following manner:[5]

| Age | Rate of Death Expressed as a Fraction | Rate of Death Expressed as a Decimal |
|---|---|---|
| 0 | 80/10,000 | 0.0080 |
| 1 | 90/30,000 | 0.0030 |
| 2 | 600/150,000 | 0.0040 |
| 3 | 360/80,000 | 0.0045 |

The rate of mortality ($q_x$) at any given age is the quotient of the number of deaths and the corresponding exposure for the period of study.[6] The rate represents the probability that a person who has just attained a given age will die before he or she attains the next age. The rate of mortality is usually expressed in terms of the number of deaths per thousand.

The mortality table may be constructed by using an arbitrary number of persons, known as the **radix**, assumed to be alive at the youngest age for which death rates are available, and successively applying the mortality rates at each age. Applying the death rates developed above to an arbitrary radix of 10,000,000 will illustrate the process:

| (1) | (2) | (3) | (4) | (5) |
|---|---|---|---|---|
|  |  |  | Number of Deaths before | Number Living |
|  | Number Living | Mortality Rate | Next Age | at Next Age |
| Age | at Given Age | for Given Age | [(2) x (3)] | [(2) - (4)] |
| (x) | ($l_x$) | ($q_x$) | ($d_x$) | ($l_{x+1}$) |
| 0 | 10,000,000 | 0.0080 | 80,000 | 9,920,000 |
| 1 | 9,920,000 | 0.0030 | 29,760 | 9,890,240 |
| 2 | 9,890,240 | 0.0040 | 39,561 | 9,850,679 |
| 3 | 9,850,679 | 0.0045 | 44,328 | 9,806,351 |

[5]If the period of observation is more than one year, which it usually is, the number under observation is adjusted to reflect this fact. Thus if the period of observation was five years, one individual under observation would be observed at five successive ages, unless he or she died or the policy lapsed during the period. The deaths occurring at each age are compared with the total "exposure" at that age.

[6]The distinction between "mortality rates," as the rates above are called, and "probabilities of death" is one of preciseness of attained age. For purposes of simplification here, death rates and probabilities of death are assumed to be identical. For the construction of a mortality table, probabilities of death are necessary; they refer to rates of dying among a group of persons who have just attained a certain age of life. See Robert W. Batten, *Mortality Table Construction* (Englewood Cliffs, N.J.: Prentice-Hall, Inc., 1978).

Since the probability of dying at age 0 is 0.0080, 80,000 deaths are expected during the year among the 10,000,000 starting at age 0. This leaves 9,920,000 of the group to begin age 1. These die at the rate of three per thousand (0.0030), yielding 29,760 deaths during the year. In this way, the original 10,000,000 are reduced in number by deaths year after year until all have died. This is the basis for the statement that the mortality table represents "a (hypothetical) generation of individuals passing through time."

Since the radix of the table is arbitrary, the numbers in the columns headed "Number Living" and "Number of Deaths" are not significant in themselves.[7] They simply reflect the series of death rates, the real heart of a mortality table.

Sometimes a mortality table has an additional column showing the "expectation of life" or "life expectancy" at each age. The figure in this column opposite any age is the average number of years of life lived after attaining that age by all who reach that age, and is calculated from the following formula:

$$e_x = \sum_{t=1}^{w-x-1} \frac{l_{x+t}}{l_x}$$

where

$e_x$ = life expectancy for an individual age $x$, and
$w$ = terminal age of the mortality table being used.

Expectation of life can be a misleading term, since it has no significance for any individual. The probable future lifetime of any person depends on many factors, including his or her state of health, and may be longer or shorter than average. It is commonly supposed that life insurance companies make premium rate calculations on the assumption that everyone will live for the period of his or her life expectancy. This is not the case, as explained later in Chapters 19 and 21.

***Adjustments to Mortality Data.*** The mortality tables used by life insurers in calculating premium rates, reserves, and cash values do not reflect the precise mortality rates developed from the basic mortality data. Because the volume of experience is not uniform at all ages and is insufficient to provide completely credible or reliable statistics, two types of adjustments may be made to the derived rates: (1) the rates are smoothed into a curve (the process is known as graduation), and (2) a margin may be added to the rates in the derived curve.

**Graduation** is performed to eliminate the irregularities in the observed data that are believed not to be true characteristics of the universe from which the sample experience was extracted. One of several methods of graduation is used, depending upon the data involved and the purpose of the computation. The objective in all cases, however, is to introduce smoothness and regularity, while preserving the basic characteristics of the observed values.

[7]For the *American Experience Table*, the radix was 100,000 at age 10; for the *1941 CSO Table*, it was 1,000,000 at age 1; for the *1958 CSO Table*, 10,000,000 at age 0; and for the *1980 CSO Table*, 10,000,000 at age 0.

When the derived rates will be used as a valuation mortality table, a **margin** is added to them; it is added in the interest of safety.[8] In a mortality table used to value life policy liabilities, this means showing higher death rates than those actually expected. In an annuity valuation table, it means showing lower rates of mortality than those expected. Thus the *1980 CSO Table*, as a life insurance valuation table, had margins added to the underlying mortality rates. Margins may also be provided by adjusting the underlying data prior to the derivation of the basic rates themselves. The insertion of these margins enhances the security of life insurance contracts and is considered a sound practice.

## TYPES OF MORTALITY TABLES

*Valuation versus Basic Tables*. A **valuation mortality table** is used as the basis for calculating minimum reserves and cash surrender values. As noted above, these tables contain margins that render them conservative. The use of these tables is prescribed by law.

Valuation tables may also be used for gross premium calculation for participating, indeterminate premium, and current assumption policies. In such cases, the dividend scale or current mortality charges are based on a basic table.

A **basic mortality table** reflects the actual experience of the population from which it was drawn. No margins are added to these tables. Basic tables are commonly used for:

1. Calculation of gross premium rates

2. Development of current mortality charges for universal life and other current assumption policies

3. Development of dividend scales and actual dividend payments on participating policies

4. Mortality studies of the insurer's own experience, especially in identifying trends

5. Financial statements prepared under generally accepted accounting principles (see Chapter 32)

6. Asset share, model office, and other financial studies and projections

*Select, Ultimate, and Aggregate Tables*. Mortality tables may be classified as select, ultimate, and aggregate. These terms relate to the extent to which the data used have been affected by the underwriting process. As discussed in Chapter 4, insured lives, having passed the necessary requirements before becoming insured, show a lower rate of mortality than lives not subject to such

[8]See Chap. 20.

524     Chapter 18

scrutiny. Thus the number of deaths occurring among 10,000 insureds aged 40 who have just passed a medical examination can be expected to be lower than among 10,000 persons aged 40 who were first insured at age 30 and have been insured for ten years. It is important, therefore, for an insurer in estimating the probable mortality to know whether it has a large number of newly selected lives.

A **select mortality table** is based on data of newly insured lives only. An **ultimate mortality table** excludes these early data—usually the first 5 to 15 years following entry—and is based on the mortality among these insured lives in later policy years. The *1980 CSO Table* shown in Table 18-1 is an ultimate table. Since insurers and their regulators are usually interested in establishing conservative reserve estimates, it is generally considered safer for an insurer to compute reserve liabilities on the basis of the mortality among risks for whom the benefits of fresh medical selection have passed. An **aggregate mortality table** includes all the mortality data—the early years following entry as well as the later ones.

A select mortality table shows rates of mortality by both age and duration of insurance. Since the greatest effect of selection generally wears off in 5 to 15 years, the mortality rates are usually differentiated by duration only for such a period. An example of a select mortality table is presented in Table 18-2. The blocked ages show how the mortality rates vary by duration even though each is aged 30. The rates shown in column "6 and over" constitute the ultimate mortality level and could be used in the development of an ultimate mortality table.

Select tables are used for purposes of analysis and comparison. The basic tables prepared and published by the Mortality Committee of the Society of Actuaries from data supplied by a group of established insurers are constructed to show both select and ultimate mortality, since their primary purpose is to reflect mortality trends.

The mortality tables used in expressing participating life insurance premiums usually are ultimate tables. Select mortality is frequently used in asset share calculations, in dividend and other nonguaranteed element calculations, and in the calculation of nonparticipating gross premiums.

**TABLE 18-2     SELECT AND ULTIMATE MORTALITY TABLE**
**(RATES PER 1,000)**

| Age at Issue | 1 | 2 | 3 | 4 | 5 | 6 and Over | Attained Age |
|---|---|---|---|---|---|---|---|
| 25 | 0.71 | 0.82 | 0.88 | 0.93 | 0.97 | 1.01 | 30 |
| 26 | 0.72 | 0.82 | 0.89 | 0.96 | 1.00 | 1.06 | 31 |
| 27 | 0.73 | 0.83 | 0.92 | 0.99 | 1.05 | 1.12 | 32 |
| 28 | 0.74 | 0.84 | 0.93 | 1.03 | 1.11 | 1.21 | 33 |
| 29 | 0.74 | 0.84 | 0.97 | 1.08 | 1.20 | 1.32 | 34 |
| 30 | 0.74 | 0.86 | 1.02 | 1.16 | 1.31 | 1.44 | 35 |

Year of Insurance

*Mortality Tables for Annuities*. A mortality table based on life insurance experience is not suitable for use in connection with annuities, for several reasons. One reason is that annuities generally are not purchased by individuals in poor health. At the higher ages (particularly in the case of annuity contracts purchased by single premiums for immediate income), the rates of mortality experienced among annuitants generally are lower than among insureds under life insurance policies. A life insurance mortality table would overstate expected mortality rates.

Another important reason is that the long-term improvement in mortality rates (offset, periodically, by developments such as AIDS) provides a gradually increasing margin of safety for life insurance, but has the opposite result for annuities. In fact, it is recognized that no annuity mortality table based on past experience can be used safely. What is needed is a table that shows the (lower) rates of mortality anticipated in the future rather than the rates that have been experienced in the past. Such a table is known as a **table with projection**.

*Static Tables versus Tables with Projection*. Most life insurance mortality tables in use today are **static tables**, in that they do not provide for changes in their rates depending on the calendar year to which they apply. As the secular trend toward mortality improvement has continued, these static tables have periodically been replaced by other static tables based on more recent experience. The improvement in mortality has led to increasing margins in life insurance premiums, since the postponement in death payments enables insurers to earn additional interest on their invested funds and to collect additional premiums. In participating policies as well as indeterminate premium and current assumption nonparticipating policies these gains can be credited to policy owners via enhanced dividends or other nonguaranteed payments or benefits.

The situation has been just the reverse in connection with annuity contracts, in which improving mortality has led to smaller margins. Postponement of death has led to additional annuity payments. To avoid the large expense of frequently constructing new static tables, the traditional practice was to make an allowance for the decrease in mortality rates by using age setbacks—that is, the static table was still used, but the rates shown in the table were assumed to be those that apply to lower actual ages.[9] Setbacks of from one to four years are used by many insurers.

Annuity tables used today usually contain projection factors on different bases that can be applied to the basic table to make allowance for future reductions in mortality rates. For example, suppose that the mortality rate for 65-year-olds is expected to improve at the rate of 1 percent per calendar year. The projected mortality rate for 65-year-olds in some future calendar year, say $CY +$

---

[9]For example, a 65-year-old person may be assumed to be subject to the mortality rates of a person of 64 or 63, thus increasing the premium for a given amount of annuity income.

*N*, can be calculated from the mortality rate in an earlier calendar year, *CY*, by the following formula:

$$q_{65}^{CY+N} = q_{65}^{CY}(1 - 0.01)^N$$

The importance of providing for mortality improvement in annuity mortality tables can be seen in the fact that annuity business constitutes a majority and growing proportion of most life insurance companies' total business.[10]

*Smoker versus Nonsmoker Tables*. Separate basic and valuation mortality tables have been developed for smokers and nonsmokers, in recognition of the substantial mortality differences between the two groups. Figure 18-2 illustrates the relative mortality differences as between smokers and nonsmokers for one large U.S. reinsurer. It also shows the life expectancy for each category of smoker.

*Published Tables in Use Today*. A multitude of mortality tables is used today. The ones discussed below are used chiefly for purposes of valuing insurers' policy reserves and establishing minimum acceptable surrender values and not for rate-making.

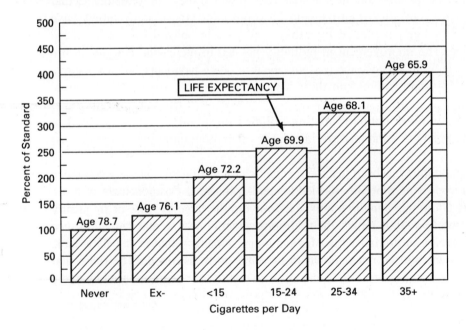

**FIGURE 18-2**

**MORTALITY RATIOS OF SMOKERS TO NONSMOKERS**
*Source:* Lincoln National Reinsurance Company

[10]Annuity business includes, in addition to individual annuities, group annuities and settlement option agreements.

*1. Life Insurance Tables.*  The *Commissioner's 1941 Standard Ordinary Table of Mortality (1941 CSO Table)* was used extensively for policies issued between 1948 and 1966. The *1941 CSO Table* is still important because much outstanding insurance is based on this table. For many years prior to the advent of the *1941 CSO Table*, the *American Experience Table of Mortality* was widely used.[11]

The *Commissioner's 1958 Standard Ordinary Mortality Table (1958 CSO Table)* was developed by the Society of Actuaries from the combined ultimate mortality experience of 15 large insurers between 1950 and 1954. At one time it was required that the *1958 CSO Table* be used as the basis for minimum reserves and nonforfeiture values in all states.[12] As of the mid-1980s, the *1980 CSO Table* (see below) had replaced the *1958 CSO Table* as the mandatory table.

The newest ordinary life tables are the *Commissioner's 1980 Standard Ordinary Mortality Tables (1980 CSO Tables)*, with separate versions for males and females.[13] These tables reflect a decline in mortality rates at most ages compared to the rates in the *1958 CSO Table*. The *1980 CSO Table*, however, reflects a slight increase in male mortality rates in the late teenage years. This increase results in higher 1980 male mortality rates at some ages, relative to the 1958 rates. The increases in male mortality rates during the late teenage years result in *declining* male mortality rates between ages 21 and 28 in the *1980 CSO Table*. By contrast, the 1980 female mortality rates always increase with age after about age 10, as is true in most other mortality tables.

The latest mortality table for industrial insurance is the *1961 Commissioner's Standard Industrial (CSI) Mortality Table*. Use of the *1961 CSI Table* is mandatory for computing minimum reserves and nonforfeiture values for industrial policies issued after 1967. There also is a table for use with group life insurance—the *Commissioner's 1960 Standard Group Mortality Table*.

*2. Annuity Tables.*  The *1937 Standard Annuity Table* formerly was used extensively for individual annuity business. The steady improvement in mortality led to the development of the *Annuity Table for 1949*, which introduced projection factors to reflect continued improvement in mortality rates. The *1955 American Annuity Table* was developed to provide reasonable rates for annual-premium deferred annuities and life income settlement options. The *Group*

---

[11]Although of little practical significance, it is historically interesting to note that the *Actuaries'* or *Seventeen Offices Table*, which in large measure preceded the *American Experience Table*, was of British origin and introduced into the United States by Elizur Wright as the standard for the valuation of policies in Massachusetts.

[12]See Chap. 22.

[13]Other *1980 CSO Tables* exist. Because of the interest in some states in gender-neutral rating and reserving, there are various merged-gender tables. Also, a ten-year select *1980 CSO Table* exists as well as a table for extended term insurance (the *1980 CET Table*). The CSO select table is based on the same ultimate data as underlie the regular *1980 CSO Tables*. The mortality rates vary not only with age and sex, but also with the number of elapsed years since the policy was issued. Finally, there is a set of nonsmoker/smoker *1980 CSO Tables*. These tables can be used in states that permit reserving and surrender value differences between smokers and nonsmokers.

**FIGURE 18-3**

**GRAPHS OF TWO MORTALITY TABLES**

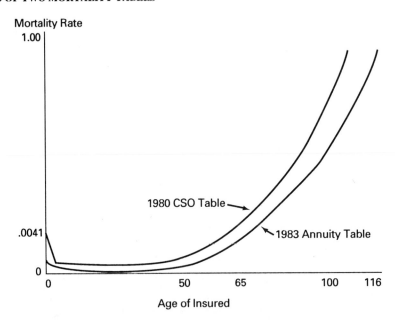

*Annuity Table for 1951* was the first table based on the experience of group annuitants and was widely used in computing rates and reserves for group annuities.

When interest rates increased to levels that were substantially higher than the level used in determining minimum reserves, new annuity business created a surplus strain for life insurance companies. Use of older annuity mortality tables gave partial relief from the surplus strain caused by low valuation interest rate ceilings, but more accurate reserves required up-to-date mortality and interest bases. Thus two new mortality tables, the *1971 Group Annuity Table* and the *1971 Individual Annuity Table*, were developed for use with the higher interest rates in setting reserves. Two new projection scales for males and one for females were also designed for use with the *1971 Group Annuity Table*.

Two further annuity mortality tables were adopted by the NAIC in 1983 and are in use throughout the United States. One table is for reserve and nonforfeiture purposes on individual annuity business—the so-called *1983 Table-a*—the other applies to group business (the *1983 GAM Table*). Figure 18-3 illustrates the mortality levels and slopes of the *1980 CSO Table* (male) and the *1983 Table-a* (for annuity mortality—males).

## APPLICATION OF THE LAWS OF PROBABILITIES TO MORTALITY

Earlier in this chapter the statement was made that risk in life insurance is measured by the application of the laws of probability to the mortality table. Now that these laws are understood and the mortality table has been explained, a few simple illustrations may be used to show this application. Suppose that it is desired to estimate the probability of a man's death within one, two, and five years from age 35. This probability, according to the laws explained earlier, is determined according to a chosen mortality table and is a fraction, the denominator of which equals the number living at age 35 and the numerator of which is the number that have died during the one, two, and five years, respectively, following that age. According to the *1980 CSO Table*, 9,491,711 men are living at age 35 and 20,028 die before the end of the year. Hence, the probability of death within one year is:

$$q_{35} = \frac{d_{35}}{l_{35}} = \frac{20,028}{9,491,711} = 0.0021$$

During the two years following the stated age, there are 20,028 + 21,217 deaths, for a total of 41,245. Therefore the probability of dying within two years (represented by $_2q_{35}$) is:

$$_2q_{35} = \frac{d_{35} + d_{36}}{l_{35}} = \frac{41,245}{9,491,711} = 0.0043$$

Similarly, the total number of deaths within five years is 114,486 (20,028 + 21,217 + 22,681 + 24,324 + 26,236). Thus the probability that a man age 35 will die within five years ($_5q_{35}$) is:

$$_5q_{35} = \frac{d_{35} + d_{36} + d_{37} + d_{38} + d_{39}}{l_{35}} = \frac{114,486}{9,491,711} = 0.0121$$

Note that this last expression could be simplified as follows:

$$_5q_{35} = \frac{l_{35} - l_{40}}{l_{35}}$$

where the difference between the number living at age 35 ($l_{35}$) and at age 40 ($l_{40}$) equals the number who died during this five-year interval.

Probabilities of survival can also be expressed by using the table. The chance of living one year following age 35 ($p_{35}$) will be a fraction, the denominator of which is the number living at age 35 and the numerator of which is the number that have lived one year following the specified age (i.e., to age 36). Thus:

$$p_{35} = \frac{l_{36}}{l_{35}} = \frac{9,471,683}{9,491,711} = 0.9979$$

The discussion in the following chapters utilizes the *1980 CSO Table* in illustrating the principles involved in rate-making. As emphasized in Chapter 2, the *1980 CSO Table* is not, however, used by life insurance companies as the primary basis for establishing premium rates. They use tables that reflect up-to-date experience (often based upon the insurer's own most recent experience) in establishing premium rates. The *1980 CSO Table* is used for reserve valuation and nonforfeiture-value purposes.

## UNDERLYING PRINCIPLES

### INTEREST

As pointed out in Chapter 2, prefunding for life insurance protection via either a fixed, level premium or a flexible premium can lead to the accumulation of large sums of money, which are often held by insurers for many years before being used to pay benefits. The funds, in large part, are invested in income-producing assets, whose earnings permit life insurance companies to charge lower premiums than would otherwise be the case. Because interest plays such a vital role in the actuarial calculations and the actual operations of a life insurance company, it is essential to consider some of the more important concepts relating to it.

*Terminology*. **Interest** may be defined as the price paid for the use of money. The original investment, referred to as the **principal amount** or simply **principal**, accumulates by the end of a specified term to a sum referred to as the **accumulated amount**. The interest earned for this particular period is the simple difference between the accumulated amount and the principal.

Abbreviations are commonly used in dealing with interest. Some of the most common ones are:

| | | |
|---|---|---|
| $I$ | = | interest amount |
| $S$ | = | accumulated amount |
| $A$ | = | principal amount |
| $i$ | = | interest rate |
| $n$ | = | number of compounding periods, often expressed in years. |

Using these abbreviations, the statement that an accumulated amount is equal to the principal amount plus interest may be expressed as $S = A + I$. The statement that interest is equal to the principal times the rate per annum may be expressed as $I = Ai$. By rewriting the statement for accumulated amount, one obtains $S = A + Ai$, or $S = A(1 + i)$. The equation $S = A(1 + i)$ states that the amount to which the principal will accumulate in one year at a given interest rate is equal to the principal multiplied by the sum of one plus the interest rate.

Interest that is credited or paid only on the original principal is described as **simple interest**. In many cases, as is the case for life insurance calculations, interest earnings will be left with the original principal to itself earn interest. When interest is not distributed but used to earn additional funds, it is described as **compound interest**.

*Compound Interest Functions*. Four basic compound interest functions are used in insurance mathematics. An understanding of these functions is important for anyone interested in insurance or any other area of finance.

*1. Accumulated Value of 1.* The amount to which a principal will accumulate in one year at a given rate per annum has been expressed as $S_1 = A(1 + i)$. If this amount were invested for an additional year, the interest for the second year would be $i$ times $S_1$. The amount at the end of the second year could then be expressed as:

$$S_2 = S_1 + iS_1$$
$$= S_1(1 + i)$$
$$= A(1 + i)^2$$

Still using simple algebra, the accumulated value of $A$ at the end of $n$ years may be expressed as $S = A(1 + i)^n$. Since interest tables show the value for a principal of one, the values $(1 + i)^n$ may be found in the appropriate interest table and multiplied by the principal amount to determine the future value. Table A1-1 in the Appendix provides these compound interest factors at various interest rates.

*2. Present Value of 1.* In all financial areas, it is often necessary to provide a set amount of money at the end of some specified period of time. To achieve this goal, a sum of money is invested today. The principal that must be invested now to accomplish some objective in the future is referred to as the **present value**.

Since $S = A(1 + i)^n$, it is only necessary to divide both sides of this equation by $(1 + i)^n$ to determine the expression $A = S/(1 + i)^n$. Thus to determine the present value of the amount—that is, the principal—it is only necessary to divide the amount $S$ by $(1 + i)^n$.

Of course,

$$\frac{S}{(1 + i)^n} = S\left[\frac{1}{1 + i}\right]^n$$

The symbol $v$ is commonly used for $\left[\frac{1}{1 + i}\right]$. Thus

$$v^n = \left[\frac{1}{1 + i}\right]^n$$

Tables for the value $v^n$ at various interest rates are available. Table A1-2 in the Appendix is such a table. The figures given in these tables are commonly referred to as the present value of 1 rather than $1/(1 + i)^n$ or $v^n$. Present value tables were developed so that multiplication rather than division could be performed to obtain present value results.

*3. Accumulated Value of 1 per Year.* Suppose that an investment of $1 is made at the beginning of each year for three years. To determine the accumulated amount at the end of three years, it is only necessary to add the amounts to which each of the payments will grow. The first $1 will grow to an amount of $(1 + i)^3$. The second $1 will grow to an amount of $(1 + i)^2$, and the third $1 will grow to an amount of $(1 + i)$. The total amount at the end of three years may be expressed as:

$$\ddot{s}_{\overline{3}|} = (1 + i) + (1 + i)^2 + (1 + i)^3$$

where

$$\ddot{s}_{\overline{n}|}$$

is the symbol for the accumulated value at the end of $n$ years of 1 invested at the *beginning* of each year for $n$ years.[14] In general,

$$\ddot{s}_{\overline{n}|} = \sum_{t=1}^{n} (1 + i)^t = (1 + i) + (1 + i)^2 + \ldots + (1 + i)^{n-1} + (1 + i)^n$$

Table A1-3 in the Appendix gives tables of $\ddot{s}_{\overline{n}|}$ at various interest rates.

*4. Present Value of 1 per Year.* Another common compound-interest problem is to determine what principal (i.e., present value) should be invested now to provide equal annual payments at the *end* of each year for the next $n$ years. The total present value of the payments is computed by summing the present value of each payment. For example, suppose that we wish to find the present value of $1 payable at the end of each year for three years. The present values of the first, second, and third payments are $v^1$, $v^2$, and $v^3$, respectively. The total present value may be expressed as:

$$a_{\overline{3}|} = v^1 + v^2 + v^3$$

where $a_{\overline{n}|}$ is the symbol for the present value of 1 paid at the end of each year for the next $n$ years.[15] In general, then,

$$a_{\overline{n}|} = \sum_{t=1}^{n} v^t = v + v^2 + \ldots + v^{n-1} + v^n$$

Table A1-4 in the Appendix gives tables of $a_{\overline{n}|}$ at various interest rates.

## ANNUITIES

An **annuity** is simply a series of payments (or receipts).[16] Usually, the payment is a constant amount and the intervals are regular, such as, for example, $100

[14]The notation $\ddot{s}_{\overline{n}|}$ is commonly read as: "s double-dot angle n." The two dots above the s mean that payments are made at the beginning of each period. An s without the two dots means that the payments are made at the end of each period.

[15]The $a_{\overline{n}|}$ notation is commonly read as "a angle n." The absence of the two dots above the a indicates that payments are made at the end of each period. See footnote 14.

[16]A series of payments to a payor is a series of receipts to the recipient.

payable at the end of each month for 10 years, or $5,000 payable at the end of each year for 20 years. The annuity payment may be certain or it may be contingent on a particular person being alive. The former annuities are called **annuities certain**. The latter are called **life annuities**. A life annuity for a set term of years (but terminating if and when the individual dies during the set term) is called a **temporary life annuity**. An annuity that pays for as long as either or both of two persons is alive is a **joint and survivor annuity**.

When the annuity payments are assumed to be made at the *beginning* of each period, the annuity is referred to as an **annuity due.** Its symbol is

$$\ddot{a}_{\overline{n}|}$$

Annuity theory plays an important role in actuarial calculations, because premium payments to a life insurance company by a policyowner constitute an annuity due to the insurer.

## ASSUMPTIONS UNDERLYING RATE COMPUTATIONS

When the problem of life insurance rate computation is approached, several questions arise at once, and the answers to these questions directly influence the results obtained. For instance, how often will the premium be paid? Annually, semiannually, or otherwise? For how long will premiums be paid? For 5, 10, 20 years, or for life? There are additional questions: What disposition will be made of funds between the time they are received and the time they are paid out? How will mortality rates be determined for periods of less than one year's duration in case, for instance, monthly premiums are decided upon, since standard mortality tables give only yearly rates of mortality? Clearly, these and many other questions must be answered before the computation of rates can be accurately made.

Premiums may be paid in a single cash sum, called a single premium, which pays for the entire risk incurred during the term of the policy, or they may be paid over a period equal to or less than the life of the contract. Many policies are purchased by an annual premium. In this connection, two simplifying assumptions usually are made: (1) premiums are paid at the beginning of each policy year, and (2) claims are paid at the end of the policy year in which the policy matures.[17] Accordingly, if a policy is purchased by a single premium, this sum is to be paid at the inception of the risk. In the case of level annual premiums, the first payment is to be made on the date of issue of the policy, and equal amounts are then paid annually thereafter on the anniversary of this date.

It is evident in the case of single premiums, and it is true only to a lesser degree with annual premiums, that the insurer will have possession of the funds for some time before being called upon to pay claims. Amounts in excess of that

[17]Of course, insurers do not actually wait to pay death claims until the end of the policy year. They are paid promptly. The assumption that they are paid at the end of the year simplifies the analysis while not doing harm to the concepts.

needed to meet current expenses and other policy obligations are invested and earn interest while in the insurer's possession. These interest earnings are an important source of the funds available to pay claims. Since the insurer does not know the rates of interest to be earned in the future, it is necessary to assume a rate that is reasonably certain of being earned each year throughout the potentially long life of a policy.[18]

In determining the interest rate to be assumed in computing guaranteed maximum premiums (or choosing a guaranteed minimum interest rate under current assumption policies), it is necessary to select a rate that the insurer is reasonably sure of earning each year over a long period of years. The assumption that 9 or 10 percent could be earned might be disastrous, for although the insurer might earn that rate or more in some years, the rate might decrease. If the insurer failed to earn the assumed 9 or 10 percent rate, it would need to make up the difference from surplus accumulated in previous years, or, in the absence of the latter, it might become insolvent. Insurers issuing participating or current assumption nonparticipating insurance policies generally select a conservative interest rate, with the intention and expectation of returning to the policyowner, through dividends or otherwise, earnings in excess of the rate selected. A typical rate used by companies for original rate computations might be 4 to 5 percent. The rate chosen may make little difference (other things being the same), as long as it is neither too high (which could endanger solvency) nor too low (which could produce an uncompetitively high premium), since much of the excess earnings under most cash-value policies sold today eventually will be paid or credited to policyowners.

The second simplifying assumption sometimes made is that claims are paid at the end of each policy year. If there is a fairly even distribution of deaths throughout the policy year (roughly equivalent to all deaths at the middle of year), the payment of claims would occur on the average six months after death.[19] Thus the assumption of paying death claims at the end of the year is too generous, to the extent of six months' interest in discounting claims. If premium rates are computed at 5 percent, this would mean a loss to the insurer of $250 on a $10,000 policy. Even so, many insurers calculate net premiums on the assumption that claims are paid at the end of the year. The error introduced typically is corrected by a small adjustment in the expense-loading formula or in the timing of interest credits.

The assumption of when in the policy year deaths occur is financially significant to insurance companies primarily in the case of policies with

---

[18]Amounts actually earned in excess of those assumed can be credited to the policyowner via dividends under participating policies, via lower premiums on indeterminate premium policies, and via higher cash-value interest credits on universal life and other current assumption policies.

[19]In the early experience of life insurance companies, this was not far from the truth, for it took about three months to establish proof of death, and old policies allowed the insurer three months after proof before the claim was payable. At present, however, claims are paid promptly. One prominent insurer, for instance, advertises that over 95 percent of its claims are paid within one working day of receipt of proof of death.

premiums that are payable at more frequent intervals than once a year. In the case of monthly premiums, if only one-twelfth of the annual premium has been collected in the first month, but one-sixth of the year's total mortality costs occur during the first month, the insurer will have to use its surplus funds to pay losses. With some mortality tables, this situation occurs during the first ten years of life, when the mortality rate is decreasing and proportionately more deaths occur at the beginning of the year than toward the end of the year. At other ages, the mortality rate generally increases, and the discrepancy between the assumption of uniform deaths and the actual situation is favorable to the insurer.

In addition to these assumptions, the following must be known to compute premium rates in life insurance:

1. The age of the insured

2. The sex of the insured (where this is a permitted factor)

3. The benefits to be provided

4. The mortality table to be used (possibly involving separate tables for smokers and nonsmokers)

5. A rate of interest

6. An amount to cover the insurer's expenses for operation, profits, and a margin for contingencies

Also, an estimate is needed as to the proportion of policyowners whose contracts terminate each year for reasons other than death or policy maturity. Together, all of these assumptions are used to test the tentative gross premiums through asset-share studies (discussed in Chapter 21).

## INTERACTION OF PROBABILITY, MORTALITY, AND INTEREST CONCEPTS

As pointed out earlier, the process of obtaining the present value of a dollar payable at a specified time in the future is referred to as **discounting**. Assuming that the payment of the dollar in the future is not a certainty but is contingent on some insured individual being alive, it is necessary to reduce the present value of the future dollar still further, reflecting the probability that the individual will be alive to pay it. The process of discounting for probability is referred to as taking an **expected value**.

For example, assume that it is desired to know the value today of a promise to pay $1,000 in 20 years if a male now aged 30 is alive at that time. Assume money is valued at 6 percent and that *1980 CSO* mortality rates apply. From referring to Table A1-2, we know that the value today of $1,000 to be paid in 20 years (ignoring the survival probability) is found by multiplying the present value factor (at 6 percent and 20 years) by $1,000. Thus $1,000 x 0.312 = $312.

The probability that a male aged 30 will live for 20 years, $_{20}p_{30}$, is the ratio of the number living at age 50 ($l_{50}$) to the number living at age 30 ($l_{30}$), that is,

$l_{50}/l_{30}$ or, referring to Table 18-1, 8,966,618 ÷ 9,579,998, which equals 0.936. Thus the present *expected* value of the $1,000 to be paid at age 50 is found by taking the product of the present value and the expected value—that is, $312 x 0.936 = $292. This represents the value (or worth) today of the future promise, based on the stated assumptions.

If expenses are ignored and the net premium rate for a life insurance policy is calculated, at date of issue the present value of all future expected premiums must be equal to the present value of all future expected benefits, where values are discounted for both interest and mortality. In word form, therefore, we observe that at issue date for any life insurance policy:

Present expected value                Present expected value

of future premiums (PVFP) = of future benefits (PVFB)

This relationship is illustrated in Table 18-3 for a hypothetical $1,000 ordinary life policy issued to an 80-year-old male. Column 1 shows the net level annual premium that hypothetically would be paid at the beginning of each year if the insured were alive then. Column 2 shows present value factors, where the factor for the first year is 1 since the premium is paid now. Column 3 shows probabilities of survival to the attained age shown. Column 4 lists the present expected values for each premium payment. The $698.96 total at the bottom of column 4 is the total present expected value of all future premiums.

Column 5 shows yearly death benefits payable. The figures in column 6, the discounts for interest, are smaller than the corresponding figures in column 2 because death benefits are assumed to be paid at the end of the year, whereas premiums are paid at the beginning of the year. Hence death benefits are discounted for one year more than are premiums. Whereas column 3 shows the probability of survival to pay the premium at each age, column 7 shows the probability of dying and, therefore, the likelihood of payment of the death benefits at each age. Column 8 shows yearly present expected values of each future benefit. The total of $698.96 at the bottom of column 8 is the total present expected value of all future death benefits and is the same as the present expected value of all future premiums. Thus at date of issue we see that PVFP = PVFB.

Table 18-3 reflects the interaction of probability, mortality, and money concepts. Each of these elements has been included in its proper place and has been combined with the other elements according to a precise mathematical blend. The result is that based on the given assumptions as to mortality and interest, an insurance contract represents an equal exchange of *expected* value between the policyowner and the insurer. The policyowner pays the premiums. The insurer agrees to pay the stated death benefits, and the present expected values are equal. The following chapters consider premium calculations in detail. It is important not to lose sight of this basic goal in all insurance contracts: the exchange of equal expected values at date of issue.[20]

[20]This statement, of course, ignores insurer loadings.

**TABLE 18-3    $1,000 ORDINARY LIFE POLICY FOR MALE, AGED 80 (*1980 CSO TABLE*, 6% INTEREST)**

| | Premiums | | | | Benefits | | | |
|---|---|---|---|---|---|---|---|---|
| (1) | (2) | (3) | (4) | (5) | (6) | (7) | (8) |
| | Interest | Probability | Present Expected | | Interest | | Present Expected |
| Level | Discount | of | Value of | | Discount | Probability | Value of |
| Attained | Annual | Factor | Survival | Premiums | Death | Factor | of Death | Benefits |
| Age (x) | Premium | $(v^{t-1})$ | $({}_tp_{80})$ | [(1) x (2) x (3)] | Benefit | $(v^t)$ | $(d_x/l_{80})$ | [(5) x (6) x (7)] |
| 80 | $131.42 | 1.0000 | 1.0000 | $131.42 | $1,000.00 | 0.9434 | 0.0988 | $ 93.25 |
| 81 | 131.42 | 0.9434 | 0.9012 | 111.72 | 1,000.00 | 0.8900 | 0.0969 | 86.20 |
| 82 | 131.42 | 0.8900 | 0.8043 | 94.07 | 1,000.00 | 0.8396 | 0.0943 | 79.18 |
| 83 | 131.42 | 0.8396 | 0.7100 | 78.34 | 1,000.00 | 0.7921 | 0.0911 | 72.13 |
| 84 | 131.42 | 0.7921 | 0.6189 | 64.43 | 1,000.00 | 0.7473 | 0.0868 | 64.87 |
| 85 | 131.42 | 0.7473 | 0.5321 | 52.26 | 1,000.00 | 0.7050 | 0.0814 | 57.38 |
| 86 | 131.42 | 0.7050 | 0.4507 | 41.76 | 1,000.00 | 0.6651 | 0.0749 | 49.79 |
| 87 | 131.42 | 0.6651 | 0.3759 | 32.85 | 1,000.00 | 0.6274 | 0.0675 | 42.34 |
| 88 | 131.42 | 0.6274 | 0.3084 | 25.43 | 1,000.00 | 0.5919 | 0.0596 | 35.28 |
| 89 | 131.42 | 0.5919 | 0.2488 | 19.35 | 1,000.00 | 0.5584 | 0.0516 | 28.80 |
| 90 | 131.42 | 0.5584 | 0.1972 | 14.47 | 1,000.00 | 0.5268 | 0.0437 | 23.04 |
| 91 | 131.42 | 0.5268 | 0.1535 | 10.63 | 1,000.00 | 0.4970 | 0.0364 | 18.08 |
| 92 | 131.42 | 0.4970 | 0.1171 | 7.65 | 1,000.00 | 0.4688 | 0.0297 | 13.92 |
| 93 | 131.42 | 0.4688 | 0.0874 | 5.39 | 1,000.00 | 0.4423 | 0.0238 | 10.52 |
| 94 | 131.42 | 0.4423 | 0.0636 | 3.70 | 1,000.00 | 0.4173 | 0.0188 | 7.86 |
| 95 | 131.42 | 0.4173 | 0.0448 | 2.46 | 1,000.00 | 0.3936 | 0.0148 | 5.82 |
| 96 | 131.42 | 0.3936 | 0.0300 | 1.55 | 1,000.00 | 0.3714 | 0.0115 | 4.29 |
| 97 | 131.42 | 0.3714 | 0.0185 | 0.90 | 1,000.00 | 0.3503 | 0.0089 | 3.11 |
| 98 | 131.42 | 0.3503 | 0.0096 | 0.44 | 1,000.00 | 0.3305 | 0.0063 | 2.09 |
| 99 | 131.42 | 0.3305 | 0.0033 | 0.14 | 1,000.00 | 0.3118 | 0.0033 | 1.02 |
| | | | | $698.96 | | | | $698.96 |

# APPENDIX 18-1
## ACCUMULATED VALUE OF 1, AT VARIOUS INTEREST RATES

| Years n | 3.0% | 4.0% | 5.0% | 5.5% | $(1+i)^n$ 6.0% | 7.0% | 8.0% | 9.0% | 10.0% |
|---|---|---|---|---|---|---|---|---|---|
| 1 | 1.030 | 1.040 | 1.050 | 1.055 | 1.060 | 1.070 | 1.080 | 1.090 | 1.100 |
| 2 | 1.061 | 1.082 | 1.103 | 1.113 | 1.124 | 1.145 | 1.166 | 1.188 | 1.210 |
| 3 | 1.093 | 1.125 | 1.158 | 1.174 | 1.191 | 1.225 | 1.260 | 1.295 | 1.331 |
| 4 | 1.126 | 1.170 | 1.216 | 1.239 | 1.262 | 1.311 | 1.360 | 1.412 | 1.464 |
| 5 | 1.159 | 1.217 | 1.276 | 1.307 | 1.338 | 1.403 | 1.469 | 1.539 | 1.611 |
| 6 | 1.194 | 1.265 | 1.340 | 1.379 | 1.419 | 1.501 | 1.587 | 1.677 | 1.772 |
| 7 | 1.230 | 1.316 | 1.407 | 1.455 | 1.504 | 1.606 | 1.714 | 1.828 | 1.949 |
| 8 | 1.267 | 1.369 | 1.477 | 1.535 | 1.594 | 1.718 | 1.851 | 1.993 | 2.144 |
| 9 | 1.305 | 1.423 | 1.551 | 1.619 | 1.689 | 1.838 | 1.999 | 2.172 | 2.358 |
| 10 | 1.344 | 1.480 | 1.629 | 1.708 | 1.791 | 1.967 | 2.159 | 2.367 | 2.594 |
| 11 | 1.384 | 1.539 | 1.710 | 1.802 | 1.898 | 2.105 | 2.332 | 2.580 | 2.853 |
| 12 | 1.426 | 1.601 | 1.796 | 1.901 | 2.012 | 2.252 | 2.518 | 2.813 | 3.138 |
| 13 | 1.469 | 1.665 | 1.886 | 2.006 | 2.133 | 2.410 | 2.720 | 3.066 | 3.452 |
| 14 | 1.513 | 1.732 | 1.980 | 2.116 | 2.261 | 2.579 | 2.937 | 3.342 | 3.797 |
| 15 | 1.558 | 1.801 | 2.079 | 2.232 | 2.397 | 2.759 | 3.172 | 3.642 | 4.177 |
| 16 | 1.605 | 1.873 | 2.183 | 2.355 | 2.540 | 2.952 | 3.426 | 3.970 | 4.595 |
| 17 | 1.653 | 1.948 | 2.292 | 2.485 | 2.693 | 3.159 | 3.700 | 4.328 | 5.054 |
| 18 | 1.702 | 2.026 | 2.407 | 2.621 | 2.854 | 3.380 | 3.996 | 4.717 | 5.560 |
| 19 | 1.754 | 2.107 | 2.527 | 2.766 | 3.026 | 3.617 | 4.316 | 5.142 | 6.116 |
| 20 | 1.806 | 2.191 | 2.653 | 2.918 | 3.207 | 3.870 | 4.661 | 5.604 | 6.727 |
| 21 | 1.860 | 2.279 | 2.786 | 3.078 | 3.400 | 4.141 | 5.034 | 6.109 | 7.400 |
| 22 | 1.916 | 2.370 | 2.925 | 3.248 | 3.604 | 4.430 | 5.437 | 6.659 | 8.140 |
| 23 | 1.974 | 2.465 | 3.072 | 3.426 | 3.820 | 4.741 | 5.871 | 7.258 | 8.954 |
| 24 | 2.033 | 2.563 | 3.225 | 3.615 | 4.049 | 5.072 | 6.341 | 7.911 | 9.850 |
| 25 | 2.094 | 2.666 | 3.386 | 3.813 | 4.292 | 5.427 | 6.848 | 8.623 | 10.835 |
| 26 | 2.157 | 2.772 | 3.556 | 4.023 | 4.549 | 5.807 | 7.396 | 9.399 | 11.918 |
| 27 | 2.221 | 2.883 | 3.733 | 4.244 | 4.822 | 6.214 | 7.988 | 10.245 | 13.110 |
| 28 | 2.288 | 2.999 | 3.920 | 4.478 | 5.112 | 6.649 | 8.627 | 11.167 | 14.421 |
| 29 | 2.357 | 3.119 | 4.116 | 4.724 | 5.418 | 7.114 | 9.317 | 12.172 | 15.863 |
| 30 | 2.427 | 3.243 | 4.322 | 4.984 | 5.743 | 7.612 | 10.063 | 13.268 | 17.449 |
| 31 | 2.500 | 3.373 | 4.538 | 5.258 | 6.088 | 8.145 | 10.868 | 14.462 | 19.194 |
| 32 | 2.575 | 3.508 | 4.765 | 5.547 | 6.453 | 8.715 | 11.737 | 15.763 | 21.114 |
| 33 | 2.652 | 3.648 | 5.003 | 5.852 | 6.841 | 9.325 | 12.676 | 17.182 | 23.225 |
| 34 | 2.732 | 3.794 | 5.253 | 6.174 | 7.251 | 9.978 | 13.690 | 18.728 | 25.548 |
| 35 | 2.814 | 3.946 | 5.516 | 6.514 | 7.686 | 10.677 | 14.785 | 20.414 | 28.102 |
| 36 | 2.898 | 4.104 | 5.792 | 6.872 | 8.147 | 11.424 | 15.968 | 22.251 | 30.913 |
| 37 | 2.985 | 4.268 | 6.081 | 7.250 | 8.636 | 12.224 | 17.246 | 24.254 | 34.004 |
| 38 | 3.075 | 4.439 | 6.385 | 7.649 | 9.154 | 13.079 | 18.625 | 26.437 | 37.404 |
| 39 | 3.167 | 4.616 | 6.705 | 8.069 | 9.704 | 13.995 | 20.115 | 28.816 | 41.145 |
| 40 | 3.262 | 4.801 | 7.040 | 8.513 | 10.286 | 14.974 | 21.725 | 31.409 | 45.259 |
| 41 | 3.360 | 4.993 | 7.392 | 8.982 | 10.903 | 16.023 | 23.462 | 34.236 | 49.785 |
| 42 | 3.461 | 5.193 | 7.762 | 9.476 | 11.557 | 17.144 | 25.339 | 37.318 | 54.764 |
| 43 | 3.565 | 5.400 | 8.150 | 9.997 | 12.250 | 18.344 | 27.367 | 40.676 | 60.240 |
| 44 | 3.671 | 5.617 | 8.557 | 10.546 | 12.985 | 19.628 | 29.556 | 44.337 | 66.264 |
| 45 | 3.782 | 5.841 | 8.985 | 11.127 | 13.765 | 21.002 | 31.920 | 48.327 | 72.890 |
| 46 | 3.895 | 6.075 | 9.434 | 11.739 | 14.590 | 22.473 | 34.474 | 52.677 | 80.180 |
| 47 | 4.012 | 6.318 | 9.906 | 12.384 | 15.466 | 24.046 | 37.232 | 57.418 | 88.197 |
| 48 | 4.132 | 6.571 | 10.401 | 13.065 | 16.394 | 25.729 | 40.211 | 62.585 | 97.017 |
| 49 | 4.256 | 6.833 | 10.921 | 13.784 | 17.378 | 27.530 | 43.427 | 68.218 | 106.719 |
| 50 | 4.384 | 7.107 | 11.467 | 14.542 | 18.420 | 29.457 | 46.902 | 74.358 | 117.391 |

# APPENDIX 18-2
## PRESENT VALUE OF 1, AT VARIOUS INTEREST RATES

$(V)^n$

| Years n | 3.0% | 4.0% | 5.0% | 5.5% | 6.0% | 7.0% | 8.0% | 9.0% | 10.0% |
|---|---|---|---|---|---|---|---|---|---|
| 1 | 0.971 | 0.962 | 0.952 | 0.948 | 0.943 | 0.935 | 0.926 | 0.917 | 0.909 |
| 2 | 0.943 | 0.925 | 0.907 | 0.898 | 0.890 | 0.873 | 0.857 | 0.842 | 0.826 |
| 3 | 0.915 | 0.889 | 0.864 | 0.852 | 0.840 | 0.816 | 0.794 | 0.772 | 0.751 |
| 4 | 0.888 | 0.855 | 0.823 | 0.807 | 0.792 | 0.763 | 0.735 | 0.708 | 0.683 |
| 5 | 0.863 | 0.822 | 0.784 | 0.765 | 0.747 | 0.713 | 0.681 | 0.650 | 0.621 |
| 6 | 0.837 | 0.790 | 0.746 | 0.725 | 0.705 | 0.666 | 0.630 | 0.596 | 0.564 |
| 7 | 0.813 | 0.760 | 0.711 | 0.687 | 0.665 | 0.623 | 0.583 | 0.547 | 0.513 |
| 8 | 0.789 | 0.731 | 0.677 | 0.652 | 0.627 | 0.582 | 0.540 | 0.502 | 0.467 |
| 9 | 0.766 | 0.703 | 0.645 | 0.618 | 0.592 | 0.544 | 0.500 | 0.460 | 0.424 |
| 10 | 0.744 | 0.676 | 0.614 | 0.585 | 0.558 | 0.508 | 0.463 | 0.422 | 0.386 |
| 11 | 0.722 | 0.650 | 0.585 | 0.555 | 0.527 | 0.475 | 0.429 | 0.388 | 0.350 |
| 12 | 0.701 | 0.625 | 0.557 | 0.526 | 0.497 | 0.444 | 0.397 | 0.356 | 0.319 |
| 13 | 0.681 | 0.601 | 0.530 | 0.499 | 0.469 | 0.415 | 0.368 | 0.326 | 0.290 |
| 14 | 0.661 | 0.577 | 0.505 | 0.473 | 0.442 | 0.388 | 0.340 | 0.299 | 0.263 |
| 15 | 0.642 | 0.555 | 0.481 | 0.448 | 0.417 | 0.362 | 0.315 | 0.275 | 0.239 |
| 16 | 0.623 | 0.534 | 0.458 | 0.425 | 0.394 | 0.339 | 0.292 | 0.252 | 0.218 |
| 17 | 0.605 | 0.513 | 0.436 | 0.402 | 0.371 | 0.317 | 0.270 | 0.231 | 0.198 |
| 18 | 0.587 | 0.494 | 0.416 | 0.381 | 0.350 | 0.296 | 0.250 | 0.212 | 0.180 |
| 19 | 0.570 | 0.475 | 0.396 | 0.362 | 0.331 | 0.277 | 0.232 | 0.194 | 0.164 |
| 20 | 0.554 | 0.456 | 0.377 | 0.343 | 0.312 | 0.258 | 0.215 | 0.178 | 0.149 |
| 21 | 0.538 | 0.439 | 0.359 | 0.325 | 0.294 | 0.242 | 0.199 | 0.164 | 0.135 |
| 22 | 0.522 | 0.422 | 0.342 | 0.308 | 0.278 | 0.226 | 0.184 | 0.150 | 0.123 |
| 23 | 0.507 | 0.406 | 0.326 | 0.292 | 0.262 | 0.211 | 0.170 | 0.138 | 0.112 |
| 24 | 0.492 | 0.390 | 0.310 | 0.277 | 0.247 | 0.197 | 0.158 | 0.126 | 0.102 |
| 25 | 0.478 | 0.375 | 0.295 | 0.262 | 0.233 | 0.184 | 0.146 | 0.116 | 0.092 |
| 26 | 0.464 | 0.361 | 0.281 | 0.249 | 0.220 | 0.172 | 0.135 | 0.106 | 0.084 |
| 27 | 0.450 | 0.347 | 0.268 | 0.236 | 0.207 | 0.161 | 0.125 | 0.098 | 0.076 |
| 28 | 0.437 | 0.333 | 0.255 | 0.223 | 0.196 | 0.150 | 0.116 | 0.090 | 0.069 |
| 29 | 0.424 | 0.321 | 0.243 | 0.212 | 0.185 | 0.141 | 0.107 | 0.082 | 0.063 |
| 30 | 0.412 | 0.308 | 0.231 | 0.201 | 0.174 | 0.131 | 0.099 | 0.075 | 0.057 |
| 31 | 0.400 | 0.296 | 0.220 | 0.190 | 0.164 | 0.123 | 0.092 | 0.069 | 0.052 |
| 32 | 0.388 | 0.285 | 0.210 | 0.180 | 0.155 | 0.115 | 0.085 | 0.063 | 0.047 |
| 33 | 0.377 | 0.274 | 0.200 | 0.171 | 0.146 | 0.107 | 0.079 | 0.058 | 0.043 |
| 34 | 0.366 | 0.264 | 0.190 | 0.162 | 0.138 | 0.100 | 0.073 | 0.053 | 0.039 |
| 35 | 0.355 | 0.253 | 0.181 | 0.154 | 0.130 | 0.094 | 0.068 | 0.049 | 0.036 |
| 36 | 0.345 | 0.244 | 0.173 | 0.146 | 0.123 | 0.088 | 0.063 | 0.045 | 0.032 |
| 37 | 0.335 | 0.234 | 0.164 | 0.138 | 0.116 | 0.082 | 0.058 | 0.041 | 0.029 |
| 38 | 0.325 | 0.225 | 0.157 | 0.131 | 0.109 | 0.076 | 0.054 | 0.038 | 0.027 |
| 39 | 0.316 | 0.217 | 0.149 | 0.124 | 0.103 | 0.071 | 0.050 | 0.035 | 0.024 |
| 40 | 0.307 | 0.208 | 0.142 | 0.117 | 0.097 | 0.067 | 0.046 | 0.032 | 0.022 |
| 41 | 0.298 | 0.200 | 0.135 | 0.111 | 0.092 | 0.062 | 0.043 | 0.029 | 0.020 |
| 42 | 0.289 | 0.193 | 0.129 | 0.106 | 0.087 | 0.058 | 0.039 | 0.027 | 0.018 |
| 43 | 0.281 | 0.185 | 0.123 | 0.100 | 0.082 | 0.055 | 0.037 | 0.025 | 0.017 |
| 44 | 0.272 | 0.178 | 0.117 | 0.095 | 0.077 | 0.051 | 0.034 | 0.023 | 0.015 |
| 45 | 0.264 | 0.171 | 0.111 | 0.090 | 0.073 | 0.048 | 0.031 | 0.021 | 0.014 |
| 46 | 0.257 | 0.165 | 0.106 | 0.085 | 0.069 | 0.044 | 0.029 | 0.019 | 0.012 |
| 47 | 0.249 | 0.158 | 0.101 | 0.081 | 0.065 | 0.042 | 0.027 | 0.017 | 0.011 |
| 48 | 0.242 | 0.152 | 0.096 | 0.077 | 0.061 | 0.039 | 0.025 | 0.016 | 0.010 |
| 49 | 0.235 | 0.146 | 0.092 | 0.073 | 0.058 | 0.036 | 0.023 | 0.015 | 0.009 |

# APPENDIX 18-3
## ACCUMULATED VALUE OF 1 PER YEAR, AT VARIOUS INTEREST RATES

$i_{TT}$

| Years n | 3.0% | 4.0% | 5.0% | 5.5% | 6.0% | 7.0% | 8.0% | 9.0% | 10.0% |
|---|---|---|---|---|---|---|---|---|---|
| 1 | 1.030 | 1.040 | 1.050 | 1.055 | 1.060 | 1.070 | 1.080 | 1.090 | 1.100 |
| 2 | 2.091 | 2.122 | 2.153 | 2.168 | 2.184 | 2.215 | 2.246 | 2.278 | 2.310 |
| 3 | 3.184 | 3.246 | 3.310 | 3.342 | 3.375 | 3.440 | 3.506 | 3.573 | 3.641 |
| 4 | 4.309 | 4.416 | 4.526 | 4.581 | 4.637 | 4.751 | 4.867 | 4.985 | 5.105 |
| 5 | 5.468 | 5.633 | 5.802 | 5.888 | 5.975 | 6.153 | 6.336 | 6.523 | 6.716 |
| 6 | 6.662 | 6.898 | 7.142 | 7.267 | 7.394 | 7.654 | 7.923 | 8.200 | 8.487 |
| 7 | 7.892 | 8.214 | 8.549 | 8.722 | 8.897 | 9.260 | 9.637 | 10.028 | 10.436 |
| 8 | 9.159 | 9.583 | 10.027 | 10.256 | 10.491 | 10.978 | 11.488 | 12.021 | 12.579 |
| 9 | 10.464 | 11.006 | 11.578 | 11.875 | 12.181 | 12.816 | 13.487 | 14.193 | 14.937 |
| 10 | 11.808 | 12.486 | 13.207 | 13.583 | 13.972 | 14.784 | 15.645 | 16.560 | 17.531 |
| 11 | 13.192 | 14.026 | 14.917 | 15.386 | 15.870 | 16.888 | 17.977 | 19.141 | 20.384 |
| 12 | 14.618 | 15.627 | 16.713 | 17.287 | 17.882 | 19.141 | 20.495 | 21.953 | 23.523 |
| 13 | 16.086 | 17.292 | 18.599 | 19.293 | 20.015 | 21.550 | 23.215 | 25.019 | 26.975 |
| 14 | 17.599 | 19.024 | 20.579 | 21.409 | 22.276 | 24.129 | 26.152 | 28.361 | 30.772 |
| 15 | 19.157 | 20.825 | 22.657 | 23.641 | 24.673 | 26.888 | 29.324 | 32.003 | 34.950 |
| 16 | 20.762 | 22.698 | 24.840 | 25.996 | 27.213 | 29.840 | 32.750 | 35.974 | 39.545 |
| 17 | 22.414 | 24.645 | 27.132 | 28.481 | 29.906 | 32.999 | 36.450 | 40.301 | 44.599 |
| 18 | 24.117 | 26.671 | 29.539 | 31.103 | 32.760 | 36.379 | 40.446 | 45.018 | 50.159 |
| 19 | 25.870 | 28.778 | 32.066 | 33.868 | 35.786 | 39.995 | 44.762 | 50.160 | 56.275 |
| 20 | 27.676 | 30.969 | 34.719 | 36.786 | 38.993 | 43.865 | 49.423 | 55.765 | 63.002 |
| 21 | 29.537 | 33.248 | 37.505 | 39.864 | 42.392 | 48.006 | 54.457 | 61.873 | 70.403 |
| 22 | 31.453 | 35.618 | 40.430 | 43.112 | 45.996 | 52.436 | 59.893 | 68.532 | 78.543 |
| 23 | 33.426 | 38.083 | 43.502 | 46.538 | 49.816 | 57.177 | 65.765 | 75.790 | 87.497 |
| 24 | 35.459 | 40.646 | 46.727 | 50.153 | 53.865 | 62.249 | 72.106 | 83.701 | 97.347 |
| 25 | 37.553 | 43.312 | 50.113 | 53.966 | 58.156 | 67.676 | 78.954 | 92.324 | 108.182 |
| 26 | 39.710 | 46.084 | 53.669 | 57.989 | 62.706 | 73.484 | 86.351 | 101.723 | 120.100 |
| 27 | 41.931 | 48.968 | 57.403 | 62.234 | 67.528 | 79.698 | 94.339 | 111.968 | 133.210 |
| 28 | 44.219 | 51.966 | 61.323 | 66.711 | 72.640 | 86.347 | 102.966 | 123.135 | 147.631 |
| 29 | 46.575 | 55.085 | 65.439 | 71.435 | 78.058 | 93.461 | 112.283 | 135.308 | 163.494 |
| 30 | 49.003 | 58.328 | 69.761 | 76.419 | 83.802 | 101.073 | 122.346 | 148.575 | 180.943 |
| 31 | 51.503 | 61.701 | 74.299 | 81.677 | 89.890 | 109.218 | 133.214 | 163.037 | 200.138 |
| 32 | 54.078 | 65.210 | 79.064 | 87.225 | 96.343 | 117.933 | 144.951 | 178.800 | 221.252 |
| 33 | 56.730 | 68.858 | 84.067 | 93.077 | 103.184 | 127.259 | 157.627 | 195.982 | 244.477 |
| 34 | 59.462 | 72.652 | 89.320 | 99.251 | 110.435 | 137.237 | 171.317 | 214.711 | 270.024 |
| 35 | 62.276 | 76.598 | 94.836 | 105.765 | 118.121 | 147.913 | 186.102 | 235.125 | 298.127 |
| 36 | 65.174 | 80.702 | 100.628 | 112.637 | 126.268 | 159.337 | 202.070 | 257.376 | 329.039 |
| 37 | 68.159 | 84.970 | 106.710 | 119.887 | 134.904 | 171.561 | 219.316 | 281.630 | 363.043 |
| 38 | 71.234 | 89.409 | 113.095 | 127.536 | 144.058 | 184.640 | 237.941 | 308.066 | 400.448 |
| 39 | 74.401 | 94.026 | 119.800 | 135.606 | 153.762 | 198.635 | 258.057 | 336.882 | 441.593 |
| 40 | 77.663 | 98.827 | 126.840 | 144.119 | 164.048 | 213.610 | 279.781 | 368.292 | 486.852 |
| 41 | 81.023 | 103.820 | 134.232 | 153.100 | 174.951 | 229.632 | 303.244 | 402.528 | 536.637 |
| 42 | 84.484 | 109.012 | 141.993 | 162.576 | 186.508 | 246.776 | 328.583 | 439.846 | 591.401 |
| 43 | 88.048 | 114.413 | 150.143 | 172.573 | 198.758 | 265.121 | 355.950 | 480.522 | 651.641 |
| 44 | 91.720 | 120.029 | 158.700 | 183.119 | 211.744 | 284.749 | 385.506 | 524.859 | 717.905 |
| 45 | 95.501 | 125.871 | 167.685 | 194.246 | 225.508 | 305.752 | 417.426 | 573.186 | 790.795 |
| 46 | 99.397 | 131.945 | 177.119 | 205.984 | 240.099 | 328.224 | 451.900 | 625.863 | 870.975 |
| 47 | 103.408 | 138.263 | 187.025 | 218.368 | 255.565 | 352.270 | 489.132 | 683.280 | 959.172 |
| 48 | 107.541 | 144.834 | 197.427 | 231.434 | 271.958 | 377.999 | 529.343 | 745.866 | 1056.190 |
| 49 | 111.797 | 151.667 | 208.348 | 245.217 | 289.336 | 405.529 | 572.770 | 814.084 | 1162.909 |
| 50 | 116.181 | 158.774 | 219.815 | 259.759 | 307.756 | 434.986 | 619.672 | 888.441 | 1280.299 |

# APPENDIX 18-4
## PRESENT VALUE OF 1 YEAR, AT VARIOUS INTEREST RATES

| Years n | 3.0% | 4.0% | 5.0% | 5.5% | 6.0% | 7.0% | 8.0% | 9.0% | 10.0% |
|---|---|---|---|---|---|---|---|---|---|
| 1 | 0.971 | 0.962 | 0.952 | 0.948 | 0.943 | 0.935 | 0.926 | 0.917 | 0.909 |
| 2 | 1.913 | 1.886 | 1.859 | 1.846 | 1.833 | 1.808 | 1.783 | 1.759 | 1.736 |
| 3 | 2.829 | 2.775 | 2.723 | 2.698 | 2.673 | 2.624 | 2.577 | 2.531 | 2.487 |
| 4 | 3.717 | 3.630 | 3.546 | 3.505 | 3.465 | 3.387 | 3.312 | 3.240 | 3.170 |
| 5 | 4.580 | 4.452 | 4.329 | 4.270 | 4.212 | 4.100 | 3.993 | 3.890 | 3.791 |
| 6 | 5.417 | 5.242 | 5.076 | 4.996 | 4.917 | 4.767 | 4.623 | 4.486 | 4.355 |
| 7 | 6.230 | 6.002 | 5.786 | 5.683 | 5.582 | 5.389 | 5.206 | 5.033 | 4.868 |
| 8 | 7.020 | 6.733 | 6.463 | 6.335 | 6.210 | 5.971 | 5.747 | 5.535 | 5.335 |
| 9 | 7.786 | 7.435 | 7.108 | 6.952 | 6.802 | 6.515 | 6.247 | 5.995 | 5.759 |
| 10 | 8.530 | 8.111 | 7.722 | 7.538 | 7.360 | 7.024 | 6.710 | 6.418 | 6.145 |
| 11 | 9.253 | 8.760 | 8.306 | 8.093 | 7.887 | 7.499 | 7.139 | 6.805 | 6.495 |
| 12 | 9.954 | 9.385 | 8.863 | 8.619 | 8.384 | 7.943 | 7.536 | 7.161 | 6.814 |
| 13 | 10.635 | 9.986 | 9.394 | 9.117 | 8.853 | 8.358 | 7.904 | 7.487 | 7.103 |
| 14 | 11.296 | 10.563 | 9.899 | 9.590 | 9.295 | 8.745 | 8.244 | 7.786 | 7.367 |
| 15 | 11.938 | 11.118 | 10.380 | 10.038 | 9.712 | 9.108 | 8.559 | 8.061 | 7.606 |
| 16 | 12.561 | 11.652 | 10.838 | 10.462 | 10.106 | 9.447 | 8.851 | 8.313 | 7.824 |
| 17 | 13.166 | 12.166 | 11.274 | 10.865 | 10.477 | 9.763 | 9.122 | 8.544 | 8.022 |
| 18 | 13.754 | 12.659 | 11.690 | 11.246 | 10.828 | 10.059 | 9.372 | 8.756 | 8.201 |
| 19 | 14.324 | 13.134 | 12.085 | 11.608 | 11.158 | 10.336 | 9.604 | 8.950 | 8.365 |
| 20 | 14.877 | 13.590 | 12.462 | 11.950 | 11.470 | 10.594 | 9.818 | 9.129 | 8.514 |
| 21 | 15.415 | 14.029 | 12.821 | 12.275 | 11.764 | 10.836 | 10.017 | 9.292 | 8.649 |
| 22 | 15.937 | 14.451 | 13.163 | 12.583 | 12.042 | 11.061 | 10.201 | 9.442 | 8.772 |
| 23 | 16.444 | 14.857 | 13.489 | 12.875 | 12.303 | 11.272 | 10.371 | 9.580 | 8.883 |
| 24 | 16.936 | 15.247 | 13.799 | 13.152 | 12.550 | 11.469 | 10.529 | 9.707 | 8.985 |
| 25 | 17.413 | 15.622 | 14.094 | 13.414 | 12.783 | 11.654 | 10.675 | 9.823 | 9.077 |
| 26 | 17.877 | 15.983 | 14.375 | 13.662 | 13.003 | 11.826 | 10.810 | 9.929 | 9.161 |
| 27 | 18.327 | 16.330 | 14.643 | 13.898 | 13.211 | 11.987 | 10.935 | 10.027 | 9.237 |
| 28 | 18.764 | 16.663 | 14.898 | 14.121 | 13.406 | 12.137 | 11.051 | 10.116 | 9.307 |
| 29 | 19.188 | 16.984 | 15.141 | 14.333 | 13.591 | 12.278 | 11.158 | 10.198 | 9.370 |
| 30 | 19.600 | 17.292 | 15.372 | 14.534 | 13.765 | 12.409 | 11.258 | 10.274 | 9.427 |
| 31 | 20.000 | 17.588 | 15.593 | 14.724 | 13.929 | 12.532 | 11.350 | 10.343 | 9.479 |
| 32 | 20.389 | 17.874 | 15.803 | 14.904 | 14.084 | 12.647 | 11.435 | 10.406 | 9.526 |
| 33 | 20.766 | 18.148 | 16.003 | 15.075 | 14.230 | 12.754 | 11.514 | 10.464 | 9.569 |
| 34 | 21.132 | 18.411 | 16.193 | 15.237 | 14.368 | 12.854 | 11.587 | 10.518 | 9.609 |
| 35 | 21.487 | 18.665 | 16.374 | 15.391 | 14.498 | 12.948 | 11.655 | 10.567 | 9.644 |
| 36 | 21.832 | 18.908 | 16.547 | 15.536 | 14.621 | 13.035 | 11.717 | 10.612 | 9.677 |
| 37 | 22.167 | 19.143 | 16.711 | 15.674 | 14.737 | 13.117 | 11.775 | 10.653 | 9.706 |
| 38 | 22.492 | 19.368 | 16.868 | 15.805 | 14.846 | 13.193 | 11.829 | 10.691 | 9.733 |
| 39 | 22.808 | 19.584 | 17.017 | 15.929 | 14.949 | 13.265 | 11.879 | 10.726 | 9.757 |
| 40 | 23.115 | 19.793 | 17.159 | 16.046 | 15.046 | 13.332 | 11.925 | 10.757 | 9.779 |
| 41 | 23.412 | 19.993 | 17.294 | 16.157 | 15.138 | 13.394 | 11.967 | 10.787 | 9.799 |
| 42 | 23.701 | 20.186 | 17.423 | 16.263 | 15.225 | 13.452 | 12.007 | 10.813 | 9.817 |
| 43 | 23.982 | 20.371 | 17.546 | 16.363 | 15.306 | 13.507 | 12.043 | 10.838 | 9.834 |
| 44 | 24.254 | 20.549 | 17.663 | 16.458 | 15.383 | 13.558 | 12.077 | 10.861 | 9.849 |
| 45 | 24.519 | 20.720 | 17.774 | 16.548 | 15.456 | 13.606 | 12.108 | 10.881 | 9.863 |
| 46 | 24.775 | 20.885 | 17.880 | 16.633 | 15.524 | 13.650 | 12.137 | 10.900 | 9.875 |
| 47 | 25.025 | 21.043 | 17.981 | 16.714 | 15.589 | 13.692 | 12.164 | 10.918 | 9.887 |
| 48 | 25.267 | 21.195 | 18.077 | 16.790 | 15.650 | 13.730 | 12.189 | 10.934 | 9.897 |
| 49 | 25.502 | 21.341 | 18.169 | 16.863 | 15.708 | 13.767 | 12.212 | 10.948 | 9.906 |
| 50 | 25.730 | 21.482 | 18.256 | 16.932 | 15.762 | 13.801 | 12.233 | 10.962 | 9.915 |

# Chapter 19

# NET PREMIUMS

## INTRODUCTION

With the preceding life insurance mathematical principles as a base, it is now possible to illustrate one process by which life insurance and annuity premiums are calculated.[1] The process shown includes the calculation of net premiums for term, whole life, endowment, and annuity policies, to which amounts to cover expenses, profits, and contingencies are added to develop a gross premium rate structure. Net premiums take into account interest and mortality factors only. This study begins by first determining the net single premium, from which the net annual premium can be found. Next, various methods of loading to ascertain a gross premium rate schedule will be studied.[2]

## NET SINGLE PREMIUMS

### THE CALCULATION PROCESS

The computation of net premium rates for life insurance generally requires information as to (1) the age and sex of the insured, (2) the benefits to be provided, (3) the mortality rates to be used, and (4) the rate of interest assumed. In the computations that follow,

---

[1] Another process was illustrated in Chap. 2.

[2] This procedure is not always followed, but in any case, the gross premium is ordinarily tested by asset-share studies under realistic assumptions. See Chap. 21.

mortality will be assumed to be that of the *1980 CSO Table*; the rate of interest assumed will be 5 percent; the face amount of the policy, $1,000; and the insured a male. The age of the insured will be stated in each instance.[3]

## TERM INSURANCE

Term insurance is the simplest type of life insurance. Term policies usually cover a set period and promise to pay the sum insured if the insured dies within this period. (Nothing is paid if death does not occur during the designated term.) Yearly renewable term (YRT) policies, which are discussed in Chapter 4, are the simplest forms of term life insurance and offer an excellent opportunity to explain the elements of rate-making.

Suppose that the net single premium is to be ascertained on a one-year term life insurance policy of $1,000 on a male aged 45. Immediate use will now be found for two assumptions mentioned in Chapter 18—that premiums are paid at the beginning of each policy year and that matured claims are paid at the close of the policy year. The question is: What amount of money must be paid at the beginning of the year by policyowners to enable the insurer to pay $1,000 at year-end for each insured who dies during the period, and the amount is held at interest until the claim is paid? The insurer is interested in the probability of having to pay the death claim—in other words, in the chance of a 45-year-old male dying during the year. This will be determined by means of the mortality table shown in Table 18-1.

Suppose that an insurance company issued 9,210,289 (number living at age 45) one-year term policies to males aged 45. If the actual mortality experienced among this group coincided with the experience expected under the mortality table, there would be 41,907 deaths during the year. Since each of these deaths represents a liability of $1,000 to the insurer, and since the claims are assumed to be payable at the close of the year, the insurer must have on hand at that time $41,907,000 to pay claims. This entire amount, however, need not have been collected from the policyowners, since they were required to pay their premiums at the beginning of the year and the insurer was able to invest the money at interest for one year at, say, 5 percent. One dollar discounted for one year at 5 percent interest equals $0.952. Therefore the insurer needs to have on hand at the beginning of the year only $39,895,464 (0.952 x $41,907,000), in order to have at the end of the year sufficient funds to pay $1,000 for each of the 41,907 deaths. To obtain the premium each individual should pay, it is only necessary to divide the total fund by the group of 9,210,289 to be insured:

$$\$39,895,464 \div 9,210,289 = \$4.33$$

---

[3] The reader is reminded that, the *1980 CSO Table* is not generally used for rate-making; it is used for valuing insurance companies' policy liabilities. Insurers use up-to-date mortality experience in deriving premiums to be charged.

The net single premium for a one-year term insurance policy at age 45, or the amount of money that must be paid at the beginning of the year to supply each individual's contribution to the death losses of the group for the year, is, therefore, $4.33.[4]

The same problem may be approached in a different way and a formula stated for determining costs. An estimated 41,907 males aged 45 will die out of the group of 9,210,289, based on the mortality table used here. This is equivalent to saying that the probability of death during the forty-fifth ($q_{45}$) year is 41,907/9,210,289 or 0.00455. The expected value of a death claim for an insured is, therefore, $1,000 x 0.00455, or $4.55. This is the value needed at the end of the year, and money is valued at 5 percent. The amount to be paid by the insured at the beginning of the year will be $4.55 discounted for one year at 5 percent, or $4.55 x 0.952, which equals $4.33. This may be summarized as follows:

$$(\$1,000)(\frac{41,907}{9,210,289})(0.952) = \$4.33$$

which, in actuarial notation, can be written:

$$(1,000)(q_x)(v) = (1,000)(\frac{d_{45}}{l_{45}})(v)$$

It should not be assumed from this that an insurance company can insure a single person only. Instead, it should deal with a group sufficiently large to ensure that the law of large numbers can operate reasonably. It does not, however, need to insure this entire group with the same kind of policy or at the same age. Results will be satisfactory if the entire group of insureds, including all ages and all kinds of policies, is sufficiently large.

The method used here in determining the premium rate embodies the following process: multiply the probability of the occurrence of the event insured against by the amount of the policy, and then multiply by the value of 1 discounted for one year at the assumed rate of interest. This is a **present expected value**. It is an *expected value* because it is based on probabilities, and it is a *present value* because it is discounted for interest (the time value of money).

To continue, suppose that it is desired to compute the net single premium for a five-year term life insurance policy issued to a male aged 45—that is, the amount of money that, paid in a single sum at age 45, will purchase insurance against death at any time within the next five years. Two facts are apparent: (1) the premium is paid only once, in a single sum at policy inception, and (2) death claims will be paid at the end of the year in which death occurs, not at the end of the five-year period. This latter fact has an important bearing on the interest earned and, therefore, on the method of computing the cost.

---

[4]This method of determining individual net single premiums has been termed the **aggregate approach**, since it emphasizes the total fund necessary to meet death claims as they occur. An alternative approach, which is discussed next, is usually referred to as the **expected value approach**. The methods are equally correct.

Manifestly, the cost cannot be correctly determined by multiplying the total probability of dying during the five years by the face amount of the policy and discounting this amount in one operation, since some of the money collected will draw interest for only one year, another part will earn interest for two years, and so on. It is necessary to compute each year's mortality costs separately. The probabilities insured against in this case are the chances that a male aged 45 will die during the first year, during the second year, the third year, and so on. In actuarial notation, these probabilities would be found as follows:

$$\frac{d_{45}}{l_{45}} = \frac{41,907}{9,210,289} = 0.00455$$

$$\frac{d_{46}}{l_{45}} = \frac{45,108}{9,210,289} = 0.00490$$

$$\frac{d_{47}}{l_{45}} = \frac{48,536}{9,210,289} = 0.00527$$

$$\frac{d_{48}}{l_{45}} = \frac{52,089}{9,210,289} = 0.00566$$

$$\frac{d_{49}}{l_{45}} = \frac{56,031}{9,210,289} = 0.00608$$

Each of these figures must be multiplied by the insurance amount and by the present value of 1, discounted in each instance by the length of time the money is held. The money available for the first year's claims will be held for one year; for the second year's claims, two years; and so on, the funds for the last year's claims being held five years. The relevant discount factors for one, two, three, four, and five years at 5 percent interest are, respectively, 0.9524, 0.9070, 0.8638, 0.8227, and 0.7835. The cost of the five years of insurance, therefore, can be calculated as shown in Table 19-1.

This computation shows that, ignoring expenses, taxes, and so on, $22.74 paid to the insurer by each policyowner and placed at 5 percent interest will furnish enough money to pay all the expected death claims on this five-year term policy. By simply continuing the process of calculating the cost of insurance on a per-year basis, the net single premium for a term insurance contract of any longer duration may be determined.

## WHOLE LIFE INSURANCE

A whole life policy provides coverage for the whole of life as defined by the mortality table used to calculate premiums, promising to pay the face amount whenever death occurs. This policy is like the term contracts just considered with the exception that, instead of being limited to a set number of years, it continues to the end of the mortality table. Since the *1980 CSO Table* assumes that all males die by the end of their one-hundredth year, the maximum possible age for which the cost of insurance against death needs to be calculated is 99. (If the insured attains the mortality table's terminal age the face amount is paid as if the insured had died.) The net single premium on a whole life policy issued at male age 45 must, therefore, provide against the possibility that the

**TABLE 19-1    ILLUSTRATIVE NET SINGLE-PREMIUM CALCULATION FOR FIVE-YEAR TERM INSURANCE (MALE, AGED 45, *1980 CSO* MORTALITY, 5 PERCENT INTEREST)**

| Policy Year (t) | Age (x) | Calculation | Year's Cost of Insurance |
|---|---|---|---|
| 1 | 45 | $(\$1,000)\left[\dfrac{d_{45}}{l_{45}}\right](v) = (\$1,000)(0.00455)(0.952)$ | $= \$4.33$ |
| 2 | 46 | $(\$1,000)\left[\dfrac{d_{46}}{l_{45}}\right](v^2) = (\$1,000)(0.00490)(0.907)$ | $= 4.44$ |
| 3 | 47 | $(\$1,000)\left[\dfrac{d_{47}}{l_{45}}\right](v^3) = (\$1,000)(0.00527)(0.864)$ | $= 4.55$ |
| 4 | 48 | $(\$1,000)\left[\dfrac{d_{48}}{l_{45}}\right](v^4) = (\$1,000)(0.00566)(0.823)$ | $= 4.66$ |
| 5 | 49 | $(\$1,000)\left[\dfrac{d_{49}}{l_{45}}\right](v^5) = (\$1,000)(0.00608)(0.784)$ | $= 4.76$ |
| | | TOTAL (net single premium) | $\$22.74$ |

insured will die during his forty-fifth year, his forty-sixth year, his forty-seventh year, and so on, during every year up to and including his one-hundredth year. The separate probabilities insured against number 55—that is, for ages 45 to 99 inclusive.

The chance of dying in each separate year $(d_{x+t-1}/l_x)$ is multiplied by the face amount of the policy ($1,000), and this amount is discounted for the number of years between the issue of the policy (i.e., the payment of the single premium) and the payment of death claims. Table 19-2 illustrates the calculations.

This $270.84 is the present value of this policy's share of all the expected death claims payable from age 45. It is, therefore, the net single premium that will purchase a whole life policy issued at age 45, based on the stated assumptions. It is true that a few men outlive their one-hundredth year, but since the computations assume that the insured will not have survived this age, and since sufficient money will have been accumulated to pay the claim at the close of the one-hundredth year of life, the policy may then be terminated for its full face amount at that time.

Note that the probabilities of death used in the net single-premium calculation are not the same as the yearly death probabilities shown in Table 18-1. An understanding of this difference is crucial. The death probabilities shown in column 3 of Table 18-1 give the probabilities of death *for a person who has attained the stipulated age*, whereas the death probabilities used in the above calculation give the probabilities of *dying in various future years for a person now aged 45*.

An examination of the two death probabilities at age 99 illustrates this important difference. The probability of a 99-year-old male dying within his next

**TABLE 19-2    ILLUSTRATIVE NET SINGLE-PREMIUM CALCULATION FOR WHOLE LIFE INSURANCE (MALE, AGED 45, *1980 CSO* MORTALITY, 5 PERCENT INTEREST)**

| Policy Year ($t$) | Age ($x$) | Calculation | | Year's Cost of Insurance |
|---|---|---|---|---|
| 1 | 45 | $(\$1,000)\left[\dfrac{d_{45}}{l_{45}}\right](v) = (\$1,000)(0.00455)(0.952)$ | = | \$4.33 |
| 2 | 46 | $(\$1,000)\left[\dfrac{d_{46}}{l_{45}}\right](v^2) = (\$1,000)(0.00490)(0.907)$ | = | 4.44 |
| 3 | 47 | $(\$1,000)\left[\dfrac{d_{47}}{l_{45}}\right](v^3) = (\$1,000)(0.00527)(0.864)$ | = | 4.55 |
| • | • | • | • | • |
| • | • | • | • | • |
| • | • | • | • | • |
| 53 | 97 | $(\$1,000)\left[\dfrac{d_{97}}{l_{45}}\right](v^{53}) = (\$1,000)\left[\dfrac{29,054}{9,210,289}\right](0.075)$ | = | 0.24 |
| 54 | 98 | $(\$1,000)\left[\dfrac{d_{98}}{l_{45}}\right](v^{54}) = (\$1,000)\left[\dfrac{20,693}{9,210,289}\right](0.072)$ | = | 0.16 |
| 55 | 99 | $(\$1,000)\left[\dfrac{d_{99}}{l_{45}}\right](v^{55}) = (\$1,000)\left[\dfrac{10,757}{9,210,289}\right](0.068)$ | = | 0.08 |
| | | TOTAL | | \$270.84 |
| | | (net single premium) | | |

year of life is shown as 1 (a certainty) in Table 18-1. In other words, a person who has attained age 99 is, according to this mortality table, certain to die during the next year. On the other hand, the probability of a 45-year-old dying during his ninety ninth year is $d_{99}/l_{45}$ or $10,757 \div 9,210,189$ or $0.00117$—a small likelihood. This suggests that our 45-year-old male is highly *unlikely* to die during his ninety-ninth year. Why? It is highly unlikely that he will live to attain such an advanced age in the first instance. (The only way that he could die then is if he survives to age 99!)

The net single-premium calculation for a whole life policy, in essence, apportions the probability of dying (a certainty) over the various years remaining in one's life. Thus if the death probabilities in the above whole life net single-premium computation are summed, they would equal one. By contrast, a summation of the Table 18-1 yearly death probabilities would have no meaning.[5]

[5] Indeed, they would sum to greater than 1! This is also the reason why a comparison of YRT rates to age 100 and the level premium for an ordinary life policy is not meaningful mathematically, without adjustment of the YRT premiums for the probabilities of survival. See Robert E. Cooper, "The Level Premium Concept: A Closer Look," *Journal of the American Society of Chartered Life Underwriters*, Vol. XXX (July 1976).

## ENDOWMENTS

Although endowment insurance is not very popular in the United States,[6] several important life insurance principles are illustrated in endowments. For this reason, an understanding of the way they function mathematically is important.

*Pure Endowments.* A **pure endowment** promises to pay the face amount if, and only if, the insured survives a specified period. Thus a five-year pure endowment would pay the policy face amount if the insured is living five years from the date of issue. Table 18-1 shows, for example, that of the 9,210,289 males living at age 45, 8,966,618 are still living at age 50. Thus the probability of a male aged 45 surviving for five years, symbolized $_5p_{45}$, is:

$$_5p_{45} = \frac{l_{50}}{l_{45}} = \frac{8,966,618}{9,210,289} = 0.97354$$

Stated differently, the probability of the occurrence of the event insured against is 0.97354. Since the money paid as a single premium for a five-year endowment would be held for five years before the policy matures, the formula for determining the net single premium for a $1,000 pure endowment policy (at 5 percent interest) is:

$$\text{NSP} = (\$1,000)(_5p_{45})(v_5) = (\$1,000)(0.97345)(0.784) = \$762.77$$

A clear distinction must be made between a pure endowment and a savings account that is left to accumulate at an agreed rate of interest. The insured cannot obtain possession of the money invested in a pure endowment before the expiration of the endowment period. Nothing is returned if the insured should die during this period. The money remains in the fund needed to pay the survivors. A bank savings account, on the other hand, is not lost through death of the saver. This fact makes it possible to divide the $1,000 that will be paid *in case of survival through the endowment period* into two funds, one of which might be called an **investment fund** and the other a **benefit of survivorship** fund. The investment fund element of our five-year pure endowment will equal $762.77 plus interest compounded for five years at 5 percent. Using the formula for the accumulated value of 1 per year produces these results:

$$S = (A)(1.05)^5 = (\$762.77)(1.276) = \$973.29$$

This $973.29 is the amount that would be obtained by investing the net single premium of this pure endowment policy at 5 percent interest for five years. The remainder of the $1,000, or $26.71, comprises the survivor's share of the amounts left by those insureds who died before their policies matured—the benefit of survivorship contribution. The possibility of losing the entire amount of one's investment by death before the endowment period has expired makes the pure endowment a policy that finds little favor with the insuring public in the U.S.[7] For this reason, it is combined with, or constitutes a feature of, some other kind

---

[6] See Chap. 4. The U.S. tax law definition of life insurance has further decreased the popularity of endowments. (See Chap 13.)

[7] In some jurisdictions, pure endowment contracts are prohibited by law. They are sold in other countries.

of policy. It is interesting to note that a life annuity is merely a series of pure endowments (see below).

*Endowment Insurance.* An **endowment** promises to pay a certain sum in case the insured dies within the term of the policy, or (usually) a similar sum at the end of the term in case of survival. This contract includes the pure endowment feature just discussed and, in addition, insurance against death during the term of the endowment. Thus a five-year endowment insurance policy issued at male age 45 will pay the face amount if the insured dies during the first, second, third, fourth, or fifth years, or it will pay the same sum at the end of the endowment period. The net single premium for these two promises can be found by adding the net single premium for five years of term life insurance coverage and the net single premium for a five-year pure endowment. Based on our assumptions, the net single premium for the five-year pure endowment is $762.77 and for the five-year term it is $22.75 for a total of $785.52.

There are other types of endowment contracts: partial endowments, semi-endowments, and double endowments. They differ from the above policy in that the amount due on survival (i.e., the pure endowment element) differs from the amount paid on death.[8]

## POLICIES INVOLVING MORE THAN ONE LIFE.

The policies illustrated here involve only one life. Life insurance companies also issue policies that cover risks on two or more lives; joint life and second-to-die policies are examples.[9] The computation of premium rates for these policies follows the same principles as for single-life policies. The critical difference in computation relates to the probability of the occurrence of the insured event. Thus with a joint-life policy that pays the face amount on the death of *either* of two insureds, the probability of the insurer paying a claim can be derived by summing the compound probabilities of an insured event occurring.

Thus the insurer will have to pay the claim under a joint life policy if any one of three combinations of events occurs:

1. Insured A lives $(p_x^A)$ and insured B dies $(q_x^B)$.

2. Insured A dies $(q_x^A)$ and insured B lives $(p_x^B)$.

3. Insured A dies $(q_x^A)$ and insured B dies $(q_x^B)$.

The probability of the occurrence of the first combination of events is given by the compound probability:

$$(p_x^A)(q_x^B)$$

---

[8] Note that the so-called deposit term life insurance policy discussed in Chap. 4 is, in reality, a term policy with a modest pure endowment feature.

[9] See Chap. 7.

The probability of the second and third events occurring is given, respectively, by:

$$(q_x^A)(p_x^B)$$

$$(q_x^A)(q_x^B)$$

The sum of the three compound probabilities gives the probability of the occurrence of an insured event—the figure that would be used in each year's probability of death (i.e., claim payment).

Second-to-die policies pay the face amount only on the death of the second of two insureds. Conditional probability calculations, which are beyond the scope of this introductory treatment, are necessary to derive such premiums.

## LIFE ANNUITIES

The remaining class of contracts to be analyzed is known as life annuities. Life annuities promise to pay the possessor a stated income at intervals of one year or, more frequently, during the annuitant's lifetime. They furnish a type of investment whereby the recipient can be assured of an income for life.

Annuities covering a single life are ordinarily of two kinds—immediate and deferred. An **immediate life annuity** begins payments one period hence. A **deferred life annuity** begins payments more than one period hence. Annuities may be temporary (that is, limited to a term of years during the lifetime of the annuitant); they may continue for the whole of life; or they may promise a minimum number of payments irrespective of whether the annuitant is living. Each of these contracts will be considered in turn.

*Immediate Life Annuities.* An immediate temporary life annuity of $100, purchased, say, at age 70 and continuing for a period of ten years will promise to pay the annuitant $100 one year from the date of purchase, if he or she is then living, and $100 at each anniversary of that date, if he or she is still living, until ten payments have been made. The cost of this contract will be the net single premium (present expected value) at age 70 for the payments of the sums promised to the annuitant. Since a payment is made to the annuitant at the end of each year, the cost for each year must be determined separately and these amounts summed to obtain the net single premium. This annuity is equivalent to a series of 10 pure endowments, the first maturing in one year from date of purchase, the second in two years, the third in three years, and so on, until the ten payments have been made.

Although the formulas are equivalent to those for insurance, the mortality table is different, since insurance companies find that annuity mortality experience produces lower mortality rates than does insurance mortality experience. The *1983 Individual Annuity Mortality Table for Males (1983 Table a)*, without projection, as shown in Table 19-3, is a table that is widely used for annuity valuation.[10] According to this table, the probability that the first annuity payment will be made equals the probability that a man aged 70 will survive one year ($p_{70}$), or it can be expressed in the form of a fraction, $l_{71}/l_{70}$, which equals 7,747,883/7,917,079. The $100 paid in case of survival is paid one year from the date of purchase of the annuity, and, therefore, the net cost of the first payment will be the value of this sum discounted for one year at 5 percent and multiplied by the probability of survival. The process is continued through the second, third, and following years as shown in Table 19-4.

If the contract issued at male age 70 promises to pay an annuity for the whole of life, the computations must continue throughout the annuity mortality table, which in the case of the *1983 Table a*, is through age 115. The computation of the cost of this whole life annuity is shown in Table 19-5 (the first ten years being the same as for the term annuity just computed).

If this same annuity guaranteed that the first five payments were to be certain—that is, not affected by the death of the annuitant before their completion—this fact would have to be taken into consideration in computing the net cost. The distinction would lie in the fact that these five payments would not be affected by death, or, in actuarial terms, the probability of payment would be a certainty, or 1. Therefore the first five payments would be discounted for interest only. The sixth and all subsequent payments would depend on the probability of survival, and their net cost would therefore be computed in the same manner as above for the pure life annuity.

***Deferred Life Annuities.*** Immediate life annuities are usually purchased by persons of advanced age, and they contemplate the payment of benefits at periodic intervals following the date of issue. Some persons are interested in a **deferred life annuity,** an annuity contract that can be purchased by annual sums paid during their wage-earning years. It bears a close resemblance to private pension plans, under which money is accumulated year by year in small amounts from the wages of the employees and contributions by the employer, and this money is paid periodically during the lifetime of the employee after he or she has attained retirement age.

The traditional deferred life annuity was usually purchased by an annual premium. Of course, flexible-premium deferred annuities may be purchased with any desired, reasonable premium pattern. It is also possible to pay for such a contract by a single premium paid at the date of purchase of the contract.

Assume that it is desired to find the net single premium payable for a male, aged 40, that will purchase the right to receive a whole life annuity of $100 beginning at age 70. There are two possible ways of approaching the problem. It may be asked: What is the amount of money that must have been accumulated

[10] The authors have computed this table complete with $l_x$, $d_x$ and $p_x$ values, using a radix of 10,000,000 lives at age 5.

**TABLE 19-3  1983 INDIVIDUAL ANNUITY MORTALITY TABLE (MALE LIVES)**

| Age (x) at Beginning of Year | Number Living at Beginning of Year (l_x) | Number Dying during Year (d_x) | Yearly Probability of Dying (q_x) | Yearly Probability of Surviving (p_x) |
|---|---|---|---|---|
| 5 | 10,000,000 | 3,770 | 0.000377 | .999623 |
| 6 | 9,996,230 | 3,499 | 0.000350 | .999650 |
| 7 | 9,992,731 | 3,328 | 0.000333 | .999667 |
| 8 | 9,989,403 | 3,516 | 0.000352 | .999648 |
| 9 | 9,985,887 | 3,675 | 0.000368 | .999632 |
| 10 | 9,982,212 | 3,813 | 0.000382 | .999618 |
| 11 | 9,978,399 | 3,931 | 0.000394 | .999606 |
| 12 | 9,974,468 | 4,040 | 0.000405 | .999595 |
| 13 | 9,970,428 | 4,138 | 0.000415 | .999585 |
| 14 | 9,966,290 | 4,236 | 0.000425 | .999575 |
| 15 | 9,962,054 | 4,333 | 0.000435 | .999565 |
| 16 | 9,957,721 | 4,441 | 0.000446 | .999554 |
| 17 | 9,953,280 | 4,559 | 0.000458 | .999542 |
| 18 | 9,948,721 | 4,696 | 0.000472 | .999528 |
| 19 | 9,944,025 | 4,853 | 0.000488 | .999512 |
| 20 | 9,939,172 | 5,019 | 0.000505 | .999495 |
| 21 | 9,934,153 | 5,215 | 0.000525 | .999475 |
| 22 | 9,928,938 | 5,421 | 0.000546 | .999454 |
| 23 | 9,923,517 | 5,656 | 0.000570 | .999430 |
| 24 | 9,917,861 | 5,911 | 0.000596 | .999404 |
| 25 | 9,911,950 | 6,165 | 0.000622 | .999378 |
| 26 | 9,905,785 | 6,439 | 0.000650 | .999350 |
| 27 | 9,899,346 | 6,702 | 0.000677 | .999323 |
| 28 | 9,892,644 | 6,964 | 0.000704 | .999296 |
| 29 | 9,885,680 | 7,226 | 0.000731 | .999269 |
| 30 | 9,878,454 | 7,498 | 0.000759 | .999241 |
| 31 | 9,870,956 | 7,759 | 0.000786 | .999214 |
| 32 | 9,863,197 | 8,029 | 0.000814 | .999186 |
| 33 | 9,855,168 | 8,308 | 0.000843 | .999157 |
| 34 | 9,846,860 | 8,626 | 0.000876 | .999124 |
| 35 | 9,838,234 | 9,022 | 0.000917 | .999083 |
| 36 | 9,829,212 | 9,515 | 0.000968 | .999032 |
| 37 | 9,819,697 | 10.134 | 0.001032 | .998968 |
| 38 | 9,809,563 | 10.928 | 0.001114 | .998886 |
| 39 | 9,798,635 | 11.915 | 0.001216 | .998784 |
| 40 | 9,786,720 | 13.124 | 0.001341 | .998659 |
| 41 | 9,773,596 | 14.582 | 0.001492 | .998508 |
| 42 | 9,759,014 | 16.327 | 0.001673 | .998327 |
| 43 | 9,742,687 | 18.375 | 0.001886 | .998114 |
| 44 | 9,724,312 | 20.703 | 0.002129 | .997871 |
| 45 | 9,703,609 | 23.279 | 0.002399 | .997601 |
| 46 | 9,680,330 | 27.069 | 0.002693 | .997307 |
| 47 | 9,654,261 | 29.050 | 0.003009 | .996991 |
| 48 | 9,625,211 | 32.177 | 0.003343 | .996657 |
| 49 | 9,593,034 | 35.437 | 0.003694 | .996306 |
| 50 | 9,557,597 | 38.775 | 0.004057 | .995943 |
| 51 | 9,518,822 | 42.178 | 0.004431 | .995569 |
| 52 | 9,476,644 | 45.602 | 0.004812 | .995188 |
| 53 | 9,431,042 | 49.023 | 0.005198 | .994802 |
| 54 | 9,382,019 | 52.455 | 0.005591 | .994409 |
| 55 | 9,329,564 | 55.921 | 0.005994 | .994006 |
| 56 | 9,273,643 | 59.435 | 0.006409 | .993591 |
| 57 | 9,214,208 | 63.016 | 0.006839 | .993161 |
| 58 | 9,151,192 | 66.712 | 0.007290 | .992710 |
| 59 | 9,084,480 | 70.695 | 0.007782 | .992218 |
| 60 | 9,013,785 | 75.157 | 0.008338 | .991662 |
| 61 | 8,938,628 | 80.296 | 0.008983 | .991017 |
| 62 | 8,858,332 | 86.280 | 0.009740 | .990260 |
| 63 | 8,772,052 | 93.247 | 0.010630 | .989370 |

**TABLE 19-3** (CONTINUED)

| Age (x) at Beginning of Year | Number Living at Beginning of Year $(l_x)$ | Number Dying during Year $(d_x)$ | Yearly Probability of Dying $(q_x)$ | Yearly Probability of Surviving $(p_x)$ | Age (x) at Beginning of Year | Number Living at Beginning of Year $(l_x)$ | Number Dying during Year $(d_x)$ | Yearly Probability of Dying $(q_x)$ | Yearly Probability of Surviving $(p_x)$ |
|---|---|---|---|---|---|---|---|---|---|
| 64 | 8,678,805 | 101.230 | 0.011664 | .988338 | 94 | 1,139,728 | 203.484 | 0.178537 | .821463 |
| 65 | 8,577,575 | 110.230 | 0.012851 | .987149 | 95 | 936.244 | 179.023 | 0.191214 | .808786 |
| 66 | 8,467,345 | 120.228 | 0.014199 | .985801 | 96 | 757.221 | 155.019 | 0.204721 | .795279 |
| 67 | 8,347,117 | 131.192 | 0.015717 | .984283 | 97 | 602.202 | 131.955 | 0.219120 | .780880 |
| 68 | 8,215,925 | 143.072 | 0.017414 | .982586 | 98 | 470.247 | 110.383 | 0.234735 | .765265 |
| 69 | 8,072,853 | 155.774 | 0.019296 | .980704 | 99 | 359.864 | 90.646 | 0.251889 | .748111 |
| 70 | 7,917,079 | 169.196 | 0.021371 | .978629 | 100 | 269.218 | 72.933 | 0.270906 | .729094 |
| 71 | 7,747,883 | 183.214 | 0.023647 | .976353 | 101 | 196.285 | 57.337 | 0.292111 | .707889 |
| 72 | 7,564,669 | 197.672 | 0.026131 | .973869 | 102 | 138.948 | 43.883 | 0.315826 | .684174 |
| 73 | 7,366,997 | 212.427 | 0.028835 | .971165 | 103 | 95.065 | 32.548 | 0.342377 | .657623 |
| 74 | 7,154,570 | 227.472 | 0.031794 | .968206 | 104 | 62.517 | 23.262 | 0.372086 | .627914 |
| 75 | 6,927,098 | 242.767 | 0.035046 | .964954 | 105 | 39.255 | 15.909 | 0.405278 | .594722 |
| 76 | 6,684,331 | 258.222 | 0.038631 | .961369 | 106 | 23.346 | 10.325 | 0.442277 | .557723 |
| 77 | 6,426,109 | 273.669 | 0.042587 | .957413 | 107 | 13.021 | 6.294 | 0.483406 | .516594 |
| 78 | 6,152,440 | 288.863 | 0.046951 | .953049 | 108 | 6.727 | 3.559 | 0.528989 | .417011 |
| 79 | 5,863,577 | 303.469 | 0.051755 | .948245 | 109 | 3.168 | 1.835 | 0.579351 | .420649 |
| 80 | 5,560,108 | 317.071 | 0.057026 | .942974 | 110 | 1.333 | 846 | 0.634814 | .365186 |
| 81 | 5,243,037 | 329.216 | 0.062791 | .937029 | 111 | 487 | 339 | 0.695704 | .304296 |
| 82 | 4,913,821 | 339.452 | 0.069081 | .930919 | 112 | 148 | 113 | 0.762343 | .237657 |
| 83 | 4,574,369 | 347.231 | 0.075908 | .924092 | 113 | 35 | 29 | 0.835056 | .164944 |
| 84 | 4,227,138 | 351.825 | 0.083230 | .916770 | 114 | 6 | 5 | 0.914167 | .085833 |
| 85 | 3,875,313 | 352.603 | 0.090987 | .909013 | 115 | 1 | 1 | 1.000000 | .000000 |
| 86 | 3,522,710 | 349.178 | 0.099122 | .900878 | | | | | |
| 87 | 3,173,532 | 341.399 | 0.107577 | .892423 | | | | | |
| 88 | 2,832,133 | 329.422 | 0.116316 | .883684 | | | | | |
| 89 | 2,502,711 | 313.825 | 0.125394 | .874606 | | | | | |
| 90 | 2,188,886 | 295.252 | 0.134887 | .865113 | | | | | |
| 91 | 1,893,634 | 274.336 | 0.144873 | .855127 | | | | | |
| 92 | 1,629,298 | 251.686 | 0.155429 | .844571 | | | | | |
| 93 | 1,367,612 | 227.884 | 0.166629 | .833371 | | | | | |

**TABLE 19-4    ILLUSTRATIVE NET SINGLE-PREMIUM CALCULATION FOR A TEN-YEAR IMMEDIATE LIFE ANNUITY (MALE, AGED 70, *1983 CSO TABLE A* MORTALITY, 5 PERCENT INTEREST)**

| Policy Year ($t$) | Age ($x$) | Calculation | Cost of Year's Annuity Payment |
|---|---|---|---|
| 1 | 70 | $(\$100)\left[\dfrac{l_{71}}{l_{70}}\right](v) = (\$100)\left[\dfrac{7,747,883}{7,917,079}\right](0.952) \quad =$ | \$93.20 |
| 2 | 71 | $(\$100)\left[\dfrac{l_{72}}{l_{70}}\right](v^2) = (\$100)\left[\dfrac{7,564,669}{7,917,079}\right](0.907) \quad =$ | 86.67 |
| 3 | 72 | $(\$100)\left[\dfrac{l_{73}}{l_{70}}\right](v^3) = (\$100)\left[\dfrac{7,366,997}{7,917,079}\right](0.864) \quad =$ | 80.38 |
| $\bullet$ | $\bullet$ | $\bullet \qquad \bullet$ | $\bullet \qquad \bullet$ |
| $\bullet$ | $\bullet$ | $\bullet \qquad \bullet$ | $\bullet \qquad \bullet$ |
| $\bullet$ | $\bullet$ | $\bullet \qquad \bullet$ | $\bullet \qquad \bullet$ |
| 8 | 77 | $(\$100)\left[\dfrac{l_{78}}{l_{70}}\right](v^8) = (\$100)\left[\dfrac{6,152,440}{7,917,079}\right](0.677) \quad =$ | 52.60 |
| 9 | 78 | $(\$100)\left[\dfrac{l_{79}}{l_{70}}\right](v^9) = (\$100)\left[\dfrac{5,863,577}{7,917,079}\right](0.645) \quad =$ | 47.74 |
| 10 | 79 | $(\$100)\left[\dfrac{l_{80}}{l_{70}}\right](v^{10}) = (\$100)\left[\dfrac{5,560,108}{7,917,079}\right](0.614) \quad =$ | 43.11 |
| | | TOTAL (net single premium) | \$667.29 |

by the insurer by the time the annuity begins? This is equivalent to asking how much money must be available at age 70 to furnish \$100 annually during life, the first payment to be made when the annuitant reaches age 70. The problem at this point is, therefore, identical to that of the immediate whole life annuity just discussed, with the single exception that here the first \$100 payment is made at age 70, whereas in the former case, the first payment was made at age 71. Therefore the insurance company must have on hand at the time the annuitant becomes 70 years of age the amount of money necessary to purchase an immediate life annuity, the first payment being made at age 70. Taking the figures from the previous computations, we find a new net single premium of \$936.18 + \$100.00, or \$1,036.18. This amount may be considered as the net cost *at age 70* of a whole life annuity *due*, the first payment of which is made to the annuitant at that age.

**TABLE 19-5    ILLUSTRATIVE NET SINGLE-PREMIUM CALCULATION FOR AN IMMEDIATE WHOLE LIFE ANNUITY (MALE, AGED 70, *1983 CSO TABLE A MORTALITY*, 5 PERCENT INTEREST)**

| Policy Year (t) | Age (x) | Calculation | | Cost of Year's Annuity Payment |
|---|---|---|---|---|
| 1 | 70 | $(\$100)\left[\dfrac{l_{71}}{l_{70}}\right](v) = (\$100)\left[\dfrac{7,747,883}{7,917,079}\right](0.952)$ | $=$ | \$93.20 |
| 2 | 71 | $(\$100)\left[\dfrac{l_{72}}{l_{70}}\right](v^2) = (\$100)\left[\dfrac{7,564,669}{7,917,079}\right](0.907)$ | $=$ | 86.67 |
| 3 | 72 | $(\$100)\left[\dfrac{l_{73}}{l_{70}}\right](v^3) = (\$100)\left[\dfrac{7,366,997}{7,917,079}\right](0.864)$ | $=$ | 80.38 |
| . | . | . | . | . . |
| . | . | . | . | . . |
| . | . | . | . | . . |
| 43 | 112 | $(\$100)\left[\dfrac{l_{113}}{l_{70}}\right](v^{43}) = (\$100)\left[\dfrac{35}{7,917,079}\right](0.123)$ | $=$ | 0.00* |
| 44 | 113 | $(\$100)\left[\dfrac{l_{114}}{l_{70}}\right](v^{44}) = (\$100)\left[\dfrac{6}{7,917,079}\right](0.117)$ | $=$ | 0.00* |
| 45 | 114 | $(\$100)\left[\dfrac{l_{115}}{l_{70}}\right](v^{45}) = (\$100)\left[\dfrac{1}{7,917,079}\right](0.111)$ | $=$ | 0.00* |

TOTAL    \$936.18
(net single premium)

*Less than 0.0005

The amount payable by a man at age 40 that will furnish this sum (\$1,036.18) at age 70 is the present value of this sum discounted for 30 years at the assumed interest rate:

$A = (S) \times (v^{30}) = (\$1,036.18) \times (0.231) = \$239.36$

A deferred annuity is almost always purchased on a basis whereby payments (single or periodic) made during the accumulation period are not forfeited in the event of death. The above calculation is based on this premise. If the cost of this contract taken out at age 40 had been computed on the assumption that the single premium paid at age 40 or the level annual premiums paid from ages 40 to 70 were forfeitable (i.e., the purchaser relinquished any right to his or her contributions in case he or she failed to survive to age 70), the calculation would further discount the \$239.36 figure for the probability of survival from age 40 to 70.

# NET LEVEL PREMIUMS

## THE LEVEL-PREMIUM SYSTEM

Insurance policies may be purchased by a single cash sum or by periodic payments made monthly, quarterly, semiannually, or annually, and, with flexible-premium contracts, as often or infrequently as desired. Because of premium outlay considerations, policies ordinarily are purchased by periodic premiums. With traditional forms of life insurance, the determination of level premiums is made after the single premium has been ascertained.

If policyowners are given the choice of payment for insurance by single or annual premiums, the amounts of the latter must be determined on such a basis that the insurer will receive equivalent value under each method of payment. Since the manner of computing the net single premium is known, the problem can be solved by finding a series of net annual level premiums that are mathematically equivalent to the net single premium. Such premiums will be paid during the life of the insured or for a limited number of years, but they always *cease upon his or her death*. Note that this is the definition of a life annuity.

It is helpful to view annual premiums as annuities. They differ, however, in four important respects from the annuities thus far considered. First, they are paid *by* the policyowner *to* the insurer, whereas regular annuities are paid *by* the insurer *to* the annuitant. Second, annuities are ordinarily purchased by single or annual premiums. If annual premiums are analogous to annuities, what does the insurer offer the policyowner as consideration for the series of annuity (premium) payments? It promises a cash payment (the policy face amount) upon the happening of the insured event.

Third, annuitant mortality is considerably lower than insurance mortality. This consideration, however, does not apply to the annuities represented by the annual level premiums, and regular insurance mortality tables are used in the calculations regarding life insurance annual level premiums. Obviously, life insurance purchasers will have the mortality experience of insureds, not that of annuitants.

Fourth, the time when annual level premiums and annuity payments begin is different. The immediate life annuity pays the first annual income installment one year from the date of contract issue. In practice, the first annual premium is payable when a life insurance policy is issued, and not one year later, as is the case with annuities. Thus the series of premium payments is a life annuity due.

The net level premium cannot be obtained simply by dividing the net single premium by the number of agreed-upon installments. The net single premium is a discounted expected value, and the net annual level premium must reflect (1) the possibility that the insured may die and not pay future premiums and (2) the smaller sum that will be invested at compound interest, with the resultant loss of interest earnings to the insurer.

The problem stated previously may now be restated in the following terms: The series of net annual level premiums will be a life annuity due that is equivalent to the net single premium.

## COMPUTATION OF THE NET ANNUAL LEVEL PREMIUM

*Term Insurance.* In computing net annual level premiums, one can begin by ascertaining the net single premium. The second step would be to define the *premium payment period* over which annual premiums are to be paid and for which the *life annuity due* is to be ascertained.

An example will help clarify the issues. Assume that we seek the net annual level premium for purchasing a five-year term insurance policy of $1,000 at male age 45 using the *1980 CSO Table* and 5 percent interest. It was found earlier that the net single premium on this policy was $22.74. Beginning at date of issue, the annual level premium will be paid over a five-year period, or until prior death, and it is, therefore, a *five-year temporary life annuity due.*

Since the amount of the annual level premium is the unknown quantity, it will be impossible to proceed directly to the computation of its present value, but it is feasible to take any assumed premium, such as $1, and compute the present value of an annuity due for this amount. An annuity due of $1 on the policy in question equals a temporary immediate annuity for four years plus $1 paid initially (making it an annuity due). Note that the *1980 CSO Table*, not the *1983 Table a,* would be used, because the calculation is required for a life insurance policy.

The calculation for the present value of the five-year life annuity due is shown in Table 19-6. The 4.504 total is the present expected value equivalent of 1 per year for five years. Thus an annual premium of $1 for this period would purchase any policy the net single premium of which was equal to $4.504. The net single premium on the policy in question was found to be $22.74. If the present value of the above annuity due is divided into the net single premium on this policy, the resultant factor would show how many times the annual level premium of $1 must be taken to obtain an annual level premium, the present value of which will equal the net single premium. From this analysis, it is possible to state a general rule for ascertaining the net annual level premium on any policy: *Divide the net single premium by the present value of a temporary life annuity due of 1 for the premium-paying period.* Thus

$$NLP = \frac{NSP}{PVLAD \text{ of } 1 \text{ for } PPP}$$

The net annual level premium on a five-year term insurance policy of $1,000 issued at age 45 is, thus, $5.05, computed as follows:

$$NLP = \frac{NSP}{PVLAD \text{ of } 1 \text{ for } PPP} = \frac{\$22.74}{4.504} = \$5.05$$

**TABLE 19-6**     ILLUSTRATIVE FIVE-YEAR LIFE ANNUITY DUE CALCULATION (MALE AGED 45, *1980 CSO* MORTALITY, 5 PERCENT INTEREST)

| Policy Year ($t$) | Age ($x$) | Calculation | | Year's Present Expected Value |
|---|---|---|---|---|
| 1 | 45 | 1 due immediately | $=$ | 1.000 |
| 2 | 46 | $\left[\dfrac{l_{46}}{l_{45}}\right](v) = \left[\dfrac{9,168,382}{9,210,289}\right](0.952)$ | $=$ | 0.948 |
| 3 | 47 | $\left[\dfrac{l_{47}}{l_{45}}\right](v^2) = \left[\dfrac{9,123,274}{9,210,289}\right](0.907)$ | $=$ | 0.898 |
| 4 | 48 | $\left[\dfrac{l_{48}}{l_{45}}\right](v^3) = \left[\dfrac{9,074,738}{9,210,289}\right](0.864)$ | $=$ | 0.851 |
| 5 | 49 | $\left[\dfrac{l_{49}}{l_{45}}\right](v^4) = \left[\dfrac{9,022,649}{9,210,289}\right](0.823)$ | $=$ | 0.806 |
| | | | TOTAL | 4.504 |

***Ordinary Life Insurance.*** The net single premium for a whole life policy of $1,000 issued at age 45 is $270.84, according to the earlier figures. To find the net annual level premium for an ordinary life policy, this sum must be divided by the present value of a life annuity due of 1 for the whole of life, since premiums are paid annually through the life of this policy. The method of ascertaining the present value of the life annuity due of 1 is shown in Table 19-7.

Thus the net annual level premium for an ordinary life policy of $1,000 issued at male age 45 with *1980 CSO Table* mortality and on a 5 percent basis is $17.69. This result is obtained as follows:

$$\frac{\$270.84}{15.312} = \$17.69$$

***Limited-Payment Whole Life Insurance.*** If paying for the above whole life policy is desired over a period that is less than the whole of life, it is necessary to compute the annual level premium that, continued for the desired premium payment period or ceasing upon prior death, will purchase this policy. In accordance with the formula, the annual level premium for a 20-year payment period would be found by dividing into the net single premium the present value of a *temporary* life annuity due for a term of 20 years following age 45. The calculation of the present value of this life annuity due at male age 45 for 20 years is shown in Table 19-8.

The net annual level premium, therefore, for a 20-payment whole life policy issued at male age 45 is $270.84 ÷ 12.333, or $21.96.

Note that in all cases, the net single premium for the whole life policy (the numerator in the formula) is the same regardless of the premium-paying period selected. In the case of a 30-payment whole life or a life-paid-up-at-65 policy,

**TABLE 19–7   ILLUSTRATIVE WHOLE LIFE ANNUITY DUE CALCULATION (MALE, AGED 45, *1980 CSO* MORTALITY, 5 PERCENT INTEREST)**

| Policy Year ($t$) | Age ($x$) | Calculation | | Year's Present Expected Value |
|---|---|---|---|---|
| 1 | 45 | 1 due immediately | = | 1.000 |
| 2 | 46 | $\left[\dfrac{l_{46}}{l_{45}}\right](v) = \left[\dfrac{9,168,382}{9,210,289}\right](0.952)$ | = | 0.948 |
| 3 | 47 | $\left[\dfrac{l_{47}}{l_{45}}\right](v^2) = \left[\dfrac{9,123,274}{9,210,289}\right](0.907)$ | = | 0.898 |
| . | . | . | . | . |
| . | . | . | . | . |
| . | . | . | . | . |
| 53 | 97 | $\left[\dfrac{l_{97}}{l_{45}}\right](v^{52}) = \left[\dfrac{60,504}{9,210,289}\right](0.079)$ | = | 0.001 |
| 54 | 98 | $\left[\dfrac{l_{98}}{l_{45}}\right](v^{53}) = \left[\dfrac{31,450}{9,210,289}\right](0.075)$ | = | 0.000* |
| 55 | 99 | $\left[\dfrac{l_{99}}{l_{45}}\right](v^{54}) = \left[\dfrac{10,757}{9,210,289}\right](0.072)$ | = | 0.000* |
| | | | TOTAL | 15.312 |

*Less than 0.0005

the same principle would be followed—that is, dividing the net single premium ($270.84 at male age 45) by the present value of a life annuity due for the appropriate premium-paying period. This is because the net single premium is a measure of the present value of future expected policy benefits and is blind to the actual policy premium payment method.

*Deferred Annuity.* Deferred annuities often are paid for by flexible, periodic premiums or, less commonly, by fixed, periodic premiums. Even when premiums are flexible, the contract holder often will choose to pay a level amount into the annuity, with the idea of building to a future target sum. In theory, premiums may continue through the entire period of deferment, or, as in the case of the whole life policy described above, they may be limited to a stated number of years. As with life insurance premiums, the annual level premium on these contracts is paid only while the insured is alive. If, therefore, the deferred annuity issued at age 40 begins the payment of an annual income of $100 at age 70 and if the net single premium for it is $239.36 (see above), the annual premium on this policy may be paid until one year prior to the beginning of the annuity (until the holder of the contract is 69). In this case, the series of annual

**TABLE 19-8    ILLUSTRATIVE 20-YEAR LIFE ANNUITY DUE CALCULATION (MALE, AGED 45, *1980 CSO* MORTALITY, 5 PERCENT INTEREST)**

| Policy Year ($t$) | Age ($x$) | Calculation | | Year's Present Expected Value |
|---|---|---|---|---|
| 1 | 45 | 1 due immediately | = | 1.000 |
| 2 | 46 | $\left[\dfrac{l_{46}}{l_{45}}\right](v) = \left[\dfrac{9,168,382}{9,210,289}\right](0.952)$ | = | 0.948 |
| 3 | 47 | $\left[\dfrac{l_{47}}{l_{45}}\right](v^2) = \left[\dfrac{9,123,274}{9,210,289}\right](0.907)$ | = | 0.898 |
| . | . | . | . | . |
| . | . | . | . | . |
| . | . | . | . | . |
| 18 | 62 | $\left[\dfrac{l_{62}}{l_{45}}\right](v^{17}) = \left[\dfrac{7,814,753}{9,210,289}\right](0.436)$ | = | 0.370 |
| 19 | 63 | $\left[\dfrac{l_{63}}{l_{45}}\right](v^{18}) = \left[\dfrac{7,814,753}{9,210,289}\right](0.416)$ | = | 0.346 |
| 20 | 64 | $\left[\dfrac{l_{64}}{l_{45}}\right](v^{19}) = \left[\dfrac{7,503,368}{9,210,289}\right](0.396)$ | = | 0.322 |
| | | | TOTAL | 12.333 |

premiums becomes a temporary annuity due for a term of 30 years—ages 40 to 69 inclusive. The amount of this net annual premium would be found, therefore, by dividing the net single premium by the present value of an annuity due of 1 computed for a 30-year term.

The present value of a 30-year annuity due is 16.141, the present value of an annual level premium of $1 paid over the same term as the premiums on the deferred annuity. This figure divided into the net single premium for the deferred annuity gives a net annual level premium:

$$\frac{\$239.36}{16.141} = \$14.83$$

Note that, unlike the life insurance premium calculation, the divisor is not a *life* annuity due since almost no deferred annuities involve life contingencies during the accumulation period.

# Chapter 20

# LIFE INSURANCE RESERVES AND CASH VALUES

One of the most difficult subjects for the layperson to appreciate in connection with the administration of a life insurance company is the need for the existence of the enormous assets possessed by the companies. The great majority of these assets is needed to back the insurer's liabilities to its policyowners and contractholders. Without these assets, the security of life insurance protection as we know it would not be possible. One of the chief liabilities is known as the policy reserve. As discussed briefly in Chapter 2, cash surrender values are related to reserves in that they represent policyowners' demand claims against the insurer's assets. This chapter discusses both reserves and surrender values in more detail.

## RESERVES

Some 80 percent or more of the total funds held by U.S. life insurance companies represents funds held to support their reserve liabilities. These vast resources justify a careful analysis of the nature and purposes of the reserve liabilities.

### ORIGIN AND DEFINITION OF THE RESERVE

Previously, it was stated that life insurance policies may be purchased by a single payment, by fixed annual premiums paid over a period of years, or by flexible premiums. It was also pointed out that mortality rates generally increase with increasing age. Thus in the early policy years, fixed-level premiums and (often) flexible premiums paid exceed the annual cost of insurance. In later years, the reverse may be true. The excess funds not used immediately to pay policy claims and expenses must be recognized by the

557

insurer and preserved for the benefit of all the policyowners until they are needed at some future date. In a similar manner, when a policy is purchased by a single premium, this premium becomes the policyowner's only contribution toward claims to be paid and expenses incurred under contracts of the class, and a large share of this single premium must be held by the insurer to meet future obligations.

The **statutory reserve** is the amount that, together with future net premiums and interest, will be sufficient, according to the valuation assumptions, to pay future claims. This is the prospective definition of the reserve. Statutory reserve calculations effectively ignore insurer expenses and lapse rates, being based instead solely on state-sanctioned mortality and interest assumptions and on the nature of policy benefits and method of calculation. Another way of viewing the reserve is the retrospective view, under which the reserve is considered as the difference between the accumulation at interest of the net premiums received in the past and the accumulation at interest of the claims paid, according to the valuation assumptions.

Reserve calculations (valuations) of policy liabilities require the use of a mortality table and an interest rate. It is then necessary to calculate the net premium on the basis of the table and rate selected and in the manner that has been described in Chapter 19.[1] With the selection of the policy duration for which the reserve is needed, the calculation may proceed, using either the prospective or retrospective method. The retrospective and prospective approaches are merely different ways of viewing the same issue, and, therefore, with the same underlying assumptions, they will always yield identical results.

The retrospective (and therefore the prospective) reserve has no relationship with the insurer's actual past experience. It is always calculated on the assumption that experience has been in accordance with the mortality table selected and interest rate assumed. The term *reserve* has come to have a technical meaning in life insurance, because the states' minimum reserve standards establish definite methods of valuing policy liabilities.[2]

The word *reserve* is somewhat misleading, since it is not used here as it is used in the usual commercial dealings, where *reserve* is often synonymous with *surplus*. The policy reserve of a life insurance company is a liability. It is a measure of the value of obligations to policyowners. As brought out in the following discussion, if the insurer underestimates its policy reserves, or fails to maintain sufficient assets to back its reserves, it eventually may be unable to pay claims. Of a life insurance company's liabilities, the policy reserve often is the most important one.

---

[1] It is also necessary to select a specific valuation method (see later in this chapter).
[2] See "Regulation of Reserves and Cash Values" later in this chapter.

## METHODS OF CALCULATION

*Retrospective Method.* The retrospective method may be explained in terms of either a group or individual approach.

*1. Group Approach.* The reserve arises from the payment of a net (valuation) premium in excess of that needed to meet current mortality costs. Under this approach, premiums in the early policy years usually are more than sufficient to pay the death claims that are assumed; they create a fund that can be used in later policy years, when death rates rise sharply and premiums alone may be insufficient to meet the then current claims. The retrospective reserve can be thought of as an unearned net premium reserve. It represents the provision in early premiums for advance funding of the benefits of surviving insureds, and is shown on the insurer's financial statement as a liability item.[3]

*2. Individual Approach.* The retrospective reserve valuation method also may be illustrated with reference to an individual policy. The retrospective terminal reserve for any particular policy year can be obtained by adding the *net premium* for the year in question to the *terminal reserve* of the preceding year, increasing the combined sum (called the *initial reserve*) by one year's interest at the assumed rate, and deducting the *cost of insurance* for the current year utilizing the assumed mortality table.

Consideration of the process by which this reserve is built involves an understanding of the cost of insurance concept. Reference was made in previous chapters to the **net amount at risk**, which is the death benefit less the terminal reserve at the end of the policy year.[4] When an insured dies, the reserve held for the policy is no longer required. Under this approach, the value of assets corresponding to that reserve is considered to be freed to help pay the claim. The balance of the claim (the net amount at risk) is paid through charges against all policies in the group, including those that mature as a death claim.

The contribution each insured must make as his or her pro-rata share of death claims in any particular year—the **cost of insurance**—is determined by multiplying the net amount at risk at the end of the year in question by the tabular probability of death during that year. This procedure, of course, is identical in concept to that in which the mortality charge of a universal life (UL) policy is determined.

*Prospective Method.* Although the retrospective method of computation provides a clear exposition of the origin and purpose of the reserve, it typically is not used. The prospective method is more commonly used.

As mentioned earlier, the reserve is the balancing factor in the basic insurance equation—that is, in prospective terms, the reserve is the difference

---

[3]A simplified example was given in Chap. 2.
[4]See Chap. 2.

between the present value of expected future benefits and the present value of expected future net premiums. (Of course, the assumptions underlying the calculation may or may not be reasonable.)

At the inception of a contract, the present value of future benefits (PVFB) equals exactly the present value of future net premiums (PVFP). Thus

$$PVFB = PVFP \quad \text{(at date of issue)}$$

As soon as the contract goes in force and the first premium has been paid, the present value of future benefits almost always exceeds the present value of future net premiums.[5] This should be apparent, since fewer premiums remain to be paid and the present value of future benefits is greater because the policy is nearer to maturity. The difference between these two quantities is a measure of the obligation (reserve) of the insurer. Thus

| Net level terminal reserve (age of valuation) | = | PVFB (age of valuation) | − | PVFP (age of valuation) |
|---|---|---|---|---|

It has already been shown that the net single premium (NSP) for a given policy is equal to the present value of future expected benefits, so the above equation may be written as

| Net level terminal reserve (age of valuation) | = | NSP (age of valuation) | − | PVFP (age of valuation) |
|---|---|---|---|---|

The present value of future net premiums necessarily must equal the net level annual premium (NLP) for the contract under consideration, multiplied by the present value of a life annuity due (PVLAD) of 1 for the remaining premium-paying period. Finally, then, the equation may be written in word form as follows:

| Net level terminal reserve ( age of valuation) | = | NSP (age of valuation) | − | NLP (age of issue) | × | PVLAD of 1 for remaining premium-paying period |
|---|---|---|---|---|---|---|

The same approach may be illustrated more analytically and concisely as follows:

$$_tV_x = 1{,}000A_{x+t} - (P_x)\ddot{a}_{\overline{x+t}|}$$

where $_tV_x$ is the net level terminal reserve for an ordinary life policy issued at age $x$ at the end of any number of years $t$, $P$ is the net level premium, and the other variables have the same meaning as discussed in Chapter 19.

[5]This statement is true in general for ordinary life policies, but not for the first-year terminal reserve of an issue age 0 ordinary life policy on the *1958 CSO Table*. The statement also can be inaccurate for level-premium decreasing term insurance.

The manner in which the present value of future benefits and the present value of future net premiums diverge to create the necessity for a reserve is illustrated in Figure 20-1 (not drawn to scale). The computation of the present value of future net premiums involves the determination of the original net level annual premium applicable to the contract, which is multiplied by the present value of a temporary life annuity due of 1 for the remaining premium-paying period.

By way of further illustration, the computation of the twentieth-year net level terminal reserve on a 15-payment whole life policy issued at age 35 is:

$$\text{Net level} \atop \text{terminal reserve}_{55} = NSP_{55} - (NLP_{35})(PVLAD_0)$$
$$_{20}V_{35} = NSP_{55} - (NLP_{35})(0)$$
$$= NSP_{55}$$

The result illustrates the principle that, since no further premiums are due on a paid-up policy, the reserve must equal the present value of future benefits, which can be measured by the net single premium of the policy at the attained age of valuation. The principle is even more graphically illustrated by the single-premium policy, which is paid up after the payment of the first premium. Thus a single-premium whole life policy issued at male age 35 would produce a twentieth-year reserve identical to that of the twentieth-year reserve on the preceding 15-pay whole life policy, both of which would equal the net single premium for a whole life policy at male age 55. The reserves at a given attained age on all paid-up policies of the same type and amount and calculated under the same assumptions must be equal to each other, at the age of valuation, and they all must equal the net single premium for that generic type of policy.

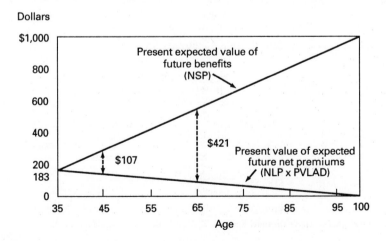

**FIGURE 20-1**

**SOURCE OF THE RESERVE: PROSPECTIVE METHOD FOR ORDINARY LIFE POLICY, $1,000 FACE AMOUNT (AGE 35, *1980 CSO TABLE*, 5% INTEREST, NET LEVEL PREMIUM RESERVE)**

For a policy not yet paid up, consider the tenth-year net-level reserve on a 20-payment whole life policy issued at age 25. It would be formatted as follows:

$$\text{Net level terminal reserve}_{45} = \text{NSP}_{45} - \text{NLP}_{35} \times \text{PVLAD of 1 for 10 years}_{45}$$

Table 20-1 shows the actual computation of reserves for this policy and for two other policies issued at age 25, utilizing the principles developed here and in the previous chapter.

**TABLE 20-1     COMPUTATION OF PROSPECTIVE NET LEVEL RESERVES**
*(1980 CSO TABLE*, 5% INTEREST)*

| Age | Net Single Premium Per $1,000 | | | Payment Value of Life Annuity Due of 1 | | |
|-----|-------|--------|--------|------|----------|----------|
|     | Whole Life | 20-Year Endowment | 10-Year Endowment | Life | 20 Years | 10 Years |
| 25 | $124.316 | $386.254 | $616.655 | 18.389 | 12.889 | 8.050 |
| 35 | 183.559 | 393.167 | 617.928 | 17.145 | 12.743 | 8.023 |
| 45 | 270.840 | 412.730 | 622.701 | 15.312 | 12.333 | 7.923 |
| 55 | 387.005 | 457.051 | 634.199 | 12.873 | 11.402 | 7.682 |

| Net level terminal reserve (age of valuation) | = | NSP (age of valuation) | − | NLP (age of issue) | × | PVLAD of 1 for remaining premium-paying period |
|---|---|---|---|---|---|---|

*Computation*

1.  Twentieth-Year Net Level Terminal Reserve, Ordinary Life Issued at Age 25:

    Net level reserve $_{45}$ = NSP$_{45}$ − (NLP$_{25}$ × PVLAD of 1 for life $_{45}$)

    $$= \$270.840 - \frac{\$124.316}{18.387} \times 15.312$$

    $$= \$167.33$$

2.  Tenth-Year Net Level Terminal Reserve, 20-Payment Whole Life Issued at Age 25:

    Net level reserve $_{35}$ = NSP$_{35}$ − (NLP$_{25}$ × PVLAD of 1 for 10 years $_{35}$)

    $$= \$183.559 - \frac{\$124.316}{12.889} \times 8.023$$

    $$= \$106.33$$

3.  Tenth-Year Net Level Terminal Reserve, 20-Year Endowment Issued at Age 25:

    Net level reserve $_{35}$ = NSP$_{35}$ − (NLP$_{25}$ × PVLAD of 1 for 10 years $_{35}$)

    $$= \$617.928 - \frac{\$386.254}{12.889} \times 8.023$$

    $$= \$377.49$$

## TERMINAL, INITIAL, AND MEAN RESERVES

Depending on the point of time within the policy year when valuation occurs, reserves may be classified as terminal, initial, and mean. The calculations illustrated earlier have been concerned primarily with the **terminal reserve**— that is, the reserve at the end of any given policy year. The **initial reserve**, the reserve at the beginning of the policy year, equals the terminal reserve for the preceding year increased by the net annual premium (if any) for the current year. The **mean reserve** is the arithmetic average of the initial reserve and the terminal reserve for any year of valuation. As discussed in Chapter 21, the initial reserve is used principally in connection with the determination of dividends under participating policies. The initial reserve generally is selected as the basis for allocation of interest earnings in excess of those assumed in the reserve.

The terminal reserve also is used in connection with dividend distributions, since mortality savings are allocated on the basis of the net amount at risk, and the terminal reserve is used to determine the net amount at risk. The terminal-reserve concept also is used to determine nonforfeiture values, although a so-called adjusted premium is used rather than the net premium in such determinations.[6] The terminal reserve also is used in connection with the form of reinsurance based on yearly renewable term insurance for the net amount at risk.[7]

The mean reserve is used in connection with the annual statements of life insurance companies. Since policies are written at different points throughout the year and insurer annual statements are prepared as of December 31, it can be complicated and expensive to attempt a precise reserve calculation for each individual policy. Consequently, for purposes of the annual statement, it is generally assumed that policy anniversaries are uniformly distributed throughout the calendar year of issue, and the mean reserve is used for these valuation purposes.

## SIGNIFICANCE OF ACTUARIAL ASSUMPTIONS

In measuring or valuing its liabilities under outstanding contracts, a life insurance company must make assumptions as to the rate of mortality among its insureds and the rate of earnings on the assets standing behind the reserves. These assumptions are reflected in the mortality table and rate of interest assumed in making the valuation and the purpose for which the valuation is made, all of which are themselves constrained by state and federal (tax) laws. The preceding discussion assumed the *1980 CSO Table* and 5 percent interest. Other assumptions, however, can be and are used in reserve valuations. It is

[6]See later in this chapter.
[7]See Chap. 24.

**TABLE 20-2    NET LEVEL TERMINAL RESERVES PER $1,000, DIFFERENT MORTALITY TABLES**
*(1941, 1958, AND 1980 CSO MORTALITY TABLES, 5% INTEREST, ISSUED AT MALE AGE 35)*

| Ordinary Life | | | | Endowment at Age 65 | | | |
|---|---|---|---|---|---|---|---|
| Duration (Years) | 1941 CSO | 1958 CSO | 1980 CSO | Duration (Years) | 1941 CSO | 1958 CSO | 1980 CSO |
| 1 | $ 11.01 | $ 10.06 | $ 9.15 | 1 | $ 16.71 | $ 16.51 | $ 16.24 |
| 10 | 125.57 | 117.60 | 106.90 | 10 | 199.86 | 200.48 | 197.63 |
| 20 | 283.07 | 269.83 | 249.19 | 20 | 497.23 | 502.04 | 500.21 |
| 30 | 459.52 | 443.84 | 420.57 | 30 | 1,000.00 | 1,000.00 | 1,000.00 |
| 50 | 769.48 | 750.08 | 749.22 | | | | |
| 60 | 872.51 | 869.15 | 868.32 | | | | |

important, therefore, to consider the impact on reserves of the choice of the mortality table and interest table used.

*Mortality.* In practice, it frequently is impossible to determine which of two mortality tables will result in larger reserves at a given age and duration simply by reviewing the mortality rates. A change in mortality not only affects the number of deaths at a given age, but it also affects the number surviving at subsequent ages. Under the net level premium method, the effect of a change in mortality is somewhat spread over the premium-paying period. Because the impact of a change in mortality is not uniform from age to age and duration to duration, it may result in either an increase or a decrease in reserve at any given age and duration. The simplest way to analyze the effect of a change in mortality is to calculate the reserves on both mortality bases for representative plans and issue ages. Without actually calculating the reserves, the determination of the effect on reserves of a change in mortality assumptions is a complex mathematical problem and is beyond the scope of this volume.[8] Table 20-2 shows a comparison of reserves under the *1941 CSO Table*, the *1958 CSO Table*, and the *1980 CSO Table*, assuming an interest rate of 5 percent in each case.

*Interest.* The impact on reserves of a change in the interest assumption can be easily visualized. If the rate of interest assumed is decreased, the result will be an increase in reserves. This may be explained simply by the fact that the smaller anticipated earnings must be offset by a larger reserve at any point in time. The impact of a change in interest assumptions on the reserves of an individual contract utilizing the *1980 CSO Table* is presented in Table 20-3.

An explanation of the impact of the change in interest assumption in terms of the conventional prospective and retrospective methods of calculation is not as easily grasped. Such an explanation is complicated by the fact that both the assumed earnings on the assets backing the reserve and the net premiums are

[8]See C. Wallace Jordan, Jr., *Life Contingencies*, 2nd ed. (Chicago: Society of Actuaries, 1967), pp. 118-123.

TABLE 20-3    NET LEVEL TERMINAL RESERVES PER $1,000,
VARYING RATES OF INTEREST
(ORDINARY LIFE, *1980 CSO TABLE*,
MALE AGE 35)

| Duration (Years) | Rate of Interest | | |
|---|---|---|---|
| | 3% | 5% | 6% |
| 1 | $ 13.32 | $ 9.15 | $ 7.63 |
| 10 | 145.56 | 106.90 | 91.93 |
| 20 | 315.30 | 249.19 | 221.77 |
| 30 | 496.89 | 420.57 | 386.81 |
| 50 | 799.91 | 749.22 | 724.36 |
| 60 | 898.60 | 868.32 | 852.84 |

affected by the change, and the net effect on these modifications leads to the final reserve level. Even so, in general, we observe that the prospective approach utilizes a present value calculation. The higher the interest rate used in any present value calculation, the lower the present value, *ceteris paribus*. Thus, with reserve (and cash value) derivation, the higher the interest rate used, the lower the values, other things being held constant.

*Plan of Insurance.* The relative net level reserves for various plans of whole life insurance based on the indicated assumptions are illustrated in Figure 20-2. The figure illustrates that all limited payment policies (assuming the same age of issue, amount, and underlying assumptions) have the same reserves after they are paid up. In terms of the formula discussed earlier, the temporary life annuity due becomes zero after all premiums have been paid, and the reserve becomes the net single premium in question at the insured's attained age.

## MODIFIED RESERVES

Ideally, each class of policies should pay its own costs. From the standpoint of the insurer, however, the problem of meeting the expense when it occurs is of greater immediate importance. The primary difficulty is that the expenses of the first policy year greatly exceed those of any subsequent year and frequently exceed the entire premium. That first-year expenses are high can be seen by considering that selling expenses, such as agents' commissions and expenses of physical examinations, of approving applications, and of preparing policies for issue, as well as the expenses of setting up records for new policies, are all incurred in the first policy year.

Thus the major problem of the incidence of expense is that policies typically cannot pay their first-year expenses from the amount available from the first premium. These expenses must be met when incurred, yet the insurer faces the necessity of maintaining a reasonable premium level, of paying death claims during the year, and of holding in reserve the remainder of the net premium.

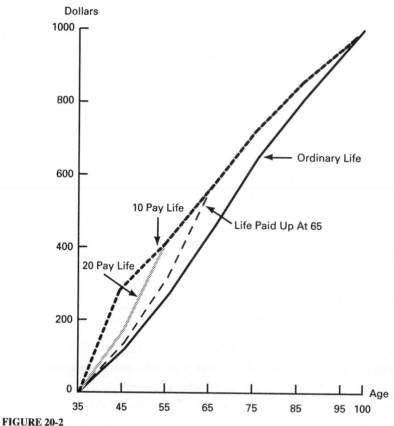

**FIGURE 20-2**

**NET LEVEL TERMINAL RESERVES FOR VARIOUS WHOLE LIFE POLICIES ($1,000, MALE, AGE 35, *1980 CSO TABLE*, 5% INTEREST)**

Consider, for example, an ordinary life policy whose gross premium per $1,000 is $13.39 at age 35. Its valuation net premium of $10.71 (using the *1980 CSO Table* and 5 percent interest) would be increased at 5 percent interest to $11.25 at the close of the policy year. Of this amount, $2.10 is necessary to pay the estimated cost of insurance for the year. Thus $9.15 ($11.25 − $2.10) constitutes a measure of the assets that should be earmarked (reserve) in anticipation of future claims against the policy. Under this statutory approach, the loading of $2.68 ($13.39 − $10.71) is the only portion of the first premium available to pay the first year's expenses, and this would be insufficient.

These first-year costs must be provided from some outside source, or some modification of the system of level reserve valuation must be made. For an old and well-established insurer with a large surplus, the solution to the problem is comparatively simple, for it can pay expenses of new business from surplus and depend on replacing the amount from margins in the loadings of the later premiums. This, however, is not possible for new and small companies, for they have less surplus from which to borrow to supply the demands of a rapidly increasing business.[9]

Another possible way of dealing with this problem is through some modification of the system of valuing reserves, whereby the policy reserve of the first year or of the first few years can be reduced. The two important methods of modifying full net level terminal reserves used in the United States are known as the **full preliminary term method** and the **commissioners' reserve valuation method**.

*Full Preliminary Term Method.* The germ of the full preliminary term concept was introduced into the United States from Europe. The technique entails treating the first year of insurance as term insurance, irrespective of the type of contract actually involved, and assuming that the original contract goes into effect at the beginning of the second policy year. Hence, "preliminary term" is a logical name for it.

This method of valuation provides that the first year's premium under any form of policy will pay for term insurance for one year and that the regular policy for reserve purposes will come into operation one year later than the age of issue, and will be for a one-year-shorter premium-payment period. By this means, the insurer need not earmark against the policy liability (terminal reserve) any portion of the first-year premium; the entire premium becomes available for payment of first-year claims and expenses. Since the amount required for first-year claims is the net premium for one-year term insurance (typically a relatively small amount), the amount available to cover expenses is the excess of the gross premium over the one-year term net rate.

For example, the net level premium on an ordinary life policy at male age 35 (using the *1980 CSO Table* and interest at 5 percent) is $10.71. The net premium for one-year term insurance at age 35 is $2.11 ($1,000 x 0.00211). Thus the excess amount released to help defray first-year expenses would be $8.60 ($10.71 − $2.11). On the 20-payment whole life plan at the same age, the corresponding excess is $12.29, whereas on an endowment-at-age 65 plan, it is $15.33. The net premium for the later years of the policy is then increased and the loading is correspondingly reduced, since the gross premium paid by the policyowner does not change. The net premium becomes that for insurance issued at an age that is one year higher, at a date one year later, and for a term that is one year shorter.

The reserves held on the policy for the second and last years are the reserves based on this new net premium. Thus an ordinary life policy's reserve at the end of the first year would be zero. The reserve at the end of the *second* year would be equal to that of the *first* year terminal reserve for an ordinary life

---

[9]Smaller insurers often rely on reinsurance to provide some relief from the strain on surplus caused by new business (see Chap. 24).

policy issued at age 36. The renewal (age 36) net premium equals the net level premium for age 36, and it is sufficient to provide benefits for an ordinary life policy issued at age 36 with level net premiums. The remainder of the gross premium is available each renewal year for expenses.

The net effect of the full preliminary term method compared to the net level method is to defer funding the first-year reserve and amortize this amount over the remaining premium-paying period of the contract. This method of valuation makes no distinction between various types of cash-value contracts.

For most low-premium policies written by a typical life insurance company, the additional first-year loading made available by treating the first year of insurance as term insurance is inadequate to fully cover substantial first-year expenses. The remainder of the amount needed must be drawn from assets backing the insurer's surplus. Thus it is possible for a rapidly growing company to have a capacity problem, despite the fact that it is using the preliminary term plan.

On higher-premium plans, on the other hand, the first-year reserve borrowed is correspondingly greater, since the cost of one-year term insurance remains the same. The logic of this position has led regulatory authorities to prescribe the use of some modification of the full preliminary term method of valuation, the most important of which is the commissioners' reserve valuation method.

***Commissioners' Reserve Valuation Method.*** The Commissioners' Reserve Valuation Method (CRVM) in effect makes the 20-payment whole life policy the maximum basis on which deferred reserve funding is permitted, and, in doing so, it divides policies into two groups:

1. The full preliminary term method is used if the net premium for the second and subsequent years of the plan does not exceed the corresponding modified net premium for a 20-payment whole life plan.

2. For plans with higher premiums, the additional amount for expenses is limited to approximately the same amount as is permitted under the preliminary term method for a 20-payment whole life policy. It is not exactly the same as the 20-payment life amount in the case of policies that require more or less than 20 years' premiums, because the amount "borrowed" is "repaid" by a level premium payable for each year of the premium-paying period, including the first.

For example, for ordinary life at male age 35, the CRVM calls for the full preliminary term method, because the net premium at male age 36 is less than the corresponding 20-payment life preliminary term basis premium for the second and subsequent years of $15.46 (i.e., the 19-payment life rate at male age 36).

In the case of the endowment at age 65 issued at male age 35, however, the modified method applies, since the rate at male age 36 for an endowment at age 65 of $18.32 exceeds the 19-payment life rate at male age 36 of $15.46. The additional amount available for expenses is found to be $12.29 (following the method described in paragraph 2); this amount is equal to that given earlier for the 20-payment life plan under the preliminary-term plan. If the premium-paying period differs from 20 years, however, the result will be slightly different. Table 20-4 presents terminal reserve values under the several methods of valuation discussed above, using 5 percent interest.

## OTHER RESERVES

*Deficiency Reserves.* In the past, if gross premiums charged by a life insurance company for a particular class of policies were less than the valuation net premiums, the insurer was required to maintain a supplemental reserve, called a **deficiency reserve**. Valuation net premiums historically have been considerably less than gross premiums. In recent years, however, continued improvement in mortality and increasing price competition brought gross premiums levels down to or even below valuation net premiums. The establishment of deficiency reserves was particularly difficult for smaller insurers with limited surplus.

Deficiency-reserve requirements (or their equivalent) are founded on the theory that the use, in the prospective reserve formula, of a valuation net-level premium larger than the actual gross premium overstates the present value of expected future premiums and, consequently, understates the amount of the reserve. The deficiency is represented by the present value of the expected excess of the valuation net premium over the gross annual premium.

State law no longer requires the establishment of deficiency reserves as such. Rather, the law defines a new minimum required reserve as the present value of expected future benefits less the present value of expected future

**TABLE 20-4**  **TERMINAL RESERVES PER $1,000, VARIOUS METHODS OF VALUATION** (*1980 CSO TABLE*, 5% INTEREST, MALE, AGE 35)

| Plan | Policy Year | Full Preliminary Term Method | Commissioners' Reserve Valuation Method | Net Level Premium Method |
|---|---|---|---|---|
| Ordinary life | 1 | $ 0.00 | $ 0.00 | $ 9.15 |
| | 5 | 40.42 | 40.42 | 49.20 |
| | 10 | 98.66 | 98.66 | 106.90 |
| | 15 | 165.90 | 165.90 | 173.54 |
| | 20 | 242.25 | 242.25 | 249.19 |
| 20-Payment life | 1 | 0.00 | 0.00 | 13.04 |
| | 5 | 59.62 | 59.62 | 70.83 |
| | 10 | 148.35 | 148.35 | 156.71 |
| | 15 | 255.93 | 255.93 | 260.67 |
| | 20 | 387.01 | 387.01 | 387.01 |
| Age 65 endowment | 1 | 0.00 | 3.01 | 16.24 |
| | 5 | 73.55 | 76.33 | 88.59 |
| | 10 | 184.38 | 186.83 | 197.63 |
| | 15 | 321.21 | 323.26 | 332.24 |
| | 20 | 491.96 | 493.49 | 500.21 |

valuation net premiums calculated by the method (commissioners' or net level) actually used in computing the reserve for the policy, but using the minimum valuation standards of mortality and rate of interest. The gross premium on the policy is substituted in this reserve calculation at each contract year in which it is less than the valuation net premium. If the reserve calculated in this way is larger than the reserve otherwise required, it becomes the minimum reserve for the policy. In practice, however, the term *deficiency reserve* is still used to denote these special situations.

*Reserves for Individual Deferred Annuities.* There are three basic forms of annuity policies: the flexible- or fixed-premium deferred annuity, the single-premium deferred annuity, and the single-premium immediate annuity. When any annuity becomes income paying, it is reserved on the basis of a legally recognized mortality table and interest rate, using the annuitant's attained age and the monthly income, and taking into account any minimum benefit guarantees. The mortality standard generally used is more conservative than that used for life valuation. (*Conservative* for life insurance means higher mortality rates, while *conservative* for annuities means lower mortality rates.)

Annual-premium deferred annuities are policies in which the owner pays annual premiums during an accumulation period until such time as the annuitant begins to receive income. These annual premiums may be a specified amount or they may be subject to the discretion of the owner under flexible-premium annuities. At income commencement, an annuitant receives the monthly income based on the cash value of the policy at that time and an annuity factor for the annuitant's attained age.

In 1976 a **Commissioners' Annuity Reserve Valuation Method** was defined. It requires the comparison of the present value of future guaranteed benefits at each duration to the present value of future required premiums at that duration. The greatest excess revealed by these comparisons is the minimum reserve for the contract. Supplementary contracts involving life contingencies generally are valued according to the mortality and interest basis upon which the payments were calculated.

*Reserves for Paid-Up Contracts.* Under contracts in which no further premiums will be received, reserves are merely valuation net premiums (i.e., the present value of future benefits). This would include (1) single-premium life and endowment contracts, (2) individual life annuities, (3) paid-up life and endowment policies, and (4) supplementary contracts issued to beneficiaries in lieu of a lump-sum payment.

*Reserves for Second-to-Die Policies.* The procedure for deriving these reserves is identical conceptually to that for single-life policies. An adjustment, however, is necessary in the calculation to recognize the conditional probabilities involved with two insureds. Reserves under second-to-die policies are low while both insureds are alive. When one insured dies, however, required reserves increase substantially since the policy, at that point, becomes, in effect, a regular single-life policy.

*Reserves for Substandard Policies.* In the case of substandard policies, an additional reserve liability is recognized to anticipate the additional mortality risk over that expected for a standard policy. This reserve is calculated by any one of numerous methods, and the approach followed varies from insurer to insurer.

Similarly, the adverse selection reflected in the mortality experience under group and term conversions may be recognized by establishing an additional reserve for the extra mortality experienced. Reserving for these items is not uniform.

*Reserves for Special Benefits.* State laws require that a minimum reserve liability be maintained for accidental death and waiver of premium benefits, and an appropriate liability for supplementary contracts without life contingencies, dividend accumulations, and similar benefits.

Accidental death benefit minimum reserves are determined in a similar manner to ordinary policy reserves, using a mortality table (the *1959 Accidental Death Benefits Table*) based on accidental deaths.

Reserves for waiver of premium are, of course, based upon appropriate morbidity and mortality tables. These form the basis for predicting the joint probability of dying or becoming disabled, and, assuming that the waiver of premium annuity has been entered upon, the joint probability of death or recovery.

Supplementary contracts without life contingencies, dividend accumulations, premiums paid in advance, and similar benefits are easily valued, since they involve only compound interest calculations.

*Voluntary Reserve.* In addition to the specific policy/benefit reserves (legal and voluntary) held to meet specific policy obligations, life insurance companies set aside various voluntary reserves that really represent earmarking of surplus for particular purposes and may not be liabilities.

## CASH VALUES

Whether the reserve derives from a level-premium or a flexible-premium policy, the result is the same—prefunded mortality charges. What is an appropriate, fair disposition of these prefunded charges if the policyowner surrenders his or her policy? Clearly, under these circumstances, the insurer no longer requires the assets backing the reserve liability, since its future liability under the policy ceases. Experience has shown that it is not necessary, for the protection of the insurer or other policyowners, to insist that the terminating policyowner forfeit an amount equal to the policy's entire reserve. The practice in the United States is to permit the policyowner who surrenders his or her policy to receive a cash surrender value.

Although the practice of allowing a cash surrender value in some form is old, for many years the matter was entirely optional on the part of U.S. insurers. At one time, some insurers voluntarily granted cash surrender values while others did not. All U.S. states today, however, have nonforfeiture laws that define the minimum amount that must be returned upon policy surrender. Many insurers provide cash surrender values that exceed the legal minimums.

Insurer practice in determining the proper value to be granted discontinuing policyowners is based on certain principles. Before examining the Standard Nonforfeiture Law, these principles are considered briefly.

## CONCEPTS OF EQUITY

The actual treatment of withdrawing policyowners generally can be based on any one of three possible concepts of equity. One view is that the policyowner should receive nothing, on the grounds that the sole function of a life insurance contract is to provide certain designated benefits in the event of the insured's death or survival to the maturity date of an endowment policy. Under this approach, the policyowner bears the primary risk of loss associated with policy termination. Premiums could be discounted for anticipated surrenders (or dividends could be increased on participating policies) and the forfeiture thereby reflected in a reduction in the cost of insurance. In the early days of the U.S. insurance business, this view generally was accepted and applied, in many cases without an adjustment in the contract premium. Such practices led to the introduction of nonforfeiture legislation, and this approach probably would be difficult to sell today in the absence of complete, effective buyer disclosure. Discussions have taken place at the regulatory level about the possibility, for example, of allowing no cash values within whole life policies but, to date, they have not resulted in any relaxation of past nonforfeiture standards. It is worth noting that cash values remain purely optional in many other national markets, although the accepted practice is to provide them.

At the other extreme, it might be considered that the withdrawing policyowner is entitled to the return of all premiums paid (less dividends), plus interest at the contractual rate, less a pro-rata share of assumed death claims—that is, to the full reserve under the contract, irrespective of the policy year in which the surrender occurs. This view, of course, ignores the incidence of expense and assumes that unamortized acquisition expenses under policies surrendered during the early years after issue should be borne by persisting policyowners or charged to the insurer's general surplus or the agent's commission.

Proponents of this view note that a substantial proportion of purchasers of cash-value policies terminate their policies within the first few policy years, even though it is accepted wisdom that these policies should be purchased only for long-term needs. A high rate of early policy termination results in substantial consumer loss—loss that arguably is traceable, to a large degree, to the policy not having been suitable to the customer in the first instance. This unsuitability could have stemmed from improper or incomplete counseling during the sales process, from the policy offering poor value, or from a host of other reasons. Of course, unforeseen changes in the consumer's circumstances also undoubtedly increases the rate of early policy termination.

This view of equity insists, in effect, that terminating policyowners should receive the full policy reserve and that the insurer and, perhaps, the agent should be held primarily accountable for early policy terminations. This accountability would take the form of having the insurer (via a charge to surplus) and also the agent (through a charge against his or her commission) bear the costs of early surrender.

This view received support through a report issued by the Committee on Consumer Policy of the Organization for Economic Cooperation and Development (OECD). After noting that a frequent cause of consumer concern in several countries arises from the low amount of surrender value granted in early policy cancellations, the report goes on to conclude:

> Further consideration should therefore be given to either greater disclosure of surrender values in the early years or to a reasonable burden-sharing which better balances the interest of the [insurance] company, the agent and the policy-holder and which gives the agent more of an incentive to counsel the consumer about the long-term nature of the contract.[10]

According to this concept, insurers and agents, by having a greater financial stake in whether a policy terminates early, will do a better job of matching policy to customer needs and a better job of disclosure. With this view, the insurer (and possibly, the agent) bears the primary risk of loss associated with policy termination. A modified form of this approach would have the acquisition expenses due to early terminations borne partially by the insurer, agent, and persisting policyowners, and partially by the terminating policy-owners themselves. This would result in a surrender value of something less than the full reserve but more than the asset share (see below), until the acquisition expenses had been fully amortized, after which it would equal the full reserve.[11]

---

[10]*Consumers and Life Insurance* (Paris: OECD, 1987), p. 38.

[11]Key to any discussion about who ultimately bears the cost burden associated with early policy terminations is an understanding of the elasticities of demand and supply of each of the stakeholders (a discussion that is beyond the scope of this text). It is worth noting, however, that because of elasticity differences, the cost may not be borne ultimately by the apparent person or entity. For example, were it the intent to have insurer surplus absorb the costs of early termination, it would be unclear whether those costs were ultimately borne by the insurer stockholders in the form of lower dividends, by the policyowners in the form of higher premiums, or by the insurer's employees or agents in the form of lower wages and commissions.

The third concept of equity, and the one generally applied, is that withdrawing policyowners should receive a surrender value that is as nearly as possible equivalent to their contribution to the funds of the insurer, less (1) the cost of protection received, (2) any expenses incurred by the insurer in establishing and handling the policy, and (3) perhaps a contribution to insurer surplus. This view has as its objective that the withdrawal of a policyowner should neither benefit nor harm continuing policyowners in a substantial way. Under this concept, the amount received by the withdrawing policyowner would be based on the pro-rata share of the assets accumulated by the insurer on behalf of the classification of policies to which his or her policy belongs—that is, the asset share.

## Reasons Justifying Paying Less Than the Asset Share

The asset share value equals the pro-rata share of the assets accumulated by the insurer on behalf of the block of policies to which a particular policy belongs. This value reflects the incidence of expense and its relationship to policy duration. It has been argued that the actual cash surrender benefit may be somewhat less, for several reasons, including (1) adverse financial selection, (2) adverse mortality selection, (3) contribution to a contingency reserve or profits, and (4) cost of surrendering the policy.

*Adverse Financial Selection.* A reason advanced for not allowing the policyowner to obtain the full asset share on the policy at any time is the possibility that during periods of financial stringency or business depression, policyowners may avail themselves of the privilege of surrendering their policies to such an extent that the insurer's financial standing may be weakened, to the detriment of remaining policyowners. In normal times, life insurance companies have an excess of income over expenditures that is more than sufficient to meet demands for loans and cash surrender values. During difficult economic times, however, demands by policyowners may be so great that it becomes necessary to liquidate assets at depressed prices. The option of the policyowner to demand the policy's cash surrender value at any time also necessitates a more liquid investment policy than would otherwise be required.[12] Many insurers believe that the policyowners who surrender their policies should be charged with the loss of investment earnings (including capital losses) arising from their actions, and they take this into account in establishing the termination value.

*Adverse Mortality Selection.* An additional argument for granting a surrender value that is less than the full asset share (although some writers question its importance) relates to the adverse mortality selection that is assumed

---

[12]See Chap. 30 for a discussion of the financial nature of insurers' obligations. Insurers have the legal right to postpone payment of the cash surrender value for a period of six months. From a practical standpoint, however, this right should be invoked only under the most severe financial circumstances.

to be brought about by the allowance of liberal surrender values. The position taken by the supporters of this view is that a life insurance policy is a unilateral contract, to which the insurer always must adhere, but which the policyowner has the option of terminating at any time. Whenever, therefore, the payment of premiums seems a hardship, healthy insureds not feeling the immediate need for insurance, may have no hesitancy in discontinuing coverage. Insureds in poor health will, on the contrary, appreciate fully the value of their insurance and will exert themselves to the utmost to pay the premium. Hence, according to this view, policies on the good risks are likely to lapse on a larger scale if surrender values are liberal, while impaired risks will stay with the insurer. The result is a reduction in the average vitality of remaining policyowners. It is therefore argued that terminating policyowners should receive less than the pro-rata share of their policies, in order to provide a fund to meet the higher death rate among the poorer risks that remain. Although the argument is logical, this tendency has been difficult to substantiate statistically.

*Other Reasons.* Some insurers believe that each contract should make a permanent contribution to the insurer's surplus, both to absorb adverse fluctuations and to enhance the insurer's overall financial security and profitability. To the extent that such a permanent contribution is required, the surrender value should be reduced.

In a stock insurer, an adjustment may be made in the surrender value to account for that policy's contribution to profits, in recognition of the risk borne by stockholders' investments. Finally, a certain amount of expense is incurred in processing the surrender of a policy. Some insurers adjust the surrender value to reflect this factor, rather than taking it into account in their premium-loading formula.

## REGULATION OF RESERVES AND CASH VALUES

All states in the United States have laws that stipulate the requirements that insurers must meet in calculating reserves and cash surrender values. These laws have the effect of establishing minimum values below which insurers may not venture in establishing reserves and surrender values. The **Standard Valuation Law** defines the minimum reserves for life insurance and annuity contracts. The **Standard Nonforfeiture Law** defines minimum cash surrender values. Insurers are free to maintain reserves at a level higher than those required by the valuation laws and they may have higher surrender values than those required by the nonforfeiture laws, but values cannot be lower. Most states' laws are patterned closely after the 1980 NAIC model laws which are discussed below.

The basis for both reserve and surrender value computation is stated in terms of the mortality table to be used, the maximum rate of interest to be assumed, and the method to be applied. The requirements differ as between life insurance and annuities and as among ordinary, group, and industrial life insurance. Supplementary agreements relating to proceeds left with the insurance company are subject to special rules.

## BACKGROUND

Early nonforfeiture laws were enacted to prevent the forfeiture of equities built in level-premium policies, and early valuation laws were designed to ensure company solvency. Traditionally, the surrender values required to be returned have been called **nonforfeiture values**, and the form in which these values may be taken is referred to as **nonforfeiture options**.[13]

Prior to 1948, the legal minimum standard in most states for computing reserves and surrender values for ordinary insurance was the *American Experience Table* and 3 1/2 percent interest. The minimum basis (mortality table) for valuing reserves and surrender values for newly issued ordinary policies was changed in 1948 to the *1941 CSO Table*. Previously, nonforfeiture benefits were linked directly to reserves, whereas under the 1948 law this close tie-in was obviated, with the result that greater equity could be maintained between insureds at different ages and also with respect to different plans of insurance. The elimination of the former linkage recognized that reserves are an aggregate measure of future liabilities, whereas nonforfeiture values are meant to recognize to some degree the policyowner's interest in a particular contract. The 1948 law also established a new method for calculating nonforfeiture values. Variations of this method have been used since that time.

The use of the *1958 CSO Table* and 3 1/2 percent interest was made mandatory for reserves on ordinary policies issued on or after January 1, 1966. The interest rate was changed to 4, and later to 4 1/2 percent.

Minimum surrender values could be based on 5 1/2 percent interest for annual premium policies, and on either 5 1/2 percent or 6 1/2 percent for single-premium policies. Changes in 1972 updated the valuation mortality tables for both group and individual annuities. Under 1976 amendments, the maximum nonforfeiture interest rate that could be used was 1 percent higher than the statutory interest rate specified for determining minimum reserves.

In spite of seemingly continual updating of the earlier valuation and nonforfeiture laws, the need for further changes appeared to be constant. Each time a change in mortality tables or interest rates was needed, an amendment was necessary in every state's valuation and nonforfeiture laws. This was both a time-consuming and expensive process. It was widely recognized that the *1958 CSO Table* was out of date and that with interest rate volatility, further changes would be needed in the interest rate assumptions.

---

[13]See Chap. 9.

## THE 1980 VALUATION AND NONFORFEITURE LAWS

In response to these converging problems, a revised NAIC **Model Standard Valuation Law** and a revised NAIC **Model Standard Nonforfeiture Law** were adopted by the NAIC in 1980, the effects of which were intended to introduce greater flexibility into the laws and to render them more suitable for contemporary conditions. All jurisdictions in the United States adopted the new NAIC models or close variations thereof.

The revised laws had no effect on life insurance policies and individual annuity contracts in force prior to the change in laws. They did not affect the reserves that had already been set up on existing group annuity–type contracts, but the future growth of these reserves could be affected.

***Changes from Earlier Laws.*** Three important aspects of the 1980 model laws deserve comment: (1) dynamic maximum interest rates, (2) new mortality bases, and (3) certain technical changes.

1. *Dynamic Interest Rates.* The 1980 model laws define the maximum interest rates that can be used to calculate reserves and nonforfeiture benefits on a dynamic basis. The maximum permitted interest rate is automatically adjusted if a recalculation produces a significant change. The laws make use of the *Moody's Corporate Bond Yield Average—Monthly Average Corporates*, as published by Moody's Investors Service, Inc., as the applicable index. The maximum interest rates themselves, however, depend on the type of insurance contract, and they may be much smaller than this composite yield rate. These maximum interest rates are recalculated at 12-month intervals. The maximum interest rate for a particular life insurance policy or individual annuity contract is fixed at its date of issue. A change in the maximum interest rate applies only to newly issued life insurance policies or individual annuity contracts—not to those already in force.

The dynamic interest basis is an improvement over previous methods, in that it automatically can adjust maximum interest rates to current conditions without the need for legislative action. Of course, the laws permit an insurance company to use lower interest rates than the permitted maximums if it wishes to do this.

2. *Mortality Tables.* The model laws make use of revised mortality tables for individual life insurance, which were developed by a Society of Actuaries committee. These tables are constructed separately for males and females, for smokers and nonsmokers, and they are styled as the *Commissioners 1980 Standard Ordinary Mortality Tables*, the *Commissioners 1980 Standard Ordinary Mortality Table with Ten-Year Select Mortality Factors,* and the *Commissioners 1980 Extended Term Insurance Tables.*[14]

---

[14]There are other specialized *1980 CSO Tables* (see Chap. 18).

The model laws also contain a procedure whereby new mortality tables developed in the future can become effective in a state without being specifically named in the text of the laws. First, the NAIC must adopt any such new tables. These new tables must then be approved through a regulation promulgated by the Commissioner of Insurance for the state. The new mortality tables can be tables for individual life insurance or tables for other classes of contracts described in the laws.[15]

3. *Certain Technical Changes.* The model laws contain many technical changes, although the fundamental calculation processes remained unchanged. This summary identifies only a few of the changes.

The laws changed the formula for the expense allowance used in the Standard Nonforfeiture Law for life insurance, so as to reflect current patterns of expenses more accurately. The laws allow the state's Commissioner of Insurance to promulgate regulations describing appropriate minimum reserves and minimum nonforfeiture benefits for certain new or complex plans of life insurance that might not have been contemplated when the laws were originally written. The laws also cause the minimum reserves and minimum nonforfeiture benefits for some life insurance policies in the early policy years to be increased over what they would be otherwise, in certain cases when the plan provides relatively high guaranteed benefits or cash values in one or more of the later policy years.

*Requirements.* As mentioned earlier, valuation and nonforfeiture laws stipulate: (1) the mortality table to be used, (2) the maximum interest rate to be assumed, and (3) the method to be applied. The maximum interest rates permitted vary as between annuities and life insurance, and, within each of these categories, based on duration and plan types. The permissible maximums change periodically in accordance with changes in Moody's bond yield figures, as discussed above. The longer the policy duration, the lower the maximum permissible interest rate, *ceteris paribus*. Maximum rates to be used for valuation (reserve) calculation purposes are lower than permissible maximums to be used for nonforfeiture (cash value) calculation purposes.

The nonforfeiture law stipulates that the nonforfeiture interest rate cannot exceed 125 percent of the reserve interest rate. Of course, insurance companies are free to use rates that are lower than the maximum permitted in law, and many do so in the interest of conservatism.

The valuation laws stipulate that the method used for calculating minimum reserves can be the CRVM (discussed earlier). The net-level-premium method, in other words, is not required, but it may be used since it develops higher reserves than the CRVM.

The minimum nonforfeiture value at any policy duration is the present value of the future benefits under the policy less the present value of future *adjusted*

---

[15]New mortality tables were being devised as this book was going to press.

premiums. This definition is essentially the prospective reserve formula utilizing an adjusted premium in lieu of the valuation net level premium. The **adjusted premium** is the level premium necessary to pay the benefits guaranteed by the policy (the net level premium) *plus* the level equivalent of a defined special **first-year expense allowance**.

Under pre-1980 laws, the maximum allowance for special first-year expenses was defined as a constant of $20 per $1,000 of insurance, plus a percentage (40 percent) of the adjusted premium for the policy, and a percentage (25 percent) of either the adjusted premium for the policy or the adjusted premium for a whole life policy issued at the same age for the insurance amount, whichever was less. According to the previous legislation, the first-year expense allowance could not exceed $46 per $1,000 of insurance. With this earlier formula, the percentage allowance was a function of the adjusted premium—the item being sought.

This circularity was removed by the 1980 changes which made the formula a function of the net premium rather than the adjusted premium. Thus under the law, the maximum allowance is defined as 125 percent of the lesser of (1) the nonforfeiture net level premium or (2) $40 per $1,000; plus a constant of $10 per $1,000 of insurance. This approach simplified the calculation. The maximum first-year expense allowance per $1,000 face amount is, therefore, $60 (1.25 x $30 + $10).

*Illustration of Adjusted-Premium Method*. The first step in deriving surrender values under the Standard Nonforfeiture Law is to determine the special first-year expense allowance. This may be based on the insurer's expense situation, competitive pressures, or other considerations, but it is limited to the maximum amount permitted under the law.

The second step in the process is to calculate the adjusted premium. This may be approached from two standpoints. It may be regarded as the net annual level premium required to amortize a principal sum equal to the present value of the benefits under the policy and the special first-year expense allowance. Thus the present value of future benefits (PVFB) for an ordinary life policy issued at male age 35 (based on the *1980 CSO Table* and interest at 5 1/2 percent) equals the net single premium for such a policy, or $159.59. The net level premium is $9.90. The maximum special first-year expense allowance for such a policy is, therefore, $22.38.[16] The total of $159.59 and $22.38 yields a principal sum of $181.97. The net annual level premium that will amortize this sum may be obtained by dividing $181.97 by 16.121, the present value at 5 1/2 percent of a life annuity due of 1 as of age 35. The result, $11.29, is the adjusted premium.

The second way of considering the adjusted premium is as the sum that is obtained by adding to the regular net annual level premium the annual amount needed to amortize the special acquisition expenses over the premium-paying

[16](1.25)($9.90) + $10.00 = $22.38.

period. Thus, by dividing $22.38 (the maximum special first-year expense allowance) by the present value of a life annuity due of 1 for the premium-paying period, 16.121, the annual amount of $1.39, is obtained, which, when added to the net level premium for an ordinary life policy issued at male age 35, $9.90, gives $11.29, the same adjusted premium determined above.

The final step in determining the minimum surrender value is to substitute the adjusted premium for the regular net level premium in the formula employed in the computation of prospective reserves. The following summary of the calculation of the tenth-year minimum nonforfeiture value for an ordinary life policy issued at male age 35 (*1980 CSO Table* and 5 1/2 percent) will illustrate the application of the principles developed here:

$$
\begin{aligned}
&\begin{array}{lll}
\text{NFV} & \text{present value} & \text{present value} \\
\text{(age of} & = \text{future} & - \text{of future} \\
\text{valuation)} & \text{of benefits} & \text{adjusted premiums}
\end{array}
\\[1em]
&\begin{array}{lll}
\text{NFV} & \text{NSP} & - \left[ \left( \dfrac{\begin{array}{l}\text{NSP} \quad\quad \text{special} \\ \text{(original} + \text{expense} \\ \text{age)} \quad\quad \text{allowance}\end{array}}{\text{PVLAD of 1 PPP}} \right) \left( \begin{array}{l}\text{PVLAD of 1} \\ \text{for remaining} \\ \text{premium} \\ \text{paying period}\end{array} \right) \right] \\
\text{(age of} & = \text{(age of} & \\
\text{valuation)} & \text{valuation)} &
\end{array}
\\[1em]
&\text{NFV}_{45} \quad = \quad \text{NSP}_{45} \quad - \left[ \left( \dfrac{\begin{array}{l}\quad\quad\quad \text{special} \\ \text{NSP}_{35} + \text{expense} \\ \quad\quad\quad \text{allowance}\end{array}}{\text{PVLAD of 1 PPP}} \right) \left( \begin{array}{l}\text{PVLAD of 1} \\ \text{for life at} \\ \text{age 45}\end{array} \right) \right]
\\[1em]
&\quad\quad\quad = \quad \$242.87 - \left( \dfrac{\$159.59 + \$22.38}{16.121} \right) (14.523)
\\[1em]
&\quad\quad\quad = \quad \$78.94
\end{aligned}
$$

Note that the only difference between this formula and the minimum reserve formula utilized earlier is the addition of the expense factor to the original net single premium, resulting in a net level adjusted premium. Thus in prospective terms, the nonforfeiture value is the present value of future benefits less the present value of future adjusted premiums.

*Modifications of the Adjusted-Premium Method.* The above illustration demonstrates the calculation of minimum surrender values under a 5 1/2 percent interest assumption. As mentioned earlier, many companies provide surrender values in excess of the minimums of the law. This may be accomplished by (1) assuming lower first-year expenses than the maximum permitted, (2) assuming the maximum expenses and amortizing them over a shorter period or at an uneven rate over the premium-paying period, (3) assuming a lower rate of interest than that permitted by law, or (4) a combination of the above.

If lower first-year expenses are assumed, the adjusted premium will be smaller, making the present value of future adjusted premiums smaller and resulting in larger surrender values. Similarly, in the case of amortizing the maximum permitted excess first-year expense allowance over a shorter period or at an uneven rate, the adjusted premium is itself adjusted, resulting in appropriately modified surrender values. In those cases when the premium is adjusted to produce surrender values, the modified adjusted premium is known as a **nonforfeiture factor**. Similarly, the term **adjusted-premium method** refers to the derivation of minimum values only. Where larger values are derived through the use of nonforfeiture factor(s), the term **standard nonforfeiture-value method** is applied. The law requires only that values provided be no less than those derived by the adjusted-premium method.

Table 20-5 illustrates the variation in cash surrender values with changes in the interest assumption only, holding mortality and expense allowances constant. The interest assumption is of great importance in determining the level of surrender values, especially at early policy durations. Table 20-6 shows how results differ under various mortality tables, with each using the adjusted-premium method and interest at 5 percent.

## REQUIREMENTS FOR NONTRADITIONAL PRODUCTS[17]

The valuation and nonforfeiture laws permit state insurance commissioners to promulgate special reserve and surrender requirements for policies whose cost and benefit structures do not fit easily into the classical mold. Some commissioners have taken advantage of this legislative opportunity by

**TABLE 20-5 EFFECT OF INTEREST RATE ASSUMPTION ON SURRENDER VALUES (ORDINARY LIFE, MALE, AGE 35, $1,000 BASIS, BASED ON 1980 NAIC MODEL LAW)**

| | Interest Rate | | | |
|---|---|---|---|---|
| End of Policy Year | 3% | 5% | 7-1/2% | 9% |
| 1 | $ 0 | $ 0 | $ 0 | $ 0 |
| 2 | 0 | 0 | 0 | 0 |
| 3 | 13.33 | 5.78 | 0 | 0 |
| 4 | 27.92 | 16.20 | 6.70 | 2.89 |
| 5 | 42.79 | 26.97 | 14.04 | 8.81 |
| 10 | 121.05 | 86.02 | 56.02 | 43.04 |
| 15 | 205.63 | 154.21 | 108.01 | 87.82 |
| 20 | 295.66 | 231.63 | 171.28 | 143.81 |
| 25 | 388.53 | 316.33 | 245.01 | 211.21 |
| 30 | 482.45 | 407.03 | 329.03 | 290.58 |

[17]This section draws on Douglas C. Doll, "Universal Life: A Product Overview, *SOA Study Note 340-41-91* (Itasia, Ill.: Society of Actuaries, 1991), pp. 10-11.

| TABLE 20-6 | EFFECT OF MORTALITY ASSUMPTION ON SURRENDER VALUES (ORDINARY LIFE, MALE, AGE 35, $1,000 BASIS, INTEREST AT 5%, BASED ON 1980 NAIC MODEL LAW) |
|---|---|

| End of Policy Year | 1941 CSO | 1958 CSO | 1980 CSO |
|---|---|---|---|
| 1 | $   0 | $   0 | $   0 |
| 2 | 0 | 0 | 0 |
| 3 | 6.51 | 7.22 | 5.78 |
| 4 | 18.90 | 18.73 | 16.20 |
| 5 | 31.64 | 30.62 | 26.97 |
| 10 | 100.64 | 95.60 | 86.02 |
| 15 | 178.05 | 169.71 | 154.21 |
| 20 | 262.63 | 251.62 | 231.63 |
| 25 | 352.29 | 339.45 | 316.33 |
| 30 | 444.11 | 429.98 | 407.03 |

stipulating special requirements for universal life (UL) and current assumption whole life (CAWL) insurance plans. These special requirements usually are patterned after the NAIC **Universal Life Model Regulation**, so discussion will center on this model.

In viewing reserve and surrender value requirements for UL policies, it should be recognized that the UL account value mechanism is the cost structure of the policy. The guarantees of interest, mortality, and expense charges take the place of the premium rate in more traditional forms of insurance.

There has been much debate as to how the standard laws should be applied to universal life. The flexible-premium aspect means that future premiums and policy benefits are not determinable at issue or at valuation, so the traditional methodology of "present value of future benefits minus present value of future adjusted premiums" does not appear applicable. The regulation solved this quandary in different ways for valuation and nonforfeiture.

For valuation, the regulation defines a future premium to use for calculating reserves, based on the level premiums needed at issue to endow the contract at its maturity date. The reserve calculations require that a projection of future benefits be made, using the fund value at the valuation date and assumed future premiums. This policy-by-policy projection requires extensive computer use. Some products' parameters permit simplified calculations. In many cases, it can be demonstrated that the cash surrender value is as large as the reserve, so separate reserve calculations need not be performed.

For UL nonforfeiture, the regulation breaks with the methodology required in the Standard Nonforfeiture Law and bases minimum values on a retrospective accumulation. Minimum required cash surrender values equal the accumulation, at interest, of premiums less acquisition and administrative expense charges, mortality and other benefit charges, service charges, and deductions for partial withdrawals. Acquisition expense charges are limited to the allowance provided in the Standard Nonforfeiture Law for a fixed-premium, fixed-benefit plan that would endow for the specified amount at the policy maturity date. Surrender charges are permitted and may not exceed any unused, unamortized acquisition expense allowance plus any excess interest credited in the previous 12 months. There are no limits on administrative, benefit or service charges. There is no minimum interest rate.

The section specifying surrender values for current assumption whole life plans differs from that for UL policies and basically is a restatement of the nonforfeiture law, with an explanation of future guaranteed benefits as indicated by the following quote from the regulation:

> Future guaranteed benefits are determined by (1) projecting the policy value, taking into account future premiums, if any, and using all guarantees of interest, mortality, expense deductions, etc., contained in the policy or declared by the insurer; and (2) taking into account any benefits guaranteed in the policy or by declaration which do not depend on the policy value.

The last term, referring to benefits guaranteed that do not depend on the policy value, may seem odd. Policies may have guarantees in addition to those of the account value. Many policies utilize such guarantees. They usually are found in policies in which the account value will not support whole life benefits on a guaranteed basis. The policy form will contain an additional guarantee that the policy will prove to be whole life, regardless of the performance of the account value. Obviously, if the guaranteed plan of insurance is whole life, then the minimum cash surrender values must be those of whole life. With these secondary guarantee forms, the minimum surrender value can be greater than the full account value.

The regulation has been adopted by a handful of states only. A few states have adopted variations of the model regulation. The state of New York passed legislation with nonforfeiture provisions that are substantially different from those of the model regulation. Most states have not adopted the regulation for two reasons. First, these states accept policies that meet the regulation requirements, even though they have not adopted the regulation; thus there is little incentive to promulgate the regulation in these states. Second, several state insurance departments are dissatisfied with the model regulation's valuation and nonforfeiture provisions.

The method for calculating minimum reserves is the same for both CAWL and UL plans, and is prospective in nature. The calculation procedure is complex, and there is concern that the regulation method is too complicated, difficult, and costly to apply and verify. There also is concern that, more so than for traditional whole life products, the reserves ought to be affected by cash surrender values after the valuation date—for example, any short-term cash-value guarantees that are more liberal than those within the valuation law should be recognized in the reserve liability. This is an attempt to apply annuity-type valuation procedures to a life product, and it may be prompted by the perception of universal life as a combination of term life insurance plus a side fund rather than an integrated life product. Several proposals have been made to revise the valuation provisions of the regulation, but none has received much support.

Regulators have been more concerned with nonforfeiture values. The lack of limits on charges and interest credits is perceived by many to produce no meaningful minimum cash surrender values. This possibility is acknowledged in the regulation: "If benefit charges are substantially level by duration and develop low or no cash values, then the Commissioner shall have the right to require higher cash values." Some regulators prefer to have explicit maximum benefit charges and minimum interest rates, or a minimum interest rate of 3 percent, or both. Proposals to place these limits in the regulation have met significant resistance from life insurance companies which perceive them as a form of rate regulation.

## THE 1990 STANDARD VALUATION LAW AMENDMENTS

In 1990 the NAIC adopted an amended version of its 1980 Standard Valuation Model Law. Implementing model regulations were adopted in 1991. This new model, effectively a restatement of the 1980 model law, differs in one important respect. It requires the filing of an **actuarial opinion** about selected aspects of the insurer's operations. Every insurer must establish the position of **appointed actuary**. The appointed actuary is responsible for annually rendering opinions as to "whether the reserves and related actuarial items . . . are computed appropriately, are based on assumptions which satisfy contractual provisions, are consistent with prior reported amounts and comply with applicable laws of the state."

Larger insurers and insurers that do not meet certain financial tests must also file their appointed actuary's opinion as to whether reserves and related actuarial items, in light of the insurer's assets, make adequate provision for the anticipated cash flows required by the insurer's contractual obligations and related expenses. Extensive cash flow testing is required to render this opinion.

The model law establishes minimum standards for the appointed actuary and seeks to provide him or her with greater independence. The actuary may, however, be a company employee.

While specifying detailed minimum reserve standards, the law further requires insurers to maintain sufficient aggregate reserves for the appointed actuary to be able to render the required opinion. This requirement means that insurers should maintain greater reserves than those resulting from the minimum reserve standards if, in the actuary's opinion, they are necessary.

This model law provides regulators with another tool for evaluating insurer solidity. As noted in Chapter 34, the United Kingdom, Canada, and other countries have a history of relying upon the accounting and actuarial profession for insurer financial monitoring.

# Chapter 21

# GROSS PREMIUM RATE STRUCTURES AND NONGUARANTEED POLICY ELEMENTS

The concept of the net premium was analyzed in the preceding chapters. An insurer must, however, collect premiums that, supplemented by interest, will enable it to meet all costs under the contract, including the policy's share of the insurer's operating expenses and perhaps a permanent contribution to surplus. The charges intended to meet these multiple objectives are referred to as the gross premium rate structure. The premiums actually paid by policyowners are determined from this rate structure.

One should not examine gross premium rate structures without also recognizing that most cash-value policies sold today in the United States provide for some mechanism of lowering the effective cost of policies below that inherent in the guaranteed assumptions. Historically, the payment of dividends under participating policies has served this function. Today there are other techniques, such as excess interest credits and indeterminate premium rate structures.

## GENERAL CONSIDERATIONS IN DERIVING GROSS PREMIUMS

A gross premium may be regarded as either (1) the valuation net premium increased by an amount called loading or (2) a sum derived independently of the valuation net premium and based on all factors that enter into a gross premium computation (i.e., mortality, interest, expenses, lapse rates, contingency allowance, and an allowance for a contribution to surplus or profit). The gross premiums of mutual insurers historically were derived by using the first method, whereas the premiums of stock insurers typically were derived by the second method. In recent years there has been a trend toward use of the second approach by both stocks and mutuals, and the second approach typically is followed in establishing the structure of charges and credits under universal life (UL) policies.[1] This trend toward selecting a gross premium level first and then working back to design a policy that can be supported by that premium level reflects the increasing importance of competitive forces in deriving gross premiums.

The combination of mortality, expense, and surrender charges and interest credits is a UL policy's rate structure. The only difference conceptually between UL and traditional forms is that the structure is unbundled under UL and other similar policies, and it is bundled under the more traditional forms. For purposes of discussion, it should be understood that for UL and other similar, unbundled policies, the account value mechanism serves the same function as and, in effect, is the same as the gross premium rate structure under more traditional forms of life insurance.

## BASIC CRITERIA AND PARAMETERS

In developing a gross premium rate structure for a block of policies, considerations such as adequacy, equity, legal limitations, competition, and specific insurer objectives all enter into the process. Adequacy clearly is the most important requirement of a gross premium rate structure, because insurer solvency can be jeopardized by inadequate charges. Equity in a premium structure primarily is for the benefit of the policyowners, although there is a practical limit to the degree of equity that can be attained. Charges must not be in conflict with any law. Deficiency reserve statutes or their equivalent may indirectly influence premium charges for practical reasons.[2] Competition will, obviously, affect an insurer's premium rates. In setting growth and profit goals, other objectives, such as markets selected, products emphasized, or compensation philosophy, can all affect the gross premium rate structure that is finally adopted.[3]

## NATURE OF INSURANCE COMPANY EXPENSES

In discussing insurer expenses, the first step is to divide them into investment expenses and insurance expenses. **Investment expenses** include the costs of making, handling, and protecting investments. Since they are related directly to the production of investment income, they are deducted from the gross investment income. They are, therefore, taken into account in determining the net

---

[1] Risk theory can be the basis for premium development. See R. E. Beard, T. Pentikäinen, and E. Pesonen, *Risk Theory*, 3rd ed. (New York: Chapman and Hall, 1984), and Hans U. Gerber, *An Introduction to Mathematical Risk Theory* (Homewood, Ill.: Richard D. Irwin, Inc., 1979).

[2] See Chaps. 4 and 20.

[3] See Chap. 33 for a discussion of product development in the context of an insurer's marketing plan.

rates of interest to be used in calculating premium or excess interest credits and are not considered explicitly in connection with the loading.

**Insurance expenses** are those of a noninvestment nature and may be classified in various ways, depending on the purpose they serve. The costs of procuring, underwriting, and issuing new business—including commissions attributable to the first year's premiums—are regarded as **first-year expenses.** The various costs of maintaining and servicing outstanding policies, as well as renewal commissions, are regarded as **renewal expenses. Claims expenses** include claim litigation costs and appropriate amounts for salaries, rent, utilities, and so on, all of which are attributable to the claim department. Finally, there is what may be labeled **administrative expenses,** which include expenses such as salaries, rent, and utilities; and these are attributable to the nonclaim, nonmarketing executive and administrative functions.

For purposes of determining a proper amount of loading, these various insurance expenses may be assigned to three major groups:

1. Expenses that vary with the amount of premiums—for example, agent's commissions and premium taxes

2. Expenses that vary with the amount of insurance —for example, underwriting costs tend to vary with policy size

3. Expenses that vary with the number of policies—for example, the cost of preparing policies for issue, establishing the necessary accounting records, and sending of premium notices.

There are two major problems associated with reflecting expenses in the rate structure: (1) achieving the equitable distribution of expenses among different classes of policies and among policyowners of different ages—that is the problem of making each policy pay its own cost, and (2) recognizing when the expense is incurred. The solution to these problems is complicated by the objectives of complying with statutory requirements, maintaining a consistent policy regarding surrender values and dividends, accommodating those expenses that do not fall neatly into one of the groups, and meeting the competition. The problems may be complicated further by the desired premium-payment pattern. For example, with UL policies, the front-end or back-end loads or other hidden charges (e.g., mortality or interest margins) are not likely to track the actual incidence of expense. On the other hand, UL and other unbundled products can facilitate the matching of expense charges to expenses incurred. The UL premium rate structure, unlike that of more traditional policies, is not constrained to a fixed, level-premium pattern, and this potentially eases the incidence of expense-matching problems.

Because the objectives of adequacy and equity are sometimes in conflict with the objective of maintaining or improving the competitive position of the insurer, the final gross premium rate structure normally represents a compromise. Nevertheless, in the aggregate, adequacy must be maintained.

## NATURE OF LOADING

An equitable system of loading should result in every policyowner paying the expenses properly attributable to his or her policy. The foregoing analysis of insurance company expenses suggests that loading should consist partly of a percentage of premium charge, partly of a charge for each $1,000 of insurance, and partly of a charge for each policy. In fact, the expense charges of many UL and other unbundled products are structured in this tripartite manner. Many unbundled products, however, omit one or more of the three elements in their expense charges, with some having no identifiable expense charges. In the latter situation, of course, the insurer's expenses must be met from margins built into the mortality charges and interest credits.

The expense-loading formulas of more traditional forms of life insurance often convert the "per-policy" expense element to a "per $1,000" charge by relating it to the average-size policy issued. To meet competition and to provide greater equity between classes of policies where the average-size policy issued varies considerably, most insurers assume a separate average-size policy for each policy band (see below) or for the principal plans of insurance and age groups in their premium calculations.

The loading formula includes, in addition to an allowance for expenses, a provision for contingencies and a margin for contribution to surplus or profits. With the per-policy expenses converted to an "amount per $1,000 basis," the hypothetical loading formula may be reduced to two factors: (1) a percentage of the premium and (2) a constant per $1,000.

## DEVELOPING THE TENTATIVE GROSS PREMIUM RATE STRUCTURE

Although the gross premium rate may be viewed as a net premium augmented by an amount called loading, it is more frequently regarded as an amount derived independently of the valuation net premium and based on all the factors that enter into the gross premium. The five elements basic to the calculation are: (1) the expected amount and incidence of claims, (2) an appropriate rate of investment return, (3) withdrawal rates and amounts withdrawn, (4) amounts and incidence of expenses, and (5) a margin for contributions to surplus or profit. Under traditional policy forms, assumptions as to each of these elements can be selected, a formula embodying all of them derived, and a premium rate calculated. Under unbundled product forms, assumptions are still required but the possibility of offsetting one element (e.g., decreased expense charges) with another (e.g., increased mortality charges) complicates the analysis. In any event, with both bundled and unbundled product forms, the tentative gross premium rate structure is tested by asset-share studies to be certain it is consistent with insurer objectives. Therefore, its method of development is not critical.

The determination of unit expense rates involves both the amount of expense incurred, as shown by cost evaluations, and the time of its occurrence. Although the derivation of the individual unit expense rates is beyond the scope of this volume, a few additional comments are appropriate. Claim expenses and the costs of paying surrender values, dispensing policy loans, processing beneficiary changes, and other service activities may be accounted for separately and treated as additional benefits. If this is done, the cost of writing the policy and establishing records would be assessed on a per-policy basis; valuation fees paid the state insurance department would be on a per-$1,000 basis; and underwriting expenses would be split two ways, with one part on a per-$1,000 basis and one part on a per-policy basis. Salaries would be allocated on the basis of the nature of the work done, using time studies or other appropriate measures. Utilities usually follow the salary distributions.

Once all unit expenses are developed, they are then combined to give a pattern of (1) per-policy, (2) per-$1,000, and (3) percentage expenses separately for the first year and renewal years. The unit expense rates developed on the basis of careful cost evaluations can be tested for accuracy by applying them to appropriate insurer functions. If this application results in total expenses approximating those actually incurred, it may be presumed that they do in fact represent the insurer's operating costs. Judgment modifications can be made, depending on management's optimism or pessimism regarding the future.

Having determined the present value of all expenses and spread them over the premium-paying period, it is only necessary to include a margin for profit and contingencies and (in the case of participating insurance) dividends, to produce the tentative gross premium. Table 21-1 presents a set of hypothetical expense factors reflecting the principles discussed.

For participating insurance, it is customary to insert an additional allowance in the loading for the specific purpose of creating a surplus from which dividends can be paid. In addition, in most cases, provision is made for a minimum dividend to be augmented by favorable deviations from the

**TABLE 21-1     HYPOTHETICAL EXPENSES**

| | First Year | | | Renewal | | | | |
| | | | | | | Percentage Premium by Duration (Years) | | |
| Expense Item | Per Policy | Per $1,000 | Percent Premium | Per Policy | Per $1,000 | 2-9 | 10-15 | 16-20 |
| --- | --- | --- | --- | --- | --- | --- | --- | --- |
| Premium taxes | | | 2.0 | | | 2.0 | 2.0 | 2.0 |
| Commissions | | | 60.0 | | | 7.3 | 5.0 | 3.0 |
| Expense allowance | | | 20.0 | | | 2.7 | 1.8 | 1.1 |
| Medical and inspection | $22.15 | $0.90 | | | | | | |
| Acquisition | 20.93 | 0.21 | 14.0 | | | | | |
| Maintenance | 22.12 | 0.05 | — | $22.12 | $0.05 | — | — | — |
| | $65.20 | $1.16 | 96.0 | $22.12 | $0.05 | 12.0 | 8.8 | 6.1 |

Claim expense:     $32.25 per policy plus $0.20 per $1,000

conservative assumptions underlying the premium rate. Such decisions involve broad managerial policy and vary from company to company. A moderate provision might be 5 percent of the gross premium or, alternatively, the equivalent amount expressed per premium dollar and per $1,000. The loading formula for participating business usually is expressed in terms of the tabular (the reserve basis) net premium.

## TESTING THE TENTATIVE GROSS PREMIUM RATE STRUCTURE

A gross premium rate structure derived by applying a loading formula to a set of net premiums commonly is only tentative and is tested at various issue ages. The purpose is to determine whether, under realistic assumptions as to mortality, investment earnings, expenses, and terminations, the rate structure would develop sufficiently high asset accumulations to provide the surrender values and death and other benefits promised under the contract, to meet the legal requirements and to assure that the resulting net costs are competitive, reasonable, and consistent.

### ASSET-SHARE CALCULATIONS

It will be recalled from Chapter 2 that these tests are based on the asset-share model. The purpose is to determine, for any block of policies (with the same plan and ratebook), the expected fund per $1,000 of insurance held by the insurer at the end of each policy year after payment of all policy benefits and expenses, taking into consideration all premiums paid and expected (realistic) investment earnings. Each year's accumulated fund, divided by the number of surviving and persisting insureds, produces the asset share. Asset-share studies are simulations of expected experience for blocks of policies using the best estimates of anticipated operating experience.[4] The purpose of such an asset-share calculation is to determine if the individual elements of the policy are well balanced and will produce acceptable results for both the insurance company and policyowners. The gross premium rate structure is only one of the many factors being evaluated.

By comparing the asset share at each duration with the comparable cash surrender value and reserve, the insurer can evaluate the adequacy and equity of the tentative gross premium rate structure. From an accounting standpoint, the amount taken from surplus to cover excess first-year expenses for a given block of policies is not fully recovered until the asset share equals the reserve. Up to that point, funds must be "borrowed" from surplus. The extent of the strain on

---

[4]Asset-share studies also are made using historical data. This asset-share research is an integral part of monitoring developing experience and, for insurers writing participating insurance, evaluating the adequacy and appropriateness of dividend scales.

surplus may be mitigated through a modified reserve system.[5] Determination of the duration at which the full policy reserve is to be accumulated (when the asset share equals the reserve) is a management decision influenced by the competitive situation. The length of time over which this takes place (while the insurer has a "book" loss on the block of policies) is known as the **validation period**. The shorter the period, the larger must be the gross premium or the lower must be policy benefits or margins for contingencies or profit.

It is not unusual for a well-established insurer to take 8 to 12 years to amortize the acquisition expenses of a particular class of policies. Insurers with a large volume of new business relative to their total volume in force or insurers that expect termination rates to be high may amortize their acquisition expense within a period of five years or less.

Most insurers expect policies to make some permanent contribution to surplus, the extent being a management decision limited by considerations of safety, equity, and competition.[6] The actual contribution as opposed to the book contribution of a block of policies (negative or positive) depends on the relationship between the asset share and the surrender value of the policy. When a policy is terminated by surrender, the reserves are released, because, of course, the company is not required to maintain a reserve liability on its balance sheet for policies that are no longer in force. If the asset share exceeds the surrender payment, the company has a real gain. This typically occurs after the first few (e.g., 3 to 10) policy years. The asset share commonly is less than the surrender value in the early policy years, so the insurer has a real loss from surrenders during this period.[7] Determining the point at which the asset share for a block of policies should equal or exceed the surrender value is an important management decision. Once a surrender has occurred, the impact of that policy on the insurer's gain or loss is fixed.

If the asset shares produced by the tentative gross premium rate structure are deficient in the light of insurer objectives, the premiums may be increased or some specific item of expense or outgo (e.g., dividends, cash values, expenses) decreased. If the fund accumulation appears excessive, premiums can be reduced or benefits increased.

## SELECTION OF MOST PROBABLE ASSUMPTIONS

If the asset-share calculations are to be a reasonable test of premium adequacy and equity between blocks of policies, the factors entering into the calculation must be chosen with great care. The assumptions underlying any mathematical model are critical to its effectiveness as a predictive device.

[5]See "Modified Reserve Systems" in Chap. 20.

[6]The state of New York regulates the contribution that participating policies can make to surplus in the aggregate.

[7]This statement is not true for so-called lapse-supported policies (see later in this chapter).

*Mortality.* Selection of the most probable assumption as to future mortality is complicated by the secular trend toward mortality improvement. It might be argued that the asset-share study should reflect anticipated improvement in future mortality. The majority of insurers do not reflect this anticipated improvement in their computations, but they do test under varying mortality scenarios. Regardless of this feature, all insurers utilize the latest available experience.

The best source of information on current trends, incidence, and levels of mortality among ordinary insureds has been the *Reports* of the Committee on Mortality under Ordinary Insurance and Annuities, published annually by the Society of Actuaries. These data are compiled by the committee from statistics supplied by a number of the largest life insurance companies. The experience is published on a select and ultimate basis. The death rates generally are shown for all ages on juvenile lives, but only at quinquennial age groups with respect to adult lives. Periodically, the committee publishes a graduated mortality table based on these data. Most larger insurers use mortality from their own experience, and many insurers rely on their reinsurers for guidance on mortality rates.

*Interest.* Determining the rate of interest to be used in asset-share calculations involves estimates of investment returns over the next 20 or more years. These estimates must be made with knowledge that the long-range impact of interest on life insurance is great. From the standpoint of the shareholder in a stock company, the leverage based on the margin between actual and assumed interest rates is enormous.

The rate selected normally will fall within a range of possible rates, the upper limit of which (during a period when interest rates are increasing) is the rate being earned on new investments, and the lower limit the valuation rate of interest for policies currently being issued. For both mutual and stock insurers, allowance is made in selecting these rates for the impact of U.S. federal income taxes.[8] Furthermore, recognition can be given to the possibility of changes in earned interest rates in future years. For example, a higher interest rate might be assumed for policy years 1 to 10, with a lower rate assumed thereafter.

*Operating Expenses.* Mutual and stock insurers compute their expense rates in a similar manner. The average size of new policies is computed by plan and age at issue, and it is applied to the constant expense per policy to permit the expression of expense rates in terms of a percentage of the premium plus a number of dollars per $1,000 of insurance. Since the expense factors are based on the average collection frequency of the insurer's business, the expenses within the asset-share study must be adjusted to reflect the estimated proportions of the

---

[8]A potentially significant problem arises for life insurers when products are priced assuming a particular tax burden and the federal government (with respect to income tax) or the state (with respect to premium taxation) increases insurers' taxes. Depending on the types of products, insurers may not be able easily to adjust experience participation to accommodate the increase.

types of premium payment frequency. If the tentative gross premium rate schedule was based on a detailed analysis of current expenses, these same expense rates could be used as a basis for estimating future expenses. Otherwise, a detailed cost study must precede the asset-share calculation.

*Termination Rates*. Predicting future lapse (termination) rates usually is a difficult task. The difficulty is caused by the extreme fluctuations over the years, largely as a result of economic conditions. Although for many insurers lapse rates may not be as important to the adequacy test as are the other three factors, for other insurers the financial implications can be significant.

As in the case of the other factors, it is customary to use termination rates based on the insurer's individual experience, although published studies provide a guide.[9] Termination rates are influenced by many factors, including the quality of the agency force, age of issue, amount of premium, frequency and method of premium payment, as well as income levels and other economic conditions of the likely customers for the policy. In practice, termination rates usually are differentiated by plan of insurance, age of issue, and frequency and method of premium payment. Under most plans, they are highest during the first two years and lower thereafter. Lapse rates for UL policies have tended to be somewhat more uniform from year to year.

Ordinarily, the higher the lapse rates, the lower the insurer's profit (or surplus contribution) and, therefore, the lower the dividends or other nonguaranteed policy benefits. This is the result whenever the asset share is less than the cash surrender value. Recently, however, some insurers have designed and sold policies wherein the higher the lapse rates, the *higher* the profit. Some survivorship life policies and policies with interest rate bonuses are designed in this fashion. The insurer designs products such that the surrender values are less than the corresponding asset share. The hope is that lapse rates will be sufficiently high so that gains from surrenders can be used to augment later-year policy values. The problem with these **lapse-supported policies** is that lower-than-expected lapse rates can result in lower future asset shares and, therefore, potentially lower product value.

Termination rates are necessary in premium calculations because of the disparity between cash surrender values and asset shares. If surrender values exactly equaled each year's asset share, lapse rates could be ignored for purposes of calculating asset shares but would remain important to overall insurer profitability and asset growth.

---

[9]See M. A. Linton, *The Record of the American Institute of Actuaries*, Vol. 13 (1924), pp. 283-316; see also C. F. B. Richardson and John M. Hartwell, *Transactions of the Society of Actuaries*, Vol. 3 (1951), pp. 338-372; and Ernest J. Morehead, "The Construction of Persistency Tables," *Transactions of the Society of Actuaries*, Vol 12 (1960), pp. 545-563.

## SPECIAL UNIVERSAL LIFE PRICING CONSIDERATIONS[10]

The pricing of universal life (UL) is complex. The flexible nature of UL brings with it the need for additional assumptions. The premium payment pattern can vary. The benefit pattern, also, can vary according to changing specified amounts and type of coverage. Withdrawals or policy loan activity may result from client investment antiselection. Changing margins of interest earned over interest credited imply that adjustments will have to be made periodically. Inflation and other economic factors are likely to remain in a state of flux. Prudence requires that various scenarios be tested for each of these assumptions.

Of course, from this vast set of possible alternatives, only the most realistic scenarios can reasonably be examined. In doing so, it is important to determine the sensitivity of asset share and other profit studies to deviations from the assumptions and equally important to monitor actual experience and to compare it with expected results.

The original UL concept was that product loads would match product expenses and that the result would be a significantly lower expense persistency risk to the insurance company. This was true for the first few products introduced, but most products since then have had first-year expense assumptions that were larger than expense loads, with excess expenses covered eventually by mortality margins, interest margins, and surrender charges.

*Source of Profit Analysis*. Although not all costs will be covered by corresponding direct charges, it is important to balance the sources of margin so that most scenarios of premiums and persistency will result in acceptable profit results. Otherwise, policyowner antiselection might cause profits to be less than anticipated. This requires that the pricing actuary be aware of and measure each of these sources of profits:

1. Interest earned less interest credited

2. Cost of insurance charges less death benefits paid

3. Expense charges less expenses and commissions

4. Surrender charges

The source of profit analysis is easier to interpret when calculated using the policy's gross cash (fund) value as the reserve basis. If actual reserves are different than the cash value, net profits should include a reserve adjustment factor.

*Asset/Liability Analysis.* Universal life carries a risk of interest rate antiselection. If external interest rates are higher than the rate credited to the cash value, the policyowner may withdraw the cash value (via lapse or partial

---

[10]This section draws on Douglas C. Doll, "Universal Life: A Product Overview," *SOA Study Note 340-41-91* (Itasca, Ill.: Society of Actuaries, 1991), pp. 16-17.

withdrawal) and invest it elsewhere. If the assets held by the insurer have a reduced market value (which is likely if interest rates have risen), the insurer suffers a capital loss if these assets have to be sold. This risk is not unique to UL. It is argued, however, that, because of the attention paid to the credited interest rate, UL policies are more subject to this risk than are other life insurance policies. Prudence dictates that the actuary perform an analysis of the UL product combined with the possible investment and interest crediting strategies under different interest scenarios, to determine the appropriate strategies and the appropriate charge to make for the interest rate risk.

## SAMPLE ASSET-SHARE CALCULATION

The process by which a gross premium rate schedule is tested was illustrated with an example in Chapter 2, shown in Table 2-6. This table is reproduced below as Table 21-2. It may be recalled that the gross premium for the ordinary life policy being tested was $15 per $1,000 and that cash values (column 7) were calculated on the basis of the *1980 CSO* mortality and 5 1/2 percent interest, and that net level terminal reserves (column 18) were used (at 5 percent and *1980 CSO*).

Other needed assumptions included expected death (column 3) and withdrawal rates (column 4), expected expenses (column 6), and illustrated dividends (column 8). A net investment earnings rate of 8 percent was assumed to be reasonable over the next 20 years. Column 17 gives the yearly asset shares for the hypothetical policy being tested, with column 19 providing the anticipated net surplus position of the insurer for this policy.[11]

The assumptions used in an asset-share calculation are supposed to represent the best estimates of what the actual experience will be. Invariably, however, actual results deviate from those assumed. Insurers expect this. As a result, they conduct several asset-share calculations with various underlying assumptions. This enables the actuary to judge the sensitivity of the results under varying possible future conditions.

Tables 21-3 through 21-9 indicate the sensitivity to change of the hypothetical asset-share calculation illustrated in Table 21-2 by showing the impact on the calculation of the following changes in assumptions and benefits:

1. Interest rate decreased from 8 percent to 7 percent

2. Mortality Increased by 20 percent

3. Expenses increased by 5 percent

4. Gross premium increased from $15.00 to $15.50

---

[11]No further discussion of the example based on the stated assumptions is presented here (see Chap. 2 for such a discussion).

**TABLE 21-2     ASSET-SHARE CALCULATION, $1,000 ORDINARY LIFE ISSUED AT MALE, AGE 35 ($15 RATE PER $1,000)**

| (1) Policy Year | (2) Number Paying Premiums at Beginning of Year | (3) Number Dying[a] | (4) Number Withdrawing[b] | (5) Number Alive at End of Year after Withdrawals [(2)-(3)-(4)] | (6) Expense Rate per $1,000 | (7) Cash Value per $1,000 on Withdrawal[c] | (8) Dividend per $1,000 |
|---|---|---|---|---|---|---|---|
| 1 | 100,000 | 88 | 10,000 | 89,912 | $22.00 | $ 0.00 | $ 0.00 |
| 2 | 89,912 | 92 | 5,394 | 84,426 | 2.25 | 0.00 | 0.50 |
| 3 | 84,426 | 101 | 4,221 | 80,104 | 2.25 | 4.31 | 1.00 |
| 4 | 80,104 | 111 | 3,524 | 76,469 | 2.25 | 13.91 | 1.50 |
| 5 | 76,469 | 118 | 3,058 | 73,293 | 2.25 | 23.86 | 2.00 |
| 6 | 73,293 | 132 | 2,638 | 70,523 | 2.25 | 34.16 | 2.50 |
| 7 | 70,523 | 142 | 2,256 | 68,125 | 2.25 | 44.81 | 3.10 |
| 8 | 68,125 | 152 | 1,975 | 65,998 | 2.25 | 55.82 | 3.70 |
| 9 | 65,998 | 164 | 1,781 | 64,053 | 2.25 | 67.19 | 4.30 |
| 10 | 64,053 | 175 | 1,601 | 62,277 | 2.25 | 78.94 | 5.90 |
| 11 | 62,277 | 198 | 1,494 | 60,585 | 2.25 | 91.05 | 6.60 |
| 12 | 60,585 | 212 | 1,393 | 58,980 | 2.25 | 103.56 | 7.30 |
| 13 | 58,980 | 226 | 1,297 | 57,457 | 2.25 | 116.46 | 7.90 |
| 14 | 57,457 | 240 | 1,206 | 56,011 | 2.25 | 129.78 | 8.50 |
| 15 | 56,011 | 256 | 1,120 | 54,635 | 2.25 | 143.51 | 9.20 |
| 16 | 54,635 | 273 | 1,092 | 53,270 | 2.25 | 157.66 | 9.90 |
| 17 | 53,270 | 293 | 1,065 | 51,912 | 2.25 | 172.19 | 10.60 |
| 18 | 51,912 | 315 | 1,038 | 50,559 | 2.25 | 187.10 | 11.40 |
| 19 | 50,559 | 340 | 1,011 | 49,208 | 2.25 | 202.35 | 12.20 |
| 20 | 49,208 | 368 | 984 | 47,856 | 2.25 | 217.92 | 13.00 |

| (1) Policy Year | (9) Fund at Beginning of Year [(16) Prior Year] | (10) Premium Income [($15.00)x(2)] | (11) Expense Disbursements [(2)x(6)] | (12) Death Claims Paid [$1,000x(3)] | (13) Amounts Paid on Surrender [(4)x(7)] | (14) Total Dividends Paid [(5)x(8)] |
|---|---|---|---|---|---|---|
| 1 | $ 0 | $1,500,000 | $2,200,000 | $ 88,000 | $ 0 | $ 0 |
| 2 | −847,520 | 1,348,680 | 202,302 | 92,000 | 0 | 42,213 |
| 3 | 184,874 | 1,266,390 | 189,959 | 101,000 | 18,185 | 80,104 |
| 4 | 1,158,880 | 1,201,560 | 180,234 | 111,000 | 49,019 | 114,704 |
| 5 | 2,075,460 | 1,147,035 | 172,055 | 118,000 | 73,965 | 146,586 |
| 6 | 2,952,205 | 1,099,395 | 164,909 | 132,000 | 90,126 | 176,308 |
| 7 | 3,793,912 | 1,057,845 | 158,677 | 142,000 | 101,091 | 211,188 |
| 8 | 4,608,568 | 1,021,875 | 153,281 | 152,000 | 110,248 | 244,193 |
| 9 | 5,402,814 | 989,970 | 148,496 | 164,000 | 119,667 | 275,428 |
| 10 | 6,178,176 | 960,795 | 144,119 | 175,000 | 126,377 | 367,434 |
| 11 | 6,878,629 | 934,155 | 140,123 | 198,000 | 136,030 | 399,861 |
| 12 | 7,544,662 | 908,775 | 136,316 | 212,000 | 144,255 | 430,544 |
| 13 | 8,187,202 | 884,700 | 132,705 | 226,000 | 151,050 | 453,910 |
| 14 | 8,814,332 | 861,855 | 129,278 | 240,000 | 156,514 | 476,094 |
| 15 | 9,428,453 | 840,165 | 126,025 | 256,000 | 160,729 | 502,642 |
| 16 | 10,024,390 | 819,525 | 122,929 | 273,000 | 172,162 | 527,373 |
| 17 | 10,595,210 | 799,050 | 119,858 | 293,000 | 183,387 | 550,267 |
| 18 | 11,137,980 | 778,680 | 116,802 | 315,000 | 194,213 | 576,273 |
| 19 | 11,645,660 | 758,385 | 113,758 | 340,000 | 204,581 | 600,338 |
| 20 | 12,114,990 | 738,120 | 110,718 | 368,000 | 214,430 | 622,128 |

**TABLE 21-2**      *(CONTINUED)*

| Policy Year | (15) Interest Earned during Year $\{0.08[(9)+(10) -(11)-1/2(12)]\}$ | (16) Fund at End of Year $[(9)+(10)-(11)-(12) -(13)-(14)+(15)]$ | (17) Asset Share at End of Year: $[(16) \div (5)]$ | (18) Reserve[d] at End of Year | (19) Surplus per $1,000 at End of Year $[(17)-(18)]$ |
|---|---|---|---|---|---|
| 1  | $-59,520  | $-847,520  | $-9.43 | $  9.15 | $-18.58 |
| 2  | 20,229    | 184,874    | 2.19   | 18.65   | -16.46  |
| 3  | 96,864    | 1,158,880  | 14.47  | 28.49   | -14.03  |
| 4  | 169,976   | 2,075,460  | 27.14  | 38.68   | -11.54  |
| 5  | 239,315   | 2,952,205  | 40.28  | 49.20   | -8.92   |
| 6  | 305,655   | 3,793,912  | 53.80  | 60.07   | -6.27   |
| 7  | 369,766   | 4,608,568  | 67.65  | 71.25   | -3.61   |
| 8  | 432,093   | 5,402,814  | 81.86  | 82.79   | -0.93   |
| 9  | 492,983   | 6,178,176  | 96.45  | 94.67   | 1.78    |
| 10 | 552,588   | 6,878,629  | 110.45 | 106.90  | 3.55    |
| 11 | 605,893   | 7,544,662  | 124.53 | 119.48  | 5.05    |
| 12 | 656,890   | 8,187,202  | 138.81 | 132.43  | 6.38    |
| 13 | 706,096   | 8,814,332  | 153.41 | 145.75  | 7.66    |
| 14 | 754,153   | 9,428,453  | 168.33 | 159.45  | 8.88    |
| 15 | 801,167   | 10,024,390 | 183.48 | 173.54  | 9.94    |
| 16 | 846,759   | 10,595,210 | 198.90 | 188.01  | 10.89   |
| 17 | 890,232   | 11,137,980 | 214.56 | 202.83  | 11.73   |
| 18 | 931,389   | 11,645,660 | 230.34 | 217.99  | 12.35   |
| 19 | 969,623   | 12,114,990 | 246.20 | 233.45  | 12.75   |
| 20 | 1,004,672 | 12,542,510 | 262.09 | 249.19  | 12.90   |

[a]Deaths are based on select and ultimate experience mortality table. Deaths are assumed to occur in middle of policy year on the average.

[b]Withdrawals are based on Linton A lapse rates and assumed to occur on anniversary at end of policy year.

[c]Cash values using *1980 CSO Table* at 5-1/2% interest.

[d]Net-level-premium reserves using *1980 CSO Table* at 5% interest.

5. Dividends reduced by 10 percent each year

6. Cash values increased

7. Lapse rates doubled

In examining these tables, it is instructive to note the impact on the validation period in each case (see column 19). Similarly, note the point at which the block of policies would begin realizing a gain from surrenders (i.e., the time at which the asset share exceeds the surrender value).

Practically, of course, more than one factor may be adjusted simultaneously to examine the effects of the combined changes. When a combination of adjustments is made, the strength and direction of change in asset-share values cannot always be determined intuitively. As mentioned above, computers permit a wide range of experimentation in finding a combination of factors that are compatible with the insurer's objectives.

598     Chapter 21

| (1) | (17) | (18) | (19) | (20) |
|---|---|---|---|---|
| | | | | Surrender |
| | | | Surplus | Gain |
| | Asset | | per $1,000 | per $1,000 |
| | Share | Reserve | at End | at End |
| Policy | at End | at End | of Year | of Year |
| Year | of Year | of Year | [(17)-(18)] | [(17)-(7)] |
| 1 | $ −9.34 | $ 9.15 | $ −18.49 | $ −9.34 |
| 2 | 2.25 | 18.65 | −16.40 | 2.25 |
| 3 | 14.39 | 28.49 | −14.11 | 10.08 |
| 4 | 26.78 | 38.68 | −11.90 | 12.87 |
| 5 | 39.46 | 49.20 | −9.74 | 15.60 |
| 6 | 52.35 | 60.07 | −7.72 | 18.18 |
| 7 | 65.36 | 71.25 | −5.89 | 20.55 |
| 8 | 78.52 | 82.79 | −4.27 | 22.70 |
| 9 | 91.81 | 94.67 | −2.86 | 24.62 |
| 10 | 104.23 | 106.90 | −2.67 | 25.29 |
| 11 | 116.44 | 119.48 | −3.05 | 25.39 |
| 12 | 128.52 | 132.43 | −3.91 | 24.97 |
| 13 | 140.57 | 145.75 | −5.18 | 24.11 |
| 14 | 152.56 | 159.45 | −6.89 | 22.78 |
| 15 | 164.34 | 173.54 | −9.19 | 20.84 |
| 16 | 175.91 | 188.01 | −12.10 | 18.25 |
| 17 | 187.17 | 202.83 | −15.65 | 14.98 |
| 18 | 197.95 | 217.99 | −20.03 | 10.85 |
| 19 | 208.13 | 233.45 | −25.32 | 5.78 |
| 20 | 217.58 | 249.19 | −31.60 | −0.33 |

TABLE 21-3     ASSET-SHARE CALCULATION WITH 7% INSTEAD OF 8% INTEREST RATE

## OTHER ASPECTS

### FRACTIONAL PREMIUMS

The calculations earlier in this text illustrate the determination of an annual premium. It would be possible to follow the same principles for any unit of time, but the existing mortality tables are not graded for periods of less than a year. When the policyowner pays premiums other than annually, a carrying charge is added to the fractional premiums, based on the company's experience.

The purpose of the carrying charge is to reimburse the insurance company for the additional expense associated with more frequent premium collection, to offset the loss of interest stemming from the deferment of part of the year's premium, and to compensate for the higher lapse rates that may arise when premiums are paid other than annually. In addition, the carrying charge is sometimes viewed as including an element of life insurance, because companies disregard any remaining fractional premiums in the year of death.

TABLE 21-4        ASSET-SHARE CALCULATION WITH A
                  20% INCREASE IN MORTALITY

| (1) | (17) | (18) | (19) | (20) |
|---|---|---|---|---|
| | | | | Surrender |
| | | | Surplus | Gain |
| | Asset | | per $1,000 | per $1,000 |
| | Share | Reserve | at End | at End |
| Policy | at End | at End | of Year | of Year |
| Year | of Year | of Year | [(17)-(18)] | [(17)-(7)] |
| 1 | $-9.64 | $ 9.15 | $ -18.79 | $ -9.64 |
| 2 | 1.73 | 18.65 | -16.92 | 1.73 |
| 3 | 13.68 | 28.49 | -14.81 | 9.37 |
| 4 | 25.95 | 38.68 | -12.73 | 12.04 |
| 5 | 38.62 | 49.20 | -10.58 | 14.76 |
| 6 | 51.55 | 60.07 | -8.51 | 17.39 |
| 7 | 64.74 | 71.25 | -6.52 | 19.93 |
| 8 | 78.18 | 82.79 | -4.62 | 22.36 |
| 9 | 91.87 | 94.67 | -2.80 | 24.68 |
| 10 | 104.83 | 106.90 | -2.07 | 25.90 |
| 11 | 117.69 | 119.48 | -1.80 | 26.64 |
| 12 | 130.58 | 132.43 | -1.85 | 27.02 |
| 13 | 143.58 | 145.75 | -2.17 | 27.12 |
| 14 | 156.68 | 159.45 | -2.77 | 26.90 |
| 15 | 169.78 | 173.54 | -3.76 | 26.27 |
| 16 | 182.85 | 188.01 | -5.15 | 25.19 |
| 17 | 195.83 | 202.83 | -7.00 | 23.63 |
| 18 | 208.54 | 217.99 | -9.45 | 21.43 |
| 19 | 220.88 | 233.45 | -12.57 | 18.53 |
| 20 | 232.76 | 249.19 | -16.43 | 14.84 |

A fractional premium often is calculated by multiplying the annual premium by a specified factor and, sometimes, adding to the result a flat dollar amount. Common factors for semiannual premiums are 0.51, 0.515, and 0.52; for quarterly premiums they are 0.26, 0.2625, and 0.265; and for monthly premiums, 0.0875, 0.0883, and 0.09.

## RETURN OF PREMIUM POLICIES

Policies sometimes include a provision whereby, on the death of the insured, an additional death benefit equal to the sum of the premiums paid will be paid to the beneficiary if death occurs within a stipulated time period. In actuality, of course, the insurer does not return the paid premiums. It simply calculates its premiums on the basis that the amount of life insurance protection each year equals the policy face amount plus an additional death benefit equal to the then sum of the premiums paid to date.

| TABLE 21-5 | | ASSET-SHARE CALCULATION WITH 5% EXPENSE INCREASE | | |
|---|---|---|---|---|
| (1) | (17) | (18) | (19) | (20) |
| | | | | Surrender |
| | | | Surplus | Gain |
| | Asset | | per $1,000 | per $1,000 |
| | Share | Reserve | at End | at End |
| Policy | at End | at End | of Year | of Year |
| Year | of Year | of Year | [(17)-(18)] | [(17)-(7)] |
| 1 | $-10.75 | $ 9.15 | $ -19.90 | $ -10.75 |
| 2 | 0.54 | 18.65 | -18.11 | 0.54 |
| 3 | 12.46 | 28.49 | -16.03 | 8.15 |
| 4 | 24.75 | 38.68 | -13.93 | 10.84 |
| 5 | 37.45 | 49.20 | -11.75 | 13.59 |
| 6 | 50.50 | 60.07 | -9.57 | 16.33 |
| 7 | 63.83 | 71.25 | -7.42 | 19.03 |
| 8 | 77.49 | 82.79 | -5.31 | 21.66 |
| 9 | 91.46 | 94.67 | -3.21 | 24.27 |
| 10 | 104.78 | 106.90 | -2.13 | 25.84 |
| 11 | 118.11 | 119.48 | -1.38 | 27.06 |
| 12 | 131.56 | 132.43 | -0.87 | 28.00 |
| 13 | 145.24 | 145.75 | -0.51 | 28.78 |
| 14 | 159.16 | 159.45 | -0.29 | 29.38 |
| 15 | 173.20 | 173.54 | -0.33 | 29.69 |
| 16 | 187.39 | 188.01 | -0.62 | 29.73 |
| 17 | 201.68 | 202.83 | -1.15 | 29.48 |
| 18 | 215.93 | 217.99 | -2.05 | 28.83 |
| 19 | 230.09 | 233.45 | -3.36 | 27.73 |
| 20 | 244.07 | 249.19 | -5.11 | 26.16 |

## PREMIUM RATES GRADED BY POLICY SIZE

Certain expenses vary with the number of policies. If the premium formula were to incorporate a constant for this element that did not vary by amount of insurance, the premium rate per $1,000 would decline as the face of the policy increased.

Two quantity discount systems have developed in which size classifications are used. Under the **band system**, a number of "size bands," often three to five, are established, with different premium rates applying within each band. The following might be typical under this system:

| Size Band | Premium per $1,000 for a Particular Plan and Age |
|---|---|
| $ 25,000—$ 99,999 | $ 14.00 |
| 100,000— 249,999 | 13.00 |
| 250,000— 499,999 | 12.50 |
| 500,000— 999,999 | 12.25 |
| 1,000,000 and over | 12.00 |

**TABLE 21-6    ASSET-SHARE CALCULATION WITH GROSS PREMIUM INCREASED FROM $15.00 TO $15.50**

| (1) | (17) | (18) | (19) | (20) |
|---|---|---|---|---|
| | | | Surplus | Surrender Gain |
| | Asset | | per $1,000 | per $1,000 |
| | Share | Reserve | at End | at End |
| Policy | at End | at End | of Year | of Year |
| Year | of Year | of Year | [(17)-(18)] | [(17)-(7)] |
| 1 | $ -8.83 | $ 9.15 | $ -17.98 | $ -8.83 |
| 2 | 3.46 | 18.65 | -15.20 | 3.46 |
| 3 | 16.48 | 28.49 | -12.02 | 12.17 |
| 4 | 29.98 | 38.68 | -8.70 | 16.07 |
| 5 | 44.04 | 49.20 | -5.16 | 20.18 |
| 6 | 58.58 | 60.07 | -1.48 | 24.42 |
| 7 | 73.56 | 71.25 | 2.30 | 28.75 |
| 8 | 89.01 | 82.79 | 6.21 | 33.19 |
| 9 | 104.96 | 94.67 | 10.29 | 37.77 |
| 10 | 120.46 | 106.90 | 13.55 | 41.52 |
| 11 | 136.19 | 119.48 | 16.71 | 45.14 |
| 12 | 152.31 | 132.43 | 19.87 | 48.75 |
| 13 | 168.92 | 145.75 | 23.17 | 52.46 |
| 14 | 186.07 | 159.45 | 26.62 | 56.29 |
| 15 | 203.67 | 173.54 | 30.14 | 60.17 |
| 16 | 221.82 | 188.01 | 33.81 | 64.16 |
| 17 | 240.51 | 202.83 | 37.69 | 68.32 |
| 18 | 259.68 | 217.99 | 41.69 | 72.58 |
| 19 | 279.31 | 233.45 | 45.86 | 76.96 |
| 20 | 299.42 | 249.19 | 50.23 | 81.50 |

Under the **policy fee system,** the premium for a policy is expressed as the product of the policy amount and a basic rate per $1,000, plus a flat amount (known as the policy fee). For a particular plan and age, the premium might be $12.00 per $1,000 plus a flat $25. Thus the premium is $265 for a $20,000 policy, $625 for a $50,000 policy, and $1,225 for a $100,000 policy.

With both systems, the loading formula is modified so that the expense amount deemed to be independent of size is treated accordingly in determining the premium. The total amount necessary to cover expenses is not changed by such gradations, and the lower-amount policies must of necessity pay a higher rate to offset the discount granted to the larger-amount policies. Insurers most often use a policy fee with a banded system.

## SURPLUS AND ITS DISTRIBUTION

The earlier chapters made it clear that life insurance policies often contain elements that are not wholly guaranteed. Participating life insurance policies sold

**TABLE 21-7    ASSET-SHARE CALCULATION WITH
10% REDUCTION IN DIVIDENDS**

| (1) | (17) | (18) | (19) | (20) |
|---|---|---|---|---|
| | | | | Surrender |
| | | | Surplus | Gain |
| | Asset | | per $1,000 | per $1,000 |
| | Share | Reserve | at End | at End |
| Policy | at End | at End | of Year | of Year |
| Year | of Year | of Year | [(17)-(18)] | [(17)-(7)] |
| 1 | $ −9.43 | $ 9.15 | $ −18.58 | $ −9.43 |
| 2 | 2.24 | 18.65 | −16.41 | 2.24 |
| 3 | 14.62 | 28.49 | −13.87 | 10.32 |
| 4 | 27.47 | 38.68 | −11.21 | 13.56 |
| 5 | 40.85 | 49.20 | −8.35 | 16.99 |
| 6 | 54.69 | 60.07 | −5.38 | 20.52 |
| 7 | 68.95 | 71.25 | −2.30 | 24.14 |
| 8 | 83.69 | 82.79 | 0.89 | 27.86 |
| 9 | 98.91 | 94.67 | 4.24 | 31.72 |
| 10 | 113.77 | 106.90 | 6.87 | 34.84 |
| 11 | 128.88 | 119.48 | 9.39 | 37.83 |
| 12 | 144.37 | 132.43 | 11.93 | 40.81 |
| 13 | 160.35 | 145.75 | 14.60 | 43.89 |
| 14 | 176.88 | 159.45 | 17.42 | 47.10 |
| 15 | 193.86 | 173.54 | 20.32 | 50.35 |
| 16 | 211.39 | 188.01 | 23.38 | 53.73 |
| 17 | 229.46 | 202.83 | 26.63 | 57.26 |
| 18 | 248.00 | 217.99 | 30.02 | 60.90 |
| 19 | 267.02 | 233.45 | 33.57 | 64.67 |
| 20 | 286.51 | 249.19 | 37.32 | 68.59 |

in the United States have always been characterized by their nonguaranteed aspect—that is, by dividends.[12] With the advent of indeterminate premiums and charges and of excess interest credits (all on nonparticipating policies) the entire area of nonguaranteed policy elements has assumed greater prominence.

The actuarial aspects of the ways insurers determine excess interest credits and mortality and expense charges are not covered as thoroughly in the literature as that covering surplus distribution. In many ways, however, they are the same. Each shifts portions of the risk of deviations in interest, mortality, and expense experience from the insurer to the policyowner. This shift permits insurers to offer potentially better valued products since they need not guarantee a fixed, rigid benefit package and attendant prices for decades into the future.

As discussed in earlier chapters, current assumption nonparticipating products differ from participating products primarily in the mechanism by which

---

[12]Participating policies sold in many other countries are referred to as **with profits** policies. These policies pay **bonuses** rather than dividends. Correspondingly, nonparticipating policies—in U.S. terminology— are known elsewhere as **without profits** policies.

**TABLE 21-8**          **ASSET-SHARE CALCULATION WITH**
                        **INCREASED CASH VALUES**

| (1) | (17) | (18) | (19) | (20) |
|---|---|---|---|---|
| | | | | Surrender |
| | | | Surplus | Gain |
| | Asset | | per $1,000 | per $1,000 |
| | Share | Reserve | at End | at End |
| Policy | at End | at End | of Year | of Year |
| Year | of Year | of Year | [(17)-(18)] | [(17)-(7)] |
| 1 | $ −9.43 | $ 9.15 | $ −18.58 | $ −9.43 |
| 2 | 2.19 | 18.65 | −16.46 | 2.19 |
| 3 | 14.39 | 28.49 | −14.10 | 8.61 |
| 4 | 26.95 | 38.68 | −11.73 | 10.75 |
| 5 | 39.93 | 49.20 | −9.27 | 12.96 |
| 6 | 53.26 | 60.07 | −6.81 | 15.17 |
| 7 | 66.89 | 71.25 | −4.36 | 17.35 |
| 8 | 80.85 | 82.79 | −1.94 | 19.51 |
| 9 | 95.16 | 94.67 | 0.48 | 21.65 |
| 10 | 108.83 | 106.90 | 1.92 | 22.81 |
| 11 | 122.53 | 119.48 | 3.05 | 23.64 |
| 12 | 136.40 | 132.43 | 3.96 | 24.25 |
| 13 | 150.52 | 145.75 | 4.77 | 24.74 |
| 14 | 164.91 | 159.45 | 5.46 | 25.11 |
| 15 | 179.48 | 173.54 | 5.94 | 25.26 |
| 16 | 194.23 | 188.01 | 6.22 | 25.21 |
| 17 | 209.14 | 202.83 | 6.31 | 24.95 |
| 18 | 224.07 | 217.99 | 6.08 | 24.37 |
| 19 | 238.97 | 233.45 | 5.52 | 23.45 |
| 20 | 253.78 | 249.19 | 4.60 | 22.15 |

experience deviations are addressed.[13] For the indeterminate aspects of current assumption policies, the insurer typically examines its *current and likely future* operating experience in light of the competitive environment to decide upon the current year's *explicit* mortality and expense charges and excess interest credits.[14]

For participating products, the insurer typically examines the product's *past and current* operating experience in light of the competitive environment, to decide upon the current year's *implicit* mortality and expense charges and excess interest credits.[15] Because participating products involve greater reliance on past rather than probable future experience, their nonguaranteed element (dividends) tends to be more stable than the nonguaranteed elements (excess interest credits, mortality charge deviations, and possibly expense variations) of current assumption nonparticipating products.

[13]See chaps. 2, 6, and 9.

[14]Of course, not all policy elements necessarily would be indeterminate. Often, only the interest and mortality elements are subject to annual redetermination (see Chap. 6).

[15]With participating products, the insurer normally considers all three of these aspects of product pricing in determining the amount of surplus to be distributed.

TABLE 21-9          ASSET-SHARE CALCULATION WITH
                    WITHDRAWAL RATES DOUBLED

| Policy Year | Asset Share at End of Year | Reserve at End of Year | Surplus per $1,000 at End of Year [(17)-(18)] | Surrender Gain per $1,000 at End of Year [(17)-(7)] |
|---|---|---|---|---|
| 1 | $ −10.61 | $ 9.15 | $ −19.76 | $ −10.61 |
| 2 | 0.94 | 18.65 | −17.72 | 0.94 |
| 3 | 13.58 | 28.49 | −14.91 | 9.27 |
| 4 | 26.79 | 38.68 | −11.89 | 12.88 |
| 5 | 40.69 | 49.20 | −8.52 | 16.83 |
| 6 | 55.13 | 60.07 | −4.93 | 20.97 |
| 7 | 70.09 | 71.25 | −1.16 | 25.28 |
| 8 | 85.59 | 82.79 | 2.79 | 29.77 |
| 9 | 101.69 | 94.67 | 7.02 | 34.50 |
| 10 | 117.41 | 106.90 | 10.50 | 38.47 |
| 11 | 133.46 | 119.48 | 13.97 | 42.41 |
| 12 | 150.00 | 132.43 | 17.56 | 46.44 |
| 13 | 167.14 | 145.75 | 21.39 | 50.68 |
| 14 | 184.91 | 159.45 | 25.46 | 55.13 |
| 15 | 203.27 | 173.54 | 29.73 | 59.76 |
| 16 | 222.34 | 188.01 | 34.34 | 64.69 |
| 17 | 242.19 | 202.83 | 39.36 | 69.99 |
| 18 | 262.77 | 217.99 | 44.78 | 75.67 |
| 19 | 284.10 | 233.45 | 50.65 | 81.75 |
| 20 | 306.27 | 249.19 | 57.08 | 88.35 |

The following discussion deals primarily with surplus distribution under participating policies. Many aspects, however, are also applicable to current assumption products.

## NATURE OF SURPLUS

Guaranteed life insurance premiums are calculated conservatively. This is essential if an insurer is to avoid jeopardizing its long-term viability. Consequently, it is expected that insurers over time will show a gain from operations. The immediate result of a gain is to increase the insurer's surplus position. The size and disposition of this gain depends, among other factors, on whether the business written is on a participating basis; a guaranteed cost, nonparticipating basis; or a current assumption, nonparticipating basis.

In the aggregate, statutory surplus will develop only if an insurer accumulates funds in excess of those needed to establish policy reserves and other liabilities.[16] Surplus arises from favorable deviations from the assumed

---

[16]Insurers' decisions regarding surplus distribution to policyowners are heavily influenced by the statutory accounting procedures required by state insurance regulators. As a result, these decisions focus on *statutory surplus* as opposed to surplus as measured by a realistic assessment of the insurer's cash flows. The difference in approaches should not affect the ultimate amount of surplus generated by a block of policies—only the time of its recognition.

experience as to mortality, interest, and loading contained in the gross premium. These constitute the primary sources of additions to surplus and usually are designated as mortality savings, excess interest, and loading savings. The word savings is used here to connote both the residue arising from operations that were more efficient and economical than anticipated and margins intentionally provided in fixing the gross premium rate schedule. Even though insurers usually make participating premiums conservative, capable management can make a significant difference by adding yearly amounts to surplus.

An insurer's statutory surplus arising from a given block of policies consists of the sum of the excess interest, mortality savings, and savings from loading, plus gains from minor sources. For some policies, ages at issue, and durations, some or all of the three gains could be negative. In particular, the savings from loading are almost always negative in the first policy year, when the insurer's expenses are high.

*Gains from Investment Earnings.* Since life insurance policies often are written for a long term of years, it is essential that insurers assume a conservative rate of interest for their net premium and reserve computations to assure its being earned throughout the life of the contract. If an insurer bases its reserves on the assumption that it will earn 5 percent but actually earns 7 percent, that 2 percent difference represents the excess of investment earnings over the return necessary to maintain reserve liabilities, and it may be returned to the policyowners who were responsible for its existence, if this is considered advisable.

*Gains from Mortality.* This gain arises because life insurance companies in the United States ordinarily do not experience mortality that is as heavy as that indicated by the mortality table employed by them in reserve calculations. Because the reserve mortality table is deliberately made conservative, it is natural that a surplus gain normally results from operations. Too much reliance should not be placed on a single year's mortality experience, however, since it tends to fluctuate from year to year. In the interest of stability and safety, therefore, most insurers average mortality experience over a period of years. Any surplus gain does not necessarily mean that the block of policies is profitable. The surplus gain or loss relates actual experience to the reserve liability value, which usually is conservative.

*Gains from Loading.* Sound insurance company management dictates that the gross premium should be more than sufficient to meet normal requirements, so that the insurer and its policyowners may be protected against exceptional conditions. In fact, as pointed out above, the loading on participating policies frequently includes an amount for policyowner dividends together with gains from other sources. Competitive conditions—especially in the matter of agents' commissions—as well as inflationary pressures on expenses, have at times caused expenses to exceed loadings in the aggregate. This has been a particular challenge for insurers selling universal life policies. In recent years, life insurance companies have made a marked effort toward more economical management.

***Gains from Surrenders.*** Cash surrender values, as previously explained, normally are less than policy reserves. The difference between (1) reserves released as a result of surrender and (2) surrender values allowed constitutes another source of surplus gain. Such a gain frequently represents, in whole or in part, amounts returned to surplus that originally were taken from it to establish the reserves. In general, a surplus gain from surrenders will be a "paper" gain—a repayment of previously borrowed surplus—where the asset share is less than the policy surrender value. The gain will be "real" when the asset share is greater than the surrender value. Real gains derived from this source are generally used to offset expenses when calculations are made to apportion the divisible surplus to policyowners.[17]

## DISTRIBUTION OF SURPLUS

***Divisible Surplus.*** Following each year's operations, a United States insurer must determine how much of the total surplus (previously existing surplus plus additions for the year) should be retained as a contingency fund or other special surplus appropriation and how much should be distributed to policyowners. No fixed relationship may exist between the surplus gain in a particular calendar year and the dividends distributed to policyowners on the next policy anniversaries. The directors or trustees of the insurer, as a matter of business judgment, make the decision. The amount earmarked for distribution is designated as divisible surplus, and once set aside by action of the directors or trustees, it loses its identity as surplus and becomes a liability of the insurer.

In deciding the portion of the total surplus that should be retained as contingency funds, a balance must be maintained between the need for a general contingency fund and the competitive advantages of a liberal dividend scale. When the surplus earned for any given year is insufficient to permit the insurer to maintain its current dividend scale, management may decide to use a portion of the general contingency fund for this purpose.[18] On the other hand, if, during a temporary period, additions to surplus are more than adequate to support the existing dividend scale, the excess often is added to the general contingency fund to avoid the expense and complications involved in changing the scale. If the

---

[17] In the apportionment of surplus, as explained in a later section, it is more practical to treat all surpluses as coming from the three main sources previously mentioned: loading, interest earnings, and mortality. Surplus from other sources, such as forfeitures and appreciation in the values of assets, is, therefore, not treated separately, but instead is considered in connection with expenses and interest earnings, respectively.

An exception to this general statement occurs with lapse-supported policies when the gain from surrender is explicitly counted upon to support future policy values.

[18] An insurer may earmark a special fund for dividend fluctuations, but the principle is the same.

excess is substantial and is expected to continue over a reasonable period, competitive considerations will usually lead to a change in the scale.

In the interest of security of the benefits and good management, life insurance companies maintain surplus and general contingency funds that bear a reasonable relationship to liabilities. As policy reserves increase through new business and the natural accretion under older policies, surplus and general contingency funds should also increase. With many insurers, each policy is expected to make a permanent contribution to the insurer's surplus. These contributions enable insurers to fulfill their contractual obligations even in the face of a catastrophe of the type that may occur only once in several decades. Thus over the lifetime of a class of policies, aggregate dividend distributions[19] made often will be somewhat less than the contributions of the class to surplus. On the other hand, some insurers' dividend practices result in substantially complete liquidation of each generation's contributions to surplus by the time that generation of policies is eliminated from the books.

Although insurers may, in the absence of legislation, use their discretion in determining the amount of surplus to be distributed, some states regulate this matter by statute. New York limits the amount of surplus an insurer can retain on its participating business to an amount not exceeding $850,000, or 10 percent of its policy reserves and other policy liabilities, whichever is the greater amount. The purpose of this legislation is to prevent insurers from retaining more surplus than is judged necessary to offset factors such as fluctuations in the mortality rate and interest earnings that may interfere with the payment of stable dividends. This limitation grew out of abuses identified during the 1906 Armstrong investigation in New York.[20] Many commentators today question whether such limitations serve the public interest and are warranted, especially given the great concern over insurer solvency.

*Frequency of Distribution*. Unlike the situation in many other countries, in the United States surplus is distributed annually on practically all participating policies sold. This is required by statute in many states. There are still a few policies on which deferred dividends are paid.

**Deferred dividends** are dividends payable only at the close of a stipulated number of years, such as 5, 10, 15, or 20. Policies providing for payment of dividends in this manner are commonly called deferred-dividend, accumulation, distribution, or semitontine policies.[21] According to the underlying principle of the plan, policyowners who fail to continue premium payments to the end of the designated period (because of death, surrender, or lapse) lose the dividends they

---

[19]This includes, in addition to the usual dividends distributed annually, extra dividends and terminal dividends (see below).

[20]See Chap. 3

[21]Interest-rate bonuses under current assumption policies are similar in effect to deferred dividends under participating policies. **Retroactive bonuses** provide that, after a predefined time period, e.g., 10 years, a bonus interest rate will be retroactively applied to all previous periods. **Prospective bonuses** provide that, after a predefined time period, future interest credits will be augmented by a bonus rate.

would have received under the annual-dividend plan. The lost dividends revert to the policyowners who continue their premium payments throughout the deferred-dividend period.

The traditional deferred-dividend plan lost favor with the United States public, having been almost wholly superseded by the annual-distribution system. The latter plan, it is argued, is well adapted to the policyowner who wishes to keep his or her net annual outlay to the lowest possible amount, and it also serves to encourage managerial economy, since extravagance could be revealed by a reduction in the annual-dividend distribution.

The deferred system in a modified form is still used to some extent in Canada and elsewhere.[22] Under Canadian law, for example, dividend distributions may be made every five years, but the amount of surplus set aside for deferred dividends during a five-year period must be carried as a liability until it is paid. Most Canadian insurers pay an interim dividend in the event of death during the period, but not in the event of lapse or surrender.

*The Contribution Principle*. The allocation of divisible surplus among policyowners is a complex matter. Equity is the basic objective, but consideration must be given to competition, flexibility, and simplicity. That the allocation should be competitive is obvious. Flexibility can be viewed as a facet of equity, since adaptability to changing circumstances is essential if equity is to be attained. Simplicity is desirable both from an expense viewpoint and from the viewpoint of understanding by agents and policyowners. The earlier discussion of the sources of surplus would suggest that one way of obtaining reasonable equity would be *to return to each class of policyowners a share of the divisible surplus proportionate to the contribution of the class to the surplus*. This concept is known as the **contribution principle**. The principle does not require the return of all or even most surplus. It merely requires that whatever the amount of divisible surplus, it be allotted to policyowners in the approximate proportion in which they contributed to it. This principle underlies the equity implicit in participating insurance.

*The Three-Factor Contribution Method*. The contribution principle provides the underlying philosophical base for surplus distribution in the United States. The most widely used approach for applying the principle is referred to as the **three-factor contribution method**.[23]

---

[22]In the United Kingdom and in many other countries, divisible surplus (bonuses) under participating (with-profits) policies (see footnote 12) are declared at the insurer's discretion or as required by law at fixed intervals that are often greater than a single year. A **reversionary bonus** is commonly used, whereby the divisible surplus is used to increase the policy's face amount (the **sum assured**) and its surrender value. The amount is often calculated as a percentage of the face amount without regard to the insured's age or the time that the policy has been in force. Sometimes an additional or **terminal** (or **capital**) **bonus** is paid on policy maturity, the intent of which is to allow the policyowner to share more equitably in the favorable operations of the insurer (**office**).

[23]Another method of computing dividends is the so-called experience-premium method, which is used by many insurers in the United States. Its purpose is to avoid decreases in dividends on any plan, even with a low excess-interest factor. See Joseph B. Maclean, *Life Insurance*, 9th ed. (New York: McGraw-Hill, 1962), pp. 159-160.

This method is based on an analysis of the sources of insurer surplus and develops dividends that vary with the plan of insurance, age of issue, and duration of the policy. In the interest of simplicity, consideration usually is limited to the three major sources of surplus: excess interest, mortality savings, and loading savings. When special benefits are involved, such as disability and accidental death, an additional factor sometimes is included for these features.

*1. The Formula.*[24] Generally the three-factor contribution method may be expressed as:

$$D_t = I_t + M_t + E_t$$

where
$D_t$ = dividend per $1,000 payable at the end of policy year $t$
$I_t$ = excess interest factor for policy year $t$
$M_t$ = mortality savings factor for policy year $t$
$E_t$ = expense savings factor for policy years $t$

Each of the three factors, in turn, can be determined by the following formulas:

$$I_t = (i'_t - i_t)(_{t-1}V_x + {}_tP_x)$$
$$M_t = (q_{x+t-1} - q'_{x+t-1})(1{,}000 - {}_tV_x)$$
$$E_t = ({}_tG_x - {}_tP_x - {}_te_x)(1 + i'_t)$$

where
$x$ = age of issue
$i'_t$ = dividend interest rate in policy year $t$
$i_t$ = reserve interest rate in policy year $t$
${}_tV_x$ = $t^{th}$ policy year's terminal reserve per $1,000 for a policy issued at age $x$
${}_tP_x$ = $t^{th}$ policy year's valuation annual premium per $1,000 for a policy issued at age $x$
$q_x$ = reserve mortality rate at age $x$
$q'_x$ = dividend mortality rate at age $x$
${}_tG_x$ = $t^{th}$ policy year's gross annual premium per $1,000 for a policy issued at age $x$
${}_te_x$ = $t^{th}$ policy year's expense charge per $1,000 for a policy issued at age $x$

The following sections consider briefly the operation of the preceding formula. The discussion of each factor includes a sample calculation for that factor. The sample is based on a hypothetical $10,000 ordinary life policy issued 15 years ago to a male *then* aged 25. The gross annual premium is $170.00 ($17.00 per $1,000). Net-level terminal reserves are assumed to be calculated on the *1958 CSO Table*, with interest of 3 percent. The valuation net annual premium calculated on these assumptions is $11.28 per $1,000. Policy reserves per $1,000 face amount at the end of the fourteenth and fifteenth policy years are $162.97 and $176.80, respectively.

24. See Joseph M. Belth, "Distribution of Surplus to Individual Life Insurance Policy Owners," *The Journal of Risk and Insurance*, Vol. 45 (March 1978), pp. 10-11.

*2. Interest Factor.* The interest factor $(I_t)$ is the simplest element of the dividend, consisting of the excess interest on, usually, the initial reserve for the policy period at the end of which the dividend is payable.[25] Recall that the initial reserve is the previous year's terminal reserve $(_{t-1}V_x)$ plus the valuation net level premium $(_tP_x)$.

Assume that the dividend interest rate is 8 percent for this policy.[26] Under these circumstances, the rate of excess interest $(i_t' - i_t)$ would be 5 percent. Thus on the $10,000 ordinary life policy issued at male age 25 that had been in force 15 years, the interest factor of the dividend would be calculated as follows:

$$
\begin{aligned}
I_t &= (i_t' - i_t)(_{t-1}V_x + _tP_x) \\
I_{15} &= (i_{15}' - i_{15})(_{14}V_{25} + _{15}P_{25}) \\
I_{15} &= (0.08 - 0.03)(\$162.97 + \$11.28) \\
I_{15} &= (0.05)(\$174.25) \\
I_{15} &= \$8.71
\end{aligned}
$$

The interest factor has a strong influence on the dividend, particularly at long durations where the initial reserve is large.

Although the interest factor is simple in concept, several complications arise in application. Several bases can be and are used to compute the rate of investment yield.[27] For purposes of asset-share studies underlying the dividend formula, it is common to use a base consisting of the interest-bearing liabilities and surplus. Interest-bearing liabilities include policy reserves, funds held under settlement agreements, dividend accumulations, and advance premiums.[28] If certain items, such as dividend accumulations, have a minimum guarantee, some insurers credit these items with the guaranteed rate only and increase the net effective rate for regular policy dividend purposes. The final rate utilized in the dividend formula may well be less than the rate used in the asset-share studies. This results in a contribution to the assets backing the general contingency reserves, part of which ultimately may be distributed as a terminal dividend (see below).

With many insurers, the excess-interest factor reflects the general trend of the insurer's investment earnings and would be set at a level that, according to the insurer's best judgment, should be appropriate for several years. For short periods of time, the factor could be based on a rate higher than that actually being earned.[29]

---

[25] Many insurers utilize the mean reserve on premium-paying policies and the initial reserve on policies when premiums have been fully paid.

[26] Actual dividend interest rates can vary significantly from insurer to insurer.

[27] For example, the base logically could be ledger assets, admitted assets, or invested funds.

[28] Most insurers permit policyowners to prepay premiums by discounting them at a given rate of interest. The discounted premiums so paid are applied at the appropriate premium-due dates. If the insured dies, all unapplied premiums (less unearned discount) are paid to the beneficiary.

[29] In the interest of showing more competitive-seeming illustrations, some insurers are said to include an element of optimistic interest projection in their dividend formulas.

Some insurers vary the dividend interest rate by the length of time the policy has been in force. These insurers artificially segregate policies into different "generations" and use a dividend interest rate for each generation, that is based on the investment return on the assets accumulated on behalf of that generation. Thus different generations easily could be credited with different interest rates. This **investment generation method** of investment income allocation tends to produce a dividend pattern that can change rapidly as earnings change, especially for generations of only a few years duration.

Other insurers base their dividend interest rate on the average investment return of their entire asset portfolio. This **portfolio average method** does not segregate policies into generations; instead it uses the same dividend interest rate for all participating policies. This method produces a more stable dividend pattern than one based on the investment generation method. Both of these methods of investment income allocation, as discussed in earlier chapters, have been the subject of discussion and debate, and they render cost comparisons between these policies more difficult.[30] Questions have been raised about possible incomplete disclosure and the possibility of an insurer switching from one method to the other, depending on market rate changes.[31]

Many insurers tie their dividend interest rate directly or indirectly to the policy loan rate or activity. Thus under the **direct recognition approach** discussed earlier, the excess interest rate is influenced directly by any policy loan activity and rate.[32] If a policyowner borrows heavily under his or her policy at a favorable interest rate relative to the market rate, this could cause lower dividends.

The treatment of capital gains and losses on assets also can vary among insurers. Some insurers take these into account in fixing the dividend interest rate when they reflect actual market transactions as opposed to unrealized gains or losses arising out of adjustments in book value. The more common practice, however, is to transfer these gains and losses to an investment fluctuation fund or to a general contingency reserve, where over a period of time the gains and losses offset each other to some degree. This stabilizes net interest earnings.

Insurers also differ in the treatment of investment expenses. They particularly differ in their treatment of general overhead expenses and federal income taxes. This can make a significant difference and although it should not affect the aggregate amount of surplus distributed, it does affect the pattern of distribution between blocks of policies.

Under the three-factor contribution approach, the correct base against which to apply the dividend interest rate is the initial reserve less one-half a

[30]See Chaps. 6, 9, and 10.

[31]The NAIC Model Life Insurance Disclosure Regulation requires insurers to disclose their practices in this regard.

[32]See Chaps. 6 and 9.

year's cost of insurance. The difference between this theoretically correct base and the mean reserve is small. Although the mean reserve would be a more accurate measure of the policy funds available for investment, the difference in results is so insignificant that most insurers continue to use the initial reserve without the adjustment for one-half year's cost of insurance.

With a constant dividend interest rate, the excess-interest contribution increases with duration if reserves increase. At all ages of issue and durations, it is larger for higher-premium than for lower-premium policies. Thus assuming the same duration and age of issue, excess interest makes a greater contribution to the dividend of a 20-pay whole life policy than to the dividend of an ordinary life policy, particularly at longer durations. The interest factor has a strong influence on the dividend.

*3. Mortality Factor.* The mortality factor in the three-factor formula can be derived by multiplying (1) the difference between the mortality rate used for reserve computation ($q_x$) and the (usually) lower rate to be used for dividend purposes $q'_x$ by (2) the year's net amount at risk ($1,000 - {}_tV_x$). In a continuation of the earlier example, the mortality savings for the 15-year-old ordinary life policy, with reserves based on the *1958 CSO Table* and 3 percent interest, would be calculated (assuming $q'_{39} = 0.00225$) as follows:

$$
\begin{aligned}
M_t &= (q_{x+t-1} - q'_{x+t-1})(1,000 - {}_tV_x) \\
M_{15} &= (q_{39} - q'_{39})(1,000 - {}_{15}V_{25}) \\
M_{15} &= (0.00325 - 0.00225)(\$1,000 - \$176.80) \\
M_{15} &= (0.001)(\$823.20) \\
M_{15} &= \$0.82
\end{aligned}
$$

Many insurers express the mortality savings factor as a percentage of the assumed cost of insurance.[33] The percentage for any block of policies generally depends only on the attained age of the insured and the insurer's experience among all insureds at that age and duration. The mortality factor of the formula normally takes the form of a scale of percentages of the assumed cost of insurance, decreasing with attained age, and reflecting the insurer's actual mortality table assumed in calculating reserves. The scale of percentages may range from a high of 40 to 50 percent at the younger ages to a low of 5 to 10 percent at the older ages. Since mortality experience under term policies often is considerably different age by age than under cash-value plans, a separate scale of mortality savings often would be applied to these classes of policies.

The percentage utilized in the final dividend calculation normally is based on the ultimate mortality experience under the insurer's basic mortality table, although select experience is utilized in the asset share underlying the development of the dividend distributions. Otherwise, a decreasing dividend scale by duration could result because of large mortality savings at early

[33]See Chap. 20.

durations. The savings from the effect of selection are assumed to be applied toward the payment of excess first-year expenses and, hence, are distributed indirectly in accordance with the method used to assess expenses to the various blocks of policies.

With the increasing incidence of deaths because of acquired immunodeficiency syndrome (AIDS), insurers have made appropriate adjustments within their dividend formulas. Most AIDS deaths and therefore attendant insurer death claims are of males from 20 to 40 years of age. The mortality factors for policies on males in this age range are, therefore, adjusted downward by many insurers, to account for the increased mortality.

The mortality contribution normally is smallest on the higher-premium plans and higher ages of issue since the net amounts at risk are smaller. With advancing duration, a declining percentage factor is applied to a steadily smaller net amount at risk and, hence, in the usual case, a smaller cost of insurance. The higher the premium (because of plan or age at issue), the more pronounced is the decline in mortality savings. This is not invariably so, however. The cost of insurance actually increases at the higher ages under certain types of policies. In these cases, the increase in the rate of mortality more than offsets the decrease in the net amount at risk, resulting in an increased mortality cost for the year. In general, however, the mortality factor results in a decreasing contribution with greater durations.

In contrast to the interest factor, the mortality contribution is highly significant for term insurance policies. The percentage factor is applied to a larger net amount at risk and, hence, cost of insurance, resulting in a relatively greater proportionate contribution to the dividends distributable to term policies.

4. *Loading Factor.* The loading factor $(E_t)$ of the dividend consists of the difference between (1) the gross premium and (2) the valuation net premium and an expense charge, with the difference taken as a year-end figure by increasing the amount for a year's interest at the dividend interest rate. In the example, the gross premium per \$1,000 is \$17.00 and the valuation net annual premium is \$11.28. Assume that the fifteenth year's expense charge is \$5.00. The expense savings factor for the example would, therefore, be calculated:

$$
\begin{aligned}
E_t &= ({}_tG_x - {}_tP_x - {}_te_x)(1 + i'_t) \\
E_{15} &= ({}_{15}G_{25} - {}_{15}P_{25} - {}_{15}e_{25})(1 + i'_{15}) \\
E_{15} &= (\$17.00 - \$11.28 - \$5.00)(1 + 0.08) \\
E_{15} &= (\$0.72)(1.08) \\
E_{15} &= \$0.78
\end{aligned}
$$

Thus the expense factor for policy year 15 is \$0.78.

The assessment of expenses probably presents one of the greatest difficulties connected with the distribution of surplus, as discussed earlier in this chapter. In general, the expense charge frequently is in the form of a percentage of the premium and a constant of so many dollars per $1,000 of face amount. The constant may vary to allow for differences in the average amount of policy by plan of insurance. The percentage element of the expense charge usually is on a decreasing basis, at least for the first few years, to reflect the lower expenses after the first two years. There are wide differences among insurers, both in gross premiums charged and in the manner of computing the expense charge. Consequently, the importance of the loading factor varies considerably, the amount being much higher in an insurer with "high" gross premiums than in an insurer utilizing "low" gross premiums. The pattern in most cases, however, is for the loading contribution to increase for the first few years and thereafter to increase slightly or remain roughly constant.

Combining each of the three factors, the fifteenth year's dividend per $1,000 face amount for the hypothetical policy is therefore:

$$
\begin{aligned}
D_t &= I_t + M_t + E_t \\
D_{15} &= I_{15} + M_{15} + E_{15} \\
D_{15} &= \$8.71 + \$0.82 + \$0.78 \\
D_{15} &= \$10.31
\end{aligned}
$$

5. *Dividend Pattern.* For most plans of whole life insurance, the annual dividend under the contribution plan usually increases with duration. This is entirely aside from an increase in the scale itself. The normal increase of dividends with duration occurs because the interest factor normally increases with duration. In the usual case, this more than offsets the tendency of the mortality and loading factors to decrease with duration, but this is not always so. An unfavorable investment market may well cause just the opposite to occur, as happened in the 1940s, when the average rate of return dropped to below 3 percent. Also, the fact that many insurers have switched to the investment generation method of interest allocation renders dividend patterns less stable.

***Special Forms of Surplus Distribution.*** United States insurers pay extra dividends or terminal dividends in addition to the regular annual dividends. An **extra dividend** may consist either of a single payment made after a policy has been in force a specified number of years or of a payment made periodically at stated intervals. The single-payment extra dividend is generally used when no first-year dividend is paid, the extra dividend serving as a substitute. This practice has the practical advantage of reducing the surplus strain of initial expenses, and it also may have a tendency to reduce the first-year lapse rate. It has the effect of assessing a larger share of first-year expense against policies that terminate prior to the time when the extra dividend is paid.

Extra dividends paid periodically (say, at every fifth year) have little justification in theory unless regular dividends have been calculated on a conservative basis and equity insists that extra dividends be paid periodically to the policyowners as the experience develops. A practical advantage, however, is that illustrative net costs over a period of years are reduced by these extra amounts; only those policies remaining in force get the additional payments. This is particularly true of an extra dividend payable only at the end of the twentieth year.

Some insurers pay a **terminal dividend** in the event that a policy terminates by maturity, death, or surrender. In most cases, these dividends are payable only if the policy has been in force for a minimum length of time. Terminal dividends, in theory, have the purpose of returning to terminating policyowners part of the general surplus to which they have contributed, or adjusting for a guaranteed cash-value that is something less than the asset share. Some insurers, however, in effect use terminal dividends as a means of making their policies appear more attractive from a cost standpoint than they really are. This occurs when an insurer uses particularly high terminal dividends only at the duration required for cost index calculation purposes.[34]

The distinction between a postmortem or mortuary dividend and a terminal dividend payable at death is important. A **postmortem dividend** is payable at death, but either it is paid in proportion to the part of the policy year of death for which premiums have been paid or it represents a one-time distribution of surplus, mainly on term insurance, in lieu of dividends on each policy anniversary while the insured was living.

*Practical Considerations.* In establishing a scale of dividends, several practical considerations impinge on the decisions made. For example, the dividend scale should be satisfactory to existing policyowners. They probably would have been conditioned by the existing scale to a pattern of dividends, and significant changes, as a practical matter, normally would be accomplished by a series of adjustments. Also, the net cost position of the insurer under a proposed scale must be checked against the position of competitors to avoid dissatisfaction among the agency force and to assure a competitive product from the buyer's viewpoint. Similarly, the administrative cost of developing and implementing a new scale must be considered. At some point, the increased cost of greater theoretical equity outweighs the benefit involved. These and other practical considerations are an integral part of the process of establishing a scale of dividends for participating contracts.

The various options under which dividends may be taken were discussed in Chapter 9. In Chapters 6 and 9 some of the problems related to "frozen" dividend scales and the comparability of dividend scales were discussed.

[34]See Chap. 10.

# Chapter 22

# THE MATHEMATICS OF HEALTH INSURANCE

Premiums for individual health insurance policies are affected by many factors, such as the rates of morbidity, interest, expense, and lapse. Other factors, however, such as the method of selling, the underwriting philosophy, and the claims administration policy, as well as the overall philosophy and objectives of the insuring company, may result in a different experience by insurers issuing similar types of coverage. Similarly, changes and variations in hospital administration and medical practice, both geographically and from time to time in the same locality, and the impact of varying regulatory, economic, and business conditions make it difficult to predict reliably the future net annual claim costs.

## PRINCIPLES OF RATE-MAKING

### THE RATING PROCESS

Rate-making involves the analysis of available data and the development for the various classifications of insureds of premium rates that are *adequate, reasonable*, and *equitable*. Thus, in pricing benefits, insurers classify insureds according to characteristics such as age, sex, geographic area, and occupation, depending upon the type of benefit involved as well as legal and competitive constraints. These classifications are considered necessary if reasonable equity between policyowners is to be realized.

If all insureds were charged an average premium rate regardless of the loss exposure presented by a particular individual, serious antiselection by those with a high exposure would result, and individuals with a lower loss exposure would not purchase the insurance. There are, however, practical limitations on the process of refining classifications in the interest of equity. As in life insurance, the parameters are established by the increasing administrative expense of dealing with multiple classes and the need to have a sufficient volume of business within a class to provide reliable experience and stability in the rate structure.

Competition usually is relied upon to keep premium rates reasonable in relation to the benefits provided, but this is not always the case. Some states require filing of health insurance rates, and an increasing number of states require approval of premium rates on individual policies.

Adequacy is arguably the most important criterion against which a premium rate should be measured. When a new type of coverage with unreliable experience is being introduced, the margin of safety built into the premium is larger than in an established type of coverage that has its own body of experience. In addition to developing premium rates for new policies, there is the problem of revising rates on existing individual policies when they are issued on an adjustable-premium, guaranteed-renewable basis. As discussed below, insurers normally test the level of their premiums with asset-share studies, utilizing various assumptions as to expense rates, lapses, morbidity, mortality, and interest.

## MEASURES OF MORBIDITY EXPERIENCE

In establishing premium rates for any type of health insurance coverage, it is necessary to begin by providing a measure of the expected net annual claim cost per policy.

*Unit Benefit Costs*. The net annual claim cost of any benefit is the product of the frequency of occurrence and the amount of the average claim (severity). The unit benefit cost method entails the calculation of the cost of providing a unit benefit, so that the net annual claim cost of benefits actually provided can be determined by multiplying the unit benefit cost by the appropriate benefit amount.

The unit of exposure may be $1 of daily hospital benefit, $1 of monthly income disability benefit, a standard maximum surgical schedule, or other suitable units selected. Unit costs can be broken down to reflect the combination of age, sex, occupation, geographic location, and other factors.

It is possible to obtain the net annual claim cost without separately determining the frequency and average amount of claim for the benefit under consideration.[1] For example, all hospital miscellaneous benefits paid during the year under policies providing the same maximum benefit can be divided by the

---

[1] It can be done the other way, however, using one body of data for frequency and another for claim size.

appropriate exposure to determine the average annual claim cost per life. In a similar manner, if interest is ignored, the net annual claim cost per dollar of monthly income, under disability income insurance with a particular elimination period and maximum benefit limit, may be determined by dividing the value of total incurred claims at each age of disablement by the total monthly indemnity exposed. The result is the same as the rate of disability (frequency) multiplied by the value of the disabled life annuity, computed without interest (average amount of claim).

*Continuance Tables*. The determination of (1) the expected claim frequency among insured lives and (2) the average claim value are two important problems that confront the actuary. The mathematical measurement of the effect on claims cost of various elimination periods usually is handled by developing a **continuance table**, which shows the probabilities of claim continuance for various durations or amounts.[2]

Hospital confinement, for example, may be expressed as the number of patients remaining in the hospital at the end of *t* days out of an assumed initial number of patients confined to a hospital, such as 10,000. Figure 22-1 reflects a study of the probability of continuance of hospital confinement among 10,000 lives confined (adult males).

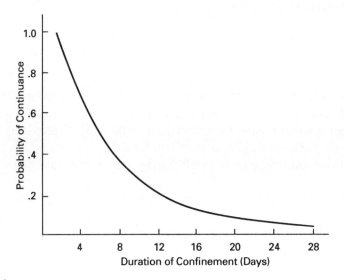

**FIGURE 22-1**

**PROBABILITY OF CONTINUATION OF HOSPITAL CONFINEMENT AMONG 10,000 LIVES CONFINED (ADULT MALES)**

---

[2]For an explanation of the development and utilization of continuance tables, see Edwin L. Bartleson et al., *Health Insurance*, 2d ed. (Chicago: Society of Actuaries, 1968), pp. 192–196.

In disability income insurance, the elimination period has a dramatic effect on the rate level required. Figure 22-2 reflects a study of the probability of continuance of disability among 10,000 lives disabled at age 40.

In a similar manner, a major medical continuance table could express the probability that the claim experience will equal or exceed various dollar levels, from which the effect of varying deductibles and varying maximum amounts could be determined.

Continuance tables are helpful in computing the average-sized claim. These average claim values, in combination with the expected claim frequency (rate of claims), produce the expected net annual claim cost for the pattern of benefits under consideration. The method is easy to apply in practice when a single benefit, such as a monthly disability income benefit, is being considered. When benefits are combined in various ways with different elimination periods and different maximum benefit limitations, the problem of measuring the expected net annual claim cost becomes exceedingly complex.

***Net Level Premiums.*** The net level premium for a disability income contract, as in the case of life insurance, is the level annual payment needed to pay benefits (1) if future claims exactly follow the average claim amounts assumed, as well as the frequency rates shown in the morbidity tables adopted; (2) if deaths among persons insured occur at the rates given by the assumed mortality table; and (3) if the rate of interest earned is that assumed in the rate basis. Thus the net level premium at date of issue is found as follows:

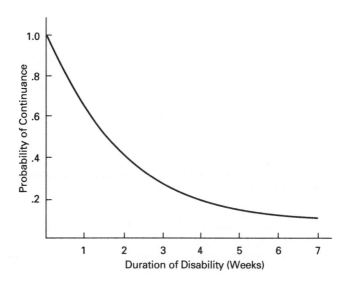

**FIGURE 22-2**

**PROBABILITY OF CONTINUATION OF DISABILITY AMONG 10,000 LIVES DISABLED AT AGE 40 (ADULT MALES)**

$$NLP = \frac{\text{present value of future net annual claim costs}}{\text{present value of a life annuity due of 1 for the premium-paying period}}$$

The present value of future net annual claim costs is the value at date of issue of all benefits that are expected to be paid until the termination date of the contract, appropriately discounted with interest. Table 22-1 illustrates the calculation of a net level premium for a five-year term, guaranteed-renewable hospital expense policy issued to a male aged 60.

***Loss Ratios.*** This method of establishing the level of morbidity costs is based on the ratio of benefits incurred to premiums earned. It is an acceptable method for developing premium rates on business issued on a one-year term basis, but not for business issued on a level-premium basis. The loss-ratio method should be used with great caution when comparing morbidity costs among different insurers. These comparisons can be misleading because of differences in (1) premium levels for the same types of benefits, (2) types of policies with varying benefits, (3) reserve requirements, (4) lapse rates, or (5) rates of insurer growth.[3]

**TABLE 22-1**   **ILLUSTRATIVE CALCULATION OF NET LEVEL PREMIUM FIVE-YEAR GUARANTEED-RENEWABLE HOSPITAL EXPENSE POLICY (MALE, AGED 60)**

| (1) | (2) | (3) | (4) | (5) | (6) |
|---|---|---|---|---|---|
| Attained Age | Annual Claim Cost during Year Following Attained Age | Average Period from Date of Issue of Contract to Commencement of Claim (Years) | Proportion of Those Insured Who Will Survive Average Period | Amount of 1 Discounted at 4 1/2% per Annum for Average Period | Present Expected Value of Claim Cost [(2)x(4)x(5)] |
| 60 | $18.10 | 0.5 | 0.9898 | 0.9782 | $17.525 |
| 61 | 18.70 | 1.5 | 0.9688 | 0.9361 | 16.959 |
| 62 | 19.32 | 2.5 | 0.9462 | 0.8958 | 16.376 |
| 63 | 19.96 | 3.5 | 0.9222 | 0.8572 | 15.779 |
| 64 | 20.62 | 4.5 | 0.8965 | 0.8203 | 15.164 |

Total of column 6, present value of future annual claim costs    $81.803

Present value of a five-year temporary life annuity due of 1 at age 60 (*1980 CSO Table*, 4 1/2%)    4.436

$$\text{Net level premium} = \frac{\$81.803}{4.436} = \$18.44$$

---

[3]See John B. Cumming, "Regulatory Monitoring of Individual Health Insurance Policy Experience," *Transactions of the Society of Actuaries*, Vol. 34 (1982), pp. 617–634.

# GROSS PREMIUMS[4]

The gross premium must provide for benefits, expenses, and contingency margins in the event that claims and expenses are higher than anticipated. Gross premiums usually are calculated on the assumption that they will be paid annually, but they may be paid semiannually, quarterly, or monthly. On many individual health insurance policies, gross premiums are paid on a level basis, which means that the same premium is payable each year, from the date of issue to the end of the term period of the policy, such as to age 65. Gross premiums also may be developed on a one-year term basis or a step-rate basis. Several insurers issue comprehensive major medical benefits when the premiums increase each year to keep pace with annual increases in medical costs.

*Factors Affecting the Premium*. The premium rates for a particular benefit depend on (1) morbidity, (2) expenses, (3) persistency, (4) interest, and (5) contingency margins.

*1. Morbidity*. In dealing with mortality rates, the only element considered is the number of deaths during a year compared with the total number of persons exposed in the class. In contrast, in the measurement of morbidity, the annual claim cost for a given age-sex-occupational class is the product of (a) the annual frequency of a particular event and (b) the average claim when such an event occurs. For example, the annual frequency of hospitalization for a given age and sex might be 10 percent, the average duration of the hospital stay might be seven days, and therefore the annual claim cost for a $100 daily hospital benefit would be $70 (0.1 x 7 x $100).

In health insurance, although mortality is a consideration, the primary consideration is the morbidity cost. Annual claim costs may vary, depending upon the kind and amount of benefits, according to such factors as age, sex, occupational class, and geographical area. Inasmuch as most policies contain more than one benefit, it is necessary to obtain separate annual claim costs for each type of benefit.

Most morbidity tables used to calculate net annual claim costs of disability income benefits exclude the experience during the calendar year that a policy is issued. Attempts to identify the influence of underwriting on experience by policy year (select experience) have not been very successful, in contrast to the success of the practice for life insurance. The pattern of select experience under disability insurance is quite different from that for mortality under individual life policies. At age 40 and under, the benefits of selection in the early policy years are almost negligible. This probably is due to the fact that for ages below 40, sickness costs tend to increase by policy duration, but accident costs tend to decrease by policy duration.

---

[4]This section draws from *Individual Health Insurance, Part B* (Washington, D.C.: Health Insurance Association of America, 1992) pp. 81–101.

It is even more important to note that there is apparently substantial selection against the insurer by those applying for disability income policies whose elimination periods and maximum durations are relatively short. Studies show that at ages 50 to 65 there is a substantial increase in morbidity by policy duration that continues until the coverage terminates. Applicants who become insured in their twenties and thirties develop a higher level of morbidity after age 50 than those applicants who become insured after age 50. Furthermore, the experience varies considerably, depending on the type of benefit under consideration. The experience is further complicated in the case of medical expense insurance by the continuing inflation in the cost of medical services, and in the case of disability insurance, by the U.S. economy.

Obviously, consideration should be given to the relationship of select to ultimate experience in establishing gross premiums, so that the premiums for insurance issued at advanced ages may properly reflect the savings from selection.

*2. Expenses.* To obtain suitable expense rates for determination of premium rates, it is necessary to make detailed cost studies in which the various expense items are expressed as (a) a percentage of the premium (e.g., premium taxes and agents' commissions); (b) an amount per policy (e.g., cost of underwriting and issuing a policy); or (c) an amount per claim paid (e.g., cost of investigating and verifying a claim). Because of the nonlevel commission rates, the per-premium types of expenses usually are larger in the first policy year, decrease during the next few policy years, and then are level for the remaining policy duration. The per-policy types of expenses are much larger in the first policy year, reflecting the cost of underwriting and issuing of the policy. The per-policy type of expense after the first policy year is relatively constant, except for the impact resulting from inflation.

*3. Persistency.* The **persistency rate** for a group of policies is defined as the ratio of the number of policies that continue coverage on a premium-due date to the number of policies that were in force as of the preceding due date. Thus, if out of 100 policies that are issued, 75 policies are in force on the first policy anniversary, the first-year annual persistency rate is 75 percent. The persistency rate usually improves with policy duration, and for some types of coverage the annual persistency rate will be 95 percent or higher after the fifth policy year. Naturally, other factors affect persistency rates. In general, persistency rates usually are higher at the older issue ages and better for the less hazardous occupations. Persistency usually is better in connection with major medical expense and disability income coverages than on basic hospital expense coverages.

Lapses are important in health insurance rating for two reasons. First, expenses are higher during the first year than in subsequent years because of the expenses of issuing the policy or certificate and because of the typically higher first-year commission rate. Also, claim rates under health insurance tend to increase as the age of the insured increases. In view of these factors, which vary by age at issue and policy duration, the premium-rate level will depend on the rate of lapse.

*4. Interest.* When a level premium is used, the insurer will have, after the first few policy years, an accumulation of funds arising from the excess of premium income over the amounts paid for claims and expenses. As in level-premium life insurance, the funds accumulated during the early policy years will be needed in the later policy years, when the premium income is not sufficient to pay claims and expenses. In computing premium rates, therefore, it is necessary to assume a suitable interest rate to reflect the investment earnings on these accumulations.

Interest rates are of less significance in the calculation of health insurance premiums than in calculating life insurance premiums. The ratio of claims to premiums under health insurance during the early policy years is substantially greater than under level-premium life insurance. Accordingly, more of the premium is used for claim payments soon after it is received by the insurance company, and it is, therefore, not available for investment and the accumulation of substantial reserves, as is the case with level-premium life insurance. It is important to consider interest in measuring the average claim cost under long-term disability income coverage. The value of the disability annuity can be significantly reduced because of the interest discount.

*5. Contingency Margins.* As with insurance premium rates, it is necessary to introduce a margin for contingencies into the premium-rate calculation. One method of doing so is to calculate a premium on the basis of most probable assumptions and then increase the premium by a percentage to provide some margin for contingencies. Another method is to introduce conservative morbidity, expense, persistency, and interest assumptions and determine a premium on that basis. Both approaches can produce approximately the same aggregate results.

***Derivation of the Gross Premium.*** Having determined for a particular type and amount of benefit all the assumptions for a given issue age, sex, occupational class, area, and so on, as to morbidity, expenses, persistency, and interest rate, the actuary estimates what the gross premium will be. This tentative gross premium is tested against realistic expense, claim, persistency, and interest assumptions over an arbitrary period, commonly 20 years. If the tentative gross premium produces a fund accumulation that is too high or too low at the end of the projected period, based on the insurer's objectives, an adjustment is made in the tentative premium to establish the appropriate gross-premium level needed to support the particular policy under consideration.[5] In the case of participating

[5]With the appropriate assumptions and parameters, it also is possible to solve the asset-share formula, with the gross premium as the unknown, and thus to derive the appropriate gross premium directly. For a detailed description of how asset shares are used to determine premium rates, see Health Insurance Association of America, *Individual Health Insurance, Part B* (New York: HIAA, 1992), Chapter 3.

policies, if it is subsequently determined that the accumulated fund at any time, together with future premiums, exceeds the amount needed to pay future claims and expenses, dividends may be paid. Similarly, if the policies are nonparticipating, the insurer will realize a profit that it is entitled to for insuring the risk. In general, the margins in the premium rates are smaller on nonparticipating policies than on participating policies. Margins should be larger on noncancelable policies because premiums cannot be increased.

Gross premiums usually are not derived for every age by the method described above but possibly for every decennial age, such as ages 20, 30, 40, 50, and 60. Premiums for intervening ages can then be derived by fitting a curve through the premiums for these ages. Another approach utilized by some insurers is to determine for each plan the net level premiums (based only on morbidity, mortality, and an interest rate) for each age and to find a loading formula, usually in the form of a constant plus a percentage of the net level premium, that will approximately reproduce the gross premiums that are obtained for decennial ages.

*Significance of Judgment.* The morbidity statistics used by an actuary assigned to compute health insurance rates for an insurer about to enter the business may come from several sources and may involve several modifications of the basic data based on experience and judgment. In view of the lack of reliable data and the multiplicity of factors producing variable cost levels, informed judgment plays an important part in health insurance rate-making. A comparison of the gross premiums charged by other insurers for similar benefits can help an insurer determine whether the premiums it contemplates charging are competitive.

## ANNUAL CLAIM COSTS

The net annual claim cost can be viewed as the product of the claim frequency and the average claim value. Since many types of benefits with varying claim values are issued in the field of health insurance, it is necessary to consider each type of benefit separately in developing the necessary formulas and in applying the appropriate morbidity data for rate-making purposes.

## ACCIDENTAL DEATH AND DISMEMBERMENT

If $r_x$ represents the accidental-death rate at age $x$, if the principal-sum death and dismemberment benefit provided is $1,000, and if $k$ equals the percentage of total claims that are dismemberment claims, then an equation that expresses the pure annual premium $P_x$ for accidental death and dismemberment is:

$$(1 - k)P_x = \$1,000r_x$$
$$P_x = \frac{\$1,000r_x}{1 - k}$$

Dismemberment claims usually represent about 10 percent of total accidental death and dismemberment claims. This can be expressed as $k = 10$ percent and

$$P_x = \frac{\$1,000r_x}{0.90}$$

Since accidental-death rates vary only slightly with age at most ages at which this benefit is issued, the same premium is usually charged at all issue ages. Another method is to charge the same premium rate for all issue ages less than age 45. For higher issue ages, premiums increase with issue age.

## MEDICAL EXPENSE BENEFITS

*Hospital Room and Board Benefits.* The average net annual claim cost varies considerably with the type of hospital benefit, the level of benefit provided, the maximum duration of hospitalization benefits, and the age and sex of the insured. Separate net annual claim costs may be developed from available statistics for males, females, and children, on the basis of $1 of hospital benefits payable for varying maximum durations. Occupational hazards and variations in claim costs by geographic area may be recognized by adjusting the net annual claim cost. This method might be used on individual health insurance. With group insurance, adjustment factors might be applied to the gross premiums.

*Hospital Miscellaneous Expense Benefits.* The hospital miscellaneous expense benefit is intended to provide coverage for hospital services not covered by the room and board benefit. Net annual claim costs may be developed from available statistics. These claim costs vary by age and sex for adults but not for children.

Hospital room and board and miscellaneous expense benefits, until recently, were determined without regard to geographic location. Since with regular hospital and surgical coverage, consumers buy a fixed amount of daily benefit, they tend to buy what is needed for their area, and geography was not considered very important. The trend today is toward using net annual claim costs for miscellaneous hospital coverages that vary by geographic location. This trend has developed since the introduction of major medical coverage, where experience studies have confirmed the necessity for such refinement to establish equity between various policyowners, both for individual and group coverages.

*Maternity Benefits.* Maternity benefits normally are dealt with separately, since they have a separate cost pattern. Under individual policies, if the maternity benefit is included as an optional benefit that may be removed by the policyowner at any time, a gross annual premium of as much as $10 per $100 of maternity benefit may be considered appropriate.

*Surgical Benefits.* The surgical benefit schedules in common use are fairly standard, and the costs of providing these standard benefits are fairly well established. In addition, the relative frequencies of certain procedures have been recorded on a basis that is unrelated to the benefit schedule. It is possible, therefore, to develop rates for varying surgical benefits quite reliably. The process includes examining enough claims to determine the expected average claim cost under the new schedule as compared with the standard schedule, and adjusting the rate used for the standard schedule by multiplying it by the ratio of the average net annual claim cost under the new schedule to the average net annual claim under the original schedule. Such cost variations for nonmaternity surgical benefits usually are determined separately for adult males, adult females, and children. The additional cost for obstetrical claims is determined separately.

*Major Medical Benefits.* The most difficult part of determining realistic rates for major medical coverage, whether on an individual or a group basis, has been the problem of adjusting available morbidity statistics, many of which have been developed from base-plan coverages, to the types of benefits provided under major medical coverage. Factors other than the age and sex of covered persons that influence the cost of benefits include:

1. The effect of inflation, increased utilization, and better technology on medical care costs.

2. The effect on benefit costs of increased earnings of the insured.

3. The effect of geographic area on benefit costs for both employee and dependent coverages.

4. The effect on benefit costs of various recognized deductibles and percentage participation (coinsurance) factors.

5. The difference in the level of cost between "per-illness" plans and "all-cause" plans.

6. The effect on benefit costs of inside limits, such as (a) a maximum hospital daily room and board benefit or (b) a maximum surgical fee schedule. These limits tend to affect the utilization of private-room facilities in the hospital as well as the amount payable for standard surgical procedures. The charges for these items may vary greatly depending on the geographical location and the nature of the individual hospital confinement or surgical procedure required.

*Cost Variations by Benefit Type.* The cost variations according to the type of benefit are illustrated in the following tables, which show annual claim costs for hospital and surgical, maternity, major medical, and disability income benefits.

Table 22-2 shows that the annual claim costs for hospital and surgical benefits generally increase by age. The annual claim costs for females are higher than for males at some ages and for certain benefit types, but lower at others. Usually, no distinction is made by sex or age in deriving the annual claim costs for children.

Table 22-3 shows annual claim costs for a $100 maternity benefit. The cost of maternity benefits decreases by age. The cost of the benefits during the first policy year will be low because of the effect of the maternity waiting period (usually ten months). The maternity claim rates at the younger ages are much greater than at the older ages, and therefore the cost of the maternity benefits is higher at the younger ages. If the maternity benefit is included on an optional basis, however, there is likely to be antiselection by the insured, and therefore the claim cost probably will not vary by the age of the insured.

Table 22-4 shows the annual claim costs for one plan of major medical benefits. The costs of the benefits increase with age, but the increase by age is much greater for major medical benefits than for the basic hospital and surgical benefits shown in Table 22-2. As indicated in the heading for Table 22-4, the costs shown are for a particular plan. They will be different for other plans, depending upon their specifications.

It must be kept in mind that studies of morbidity experience are based on experience that is already out of date, and since morbidity costs that are applicable to the future are needed, it is necessary, particularly when it comes to major medical coverages, for the actuary to use projection or trend factors.

There is a variation in the cost of medical care by geographical area. Under hospital and surgical expense coverages, benefits usually are subject to a daily hospital benefit limit and to a surgical schedule, and, therefore, there usually is no need to vary premium rates by area. In the case of major medical expense

**TABLE 22-2**    **ANNUAL CLAIM COSTS FOR CERTAIN HOSPITAL AND SURGICAL BENEFITS**

| Attained Age | $1.00 Daily Hospital Benefit, Maximum Benefit Period 90 Days | | Miscellaneous Hospital Expense Benefit, $200 Maximum Benefit | | $100 of Maximum Surgical Benefit Standard Schedule | |
|---|---|---|---|---|---|---|
| | Male | Female | Male | Female | Male | Female |
| 25–29 | $6.59 | $5.82 | $7.14 | $14.00 | $1.02 | $2.12 |
| 30–34 | 7.01 | 6.21 | 8.80 | 16.58 | 1.14 | 2.56 |
| 35–39 | 7.55 | 6.79 | 12.43 | 23.82 | 1.31 | 2.78 |
| 40–44 | 8.10 | 7.28 | 13.92 | 25.51 | 1.60 | 2.91 |
| 45–49 | 8.45 | 7.70 | 16.14 | 26.31 | 2.08 | 3.05 |
| 50–54 | 8.82 | 8.19 | 20.07 | 27.15 | 2.82 | 3.29 |
| 55–59 | 9.31 | 8.75 | 24.11 | 27.93 | 3.89 | 3.67 |
| 60–64 | 9.82 | 9.12 | 28.27 | 29.51 | 5.23 | 4.23 |
| | Child | | Child | | Child | |
| All ages | $5.37 | | $9.01 | | $0.99 | |

*Source: Transactions of the Society of Actuaries—1983 Reports.*

| TABLE 22-3 | ANNUAL CLAIM COST FOR $100 MATERNITY BENEFIT | |
|---|---|---|

| Attained Age | Annual Claim Costs |
|---|---|
| 20–24 | $23.50 |
| 25–29 | 18.30 |
| 30–34 | 8.70 |
| 35–39 | 3.00 |
| 40–44 | 0.70 |
| 45–49 | 0.10 |

*Source: Transactions of the Society of Actuaries—1979 Reports.*

coverages, however, the cost of the benefits will be higher in high-cost areas. To a certain extent, this can be controlled by using so-called inside limits for room and board benefits, and by using a surgical schedule. If inside limits are not used, premium rates often are varied by geographical area. For a major medical policy providing comprehensive medical expense benefits, with no inside limits, the cost of the benefits in the highest-cost areas of the United States is about three times higher than in the lowest-cost areas.

## DISABILITY INCOME BENEFITS

The annual claim costs for a disability income benefit vary significantly by occupational class. Table 22-5 shows the annual claim costs for one particular disability income plan. The costs vary according to age, sex, occupational class, elimination period, and maximum duration of benefits. If the elimination period and maximum duration of benefits are different for sickness benefits than for accident benefits, it is necessary to develop separate costs for accident and for

| TABLE 22-4 | ANNUAL CLAIM COSTS—MAJOR MEDICAL EXPENSE BENEFITS ($500 DEDUCTIBLE AMOUNT, $10,000 MAXIMUM AMOUNT, 75% COINSURANCE, NO HOSPITAL ROOM AND BOARD LIMIT, CALENDAR DURATION 3 AND LATER) | |
|---|---|---|

| Attained Age | Annual Claim Costs | | |
|---|---|---|---|
| | Male | Female | Child (All Ages) |
| 35–39 | $ 86.82 | $ 71.59 | $27.42 |
| 40–45 | 94.09 | 113.54 | |
| 45–49 | 116.85 | 152.16 | |
| 50–54 | 165.37 | 163.00 | |
| 55–59 | 220.94 | 190.05 | |
| 60–64 | 272.18 | 249.06 | |
| 65–69 | 303.86 | 326.74 | |

*Source: Transactions of the Society of Actuaries—1979 Reports.*

| TABLE 22-5 | ANNUAL CLAIM COSTS PER $100 OF MONTHLY DISABILITY INCOME BENEFIT (MAXIMUM BENEFIT PERIOD, ONE YEAR; SEVEN-DAY ELIMINATION PERIOD) |
|---|---|

| Attained Age | Annual Claim Costs | | |
|---|---|---|---|
| | Accident | Sickness | Accident and Sickness |
| *Male—Occupation Group I* | | | |
| Under 30 | $13.12 | $4.31 | $17.43 |
| 30–39 | 6.48 | 10.65 | 17.13 |
| 40–49 | 7.60 | 11.84 | 19.44 |
| 50–59 | 6.69 | 22.04 | 28.73 |
| 60–69 | 5.17 | 35.47 | 40.64 |
| *Male—Occupation Group II* | | | |
| Under 30 | $8.89 | $5.69 | $14.58 |
| 30–39 | 11.59 | 9.55 | 21.14 |
| 40–49 | 11.86 | 15.18 | 27.04 |
| 50–59 | 11.33 | 30.27 | 41.60 |
| 60–69 | 9.24 | 46.81 | 56.05 |
| *Female—Occupation Group I* | | | |
| Under 30 | $ 1.64 | $ 9.00 | $10.64 |
| 30–39 | 4.26 | 12.30 | 16.56 |
| 40–49 | 6.76 | 14.80 | 21.56 |
| 50–59 | 6.74 | 18.52 | 25.26 |
| 60–69 | 12.31 | 24.88 | 37.19 |

*Source: Transactions of the Society of Actuaries—1984 Reports.*

sickness. Occupation Group I shown in the table covers white-collar types of occupation classes, and Occupation Group II covers blue-collar types of occupation classes.

## PREMIUM-RATE VARIABLES

The inability to work because of accident or sickness is subjective in nature and involves an attitude as well as a physical or mental impairment. Since disability is at least partially a state of mind, experience is subject to many factors, including the level of unemployment, the attitude of insurers, individuals' work ethics and their attitudes toward retirement, and the attitudes of physicians who certify disability. In an attempt to cope with these problems, insurers underwrite health insurance coverage carefully and use several risk classification factors, as discussed below.

## AGE AND SEX CLASSIFICATIONS

Age is of major importance in almost all forms of health coverage, as previously discussed. The premium rates for females for hospital, surgical, and medical expense benefits and disability income benefits are higher than for males, at the younger ages. With increased age, however, the costs become lower for females. For group insurance—but not for individual insurance—the relationship also varies between employed females and dependent females. Female group rates may be calculated as a percentage increase over the male rate or they may be based on an analysis of actual experience of female lives.

Disability income benefits usually are issued to regularly employed persons only. The rates for females generally range from 1 1/2 to 2 times the male rate.

## OCCUPATIONAL CLASSIFICATIONS

Most hospital and surgical plans do not pay benefits for work-related illness or injury that would be payable under workers' compensation. Since this exclusion eliminates much of the adverse effect of hazardous occupations, it is customary to charge the same premium for hospital and surgical benefits regardless of occupation. Industry loadings are, however, used for group insurance.

Accidental death and dismemberment benefits and disability income benefits may be issued on an occupational basis. In these cases, it is customary to subdivide the various occupations into at least three classes, with appropriate extra premiums depending on the degree of extra morbidity expected. Some occupations may be eliminated entirely because of an extreme occupational hazard.

## GEOGRAPHICAL AREA CLASSIFICATIONS

Within the United States, the location of the insured individual is rarely a factor for determining premium rates for disability income or accidental-death insurance. The indications are, however, that there are cost variations by area on disability income. Therefore the actuary often will determine whether the variations are significant enough to introduce them into the premium structure. Geography is more significant in major medical insurance costs mainly because of wide variations in hospital rates and other medical care expenditures. Variations in claim frequency also occur in some areas.

## ELIMINATION PERIODS

The elimination of income benefits for varying periods (such as 7, 14, 30, 60, 90, 120, 180, or 365 days) is a method used to provide benefits that suit the various income-replacement needs of insureds in the event of disability. Many persons have underlying employer-provided or other disability plans that cover the first several weeks of disability. The cost of benefits decreases as the elimination period increases.

If a continuance table is used for disability income benefits, it is easy to make the necessary adjustments in rates for various elimination periods. Ideally, however, there should be a continuance table for each elimination period, since the experience for policies with different elimination periods differs.

Through the use of a deductible, major medical policies often provide for the elimination of the first dollars of hospital or medical expenses incurred. The amount of the deductible depends on the type of plan being offered. In group insurance, major medical coverage often provides for payment of all covered physician's hospital charges (usually at semiprivate room rate) at a rate of 80 percent, but with a maximum "out-of-pocket cap" of $1,000 on the insured's payment. After the insured has incurred the out-of-pocket expenses, the insurer pays 100 percent of all further covered expenses. Benefits would be subject to a deductible of $50 to $250 or more. It is customary to provide a fixed maximum benefit of $500,000, $1,000,000 or more, except for certain inside limits. A few insurers issue comprehensive major medical benefits on individual policies with benefits similar to those described above for group insurance, although, in general, benefits provided under individual policies tend to be less liberal than those provided under group plans.

## DEPENDENT CLASSIFICATIONS

For individual insurance, it is customary to charge a rate for each child rather than a rate for all children, as is done in group insurance.[6] The premium for children varies by type of plan, but not by age or sex. The hospital stay usually is short for most surgical procedures performed on children; therefore, the level of miscellaneous benefits provided by the plan affects the claim cost most dramatically and may vary the relationship between the cost of coverage for adults and for children.

The premium rate for dependent coverage under group insurance depends on the age of the employee and may or may not be independent of industry, depending upon the insurer. For group coverages, as opposed to individual coverage, there is no additional charge for children after the first charge, whether the plan is a basic hospital and surgical or major medical one. Although charging for each additional child would produce greater equity, it complicates administrative procedures. Since a portion of the premium normally is paid by the employer, the insured employees still receive equitable treatment under a properly designed group plan covering their dependents.

---

[6]In major medical coverage, it is feasible to use an all-children rate on individual insurance because of the cost-reduction effect of a large deductible. This effect is lacking in basic individual coverages, and, hence, a per-child rate usually is considered necessary.

## OTHER PREMIUM CLASSIFICATIONS

Smokers exhibit higher morbidity experience than nonsmokers. As a result, many insurers have adopted premium differentials for smokers and nonsmokers. The differential ranges from 6 to 10 percent.

Increasingly, insurers issue individual noncancelable disability income or guaranteed-renewable medical expense policies to impaired risks, subject to the payment of an extra premium. Numerical morbidity ratings have been established for each insurable impairment, and these vary from approximately 125 percent to 300 percent. Two ratings are required for each impairment—one for accident-only policies and another for accident and sickness, including hospital and surgical and major medical coverage. Some impairments are standard for accident coverage only, but are rated for accident and sickness coverage.

Some relatively undesirable hospital and surgical risks can be accepted for disability income coverage if there is, say, at least a 30-day elimination period. On the other hand, there are some poor disability income risks who are acceptable hospital risks.

## HEALTH INSURANCE RESERVES AND OTHER LIABILITIES

In health insurance, as in life insurance, it is important that proper provision be made in the insurer liabilities for all the obligations assumed by the insurer under its contracts, irrespective of whether it is required by law. Liability accounts are established for present or future claims against the insurer's assets that must come from the premiums already received. **Reserve** is the term used to refer to the amount of the insurer's liability to fulfill future contingencies and unpaid liabilities already incurred.

Health insurance reserves and other liabilities may be broadly classified as follows:

1. **Policy reserves** refer to the amounts necessary for the fulfillment of contract obligations as to future claims, which include pro-rata unearned premium reserves and additional reserves for level-premium policies.

2. **Claim reserves and liabilities** include the amounts necessary to cover payments on claims already incurred.

3. **Expense liabilities** include the amounts necessary to pay expenses and taxes under obligations incurred by the insurer from operations prior to the annual statement date.

Table 22-6 shows a hypothetical insurer statement illustrating the various health insurance reserves and liabilities discussed below.[7]

---

[7]In the Life Insurance Company Annual Statement Form, provision is made for a breakdown of health insurance reserves in Exhibit 9, and liability for policy and contract claims in Exhibit 11 (see Chap. 32).

**TABLE 22-6**      **XYZ INSURANCE COMPANY ANNUAL STATE-MENT OF FINANCIAL CONDITION, DECEMBER 31, 19XX**

| | |
|---|---:|
| Assets: | |
| Cash | $  170,000 |
| Bonds | 675,000 |
| Stocks | |
|     Preferred | 75,000 |
|     Common | 25,000 |
| Real estate owned | 40,000 |
| First-mortgage loans | 316,000 |
| Premiums due and unpaid | 43,000 |
|     Total assets | $1,344,000 |
| Liabilities, capital, and surplus: | |
| Unearned premium reserve | $  320,000 |
| Net-level-premium reserves | |
|     (additional reserve for | |
|     noncancelable policies) | 35,000 |
| Premiums paid in advance | 40,000 |
| Liability for claims in course of settlement | 140,000 |
| Liability for claims incurred | |
|     but unreported | 50,000 |
| Present value of future amounts | |
|     due on claims | 110,000 |
| Reserve for future contingent benefits | 20,000 |
| Liability for dividends declared | 20,000 |
| Liability for expenses and taxes due | |
|     and accrued | 85,000 |
| Asset valuation reserve | 36,000 |
| Capital | 250,000 |
| Unassigned surplus | 238,000 |
|     Total liabilities, capital, and surplus | $1,344,000 |

## POLICY RESERVES

*Unearned Premium Reserves.* In determining the amount of the unearned premium reserve to be included in the annual statement, the pro-rata portion of the full gross premium from the statement date to the end of the period for which premiums have been paid on the policy is required to be set up as a reserve, regardless of the renewal provisions of the policy. In establishing the appropriate amount, approximation methods often are used. It is often assumed that premium-due dates are distributed uniformly over the year so that, on the average, one-half of the total premiums in force, regardless of the mode of premium payment, are unearned as of the end of the year. This normally is the largest item among the policy reserves, unless the insurer has large amounts of noncancelable or guaranteed-renewable business.

The unearned gross-premium reserve automatically provides a reserve allowance for the payment of expenses that will be incurred after the statement date, as well as for the benefit payments that will be incurred and must be paid from premiums already received. Premiums paid on or before the statement date but due after the statement date are classified separately as premiums paid in advance.[8]

*Additional Reserves for Noncancelable and Guaranteed-Renewable Policies*. Noncancelable and guaranteed-renewable health insurance policies usually provide coverage to a specified age, such as 60 or 65, and often are issued on the basis of level premiums payable each year after the date of issue. Because of increasing morbidity costs as age increases and the use of a level premium, excess funds are accumulated in the early years (measured by the reserve liability). These funds eventually are consumed through increased claim costs by the expiration date of the benefits, in much the same manner as reserves on term-to-age-65 life insurance policies build in the early years and decrease to zero at age 65. As in life insurance, the so-called active life reserve, calculated prospectively, is equal to the difference between the present value of future benefits and the present value of future premiums.

The *1985 Commissioners Disability Tables,* adopted by the National Association of Insurance Commissioners in 1985, are the minimum standard for the valuation of disability income benefits due to accident and sickness for policies issued on or after January 1, 1987. For accidental-death benefits, the minimum standard is the *1959 Accidental Death Benefit Table*.

As in the case of life insurance, to establish a minimum standard for reserves, state regulatory authorities specify particular morbidity and mortality tables and a maximum rate of interest. For health insurance benefits, insurers are permitted to use as an interest assumption the maximum rate currently permitted by law for the valuation of new life contracts, and for mortality, any table permitted by law in the valuation of currently issued life insurance. Insurers may use a net-level or a one- or two-year preliminary-term method of valuation for active-life reserves. Although the additional reserve is required only on noncancelable or guaranteed-renewable policies or on policies in which the right of nonrenewal is limited, the need for this reserve exists on any level-premium type of coverage in which the incidence of cost increases with advancing age.

## Claim Reserves

There are many acceptable methods of estimating the insurer's liability for outstanding claims that have not been paid in full on the annual statement preparation date. Any method selected to determine the amount of outstanding claim liability should be one that assures adequacy and fairly reflects the actual liability, which will later be developed, after sufficient time has passed to permit the insurer to tabulate the actual results that occur subsequent to the statement date.

---

[8]Advance premiums are not a part of the unearned premium reserve but appear as a separate liability, because the premiums paid are not yet due. The insured may change his or her mind and request the return of the premiums, and therefore sound accounting practice indicates separate treatment.

*Present Value of Amounts Not Yet Due on Claims*. Because of the problem of determining the reserve liability for disabled lives, disability income benefits provide the best example of the complicated nature of health claim-liability items. As the rate of recovery decreases with increasing duration of disability, the value of the claim annuity for a long-duration benefit period normally increases, until the value of the claim annuity reaches a peak, and then it gradually decreases to the end of the period for which benefits are payable. In estimating this liability item as of the valuation date, it is, therefore, desirable to show for each claim the age at date of disability, the number of months or years the claimant has been disabled, and the number of years of benefit remaining, in order to be able to apply the appropriate claim annuity factor to the monthly benefit amount being provided. If the monthly income is not payable for more than one year, the claim annuity valuation factors may be based on an average age and on average durations that vary with the type of benefit being considered.

Hospital, surgical, and medical expense benefits are usually settled in a single sum, and it is not practical to obtain the claim liability for each claim. Instead, by making a reconciliation of previous years' claims, one can develop a factor such that by applying the factor to the cash claims payable during the calendar year, a reasonable estimate can be made of the claim liability at the end of the year.

*Claims Due and Unpaid*. This item normally is small or nonexistent for health insurance claims. Most insurers pay amounts due on a claim as soon as the amount can be determined and the claim approved.

*Claims in the Course of Settlement*. The liability shown for this item is based on claims on which notice of claim has been received, but on which all the proofs of loss or other documentation have not been received, so that the claim cannot be approved on the statement date. Some insurers examine each claim individually and prepare a list showing each item involved. Others use approximate methods. One method is to add the total amount of outstanding claims and apply to it a factor obtained from the experience on previous valuation dates. Another method is to analyze a sample of claims and determine a percentage factor that is applied to the total liability for claims, including both accrued and unaccrued amounts.

*Claims Incurred but Not Reported*. Experience will show that many claims that were actually incurred prior to the statement date are paid after that date each year, because the insurer had no knowledge of the claim until after the statement date. It is usual to tabulate these claims each year and relate the amount to some base, such as volume of business in force or earned premiums on the type of coverage involved. The total liability for incurred but unreported claims is divided into two parts: accrued and contingent. The accrued liability is reported as "incurred but unreported," as part of the policy claim liability. The contingent liability accruing after the valuation date is included under the heading of "Present Value of Amounts Not Yet Due on Claims."

## LIABILITY FOR EXPENSES

It is necessary to provide in insurer liabilities a reasonable estimate of the claim expenses that will be paid on unpaid losses incurred prior to the statement date. This liability may be computed as a cost per claim, as a percent of the liabilities for claims incurred, or as a combination of both. In major medical coverage, where the cost of settling claims may be much higher per claim than under base-plan coverage, it usually is necessary to develop separate factors for each type of coverage, based on actual cost studies.

Other than claim expenses, the reserve for expenses may be accounted for in the unearned gross-premium reserve, or, if this reserve is not adequate, an additional amount may be established in the expense liability. This situation might occur during the first year if unpaid commissions or other expenses end up being greater than the loading provided in that year's premium calculation.

## GROUP RESERVES AND LIABILITIES

An insurer's liabilities under group health contracts create the need for the same types of policy and claim reserves as for individual health insurance contracts. The amounts of the reserves, however, usually are smaller. In general, premiums are paid monthly under group health contracts, and the insurer reserves the right to adjust premium rates on any policy anniversary. Nevertheless, it is important to keep the level of premiums and, therefore, the insured's costs on a stable basis.

## OTHER RESERVES AND LIABILITIES

On the statement date, participating health insurance policies will have dividends declared that will not be payable until after the statement date. This **liability for dividend payable** should be set up as a liability on the statement date.

**Contingency reserves**, which are not liabilities, are sometimes established on a voluntary basis to allow for the possibility of an upward trend in claim costs or an unusual occurrence. In state disability plans, these reserves may be established to offset decreasing premiums, without a corresponding decrease in liability. This treatment may be necessary because premiums are paid on current wages while benefits depend on wages during a base period. Some states require the accumulation of a contingency reserve for group health business.

## SURPLUS DISTRIBUTION

Individual health insurance policies are issued on both a nonparticipating and participating basis. Overall experience (except for some disability income policies) has not been favorable, and therefore dividends have either not been payable or the amount payable has been small. Group health insurance policies are virtually always participating through a variety of experience-rating devices. The concepts underlying both dividends and experience rating are similar, but may differ somewhat in basic philosophy. In any case, the process should take into consideration the surplus position of the policyowner or class, the extent to which losses are pooled (averaged) among cases, the expenses incurred as between policyowners or classes, and the total surplus available for distribution.

## INDIVIDUAL POLICIES

In the case of individual policies, funds are accumulated separately for each class of policy (sometimes referred to as policy form). In this way, the amount of surplus accumulated for any dividend class is ascertainable. The dividend formula usually is simple, taking into account only broad equities. For example, for policies that have been in force for, say three years, a specified percentage of the premiums (varied in some insurers by duration) may be returned as a dividend. In connection with dividends, the asset-share calculation is used principally as a test of the adequacy of the accumulation for any dividend class. As pointed out earlier, the adequacy of the insurer's contingency reserve for this type of business will affect the proportion of current earnings that is added to the contingency reserve for a particular class of policies.

## GROUP POLICIES

An approach similar to that used for individual classes is used in dealing with small group cases. Groups are classified, and surplus distribution is determined through the use of fund accounts for each class of groups. Again, only a limited number of variables is considered. In small cases, morbidity experience must be averaged, because of the low credibility of the individual case's experience. Expenses are relatively high, but because of the smaller-size discounts granted these cases, they may develop reasonable dividend distributions over a period of time.

For the larger group health cases, it is practicable to develop the appropriate dividend or premium refund through the use of fund accounts. As in the case of life insurance, this involves the accumulation from date of issue of the premiums paid, increased in some cases by interest earnings. From this amount, losses incurred, accumulated expenses incurred directly or allocated to the case, and allowances for contingencies and profit are deducted. From this net accumulation, total dividends paid previously are deducted, and the result is the surplus amount available for distribution.

The chief problems in large group cases involve the development of unit expense charges for indirect expense items, the determination of the period of amortization of acquisition expenses, and the individual-case contribution to contingencies or profits. In all but the largest cases, it is necessary to establish a limit on the maximum level of losses considered in the experience-rating formula. This usually is achieved by imposing a limit on an aggregate basis or, in some cases, an aggregate limit and a maximum for a single claim during a given experience period.

In all cases, the experience-rating formula considers (1) premiums paid, (2) incurred losses (modified by loss limits and credibility), (3) direct and allocated expenses, and (4) allowances for contingencies and profits.

# Chapter 23

# LIFE AND HEALTH
# INSURANCE UNDERWRITING: I

## THE PURPOSE OF UNDERWRITING

In any insurance plan, each insured person contributes to a common fund, from which amounts are paid to or on behalf of the unfortunate ones who suffer covered losses. To maintain equity among different insured classes, each insured should contribute according to the expected loss probabilities that he or she transfers to the common fund. If one person is allowed to pay less than his or her fair share, it necessitates an overcharge against other persons. In each instance, therefore, the insurance company should estimate the expected loss exposure presented to it by the insured and charge a premium for it commensurate with that risk. This can be accomplished only with careful selection and classification of risks.

In any group of individuals of the same age, some are near death, some have impaired health, some are exposed to unusual risks of death or ill health because of occupation or other activity, the great majority are in good health, and a few are free of even the slightest impairment. Knowledge and understanding of the way the various factors influence mortality and morbidity enable the company to classify insureds into groups that will give relative mortality and morbidity rates close to those that are anticipated.[1] The groups subject to a higher-than-average mortality are said to be substandard.

Two views of anticipated relative mortality are depicted in Figures 23-1 and 23-2. Both figures show insurers' perceptions of distribution of relative mortality for a

[1] Pearce Shephard and Andrew C. Webster, *Selection of Risks* (Chicago: The Society of Actuaries, 1957), p. 2.

**FIGURE 23-1**

**ANTICIPATED MORTALITY BASED ON RISK CHARACTERISTICS *EXCLUDING SMOKING* REPRESENTED IN A RANDOMLY SELECTED GROUP OF THE SAME AGE AND SEX, WITH 100 PERCENT REPRESENTING AVERAGE MORTALITY FOR GROUP**

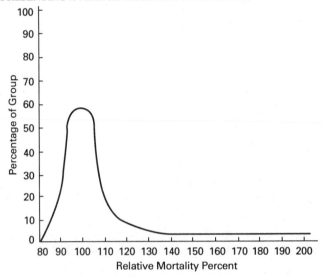

randomly selected group of persons of the same age and sex. In each case, 100 percent represents average mortality for the group.

Figure 23-1 gives a view of insurers' anticipated mortality as implicit in their traditional pricing structure and underwriting practices. No segregation is made in pricing or underwriting between persons who smoke cigarettes and those who do not smoke.

Figure 23-2, on the other hand, depicts a more contemporary view of insurers' anticipated relative mortality as made implicit in their pricing and underwriting. In this case, the classification scheme employed recognizes differences in anticipated mortality between smokers and nonsmokers.

The figures portray the wide range of anticipated future mortality for a group of persons. Clearly, all should not be offered insurance on the same terms. Life insurance companies must establish ranges of mortality (and morbidity) expectations within which proposed insureds would be regarded as average, and hence insurable at standard premium rates, or, conversely, the limits beyond which they would be considered substandard and subject to higher rates or policy restrictions or denied insurance altogether.

The development of the bimodal distribution in current experience as shown in Figure 23-2 is intended to reflect current practice as it relates to the need for two "standard" classifications. Those who smoke exhibit higher mortality, age by age, than those who do not smoke. As the body of mortality experience has developed, more and more companies have begun implementing two standard classifications, one for smokers and one for nonsmokers (see below). Some

**FIGURE 23-2**

**ANTICIPATED MORTALITY BASED ON RISK CHARACTERISTICS *INCLUDING SMOKING* REPRESENTED IN A RANDOMLY SELECTED GROUP OF THE SAME AGE AND SEX, WITH 100 PERCENT REPRESENTING AVERAGE MORTALITY FOR GROUP**

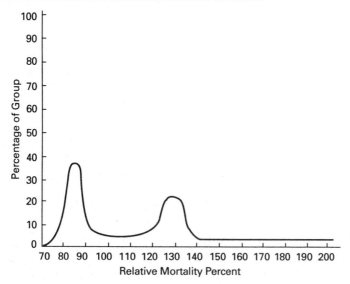

companies have established "super standard" or preferred classifications that permit them to charge rates based on better-than-average anticipated mortality. In addition to establishing the limits for the various classes of risk, the company must adopt procedures that permit proposed insureds to be properly classified.

The process is complicated by the fact that persons applying for life insurance do not constitute a randomly selected group as depicted in Figure 23-1. The decision by individuals to apply for insurance may be based on their knowing or suspecting more about their health than the company does. It is only natural for individuals to "decide" on the basis that is most favorable to themselves. This tendency, known as **adverse selection** or **selection against the company,** appears whenever an individual has freedom to buy or not to buy, to choose the amount or plan of insurance, and to persist or to discontinue as an insured. A major purpose of underwriting is to protect the company against such adverse selection. More broadly stated, the purpose of underwriting is to ensure that insurance is issued on such terms and conditions and at such a premium as to reflect accurately the degree of risk presented to the insurer.

The term underwriting, commonly used throughout the insurance business, implicitly incorporates two essential elements: (1) selection and (2) classification. **Selection** is the process whereby an insurer evaluates individual applications for insurance to determine the degree of risk represented by the proposed insured. **Classification** is the process of assigning a insured to a group of individuals of approximately the same expected loss probabilities. The principles and factors underlying a given company's underwriting philosophy are outlined in the following section.

## UNDERWRITING PHILOSOPHY

Certain fundamental principles and factors govern sound selection and classification procedures. Some are mutually inconsistent, but they must be considered in the formulation of an underwriting philosophy. The life insurance company's philosophy directly reflects the resultant balance among these opposing principles and considerations.

## THE STANDARD GROUP—NONSMOKERS AND SMOKERS

An accepted principle is that the standard group—those regarded as average and insurable at standard rates—should be broad enough to encompass a great percentage of insureds. The justification for this principle lies in the desire to have a group large enough to assure stable, predictable mortality (morbidity) experience and to minimize the administrative costs of having multiple classes. Evidence of this in practice is the fact that currently 93 percent of the applications for ordinary insurance are accepted at standard rates.[2]

Overexacting standards and procedures could result in an excessive number of rejections and rated cases. This could undermine the morale of salespersons, tend to increase the cost of operation, and involve public relations considerations. Appraisal of an individual's expected mortality or morbidity cannot be exact in any case. Apart from the practical considerations mentioned, the broader the base of standard risks, the more stable will be the mortality or morbidity experience of the standard group. The extension of this principle is limited by considerations of equity and competition.

While an important underwriting objective is to have the majority of insureds fall within the standard group, change is continuing to cause a split of the standard group into two or more classes, as illustrated in Figure 23-2. This split has been caused by a recognition within many companies' pricing structures and underwriting procedures of the higher mortality of smokers. This has led, in effect, to the establishment of two (and in some cases more than two) standard classes.

In practice, companies have reflected this mortality differential through offering lower premiums to the better risks—that is, non–cigarette smokers. Some companies offer nonsmokers with additional favorable risk characteristics (e.g., a favorable cardiovascular risk profile) an additional discount.

---

[2]Of the remaining 7 percent, only 3 percent are declined, with the remaining 4 percent being offered substandard rates. See *1992 Life Insurance Fact Book* (Washington, D.C.: American Council of Life Insurance, 1992), p. 117.

## THE SUBSTANDARD GROUPS

The substandard classes or gradations of risk to be recognized in a company's premium-rate structure are a function of the balance between the need, on the one hand, (1) to minimize the number of classifications for the purposes of stability in mortality and morbidity experience and administrative efficiencies and, on the other, (2) to maximize the number of classifications to avoid competitive disadvantages and to achieve reasonable equity. Naturally, the size of the company, marketing objectives, product type, and other company policies are involved in the decision to provide substandard insurance and in the classifications to be established. (This question is addressed more fully in Chapter 24.) When a given risk factor leads to a significantly large substandard group (e.g., smokers), creation of two standard classifications is considered desirable by many companies.

## BALANCE WITHIN EACH CLASS

Having defined its risk classifications, a company should maintain a reasonable balance among the insureds accepted in each classification. If the overall mortality experience within each classification is to approximate the predicted average for the group, every insured within that class whose mortality experience is expected to be higher than average must be offset by one whose experience is expected to be lower than average.

Maintaining the proper balance within a standard classification is a difficult task. In considering a borderline application, a home office underwriter is tempted, because of agency pressures, desire for business, and human nature, to approve the application for the lowest possible rating. This is evidenced by the fact that studies consistently show that the distribution of risks within each substandard classification is skewed toward the top limit of the class. This fact is considered, of course, in establishing the premium rate for the class, but it demonstrates the human element in the underwriting process.

## EMPHASIS ON THE MAJOR RISKS

The underwriting process is concerned primarily with significant risk exposures that are not common to all persons seeking insurance. Risk exposures that are common to the applying group operate to increase the mortality among all lives and are reflected in the general mortality levels assumed.

Airline travel is so widespread that the accidental deaths or disabilities that result are regarded as a part of the general hazards of life and provided for in the general mortality levels underlying the rate structures. Relatively fewer persons, however, are private airplane pilots, and it is the additional air time of engaging in piloting a private plane that would be of concern from an underwriting standpoint. Underwriters do ignore factors that produce some extra mortality, but none of these (e.g., driving, moderate overweight, or moderately elevated blood pressure) produce sufficient extra mortality to be rated substandard. These same factors, however, cannot be ignored if the problem is severe (poor driving record, gross overweight, or significantly elevated blood pressure). In sum, the process of underwriting constantly strives to ascertain significant risk factors that set a given proposed insured apart from the average member of a group. Where a given risk factor (e.g., smoking) is identified as setting a substantial proportion of the group apart from other members of the group, a separate standard classification often is indicated.[3]

## EQUITY AMONG INSUREDS

The manner in which insureds are rated must recognize the principle of equity. Some grouping of insureds is desirable in order to have a reasonable volume of experience within a given classification and because of expense considerations. On the other hand, to be satisfactory to the proposed insured and the company, the spread between the worst and best risks within a classification should not be so broad as to produce significant inequity or hinder a company in competition. In practice, the width of rating classes tends to vary directly with the degree of substandard rating, with which, in turn, the accuracy of predicted extra mortality also varies. Hence, the width of class is to some extent a function of the dependability of the available mortality data on impaired lives. Differences between companies, in practice, are the result of different judgments as to what is the best overall policy.

Risk classification is a process of differentiating, or discriminating, among groups of individuals so that each insured contributes in proportion to the anticipated (expected) loss exposure that he or she brings to the group. Equity calls for equivalent treatment (classification) of equivalent risks. This requires not only that equal classes be treated equally but also that unequal classes not be treated equally.[4]

Historically, the practice of charging individuals applying for life insurance according to their relative risks of dying or becoming disabled has been viewed as fair by a majority of the public. In recent years, however, public acceptance of the fairness of risk classification has been both variable and declining. A recent survey showed that while 47 percent of those surveyed believe it is fair to price life insurance according to one's risk of dying, fully 39 percent viewed it as unfair.[5]

---

[3]Separate standard classifications within one company are not new. Companies writing industrial and ordinary insurance have traditionally used different standard pricing that reflects the significant differences in anticipated mortality between the two life and health insurance markets. Similarly, except where legislation prohibits differentiation in pricing on the basis of sex, there are, in effect, two standard classes based on this risk factor.

[4]*Griggs vs. Duke Power Co.*, 401 U.S. 424 (1971).

[5]*MAP 1992* (Washington, D.C.: American Council of Life Insurance, 1992), p. 55.

**FIGURE 23-3**

**PROPORTION OF RESPONDENTS INDICATING USE OF FACTOR AS BEING FAIR**

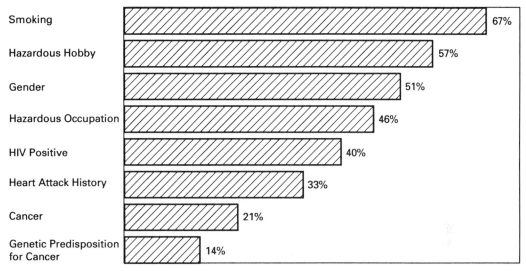

*Source:* ACLI, *Map 1990.*

Recent studies of public attitudes toward risk classification show that the public tends to accept as fair, risk factors over which individuals have some degree of choice (e.g., hazardous hobbies or smoking), and tends to perceive as unfair risk factors over which they have no real control as an individual (e.g., heart attack history or cancer). Figure 23-3 presents a summary of the *MAP 1990* survey findings of public support for the use of several specific risk classification guidelines by life insurance companies.[6]

In contrast with social insurance, risk classification is a fundamental principle of private insurance. In the case of social insurance, in which coverage and participation are mandatory, adverse selection is not a problem and the issue of individual equity is far less important. With private insurance, however, some adverse selection is inevitable, and reasonable individual equity is essential to the successful operation of the insurance mechanism. Risk classification is the *sine qua non* of private insurance. Without it, the voluntary private insurance market as we know it today could not function.

## RECOGNITION OF UNDERLYING MORTALITY ASSUMPTIONS

Risk classification reflects the mortality levels assumed in determining the premium rate applied. If the proposed insured is to be considered at standard rates, the expected mortality experience must be comparable to that used in determining these rates.

[6]*MAP 1990.*

In practice, some companies (especially large ones) continually study their mortality experience and evaluate their classification rules. They review their experience on lives accepted as standard and compare their experience on impaired lives with the standard experience. Based on this study and analysis, each company adjusts its classification rules where indicated. The basic objective is to assure reasonable homogeneity within a given classification.

Since insured experience is made up of selected lives, the underwriting that is to be exercised in the future should at least be as effective as that used in the past, if mortality is to be similar to that provided for in the premium rate structure. A situation of generally improving mortality, however, might permit acceptance of some impaired lives without exceeding the mortality assumed in the premium calculations. Such action, however, would adversely affect the company's competitive position if other companies continued to accept only standard risks at their standard rates.

## FACTORS AFFECTING THE RISK

In deciding whether to issue life insurance (selection), and if so, on what terms and conditions and at what price (classification), life insurance companies examine several factors to ensure that policyowners are treated equitably and to guard against them being charged either excessive or inadequate rates for the insurance coverage. Underwriting, therefore, is an essential link through which the three objectives of rate-making—that rates be adequate, equitable, and not excessive—are obtained. This section reviews the chief factors examined by life insurers in underwriting life insurance and health insurance.

### THE LIFE INSURANCE RISK

*Age.* Expected future mortality is highly correlated with age. The older a person, other things being the same, the greater the likelihood of death.[7] Age, therefore, is a key factor in determining the rate an individual is to be charged for life insurance. Age is rarely a selection factor, however, except for individuals who are of advanced age or, with some types of insurance, very young. Some insurers may use age alone to deny some types of insurance to older persons (e.g., those who are past age 75). This may occur because the insurer believes its statistical base to be too small to permit proper rating, because the insurer has insufficient confidence in its underwriting process for advanced ages, or because the insurer believes the premium rate it would be required to charge is too high for marketing purposes.

---

[7] In fact, chronological age is a proxy for biological age. Medical science does not as yet possess sufficiently accurate, low cost means of determining one's biological age so one's chronological age is used as a convenient substitute.

The applicant is not required to furnish proof of age at the time he or she applies for insurance, since (1) such a requirement could cause delay, (2) few persons misstate their age, (3) proof is usually easily obtained if needed, and (4) the misstatement of age clause handles those situations where a problem arises.[8]  In the case of an immediate annuity, under which it would be impractical to adjust the amount of the benefits if a misstatement of age is discovered at the time of the annuitant's death, proof of age usually is required at the time of annuity purchase.

*Sex.* The gender of proposed insureds, like their age, is rarely used as a selection factor but it is routinely used as a classification (rate-setting) factor with respect to individual life insurance. Yearly probabilities of death of females are less than the yearly probabilities of death of similarly situated males. As a result, the majority of insurers in most states charge lower life insurance premium rates and higher annuity rates for females than for males. This was not always true: several decades ago insurers charged men and women the same rates because of "the frailty of women and the hazards of childbirth." Increasingly accurate statistics, competition, and a widening mortality gap between the two sexes caused insurers to alter this practice.

While mortality statistics clearly show a difference in death rates between men and women and, therefore, can be used *statistically* to justify charging different rates for men and women, other important considerations have arisen. The question  now being debated is:  Is it *socially* acceptable to charge men and women different rates for life insurance (and annuities)?  The state of Montana concluded that it is not socially acceptable and banned the use of gender as a rating factor. Legislation has been introduced in other states to accomplish the same objective, although to date no other state has followed Montana's lead. The issue is one of statistical relevance versus social policy.[9]

*Medical Aspects.* (1) *Physical Condition.* The physical condition of a proposed insured is of basic significance in underwriting. One of the determinants of physical condition is build.[10]  Build includes height, weight, and distribution of the weight. Experience has shown that overweight increases the likelihood of death at all ages. While moderate overweight may not, in and of itself, have a ratable effect, it can magnify the significance of other physical ailments, such as cardiac conditions.

[8]See Chap. 8.

[9]See Mary W. Gray, "The Case for Nondiscrimination in Insurance," *Journal of Insurance Regulation*, Vol. 2 (Sept. 1983), pp. 3–10, and Barbara J. Lautzenheiser, Jo Conway Roberts, and Marvis A. Walters, "H.R.100/S.372:  Are They Necessary?" ibid, pp. 11-19. See also Patricia L. Scahill, "Actuarial Aspects of Sex Discrimination," *SOA Part 9 Study Note* (Itasca, Ill.:  Society of Actuaries, 1984).

[10]The first comprehensive statistical study of the relationship between build and mortality covered the experience on policies issued by the principal companies from 1885 through 1908 and was published in 1913 as the *Medico-Actuarial Mortality Investigation*. The most recent investigation undertaken by the Society of Actuaries and the Association of Life Insurance Medical Directors of America encompassed the ordinary issues of 25 companies for the years 1954 to 1972 and published in 1979 in a study entitled Build and Blood Pressure Study, 1979. A related investigation, *Medical Impairment Study*, was published in 1983.

Most companies use a table showing average weights according to height, age, and sex. The table is then extended to other weights, and expected extra mortality is shown as a percentage of standard. At the best weights—less than the average—the tables indicate a better-than-average expected mortality rate.

Other aspects of a proposed insured's physical condition also are important. Companies know from experience that future mortality experience will depend, in varying degrees, upon abnormalities in one or more of the important systems of the body—that is, the nervous, digestive, cardiovascular, respiratory, or genitourinary systems, and glands of internal secretion. The defects and disabilities that may be found in the organs of the body and the methods of ascertaining them are necessarily medical in character. No attempt is made to explain them here. However, some of the more common of these that usually increase the risk may be mentioned. Thus an examination of the circulatory system may reveal elevated blood pressure, a heart murmur, or a high or irregular heart rate. An analysis of the urine may disclose the presence of albumin, sugar, or red blood cells. Indications of any of these or similar conditions necessitate further examination before the application can be accepted on terms satisfactory to both parties.

Coronary risk factors are used by many companies in their overall assessment of expected mortality. Factors such as low blood cholesterol, optimal blood pressure, and non–cigarette smoking contribute significantly to improved mortality from heart disease.

Acquired immune deficiency syndrome (AIDS) is important to life and health insurers because of its rapid spread and (to date) always fatal effect. Insurers desire to treat AIDS as any other medical condition for individual underwriting purposes. This means being able to have proposed insureds tested for the presence of the AIDS virus antibodies, which would indicate exposure to the virus. The right to test persons applying for individual life and disability income insurance for exposure to the AIDS virus has been generally accepted in all jurisdictions. Issues that previously existed about unfair discrimination and test result confidentiality have largely been resolved. Insurers test solely on the basis of age, amount of insurance, and medical history, and they have established procedures to safeguard confidentially. The right of insurers to test persons applying for individual or group medical expense coverage for exposure to the AIDS virus remains a controversial issue, and some jurisdictions prohibit this testing.

*(2) Personal History.* Insurance companies inquire into facets of the proposed insured's background that could have a bearing on his or her expected mortality. This investigation may include the individual's health record, habits, driving violations, and amount of insurance already owned.

The health record is usually the most important of the personal history factors. If the individual has in the past suffered a serious illness or accident, an appraisal of its probable effects on future life will be made. The appraisal frequently will require that, in addition to the medical history given by the proposed insured, reports be obtained from personal physicians and hospitals.

Insurance history is important. The proposed insured may have been refused life insurance by some insurer or offered insurance under special terms. If so, this fact may imply an extra hazard that existed formerly and may still be present and should be investigated. In some jurisdictions, legal restrictions prohibit the basing of an adverse action solely on information of any previous such action by another company. In any event, sound underwriting practice dictates that the company make every effort to establish for itself the proposed insured's insurability. Also, the individual may have such a large amount of insurance already in force on his or her life that a request for more may be indicative of speculation, if not justified by present income and finances.

*(3)* *Family History.* Family history is considered important by some companies because of the transmission of certain characteristics by heredity. If the history shows that most members of the family have lived to old age without incurring heart disease, cancer, diabetes, and other serious diseases, it may be inferred that the proposed insured will be less susceptible to these diseases. In many companies, however, family history is not used directly in classification, unless it reveals a characteristic that also appears in some form in the proposed insured. For example, two or more deaths below age 60 because of cardiovascular disease in the family may suggest a need for an additional debit[11] in the case of an individual with elevated blood pressure or only a small debit in the absence of elevated blood pressure or other impairments of the cardiovascular system.

***Financial Status.*** The financial status of an applicant for life insurance is critical from an underwriting standpoint. The amount of insurance should be compatible with the anticipated amount of loss. The basis of financial underwriting is to establish that the amount of insurance issued will compensate for an untimely loss, but not provide a profit to someone.

The first consideration is to establish that an insurable interest exists. Regardless of legal requirements, the underwriter must relate the applicant's and the beneficiary's interest to a logical need and potential financial loss. Determining the motivation for the proposed insurance is a primary factor in financial underwriting. This is best demonstrated by a well-established purpose, logical beneficiary, and reasonable amount in relation to the insured's (and if different from the insured, the policyowner's) financial status. When the motivation is questionable, it is essential to resolve any doubts and establish that the purchase is not speculative (see below).

Perhaps the most common underwriting guideline used by many companies is a formula with which one determines the maximum reasonable face amount of

---

[11]See Chap. 24.

**TABLE 23-1**      UNDERWRITING GUIDELINE FOR MAXIMUM INSURANCE AMOUNT (TIMES INCOME RULE)

| Age | Times Income | Age | Times Income |
|---|---|---|---|
| 25 and under | 18 | 46–50 | 10 |
| 26–30 | 16 | 51–55 | 9 |
| 31–35 | 14 | 56–60 | 7 |
| 36–40 | 13 | 61–65 | 5 |
| 41–45 | 12 | Over 65 | 4 |

insurance that will be purchased on most wage earners. This amount is determined by multiplying the proposed insured's annual income by a multiple that is a function of age. Table 23-1 presents a typical underwriting manual guideline. Such a rule is a guideline, not a hard and fast standard. All facts surrounding the case should be considered in establishing an acceptable level of insurance.

***Antiselection and Speculation.*** Some applicants withhold or misrepresent information when they apply for insurance. Others seek insurance while knowing or suspecting the existence of an adverse condition that the company does not know about, in the hope that the condition will not be discovered. Therefore, for larger amounts of insurance, companies make independent investigations about all aspects of insurability, including not only those previously discussed but also character and financial standing. Information sought about character includes business as well as personal activities. The applicant's reputation for meeting obligations and for fairness in dealings may indicate the type of moral risk that is involved in his or her insurance. Financial status, as represented by personal net worth, size and sources of income, and permanency of the income, is probably as important as any factor. Even when the amount of insurance applied for is not large, if the applicant appears to have sufficient protection already, the case will bear close investigation.

Speculation must be avoided, not only when the insured takes out insurance on his or her own life, but when one person wishes to insure the life of another. Although the law gives an individual an unlimited insurable interest in his or her own life, the need for insurance, as determined from such factors as financial status and dependents, largely governs the maximum amount the company will sell to an individual. If the insurance is applied for by one person on the life of another, companies also want to know about the insurable interest and the extent of the economic loss that the death of the insured would cause the applicant. Applications for life insurance for speculative purposes are rare when compared with the total insurance sold, but the cases are frequent enough to be of importance. Individual cases have involved millions of dollars. Also, a company has a legal responsibility to protect against speculation by an individual who does not have an insurable interest in the life of another, because it could be sued for damages if the amount of insurance was possibly a contributing factor in the insured's death.

Today, most companies will insure children at birth. The mortality experience for this class of business has been excellent. Some companies will issue whatever amounts are reasonable on a child's life, provided that the parents (if they are insurable) have a suitable insurance program and provided that all children in the family are insured for comparable amounts. The underwriting problem is to guard against one child being selected for insurance.

Comparatively few persons at advanced ages can qualify as good risks. The earning power of such individuals usually has decreased or ceased, thus reducing the insurable value and the need for protection. Companies insure older persons only after careful underwriting, and then usually to provide liquidity to meet estate taxes and other cash needs following the death of a person with substantial property holdings. Whether intentional or not, insurance of older persons by those on whom they are dependent is often speculative, and is therefore approached with caution by insurers.

*Tobacco Use.* Whether an individual smokes cigarettes, cigars, or a pipe is today by itself an important risk factor. In the past, smoking or other tobacco use was considered, but only rarely, to be a factor of importance by itself. For example, if a person had a respiratory problem and smoked, the underwriting decision might be less favorable than if an otherwise similarly situated individual had the same medical problem and did not smoke. Smoking unaccompanied by any other negative factor, however, was not a cause for a less favorable rating.

Insurers now understand that smoking or other tobacco use, even in the absence of any other negative factor, causes expected future mortality to be worse than the average, and the degree of variation is of such significance as to warrant separate classification. So important is this factor that the average female smoker can be expected to exhibit higher mortality than the average nonsmoking male of the same age. Smoking aggravates many other health problems. As a result, as indicated before, most insurers now have separate rates for smokers and nonsmokers and factor smoking habits into overall risk assessment.

Information regarding smoking habits is elicited on the application and verified through medical and nonmedical (e.g., consumer reporting agency) sources. Verification has proven difficult, with many persons misrepresenting the fact that they smoke.[12]   In persons applying for large amounts, smoking habits are verified by testing urine for the presence of nicotine.

Most insurers subdivide the standard group into about 75 percent nonsmokers, who experience about 85 percent relative mortality, and 25 percent smokers, who experience about 150 percent relative mortality. This differential varies by age; in the 40–49 age group, cigarette smokers experience twice the mortality rates of nonsmokers.

---

[12]Recently, the Third Circuit of Appeals ruled that New York Life Insurance Co. could avoid paying a claim on a smoker who lied on the application about his habit, even though he died of a nonsmoking-related cause. *New York Life Insurance Company v. Johnson*, 923 F. 2d. 279 (Third Circuit, 1991).

A few companies still call their nonsmoker class "preferred" and require that additional criteria such as build be met. The nonsmoker group, however, is not a "super standard" group. Assuming a continuing decline in the proportion of the smoking population, the nonsmoker will effectively become standard, with smoking becoming a risk factor leading to a substandard classification.

*Alcohol and Drugs.* Information is usually sought regarding the proposed insured's use of habit-forming drugs and intoxicating beverages. If the individual uses alcoholic beverages in large amounts, he or she may be declined or offered substandard insurance, depending upon the degree of use. Use of alcohol in moderation is considered normal. Use of drugs not prescribed by a physician or drug abuse may call for a declination, depending upon the type of drug. A history of misuse or unsupervised use may require an extra rating, depending upon the length of time since the drug or drugs were used, the nature of the treatment given, and whether there has been participation in a continuing support program (e.g., Alcoholics Anonymous).

*Occupation.* Occupational hazards are not as important today as they were in the past, although in certain cases they can be. They may increase the risk in at least three different ways. First, the occupation may present an environmental hazard, such as exposure to violence, irregular living, or a temptation to experiment with drugs or overindulge in alcohol. Second, the physical conditions surrounding an occupation can have a decided bearing upon health and longevity, as in the case of persons who work in close, dusty, or poorly ventilated quarters or are exposed to chemical toxins. Finally, there is the risk from accident, such as is faced by professional auto racers, crop dusters, and professional divers.

An individual who has recently changed from a hazardous occupation to a safer form of employment must be underwritten carefully, since he or she may still retain ill effects from the earlier employment or because the change may have been prompted by a health factor. Also, such a person is more likely than a person without such a history to return to the former occupation. The usual practice is to ignore prior occupation if the individual has been removed from it for a period of one or more years. Because of increased attention to job safety and working conditions, ratings have been reduced or eliminated for many occupations.

*Hazardous Sports and Avocations.* Persons with a high standard of living and searching for new ways to spend their leisure time often resort to hobbies and avocations. Such activities as scuba diving, mountain climbing, competitive racing, hang gliding, and skydiving clearly can involve a significant additional hazard to be considered in the underwriting process. If a hazard causes increased expected mortality and the individual is insurable on some basis, he or she usually is charged a flat extra premium commensurate with the risk. In states where it is permitted, a rider excluding death resulting from participation in the hazardous activity may be employed occasionally.

*Aviation.* It is usual to ask in the application if the proposed insured engages in aviation activities. As previously noted, flights as a fare-paying passenger on regularly scheduled airlines are not sufficiently hazardous to affect the risk, particularly since such travel has become so widespread. Where there may be a definite aviation hazard involving commercial, private, or military flying, the proposed insured may be requested to complete a supplementary questionnaire devoted entirely to this subject. The company may then charge an extra premium to compensate for the aviation hazard, or, infrequently, this cause of death may be excluded from the policy entirely. If the risk is excluded and if death occurs because of aviation activities, the company is liable only for a return of premiums paid or the reserve accumulated on the policy, or, sometimes, whichever of the two produces the larger figure. Most scheduled airline and private pilots are issued standard insurance without aviation restrictions. Those who participate in other types of flying, where the hazards are more extensive, are underwritten on the basis of experience and exposure and may be charged an extra premium or issued coverage with an exclusion clause.

*Military Service.* In the absence of hostilities, contracts are issued to military personnel with no exclusions or limitations. The adverse selection involved when individuals are engaged in or facing military service during a period of armed conflict can constitute an underwriting problem. Underwriting action taken in the past included outright declination, a limitation on the amount of insurance issued, or the attachment of a war clause that limits the insurer's obligation to the refund of premiums paid with interest, depending on the cause of death.[13] The war clause was used extensively during World War II in policies issued to military personnel. The clause was also used during the Korean conflict, primarily for military personnel going to Korea or for members of particularly hazardous combat forces. It generally was not used during the Vietnam War. In any event, when hostilities cease, war clauses are routinely canceled and cannot be reactivated.

*Residence.* The mortality rate in most developing countries is higher than in most developed countries, primarily because of climate and general living conditions. Individuals moving to a developed country from a developing country may already have been adversely affected by these conditions. When a proposed insured intends to reside in a developing country, the possible increased hazards of climate, general living conditions, and political unrest must be considered. A flat extra premium rate may be charged.

Another concern in underwriting individuals residing or who have resided in other countries is the inability to develop the full extent of underwriting information. It is difficult, generally, to obtain investigative reports, attending physicians' statements, and other underwriting information on a timely basis.

[13]See Chap. 8.

An additional problem with foreign residents is that restrictions on claims investigations may be such that, for all practical purposes, both the contestable and suicide provisions may have been essentially waived at the time of issue. Also, currency restrictions may make it difficult for the insured to pay premiums.

## THE HEALTH INSURANCE RISK

In underwriting individual health insurance—just as with life insurance—the hazards that affect the probability of loss must be evaluated. In contrast to life insurance, in health insurance the multiplicity of benefit types has an important bearing on the evaluation of the hazards. The claim rates and the average severity of the claims are affected by many of the same factors as those discussed for the life risk, but their significance varies. To avoid duplication, the following discussion on selection and classification in health insurance attempts to concentrate on the unique aspects of individual health insurance underwriting.

*Age.* Age affects annual claim costs differently, depending on the type of benefit involved, although both frequency and severity generally increase with advancing age for all types of benefits. In the case of long-term disability, the increase in risk can be as rapid as that found in death rates. For medical expense coverages and short-term disability income contracts, the increase is not marked until about age 55. Thus guaranteed-renewable and noncancelable disability income policies and life insurance disability riders are usually issued with premiums graded according to age of issue. Other types of policies, such as those that are optionally renewable by the insurance company, sometimes utilize a flat premium from, say, ages 18 to 55, with sharply higher rates utilized for renewals or new issues at higher ages. In the past, policies have not been available at ages much beyond 60, although in recent years medical care expense coverage has been extended increasingly to older ages. Normally, little need exists for income-replacement coverage at advanced ages, since some form of retirement income is available to most insureds. Some disability policies provide for continuance to age 75 or even for the insured's lifetime, subject only to full-time employment.

Adverse selection is a severe problem at older ages, but considerable medical expense protection is provided for retiring persons under group policies and under federal Medicare coverage. Most individual policies are limited as to amount and type of coverage after a certain age, such as 65 or 70, although some companies have made lifetime coverage available. Most companies now offer Medicare supplement policies that pay the expenses not covered by Medicare.

*Sex.* Gender, as in the case of life insurance policies, is of considerable significance in health insurance underwriting. Females show higher disability rates than males at all but the upper ages (e.g., 55 and older) in most studies. This is true even for policies that exclude or limit coverage of pregnancy, miscarriage, abortion, and similar occurrences. In the past, underwriters believed that these higher rates were due to a greater hazard of malingering in connection with women, since they were not normally the primary breadwinners. Also, companies were reluctant to issue disability income coverage to working women because their employment traditionally was often temporary and intermittent. Wherever issued, such coverage frequently provided shorter and lower income benefits than those issued to men. Life insurance disability income riders and long-term noncancelable disability income policies were seldom issued to women. For all types of policies, women were usually charged a higher rate than men, even if the maternity risk was excluded. When such coverage was included, rates for the childbearing ages were even higher. These practices, based on the higher rates of disability actually experienced, were almost universal.

Currently, however, as a result of a more enlightened view by insurers resulting from greater competition and because of legislation and regulation in the area of civil rights, sex has virtually ceased to be a selection determinant. Companies now offer the same policy benefits and provisions to men and to women at a unisex rate, and often with an exclusion or limitation for normal pregnancy. A few companies, however, charge sex-distinct rates.

***Medical Aspects.*** To evaluate a proposed insured for health insurance, it is necessary to consider both his or her health history and current physical condition. This evaluation is done primarily by estimating the probable influence of current impairments and previous medical histories on future claims.

*1. Medical History.* The importance the underwriter attaches to a history of past illness or accident will vary, depending upon the nature of the condition and its severity, the frequency of attacks, the degree of permanent impairment, and the length of time that has elapsed since recovery. This is important for both accidental injury and sickness coverages. For example, a history of epilepsy or vertigo would increase the probability of accidents, and diabetes, obesity, or cardiovascular conditions would increase the duration of disability from injury or sickness.

Particular attention is paid to chronic conditions in which the probability of recurrence is high. Less attention is necessary for acute conditions, even if they are quite serious, if recovery has been good, permanent impairment is not evident, and a reasonable time has elapsed without recurrence. Thus a chronic condition such as asthma will be regarded more seriously than a history of kidney stones or gall bladder trouble. Naturally, conditions that are both chronic and serious, such as heart disease, poorly controlled hypertension, and cancer, will be underwritten very carefully and may require declination if coverage on an extra premium basis cannot be offered.

*2. Physical Condition.* Obviously, the present and potential physical condition of the proposed insured is important. The present physical condition and past health record must be evaluated to predict the probability of future disability. Naturally, an individual who is currently disabled or undergoing medical treatment for a significant ailment at the time of application is not eligible for insurance against losses resulting from the currently existing impairment.

*Fitness,* as evidenced by blood pressure and pulse as well as weight, is of considerable significance. Thus while obesity and elevated blood pressure are not disabling in and of themselves, they are considered indicators of a higher future incidence of cardiovascular impairment. Obesity can also complicate any future surgical procedures or disabilities due to any cause and can increase the time needed for recovery. As in the case of life insurance, cigarette smoking also is recognized as a significant underwriting factor. Many companies use separate health insurance premium rates for smokers and nonsmokers.

*Underweight,* especially if marked, is also an underwriting consideration that should be viewed in the light of the proposed insured's history—as in the case of ulcer, bronchitis, frequently recurring colds or pneumonia, and colitis. It could also be an indication of an undiagnosed condition that would call for a medical examination by the company. Underweight in and of itself, however, is usually not significant.

*3. Family History.* The application may request information on the age and health status of living parents, brothers, and sisters, and on age at death and cause of death for those who are deceased. While family history is usually of little significance in underwriting health insurance, it is sometimes taken into account, especially when evaluating an applicant who shows early signs of cardiovascular disease or diabetes.

*Financial Status.* The financial status of the proposed insured can be a prime underwriting consideration for individual health insurance coverages.

*1. Plan of Insurance.* One of the most important factors affecting actual claim rates is the type of policy and amount of benefit. In this regard, the definition of disability itself is important (for instance, "own occupation" or "any occupation," or whether the disability must be total or can be partial).[14] In medical expense coverages, the definition of claim eligibility may be in terms of admission to a hospital, treatment by a physician, or the incurring of an expense. The length of the elimination period, the benefit period, the amount of the deductible, and the extent of percentage participation (coinsurance) can be major factors in determining claim rates for disabilities of short duration.

In contrast to the differences in rates due to different definitions of covered events, differences in types and amounts of benefits will produce different claim rates. This can be a reflection of moral hazard. Under exactly the same definition of disability and elimination period, for example, higher claim rates result for a disability income benefit than for a waiver-of-premium benefit. In general, the greater the prospective benefit in terms of both amount and duration, the greater will be the claim rate, other things being equal. Naturally, when the potential

[14]See Chap. 17.

benefit exceeds the loss, particular difficulties arise. In such a case, the insured can make a profit from disability, and this means that the motivation for malingering and a slow recovery will be greatest.

The underwriter's primary concern with differences in disability definition is to be careful in applying appropriate criteria to specific types of insurance. When a policy or life insurance disability rider is noncancelable, stricter standards are usually applied in initial underwriting. There can be no renewal underwriting, as is possible with optionally renewable individual health insurance. More conservative standards must also be applied to contracts providing high benefits in regard to amount or duration, or both. Similarly, stricter standards are applied to policies covering sickness than to those covering accidental injury only.

In practice, the strictest underwriting standards are applied to the long-term, noncancelable disability income policies and to life insurance disability riders. In the case of medical expense coverage, similar high standards are applied to major medical expense contracts. Disability income contracts and medical expense contracts renewable at the option of the company are underwritten more liberally. The most lenient underwriting standards are applied to industrial and limited policies in which benefit amounts are small and durations are short.

There is growing conviction in the industry that more exacting standards should be applied to all plans regardless of renewability provision, since the main claim problem is the large continuing claim rather than repeat claims. Once an insured is on claim status, it really does not matter if the contract is noncancelable or optionally renewable.

2. *Relation of Insurance to Loss.* The most significant underwriting safeguard against moral hazard is a reasonable relationship between the insurance benefit and the amount of potential loss. Underwriters believe the insured should share in the loss to some extent. This may be accomplished by limited benefit periods, limitations on the amount of insurance issued, and policy provisions limiting the amount that may be collected in relation to the loss.

In medical expense coverages, for example, the amount of benefit for each type of expense usually is limited and stated in the contract. Also, some policies exclude such expenses as nurses' fees and the cost of drugs, appliances, prosthetics, and blood plasma.

In major medical expense policies, such items as dental services, services in government hospitals, and services primarily for rest or diagnosis usually are not covered. These contracts also commonly include deductible and percentage participation (coinsurance) provisions. The deductible serves mainly to avoid duplication with underlying basic policies, but the coinsurance provision causes the insured to participate directly (to the extent of 20 to 25 percent) in loss payments above the deductible.

Disability income contracts rely mainly on limiting the amount of benefit in relation to earned income. Companies will not issue coverage for more than a portion of the proposed insured's earned income. This portion may be a straight percentage of earned income or a percentage plus or minus a stated amount. It was not uncommon in the past to insure as much as 75 or 80 percent of the insured's earned income, but with disability benefits being offered by the federal and some state governments, this percentage has rapidly decreased. Because of the effect of taxes on take-home pay, companies will insure a larger percentage of income at the lower range of their issue limits charts than they will on higher incomes.

In addition to setting an amount limit based on percentage of income, most life insurance companies establish a maximum issue and participation limit—the overall maximum amount of disability coverage they will participate in writing on any one individual regardless of income. This amount usually varies by class. Many companies have a maximum limit that is as high as $20,000 per month on the best class of risks, and a few will consider even higher amounts.

Most companies also will test the need and incentive to return to work by scrutinizing the individual's unearned income and net worth. This financial analysis can be very important when application is made for sizable amounts of disability insurance.

For those with higher incomes and coverages involving long benefit durations, noncancelable or guaranteed-renewable features, and life insurance disability income riders, even stricter standards are applied. In noncancelable policies, the **average earnings clause** is occasionally used,[15] particularly when the benefit duration is long. Most companies do not use the clause, and since it takes no account of take-home pay, it is of limited value anyway. Benefit prorating provisions are rarely found in medical expense policies, and there is no protection against duplication of benefits in the usual policy. State laws often prohibit individually issued medical expense policies from having coordination-of-benefit clauses. Rising health insurance claims and the rising level of disability claims under Social Security have directed attention to the underwriting problems in these areas, and safeguards against these situations are being sought.

***Occupation.*** The probability of disablement is materially affected by occupation, particularly as regards the perils of accidental injury. Certain occupations, such as heavy construction, logging and mining are usually considered uninsurable on an individual basis. The duties of an occupation will also affect a claimant's ability to work, and this, as well as the accident peril, is a basis for classifying and rating occupations. For example, after becoming disabled by a lower back condition, it would be easier for a desk clerk than, say,

---

[15]This clause provides that if the total benefits under all valid disability income policies exceed the average monthly earnings of the insured over the previous two years or his or her current monthly earnings, whichever is greater, then the company will pay only such a portion of the amount of benefit due as the amount of such earnings bears to the total benefits under all such policies.

a construction worker to return to work. Experience has indicated that the incentive to malinger is greater among certain lower-paid occupations where the work is repetitive and unchallenging than among business owners and professionals. This factor is of significance mostly in connection with disability income coverage.

For disability income, insurable occupations are classified into broad groups of about the same average claim cost, with appropriate scales of premium rates applying to each class. The number of classes may vary from four to six, depending on the type of company and the types of coverage provided. There is some diversity among companies in this regard.

The complexity of occupational classifications is greatest in the noncancelable policies. Limited and industrial contracts are usually sold at a uniform rate for all occupations, with some being excluded by policy provisions. Some companies restrict sales of noncancelable policies to occupations with relatively favorable experiences. Most companies have limitations as to benefit periods and amounts available to the less favorable occupations.

***Antiselection and Speculation.*** Antiselection and speculation are particularly serious problems in health insurance. The subjective nature of the disability status and the difficulties in defining the insured events complicate the problem considerably. In underwriting a disability application, the underwriter must make subjective evaluations that take into consideration such nebulous factors as motivation to work, occupational stability, and the financial situation of the proposed insured. For example, the owner of a small profitable business who knows that continued profitability depends on his or her being on the job every day may have a much stronger motivation to return to work than an individual whose business may be on the verge of collapse. The underwriter must make a subjective evaluation as to which individual will be disabled longer in the event of an accident or sickness, and which one will be more inclined to malinger and take unfair advantage of any benefit provisions.

The character of the insured is one of the important determinants of claim rates. Insurers must contend with such conditions as psychosomatic illness, accident proneness, and hypochondria, as well as deliberate malingering. The underwriter must be careful to avoid **overinsurance.** In addition to the basic safeguard of limiting the amount of benefit to something less than the insured's take-home pay and avoiding duplicate hospital coverages, companies scrutinize all aspects of the underwriting process for evidence of moral hazard.

An applicant who voluntarily approaches a company for insurance requires careful consideration. Experience has indicated that there is a better-than-average chance that he or she has knowledge of some condition that will make the insurance particularly valuable to him or her—that is, there exists selection against the insurer. In most cases where the occupation is characterized by unstable earnings, work performed exclusively or primarily at home, irregular and seasonable work, or any connection with illegal or dubious activities, underwriters hesitate to approve the application. Such activities as dishonest or questionable business practices or ethics, questionable associates, criminal activity, and poor personal habits all present danger signals. Poor personal habits include gambling, excessive drinking, and use of addictive drugs. Any evidence of fraud or misrepresentation in the application is also considered significant.

*Other Factors.* Other factors that affect physical hazards to some degree include foreign travel or residence, habits, and avocations. Foreign travel or residence is considered in underwriting health risks because of the difficulty in claim administration and in obtaining underwriting data. Habits of drug addiction or excessive use of alcohol are, of course, quite significant. These affect both the physical and moral hazard and normally lead to rejection. Exclusion riders are usually used for individuals who participate in particularly hazardous sports. Private aviation activities are excluded by policy wording from some disability contracts in which an accidental-death benefit is included in the contract. For those companies granting unrestricted aviation coverage, such activities, including the type and frequency of flying, become an underwriting consideration.

## METHODS OF RISK CLASSIFICATION

Once underwriting information about a proposed insured has been assembled, it must be evaluated and a decision must be reached as to whether the individual is to be accepted at standard rates with or without a preferred risk or nonsmoker discount, treated as a substandard but acceptable risk, or rejected entirely. Occasionally, a risk is postponed for a period of time until the effect of a condition or impairment is resolved. For instance, if the proposed insured is expecting to undergo imminent surgery, a decision could be postponed until after the surgery.

Ideally, the selection and classification system used by a company should (1) measure accurately the effect of each factor affecting the risk; (2) assess the combined impact of interrelated factors including the conflicting ones; (3) produce equitable results; and (4) be relatively simple and inexpensive to operate. Two basic systems are used in the United States in an effort to accommodate these concerns: the judgment method and the numerical rating system.

## The Judgment Method

Originally and for many years companies used the judgment method of rating. Under this method, the company depended upon the combined judgment of those in the medical, actuarial, and other areas who were qualified for this work. The judgment method of rating functions effectively when there is only one unfavorable factor to consider or when the decision to be made is simply whether to accept the proposed insured at standard rates or to reject him or her entirely. Where multiple factors (some possibly in conflict) are involved or a proper substandard classification is needed, it leaves something to be desired. Moreover, it requires the use of highly skilled personnel to achieve proper risk appraisal with consistency of treatment. To overcome the weakness of the judgment method of rating, the life insurance business developed the numerical rating system.[16]

## THE NUMERICAL RATING SYSTEM

The numerical rating system is based on the principle that a large number of factors enters into the composition of a risk and that the impact of each of these factors on longevity can be determined by a statistical study of lives possessing that factor. Under this plan, 100 percent represents a normal or standard risk, one that is physically and financially sound and has a need for the insurance.

Each of the factors that might influence a risk in an unusual way is considered a debit or a credit. Values are assigned to the individual factors. For example, if the mortality of a group of insured lives reflecting a certain degree of overweight, or a certain degree of elevated blood pressure, has been found to be 150 percent of standard risks, a debit (addition) of 50 percentage points will be assigned to this degree of overweight or blood pressure.

Judgment still enters into the operation of the numerical system, primarily in the assignment of numerical values to each factor and, when it occurs, in determining the effect of two or more factors that are related to each other in some way. When two factors are so related that one affects the other, judgment and past experience may dictate an addition that is greater or smaller than the mere addition of the numerical factors. For example, if family history shows several early deaths from heart disease, this adverse factor may be nullified somewhat by a good physical condition, good build, normal electrocardiograms, and similar favorable factors. On the other hand, this type of family history plus findings of obesity or elevated blood pressure will probably warrant a larger addition than the sum of the two adverse factors.

The system in practice is applied with common sense and has the advantages of greater consistency of treatment and of permitting lay underwriters to process all applications other than those requiring detailed medical analysis. This reduced reliance on physicians in underwriting helps minimize the expense of the underwriting process.

A hypothetical illustration will help make clear the operation of the numerical rating system. Suppose that an attorney, aged 35, applies for a universal life policy. Information obtained by the company reveals the following facts: height, 5 feet, 9 inches; weight, 205 pounds; family history, better than average; habits, good; personal history shows medical attention for slightly elevated blood pressure. A paramedical examination is requested and the

---

[16]See Arthur H. Hunter and Oscar H. Rogers, "The Numerical Method of Determining the Value of Risks for Insurance," *Transactions of the Actuarial Society of America*, Vol. XX, Part 2 (1919).

individual's blood pressure is found to be 150/90. An attending physician's report is obtained to provide details on the extent of elevation and the response to treatment. From tables developed for this purpose, the company will first ascertain the basic rating for this individual, which depends upon the build. In this case, the basic rating, according to the company's table, is 125, because the individual is overweight. In other words, the obesity in a case like this is expected to result in mortality that equals 125 percent of average. To this basic figure, 75 is added for elevated blood pressure. The total is 200. On the other hand, a credit of 10 is allowed for a favorable family history. The net result, 190, represents an expected mortality that is 90 percent greater than that expected for standard risks. The analysis is summarized as follows:

| Factor | Base = 100 | Debits | Credits |
|---|---|---|---|
| Build: overweight | | 25 | |
| Personal history: blood pressure | | 75 | |
| Family history | | | 10 |
| Total | | 100 | 10 |
| | Rating = 190 | | |

The ratings obtained by this method range in most companies from a low of 75 to a high of 500 or more. In most companies, the ratings that fall between 75 and 125 are classified as standard. Some companies may broaden the standard category to include ratings up to 130 or 140, particularly at the younger ages. Proposed insureds who produce a rate in excess of the standard limit are either assigned to appropriate substandard classes or declined.

The scale of ratings produced by the numerical rating system might be classified in a particular company as follows:

| Standard / Substandard | | /Uninsurable |
|---|---|---|
| 75  85  100  115  125  135  145  155 | ••••• | 485      500 |

Some companies' ratings extend to as high as 1000 percent. Generally, ratings of over 500 percent are classified as experimental underwriting.

There can be wide differences in underwriting decisions among competing life insurance companies, and these can be explained in two ways. First, the size of the numerical debits in their impairment manuals may differ. Second, their judgment in assessing debits and credits may differ. In addition, some numerical measures of impairments or variations of impairments do not appear in the manuals.

## USE OF THE COMPUTER IN UNDERWRITING

For some years, managers of life insurance underwriting departments have utilized the computer to relieve the underwriter of many clerical operations associated with application screening. Certain application data, including answers to underwriting questions, can be input by personnel at agency offices that process applications received from agents or by home office personnel. The computer can identify answers that raise possible underwriting problems. The computer, in effect, underwrites the application and eliminates the need for a normal underwriting review, unless problems are identified.

The percentage of applications that can be computer-rated depends upon the amount of data input and the sophistication of the computer program in identifying and even rating adverse data. At a minimum, the computer can identify "yes" or "no" answers. If the answers are all "no," the application can be approved. At the other extreme, the computer can calculate the mortality debits for build, blood pressure, and other numerical measurements, and show on a screen the details to a "yes" answer, so that the underwriter does not need to await receipt of the written application before completing underwriting action.

The electronic underwriting manual is also a new procedure that assists in the underwriting process. Data from a typical paper underwriting manual is transferred to a disk format for use on a personal computer. A stand-alone personal computer (PC) or a computer that is part of a network can be used.

The underwriter typically inputs either the full name of or an abbreviation for an impairment, and all information pertaining to that impairment appears on the monitor. The typical screen provides a description of the disorder, a list of suggested requirements necessary for evaluating the disorder, positive and negative risk factors, and a range of ratings that the underwriter uses to develop a mortality assessment. Use of the diskette makes updating quick, simple, and less costly.

Also available are expert system programs that calculate specific mortality ratings for the underwriter after particular data from medical exams, attending physicians' statements, blood profile results, EKG interpretations, and the like have been coded into a PC. These programs also suggest additional requirements that should be secured and the positive and negative risks factors that the underwriter should be cognizant of when deriving the final mortality assessment.

Systems like these develop a judgment base so that the program can remember different situations and act accordingly. Most of them do not have the authority to reject an application; for the time being, this is the exclusive province of the underwriter. Expert systems are intended to provide consistency, cost savings, and quick turnaround time.

# Chapter 24

# *L*IFE AND *H*EALTH *I*NSURANCE *U*NDERWRITING: II

## CLASSIFYING SUBSTANDARD RISKS

In the classification of substandard life and health insurance, provision must be made for higher than standard mortality or morbidity. This may be done by charging an extra premium in addition to the standard premium or by other methods. The methods are discussed below, first with reference to life insurance, then health insurance.

## LIFE INSURANCE ON SUBSTANDARD RISKS

Statistical information on past experience is essential to develop an equitable basis for providing insurance on lives subject to different impairments. Companies have accumulated considerable statistics on impairments that aid them in estimating their influence on mortality. Similarly, the wide experience of reinsurers, especially with substandard risk appraisal, has assisted direct-writing companies in establishing sound underwriting systems.

Companies use two types of statistics on past experience. Experience under life insurance policies is useful, but often it is not available in sufficient quantity, particularly when it comes to impairments that occur infrequently and that are associated with mortality so high that insurance is unobtainable at a reasonable price. Articles in medical journals are useful to underwriters in that they provide data on impairments for which insurance is not available or for which insurance experience is not sufficiently current to reflect the results of new medical developments.

Some companies use reinsurance extensively to seek standard insurance on risks that are substandard by their own underwriting standards. Some reinsurance companies pursue this business aggressively. They are willing to assume risks that a direct-writing company, concerned about maintaining competitive pricing for standard risks, is not willing to assume.

***Incidence of Extra Mortality.*** Although a number of factors may cause a proposed insured to be rated substandard, more than 82 percent are so rated because of various physical impairments such as heart murmurs, obesity, diabetes, and elevated blood pressure.[1] However rating systems for substandard insurance do not precisely follow over time the pattern of extra mortality of each impairment. This would be difficult and probably impracticable, because knowledge of substandard mortality is insufficiently developed. Absolute equity is an objective to be sought; it is not attainable.

The majority of companies, therefore, categorize substandard insureds into three broad groups: (1) those in which the number of extra deaths is expected to remain at approximately the same level in all years following the issue of the policy; (2) those in which the number of extra deaths is expected to increase as insureds grow older; and (3) those in which the number of extra deaths is expected to decrease with time. Examples of the constant type of extra deaths would be persons with a hazardous avocation or occupation. An example of increasing extra mortality would be a person with diabetes, whereas a person who had just undergone a supposedly successful operation would be representative of the decreasing category. Such a classification permits companies to assess premiums according to the incidence of the extra deaths. If companies expect the same number of extra deaths to occur in two groups over a particular period of time, but also expect the timing to be different, different types of extra premiums will be needed for the extra mortality in the group in which the extra deaths occur early (decreasing) compared to those needed for the group in which the deaths occur later (increasing).

***Methods of Rating.*** Several methods exist for rating impaired lives. In general, an effort is made to adapt the method to the type of exposure represented by the impaired individual, but departures from theoretically correct treatment are made for practical reasons. The objectives in establishing an extra-premium structure are that it be: (1) equitable between impairments and between classes, (2) easy to administer, and (3) easily understood by agents and the consumer public. Several of these premium structures are discussed below.

---

[1] Based on a 1984 study of ordinary insurance, the proportion was 73 percent. The reasons for extra ratings in this same study showed the following distribution: cardiovascular renal disease or its symptoms, 36 percent; weight problem, 14 percent; other medical reasons, 32 percent; occupation and other reasons, 18 percent. See American Council of Life Insurance, *1992 Life Insurance Fact Book* (Washington, D.C.: American Council of Life Insurance, 1992 ), p. 118.

*1. Multiple Table Extra.* By far the most common method used for substandard insurance is the multiple table extra method. Substandard risks are divided into broad groups according to their numerical ratings, and premium rates or mortality charges are based on mortality rates that correspond to the average numerical ratings in each class. Most companies use the same nonforfeiture values and dividends as they do for standard risks. Some companies do not permit the extended term insurance option on highly rated cases.

Generally, numerical ratings of up to approximately 125 are considered standard, and policyowners with these ratings pay the same premium rates. The procedures for establishing a substandard class are identical, except that the average rating of each additional substandard class is progressively higher than that for the standard class. Companies usually provide for at least 4 and sometimes as many as 6 or 7 substandard classes when special nonforfeiture values are used, and as many as 16 classifications when standard values are used. Proposed insureds are then placed in the appropriate class (standard or substandard) in accordance with their numerical ratings. The average numerical rating within these classes may range from about 125 to 500, or even higher. An example of a scale of substandard classifications is shown in Table 24-1.

Under this method, a special mortality table is developed for each substandard classification that reflects the experience of each, and a set of gross-premium rates is computed for the classification. Table 24-2 shows illustrative gross-premium rates for an ordinary life contract under different scales of substandard mortality classifications. The standard rates are also shown for purposes of comparison.

These rates are not necessarily representative of the rates charged by any company, but they do show the relationship between rates for different substandard classes. Companies also vary premium rates for substandard risks by plan, with the extra charges being lower for the higher cash-value plans, other

**TABLE 24-1     ILLUSTRATIVE SCALE OF SUBSTANDARD MORTALITY CLASSIFICATIONS**

| Table | Mortality (%) | Numerical Rating |
|-------|---------------|------------------|
| 1     | 125           | 120–135          |
| 2     | 150           | 140–160          |
| 3     | 175           | 165–185          |
| 4     | 200           | 190–210          |
| 5     | 225           | 215–235          |
| 6     | 250           | 240–260          |
| 7     | 275           | 265–285          |
| 8     | 300           | 290–325          |
| 10    | 350           | 330–380          |
| 12    | 400           | 385–450          |
| 16    | 500           | 455–550          |
| -     | -             | Over 550         |

**TABLE 24-2      ILLUSTRATIVE PARTICIPATING GROSS-PREMIUM RATES (ORDINARY LIFE, MALE, NONSMOKER)**

| Age | Rates for Standard Risks | Table 1 120%–135% | Table 2 140%–160% | Table 3 165%–185% | Table 4 180%–210% |
|---|---|---|---|---|---|
| 15 | $ 8.19 | $ 8.94 | $ 9.69 | $10.44 | $11.19 |
| 20 | 9.12 | 10.02 | 10.92 | 11.81 | 12.72 |
| 25 | 10.46 | 11.49 | 12.51 | 13.54 | 14.56 |
| 30 | 12.45 | 13.75 | 15.15 | 16.45 | 17.65 |
| 35 | 14.82 | 16.45 | 18.07 | 19.70 | 21.32 |
| 40 | 18.08 | 20.01 | 21.93 | 23.86 | 25.78 |
| 45 | 22.25 | 24.70 | 27.15 | 29.60 | 32.05 |
| 50 | 28.43 | 31.46 | 34.48 | 37.51 | 40.53 |
| 55 | 36.48 | 40.23 | 43.98 | 47.73 | 51.48 |
| 60 | 47.22 | 51.80 | 56.37 | 60.95 | 65.52 |
| 65 | 62.05 | 67.25 | 72.45 | 77.65 | 82.85 |

things being equal. The substandard premiums are lower for high cash-value plans because of the decreasing net amount at risk over the life of the policy. Also except for level term plans, substandard premiums do not increase in proportion to the degree of extra mortality involved, because, for cash-value products, the loading does not increase in proportion to the degree of extra mortality involved. Universal life extra premiums are based on the net amount at risk and, depending on plan design, could either be equivalent to term or to ordinary life extra premiums.

Multiple table extra ratings do not differentiate among the various types of substandard risks with different incidences of extra mortality (i.e., increasing, decreasing, or constant). The assumption of a constant percentage of the standard mortality rates implies a number of extra deaths per thousand that increases with age for all types of cases rated on this basis. Although this method theoretically may not exactly reflect the incidence of extra risk, the procedure is justified on an expense basis, and, on the average, it is reasonably accurate. Many companies use the multiple table extra method for some impairments and flat (usually temporary) extras for others.

Notwithstanding the fact that many companies write insurance on persons subject to 500 percent of standard mortality, there is a point beyond which the degree of extra mortality is so high and the number of similar risks so limited that companies do not wish to insure those persons even when they have reasonable reinsurance facilities. As the ratings increase, fewer applicants are normally willing to pay the necessarily higher premiums (or mortality charges), and the ones who are willing may know, somehow, that they are even worse risks than the company has estimated. As the premium is increased for a policy of individual insurance, the likelihood of adverse selection increases markedly.

*2. Flat Extra Premium.* This method is used when the extra mortality, measured in additional deaths per thousand, is expected to be constant, either for a temporary period or permanently, and when it is largely independent of age. Under this method, a regular policy is issued, but a constant extra premium is charged to provide for the additional expected mortality. The policy is treated as standard for the purpose of dividends and nonforfeiture values.

The method is appropriate for most hazardous occupations and avocations, since much of the extra mortality is of an accidental nature and independent of age. It is also appropriate for covering temporary extra mortality (for a specified period) as when most of the extra risk falls in the early years after an operation or when there is a particular event such as a coronary thrombosis. Coronary ratings are typically made up of a table rating plus a temporary flat extra premium.

*3. Other Methods.* In addition to the methods already discussed, another method of treating substandard insureds is to provide a limited death benefit equal to a refund of premiums if death occurs in the first few years (typically first two years). This limited death benefit, together with a higher standard premium, is used by some companies that offer insurance by mail, with little or no underwriting, usually to older age groups (over 50).

Another common form of limited death benefit contract is a graded death benefit, with the graded amount payable increasing in each of the first three to five years, after which the full death benefit is payable.

Companies sometimes have been willing to treat proposed insureds who would have been substandard as standard risks, if the policy applied for is of a relatively high premium variety. Such a policy would have a higher reserve than lower-premium forms, thus lessening the risk assumed by the insurer. It is assumed that there is less antiselection with high-premium plans. Some companies refuse to issue term plans at high ratings, such as ratings above 250 or 300 percent, primarily because of concern about adverse selection, particularly at each premium-due date, when the better risks have less incentive to continue the policy.

***Improvement in Expected Mortality.*** After a policy has been issued substandard under the permanent flat-extra-premium or multiple table extra method, the insured may become eligible to purchase insurance at standard rates or under better terms than those governing the rated policy. Under such circumstances, insureds expect reconsideration. Many ratings are automatic in the sense that the rating is reduced in conjunction with the new underwriting evidence on a repeat sale that has a lower or no rating. Many companies enclose a notice with the policy informing the insured that they will consider reducing or removing the rating on or after a specific anniversary, and some also enclose a reminder in the premium mailing on that anniversary. Most reconsiderations are noncompetitive, but some may be triggered by an offer of standard insurance made by another company.

To prevent insured persons from withdrawing, companies generally make some provision for handling these improvements. For the company to remove the extra charge without loss to itself, the extra charge in the first instance must have been computed with data from which the improved lives were eliminated at the point where their ratings were removed. If the extra premium for the impairment was calculated from data that included lives that had improved, the company theoretically should not remove the extra charge. In this latter case, some of the insureds would no doubt improve, but others will grow worse, and since the company could not increase the charges against those that deteriorate, it should not reduce charges for those who improve. As a practical matter, most companies will reduce or remove a rating if they receive evidence that the risk has improved.

When an apparent reduction in expected mortality is due to a change in residence, occupation, or avocation, some companies require a probationary period of one or two years prior to rating removal. At the end of this period, the company makes a retroactive refund of the extra premium dating from the time the change occurred. This protects the company against the possibility that the insured will return to the former occupation, avocation, or residence. For practical reasons, however, some companies make the change without such a probationary period.

## HEALTH INSURANCE ON SUBSTANDARD RISKS

As in the case of life insurance, the health insurance company can either reject an application, accept it at standard rates on a regular policy form, accept it on a higher premium plan, or accept it on a regular policy form with an extra premium. In recent years, there have been significant advances in the underwriting of impaired risks for health insurance, so that today only a small proportion of these risks is ineligible for insurance on some basis. In addition to those used in life insurance, techniques for handling impaired risks include the use of exclusion riders and limitations on policy benefits.

*Exclusions.* In contrast with life insurance, in which only war or aviation clauses are used, exclusions are a common method of handling physical impairments in health insurance. An exclusion rider is an endorsement attached to a policy that excludes from coverage any loss arising from a named disease or physical impairment. After such losses have been excluded and other aspects of the case have been deemed normal, full coverage can be issued for other types of losses at standard rates. The exclusion may be somewhat broader than the condition that leads to its use. For example, a proposed insured with a history of kidney stones might be offered a policy excluding all diseases of the kidneys or genitourinary tract. Such an approach is considered essential because a kidney stone condition might aggravate another related disease, and it also avoids possible problems if a claim based on a slightly different manifestation of the same condition is filed.

Although a broad exclusion rider impairs the value of the coverage, it is usually far preferable to the alternative. The only alternative often is declination if the condition is one that would be impossible to price accurately (such as a highly subjective condition). Furthermore, from the company's standpoint, the existence of the impairment can often produce disability, even from unrelated ailments. Conditions that commonly require waivers include back injuries, appendicitis, hernias, and optionally elective surgical procedures. If, however, in the case of disability insurance, a long elimination period is requested, many conditions such as hernias and appendicitis may not require waivers.

*Extra Premiums.* Most companies offer full coverage to certain impaired risks at an extra premium. Some companies offer coverage only on selected impairments or selected plans; others offer on all bases. Some reduce benefits, increase the elimination period for certain impairments, charge an extra premium, or utilize one or more of these features in combination. Companies void the preexisting condition exclusion in the policy with respect to an impairment for which an extra premium is charged.

There are a multitude of problems in obtaining morbidity statistics that accurately reflect increased expected morbidity. Yet the prospect of offering broad coverage for preexisting conditions that could cause disability or hospitalization has encouraged many companies to change their underwriting practices and grant more complete coverage for an extra premium. Many impairments that could not be satisfactorily covered in the past because they either were too broad in scope or had too many systemic complications (such as many heart conditions or diabetes) can now be covered for a price. The use of the extra-premium approach, however, does not eliminate the need for exclusions. Although exclusions are probably resorted to less frequently, there are still problems in granting unrestricted coverage in all instances.

*Modification of Type of Coverage.* The third major method of handling impaired health risks is to modify the type of policy. In the case of borderline applications, health insurance underwriters frequently settle the problem by offering a different and more limited form of coverage. This limitation may be a lower amount, a shorter benefit period, or a longer elimination period. This last device is particularly useful for cases in which the medical history involves short-term disabilities only.

*Renewal Underwriting.* Renewal underwriting is concerned with the health history of the insured and also changes in occupation, income, residence, or habits, all of which may have made him or her an undesirable risk. With optionally renewable policies, the company has an opportunity to reevaluate its insureds periodically. Some companies do not avail themselves of their right to reunderwrite optionally renewable policies unless or until the loss ratio for that particular group of policies reaches a point where action must be taken.

Cancellation and reunderwriting seem unfair to some persons. It is said that the insured often does not fully understand the terms of the contract or, if he or she understands them, does not appreciate their full importance. This is one reason so many insurers charge more and guarantee renewal of their policies to a specified age, rather than emphasizing one-year term plans.

## SPECIAL UNDERWRITING PRACTICES

Usual underwriting practices are relaxed in several areas. In the process, special underwriting concerns are created. The following discussion is intended to explain how reasonable results can be obtained in these areas.

### NONMEDICAL LIFE INSURANCE

A substantial proportion of all new life insurance in the United States is written without the benefit of a medical or paramedical examination.[2] The expression **nonmedical life insurance** normally refers to ordinary insurance sold in this manner.

In one sense, the use of the term is unfortunate since it sometimes conveys the (erroneous) idea that the insurance is issued without any medical information. Of course, this is not the case. Medical information is still sought, but it is gathered from the proposed insured by the agent seeking answers to the application questions (and possibly from attending physician statements and other sources). The term *nonmedical* should be understood to be synonymous with *no physical examination required.*

For many years, the medical examination was considered a necessity. Toward the end of the nineteenth century, life insurance companies in England began to experiment with nonmedical underwriting on a limited basis. Not until 1921, however, did several Canadian companies begin to experiment with nonmedical underwriting as it is practiced today. The motivation for the development was a shortage of medical examiners, particularly in the rural areas, and the desire to reduce the expense rate on the predominantly small policies issued at that time. The practice spread to U.S. companies about four years later and is firmly entrenched today in Canada, the United States, and elsewhere.

Although nonmedical underwriting lessens the demands on the medical profession and facilitates the sale and processing of an application, the primary justification for it lies in expense saving. As long as the expenses saved by elimination of the medical examination are greater than the cost of any extra mortality incurred because of its elimination, it is economically sound. Actuarial

---

[2]About two out of every three policies of ordinary insurance are written on a nonmedical basis. These policies account for approximately one-third of the amount of new ordinary insurance written.

studies underlie the nonmedical rules utilized by life insurance companies. Modifications are made in these rules from time to time as indicated by emerging experience, including the increasing costs of medical examinations in recent years.

Perhaps the most important safeguard built into the nonmedical underwriting rules is a limit on the amount available on any one insured. In the early days, this limit was $1,000. When experience proved to be more favorable than anticipated, the limits were gradually raised. During the 1970s, many companies provided up to $100,000 or higher on a nonmedical basis (subject to age limitations), and virtually all issued $50,000 on that basis.

In the 1980s, nonmedical limits exploded. Some companies had limits as high as $500,000 at the younger ages (through age 30) and at least one company had a $1,000,000 maximum. The maximum age generally held at 40 or 45. The reasons for this dramatic change were the effects of inflation on underwriting expenses, continuing reduction in deaths from natural causes at the younger ages, and high interest rates that decreased substantially the present value of the extra mortality from not obtaining a medical exam.

Usually, these large amounts of nonmedical insurance were underwritten without blood testing. Today, the situation has changed. The impact of AIDS and lower interest rates has led to significantly lower blood testing limits. Currently, most companies require a blood test for amounts of $100,000 or more and some companies have a lower limit. Also, nonmedical limits have been reduced at the younger ages.

A second safeguard built into nonmedical rules is a limit on the ages at which the insurance will be issued. Nonmedical insurance is not regularly available beyond age 50 or 60, except in special situations, such as a salary savings group where the age limits might be higher. Most companies impose no lower age limit, offering it down to age zero.

Other safeguards include the general limitation of nonmedical insurance to medically standard risks. Companies will usually consider occupations in which the extra hazard is largely accidental as well as all aviation and avocation exposure on a nonmedical basis. Some companies offer nonmedical coverage to higher ages or for larger amounts if the proposed insured has completed a comprehensive physical within the past six months or one year and the results are available from the attending physician. In addition to the expansion of nonmedical underwriting, there has also been expanded use of simplified underwriting in which only a few medical history questions are asked.

The application form used for nonmedical insurance contains the questions that would normally be asked by the medical examiner as well as the usual questions completed by the agent under a medical application. In the cases in which adverse medical information is developed from these or other sources, the company may request a paramedical examination or attending physicians' statements, or, at times, it may require a complete medical examination. This occurs with an estimated 10 percent of nonmedical applications.

## GUARANTEED ISSUE INSURANCE

One of the important contractual arrangements under which retirement benefits are provided to employees is the individual contract pension trust. Under this arrangement, benefits are provided through retirement annuity or retirement income contracts purchased by the employer, through a trustee, for each of the employees eligible to participate in the pension plan. Traditionally, when retirement income contracts were used, each employee had to furnish evidence of insurability in the form of a satisfactory medical examination. Many companies today underwrite such plans on a nonmedical basis. In fact, the arrangement goes beyond the conventional concepts of nonmedical insurance. If the *group* is acceptable, the insurance company dispenses with individual underwriting and agrees in advance to accept applications for insurance on all employees who are actively at work. This practice is known as **guaranteed issue**. With this arrangement, there is no underwriting of individuals's lives; being actively at work is the only requirement.

The mortality experience on these arrangements is higher than usual mortality, as would be expected. To offset the anticipated extra mortality under guaranteed issue plans, many companies pay lower commissions, and either charge a higher premium or classify the policies separately for dividend purposes.

## REINSTATEMENTS AND POLICY CHANGES

When a life insurance policy lapses for nonpayment of premium within the grace period, the policyowner has the contractual right to apply for policy reinstatement.[3] The owner must pay past-due premiums, plus provide evidence of insurability that is satisfactory to the insurer. Evidence of insurability is typically provided via a reinstatement application. This application is a shortened version of the original application and is completed with minimal effort and time. Underwriting requirements commonly are less strict for recently lapsed policies and the entire process is streamlined. For policies that have been lapsed for a longer time and for which reinstatement is sought, the underwriting procedure more closely resembles that for a new insurance policy.

Underwriting also may be required in connection with certain policy changes. In general, an insurer will require evidence of insurability on any policy change that increases the policy's net amount at risk, except of course, when the change is one guaranteed by the contract (e.g., automatic face amount increases under a cost-of-living-adjustment rider). Thus if a policyowner wishes to increase the policy face amount under a universal life or other policy, evidence of insurability ordinarily will be required.

[3]See Chap. 8.

Also, if it is desired to add additional benefits—such as waiver of premium, accidental death benefit, or guaranteed insurability option—to an existing policy, the insurer typically will require evidence of insurability. Similarly, underwriting and additional requirements are necessary to reduce or remove the extra premium on a rated policy. In each case, the essential purpose is to avoid adverse selection.

## HIGHLY IMPAIRED RISKS

In some cases, individuals with significant impairments have opportunities to obtain insurance at a cost they can afford even though the original application may have been declined by one or more companies. These opportunities can be found with companies that specialize in this market.

Specialist brokers often have arrangements with a large number of these specialist companies and can readily identify the company likely to make the best offer for a specific impairment. Insurers often have a business arrangement with substandard specialist companies or brokers to assist their agents in obtaining coverage through an alternate source. A proposed insured should not be unduly discouraged by a declination from one company, since considerable variation in underwriting judgment can exist even among the companies specializing in highly impaired risks.

## SOURCES OF INFORMATION CONCERNING LIFE AND HEALTH INSURANCE RISKS

An insurer may utilize several sources in obtaining information about a proposed insured, including: (1) the application, (2) a physical examination, (3) laboratory testing, (4) the agent, (5) attending physicians, (6) consumer reporting agencies, and (7) the Medical Information Bureau. The data from these sources overlap. The "double check" is justified by experience. The federal Fair Credit Reporting Act of 1970 and individual state Fair Insurance Information Practices laws have established procedures for the collection and disclosure of certain underwriting information to ensure fair and equitable treatment of the consumer with regard to confidentiality, accuracy, disclosure, and proper use.

## THE APPLICATION

Although application forms are by no means uniform in their content or arrangement, they generally consist of two parts. Part I of *life insurance* applications contains questions requesting information regarding: name, present and past home and business addresses, occupation, sex, date of birth, name and relationship of beneficiary, amount and kind of insurance for which application is being made, amount of life insurance already carried, driving record, past modifications or refusal to issue insurance, past and contemplated aviation activities, avocations, and plans for foreign residence or travel. In addition, the company will ask if the life insurance applied for is intended to replace insurance in force. This is required by most states over the applicant's signature.

Part I of the *health insurance* application consists of certain information about the proposed insured and members of his or her family. It reveals whether a family policy is being applied for and has a description of the policy for which application is being made. The application form is usually quite detailed and complete for noncancelable, guaranteed renewable, and optionally renewable insurance, but less so for industrial and limited policies. In its most complete form, it will include the individual's name, address, sex, occupation, business, and employer. Normally, it will also call for information as to present earnings and health insurance carried in all companies, including the one to which application is being made as well as replacement intentions, if any. Any life insurance in force must be listed, particularly if any disability income riders are involved. Such coverages must, in many cases, be described completely, including any applicable waiting periods and deductibles. The applicant is required to state whether any life or health company has ever rejected or modified his or her application, canceled or refused to renew a policy, or refused payment of a claim, as well as the reason for any such treatment.

Part II of both life and health insurance applications consists of medical history, furnished by the proposed insured to the medical or paramedical examiner or, if the policy is applied for on a nonmedical basis, to the agent, in response to questions that the latter is instructed to ask. Thus questions are asked regarding the illnesses, diseases, injuries, and surgical operations experienced in the last ten years, and regarding every physician or practitioner whom the proposed insured has consulted in the past five (or some other number of) years. Other questions relate to the present physical condition. All companies ask questions relating to the proposed insured's use of alcohol, tobacco, and drugs. Finally, questions may be asked about the individual's parents and siblings, including the number who are living, their present health condition, and the date and cause of any deaths that have occurred.

Some companies use "simplified underwriting" for applicants at younger ages and for smaller amounts that have a lesser mortality or morbidity risk; in these cases, in order to save time, only a few questions of a nonmedical nature are asked. This process is similar to that of a regular Part I application, but the medical history questions, which usually make up Part II, are condensed into only a few, less-detailed questions. This can be done because medical history at younger ages (where simplified underwriting is primarily used) is generally not very extensive or significant.

## THE MEDICAL (OR PARAMEDICAL) EXAMINATION

If a physical examination is necessary, the proposed insured's answers to the Part II medical history questions are recorded by the physician or paramedic. Also, the physician or paramedic reports the findings on the current medical examination. The examination by a paramedic might include height and weight measurements, chest and abdomen measurements, a blood profile, test for exposure to the AIDS virus, and a urinalysis that includes testing for nonprescription drug use. A regular medical exam might include all of these items plus an examination of the condition of the heart, lungs, and nervous system. In the case of larger life and disability policies, more detailed information involving complete blood and urine testing, electrocardiograms, pulmonary functions tests, and chest x-rays may be requested.

The medical examination in not foolproof. Many serious medical conditions can be detected only through sophisticated tests or invasive procedures that are inappropriate for insurance underwriting and therefore can pass undetected. Also, some individuals go to considerable effort to appear at their best through rest and diet, and may deliberately or unintentionally not disclose important items of health history. Only through the use of available information from all sources can an underwriter create an accurate picture of the individual and arrive at a fair decision.

Insurance companies routinely use paraprofessionals in lieu of physicians. Paramedical-type centers operate in many areas of the country, although the vast majority of paramedical examinations are undertaken in the proposed insured's home or office. Technicians will take the individual's medical history and take measurements and readings as mentioned above. An electrocardiogram may be taken, and blood and urine may be collected. In addition, some centers have medical doctors available. The increasing popularity of paramedical facilities can be attributed mainly to a combination of cost savings and a shortage of physicians to administer insurance exams. Most insurance companies using this service use it for policies that do not exceed a certain size but go beyond the company's nonmedical limits, or in lieu of a second medical exam (when one is required).

In health insurance, a medical examination is used regularly in applications for large amounts of long-term disability income coverage and life insurance disability income riders, and sometimes for major medical coverage at the older ages. In most other types of health insurance, it is used in doubtful cases. It is virtually never used with limited policies. In general, the frequency of medical examination use and the detail involved are not as great for health insurance applications as for life cases, because of expense considerations.

## LABORATORY TESTING

The scope of blood and urine testing for life and health insurance has increased dramatically in recent years, principally because of concern over excess claim exposure due to AIDS and illegal drug use. Insurers have found that this testing is cost justified, even at low levels of coverage in some cases. A side effect of this increased testing has been the increased availability of other useful information for risk selection purposes such as liver enzymes, lipids, and glucose levels.

A menu approach to testing offered by testing laboratories allows insurers to customize the testing of the blood and urine. The options for a venous blood draw range from a complete profile with 20 or more chemistries to a "miniprofile" that provides chemistries in key areas only, such as AIDS antibody testing, glucose tolerance, liver function, and lipids. More limited testing is also available with finger stick methods of collection such as the "microprofile" or dried blood spot testing.

Urine specimens are routinely collected at the same time as the blood specimen, and traditional urine tests have been expanded to include testing for controlled substances, medications, and nicotine. Additionally, urine testing is now available for the AIDS virus and is being utilized by some companies. Saliva testing is being investigated as a possible testing vehicle. The newer testing methods are not approved for use in all jurisdictions and tend to be used more frequently at lower limits to expand insurers' testing programs.

Recently, a great deal of research and discussion relating to genetic testing has taken place. Advances in genetic research mean that new information will be available on a variety of genetic illnesses. The life insurance industry's position is to treat genetic tests used by medical professionals in diagnostics, treatment, and preventive medicine no differently from any other medical tests used in clinical medicine.

Presently, insurers claim to be in no rush to use genetic testing. Nevertheless, the industry plans to follow the developing research and, at the appropriate time, introduce genetic testing, as it has with other medical advances, as an underwriting tool.

## THE AGENT'S REPORT

Most companies include on the back of the Part I application certain questions that the agent answers. Companies will usually ask the agent how long he or she has known the proposed insured and whether he or she knows of any adverse information. The agent may also be asked to express an opinion about his or her knowledge of the individual's financial standing, character, and environment.

When a company does not require an agent's report, it relies on its general instructions to its agents to prevent them from writing applications on persons who are unacceptable risks. If the agent believes the risk is doubtful, he or she may be instructed to submit a preliminary inquiry. If the individual has ever been refused insurance by any company, the agent may be instructed to report this fact to the company.

## ATTENDING PHYSICIAN STATEMENTS

The attending physician statement (APS) is used when the individual application or the medical examiner's report reveals conditions or situations, past or present, about which more information is desired. It may reveal additional health conditions or the names of additional physicians not reported in the application.

Because legal considerations prevent a physician from divulging information without the consent of the patient, this consent is always obtained. The applicant or proposed insured always signs an authorization at the time of application, and a copy of this is sent to the physician with the request for information. Standards exist in some states for these authorizations, as well as restrictions as to the extent to which information obtained with them may be disclosed to others. The APS is considered by many to be the single most important source of underwriting information.

## CONSUMER REPORTS

Life insurance companies obtain consumer reports or investigative consumer reports on all persons who apply for relatively large amounts of insurance. In the case of modest amounts (say $100,000 and less) and at the younger ages, many companies do not routinely obtain such reports. The reports can provide information bearing on the insurability of the proposed insured. Most companies use the services of **consumer reporting agencies** that maintain a staff to make such reports for these and other (e.g., employment) purposes.

A **consumer report** is defined by the federal **Fair Credit Reporting Act** (FCRA) as a written, oral, or other communication of any information by a consumer reporting agency that has a bearing on the consumer's creditworthiness, credit standing, credit capacity, character, general reputation, personal characteristics, or mode of living, and which is expected to be used in whole or in part to establish eligibility for insurance.[4] An **investigative consumer report** is a consumer report for which information is obtained from personal interviews with neighbors, friends, associates, or others acquainted with the consumer.[5]

When the company receives an application, if its rules call for a consumer report, one is promptly ordered, giving the applicant's name, age, sex, occupation, and places of residence and business. In some companies, the request for the report is made by the field agency. The report is then sent directly to the home office. The FCRA requires that the applicant be notified that such a consumer report may or will be made. The notification may be part of the application form, or it may be a separate notice.

When the amount of insurance is not particularly large, the investigator will make a rather general inquiry into the habits, character, financial condition, occupation, avocations, and health of the applicant. If the amount of insurance is large or if there is concern about possible adverse selection, a more careful and detailed report (the *investigative* consumer report) may be obtained, particularly

---

[4]FCRA, § 603(b). Consumer reports are also used for credit and employment purposes.
[5]FCRA, § 603(e).

regarding financial information, and more informants may be contacted. To obtain the necessary information for an investigative report, the investigator may interview the applicant's employer, neighbors, banker, accountant, business associates, others who may be able to contribute the information desired, and often also the applicant. The investigator will also check public records.

In lieu of consumer reports from outside investigative agencies, many companies rely on personal history interviews. During these interviews, which are conducted by personnel of the insurer directly with the applicant, the interviewer completes a questionnaire. As companies are becoming more comfortable with the results of these interviews, this format is being used for increasingly larger amounts.

## THE MEDICAL INFORMATION BUREAU

Another source of information regarding insurability is the Medical Information Bureau (MIB). A membership association of virtually all U.S. life insurance companies, it acts as a repository for confidential data, primarily of a medical nature, on individuals who apply for life or health insurance to member companies.

Member companies are required to code and report to the MIB certain medical impairments covering a broad spectrum of health conditions found during the underwriting process. Only data obtained from a medical source or directly from the applicant are to be reported as medical codes. A limited number of nonmedical codes exist, such as adverse driving record, aviation, hazardous sport activities, or known or suggested association with criminal activities, which are reportable because they may be considered significant by home-office underwriters. Member companies do not indicate their underwriting decisions in their reports to the MIB, nor do they state the amount or type of insurance applied for.

Member companies screen proposed insureds against MIB computer data files. If an impairment code is found, the company attempts to substantiate the code through its own investigation. If it fails to substantiate the recorded condition, it can submit a request for details through the MIB to the original reporting company. The original reporting company furnishes whatever details (if any) it wishes. MIB rules and many state laws stipulate that a member may not take any unfavorable underwriting action wholly or in part on the basis of MIB information. Such information is to serve only as an "alert" to the member. Using other sources, the member is expected to substantiate any unfavorable underwriting action by corroborating data regarding a particular condition. The MIB also provides the dates of database inquiries. This alerts companies to the possibility that the proposed insured may be avoiding certain underwriting requirements by applying for smaller amounts in several companies rather than for a large amount in one company.

A service provided by MIB that is of special interest to health insurers is the **Disability Income Record System** (DIRS). The purpose of this system is to provide information about applications for disability income insurance that will assist insurers in recognizing situations involving potential overinsurance.

The DIRS employs a central file that records certain nonmedical information about disability applications processed by the subscribing companies. When a member receives an application for disability income insurance involving a monthly disability income benefit of $300 or more with a benefit period of at least 12 months, it sends this information to the DIRS file. This information, retained in the file for five years, is made available to any other member company to which an individual may apply for disability income insurance.

The various state insurance-related privacy laws require that an individual be informed in writing before he or she has completed the application for insurance, that the company may report information to the MIB. The applicant is also advised how to obtain disclosure of his or her MIB file and dispute its accuracy. An authorization is signed permitting an inquiry to MIB. MIB disclosure and disputed accuracy procedures are set forth in the federal Fair Credit Reporting Act and state privacy requirements.

## LAWS AFFECTING UNDERWRITING

As discussed above, the underwriting process involves the collection and use of personal information concerning individuals who apply for life and health insurance. This fact has led to public concern about how insurers use this information, as well as about the confidentiality with which it is maintained. The federal FCRA, discussed earlier, was one of the first federal laws that addressed these concerns. Other federal and state laws and regulations place limits on insurers' freedoms with respect to the collection, maintenance, use, and disclosure of personally identifiable information on consumers. Each of the more important ones is discussed below.

## THE FAIR CREDIT REPORTING ACT

The federal FCRA was one of the first important laws to affect life insurance companies' information-gathering practices. It requires users of investigative consumer reports to notify the individual who is the subject of such a report that the report will be or has been requested. The user—in this case, the insurer—also must advise the consumer that he or she has the right to request disclosure of the nature and scope of the investigation.

A second requirement of the FCRA imposes a duty on the user of any consumer report to supply the subject consumer with the name and address of the consumer reporting agency if any action is taken to the consumer's detriment *and* the report contributed in whole or in part to the decision. This requirement applies whenever insurance (or credit) is denied or the charge increased because of information contained in the report. The consumer may then request disclosure.

In general, every consumer reporting agency (CRA), when it is requested to do so, must disclose to the consumer the nature and substance of all information (except medical information) contained in his or her file. Not only must the information itself be disclosed, but the CRA must also advise the consumer of the CRA's sources, although it need not disclose sources used solely to compile an investigative consumer report. While the FCRA does not give consumers the right to see and obtain copies of the report (only to learn the "nature and substance" thereof), in practice, however, CRAs routinely permit the consumer to see and to obtain actual copies of the report.

If the consumer disputes the completeness or accuracy of an item of information in his or her file, the CRA must reinvestigate within a "reasonable period of time" to ascertain the accuracy of the disputed information. If the reinvestigation proves the file information to be inaccurate or if it cannot be substantiated, the disputed data must be deleted. If, on the other hand, the reinvestigation fails to resolve the dispute, the consumer has the right to file a statement of up to 100 words presenting his or her side of the contested matter. Thereafter, the statement or a clear summary thereof must accompany the consumer report.

Several states have their own Fair Credit Reporting Acts. Generally, they track the federal law, except for extending certain additional rights to consumers or for limiting CRA's actions in some ways.

## THE NAIC MODEL PRIVACY ACT[6]

In 1979 the National Association of Insurance Commissioners adopted the NAIC **Insurance Information and Privacy Protection Model Act** (NAIC Model Privacy Act). It was revised in 1980 and again in 1981 and has since been adopted by about a dozen states. However its importance extends beyond these states' borders, since most insurers comply with the act's requirements, even in those states that have not enacted the law.

The NAIC Model Privacy Act is both a lengthy and a complex document. As a result, space permits only an overview of its significant provisions.[7] The act clearly and purposely is patterned after the insurance recommendations contained in the Privacy Protection Study Commission (PPSC) Report.[8]

[6]This section draws from Harold Skipper, Jr., "An Analysis of the NAIC Model Privacy Act," *Best's Review*, L/H ed., Vol. 80 (Mar. 1980).

[7]See James W. Newman, Jr., "A Description and Explanation of the NAIC Insurance Information and Privacy Protection Model Act," *Journal of Insurance Regulation*, Vol. I (Mar. 1983), pp. 352–377, for a more complete discussion of the act.

[8]Privacy Protection Study Commission, *Personal Privacy in an Information Society* (Washington, D.C. G.P.O., 1977), pp. 188–222.

The act may be divided arbitrarily into three areas. The first (sections 1 and 2) specifies the scope of the act and gives key definitions. The second (sections 3–13) contains the act's operative provisions, wherein the obligations imposed upon insurers, agents, and insurance consumers reside. The third (sections 14–24) contains the NAIC Model Privacy Act's enforcement and immunity provisions.

Thus, within the first area the act establishes that, with respect to life/health insurance, the residency of the individual determines the applicable state law. The task force that drafted the act hoped that this approach would avoid any problem with conflict of laws.

Within the second major area of the act (the operative sections 3–13) are found, in some form, most of the insurance recommendations of the PPSC. Thus the NAIC Model Privacy Act prohibits the use of pretext interviews except in certain claim situations. The act requires that a notice of an insurer's information practices be given to applicants and to certain policyowners.

The act mandates that insurers and agents specify clearly to an individual those inquiries that elicit information desired solely for marketing, research, or other purposes that are not directly related to the insurance transaction at hand. It also mandates minimum standards for disclosure authorization forms used by insurance institutions, agents, and insurance-support organizations.

Individuals are given the right under the act to be interviewed in connection with the preparation of any investigative consumer report. Certain persons are given a right of access to personal information on them maintained by insurers, agents, and insurance-support organizations. A corresponding right to request correction also is provided.

The act requires insurers to advise individuals of the reasons for any adverse underwriting decision affecting them and, if it is requested, to provide individuals with the information upon which the decision is based. The Model Act further stipulates that no insurer or agent may base an adverse underwriting decision on the mere fact of a previous adverse underwriting decision. It also provides that no insurer should base an adverse underwriting decision on personal information received from an insurance-support organization whose primary source of information is insurance institutions (e.g., the MIB).

Section 13, dealing with disclosure limitations and conditions, is the most complex section of the act. This section specifies the circumstances under which insurers, agents, and insurance-support organizations may disclose information about an individual without the individual's consent.

The third major area specifies the power given the insurance commissioner under the act and the remedies available to him or her. This area also provides that any person who is subject to an order of the commissioner has the right to obtain a review of such order through the appropriate county court. Violations of cease and desist orders are punishable by fine and/or suspensions or revocation of an insurer's or agent's license.

## REGULATIONS AND LAWS RELATED TO UNFAIR DISCRIMINATION

In addition to the limitations on a life insurance company's freedom to contract discussed earlier, there are various prohibitions in state laws against discrimination among persons applying for insurance. Most states have laws that provide that life insurance companies may not discriminate unfairly among individuals of the same class and with equal expectation of life in premiums, policy terms, benefits, or dividends. State laws also prohibit unfair discrimination because of sex, marital status, race, religion, or national origin. Some states prohibit discrimination because of sexual preference, as well.

The issue of unfair discrimination based on sex continues to be important to the insurance business. The implications of the U.S. Supreme Court's decision on the *Norris* case (prohibiting the use of sex-distinct mortality tables in an employer's voluntary deferred compensation plan) remains unclear, except for employer-sponsored plans.[9]

Montana became the first (and at this writing remains the only) state to prohibit the use of sex as a rating factor in individual insurance, including individual life and health insurance. Massachusetts issued a regulation to the same effect, but it was later overruled by that state's supreme court. In the federal and state legislatures and courts, efforts continue, by those who oppose using sex as a rating factor, to proscribe its use.

The argument by opponents of sex-based pricing is that, irrespective of statistics, it is unfair from a social standpoint. The insurance industry and others contend that use of sex-based pricing is not only justified (actuarially, women as a group live longer than men as a group), but also that to fail to recognize a price difference would itself be unfair discrimination.

The NAIC adopted a **Model Regulation to Eliminate Unfair Sex Discrimination** in 1976, and the majority of states have regulations or other requirements that are similar to those embodied in this NAIC model regulation. The regulation does not prohibit use of sex-based pricing; rather, it prohibits the denial of insurance coverage or benefits on the basis of sex or marital status.

The NAIC also adopted a **Model Regulation on Unfair Discrimination in Life and Health Insurance on the Basis of Physical or Mental Impairment.** The regulation prohibits refusal or limitation of coverage or rate differentials based solely on physical or mental impairment, unless the refusal, limitation, or rate differential is based on solid actuarial principles or reasonably anticipated experience. Several states have adopted regulations or passed laws in this area.

A companion regulation, the NAIC **Model Regulation on Unfair Discrimination on the Basis of Blindness or Partial Blindness,** has been adopted, in one form or another, in most states. The regulation stipulates that the refusal to insure or to continue to insure, or the limitation on the amount, extent

---

[9]*Arizona Governing Committee v. Norris*, 77, L.Ed.2d. 1236 (July 1983).

or kind of coverage available to an individual, or the charging of a different rate solely on the basis of blindness or partial blindness constitutes an unfair discrimination under the state's Unfair Trade Practices Act. The regulation enjoys strong insurance industry support.

## REINSURANCE OF LIFE INSURANCE RISKS

**Reinsurance** may be defined as a device by which a life insurance company transfers all or a portion of its exposure under a life insurance policy to another company. It is insurance for the insurer. The company that issued the policy originally is known as the **direct-writing** or **ceding company**. The company to which the risk is transferred is the **reinsurer** or **assuming company.**

### PURPOSES OF REINSURANCE

Although the primary purpose of reinsurance is to avoid too large a risk concentration within one company, it also may be used to take advantage of the underwriting judgment of the reinsurer, to transfer all or certain classes of substandard business,[10] to reduce the strain on surplus caused by writing new business, to stabilize the overall mortality experience of the ceding company, or, in the case of newly organized or smaller companies, to obtain advice and counsel on underwriting procedures, rates, and forms. A company also must provide its agency force with competitive facilities and needs reinsurance to permit acceptance of the cases written by its agents, regardless of the amounts involved.

Reinsurance also is used regularly by most companies as a means of obtaining better underwriting offers for proposed insureds who do not qualify for a standard or a moderately substandard offer under their own underwriting standards. Some reinsurers with liberal underwriting philosophies aggressively seek this type of business. Typically, the ceding company will retain only a small or no portion of the risk. Some reinsurers require a ceding company to maintain a portion of the risk on facultative cases (see below).

### THE CONCEPT OF RETENTION

A life insurance company deals with a type of risk that, in the aggregate, may be measured and predicted with a remarkable degree of accuracy, the closeness of the approximation depending on the number and homogeneity of the individuals

---

[10]Life reinsurance also may be undertaken to transfer all or a specific portion of a company's existing liabilities to the reinsuring company, including the administration of these policies directly with policyowners. This is known as **assumption reinsurance** and might be utilized when a company wishes to withdraw from business entirely or from a particular territory. Alternatively, specified blocks of business may be reinsured under **portfolio reinsurance.** Questions have arisen as to whether direct-writing companies should be able to make such transfers without policyowner consent. NAIC inquiries into the issue are expected to result, at the least, in more informed policyowners.

in the group. On the other hand, the exposure of one individual may be $300,000 and the exposure of another, $25,000. The probability of death for each may be the same, but the impact on the surplus of a company because of death clearly would be much greater with the $300,000 policy.

With a recently organized or small company, the need for a maximum limit on the amount of insurance it will retain for its own account on any individual life should be obvious. In companies with a relatively small total number of insureds, mortality experience can fluctuate widely from year to year. In such companies, the surplus funds available to absorb unusual losses usually are small, and a single large death claim or several significant claims might have a marked adverse effect on operations for the year. As a company increases in size because of an increasing total volume of insurance in force and increasing surplus funds, the chance of significant fluctuations in its overall mortality experience will decrease (thanks to the law of large numbers), and the company's ability to absorb unusual losses will increase. Thus it can gradually and safely increase its maximum retention on any one life.

There is no simple formula for fixing a retention limit, since it depends on a number of factors that are peculiar to a company's economic position and manner of operation. Such factors include: (1) the size of the company's unallocated surplus, (2) the quality of its agency force, (3) the quality of the home-office underwriting staff, (4) the distribution of insurance in force (by amount, number of policies, sex and age, proportion of substandard, etc.), and (5) the probable distribution of new business and average amount per policy.[11] In general, the smaller the group of units exposed to loss and the less homogeneous they are, the sharper and more sudden can be the fluctuations, and, therefore, the lower should be a company's limit of retention. Limits range from $25,000 in small, recently established companies to $20,000,000 or more in the largest companies. There are usually various limits within a given company, depending upon age at issue, substandard classification, and, sometimes, plan.

## REINSURANCE ARRANGEMENTS

The traditional plans of reinsurance developed to deal with individual risks may be broadly classified as proportional reinsurance and nonproportional reinsurance plans. Under **proportional reinsurance** plans the reinsurer and the ceding company share both premiums and claims on a given risk in a specified proportion. In contrast, **nonproportional reinsurance** provides for the reinsurer to pay a claim only when the amount of loss exceeds a specified limit (excess of loss coverage). Nonproportional reinsurance plans have the objective of

---

[11]A study by Kwangbong Lee, Bruce A. Palmer, and Harold D. Skipper, Jr., "An Analysis of Life Insurer Retention Limits," *The Journal of Risk and Insurance,* Vol. LIX (June 1992), found insurer size to be the most important determinant of insurer retention limits. Other factors included the insurer form (stock or mutual), the insurer's relative new business emphasis, average policy size, and the insurer's relative emphasis on term life insurance.

stabilizing the overall mortality experience of the ceding company. Nonproportional reinsurance usually takes one of three forms: stop-loss reinsurance, catastrophe reinsurance, or spread-loss reinsurance.[12] The basic characteristic that differentiates nonproportional plans from traditional proportional reinsurance plans is that they relate the reinsurer's liability to some measure of overall experience on all or specified blocks of the ceding companies' business, rather than to individual or specified policies of insurance. In addition, the proportion in which the ceding company and the reinsurer will share losses under nonproportional reinsurance is not determinable in advance. These forms are adaptations of property and liability reinsurance and are not widely utilized in the life field. In view of the predominance of proportional reinsurance, the remainder of this discussion relates to this form.

*Agreements.* Reinsurance may be arranged on a facultative or an automatic (also called treaty) basis. Under the **facultative** plan, each application is underwritten separately by the reinsurer. When the direct-writing company receives an application for a policy for more than the amount it wishes to assume, it negotiates with one or more reinsurers for a transfer of that part of the insurance that is in excess of the amount the company wishes to retain. Copies of the ceding company's application papers are sent to the reinsurer(s) for evaluation. The reinsurer (or reinsurers) then makes its own underwriting judgment and advises the ceding company.

The facultative method has certain advantages. It is flexible, and questions about the developed underwriting information can be discussed in the reinsurance negotiations. The original insurer also obtains the advice of the reinsurer with which it negotiates. The major disadvantages are the additional time required for completing the transaction, which may result in loss of business to competitors, and a higher cost per $1,000 for such coverage.

The **automatic** plan provides that the direct-writing company *must* transfer an amount in excess of its retention of each applicable insurance policy to the reinsuring company immediately upon payment of premium and the issuance of the policy. The reinsurer *must* accept the transfer that falls within the scope of the agreement. The treaty always provides that not more than a certain amount per policy may be transferred to the reinsurance company, and the agreement may provide for a distribution of the excess to more than one reinsuring company. The usual "split account" system may be based on percentage shares of each reinsured policy or on the first letter of the insured's surname (e.g., reinsurer 1 gets letters A–K and reinsurer 2 gets L–Z). When an application exceeds the limits of automatic treaties, facultative reinsurance is secured.

---

[12]**Stop-loss reinsurance** becomes payable if and when the aggregate death claims experienced by the ceding company in a year exceed some predetermined level. **Catastrophic reinsurance** covers multiple insured deaths arising from a single accident or other occurrence. Under **spread-loss reinsurance,** excess claims in a year are covered by the reinsurer, which is then, in effect, reimbursed over a period of time, and which allows the ceding company to spread its loss over several years.

With proportional reinsurance arrangements, the original insured is not a legal party to any reinsurance contracts that may result. He or she must look solely to the direct-writing company for any payments to which he or she is entitled under the policy, and the direct-writing company is liable for such payments, regardless of the existence and terms of any reinsurance contracts to which it may be a party.

*Plans.* There are two general methods for determining a reinsurer's liability in case of a loss under either facultative or automatic agreements. One of these is the **coinsurance plan,** under which the reinsurer assumes a share of the risk according to the terms that govern the original policy. If a loss occurs, the reinsurer is liable for a part thereof, which is determined by the size of the insurance assumed in relation to the original insurance amount.

Thus if the reinsurer has accepted one-half of the original insurance, it becomes liable for one-half of any loss. In return for this guarantee, the reinsurer receives a prorata share of the original premium less a ceding commission and allowance, the purpose of which is to reimburse the direct-writing company for an appropriate share of the agent's commissions, premium taxes paid, and a portion of the other expenses attributable to the reinsured policy. Similarly, the reinsurer reimburses for a proportionate share of dividends paid. In general, the reinsurance contract is a duplicate of that entered into by the original company with the insured. In essence, the ceding company and the reinsurer share a risk (premiums and claims) according to agreed proportions with reinsurance rates being derived from the original rates charged the policyowner.

Another plan of reinsurance is the **yearly renewable term plan.** This plan is particularly appropriate for smaller ceding companies, since it results in larger assets for these companies and is simpler to administer than the coinsurance plan. Under this plan, the reinsurer assumes the reinsured policy's net amount at risk for the amount in excess of the ceding company's retention. The ceding company pays premiums on a yearly renewable term basis. Thus for policies with declining net amounts at risk, a decreasing amount of reinsurance is purchased each year. If a loss occurs, the reinsurer is liable for the amount that it has assumed that year, and the ceding insurer is liable for its retention plus the full reserve on the reinsured portion of the policy. Premium rates for yearly renewable term reinsurance are established independently of the premium charged the policyowner.

In the interest of permitting a company to retain control over the funds arising out of its own policies, a **modified coinsurance plan** has been developed. Under this arrangement, the ceding company pays the reinsurer a proportionate part of the gross premium, as under the conventional coinsurance plan, less commissions and other allowances, premium taxes, and overhead allocable to reinsured policies. At the end of each policy year, the reinsurer pays to the ceding company a reserve adjustment that is equal to the net increase in the reserve during the year, less one year's interest on the total reserve held at the beginning of the year. The net effect of the plan is to return to the ceding company the bulk of the funds developed by its policies.

Modified coinsurance can be considered as yearly renewable term on a calendar-year basis, since the reinsurer, after paying the reserve adjustment, cash surrender values, and commissions and allowances, is left with only a risk premium. Aside from the reserve adjustment, the modified coinsurance follows that of the regular coinsurance plan. Table 24-3 provides a comparative analysis of the three basic reinsurance plans.

**TABLE 24-3      COMPARATIVE ANALYSIS OF REINSURANCE PLANS**

| Plan | Amount of Reinsurer's Liability in Case of Death | Responsibilities of Reinsurer | Allocation of Premium | Advantages |
|---|---|---|---|---|
| Yearly renewable term | Net amount at risk on portion of original policy reinsured[a] (reinsured amount tracks policy's net amount at risk above retention) | Reserves: yearly renewable term reserves only<br>Nonforfeiture value: none<br>Dividends: none | Premium to reinsurer equals net amount at risk times yearly renewable term rate for attained age (first-year rate may be 50% of renewal or less, to recognize insurer's high, first-year expenses) | Preferred by majority of companies; allows greater amount of asset retention and more premium for investment<br>Simplicity, inexpensive to administer |
| Coinsurance | Face amount on portion of original policy reinsured[a] (reinsured amount tracks policy's face amount in excess of retention) | Reserves: pro rata share<br>Nonforfeiture values: prorata share (reinsurer usually does not participate in policy loans)<br>Dividends: prorata share | Premium to reinsurer equals prorata share of gross premium less allowances | Preferred by companies with high acquisition costs for term plans<br>Reinsurer shares in surplus drain of new business by absorbing a proportion of the initial expense and reserve liability |
| Modified co-insurance | Same as coinsurance | Reserves: none<br>However at end of policy year, reinsurer pays to ceding company net amount of increase in reserves during year, less growth due to required interest<br>Nonforfeiture values: none, because reserves are held by ceding company<br>Dividends: prorata share | Premium to reinsurer equals prorata share of gross premium less allowances | Same as coinsurance above, but also cash value plans, plus return to ceding company of bulk of funds developed by policies<br>Original insurer's assets not diminished |

[a]In most cases, the portion of the original policy reinsured equals the face amount of the original policy minus the ceding company's retention limit. In some cases under facultative agreements, however, the ceding company might retain less than its usual retention limit.

## SOURCE OF FUNDS

Table 24-4 includes an example of the distribution of liability between a direct-writing company and a reinsurer with respect to a $100,000 ordinary life policy issued to a 35-year-old male reinsured under the coinsurance, yearly renewable term, and modified coinsurance plans. In each case, a retention of $25,000 is assumed.

## REINSURANCE OF HEALTH INSURANCE RISKS

Some health insurance coverages (e.g., major medical and disability income plans) involve substantial liability. As in the case of life insurance, reinsurance is utilized to avoid disruptive fluctuations in experience and company operating

**TABLE 24-4**  SOURCE OF FUNDS FOR PAYING A DEATH CLAIM UNDER THE COINSURANCE, YEARLY RENEWABLE TERM, AND MODIFIED COINSURANCE PLANS (ORDINARY LIFE, MALE, AGED 35, POLICY AMOUNT $100,000, $25,000 RETENTION)*

| Year | Direct Writer | | Reinsurer | | Total |
|---|---|---|---|---|---|
| | Reserve | Surplus | Reserve | Surplus | |
| | | | Coinsurance | | |
| 1 | $ 228.50 | $24,771.50 | $ 685.50 | $74,314.50 | $100,000 |
| 2 | 466.25 | 24,533.75 | 1,398.75 | 73,601.25 | 100,000 |
| 3 | 712.25 | 24,287.75 | 2,136.75 | 72,863.25 | 100,000 |
| 4 | 966.75 | 24,033.25 | 2,900.25 | 72,099.75 | 100,000 |
| 5 | 1,230.00 | 23,770.00 | 3,690.00 | 71,310.00 | 100,000 |
| 10 | 2,672.50 | 22,327.50 | 8,017.50 | 66,982.50 | 100,000 |
| 20 | 6,229.50 | 18,770.50 | 18,688.50 | 56,311.50 | 100,000 |
| | | | Yearly Renewable Term | | |
| 1 | $ 914.00 | $24,771.50 | $ 0.00 | $74,314.50 | $100,000 |
| 2 | 1,865.00 | 24,533.75 | 0.00 | 73,601.25 | 100,000 |
| 3 | 2,849.00 | 24,287.75 | 0.00 | 72,863.25 | 100,000 |
| 4 | 3,867.00 | 24,033.25 | 0.00 | 72,099.75 | 100,000 |
| 5 | 4,920.00 | 23,770.00 | 0.00 | 71,310.00 | 100,000 |
| 10 | 10,690.00 | 22,327.50 | 0.00 | 66,982.50 | 100,000 |
| 20 | 24,918.00 | 18,770.50 | 0.00 | 56,311.50 | 100,000 |
| | | | Modified Coinsurance | | |
| 1 | $ 228.50 | $24,771.50 | $ 685.50 | $74,314.50 | $100,000 |
| 2 | 1,186.02 | 24,533.75 | 678.98 | 73,601.25 | 100,000 |
| 3 | 2,180.94 | 24,287.75 | 668.06 | 72,863.25 | 100,000 |
| 4 | 3,210.34 | 24,033.25 | 656.66 | 72,099.75 | 100,000 |
| 5 | 4,275.25 | 23,770.00 | 644.74 | 71,310.00 | 100,000 |
| 10 | 10,127.76 | 22,327.50 | 562.24 | 66,982.50 | 100,000 |
| 20 | 24,612.90 | 18,770.50 | 305.10 | 56,311.50 | 100,000 |

*Assumes the *1980 CSO Table*, 5%, NLP reserve method, and claim paid on last day of policy year prior to any reserve payment from the reinsurer to the direct writer.

results. Reinsurance is also used for experimental coverages or for the writing of unusual lines with an inadequate spread of risk.

## PROPORTIONAL REINSURANCE[13]

As pointed out above, reinsurance methods involve sharing the risk on either a proportional or nonproportional basis. Proportional reinsurance can be expressed either as quota share or surplus share. Under the **quota-share** method, the insurer and the reinsurer share in a predetermined proportion of every risk underwritten in a specified category. Thus a company might reinsure 40 percent of every risk written on a certain policy form, regardless of the size of the risk. This basis also could apply to the company's entire health insurance portfolio or to one specific benefit among several benefits offered. In certain cases (e.g., experimental coverage), the ceding company might want the reinsurer to participate in a relatively large share of the risk.

In **surplus-share** reinsurance, the reinsurer assumes the liability above a predetermined dollar amount called the ceding company's retention. For example, a ceding company might retain up to $100,000 of accidental death benefit on any one life. Amounts in excess of this retention would be reinsured. When a disability income policy is involved, a company might retain $2,000 a month. Once the retention is selected, the reinsurer shares proportionately in the risk. Thus if a disability policy is issued for $4,000 a month and the retention is $2,000 a month, 50 percent of all payments are reinsured. Similarly, if the policy is for $8,000 a month, 75 percent of all payments would be reinsured. This method of reinsurance perhaps is the best means of leveling out marked or chance fluctuations in experience, especially when an insurer does not have the proper spread of risk on large cases.

A relatively small portion of an insurer's business typically is reinsured, with this portion made up of the large risks that are potentially less desirable, especially for disability income and accidental death. In such cases, involving greater potential adverse selection and malingering, underwriters exercise greater care in selection and greater care is also exercised in handling such claims.

## EXCESS-OF-LOSS REINSURANCE

With **excess-of-loss reinsurance,** a reinsurer reimburses a portion of the claim payments of the ceding insurer, but only after the ceding insurer had made payments for a specified number of months of total disability or after its retention, expressed in dollars, is exceeded. In **excess-of-time** (extended elimination) **reinsurance**, the extended-wait period extends beyond the elimination period found in the policy itself. The extended-wait period can be

---

[13]This and the following section are based upon *Individual Health Insurance*, Part A (Washington, D.C.: Health Insurance Association of America, 1992), pp. 149–154.

one, two, five, or even ten years under this plan before the reinsurer becomes responsible for payment. The reinsurer's share of such claim payments after the extended-wait period may be 70 to 80 percent of the monthly benefit. This reinsurance covers total disability benefits only and does not cover any other benefit of the policy, such as partial disability. It is not unusual to combine extended-wait with other types of reinsurance, such as surplus-share.

As in the case of life reinsurance, an automatic reinsurance agreement is often used, or it may be combined with automatic and facultative segments. (The latter is more common.) A facultative arrangement would have no automatic provision, and each case would be underwritten by the reinsurer.

# Chapter 25

# SOCIAL INSURANCE

This chapter begins a four-chapter discussion on employee benefit plans, with an emphasis on insured plans. A brief overview of employee benefit plans is first presented, followed by a discussion of the various social insurance programs in existence today in the United States. Chapter 26 is devoted to group insurance principles and to group life insurance while Chapter 27 covers medical care costs and benefits. The discussion in Chapter 28 on retirement plans completes the employee benefit plan presentation.

## INTRODUCTION TO EMPLOYEE BENEFIT PLANS

Government, employers, and individuals all play a role in the economic security of families and individuals. Employee benefit plans have an important place in this process of providing financial security.[1] Employee benefit plans may be defined as employer-sponsored plans that provide benefits if employees die, become sick or disabled, or lose their earnings as a result of retirement or unemployment. These benefits have become a significantly increasing part of the system of total compensation provided by U.S. employers. Along with other elements of a company's compensation system, these employee benefits should be effectively planned, coordinated, and balanced to help meet the objectives of both employees and the employer.

---

[1] For an excellent review of employee benefit plans, see Employee Benefit Research Institute, *Fundamentals of Employee Benefit Programs,* 4th ed. (Washington, D.C.: EBRI, 1990).

According to the U.S. Chamber of Commerce survey, the average payment of its members for employee benefits was 39.2 percent of payroll in 1991, up from 38.4 percent the previous year.[2] The average payment in 1991 was $13,126 per year per employee. The cost of employee benefits during 1991 was distributed as follows: medical and medically related benefits 26.4 percent; payment for time not worked 26.4 percent; legally required benefits ( including Old-Age Survivors, Disability and Health Insurance (OASDHI), Railroad Retirement, Unemployment Compensation, Workers' Compensation and Statutory Disability Benefits) 22.7 percent; retirement and savings plans 15.3 percent; life insurance 1.3 percent; paid rest periods 5.6 percent; and miscellaneous (discounts, educational assistance, and so forth) 2.3 percent.

The total cost of life and health insurance was 12.6 percent of payroll. This is a 0.7 percent increase from 11.9 percent in 1990. Employees have absorbed 38 percent of the increase in medical insurance costs between 1990 and 1991. This was a significant change from 1990 when employers absorbed virtually the entire cost of health insurance premiums. In addition, 73 percent of the firms in the survey indicated that they had either raised or instituted a deductible. This shift of medical care costs from the employer to the employee represents one of the responses of employers to rapidly increasing medical care costs.

The term *employee benefits* has many definitions.[3] This volume, however, will deal only with (1) income maintenance during periods when regular earnings are interrupted because of death, disability, retirement, or unemployment and (2) benefits to meet medical expenses associated with illness or injury.

## SOCIAL INSURANCE PROGRAMS

As suggested above, governments play an important role in providing economic security to families and individuals. Social insurance programs develop primarily in response to a perceived need by society for certain types of economic security measures for which neither individuals themselves nor private insurers can (or will) provide adequate coverage. Since the introduction of the U.S. Social Security program in 1935, many citizens have come to expect the government to provide at least a minimum level of protection against the financial consequences of premature death, old age, disability, and unemployment.

---

[2]Chamber of Commerce of the United States, *Employee Benefits 1992*. This study is updated annually.

[3]See, Burton T. Beam, Jr., and John J. McFadden, *Employee Benefits*, 3rd. ed. (Dearborn, Mich: Financial Publishing, Inc., 1992), pp. 3-5.

For the great majority of U.S. citizens, the most important form of household wealth is the anticipated Social Security retirement benefits. The introduction of Medicare has enhanced the significance of this source of wealth. Even so, a host of public policy issues has been debated since the start of Social Security.

The U.S. system is based on social adequacy rather than on individual equity concepts.[4] Social adequacy means that benefits paid provide a certain minimum standard of living to all contributors. Individual equity means that contributors receive benefits directly related to their contributions. The present U.S. system provides benefits on a basis that falls between these two definitions but with a heavy emphasis on the former. Thus benefits are heavily weighted in favor of lower-income groups, individuals with large families, and persons who were near retirement when they were first covered by Social Security. The purpose of the social adequacy principle is to provide a minimum floor of benefits to all groups.

Since private insurance operates on the individual equity principle, the issue of providing retirement and other benefits through either public or private means has been an ongoing debate. Disagreements over the impact of Social Security on the U.S. savings rate continue.[5] In central and eastern Europe, where Social Security systems first developed, proposals are under consideration to abolish the extensive governmental retirement systems, replacing them with private security systems.[6] In the United States, there has been a debate over making OASDHI voluntary.[7] Others have argued that in light of the greater longevity of women, the increasing divorce rate, and the aging of the population generally, the adequacy of the combined public and private approach is questionable.[8] Other issues include intergenerational equity and concern over the ability of the government system to pay promised benefits when this generation of workers retires.[9]

A recent study suggests that the notion that government cannot operate

[4]The classic paper on the issue of social adequacy is the one by Reinhard A. Hohaus, "Equity, Adequacy and Related Actions in Old-Age Security," in William Haber and Wilbur J. Cohen, eds., *Social Security: Program, Problems and Policies* (Homewood, Ill: Richard D. Irwin, 1960), pp. 61-63.

[5]See P. A. Diamond, "A Framework for Social Security Analysis," *Journal of Public Economics* (Aug. 1977), pp. 275-298; Martin Feldstein, "Social Security, Induced Retirement, and Aggregate Capital Accumulation," *Journal of Political Economy*, Vol. 82, No. 31 (Oct. 1974), pp. 905-926; Dean R. Leimer and Selig D. Lesnoy, "Social Security and Private Saving: New Time-Series Evidence," *Journal of Political Economy*, Vol. 90, No. 3 (June 1982), pp. 606-629; and Martin S. Feldstein, "Social Security and Private Saving: Reply," *Journal of Political Economy*, Vol. 90, No. 3 (June 1982), pp. 905-926.

[6]Steve A. Hanke, "Private Social Security: The Key to Reform in Eastern Europe," *Contingencies* (July/Aug. 1991), pp. 18-21.

[7]See Wilbur J. Cohen and Milton Friedman, *Social Security: Universal or Selective? National Debate Series* (Washington, D.C.: American Enterprise Institute, 1972).

[8]Alan J. Auerbach and Laurence J. Kotlikoff, "Life Insurance for the Elderly: Adequacy and Determinants," in *Work, Health and Income Among the Elderly*, Gary Burtless, ed. (Washington, D.C.: Brookings Institution, 1987), pp. 231-261.

[9]Merton C. Bernstein and Joan Brodshang Bernstein, *Social Security: The System that Works* (New York: Basic Books, Inc., 1988). See Chapter 14 discussion on retirement.

programs efficiently and inexpensively is untrue. Tables 25-1 and 25-2 show that the ratio of administrative expenses of the Social Security program relative to benefit outgo was 1.28 percent in 1990, and to contribution income it was 1.10 percent. The author concludes:

> This analysis clearly shows that the various portions of the Social Security program have, over the decades, been operated at a very low administrative cost. In fact, it is most likely that such costs have been somewhat too low and that the beneficiaries deserve better service and could well be willing to bear the slight additional amount needed. Significant improvements in the public understanding of the Social Security program and public confidence in the program's financial health could undoubtedly be achieved if the ratio of administrative expenses to contribution income were, say 1.25 percent instead of the actual 1.10 percent which occurred in 1990.[10]

**TABLE 25-1    ADMINISTRATIVE EXPENSES OF SOCIAL SECURITY PROGRAM RELATIVE TO BENEFIT OUTGO, 1990 (DOLLAR FIGURES IN MILLIONS)**

| Program | Administrative Expenses | Benefit Outgo | Ratio |
|---|---|---|---|
| Old-age and survivors insurance | $1,563 | $222,987 | 0.70% |
| Disability insurance | 707 | 24,829 | 2.85 |
| Old-age, survivors, and disability insurance | 2,270 | 247,816 | 0.92 |
| Hospital insurance | 758 | 66,239 | 1.14 |
| Supplementary medical insurance | 1,519 | 42,468 | 3.58 |
| Total medicare | 2,277 | 108,707 | 2.09 |
| Total programs | 4,547 | 356,523 | 1.28 |

**TABLE 25-2    ADMINISTRATIVE EXPENSES OF SOCIAL SECURITY PROGRAM RELATIVE TO CONTRIBUTION INCOME, 1990 (DOLLAR FIGURES IN MILLIONS)**

| Program | Administrative Expenses | Contrib. Income | Ratio |
|---|---|---|---|
| Old-age and survivors insurance | $1,563 | $270,290 | 0.58% |
| Disability insurance | 707 | 27,908 | 2.53 |
| Old-age, survivors, and disability insurance | 2,270 | 298,198 | 0.76 |
| Hospital insurance | 758 | 71,922 | 1.05 |
| Supplementary medical insurance | 1,519 | 44,355 | 3.42 |
| Total medicare | 2,277 | 116,277 | 1.96 |
| Total programs | 4,547 | 414,475 | 1.10 |

*Source*: Robert J. Myers, "Can the Government Operate Programs Efficiently and Inexpensively?" *Contingencies* (Mar./Apr. 1992), p. 15.

[10]Robert J. Myers, "Can the Government Operate Programs Efficiently and Inexpensively?" *Contingencies* (Mar./Apr. 1992), pp. 15-17.

It is beyond the scope of this text to discuss these issues in detail, but they are important public policy questions.

Social insurance programs in the United States may be put into four categories:

1. Old-age, survivors, disability, and health insurance

2. Unemployment insurance

3. Workers' compensation insurance

4. Temporary disability insurance

These social insurance programs play a significant role in employee benefit planning. The largest insurance expenditure for most employees is their contribution to Social Security. Furthermore, almost 25 percent of the dollars United States employers spend on benefits for their employees is used for legally required payments to social insurance programs. Finally, these programs form the foundation on which many individual insurance plans and employee benefit plans are built.

The emphasis in this text is on private employee benefit programs. Social Security, however, is so significant, both in terms of its own benefit structure and its impact on private plan design, that a reasonably detailed overview of this program seems essential. A brief overview of the other social insurance programs also is included.

## OLD-AGE, SURVIVORS, DISABILITY AND HEALTH INSURANCE PROGRAM

The Social Security Act of 1935, inspired largely by the severe business depression of 1930 to 1936, gave the United States an old-age benefit system for the first time.[11] This depression highlighted the reasons such a government plan of protection was needed: (1) the national economy had gradually been transformed from an extended family, self-sufficiency basis, where the aged contributed to family support, to a complex urban system under which the self-sufficiency of the nuclear family largely ceased; (2) there was an increasing need, under the new urban system, for the old to have money for room and board without their having the opportunity to earn a living; (3) the increasing specialization and efficiency of industrial establishments made it difficult for the old to retain their jobs and next to impossible for them to secure new jobs if the old ones were lost; and (4) there was a rapid increase, both absolutely and

---

[11] The 1935 Social Security Act was a broad attack on the problems of financial insecurity. In addition to old-age insurance benefits, the act covered areas such as aid to the blind, orphans, and aged, and unemployment insurance. This discussion is concerned with the present system only. For an extensive study of Social Security, see Robert J. Myers, *Social Security* (Homewood, Il.: Richard D. Irwin, 1985). See also *History of the Provisions of Old-Age, Survivors, Disability, and Health Insurance, 1935-1989* U.S. Department of Health and Human Services, Social Security Administration, Office of the Actuary (Mar. 1990).

relatively, in the number of old persons in the population. At first, benefits were available only to the worker, but in 1939 the system was enlarged to provide insurance protection to the worker's family also. The new enlarged system then assumed the name of Old-Age and Survivors Insurance (OASI).

Several amendments were made in the 1940s and 1950s, the effects of which were to expand the system and increase benefits. Amendments in 1956 made disability income part of the bundle of benefits provided in the act, changing the name to Old-Age, Survivors, and Disability Insurance (OASDI).

Further amendments and benefit increases were made throughout the 1960s and 1970s. The 1965 amendments introduced, among other things, a new Title XVIII to the Social Security Act. This title initiated a health insurance program for the aged, popularly referred to as Medicare, thus changing the name to the Old-Age, Survivors, Disability, and Health Insurance (OASDHI) program—its current name.

## COVERAGE

Coverage for Old-Age, Survivors, and Disability Insurance is conditioned on attachment to the labor market. Unlike many social insurance programs in other countries, the United States program is not based on the principle of universal coverage of all citizens, but rather only of those who are employed.

Virtually all occupations are covered, although certain occupations are subject to special eligibility rules because of administrative or constitutional reasons. Covered on an elective basis are state and local government employees who are covered under a retirement system, and ministers. Presently, about 95 percent of the employed are covered under OASDI and must pay Social Security taxes.

## ELIGIBILITY FOR BENEFITS

The benefits derived from OASDI depend upon the insured status of the individual worker. There are three types of insured status: (1) fully insured, (2) currently insured, and (3) disability insured. Determination of an individual's insured status depends upon his or her number of **quarters of coverage** and, in some instances, when they were earned.

For 1993, a quarter of coverage is given for each full $590 unit of annual earnings on which Social Security taxes are paid, up to a maximum of four quarters per year. This earnings amount is adjusted annually according to changes in the national wage level.

*Fully Insured Status.* An individual can attain **fully insured** status by being credited with either (1) 40 quarters of coverage earned at any time after 1936 or (2) at least one quarter of coverage (whenever earned) for every calendar year elapsing after 1950 (or after the year in which the worker attains age 21, if later), up to the year in which he or she reaches age 62 or, if earlier, dies or becomes disabled. A worker who fulfills the first requirement remains fully insured even if he or she spends no future time in covered employment. A minimum of six quarters of coverage is required in any case. Subject to certain requirements set forth in law, a year during which a worker is disabled does not adversely affect his or her eligibility for fully insured status.

*Currently Insured Status.* An individual can attain **currently insured** status by being credited with a minimum of six quarters of coverage during the 13-quarter period ending with the quarter in which he or she dies. Fully insured status is related to the length of attachment and currently insured status to the recency of attachment related to the labor market.

*Disability Insured Status.* An individual worker is eligible for cash disability benefits if he or she (1) is fully insured; (2) has at least 20 quarters of coverage out of the last 40 quarters prior to disability; and (3) has been disabled for at least five months by a disability that is so serious that it prevents him or her from engaging in "any substantial gainful activity" and has lasted or may be expected to last at least 12 months or to result in death. For persons born in 1962 or later, the coverage requirements are reduced. The disabled individual also must be willing to accept state vocational rehabilitation services.

## BENEFIT AMOUNTS[12]

To understand the Social Security benefit structure, one must understand certain key concepts and terms in the law that determine benefit amounts.

*Primary Insurance Amount.* All monthly income benefits are based on the worker's **primary insurance amount** (PIA), which is the monthly amount paid to a retired worker at normal retirement age (currently age 65) or to a disabled worker. The primary insurance amount, in turn, is based on the worker's **average indexed monthly earnings** (AIME).

*Average Indexed Monthly Earnings.* Prior to the 1977 amendments to the Social Security Act, there was a technical flaw in the provision for computing benefits. The way the original legislation was written, covered workers could benefit twice during certain types of inflationary conditions. First, the benefit scale was adjusted upward to reflect the price inflation. Second, as wages tended to increase during inflationary periods, higher wages also would produce still higher future benefits. These two elements could, under some circumstances, more than offset the effect of the changing factors in the weighted benefit formula. The result was that workers retiring in the future could, under some

---

[12]This section draws on George E. Rejda, *Social Security and Economic Security*, 4th ed. (Englewood Cliffs, NJ: Prentice-Hall, Inc., 1991), pp. 99-104.

circumstances, receive retirement benefits eventually exceeding 100 percent of their earnings in the year prior to retirement. Naturally, long-run costs would have increased significantly. The AIME basis for determining benefits was developed in response to this unintended result of the earlier legislation.

This wage-indexing method is designed to ensure that monthly cash benefits will reflect changes in wage levels over the worker's lifetime so that the benefits paid will have a relatively constant relationship to the worker's earnings before retirement, disability, or death. The result is that workers who retire today and workers who will be retiring in the future will have about the same proportion of their earnings replaced by Social Security retirement benefits.

Earnings are indexed by multiplying the actual earnings subject to Social Security taxation for the year being indexed by the ratio of (1) average national wage for the second year before the worker reaches age 62 or, if earlier, becomes disabled or dies, to (2) average national wage for the year being indexed. For example, assume that George retired at age 62 in 1993. The significant year for setting the index factor is the second year before he attained age 62 (1991). If George's actual taxable wages were $5,000 in 1956, this amount is multiplied by the ratio of the average national wage ($21,811.60) in 1991 to the average national wage ($3,532.36) in 1956. Thus George's indexed earnings for 1956 would be calculated as follows:

$$\frac{\text{Actual Earnings}}{\text{in 1956}} \cdot \frac{\text{average annual wages in 1991}}{\text{average annual wages in 1956}} \cdot \frac{\text{Indexed Earnings}}{\text{for 1956}}$$

and

$$\$5,000.00 \cdot \frac{\$21,811.60}{\$3,532.36} = \$30,873.98$$

A similar calculation is carried out for each year in the measuring period, except that earnings for and after the indexing year are counted in actual dollar amounts. The adjusted earnings then are used to determine the worker's primary insurance amount.

To obtain the AIME, one must first calculate the number of years elapsing between (1) the first day of the year in which the insured reached age 22 or January 1, 1951, if later, and (2) the year before the insured becomes 62 or, if earlier, dies or becomes disabled. Five is arbitrarily subtracted from this result.[13] This further result is converted from years into months.

The worker's indexed covered earnings are then calculated for the relevant time period, following the procedure illustrated above. These earnings, prior to indexing, are subject to year-by-year maximums, shown in Table 25-3. The years with the highest indexed earnings are used, but if the individual does not

[13]For persons disabled before age 47 the number of drop-out years is four for ages 42 to 46, three for ages 37 to 41, two for ages 32 to 36, one for ages 27 to 31, and none for ages under 27.

have as many years with earnings as must be used, zeros must be used for the remaining years. The periods during which an insured individual is totally disabled are omitted in the calculation of the number of years used in determining the average indexed monthly earnings. The effect of the drop-out and disability freeze provisions is to increase the average indexed monthly earnings and, consequently, the benefits to be provided. In retirement cases, the number of years used cannot be less than five. Earnings in any years after 1950 can be used, including years before age 22 and years after age 61.

*PIA Formula.* After the worker's AIME is established, a weighted formula is used to determine the primary insurance amount. Based on the 1993 benefit formula, which is applicable to persons who attain age 62 in 1992 (or workers under age 62 who die or become disabled in 1992), the PIA is determined as follows:

90 percent of the first $401 of AIME

+

32 percent of the next $2,039 of AIME

+

15 percent of the AIME in excess of $2,420

The formula break points are adjusted annually to reflect changes in average wages in the national economy. In addition, the benefit amount resulting from application of the formula is subject to the automatic cost-of-living provisions (see below) for the year of attainment of age 62 (or prior death or disability).

*Automatic Cost-of-Living Adjustment.* Monthly cash benefits are adjusted automatically for specified changes whenever the Consumer Price Index (CPI)

**TABLE 25-3**      **MAXIMUM COVERED EARNINGS TO BE USED IN CALCULATING AVERAGE INDEXED MONTHLY EARNINGS**

| Period | Amount | Period | Amount |
|---|---|---|---|
| 1937–50 | $ 3,000 | 1980 | $25,900 |
| 1951–54 | 3,600 | 1981 | 29,700 |
| 1955–58 | 4,200 | 1982 | 33,400 |
| 1959–65 | 4,800 | 1983 | 35,700 |
| 1966–67 | 6,600 | 1984 | 37,800 |
| 1968–71 | 7,800 | 1985 | 39,700 |
| 1972 | 9,000 | 1986 | 42,000 |
| 1973 | 10,800 | 1987 | 43,800 |
| 1974 | 13,200 | 1988 | 45,000 |
| 1975 | 14,100 | 1989 | 48,000 |
| 1976 | 15,300 | 1990 | 51,300 |
| 1977 | 16,500 | 1991 | 53,400 |
| 1978 | 17,700 | 1992 | 55,500 |
| 1979 | 22,900 | 1993 | 57,600 |

increases during the measured period.  Benefits are increased by the same percentage (rounded to one-tenth of 1 percent) as the percentage by which the CPI for the cost-of-living computation quarter exceeds the CPI for the later of: (1) the most recent cost-of-living computation quarter or (2) the most recent calendar quarter in which a general benefit increase became effective.  If the cost-of-living adjustment is made, the taxable earnings base and earnings test (discussed below) also are automatically adjusted.[14]

The cost-of-living provision is valuable since, with its use, the real purchasing power of the cash benefits tends to be maintained during inflationary periods.  In view of the political sensitivity of Social Security benefits, it is not surprising that if the CPI declines during the measuring period, benefits are not changed (but subsequent increases are then based on the CPI level before the decline).

*Maximum Family Benefits.* There is a limit on the maximum monthly benefits that can be paid to a family based on the earnings record of one person.  For persons disabled in 1983 and later, the maximum family benefit is the lower of (1) 85 percent of the worker's AIME (or actual PIA if higher) or (2) 150 percent of the PIA.  The maximum family benefit for persons who reach age 62 and retire in 1993 or who die before age 62 in 1993 is based on the following formula:

150 percent of the first $513 of PIA

+

272 percent of the next $227

+

134 percent of the next $226

+

175 percent of the PIA in excess of $966

Whenever the total monthly benefits payable to all beneficiaries on the basis of one worker's earnings record exceed the maximum allowed, each dependent's or survivor's benefit is reduced proportionately (but not the worker's benefit), to bring the total within the maximum.

## NATURE OF BENEFITS

The OASDI program provides retirement, survivor, and disability benefits.  As pointed out above, all benefits are based on the insured worker's primary insurance amount.

---

[14]The maximum earnings base is adjusted annually based on changes in average wages in the national economy if benefits are increased according to the automatic cost-of-living provisions. Rejda, *Social Security and Economic Security*, pp. 101-102.

*Retirement Benefits*. The insured worker's retirement benefit, a life income, is referred to as the old-age insurance benefit and is equal to 100 percent of the worker's PIA for retirement at the **normal retirement age** (NRA).  NRA is 65 until the year 2003.  It slowly increases then until it reaches 67 in 2027.[15]  The spouse of a retired worker is entitled to a benefit (**wife's/husband's benefit**) equal to 50 percent of the worker's PIA if he or she is at the NRA or older at the time of claim,[16] or regardless of age, if the spouse has under his or her care a dependent and unmarried child of the worker under age 16, or regardless of age if the child is disabled before age 22.

In addition, each unmarried child under 18 (or under 19 if the child is attending a primary or secondary educational institution on a full-time basis) or disabled before age 22 is entitled to a benefit (**child's benefit**) equal to 50 percent of the worker's PIA.  The total benefits payable to a retired individual and his or her dependents are subject to the overall family maximums.  Retirement benefits are available only to fully insured workers.

*Survivor Benefits*. The unremarried spouse of a deceased, fully insured worker can be entitled to survivor benefits as early as age 60.  He or she is entitled to 100 percent of the deceased worker's PIA if he or she waits until the NRA or later to receive benefits.  These **widow's/widower's benefits** that are claimed between ages 60 and the NRA are reduced proportionately.  The NRA for widows and widowers increases beyond age 65 for those attaining age 60 by 2000 and gradually rises to 67 for those attaining age 60 in 2022 (i.e., becoming 67 in 2029).  If the widow/widower is aged 50 to 59 and also disabled, she or he can be entitled to a disability benefit.  Regardless of age, if a widow/widower has under her or his care a dependent and unmarried child under age 16 of a worker or a child disabled before age 22, he or she is entitled to a benefit (**mother's/father's benefit**) equal to 75 percent of the PIA.

In addition, a dependent and unmarried child under age 18 (or under 19 if the child is attending a primary or secondary educational institution on a full-time basis) or regardless of age, if disabled before age 22, is entitled to a benefit (**child's benefit**) that is equal to 75 percent of the primary insurance amount. Dependent parents who are 62 and over are each entitled to a benefit (**parent's benefit**) that is equal to 75 percent of the PIA.[17]  The same maximum family

---

[15]A man or woman who retires as a worker when the NRA is 65 can elect to retire at age 62 with a permanently reduced benefit equal to 80 percent of his or her full benefit (PIA).  When the NRA increases to above 65, the reduction for early retirement increases (and the factor for age 62 is 70 percent when the NRA is 67).  Benefits are prorated for retirement between ages 62 and the NRA.

[16]The spouse of a retired worker, when the NRA is 65, may qualify for benefits as early as age 62, but with a reduced benefit: 75 percent of the full benefit is payable at age 62, and proportionately more if benefits are first claimed between ages 62 and 65.  When the NRA increases to above 65, the reduction for early retirement increases (and the factor for age 62 is 65 percent when the NRA is 67).

[17]If only one parent is entitled to this benefit, the benefit is 82 1/2 percent of the deceased's primary insurance amount.

benefit applies as in retirement cases. In addition to the income benefits, on the death of the worker who was living with a spouse or who leaves a spouse or child immediately entitled to monthly benefits, a lump-sum benefit of $255 **(death benefit)** is paid.

All of these survivorship benefits are available to the dependents of a fully insured worker. The dependents of a currently insured worker are eligible only for (1) the mother's/father's benefits; (2) the survivor child's benefit; and (3) the lump-sum death benefit.

*Disability Benefits.* The disability income benefit is equal to 100 percent of the primary insurance amount, but it continues only for as long as there is disability. The determination of disability is made by state agencies, with the Social Security Administration having the right of review. The determination of continuance of disability is made by the Social Security Administration.

Monthly payments are made to the dependents of persons receiving disability insurance benefits. The dependents eligible for these benefits are the same as the ones who would qualify as dependents of persons receiving retirement benefits. Since legislation in 1980, a lower family maximum benefit has applied in disability cases than in retirement and survivor cases (namely, the lower of 150 percent of PIA or 85 percent of AIME, but not less than the PIA).

The 1980 amendments accented the importance of rehabilitation in the disability program. Thus a disabled beneficiary who performs services despite severe handicaps can continue to receive benefits for 12 months. In addition, the law provides a three-month period of adjustment for beneficiaries who medically recover from their disabilities.

An unmarried child of a deceased, disabled, or retired worker who is disabled prior to age 22 is eligible for a cash disability benefit at age 18 or after. The child's disability benefits are payable for as long as the disability continues and are the same as the benefit received by a dependent child of a disabled, retired, or deceased worker. Also, a mother's/father's benefit is payable to the parent who has in his or her care a disabled child receiving benefits. This applies if he or she is a spouse of a disabled, retired, or deceased worker. The rehabilitation features of the disability program also apply to a disabled child. Blind persons are eligible for disability benefits even if not currently insured.

## REDUCTIONS AND OTHER BENEFIT CHANGES

A Social Security beneficiary can be subject to a total or partial reduction in benefits under certain situations.

*Earnings Test.* Benefits are reduced for Social Security beneficiaries under the age of 70 if they have earnings from work that exceed a specified level. If an eligible person is, in 1993, aged 65 to 69 and receives earnings of more than

$10,560 a year[18] from covered or noncovered employment, some or all benefits will be lost for that year.  Earnings of $10,560 or less cause no loss of benefits.  There is a loss of $1 in benefits for every $3 of earnings on the portion of earnings over $10,560 (for persons under age 65, the loss is $1 of benefits for every $2 of earnings over $7,680).  However, no benefits are lost for any month in the first year of retirement in which the individual neither earns more than one-twelfth of the annual exempt amount in wages nor renders substantial services in self-employment.  The earnings test applies to all beneficiaries under age 70, except disabled beneficiaries.

The earnings of a person who is receiving benefits as a dependent or as a survivor affect only his or her own benefits, and not payments to other members of his or her family.  Thus if the wife of a deceased worker loses her benefit because of the earnings test, her children (if they are under age 18, disabled since age 18 or until they are age 19 if they meet the school-attendance requirement) will continue to receive their benefits.

*Dual Eligibility.*  A person eligible for more than one benefit will receive in effect the highest benefit for which application has been made.  Thus a wife, eligible in her own right as an insured worker, can draw benefits under her husband's insured status only to the extent that they exceed the amount of her old-age benefit.  Also, the benefits for a spouse of a retired, disabled, or deceased insured worker are reduced by two-thirds of any pension that such spouse earned from a retirement system for government employees that was not coordinated with Social Security.

*Delayed Retirement.*  A worker receives a special increase in his or her old-age benefits for each month that he or she delays retirement between the NRA and age 70.  For persons who attained age 65 in 1982 to 1989, this increase was at the annual rate of 3 percent; for attainments of age 65 in 1990 to 1991, it was 3 1/2 percent.  Thereafter the increase is 4 percent for 1992 to 1993 attainments and 8 percent for attainments of the NRA in 2009 (then age 66) and after.  Work beyond retirement age frequently results in a higher AIME.  Years worked after age 62 can be selected as years of highest earnings.[19]

*Changes in Family Status.*  Social Security benefits are terminated when changes in family status, such as marriage or divorce, alter the conditions under which payments are made.  For example, payments to a nondisabled child stop when he or she reaches age 18, or 19 if the child is attending high school, and payments to a widow or widower generally stop if she or he remarries (but not if the beneficiary is 60 years or over).

---

[18]For beneficiaries who are under 65 in 1993, the limit is $7,680.  This amount increases automatically in accordance with changes in the general level of wages.

[19]See *Social Security Manual* (Cincinnati, Ohio:  The National Underwriter Company, 1993), Section F27.

*Other.* Failure to file for benefits after eligibility may deprive a person of benefits for a period of time. The act grants monthly benefits retroactively for a period of 6 months (12 months for disability cases). The individual also has a responsibility, periodically, to check into the accuracy of the Social Security Administration's records relating to his or her account. Benefits also may be lost because of certain work performed outside the United States and/or because an individual is convicted of certain subversive crimes.

*Taxation of Social Security Benefits.* As a result of 1983 amendments, part of Social Security benefits may be subject to federal income taxation. Beginning in 1984, up to one-half of Social Security benefits is included in the gross income of beneficiaries whose modified adjusted gross income exceeds certain base amounts. The base amounts are $25,000 for a single taxpayer, $32,000 for married taxpayers filing jointly, and zero for married taxpayers filing separately. The amount included is 50 percent of this excess. As this book was going to press, discussions were taking place about possibly increasing the amount of benefits subject to income taxation.

## MEDICARE PROGRAM

The 1965 amendments in the Social Security Act added Title XVIII, thereby initiating a health insurance program for the aged. Medicare represented one of the most sweeping changes ever made in the Social Security system.[20]

**Medicare** is, in general, a two-part program of federal health insurance. Under **Part A**, the Hospital Insurance Plan, essentially all persons aged 65 or over and all persons who have been receiving Social Security disability benefits for at least two years are covered for extensive hospitalization benefits.[21]

*Part B*, which is optional, provides a supplementary program for surgical and physician's care, and certain other benefits, for persons over age 65 and all persons who have been receiving Social Security disability benefits for at least two years. Eligible persons must pay a monthly premium of $36.60 in 1993 for this coverage. The premium will change yearly.

Medicare is secondary in payment to private group health insurance or liability insurance in some cases [e.g., to liability insurance under automobile policies, to group health insurance for chronic renal disease for the first 12 months, and to group health insurance for persons actively at work (and their spouses) for employers with 20 or more employees].

---

[20]The 1972 amendments extended Medicare to persons under age 65 who receive Social Security or railroad retirements benefits based on long-term disability for at least 24 months or who have chronic renal disease and require hemodialysis or a kidney transplant.

[21]All persons eligible to receive Social Security benefits because they are at least age 65, a worker (even if not actually retired), a spouse, or a survivor, or because they have been receiving benefits based on disability for at least 24 months are automatically eligible for health insurance benefits. All other persons (with minor exceptions) can buy this protection by paying premiums ($192 per month in 1992), providing they also enroll in Part B of the program.

***Hospital Insurance.***  The basic hospital-plan benefits include the following:

1. *Inpatient hospital services* for up to 90 days in each *benefit period.* There also is a provision for a lifetime reserve of 60 days that can be used after the 90 days in a *spell of illness.* In 1993 the patient pays a deductible amount of $676 for the first 60 days, plus coinsurance of $169 a day for the next 30 days for each spell of illness, plus coinsurance of $338 a day for the lifetime-reserve days.  Hospital services include all those ordinarily furnished by a hospital to its inpatients.  However, payment is not made for private-duty nursing or for the hospital services of physicians except by medical or dental interns or residents in training under approved teaching programs.  Inpatient psychiatric hospital service is included, but a lifetime limitation of 190 days is imposed.

2. *Posthospital skilled nursing care* (in a facility having an arrangement with a hospital for the timely transfer of patients and for furnishing medical information about patients) after a patient is transferred from a hospital (after at least a three-day stay) for up to 100 days in a benefit period.  In 1993, after the first 20 days, patients pay coinsurance of $84.50 a day for the remaining days of care in a spell of illness.

3. *Home health services* on an unlimited-visit basis, without a requirement of prior hospitalization.  The recipient must be in the care of a physician and under a plan established by a physician.  These services include intermittent nursing care, therapy, and the part-time services of a home health aide.  The patient must be homebound, except that when certain equipment is used, the individual can be taken to a hospital, extended-care facility, or rehabilitation center to receive some of these covered home health services in order to get the advantage of the necessary equipment.

4. *Hospice care* for terminally ill patients.

A **benefit period** is considered to begin when the individual enters a hospital, and it ends when he or she has not been an inpatient of a hospital or skilled nursing facility (including rehabilitation services) for 60 consecutive days. The deductible amounts for inpatient hospital care are increased to keep pace with increases in hospital costs.  The daily coinsurance amounts for long hospital stays and skilled nursing care benefits are correspondingly adjusted.

***Supplementary Medical Insurance***.  Subject to a $100 annual deductible and a 20 percent participation (coinsurance) of covered expenses (subject to a maximum of the standard charges recognized by Medicare) above the deductible, the supplementary plan provides the following benefits:

1. *Physicians' and surgeons' services*, whether furnished in a hospital, clinic, office, home, or elsewhere.

2. *Home health services*, without limit (identical to those covered under hospital insurance, which provides such benefits if the person is covered thereunder) are available and are not subject to cost-sharing provisions.

3. *Medical and health services,* including diagnostic X-ray, diagnostic laboratory tests, and other diagnostic tests; X-ray, radium, and radioactive-isotope therapy; ambulance services; surgical dressings and splints, casts, and other devices for reduction of fractures and dislocations; rental of durable medical equipment, such as iron lungs, oxygen tents, hospital beds, and wheelchairs used in the patient's home; prosthetic devices (other than dental) that replace all or part of an internal body organ; braces and artificial legs, arms, and eyes; physical therapy treatments; and so on. In some instances, certain services are not subject to the deductible and coinsurance provisions (e.g., diagnostic laboratory tests).

4. *Psychiatric care,* subject to a special limitation on outside-the-hospital treatment of mental, psychoneurotic, and personality disorders. Payment for such treatment during any calendar year is limited, in effect, to 50 percent of the expenses.

The program recognizes only the so-called "reasonable charges" for services. Thus not all physician charges may be reimbursable under the program. If any of the services outlined above are covered under the basic hospital plan, they are excluded from coverage under the supplementary plan. The law provides for special rules regarding enrollment periods and the time when coverage commences. Figure 25-1 summarizes Medicare benefits as of January 1, 1993.

## FINANCING OASDHI

*OASDI.* The Old-Age, Survivors, and Disability Insurance System is financed on a contributory basis, shared equally by employee and employer.[22] The employee pays a tax on the wages he or she receives, and the employer pays a tax on its payroll. The 1993 rate of contribution is 6.2 percent of covered wages and of payroll, for a total contribution of 12.4 percent of covered payroll (present law schedules no change in this rate in the future). The tax in 1993 for OASDHI is calculated on the first $57,600 of wages paid to an employee. The maximum taxable earnings rise with earnings trends. The employer withholds the employee's tax from his or her pay and remits the employee's tax and its own tax to the United States District Director of Internal Revenue.

The tax pattern is somewhat different for self-employed persons covered under the act. To finance this phase of the program, self-employed individuals pay a tax equal to the combined employer/employee rate, but with a special federal income tax deduction of 50 percent of the Social Security self-employment tax. This tax, 12.4 percent in 1993, is imposed on self-employment income up to the same maximum amount as in the employer/employee tax. The self-employed person pays his or her tax on the basis of a special schedule attached to the federal income tax return.

[22]The Federal Insurance Contributions Act (FICA), Chap. 21, Internal Revenue Code.

**FIGURE 25-1    SUMMARY OF MEDICARE BENEFITS**

| TABLE OF MEDICARE BENEFITS*  Effective after January 1, 1993 | | | |
|---|---|---|---|
| MEDICARE BASIC PLAN: HOSPITAL INSURANCE–  COVERED SERVICES PER BENEFIT PERIOD (1) | | | |
| Service | Benefit | Medicare Pays | A Person Pays** |
| HOSPITALIZATION  Semiprivate room and board, general nursing and miscellaneous hospital services and supplies | First 60 days | All but $676 | $676 |
| | 61st to 90th day | All but $169 a day | $169 a day |
| | 91st to 150th day* | All but $338 a day | $338 a day |
| | Beyond 150 days | Nothing | All costs |
| POSTHOSPITAL SKILLED NURSING FACILITY CARE  In a facility approved by Medicare. A person must have been in a hospital for at least 3 days and enter the facility within 30 days after hospital discharge. (2) | First 20 days | 100% of approved amount | Nothing |
| | Additional 80 days | All but $84.50 a day | $84.50 a day |
| | Beyond 100 days | Nothing | All costs |
| HOME HEALTH CARE | Unlimited as medically necessary | Full cost | Nothing |
| HOSPICE CARE | Two 90-day periods and one 30-day period (and possible extensions) | All but limited costs for outstanding drugs and inpatient respite care | Limited cost sharing for outpatient drugs and inpatient respite care |
| BLOOD | Blood | All but first 3 pints | For first 3 pints |

\*   60 Reserve days may be used only once, days used are not renewable.
\*\* These figures are for 1993 and are subject to change each year.
(1) A benefit period begins on the first day a person receives service as an inpatient in a hospital and ends after he or she has been out of hospital or skilled nursing facility for 60 days in a row.
(2) Medicare and private insurance will not pay for most nursing home care. A person pays for custodial care and most care in a nursing home.

| MEDICARE SUPPLEMENTAL PLAN: MEDICAL INSURANCE–  COVERED SERVICES PER CALENDAR YEAR | | | |
|---|---|---|---|
| Service | Benefit | Medicare Pays | A Person Pays** |
| MEDICAL EXPENSE  Physician's services, inpatient and outpatient medical service and sup-plies, physical and speech therapy, ambulance, etc. | Medicare pays for medical expenses in or out of the hospital. Some insurance poli-cies pay less (or nothing) for hospital outpatient medical services in a doctor's office. | 80% of approved amount (after $100 deductible), with some exceptions (when no cost-sharing) | $100 deductible* plus 20% of balance of approved amount (plus any charge above approved amount)** |
| HOME HEALTH CARE | Unlimited as medically necessary | Full cost | Nothing |
| OUTPATIENT HOSPITAL CARE | Unlimited as medically necessary | 80% of approved amount (after $100 deductible) | Subject to deductible plus 20% of balance of approved amount |
| BLOOD | Blood | 80% of approved amount (after first 3 pints) | For first 3 pints plus 20% of balance of approved amount |

\*   Once a person has $100 of expense for covered services in 1993, the deductible does not apply to any further covered services received for the rest of the year.
\*\* A person pays for charges higher than the amount approved by Medicare unless the doctor or supplier aggrees to accept Medicare's approved amount as the total charge for services rendered.

*Source: Social Security Manual* (Cincinnati, Oh: The National Underwriter Company, 1993), p. 174.

*Medicare.* The basic Hospital Insurance Plan (Part A) is financed by a separate Hospital Insurance tax imposed upon employers, employees and self-employed persons. The maximum earnings base is $135,000 in 1993 in contrast to the maximum of $57,600 for OASDI. For 1993 (and after), the rates of the Hospital Insurance tax are 1.45 percent for employees and 1.45 percent for employers and 2.90 percent for self-employed persons. As in the case of the OASDI tax, there is a special federal income tax deduction of 50 percent of the Hospital Insurance self-employment tax. This income tax deduction is designed to treat the self-employed in much the same manner as employees and employers are treated for Social Security and income tax purposes under present law.

Supplementary Medical Insurance (Part B) is voluntary and is financed through premiums paid by individuals who enroll and through funds from the federal government. For 1993, each person who enrolls must pay a basic premium of $36.60 per month through December 1993, and the federal government pays about three times as much as a matching amount from general revenues. The monthly premium is scheduled to increase to $41.40 in 1994, and $46.10 in 1995. The monthly premiums are, of course, in addition to the deductible and coinsurance amounts paid by the patient.

When paid, the funds collected for the several programs are allocated to the Old-Age and Survivors Insurance Trust Fund, the Disability Insurance Trust Fund, the Hospital Insurance Trust Fund, and the Supplementary Medical Insurance Trust Fund. They are managed by boards of trustees consisting of the secretaries of the Treasury, of Labor, and of Health and Human Services and two public trustees. The Secretary of the Treasury is known as the managing trustee and has wide powers of management over the trust funds. The funds must be invested in securities that are the direct obligation of or guaranteed by the United States government. Funds are disbursed from these accounts to cover benefit payments and administrative expenses.

The Social Security program is essentially a partially funded system. Current payroll taxes and other contributions received by the program are used to pay the current benefits of persons who, for the most part, are no longer paying Social Security taxes because of disability or retirement, and the excess of income over expenditures is invested in government bonds. Private sector insurance retirement plans are based on considerably more advance funding whereby assets are accumulated from current contributions to pay the future benefits of those making the contributions.

The Social Security program does have limited reserves to serve as emergency funds in periods when current benefit expenditures exceed current contributions, such as in times of recession. However, these reserves are currently relatively small (they are enough to cover one year's expenditures, but estimated to be larger in the future—about four years' expenditures some 25 years hence) and could pay benefits for only a limited time if contributions to a trust fund ceased.

## CURRENT FINANCIAL CONDITION OF SOCIAL SECURITY AND MEDICARE

A serious short-range financing crisis confronted the OASDI program in the early 1980s, largely as a result of the adverse economic conditions then (and the financing under the 1977 Act being based on moderately optimistic economic assumptions).[23] The 1983 amendments (which were based largely on the recommendations of the bipartisan National Commission on Social Security Reform) attempted to establish the program on a sound financial basis at least for the 1980s, and it was hoped for the next 20 to 30 years as well. Furthermore, the objective was to provide anticipated long-range financing (up to the mid-2000s). These amendments made many changes to accomplish this result: extending coverage to almost all categories of workers previously not covered, delaying cost-of-living adjustments of benefits for six months each year, making up to 50 percent of benefits subject to income tax for high-income persons, raising the normal retirement age on a deferred gradual basis, and advancing some of the previously-scheduled increases in the tax rates. As this text goes to press, consideration is being given to raise the income tax paid by higher-income persons.

Many believe that Medicare will be confronted by a financing crisis within the next decade, primarily because medical care costs are continuing to escalate to the point where they will soon constitute over 15 percent of the U.S. gross domestic product. The increasing proportion of elderly people in the population and the current decline in productivity are expected to exacerbate the problem.[24]

Whatever direction is taken in connection with health care proposals and other recommended modifications of the overall Social Security program, the Social Security Act marks a milestone in the evolution of the United States. Its influence on the economic security of the people of the United States is significant and pervasive.

## OTHER U.S. SOCIAL INSURANCE PLANS

This section provides an overview of (1) unemployment insurance, (2) workers' compensation insurance, and (3) temporary disability insurance.[25] Unemployment insurance is a joint federal-state program, and workers' compensation insurance and temporary disability laws are individual state programs.

[23]Robert J. Myers, "Social Security and the Federal Budget: Some Mirages, Myths, and Solutions," *Journal of the American Society of CLU & ChFC* (Mar. 1989), pp. 58-63.

[24]In December 1989, the Advisory Council on Social Security convened a panel of technical experts to review the assumptions and methodology used to project the future financial status of the OASDI programs. The panel was also asked to review measures of the financial soundness of the OASDI system. The panel's report was submitted on August 17, 1990. See *The Social Security Technical Panel Report to the 1991 Advisory Council on Social Security* (Washington, D.C.: 1991 Advisory Council on Social Security).

[25]For a comprehensive discussion of these programs, see George E. Rejda, *Social Insurance and Economic Security*, 4th ed. (Englewood Cliffs, N.J.: Prentice-Hall, Inc., 1991), Chaps. 9, 11, 12, 13, and 14.

## UNEMPLOYMENT INSURANCE

In contrast with OASDHI, unemployment insurance is financed and administered primarily by the states, with some federal participation. The Social Security Act of 1935 provided for a payroll tax to be levied on covered employers in all states. The act was intended to motivate the individual states to establish unemployment insurance programs under guidelines issued by the federal government. This was accomplished by granting a credit against up to 90 percent of the federal tax if a state established an acceptable program based on the federal guidelines. All states now have these unemployment insurance programs.

Unemployment insurance programs have several objectives: (1) to provide periodic cash income to workers during temporary periods of involuntary unemployment; (2) to help the unemployed find jobs; (3) to encourage employers to stabilize employment; and (4) to help stabilize the economy during recessionary periods.

*Coverage and Benefits.* Although the detailed requirements vary from state to state, the pattern of requirements that must be met to be eligible to receive unemployment benefits includes: (1) having a recent, prior attachment to the labor force (usually 52 weeks or four quarters); (2) being able to work and being available for work; (3) actively seeking work; (4) being free from disqualification (e.g., discharge for misconduct); and (5) satisfying a prescribed waiting period (usually one week). Unemployed workers are required to register at local unemployment offices, and officials of the U.S. Employment Service provide assistance in finding suitable jobs.

In most states, regular unemployment insurance benefits are paid for a maximum of 26 weeks. The basis for determining the amount of the weekly benefit payment varies, but in one way or the other it reflects the individual compensation during a base period just prior to unemployment. Benefits in all states are subject to minimum and maximum amounts. Minimum weekly benefits typically range from $5 to $50 and maximum weekly benefits from $100 to $300.[26]

During periods of high unemployment, some workers exhaust their regular unemployment benefits. A federal-state program of **extended benefits** has been established that pays additional benefits to these workers. The state must extend the benefit duration by 50 percent up to a maximum of 13 weeks. The costs of the extended benefits are shared equally by the federal government and the states.

*Financing of Benefits.* State unemployment insurance programs are financed largely by payroll taxes paid by employers on the covered wages of

---

[26]Beam and McFadden, *Employee Benefits*, p. 57.

employees.[27] All tax contributions are deposited into a Federal Unemployment Trust Fund administered by the Secretary of the Treasury. Each state's separate account is credited with its unemployment-tax contributions and the state's share of investment income. Unemployment benefits are paid from each state's account.

As of January 1993, each covered employer had to pay a federal payroll tax of 6.2 percent on the first $7,000 of annual wages paid to each covered employee. Employers can apply as a credit toward the federal tax any state contributions paid under an approved unemployment insurance program and any tax savings under an approved experience-rating plan. The maximum credit is 5.4 percent, leaving 0.8 percent to be paid to the federal government. Many jurisdictions use a taxable wage base in excess of the $7,000 federal standard and have a higher tax rate.

All states use a method of **experience rating** whereby an employer whose employment record is volatile has a higher tax rate than an employer whose employment record has been stable. The theoretical basis for using experience rating is to provide a financial incentive to employers to stabilize their employment. Many cyclical and seasonal firms, however, have little control over their employment and see little financial incentive for them to stabilize employment.

## WORKERS' COMPENSATION INSURANCE

Workers' compensation is based on the principle of liability without fault. The employer is held absolutely liable for the occupational injuries or diseases suffered by the workers, regardless of who is at fault. Disabled workers are paid for their injuries according to a schedule of benefits established by law. Employees are not required to sue their employers to collect benefits. The full cost of providing workers' compensation benefits ordinarily is borne by the employer. The political hope was that this cost would be included in the cost of production and passed on to the consumer. In practice, the ultimate burden of the cost will be borne by the employees (through lower wages), the firm's owners (through lower returns), or the firm's customers (through higher prices), depending on the demand and supply characteristics (elasticity) of each.

*Coverage and Benefits.* The key criterion for coverage under workers' compensation laws is that accidental occupational injuries or death must arise out of, and be in the course of, covered employment. Self-inflicted injuries and accidents resulting from an employee's intoxication or willful disregard of safety rules usually are excluded. Illnesses resulting from occupational diseases are covered in all states. Some states, however, cover only those diseases

---

[27]In four states—Alabama, Alaska, New Jersey, and Pennsylvania—employees must also contribute.

specifically listed in the law. Workers' compensation laws provide (1) medical care reimbursement, (2) disability income, (3) death benefits, and (4) rehabilitation benefits. Benefit levels vary significantly from state to state.

*Financing.* Employers can comply with the law by purchasing a workers' compensation policy, by self-insuring, or by obtaining insurance from a monopolistic or competitive state fund. Most employers purchase workers' compensation policies from private insurance companies. The policy guarantees the benefits that must be legally provided to workers who are occupationally disabled.

Self-insurance is allowed in most states. Many large firms prefer to self-insure their workers' compensation losses, in the hope of avoiding some of the administrative costs associated with workers' compensation contracts. In such cases, the employer must obtain administrative approval and usually is required to post a bond or other security.

Workers' compensation insurance can be purchased from a state fund in 19 states. In six of these states, covered employers must purchase the workers' compensation insurance from a monopolistic state fund. In the other 13 states, the insurance may be purchased from a state fund or private insurers.

Workers' compensation premiums are calculated as a percentage of payroll and are based upon the occupational classes of workers. Larger employers with workers' compensation premiums above a specified amount are subject to experience-rating. Under experience-rating, employers are encouraged to take an active interest in employee safety, since injuries and fatalities directly impact their workers' compensation premiums.

## TEMPORARY DISABILITY INSURANCE

Five states—California, Hawaii, New Jersey, New York, and Rhode Island—and Puerto Rico have temporary disability benefit plans. Under these laws, employees can collect disability income benefits regardless of whether their disability begins while they are employed. These benefits are not provided for disabilities covered under workers' compensation laws. From a benefit standpoint, these laws (except in New York) generally are patterned after the state unemployment insurance law.

Employees contribute to the cost of the plans in all six jurisdictions. In two of them, California and Rhode Island, only employees contribute. Except for Rhode Island, which has a monopolistic state fund, an employee may obtain coverage from either a competitive state fund or private insurers. The laws require that private coverage must provide benefits that are at least as liberal as those prescribed under the law. In effect, these plans are compulsory group health plans similar to the voluntary plans in effect in many businesses. Self-insurance generally is permitted.

## INTERNATIONAL SOCIAL INSURANCE PROGRAMS[28]

Economic security is, of course, a universal problem for all countries and societies. Every developed country and most developing countries have social security programs that respond to the needs government perceives to be inadequately met by individuals or private insurers. What is a proper and adequate social security system for one country is obviously not necessarily satisfactory for another country. Much depends on economic, demographic, social, and even philosophical conditions.

Coverage may be universal, based on labor force attachment, or limited in other ways (e.g., self-employed and high-salaried employees may be excluded). In some countries, separate plans were developed for white-collar and manual workers, although they eventually were combined. It is a common practice to have a separate system for government employees, but in some countries these workers are covered by the general program.

The provision of medical care through social security systems may be much more necessary in economically poor countries than in well-developed countries. The demography of a country can also have a significant effect on the character of a country's social security system. For example, when there is a high mortality rate in a country, the accompanying conditions lead to relatively low retirement ages for old-age pensions. A country with low earnings levels, with most people at bare subsistence levels, and with little personal savings may have a benefit level that is relatively higher (in relation to wages) than that required in economically more developed countries.

In many developing countries, the extended family still plays an important role. The elderly and disabled are taken care of by the younger, active members of the family. Any social benefits provided in these nations are often large lump-sum payments under a so-called provident fund plan,[29] rather than periodic payments. However, with growing industrialization and urbanization, these countries may well need the more usual type of social security benefit programs.

In most countries, the first form of social security was workers' compensation, because of employers' legal responsibilities in many of these cases. Today, all developed countries and many other countries have systems that provide more social security programs (benefits) than does the United States. This is particularly the case in regard to medical care benefits, cash sickness payments and maternity benefits and family allowances. On the other hand, unemployment insurance is not widespread outside economically developed countries. In a growing number of economically advanced countries, provision is

---

[28]This section draws on Robert J. Myers, *Social Security*, 3rd ed. (Homewood, Ill.: Richard D. Irwin, Inc., 1985), Chap. 17. See also Dimitri Vittas and Michael Skully, *Overview of Contractual Savings Institutions, Working Papers* (World Bank, Mar. 1991).

[29]Vittas and Skully, *Overview of Contractual Savings Institutions*, pp. 8-12.

made for automatically increasing the benefit level in accordance with changes in the price level and other economic conditions.

In most countries, social insurance systems are financed by taxes or contributions (which are not necessarily equal) from three parties: the worker, the employer, and the government. In some countries, the social insurance system has difficulty in getting the government to pay its required contribution. The combined level of contributions to systems with a broad span of benefits at high levels runs up to as much as 40 percent or more of payroll. In some cases, the government's share can be quite significant, with the funds coming from general taxation.

A U.S. citizen or resident employed by a U.S. employer is covered by U.S. Social Security and is subject to that tax whether working in this country or abroad. Special rules for U.S. taxpayers may let an individual be covered while working for non-U.S. companies that are subsidiaries of U.S. companies as well. The United States has entered into totalization agreements—social security treaties—with many European countries and Canada to eliminate dual social security coverage and taxation. Both the employer's and the employee's contributions fall within a totalization agreement, when one applies. If an individual is not subject to U.S. coverage, he or she cannot be exempt from foreign coverage. In fact, totalization agreements go to some lengths to ensure that an employee will be covered by at least one system.

Although the details differ, much can be learned from cross-country comparisons. The International Social Security Association, under the sponsorship of the U.S. Social Security Administration, conducts an annual survey on developing world trends.[30] Other important sources of information include the International Labor Office and other international organizations, such as the Permanent Inter-American Social Security Committee, the Organization of American States, the Organization for Economic Cooperation and Development, and the European Community.

[30]U.S. Department of Health and Human Services, *Social Security Programs throughout the World* (updated periodically).

# *Chapter 26*

# *G*ROUP *I*NSURANCE

Originating in the early years of this century to provide life insurance benefits, the group approach has been applied to an increasing variety and number of groups and is now utilized to provide a wide range of employee benefits. Group insurance is the youngest branch of the life insurance business. Over 750,000 plans of group life insurance are in force in the United States, covering some 165 million persons and providing over $4,057.6 billion of protection.[1] These figures, which represent 40 percent of all life insurance in force, do not reflect the development of other group areas, especially group health insurance and group annuities. Taken in the aggregate, the group business is a major segment of the life insurance industry.

## GROUP INSURANCE FUNDAMENTALS

Group insurance is a means through which groups of persons who have a business or professional relationship to the contract owner are provided coverage under a single contract. The accepted meaning of group insurance is not as elementary as this definition might suggest. What is considered group insurance today might not have been considered group insurance several decades ago. Over time, innovative underwriting techniques of group insurers and liberalized regulatory actions have broadened the definition.

    A sound understanding of group insurance and the scope of group products can be acquired only through a discussion of its distinguishing characteristics, its differences

[1] 1992 *Life Insurance Fact Book* (Washington, D.C.: American Council of Life Insurance, 1992), pp. 30–31. Unless noted to the contrary, all statistical aggregates used in this section are taken from this source.

from and similarities to other forms of insurance, and a reasonably detailed examination of each of its components. Achieving such a comprehension of group life and health insurance is the objective of this and the following chapter.

## DISTINGUISHING CHARACTERISTICS

In a comparison of group insurance with other forms of insurance written by life insurance companies, several distinguishing features are evident: (1) the substitution of group underwriting for individual underwriting, (2) the use of a master contract, (3) lower administrative cost, (4) flexibility in contract design, and (5) the use of experience-rating.[2]

*Group Underwriting.* Probably the most significant distinguishing characteristic of group insurance is the substitution of group underwriting for individual underwriting. In group cases, no individual evidence of insurability is usually required, and benefit levels can be substantial, with few, if any, important limitations.[3]

Group underwriting normally is not concerned with the health aspect or other insurability aspects of any particular individual. Instead, it aims to obtain a group of individual lives or, what is even more important, an aggregation of such groups of lives that will yield a predictable rate of mortality or morbidity. If a sufficient number of groups of lives is obtained, and if these groups are reasonably homogeneous in nature, then the mortality or morbidity rate will be predictable. The point is that the group becomes the unit of underwriting, and insurance principles may be applied to it just as in the case of the individual. To assure that the groups obtained will be reasonably homogeneous, the underwriting process in group insurance aims to control adverse selection by individuals within a given group.

In underwriting group insurance, then, certain important features should be present that either are inherent in the nature of the group itself or may be applied in a positive way to avoid serious adverse selection. These are reviewed below.

*1. Insurance Incidental to Group.* The insurance must be incidental to the group; that is, the members of the group must have come together for some purpose other than to obtain insurance. For example, the group insurance furnished to the employees of a given employer must not be the feature that motivates the formation and existence of the group.

---

[2]For a comprehensive study of group insurance, see Burton T. Beam, Jr., and John J. McFadden, *Employee Benefits* (Homewood, Ill.: Dearborn Financial Publishing, Inc., 1992). See also Health Insurance Association of America, *Group Life and Health Insurance*, Part A, Part B, and Part C (Washington, D.C.: HIAA, 1992).

[3]In recent years, there has been a trend toward large amounts of group life coverage on individual lives, with a consequent increase in utilization of evidence of insurability, as in the case of ordinary insurance. Another exception is the underwriting of small groups (fewer than 10 lives). Some form of individual evidence of insurability usually is required for these groups. (These cases are treated later in this chapter.)

*2. Flow of Persons Through Group.* There should be a steady flow of persons through the group; that is, there must be an influx of new young lives into the group and a flow out of the group of the older and impaired lives. With groups of actively working employees, it may be assumed that they are in average health.

*3. Automatic Determination of Benefits.* Group insurance underwriting requirements commonly insist on an automatic basis for determining the amount of benefits on individual lives, beyond the control of the employer or employees. If the amount of benefits taken were completely optional, it would be possible to select against the insurer, since those in poor health would tend to insure heavily and the healthy ones might tend to elect minimum coverage.

As the group mechanism has evolved, however, insurers have responded to demands from the marketplace, particularly larger employers, for more flexibility in the selection of benefits. This flexibility typically is expressed in optional amounts of life insurance in excess of basic coverage provided by the employer and in extra health insurance benefits in excess of the employer's basic program.

Also, the increasingly popular **cafeteria plans** allow participating employees to select among an array of benefits using a predetermined allowance of employer funds. The individual may select, subject to certain basic coverages being required, a combination of benefits that best meets his or her individual needs.

*4. Minimum Participation by the Group.* Another underwriting control is the requirement that substantially all eligible persons in a given group be covered by insurance. In contributory plans (see below), generally at least 75 percent of the eligible employees should join the plan if coverage is to be effective. In the case of noncontributory plans, 100 percent participation is required.[4] By covering a large proportion of a given group, the insurance company gains a safeguard against an undue proportion of substandard lives.

*5. Third-Party Sharing of Cost.* A portion of the cost of a group plan ideally should be borne by the employer or some other third party, such as a labor union or trade association. The noncontributory employer-pay-all plan is simple, and it gives the employer full control over the plan. It provides for insurance of all eligible employees and thus eliminates any difficulties involved in connection with obtaining the consent of a sufficient number of employees to meet minimum participation requirements. Also, there is no problem of distributing the cost among the various employees, as in the contributory plan.

The contributory plan is usually designed to be less costly to the employer. Hence, with employee contributions, the employer is likely to arrange for more adequate protection for the employees. It can also be argued that if the employee contributes toward his or her insurance, he or she will be more impressed with its

---

[4]In cases where employees refuse the insurance for religious or other reasons that do not involve any elements of selection, this rule is relaxed.

value and will appreciate it more. On the other hand, the contributory plan has a number of disadvantages. Its operation is more complicated, and this at times increases administrative costs considerably. Each employee must consent to contribute toward his or her insurance, and, as stated before, a minimum percentage of the eligible group must consent to enter the arrangement. New employees entering the business must be informed of their insurance privilege. If the plan is contributory, employees may not be entitled to the insurance until they have been with the company for a period of time (e.g., one month). If they do not agree to be covered by the plan within a period of 31 days, they must provide satisfactory evidence of insurability to become eligible. Some noncontributory plans also have these probationary periods.

*6. Efficient Administrative Organization.* A single administrative organization should be able and willing to act on behalf of the insured group. In the usual case, this is the employer. In the case of a contributory plan, there must be a reasonably simple method, such as payroll deduction, by which the master policyowner can collect premiums. An automatic method is desirable from both an administrative and an underwriting standpoint.

A number of miscellaneous controls of underwriting significance are typically used in group insurance plans, but the discussion above will permit an appreciation of the group underwriting theory. The discussion applies to groups with a large number of employees. A majority of the groups, however, are not large. The group size is a significant factor in the underwriting process. In smaller plans, more restrictive underwriting practices relating to adverse selection are used. These may include less liberal contract provisions, simple health status questions, and, in some cases, detailed individual underwriting of group members.

***Master Contract.*** A second characteristic of group insurance is the use of a master contract, with or without certificates of insurance, in lieu of individual policies. Such booklet-certificates provide information on the plan provisions and claim filing requirements and serve as the insured person's evidence of insurance coverage. The use of certificates and a master contract constitutes one of the sources of economy under the group approach. The master contract is a detailed document setting forth the contractual relationship between the group contract owner and the insurance company. The insured persons under the contract, usually employees and their beneficiaries, are not actually parties to the contract, although they may enforce their rights as third-party beneficiaries. The four-party relationship (employer, insurer, employee, and beneficiaries and dependents) found in a group insurance plan can create a number of interesting and unusual problems that are common only to group insurance.

***Lower Cost.*** A third feature of group insurance is that it should be lower-cost protection than that which is available in individual insurance. The nature of the group approach permits the use of mass-distribution and mass-administration methods that afford group insurance important economies of operation that are not available in individual insurance. These economies are more significant in larger cases. In some smaller-group cases, administrative unit expenses could conceivably exceed those of individual insurance. Also, since lack of individual underwriting leads to average costs, a given healthy individual can perhaps buy individual term life insurance at a lower cost. Employer subsidization of the cost is a critical factor in group insurance plan design.

Probably the most significant savings in the cost of marketing group life insurance lies in the fact that group commissions absorb a much smaller proportion of total income than commissions for individual contracts. The marketing system relieves the agent or broker of many of the duties, responsibilities, and expenses normally connected with selling and servicing of individual insurance. Because of the large premiums involved in many group insurance cases, the commission rates are considerably lower than for individual contracts and are usually graded downward as the size of the premium for the case increases.

Some large-group insurance buyers deal directly with insurance companies and commissions are eliminated. In these cases, however, fees frequently are paid to the consultants involved.

The nature of the administrative procedures permits simplified accounting techniques. The mechanics of premium collection are less involved, and experience refund procedures are much simplified, because there is only one party with which to deal—the master contract owner. Of course, the issuance of a large number of individual contracts is avoided, and, because of the nature of group selection, the cost of medical examinations and inspection reports is minimized. Also, state insurance department filings and other regulatory requirements are minimized. Finally, administrative procedures are simplified on group term life, since a large proportion of group coverage is on a term basis as opposed to a cash-value form, which requires special records for reserve and nonforfeiture-value purposes.

*Flexibility.* In contrast with the situation in which there is an individual contract, which must be taken essentially as written, the larger contract owner usually has options in the design and preparation of the group insurance contract. Although the contracts follow a pattern and include certain standard provisions, there is considerably more flexibility here than in the case of individual contracts. The degree of flexibility permitted is, of course, a function of the size of the group involved. The group insurance program usually is an integral part of an employee benefit program, and, in most cases, the contract can be molded to meet the objectives of the contract owner, as long as the requests do not entail complicated administrative procedures, open the way to possibly serious adverse selection, or violate legal requirements.

*Experience-rating.* Another special feature of group insurance is that premiums often are subject to experience-rating. The experience of the individual group may have an important bearing on dividends or premium-rate adjustments. The larger, and hence, the more reliable the experience of the individual group, the greater is the weight attached to its own experience in any single year. The knowledge that net premiums after dividends or premium-rate adjustments will be based on the employer's own experience gives the employer a vested interest in maintaining a favorable loss and expense record. For the largest employers, insurers often agree to complicated procedures to satisfy the employer's objectives, since most such cases are experience-rated and reflect the increased cost.

Some insurers experience-rate based on the class or type of industry, or even based on the type of contract. For small groups, most insurance companies use **pooled rates,** under which a uniform rate is applied to all such groups, although it is becoming more common to apply separate pooled rates for groups with significantly better or worse experience than that of the total class. The point at which a group is large enough to be eligible for experience-rating varies from company to company, based on that insurer's book of business and experience. The size and frequency of medical claims varies considerably among geographic regions of the United States and must be considered in determining a group insurance rate. The composition (age, sex, and income level) of a group will also affect the experience of the group and, similarly, will be an important underwriting consideration.

## ADVANTAGES AND LIMITATIONS OF GROUP MECHANISM

*Advantages.* The group insurance mechanism has proved to be a remarkably effective solution to the need for employee benefits for a number of reasons. The utilization of mass-distribution techniques has extended protection to large numbers of persons with little or no life or health insurance. The increasing complexity of our industrial/service economy has brought increasingly large numbers of persons together, and the group mechanism has enabled the life insurance industry to reach vast numbers of individuals within a relatively short period and at low cost. Group insurance also has extended protection to a large number of uninsurable persons. Equally important has been the fact that the employer usually pays a large share of the cost. Moreover, the deductibility of employer contributions and the favorable tax treatment of the benefits to employees make it a tax-effective vehicle with which to provide benefits.

Another significant factor, and one of the more cogent motivations for the rapid development of group insurance, has been the continuing federal role in the security benefits area. Within the U. S., the federal Old-Age, Survivors, Disability and Health Insurance program has expanded rapidly, but many observers believe that had not group insurance provided substantial sums of life insurance, health insurance, and retirement protection, the social insurance plan would have developed even more rapidly.

*Limitations.* From the viewpoint of the employee, group insurance has one great limitation—the temporary nature of the coverage. Unless an employee converts his or her coverage to an individual policy (which usually is more expensive and provides less liberal coverage), the employee loses his or her insurance protection if the group plan is terminated, and, often also, at retirement because employment is terminated.[5]

Group life and health protection is continued after retirement in a significant proportion of cases today, but often at levels that are reduced from those available to the employed worker. Recently, with the introduction of a new accounting standard (FAS 106) requiring that the cost of such benefits be accrued, an increasing number of employers have discontinued postretirement life and health benefits entirely. When such continued protection is not available, however, the temporary nature of the coverage is a serious limitation. Retiree group health insurance often is provided as a supplement to Medicare.

Another problem of potential significance involves individuals who may be lulled into complacency concerning their life insurance programs by having large amounts of group life insurance during their working years. Many of these persons fail to recognize the need for, or are unwilling to face the cost of, individual life insurance. Perhaps of even greater significance is the fact that the flexibility of the group approach is limited to the design of the master policy and does not extend to the individual covered employees. Furthermore, group plans typically fail to provide the mechanism for any analysis of the financial needs of the individual—a service that is normally furnished by the agent or other advisor. Many agents, however, discuss group insurance coverage with individuals as a foundation for discussing the need for additional amounts of individual life insurance.

## Types of Eligible Groups[6]

The types of groups eligible for group insurance coverage have broadened significantly over the years. This wider eligibility is reflected in both statutory regulations and the underwriting philosophy of group writing insurers. Group insurance is permitted today for types of groups that did not even exist in the early days of its development, and it is written on some types of groups whose applications would not have even been given consideration when the product was first introduced. The NAIC Model Group Insurance bill permits coverage on four specific categories of groups. Many states permit coverage on additional types of groups not identified in the NAIC model bill.

---

[5]The 1985 Consolidated Omnibus Reconciliation Act (COBRA) requires group health coverage to be extended for up to 36 months for certain "qualifying events." Termination of employment is a qualifying event, but termination of the group plan typically is not. (See Chapter 27.)

[6]This section draws from Robert W. Batten, George H. Hider, et al., *Group Life and Health Insurance*, Vol. 1, pp. 36–38 Copyright ©1979, LOMA (Life Office Management Association, Inc.). Adapted with the permission of the publisher.

*Employees of a Single Employer.* The employees of a single employer comprise the first category mentioned in the NAIC model bill. An employer may be a sole proprietorship, a partnership, or a corporation. Also, employees may not only include the immediate employees of the employer, but several other categories as well. The single-employer group is by far the dominant type of group that is provided group insurance coverage.

*Debtor-Creditor Groups.* Group credit insurance (life and disability income) has grown rapidly, reflecting our credit-oriented society. The contract owner in these plans is the creditor, such as a bank, a small-loan company, a credit union, or any business that has significant accounts receivables, including those that rely heavily on credit card customers. The insurance benefits are payable to the master contract owner rather than to the individuals who are insured or their beneficiaries. If the debtor dies or becomes disabled, the insurance proceeds generally pay the indebtedness that provided the basis for the coverage. Debtors usually must be under a binding, irrevocable obligation to repay the indebtedness for coverage to be effected.

*Labor Union Groups.* Members of labor unions may be covered under a group contract issued to the union itself. The insurance must be for the benefit of persons other than the union or its officials. In practice, generally, the entire premium may not be paid directly by member contributions. It is common, however, for payment to be made from funds partially contributed to the union by members specifically for their insurance and partially by the union from its own funds. In some cases, the union pays the total premium from its own funds.

Group contracts often are written on multi-employer groups and issued to the trustees of a fund created through collective bargaining processes. This arrangement is typically established by two or more employers in the same or a related industry, by one or more labor unions, or even jointly by employers and labor unions. The Taft-Hartley Act prohibits employers from turning over funds for employee welfare plans directly to a union—hence, the need for a separate trust and its trustees to serve as the group contract owner and decision-maker.

*Multiple-Employer Trusts.* **Multiple-employer trusts (METs),** often referred to as **multiple-employer welfare arrangements (MEWAs),** market group benefits to employers who have a small number of employees. METs may be sponsored by life insurance companies, independent administrators, or two or more employers in the same industry. The sponsor designs the plan, selects the employers (or other groups) that will be permitted to participate, and usually handles the administration. Each such trust also must have a trustee (often the trust department of a bank).

All financial transactions flow through and are accounted for by the trust. The member employers pay premiums to the sponsoring organization, which uses the money to purchase a group contract. The entire group of employers is experience-rated, thereby permitting greater credibility to be given to the group's own experience.

Self-insured METs assume the responsibility of making claim payments through a third-party administrator. They should assess adequate premiums (contributions) and maintain appropriate reserves. In the early development of METs, this was not always done properly and a number of METs became bankrupt. For several years, state insurance departments had tried to terminate mismanaged METs, but the administrators of these plans argued that they were exempted from state regulation by the Employee Retirement Income Security Act (ERISA). As a result, in 1992 the U.S. Congress enacted legislation that requires self-insured METs to meet state insurance regulations concerning the adequacies of contributions and reserve levels.

METs (MEWAs) have proven to be a source of regulatory confusion, enforcement problems, and even fraud. A U. S. General Accounting Office (GAO) report[7] showed that between January 1988 and June 1991, METs left some 398,000 participants and their beneficiaries with over $129 million in unpaid claims and many other participants without insurance. More than 600 METs failed to comply with state insurance laws, and some violated criminal statutes.

The GAO report confirmed that state efforts to regulate METs, enforce state laws, and recover unpaid claims were hindered because the states could not identify METs operating within their jurisdictions. Furthermore, when complaints did come to the attention of state regulators, they were frequently frustrated, because METs asserted that they were exempt under ERISA. In 1982, Congress enacted legislation to permit states to shut down mismanaged METs. The legislation (amended in 1983), however, did not completely resolve the problems in this area. Moreover, the Department of Labor was sometimes slow in responding to state questions.

The GAO report recommended that the Department of Labor develop a mechanism to help states identify METs and improve procedures to respond to questions about such issues as ERISA exemption and state regulatory authority, thus enabling states to deal with problem METs more aggressively. The net effect has been a significant reduction in the number of self-funded METs.

*Miscellaneous Groups.* As suggested earlier, many other types of groups not specifically identified in the NAIC model bill are eligible for group insurance through company underwriting practice and enabling state laws. These include trade associations, professional associations, college alumni associations, veteran associations, religious groups, customers of large retail chains, and savings account depositors, among many others.

## GROUP LIFE INSURANCE

Group life insurance is one of the most common forms of employee benefit plans offered in the United States. Over 40 percent of all life insurance in force (by

[7]Employee Benefits: MEWA Regulation; GAO HRD-92-40 (March 1992).

face amount) in the U.S. is on a group basis. The average amount of group life insurance in force per certificate is over $28,700. Almost 85 percent of group life coverage is accounted for by employer-employee groups.

## NATURE OF COVERAGE

In addition to the eligibility of the group itself, other criteria are involved in coverage under a group life insurance contract. Since the individual-employer group is by far the most prevalent type of group that is being provided group life insurance benefits, the remainder of this discussion of group life insurance is directed principally toward this type of group.

*Minimum Size and Proportion.* Many years ago, insurers believed that a minimum of 50 lives was necessary to qualify for group life coverage and state law reflected this belief. Today states permit groups to be insured with ten or fewer lives. State laws also stipulate the minimum proportion of the eligible employees that should be insured under a group life contract.

Requirements of this nature assure that there will be the maintenance of a reasonable average age, with a view to preventing a rise in total premiums from year to year, and they also protect the insurance company against the group becoming substandard through adverse selection. Also, the larger the group, the less the expense per person insured. For these reasons, insurance companies usually prescribe a minimum number of employees to be covered for group life insurance. In general, for employer-pay-all (noncontributory) plans, insurers usually require that all employees or all of any class thereof, as determined by the conditions of employment, must be insured. When employees contribute a portion of the premium (i.e., in a contributory plan), at least 75 percent of the employees must be included under the plan.[8]

*Individual Eligibility Requirements.* In general, only regular, active, full-time employees are eligible for group life insurance. All such employees, or all such employees in certain classes determined by conditions pertaining to their employment (e.g., "all salaried employees" or "all hourly paid employees"), must be included in the group as eligibles.

Another individual eligibility requirement for coverage is that an employee must be actively at work and must work no fewer than the normal number of hours in a work week at his or her job on the date when he or she becomes eligible for coverage. The requirement assures a reasonable minimum of health and physical well-being and protects the insurer against serious adverse selection.

---

[8]As the types and sizes of groups covered have expanded, the minimum participation requirements have become a function of size, legal requirement, and rate basis. So-called association cases commonly insure less than 75 percent of the eligible group, reflecting a somewhat higher rate basis than normally used on employer groups. Similarly, in the 10 to 25 life range, many companies require a participation of 85 percent. Participation levels below 75 percent are often allowed with simplified short-form health questionnaires on each individual.

A waiting or **probationary period** often is applied to new employees (usually one to six months) before they become eligible for insurance. The probationary period minimizes the record-keeping and administrative expenses involved in setting up records for employees who remain with the employer for a short period, although with the widespread use of computers, this consideration is less important than formerly.

After the completion of the probationary period, under a noncontributory plan the employee automatically is covered. Under a contributory plan, the employee is given a period of time, known as the **eligibility period,** during which he or she is entitled to apply for insurance without submitting evidence of insurability. This period is limited, usually to 31 days, to minimize selection against the insurance company by employees. For the same reason, it is customary to require evidence of insurability from employees who have discontinued their coverage and desire to rejoin the plan. If the plan is written on a noncontributory basis, these rules do not apply, since all employees (or all employees within the designated classes) automatically are covered unless they specifically decline coverage.

*Duration of Coverage.* Once the insurance becomes effective for a particular employee, the protection continues for as long as he or she remains in the service of the employer (assuming, of course, that the employer maintains the plan in force and the employee continues to pay any contributory premium required). The master contract usually gives the employer the right to continue premium payments for employees who are temporarily off the job, provided that the employer does so on a basis that precludes individual selection. Upon permanent termination of service, the employee's coverage continues for 31 days beyond the date of termination. This extension of coverage gives the employee an opportunity to replace the expiring protection with individual insurance, to obtain employment with another firm with group insurance, or to convert the expiring term insurance to a cash-value form of insurance.

Many plans continue coverage after retirement, and provide at least enough life insurance to cover the employee's last illness and funeral expenses. In the past, many plans continued full benefits on retired lives, with no special provision for prefunding the rapidly rising costs as the number of covered retired employees increased. The cost of providing this life insurance coverage can be very high, and new accounting standards require employers to accrue these expenses yearly instead of expensing them on a pay-as-you-go basis. (See discussion under "Postretirement Coverage" below.)

## BENEFITS

*Approaches to Benefit Amounts.* To minimize adverse selection, the amount of group life insurance for which an employee is eligible usually is determined by a system that precludes the employee from selecting the coverage amount. Traditionally, this system used one or more of four bases for determining the amount of group coverage: (1) a set dollar amount for all employees; (2) a function of employee compensation; (3) a function of employees' position; or (4) a function of each employee's length of service. Any life insurance benefit schedule that tends to discriminate in favor of highly compensated or executive employees can cause the loss of important tax benefits.

*1. Fixed Amount.* The use of a fixed-amount benefit plan places all employees in one category. It has the advantage of simplicity, but it also has the important disadvantage of placing all employees on an equal level. If group insurance is to serve as a means of rewarding workers in the interest of less turnover (and this is one of the strong arguments for it), it seems neither wise nor fair that low-paid or new employees should obtain the same benefits as those who are skilled or have served the employer for years. However, the fixed amount plan greatly minimizes adverse selection and stabilizes cost. This type of benefit has been used principally in conjunction with union welfare funds.

*2. Amount of Compensation.* Most group life plans base the amount of insurance on employees' earnings. The plan could be based on any common earnings unit. Most plans utilize a benefit formula that is a multiple of earnings, usually rounded to the nearest $1,000. Multiples of 1, 1 1/2, and 2 times earnings are common. The trend is to higher amounts and multiples of 3, 4, and 5 times salary are not uncommon among plans offered by large employers, particularly when some choice is involved, such as under cafeteria plans.

*3. Position.* When the salary or wage is difficult to determine in advance, as in the case of pieceworkers or salespersons, the insurance may be set according to the position held by the employee. Thus officers, superintendents, and managers may receive $50,000 each; foremen and salespersons $30,000 each; and all other employees $20,000 each. This approach tends to reflect need and ability to pay.

*4. Service.* Under the so-called service plan, the amount of protection is increased in accordance with the length of time that the employee has been in the employer's service. Since the plan provides increasing amounts of insurance based upon length of service, it tends to result in progressively higher premium costs. In view of the cost implications and the enactment of the Tax Equity and Fiscal Responsibility Act of 1982 (TEFRA), service plans have virtually disappeared.

*5. Combination.* To benefit its most valuable employees, an employer may adopt a plan in which amounts of group term life insurance are determined on the basis of both salary and length of service. Such a plan would determine the amount of insurance to which an employee is entitled by multiplying the employee's annual salary by the product of the appropriate salary and years of service factors. For the reasons mentioned above, this approach is seldom used today.

*Minimum and Maximum Amounts.* Regardless of the plan used, some provision always is made to keep the amounts of insurance extended to executives and others with high salaries in line with the total amount of protection extended to the whole group. Thus while some insurers will not write less than $2,000 on any one insured, most require at least $5,000 or $10,000—and even more on small groups. In addition, insurers will not write more than a certain maximum amount, which is determined by both the number of persons insured and the average amount of insurance per employee. In the past, state-mandated maximums were common.

Underwriting limitations on amounts are necessary in smaller groups, to minimize adverse selection. In larger groups, where the group's individual experience has a strong effect on the level of dividends, a maximum is highly desirable to avoid undue fluctuations in cost from year to year.[9]

Virtually any company will write as much as $100,000 on an individual life under proper underwriting circumstances, and, in some cases, as high as $1,000,000 and over is provided on individual lives. Many insurance companies permit individual amounts in excess of their normal maximums, provided that evidence of insurability is submitted for the excess amounts or that other safeguards are established to protect against severe adverse selection.[10] The willingness of some insurance companies to superimpose a schedule of life insurance benefits on an already existing plan provided by another insurer has led to the writing of amounts of group life insurance on a single life that are far beyond what one insurer's underwriting rules will permit.

*Conversion Privilege.* An insured employee has the privilege of converting his or her group life insurance protection to an individual policy of cash-value insurance under certain conditions. Normally, the employee may convert, within 31 days after termination of employment or cessation of membership in an eligible classification, to one of the insurer's regular cash-value forms at standard rates for his or her attained age. The most significant advantage to the employee lies in the fact that no evidence of insurability is required.[11]

---

[9] In many cases, companies will place a maximum on the amount of coverage on a single life that will be charged to the experience of the individual case, with any excess coverage being pooled among cases.

[10] Other safeguards include consumer reports on one or more individuals, extra premiums charged on the case, excess amounts reinsured, special reserves built for the case, and excess-amount risks pooled for experience purposes.

[11] A conversion privilege also is available on the termination of the master contract but under far more restrictive conditions. In view of the importance of group insurance as a factor in the security of most employees, some liberalization of the conversion privilege upon termination of the master contract would be desirable. Although adverse selection is a problem, the improved service to insured employees would appear to justify a continuing effort to liberalize the conversion privilege.

The death benefit provided under a group life insurance contract is continued during the conversion period (usually 31 days) after an employee withdraws from the eligible group. If the employee dies during this period, a death benefit is paid under the group policy, and any premiums that may have been paid on a conversion policy are returned.

*Waiver of Premium Benefits.* A waiver of premium clause commonly is used in group life contracts. As long as the insured proves his or her disability periodically, this clause provides that coverage will continue indefinitely with no payment of premium from the employer or, if the plan is contributory, from the employee.

Larger employers often eliminate the waiver of premium provision under their group life contracts and substitute the employer's continuing premium payments. This provides the employer the cash flow advantage of paying ongoing premiums instead of incurring a claim charge (typically 75 percent of the face amount). Of course, if the employer changes insurers, it will need to be assured that the new insurer accepts the disabled lives, since the new company would normally not accept these risks. In addition, waiver typically applies only when disability occurs prior to the employee's sixtieth (or sixty-fifth) birthday, and the amount of insurance continued under waiver is sometimes reduced as the disabled person attains specified ages such as 65 or 70. Some plans even reduce continued amounts to zero at specified ages.

## PLANS OF INSURANCE

*Yearly Renewable Term Insurance.* The basic plan of insurance under which group life insurance is provided is yearly renewable term insurance—the same coverage that is provided through individual policies. With respect to any covered employees, the protection technically expires at the end of each year, but it is renewed automatically without evidence of insurability. As in the case of individual coverage, the premium rate per $1,000 of protection increases at an increasing rate from year to year. Despite this, the employee's contribution (if the plan is contributory) usually remains at the same level regardless of his or her attained age. The level contribution by the employee is practicable because the employer absorbs the portion of the cost that is in excess of the employee's annual contribution. Thus the employer's contribution for any individual employee usually increases year by year. On the other hand, the employer's total contribution to the plan may well remain stable or even decline, depending upon the benefit formula, the age and sex composition of the group, and the experience of the plan.

The simplest way to comprehend the relative roles of the employer and employees in financing a term plan is through the calculation of an average annual premium for a hypothetical plan. This is presented in Table 26-1 for the first year of group term insurance. Each employee is assumed to be a male and to have insurance equal to two times salary, subject to a maximum of $100,000.

The first step in calculating the average annual premium is to determine the total premium payable at each age represented by the group of covered employees. The sum of these values, as shown in Table 26-1, is $81,448.50. To this sum must be added a "policy constant" expense charge, which is $2.40 per year per $1,000, but is applied only to the first $40,000 of insurance. This recognizes the minimum expenses that are associated with any group. The total aggregate annual premium, then, is $81,544.50, and it is only necessary to apply an "advance expense adjustment factor" (based on the size of the premium and the number of lives involved) to derive the initial annual premium. In this instance, the group qualifies for a 35 percent discount, and the initial annual premium is $53,003.92. The final step in deriving the average annual premium per $1,000 involves dividing $53,003.92 by the number of $1,000 units of insurance—namely, 7,550—which gives $7.02. Assuming that the employee's contributions are $3.50 per $1,000, the employer must bear the difference of $3.52 per $1,000, or $26,576.00. In practice, these premiums and contributions normally would be converted to a monthly basis.[12]

**TABLE 26-1     CALCULATION OF AVERAGE ANNUAL PREMIUM PER $1,000 OF GROUP TERM LIFE INSURANCE**

| Attained Age | Number of Employees | Insurance per Employee | Total Amount of Insurance | Annual Premium per $1,000 | Total Premium |
|---|---|---|---|---|---|
| 20 | 5 | $15,000 | $75,000 | $2.75 | $206.25 |
| 25 | 5 | 35,000 | 175,000 | 2.97 | 519.75 |
| 30 | 10 | 45,000 | 450,000 | 3.15 | 1,417.50 |
| 35 | 10 | 55,000 | 550,000 | 3.74 | 2,057.00 |
| 40 | 20 | 70,000 | 1,400,000 | 5.28 | 7,392.00 |
| 45 | 20 | 80,000 | 1,600,000 | 8.08 | 12,928.00 |
| 50 | 20 | 90,000 | 1,800,000 | 12.51 | 22,518.00 |
| 55 | 10 | 100,000 | 1,000,000 | 19.55 | 19,550.00 |
| 60 | 5 | 100,000 | 500,000 | 29.72 | 14,860.00 |
| Totals | 105 | | $7,550,000 | | $ 81,448.50 |

| | |
|---|---|
| Total Annual Premium | $81,448.50 |
| Additional for "policy constant" (40 x $2.40) | 96.00 |
| Aggregate annual premium | 81,544.50 |
| Advance expense adjustment (35%) | -28,540.58 |
| Initial annual premium | 53,003.92 |
| Average annual premium per $1,000 ($53,003.92 ÷ 7,550) | $7.02 |

*The 1961 Standard Group Life Insurance Premium Rates (1960 Commissioners Standard Group Table of Mortality at 3 percent, loaded by basic loading percentage).

[12]Not all insurers calculate group life rates exactly as presented. Many insurers would in fact find premiums based on Table 26-1 to be uncompetitive in today's market. Insurers use a variety of factors to load or reduce their rates: male-female mix, average amount of insurance, whether insurance is noncontributory, and the type of industry.

If the experience under a pooling arrangement of small-size employers is favorable, the dividend or retroactive rate adjustment will reduce the employer's cost. Under some plans, the dividend might equal and occasionally exceed the employer's contribution. In the latter instance, the excess of the dividend is at times applied in some manner for the benefit of the employees. This is required by law in some states.

Group insurance premiums are paid monthly by the employer. Other premium modes are possible, but quarterly premiums are used only with small groups. All adjustments in the amount of insurance during the year—arising out of new employees, terminations, and reclassifications—are made on the basis of the average monthly premium rate, regardless of the actual ages of the employees involved. At the end of each policy year, a new average monthly premium is computed. With small groups, however, age-graded rates are commonly used to properly reflect changes in the age distribution on a month-to-month basis, and to avoid the possibility of substantial average rate changes at renewal.

Group term insurance rates are guaranteed for one year only. From a practical standpoint, insurers try to avoid rate increases, because they are disturbing to the contract owner, and, whenever possible, they prefer to make adjustments in cost through the experience-rating process.

When group term life plans are on a contributory basis, employee contributions frequently are at a uniform rate per $1,000, regardless of age. In regard to setting the level of contributions, an important principle is that the cost to the employees is such that the insurance is an attractive buy in comparison with insurance that is available to them under individual policies.

Most states require that the employer pay at least a portion of the premium for group term insurance, and a few states impose limitations on the amounts that may be paid by any employee. The most common restriction limits the contribution to the greater of 60 cents per month per $1,000 of coverage or 75 percent of the premium rate for that employee.

*Cash-Value Life Insurance.* Group life insurance that continues after retirement is available through three categories of products. Group paid-up insurance and group ordinary insurance have been available for a number of years, and if they are properly designed, they may qualify for favorable tax treatment under Internal Revenue Code (IRC) Section 79. Neither group paid-up insurance nor group ordinary insurance has been widely accepted. A new product, group universal life insurance, which can also provide postretirement life insurance coverage, has been well received.

*1. Group Paid-Up.* At one time, the group term plus paid-up approach was the most popular plan for providing postretirement life insurance coverage. This plan is a combination of accumulating units of single-premium whole life insurance and decreasing units of group term life insurance. The combination provides the same death benefits as do regular employer group term plans. Each paid premium consists of the individual employee's contribution and the employer's contribution. Employee contributions usually are applied to purchase increments of paid-up single-premium whole life insurance, the amount of which is determined by the individual employee's attained age and the contribution amount. The employer's contribution is applied to provide an amount of decreasing term insurance, which, when added to the accumulated face amounts of the paid-up whole life insurance purchased by the employee, equals the total amount for which he or she is eligible.

Ordinarily, at retirement the portion of the insurance that is still on a term basis is discontinued, and the paid-up insurance remains in force for the balance of the employee's lifetime. The employee may have the right to convert the term portion. When employees terminate employment prior to retirement, similar provisions apply. They may withdraw the surrender value in cash if they wish to terminate the insurance entirely. There is relatively little interest in this coverage today.

*2. Group Ordinary.* There is no typical group ordinary insurance product. Rather, the terminology is used to describe any traditional product (except group paid-up insurance) that provides cash-value life insurance to a group of employees and that will qualify for favorable income tax treatment under IRC Section 79. The cost of the term portion of the coverage is paid by the employer, and the cash-value portion, which the employee may be able to decline, generally is paid by the employee.

In general, federal income tax treatment of the term life insurance portion of group paid-up insurance and group ordinary insurance is essentially the same as it is for group term life insurance. The portion of any employer contributions paid for the cash-value portion of the insurance is taxable to the employee as additional compensation. The sale of this type of coverage has been minimal in recent years.

*3. Group Universal Life.* Today, numerous companies market a group universal life product (GULP). These products include the typical guaranteed interest rate, fixed death benefit and loan options, plus the flexibility and potential returns that are associated with new life products. Universal life is particularly attractive in light of the new Financial Accounting Standard No. 106, which requires that plan sponsors report the liability of future postretirement life insurance benefits on an accrual accounting basis. Employers wishing to prefund their liability on a more favorable tax basis may consider the use of life insurance products.

Overall, GULP works much the same way as individual universal life. As a group program, however, it does differ in certain ways.[13]

---

[13]See Beam and McFadden, *Employee Benefits*, Chapter 7. See also Chapter 6 for a discussion of individual universal life insurance.

- Coverage generally is issued up to some limit without evidence of insurability. While limits do vary (depending on specific plan provisions, the size of the participating group and the insurer's underwriting standards), such coverage usually is high enough to meet most employees' needs.

- Policies typically are available on a low or no-commission basis.

- Administrative charges should be lower than those assessed for individual coverage.[14]

Another (less positive) difference is that the use of group underwriting standards to limit adverse selection may cut into GULP's flexibility to some extent. Active employment, for example, is likely to be a prerequisite for participation, and minimum and maximum amounts of coverage (e.g., from one to four times pay) usually are prescribed. Some proof of insurability also may be required for large amounts. The plans typically are employee-pay-all. Nevertheless, the overall plan design remains highly flexible.

GULP can be an inexpensive, convenient way to purchase portable cash-value life insurance. Employees have a chance to invest—at attractive interest rates—in a tax-favored vehicle. Since other forms of capital accumulation have been limited by recent tax law changes, GULP has become more and more popular.

*Supplemental Life Insurance.* To provide flexibility to employees in tailoring group life insurance protection to their needs, supplemental life insurance sometimes is made available as part of a group life insurance plan. The supplemental coverage normally is contributory and may have age-banded rates, with the number of options available based on the underwriting requirements of the life insurance company, the wishes of the employer, and applicable statutory requirements. The term **voluntary life insurance** is frequently used to denominate plans in which each employee can choose an amount of additional insurance in increments up to a maximum that is based on the employee's earnings (e.g., three times salary).

## TAXATION OF GROUP TERM LIFE INSURANCE

While the tax treatment of group insurance premiums paid by an employer is relatively straightforward, the income tax treatment to covered employees is more complex. In general, premiums paid for employees' group insurance are deductible by the employer. Premiums paid by sole proprietors and partners for group insurance on their own lives, however, are not deductible, since they are not considered employees.

*Employee Income Taxation.* Under current law, the cost of the first $50,000 of employer-provided group term life coverage is income-tax-exempt to

---

[14]Burton T. Beam and Edward E. Graves, "Group Universal Life Insurance," *Journal of the American Society of CLU & ChFC* (January 1987), pp. 46-52.

the employee. Amounts in excess of $50,000 may invoke taxable income. If the employee contributes toward the cost of the insurance, all of his or her contributions are allocable to the coverage provided in excess of $50,000. This is advantageous since it reduces or even eliminates any income tax consequences to the employee for having group coverage in excess of $50,000.

The economic benefit flowing to employees who enjoy coverage in excess of $50,000 is calculated on a monthly basis. The following procedural outline illustrates both the calculation of the amount taxable to the employee and the offset of any employee contributions:

(1) Find the total amount of group term life insurance coverage for the employee in each calendar month of a taxable year.

(2) Subtract $50,000 from each month's coverage.

(3) Apply the appropriate rate from the Uniform Premium Table (Table 26-2) to any balance for each month.

(4) From the sum of the monthly cost, subtract total employee contributions for the year.

An example will illustrate the application of this approach. Assume that José, age 56, is provided $150,000 of group term life insurance coverage throughout the year by his employer, and that he contributes $15 per month ($0.10 per $1,000) toward this coverage. The procedure to derive José's taxable income from the employer providing this protection would be as follows:

|          | Amount of coverage              | $150,000 |
|----------|---------------------------------|----------|
| Less:    | Exempt amount                   | -50,000  |
| Equals:  | Excess over exempt amount       | $100,000 |
|          |                                 |          |
|          | Excess over exempt amount       | $100,000 |
| Times:   | Uniform Premium Table rate      | x 0.75   |
|          | Tentative monthly taxable income | 75.00   |
| Times:   | Months of coverage              | x 12     |

**TABLE 26-2    UNIFORM PREMIUM TABLE I\***

($1,000 of Group-Term Life Insurance Protection)

| | |
|---|---|
| Under 30 | $0.08 |
| 30 to 34 | 0.09 |
| 35 to 39 | 0.11 |
| 40 to 44 | 0.17 |
| 45 to 49 | 0.29 |
| 50 to 54 | 0.48 |
| 55 to 59 | 0.75 |
| 60 to 64 | 1.17 |
| 65 to 69 | 2.10 |
| 70 and above | 3.76 |

The employee's age for purposes of the Uniform Premium Table is his or her attained age on the last day of the taxable year.

\*IRC §79.

| | | |
|---|---|---|
| Equals: | Tentative yearly taxable income | $ 900.00 |
| | Tentative yearly taxable income | $ 900.00 |
| Less: | Employee contributions | -180.00 |
| | ($15/month x 12 months) | |
| Equals: | Taxable economic benefit | $ 720.00 |

The above tax treatment assumes that certain conditions specified by IRS Code Section 79 and related regulations (see below) have been met. In designing a plan to meet these requirements, there are two areas of special concern: (1) the groups covering fewer than ten employees and (2) the nondiscrimination rules of Code Section 79(d).

*Under Ten Lives/Ten or More Lives.* When a group has fewer than ten lives, underwriting and amounts of insurance are both limited by IRS Regulation 1.79-1(c), which requires that all full-time employees who provide required satisfactory evidence of insurability must be included, unless they explicitly state their intention not to participate. The formula for determining the amount of life insurance is prescribed, and underwriting is restricted to a medical questionnaire. No physical examination is permitted.

Where 10 or more lives are involved, the basic rule is that regular underwriting is permissible and the amount of insurance for each employee can be computed under any formula that precludes individual selection.

*Nondiscrimination Rules.* Under the Tax Equity and Fiscal Responsibility Act of 1982 (TEFRA),[15] the exemption from income taxation of the cost of the first $50,000 of group term life insurance is not available to key employees if the plan discriminates in their favor as to either eligibility or type and amount of benefit. The law and accompanying regulations provide detailed definitions of what constitutes a key employee and discrimination.

Benefits are not considered discriminatory if all benefits available to key employees are also available to all participants. Furthermore, benefits will not be considered discriminatory merely because they bear a uniform relationship to total compensation or the basic rate of compensation of each employee.

*Other Tax Aspects.* As with individual coverages, death proceeds payable under group life insurance are received income-tax-free, whether they are received from term or cash-value group insurance.[16] The general rules for including life insurance proceeds in the gross estate for federal estate tax purposes apply.[17] An employee can assign all incidents of ownership in group life insurance, as long as both the master policy and applicable state law permit it.

[15]Section 79.
[16]IRC §101(a). See Chap. 13.
[17]See Chapter 13.

## POSTRETIREMENT COVERAGE

Three general approaches have been used to provide life insurance protection to retired employees: (1) continuation of a portion of the term life insurance; (2) retired lives reserve (RLR); and (3) cash-value life insurance. Continuation of a portion of the group term life insurance is straightforward. Unless the original amount of coverage is modest, the coverage to be continued often is a flat dollar amount, such as $5,000 or $10,000, or it varies from 25 to 50 percent of the former coverage. The other two approaches deserve further consideration.

*Retired Lives Reserve.*[18] A retired lives reserve (RLR) is a group product that has the basic objective of providing continuing life insurance beyond retirement. RLR consists of two basic elements: (1) term insurance (usually annually renewable to age 100) that qualifies as group term insurance under IRC Section 79 and (2) a reserve that will be accumulated, prior to retirement, and is to be used to pay premiums on the term insurance after retirement. Under a properly designed plan, an employer can make tax deductible contributions to the fund on behalf of employees and the contributions are not taxable income to the employees. The fund may be administered through a trust or by a life insurance company. As long as any employees under the plan are alive, the reserve cannot revert to the employer. If the employee dies or quits before retirement, the reserve value is used to fund future costs for others in the plan.

The employer may deduct the portion of the premium credited to any retired lives reserve fund (see below) for continuing coverage on retired employees. However, the amount added to the retired lives reserve must be no greater than the amount required to allocate the cost over the working lives of the employees, and the contract owner must have no right to capture any portion of the reserve so long as any active or retired employees remain alive. Similarly, a corporation's nonrefundable contributions to an employees' trust to provide group health and group term life insurance for both active and retired employees is deductible under Code Section 162. Contributions by the employer that are applied toward the savings portions of group cash-value plans are deductible by the employer, but taxable currently to the employee.

The Tax Reform Act of 1984 introduced additional constraints on the use of retired lives reserves that have materially reduced interest in and utilization of retired lives reserves. For example, the law made deductions for contributions on behalf of key employees contingent on the plan being nondiscriminatory under Section 79 (see taxation discussion above) and generally limited the amount of coverage to $50,000.

*Cash-Value Life Insurance.* Postretirement life insurance coverage also is funded through the use of various cash-value life insurance plans. These plans, discussed earlier, provide a means of prefunding the high mortality costs experienced in postretirement years.

[18]For a comprehensive discussion of RLR, see Beam and McFadden, *Employee Benefits*, pp. 124-130.

## TERMS OF CONTRACTS AND CERTIFICATES

Various important features of group life insurance policies have already been discussed. In connection with the term of the contract and renewal, when the policy is a group term life plan, the insurance company cannot refuse to renew each year if the employer wishes to continue the contract and pay the premiums. The premium rates, however, may be increased to such an extent that, for all practical purposes, the right to renew may not be of any value.

The master policy also provides that if at any time the number of employees does not equal the required number (e.g., ten), or if the plan is contributory and the required minimum percentage (e.g., 75 percent) of employees is not covered under the plan, the contract may be canceled.

Also, the laws in most states require certain standard provisions. Thus the employer must deliver to the employee a certificate showing the amount of insurance and the name of the beneficiary, and containing a conversion clause. Another required clause provides for an adjustment of premiums and insurance in case the age of an employee has been misstated. If the age has been overstated, the employer will receive a refund. If the age has been understated, the employer will be required to pay the amount by which past premiums have been deficient. Note that this method of adjusting policies for misstated ages differs from the adjustment made in individual life policies.

Group life insurance policies also contain an incontestable clause, although it is of less significance than in individual insurance. In addition, the policy usually provides for (1) a grace period of 31 days in connection with premium payments; (2) a right to have death proceeds paid in installments; (3) the necessity of making claims within one year following the last premium payment for the employee in question; (4) continued insurance, for the period provided by the contract, on laid-off employees, provided the employer continues to pay the necessary premium; (5) waiver of premium for an employee with disability commencing prior to age 60; and (6) extension of the insurance to employees who are eligible, but have been erroneously reported ineligible.

## SUPPLEMENTAL COVERAGES

Supplemental benefits may be added to group term life insurance contracts through the use of riders. These riders may include (1) accidental death and dismemberment insurance, (2) survivor income benefits, and (3) dependent life insurance. These coverages also may be written as separate contracts.

*Accidental Death and Dismemberment Insurance.* Many group life insurance contracts provide accidental death and dismemberment (AD&D) coverage. AD&D insurance provides a benefit if an employee dies, loses the sight of one or both eyes, or loses a hand or a foot directly and solely as a result of an accidental bodily injury. Although it can be written on a nonoccupational basis only, AD&D insurance usually is written as 24-hour coverage, particularly for small groups.

The benefit structure of AD&D coverage is based on an amount called the **principal sum**, which is typically equal to the coverage under the basic group life insurance contract. In the event of accidental death, the benefit is equal to the principal sum. In addition to this accidental death benefit, a benefit schedule is provided in the contract that relates types of injuries to the principal sum. Thus, for example, in the case of loss of both hands, both feet, or both eyes, the principal sum is payable. Similarly, one-half the principal sum is payable for the loss of one hand, foot, or eye.

The amount of insurance for accidental death usually is payable in a lump sum (although installment payments may be requested) to the designated beneficiary. For other losses, payment is made to the employee. Accidental death and dismemberment benefits normally cease at retirement, even if the basic life insurance coverage continues.

Under some plans, an elective benefit that is called **voluntary AD&D** that is not part of a regular group life insurance program is available. Employees usually pay all or almost all of the premium, and the employer's payroll deduction facilities are used for collecting the employee's contributions. The benefits of voluntary AD&D are essentially the same as those of basic AD&D, the most significant differences being in the substantial amounts of coverage available and the employee's privilege of selecting the amount of coverage.

*Survivor Income Benefits.*   Survivor income benefits are a form of monthly income that becomes payable upon the death of an employee who may be covered under either a pension plan[19] or a group life insurance plan. Three characteristics distinguish true survivor income benefits from the more traditional types of group life insurance: (1) the proceeds are payable in the form of monthly income only; (2) the covered employee does not name his or her beneficiary, since benefits are payable only to specified beneficiaries; and (3) benefits usually are payable only as long as there is a living survivor beneficiary and, in some cases, may cease on remarriage.

Although specific provisions vary from insurer to insurer, the survivor benefit income product is designed around the above three characteristics, with special features aimed at meeting the needs of employees with the greatest family responsibilities. For example, one insurer markets the following survivor income benefit product:

1. Single employees are not eligible for survivor benefits.
2. Permissible beneficiaries include only an employee's spouse and children.
3. Benefits normally are expressed as a percentage of the employee's pre-death earnings and are payable in two forms: a spouse benefit

[19]See Chap. 28.

and a children's benefit. The most common spouse-benefit percentage is between 20 and 40 percent of an employee's pre-death earnings, and the children-benefit percentage usually is significantly lower.

4. The spouse benefit normally is payable until the spouse reaches age 62 or 65. The children's benefit is payable until the youngest unmarried child reaches age 19 or, alternatively, age 23, if the child is in school.

5. The benefit ceases if the spouse remarries or dies before the end of the benefit period. When the youngest unmarried child reaches the limiting age for children, the children's benefit ceases.

Although the survivor income benefit is included in a relatively small percentage of plans, proponents believe that the plans can play an important role in augmenting the amount of insurance protection for the family.

*Dependent Life Insurance.* Group life insurance contracts commonly provide coverage on the lives of employees' dependents. The law in all jurisdictions permits employers to extend group term life insurance to the employee's spouse and eligible children. The amounts of dependent life insurance usually are small in relation to the amount of insurance on employees. The definition of dependents usually includes an employee's unmarried dependent children over, say, 14 days of age but under some specified age, such as 19. The employee is automatically the beneficiary under the coverage.

Many states limit life insurance benefits on dependents. These limits usually restrict the amount of insurance on the spouse to a maximum amount and frequently provide that in no event can the spousal benefit be more than 50 percent of the benefit provided the employee. Spousal benefits of $1,000, $2,000, and $5,000 are still very common. Children's benefits also are restricted in many jurisdictions.

## GROUP DISABILITY INCOME INSURANCE

Group insurance can be written to provide virtually any combination of health insurance benefits. As with individual policies, group health insurance benefits may be broadly classified as (1) disability income and (2) medical expense. Since medical expense benefits will be discussed in detail in the next chapter, this discussion will relate to disability income benefits. There are two approaches to providing disability income benefits: short-term disability and long-term disability.[20]

## SHORT-TERM DISABILITY

Short-term disability coverage is intended as income replacement for a relatively short period of time, and it is most often payable from the first day of disability

[20]See Chaps. 16 and 17 for more details on disability income insurance.

resulting from an accident and from the eighth day of disability resulting from sickness. (Many other combinations of waiting periods are also utilized.) Income benefits for both accident and sickness usually are payable for up to 13, 26, or 52 weeks. U.S. federal law requires that pregnancy be treated the same as a sickness under all fringe benefit plans for employers with 15 or more employees. Many states have stricter requirements than the federal requirement. The cost impact of these laws can be substantial.

## Long-Term Disability

Long-term disability benefits are provided in recognition of the continuing need for income for the duration of a long-term disability arising from either accident or sickness, and without regard to whether it is job-connected. The definition of disability usually requires total disability. However, some companies include a **residual disability benefit** and a **presumptive disability** clause in their contracts. Under the residual benefit clause, the insured does not have to be totally disabled to qualify for benefits. For example, if disability reduces an insured's income by at least 20 percent in the first two years, the plan pays a proportionate benefit. This residual disability and temporary recovery benefits are consistent with the increasing emphasis on rehabilitation services as part of plan benefits. Under the presumptive benefit provision, the total loss of sight, speech, hearing, or two or more limbs automatically qualifies the individual for long-term disability benefits. The usual elimination period is waived. The presumptive disability benefit provision is not common.

Benefits normally are not provided until the expiration of an elimination period, which may run from 7 days to 12 months, and they are often designed to provide long-term disability income protection upon cessation of the short-term disability benefit coverage. Assuming that there is a continuation of disability, benefits usually continue until age 65, but alternative approaches, such as two or five year's coverage, or lifetime accident coverage, are not uncommon. The size of the group is a most important underwriting consideration. With large groups, considerable latitude in underwriting is prevalent. Another important underwriting consideration for long-term disability is the nature of work performed by the group. Blue-collar groups are underwritten with considerable caution.

## Taxation of Disability Income Benefits

As with all types of health insurance benefits, premiums (or other employer contributions) paid by an employer for disability income insurance for employees are generally tax deductible by the employer and are not taxable income to the employee for federal income tax purposes. Employee contributions, on the other hand, are not tax deductible by the employee. It is consistent with these two rules that the payment of benefits under an insured plan or a noninsured salary continuation plan will result in the receipt of taxable income by the employee, to the extent the benefits received are attributable to employer contributions. Thus if the employer pays 75 percent of the monthly premium and the employee pays 25 percent, 25 percent of any benefits received will be tax free and 75 percent taxable.

## ALTERNATIVES FOR GROUP INSURANCE PLAN FUNDING

### INTRODUCTION

During the 1960s, with rare exceptions, the arrangement under which group benefit plans were funded was the traditional group insurance contract. In the 1970s and 1980s many corporations experienced reduced profits and cash flow problems. At the same time, benefit programs became more liberal, with accompanying premium increases. Escalating health care inflation and greater utilization increased the cost of providing health insurance benefits. During the same time period, the cost of borrowing money for corporate purposes rose to historic highs. These developments gave risk managers and other financial officers a reason to investigate alternate financing mechanisms for their benefit programs.

Generally, employers were (and are) interested in examining alternative methods of financing benefit programs for one or more of the following reasons:

1.  To control and use reserve funds that would normally be available to the insurance company under a conventional insured plan

2.  To reduce or eliminate payment of state premium taxes and insurer risk, profit, and contingency charges that normally are part of the cost of a conventional insured plan

3.  To exercise more control over their plan design by avoiding state insurance mandates and requirements

4.  To participate more fully in their own favorable experience

5.  To enjoy improved cash flow via more immediate recognition of their own experience.

In response to these developments, a number of techniques have been developed by insurers that modify conventional methods of funding group insurance, but offer a reasonable guarantee of comparable benefits.

### FULLY INSURED PLAN VARIATIONS

*Retrospective Premium Arrangements.* Under a **retrospective premium arrangement**, premiums are set realistically to cover expected claims and expenses without the margin for contingencies usually included to cover higher-than-expected levels of either. In lieu of the premium margin, there is an agreement under which the insurer reserves the right to collect additional premiums at the end of the contract year if claims and expenses are higher than the premiums paid. The additional premium usually is limited so that the amount paid will not be greater than that which would have been required under the insurer's premium schedule had the margin been included.

*Cost-Plus.* Cost-plus funding offers the employer another funding alternative for group benefits. By assuming a portion of the risk normally assumed by an insurer, the employer may achieve lower charges, with the insurer remaining the guarantor of benefits. The reserves normally held by the insurer (less about one-third for claims-reporting lag) can be held by the employer, and this increases the options for the use of money. Money that in a conventionally insured plan would have been returned as a dividend is never paid out by the employer.

Through a cost-plus plan the employer assumes the cost of the benefit payments and administrative expenses of the plan on a month-to-month basis, up to specified annual deferred and stop-loss limits. In using this funding method, certain values of a conventionally insured plan are lost. Monthly budgeting is more difficult with the loss of a fixed, level premium, and cash flow will be less predictable in the short run. Upward claim fluctuations may mean a greater plan cost in some years than would have been the case with an insured, guaranteed plan. Also, financial responsibility for terminal (runoff) claim liability beyond a minimum established reserve is assumed by the employer.

*Extended Grace Period.* Another way of increasing the cash flow for the contract owner is to extend the usual 31-day grace period for the payment of premiums by an additional 30 to 60 days. This permits the contract owner to retain the use of two or three months' premium, thus permitting the employer, effectively, to retain a substantial portion of the reserves normally held by the insurer.

*Release of Reserves.* An insurer, on request, may agree to release the reserves it is holding on the employer's contracts. Since liability for benefits due after termination of the contract remains with the insurer, the insurer usually will require a letter of credit for the amount of the reserves released or audited acceptable financial statements from the contract owner.

*Flexible Funding Life Insurance.* Flexible funding is a cost-plus approach to funding life insurance. Under this arrangement, the contract owner's monthly premium is equal to the claims paid in the previous month plus reserve adjustments, premium taxes, and the insurer's expense charges. The contract owner may accept liability for all claims or the plan may limit the contract owner's liability to what the premium would have been under a conventional fully insured arrangement.

## ALTERNATIVES TO FULLY INSURED PLANS

The concept of an employer self-funding a benefit plan as an alternative to an insured plan is really not new. Health benefit programs initially were self-funded, and self-funding has been a vehicle commonly used by employers for workers' compensation benefits.

In evaluating whether to adopt self-funding, it is of primary importance to consider the size of the group. In considering the cost of self-funding versus insurance, the financial manager weighs the advantages against the cost of additional management and administrative resources required and, if an outside claims administrator is used, loss of insurance company expertise in such areas as claims payment and cost containment. Also, the importance of current cash flow to the employer, the additional risk under some cash flow arrangements, and employee reaction to self-funding all must be factored into the analysis.

*Minimum Premium Plans.* **Minimum premium plans** (MPPs) create a partially self-funded arrangement that has premium tax savings for the employer as one of its primary objectives. Under an MPP the contract owner assumes liability for all but the largest claims or very unfavorable total experience of the plan.

An individual stop-loss arrangement, which is part of such plans, limits the contract owner's liability for any insured individual's claims within a specific time period to a predetermined dollar maximum. Amounts over this maximum (the individual or specific stop-loss limit) do not count toward claims that are funded by the contract owner. Also, an aggregate stop-loss limit applies to the aggregate of all claims during the plan year. It is typically calculated at 100 percent (sometimes 105, 110, or 115 percent) of the projected claims level that the insurer would have used had it computed a premium for a conventional fully insured plan. Claims over the aggregate stop-loss limit are paid from insurer funds. Premiums to cover losses over the stop-loss limits, to maintain reserves, and to cover operating costs are paid to the insurer.

Under an MPP, the employer/contract owner deposits funds, as needed, to a special bank account to cover claims funded by the contract owner. The insurer, acting as agent of the contract owner, pays claims out of the special account first. The insurer continues to provide the same services, assumes the same risks, and, unless some special arrangement is made, holds essentially the same claim reserves as those under a conventional fully insured plan. The reserves must be maintained, since, on termination of the group plan, the insurer is still responsible, as under a fully insured plan, to pay all covered outstanding claims. In some minimum premium plans, however, the contract owner agrees to assume responsibility for all outstanding claims upon discontinuance of the plan. In such cases, the need for the insurer to maintain reserves is removed, although the insurer can be at risk upon contract owner bankruptcy.

Most states assess premium taxes only on premiums received by the insurance company for payment of claims under an insurance contract. Thus, by channeling most of the claim funds directly from the contract owner to the covered individuals, an MPP makes it possible to avoid premium taxes on approximately 80 to 90 percent of claims costs.

*Administrative Services Only.* Under an **administrative services only (ASO)** self-insurance arrangement, the insurer reviews claims and makes payment from the employer's funds and provides administration services. In the usual case, full administrative, underwriting, and actuarial services are provided as well. There is, however, no insurance and, therefore, no insurance contract is involved. The ASO agreement is a service contract between the insurer as administrator and the employer as buyer. It specifies the services to be provided by the insurer, the rights and obligations of both parties, and the administrative fees involved. Similar arrangements can be made with a third-party administrator (TPA) rather than an insurer.

The employer who chooses ASO frequently purchases stop-loss insurance on medical care expenses from an insurer as protection against the risk of catastrophic losses. As with minimum premium plans, stop-loss insurance purchased with an ASO contract can take the form of either individual or aggregate stop-loss insurance or both (aggregate insurance is typically calculated at 115 to 130 percent of projected claims).

*Letters of Credit.* Although a letter of credit is not itself a cash flow option, it is sometimes required as a security measure to protect the insurance company, because of the risk inherent in several alternate funding arrangements. It is a document issued by a bank to the insurer to guarantee the contract owner's promise to pay monies due under such funding arrangements. The bank receives a fee for this credit-guarantee service.

Table 26-3 shows various funding methods available and summarizes the handling of the key cost components under each.

**TABLE 26-3    GROUP BENEFIT FUNDING METHODS**

|  | Premium Rates | Reserves | Risk | Retention |
|---|---|---|---|---|
| Insured conventional | Established and guaranteed for a stated period (usually 12 months) | Established and held until plan ceases | Assumed by insurer above premium income | Commissions, administrative expense, risk charge, and taxes |
| Insured retrospective premium rating | Established at a level lower than conventional, with provision for lump-sum additional payment | Established and held until plan ceases | Assumed by insurer above premium income, including retrospective limit | Commissions, administrative expense, risk charge, interest loss, and taxes |
| Insured cost-plus | None or only for first year; premium is equal to paid claims plus insurer charges | Partially established, perhaps in the form of a deposit, and held until plan ceases | Assumed by insurer in excess of a generally conservative stop-loss point | Commissions, administrative expense, lower risk charge, interest loss, and taxes |
| Partially self-funded minimum premium plan | Covers all charges by the insurer; includes amounts needed to fund the insured part of the risk, reserve charges, insurer administrative expense, taxes on premiums received by the insurer, and stop-loss rates | Established on both the insured and self-funded portions of the plan; these reserves are held by either the insurer or the contract owner until the plan ceases | Assumed by insurer for amounts in excess of pre-determined premium and plan contributions; in event of termina-tion of the plan, the run-out claims are insured by the insurer or self-funded by the contract owner | Commissions, administrative expense, risk charge, and taxes on only the premium received by the insurer where permitted by state law |
| Self-insurance with administrative services only | None or used only for cost analysis and any stop-loss rates | None or used entirely by employer for cost accounting and tax purposes | Assumed by employer | Administrative expense; consultant fees may be borne separately by employer |

# Chapter 27

# HEALTH CARE PLANS

## THE HEALTH CARE ENVIRONMENT IN THE UNITED STATES

As the cost of health care has continued to escalate, health care benefits have become an increasingly valuable employee benefit. Nearly three in four employees in the United States are covered by an employer-sponsored health insurance plan, with coverage being more common among medium-sized employers and large employers than among small employers. Two primary types of medical expense plans are offered by employers: (1) traditional fee-for-service plans offered by insurance companies and many self-insured employers and (2) prepaid plans, such as those provided by health maintenance organizations (see below). As medical care costs have risen dramatically, cost containment has become a critical concern for insurers, plan sponsors, and covered employees. Despite a decade of innovation and effort, attention continues to be focused at both the public and corporate policy levels on the issue of cost containment.[1]

### MEDICAL CARE COST TRENDS

The rate of increase in U.S. health care expenditures throughout the 1980s and into the 1990s was significantly higher than the increases in general inflation, population growth, and the overall increase in the gross domestic product (GDP). Increases in health care costs have consistently been in double digits—that is, at a rate two times that of inflation. Health care costs consumed over 14 percent of U.S. GDP in 1992. Other countries—

---

[1]For a comprehensive review of health insurance plans, see Burton T. Beam, Jr. and John J. McFadden, *Employee Benefits* (Homewood, Ill.: Dearborn Financial Publishing, Inc., 1992) and HIAA, *Group Life and Health Insurance*, Part A, Part B, and Part C (Washington, D.C.: Health Insurance Association of America, 1992).

even those with universal health care systems—spend less on health care than does the United States, as Figure 27-1 shows. Even worse, many employer-sponsored indemnity plans are experiencing annual cost increases on the order of 20 to 25 percent as a result of increases in the number of units being bought (utilization) and the shifts in cost from Medicare and indigent care and other cost-increasing mechanisms.

As a nation, the United States has experienced a constant and dramatic increase in the demand for and cost of health care services. When the fundamental factors driving both utilization and unit prices are analyzed, there is no reason to believe that this situation will moderate in the near term. Although all indications point to demand and costs increasing in the future, the fact that employees and many employers, providers, and politicians would like to do something about controlling costs should lead to a slowing of the increase in health care costs.

## CAUSES OF HEALTH CARE INFLATION

As individuals live longer, they are consuming more and more medical services. Across all demographic groups, demand has increased for quality health care and state-of-the-art treatment. It is projected that the population aged 75 and older will increase four times faster than that under age 65. Many elderly people have chronic, disabling illnesses. It is anticipated that institutional care will increase, and hospital care and nursing home care are expected to consume an even larger share of personal health care spending.

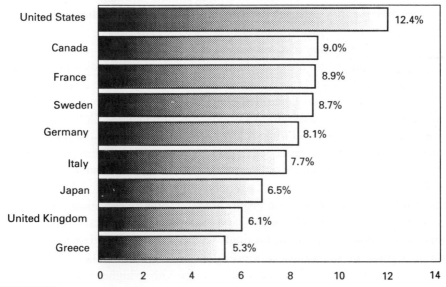

**FIGURE 27-1**

**HEALTH EXPENDITURES AS A PERCENT OF GROSS DOMESTIC PRODUCT, 1990**
*Source*: OECD

The rapid advances in sophisticated, expensive diagnostic and therapeutic technology have helped fuel the growth in health care expenditures. For example, in 1950 cataract surgery as it is known today did not exist. Today physicians using lasers and other advanced surgical techniques save the sight of over one million individuals each year, but at a cost of $3 billion. Until recently, many physicians were obtaining ownership in facilities that operate this new equipment, making referrals to these facilities, and sharing in their profits. The American Medical Association recently ruled that such activity is unethical and involvement on the part of physicians will undoubtedly decline.

Despite a continuing reduction in the amount of inpatient care, dramatic increases in the price per episode of inpatient care have also contributed to medical inflation. As overall hospital utilization continues to decline, fewer patients must carry the load of a greater portion of each hospital's total overhead.

Both the utilization and the cost of ambulatory care (care for the hospital outpatient and in the physician's office) are increasing at a rapid pace. In the United States, most surgery that should be done on an ambulatory basis is done that way. The number of visits to physicians' offices and of tests taken with expensive equipment has risen. The shift to outpatient surgery has been accompanied by a dramatic increase in the volume of these procedures. More individuals are having operations as outpatients than when these operations were available on an inpatient basis only.

Another source of the cost increase is the weak balance of supply and demand of medical services. Frequently, the demand for services is controlled by the provider, such as a physician who has significant influence on the procedures performed on a patient. Research indicates that typical abused procedures include Cesarean sections, hysterectomies, heart bypass surgery, and imaging diagnostic procedures.

Increased legal activity has also increased costs. Malpractice suits are routinely filed for everything from allegedly faulty diagnoses to mishandled child deliveries, and awards often include substantial amounts for noneconomic losses as well as for economic losses. Malpractice premiums have soared to cover possible lawsuits, and service providers pass along the costs in higher fees. Defensive medicine aimed at reduced vulnerability to lawsuits has also brought a sharp increase in procedures that some consumer advocates believe are unnecessary.

Cost shifting, another component of increased cost in employer-sponsored health plans, is the result of other payors not reimbursing providers at levels that are sufficient to recover cost and make a profit. Medicare, the federal insurance program for elderly people, disabled people, and patients with end-stage renal disease, limits the amount it will pay to hospitals and other providers. Hospitals and doctors tend to make up for the lost revenue by increasing fees to others. Any person or organization actually paying charges ends up with a higher bill. Bad debts, indigent care, inadequate Medicaid reimbursement, and discounted rates for contracting health maintenance organizations (HMOs) and preferred provider organizations (PPOs) also add to the cost shifts to the noncontracting plans. As a result, there have been dramatic rate increases in nonnegotiated hospital rates. This is why some plans experience 25 percent inflation while others experience single or low double-digit increases. Other factors that increase costs include excess hospital capacity, varying medical practice standards, overuse of specialist physicians, and a focus on acute care rather than on preventive care. Figure 27-2 provides a broad breakdown of the factors causing increasing costs in health care.

## EMPLOYER RESPONSES TO RISING COSTS

Until recently, employers responded to these rapidly increasing costs by raising the share of costs paid by employees or by trying to cap the employer's contribution (cost). These efforts included:

- Increased employee contributions
- Increased employee out-of-pocket expenses (e.g., increased deductibles, raised coinsurance percentages, greater use of internal limits on certain types of benefits)
- Introduction of flexible benefit plans (see below), whereby the employee chooses from a variety of life insurance, medical care, and other benefits provided by a fixed employer contribution
- Termination of the plan itself

All of these responses can be considered passive in the sense that they manage an important human resource problem. Today more and more larger employers are approaching the problem positively by attempting to manage the

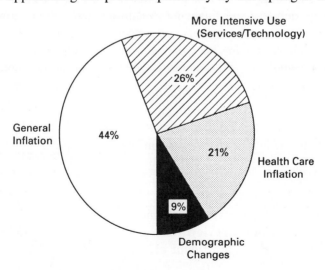

**FIGURE 27-2**

**FACTORS CAUSING INCREASING COST OF HEALTH CARE.**
*Source: Health Care Financing Administration, 1991*

medical care benefits provided to their employees as part of their overall employee benefit program. Employers are responding to increases in plan costs by initiating some or all of the following actions in relation to their health benefit plans:

- Reducing coverage through increased deductibles, out-of-pocket limits, and maximum amounts, including maximums for coverages such as mental health and chemical dependency
- Redesigning benefits to create incentives for more efficient utilization of health care resources
- Evaluating the administration of the plan
- Evaluating the financing of the plan
- Investigating the use of alternative delivery and reimbursement systems such as HMOs, PPOs, and exclusive provider organizations (EPOs)

Although all of these activities have contributed to more effective management of employer health care dollars, to date the greatest attention has been placed on benefit redesign. As changes have taken place, the concept of managed care has evolved.

## MANAGED CARE

As health care costs have escalated and cost containment efforts have been emphasized, benefit redesign, alternative delivery systems, self-insurance, and other developments have led to the emergence of the concept of **managed care**, which has had a profound impact on health insurance. During the past five to ten years, the health care delivery and financing system has evolved at a pace few anticipated, as it largely responded to the acute concern about the ever-rising cost of care. The most visible change has been the explosive development of managed care delivery systems, of which HMOs and PPOs are the best-known examples.

*Definition of Managed Care.* Managed care, which integrates the financing and delivery of appropriate health care services, means different things to different persons, but it is agreed that it has three major objectives. They are: (1) to ensure access to medically needed care in the most appropriate and cost-effective manner; (2) to provide coordination and continuity of medically necessary health services to the patient; and (3) to assist the patient in achieving his or her full potential for restored health.

Managed care involves the active management of the services and providers in health care plans. **Utilization review** (also called utilization management) programs constitute the most significant element of managed care. These programs usually include (1) preadmission certification, (2) concurrent and continued stay review, (3) discharge planning, (4) catastrophic case management, and (5) data management and reporting (see below). Other managed care options most commonly found in health insurance plans (financed either by insurers or self-funded) include the previously mentioned **health maintenance organizations** (HMOs) and **preferred provider organizations** (PPOs), which sometimes are referred to as alternative delivery (of treatment) systems.

*Managed Care Delivery Systems.*     When a person covered by traditional health insurance needs medical care, he or she seeks the services of a physician, who attempts to diagnose the illness and to select the appropriate course of treatment. In attempting to remain neutral in the medical decision-making process, traditional insurance has inflated health care costs by increasing demand for services. Since physicians traditionally are paid a fee for each service they provide and hospitals historically have been reimbursed on a cost basis, neither type of provider has had any economic incentive to minimize the resources that are used to treat patients. Alternative delivery systems, on the other hand, provide incentives to consider the relative costs of alternative approaches to treatment.

As pointed out above, managed care implies continual monitoring of the utilization of services to covered individuals for the purpose of determining whether patterns of medical practice are appropriate and cost-effective. Managed care provides oversight, supervision, and feedback to providers in regard to their behavior and the aggregate expenditures on behalf of an enrolled group.

In addition to their role in health care cost containment, managed care delivery systems give health care financing organizations a choice among providers who compete for their health care business. Some believe that competition for payors' health care dollars creates incentives for providers to deliver health care more effectively while maintaining a high standard of care. Others are concerned that competition among alternative health care systems may actually increase costs or reduce quality. Competing alternative health care financing organizations may seek to attract members who are less costly to treat. If health care payors seek to distinguish themselves by the amenities they offer in order to attract healthier members, competition may promote inflation rather than cost containment.

Most managed care plans reduce enrollees' out-of-pocket costs by lowering or eliminating copayments and deductibles, and they may offer broader and deeper coverage of preventive care services than is offered by traditional group insurance plans. In addition, managed care plans may appeal to a younger, more mobile, healthier population that is less likely to have established relationships with traditional insurance plans.

While it is difficult to measure the quality of medical care and patients may feel uncertain about their ability to select among providers, managed care delivery systems do have to compete against standards set by providers under traditional plans. At the same time, competition among financing organizations seeking to attract lowest-risk patients may leave higher-risk persons without any plan willing to accept them. Other things being equal, providers of health care services prefer higher-risk patients, except where fees are capitated as in an HMO. As discussed below, HMOs provide services for members who pay a fixed periodic premium in advance for the services of participating physicians, cooperating hospitals, and other health care providers.

HMOs enroll more than 14 percent of the population, with six states having more than 20 percent of their population in HMOs. Large HMOs (with more than 100,000 members) are growing at a rapid pace. Although there are 84 HMOs in the United States that have more than 100,000 members each, 85 percent of all HMOs have fewer than 100,000 enrollees.[2]

The structures of HMO plans are becoming hybrid and more diversified. Among plans that are more than three years old, over one-half have added PPOs, traditional indemnity options, open-ended options, or employee assistance programs to assist individuals with substance abuse or mental health problems. PPOs (see below), primarily a development of the 1980s, also are growing rapidly. PPOs increased from 572 in 1987 to 978 in 1991.

The recent rapid growth of managed care plans reflects the recognition by major employers and insurers that ways must be found to reduce costs while assuring that patients get appropriate care. Insurers increasingly recognize that traditional fee-for-service indemnity plans do not provide mechanisms for containing costs. As a consequence, many insurers have made major commitments to develop and sustain comprehensive managed care systems. Figure 27-3 depicts the growth of managed care in the commercial health insurance industry.

## FEDERAL REGULATION

Many aspects of federal regulation have affected the establishment and character of group insurance plans. The most important of these include the Age Discrimination in Employment Act, the Civil Rights Act, the Employee Retirement Income Security Act, the Social Security Act, the Health Maintenance Organization Act, the Consolidated Omnibus Budget Reconciliation Acts of 1985, 1986, and 1990, the Americans with Disabilities Act, and the Internal Revenue Code. The Social Security Act was discussed in Chapter 25 and nondiscrimination rules are discussed throughout Chapters 26, 27, and 28. As background for this chapter, the other laws are discussed briefly.

The **Age Discrimination in Employment Act**, enacted in 1967, was amended in 1986 to eliminate the upper-age limitation from the prohibition against age discrimination for most working persons. With some exceptions, such as in the case of senior executives, compulsory retirement is no longer allowed. In 1990 Congress explicitly placed employee benefits under the provisions of the Age Discrimination in Employment Act, requiring these benefits to be continued

---

[2]*1992 Source Book of Health Insurance Data,* (Washington, D.C.: Health Insurance Association of America, 1992), p. 21.

**FIGURE 27–3**

**GROWTH OF MANAGED CARE IN THE U.S. COMMERCIAL HEALTH INSURANCE INDUSTRY (1982-1990). PERCENTAGE OF GROUP BUSINESS.**
*Source: HIAA Managed Care Survey, 1991*

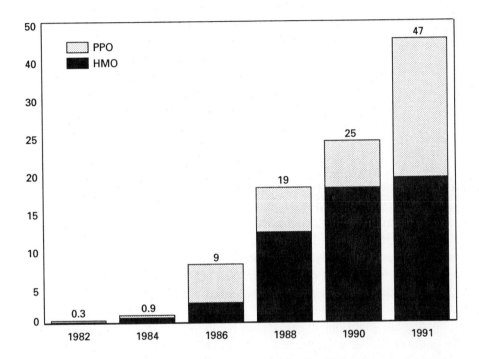

for older employees. The act currently permits a reduction in the level of some benefits for older workers, provided the cost of providing older employees with the specific benefits is no greater than the cost of providing similar benefits for younger employees. Medical expense coverage, however, cannot be reduced. These restrictions apply only to benefits for active employees; there are no requirements under the act that any benefits be continued for retired workers. In contrast to the situation pertaining to other benefits, employees over age 65 cannot be required to pay any more for their medical expense coverage than is paid by employees under age 65.

A 1978 amendment to the **Civil Rights Act** requires that women affected by pregnancy, childbirth, or related medical conditions be treated in the same way as other persons for employment-related purposes. The amendment, known as the **Pregnancy Discrimination Act**, applies only to insured and self-funded benefit plans of employers with 15 or more employees. Although employers with fewer employees are not subject to the provisions of the amendment, they may be subject to comparable state laws.

The **Employee Retirement Income Security Act** (ERISA) clarified and reserved to the federal government the authority to regulate employee benefit plans. While ERISA's provisions primarily address the activities and responsibilities of employer-sponsored pension plans, the law also establishes federal authority over employee welfare plans, including health insurance benefits. ERISA's most important provisions relating to employer-sponsored health insurance plans include the preemption of all state laws regulating employee benefit plans. This situation is an important attraction of self-funding. As amended, other provisions of ERISA exclude employer welfare plans from the funding and coverage provisions that govern pensions and require that employer-sponsored health insurance plans allow employees and their dependents whose coverage is terminated under most circumstances to continue to be covered by the employer plan. As discussed earlier in Chapter 26, ERISA also gives to the states regulatory authority to impose and enforce financial standards for multiple-employer welfare arrangements, including multiple-employer trusts.

For employers with 20 or more employees, the **Consolidated Omnibus Budget Reconciliation Acts of 1985, 1986, and 1990** (COBRA) require that group health plans (including dental plans) allow employees and certain beneficiaries to elect to have their current health insurance coverage extended, at group rates, for up to 36 months following a "qualifying event" that results in the loss of coverage. Failure to comply with the act results in an employer losing the income tax deduction for the cost of the health plan. The employer may also be subject to civil penalties, and highly compensated employees are taxed on employer contributions made on their behalf.

The following are qualifying events if they result in the loss of coverage by an employee or the employee's spouse or dependent child:

- The death of the covered employee
- The termination of the employee except for gross misconduct
- A reduction of the employee's hours so that the employee or dependent is ineligible for coverage
- The divorce or legal separation of the covered employee from his or her spouse
- The employee's eligibility for medicare (for spouses and children)
- A child's ceasing to be an eligible dependent under the plan

Under the act, any employee, spouse, or dependent child who loses coverage because of any of these events is entitled to elect continued coverage without providing evidence of insurability. The beneficiary must be allowed to continue coverage that is identical to that provided to employees and dependents to whom a qualifying event has not occurred.

Under COBRA, the cost of the continued coverage may be passed on to the qualifying beneficiary, but it cannot exceed 102 percent of the total cost to the plan for the period of coverage for a similarly situated active employee to whom a qualifying event has not occurred. The continuation of coverage is not automatic; it must be elected by a qualifying beneficiary. COBRA does not apply to group life insurance.

The 1990 **Americans with Disabilities Act** will have a major impact on employment practices, but employee benefits are largely exempt from its provisions. The act, however, does impose some restrictions on employers with respect to employee benefits. For example, a person with a disability that does not pose increased risks cannot be denied coverage or be subject to different terms based on the disability alone. It appears, however, that employers can deny coverage or require higher employee contributions based on medical underwriting.

## Postretirement Welfare Costs[3]

After a long study, the Financial Accounting Standards Board (FASB) issued FAS 106. This new standard, issued in December 1990, effectively ended the pay-as-you-go *accounting* for nonpension benefits for retirees. The new rule does not change the actual cost of providing welfare benefits to retirees. At the same time, it will have a significant adverse effect on earnings for many companies. Employers must calculate the cost of providing lifetime coverage to all active and retired employees as a current lump-sum value and begin expensing a designated portion of that amount over employees' working years. Although the financial impact will vary from company to company (depending on such factors as employee demographics and benefit plan provisions), many employers can expect as much as a tenfold increase in current accounting expense for medical benefits. This change in accounting treatment will force employers to recognize that retiree medical coverage is an expensive benefit.

The change in accounting treatment also does not directly affect funding decisions. There is, as yet, no legal requirement or fully tax-qualified vehicle available to prefund retiree welfare plans. Employers could choose to maintain pay-as-you-go financing while moving ahead to accrual-based accounting. Assuming the employer wishes to consider advance funding, there are a number of vehicles available. In selecting a vehicle for advance funding, employers must consider three key questions:

- Can employers take a tax deduction on contributions to the plan?
- Does the income from plan investments accumulate tax free?
- Are plan participants taxed on their benefits when received?

If these criteria are used, none of the available funding vehicles meets all of an employer's needs. The following discussion summarizes these vehicles briefly.

[3]This section draws on *Postretirement Welfare Benefits—Arriving at a Manageable Solution* (Atlanta, Ga.: Towers Perrin, 1991).

*The 501(c)(9) VEBA Trust.*     The **Voluntary Employees Beneficiary Association** (VEBA), described in Section 501(c)(9) of the Internal Revenue Code, is a trust established to provide sickness and accident benefits to employees. Once a common funding mechanism for retiree welfare benefits, its popularity waned with passage of the Deficit Reduction Act of 1984, which imposed a tax on the investment income from assets held for postretirement health benefits and limited employers' tax deductions on contributions to both retiree health and life insurance plans.

*The 401(h) Pension Plan Trust.*     This trust is a special account established within a company's defined benefit pension plan to pay for medical and life insurance benefits. Investment income from such a trust is tax sheltered and contributions are tax deductible. Employers, however, are allowed to use only one-third of the amount they contribute to their pension plan. This limitation is intended to ensure that other retiree benefits remain subordinate to pension benefits. Thus those with well-funded pension plans will only have limited opportunity to make tax-deductible contributions.

Employers with a significant pension surplus and cash flow concerns may find this vehicle relatively attractive, since under the 1990 Omnibus Reduction Act (OBRA), they can transfer annually part of their surplus pension assets to their 401(h) accounts to cover current retiree medical expense payments. Most employers, however, are likely to be put off by the significant restrictions associated with this vehicle.

In a variation on the pension plan trust, an employer can establish a separate 401(h)-like account within its profit-sharing plan and allow employees to elect irrevocably to put a portion of their profit-sharing allocation into the account to purchase health insurance after retirement. The IRS has not yet ruled on whether employees would be taxed on receipt of benefits from such an account.

*Other.*     Corporate-owned life insurance (COLI), trust-owned life insurance (TOLI), and VEBA-owned life insurance (VOLI) are individual or group contract arrangements through which employers can fund retiree welfare benefits. Although all three are tax effective under current law, possible future tax rule changes could significantly limit their attractiveness, particularly the policies that have little flexibility. Employers may also find it administratively burdensome to maintain numerous individual insurance contracts. In addition, COLI arrangements are not considered plan assets under FAS 106 because the assets are not segregated and restricted for retiree welfare benefits.

The remainder of this chapter presents an overview of the providers of health insurance benefits in the United States, the typical health insurance benefits that are available under health insurance contracts, and a review of plan design components and systems of cost control that have developed. With this background, a review of coverage arrangements in group health insurance is presented. The chapter concludes with an overview of the current public policy debate in the field of health care financing.

## HEALTH INSURANCE PROVIDERS

Health insurance in the United States is available from five principal sources: (1) commercial insurers, (2) Blue Cross and Blue Shield organizations, (3) HMOs, (4) self-insured plans, and (5) federal or state governments. Each is briefly discussed below.[4]

Measured either by number of persons covered or the dollars involved, health insurance is the most significant type of group insurance. For most employers, the cost of providing group medical expense insurance is several times as great as the combined cost of life and disability income insurance.

### COMMERCIAL INSURANCE COMPANIES

Approximately 1,000 U.S. commercial insurers write some form of health insurance.[5] These stock and mutual corporations are organized as life, casualty, or health insurance companies to provide medical expense and disability income insurance on a group or individual basis. The health insurance policies of commercial insurers generally provide for payment of benefits directly to the insured, unless the insured has specifically assigned payment to the designated provider of medical services.

Although approximately 700 insurers write group insurance, virtually all health insurance coverage is written by less than 100 companies. More than one-half of this coverage is written by approximately 30 commercial insurers. More than 180 million persons are covered under policies issued by commercial insurers.

### BLUE CROSS AND BLUE SHIELD PLANS

The Blue Cross and Blue Shield Association coordinates the 53 Blue Cross/Blue Shield plans that operate statewide or regionally across the nation as nonprofit hospital and medical service corporations.[6] These plans dominate the market for basic medical expense coverage in many geographic areas, primarily because of lower premiums as a consequence of a favored tax status and close ties to the hospitals and organized medical societies in the localities that they serve. Major medical insurance and group dental insurance are often available from Blue Cross/Blue Shield plans. Over 70 million persons were covered under Blue Cross and Blue Shield plans in 1991.

---

[4]For a thorough analysis of health insurance providers, see Beam and McFadden, *Employee Benefits*, Chap. 9.

[5]Because of the more detailed treatment of commercial insurers in Chaps. 11 and 29, this discussion of commercial insurers is brief.

[6]In addition to the 53 plans that jointly write Blue Cross/Blue Shield coverage, there are eight separate Blue Cross plans and 13 separate Blue Shield plans.

**Blue Cross** plans are nonprofit hospital expense prepayment plans. Most plans were organized by hospitals in the area served by the plan. Historically, member hospitals usually elected the board of directors, which normally included members from the public and the medical profession, as well as hospital administrators. Today the composition of the boards has changed significantly to reflect more business and consumer representation.

The plans provide for hospital care on a service-type basis, whereby Blue Cross enters into contracts separately with member hospitals for certain types and amounts of hospital services and then reimburses the hospital directly for the covered services rendered to plan subscribers. The subscriber, the Blues' term for the insured, is billed only for services not covered by the Blue Cross certificate and, unlike the situation with commercial health insurance, there usually is no direct payment to the covered person.

The majority of Blue Cross plans are coordinated with Blue Shield plans. **Blue Shield** plans are nonprofit organizations offering prepayment coverage for surgical and medical services performed by a physician. Independently organized on a state or regional basis, these plans are members of the National Association of Blue Cross and Blue Shield Plans and are now commonly controlled locally by a board of directors representing both consumers and the medical profession. As in the case of Blue Cross, each plan operates autonomously, but the National Association has developed a set of comprehensive contract definitions to assure common administration from plan to plan for subscribers in large national or multistate groups. In recent years there has been a consolidation of more than one-half of the Blue Cross and Blue Shield plans. In some cases, this has involved a complete merger; in others, the consolidation has been partial, involving a single staff but separate governing boards.

The typical Blue Shield plan provides benefits that are similar in nature to those provided under the surgical and physicians' expense benefit provisions of the commercial health insurance policy. Blue Cross/Blue Shield major medical coverage is available on both a group and an individual basis. The major medical plans resemble those of commercial insurers. A deductible is involved and the subscriber usually must pay a 20 percent coinsurance until out-of-pocket expenses reach a certain amount, after which no coinsurance applies. The benefit maximum for major medical expense may be $250,000 or more. Many, if not most, Blue Cross/Blue Shield plans offer comprehensive major medical insurance (see below) for their local groups.

The distinct advantage enjoyed by Blue Cross/Blue Shield has been the favorable tax treatment given these organizations. While commercial insurers have long been subjected to federal income taxes, a variety of state taxes (including a significant tax on premiums received), and even certain local taxes, Blue Cross/Blue Shield organizations traditionally have been virtually immune from the burden of significant state taxes and they are afforded favorable treatment under the federal income tax laws. The trend at the state level seems to be to tax the Blues as any other health insurer, and the Tax Reform Act of 1986 eliminated their complete exemption from federal income tax. Although the tax act eliminated complete exemption, various deductions that can be taken result in an average effective tax rate for Blue Cross and Blue Shield plans that is below the average tax rate for insurance companies.

## HEALTH MAINTENANCE ORGANIZATIONS

Perhaps the most significant recent development in the financing and delivery of prepaid physician and hospital care in the U.S. has been the growth of HMOs.[7] An HMO provides a wide range of comprehensive health care services for members who are normally enrolled on a group basis and who typically pay a fixed periodic premium in advance for the services of participating physicians and cooperating hospitals. HMOs differ from traditional insurance indemnity plans in that they are both the financing *and* servicing mechanism. They emphasize preventive medicine and early treatment through prepaid routine physical examinations and diagnostic screening techniques. At the same time, they provide complete hospital and medical care for sickness and injury.

The 1973 federal legislation and later amendments in 1976 essentially provided for substantial government funding through grant arrangements to encourage the establishment of health maintenance organizations. The most important support for development of HMOs came from the law's requirement that certain employers must offer their employees the option of coverage by an HMO as an alternative to traditional forms of insurance. This requirement ceases on October 1, 1995. HMOs have become a significant factor in the health care industry. By the early 1990s the various types of HMOs had grown to almost 600 operational units, enrolling more than 14 percent of the U.S. population.

Health maintenance organizations are basically prepaid group practice plans that have an agreement with one or more hospitals for admission of enrolled members on a service-type basis. A group of physicians is also organized into a cooperative to provide complete office and hospital care. They may (1) practice in a clinic setting as salaried staff of the HMO, (2) provide individual care in their own offices, or (3) operate in a full group practice for salary or on a capitated basis. Over one-half of existing HMOs are organized as full group practices in the latter arrangement. Most HMOs accept enrollment only from clearly designated groups, such as employees of any of several employers or residents of a particular locality, although some may permit enrollment from the general population on an individual basis. The plans are designed to provide an economic incentive to accept focused access to health care providers. The development of HMOs also facilitated the general development of managed care as a significant cost containment concept.

[7]For an excellent review of the types of managed health care organizations, see Peter R. Kongstvedt, ed., *The Managed Health Care Handbook* (Rockville, Md.: Aspen Publishers, Inc., 1989), Chap. 2.

Until recent years, most HMOs were operated as nonprofit organizations. The majority of new HMOs, however, are for-profit organizations. Although many subscribers are covered by HMOs that have been sponsored by consumer groups, a sizable and growing portion are covered by plans sponsored by insurance companies or Blue Cross/Blue Shield organizations. Physicians, hospitals, and labor unions also sponsor such plans.

Some insurers view HMOs as competitors and are critical of insurance companies that sponsor them. Others view them as a viable alternative method of financing and delivering health care that can be offered to employers as one of the products in their portfolio. A few insurers and Blue Cross/Blue Shield plans are now providing multiple-option plans (i.e., HMO or an indemnity plan with a PPO) under a single medical expense contract. This arrangement simplifies the administration of the plans, and, normally, the entire contract is subject to experience-rating.

## SELF-INSURED PLANS

As discussed in Chapter 26, employers have increasingly adopted funding methods that are alternatives to the traditional fully insured group insurance contract. Both medical expense and disability income insurance are made available through self-insured or self-funded plans of employers, labor unions, and fraternal or cooperative groups. These plans may require that enrolled members share in the funding through dues or contributions. The benefits provided under these plans are similar to those of commercial group insurance contracts, but usually they are in the amount that is desired and affordable by a specific group of individuals.

Larger employers, particularly those with employees in more than one state, are likely to provide benefits through a trust governed by ERISA. Since ERISA preempts state insurance laws under certain conditions, employers that use a trust or self-funding arrangement do not have to provide the specific insurance benefits mandated in a number of states. The additional costs of providing mandatory benefits, which often differ from state to state, have led to an increase in self-insured groups. Insurance companies may service these groups under administrative service only (ASO) arrangements or by minimum premium plans (MPP), as discussed in Chapter 26.

The continuing rise in health care costs is causing more and more employers to move to self-insurance. A recent survey found that more than two-thirds of employers surveyed said that they self-insured their group health plans.[8]

In general, the vast majority of large employers moved to some form of self-insurance in the 1970s and early 1980s. However, as health insurance premiums have continued to rise, small and midsize employers have increasingly

---

[8]A. Foster Higgins & Co., Inc., *1992 Survey of Group Medical Plans.*

also turned to self-insurance. In the survey cited above, 44 percent of small employers (fewer than 500 employees) and 75 percent of midsize companies (between 1,000 and 2,499 employees) reported self-insuring their plans. Other current data reinforce these findings.

## FEDERAL AND STATE GOVERNMENTS

Over 40 percent of U.S. health care expenditures is spent at all levels of government for health and medical programs, including funding of research projects and construction of medical facilities. Expenditures of the federal government were more than double those at the state and local levels.

The majority of federal spending for health services is directed to six major groups: persons eligible for Medicaid, persons eligible for Medicare, military personnel and their dependents, veterans, federal civilian employees, and native Americans. The major part of state spending for health services is paid toward workers' compensation medical expenses, state contributions to Medicaid, and the public health programs of the nation's 53 official state health agencies.

While most of the government programs are directed toward the indigent or to selectively defined groups, several important programs apply to the general public. These programs, discussed in Chapter 25, are Medicare for medical expenses, Social Security for disability, workers' compensation, and, in five states and Puerto Rico, temporary disability plans.

## COMPREHENSIVE HEALTH INSURANCE PLANS

Group health insurance refers to arrangements in which coverage is provided for groups of individuals under a single master contract issued to a group contract owner. The contract owner may be an employer, an association, a labor union, a trust, or any other legitimate entity that was not organized solely for the purpose of obtaining insurance. Members of larger groups generally obtain coverage without having to furnish evidence of insurability, but this evidence usually is required for groups of less than ten lives. Group health insurance plans generally cover the group member, his or her spouse, and any dependent children.

Group insurance can be written to provide virtually any combination of health insurance benefits. As with individual policies, group health insurance benefits may be broadly classified as (1) medical expense insurance and (2) disability income.

In the past, the basic hospital-surgical plans consisted of separate benefits for hospital expenses, surgical expenses, and physician's charges. Coverage was limited and many types of medical expenses were not covered. Over time, basic coverages for other types of medical expenses were developed and employers began to provide more extensive benefits to employees. These basic coverages offered by private insurers (commercial insurers and Blue Cross/Blue Shield associations) were gradually augmented by supplemental major medical plans, and today they have been supplanted by comprehensive major medical plans. Dental insurance, vision insurance, and prescription drug coverage have, for the most part, continued to be offered as separate coverages.

## MAJOR MEDICAL EXPENSE INSURANCE

Major medical expense insurance plans provide broad coverage and significant protection from large, unpredictable, and therefore unbudgetable medical care expenses. From the beginning, most such plans covered a wide range of medical care charges, with few internal limits and a high overall maximum benefit. Although they were born as a supplement to basic medical expense insurance plans, there now is a stand-alone package known as a comprehensive major medical plan.

*Supplemental Major Medical Expense Benefits.*  **Supplemental major medical expense insurance** is superimposed on a basic plan provided by an insurer or another company such as Blue Cross/Blue Shield. An insured individual is reimbursed for the charges covered under the reimbursement formulas in the basic plan as if the supplemental plan did not exist. All covered expenses not reimbursed under the basic plan are subject to a so-called **corridor deductible** before the supplemental major medical plan begins reimbursement. After this deductible amount has been satisfied, the supplemental major medical plan usually pays a percentage, such as 80 percent, of the remaining covered expenses. Thus the claimant shares in the claim cost to the extent of the deductible plus the percentage of expenses not reimbursed as a result of the coinsurance provision under the major medical formula. Figure 27-4 illustrates how a typical supplemental major medical plan works.

*Comprehensive Major Medical Expense Benefits.*  **Comprehensive major medical expense insurance** covers virtually all types of medical care services and supplies. The reimbursement formula applies to the total covered expenses, subject to a deductible. Thus a simple comprehensive plan could provide for the reimbursement of 80 percent of all combined covered expenses in a calendar year after a deductible of $300, up to a lifetime maximum of $1,000,000. The main advantages of comprehensive major medical plans are simple plan design, fewer first-dollar benefits to help control costs and utilization, and avoidance of duplicate coverage and frequent plan revisions.

A variety of modified comprehensive designs has been developed that provide some first-dollar coverage. In some plans, certain types of expenses are not subject to a deductible, such as hospital expenses, and no coinsurance is applied on the initial hospital expenses, such as the first $2,000 or $5,000. Surgeons' fees may be treated similarly, subject to a usual and customary fee limitation. It is possible to waive or modify the deductible and coinsurance features for other services, such as physicians' hospital visits and diagnostic tests, thus further matching the basic plus supplemental major medical concept. Most

**FIGURE 27-4**

**TYPICAL SUPPLEMENTAL MAJOR MEDICAL PLAN DESIGN**

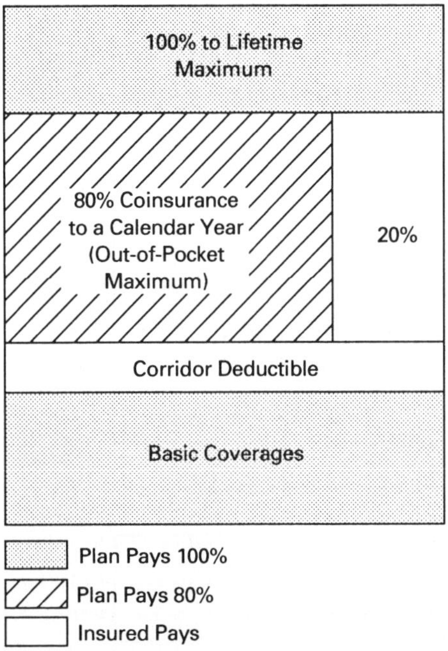

100% to Lifetime Maximum

80% Coinsurance to a Calendar Year (Out-of-Pocket Maximum)

20%

Corridor Deductible

Basic Coverages

Plan Pays 100%
Plan Pays 80%
Insured Pays

plans today have a stop-loss provision that provides a $1,000 or $2,000 maximum annual out-of-pocket cap on employee-paid expenses. The elements of a particular plan reflect both the desires of the contract owner and the underwriting practices of the insurer. Figure 27-5 illustrates a comprehensive plan both with and without first-dollar coverage on initial hospital expenses.

## FEATURES OF MAJOR MEDICAL PLANS

Supplemental and comprehensive major medical plans have common provisions, such as covered expenses, deductibles, coinsurance, and overall maximum benefits.

*Covered Expenses.*   Major medical plans cover usual and customary charges incurred for most medical care services, supplies, and treatments prescribed as necessary. Exact eligible charges and their description vary from plan to plan, but the scope of covered expenses usually includes:

- Professional services of doctors of medicine and osteopathy and other recognized medical practitioners
- Hospital charges for semiprivate room and board and other necessary services and supplies
- Services of registered nurses and, in some cases, licensed practical nurses
- Physiotherapy
- Anesthetics and their administration

**FIGURE 27-5**

**TYPICAL COMPREHENSIVE MAJOR MEDICAL PLAN DESIGN**

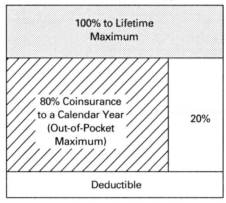

- X-rays and other diagnostic laboratory procedures
- Oxygen and other gases and their administration
- Blood transfusions, including the cost of blood when there is a charge
- Drugs and medicines requiring a prescription
- Specified ambulance services
- Rental of durable mechanical equipment required for therapeutic use
- Artificial limbs or other prosthetic appliances, but not replacement of such appliances
- Casts, splints, trusses, braces, and crutches
- Rental of a wheelchair or hospital-type bed

As pointed out below, plans normally provide coverage for confinement in skilled nursing facilities, as well as home health care expenses and hospice care expense benefits.

*Deductible.*    As with deductibles in other lines of insurance, the primary purpose of the deductible in a major medical plan is to lower premium costs. In health care insurance, this is accomplished by avoiding unnecessary utilization and eliminating small claims and the expense of handling them. In meeting the deductible amount, an accumulation period feature recognizes the fact that small, frequent medical expenditures can accumulate to a significant amount in some cases. The **accumulation period provision** defines the period of time during which incurred medical care expenses may be accumulated to satisfy the deductible.

There are a variety of deductible provisions. The type and amount of the deductible and the way it operates, as with all design aspects of a plan, reflect the contract owner's desires and the underwriting requirements of the insurer. Deductibles can be classified as all cause, per cause, corridor, and integrated.

*1. All Cause Deductible.* Under the **all cause deductible**, all expenses incurred are accumulated to satisfy the deductible, regardless of the number of illnesses or accidents giving rise to the expenses. Benefits are paid, following the satisfaction of the deductible, for expenses incurred during the remainder of the **benefit period**. The calendar year is almost universally used for both the deductible accumulation period and the benefit period. Assuming a $100 deductible, the same deductible applies to each calendar year benefit period and must be satisfied between January 1 and December 31.

In view of the fact that some insureds incur expenses early in the year and others incur expenses late in the year, a **carry-over provision** usually is included for the latter insureds. Under such a provision, expenses incurred in the last three months of a calendar year (which are applied toward satisfaction of the deductible for that year) may be carried over to be used again in satisfying the deductible for the next calendar year.

Since several members of a large family may have major expenses in one year, a **family deductible** provision usually is included that waives the deductible for all family members after any two or three of them individually have satisfied their deductibles in the same year. The all cause approach is simple to administer and easy to understand. This is an important consideration in plan design.

*2. Per Cause Deductible.* In the case of the **per cause deductible**, all expenses incurred because of the same or related causes are accumulated to satisfy the deductible, after which benefits begin. The unique characteristic of the per cause deductible is that the benefit period for each cause starts with the first expense that is used to satisfy the deductible and normally ends one or two years after the date it starts. In some plans, the benefit period is set to end two years from the date the deductible was satisfied. In the case of benefit periods that are no longer than one year, an alternate basis for terminating the benefit period is usually included. Thus the benefit period might be cut off at the end of a period of 60 to 90 days during which less than a certain amount of expenses is incurred. Once a benefit period has ended, the deductible must be satisfied again to start a new one. Although it is unlikely, an individual could have to satisfy two or more deductibles in a given twelve-month period.

The chief advantage of the per cause approach is that claims for minor, unrelated illnesses are eliminated. Use of a per cause deductible increases administrative costs. With advancing age, it often is difficult to distinguish among causes of diseases. The per cause deductible is rarely used today.

*3. Corridor Deductible.* The most common method of applying either an all cause or per cause deductible in supplemental major medical plans involves the use of a corridor deductible. The term **corridor deductible** reflects the fact that it applies after the basic plan benefits have been exhausted and must be satisfied by additional expenses incurred before the supplemental major medical benefits are payable. Thus medical expenses that exceed the amounts covered in the basic plan are covered under the supplemental major medical coverage only after the corridor deductible is satisfied. The amount of the deductible typically is $100 or $150.

*4. Integrated Deductible.* Supplemental plans also use a so-called **integrated corridor deductible**. It defines a corridor that is the greater of (1) a fairly high amount, such as $500, or (2) the basic plan benefits. For example, if the basic plan paid $625 and the stated value of the integrated deductible was $500, the deductible would be deemed to have been met and supplemental major medical benefits would be payable.

*5. Common Accident Provision.* Many major medical plans include a **common accident provision** that provides that only one deductible will have to be satisfied when two or more insured persons in the same family are injured in a common accident. In such cases, only one deductible applies to the total covered medical care expenses incurred as a result of the accident both in the calendar year in which the common accident occurred and in the following calendar year.

*Coinsurance.*     The term **coinsurance** refers to the percentage of covered expenses paid by a medical expense plan. Thus a plan with 80 percent coinsurance will pay 80 percent of covered expenses while a person who receives benefits under the plan must pay the remaining 20 percent. The term **percentage participation** is used in some plans.

The coinsurance or percentage participation provision has two objectives. It serves both to keep plan costs down and to retain the insured's financial interest in the cost of services, thereby helping to minimize unnecessary utilization of services. Under the usual provision, the insured is required to pay 20 percent for covered expenses incurred beyond the deductible. As pointed out earlier, many plans apply a cap to the coinsurance and deductible amount to be borne by the insured, by eliminating coinsurance for the balance of the calendar year after the insured has absorbed a defined dollar amount of expense.

*Maximum Benefit.*    Except for specifically identified coverage limitations, usual and customary charges for all eligible expenses are covered by the plan provisions up to the overall **maximum benefit** of the plan. As with the application of the deductible discussed earlier, the overall maximum benefit may be written on a lifetime or a per cause basis.

*1. Lifetime.* The **lifetime maximum benefit provision** applies to all covered expenses during the entire period of coverage. To avoid penalizing insureds who either have partially or wholly exhausted their benefits, but have recovered to the extent of again being acceptable insurance risks, a reinstatement provision usually is included. A typical **reinstatement provision** states that the maximum may be reinstated—after, say, $5,000 or $10,000 in benefits has been used—by submitting evidence of insurability that satisfies the insurance company. It also is common to provide some form of **automatic reinstatement**. For example, a set amount (e.g., $10,000) or set percentage (e.g., 10 percent of the full maximum) of benefits paid each year will be reinstated automatically as of each January 1. According to still another approach, there is reinstatement of some or all of the maximum if the insured does not incur medical care expenses of more than a specified amount during a given period (e.g., $500 during a six-month period). Since it is not uncommon today to find maximums as high as $1,000,000, and even unlimited benefits, the reinstatement provision has lost much of its significance.

*2. Per Cause.* A few plans contain a per cause overall maximum benefit that applies to each cause of illness or injury. A typical **per cause reinstatement provision** states that when a covered person has received benefits for any one accidental injury or any one sickness equal to the overall maximum benefit, benefits for such injury or sickness will terminate unless evidence of insurability satisfactory to the insurer is submitted. This type of limit is used only when the deductible is also applied on a per cause basis. Coverage for other unrelated injuries or sicknesses continues to be effective.

## MEDICAL EXPENSE INSURANCE BENEFITS

Medical expense insurance provides full or partial reimbursement for a wide range of health care expenses incurred by employees and their eligible dependents. The particular coverages offered by plans continue to change and expand in response to changes in health services demand and technology. Basic benefits, plan components, and coverage arrangements are discussed below.

### HOSPITAL EXPENSE BENEFITS

As in the case of individual insurance, group coverage for hospital expenses normally distinguishes between the room and board charges and expenses for other hospital services. The room and board charges typically include the cost of a room (which, usually, is semiprivate), meals, and nursing services routinely provided to all inpatients. This benefit may be expressed as a daily payment for each day of confinement up to a maximum, or as a service benefit with the benefit payment based on charges for a semiprivate room. Most hospital expense insurance plans have a special provision for intensive care, increasing the room and board benefit when use of an intensive care unit is necessary. The daily room and board benefit and charges for other necessary services and supplies resulting from a single confinement are payable under basic medical expense insurance plans up to a maximum number of days per year, such as 31, 60, 120, or 365.

Coverage of necessary services and the supplies portion of hospital expense insurance (sometimes referred to as "miscellaneous expense," "other charges," or "ancillary services") provides reimbursement for hospital charges such as drugs and medicines, diagnostic X-rays and laboratory tests, and use of an operating room and ambulance service. The hospital miscellaneous expense benefit may be written on an unscheduled basis for up to some multiple of the daily room and board rate. Some plans pay in full up to a dollar maximum (e.g., $500), with coinsurance (e.g., 75 percent) for expenses in excess of the maximum. Other plans provide full reimbursement for miscellaneous hospital expenses.

## SURGICAL EXPENSE BENEFITS

Surgical coverage provides reimbursement for physician charges for surgical procedures. Surgical expense benefits may be provided on a scheduled or nonscheduled basis. Under a **scheduled plan**, a specific payment maximum is allotted for each surgical procedure. A typical published schedule may include 100 different operations that cover each of the important categories of surgical procedures. Reimbursement for unlisted procedures is based on a scale that is proportionate to the listed procedures.

Differences among company schedules are based on (1) the amount that they allow for each procedure; (2) the overall maximum benefit for multiple procedures; and (3) the relative or proportionate value of the procedures listed in the schedule to each other.

Schedules are sometimes denominated in units rather than in dollars. These are referred to as **relative value schedules**. A factor that reflects the level of charges in a geographic area multiplied by the number of units provided for each procedure determines the maximum amount the plan will pay.

Under a **nonscheduled plan**, instead of there being a specific allowance, reimbursement of the surgeon's fees and usually the anesthetist's fee is based on the usual and customary charge for the procedure performed. A usual and customary charge—entailing a limit that is imposed on all benefits—is defined based on the normal charges for the service provided by physicians in the given geographic area. In the case of multiple operations, the benefit paid may vary depending upon whether the two or more operations involve separate incisions, are in different operative fields, or are separated in time.

## EXTENDED CARE SERVICES

*Skilled Nursing Expense Benefits.*    **Skilled nursing facility expense coverage** provides reimbursement for medical expenses incurred when an insured individual is confined in an extended care facility and requires ongoing active medical and skilled nursing care. Moving a patient from a hospital room to a less expensive extended care facility when, at the advice of a physician, medical needs relate principally to continued skilled nursing care can significantly reduce total cost.

The definition of an extended care facility is important, since the coverage is not intended to provide custodial care in institutions with little or no medical care facilities. Insurers either specify the services that must be provided or restrict coverage to institutions that are approved by Medicare as skilled nursing facilities.

The amount and extent of benefits available varies. Thus there may be a total dollar limit for each day of confinement in an extended care facility or a specific dollar limit for room and board and for necessary services and supplies. A daily limit expressed as a percentage (usually 50 percent) of the hospital room and board benefit available under hospital or major medical expense insurance coverage is used by some plans. Plans usually provide for a maximum of 30 to 200 days per confinement in an extended care facility.

Coverage is limited to individuals (1) requiring supervised medical treatment, (2) confined in an extended care facility at the recommendation of a physician, and (3) under a physician's care while confined. It is common to require hospitalization for a minimum period (e.g., three to five days) prior to confinement in an extended care facility. In addition, many plans require that confinement in the extended care facility begin within a specific period (e.g., 7 to 14 days) from the date of discharge from the hospital.

*Home Health Care Expense Benefits.*    **Home health care benefits** include costs of a variety of types of skilled care. The purpose of the coverage is to minimize institutional confinement when more comfortable and less expensive services can be provided in the patient's home.

Home health care coverage typically includes care by a physical, occupational, or speech therapist; periodic home nursing care; periodic services of a home health aide; medical social services; and care provided by a hospital intern or resident under an approved hospital teaching program. These services may be provided by a hospital or by a home health care agency.

Payment of home health benefits may require prior hospitalization or confinement in an extended care facility for the same or a related disability. In this case, covered home health care services must begin within a specified number of days following hospital or nursing home discharge.

Home health care coverage usually is limited to a maximum number of covered visits by a licensed health care professional. Thus services rendered by a person who ordinarily resides in the individual's home or who is a member of his or her immediate family, typically, would not be covered. Expenses for custodial care, meals, and general housekeeping services are usually excluded.

*Hospice Care Expense Benefits.*    A **hospice** is a program of care for the terminally ill patient and his or her family, with a focus on palliative care and social support services. Trained medical personnel, homemakers, and counselors (who make up a hospice team) help the patient and the family cope with the social, psychological, and physical stresses of death and bereavement. Most hospice care benefits may pay for additional home care and respite care for family caretakers, as well as for hospice facility care, palliative drugs and therapy, and family counselling.

Hospice coverage typically pays usual and customary charges of the hospice. The benefit period, prior to death, starts when the attending physician certifies that the patient is expected to live only six months or less. Hospice coverage ends when the patient dies or at the end of a specified period (such as 6 or 12 months), whichever occurs first. A new benefit period may be established by recertification if the patient is still living at the end of a benefit period.

A defined **period of bereavement** begins when the patient dies and typically ends 6 or 12 months after the date of death. Benefits may be limited to a specific number of counseling sessions for the surviving dependents, with a dollar maximum per session. Benefits for services that have not been recommended by an attending physician or for those that a covered individual would not legally have had to pay in the absence of coverage are excluded.

## OTHER MEDICAL EXPENSE BENEFITS

*Diagnostic X-Ray Examinations and Laboratory Tests.*    A variety of coverages is available to finance other types of health expenses. For example, most plans cover the cost of **diagnostic x-ray examinations** and **laboratory tests** when these services are rendered in a physician's office or in a hospital outpatient department.

*Physicians' Nonsurgical Fees.*    Most plans provide reimbursement for **physicians' nonsurgical fees** for acute or preventive care. Inpatient physician visits are often covered in full; outpatient or office visits (for nonpreventive care) typically are subject to cost sharing.

*Mental and Alcohol/Substance Abuse Health Care Benefits.*    Coverage for mental and alcohol/substance abuse health care benefits has increased during the past decade. In fact, it is commonly mandated by state law.

Typical reductions and limitations placed on inpatient and outpatient mental and alcohol/substance abuse health care benefits include (1) limits on the duration of a hospital stay (e.g., 30 to 60 days as opposed to 120 to 365 days for other medical care), (2) reductions in the in-year maximum or lifetime maximum ($25,000 lifetime versus $1 million in some plans), (3) ceilings on the number of outpatient health services to be covered, and (4) lower coinsurance for mental and alcohol/substance abuse compared with the coinsurance for other medical services.

## COST CONTROL COMPONENTS[9]

Comprehensive medical benefit plans are rapidly replacing basic-plus supplemental major medical plans. Compared to other types of traditional group insurance plans, a comprehensive plan is simpler to understand and easier to communicate to employees, since it applies one overall reimbursement formula to covered expenses. Even though comprehensive plans differ in detail, most have provisions that encourage the use of outpatient treatment settings and encourage more effective use of health care services through various incentives, such as fuller reimbursement for outpatient surgery compared with inpatient surgery. In designing a comprehensive health care plan, a large number of possible components is considered. These components and cost-containment techniques are discussed in this section.

### BASIC COST CONTROLS

Cost control is a key issue in medical benefit plan design. Plan provisions can take different forms. Virtually all group insurance plans have traditionally incorporated certain basic provisions intended to contain costs:

1. Deductibles
2. Coinsurance
3. Internal benefit limits
4. Coordination of benefits
5. Subrogation

Many experts believe that employees who share in health care costs should do so at the point of service (i.e., by utilizing deductibles, coinsurance, and internal benefit limits) rather than through increased premium contributions. The increased premium contribution lowers the employer's health care insurance premiums, but does not affect the overall cost of health care.

***Deductibles.*** A **deductible** is a specified amount of initial medical costs that the participant must pay before any costs are paid by the plan. Thus in a plan with a $300 deductible, the participant must pay the first $300 in expenses for covered health care services. The deductible provision usually has a family limit equal to two or three times the individual limit. After the deductible has been satisfied, the plan pays for additional health care expenses according to other plan provisions. In the past, a number of plans offered first-dollar coverage with no deductible or coinsurance required. The number of these plans has declined significantly in recent years.

[9]This analysis draws from Jerry S. Rosenbloom, editor, *The Handbook of Employee Benefits*, 2nd ed. (Homewood, Ill.: Dow Jones-Irwin, 1988) and David Aquilina et. al., *Driving Down Health Care Costs— Strategies and Solutions* (New York: Panel Publishers, Inc., 1992).

Adding or increasing the amount of deductibles and other techniques that require greater contributions by employees is a sensitive issue. A few employers vary the deductible (with minimums and maximums) with salary levels, thereby intending to insulate low-income employees from paying a large percentage of their disposable income for health care, and to ensure sufficient motivation for participants at all levels to control overutilization. Varying the deductible with salary is becoming more common as more companies develop the administrative capabilities to handle this approach.

The various cost-sharing methods (deductible, coinsurance, and premium sharing) have become common components of health benefit plans and should be regularly reviewed to reflect medical trends if participant incentives to control costs are not to diminish. A carefully designed and implemented utilization review program (see below) can help reduce the need to increase deductibles and insured's coinsurance levels. Although maintaining cost sharing at a constant proportion of total costs is necessary to help control participants' overuse of health care services, it is often not well received by employees. Utilization review and other components of a managed care program should be more effective in assuring appropriate use of health care services by plan participants and providers alike.

**Coinsurance.**   **Coinsurance,** a second active form of cost management, requires participants to pay a percentage of reasonable and customary amounts up to some ceiling, such as $1,500 or $2,000. After the deductible has been satisfied, the plans pay for 70 to 80 percent of eligible medical expenses up to this defined out-of-pocket limit. The plans pay 100 percent of additional costs after the out-of-pocket limit is reached. As is the case with deductibles, this provision usually has a family limit equal to two or three times the individual limit.

**Internal Benefit Limits.**   Many benefit plans use inside limits to provide cost sharing by plan participants. These limits may take the form of a specific dollar maximum (e.g., for hospital daily room and board charges, surgical procedures, doctors' visits, or outpatient laboratory tests and X-rays), a percentage of a maximum allowance (e.g., for anesthesia administration), or even a lifetime maximum on all benefit payments. This practice is intended to emphasize the need for the employee to restrict utilization of these selected services and to increase employee awareness of the cost involved.

Although many comprehensive medical benefit plans impose a maximum limit (typically $1 million) on the amount of insurance coverage, the difference in cost between a specified maximum limit and unlimited coverage is often insignificant in these plans. Internal limits have a greater impact on costs. Increasingly, expensive technology and procedures make higher lifetime maximums more desirable. Jumbo maximums are not usually a function of premium levels. Premium levels are more a function of short-term claims with inadequate deductibles. Factors other than cost may influence an employer's decision in selecting the maximum amount.

*Coordination of Benefits.*    The increasing numbers of dual-income families have made it common for individuals to be covered under two group insurance plans, and this sets up the potential for an individual to receive dual or double payments for the same medical bills. **Coordination of benefits (COB)** is used in virtually all group plans to prevent the recovery of more than 100 percent of actual health care expenses. The provision requires two affected insurance plans to work together so that the bills are paid, but the covered individual does not profit by receiving duplicate payments. Employee medical care plans coordinate benefits not only with other group medical insurance plans and health maintenance organizations, but they also may do so with at least the mandatory benefits under state no-fault automobile laws and Medicare.

Recently, retiree plans have introduced even more restrictive integration methods to deal with Medicare coverage situations. A method called **carve-out** or **maintenance of benefit**, which is gaining strong acceptance, limits the total reimbursement to the largest benefit of the plans. The plan's normal benefit is first calculated and Medicare's payment is then subtracted to determine the employer's final payment. A second method, called **exclusion** or **modified carve-out**, subtracts Medicare's payment from eligible expenses before plan benefits are calculated. These integration methods are rarely used with plans for active employees. Since self-insured plans do not have to satisfy state laws, carve-out plans are increasingly used by self-funded plans.

The **Tax Equity and Fiscal Responsibility Act of 1982** (TEFRA) amended the **Age Discrimination in Employment Act of 1967** to require employers with 20 or more employees to offer active employees aged 65 through 69, and their spouses of the same age, the same coverage offered to younger workers. The legislation permitted the employee to choose Medicare to be either primary or secondary.

These provisions were extended by the **Deficit Reduction Act of 1984** to include 65-through-69-year-old dependent spouses of active employees under age 65. The **Consolidated Omnibus Budget Reconciliation Act of 1985** further extended the provisions to include active employees and their dependents who were age 70 or older. The **Omnibus Reconciliation Act of 1989** made Medicare secondary to the active employee's plan, including workers' compensation. Today, therefore, Medicare is secondary for those active employees who choose to continue using as their primary plan the employer's plan, but if they choose Medicare as their primary plan, they do not receive any secondary employer benefits. For covered retirees who are eligible for Medicare, Medicare is the primary plan and the employer's plan is secondary.

*Subrogation.*    In general, **subrogation** means the substitution of one party (in this case the employer or the insurer) in place of another party (the employee or a dependent) that has a legal claim against a third party. Thus an employee benefit plan that includes subrogation provides the employer or insurer that pays a claim for which a third party is liable with the rights that a covered employee or dependent might have against the third party. Such claims might arise out of workers' compensation accidents, and the employer's insurer could receive reimbursement if the employee or the dependent received benefits under a workers' compensation statute. The time delays involved in settling claims have historically caused some insurers to be reluctant to include specific subrogation provisions in group insurance contracts, but the need for cost control has increasingly caused this provision to be included.

## SECOND SURGICAL OPINIONS

Another utilization control involves obtaining a second opinion before surgery is to be performed. **Second surgical opinion** programs may be voluntary or mandatory. Voluntary second surgical opinion programs, however, are less effective compared with programs requiring second surgical opinions for specified procedures.

Most plans with second surgical opinion programs provide 100 percent reimbursement for the consultation fee of the physician from whom the second opinion is obtained. Under these plans, payment is usually also made for any "tie-breaking" third surgical consultations and for related diagnostic X-rays and lab work. The purpose of a second surgical opinion program is to eliminate unnecessary surgery and to encourage plan participants to make a more informed decision regarding surgery.

Eligible charges incurred as a result of actual surgery are reimbursed according to the benefit levels of the group health plan (e.g., 80 percent of eligible charges). Many utilization review programs incorporate second surgical opinions by integrating the review of surgery requests into the utilization review process on a case by case basis.

While a second surgical opinion program can be useful, some studies of these programs have found few savings. Many professionals believe that the real value of second surgical opinion lies in educating participants to be better consumers of health care services, and in reducing providers' unnecessary surgery requests as a result of the knowledge that the review process exists.

## PREADMISSION TESTING AND SAME-DAY SURGERY PROVISIONS

The first day or two of hospital confinements, particularly for surgical procedures, are often devoted to necessary diagnostic tests and X-rays. These tests can be performed on an outpatient basis, thus avoiding unnecessary hospitalization. This **preadmission testing** procedure has been widely adopted.

Similarly, surgical procedures that can be completed on an outpatient basis avoid the additional cost of hospitalization. These approaches combined with preadmission certification have been well received, although some physicians and patients prefer hospitalization.

## UTILIZATION REVIEW

As cost containment efforts led to managed care, **utilization review** programs became the vehicle for coordinating a series of cost control innovations developed separately. Utilization review programs are concerned primarily with the appropriateness of care delivered in hospital settings. Most programs contain five components: (1) preadmission certification, (2) concurrent or continued stay review, (3) discharge planning, (4) catastrophic case management, and (5) retrospective review, including hospital bill audits. Utilization review is a major component of managed care.

*Preadmission Certification.*    **Preadmission certification** programs require prior review of a hospital admission for nonemergency conditions and often for outpatient surgery as well. Emergency admissions usually must be certified within 24 hours after admission. The purpose of preadmission review is to determine the appropriateness of care, and to discourage admission of patients for testing and treatment that can be performed safely and less expensively in another setting.

*Concurrent or Continued Stay Review.*    **Concurrent review** is an ongoing monitoring of a patient's hospital stay to determine whether the patient is in need of continuing inpatient treatment. A variant of concurrent review, known as chart audit, is an on-site concurrent review. This approach seems to be gaining acceptance.

Mandatory preadmission and concurrent review are rapidly becoming general practice. Employers' plan designs often establish a schedule of penalties to motivate individuals to participate in the preadmission and concurrent review programs. Some employers impose a moderate penalty for noncompliance (e.g., an additional $100 deductible) while others decrease the employer's coinsurance share to 50 percent.

*Discharge Planning.*    **Discharge planning** identifies the appropriate level of care a patient may need when a hospital setting is no longer necessary. The purpose of discharge planning is to enable patients to be released from inpatient care as soon as is appropriate. As part of the review, special equipment and nursing services to care for the patient outside of the hospital are identified.

*Catastrophic Case Management (CCM).*    Traditionally, employers have not had the opportunity to review catastrophic and high-risk claims from the perspective of total **case management**. Today **large claim management programs** (also called medical case management) are often included with utilization review programs or are available to employers from independent review organizations and many insurers. The initial stage of a serious illness (e.g., severe stroke or multiple sclerosis) or injury (e.g., major head trauma, spinal cord injury, or severe burns) is the point at which the final outcome can be changed most dramatically. With about 10 percent of claimants causing 70 percent of claims, it is essential to identify the potentially large claims early. CCM utilizes case managers (usually nurses) and consulting physicians to manage large claims closely, inclusive of using alternate care.

Firms specializing in medical case management assess the case—taking into account the patient's needs and treatment plan—manage the use of available resources, and evaluate the work environment and family situation. These case management professionals work with medical care providers to implement alternatives if and when they are appropriate. Of course, the patient and his or her attending physician always have final control over the plan of treatment.

*Retrospective Review.*    Many utilization review plans include a component that involves a **retrospective review** of large claim and utilization review processes. These reviews enable employers and health insurance providers to evaluate the utilization review process itself as well as the effectiveness of the professionals involved. These reviews also include hospital bill audits.

Data management is increasingly becoming an integral part of the managed care process. Claims data are analyzed carefully to determine a given plan's utilization rates, which, in turn, can be compared with average or target levels of utilization. This data analysis also can determine if particular health care providers are showing efficient and cost-effective practice patterns.

Data analysis can be an effective tool in a managed care program. Firms that specialize in managed care processes are quite active in servicing self-funded plans.

Thus, a **hospital bill audit** may be used to verify that a patient received all of the hospital services and items for which he or she was billed. Most errors during an audit are found among ancillary charges and intensive care services.

The process of auditing hospital bills is usually triggered by a minimum dollar figure (e.g., all bills in excess of $10,000). Although any questionable bill should be scrutinized, cost benefit analysis suggests that those with higher dollar amounts, longer lengths of stay, and more complex services should be targeted for audit. Hospital bill audit services are provided by insurance companies, third party administrators, and special utilization review organizations. Given the potential for human error, hospital bill audits can be a cost-effective means of reducing total hospital claims, thereby saving limited benefit resources.

To encourage patients to review their own bills, some plans pay patients a certain percentage of the dollar amount of any errors they find that the hospital's business office agrees are true errors. The patient deals directly with the hospital in this process and presents the business office's verification to the employer to receive the reward for his or her diligence. These programs typically limit the maximum payment to a small amount, such as $250 or $500.

## OTHER COST CONTROL PROGRAMS

*Preferred Provider Organizations.*    One of the most significant cost control programs in managed care plans is the use of preferred provider organizations. **Preferred provider organizations** (PPOs) are viewed by employers and insurance companies as a significant factor in their efforts to control rapidly rising medical care costs. PPOs developed rapidly as the need to control costs escalated and because under these programs employees maintain some freedom to choose from what can be a long list of providers. In essence, PPOs represent a compromise between the traditional fee-for-service system, in which employees have virtually complete freedom to choose individual providers at the point of service, and HMOs, in which employees are usually locked into one group of providers for all their health care needs. In the early 1990s almost 800 PPOs were in existence in the United States, and an estimated 40 million employees had the option of using them for receiving medical care.

Under the usual PPO arrangement, an employer, union, or insurer obtains price discounts or special services from a small group of health care providers in return for channeling employees or members to them. The third-party payor contracts with a group of medical care providers, who furnish services at lower than usual fees in return for prompt payment and a certain volume of patients. While PPOs are often organized by insurance companies, unions, or groups of employers, they can also be organized by the providers themselves. The contractual arrangement may accommodate either group or individual practices; it also defines the scope of medical services to be provided. In contrast with HMOs, practitioner participants in a PPO are usually paid on a fee-for-service basis as their services are used, but under a fee schedule that is the same for all participating practitioners. There is an economic incentive, under such a design, for practitioners to maximize utilization to compensate for the lower revenues from discounted fees.

As pointed out above, employees are not required to use the PPO facilities. Employees are offered either incentives or disincentives to do so, however. For example, the plan may pay 90 or 100 percent of the charges of a PPO and only 80 percent of the charges of a nonpreferred provider (incentive plan), or it may pay 80 percent for PPO providers and 50 to 70 percent for non-PPO providers (disincentive plan). The plan may also include different deductibles and coinsurance payments. Nevertheless, the employee may choose health care services outside the PPO.

**Exclusive provider organizations** (EPOs) constitute another phase of limiting choice of access to providers. EPOs provide less choice than regular PPOs, but both are more restrictive than HMOs without a PPO option. Recent EPO plans provide limited benefits (e.g., 50 percent coinsurance) for care provided without primary care physician approval, thus maintaining a limited version of the point-in-service feature in PPOs that is not generally available with HMOs. Often participants select a primary care physician (PCP) in advance as their only preferred physician. All care must be approved by the PCP. Services rendered by nonaffiliated providers are not reimbursed, so individuals belonging to an EPO must receive their care from affiliated providers or pay the entire cost themselves. Providers typically are compensated on a fee-for-service basis, utilizing a negotiated discount or fee schedule and frequently involving bonus arrangements with the physicians to encourage better utilization control.

Recently, another type of PPO, known as **point of service** (POS) plans, has evolved. Sometimes called open-ended HMOs, POS plans utilize a network of participating providers. Employees select a primary care physician, who contols referrals to medical specialists. If an employee receives care from a plan provider, the employee pays little or nothing out-of-pocket (as in an HMO) and does not file claims. Care provided by out-of-plan providers will be reimbursed, but employees must pay significantly higher copayments and deductibles. Providers may be compensated on a capitated basis or on a fee-for-service basis; however, there are usually financial incentives for providers to avoid overutilization.

Despite the rapid growth in the number of PPOs, many persons are not convinced that PPOs will significantly help control costs without sacrificing quality. PPOs are not regulated, and any entity can offer discounts without necessarily lowering the ultimate costs resulting from gross charges and increased utilization. As PPOs mature, experience seems to indicate that they and HMOs become fairly comparable in controlling medical expense costs. There are wide variations in both types of organizations. A careful analysis of quality of care, cost, and financial stability is essential in selecting a particular HMO or PPO.

*Prescription Drug Copayment Plans.*    One method used to manage prescription drug costs is to encourage the use of less expensive generic drugs instead of brand-name drugs, subject to physician approval. The average cost of generic drugs can be as much as 40 to 50 percent less than the average cost of a corresponding brand name. Employers are encouraged to obtain a listing of generic substitutes for brand-name drugs and to share this list with employees.

Most prescription drug plans provide the covered employee with an economic incentive to use generic prescription drugs by using a lower copayment (e.g., $9 for generic and $10 otherwise). The arrangement with the pharmacy may also provide an incentive to the pharmacy to dispense generic drugs.

A mail order prescription drug plan is a convenient and reasonable arrangement for long-term and maintenance drugs. A six-month supply of drugs can be dispensed by a mail order drug program, thus saving five dispensing fees and five deductibles. While mail order drug programs can save time and money, the savings may at times be negated if medication is changed or discontinued soon after a large supply has been delivered to the patient.

Prescription drug plans that use the services of local pharmacies may also offer substantial savings by using generic drugs, providing centralized claims processing, and computerized review to monitor drug interaction and prescribing patterns.

*Outpatient Surgery.*    **Outpatient** or **ambulatory surgery** is a program under which a patient has surgery performed and is released on the same day to recuperate at home. Outpatient surgery can be performed in a hospital outpatient surgery facility, a free-standing ambulatory surgery center (surgi-center), or, for minor surgery, in a primary care center or physician's office. Until recently, many health benefit plans used incentives such as 100 percent payment for surgeries performed in an outpatient setting. With the recent rapid escalation of outpatient costs (and utilization review programs designed to direct patients to cost-effective treatment without incentives), the prevalence of 100 percent incentives is decreasing.

*Health Education and Screening Programs.*    Helping employees improve their health status and reduce the probability of preventable risks is the single most significant approach to reducing the number and severity of health problems. Health promotion and disease prevention activities such as smoking cessation, high blood pressure detection and control, nutrition counseling, weight management, exercise, back injury prevention, and stress management can all be instrumental in managing health care costs.

While promotion of healthful employee habits does not necessarily require extensive company resources for the program to be effective, it does require the commitment and encouragement of top management. Some low-cost yet potentially effective activities include such efforts as encouraging exercise and weight control by establishing company running or walking teams, providing space for before- or after-work aerobics classes, providing low-fat, low-salt foods in the company cafeteria and vending machines, and holding periodic health education and screening programs to teach about and detect serious illnesses.

Savings associated with health promotion activities are not often immediate, and the higher the employee turnover rate, the smaller they are. Many researchers are convinced, however, that such activities should facilitate the achievement of a healthier work force and lower total health care expenditures.

*Employee Assistance Programs.*    **Employee assistance programs** (EAPs) provide a broad range of services, including counseling for marital and family problems, job-related problems, and emotional disturbances, as well as alcohol and drug abuse problems. To implement these programs, larger employers frequently use full- or part-time personnel for in-house counseling and referral of employees to local services. Smaller employers may establish the programs by contracting with an outside consulting service. In lieu of a formal employee assistance program, employers can also encourage self-referral by providing employees with a community resource guide.

Regardless of the approach taken, the program should be monitored periodically and evaluated for its effectiveness. Health education, wellness,

EAPs, and mental health and substance abuse programs should be carefully designed to complement each other. Much of a program's value hinges on effective communication with employees.

*Maternal and Well-Baby Care Programs.*    With the entry into the work force of an increasing number of women of childbearing age, greater emphasis has been given to maternity and children assistance programs as part of corporate health insurance plans. This interest was enhanced in 1978 by the pregnancy disability amendments to the 1964 Civil Rights Act, which require that health care benefits for maternity be the same as health care benefits for other conditions. This provision applies to employers with 15 or more employees.[10]

Medical costs for low-birth-weight and preterm babies can range from $14,000 to $30,000, compared with roughly $3,000 for the birth of a normal-weight baby.[11] In view of the costs involved, corporate prenatal programs can be cost-effective. In addition, sick babies may also delay or prevent a female employee from returning to work. These benefits include expenses associated with prenatal/obstetrical well-baby and well-child care. Services include physical visits, immunizations, well-newborn care, health education, and clinical laboratory and radiological testing.

*Birthing Centers.* Maternity care is one of the most frequent reasons for hospitalization. The birthing center concept (or hospital short-stay program for maternity) is an effective means of minimizing costs associated with routine maternity care. Birthing centers are usually free-standing facilities that are separate from a hospital. These facilities, intended for low-risk pregnancies, provide midwifery or maternity services that otherwise are generally delivered by a physician. The mother and child are discharged within 24 hours of delivery in most cases.

Although there is no clear definition of the components of a well-managed health care plan, the range of possibilities is obviously quite broad. There is mounting evidence that comprehensive plans operating under a managed-care approach can produce substantial short- and long-term savings.

## FLEXIBLE BENEFIT PLANS

There are a variety of ways to introduce flexibility into employee benefit plans. Flexible benefit plans can provide numerous benefits, one of which can be an effective cost containment tool. Two methods warrant discussion.

---

[10]Many states have adopted laws that affect insured employers of as few as one worker, but most often the number is four or six.

[11]Lifetime costs for low-birthweight and preterm babies have been estimated to be as high as $400,000. U.S. Congress, Office of Technology Assessment, as cited in Deborah J. Chollet, John F. Newman, Jr., and Andrew T. Sumner, *The Corporate Cost of Poor Birth Outcomes*, Research Report No. 92-2 (Atlanta, Ga.: Center for Risk Management and Insurance Research, Georgia State University, 1992).

## CAFETERIA PLANS

The term **cafeteria plan** refers to an employee benefit plan in which choices can be made among several different types of benefits. Section 125 of the Internal Revenue Code (IRC) provides favorable tax treatment to a cafeteria plan under which all participants are employees who may choose among two or more benefits consisting of cash and qualified benefits. Qualified benefits include most welfare benefits ordinarily resulting in no taxable income to employees if they are provided outside of a cafeteria plan. However, one normally taxable benefit—employer-paid group term life insurance in excess of $50,000—can be included. In general, except for a 401(k) plan, a cafeteria plan cannot include retirement benefits. Some benefits cannot be provided under a cafeteria plan: scholarships and fellowships, transportation benefits, educational assistance, and employee discounts.

Cafeteria plans meeting the Section 125 requirements eliminate the issue of constructive receipt. Employees have taxable income only to the extent that they elect normally taxable benefits—cash and employer-paid group term life insurance in excess of $50,000.

A common type of cafeteria plan is one that offers a basic core of benefits to all employees, plus a second layer of optional benefits that permits an employee to choose benefits beyond those of a basic benefits package. These optional benefits can be purchased with additional contributions or dollars/credits given to the employee as part of the benefit package.

In addition to this "core plus" plan, there is the cafeteria plan in which an employee has a choice among a limited number of predesigned benefit packages. The predesigned packages may have significant differences or they may be virtually identical, the major difference being in the option selected for the medical expense coverage. For example, the plan may offer two traditional insured plans, two HMOs, and a PPO. The increased choices provided to covered employees naturally leads to some adverse selection. As a result, more and more employers are integrating flexible benefits and managed care to maximize employee incentives to elect and use cost effective managed-care programs.

## FLEXIBLE SPENDING ACCOUNTS

In addition to normal cafeteria plans, Section 125 also allows employees to purchase certain benefits on a before-tax basis through the use of a **flexible spending account** (FSA). FSAs can be used by themselves or incorporated into a more comprehensive cafeteria plan. The cafeteria plans of most large employers are designed with an FSA as an integral part of the plan.

An FSA allows an employee to fund certain benefits on a before-tax basis by electing to take a salary reduction. The amount of this reduction can then be used to fund the cost of any qualified benefits included in the plan. In addition to making contributions on a pre-tax basis, one can elect at the beginning of the plan year to fund on a pre-tax basis for **dependent care accounts** and **medical spending accounts**. Once these contributions are made, changes are allowed only under specified circumstances, and unused account money is forfeited at the end of the plan year.

The growing interest in cafeteria plans on the part of employers can be traced generally to a belief that (1) employees will better perceive the value, nature, and relative costs of the benefits being provided; (2) a flexible benefit structure will meet the varying and changing needs of individual employees; (3) since cafeteria plans may involve a limiting of employer contributions, this approach will provide opportunities to control the escalating benefit levels and costs; and (4) it is an effective way to direct employees into the managed-care world of limited access to providers.

## OTHER MEDICAL EXPENSE INSURANCE PLANS

Comprehensive medical expense insurance plans represent the standard approach. Although comprehensive health insurance plans have eliminated the need for many coverages introduced as separate plans, dental insurance, vision insurance, and prescription drug coverages have, for the most part, continued to be offered as separate plans. In addition, a relatively new coverage, long-term-care insurance, is also offered as a separate product.

### DENTAL INSURANCE PLANS

One of the growing health coverages is **dental expense insurance**. The contracts of some insurance companies have been written on a comprehensive major medical basis, with all types of dental expenses, above a deductible, covered on a coinsurance basis up to a maximum dollar amount. Often, the deductible does not apply to routine oral examinations. Companies believe that these examinations are a sound investment to keep overall costs down. Many companies make available a basic dental expense program, as contrasted with the comprehensive or major medical approach. These programs represent first-dollar coverage with scheduled limits.

In most plans, the coinsurance feature follows the pattern of major medical insurance, with the percentage being set at 75 or 80 percent. Reduced coinsurance percentages, typically 50 percent, are applied to orthodontia and certain restorative work, usually involving the use of gold or other precious metals. A maximum amount of benefits is payable under the program to any one covered person. This maximum amount and how it is applied varies. For example, one type of plan provides benefits for covered expenses of up to $1,000 or $2,500 in any calendar year, or $50,000 in any lifetime. Another provides a maximum of $1,000, but not more than $500 in any one calendar year applied separately to each covered member of the family. As mentioned above, orthodontia typically is handled separately, with a separate maximum and increased participation in cost by plan members.

## VISION CARE INSURANCE PLANS

**Vision care expense coverage** is now generally available. Medical expense coverages have for a long time covered expenses for diagnosis and treatment of an illness or injury of the eye. Vision care expense plans, on the other hand, provide reimbursement for the cost of eye examinations to determine whether the individual needs glasses and, if so, for the cost of required frames and lenses. Single-vision, bifocal, and trifocal lenses usually are covered, as are contact lenses and other aids for subnormal vision. To minimize overutilization, coverage usually is limited to only one examination and one pair of lenses or contacts in any 24 consecutive months. Medical or surgical treatment, sunglasses, safety glasses, and duplication of existing lenses or frames because of breakage or loss are commonly excluded. Vision care plans are really not insurance, but rather prepayment plans.

## PRESCRIPTION DRUG EXPENSE PLANS

**Prescription drug expense coverage** reimburses drug expense with little, if any, cost to the plan participant. Streamlined approaches to administration and claims processing are essential under this coverage because of the large number of small claims involved. Prescription drug expense plans are available on both a reimbursement and a service basis. Service plans involve direct payment to the provider, usually via third-party administrative firms using identification cards presented to the pharmacist. A deductible (frequently referred to as a copayment) is typically paid by the participant ($1 to $10) at the time of the purchase. Recent advances in technology have made it commonplace to have an annual deductible (copayment) and coinsurance provision for prescription drug plans.

## LONG-TERM-CARE PLANS

As pointed out in Chapter 16, the early long-term-care (LTC) products of the insurance industry tended to be very limited in scope. For example, most policies covered nursing home benefits only if the confinement followed a hospital stay; coverage for home health services was rare. Newer policies offer nursing home and home health care without prior hospitalization. Many policies provide riders that adjust benefits annually to allow for inflation, and most policyowners have choices of elimination periods.

Long-term care is a relatively new addition to the insurance industry, and its products are still evolving to meet consumer needs. Currently, there is great variation in dollar benefits, definition of covered nursing facilities, length of time benefits are paid, limitations on coverage, and eligibility for benefits.

Because long-term-care products are unique and in a period of evolution, flexible standards have been developed. The National Association of Insurance Commissioners (NAIC) has developed model legislation that has been adopted in a number of states. The **NAIC Long-Term-Care Insurance Model Act** specifies minimum standards that products must meet to be considered long-term-care insurance. The model includes the following major provisions:

- Insurers must provide an outline of coverage, summarizing the policy.
- The individual policyowner must have a free-look period under which the policy can be canceled for any reason and the premium returned.
- Waivers denying coverage for specific health conditions are prohibited.
- Insurers may not offer substantially greater benefits for skilled nursing care than for intermediate or custodial care.
- Policies must be guaranteed renewable, although state insurance commissioners may allow cancellation in limited circumstances.

The U.S. long-term care insurance market is in its early stages of development, but it is growing steadily. There are few standard group long-term-care contracts because most of the plans in existence were designed for a specific employer. The provisions of virtually all group contracts, however, are consistent with the provisions of the NAIC Model Act. Employer interest in providing LTC benefits has increased significantly in the last few years. However, the overwhelming majority of such group LTC plans were employee-pay-all. Uncertain tax treatment of employer contributions and long-term-care benefits has clearly been a deterrent to the development of group long-term-care coverage.[12]

## TAXATION OF GROUP HEALTH INSURANCE

### MEDICAL EXPENSE INSURANCE BENEFITS

In the case of employer-provided health insurance benefits, employer contributions are deductible by the employer and are generally not taxable income to the employee. Benefits received by an employee are not taxable to an employee unless they exceed the medical expenses incurred. In self-insured medical expense reimbursement plans, benefits to highly compensated employees may be taxable if the plan discriminates in favor of these individuals. As this text goes to press, health care reform, including the taxation of health care benefits and contributions, is under consideration by the government.

---

[12]For a thorough discussion of group long-term care products, see Anita Rosen and Valerie S. Wilbur, "Long-Term Care Group Insurance Products," *Long-Term Care: Needs, Costs, and Financing* (Washington, D.C.: Health Insurance Association of America, 1992), pp. 100–116.

## DISABILITY INCOME BENEFITS

As with all types of health insurance benefits, premiums (or other employer contributions) paid by an employer for disability income insurance for employees are generally tax deductible by the employer and are not taxable income to the employee for federal income tax purposes. Employee contributions, on the other hand, are not tax deductible by the employee. It is consistent with these two rules that the payment of benefits under an insured plan or a noninsured salary continuation plan will result in the receipt of taxable income by the employee to the extent that the benefits received are attributable to employer contributions. Thus under a noncontributory plan, the benefits are included in an employee's gross income. IRC Code Section 22, however, provides a tax credit to persons who are totally and permanently disabled. This credit is taken on the employee's federal income tax return. The maximum credit is $750 for a single person and $1,125 for a married person filing jointly. Under a partially contributory plan, benefits attributable to employee contributions are received free of federal income taxation, and benefits attributable to employer contributions are includable in gross income (employees are eligible for the tax credit, however).

## HEALTH CARE FINANCING AND COVERAGE ISSUES

### STATE OF THE U.S. HEALTH CARE SYSTEM

Despite devoting a larger share of its GDP to health care (see Figure 27-1) than any other nation, the United States is one of the few developed countries that does not provide universal coverage to its citizens. The U.S. health care system is characterized by rapidly escalating costs in a competition-based market, questions about quality of care, and lack of access to health care by millions of U.S. citizens. To comprehend the state of the U.S. health care system, it is essential to understand these three problems.[13]

*Health Care Costs.*   Demand for health care is significantly influenced by the aging of the population. Over 30 million U.S. citizens are aged 65 or over. Persons over 65 use three times as much hospital services as people in younger age groups. The frequency of visits to physicians by the over-65 group is about twice the rate of persons under 65. As the population ages, this will naturally increase the pressure on the system, leading to higher costs.

Technological advances stimulate demand for health services because they make possible more kinds of treatment for more people. Technology has also had a significant impact on the shift of diagnostic and surgical procedures from

[13]For an excellent review of the U.S. health care system, see two recent studies: Dean C. Coddington, David J. Keen, Keith D. Moore, and Richard L. Clarke, *The Crisis in Health Care—Costs, Choices and Strategies* (San Francisco, Ca.: Jossey-Bass Publications, 1991), and William A. Glaser, *Health Insurance in Practice* (San Francisco, Ca.: Jossey-Bass Publications, 1991).

inpatient settings to less expensive outpatient facilities. This, in turn, has led to greater utilization, since outpatient settings are less expensive and more attractive to consumers. Although technological advances increase demand and drive costs, they also reduce costs by pushing more diagnostic and surgical procedures into outpatient settings and by enabling the early detection and treatment of conditions that could be more costly to correct if allowed to go undetected or untreated. In the final analysis, however, the ability to do more things to benefit individuals creates claims and drives costs.

Traditional health care has been financed retrospectively by third-party payors based on provider cost or charges. Such cost-based reimbursement encourages greater health care supply and utilization, as well as more expensive health care because moral hazard exists when the cost of services provided is borne by an insurer or other third party. The availability of third-party payors does not encourage a cost-effective allocation of health care resources. Both patient and physician are insulated from the financial consequences of their health care choices. Although the development of managed care has impacted costs for some segments of the market, cost shifting has minimized its impact on aggregate health care expenditures.

Another factor affecting health care costs has been the performance of unnecessary tests and procedures. Medicine is not a precise science. There are no accepted practice guidelines for a given diagnosis. Furthermore, given the U.S. public expectation of the best quality of care and the growth in the frequency of malpractice suits, the increasing practice of defensive medicine is not surprising. In fact, the remarkable increases in malpractice insurance premiums have led some specialists to leave the practice of medicine completely.

Among the factors increasing health care costs, one of the foremost is the increase in operating expenses of both hospitals and physicians. Hospital personnel costs (particularly nurses and specialists) are the most important source of hospital expense increases. Physicians' operating expense increases result from both rising malpractice insurance premiums and the administrative burden of dealing with a multiplicity of payors. It is generally agreed that hospitals with 150 beds can often operate about as efficiently as those with 300 beds, and small group practices appear to be just as efficient as large group practices; but economies of scale do apply. As excess hospital capacity has developed, downsizing has not led in all cases to an appropriate paring of staff and other expenses while maintaining quality of care and financial performance. Protecting profitability in the present market-driven system, making up for past losses, and cost shifting all impact health care costs and their distribution among payor groups.

Finally, the favorable tax treatment accorded employer-financed health benefits is believed to lead to increased costs. Since employer contributions for employee health benefits are tax deductible to the employer and not taxable as income to the employee, the effective price of providing such coverage is lower to the employer and, at the same time, a portion of the price is shifted to taxpayers generally. This tax subsidy is believed to lead to an increased demand for health care services, thereby leading to increased costs overall.

***Market-Based Competition.*** Competition in health care has become widespread since the mid-1980s. In 1983 Medicare, which provides one-sixth of the health care dollars in the United States, abandoned cost-based retrospective hospital payments and began making a fixed-price prospective payment based on the diagnosis. Prospective payment to hospitals for Medicare patients has generally accomplished its original goals. Federal expenditures have been reduced and the resulting changes in standards for Medicare hospital stays have led to a reduction in lengths of hospital stays for all patients. Hospital bed use dropped sharply and, combined with past federal incentives to build more hospitals, led to an oversupply of health care facilities in many urban areas. Physician visits to hospitalized patients also dropped significantly. Large employers aggressively have sought ways to cut health care costs. It was hoped that with market-based competition, costs would be controlled by market forces.

Health insurance companies responded to the changes in the marketplace with a flurry of innovative products, including HMOs and PPOs. Managed care moved to an important role and insurers developed strategies for responding to cost shifting by other payers. Hospitals developed marketing plans to expand their physician bases. In this environment, patients were not sure how to judge as to which physicians and hospitals were likely to provide excellent care; they continued, however, to expect favorable results and to be reassured and treated with warmth and respect. The result has been a significant increase in the complexity of the system as providers (hospitals, physicians, and other medical professionals) and payors (employers, insurers, HMOs, Medicare, and Medicaid) have developed strategies to optimize their positions within the system.

***Quality of Care.***[14] The U.S. system has some special problems in assuring quality of care. Nearly all physicians have the right to admit and treat patients in a hospital. Working out of private offices located elsewhere, large numbers of physicians constantly enter and leave the hospital building. Hospitals in a market-driven competitive system feel compelled to install technically advanced programs. Many hospitals have advanced but underutilized facilities, and many physicians perform these procedures without the high volume that is necessary to develop expertise.

There are wide variations in the individual practice styles of physicians. Some efforts have been made to identify and enforce guidelines for the best course of testing and treatment for each diagnosis. Blue Cross/Blue Shield pioneered the development of criteria and methods for paying for some but not

[14]This section draws on Glaser, *Health Insurance in Practice*, pp. 242–247.

all procedures based on both cost and clinical quality. Managed-care activity attempts to assure satisfactory care for reasonable costs, but HMOs have been primarily oriented to cost containment rather than quality assurance.

Some health economists believed that the increase in competition in the health care services market would not only lower costs but that more efficient providers would lead to higher-quality services. The fact that the payors for the most part are not the users of the services and are primarily concerned with cost control can also lead to underservicing and the use of less skilled providers.

The U.S. health care system is the costliest one in the world. Despite this, the United States ranks twelfth in life expectancy—behind Japan, Italy, France, and the Scandinavian countries. It ranks twenty-first in the number of deaths of children under age five; twenty-second in infant mortality; and twenty-fourth in the percentage of babies born with inadequate birth weight.[15] Although foreign dignitaries are brought to the United States for treatment because of the excellence of U.S. medical services, these statistics reflect a maldistribution in U.S. health care services. As mentioned above, the United States is one of the few countries that does not provide universal access to health care for all its citizens.

Two aspects are entailed in assuring quality of care. First, ways must be found to monitor and influence quality of care without interfering inappropriately with provider judgments as to diagnosis and treatment. Second, the question of universal access to health care for all U.S. citizens can no longer be ignored.

***Access to Health Care Services.***    The most significant issue facing the U.S. health care system is lack of health insurance and, as a result, access to health care. Estimated at some 37 million, the uninsured are among the country's most economically and politically vulnerable citizens.[16]

Most are poor; two-thirds are in families with incomes less than twice the federal poverty level. Three-fourths of the uninsured are workers and their dependents. Many uninsured workers are employed only part-time, and they represent a growing segment of U.S. employment. These groups generally are in poorer health than persons with health care insurance.

Health care resources are scarce relative to needs. The appetite for health care is virtually infinitely expandable. Furthermore, even if the United States increased the total resources devoted to health care (at the state or national level), there is a point at which other societal goals would force a limit to the allocation. In this context of scarcity, fair access to health care must mean universal access to a basic level of health care or a basic benefits plan.[17] There is a growing consensus that this question of access to health care services by all must be resolved.

[15]See "The Crisis in Health Insurance," *Consumer Reports* (Sept. 1990), p. 608.

[16]P. Short, A. Monweit, and K. Blauregard, *A Profile of Uninsured Americans*, DHHS Publication No. (PHS) 89-3443 (Rockville, Md.: Public Health Service, 1989).

[17]Reinhard Priester, "Universal Basic Benefits Preempt Mandated Benefits," *Benefits Quarterly* (First Quarter, 1992).

In response to the issue of access, all states have mandated benefits, but the number and types of laws vary widely. The lack of uniformity among states and the piecemeal fashion in which these laws have been enacted within each state belie any coherent or comprehensive policy objective.

Mandated benefits directly affect only a limited share of the population. They do not apply to the roughly 20 percent of the population enrolled in public health care plans such as Medicare and Medicaid. Such benefits also do not directly affect self-insured plans, which are exempt from state laws by ERISA. Also, of course, mandated benefits do not apply to uninsured persons.

Although a few states are considering universal access proposals that may serve as a model in defining a minimum benefits package,[18] in the long run this problem will have to be settled by the development of a national health care policy and appropriate congressional legislation.

## REFORM PROPOSALS

As suggested above, the present system has not solved the basic health care financing and coverage problems facing the United States. Under the present system, insurers, physicians, and hospitals have developed strategies that they believe will best ensure the success of their respective businesses. This has increased competition, but not on the basis of price. On balance, competition within the health care industry has led to cost shifting and may have increased rather than decreased costs. There is growing pressure for change in the U.S. approach to health care financing and for making health care available to all U.S. citizens. A number of reform proposals have been developed and others will undoubtedly arise. It is beyond the scope of this volume to discuss the specific proposals, but it is important to present an overview of the approaches that are under consideration to reform the U.S. health care system.[19] They include (1) employer-based, universal access proposals, (2) consumer-choice proposals, and (3) single-payor proposals.

The **employer-based, universal access model** involves use of an employer-based payment system with universal access for the currently uninsured population. Under such proposals, employers would continue to be the prime source of health insurance coverage for the majority of nonelderly U.S.

[18]See, for example, "Oregon Health Plan Stalled by Politics," *New York Times*, March 18, 1993, p. 1. A central element of the Oregon plan, which would provide universal access to health care to all its citizens, is a ranking by the state of all medical procedures, ordered by a cost-benefit formula. As proposed, only 568 of the 688 procedures listed would be covered. Even the harshest critics of the plan say that Oregon has done a service by trying to sort out which procedures are important to most people and which ones are dragging down the system with higher costs and little benefit. The Oregon list would serve as the basis for a minimm level of coverage that all employers would have to provide to their employees by 1995.

[19]The Congressional Budget Office recently published a report that illustrates three approaches to expanding insurance coverage. See *Selected Options for Expanding Health Insurance Coverage* (Washington, D.C.: Congressional Budget Office, July 1991). See also Coddington, Keen, Moore, and Clarke, *The Crisis in Health Care—Costs, Choices and Strategies*.

citizens. A variety of proposals, differing in detail, build on the existing private sector model for pricing and financing health care.

**Consumer-choice proposals** stem from a fundamental premise that the health care industry can operate efficiently like other economic sectors if true competition and market responsibility on the part of the consumer are fully developed. Proposals vary from forcing employees to pay larger shares of their own health care costs to requiring all consumers to purchase their own health insurance through vouchers and tax incentives. A significant barrier to implementing a consumer-choice (and payment responsibility) approach to health care lies in the magnitude of behavioral changes involved and their side effects.

**Single-payor proposals** are unique in that they concentrate purchasing power in a single source. Full funding under a national, single-payor system would come from the federal or state governments. One significant advantage of a single-payor system is that it would eliminate cost shifting among various payor groups. Canada has such a system.

In examining the pressures for change and the various proposals, it is likely that some form of universal access will become a reality in the 1990s. It is important to evaluate reform proposals based on a set of criteria that optimize the probability of leading to a viable health care system in the United States. The authors suggest that the following criteria, in order of importance, be utilized for this purpose:

- Delivery of high-quality care
- Cost control
- Universal access
- Minimize administrative costs
- Minimize cost shifting
- Freedom of choice offered to consumers
- Financial stability for providers

There are, of course, other factors that could be added to this list such as a single standard of health care coverage for all U.S. citizens. This ideal standard is unlikely to be attained given the present environment. To meet the concerns of providers and payors, the questions that must be answered by all proposals are (1) Who should be covered? (2) Who should pay? (3) What should be the level of payment? (4) What basic benefit package should be provided? (5) How should health care providers be selected? At the same time, government representatives are examining proposals from the standpoint of national health expenditures and its components, with implications for the federal budget and the rest of the economy. The real and perceived needs of consumers, providers, and payors, as well as of both state and federal governments, underlie the ongoing debate over reform of the U.S. health care system and its financing.

# Chapter 28

# RETIREMENT PLANS

Each person has primary responsibility for his or her own welfare, or so U.S. society decrees. Personal thrift has played and probably always will play a major role in providing for old-age security. Government efforts for the most part have been directed toward providing a basic minimum benefit, as a matter of right, through various forms of social insurance. With assurance of a minimum benefit, the employee, through individual effort, supplemented by any benefits an employer may provide, can seek to raise his or her old-age income to an adequate level. The ability to do this has been facilitated in recent years through federal income tax legislation that permits individuals to accumulate tax-favored savings for retirement purposes.

## INTRODUCTION

One of private industry's most significant contributions to old-age security lies in the development of private pension plans. Every established firm eventually must face the problem of superannuated workers, and at that point it must choose among three alternatives: (1) discharge them without a retirement income, (2) leave them on the payroll, or (3) grant them a retirement income. For business and ethical reasons, the first choice often is deemed impracticable by most large businesses, and the second procedure obscures retirement costs in the payroll. Because its flexibility permits the private pension system to meet the particular needs of various industries, a well-planned program of an employer for a company's employees is the most efficient way to take care of superannuated workers.

In making the decision to install a pension plan, an employer naturally considers the value of the increased efficiency and production arising from its installation against the cost of the program. Because of favorable tax treatment for qualified plans, the cost of a pension program to employers has been relatively low. This fact has been a significant factor in the rapid development of private pension plans in the U.S.

The rapid growth of private pension plans serves as evidence not only of the employer's interest in, but also of industry's acceptance of, the desirability of a planned pension program. As of the early 1990s, approximately 60 million individuals were participants in private pension plans with life insurance companies in the United States.[1]

## CONCEPTS OF PENSION PLAN DESIGN AND OPERATION

### IMPACT OF FEDERAL LEGISLATION

*Income Tax Law.* The U.S. federal income tax law relating to qualified pension plans is quite favorable to pension program establishment. This is because (1) employer contributions are considered ordinary and necessary business expenses that are currently deductible from corporate income in determining the income tax; (2) the earnings of a qualified pension plan are exempt from income taxation; and (3) employer contributions are not taxable to the employees as income in the years in which they are contributed, but rather at such time as they are received in the form of benefits (usually after retirement, at what is usually a lower tax rate). If the full benefit is received in a single year, it may be eligible for special favorable lump-sum income taxation. As a practical matter, few funded plans are not qualified within the meaning of the tax law.

The general requirements of a **qualified plan** may be summarized as follows: (1) a *written, legally binding arrangement* must exist and must be *communicated* to the employees; (2) the plan must be for the *exclusive* benefit of the employees or their beneficiaries; (3) it must be impossible for the principal or income of the trust to be *diverted* from these benefits to any other purpose until all liabilities have been satisfied; (4) the plan must benefit a broad class of employees and *not discriminate* in favor of officers, stockholders, or highly compensated employees; (5) the plan must meet certain *minimum requirements of participation and vesting* (nonforfeitability), as discussed below; (6) the plan must provide that in the event of a plan merger, each participant's *benefit under the resulting plan will be at least equal to the benefit* to which he or she would have been entitled prior to the merger; (7) the plan must provide that a participant's benefits under the plan *may not be assigned or alienated* except as required under a qualified domestic relations order, as discussed below; (8) the plan must stipulate *when benefit payments will commence* (and this time is subject to certain stipulated maximums); (9) if the participant is married, the plan must, under certain circumstances, *provide for a joint and survivor or survivor annuity*, as discussed below; (10) the plan must provide for *limitations in*

---

[1] *1992 Life Insurance Fact Book* (Washington, D.C.: American Council of Life Insurance,1992), p. 57.

*maximum benefits*, as discussed below; (11) the plan must provide that benefits to a participant or beneficiary *may not be decreased by reason of increases in Social Security benefits* following the earlier of the termination of employment or the commencement of receipt of benefits under the plan; and (12) the plan must provide for a *claims review procedure* if the claim of a participant or beneficiary is disallowed.

   ***Employee Retirement Income Security Act of 1974.***   In addition to the federal income tax law, the **Employee Retirement Income Security Act** of 1974 (ERISA) is exceedingly important for retirement plan design and operation. The provisions of ERISA pertaining to participation, vesting, and funding influence virtually every aspect of retirement plan design.

   *1.   Limitations on Contributions and Benefits.* Contributions to and benefits received under qualified plans are limited by ERISA. With respect to defined-benefit plans (see below), the plan must provide that the annual benefit may not exceed the lesser of (1) $115,641[2] or (2) 100 percent of the participant's highest average compensation for three consecutive years. Notwithstanding this limitation, however, ERISA permits an annual benefit of at least $10,000 for an employee if he or she has not participated in a defined-contribution plan (see below). In the event that a participant has less than ten years of service or retires prior to attaining age 65, reductions in the amount of the maximum allowable benefits under the plan must be made.

   With respect to defined-contribution plans, the annual addition to a participant's account may not exceed the lesser of (1) $30,000 or (2) 25 percent of the participant's covered compensation for the year. For purposes of the limitation, annual additions to an employee's account include employer contributions, forfeitures, and, for years beginning after December 31, 1986, 100 percent of after-tax employee contributions. If an employee participates in both a defined-benefit and a defined-contribution plan, special combined limits rules apply. The 1986 Tax Reform Act froze the defined contribution dollar limit (25 percent or $30,000) until the indexed dollar limit for defined-benefit plans reaches $120,000. After this, the defined-contribution dollar limit will be equal to 25 percent of the defined-benefit dollar limit.

   *2.   Prohibited Transactions and Fiduciary Responsibility.* ERISA imposes certain excise taxes on prohibited transactions between the trust and disqualified persons. **Prohibited transactions** include the sale, exchange, leasing, lending (except for certain loans to the participant), and furnishing of goods or services between the plan and a disqualified person. A **disqualified person** includes, among others, the employer, participant, any fiduciary of the plan, service

---

[2]For plan year 1993, this amount is adjusted annually for changes in the Social Security maximum taxable wage base.

provider, employee organization, trustee, and substantial owners of the organization. The tax is initially 5 percent of the amount involved in the transaction and is imposed on the disqualified person. The failure of the disqualified person to correct the transaction within the prescribed time results in an additional tax of 100 percent of the amount involved in the prohibited transaction. The Department of Labor, however, is authorized to provide exemptions from the prohibited transaction restrictions and has done so in many cases.

ERISA also requires that a plan fiduciary discharge its duties solely in the interest of the plan participants and their beneficiaries. In regard to its conduct, the fiduciary is held to a strict prudent-person standard. In addition, a fiduciary is personally liable for breaches by a cofiduciary that it (1) knowingly participates in or conceals, (2) enables to occur by failure to comply with its own duties, or (3) has knowledge of but fails to make a reasonable effort to remedy. ERISA also provides limitations and requirements with respect to (1) the investment of fund assets in employer securities or employer real property, (2) plan termination insurance, and (3) reporting and disclosure. Provision also is made for judicial review of an adverse decision by the Internal Revenue Service (IRS) with respect to a plan qualification.

The legal and tax details of pension plans are complex, and a complete discussion is beyond the scope of this text.[3] Because these laws and regulations play such a major role in every aspect of the creation, design, and operation of a pension plan, several general aspects are nonetheless covered below.

## PRIVATE PENSIONS: THE EMPLOYEE PERSPECTIVE

Private pension and profit-sharing plans and products are marketed more to plan sponsors/employers than they are to the employees/beneficiaries. As a result, the employer's needs are given priority in designing and financing a given plan. Thus the desire to attract and hold employees, budget limitations, tax reduction and tax shelter advantages, efficient administration, and superior investment returns are the key considerations and make up the employer's perspective. Although the needs of the average employee are considered by human resource managers, the decision-making process does not always give adequate consideration to the needs and concerns of the covered employees. The design of effective retirement plans that will stand the test of time and be fully appreciated by employees/ beneficiaries requires consideration of the employee's perspective.

As discussed in Chapter 14, the purpose of a retirement plan is to provide retiring employees with a reasonable degree of financial security. Employee concerns about the impact of inflation, the security and adequacy of Social Security benefits, the financial solidity of insurers' promises, and the employer's willingness and ability to maintain its retirement benefit program are factors that

---

[3]See Dan M. McGill and Donald S. Grubbs, Jr., *Fundamentals of Private Pensions*, 6th ed. (Homewood, Ill.: Richard D. Irwin, 1989), for a detailed treatment of private pensions. This chapter draws heavily on this volume.

should be considered in the decisions relating to pension plan design and funding. Insurers should also keep the employees' perspective in mind in developing products and services for the private pension market.

## PENSION-PLAN DESIGN

*Coverage Requirements.*    A qualified pension plan must set forth rules to determine who will be covered by the plan. Relatively few plans cover all employees of an employer. For example, employees who always work fewer than 1,000 hours per year are frequently excluded from coverage. Coverage also may be restricted to employees of a given plant or division or to employees covered by a collective bargaining agreement. Current IRS regulations require that the plan must cover at least 70 percent of all non–highly compensated employees, or the percentage of the non–highly compensated employees covered must be at least 70 percent of the percentage of highly-compensated employees benefiting under the plan.[4]

In addition to determining the class or classes of employees to be covered, pension plans may make coverage for the individual employee contingent upon a minimum length of service (eligibility period), or attainment of a certain minimum age, or both. A qualified plan can no longer exclude from eligibility employees who are hired after a specified age (such as age 60), but it can defer the normal retirement age to the fifth anniversary of participation. Numerous variations of service and age requirements for coverage may be designed, but one way or another, all are intended to reduce the cost of the plan by eliminating certain groups of employees who show a record of high turnover, deferring the retirement benefits for those hired who are close to retirement, and simplifying the administration of the plan.[5] In any case, the eligibility provisions must be drawn carefully to meet the objectives intended, taking into account the nondiscrimination requirements of the Internal Revenue Code; the Civil Rights Act of 1964, which has been interpreted to require nondiscriminatory provisions for male and female employees; and the Age Discrimination in Employment Act.[6]

A plan may not require as a condition of participation a period of service longer than one year or a minimum age of more than 21 years. However, it may require two years of service if it provides for a full and immediate vesting of all participants upon entry into the plan. Employees of all corporations, partnerships, and other businesses who are members of a controlled group are treated as if they were employees of a single employer.

[4]IRC §410(b).

[5]The purpose of deferring the retirement age for employees who are hired when they are close to retirement is to minimize the cost of a defined-benefit pension program. The cost of providing a defined-benefit pension increases with the age of the employee. In addition, an employer normally feels less responsibility for the retirement needs of a person who was in his or her service for only a few years before retirement.

[6]Generally, the Age Discrimination in Employment Act does not prohibit age provisions normally included in a qualified retirement plan, although there are some exceptions.

*Normal Retirement Age.*     Every pension plan has a **normal retirement age**. This is necessary because a fixed age or schedule of ages for retirement is fundamental in estimating costs, in determining the appropriate rate of accumulating funds for retirement benefits, and, most important, in permitting organizations and employees to plan for retirement.[7] Virtually all pension plans also make provision for early or deferred retirement, subject to certain conditions.

*Benefit Formula.*     Since an employee's standard of living normally is related to his or her earnings, it is important that retirement benefits bear a reasonable relationship to those earnings.[8] For an employee to have an adequate income at the time he or she retires, it generally has been considered necessary to have an income, including Social Security, that is approximately 70 to 75 percent of his or her average compensation in the five to ten years immediately preceding retirement.[9] The target retirement benefit, of course, varies by income level. Table 28-1 presents a current study of gross and net (of Social Security benefits) replacement ratios necessary for retirees to maintain their preretirement standard of living. Because of inflation and the fixed nature of most pension arrangements, a problem that also receives attention is maintaining the adequacy of income after retirement. Some possible approaches to this problem are: (1) cost-of-living or wage-indexed benefits and (2) periodic increases in benefits for retired employees on an ad hoc basis.

**TABLE 28-1     COMPARISON OF GROSS AND NET (OF SOCIAL SECURITY BENEFITS) INCOME REPLACEMENT RATIOS**

| | REPLACEMENT RATIOS | |
| --- | --- | --- |
| Preretirement Salary | Gross Ratios | Net Ratios |
| $15,000 | 89.6% | 24.6% |
| $25,000 | 81.7 | 26.6 |
| $40,000 | 96.8 | 36.6 |
| $50,000 | 73.3 | 39.8 |
| $60,000 | 71.4 | 43.1 |
| $70,000 | 69.8 | 45.8 |
| $80,000 | 68.1 | 46.8 |
| $90,000 | 66.5 | 47.5 |

*Source*: 1991 GSU/ACG RETIRE Project Report

[7]It is possible, of course, to establish a range of ages at which employees may retire, such as 62 to 65. In such cases, an assumption is made, in estimating costs, as to the distribution of employees retiring at each age. Many negotiated pension plans do not explicitly state one specific normal retirement age; instead they base it on years of service. This, of course, is applicable only to defined-benefit plans. Defined-contribution plans, by their nature, do not face these problems.

[8]Although the great majority of union-negotiated plans provide benefits that are tied to length of service rather than to earnings, it is assumed that the duration of employment within the collective-bargaining unit is such that the average employee will have a retirement benefit that is comparable (as a percentage of earnings) to that of salaried employees.

[9]See Bruce A. Palmer, Georgia State University/Alexander Consulting Group, Inc., *RETIRE Project Report* (The Center for Risk Management and Insurance Research, 1991).

Traditionally, benefit formulas have been placed into two broad categories: (1) defined benefit and (2) defined contribution. Under a **defined-benefit plan**, a fixed benefit is developed by the formula, and the cost will depend on the age, sex, and earnings distribution of eligible employees and the operating experience (i.e., mortality, turnover, salary increases, investment return, and expenses) of the plan. A **defined-contribution plan** establishes a rate or method of contribution by the employer only (noncontributory) or employee and employer jointly (contributory), and the amount of benefit provided for each employee varies depending on the age, contribution level, investment return, and length of covered service prior to actual retirement age and on the operating experience of the plan.

The characteristic that differentiates between the defined-benefit and the defined-contribution types of plans is that in the defined-benefit formula, the benefit is fixed and the contribution varies, whereas in the defined-contribution approach, the employer's contribution is fixed by formula (or may be determined annually in the case of a profit-sharing or stock bonus plan) and the benefit varies.

A plan using a defined-contribution formula provides an individual account for each participant and bases the employee's benefits solely on the amount contributed to the participant's account and on any expense, investment return, and forfeitures allocated to the participant's account. Since the definition of the basis for contribution(s) is completely flexible, a number of qualified plans have evolved with the dual objectives of provision of retirement income and deferral of current taxable income. These include money purchase pension plans, profit-sharing plans, 401(k) plans, stock bonus plans, and also voluntary employee contributions. When a participant becomes eligible to receive a benefit, his or her benefit equals a lump-sum distribution or an annuity equal to the amount that can be provided by the fund balance.

In addition to the defined-benefit and defined-contribution formulas, there is also a hybrid plan, often referred to as a **target-benefit** plan. Under a target-benefit plan, the projected benefit to be provided to the participant is determined as if the plan were a defined-benefit plan. The contributions necessary to fund this plan are then determined, based on assumed interest and mortality factors. Once the amount of the contribution (stated as a percentage of the participant's compensation) is determined, the plan then operates as a defined-contribution plan in that the participant is entitled upon his or her retirement to the benefits that can be purchased by the amount in his or her account, rather than the target benefit used to establish the amount of the employer's contribution to be made on his or her behalf.

Another hybrid plan, known as a **cash-balance** plan, is a form of defined-benefit plan that combines some of the features of defined-benefit plans with some features of defined-contribution plans. Each participant has an individual account that increases monthly to reflect new contributions and earned interest. This account balance is a memorandum account; employer contributions are actually deposited annually into the plan fund for each participant according to a benefit formula (e.g., 5 percent of compensation). The account earns interest as specified in the plan (e.g., a flexible rate based on the average rate on one-year Treasury bills or a fixed rate).

Cash-balance plans frequently have liberal vesting schedules (see below). When a participant leaves or retires, the vested portion of the account balance can be taken in cash or in the form of an annuity. Cash-balance plans are easier for employees to understand than defined-benefit plans. This use of liberal vesting provisions makes the plan benefits portable and naturally this is viewed favorably by participants. The employer has funding flexibility and is responsible for investment risk (features of defined-benefit plans). The accelerated vesting schedules utilized also increase the employer's costs. The use of individual accounts and easier communication with participants are typical features of defined-contribution plans.

Because of the increasing popularity of benefit formulas based on account balances, the fixed-benefit, deferred-benefit nature of a defined-benefit plan has lost some of its popularity. Although the defined-benefit formula may produce a fixed amount of benefit for a given year of service, the final retirement benefit is often a function of the employee's compensation in his or her final years of service prior to retirement. Thus the defined-benefit is not really definite as to dollar amount until it has been recomputed based on the employee's final years of pay, which frequently is based on the average of his or her last three to five years of credited service prior to retirement.

Many collective-bargaining agreements involve defined-contributions but with distinct characteristics. These so-called **Taft-Hartley plans** really are not defined-contribution plans; the benefit is defined as well as the contribution. This is an actuarial anomaly, since only by sheer coincidence could these two fixed functions remain in balance over any time period. Practically, the anomaly is resolved through periodic adjustments of the benefit scale, the contribution rate or both. These plans are considered defined-benefit plans for purposes of ERISA.

Defined-benefit formulas may be a flat dollar amount or they may be related to earnings, to service, or to a combination of earnings and service. Thus a given formula may provide a retirement benefit of $300 a month regardless of earnings or service, 30 percent of final average pay, 1.5 percent of annual pay for each year of credited service, or other formulas. In any case, where it is appropriate, earnings and service are specifically defined.

In the past, defined-benefit formulas based upon earnings frequently were integrated with Social Security benefits. An integrated benefit provided either an offset of a portion of the employee's actual Social Security benefit or a larger benefit on earnings in excess of the Social Security wage base per annum.[10] This

---

[10]A larger benefit can be provided on benefits below the Social Security wage base as well. For example, a money purchase plan (a type of defined-contribution plan) could provide that all participants receive an employer contribution of 4 percent of compensation, plus an amount equal to 7 percent of compensation for all amounts in excess of $10,000 per annum.

integration recognizes the fact that the employer makes contributions on wages up to the Social Security wage base and that Social Security benefits are weighted in favor of the lower-income groups. Under new maximum disparity regulations,[11] offsets based on Social Security Primary Insurance Amount benefits have, for all practical purposes, been eliminated.

Defined-benefit formulas based on service frequently give credit for both **past service**—that is, service prior to the installation of the plan—and **future service**. Generally, the sum-total cost of the credits granted for past service represents the **initial past-service liability** at the date of plan installation. Credit for past service is sometimes limited by counting service after a given age only, such as 35 or 40, or by limiting the number of years' credit for past service to, say, 15 or 20. The resulting benefit must not discriminate in favor of highly compensated employees. In any case, an employee's retirement benefit is the total of past- and future-service credits under the pension plan at retirement.

*Maximum Benefits.*    Before ERISA, it was not customary for plans to impose an upper limit on the benefits that would be payable (other than that implicit in a flat benefit formula). As mentioned earlier, ERISA and later amendments imposed a limit on the benefits that can be provided under a defined-benefit plan, and a limit on the contributions under a defined-contribution plan. In addition, there is a maximum limit on compensation that can be recognized in the benefit formula under qualified plans.

Additional requirements apply to contributions and benefits under a top-heavy plan. A **top-heavy plan** is one under which the value of accrued benefits for key employees (certain officers and owners) and their beneficiaries exceeds 60 percent of the value of accrued benefits for all employees and their beneficiaries. Most small plans are top-heavy. Whether a plan is top-heavy is determined each plan year.

If a plan is top-heavy, it is subject to adjustments in the maximum limits on contributions and benefits, a maximum limit on recognizable compensation, more rapid vesting, and, for non-key employees, minimum benefits or contributions. A top-heavy plan must provide at least minimum benefits or contributions for all participants who are not key employees. As a practical matter, when the requirement applies, most plans usually apply it to all employees. The passage of the Tax Reform Act of 1986, with its faster vesting requirements, $200,000 (indexed) limit on compensation, and restrictive integration rules, has made the top-heavy rules less punitive, relatively speaking.

No qualified plans may take into account compensation in excess of $200,000 in determining benefits or contributions. This $200,000 limit is subject to post-1989 cost-of-living adjustments in the same manner as the dollar limits under Section 415.[12]

---

[11]See Internal Revenue Service Regulations 1.401(a)(4) and 1.401 (L).

[12]This indexed limit was $235,840 in 1993.

***Supplemental Benefits.***    In addition to a retirement income, many pension programs include death, withdrawal, disability, or other supplemental benefits during the preretirement period. Although it is important that these supplemental benefits not be included at the expense of an adequate retirement income, they can form an important part of a well-designed employee benefit program. Naturally, which supplemental benefits are provided will depend on the personnel policy, finances, and other individual circumstances of the employer. Supplemental death benefits are subject to requirements and limitations imposed by IRS regulations on both death and disability benefits. The more commonly provided supplemental benefits are based on death or disability.

The Retirement Equity Act of 1984 provides for automatic death benefits for all vested participants—whether they are active, terminated, or retired—under defined-benefit pension plans. A death benefit in the form of a joint and survivor annuity may be waived in writing by both the participant and the spouse.

The survivor benefit can be provided directly from a trust or by the purchase of an annuity from the funds that are held under a deposit administration contract.[13] Substantial supplemental death benefits can be subject to wide cost variations unless a special insurance arrangement is used. Normally, the plan provides these benefits directly from an unallocated trust fund. Regardless of the funding used, determining the appropriate amount of the death benefits for the surviving spouse requires serious consideration on the part of the employer. In addition, the design should be simple and easy for the employee to understand.

The portion of the supplemental benefits to be provided under the retirement plan and the portion to be provided under a separate group insurance program are other decisions to be made by the individual employer, with the help of or guidance from an independent consultant, the insurance company, or both. Management has come to recognize that, to the maximum extent possible, there must be a coordination of all sources of income available to the employee from both employer and government plans. This coordination is challenging because supplemental benefits may be provided in a number of ways. Historically, coordination of all forms of employee benefits with government programs has been rather poor.

***Employee Contributions.***    Pension plans may be contributory or noncontributory. Under a **contributory plan**, the employee provides part of the funds necessary to purchase his or her benefits, with the employer assuming the remaining cost.[14] Under a **noncontributory plan**, the employer bears the total cost of the program. Today about 90 percent of all nonsavings plans are noncontributory. For many years, the majority of plans that were not the result of collective bargaining were written on a contributory basis. In many cases, such

---

[13] See the section "Deposit AdministrationContracts" later in this chapter.

[14]Sometimes a plan is referred to as contributory only if the participant is required to make contributions, and not if the contributions are voluntary.

contributions permit the installation of a plan if the employer's financial position is such that, unless they were utilized, no plan would be installed at all. In other cases, employee contributions are used to enlarge the benefits provided, or they are used on the theory that the employees' appreciation will be greater if they bear part of the cost of their benefits.

Recent laws[15] and government regulations have made the administration of contributory plans exceedingly complex, and therefore the current trend in pension plans appears to be toward noncontributory plans. In addition, the theoretical case for noncontributory plans rests largely on the **deferred-wage concept**. If retirement benefits can be regarded as deferred wages, the argument that the employer should assume the total cost of these benefits is logical. On the other hand, if they are not considered deferred wages, the rationale for unilateral financing tends to fail.

Apart from the philosophical aspects of the question, there are strong practical arguments in favor of a noncontributory approach to financing. For example, employer contributions to a qualified pension plan are deductible for income tax purposes. Employees' contributions to a pension plan (except to the extent that the contributions qualify for the limited retirement-savings deduction provided by IRC Section 219) must be made from after-tax income. A cash or deferred profit-sharing plan—referred to as a **401(k) plan** [as defined in the IRC Section 401(k)]—provides that employees may make limited pre-tax contributions to a defined-contribution plan (see below). This privilege does not apply to employee contributions to defined-benefit pension plans.

*Vesting.*    A well-established principle of pension planning is that an employee must be permitted to recover his or her contributions with interest (or adjusted for earning experience) if he or she withdraws from employment. An employee's rights in that portion of accrued benefits derived from his or her own contributions are nonforfeitable. The employee's vested or nonforfeitable percentage of the employer contributions may vary from 0 to 100 percent, depending upon the vesting schedule in the plan. The vesting schedule is usually based on length of service and, in some cases, age of the participant (e.g., full vesting upon the attainment of age 65).

The vesting provisions of pension plans can be classified on at least four different bases: the *kinds* of benefits vested, the point in *time* when the eligible benefits vest, the *rate* at which the accrued benefits vest, and the *form* in which the benefits may be taken. As to the *kinds* of benefits vested, retirement, death, and total disability are all vested when the employee enters payment status. Except for this status, however, the traditional approach has been to vest the basic retirement benefit only. As to *time*, employers may grant immediate vesting in the employer contributions, or, as usually is the case, the vesting may be deferred until certain service requirements have been met.

[15]See the Omnibus Budget Reconciliation Act of 1987.

As to the *rate* at which benefits vest, the employer's contributions may vest in full or only in part, although eventually it will have to be 100 percent. A graded vesting provision, which provides an increasing percentage of vesting based on service up to 100 percent, is in reality partly a time and partly an amount classification. Benefits derived from employer contributions must be fully vested at normal retirement age and also must meet either one of two permissible standards: (1) complete vesting of all accrued benefits after five years of recognized service or (2) a so-called three-to-seven-year standard under which accrued benefits must be at least 20 percent vested after three years of recognized service, and an additional 20 percent each year during the following four years.

The *form* of the vested benefits depends to some extent on the contractual instrument used to fund the benefits. If the plan is funded through a trust, the vested terminated employee generally retains a deferred claim against the trust fund in the amount of his or her vested benefits, or else may receive a lump-sum settlement. If the plan is funded through a contract with a life insurance company, the vested benefits may take the form of a paid-up insurance or annuity contract or a deferred claim against the plan.

The term **portable pensions** has found some acceptance in the U.S. pension literature to describe vested pension benefits that would follow the employee and be put into any new plan under which he or she is covered, or vested benefits that would be transferred to some central pension clearinghouse. Portability of pensions has, at least to a limited extent, become a reality with the enactment of ERISA, which provides for rollover contributions to an individual retirement account and to other qualified retirement plans.

Under ERISA, an individual may avoid taxation on a distribution of money or property from an individual retirement account (IRA) or qualified plan by reinvesting the money or property received, within 60 days, in another qualified IRA or plan for his or her benefit.[16] To qualify for this reinvestment, a **rollover contribution** from a qualified-plan distribution must be reduced by that portion of the distribution attributable to the employee's after-tax contributions, since all amounts in a tax-deductible IRA are to have a zero tax basis. Amounts from a disqualified retirement annuity and excess contributions to an IRA may not be rolled over into an IRA. Furthermore, an individual may roll over amounts between IRAs only once each year, even though he or she may roll over amounts from a qualified plan into an IRA more than once within a one-year period.

*Methods of Distribution.*     As pointed out above, a plan may be required to distribute benefits in the form of a joint and survivor annuity or a life annuity. Other common methods of distribution are payments in equal periodic installments for a certain term (i.e., monthly for ten years) or in a lump sum. Lump-sum distributions received after age 59 usually are eligible for favorable

---

[16]IRC § 408(d)(3).

five-year income averaging treatment, or they can be rolled over into an IRA or another qualified plan, to defer income taxes.

## METHODS OF FINANCING

### FUNDING PROCEDURE

Once the basic features of a pension plan have been determined, consideration must be given to the various techniques used to measure the contribution requirements and liabilities under a pension plan. These techniques usually are referred to as **actuarial cost methods**. The methods, of course, apply only to defined-benefit plans, since defined-contribution plans are by definition a simple accumulation of the contributions made and investment earnings thereon.

An actuarial cost method is a particular technique for establishing the amount and incidence of the annual actuarial contribution for pension plan benefits, or benefits and expenses, and the related actuarial liability. The legal instruments, such as pension contracts issued by insurance companies, under which the actuarial cost arrangements operate, are referred to as **funding media** or **funding vehicles**. Pension contracts issued by insurance companies may incorporate both the *actuarial cost method* and the pension *plan*, although there is a technical distinction. A given pension plan might have one document relating to the plan and a separate legal instrument under which the funding method operates, the plan being incorporated only by reference. With separate documents, it is possible to amend the plan and not alter in any way the funding method being employed. The essence of the funding process is the accumulation of assets to offset the liabilities arising under the pension plan as measured by the actuarial method utilized.

Prior to the enactment of ERISA, only a few plans operated on the pay-as-you-go basis.[17] Under this arrangement, retirement benefits were paid as a supplementary payroll. Payments were taken from current operating revenues and were charged to operating costs.[18] No funds were set aside in advance for the payment of pension obligations even at retirement. This type of arrangement furnished the smallest degree of security to the employee, since neither the active nor the retired employees could look to a segregated fund or a third-party guarantee for satisfaction of the pension claims. In contrast to pay-as-you-go, ERISA requires advance funding of qualified pension plans. The several patterns of advanced funding may be broadly classified as (1) benefit-allocation and (2) cost-allocation methods. Although given pension benefits can be funded by several methods, usually one or the other will be more appropriate, depending

---

[17]Under *Opinion 8,* issued in 1966 by the Accounting Principles Board of the American Institute of Certified Public Accountants, neither pay-as-you-go nor terminal funding was an accepted principle of accounting for the cost of pension plans in financial statements.

[18]Social Security benefits effectively are funded this way.

upon the benefit formula and other characteristics of the plan and the plan sponsor's funding objective.

*Benefit Allocation.*   The **benefit-allocation method** of funding, also known as the accrued benefit or single-premium method, involves the setting aside, in one sum, of the amount of money needed to fund in full one unit of benefit. In practice, this unit of benefit is almost always related to a year of service—that is, it is the benefit earned during one year of service. Thus if an employee currently earns an annual benefit at age 65 of $35, a paid-up annuity in that amount would be funded for that employee. Thereafter, this particular employee would have a paid-up annuity in the appropriate amount funded each year at an increasing cost per dollar of benefit based on his or her attained age at the time of each contribution. At retirement, this employee's income would be the total of each of these annual increments of benefits.

The benefit-allocation method assumes that the normal cost[19] of a pension plan for any particular year is precisely equal to the present value of the benefits credited to the employee participants for service during that year. Thus a funding policy geared to this cost method funds future-service benefits fully as they accrue. Past-service benefits are funded according to a schedule adopted by the employer in accordance with various schedules laid down in ERISA, usually over a period of years. The benefit-allocation method of funding is virtually always used in connection with group deferred-annuity contracts and may be used with other types of plans.

*Cost Allocation.*   The other category of funding patterns, known as the **cost-allocation method**, can be used with any type of benefit formula but is especially adaptable to the type of formula that provides a composite benefit as opposed to a series of unit benefits.

*1.   Individual Level-Cost Methods.* Under the individual level-cost method *without supplemental liability* (see below), the total benefits to be paid to an employee are estimated and the sum required to provide the benefits is accumulated through level amounts contributed over the remaining years of service. The most familiar form of the individual level-cost method is the individual level-premium method, which is employed in connection with individual and group cash-value insurance contracts. This funding method provides the benefits that would be payable to the employee if his or her rate of compensation remained unchanged to normal retirement age. The premium is a function of the entering age of the employee.

If the rate of compensation and benefits increases, an adjustment in the amount of insurance is made, and the funding of the increase in benefits is

---

[19]The **normal cost** under any actuarial cost method is the cost that would be attributable to the current year of a plan's operations if, from the earliest date of credited service, the plan had been in effect and costs had been accrued in accordance with the particular actuarial cost method.

accomplished by a separate and additional level premium, payable from the date of increase and based on the age at that time. Contracts funded by this method are written in amounts designed to provide benefits for the entire period of credited service, and, consequently, no distinction is made between past- and current-service costs—that is, the supplemental liability for past service is not separately determined and handled.

The individual level-cost method *with supplemental liability* (past-service liability determined separately) serves as the funding guide for many trust fund plans and deposit administration contracts. The rationale here is that benefits are funded at a level-amount basis over the employee participant's *entire* working lifetime. The supplemental liability for past-service benefits is separately ascertained. It may be viewed as the accumulated value (with the benefit of both interest and survivorship in service) of the normal cost contributions assumed to have been made with respect to all participants with credited past service at the time the plan is installed. Widely known as the **entry-age normal method**, this funding method permits a flexible policy with regard to funding the past-service liability.

*2. Aggregate Level-Cost Methods.* The aggregate-cost methods are analogous to the individual level-cost methods, except for the calculation of costs and contributions on a collective rather than individual basis. As in the case of the individual level-cost methods, the annual cost accruals may be determined with or without the past-service supplemental liability being determined separately.

Under this method without supplemental liability, the total employer cost of all future benefits for present employees, less employer funds on hand, is expressed as a level percentage of future payroll of present employees. Each year, as new employees enter, the level percentage must be recalculated. The actual calculation is made by dividing the present value of the future compensation of the covered employees, or the present value of the appropriate portion thereof, into the excess of the present value of future estimated benefits over plan assets. This determines what is generally called the accrual rate or aggregate-cost ratio. The cost is determined by multiplying the compensation, or appropriate portion thereof, paid during the year to employees entering into the funding calculations by the accrual rate. In contrast to this, the actuary can determine a supplemental liability (determining the past-service liability separately), to provide greater funding flexibility. Aggregate cost methods are most widely used in trusteed (noninsured) plans, although they are equally adaptable to group deposit administration and immediate participation guarantee contracts.

***Funding Requirements.*** ERISA imposes certain funding requirements that are generally limited to pension plans. Profit-sharing and stock-bonus plans are excluded from the funding requirements, as are certain defined-benefit pension plans funded on a current basis solely with individual or allocated group insurance contracts. With respect to money-purchase plans, which are defined-contribution plans, an employer is required to make contributions in accordance with the plan's contribution formula. The determination of required contributions under defined-benefit plans is more complex, but basically contributions must be sufficient to cover normal service costs and to amortize past-service costs and experience gains and losses over a specified time. Unless eligible to elect the alternative minimum funding standard account, plans must meet the requirements of the minimum funding standard account. The amortization period depends upon whether the plan was already in existence on January 1, 1974. There are separately articulated amortization schedules for experience gains and losses and for liabilities created by plan amendment or change in actuarial assumptions.

In addition, if the plan is poorly funded, a deficit reduction contribution may be required to amortize more quickly unfunded past-service liabilities. Minimum contributions are required to be deposited quarterly. Notwithstanding the foregoing rules, the employer's contribution is limited to the amount necessary to make the plan fully funded—that is, the contribution necessary to make the value of the plan assets equal to the accrued liabilities under the plan, completed on a going-concern basis or, if less, 150 percent of its current liability, over the value of plan assets.

An employer's failure to meet the minimum funding requirements will result in a nondeductible 5 percent excise tax. This tax is imposed on an annual basis on the accumulated funding deficiency. Furthermore, failure to fund the deficiency within 90 days, plus extensions, after the mailing of the deficiency notice with respect to the 5 percent tax will result in an additional tax equal to 100 percent of the funding deficiency. In hardship cases, the Secretary of the Treasury may waive the funding requirements, but the amounts so waived must be amortized over a period not to exceed 15 years.

## PENSION COSTS

Advance funding involves the setting aside of funds for the payment of pension benefits in advance of their due date. In the case of defined-benefit plans, the cost of providing the benefits must be estimated years in advance. In estimating pension costs, some of the factors that may be taken into account include (1) mortality, (2) interest, (3) expense of operations, (4) turnover, (5) age of retirement, and (6) changes in compensation. These factors vary considerably over time, so the use of the word *estimating* is appropriate.

The ultimate cost of a pension plan is equal to the benefits paid out, plus the cost of administration, less the earnings (including capital gains and losses) on any funds set aside for the payment of benefits.[20] This is not, however, the true cost to the employer. For the true cost of a plan to be obtained, this cost or net

---

[20] Some authors would include an item for "pooling gains and losses," arising out of the fact that investment and mortality results under many insured plans and some noninsured plans involve some averaging of results.

financial outlay must be adjusted for such factors as reduced labor turnover, retirement of inefficient employees, improved morale, and other less easily quantifiable benefits. Because these factors are difficult to evaluate, the net financial outlay generally is assumed to represent the cost of the plan. Since a pension plan is a long-range venture, ultimate costs cannot be accurately determined in advance. This is true even in an insured pension plan, since contracts are experience-rated,[21] and the employer's own experience will have a marked effect on the level of dividends or experience-rate credits.

The term *pension costs* is also often used to refer to financial accounting pension expense. Funding and financial accounting expense requirements for pension costs are determined under separate rules and therefore are usually different amounts. The Financial Accounting Standard No. 87 dictates the determination of pension expense for companies subject to generally accepted accounting principles, whereas the Internal Revenue Code dictates pension funding.

Virtually all life insurance companies now use the **investment year** or **new money** method of determining the rate of investment income to be credited to a given pension plan. For many years, it was standard practice to credit the account with the net rate of interest earned on the insurer's total investment portfolio—the average or portfolio rate. When interest rates rose rapidly in the 1950s, the average life insurance company portfolio rate of return lagged considerably behind the new money investment rates, placing life insurers at a competitive disadvantage with banks for pension business. The investment year method was adopted in the early 1960s to minimize the adverse selection involved and to meet the competition of the banks for pension funds.

Under the investment year or new money approach, assets acquired during a particular calendar year are treated as a separate cell or component of the general asset account. The net investment income (including realized capital gains and losses) derived from the assets in that calendar year cell is credited to the cell. The asset composition of the cell changes annually because of maturities, repayments, redemptions, sales, and exchanges. Naturally, this affects the rate of return credited to the cell.

## PENSION FINANCING VEHICLES

With regard to financing, pension plans may be classified on three bases: (1) fully insured plans, (2) noninsured plans, and (3) split-funded plans. Noninsured plans are often loosely referred to as **self-administered** or **trusteed** plans. A trust is virtually always used in noninsured plans, with a trustee or investment manager being responsible for the investment and management of the funds accumulated under the plan. On the other hand, when separate insurance policies on the lives of the covered individuals are used as a funding medium, the

[21]Plans employing individual life insurance contracts under a pension trust are not experience-rated, but instead are treated as other individual life insurance policies. See the section "Level-Premium Annuity Contracts" below.

contracts also are often held in trusts. To avoid confusion in terminology, the original distinction of insured and noninsured is used in this discussion.

*Noninsured Plan.*     The noninsured plan usually involves the establishment of a trust for the benefit of the employees. Under such defined-benefit plans, an **enrolled actuary**[22] is employed to make estimates of the contributions that should be made to the trust. A bank or insurance company invests the funds so deposited and when an employee retires, the bank or insurance company pays out a monthly check or a lump-sum amount to the retired employee on the direction of the employer. The employer assumes all the risks—investment, mortality, and expense—under the trusteed defined-benefit plan. The enrolled actuary takes no responsibility for investment and mortality results, but uses reasonable actuarial assumptions in estimating pension costs. Similarly, the trustee takes no responsibility except to invest the money in accordance with the law and its best judgment or at the direction of the employer or its investment advisors (depending on the trust indenture).

The employer is in a sense a self-insurer. Under a noninsured plan, however, the employer or, in the event of insolvency of the employer, the employee assumes risks that may be assumed by the insurance company under an insured plan. The plan provisions usually limit the employer's liability to whatever monies are in the trust. The benefits promised by a defined-benefit pension plan usually are insured at least in part by the Pension Benefit Guaranty Corporation (PBGC).[23] Since the noninsured plan is a self-insured plan, this approach carries the least risk for large companies (or groups of companies), with sufficient spread of risk to permit predictable results and to keep administrative costs reasonable. Further protection has been provided to participants by the minimum-funding requirements under ERISA, which were discussed earlier.

The trusteed approach may have advantages for those corporations large enough to self-insure the pension risk. The advantages include: (1) economy of operation, (2) greater flexibility in both funding and plan provisions, and (3) the possibility of better investment results because of greater investment freedom. Although trusteed plans are noninsured in the sense that no guarantees are provided to covered individuals, the use of insurance company services is not precluded. Several insurance companies have developed contracts that permit the use of the insurance company's investment services and, if desired, its administrative and actuarial services, but do not involve irrevocable guarantees to individuals. Investment of funds with insurance companies at a minimum guaranteed rate of return via guaranteed investment contracts is also quite popular. Even though such contracts do not fall within the traditional definition of

22 An enrolled actuary must sign the actuarial report required by ERISA. Such individuals must have met the standard and qualifications set by the Joint Board for the Enrollment of Actuaries established by the secretaries of Labor and the Treasury.

23The **Pension Benefit Guaranty Corporation** is a government corporation set up by ERISA to provide termination insurance to qualified defined-benefit plans so as to protect participants from losing pension benefits if a plan terminates or an employer becomes bankrupt. See Kenn B. Tacchino, "Exposing Pension Security Concerns," *Journal of the American Society of CLU & ChFC,* Vol. 46 (May 1992).

insured pension plans, these arrangements have proven to be an important source of business for insurance companies.

*Combination Plan.*    There are pension programs in which two or more types of contracts are combined or an employer makes use of an insurance contract in conjunction with a noninsured trusteed arrangement. All these variations are called **split-funding contracts**. Frequently, a bank is used to hold and invest a part of the monies in the active life fund, and monies may be moved from the bank to the life insurance company to provide guaranteed annuities as employees retire. If the life insurance company does not hold any of the monies prior to retirement and receives money only as employees retire to purchase the guaranteed annuities, the arrangement is called a **maturity funding contract**. In another version, a portion of the contribution is invested in cash-value life insurance policies, with the remainder of the fund held and invested by the trustee.

Noninsured pension arrangements are worthy of more comprehensive treatment, but in view of the nature of this text, the remaining discussion is concerned primarily with insured pension plans.

## INSURED PENSION CONTRACTS

Life insurance companies offer considerable flexibility in tailoring a funding vehicle appropriately to meet individual employer needs. This flexibility makes it difficult to describe the available arrangements in simple terms. In this discussion, names are attached to various types of insured pension arrangements, but it should be understood that the contracts can be modified to fit particular requirements.

Life insurance companies are in the business of accepting risks, so they are willing to underwrite several different risks associated with pension plans, and to underwrite them to varying degrees, depending upon the employer's wishes. Some of these risks are:

1. More individuals may live to retire than the mortality tables used anticipated.

2. Those who retire may live longer than the mortality tables used anticipated.

3. The rate of interest earned on investments may fall below the anticipated level.

4. There may be defaults in the investment portfolio, or it may be necessary to sell particular investments at a loss.

5. Expenses of handling the plan may be higher than anticipated.[24]

---

[24]In a well-designed employee benefit program that provides death, disability, and retirement benefits with reasonably comparable values, the actuarial experience will not be significantly different whether more employees become disabled, more die, or more live and retire. If just one function like death is isolated, obviously a higher or lower rate than expected can significantly change the experience with respect to that one plan. As companies develop more sophisticated benefit programs, the effect of risk becomes less significant.

Life insurance companies are also in the position of providing a variety of services, many of which may be varied to suit the employer's wishes. Except for certain benefit guarantees, the services provided by a life insurance company can be provided by consultants and other organizations specializing in providing services in the pension field.

## SINGLE-PREMIUM ANNUITY CONTRACTS

The insurance company probably rises to its maximum usefulness in the rather unusual situation in which the employer determines the benefit that will ultimately be payable to each of its employees and makes a single payment to an insurance company to guarantee that all these benefits will be paid as they become due. This arrangement is frequently used for a body of employees who have already retired and in the situation in which an uninsured trusteed arrangement is terminated for one reason or another, and the monies in the trust are used to purchase immediate or deferred annuities for the employees covered by the trusts. It is unusual with respect to employees who are still working. The insurance contracts written under these circumstances are commonly referred to as **single-premium group annuity contracts**.

## LEVEL-PREMIUM ANNUITY CONTRACTS

Sometimes an employer makes an estimate of the amount of pension that will be payable when the employee reaches his or her normal retirement age, and the insurance company is asked to quote a *level-amount payment* for each employee that can be guaranteed to provide the estimated amount of pension. The insurance company guarantees that if the indicated premium is paid each year until the employee retires, the insurance company will pay the indicated amount of benefit.

An arrangement of this type can be provided either through separate policies issued on the lives of the individual employees or through a master group annuity contract issued to the employer with certificates of coverage given to the employees. In either event, it is quite common to provide a life insurance feature during the period prior to retirement. When separate policies are issued on the lives of the employees, the policies generally are issued to and held by a trustee, and the arrangement is called an **individual policy pension trust**. When a group vehicle is used, it may be called a **group permanent contract**, a **level-premium group annuity contract**, or a **level-premium contract with lifetime guarantees**. Under this type of arrangement, the insurance company assumes all the risks and provides all the services, and, in particular, it guarantees a price structure.

## SINGLE-PREMIUM DEFERRED ANNUITIES

Under **group deferred annuity contracts**, the employee's pension is separated into pieces that are associated with years of employment. Thus for each year of service, the employee might be entitled to an annual pension at retirement of 2 percent of his or her year's salary, or he or she might be entitled to a flat amount, such as $50 of monthly income for each year's service. Each year, the employer then purchases a single premium unit of deferred annuity, which will become payable when the employee reaches his or her normal retirement age. The employee's pension is the sum of the units that were purchased for him or her. Once the annuity has been purchased, the insurance company assumes all the risks and provides all the services. Although the company's risk with respect to any individual may extend for 40, 50, or 60 years with respect to the premium it *has received*, the life insurance company has not guaranteed the price it will charge for additional units *to be purchased* several years in the future. It is customary, however, for the insurance company to guarantee its rate structure with respect to the first five years of the contract.

A basic characteristic of all the previously described insurance arrangements is that each employee can be told with certainty that a benefit has been purchased or is being purchased for him or her, and the life insurance company guarantees that it will be paid. The employer is in the secure position of knowing that he or she is not placing on future management the risk that the promised benefits will turn out to have been inadequately funded, and the responsibility of making up a deficiency or incurring employee dissatisfaction by reducing the promised benefits.

It is characteristic of this type of arrangement that monies are set aside to provide pensions for some employees who will not stay with the employer until they have satisfied the vesting provisions, and, furthermore, that the employer must meet each year's pension obligation (based on current service) in full. Many employers indicated a desire for some method by which the employer could have greater latitude in determining its annual payments into the pension fund, by discounting its payments to allow for the probability that some of its employees will not persist in employment, and augmenting its payments to anticipate future pay increases. For these and other reasons, both level-premium and single-premium deferred annuities are less popular today, and the deposit administration contract concept has been developed in response to these shortcomings.

## DEPOSIT ADMINISTRATION CONTRACTS

Under the **deposit administration contract**, the life insurance company takes all the risks and provides all services, but *only with respect to employees who have retired*. With respect to employees who have not yet reached their retirement dates, the life insurance company provides no direct guarantees with regard to employer contributions for employees, except that pensions will be provided to the extent that monies are available at the time the employees retire. An enrolled actuary supplies the employer with estimates of the amount of money that should be set aside each year, to make reasonably certain that sufficient funds will be available to purchase annuities for employees as they retire. These monies are turned over to the life insurance company for safekeeping and investment. The life insurance company guarantees that there will be no capital impairment and that at least a specified minimum rate of interest will be earned on the funds. It also guarantees that a particular price structure will be used to establish annuities for the employees as they retire.

The deposit administration contract sets out a schedule of annuity purchase rates and a rate of interest (both conservative) at which the monies in the contractual fund (the active life fund) will be accumulated, both being guaranteed, usually, for the first five years of the contract. After the contract has been in effect for five years, these guarantees can be changed from year to year as to future contributions. The minimum rate of interest and the rate schedules in effect at the time a dollar is paid to the insurer apply to that dollar, regardless of when it is withdrawn from the active life fund to provide an annuity. Currently, some companies guarantee purchase rates for five to ten years of *retirements*, with a right to change the annuity purchase basis for new retirees after that. Following the change, another five- or ten-year period may be applicable. The volatility of investment results has caused many companies to avoid the standard types of long-term guarantees.

The life insurance company has not assumed the risk of the number of persons who will stay with the employer until retirement, but it has assumed all the other risks listed above. The insurance company may not provide all services, since the employer or its consultant may maintain employee records, determine the amounts to be paid into the plan, and evaluate the adequacy of funds to provide for future retirements.

## IMMEDIATE PARTICIPATION GUARANTEE CONTRACT

Another popular form of contract is referred to as an **immediate participation guarantee contract** (IPG). These contracts are similar to deposit administration contracts in that the employer's contributions are placed in an unallocated fund and the life insurance company guarantees that the annuities for retired employees will be paid in full. They differ from deposit administration contracts in the extent to which and the time at which the insurance company assumes mortality, investment, and expense risks with respect to retired lives.

The IPG contract may be said to have two stages. The first or active stage continues for as long as the employer makes sufficient contributions to keep the amount in the fund above the amount required to meet the life insurance company's price to provide guaranteed annuities for employees who have retired. The contract enters its second stage if the amount in the fund falls to the so-called critical level.

In the active stage, the contract fund is charged directly with the contract's share of the life insurance company's expenses and credited directly with its share of investment income (minus a small risk charge). The fund is also credited or charged directly with the contract's share of the insurer's capital gains and losses and the investment and expense experience with respect to retired employees. If the employer allows the fund to fall to the critical level and the contract enters the second stage, the amount in the fund is used to establish fully guaranteed annuities, and the fund itself ceases to exist.

Under an IPG contract, as long as the employer's contributions are sufficient to maintain the contract in active status, the life insurance company is relieved of investment, mortality, and expense risks with respect to all employees—both active and retired ones. If and when the contract enters the second stage, all these risks are assumed by the insurance company. Of course, the insurer is under a substantial risk during the active status of the contract, since it has provided a guaranteed price structure that the employer can unilaterally decide to take advantage of at any time that it feels the probable future course of investment, mortality, and expense risks to be such that it will be to its advantage to shift the risk to the life insurance company.

Recently, some IPG contracts have been modified, eliminating the guaranteed annuity rates; instead, they provide a certificate stating that nonguaranteed payments will be made until the fund is exhausted. Under this arrangement the employer is responsible for the adequacy of funding, and employees have no assurance from the life insurance company that their benefit payments will continue until death.

## SPECIAL INVESTMENT ARRANGEMENTS

*Separate Accounts.*    During the 1960s, U.S. insurance companies secured authority to set up **separate accounts**. These accounts are held separately from the other assets of the insurer and are not subject to the usual investment restrictions on insurance companies. The insurance company issues contracts under which the investment credits directly reflect the investment results of the separate account.

During the 1970s, the most common form of separate account was one in which the funds of many contractholders were pooled for investment in common stocks. Today, however, insurance companies have pooled accounts invested in stocks, bonds, mortgages, real estate, and other assets. Also, a contractholder with a large account, who does not wish to participate in a pooled separate account, may request that the insurance company establish a separate account for the company's exclusive use.

Separate accounts also may be used to provide variable annuity benefits. Amounts placed in the account usually are converted into units, and the amount of each employee's benefit is measured in terms of units. The amount of each monthly annuity payment is equal to the product of the number of units to which the employee is entitled and the unit value for the month.

*Guaranteed Investment Contracts.*    Under **guaranteed investment contracts** (GICs), the insurance company accepts from a qualified retirement plan a specific amount of money, usually $100,000 or more, and agrees to refund the money at a fixed date (one to 15 years) in the future. Interest is guaranteed for the life of the contract, usually at rates that are competitive with other long-term, fixed-income investments. The interest may be paid at fixed intervals or held to compound until the termination date of the contract.

Since the fixed term of the contract is one of its key features, substantial penalties usually are imposed for premature withdrawal (if it is allowed at all). Expenses of the insurance company often are expressed as a small subtraction from the gross interest rate quoted.

There are two types of GICs: the bullet GIC and the window GIC. The **bullet GIC** is structured to accept a single-sum deposit (generally $100,000 or more) for a specified period of time (usually three to seven years). The bullet GIC guarantees principal and interest at a stipulated rate, and it is agreed that the principal and interest will be returned at a specified date or dates. Both the amount of money deposited and the lock-in period are a function of the pension fund manager's investment strategy. Bullet GICs are usually marketed to defined-benefit plans, because they fit well with the timing of contributions from these plans, which are generally quarterly. The relative inflexibility associated with making contributions to a bullet GIC led to the creation of the other basic GIC type, known as a window GIC.

The **window GIC** is designed to help meet the need for periodic contributions inherent in some defined-contribution plans, which credit an employee's account balance with the plan contribution (frequently monthly or semimonthly) as salaries are paid. To accommodate periodic variable contributions, a window period is established. When a window GIC is used, the interest guarantees are locked in immediately, but the timing of contributions is usually left open for up to a year. Under a window GIC, the amounts contributed and the withdrawal amounts are not known. Under defined-contribution plans, the exact yearly contribution is known only at the end of the plan year. The window GIC provides flexibility to accommodate the periodic contributions. The bullet GIC, on the other hand, suits a defined-benefit plan, since, under these plans, the precise plan contribution is actuarially determined once a year.

Each basic GIC (bullet or window) can be modified to meet specific needs of a given pension plan. For example, it is not unusual to design a window GIC to guarantee the first-year rate, but to leave years two through five open during the first year. Another variation of the window GIC is the provision that allows the insurance company to accept contributions up to a certain dollar amount rather than for a window period. Similarly, the basic design of a bullet GIC can be modified to allow the plan sponsor to lock in current rates for a deposit to be made on an agreed-upon future date. Other design adjustments are possible.

In general, GICs in their various forms have been a significant investment vehicle for pension plans over the last 20 years. In the early 1990s, confidence in

GICs was seriously shaken by the financial troubles of some insurance companies that were affected by defaults of junk bonds they purchased in the 1980s and poor mortgage loan results. GICs do not generally enjoy the status of "insurance," and therefore they are not entitled to state guarantee fund coverage in the event of defaults.

## OTHER RETIREMENT PLANS

### PROFIT SHARING PLANS

**Profit-sharing plans** are a type of defined-contribution plan. Those that are intended for retirement income purposes can present a challenge for employees, since the amount available to provide an income at retirement usually is not known before retirement. Annually, each employee is allocated a share of the amount of profits contributed to the profit-sharing plan. Each employee's share is usually accounted for procedurally as with regular employee contributions, although the return of the amount in an employee's account in the event of termination of employment may be dependent upon a vesting provision. Although it is relatively rare for this to occur, the amounts of money made available each year may be used as single premiums to purchase whatever amounts of annuity can be provided on the basis of a price structure guaranteed by an insurance company.

Profit-sharing plans were originally introduced to share profits with employees, with the goal of improving productivity. They were adapted to provide retirement benefits in order to avoid the cash flow problems that a qualified pension plan creates by virtue of mandatory annual contributions. Also, the employer retains a certain amount of control over the level of annual contributions made to the plan and the allocation formula used. Plans may also be designed to allow employees to withdraw funds from participant accounts, but they must allow this flexibility to all participants. Allocation formulas cannot favor highly compensated or long-service employees, or both. The Tax Reform Act of 1986 removed the restriction that profit-sharing plans must have current or accumulated profits for the employer to be able to make a profit-sharing contribution in a given year.

Although profit-sharing plans fall under the defined-contribution category and share all the defined-contribution characteristics, the IRS regulations are somewhat more liberal in certain areas. The deduction for employer contributions to a profit-sharing plan is limited to 15 percent of the aggregate participant payroll. Any one participant is eligible to receive a contribution up to the defined-contribution limit of 25 percent of salary or $30,000.

Profit-sharing plans are frequently installed with other defined-benefit or money-purchase pension plans. For example, an employee might institute a 15 percent profit-sharing plan and a 10 percent defined-contribution pension plan. This approach retains some flexibility while assuring a minimum level of benefits for participants.

   If the profits allocated to each employee are placed in individual accounts for them under noninsured trusts, their accumulation at retirement may be used to purchase a guaranteed annuity under an arrangement similar to that of the maturity funding contract described earlier. Many insurance companies have developed both group and individual contracts that function during the accumulation phase somewhat like the noninsured trust and at retirement like a maturity funding contract.

## Keogh Plans

For many years there were restrictions on the participation of partners and proprietors in qualified retirement programs. Special plans called **Keogh** or **HR-10 plans** were used to cover partners or proprietors—that is, self-employed individuals. After 20 years of the campaign for parity between self-employed and corporate retirement plans, the Tax Equity and Fiscal Responsibility Act of 1982 (TEFRA) finally granted this parity to all new and old retirement plans established by self-employed businesses. With that parity came the ability of self-employed businesses to maintain the same types of defined-benefit and defined-contribution plans as were available previously only to corporations. Existing Keogh plans were amended to comply with the new law and became essentially regular pension and profit-sharing plans. In time, the need for the term *Keogh plan* will disappear.

## Individual Retirement Accounts

**Individual retirement accounts** were first created by ERISA to encourage retirement savings by persons who were not actually participating in qualified pension, profit-sharing, or Keogh plans. Under current law, anyone can set up an IRA, irrespective of whether he or she is covered by a qualified plan. IRA contributions, however, are deductible from current taxable income only if the person making them is not covered by a qualified plan. If the person is covered by a qualified plan, a portion of the contribution may be deductible, depending on the individual's earnings level and marital status. Investment earnings on all contributions (irrespective of whether they are deductible) accumulate tax free until distributed. The source of the funds contributed to an IRA does not determine eligibility or deductibility, so long as the contributing individual has includable compensation that is at least equal to the amount of the contribution (see below).

   *Types of IRAs.*   A **regular IRA** is one established by an individual to provide retirement income for himself or herself. For taxable years after December 31, 1981, any person could contribute 100 percent of annual *earned* income to a regular IRA up to a maximum contribution of $2,000 year. Since the primary purpose of IRAs is to provide income during retirement, there are significant penalties for withdrawal of funds prior to that time. The minimum age at which distribution can be made without penalties is 59 1/2. If death or disability occurs prior to that age, however, the IRA can be distributed to the survivors or individuals without any penalty for early withdrawal.

The Tax Reform Act of 1986 (TRA86) enlarged the scope of the IRA provisions by allowing working employees who are eligible for regular IRAs to establish **spousal IRAs** for their *nonworking spouses*.[25] If an individual establishes *both* a regular and a spousal IRA, the total *combined* contribution is limited to $2,250 per year. Although contributions can be apportioned between the regular and the spousal IRAs in any proportion desired, no more than $2,000 a year can be placed in any one account. TRA86 at the same time contracted the scope of the IRAs by restricting deductible contributions by employees covered under qualified plans and those whose income exceeds specified limits. If the adjusted gross income of an individual (or married couple if a joint return is filed) exceeds the $25,000 ($40,000) limit under the law, the $2,000 IRA limit is reduced in increments of $200 per $1,000 of additional adjusted gross income, becoming zero at $35,000 ($50,000). (See Figure 28-1.)

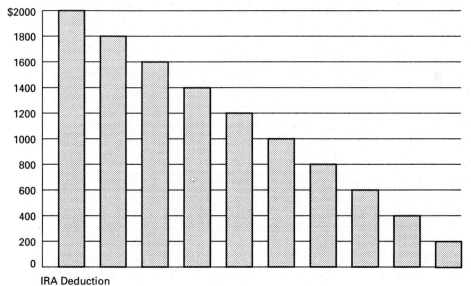

**SINGLE INCOME**
$25,000  26,000  27,000  28,000  29,000  30,000  31,000  32,000  33,000  34,000  35,000

**MARRIED INCOME**
$40,000  41,000  42,000  43,000  44,000  45,000  46,000  47,000  48,000  49,000  50,000

IRA Deduction

**FIGURE 28-1**

**HOW THE IRA DEDUCTION IS PHASED OUT WITH INCOME.**

[25]The maximum of $2,000 or 100 percent of annual earned income of the working spouse applies, as in the case of the regular IRA.

*IRA Funding Instruments.*    ERISA authorized three different funding instruments for IRAs: (1) individual retirement accounts, (2) individual retirement annuities, and (3) individual U.S. retirement bonds. The third type (the IRA bond) was based on a special issue of government savings bonds originally authorized but not offered since April 30, 1982. The bonds were discontinued, primarily due to a lack of interest on the part of investors.

Of the two presently available types of IRA funding instruments, individual retirement accounts are by far the most popular. At the present time, more than 90 percent of all IRAs are invested in some form of individual retirement account. This particular type of IRA takes one of three distinct forms. One form is a **bank trust** or **custodial account**, whereby contributions usually are invested in one or more of the bank's interest-bearing instruments or, in some cases, self-directed accounts. This form of IRA generally is offered by commercial banks, mutual savings banks, credit unions, and savings and loan associations. A second form also involves a trust or custodial account, whereby investments generally are made exclusively in **mutual fund** shares, usually within a specific family of funds. The third form is a trust arrangement offered by stockbrokers, called a **self-directed account**. Under this form of IRA, the owner is permitted to select and manage his or her own individual investments from the wide range of stocks, bonds, mutual funds, and direct participation programs that are available from the investment dealer. Mutual fund and broker accounts technically use a bank as a trustee, but the bank's role is purely technical and the investor views the fund or broker as the sponsor of the IRA.

The other type of authorized IRA is the **individual retirement annuity**. Individual retirement annuities generally are either fixed- or variable-annuity contracts that are issued by insurance companies. These contracts are flexible-premium deferred annuities. That means that a series of equal or differing contributions may be made periodically under the contract.

Since these insurance contracts are restricted and nontransferable to meet the necessary IRA requirements, no trustee or custodian is required. When the participant or beneficiary reaches retirement age, the contract may then be used to provide a regular income payment by one of several methods provided for in the terms of its settlement-option provisions. Because the laws governing IRAs specifically prohibit IRA investment in life insurance, such policies may not be used for any type of IRA.

*Rollover IRAs.*    Individuals wishing to change the funding instruments under which their IRAs are invested can do so by utilizing a **rollover IRA**. The annual contribution limits for regular and spousal IRAs do not apply to rollover IRAs, but to avoid taxation as a premature withdrawal, the rollover must be completed within 60 days of the withdrawal.

There is considerable interest in strengthening the role of some types of IRAs, in response to the desire to encourage long-term savings to meet the retirement and long-term-care needs of the aging U.S. population.

## SIMPLIFIED EMPLOYEE PENSION PLANS

For tax years beginning after 1978, an employer may establish a **simplified employee pension** (SEP). Frequently, these arrangements are referred to as SEP-IRAs because they use an IRA funding vehicle. Basically, a SEP is a written plan that requires the employer to make contributions, based on a formula contained in the plan, for all employees who have attained the age of 21 and who have performed service [and earned more than $374 (indexed as of 1992) in compensation] for the employer during at least three of the preceding five calendar years. Funds contributed to the SEP by the employer are allocated directly into IRAs maintained for each plan participant.

The amount of contribution that can be made for each employee covered by the plan may not exceed the lesser of 15 percent of the employee's covered compensation or $30,000, compared to a maximum of $2,000 with an IRA. In addition, the plan may be integrated with Social Security, although the method of integration is slightly different from a profit-sharing or money-purchase plan. SEPs were developed with the intention of simplifying the administration and reporting requirements for the employer. As a result, SEPs have been widely used by self-employed persons.

Typically, it is the employer who funds the SEP, but the Tax Reform Act of 1986 created the **salary reduction SEP**. If a salary reduction SEP is used, the maximum by which an employee can reduce his or her salary to fund the SEP is the lesser of 25 percent of compensation or $7,979 (as indexed). The SEP can be designed to use both employer contributions and salary reduction employee contributions.

## EMPLOYEES OF CHARXLE ORGANIZATIONS, EDUCATIONAL INSTITUTIONS, AND OTHER PUBLIC BODIES

Employees of a charitable organization (described in Section 501(c)(3) of the Internal Revenue Code) which is exempt from tax under Section 501(a), and employees of a public educational institution and certain other public bodies are entitled to special tax treatment on monies used by their employer to purchase an annuity for them. Federal tax law and regulations provide that such an employer may agree with the employee to have a portion of the money that would otherwise be part of his or her pay set aside by the employer in an annuity contract for him or her. These funds eventually will be subject to tax, but not until the money, with accumulated interest, is actually received, either as a cash withdrawal or as annuity payments. The funds are commonly called **403(b) annuities** (from the applicable section of the Internal Revenue Code), **tax-sheltered annuities** (TSAs), or **tax-deferred annuities** (TDAs).

The regulations governing the maximum amount of money that may be set aside each year on behalf of an employee are quite complex. In general, however, the maximum contribution payable on behalf of an employee is equal to 20 percent of his or her current year's total compensation (after salary reductions), times the total period of employment with his or her employer (expressed in years and fractions thereof), less the sum of prior contributions and certain other tax-deferred employer contributions on his or her behalf. The Tax Reform Act of 1986 imposed an overall contribution limit of $9,500. Tax-deferred annuities are also subject to nondiscrimination rules. Various types of insurance contracts (individual and group) are used as the funding vehicles for these annuities, which have proven to be a substantial source of business for many insurance companies.

Employees of other public bodies such as states, counties, or municipalities enjoy a similar device, referred to as a **section 457 deferred compensation arrangement**. Under this arrangement, the employer agrees with each employee to reduce his or her pay by a specified amount and to invest the deferrals in one or more investment outlets that may include insurance products. The amounts so deferred, plus investment earnings, will be distributed to the employee on death, retirement, or other termination of employment. The key difference between section 457 plans and 403(b) plans is that the investments in a section 457 plan are owned by the employer and the deferral limits are different. The employee looks to the public entity for satisfaction of his or her benefit claim, and not to the insurance company or other investment outlet. Deferred annuities, which may be fixed or variable, are popular in these deferred-compensation plans.

## EMPLOYEE SAVINGS PLANS

In recent years many employers have introduced one or more types of employee savings plans to supplement other existing retirement plans. A savings plan is a defined-contribution plan under which employees have separate accounts. Usually, qualified savings plans are designed as profit-sharing plans, because only a profit-sharing plan permits account withdrawals during employment, and this is an important feature of the plan if it is to be a flexible savings medium for employees. Thus in general, a savings plan can be viewed as a contributory profit-sharing plan. Thrift plans and 401(k) plans are two forms of such employee savings arrangements.

*Thrift Plans.* A **thrift plan** is designed to encourage employees to save from after-tax income. An employee, for example, might be permitted to contribute up to 10 percent of his or her salary to the plan. All investment earnings accumulate tax free until distribution, although the employee contribution itself is not tax deductible. Withdrawals from thrift plans are permitted under conditions specified in the plan by the employer. These amounts, however, may be subject to a 10 percent premature distribution tax. These conditions usually reflect the employer's view of the plan as a long-term savings program.

Most thrift plans provide for partial matching of employee contributions by employers. The employer usually contributes 50 cents for each dollar of employee contributions, although other matching arrangements are used. Most plans, however, will not provide for matching of contributions in excess of 6 percent of an employee's salary. Employees frequently are given some choice about how the funds in their thrift plan accounts are invested; usually they allocate their contributions among various types of investment funds (e.g., money market, corporate bonds, or stock). Many traditional thrift plans have been changed to 401(k) plans to permit employee pre-tax salary reductions (see below).

*401(k) Plans.*    Another employee savings plan, usually referred to as a **401(k) plan**, also allows for partial matching of employee contributions by employers. A major difference between the two plans, however, is that a 401(k) plan provides *current* as well as future tax savings for employees. Under a 401(k) plan, employees agree to defer a percentage of *pre-tax* income. The money arising from this decision reduces current (taxable) salary and is placed directly in the 401(k) plan by the employer. The 401(k) contribution is considered to have been made by the employer and is, therefore, generally not treated as part of an employee's taxable income for federal income tax purposes.[26]

The maximum reduction in salary permitted under 401(k) plans is indexed (and was $8,994 in 1993). All employee contributions are 100 percent vested, regardless of the vesting schedule applicable to any employer contributions. As in the case of a thrift plan, all investment income earned under a 401(k) plan accumulates tax free until it is distributed. Furthermore, upon distribution (which is as a lump sum), present law permits employees to use the five-year income averaging rule. The employee may decrease or even eliminate future contributions simply by changing his or her salary reduction agreement.

The 401(k) arrangement is a popular employee benefit. Employees gain tax and other advantages, and employers save on unemployment taxes and workers' compensation insurance premiums, because of the reduction in their employees' salaries. On the other hand, the IRS has established stricter rules for 401(k) plans; the nondiscrimination and the withdrawal provisions, in particular, are very stringent. No withdrawals from 401(k) plans are allowed before age 59 1/2, except for participants who die, become disabled, retire, change jobs, or suffer financial hardship. Withdrawals may also be permitted in the case of certain plan terminations and certain sales or disposition of corporate assets as stocks. Some 401(k) plans permit loans to employees, but with the passage of TEFRA in 1982, loans are limited to the lesser of $50,000 or 50 percent of the vested value of an employee's account.

## MULTINATIONAL POOLING OF EMPLOYEE BENEFITS[27]

Prior to 1960, multinational corporations had not clearly recognized the need to organize their international benefit plans on a coordinated basis. Today at least

[26]Although 401(k) contributions are not subject to federal income taxes, a few states and municipalities do tax them. Effective January 1, 1984, 401(k) contributions became subject to Social Security taxes.

[27]This section draws on M. Thakkar, *Multinational Pooling* (Zurich: Swiss Reinsurance Company, 1992).

11 active insurance networks compete in the field and new competitors are proposing to enter it. All of these major networks operate on a worldwide basis, providing insurance facilities in up to 140 countries. Each major network currently underwrites somewhere between 50 and 460 multinational contracts. The total number of multinationals using network facilities is, of course, smaller than the addition of these network contracts would suggest, since many multinationals use the facilities of more than one insurance network. According to some estimates, the total premium volume generated with these networks from multinational business is more than $2 billion. Over 20 consulting and brokerage firms are actively engaged in international benefits consulting. These figures not only indicate the volume of business being transacted on a multinational basis, but they also demonstrate the acceptance of the multinational pooling concept that has occurred since its introduction over 30 years ago. During this period, it has become an effective risk management tool not only in terms of cost savings but also as an efficient means of obtaining information on benefit plans in other countries.

The underlying concept of multinational pooling is simple. It involves the implementation of host country benefit plans of a multinational corporation, according to local laws and practices, with a superimposed umbrella contract that attempts to treat the different local units as if they were a single entity. Multinational pooling is thus a system under which insurance coverages in various countries are brought together into one pool. The purpose of establishing such an arrangement is to permit a reduction in the administration expenses and risk charges of insurers through experience-rating of the pool, whereby groups of employees in different countries are assessed as a single group in underwriting terms.

Experience-rating is an accounting system under which the costs ultimately charged to a group contractholder are determined largely by the group's own mortality and morbidity experience and not by the overall experience of the insurer's group portfolio, which would include a large number of other contractholders. Experience-rated group contracts have been common in North America for many years. For multinational pooling, this technique was applied to contracts issued by a network of insurers in different countries that were, however, linked in a common pool. This adaptation was necessary because, in many countries, local insurance companies are strictly regulated by supervisory authorities or by cartel arrangements that inhibit local experience-rating of group contracts. In addition, in countries with keen competition and where insurance companies are free to determine their own investment policies, premiums, reserve levels, and dividend formulas, local contracts are often issued on the basis of lowest possible premium rates without dividends or other experience participation.

Different networks have somewhat different requirements for installing standard pooling arrangements. In general, however, the minimum conditions may include:

1. Implementation of local group contracts in at least two countries
2. Minimum size of the pool in terms of a certain minimum number of lives (e.g., 100 or 300) or a certain minimum volume of annual premium (e.g., $ 20,000)

In recent years, under competitive pressures, networks have started offering what are known as small group pools in which their minimum conditions for standard pools are not met. A variation is a "time" pool in which, for groups smaller than the standard size, pooling is offered over an extended length of time, such as three or five years, instead of on an annual basis.

# Chapter 29

# LIFE INSURANCE COMPANY ORGANIZATION AND MANAGEMENT

Organizations that provide life and health insurance may be classified broadly as (1) commercial, (2) governmental, and (3) other. The characteristics of governmental, savings bank, fraternal and certain nonprofit organizations that provide death, accident, sickness, and retirement benefits have been presented throughout this text.[1]

The majority of the life and health insurance in force in the private sector of the U.S. economy has been issued by commercial life insurance companies, several aspects of which were discussed in Chapter 11. Just as the greatest portion of this volume has been concerned with the contracts, coverages, and practices of commercial life insurance companies, so this chapter is devoted primarily to a discussion of the organizational, financial, and management characteristics of this class of companies.

Commercial life insurance companies commonly are classified as stock or mutual companies. The distinguishing characteristic of a **stock life insurance company** is its stockholders. If a company has stockholders, it is a stock company. If the policyowners have ownership rights in the insurer, it is a **mutual life insurance company**, irrespective of the kinds of policies it issues.

At mid–year 1991, there were 2,127 U.S. commercial life insurers doing business; of these, 2,012 were stock and 115 were mutual companies.[2] Figure 29-1 shows that mutual insurers generally are larger than stock life insurers, with 43.8 percent of the assets of all U.S. life insurance companies and 39.4 percent of the life insurance in force.

---

[1]See Chap. 11 for a discussion of fraternals, savings banks, and various government plans as providers of life insurance; see Chap. 27 for a discussion of Blue Cross/Blue Shield and health maintenance organizations, and Chap. 25 for a discussion of government as a provider of social insurance benefits.

[2]Unless otherwise noted, all statistical aggregates used in this chapter are taken from *1992 Life Insurance Fact Book* (Washington, D.C.: American Council of Life Insurance, 1992).

**FIGURE 29-1**

**MUTUAL AND STOCK LIFE INSURERS RELATIVE SHARE OF ASSETS
AND LIFE INSURANCE IN FORCE**
*Source:* 1992 *Life Insurance Fact Book* (Washington, D.C.: American Council of Life Insurance, 1992),
pp. 107–108.

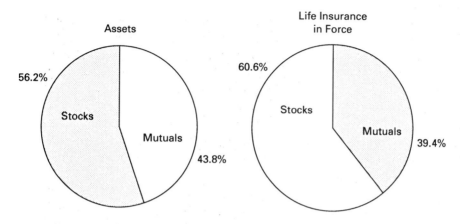

Until recently they were dominant with respect to life insurance in force, their share having declined from 62 percent in 1960. During this time period, the number of stock insurers increased from 1,273 in 1960 to 2,078 in 1991; this changed both the market shares of stock and mutual insurers, but, perhaps more importantly, it changed the life insurance industry's ability to respond to the deregulation of the financial services marketplace.

As discussed below, stock insurers have greater access to the capital markets and more corporate structural flexibility than do mutuals. Faced with increased competition from outside the insurance industry, stock insurers consider themselves to be better positioned to respond to changes in the marketplace. Mutual companies are a form of consumer cooperative in which consumers, rather than investors, own or control the organization. In important respects the structure and behavior of mutuals are closer to those of nonprofit firms than to those that characterize other consumer cooperatives. For example, the board of directors of a mutual is essentially self-appointing, the policyowners have no effective right to distribute to themselves the accumulated surplus of the company and mutual insurers. Like many nonprofit educational and religious organizations, mutual insurers accumulate large surpluses with which they can somewhat insulate themselves from market pressures. In few other industries do consumer cooperatives account for such a large share of the market.

No well accepted theory explains the prominent role of the mutual form in the life insurance industry. In a recent effort to do so, one author suggested that firms are organized as consumer cooperatives only when two broad conditions are satisfied: (1) there is market failure of a relatively severe nature in the firm's product market, and (2) consumers are able to assume effective control without incurring excessive costs. After analyzing the development of mutuals and stock insurers, and noting the rise of mutuals after a period of consumer abuse,[3] he concluded that "mutual companies seem to have been important historically, not in protecting consumers from simple price exploitation, but rather in avoiding opportunistic behavior on the part of sellers in a situation in which adequate contractual safeguards could not be established."[4] In fact, organizational form has become an important issue, with considerable interest and discussion surrounding the question of demutualization (see below).

## LIFE INSURANCE COMPANY FORMATION

Although it is theoretically possible for the life insurance business to be undertaken by an individual or by a partnership, the form of organization should be one that provides both permanence and a high degree of security of payment. A corporation has the inherent characteristics for meeting these requirements, and, under the various state insurance laws, it is the only form of business organization permitted to undertake a life insurance business.

Thus from a practical and legal viewpoint, the operation of a life insurance business in the United States requires the formation of a corporation. Both stock and mutual insurers are organized as corporations.

## STOCK LIFE INSURERS

A stock life insurance company is one that is organized for the purpose of making profits for its stockholders. Traditionally, stock insurers have issued **guaranteed-cost, nonparticipating policies**, in which the policyowners shared neither in any savings or profits nor in any losses that might arise in the operation of the business. Every policy element was fixed at issue. Stock insurers sometimes issued **participating** policies, on which dividends could be paid to policyowners. When stock companies issue participating policies, some states impose limitations on the extent to which the stockholders of the company may benefit from the participating business.[5] The majority of states, however, impose no special regulation upon the participating insurance sold by stock insurers.

With the introduction of the various forms of **current assumption, nonparticipating policies**, the distinction between stock and mutual companies on the basis of participation has become less relevant. Virtually all individual

---

[3]See the discussion of The Armstrong Investigation in Chap. 3.

[4]See Henry Hansmann, "The Organization of Insurance Companies: Mutual versus Stock," *Journal of Law, Economics, and Organization* 1:1 (1985), pp. 125-153.

[5]For example, the state of New York provides that profits on participating policies and contracts be limited to the larger of (1) 10 percent of gains on such policies or (2) 50 cents per year per $1,000 of participating business. See §216, *New York Insurance Law*. Similar limitations exist in Canada, the United Kingdom, and other countries.

cash-value policies sold today "participate" in insurers' operational performance in one way or another. Corporate coverage product lines (e.g., group insurance and pensions) of stock companies also have been indistinguishable from those of mutual companies for some time.

The life insurance business is highly specialized and is subject in every state to special insurance laws. As in other respects, the formation of a life insurance corporation is regulated by these insurance laws. Under the state insurance laws, a company must have a minimum amount of capital and surplus before it can secure a license to operate as a life insurance company. For instance, under New York state law, a stock life insurance company must have a minimum of $2 million capital and a paid-in initial surplus that is at least equal to the greater of $4 million or 200 percent of its capital. Every such company must at all times maintain a minimum capital of $2 million. These minimum capital requirements are intended to ensure that the new insurer can make the deposits required to become licensed,[6] has sufficient funds for normal operations, and has a contingency fund to meet any adverse fluctuations in experience that occur during the initial development period.[7] Once the stock has been subscribed and the various state requirements met, the insurer can be organized by the stockholders and begin business.

## MUTUAL LIFE INSURERS

A mutual life insurance company also is a corporation, but it has no capital stock and no stockholders. The policyowner in a mutual company is both a customer *and*, in a sense, an owner of the insurer, in contrast to the policyowner in a stock company, who is a customer only. The policyowner in a mutual insurer is a member of the insurer and has the right to vote in the election of the board of directors or trustees.

Technically, the assets and income of a mutual insurer are owned by the company. The policyowners usually are considered to be contractual creditors, with the right to vote for directors as provided for by law. The insurer is administered, and its assets are held, for the benefit and protection of the policyowners and beneficiaries either as reserves, surplus, or contingency funds, or they are distributed to them as dividends to the extent that the board of directors (trustees) deems such action warranted as a result of the insurer's experience. Thus in a mutual insurer, the policyowner pays a typically fixed premium stated in his or her policy (usually higher than the premium for a similar guaranteed cost contract of a stock insurer), but the actual or net cost to the policyowner will depend on the dividends or other credits allocated to his or

---

[6]See Chap. 34.

[7]The National Association of Insurance Commissioners has developed a risk-based capital formula for measuring the capital adequacy of life insurance companies. This formula applies to insurer annual statements filed for 1993. (See Chaps. 32 and 34).

her policy each year by the board of directors. The fixed premium stated in the contract is the initial outlay and represents the maximum, but the final actual net outlay is less by the amount of dividends paid or interest credited on the contract.

Normally, mutual insurers issue only *participating* policies. Sometimes, they also issue nonparticipating policies, but these policyowners, as with policyowners of stock companies, are simply customers of the mutual company. As suggested earlier, the traditional emphasis on participation versus nonparticipation as a characteristic distinguishing a mutual from a stock insurer is no longer valid.

The organization of a new mutual insurer presents some serious practical problems. As in the case of a stock company, funds are needed to cover the expenses of operation, make the required deposits with the state insurance department, and provide a surplus or contingency fund to meet any unusual fluctuations in experience before the insurer has had time to accumulate these funds from its operations.

In the case of a stock insurer, funds for all these purposes are obtained from the sale of stock, but in a mutual insurer, the only sources of funds at the beginning are the first premiums paid in by the original member policyowners or funds borrowed to establish the insurer. The lack of profit incentive is undoubtedly a significant factor in explaining why relatively few mutual insurers are formed, but, in addition, the statutory requirements for the formation of a new mutual life insurance company are exceedingly stringent. For instance, the state of New York does not permit a mutual company to begin operation as a going concern unless it has applications for not less than $1,000 each from 1,000 persons, with the full amount of one annual premium for an aggregate amount of $25,000, plus an initial surplus of $150,000 in cash. It should be apparent that there would be great difficulty in finding a large number of individuals who are insurable and who are willing to apply for insurance in, and to pay the first premium to, an insurer that is not yet in existence and not yet able to issue policies.

These difficulties of organization of a new mutual life insurance company are so great that none has been organized in the United States for many years, and no new mutual insurer is likely to be formed. The only practical way of organizing a new life insurance company in the United States is on a stock basis. After it has been fully established and has attained adequate financial stability, a stock insurer can be converted into a mutual company.[8]

## LIFE INSURER ESTABLISHMENT

In general, the procedures for organizing insurance companies in the several states are similar, and the pattern prescribed by the law of New York is

[8]Many of the large mutual companies in existence today (e.g., Metropolitan and Prudential) were, in fact, originally stock companies that were mutualized. At one time, some states provided for a guaranty capital put up temporarily by the persons interested in forming a mutual insurer. This guaranty capital was to be retired as soon as the mutual insurer's operations stabilized financially. Sometimes the stock remained outstanding for some period while the company operated on the mutual idea.

representative of the general procedure. In that state, the incorporators (at least 13 persons) first apply to the state for a charter that sets forth the name of the insurer, its location, the type of business to be transacted, its powers and how they will be exercised, the method of internal control, the amount of capital (if a stock company), and any other essential particulars. In addition to advertising in a prescribed manner their plan to incorporate themselves as an insurance company, the organizers file a "certificate of intention" and a copy of the charter with the superintendent of insurance before they become a corporation. They then receive subscriptions to the capital if the insurer is to be a stock company, or they receive applications for insurance and the premiums therefor if the insurer is to be a mutual. They may still not issue policies. When the legal minimum capital has been subscribed, or when the premiums on the necessary minimum amount of insurance (in the case of a mutual insurer) have been paid in, and when the statutory deposit has been made with the superintendent, the organization may be completed.

At this point, the subscribing stockholders or initial applicants for insurance elect the directors, who in turn authorize the issuance of the stock or the policies, as the case may be. At this organizational meeting, the owners adopt bylaws covering such matters as the duties of officers and committees, regulations on investments, maximum amount of insurance to be written on a single life, the territory in which business is to be transacted, and so on. The newly elected directors then meet to elect officers and set up committees of the board to take charge of particular departments of the general administration of the insurer, delegating powers appropriately. At this point—assuming that the company's application for a license to do business in the state has been approved by the state insurance department—staff, supplies, and equipment may be secured and business formally begun.

## CONVERSION FROM ONE TYPE OF INSURER TO ANOTHER

### MUTUALIZATION OF STOCK INSURERS

Some stock insurers have been converted from stock form into mutual form through a procedure that is called mutualization.[9] In essence, **mutualization** involves the retirement of the outstanding capital stock of the insurer, coupled with the transfer of control of the insurer from the stockholders to the policyowners. The motivations for such a move vary widely, including, for example, a desire to prevent control of the company from falling into undesirable hands through a change in stock ownership.

The officers of the insurer usually initiate mutualization proceedings by submitting a proposal to the board of directors. The key factor is, of course, the price to be paid for each share of stock and the manner of payment. The price must

[9]In the past 25 years, 16 insurers have converted from the status of a mutual company to a stock company and two stock companies have converted to mutuals (see *1992 Life Insurance Fact Book*, p. 108).

be attractive enough from the viewpoint of the stockholders to induce them to relinquish their rights of ownership and control. On the other hand, from an insurer's viewpoint, the price must be limited practically by the fact that the remaining surplus, after mutualization, must be adequate to permit sound operation. Sometimes, it is quite important that the payment for the shares be spread over a long period of time so as not to impose an undue burden on current surplus.

If the plan (including the price to be offered to the stockholders) is approved by the board of directors, it must be submitted to the state insurance department for the approval of the commissioner of insurance. Assuming that the proposed plan is approved, it will then be submitted to the policyowners and stockholders in accordance with the requirements of the applicable state insurance law.

In executing a mutualization plan approved by the necessary majorities, the company takes up the stock to the extent that is is feasible to do so. Some of the stockholders may object to the plan for one reason or another, and the process of taking up stock usually will require some time. As the stock is bought up, it is not canceled but rather transferred to trustees for the policyowners, who vote the stock in their behalf. Normally, a substantial majority of the total stock can be purchased immediately, so that effective ownership and control are obtained by the policyowners. Ultimately, when all the shares of stock have been purchased, the stock may be canceled and the insurer becomes fully mutualized.[10]

## CONVERSION OF A MUTUAL COMPANY TO A STOCK COMPANY[11]

In the past 25 years, 16 companies have converted from the status of a mutual company to a stock company through a process known as **demutualization**. Most demutualizations had been of smaller insurers, until, in the mid-1980s, a large U.S. life insurer announced its decision to demutualize.[12]

Most of the larger mutual life insurance companies indicate a lack of interest in demutualization. In 1987, the Society of Actuaries published a report on demutualization in which a task force of the Society presented the results of a three-year study of the actuarial and other issues involved in a mutual life insurer demutualization. The work of the task force concentrated on three principal aspects of a mutual life insurer demutualization: (1) maintenance of reasonable policyowner dividend expectations, (2) the aggregate amount of compensation to policyowners in exchange for their membership rights, and (3) the allocation of this aggregate amount of compensation among participating policyowners.[13]

Following this report, legislation was adopted in New York in 1988 to allow a mutual insurer to convert to a stock company. Since then additional states have

[10]For a study of mutualizations, see Linda Pickthorne Fletcher, "Mutualization of Stock Life Insurance Companies" (Ph.D. dissertation, University of Pennsylvania, 1964).

[11]This discussion draws on Harry D. Garber, "Demutualization: Wave of the Future or a Passing Fad?" *The Journal of the American Society of CLU & ChFC*, Vol. 40 (March 1986).

[12]See "Union Mutual Takes the Plunge," *Best's Review*, Life/Health ed., Vol. 89 (Jan. 1985), p. 30.

[13]*Report of the Task Force on Mutual Life Insurance Company Conversion* (Itasca, Ill.: July 1987).

adopted permissive legislation. In 1988 the Maccabees Mutual Life Insurance Company converted to stock form pursuant to the Michigan statute. Union Mutual successfully completed its demutualization and legally became a stock company in 1989, as did the Equitable Life Assurance Society in 1992.[14] In 1991 a Massachusetts statute was signed into effect providing for conversions of mutual companies into stock form. Although no Massachusetts domiciled life insurance company has publicly indicated an interest in demutualizing, the legislation is of particular interest given the number of mutual companies domiciled in Massachusetts. As deregulation of the financial services business continues, this question most likely will continue to be a critical part of the long-term corporate strategy for many mutual life insurance companies.

In a conversion action, the mutual life insurance company literally is transformed into a shareholder-owned enterprise through a process in which policyowner membership rights are exchanged for valuable consideration (i.e., cash, additional benefits, or, possibly, common stock in the resulting stock company). If the company wishes to raise new equity capital (which is one of the principal reasons for a conversion action), that step may be taken at the time of conversion or at some later date. If new capital is raised on the conversion date, ownership of the insurer will be shared between the former policyowner-members and the new shareholders. If no new capital is raised, the former policyowner-members initially will own all of the shares of the company.

In some cases, the conversion action may be taken so that the converted mutual insurer might be acquired by another company. In this case, the consideration to policyowner-members usually will be in the form of cash or additional benefits.

The converting mutual company may wish to go through a restructuring in which an upstream holding company (see below) is created. The parent holding company would own all of the shares of the converted insurance company, the policyowner-members would receive shares of the holding company, and the shares sold to the public also would be shares of the holding company.

The demutualization process involves three distinct approval phases. The first is the decision by the insurer's board of directors (trustees) that a conversion is important to the company's future progress, and that the conversion plan is in the interest of policyowners. Although state legal requirements vary, the board's action usually requires approval of a super-majority of the directors.

The second approval required usually is that of the insurance commissioner of the insurer's domiciliary state. The purpose is to assure that the proposed conversion plan meets the various requirements of state law, including, but not limited to, the provision for future policyowner dividends, the fairness of the total amount of the consideration to policyowners in exchange for their membership

---

[14]The Equitable, in completing its demutualization process, raised $450 million in its initial public offering. A French insurer, AXA-Midi, also invested $1 billion in the Equitable in exchange for notes, which were subsequently converted into stock, giving the French insurer 49 percent ownership.

rights, the allocation of that amount among policyowners, the fairness of the amounts paid by non-policyowner shareholders (particularly in the case of a proposed acquisition of the insurer by another entity), and limitations on acquisitions of stock by officers and directors. The insurance department most likely will employ actuarial, legal, investment banking, and accounting consultants to review the conversion plan and to advise the commissioner. Almost always there will be a public hearing to permit interested parties to present concurring and opposing views with respect to the proposed plan. After the hearing, the commissioner will either approve the conversion plan as submitted, approve the plan with amendments, or reject the plan. Approval or, at least, a "nonobjection" basis by insurance regulatory authorities in other states in which the insurer is licensed also may be required.

Once the insurer and the insurance commissioner have agreed on a conversion plan, it is submitted to policyowners for their approval. The degree of support required depends on state law, but a typical requirement is that two-thirds of those voting must approve the conversion plan. Before voting, all policyowners receive a comprehensive set of materials describing the conversion plan and presenting the specific dollar amount of consideration, or the number of shares (or the basis on which this number would be determined) that the policyowner will receive in exchange for the surrender of his or her membership rights. If a favorable vote is received, the mutual life insurance company can then proceed with the conversion action.

A key and complex question concerning demutualization action is how it will affect the insurance coverages of persons with participating policies. The conversion action should not have a materially adverse impact on the insurer's ability either to meet the policy guarantees or to pay policyowner dividends on a scale that is comparable to the dividends that would have been paid in the absence of demutualization.

The primary reason a mutual life insurance company would consider demutualization is to obtain access to equity capital and related financing alternatives (convertible debentures, warrants, preferred stock). This reason is becoming increasingly important. As the integration of the financial services industry accelerates, the requirements for capital growth and capital investments multiply. Besides there being a possible desire to enhance the firm's margin of solvency through an influx of new capital, there is also the need to make major capital investments in (1) computer systems, equipment, and facilities, (2) the growth of sales and distribution capabilities, and (3) acquisitions that broaden product offerings, increase scale, bring access to new customers and new markets, and so on.[15] Without such investments, some mutual insurers would find

---

[15] As in any industry, economic theory suggests that the magnitude of cost economies varies with the scale and mix of outputs. A recent study using a multiproduct cost function showed increasing overall scale economies for all but the largest agency companies, which displayed approximately constant returns to scale. See Martin F. Grace and Stephen G. Timme, "An Examination of Cost Economies in the United States Life Insurance Industry," *The Journal of Risk and Insurance*, Vol. 59 (Mar. 1992).

that they are unable to keep pace and would suffer an inevitable decline in competitive position and vitality, to the detriment of the policyowner-members.

For mutual and stock life insurance companies, the main source of equity capital has been and will continue to be retained earnings from their insurance operations. To the extent that retained earnings cannot provide all of the capital required (and today's competitive markets place limits on the amount of retained earnings available from existing business), insurers must access the capital markets for new equity or debt funds. Stock companies have available the full range of public market financing options. Mutual companies today can obtain capital funds through debt but have very limited access to equity capital. For some mutual insurers, this limited access may not be sufficient.

A second interest in demutualization could stem from the enhanced corporate structure flexibility it would permit. A basic structural advantage of the stock life insurance company form is that it permits formation of an upstream holding company (see below). Through this mechanism the company can (1) limit the impact of insurance regulatory controls and restrictions on noninsurance operations and (2) permit acquisitions of insurance companies to be made without diminution of statutory surplus.

The latter benefit, which may be particularly important in the present industry consolidation phase, requires a brief explanation. If a life insurance company acquires another insurance company, the excess of the purchase price over the acquired company's statutory surplus must be charged immediately to the statutory surplus of the acquiring company. If the acquisition is made by an upstream holding corporation, however, there is no charge to the statutory capital of either insurance company. Since the market values of most stock life insurance companies are well in excess of their respective statutory book values, this requirement places severe limitations on the ability of mutual life insurance companies to make necessary acquisitions of stock insurance companies (both of the life as well as the property and liability type).

These are the two key reasons for a mutual company to consider demutualization. There are three other oft-mentioned reasons, which for most insurers will be less important. First, stock companies report their financial results on a generally accepted accounting principles (GAAP) basis. Converting mutual companies would be able to use a comparable financial reporting basis— one that may conform much more closely to their internal management reporting basis. Second, the present federal income tax law for life insurance companies includes for mutual companies an "add-on" tax element that can constitute a major share of the company's total tax. Although the federal tax savings from conversion could be significant, the converted insurer most likely will have to pay cash dividends to shareholders that could consume all or a major part of these tax savings. Finally, availability of common stock increases compensation flexibility and permits acquisitions to be done for stock (and without tax consequences to the seller).

As the inexorable consolidation of the financial services industry proceeds, mutual life insurance companies will be subject to increasing competitive pressure. In anticipation of times of even greater competition, mutual companies naturally focus on the legal or structural matters that might offer significant advantages to their nonmutual competitors; prominent among these advantages is the ability to raise equity capital and to form an upstream noninsurance holding company on equal terms in the future with shareholder-owned companies. These advantages underlie the active interest of some mutual life companies in having demutualization legislation enacted. Most insurers are not sure that they will ever seek to convert to stock company status, but they want to have the option available if, and when, it is needed.

Having legislation on the books is one thing; deciding to demutualize is quite another. The determination as to whether an insurer should seek to convert will be an individual insurer decision based on the insurer's position in the market, its business goals, its capital position and needs, and the likelihood and ability to achieve these goals without undertaking the wrenching course of demutualization. The analysis work required for such a decision is burdensome and ordinarily will not be undertaken unless it is believed to be necessary.

As competition has tightened in the financial services marketplace, margins have declined, and demand for capital has increased, more mutual life insurance companies will be required to consider seriously whether conversion represents a necessary strategic action.[16] The globalization of financial services and investment also will be a significant consideration.

## HOLDING COMPANIES

In recent years, the use of holding companies has been the central theme of the intercorporate reorganizations that have occurred in managements' attempts to help their organizations improve their earnings and long-term growth possibilities through diversification. The deregulation of the financial services area has enhanced this development. For the most part, the holding companies are financial corporations that own or control one or more insurers, mutual-fund broker-dealer organizations, mutual-fund investment companies, consumer finance companies, and other financially related corporations. Some stock life insurance companies are owned or controlled by nonfinancial holding companies and conglomerates that group together in unrelated fields. Figure 29-2 illustrates three approaches to holding company structures.

The relationship of mutual insurance companies to the holding-company device is different from that of the stock insurance company. A holding company formed by one or more stock companies is commonly called an **upstream**

---

[16]See "Thin Cushions," *Forbes* (Sep. 19, 1989), p. 40.

**FIGURE 29-2**

**HOLDING COMPANY STRUCTURES**

Vertical Holding Company Structure

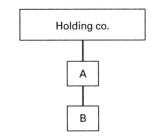

Horizontal Holding Company Structure

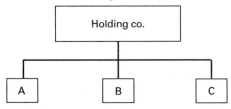

Combination Holding Company Structure

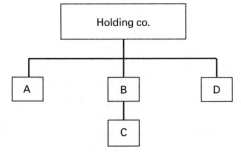

**holding company**. The holding company sits at the top of the intercorporate structure. It is owned by the stockholders, and, in turn, it owns subsidiaries. A **downstream holding company** is usually formed by a mutual insurance company. It sits in the middle of the intercorporate structure. It is owned wholly or in part by the mutual that sits at the top, and it owns subsidiaries. Figure 29-3 illustrates these two holding companies' structures.

The significance of the distinction is that the downstream holding company presents few regulatory problems to state insurance departments, because the parent mutual is directly subject to insurance regulation. As a consequence, a downstream holding company is a viable device only if the parent mutual has a strong surplus position, and, under present laws, it does not have the flexibility available to an upstream holding company.

**FIGURE 29-3**

**UPSTREAM VERSUS DOWNSTREAM HOLDING COMPANY**

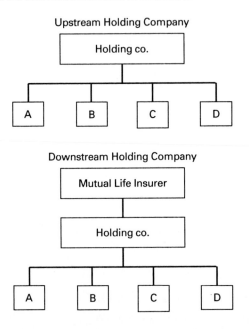

The large mutual life insurance company with a significant surplus position is capable of diversification through acquisition or otherwise by simple management decision, provided that the activity is permitted by the state insurance department. In 1969 the state of New York enacted legislation that relaxed restraints regulating insurance-related holding companies.[17]

These changes related to the formation and acquisition of subsidiaries, disclosure of intercorporate relationships among parents and subsidiaries and their affiliates to the superintendent of insurance, the liberalization of investment regulations, and greater freedom in raising capital through the sale of senior securities and securities convertible into equities. The greater flexibility provided by this legislation minimized the need, at that time, for large mutual insurers to create holding companies. As discussed earlier, competition within and deregulation of the financial services marketplace, however, has raised concerns over the ability of most mutual insurers to compete effectively in the new environment in which access to equity capital and related financing alternatives is becoming increasingly important. Since mutual life insurance companies have no stock outstanding to exchange for stock in a holding company or for a holding company or conglomerate to acquire, the problems of upstream diversification and control of mutual insurers by holding companies cannot occur. In addition,

[17]See New York Insurance Law, Chap. 190, §6.

although mutual life insurance companies can engage in downstream diversification (by organizing a holding company), restrictive insurance laws in many states make this impractical.[18] In face of the greatly increased competition both within and from outside the traditional life insurance business, this situation has created interest in demutualization.

## CORPORATE GOVERNANCE

The U.S. Securities and Exchange Commission (SEC) has a major influence on corporate governance of U.S. companies, including insurers. Corporate governance is regulated primarily through the SEC's proxy rules. These rules require disclosure to shareholders concerning the structure, composition, and function of corporate boards of directors and their committees. In particular, companies are required to disclose sufficient details concerning director and nominee relationships with the company and its customers and suppliers to enable shareholders to meaningfully assess director independence. Disclosure is required concerning (1) standing audit, compensation, and nominating committees; (2) director attendance at meetings; (3) director resignations; (4) shareholder proposals; and (5) settlement of election contests. The purpose of these rules is to make appropriate information available to shareholders, enabling them to assess the performance of their directors, and to facilitate informed voting. The SEC has recently expanded and improved the disclosure of senior management compensation.

While the actions of the SEC directly affect only stock life insurance companies that file reports with the SEC and the mutual companies that market equity products through registered separate accounts, other initiatives in the corporate governance arena have been directed specifically at mutual life insurance companies. A number of difficult, sensitive issues concerning mutual companies have surfaced at hearings, including, for example, whether policyowners have proprietary interests in the company and whether disclosure should be required of dividend distribution policies.

## HOME OFFICE ORGANIZATION AND ADMINISTRATION

### ORGANIZATION

Fundamentally, the organization of a life insurance company home office follows the pattern of other corporations that are concerned with the collection, investment, and disbursement of funds. Organization in general has three main elements: (1) levels of authority, (2) departmentalization, and (3)

---

[18]With downstream diversification, the parent company (whether it is a mutual or stock company) would be subject to direct control by insurance regulatory authorities.

functionalization. Each of these elements plays an important role in establishing an efficient organizational structure and in ensuring efficient coordination of effort within that structure.

The organization of a life insurance company is no different in its possession of these elements. In terms of total organizational structure, life insurance companies are most frequently line-staff-functional organizations. Individual segments of a life insurance company, however, may be organized on a line basis, with all operations placed directly under the control of the manager. The agency department, on the other hand, normally is organized on a line and staff basis, whereby the agency vice president is supported by line assistants (e.g., directors of agencies) and also staff assistants (e.g., directors of research and training).

Insurers differ widely by size, objectives, fields of operation, and other factors. Their actual organizational patterns also differ, since many insurers' organizational patterns have developed as a matter of evolution. Subject to this limitation, it is the purpose of this section to outline the more important official positions, committees, and departments of the average well-established life insurance company, and to describe briefly their respective functions and duties.

*Levels of Authority.*     As illustrated in Figure 29-4, there usually are four levels of authority in a life insurance organization. The board of directors and its various committees are, of course, the top or directorial level of authority. The president and senior officers of the company are found at the executive level. In addition to serving as part of the executive management team, the senior executive officers are given authority and responsibility for particular functions. Each of the vice presidents has subordinates at the managerial level who are responsible for the day-to-day functions of their departments. These subordinate managers, who may serve in line, staff, or functional relationships, make decisions on all matters within the limits of authority delegated to them. Finally, the supervisors in charge of subdivisions of the departments are found at the supervisory level of authority.

*The Board of Directors.*     The board of directors and the several committees of the board constitute the top level of authority in a life insurance company. In a mutual company, the directors typically are elected by the policyowners from among their own number, whereas in a stock company, they are elected by the shareholders. Whatever the method of election, the board possesses complete supervisory powers over those who manage the insurer. It is empowered not only to select the president and other principal officers, but to delegate to them such powers as it sees fit. It also meets at stated intervals to approve or disapprove the recommendations of officials and the findings of committees, and to consider and pass judgment upon all important matters concerning the general business conduct of the insurer. Since the transactions of a life insurance company assume a great variety of forms, it usually is considered desirable that the board be composed of individuals who possess varying, wide experience.

**FIGURE 29-4**

**LEVELS OF AUTHORITY**

DIRECTORIAL

EXECUTIVE

MANAGERIAL

SUPERVISORY

To expedite the proper fulfillment of its functions and to bring its members into close touch with the business affairs of the insurer, the board divides itself into a number of standing committees. In many companies, the president and other officers are members of the board of directors and hence are entitled to membership on important committees. If the executive officers are not directors, they are invited to various meetings in an advisory capacity. These committees vary in the different insurers, but usually they include an executive or insurance committee, a finance committee, a claims committee, and an audit committee. The executive committee, consisting of the president and certain members of the board, considers such matters as bear a vital relation to the general business policy of the insurer. For example, the committee determines the kinds of insurance contracts the company will sell, the provisions of the contracts, the premium rates, the territory in which the company will operate, and so on.

The finance committee—consisting of the president, the chief investment officer, the treasurer of the company and a certain number of the directors—exercises supervisory control over the company's investment policy and practices. In larger companies, it is quite common to have a separate committee to deal with real estate and mortgage loans. The claims committee has general control over the payment of claims, and, in particular, it determines policy in regard to doubtful or contestable claims. The audit committee, usually made up of nonemployee directors, maintains general supervision over the company's accounting system and records. Its objective is to give additional assurance regarding the integrity of (a) financial information used by the board in making decisions and (b) financial information distributed to outsiders. In the case of stock companies, it has become a widespread practice also to establish a compensation committee of nonemployee directors, to oversee the insurer's compensation policies and to approve specifically the compensation of senior management.

In general, the officers of the company who carry on its active management initiate action, the function of the directors being to approve or disapprove the recommendations made. For the most part, directors' committees are guided by the recommendations of the officers of the insurer who are directly concerned.

This is particularly true in the case of committees that deal with technical details of the business.

*Executive Officers.*    The executive officers are responsible for carrying out the policies determined by the board of directors and for the general management of the business. These officers usually include the chief executive officer (CEO) and the president (these can be the same individual); one or more vice presidents, each of whom has charge of a department; and the treasurer. The CEO usually is entrusted by the board of directors with broad executive powers, and ideally should be well versed in financial matters and have broad life insurance experience, so as to interpret properly the results attained in the respective departments of the company, advise the board of directors in supervising the general business conduct of the company, determine the best policy for it to pursue, and direct the work of the subordinate officials. He or she also is entrusted with the duty of selecting subordinate officials and department heads. The several vice presidents, each of whom usually has charge of a department of the insurer, also must keep up with the general business operations of the company, so as to be in a position to assist the president in his or her duties, assume the president's responsibilities (or those of a ranking vice president) during his or her absence, and be prepared to assume the office in the event of promotion.

*Departmentalization.*    The operations of life insurance companies involve three basic functions: to sell, to service, and to invest. For an insurer to carry out these functions properly, it must have high-quality professional actuarial, legal, underwriting, and accounting advice. Consequently, most insurers operate within seven major functional areas:  actuarial, marketing, accounting and auditing, investments, law, underwriting, and administration.

Departmentalization simply means the division of work to be performed into logical sections or assignments. Business organizations normally are departmentalized on either a functional, a geographical, or a product basis. Examples of all three types of departmentalization are found in many life insurance companies. Thus the actuarial department is established on the basis of function, a southern department follows from a geographical viewpoint, and the ordinary or group departments are established on the basis of product. In any case, a given insurer usually will follow a single pattern. The following discussion of functional departmentalization illustrates the internal organization and activities of a life insurance company.

The **actuarial department** establishes the insurer's premium rates, establishes reserve liabilities and nonforfeiture values, and generally handles all the mathematical operations of the insurer. This department also is responsible for analyzing earnings and furnishing the data from which annual dividend scales and excess interest and other credits are established. The actuarial staff, with assistance from the legal department, designs new policies and forms and is responsible for filing them with the various state insurance departments. The department also makes mortality and morbidity studies and often supervises the underwriting practices. It works closely with the marketing department in considering policy design and other factors that affect the competitive position of the insurer's agency force. Finally, because of the importance of the technical actuarial element in group insurance and group annuities, this department frequently handles the administration of this business or exercises a considerable degree of functional responsibility over it. The role of the actuary is vital to the operation of a life insurance company. In many smaller companies, the actuary in effect serves as executive vice president and exercises considerable influence over all areas of operations.

The **marketing department** is responsible for the sale of new business, the conservation of existing business, and certain types of service to policyowners. This department supervises the activities of the company's agents and also is responsible for advertising; sales promotion; market analysis; recruiting, selection, and training of agents; and controlling agency costs. (See Chapter 33.)

The **accounting and auditing department**, under the direction of the vice president and comptroller, is responsible for establishing and supervising the insurer's accounting and control procedures. Auditing, at both the agent and home office levels, is done by an independent unit of this department, which usually has direct access to the audit committee of the board. The actual preparation of the annual statement is handled here, although the actuarial department exercises considerable functional control in this regard. The accounting department is, of course, responsible for matters concerning federal, state, and local tax laws and regulations. Also, it is responsible for expense analysis and other operational statistics that are not handled by the actuarial department.

The **investment department**, usually under the direction of an investment vice president, handles the company's investment program under policies laid down by the board of directors. Besides passing on the merits of the company's investments preparatory to presenting them to the finance committee for final approval, the department usually is the custodian of the insurer's bonds, stocks, and other investments, and is entrusted with the duty of collecting the interest and dividends earned on them. To invest the company's money in securities that are safe and yet will yield a higher return than the rate assumed for premium and reserve computation requires skill and a wide knowledge of the various classes of investments in which life insurance companies are permitted to invest their funds. The volatile interest rates experienced in recent years, coupled with innovative new products and increased competition, have enhanced the importance of highly competent investment management. (See Chapters 30 to 32.)

The **legal department** is charged with the responsibility of handling all the company's legal matters. These include, among other things, the conduct of court cases growing out of contested claims, foreclosure proceedings, and imperfect titles; ensuring the sufficiency and correctness of policy forms, agency contracts, bonds, and notes; the inspection of titles to property purchased by the company or upon which the company has granted loans; and the analysis and interpretation for the benefit of the company of the statutory and court law governing life insurance in the jurisdictions where the company operates.

The **underwriting department** is responsible for establishing standards of selection and for passing judgment on applicants for insurance. (See Chapters 23 and 24.) In some insurers, the **medical department** is given a separate status. The medical director supervises the company's medical examiners and may be the final authority to pass upon the insurability and classification of applicants. In some instances, however, general underwriting control may rest in the hands of a vice president who is not a physician. The department makes use of many underwriting specialists who are not physicians. Many underwriting decisions do not depend upon a physician's opinion, since insurability connotes more than good health.

The **administration department** is responsible for providing home office service to the company's agents and policyowners. (See below.) This usually includes the issuance of new policies, premium and commission accounting, claims, loans, surrenders, policy changes, and other similar transactions. This department also is responsible for human resources, home office planning, and other staff functions. The secretary of the company has charge of the insurer's correspondence, the minutes of the board of directors and its various committees, and the company's records.

Many companies also departmentalize on the basis of product—that is they have separate departments for ordinary, health, and group insurance, depending upon the lines they write.

In addition to committees of the board of directors, a number of interdepartmental committees may be appointed by the executive officers to coordinate the efforts of the various departments. These committees normally report their findings to the officer responsible for their appointment. Some of the interdepartmental committees that might be appointed include an insurance committee, a budget committee, a public relations or advertising committee, a human resource and employee-benefit committee, and a research committee.

Although this description of home office organization is representative, it may not actually fit any particular insurer. It is presented merely to illustrate the basis for patterns of home office organization.

## ADMINISTRATION[19]

Other chapters discuss tactical areas such as underwriting, marketing, financial statements, investments, and legal and actuarial aspects of life insurance

---

[19]This section draws from *Operations of Life and Health Insurance Companies*, Chaps. 10–11, 15–16, copyright ©1986 LOMA (Life Office Management Association, Inc.). Adapted with the permission of the publisher.

operations in considerable detail. At this point, it is appropriate to review briefly some of the significant areas of administration that are not dealt with directly in other chapters. The administrative areas discussed here include policyowner service, claims administration, information systems, and human resources.

*Policyowner Service.*    The policyowner service (POS) function is usually organized as a department under the supervision of a vice president. As competition has increased in recent years, quality service to customers has become an increasingly important aspect of effective life insurance company operations.[20]

Policyowner service departments administer the insurance contract from the time of issue until termination. In addition to responding to requests for information by policyowners, beneficiaries, and agents, POS is responsible for administering contract values, maintaining policy records, informing policyowners of developments that affect their contracts, and processing any changes requested by the policyowner. The POS department also may be responsible for policy issue, premium billing and collection, agent or broker compensation, and, at times, claims administration.

The quality of service provided by the POS department is critically important in building and maintaining effective relationships between the insurer and the agent and policyowner—an important marketing goal. In addition to policyowners and agents, beneficiaries and account holders also are served by the POS department. Even when claims administration is organized as a separate department, the POS department personnel must be prepared to answer questions such as when a claim will be paid, what is the amount of the benefit, what steps must be taken to obtain the benefit, and questions related to the optional modes of settlement. Life insurance companies also administer other accounts, such as IRAs, mutual funds, and pensions. In contrast to the usual situation with the cash-value policy, their owners need periodic investment reports and frequently request information about transferring funds between accounts, the tax treatment of transactions, and so on. This makes it necessary for POS specialists to be knowledgeable about the insurer's financial products as well as their basic individual life insurance contracts.

The development of universal life, variable life, and other interest-sensitive products has increased the demands on POS departments, because they are service-intensive. These products have a number of changeable aspects that policyowners and POS personnel monitor closely.

POS departments can be organized by function (e.g., coverage changes, reinstatements, policy values, policy loans, replacements); by product (e.g., individual insurance, group insurance, health insurance, pensions); or by customer (a specific member of the department provides all the service needs of a specific customer assigned to that individual). Some insurers organize the POS function regionally.

[20]See "The Quality Revolution," *LIMRA's MarketFacts* (July/Aug. 1991), pp. 24-39.

*Claims Administration.*   The claims administration function is usually organized according to the types of products (e.g., individual life, group life, individual health, group health, pensions) sold by the insurer. A claim unit or department may be established for each line of business. Regional claim offices are usually given authority to process and pay certain types of claims up to a specified monetary limit that varies by product line. Different limits are also established for individual claims personnel, based on the size and type of claim. Table 29-1 illustrates the concept of levels of authority granted by type of claim in a claims administration department.

Life insurance claim procedures involve (1) gathering information about the claim, the claimant, and the beneficiary; (2) investigating instances of invalid claims or possible fraud; and (3) processing the claim for payment. In addition to handling administrative procedures, claims personnel must be well trained in all aspects of the insurer's product(s) including the medical, dental, and legal aspects affecting claims administration.[21]

Claims administration is an important function both in terms of providing quality service to claimants and beneficiaries and in terms of good business practice. Ninety-nine percent of all claims are paid promptly. In cases where a claim must be denied because it is invalid or fraud is involved, the present litigious nature of U.S. society makes it essential to have well-trained personnel in all aspects of the claim administration process.

*Information Systems.*   Information systems have become the *sine qua non* of a successful financial services organization. As technology and computer applications have increased in sophistication and utility, the role of the information systems department has grown in importance. The department maintains insurer records in computerized files, facilitates the development of financial statements, and constantly responds to the insureds' needs in a changing marketplace.

There are two types of information needed by insurance companies if they are to manage effectively:  management information and operational information. **Management information** is information that managers need to formulate objectives, monitor progress toward these objectives, and generally to support the decision-making process. These are broadly referred to as decision-support systems. **Operational information** is information that employees need in all functions and departments to perform their work. Both types of information are important and should be available on a timely and accurate basis.

New product development is critically dependent on the systems capability of an insurer. Every part of the insurer is dependent on the availability of effective computer systems and software applications. The systems include data base management, word processing, and office automation systems.

---

[21]The International Claim Association has an extensive education program that includes courses in these areas.

**TABLE 29-1   LEVELS OF AUTHORITY IN A CLAIMS ADMINISTRATION DEPARTMENT**

| Type of Claim | Approval Authority |
|---|---|
| Routine claims | Examiner Trainee....................................................$ 50,000 |
| | Examiner.................................................................$200,000 |
| | Senior Claims Examiner .......................................$300,000 |
| | Assistant Manager...........................................no restrictions |
| | Manager.............................................................no restrictions |
| Claims that involve the contestability provision or the accidental death benefit provision | Examiner Trainee .............................................no authority |
| | Examiner...............................................................$ 50,000 |
| | Senior Claims Examiner .......................................$200,000 |
| | Assistant Manager...........................................no restrictions |
| | Manager.............................................................no restrictions |
| Claims that involve suspicion of fraud or unusual legal complications | Examiner Trainee .............................................no authority |
| | Examiner.............................................................no authority |
| | Senior Claims Examiner....................................no authority |
| | Assistant Manager................................................$200,000 |
| | Manager ...............................................................$1,000,000 |

*Source*: Life Office Management Association, *Life Insurance Company Operations* (Atlanta, GA: LOMA, 1986).

***Human Resources.***   The availability of competent, effective human resources in an organization is critical to its operation. Their creativity, intelligence, resourcefulness and diligence are essential to any company's success, regardless of the availability of other resources such as money, technology, and information. Life insurance companies are no different.

The human resource department has the responsibility of assuring that there is an appropriate supply of qualified personnel to manage the company effectively in light of its philosophy and objectives. This includes activities such as job analysis, job structuring, human resource planning, recruitment, selection, placement, training and professional development, performance appraisal, and compensation planning and administration. The human resource department also administers all employee benefits and other services provided to the company's employees.

The steady growth in the legal and regulatory rules in all areas of human resource activity has made the management of human resources more complicated. This complexity is enhanced considerably for those companies doing business internationally. The human resource function has assumed a much more central role than it had in the past.

## LIFE INSURER MANAGEMENT

Planning along with decision-making is a primary function of management. The first step in providing a foundation for guiding decision-making and goal setting is for senior management and the board of directors to define an overall corporate mission—the overall objectives of the company.

## ESTABLISHING A CORPORATE MISSION[22]

Strategic planning is intended to allow managers to forecast the future and to develop courses of action that will result in a successful future for a company. **Strategic planning** can be defined as a process involved with the allocation of resources in order to achieve a firm's current and future mission and objectives in a dynamic and competitive business environment. Strategic planning can be contrasted with **operational planning**—planning designed to guide an organization's day-to-day activities. Operational planning is tactical; it describes methods to be used at various levels in the organization in order to achieve lower-level objectives and ultimately to accomplish major corporate objectives.

The most general strategic plan is a purpose or a mission. A **mission** can be defined as the fundamental, unique purpose that sets a business apart from other firms of its type and identifies the scope of its operations in product and market terms.

An effective mission statement is one with five characteristics. It should:

- include specifications of objectives that allow progress toward them to be measured;
- establish the individuality of the company;
- include a definition of the business the firm wants to be in;
- be relevant to all the firm's stakeholders; and
- be exciting and inspiring.

Once the mission statement has been carefully crafted, the next step in the strategic planning process is to establish **long-term objectives** that collectively ensure accomplishment of the company's mission. The primary corporate objective ordinarily would be the maximization of shareholder value in a stock insurer and policyowner value in a mutual company.

## VALUE-BASED PLANNING

The management of a life insurer's capital resources is central to the successful fulfillment of its mission. Key questions that every company faces include:

- How will corporate capital be allocated among many possible applications?
- What market segments and products represent the most attractive opportunities for investing in the company's future?

[22]This section draws on Andrew J. DuBrin, R. Duane Ireland, and J. Clifton Williams, *Management and Organization* (Cincinnati, Ohio: South-Western Publishing Company, 1989), p. 130.

- What constitutes an adequate rate of return for the company's investments?
- How will management performance be evaluated?

Value-based planning is increasingly used in the life insurance industry as a tool for analyzing these issues and establishing long-range strategy. Value-based planning focuses on the economic net worth of a company and its relative increase from planning period to planning period.

The value of a company is comprised of three elements: (1) current capital and surplus together with nonbenefit contingency reserves; (2) the value of expected future net cash flows from existing business; and (3) expected future net cash flows from future business. These values are defined as the present value of future cash flows discounted at a specified "hurdle" rate of return for alternative investments with similar risk characteristics. The discount rate is determined by reference to the company's cost of capital in the capital markets, and it may be adjusted to reflect the different risks associated with different products or ventures. Statutory capital and surplus are used, and net cash flow is generally defined as statutory net income since these are the only funds that may be consistently paid out to policyowners and stockholders.

A product or business venture creates value if discounted cash flows exceed the initial investment. Four broad strategies are generally available to management with respect to existing product lines and businesses:

- The product or venture can be discontinued and market share surrendered.
- Additional investment can be discontinued and market share harvested as it declines.
- Sufficient investment can be made to maintain existing market share.
- Significant investment can be made to build market share.

To determine whether value is created by the adoption of these strategies, the cash flows associated with the investment required for each strategy are discounted at the selected rate. The investment required for each strategy is the sum of the value that might be received through divesting the product or venture by sale or reinsurance agreement, and the additional capital required to adopt the strategy. When discounted cash flows exceed the required investment, value is created and adoption of the strategy is indicated. New products, ventures, and acquisitions can be tested similarly for value creation. As discussed in "Economic Value Analysis" in Chapter 32, aggregate value added during any planning or measurement period is the difference in beginning and ending values, adjusted for capital paid out in dividends and paid in through capital injections during the period.

Value-based planning is a standard for strategic and capital allocation decision-making. It serves as a rational basis for establishing the critical long-term policies that guide successful pursuit of the corporate mission:

- Establishing a long-term financial strategy that satisfies the requirements of the various constituencies (primarily customers, investors, regulators, and rating agencies) that management serves
- Determining a capital structure that is consistent with corporate policies regarding operational (premiums/surplus) and financial (debt/equity) leverage
- Allocating capital to ventures, products, and acquisitions that will create future value for policyowners and stockholders
- Identifying performance standards by which the success or failure of management action may be evaluated

In competitive businesses, the financial results depend ultimately on the success of the company in achieving a unique or predominant position in the segments of the market that it chooses to serve. This position may stem from a low-cost structure, a unique sales operation, a special underwriting or investment skill, and so on; each of these elements is important in enhancing profit. The key to the success for the company is to assure that these unique positions continue and that changes in other elements of the cost or pricing structure do not negate these positions.

In all areas of organization there are no simple answers. There are different choices, each with its own advantages and disadvantages. The choice will often depend more on the company's history, its current circumstances, or sometimes on the easy availability of information than on the merits one can determine on balance of a particular approach.

## PLANNING AND CONTROL CYCLE

All well-managed companies utilize a planning and control cycle made up of four stages: (1) strategic planning, (2) tactical planning, (3) performance monitoring, and (4) control and readjustment.[23]

These stages describe a management process without any particular time frame. The *strategic planning stage* defines the target markets, products (and services), and distribution systems that are coordinated to achieve the company's profitability and solvency objectives in light of the established overall corporate mission. These objectives must be achieved within solvency constraints defined by management in regard to cash flow and capital adequacy.

Everything in the management of a life insurer affects everything else. The effective manager must be able to see the logical interrelationships among micro

---

[23]This section draws on Stephen W. Forbes, *The Planning and Control Cycle* (unpublished paper, 1988).

decisions as they affect each other and the company's macro performance. A life insurer can be viewed as an aggregate of individual products and associated cash flows. Thus criteria employed to measure profitability can vary, but return on equity and value added are two widely used measures. The profitability criteria are often measured for strategic business units for purposes of determining relative performance, investment strategies, resource allocations, and incentive compensation.

Capital adequacy (both short- and long-term) is an important consideration in individual product design and the portfolio of products offered by a life insurance company. If statutory-required surplus is impaired, the insurer will face regulatory intervention. Rating services of various types also pay close attention to surplus levels. Thus cash flow and surplus management are important financial considerations, often serving as constraints on product design.

Once the target markets, distribution systems, and product mix meet the profitability and capital (surplus) criteria, the next stage of the planning cycle, *tactical planning*, can begin to provide the implementation of the strategic plan. The tactical plan involves the development and maintenance of all of the managerial and distribution components that are required to carry out the strategic plan within the timetables and cost constraints assumed in the product profitability and solvency models. Timely, efficient implementation is as important as good strategic planning. Realistic, achievable tactical plans must be developed for the product portfolio selected.

The third stage of the planning and control cycle is *performance monitoring*. The purpose, of course, is to determine if the insurer's strategic and tactical plans are being carried out so as to meet the profitability and solvency objectives. Effective performance monitoring systems involve a limited number of meaningful reports generated for each strategic business unit and for the company as a whole. The timing of the reports and the amount of detail depend upon the use to which the reports are put. Senior management reports are likely to take a summary form to facilitate management by exception, enabling executives to concentrate on correcting variances from planned objectives. Obviously, the quality and integrity of the data are very important.

Effective performance monitoring permits *control and readjustment*, the fourth stage of the planning and control cycle. Performance monitoring will lead to control and readjustment of tactics to achieve a given strategic plan, or readjustment of the strategic plan itself if it appears to be unattainable even after feasible adjustments have been made. This completes the cycle, in which strategic plans involving products, markets, and distribution systems are modified as experience unfolds and ideas for new products and strategies evolve as a natural part of the management process.

It is important to remember that creativity and imagination are critical to successful life insurance company management. There are always a number of ways to attack a problem strategically and tactically. The effective executive/manager will examine a number of alternative approaches, applying the technical tools at his or her disposal and at times even inventing new ones. Management is a dynamic process in which creativity is a critically important resource.

## THE FINANCIAL SERVICES MARKETPLACE[24]

The financial services industry consists of organizations that are involved in saving, lending, managing, or transferring money. Insurance companies are included in this industry.

Since the October 1987 collapse of stock markets throughout the world, events have clearly demonstrated the increased interlocking relationship among the world's financial markets. Since then, the dollar has fluctuated greatly in relation to other major world currencies, such as the yen, deutsche mark, and pound. Taken together, these two events indicate that there is a world economy in which no single economy or currency will play the dominant role enjoyed by the United States and the dollar since World War II. Clearly, globalization is one of the major forces in business today. There is now a world economy.

Globalization can be attributed in part to the explosion of information technology, which permits instant and simple cross-border transmission of financial instruments from virtually any location worldwide. The available operational capacity of the world market makes going global attractive to executives seeking profitable growth, especially when the potential in their home countries is limited.

### ECONOMIES OF SCALE AND SCOPE

Decision-makers in the insurance industry are currently being confronted with a great deal of anticipation and speculation on the structural changes that the industry worldwide is likely to undergo in the future. The liberalization and globalization trends of services inherent within the European Community (EC), the General Agreement on Tariffs and Trade, the North American Free Trade Agreement, and the overall integration of the world economy are forcing insurance companies and other organizations that offer financial services to approach a new set of strategic problems. Structural changes on both the demand and supply sides may require insurers to adjust themselves in terms of size, product mix, and international strength.

A strategically important consideration relates to the question of economies of scale and scope. Do insurer size and product mix have a decisive influence on a company's operating costs? Economic theory suggests that the concept of

---

[24]This section draws on *Industry Trade Summary: Insurance* (Washington, D.C.: U.S. International Trade Commission, 1991).

increasing returns to scale assumes that enterprises could gain considerable cost advantages through growth. The empirical question is: Do average costs of expanding insurers tend to decline or rise, or do they remain constant?

The results of a study by a major reinsurer[25] did not reveal any economic necessity for insurers to grow. The study pointed out that the versatile supply structure in the individual markets also holds considerable potential for smaller insurers with a variety of distribution systems, special product mixes, and market niches. The study reported a tendency of large insurers to maintain constant returns to scale. This indicates that expanding companies are not likely to suffer any substantial cost disadvantages once they have reached a cost level in the medium range. The study concluded that in two of the more liberalized markets (the United States and the Netherlands), the potential for increasing returns to scale was more noticeable among smaller insurers. The study, which addressed only the question of economies of scale, acknowledged that the wave of concentration through mergers and takeovers during the 1980s could be explained by other reasons, such as economies of scope, an improved access to capital markets, and the potential for synergy and rationalization.

A more recent study using a multiproduct cost function and an industry sample of 423 U.S. life insurers made estimates of cost economies for firms varying in both the scale and scope of output.[26] The results showed that most firms had significant economies of scale while the largest agency insurers exhibited approximately constant returns to scale. A significant increase in product-specific scale economies was found for accident and health and investment products in all insurers and for ordinary life in agency companies. The study also showed that mutuals did not have higher costs than stock insurers for a given scale and mix of outputs. Finally, the study results suggested that agency firms generally exhibit lower scale economies than non–agency firms, and this finding is consistent with the existence of greater scale economies in the production of products than in the distribution of the same products.

As structural changes continue to occur, considerations such as economies of scale and scope will be critical to strategic planners attempting to establish objectives relating to market share, product mix, distribution systems, and target markets.

## INSURERS AND GLOBALIZATION

Insurance operations of major companies around the world are becoming more international. Many are preparing to operate on a global basis. Already, foreign-owned U.S. domestic life insurers account for over 7 percent of total U.S. life premiums, with this percentage growing each year. The Canadians,

---

[25]"Economies of Scale in the Insurance Industry," *Sigma*, Swiss Reinsurance Company (Apr. 1991).

[26]Martin F. Grace and Stephen G. Timmie, "An Examination of Cost Economies in the United States Life Insurance Industry," *Journal of Risk and Insurance*, Vol 59 (Mar. 1992).

British, Dutch, French, Germans, Swiss, and Australians have significant U.S. financial service interests and are actively seeking additional acquisitions in the United States.

Diversified European financial institutions are preparing to compete in the EC and in the global market. They will profoundly affect the international presence of both U.S. banks and insurers. Furthermore, they will increase competitive pressures within the United States.

Until recently, only a few U.S. insurers had established offices or joint-venture businesses outside the United States. In fact, there may be no more than 200 U.S. insurers with any type of non-U.S. operations at all. U.S. companies have several strengths that should help them expand their businesses abroad. They have more experience than many non-U.S. competitors in developing innovative policies for diverse customers, in dealing with several regulatory authorities within a generally accepted set of rules, and in taking advantage of large economies of scale in the marketing and administering of insurance policies. U.S. insurers also tend to be technologically sophisticated. These strengths may be useful in the evolving single-license EC market. At the same time, U.S. insurers have seemed reluctant to begin dealing with other languages, exchange rates, differing legal systems, and cultural diversity. Also, developing a reputation for reliability in new markets requires time and the will to persevere in a market. The demands of U.S. investors for performance in the short term tends to make such perseverance difficult for U.S. companies. Although a number of large insurers have established operations in Europe and the Far East, the expansion of U.S. insurers overseas is expected to continue to develop slowly.

# Chapter 30

# *L*IFE *I*NSURER *F*INANCIAL *M*ANAGEMENT

This chapter provides the background and conceptual framework for understanding life insurance as a cash flow business and introduces interest-sensitive cash flow analysis as a primary tool for all major life insurer financial management decision-making. Until the 1980s, traditional views of life insurer financial management focused on the aggregate values of assets and liabilities, with relatively little attention to the possibility that these values could be subject to rapid and significant change as a result of changing economic conditions.

The chapter sections that follow will introduce (1) the risks that life insurers face and traditional management strategies applied during stable economic conditions; (2) the sensitivity of both asset and liability values to volatile market interest rates; (3) techniques for analyzing, understanding, and managing the interest rate sensitivity of insurer cash flow; and (4) the need to manage insurer surplus to protect against unexpected cash flow requirements. The cash flow nature of life insurance is an important prerequisite to under-standing the construction of investment portfolios (see Chapter 31) and the nature and limitations of contemporary financial reporting methods (see Chapter 32).

## LIFE INSURER RISK

### SOURCES OF LIFE INSURER RISK

Life insurance companies face many risks in the course of doing business. Mortality experience may exceed expectations, competing companies may develop more efficient operating procedures, or the credit quality of a company's asset portfolio may deteriorate. Economic developments, particularly shifting market interest rates, are also a source of risk to a life insurance company. As with any investor, these developments may affect the value of an insurer's investments. Life insurance companies are subject to additional risk because these same developments may influence the behavior of their customers, including borrowers.

The excess of a life insurance company's assets over its liabilities is known as **surplus**. Policy reserves (liabilities) are maintained to satisfy the insurer's expected obligations. As will be seen, traditional measures of expected liabilities have been inadequate to predict actual liabilities, particularly the demand liabilities for policy loans and cash surrender values.

Life insurance companies maintain surplus to protect against unforeseen obligations that could threaten the company's solvency. Sources of risk to company solvency can be grouped into four broad categories: (1) asset risk, (2) pricing risk, (3) asset/liability matching risk, and (4) miscellaneous risks. Designated as contingency risks by the Society of Actuaries' Committee on Valuation and Related Problems, these risks are designated as C-1, C-2, C-3, and C-4 risks, respectively. Surplus, therefore, also may be considered a **contingency reserve**.

**Asset risk,** or the **C-1 risk,** arises from the possibility that borrowers of insurer funds may default on their obligations to the company, or that the market value of an insurer's investment assets may decline. **Pricing risk,** or the **C-2 risk,** results from uncertainty regarding future operating results relating to items such as investment income, mortality, expenses, sales, and lapses. If an insurer's premium and investment income are based on assumptions that prove inadequate, it may not be able to meet its obligations to policyowners. As illustrated in Figure 30-1, inadequate pricing will eventually produce liabilities that exceed assets, or insolvency.

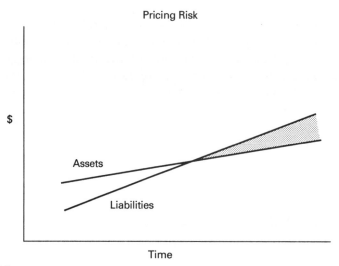

Pricing Risk

**FIGURE 30-1**

**THE IMPACT ON COMPANY NET WORTH OF INADEQUATE INSURANCE PRODUCT PRICING OVER TIME**

**Asset/liability matching risk**, or the **C-3 risk**, results from the likelihood that current policyowner cash obligations may exceed current cash income from premiums and investments. As a result, an insurer may have to sell assets at a loss or take out loans to fund cash shortages.[1] This situation can arise even though the total book value of investments is more than sufficient to satisfy the total book value of obligations. Figure 30-2 illustrates conceptually that although assets may exceed liabilities, current or cash assets may be insufficient to meet current or cash liabilities.

Other risks, referred to actuarially as **miscellaneous risks** or **C-4 risks**, are generally thought to be beyond the ability of insurers to predict and manage, but they nevertheless represent real risk to the company. These risks might include, for example, tax or regulatory changes and product obsolescence.

Surplus is designed to protect against unforeseen losses arising from these risks by absorbing operating fluctuations that may follow. Maintaining adequate surplus and controlling these risks is vital to insurer performance and policyowner security.

## TRADITIONAL RISK MANAGEMENT STRATEGIES

Historically, the hallmark of life insurer risk management in the United States and elsewhere was conservatism. After considering past experience, companies made judgments about expected future results and added safety margins to their

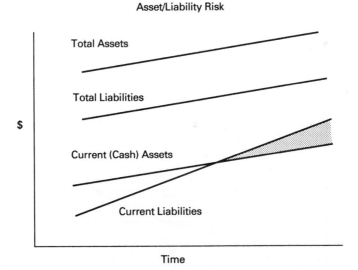

**FIGURE 30-2**

**THE IMPACT ON LIQUIDITY OF ASSET/LIABILITY MISMATCH DESPITE LONG-TERM SOLVENCY**

[1] Borrowed funds may come from traditional capital market sources such as bank loans or securities issues. Additional sales of annuities and guaranteed investment contracts may also be a source of borrowed funds. Additional whole life insurance sales are less important as a source of quick liquidity because of high acquisition costs.

pricing assumptions. Conservatism was reflected in asset management by the acquisition of high-quality investments and the broad diversification of assets. High investment yields were sought by the acquisition of what were thought to be safe, long-term investments in highly rated bonds. Higher interest rates are typically paid for investments with longer maturity periods, because of the increasing interest rate risk associated with longer-term commitments. Figure 30-3 illustrates the typical relationship of yield and term to maturity for a fixed-income investment.[2] As a result, incremental increases in term to maturity normally produce incremental increases in market value fluctuations.

Conservative interest, expense, and mortality assumptions were also used in product design and pricing. Ample premium and investment income margins were established to provide sufficient funds to meet policyowner obligations and corporate performance goals.

One of the principal risks associated with any fixed-income investment is interest rate risk, or the risk that an investment's market value may decline when interest rates rise. In the past, conservative management of the asset/liability matching risk involved the reduction of interest rate risk with a bond dedication strategy. Bond dedication refers to passive portfolio management techniques intended to fund future liabilities while reducing or eliminating interest rate risk (see next section).

Conservatism as a risk management approach served the U.S. life insurance industry well for many years. Interest rates and expenses remained relatively stable, and mortality rates typically improved from year to year. Margins used by

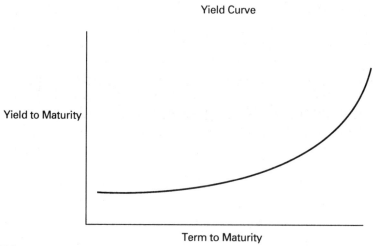

Yield Curve

Yield to Maturity

Term to Maturity

**FIGURE 30-3**

**EXPECTED SHAPE OF THE YIELD CURVE FOR FIXED-INCOME INVESTMENTS, ILLUSTRATING THE RELATIONSHIP OF SHORT- AND LONG-TERM INTEREST RATES**

[2]See discussion on interest rate risk below. Occasionally, market rates will reflect the opposite relationship and an **inverted yield curve** results.

insurers in their pricing assumptions proved sufficient to pay promised policyowner benefits, contributions to surplus, and dividends to policyowners and shareholders of stock companies.

When unfamiliar patterns of inflation and interest rates began to emerge in the United States and elsewhere, however, conservatism alone proved inadequate to maintain effective life insurer financial management. The possible range of future operating results expanded beyond the scope of the protection afforded by even the most conservative assumptions, and companies experienced severe disintermediation.

## THE CASH FLOW NATURE OF LIFE INSURANCE

### BOND DEDICATION STRATEGY

Simple bond management strategies can work in a stable interest rate environment. However, inadequacies become apparent when economic conditions become more volatile, as they did in the 1970s and 1980s. The familiar phenomenon of adverse selection, well understood in an underwriting context, became increasingly evident in policyowner behavior influencing nonclaim liabilities. As a result, effective financial management required an understanding of life insurance that recognized the simultaneous impact of changing market interest rates on the values of assets and liabilities, and on the behavior of both policyowners and company borrowers.

Until the mid-1970s, U.S. life insurance companies were able to avoid interest rate risk successfully through the use of bond dedication. **Bond dedication** refers to the construction of a bond portfolio to satisfy defined future liabilities despite the possibility of market interest rate changes. The then-prevailing character of the life insurance business made this strategy possible. Companies were able to estimate with a high degree of accuracy the number of insureds who would die in a given year and the dollar amount of claims arising from these deaths. The timing, frequency, and dollar amount of cash needs were directly tied to the timing and frequency of deaths, together with reasonably predictable policy loans and surrenders.

With predictable future policy liabilities, the higher returns available from long-term bonds could be captured without undue exposure to the adverse consequences of a upward shift in market interest rates.[3] Although the value of long-term bonds may decline when interest rates rise, the decline is irrelevant if the principal invested in the bond is not needed until maturity. Bonds have a

---

[3]Not all insurance company assets are invested in bonds, of course. This chapter in large part focuses on **marginal liquidity**. Some insurance company assets probably need not be liquid at all and may be invested in real estate and other illiquid investments. To meet current obligations, some assets must be highly liquid. Understanding the spectrum or continuum of liquidity needs is essential to effective financial management. This discussion of bonds centers on that point in the spectrum where liquidity requirements are an issue—that is, where the degree of needed liquidity is uncertain.

"memory" and their market value will approach their face value as maturity nears.[4] Figure 30-4 illustrates the general impact of different interest rate scenarios on the market value of a long-term bond.

In its simplest form, bond dedication is only possible when future liabilities are fixed in amount and timing.[5] If the amount and timing of a liability are unknown, the maturity value of a bond may not be sufficient to satisfy the liability. If the timing of a liability is not known and may arise before the maturity of the bond funding it, the bond may have to be sold before it "remembers" its value. The accurate prediction of the amount and timing of cash needs is essential to bond dedication.

In the mid-1970s, the operating character of the U.S. life insurance business changed. Historically, the timing and amount of cash requirements associated with policy loans and surrenders were reasonably predictable. Eventually, the pattern of policy loans and surrenders began to fluctuate sharply with changes in the economy. The timing and amounts of cash requirements associated with these liabilities were no longer predictable, and simple bond dedication was not possible.[6] It became necessary to consider the impact of market interest rate

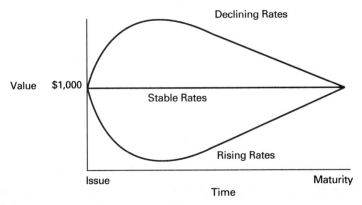

**FIGURE 30-4**

**THE IMPACT OF DIFFERENT INTEREST RATE ENVIRONMENTS ON THE VALUE OF A LONG-TERM BOND**

[4]The memory metaphor is borrowed from Marshall E. Blume, "Portfolio Management," in Marshall E. Blume and Jack P. Friedman, eds., *Encyclopedia of Investments* (Boston: Warren, Gorham and Lamont, 1982).

[5]The most basic form of bond dedication involves "cash matching" a bond portfolio with maturities and interest payments that exactly match expected liabilities. Although the discussion here of cash-matched bond portfolios is simple, in practice, more sophisticated techniques of dedication have been developed. Specifically, the concept of **duration** rather than maturity is considered. The duration concept is a measure of the potential change in market value of an asset or liability as a result of a change in market interest rates. Duration is discussed further in "Objective of Asset/Liability Management" below. Bond dedication is discussed in more detail in Chap. 31.

[6]Predicting liability cash flows remains problematical. Additional factors contributing to the unpredictable nature of liability cash flows include the unbundling of traditional life insurance products and the proliferation of new interest sensitive products, the increasing investment importance given by consumers to insurance products, and the lack of credible experience bases associated with new products such as long-term care. See *Capital Management in the Life Insurance Industry* (Atlanta, Ga Life Office Management Association, Inc.).

changes on the value of liabilities as well as assets. The primary causes of this change in consumer behavior were the deregulation of bank deposit interest rates and the onset of significant inflation in the economy.

## INFLATION, INTEREST RATES, AND CONSUMER BEHAVIOR

Interest rates are characterized as nominal and real. **Nominal interest rates** are market interest rates and are comprised of two elements: (1) a rate of return that reflects the use of the investor's money and the inherent risks of the investment, and (2) an additional rate of return, or inflation premium, that reflects the loss of purchasing power due to the expected effects of inflation. The **real interest rate** equals the nominal rate less the inflation premium.[7]

Until the early 1970s, bank deposit interest rates were regulated in the United States. Under the regulations, demand deposits such as checking accounts could pay no interest, and interest paid on time deposits such as passbook savings accounts was subject to a maximum limit. When the first postwar manifestations of serious inflation appeared, investors suffered a loss in purchasing power because interest rates did not reflect the prevailing conditions of inflation.

To provide investors with an opportunity to earn interest rates that reflect inflation, a series of consumer interest rate regulations was repealed. The most prominent of these was **Regulation Q,** which had established a ceiling on time deposit interest rates.[8] Subsequently, the Federal Reserve abandoned its attempts to control inflation by directly influencing interest rates and focused on the nation's money supply. Together with continued deregulation, these developments caused interest rates to exhibit unprecedented volatility as fears of inflation continued to influence the market.[9]

Rational investors seek the highest available return for a given level of risk. The deregulation of rates and classical market forces soon led to a proliferation of financial investments that paid current interest rates. As investors sought the higher returns then available in money market funds, certificates of deposit, and other new investments, life insurers found themselves in a vulnerable position.

## CASH FLOW ANTISELECTION

Cash flow antiselection is another manifestation of the adverse selection phenomenon. When customers have a choice in their dealings with insurers, they typically select options that are favorable to themselves and unfavorable to the

---

[7]Stephen G. Kellison, *The Theory of Interest,* 2nd ed. (Homewood, Ill.: Richard D. Irwin, 1991), pp. 298-299.

[8]Capital market interest rates applicable to government and corporate securities were not regulated. These investments were not readily available to the average consumer with relatively small sums to invest.

[9]Arnold W. Sametz, "The 'New' Financial Environment of the United States," in Edward I. Altman, Ed., *Handbook of Financial Markets and Institutions,* 6th ed. (New York: John Wiley and Sons, 1987).

insurer. Cash flow antiselection behavior can be expected, both from the company's insurance customers (its prospective and current policyowners) and borrowers (its investment customers).

Cash outflow antiselection can occur when interest rates are rising. Policyowners may withdraw funds under policy loan or cash surrender options if other investments pay higher perceived returns than their policy cash values. Bond and mortgage repayments for instruments with relatively low stated interest rates will normally be extended as long as possible when borrowers find higher rates elsewhere. The tendency of consumers to select against the company when exercising contractual cash flow options is known as **disintermediation**. If the insurer experiences a cash shortage because of disintermediation, it must sell assets when values are depressed or borrow money at high current rates to meet its cash needs.

Problems can arise during periods of declining interest rates as well. Cash inflow antiselection may develop. As interest rates decline, cash value-earnings may become more attractive than other market options.[10] Policy loans may be repaid and flexible premium income may increase. Bonds may be called and mortgages repaid when borrowers find market rates are lower than what they are currently paying. The insurer may be faced with large sums of cash to invest when rates are low, which in turn will cause overall yields to suffer.

During the late 1970s and early 1980s, many U.S. life insurance companies were heavily invested in long-term bonds when inflation and interest rates were rising rapidly. Figure 30-5 summarizes expected client behavior and company impact under different interest rate scenarios. The expected results ensued.

## DEMAND NATURE OF LOAN AND SURRENDER RIGHTS

Life insurers' historical experience with policyowner lapses and surrenders (voluntary terminations) was accumulated in an environment of stable interest rates. Voluntary termination rates were relatively insensitive to minor fluctuations in market interest rates. With the development of volatile market interest rates, it became clear that major interest rate movements would have a considerable influence on voluntary terminations.[11] Figure 30-6 illustrates the pattern of both interest rates and voluntary terminations in recent years.

---

[10]This is particularly true of companies that employ a portfolio interest crediting/dividend strategy (see Chap. 9).

[11]Patterns of interest-related disintermediation were not unknown to the life insurance industry prior to the 1970s, but the volatility of interest rates and the severity of their impact became more profound later. The *delay clause* was included in all life insurance contracts after depression-era financial stresses to help manage the impact of a "run on the company." Under this provision a company may defer cash payments, except for claims benefits, for up to six months (see Chap. 8).

**FIGURE 30-5**

**THE EXPECTED IMPACT OF DIFFERENT INTEREST RATE ENVIRONMENTS ON POLICYOWNER AND INVESTMENT CLIENT BEHAVIOR**

|  | RISING INTEREST RATES | DECLINING INTEREST RATES |
|---|---|---|
| *Expected Investment Client Behavior* | Mortgages and bonds held as long as possible | Call bonds Repay mortgages |
| *Expected Policyowner Behavior* | Make policy loans Surrender policies Suspend flexible premiums | Increase flexible premiums Repay loans Persist |
| *Insurer Impact* | Cash shortage | Cash glut |
| *Insurer Options* | Sell investment at a loss Borrow at high new money rates | Reinvest at low new money rates |

Percent

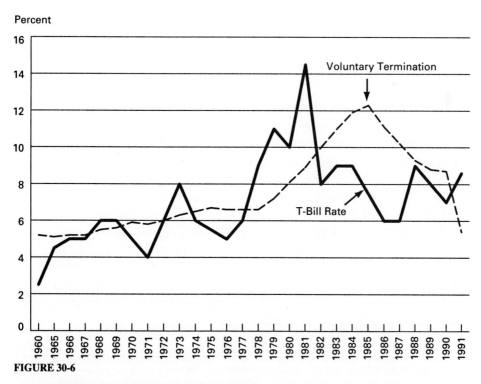

**FIGURE 30-6**

**THE HISTORICAL PATTERN OF INTEREST RATES AND VOLUNTARY TERMINATIONS**

*Source*: American Council of Life Insurance

Because of the relative historical stability of voluntary termination rates in the United States, lapses and surrenders were viewed as contract design features that provided convenience to customers, increased the marketability of life insurance products, and satisfied the requirements of state law. These contractual features had been viewed as ancillary matters when they were actually financial options with real economic value to policyowners.

The lapse and surrender option features of U.S. cash-value life insurance contracts represent book value withdrawal rights to policyowners.[12] The policyowner has the right to receive cash values on demand, in the same way a checking account owner has the right to receive the account balance on demand. Liquidity problems arose because cash values were guaranteed at book value, while the market value of investments backing the cash-value guarantee fluctuated with market interest rates. As summarized in Figure 30-6, policyowner demand for withdrawals, whether by loan or surrender, is highest at precisely the wrong time for the insurer—that is, when interest rates are rising and market values are declining.

## DEFINING ACCEPTABLE CASH FLOW RESULTS

As discussed earlier, traditional approaches to managing risk in life insurance worked well in a stable economic and improving mortality environment. The probability of loss due to asset default, inadequate pricing, and asset/liability mismatch could be effectively managed through asset diversification, conservative pricing, and simple bond dedication. Virtually all life insurer products were profitable, and the principal exposure to adverse financial performance was loss of market share.

Because of the new volatility exhibited by life insurer cash flow, it has become important to understand risk as the possible deviation of actual results from expected results. The concept of variability as a measure of risk was developed and applied to investment portfolio management in the middle of the twentieth century. Its application to the management of life insurer cash flow involves (1) the identification of key control variables and (2) the establishment of constraints that define the maximum level of variability acceptable to management.

For most life insurers, the key control variables are solvency (on both a statutory and cash-flow basis) and profitability. At a minimum, life insurers should establish constraints that are designed to avoid:

---

[12]Options in a life insurance contract form an important part of the package of benefits provided to the policyowner, and, because of the unilateral nature of life insurance contracts, the policy can be viewed as a package of options. These options provide an opportunity to select against the insurer, and policyowners should be expected to exercise the options in their own best interest. See Michael L. Smith, "The Life Insurance Policy as an Options Package," *The Journal of Risk and Insurance*, Vol. 45 (Dec. 1982), pp. 583-601.

•Regulatory intervention due to statutory insolvency

•The forced sale of assets or need to assume debt obligations to meet cash-flow solvency requirements

•Products and ventures that do not create expected value for shareholders or policyowners

To define and control the variability of solvency, liquidity, and profit-ability, effective financial management requires analytical techniques that recognize the cash-flow nature of life insurance. The use of interest-sensitive cash flow analysis is increasingly applied by life insurers to management decisions.

## ANALYZING LIFE INSURANCE CASH FLOW[13]

Historically, life insurance companies in the United States and elsewhere were managed as if they were a collection of simple assets and liabilities. As long as the market value of assets was greater than the expected value of liabilities, the insurer was thought to be solvent, and as long as premium and investment income was more than sufficient to pay current liabilities and maintain required policy reserves, the insurer was thought to be profitable.

Ultimately, as preceding sections have outlined, U.S. life insurance companies proved to be collections of complex assets and liabilities. This complexity derives from the fact that the terms *asset* and *liability* are labels that represent complex collections of expected cash flows. These terms have no real independent identity other than from the expected cash flow they represent. The stated value of a bond is a summary value of expected pay-ments of interest and principal. If the bond is in default, or if it must be sold when its market value has declined, actual cash flows will differ from expected cash flows. Similarly, the stated value of liabilities is a sum-marization of expected cash outflows. If policyowner demand for withdrawals is greater than expected, actual cash outflows will differ from expected cash outflows.

A simple statement of assets and liabilities is not a completely accurate measure of a company's financial condition, because it is based on expected cash flows derived from *static* assumptions. The real financial risk associated with life

---

[13]This section draws from *The Valuation Actuary Handbook*, and Carl R. Ohman and Michael E. Mateja, "Cash Flow Forecasting Under Different Economic Assumptions" in *Liquidity, Investments and Solvency*, Financial Planning and Control Report No. 65, copyright © 1986, LOMA (Life .Office Management Association, Inc.). Adapted with permission of the publisher.

insurer financial management is any deviation of actual from expected cash flows. A more complete understanding of the financial condition of an insurer is obtained when the impact of interest rate changes on expected cash flows is considered.

The dramatic influence of interest rate changes on the lapse and sur-render liabilities has been established. When the expected correlation of high interest rates and high inflation rates is considered, it is reasonable to conclude that virtually every aspect of life insurance company cash flow can be expected to change to some extent when market interest rates change significantly.

Effective financial management requires an understanding of the *dynamic* nature of assets and liabilities that reflects the potential deviation in expected cash flows that may arise when interest rates change. In response to the rapidly evolving financial environment, insurers are developing more sophisticated analytical techniques based on **interest-sensitive cash-flow analysis**. Building an interest-sensitive cash-flow model is a four-step process requiring (1) segmentation of the insurer's business by product line, (2) forecasting the insurer's expected liability cash flows, (3) forecasting the insurer's expected asset cash flows, and (4) testing the cash-flow results under a wide range of possible interest rate scenarios.

Traditional assumptions used in life insurance financial modeling such as commissions, expenses, mortality rates, and death benefits[14] are sup-plemented by assumptions regarding the impact of interest rate changes on various cash flows. The credibility of all financial projections, how-ever, ultimately depends on the assumptions used in developing the financial model.[15]

## SEGMENTATION BY PRODUCT LINE

Different insurance company products obviously have different cash flow patterns. For example, policyowners would be more likely to exercise policy loan options if they hold an older policy with a low interest loan rate than if they hold a new policy with a variable loan rate. To evaluate cash flow patterns effectively, then, it is necessary to consider distinct product lines independently. It is also necessary to manage different products indepen-dently.

---

[14]See chaps. 2 and 21.

[15]Some of the problems inherent in life insurance cash-flow modeling include uncertainties about (1) future economic conditions, (2) policyowner behavior with respect to relatively new (and untested) policy provisions, and (3) the market value response of investments in different interest rate situations. See *Capital Management in the Life Insurance Industry*, pp. 42-43.

Segmentation by product line is the process of independent management of different products. In the cash flow modeling process, the expected asset cash flows and liability cash flows are forecast for each product. In the management of products, an investment account is established for each line of business within the insurer's general account.

The segmented general account should not be confused with the separate account.[16] Even though a portion of general account investments may be assigned to a particular segmented product line, from a solvency perspective the assignment is a conceptual management tool only. The collective assets in the general account are available to back all liabilities supported by the general account.

In other respects, segmentation does have a practical effect on the company's policyowners. For example, interest crediting and dividend policy may be based on the investment experience of the segmented account. The implications for the company's management, therefore, include the need to ensure that investments available to the insurer are fairly allocated among different segments, that the transfer of investments from one segmented account to another is established on fair terms to policyowners of both product lines, and that intersegment loans are similarly equitable. Ultimately, the insurer's investment managers should address the specific requirements of each product, and the insurer's overall investment objectives should not hinder the prudent investment objectives established for each product line.

## LIABILITY CASH FLOWS

Understanding the impact of interest rate changes on liability cash flows is essential to effective cash flow analysis. Historically, insurers have had limited experience with lapses and surrenders within a volatile interest rate environment. Voluntary terminations, therefore, may be the most difficult liability cash flows to predict. It would be reasonable to expect voluntary terminations to increase as a function of the spread between interest rates credited on the product and alternative market rates, since consumers shift investments or replace policies to seek higher available market yields.

The clear relationship of voluntary terminations to rising interest rates was demonstrated in Figure 30-6. Other factors can be expected to influence lapse and surrender experience as well.[17] Lapse control features such as surrender charges may be effective disincentives to lapse, as may be a partial surrender

[16]See Chap. 31.
[17]Liability control strategies are discussed further below.

option. Interest crediting/dividend strategy should also help determine whether the lapse option will be attractive to policyowners.

Policy loan activity should be influenced by variable policy loan rates and direct recognition features. Potential loan activity must also be considered together with factors that influence the attractiveness of the lapse alternative.

## ASSET CASH FLOWS

The third step in interest-sensitive cash-flow modeling is the forecasting of asset cash flows. Asset types and maturities must be established and the sensitivity of interest, dividends, rents, and asset sale proceeds to changes in the interest rate environment must be considered. As discussed before, the market value of investments may decline when interest rates rise, and extreme economic conditions could result in the default of some investments.

Consideration should also be given to the asset mix. Just as interest rate changes may affect the expected cash flows from individual investments, investment strategy and the types of investments acquired will also be likely to change as interest rates change. The implications of interest rate changes would be particularly important in times of declining interest rates and cash inflow antiselection.

With flexible-premium products, premium payment patterns should change as interest rates change. Premium increases may be expected in times of declining interest rates, particularly with insurers employing a portfolio average interest crediting strategy. When interest rates rise, premiums may decrease, particularly when withdrawal control features such as variable loan rates and the surrender charges typical of newer products are present.

Strategies for dealing with negative cash flows should be evaluated and an understanding of the impact of changing interest rates developed. Unexpected negative cash flows conceivably could require the liquidation of assets or the borrowing of funds from outside sources. The expected negative cash flows associated with new product introductions would normally be well planned for and financed internally. Reinvestment strategies for positive cash flows must be considered as well.

Finally, consideration must be given to the interaction or correlation of events under different interest rate scenarios. For example, mortality antiselection should be expected during periods of high lapse rates, and extreme economic conditions such as high interest rates and unemployment could generate both asset defaults and increased disability income claims simultaneously.

## INTEREST RATE SENSITIVITY ANALYSIS

Once a determination has been reached as to the impact of changing interest rates on asset and liability cash flows, and an appropriate financial model constructed, the aggregate cash flow results are forecast under a variety of potential interest rate scenarios. At a minimum, an effective model tests results under the following general conditions:

1. Both rapidly and gradually rising interest rates

2. Both rapidly and gradually falling interest rates

3. Stable interest rates

4. Combinations of these conditions over time

It is also necessary to consider the impact of the shape of the market yield curve reflecting the relationship of short-term interest rates to long-term interest rates.

It is perhaps frustrating that interest-sensitive cash flow analysis will not produce a "correct answer." A predictable pattern of future interest rates cannot be known, since certainty is, of course, impossible. This is the nature of forecasting under conditions of uncertainty.

The usefulness of interest-sensitive cash flow analysis results from the analyst's ability to view probable results over a range of possible interest rate environments, and to identify the interest rate environments that might produce unacceptable solvency or profitability results. The analyst can then make judgments as to the probability of "troublesome" environments actually developing. When there appears to be a reasonable probability of interest rate environments developing that could adversely impact cash flow, management action is necessary. When the likelihood of adverse interest rate environments is remote, an insurer can expect profitable results under reasonable economic conditions.

Interest-sensitive cash flow analysis does not eliminate interest rate risk, but it is a helpful tool in describing risk. The insurer is able to make a reasonably informed judgment as to the level of interest rate risk it can tolerate, and to better understand the potential consequences of the risk it decides to assume.

Figure 30-7 presents the results of a hypothetical interest-sensitive cash flow analysis for a particular product. Twelve different interest rate scenarios are tested for their contribution to insurer surplus. As the results indicate, scenarios 2, 4, and 5 represent the potential for significant adverse impact to solvency and profitability. Given these results, the company is able to evaluate the probability of these troublesome environments actually developing, and to compare these results against the significant profits that may be achieved under other scenarios.

**FIGURE 30-7**

**FORECASTED PRODUCT CASH FLOWS —12 POSSIBLE SCENARIOS**

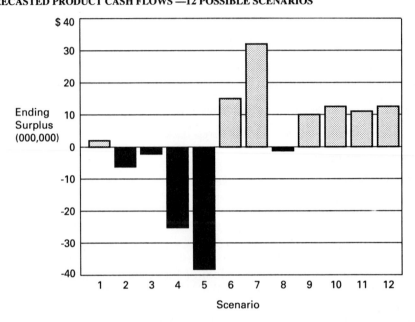

## APPLICATIONS OF CASH FLOW ANALYSIS

The most compelling reason for the development of interest-sensitive cash flow analysis has been the need to effectively manage the asset/liability matching risk. Asset/liability matching risk management is discussed in the balance of this chapter. Both *product design* and *pricing* and the construction, management, and performance measurement of *investment portfolios* are derivatives of cash flow analysis. As will be demonstrated, the importance of cash flow analysis extends to virtually every aspect of effective life insurer financial management.

In Chapter 32, statutory accounting principles (SAP) designed to measure insurer *solvency*, and generally accepted accounting principles (GAAP) designed to measure insurer *profitability*, are introduced. It will be seen that each accounting method is a static method of financial analysis, and that the sensitivity of aggregate corporate cash flows to changing interest rates must be considered to effectively evaluate the ability of an insurer to meet its future obligations and to produce profits. Performance measurement based on *economic value analysis* is derived from the cash flow model, and *value-based planning*, discussed in Chapter 29, is driven by the economic value revealed in cash flow analysis.

Additional financial management efforts requiring cash flow analysis

**FIGURE 30-8**

**FINANCIAL MANAGEMENT DISCIPLINES THAT ARE DERIVED FROM INTEREST-SENSITIVE CASH FLOW ANALYSIS**

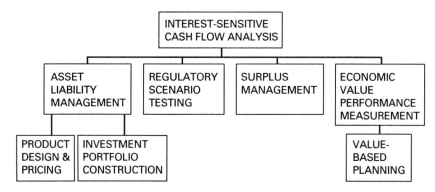

include *surplus management*, discussed below, and the *scenario testing*, which are requirements of the valuation actuary regulatory initiatives discussed in Chapter 32.

Interest-sensitive financial modeling has become critical to identifying, describing, and managing life insurer cash flows. Figure 30-8 presents interest-sensitive cash flow analysis as the central engine for the major elements of life insurer financial management. The following section discusses techniques for controlling interest-sensitive cash flows through the asset/liability management process.

## MANAGING LIFE INSURANCE CASH FLOW

Asset/liability management is a multidisciplinary undertaking. It involves both insurance product contract design and asset management. From an asset/liability perspective, the purpose of contract design is to discourage or prevent book value cash withdrawals under conditions likely to cause liquidity problems, and the purpose of asset management is to maintain an investment portfolio with sufficient liquidity to pay current obligations under a variety of economic conditions.

Because of the importance of the relationship between contract design and asset management, the actuarial and investment departments of life insurance companies are developing a closer working relationship than has been the case in the past. In some companies the position of chief financial officer has been created to manage at a senior level the activities of both the actuarial and investment departments.

The asset/liability cash flow relationship, must, of course, be integrated with the primary objectives of contract design and asset management, namely to develop marketable, actuarially sound products and to produce a maximum return on invested assets that is consistent with the company's tolerance for risk.

## OBJECTIVE OF ASSET/LIABILITY MANAGEMENT

The primary objective of asset/liability management (ALM) is to manage the impact of market interest rate changes on company cash flow. Central to the problem of ALM is the fact that interest rate shifts may have different impacts on asset and liability cash flows. This disproportionate impact may affect both liquidity (net cash flow for a given period) and surplus (cumulative net predividend cash flow for all future periods).

Net cash flow is a basic measure of liquidity for a given period:

$$\text{Asset cash flows} - \text{Liability cash flows} = \text{Net cash flow}$$

ALM in a perfect (although impractical) world is accomplished by balancing the impact of market interest rate changes:

$$\text{Asset cash flow changes} - \text{Liability cash flow changes} = 0$$

So that:

$$\text{Expected Asset Cash [Flows]} + \text{Asset Cash Flow Changes]} - \text{Expected Liability Cash [Flows]} + \text{Liability Cash Flow Changes]} = \text{Expected Net Cash Flow}$$

The impact of a change in market rates on cash flow may be either positive or negative. The degree of risk associated with an insurer's asset/liability position can be measured by the degree of variability in net cash flow produced by different market interest environments. In a perfect situation, the expected net cash flow value would remain constant through any interest rate environment, and the variability of expected cash flow, or asset/liability risk, would be 0. Asset and liability controls (discussed in the next section) are used to manage the timing and magnitude of asset and liability cash flow changes.

## THE RISK MANAGEMENT PROCESS

Common analytical methods applicable to all risk-management programs can be used to illustrate the nature of asset/liability risk management. The risk management process involves the establishment of objectives, the identification of exposures to loss, the selection of techniques for management of risk and the periodic review of the risk management strategy.

An insurer's asset/liability risk management objectives will be consistent with its primary financial objective. For most insurers, this primary financial objective is to generate growth in the economic value of the firm at a rate that is competitive with alternative uses presenting similar risk for the capital invested in the company.[18] Thus, for a given level of asset/liability risk, the insurer will test for a minimum level of expected return on its capital. The nature of the asset/liability risk is such that risk and profits are positively correlated—that is, more profits will imply more risk, and insurers should limit incremental profit-seeking activities when the probability of adverse results is inconsistent with solvency and profitability constraints.

The identification of exposures to loss is developed through the interest-sensitive cash-flow modeling process. The results of the cash flow forecast, together with the company's risk and return criteria, are used to identify asset/liability risks that are not tolerable. The intolerable risk will then be analyzed for its susceptibility to effective risk-management techniques. Depending upon its character, the risk may be avoided, transferred, retained or reduced.

*Avoidance* of asset/liability risk is warranted when a particular product will produce results that are not consistent with the company's risk and return criteria, and when the risk is not transferrable or controllable. The company will then decline to enter the market with the product. Of course, avoidance is not an option with respect to the asset/liability risk associated with in-force products.

*Transfer* of the asset/liability risk to the policyowner is the perfect asset/liability match. The new generation of variable life and annuity products passes investment experience directly through a separate account to the policyowner. In effect, withdrawal liabilities are *defined* by reference to the asset value of the separate account, and thus there is no asset/liability risk. While there has been significant growth in the market for variable products, a substantial majority of most insurers' insurance portfolios are comprised of traditional or interest-sensitive nonvariable products.[19]

---

[18]The concept of economic value and value-based planning is discussed in Chap. 29.

[19]Independent elements of the asset/liability risk may be transferred as well. Options, futures, swaps, and securitization are discussed below.

To achieve their profitability goals, most insurers find it necessary to *retain* some asset/liability risk. Competitive considerations in effect require that companies mismatch their assets and liabilities intentionally. The objective, however, is to do so on an informed basis that is consistent with the company's solvency and profitability constraints, and to control the retained risk to the extent that it is possible to do so.

The balance of this chapter is devoted to *risk reduction* techniques from the perspective of both liabilities and assets. The purpose of risk reduction is to control the probability and magnitude of adverse cash flow consequences resulting from the impact of changing market interest rates on asset and liability cash flows.

## LIABILITY CONTROLS

The purpose of liability control is to discourage or prevent book value cash withdrawals under conditions that are likely to cause liquidity problems. Liability control is accomplished during the contract design process through the inclusion of contractual provisions that create either additional cash flows to the policyowner who persists or additional cash flows to the insurer when withdrawal options are exercised.

The development of the entire new generation of current assumption products in the United States can be viewed as withdrawal liability control on a grand scale. When interest rates began to rise in the 1970s, many insurers (particularly stock companies writing guaranteed cost, nonparticipating products) had no mechanism for passing higher investment returns to policyowners. Mutual company dividend practices and regulations created delays in passing favorable results to participating policyowners. On a comparative basis, these policies were expensive, and as the practice of illustration selling gathered momentum,[20] they became highly vulnerable to replacement.

It became clear that some method of responding relatively rapidly to changing interest rates was essential to the development of competitive new products. Universal life, current assumption whole life and indeterminate premium policies are examples of the new generation of products that have mechanisms for adjusting life insurance prices as market interest rates change. When interest rates rise, interest can be credited to policyowners at rates that are competitive with other current financial instruments, and thus the incentives to withdraw are reduced or neutralized.

These experience-participation features also protect a company when

---

[20]See Chap. 33.

interest rates decline. An insurer can thereby reduce its credited interest and is not burdened with long-term interest guarantees that current investments will not adequately fund.

In addition to provisions that permit crediting of additional interest to policyowners who persist, other contract features represent disincentives to withdrawal by creating additional cash flow to the insurer when withdrawal options are exercised. Surrender charges are the most obvious example of liability controls that generate additional cash flow to an insurer when policyowners withdraw. To the extent permitted by nonforfeiture laws, charges against the policyowner's cash value are available to offset any costs associated with the surrender.

Direct recognition features reduce the amount of interest credited or dividends paid to policyowners to the extent that funds have been withdrawn under policy loan options. Interest withheld under the direct recognition agreement is available to offset any financial consequences of disintermediation.

Variable policy loan rates permit the adjustment of policy loan rates to reflect the interest rate environment existing throughout the life of the policy. The company will receive a current rate of interest for its loan and is not compelled to invest its assets at low rates agreed to years before.

Liability controls implemented by life insurers have been successful in reducing asset/liability risk. Research indicates a significant reduction in the sensitivity of policy loan demand to changes in market interest rate changes.[21]

## ASSET CONTROLS[22]

The purpose of asset control techniques is to maintain a portfolio with sufficient liquidity to pay current obligations under a variety of economic conditions, while achieving a maximum rate of return for a given level of solvency and profitability risk. Asset/liability risk is a special risk associated with the management of a financial intermediary institution that both borrows money (premiums) from its customers and reinvests the borrowed funds.

The asset/liability risk is really a particular profile of general investment risks faced by all investors, and it results from the manner in which these risks interact with the operation of an intermediary institution. The invest-

[21]James M. Carson and Robert E. Hoyt, "An Econometric Analysis of the Demand for Life Insurance Policy Loans," *The Journal of Risk and Insurance*, Vol. 59 (June 1992), pp. 239-251.

[22]This section draws from *The New Life Insurance Financial Management Structure*, copyright © 1988, LOMA (Life Office Management Association/Tillinghast). Adapted with permission of the publisher.

ment portfolio construction process is discussed in Chapter 31, but it will be seen that the asset control techniques discussed here are *investment constraints* that govern the portfolio construction process. In other words, investments must be selected that are consistent with any asset control strategy undertaken. Just as policy contract design is an important element of liability control activity, investment contract design can be an important element of asset control activity. Although more than one-half of the average life insurer's assets are purchased in the open market and obtained on the same terms as those purchased by the general investing public, a significant portion of life insurers' assets are invested in privately placed and individually negotiated corporate bonds and mortgages. These private investments can be negotiated with a view to supporting an insurer's asset/liability risk management strategy.

*Bond portfolio dedication techniques* are used to fund future liabilities while minimizing or eliminating interest rate risk. Cash matching, duration matching, and horizon matching are discussed in Chapter 31.

*Hedging transactions* are also available to transfer interest rate risk to other parties. Risk management assets—including futures, options, and swap contracts—are discussed in Chapter 31. The objective of hedging transactions is to balance any negative impact to expected cash flow resulting from interest rate changes with simultaneous risk management asset gains.

*Securitization* involves the bundling of a portfolio of assets (e.g., mortgages) into a marketable security and the subsequent sale of the portfolio in the capital market. Companies are able then to reinvest the cash proceeds into assets that are better suited to their investment needs.

The contemporary volatility of interest rates during the recent past has had a profound impact on the life insurance industry. Life companies have come to understand their business as a cash flow business, and this new understanding is apparent in virtually every aspect of their operations. Matching asset/liability cash flows has become a necessity in managing the risk associated with operating a life insurance business.

The importance of controlling the impact of changing interest rates on asset/liability cash flows is perhaps best exemplified by the entire new generation of life insurance products. Virtually every feature that distinguishes these products from their traditional predecessors (direct recognition, surrender charges, separate accounts, variable loan rates, indeterminate and flexible premium structures, and so on) is designed to control company cash flow response to changing market interest rates.

As discussed in the chapters that follow, asset/liability matching concerns influence insurer management policy in organization, investment management, product design and marketing. The regulatory environment is also rapidly changing. The asset valuation reserve, the interest maintenance reserve, the valuation actuary, and risk-based capital concepts will be seen in Chapter 32 as efforts to promote policyowner security within the context of this recognition that life insurance is a cash flow business.

## SURPLUS MANAGEMENT

The purpose of policy reserves is to ensure the availability of funds to satisfy expected liability cash flow requirements. The possibility of unexpected cash flow requirements arising from the C-1, C-2, C-3, and C-4 risks implies the need for additional funds to support any product line or business venture, and creates the need for surplus. The possibility and magnitude of unexpected cash flow requirements have increased significantly in recent decades, and the management of surplus sufficiency has become increasingly important to effective financial management of insurers.[23]

Central to the concept of surplus management is an understanding of the subjective nature of the perception of surplus. The terms *assets*, *liabilities*, and *surplus* have no meaning apart from the accounting conventions that are used to define them. This fact will become evident in Chapter 32, through a discussion of the financial information needs of various constituencies served by life insurer management, including policyowners, shareholders, rating agencies, and regulators.

Each of these constituencies has its definition of surplus as well as its own interest in surplus. Life insurer management, therefore, must view the sufficiency of surplus from the various, and sometimes inconsistent, perspectives that others bring to the concept.

As discussed above, the two most compelling financial objectives for life insurers are typically solvency and profitability—both of which are affected by a firm's operating leverage. Paradoxically, the twin objectives are best served by conflicting, and mutually exclusive, surplus management policies.

**Operating leverage** can be measured as the ratio of premium income to surplus. As operating leverage increases, two financial results are expected:

•An insurer's equity growth and return on invested capital will increase.

•The probability of insolvency increases.

In stock companies, therefore, policyowners, regulators, and rating agencies have an interest in maximum surplus, while shareholders have an interest in minimized levels of surplus. Each of these preferences is offset in part by the

---

[23]For a detailed description of the surplus management process, see *Capital Management in the Life Insurance Industry*.

expected policyowner preference for low-cost coverage and the shareholder preference for solvency. Affordable coverage and solvency are simultaneous concerns of all company policyowners. The objective of surplus management is to balance these conflicting needs in a way that satisfies the expectations of both policyowners and shareholders.

In determining appropriate surplus levels, it is useful to consider different layers of surplus that support the objectives expected by an insurer's various contingencies. Each layer represents an additional amount of required capital and includes capital represented in underlying layers.

- •**Cash flow surplus** is the minimum amount of market value required to supplement reserves in satisfying all existing contractual obligations of an insurer in the event of unexpected contingencies.

- •**Solvency surplus** is represented by the book value surplus required to maintain statutory solvency in the event of unexpected contingencies.

- •**Solidity surplus** is the additional surplus held to fund new sales, and to maintain some excess of surplus above legal requirements in the event of unexpected contingencies. Solidity surplus is necessary to satisfy the requirements of rating agencies.

- •**Benchmark** or **target surplus** is the amount of aggregate surplus required to cover cash flow contingencies, to satisfy regulatory and rating agency requirements, and to reduce the probability of insolvency to management's level of comfort.

The production and maintenance of benchmark surplus (including dividends distributed to shareholders and policyowners) constitutes the primary control variable for an insurer's solvency and profitability criteria.

Because of the risk-taking nature of insurance, measuring the profitability of a product line or venture must include the recognition of the benchmark surplus required to support the venture as well as the actual venture cash flows. In Chapter 32, the importance of benchmark surplus to product pricing and performance measurement is discussed under "Economic Value Analysis." The concept of risk-based capital can be viewed as a developing regulatory requirement of benchmark surplus and is also discussed in Chapter 32.

Amounts of capital exceeding management's required benchmark surplus level—sometimes referred to as **vitality surplus**—are available for research and development, new business diversifications, and other enterprises outside the normal operating plan of an insurer.

The surplus management process begins at the product line level with a determination of the benchmark surplus required to support the product. Product managers should project surplus requirements over a reasonable period of the expected product life span in order to determine whether required growth in benchmark surplus will be generated through product sales or will need to be acquired externally.

At the corporate level, the benchmark surplus requirements of all product lines are aggregated and comprehensive surplus strategy is established by: (1) ensuring that aggregate benchmark surplus is consistent with statutory requirements; (2) ensuring that aggregate benchmark surplus is consistent with rating agency requirements; (3) identifying the residual vitality surplus available to develop new products and ventures; and (4) establishing a strategy for the deployment of vitality surplus consistent with corporate solvency and profitability constraints.

# Chapter 31

# LIFE INSURER INVESTMENT MANAGEMENT

## INTRODUCTION

The investment function is a critically important subset of the overall financial management of a life insurance company. This chapter provides an overview of the formulation of investment strategy and the investment management process. Specifically, this chapter will (1) discuss the scope and importance of life insurer investment activity and policies; (2) identify common sources of investment risk and their special implications for a life insurer; (3) provide an overview of life insurer investment asset classes; (4) detail a value-based portfolio construction process designed to create an investment portfolio with cash flow properties that are consistent with an insurer's expected liability cash flows and asset/liability risk-management strategy; and (5) describe regulatory constraints that are applicable to life insurer investment activity.

### LIFE INSURER INVESTMENT ACTIVITY

Life insurer investment management is a significant element in the successful operation of an insurer and in its relationships with its clients. The aggregate investment activities of any country's life and health insurance industry are also a major source of capital for national economic growth. Successful asset management is a primary objective for all life and health insurers.

Life insurers fund investments in all types of corporations and make direct investments and mortgage loans for office buildings, shopping malls, apartment buildings, and other real estate. Among U.S. financial intermediary institutions, life insurance companies rank second only to commercial banks in total assets under management, and the relative contribution of funds to U.S. money and capital markets has been increasing.[1] Figure 31-1 illustrates the trend in capital contributions of life insurers, commercial banks and savings and loan associations from 1970-1991.

The total investment portfolio of a life insurance company can be separated into two categories:  (1) assets supporting the insurer's general account and (2) assets supporting separate accounts. The accounts are classified primarily according to the nature of the liabilities or obligations for which the assets are being held and invested. Assets used to support contractual obligations providing for guaranteed fixed-dollar benefit payments normally are held in the company's **general account**. Other invested assets, used to support the liabilities associated with investment risk pass-through products or lines of business (e.g., variable annuities, variable life insurance, and pension products) are held in special

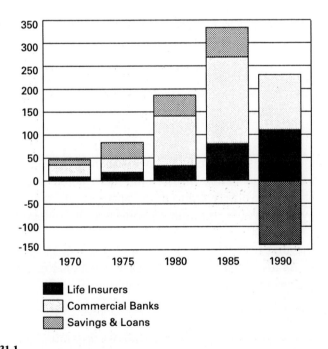

**FIGURE 31-1**

**LIFE INSURERS, COMMERCIAL BANKS, AND SAVINGS AND LOAN ASSOCIATIONS AS SOURCES OF FUNDS IN U.S. MONEY AND CAPITAL MARKETS**

*Source:* American Council of Life Insurance

[1] Because life insurance companies are far fewer in number than banks, the average portfolio of a life company is large relative to the average bank portfolio.

accounts typically labeled as **separate accounts**. Separate accounts were first used by U.S. life insurance companies in connection with their pension business in the early 1960s. A separate account is a fund established by a life insurance company and held separately from all other assets. State laws provide that assets in separate accounts may be invested without regard to the restrictions that are usually placed on the general account investments of life insurers. Thus a separate account portfolio might be comprised of only common stocks, only bonds, only mortgages, or some combination of these investments. Over 13 percent of all assets of U.S. life insurers are held in seperate accounts.

## IMPORTANCE OF INVESTMENT PERFORMANCE

Life insurer investment activities cut across all product lines and have wide significance for a company's relationship with its customers. The investment performance of the general account of a life company affects profits, dividends, and interest credits on term, traditional whole life and universal life and other current assumption products, as well as traditional annuity products and guaranteed investment contracts. Separate account performance affects variable life and annuity products and pension funds when benefits by contract depend upon investment performance and investment results are therefore passed directly to policyowners. Many insurers also offer pure investment vehicles such as money market funds, mutual funds, and other asset management services.

As discussed in Chapters 19, 20, and 21, the process of pricing insurance products, declaring dividends, and crediting interest is highly dependent on the investment returns an insurer earns. Insurers that earn above-average returns can price products more favorably than others, and insurers that earn below-average returns may not be able to retain customers in a competitive industry.

The importance of the investment management process has increased significantly in recent years. As discussed in Chapter 30, the traditional methods of life insurer financial management that were prevalent until the 1970s proved to be inadequate as economic and investment conditions began to change rapidly. Increased competition in financial services generally and the life insurance industry in particular squeezed pricing policies that were traditionally conservative. Superior investment performance is relatively more important now as a source of profits, and sales growth and profitability are more closely linked with investment performance.

The development of interest-sensitive, variable, and flexible-premium products has created significant interdependence between investment performance and product performance. Investment management has become considerably more complex since asset/liability management concerns demand the integration of investment management and product design and management into a coherent process.

Investment markets themselves have become increasingly complex because of the increased volatility of interest rates. The universe of available investment alternatives has expanded rapidly as capital markets continue to develop synthetic and derivative investment vehicles designed to address the portfolio manager's need to manage the impact of market volatility on the investment portfolio. As with all aspects of life insurer management, the investment management process has become more sensitive to the wide range of simultaneous influences that changing market interest rates can bring to investment values, product performance, and customer behavior.

## ESTABLISHING INVESTMENT POLICIES

As pointed out in Chapter 29, the board of directors or trustees has ultimate responsibility for establishing an insurer's investment policies. This responsibility is usually delegated to a finance or investment committee that is charged with developing investment policies designed to achieve the company's strategic objectives; the stated policy then guides the day-to-day activities of investment managers.

In establishing the investment policy constraints that define the parameters of the portfolio construction process, the finance or investment committee considers a number of environmental influences. These typically include general economic conditions and expected inflation, government monetary and fiscal policy, the state of various investment markets, the insurer's market posture and that of its competitors, tax liabilities, and other factors that may have an impact on investment values and policyowner behavior. Insurers operating internationally also would be concerned with currency rates, trade balances, and the geographic location of liabilities.

As discussed in the previous chapter, life insurers must address the asset/liability risk inherent in all financial intermediary activities. Investment policy for life insurers establishes a level of risk tolerance not only for individual assets and collective portfolios, but also for the risk associated with mismatched assets and liabilities. At a minimum, insurer investment objectives include meeting obligations to policyowners, maintaining the insurer's ability to compete for market share, and contributing to the growth of earnings and surplus. The primary objective is to create an investment portfolio with cash flow properties that are consistent with an insurer's expected liability cash flows and asset/liability risk-management strategy, and with its solvency and profitability constraints.

## INVESTMENT RISK

### THE SPECIAL NATURE OF LIFE INSURER INVESTMENT RISK

One of the central concepts of investment analysis is the commonly acknowledged relationship of investment risk and investment return. Greater degrees of risk associated with an investment typically imply greater returns. The objective of general investment portfolio management is to maximize investment return for a given level of risk (or to minimize risk for a desired level of return). Investment risk is generally defined as the potential variability of returns.

The traditional concept of the risk/return relationship applies to life insurers as it does to other investors. However, two aspects of the operating nature of the life insurance business require special portfolio management considerations that do not typically affect all investors. These special characteristics are revealed in the risk classifications discussed in Chapter 30.

The C-1 asset risk for insurers encompasses the same four subcategories of risk faced by all investors: (1) interest rate risk, (2) credit risk, (3) market risk, and (4) currency risk.

•**Interest rate risk** exists because the value of fixed income investments fluctuates as market interest rates change, and because the real (inflation-adjusted) rate of return may similarly fluctuate.

•**Credit risk** is the possibility that the issuer of a fixed income investment may not be able to meet its obligations due to insolvency or reorganization in bankruptcy.

•**Market risk** exists because the value of individual investments can be affected by factors that impact all investments of that class. The common stock prices of many successful companies often do not reflect their success because the stock market as a whole is not advancing.

•**Currency risk** exists because currency exchange rates relative to the U.S. dollar are not fixed, and the exchange process can increase or decrease returns associated with nondollar investments.

The C-2 insurance pricing risk incorporates the first investment aspect special to insurers and other financial intermediaries. The rate of return assumed in calculating premiums is used to discount the price of insurance to policyowners. This is an implied long-term interest rate guarantee (interest rate guarantees on interest-sensitive products are explicit). The discounting practice has two important implications: (1) to meet solvency and profitability objectives, investment returns at a minimum must equal the returns assumed in its pricing practices and (2) there are opportunities to enhance profits by achieving investment returns that exceed pricing assumptions.

The simple objective of maximizing return for a given level of asset risk must be supplemented by constraints that recognize (1) the compelling need to achieve a minimum return equal to the pricing assumption and (2) the fact that absolute yields are less important than the spread between pricing assumptions and actual earnings.

The C-3 asset/liability matching risk incorporates the second investment consideration that is special to financial intermediaries. As discussed in Chapter 30, changing market interest rates can simultaneously affect the value of a company's assets and the behavior of its customers. The investment management discipline, along with contract design, is therefore a subset of the asset/liability management process.

Despite these special characteristics, life insurers, like other investors, prefer higher returns in order to minimize the cost of insurance products and to maximize profitability objectives. When insurers seek to maximize return for a given level of risk, however, the concept of return must incorporate the idea of investment spreads, and the concept of risk must incorporate the possibilities of inadequate pricing and mismatched assets and liabilities, as well as the potential variability of investment returns.

Because of the special financial intermediary characteristics of life insurer operation and the special risk profile that results, fixed income investments make up the significant majority of a life insurer's assets. As discussed below, bond portfolio dedication techniques are used to (1) ensure returns that exceed pricing assumptions and (2) maintain an appropriate relationship between a life insurer's asset and liability cash flows.

## THE FORWARD COMMITMENT ASPECT OF INTEREST RATE RISK

Some life insurer investment opportunities, particularly private placements and mortgages, are structured so that the commitment to make an investment is followed by a period of deferral before the investment is actually funded. These commitments are known as **forward commitments** and are problematical for insurance companies because the commitment is not always mutual. The insurance company is bound to make the investment at the agreed time of funding, but the borrower is not bound to accept the loan. This is termed the **forward commitment risk**.

Life companies traditionally were able to plan ahead and make forward commitments because their cash flow was predictable, their liquidity needs were stable, and interest rates varied little. As interest rates became more volatile, forward commitments evolved into valuable call options for borrowers. If interest rates had risen when the time for funding arrived, borrowers followed through on their relatively low interest rate loans; if interest rates had fallen, they declined to accept the insurance company loan and borrowed at lower rates elsewhere.[2] To minimize the adverse impact of borrower behavior when interest

---

[2]See Robert H. Stapleford and Kenneth W. Stewart, "Introduction to the Formation of Investment Strategy," *SOA Study Note*, Course 220 (Itasca, Ill.: Society of Actuaries, 1991).

rates change, U.S. life insurers now underwrite loans made on a forward commitment basis more carefully, often charging fees for commitments and shortening the typical commitment period.

## INVESTMENT ASSETS

### U.S. LIFE INSURANCE INDUSTRY MIX OF ASSETS

U.S. life insurance companies hold assets of over $1,500 billion. The largest investment category consists of corporate bonds, representing over 40 percent of total industry assets. Real estate mortgage loans account for over 17 percent of total assets, while directly owned real estate represents 3 percent. Life insurer holdings of U.S. Treasury and federal agency securities represent another 17 percent of assets. Corporate equity holdings are almost 11 percent of total assets.

Investments in securities of other countries' governments and international agencies have always been small, amounting to $17 billion, or just over 1 percent of total assets. Investments in both long- and short-term non-U.S. corporate debt obligations represent about 2 percent of industry assets, of which a major share is in Canadian securities.

Policy loans make up another 4 percent of industry assets. These loans are taken at the option of the policyowner. Although policy loans are considered invested assets, they are not the responsibility of the investment department. Figure 31-2 shows the distribution of assets of U.S. life insurers at the end of 1991.

### INVESTMENT ASSET CLASSES[3]

This section provides an overview of the major asset types that comprise the investment portfolio of a typical U.S. life insurer, particular U.S. regulatory constraints that affect their acquisition by life insurers, and their major cash flow properties. In today's highly diverse capital markets, a virtually limitless variety of cash flow patterns can be associated with most investments; the cash flow properties discussed below are those that are most broadly offered and acquired.

As will be discussed in Chapter 32, **admitted assets** are those that qualify for listing on the insurer's statutory balance sheet. Investment regulation rules apply to these admitted assets; an insurer may hold an unrestricted amount of nonadmitted assets, but no value for minimum capital, surplus, or reserves is granted under statutory rules.

---

[3]This section draws on Kenneth M. Wright, "The Life Insurance Industry in the United States: An Analysis of Economic and Regulatory Issues," *Working Papers* (The World Bank, 1992), pp. 14-23.

**FIGURE 31-2**

**DISTRIBUTION OF ASSETS OF U.S. LIFE INSURERS FOR 1991**

*Source*: American Council of Life Insurance

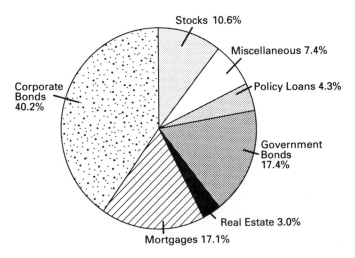

*Corporate Debt Obligations*. Fixed income obligations of corporations have been the leading investment asset for most U.S. life insurers since mid-century. As discussed above, fixed income investments are well suited to the objectives of attaining pricing assumption yields and managing the asset/liability relationship.

*1. Corporate Bonds*. Since the Second World War, the U.S. life insurance industry has funded a significant portion of the long-term capital requirements of industrial corporations, and since the 1960s it has also provided significant capital for oil and gas pipelines, aircraft, and other transportation equipment. The cash flow properties of publicly traded corporate bonds are determined primarily by periodic payment of interest at the coupon rate, and the lump-sum payment of principal at maturity. Deviations from expected cash flow can be caused by credit deterioration and default by the issuer, and prepayment of principal under call provisions. As discussed in Chapter 30, changing market interest rates can affect the market value realized if a bond is sold before maturity, as well as the probability that a bond may be called by the issuer.

Public issues of corporate bonds are rated for credit quality by rating agencies such as Standard and Poor's and Moody's. Figure 31-3 shows the rating definitions used by these agencies.

Life insurers developed and have long used a lending technique known as **private placements**. Private placements are advantageous to both issuers and life insurer investors because (1) the increased legal, accounting, and brokerage

**FIGURE 31-3**

**BOND RATINGS**

*Source*: Moody's Bond Record and Standard & Poor's Bond Guide

| Moody's | S&P | Definition |
|---------|-----|------------|
| Aaa | AAA | *High-grade investment bonds.* The highest rating assigned, denoting extremely strong capacity to pay principal and interest. Often called "gilt edge" securities. |
| Aa | AA | *High-grade investment bonds.* High quality by all standards, but rated lower primarily because the margins of protection are not quite as strong. |
| A | A | *Medium-grade investment bonds.* Many favorable investment attributes, but elements may be present that suggest susceptibility to adverse economic changes. |
| Baa | BBB | *Medium-grade investment bonds.* Adequate capacity to pay principal and interest but possibly lacking certain protective elements against adverse economic conditions. |
| Ba | BB | *Speculative issues.* Only moderate protection of principal and interest in varied economic times. |
| B | B | *Speculative issues.* Generally lacking desirable characteristics of investment bonds. Assurance of principal and interest may be small. |
| Caa | CCC | *Default.* Poor-quality issues that may be in default or in danger of default. |
| Ca | CC | *Default.* Highly speculative issues, often in default or possessing other market shortcomings. |
| C | | *Default.* These issues may be regarded as extremely poor in investment quality. |
| | C | *Default.* Rating given to income bonds on which no interest is paid. |
| | D | *Default.* Issues actually in default, with principal or interest in arrears. |

commissions associated with public offerings are avoided; (2) the issuer is certain that the entire offering will be acquired; and (3) the terms of the offering are negotiated directly, providing an opportunity for the parties to better define or customize their agreement. Private placements are less liquid and marketable than public offerings; however, insurers acquiring private placements normally expect increased yields to compensate for illiquidity.[4]

---

[4]An increasingly active secondary market for private placements has been developing among sophisticated institutional investors in recent years.

Life insurers also benefit from negotiating investment terms in a way that helps control asset/liability risk.[5] The cash flow properties of private placements can be tailored to meet the needs of both the issuer and the life insurer.

Large insurers typically employ a special staff devoted to analyzing and acquiring private placements; the analysis of private investments differs significantly from the analysis of public offerings, in large part because of the directly negotiated terms. Private placements are sometimes made to a small group or syndication of insurance companies. Participation in a syndication can be an attractive option for smaller insurers that do not have extensive research staffs and therefore rely on the investment judgment of larger companies in the group.

Through the 1960s and 1970s, life insurers acquired 75 percent or more of their corporate bond investments through private placements. In the 1980s, however, the share of private placements fell sharply, as the need for marketability of assets shifted acquisitions toward public issues. The ability to negotiate the cash flow properties of private placements directly has led to a large share of corporate bond holdings of life insurers being private placement issues.

Unlike private placements, for which a secondary market has just begun to develop, public issues are readily marketable. This became an important consideration for portfolio managers after 1980, when liquidity needs took on higher priority. As discussed in Chapter 30, liquidity needs increased because policyowners demanded policy loans or surrendered their policies to place the proceeds in other investments with significantly higher yields. The introduction of interest-sensitive insurance products after 1980 led to greater uncertainty about cash flows, and moved insurers toward more protective portfolios with higher liquidity ratios. In practice, this brought about a new interest in resalable public issues, along with a shortening of original maturities from around 20 years to about one-half that duration.

*2. Mortgage-Backed Securities.* Prior to the late 1960s, life insurers had been a major source of financing for single-family mortgages. The relative attractiveness of corporate yields, however, led to a decline in single-family residential financing, and only a few companies remain active in such direct lending.

In the late 1970s, derivative financial instruments known as **mortgage-backed securities** or **collateralized mortgage obligations** (CMOs) were developed in the capital markets. A CMO is a securitized package comprised of a large number of home loans originated by banks, savings and loans, and other originators, and by quasi-governmental agencies such as the Government National Mortgage Association (GNMA) and the Federal National Mortgage

---

[5]See Chap. 30.

Association (FNMA). Principal and interest payments of mortgages are passed through to the owners of the CMO.

The cash flow properties of CMOs differ from those of typical bonds because periodic payments of interest and principal are passed through to the bondholder, matching the self-amortizing home mortgage loan. The amount of interest and principal payments depends on the lending rate. Deviations from expected cash flows can be caused by defaults on the underlying mortgages and, in the case of variable rate mortgages, changing market interest rates. The market value of CMOs is similarly impacted by changing market interest rates.

*3. Regulation of Corporate Debt Obligations.* Because of the safety of corporate debt relative to equity investments, and because these investments are well suited to the financial management needs of life insurers, there are generally no state restrictions on the aggregate amount of corporate debt obligations that may be held as admitted assets in insurer portfolios. There are, however, restrictions with respect to the credit quality of corporate debt and to the concentration of investment in the securities of a particular issuer.

From an investment standpoint, the most important state laws are those of New York. The extraterritorial dimension of New York law requires all New York licensed insurers to comply in substance with New York investment law, even for insurers domiciled outside New York. A significant majority of all life insurance sold in the United States is sold by New York licensed companies, and hence is subject to New York investment laws. Traditionally, New York's eligibility rules for admitted bonds have involved a detailed and lengthy list of qualitative restrictions regarding the financial condition of the issuer. Because of increasing concern about the credit quality of noninvestment-grade bonds, a model NAIC law (discussed below) was enacted to provide a new approach to bond quality standards. This approach succeeds the "prudent person" rule (discussed below), adopted by New York in 1983.

The quantitative New York rules regarding concentration of investment in the securities of a particular issuer limit this investment to no more than 5 percent of the insurer's admitted assets. This requirement promotes asset quality by implicitly requiring diversification of bond investments among issuers.

**Commercial Real Estate Mortgages.** As with corporate debt obligations, commercial real estate mortgages are generally fixed income obligations. Historically, long-term commercial mortgage loans were made as an ideal way to match the long-term obligations assumed by life insurers under their whole life policies. Loan terms as long as 30 years were common. Commercial mortgages are generally illiquid investments; due to increasing liquidity requirements, the bulk of commercial mortgage lending is now closer to ten-year maturities.

Commercial mortgage loan commitments are generally made in advance of construction, and the proceeds are used to repay short-term bank construction financing. As discussed above, the forward commitment risk is increasingly being addressed by insurers through shorter commitment periods and more stringent underwriting and loan terms.

Commercial mortgages, like privately placed bonds, are directly negotiated between the insurer and borrower. The cash flow properties of mortgage loans vary widely. The negotiations represent an opportunity for insurers to match investment cash flows with expected liability cash flows, and to incorporate provisions that adjust investment cash flows to changing market interest rates.

The cash flow properties of mortgages are determined by the interest rate, principal repayment, and maturity provisions agreed upon in the loan document. The interest rate may be fixed or variable; principal may be repaid periodically or in a "bullet" or "balloon" lump sum. Additional returns supplementing earned interest are sometimes negotiated in the form of a limited equity interest or additional interest payment based upon the rental performance of the property.

Deviations from expected cash flows can be caused by default, prepayment of principal, and, in the case of variable rate mortgages, changing market interest rates. There is no significant secondary market for commercial mortgages, and most loans are held to maturity by the insurer.

State investment laws affecting admitted mortgage loans are both qualitative and quantitative in nature. The qualitative restrictions generally focus on limiting the principal amount of the loan to a stated percentage of appraised value. The limit in New York is 75 percent. Regulatory loan to value ratio requirements are applicable only at the time of the making of the loan. When real estate values are depressed, mortgages may exceed the applicable limit.

Quantitative restrictions apply to both aggregate mortgage investment as a percentage of assets (or capital and surplus), and to the percentage of assets (or capital and surplus) that may be devoted to a single property. In New York, the limits are 50 percent of assets in the aggregate and 2 percent of assets to any one property. Figure 31-4, on page 893, illustrates commercial mortgage loans as a percentage of life insurer assets from 1950 to 1991.

***U.S. Government Securities***. U.S. Government fixed income obligations, including Treasury bills (1-year maturity or less), notes (1- to 5-year maturities), and bonds (5- to 30-year maturities) are generally considered free from credit risk. Certain obligations of government agencies are similarly backed by the full faith and credit of the U.S. government. The yields on U.S. government issues are therefore less attractive than relatively more risky corporate obligations.

Following the end of World War II, government bonds were less attractive to life insurers than corporate bonds. Recent life insurer interest in U.S. government issues has grown significantly, however. The increased interest is in part due to the need to balance the unexpected high risk associated with many bonds and corporate mortgages acquired during the 1980s. Additionally, the highly liquid nature of government issues is ideal when the potential cash flow fluctuations resulting from interest-sensitive products may require the sale of assets.

The cash flow properties of U.S. government issues, like corporate obligations, are determined primarily by the coupon rate and maturity date. Because there is no credit risk, deviations from expected cash flow are possible only when an investment is sold or called before maturity. Because there is no credit risk, life insurer investment in U.S. government issues is generally unlimited. Figure 31-4 illustrates government securities as a percentage of life insurer assets from 1950 to 1991.

*Corporate Equities*. The cash flow characteristics associated with common stocks are far more variable, and therefore riskier, than those associated with fixed income obligations. As a result, U.S. life insurer interest in these investments has never been significant.

The cash flow properties of common stock are determined by the nonguaranteed, periodic payment of dividends, and by the market value of the shares. There is no maturity value for common stock.

While over relatively long time horizons common stock returns generally exhibit favorable risk-adjusted results, the irregular nature of the cash flow is considered not well suited to U.S. life insurer investment. As discussed above, U.S. life insurers need to seek relatively certain returns over specified time horizons that are consistent with their pricing assumptions and asset/liability management strategies, and the more predictable cash flow results associated with fixed income investments are generally desirable.

State investment laws historically prohibited the acquisition of common stock. Restrictions on general account investment have been somewhat liberalized, reflecting the inflation protection, diversification, and long-term performance benefits that stocks have exhibited. Relatively strict limits still apply to these investments, however. New York limits admitted common stock investment to no more than 2 percent of any issuer's stock, 0.2 percent of insurer assets in the stock of any one issuer, and 20 percent of insurer assets in the aggregate.

As discussed earlier, insurers sought, and regulators accommodated, the approval of separate accounts. Institutional clients of U. S. life insurers in the 1950s and 1960s perceived the constraints on insurer stock holdings negatively, fearing the prohibition of significant equity investments would impair the real return on long-term pension investments during times of inflation. Since separate accounts pass investment experience and risk directly to the insurer's clients, common stock holdings in separate accounts are generally not restricted. The separate account option became available to individual policyowners with the introduction of variable life insurance and annuities. Common stocks frequently comprise more than 50 percent of separate account assets.

Preferred stocks exhibit characteristics of both debt and equity investments. These shares pay a stated dividend when declared, and the preferred dividend liability must be satisfied before common stock dividends can be paid. Preferred stocks comprise less than 1 percent of life insurer assets. Figure 31-4 illustrates corporate stocks as a percentage of life insurer assets from 1950 to 1991.

***Investment Real Estate***. Direct investment or ownership in real estate is an equity investment like common stock. Real estate equity can be attractive to an insurer by producing higher current returns than equity in stocks, while providing the same opportunity for appreciation in the capital value of the investment. Real estate ownership is viewed as an attractive asset during times of inflation, since rents can be raised periodically as long as market conditions are favorable, thereby increasing property values.

The cash flow characteristics of investment real estate are determined by occupancy rates, rental fees, and operating expenses. Deviations from expected cash flow can result from tenant defaults and from variable occupancy rates.

The unpredictable cash flow properties of investment real estate are not well suited to U.S. life insurer investment needs. In recent years, real estate holdings have amounted to no more than 3 percent of total assets. About one-eighth of the total represents the value of insurer head offices and branches used for their own operations.

Investment laws limit real estate ownership, as with other invested assets. Under New York law, an insurer cannot own more than 2 percent of assets in any particular admitted property or more than 20 percent of assets in admitted real estate held for investment purposes. Up to 10 percent of admitted assets, however, can be devoted to properties used by the company, as long as total admitted real estate holdings do not exceed 25 percent. Figure 31-4 illustrates direct equity investment in real estate as a percentage of life insurer assets from 1950 to 1991.

Quantitative limits generally do not apply to real estate assets acquired through foreclosure. Regulators often require, however, that such properties be disposed of within a stipulated period of time.

***International Investments***. Investments in securities or equities issued by non-U.S. governments or nationals have been severely limited by state investment laws for many years. A number of large insurers, however, have engaged in lending abroad, although in relatively minor amounts.

***Policy Loans***. Policy loans are unique among life insurer investments for two reasons. First, policy loans are not made as the result of an investment management decision—they are options exercised at the discretion of the policyowner. Second, because loans should never exceed policy cash values, and unpaid principal amounts may be deducted from cash surrender proceeds or policy proceeds at the death of the insured, the safety of principal associated with most loans is absolute. (In the case of variable products, declining cash surrender values may reduce the value of the insurer's cash surrender collateral below the value of the loan.)

As discussed in Chapter 30, the historical experience with policy loans was troubling for life insurers, despite their safety of principal. Together with cash surrenders, they produced book value liquidity requirements that were unpredictable. With the advent of variable loan interest rates and direct recognition dividend provisions, policy loans associated with newer policies have become well suited to maintaining investment spreads and asset/liability risk management strategy.

The cash flow properties associated with principal payments and withdrawals are determined by policyowner preference; interest income is determined by the applicable loan rate in the case of variable loan rate policies, and, in the case of direct recognition policies, the effective interest is the sum of interest paid and the amount of policyowner benefit forgone in the form of the reduced dividend. Figure 31-4 illustrates policy loans as a percentage of life insurer assets from 1950 to 1991.

*Risk-Management Assets*. To minimize asset/liability risk, life insurers enter into hedging arrangements involving the use of options, futures, and swap contracts. Options and futures contracts produce gains or losses that offset gains or losses in the underlying asset portfolio, and they are also used to lock in current investment yields for premium income that will be received and invested at a future date. Swaps are used to exchange expected interest income patterns for other patterns better suited to the insurer's asset/liability matching requirements.

The price of interest rate futures and option contracts depends on an interest rate index (e.g., Treasury obligation yields). Depending on the position assumed by the insurer (i.e., long versus short, put versus call, number of contracts, and so on), a change in the interest rate index can produce cash flows to the insurer that:

•offset a decline in asset values

•offset an increase in liability values

•offset an increase in the expected purchase price of asset acquisitions
 planned for future premium receipts.

The cash flow properties of options and futures are highly speculative. Depending on the movement of market interest rates, returns may exceed the investment many times over, or the entire investment may be lost. When the net effect of interest rate movements on the value of risk-management assets and the underlying portfolio of assets and liabilities is considered, however, the result should be to reduce the variability of net cash flows, and hence risk.

Life insurers often have an advantage in purchasing fixed income investments, particularly in private placements. At the same time, the new generation of interest-sensitive insurance products provide for policy loan, surrender, and interest rate crediting liabilities of a variable-rate nature. Other capital market participants have advantages in acquiring variable-rate investments, but prefer to have fixed-rate income.

Interest-rate swaps permit an insurer to trade the fixed-rate interest payments it has a right to receive for the variable-rate interest payments another market participant will receive. The insurer's assets and liabilities are thus better

**FIGURE 31-4**

**U.S. LIFE INSURERS GENERAL ACCOUNT ASSET MIX FROM 1950 TO 1991.**

*Source*: American Council of Life Insurance

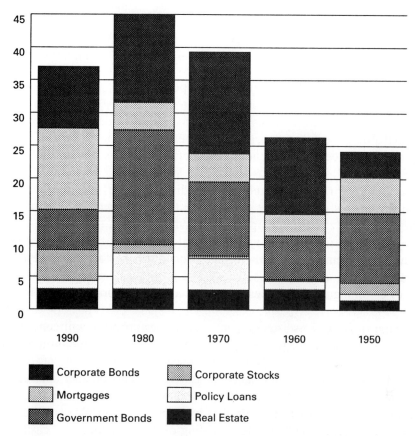

matched, while the insurer has shared its natural advantage in acquiring fixed-income investments with another participant who shares its natural advantage in variable-rate credit markets. Figure 31-4 illustrates corporate bond and mortgage-backed securities as a percentage of life insurer investment assets from 1950 to 1991.

## INVESTMENT PORTFOLIO CONSTRUCTION

Before examining the process of constructing an investment portfolio, it will be useful to review measures of investment performance. In a competitive environment, sales growth and profitability are closely related to investment performance, and investment markets have become more complex and volatile. Measuring the effectiveness of investment performance is increasingly critical to effective life insurer financial management.

## INVESTMENT PERFORMANCE MEASUREMENT

Traditional investment performance measurement has focused on achieving high yields while minimizing risk assumed for a given level of return. Refocusing performance measurement on the creation of value for shareholders and policyowners is more consistent with every insurer's primary objective, and it better promotes the construction of an investment portfolio that is consistent with the cash flow nature of the life insurance business discussed in Chapter 30.

Traditional measurement of investment performance generally involves three steps: (1) an investment yield is calculated for the asset portfolio under examination; (2) a benchmark, typically an investment index, is chosen; and (3) the portfolio yield is compared to the benchmark yield. To the extent investment yield exceeds the benchmark, performance is considered to be superior.

Because of the risk/return relationship discussed earlier, comparing an investment manager's performance to an index tends to create an incentive for the manager to select the riskiest investments available from the universe that is consistent with the insurer's investment policies. Traditional investment performance measurement also fails to take account of the fact that investment spreads may produce satisfactory solvency and profitability results without the necessity of assuming the risk necessary to exceed the performance of a market index.

Although traditional measures of investment performance will continue to be used in the financial management process, the following discussion identifies significant weaknesses in the traditional approach and describes the need for a comprehensive approach to performance measurement. This broader approach is needed for a better response to the dynamic nature of life insurer financial management discussed in Chapter 30, and it underlies a portfolio construction process that is consistent with an understanding of life insurance as a cash flow business.

Four general calculations have been widely used in the process of life insurer investment performance management. **New investment yield** measures the income yield on investments purchased during the measurement period and can be helpful in determining the marginal impact of purchase decisions. This calculation produces relatively volatile results from period to period, reflecting changing market interest rates.

**Portfolio book yield** measures the income yield on all investments, and therefore it produces relatively stable results from period to period. The current impact of prior purchase decisions is reflected. **Portfolio book income** measures aggregate cash inflows and outflows of principal and interest during the measurement period. It does not fully reflect the expected returns associated with prior purchase decisions, and its use is limited to comparisons with business plan projections. Finally, **portfolio total return** measures both income and market value changes during the measurement period.

Both the new investment and portfolio book yield measures fail to reflect fully the investment risk associated with the portfolio. Both credit risk and interest-rate risk are either ignored or inadequately reflected. New investment yield does not reflect credit or interest-rate risk, since market values are not taken into account. Portfolio book yield reflects the results of realized defaults and realized income associated with variable-rate investments, but credit deterioration and interest-rate risk are again ignored since market values are not taken into account.

Portfolio total return, because it reflects the market value of investments, is sensitive to interest rate and credit risk reflected in the market at the time of measurement, as well as income generated during the measurement period. Future interest rates and credit deterioration are not taken into account, however.

Traditional measures of investment performance at best retrospectively reflect risk realized during the measurement period, but they do not reflect changes in the prospective risk position assumed by the insurer for its future results. As discussed in Chapter 32, the economic value of a company is measured by the present value of cash flow, discounted at an interest rate reflecting both the cost of capital and the risk inherent in the company's products and ventures. If other factors remain unchanged, an increase in risk assumed by an insurer reduces the value of a company, while a reduction in risk increases its value. Since traditional measures of investment performance take no account of a change in risk profile assumed by the company, increased current yields achieved by the acquisition of risky investments may produce superior performance results by traditional methods, while at the same time reducing the value of the company.

The important issue in investment performance measurement is less whether a particular portfolio has outperformed a particular index during the measurement period, but whether the portfolio has contributed to the value of the firm. Investment portfolio construction, monitoring, and measurement must reflect potential risk, or variability of future cash flows, and they are best undertaken as integrated objectives within the context of interest-sensitive cash flow analysis discussed in Chapter 30.[6]

## THE CONSTRUCTION PROCESS

The portfolio construction process is designed to produce an investment program with cash flow properties that are consistent with an insurer's anticipated liability cash flows, pricing assumptions, and asset/liability risk-management

[6]For a detailed discussion of these issues, see William H. Panning, "The Investment Performance Paradox," *Symposium on Life Insurance Company Financial Management* (Philadelphia: S. S. Huebner Foundation, 1991).

strategy. Although the formal process may vary from insurer to insurer, five general steps are fundamental to building the portfolio effectively. The process described here is essentially a restatement of the interest-sensitive cash flow modeling process described in Chapter 30 from the perspective of the investment manager.

*1. Establish Proper Control Parameters.* Selecting an appropriate benchmark reflecting the insurer's solvency and profitability constraints for the planning of the portfolio and the measurement of its success is the first step in portfolio construction. In most situations, the objective will be to create growth in the value of the firm,[7] and a target or desired rate of growth will be established as a control parameter.

*2. Establish Portfolio Constraints.* Certain features of the investment portfolio or of insurer operations are necessarily limited for various reasons. Regulatory constraints should be obvious. Less obvious may be the need of insurers operating internationally to invest in different currencies, or limitations arising from the expected tax or financial reporting consequences of particular investment decisions.

An insurer's level of risk tolerance is established by the degree of variability in investment returns that is acceptable to management. The potential acceptable deviation of actual from expected results is always a significant constraint. The objectives of dedicated bond portfolio management techniques are discussed below and represent additional constraints for the typical life insurer.

*3. Establish Alternative Strategies.* Cash flow analysis should be conducted under a variety of possible economic scenarios. Alternative investment strategies are established to respond to the development of different market conditions. As discussed in Chapter 30, these strategies are developed in conjunction with dividend and interest-crediting strategies, as well as other responses available to the insurer.

*4. Conduct Cash Flow Analysis.* Cash flow analysis produces a range of possible outcomes that includes the expected or targeted results. The cash flow analysis includes both liability (product) cash flows and asset cash flows. The range of outcomes is examined, and strategies that produce unacceptable results are rejected. Strategies producing results that are consistent with solvency and profitability criteria and with portfolio constraints are adopted for implementation.

---

[7]Occasionally, short-term goals such as reported earnings, liquidity, or even solvency may override this objective.

5. *Monitor and Adjust Portfolio.* Monitoring the portfolio is accomplished by the periodic determination of two issues:

(1) Was actual performance during the measurement period within the distribution of acceptable outcomes?

(2) Does the distribution of possible future outcomes remain acceptable?

A negative response to either determinant signals the need for readjustment of the portfolio.

It is important that the cash flow-based portfolio construction and management process (1) avoid the unnecessary risk associated with high-yield incentives that may be embedded in an insurer's performance measurement techniques; (2) reflect the potential variability of future cash flows; and (3) reward value-creating activity rather than index-beating activity.

## BOND PORTFOLIO MANAGEMENT TECHNIQUES

As discussed above, investment risk for life insurers incorporates not only the potential variability of investment return, but also the possibilities of inadequate pricing and mismatched assets and liabilities. **Bond dedication** techniques are used to ensure that investment yields consistent with pricing assumptions and solvency and profitability constraints are achieved, and that the relationship of asset and liability cash flows remains relatively constant through changing interest-rate environments.

As discussed in Chapter 30, bond dedication involves dedicating a portfolio to servicing a prescribed set of future liabilities so that the possibility of interest-rate changes impairing the sufficiency of the portfolio to satisfy the designated liabilities will be limited or eliminated. In essence, future funds are locked-in and fluctuating interest rates should not affect the expected cash flows. While there are many variations, the most prominent dedication techniques include cash matching, duration matching, and horizon matching. Bond dedication is an asset/liability risk-reduction technique that is designed to control the anticipated cash flow properties of a portfolio servicing prescribed liability cash flows.

**Cash matching** involves the construction of a portfolio whose interest and principal payments exactly match a set of nominal liabilities. Cash matching normally requires fixed and certain liabilities. As discussed in Chapter 30, life insurer liabilities have become far less fixed and certain than had been historically the case, and the cash-matching technique has become less useful as liabilities have become more volatile.

**Duration matching** is a more sophisticated technique that takes into account the impact of market interest-rate changes on the value of an asset portfolio. The most common measure of duration, **The Macaulay Duration** is the average time point of the present values of interest and principal payments of a bond. Frederick R. Macaulay was a Scottish actuary who first proposed the concept of duration in 1938. Applied to liabilities, duration is the average time point of the present value of liability cash flows. A duration-matched set of portfolio assets and liabilities is immune to the impact of market interest rate changes. Duration matching is also referred to as **portfolio immunization.**

As discussed in Chapter 30, because bonds eventually mature, the capital value of a bond held to maturity exhibits a natural immunity to interest rate changes. Most bonds, however, pay periodic interest and the reinvestment rate affects total yield. The initial yield to maturity will be realized only if interest is reinvested at the same rate. Whenever market interest rates change, the actual yield to maturity will differ from the expected yield to maturity. Interest rate changes, however, affect bond capital values and interest on interest earnings inversely. For example, when rates rise the market price of a bond tends to decrease, but the interest on interest earnings tends to increase. The point in time where these effects are equal and opposite, precisely offsetting each other, is the Macaulay duration, measured in years. While a discussion of the financial mathematics of duration is beyond the scope of this chapter, two important, although nonintuitive, interpretations of duration are important to asset/liability management.

First, duration may be used to relate complex cash flows to simple cash flows. The duration concept can identify coupon bonds that behave like zero-coupon bonds. Since zero-coupon bonds have no cash flows before maturity, changing market interest rates do not affect the reinvestment of interest or total yield. A coupon bond of a given duration is identical mathematically to a zero-coupon bond having a maturity equal to the given duration. This property permits the matching of aggregate asset cash flows to liability cash flows without requiring the precision of a simple dedicated portfolio that is cash-matched.

Second, another form of duration, called **modified duration**, is a valuable measure of the interest-rate sensitivity of a bond's market value. There is a close relationship between a bond's duration and its price volatility. Duration is therefore valuable in conducting cash flow analyses and in preparing alternative investment strategies to respond to different interest-rate environments.[8]

**Horizon matching** is a blend of the cash- and duration-matching techniques. A short-term cash-matched portfolio is combined with a longer-term

[8]The application of duration is complicated because (a) every shift in market interest rates changes the duration of bonds and of liabilities, and portfolios must be periodically rebalanced to reflect the shift, and (b) nonparallel shifts in short- and long-term interest rates are normal, and it requires sophisticated mathematical analyses to account for the different rate movements. For a detailed discussion of duration, see Martin L. Leibowitz, "Duration and Immunization: Matched Funding Techniques," in Edward I. Atlman, ed., *Handbook of Financial Markets and Institutions,* 6th ed. (New York: John Wiley and Sons, 1987).

duration-matched portfolio. The simpler cash-matching technique is used to fund nearer-term, more certain liabilities. Duration matching for longer-term liabilities is an easier undertaking, since interest-rate changes on long-term investments are less volatile, thus requiring less adjustment and rebalancing.

Traditional dedication techniques are passive strategies designed to protect the sufficiency of the portfolio whether rates move up or down. Active strategies, by contrast, involve taking investment positions based on the assumption that rates will move in a particular direction. If the expected rate movement occurs, returns will be enhanced by capital gains; if unexpected movements occur, returns will be diminished by capital losses.

Contingent dedication techniques involve the intentional overfunding of a matched portfolio so that the investment manager is given a margin of safety with which to bet on market interest-rate movements.[9] As long as assumptions prove correct, additional returns will be achieved. If the margin of safety is eroded by losses, however, the portfolio will be shifted into a dedicated mode and active management will end.

## ASSET QUALITY AND U.S. REGULATORY INITIATIVES[10]

Since investment income to an insurer directly reduces the net cost of providing insurance, there is an inherent tension in the management of life insurer investment that results from (1) policyowner preference for affordable premiums and (2) the need for safety and the security of policyowner claims.

Safety and security of policyowner claims has been the primary stated objective of insurer investment regulation. The concept of statutory solvency discussed in Chapter 32 is intended to protect policyowners, and investment regulations are intended to promote insurer solvency. At the same time, because consumers are attracted to low-cost, high-yielding insurance products, successfully aggressive investment practices can increase an insurer's market share and profitability.

It is evident, then, that there are incentives for insurers to maximize investment income within the bounds of regulatory constraints. As mentioned above, noninvestment grade bonds, commercial mortgages, and direct real estate equity investment have underperformed expectations in recent years. There is considerable concern both within the U.S. insurance industry and among consumers over the quality of life insurer assets, and over the adequacy of current investment regulations to promote insurer solvency.

---

[9]The gambling analogy should not suggest recklessness. Contingent dedication strategies are conservative attempts to increase overall returns while continuing to maintain sufficient funds to satisfy liabilities under a reasonable range of possible interest-rate environments.

[10]This section draws on Kenneth M. Wright, "The Life Insurance Industry in the United States: An Analysis of Economic and Regulatory Issues" *Working Papers*, pp. 26-27.

As reflected in the discussion of regulatory restrictions on the admissibility of particular asset classes and assets above, traditional investment regulation has focused on qualitative and quantitative standards. Investment laws and regulations in some states set forth a number of prohibited investments. Other states use **legal lists** of permitted investments. Diversification of nonbond asset types and of particular assets is required by limiting the percentage of total assets that can be held in certain types of assets— for example, mortgage loans, common stocks, or bonds of a single issuer, and so on. These percentage restrictions are widely used in the investment laws of most states. Quantitative limits may also apply to a percentage of an issuer's securities that may be held by one insurer.

Qualitative limits relate to the quality of eligible investments. For example, the earnings of a corporate bond issuer must be in a certain ratio to the interest charges on outstanding debt or the mortgage or real estate cannot exceed a specified percentage of appraised value. In the case of common stocks, requirements may include that the stock be traded on a national exchange and have a record of paying dividends for three years. In 1983, New York abandoned its qualitative restrictions in favor of a less specific **prudent person rule** that permits investments made "with that degree of care that an ordinarily prudent individual in a like position would use under similar circumstances."

Many new investment media and industries emerged during the last few decades, and many of these were nonqualifying under existing rules. To provide some relief from these constraints, several states, including New York, provided "basket" or "leeway clauses" in their laws, thereby permitting a certain percentage of assets to be invested in any type of asset. This percentage has gradually been increased (currently, it is 10 percent in New York). The use of basket clauses allowed insurers to enter new investment areas such as equipment leasing, and oil and gas pipeline finance, and it also facilitates the use of risk-management assets such as futures and options as they were developed.

Throughout the 1980s and into the early 1990s, the quality of assets held by U.S. financial institutions, including life insurers, declined. The percentage of nonperforming bond and mortgage holdings held by insurers reached contemporary highs.

Insolvencies among U.S. life insurers have been increasingly evident in recent years. Before 1987, insolvencies numbered ten or less and involved smaller insurers with assets below $50 million. By 1989, there were more than 30 insolvencies occurring each year, many of which involved assets in the hundreds of millions of dollars. The major life insurer insolvencies in 1991 led to wide-scale public attention and calls for reform in regulatory standards. These insolvencies were directly related to investment problems arising from (1) overinvestment in noninvestment grade junk bonds that had fallen sharply in price, and (2) defaults on commercial real estate mortgage loans, leading to sizable book losses. Regulators seized the companies, in large part to halt mounting withdrawals of policyowner funds that developed after asset quality problems became widely publicized.

The decline in asset quality was due in part to aggressive investment policies developed during a highly competitive period, and in part to a general decline in the market values and performance of high-yield bonds and a weak real estate market. Although the greatest investments in junk bonds have been concentrated in a relatively small number of insurers, a drastic general reduction in the market value of junk bonds—and the publicity associated with the insolvencies in 1991 of insurers who had invested heavily in them—contributed to a movement toward investment regulation reform.

The deterioration of asset quality was generally the result of investment policies that were developed in compliance with existing regulatory restrictions. The qualitative standards associated with the regulation of corporate debt obligations did not exclude the possibility of heavy investment in noninvestment-grade bonds, and leeway clauses were used, among other reasons, to admit commercial mortgage values that would not otherwise qualify under the mortgage-specific rules.

Two regulatory initiatives are under way that would address the perceived need to control these investments more tightly. The first is addressed specifically at noninvestment-grade bonds, and the second is addressed more broadly to asset quality in general.

The purpose of the NAIC model law, **Investments in Medium Grade and Lower Grade Obligations**, is to protect the interest of the insurance-buying public by establishing limitations on the concentration of medium-grade and lower-grade obligations. The Securities Valuation Office (SVO) of the NAIC puts bonds into six quality categories, from 1, the highest, to 5, the lowest for bonds in good standing, and category 6 for bonds in or near default. **Medium-grade obligations** refers to bonds rated 3 by the SVO.[11] **Lower-grade obligations** refers to bonds rated 4, 5, or 6 by the SVO. The regulation provides that the aggregate amount of all medium- and lower-grade obligations may not exceed 20 percent of admitted assets. No more than 10 percent of admitted assets may consist of obligations rated 4, 5, or 6 by the SVO, no more than 3 percent may consist of obligations rated 5 or 6, and no more than 1 percent may consist of obligations rated 6 by the SVO.

In addition to these general limits, insurers may not invest more than an aggregate amount of 1 percent of their admitted assets in medium-grade obligations issued, guaranteed, or insured by any one institution, nor more than 0.5 percent in lower-grade obligations of any one institution. In no event may an insurer invest more than 1 percent of its admitted assets in any medium- or lower-grade obligations of any one institution. This model law has been adopted in a number of other states, with legislation pending in still others. New York has had such regulation in place for some time.

[11]See Chap. 34.

The NAIC is also developing a new model investment law, **Investments of Insurers Model Act**, similar in structure to the current regulatory scheme. It includes refinements intended to address the asset quality concerns that have developed in the industry. The most significant new provision would permit the subjective determination by a commissioner that specific investment activities endanger an insurer's solvency and would provide authorization to limit or proscribe those activities. Such a provision would considerably expand regulatory powers over investment activity.

It should be noted that while asset quality deterioration is demonstrable in the U.S. life insurance industry, the decline seems lately to have been reversed and there is considerable evidence that the financial condition of the industry, on average, is sound.[12] Regulatory reform can be expected to better suit the requirements of a changing and evolving industry, but the conservative nature of traditional solvency, accounting and investment regulations, together with management practice, has been generally responsible and successful.

---

[12]Gloria Vogel, "An Analyst's View of Insurer Insolvency," *Journal of the American Society of CLU & ChFC* (May 1992), p. 52.

# Chapter 32

# LIFE INSURER FINANCIAL REPORTING

## INTRODUCTION

The purpose of this chapter is to introduce the different financial reporting techniques that are commonly used in the life insurance industry. It will be seen that the requirements of different users of life insurer financial reports have led to the evolution of different reporting methods, some required by law or regulation and some developed for internal company purposes.

The purpose of financial reporting is to allow an assessment of the financial condition and current operating results of a company. Some companies typically undertake short-term transactions. In the sale of goods, for example, delivery and payment may take place within a short period of time. Single-year results produce a highly accurate financial report where the great majority of transactions are completed during the year.

By contrast, life insurance contracts are, on average, long-term. The current-year profitability of a block of contracts ultimately depends on results over a period of decades. Persistency, mortality, morbidity, interest, and expense experience determine whether a block of contracts will produce a profit over time.

As a result, to report the financial condition and current operating results for a life insurance company requires the construction of a valuation. A **valuation** is a measure and comparison of an insurer's assets and liabilities, and it must be based on estimates of future persistency, mortality, morbidity, interest, and expense experience.

The construction of a valuation is problematical because minor changes in the assumptions regarding future experience can produce a dramatic impact on current financial statements. Regulators require what traditionally were thought to be conservative assumptions to test the solvency of an insurer and to protect its policyowners.

In the past, this conservatism reduced the earnings and shareholder's equity in stock companies to economically unrealistic levels. As a result, separate legal requirements for reporting to regulatory authorities and shareholders have evolved.

The development and presentation of a fair life insurer valuation is further complicated by the interest-sensitive nature of insurer cash flows discussed in Chapter 30. The assumptions required by regulators were historically conservative within the context of a relatively stable interest-rate environment. As will be discussed below, the more volatile nature of contemporary interest rates raises questions about the probative value of regulatory accounting rules in solvency determination.

## FINANCIAL REPORTS

Alternative methods of calculating and presenting financial information are available. As mentioned, the needs of the user are the basis for determining the form and types of information used.

Three different life and health insurance accounting methods are required by law or regulation. The use of **statutory accounting principles** (SAP) is required by state insurance law. The use of **generally accepted accounting principles** (GAAP) is required by the Securities and Exchange Commission (SEC).[1] In addition to these financial reporting requirements, **tax basis accounting** is required by the Internal Revenue Service.[2]

In addition to accounting methods required by law to report financial results, corporate managers often require additional, internal measurement tools to manage operating results effectively and to evaluate the anticipated long-term results of management actions. **Managerial accounting** includes budgeting, cost accounting and the audit and control functions. **Economic value analysis** is used to evaluate the long-term financial results of current management actions.

As noted above, different users of life insurer financial information seek to evaluate companies from different perspectives. Their needs will differ with respect to the type and form of information they require.

---

[1] SEC regulations generally apply to companies whose shares are traded publicly and those selling variable insurance, annuity, and pension products. Some mutual companies have traditionally prepared GAAP statements for a variety of other practical reasons, including management information and comparison of performance to other companies. The Financial Accounting Standards Board develops GAAP requirements in conjunction with the American Institute of Certified Public Accountants and the SEC.

[2] Taxation of life insurance companies is discussed in Chap. 34.

## EXTERNAL USERS

*Regulators* are most interested in the solvency of an insurer and require the use of SAP in order to test a company's ability to meet its obligations to policyowners. *Investors* are interested in the return on invested capital a company can generate. GAAP accounting is required by the SEC for publicly traded stock insurers, and as a condition for listing on major stock exchanges. A sophisticated investment analysis would also include elements of economic value analysis.

*Current policyowners* and *potential customers* are interested in the solidity of the company and its ability to satisfy its future obligations, as well as its ability to maintain competitive dividends, interest crediting rates, and other nonguaranteed policy benefits. Both SAP and GAAP statements are relevant.

*Rating agencies* such as Best's, Standard and Poor's, Moody's, and Duff and Phelps report subjective opinions of insurer financial strength to policyowners and potential customers. These agencies usually rely on a variety of information sources, including management interviews.

*Creditors* are interested in the insurer's cash flow and its ability to repay debt. GAAP is helpful in predicting long-term cash flow, but SAP analysis is equally important because assets must be "free." In other words, assets are useful from the creditor's perspective only if they can be used to repay the debt. They are not useful if regulation requires that they be devoted to reserves or minimum capital and surplus requirements.

*Potential buyers* of an insurer are also interested readers of financial reports. The acquisition of a company must take into account its expected solvency and solidity positions, and the appearance of its expected SAP and GAAP financial statements. In addition, the buyer will be interested in economic value analysis that reflects the value of the insurer's distribution system, goodwill, and other features that represent opportunities for expansion and growth—that is, the vitality of the insurer.

The *Internal Revenue Service* requires that insurers prepare reports of taxable income in accordance with the Internal Revenue Code and its regulations.

A variety of other parties may also be interested in the financial condition of a life insurance company. They include employees and suppliers of the insurer, as well as the general business communities where the insurer has significant operations.

## INTERNAL USERS

The most frequent users of financial information are the insurer's management. Management must respond to the needs of each group of users of its financial reports. Therefore management decisions must be made with an understanding of the impact decisions can have on the company's SAP, GAAP, and tax-basis statements. For reasons discussed below, management, to evaluate the efficiency of invested capital, also uses managerial accounting and economic value analysis methods that differ from the financial reporting of those designed for the needs of other audiences.

Operating decisions such as product pricing and interest crediting/dividend strategy, as well as strategic decisions such as possible acquisitions or entry into new lines of business, must be analyzed with an understanding of results that will ultimately be reported to regulators, policyowners, investors, and others.

Management must also accord careful attention to financial reports derived from its statements, but issued by others. The informal regulatory role of independent rating agencies can be a significant factor in the way an insurer is viewed by its customers and investors.[3] Figure 32-1 summarizes the different accounting objectives and approaches required by principal users of life insurer financial reports.

**FIGURE 32-1**

**ACCOUNTING OBJECTIVES AND APPROACHES REQUIRED BY PRINCIPAL USERS OF LIFE INSURANCE FINANCIAL REPORTS**

| Accounting Objectives | | User | | Accounting Approach |
|---|---|---|---|---|
| Solvency | ⇒ | State insurance regulators | ⇒ | Statutory accounting |
| Solidity & profitability | ⇒ | SEC (shareholders) | ⇒ | GAAP accounting |
| Taxable income | ⇒ | Internal Revenue Service | ⇒ | Tax basis accounting |
| Operational information | ⇒ | Insurer management | ⇒ | Managerial accounting |

## LIFE INSURANCE ACCOUNTING PRINCIPLES[4]

Life insurance accounting is affected by both state regulatory requirements and generally accepted accounting principles established by the Financial Accounting Standards Board (FASB). As a result, stock life insurers are faced with the need to prepare at least two sets of mandatory financial statements with differing objectives. Although it is not generally required by law, many mutual companies also use GAAP-derived financial statements for internal management purposes.

### STATUTORY ACCOUNTING PRINCIPLES

*Objectives.* SAP financial statements are intended to present an insurer's financial condition from the viewpoint of the regulator. The main purpose is to provide proof of an insurer's solvency, or proof of its ability to meet its contractual obligations to policyowners.

---

[3]See Chap. 11.

[4]This section draws on *Life Insurance—Statutory Accounting Principles for the Life Insurance Industry* (KPMG Peat Marwick Executive Education, 1987), Chap. 7, pp. 3-4. See also Insurance Accounting and Systems Association, *Life Insurance Accounting* (Durham, N.C.: IASA, 1991).

The concept of solvency for a life insurance company has two dimensions. Economic solvency is the same as it is for any company: the ability to pay obligations when they come due. Life insurers must also be concerned with statutory solvency.

The insurer must, on an annual basis, present financial statements that meet the statutory definition of solvency in terms of investment values, reserves, and minimum capital and surplus that are defined by law. As will be discussed, economic solvency does not necessarily imply statutory solvency, and perhaps more important, statutory solvency does not necessarily imply economic solvency.

Because life insurers hold large amounts of money for the benefit of their policyowners, SAP treatment required by state law is similar to the accounting required of a trustee or fiduciary. The insurer must be able to account for all policyowner funds every time it issues its annual statement.

The insurer must also demonstrate that its assets, together with future premiums and conservative estimated interest income, will be sufficient to meet all promises to policyowners. Other sources of income, such as profits on existing or new lines of business, are not taken into account. In effect, the entire insurer is viewed as a trust account for the benefit of policyowners, and the insurer's ability to generate additional profits as an operating business, or going concern, is ignored.

An annual statement prepared according to statutory accounting principles is required in all states where an insurer is licensed to write business.[5] The statement is prepared on a calendar-year basis on forms generally developed by the National Association of Insurance Commissioners, and its accuracy is sworn to by the officers of the insurer.

Additional information is sometimes required, since some states adopt NAIC forms and regulations with changes. New York, for example, requires that the cash flows associated with certain product lines be tested under a range of differing economic scenarios.[6] Many states may require estimated statements on a quarterly or semiannual basis, and others prohibit insurers from publishing any financial statement that shows admitted assets or surplus in amounts differing from the statutory annual statement.

*Limitations.* Statutory accounting principles limit the usefulness of statutory reports in two respects. First, the stated objective of solvency determination is not well served by its static, balance sheet orientation, nor by valuation conventions that artificially stabilize reported values. Second, the solvency determination objective itself limits the usefulness of SAP to parties interested in other aspects of the financial condition.[7]

[5]See Chap. 34.

[6]See "The Valuation Actuary" later in this chapter.

[7]Ken W. Hartwell and Mark A. Milton, "Measuring Life Insurance Profitability in Today's Environment," *Financial Planning and Control Report No. 69* (Atlanta, GA: Life Office Management Association, Inc., 1988), p. 7.

One of the principal limitations of SAP solvency determination results from the "snapshot approach" it utilizes. Results are reported at a specific point in time under a set of static assumptions that ignore the possibility (indeed certainty) of changing economic conditions in the future.[8] The NAIC recently adopted a model law that requires an insurer to certify its future solvency under a variety of economic scenarios, and the role of the valuation actuary in this process is discussed later in this chapter.

Bond values are recorded on the statutory statement at amortized value (discussed below) rather than market value. This valuation convention is based on the premise that most insurer bonds are held to maturity, and that fluctuating market values would not significantly impact solvency. As discussed in Chapter 30, the simultaneous impact of changing market interest rates on asset and liability values casts considerable doubt on this assumption.

During periods of relatively high interest rates, the artificial stabilization of asset values by the amortized value convention may cause an insurer's statutory statement to exhibit a state of solvency, when in reality it would be unable to satisfy its cash obligations as they come due. Figure 32-2 illustrates the

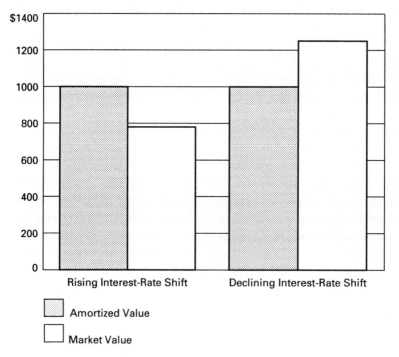

**FIGURE 32-2**

**THE RELATIONSHIP OF AMORTIZED BOND VALUES TO MARKET VALUES IN DIFFERENT INTEREST-RATE ENVIRONMENTS**

[8]See Chap. 30.

relationship of amortized values to market values in different interest rate environments. The asset valuation reserves discussed below could, under extreme conditions, contribute similar distortion in statutory reporting.

Statutory accounting also proves to be inadequate for the needs of investors and creditors because of its balance sheet orientation. First, with the exception of asset valuation conventions discussed above, SAP treatment generally examines an insurer as if it were not an operating entity, but rather a company in the process of liquidation. This results from the conservative fiduciary approach that requires accounting for all policyowner funds at all times and ignores the long-term benefits to be expected from investing in the future of the company. Second, the conservative assumptions required in the valuation of an insurer's liabilities normally do not reflect the potential profit that can be generated by in-force policies.

The solvency approach that is central to SAP tends to penalize current results without recognizing the long-term potential of a company's operations. As discussed in Chapter 2 and reflected in the sample asset share calculation, an increase in new business typically creates cash shortages in the early years of any new block of policies. Under SAP treatment, the high expenses that are associated with the writing off of acquisition costs of new business, together with reserving requirements, reduce current earnings. Lapses and surrenders, however, tend to increase current earnings under SAP rules because of the gains from surrenders created when reserves released exceed cash values paid.[9]

As a result, earnings under SAP rules are penalized as an insurer grows, with faster growth producing a greater punitive impact on earnings. Conversely, earnings can be exaggerated when an insurer is losing market share to competitors. SAP treatment also tends to penalize current earnings when an insurer invests in its distribution system or makes other capital expenditures.

The balance sheet liquidity focus of SAP is designed to prove an insurer's ability to pay future benefits that arise under its current policies, and therefore it is an inadequate tool for measuring a company's ability to generate long-term profits or for comparing results with other insurers or its own past experience.

## GENERALLY ACCEPTED ACCOUNTING PRINCIPLES

*Objectives.* While liquidity or solvency is the primary focus of statutory accounting, the principal purpose of GAAP accounting is to report financial results for a company that are comparable to those of other companies and of other reporting periods. This comparability is essential to investors who need to be able to evaluate the relative merits of alternative investments both in the insurance industry and other industries. Comparability is necessary when financial reports are used in any analysis designed to predict future financial

[9]See Chap. 21.

results. Generally accepted accounting principles are established through the issuance of Financial Accounting Standards (FAS) by the Financial Accounting Standards Board (FASB).

Quarterly and annual reports incorporating GAAP statements are required of all publicly traded companies. The most important of the required reports is Form 10-K, which annually sets forth a statement of the insurer's business, properties and business proceedings, its financial statements and supporting schedules and exhibits, and information regarding the insurer's officers and directors. Form 10-Q provides similar but less comprehensive information on a quarterly basis.

*Limitations.* While GAAP accounting is designed to *report* consistently on revenues, benefits, expenses, and current operating profit, it is often found to be inadequate as a *financial management* tool. GAAP does not recognize potential future profits on existing and future policies, and therefore it is not well suited for evaluating the long-term financial impact of current management action.

Three aspects of GAAP accounting limit its usefulness as a financial management tool.[10] These shortcomings are in large part the result of reporting the arbitrary, one-year profits of organizations that are engaged in an essentially long-term enterprise—providing insurance benefits over the whole of its customers' lives.

First, GAAP includes an accounting convention known as the **lock-in principle**, which prevents a restatement of assumptions regarding interest, expense, and mortality for policies in force and which was principally designed to deal with guaranteed-cost, nonparticipating policies. Today's product environment is largely dominated by policies that reflect actual operating experience and offer guarantees that are likely to be important only in the event of extreme interest-rate or mortality developments. The accuracy of expected results for a block of policies can be considerably improved by periodic reevaluations, and FAS 97 now effectively exempts interest-sensitive products from the lock-in principle. Lock-in continues to apply to traditional life products.

Second, as with their treatment under statutory accounting, unrealized capital gains are not recognized in the GAAP income statement. As discussed in Chapter 31, capital gains and losses are an integral element of the total return generated by an actively managed investment portfolio.

Finally, GAAP accounting in many respects does not reflect the future impact of current events. As in statutory accounting, GAAP treatment of surrenders may produce increased current-period earnings without reflecting the loss of future profits on lapsed policies, and investment in distribution systems and other capital expenditures may produce decreased current earnings without a concurrent recognition of the insurer's increased capacity to generate future profits.

---

[10]Hartwell and Milton, p. 8.

## SAP AND GAAP TREATMENT OF ACCOUNTING ITEMS

In different ways, both SAP and GAAP financial statements are derived from the same source: the Blanks Committee of the National Association of Insurance Commissioners, which develops the general form and content of all life insurance company annual statements. The SAP statement in each state follows closely the form prescribed by the NAIC, but may be considered derivative because some states have special requirements that are not incorporated in the NAIC form. GAAP statements are developed by adjustments that are made to an insurer's SAP statement.

The differences in SAP and GAAP statements are produced by the differing treatment of items that are entered into each statement. Statutory accounting treatment is governed by the applicable state law, and generally accepted accounting treatment is governed by standards established by the FASB.[11]

Differing treatment of items under SAP and GAAP can be grouped into four broad categories:

      1. Valuation of assets

      2. Valuation of liabilities

      3. Recognition of income

      4. Recognition of expense

*Valuation of Assets.* The primary differences in SAP and GAAP accounting regarding the valuation of assets involve the classification of assets that may be listed as approved assets, and the reporting of realized and unrealized capital gains and losses. Assets approved by state regulatory authorities as sound and accepted as such in the NAIC Annual Statement are known as **admitted assets**. Only the value of admitted assets may be shown on the statutory balance sheet. By contrast, all insurer assets, including nonadmitted assets that do not meet regulatory approval, are reported on the GAAP balance sheet.

As discussed below, the mandatory securities valuation reserve and, more recently, the asset valuation and interest maintenance reserves serve as means of preventing undue surplus changes in the statutory balance sheet arising from fluctuations in the market values of owned securities. There are no valuation reserves in GAAP accounting.

Increasingly, the term "fair value" is used in GAAP statements reflecting the fact that some assets have no readily available market and are valued on the basis of the combined judgment of insurer management and the insurer's independent auditors. Most nonadmitted assets under SAP fall into this category.

[11]See American Institute of Certified Public Accountants, *Audits of Stock Life Insurance Companies*, 4th ed (New York: AICPA, 1985).

*Valuation of Liabilities*. The principal differences in SAP and GAAP treatment of the valuation of insurer liabilities involve life insurance policy reserves and the payment of dividends. SAP is primarily concerned with solvency and safety of policyowner rights, and it requires the posting of reserves that are based on statutorily defined, conservative assumptions regarding mortality and interest.[12] GAAP is primarily concerned with insurer profitability, and more realistic assumptions are used with respect to mortality and interest. An insurer uses GAAP assumptions that follow its own experience or industrywide experience.

Policyowner dividends reported under SAP are limited to the anticipated liability for the insurer's following year. Because of the underlying assumption of continued company existence as a going concern, GAAP posts the present value of all expected future policyowner dividends as a liability. As dividends are paid, the balance sheet liability is reduced accordingly.

*Recognition of Income*. One of the principles of generally accepted accounting dictates that income is recognized when it is earned and not when it is received. This means that earnings should be recognized when the service (insurance protection) is provided. GAAP premiums are recognized as earned over the coverage period of policies in force, while SAP premiums are earned over the premium-paying period.

*Recognition of Expense*. SAP rules are generally based on an implicit assumption that solvency should be demonstrable if the insurer were to be liquidated during the current reporting period (excepting, again, the asset valuation conventions discussed above). As previously discussed, GAAP assumes the continued existence of the insurer as a going concern. These approaches require a significantly different treatment of the high first-year acquisition expense that is associated with issuing new policies.[13]

Although some statutory accounting relief can be provided through the use of modified reserving techniques, first-year acquisition expenses are generally charged in full to the current year's statutory income. Despite the fact that these first-year expenses are associated with policies that will generate future income, the conservative requirements of SAP do not recognize the future income that is likely to be generated.

GAAP, by contrast, assumes the continuing existence of the insurer and seeks to match the timing of expenses associated with the production of income to the period when the income is produced. GAAP thus recognizes that future income will be associated with first-year expenses, and it permits the deferral of those expenses in a way that reports the expenses ratably over a period of time. Costs related to future income are charged to future periods.

---

[12]See Chap. 20.

[13]The financial impact of significant first-year expenses is illustrated in the asset share calculation in Chap. 2.

Under GAAP, acquisition costs are capitalized as a deferred asset. In traditional policies, deferred acquisition costs (DAC) are amortized as premium income is realized and charged in future periods. In the case of current assumption policies in which premiums exceeding mortality and expense charges are considered deposits, these costs are amortized over the lives of the policies as gross profits emerge.[14] As the expenses are charged, the value of the deferred capital asset is reduced accordingly.

Figure 32-3 summarizes the important differences in SAP and GAAP treatment of different accounting items.

**FIGURE 32-3**

**COMPARISON OF SAP AND GAAP TREATMENT OF SPECIFIC ACCOUNTING ITEMS**

|  | SAP | GAAP |
|---|---|---|
| **Valuation of Assets** | | |
| Accepted values: | Admitted assets only | All assets |
| **Valuation of Liabilities** | | |
| Reserves: | Defined by law | Company and industry experience |
| Policyowner dividends: | Following year | Present value of all future dividends |
| **Recognition of income** | | |
| Premiums earned over: | Premium period | Coverage period |
| **Recognition of expenses** | | |
| First-year acquisition expense: | Full charge | Deferred and amortized |

## THE ANNUAL STATEMENT

As discussed in Chapter 34, the power of the NAIC is generally indirect in the sense that it typically develops model laws that have the force of law only when adopted by the various states, sometimes with changes. In financial reporting, the NAIC influence is more direct. It controls the standards for financial reporting through the prescribed form of annual statement, as well as the valuation of securities through the Securities Valuation Office. These responsibilities have in effect been delegated to the NAIC by the states.[15]

[14]Gross profits arise principally from investment, mortality and expense margins. Deferred policy acquisition costs are reviewed annually to determine that the unamortized portion of such costs does not exceed recoverable amounts in future periods after considering anticipated investment income. See FAS 97.

[15]For a comprehensive discussion, see Paul J. Zucconi, *Accounting in Life and Health Insurance Companies* (Atlanta, GA: Life Office Management Association, Inc., 1987), Chap 2.

The NAIC statement is not intended to be, and is not, a convenient direct source of information for policyowners, shareholders, or the general public. As a result, condensed and simplified financial statements are included in the published **annual reports** issued by companies to their policyowners and shareholders. Financial statements to shareholders are presented on a GAAP rather than a SAP basis. These statements and the excerpts from the annual reports are also used by many companies in their advertising and other publicity activities.

Any statutory figures in these reports are prepared, in part, from information in the NAIC statement. Any financial statements in the annual report are condensed versions of those in the NAIC statement and of those that might be prepared based on GAAP principles.

The scope of annual reports and the kind and detail of the information included in them vary greatly from company to company. Most of these reports contain supplementary information on the company's operations, plans, and other matters usually also found in the trade press. Among other things, there frequently is a narrative presentation of a promotional nature. If GAAP financial statements are included, there is also likely to be a reconciliation of the principal GAAP statement items with the corresponding statutory statement items.

SAP and GAAP financial statements follow the same general pattern. The following discussion of life insurer annual statements follows the form of the statutory statement. Significant differences in GAAP accounting treatment and conventions are noted.

The primary elements of the annual statement required by state insurance regulators are the balance sheet and the summary of operations. These statements are reconciled from year to year in the capital and surplus account. A cash flow statement has been required since 1985. Supplementary exhibits and schedules provide a more detailed supporting analysis of items that appear in the primary financial statements.

## THE BALANCE SHEET

The purpose of the balance sheet is to demonstrate an insurer's solvency by comparing its assets and liabilities. Under statutory accounting, if assets exceed liabilities and minimum capital and surplus, the insurer is solvent and the excess assets represent, in general corporate terms, the capital of the company. The life insurance industry designates its capital as **capital stock**, which represents funds paid into the company by shareholders, and as **surplus**, which is the remaining excess of assets over liabilities. The final accounting equation for a company's balance sheet is:

$$\text{Assets} = \text{Liabilities} + (\text{Capital Stock} + \text{Surplus})$$

Figure 32-4 illustrates the general relationship of assets and liabilities and surplus.

**FIGURE 32-4**

**CAPITAL STOCK AND SURPLUS AS THE EXCESS OF INSURER ASSETS OVER LIABILITIES**

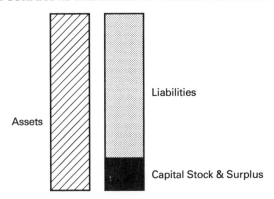

*Assets*. Insurer assets can be divided into three major categories: investment assets; other admitted assets; and deferred, due, and accrued income. Because of the regulatory concern for safety, legally prescribed methods determine permitted asset values. Asset values that exceed or do not conform to these legal methods are **nonadmitted assets**; asset values that conform to the legal requirements are **admitted assets**.

Investment assets produce interest, dividend, and rent and capital gain income.[16] Investment assets are reported in the following classes and statutory values:

•*Cash* consists of actual cash held in the insurers' offices on the date of the statement, and amounts on deposit in banks.

•*Bonds* determined by the NAIC to be in good standing are listed at their **amortized values**.[17] The market value of a bond typically differs from its par or face value because of changing market interest rates. Amortized value refers to adjustments of the original cost (original book value) by which the value is reduced or increased by successive stages until it equals the par value on the maturity date of the bond.[18] Table 32-1 illustrates the amortization process for a $1,000 bond that is two years from maturity and upon which the interest rate is

---

[16]For a description of the investment characteristics of life insurer assets, see Chap. 31.

[17]The NAIC Committee on Valuation of Securities specifies the bases for determining the eligibility of various classes of bonds for amortization. The committee submits an annual report that sets forth these requirements in great detail, and the Security Valuation Office develops a Valuation of Securities manual each year as the source for uniform treatment of securities values. It includes values for all securities, including privately placed bonds.

[18]The SEC and FASB are examining proposals that would affect the valuation of insurer fixed income investments. FAS 107 requires disclosure of the market value of fixed income investment and other assets and liabilities. A broader proposal by the SEC, under examination by the FASB, would incorporate the market value of securities into the GAAP balance sheet. If adopted, "mark to market" valuation would have a significant impact on financial reporting for all financial institutions.

6 percent (semiannual coupon rate of 3 percent). It is assumed that the bond was purchased for $1,018.81 to yield 5 percent. Bonds not in good standing are listed at current market value. Due and accrued interest on these bonds are nonadmitted assets, since the interest is reflected by the bond's market value.

**TABLE 32-1**             **AMORTIZED BOND VALUES**

| Period (half-years) | Book Value at Beginning of Half-Year | Coupon Payable at End of Half-Year | Six Months' Interest at 5% on Book Value at Beginning of Half-Year | Excess of Coupon over Interest Required (Amortization) | Book Value at End of Half-Year (Amortized Value) |
|---|---|---|---|---|---|
| 1 | $1,018.81 | $30 | $25.47 | $4.53 | $1,014.28 |
| 2 | 1,014.28 | 30 | 25.36 | 4.64 | 1,009.64 |
| 3 | 1,009.64 | 30 | 25.24 | 4.76 | 1,004.88 |
| 4 | 1,004.88 | 30 | 25.12 | 4.88 | 1,000.00 |

•*Common stocks* are listed at market value as of the date of the annual statement.

•*Preferred stocks* in good standing are valued at cost. If dividend payments are not current, market values are entered on the balance sheet. Preferred stocks not in good standing are valued at or below the market price prescribed by the NAIC.

•*Mortgage loans on real estate* are listed at unpaid principal balance unless the loan exceeds the regulatory ratio to market value of the property, typically 66.67 to 75 percent. To the extent that the unpaid balance of a mortgage loan exceeds the legal limit, the excess cost is treated as a nonadmitted asset. Overdue mortgage interest is a nonadmitted asset as well; a 90-day delinquency is generally considered overdue.

•*Real estate* is listed at book or market value, whichever is lower. Book value is original cost less accumulated depreciation, mortgages, liens, and other encumbrances under SAP rules. GAAP treatment does not record net values. Under GAAP separate asset and liability entries are made for each property.

•*Policy loans and premium notes* are valued at the unpaid principal balance of the loan at the date of the statement. To the extent that the outstanding principal balance of the loan or note exceeds the cash surrender value of the policy, the excess balance is treated as a nonadmitted asset.

•*Collateral loans* are valued at the unpaid principal balance of the loan at the date of the statement, unless the value of the loan exceeds the legal relationship to the market value of the collateral. To the extent that the unpaid principal balance of the collateral loan exceeds the legal limit, the excess cost is treated as a nonadmitted asset.

•*Risk-management assets* such as futures and options are valued at market. Most state insurance laws permit the listing of values associated with certain noninvestment assets that are closely related to the operations of the business. The most important of these *other admitted assets* are computer equipment and amounts owed to the insurer by authorized reinsurance companies. Computer equipment is generally valued at cost less accumulated depreciation under rules that may vary from state to state.

• *Deferred, due, and accrued income* is an asset category that includes investment and premium income that is due but not yet received, and policy premiums that will become due after the date of the annual statement and before the next policy anniversary date. The deferred premium asset for net premiums deferred and uncollected is established to offset the overstatement of the policy-reserve liability brought about by the difference between the assumptions as to premium payments in reserve calculations (made once a year assuming an annual premium received at midyear) and the actual modes of paying premiums. In essence, there is an overstatement of both assets and liabilities, resulting in an appropriate net liability. This item also accounts for premiums that are overdue, since the reserve is overstated in this case also.

•*Accrued interest* (in the absence of a default) is a sound asset.[19] During normal times, overdue interest is likely to be small. In periods of economic recession, overdue interest on mortgages may become sizable. In such periods, its size may be helpful in giving some indication of the quality of the mortgage portfolio. Its usefulness as such an indicator, however, is impaired by the fact that insurer practices, relative to charging off overdue interest as a nonadmitted asset, vary considerably.

Most life companies have also established **separate accounts** which are funds held separately from all other assets of the insurer. The primary purpose of separate accounts is to make investments exempt from the usual investment restrictions imposed by state law. Separate accounts are authorized by states to permit insurers to offer customers investment strategies that would not otherwise conform to insurance regulations. Separate accounts are maintained primarily for pension funds and variable life and annuity products. The customer, rather than the insurer, is responsible for all investment gains and losses. A separate account usually holds the funds of many policyowners or annuitants in a combined investment arrangement—a so-called **pooled investment account**. An individual separate account may be provided for a large corporate client, holding only its contributions.

*Liabilities*. The greatest part of a life company's liabilities is represented by policy reserves supported by assets held to fund future benefits under the company's insurance contracts. Other liabilities are also incurred in the course of operations.

---

[19] No item of overdue interest is carried as an asset on bonds in default, since the market value of these bonds reflects any interest in default.

•*Policy reserves* represent amounts needed to provide future benefits under the company's policies. Reserves are calculated on the basis of future mortality and interest assumptions.[20] These assumptions and the method of calculation are prescribed by state law in the case of statutory accounting. GAAP assumptions are derived from the insurer's best estimates based on its own experience and industry averages, and include assumptions regarding lapse rates.

•*Amounts held on deposit* are funds owed to policyowners and beneficiaries including (a) amounts held under settlement options without life contingencies; (b) dividends left to accumulate by policyowners; and (c) premiums paid in advance. Interest is credited to customers while the funds are deposited with the insurer in much the same way a bank credits interest to its depositors.

•*Dividends allocated but not yet payable* include both policyowner dividends and, in stock insurers, shareholder dividends. Under statutory accounting, the policyowner dividend liability is measured by the insurer's estimate of all dividend payments for the following calendar year. Policyowner dividend liabilities under GAAP are measured by the estimated present value of *all future dividends*. Shareholder dividends are booked at the time they are declared by the board of directors.

•*Claims incurred but not yet paid* include (a) claims due but unpaid at statement date; (b) contested claims; (c) claims in the process of being settled with beneficiaries; and (d) the estimated amount of claims incurred but unreported to the company at the date of the statement (valued on the basis of the company's past experience).

•*Amounts held for the account of others* are funds in the possession of the insurer as an agent or trustee for another. Examples include taxes and property insurance premiums of mortgagors, payroll taxes, amounts due to reinsurers, and federal income taxes due on current-year income.

•*Other amounts unpaid* include liabilities for incurred but unpaid items such as expenses and surrender values.

•*The Mandatory Securities Valuation Reserve (MSVR), Asset Valuation Reserve (AVR), and Interest Maintenance Reserve (IMR)* are statutory accounting mechanisms designed to prevent volatile fluctuations in reported surplus due to the changing market values of securities. The MSVR has been a statutory accounting mechanism since 1951, and it is being gradually replaced by the AVR and IMR during a three-year period ending in 1994.

Within limits, the valuation reserves act as buffers so that capital gains and losses are reflected in the reported reserve and do not affect reported surplus from year to year. More significant gains and losses exceeding the prescribed limits directly affect reported surplus. Absent these valuation

[20]See Chap. 21.

reserves to offset realized and unrealized capital gains and losses, the amount of reported surplus each year would fluctuate in proportion to changes in the market values of securities owned by the company. Since many insurer fixed income investments are held to maturity, and short-term fluctuations in common stock values are not reflective of the long-term value of equity investments, these fluctuations are believed by regulators to present an inappropriate statement of financial condition and could affect dividend distributions and other aspects of insurer management that depend on reported surplus.

In the case of preferred stocks in good standing and amortizable bonds, the MSVR has applied to realized capital gains and losses, and in the case of common stocks, to realized and unrealized capital gains and losses. The AVR and IMR were developed to improve the valuation reserve requirements by:

1. Expanding the focus to include real estate and mortgage loans

2. Distinguishing asset value changes due to asset quality and those due to market interest-rate changes.

The AVR replaces the MSVR and includes real estate, mortgage loans, and short-term investments as well as bonds and corporate stocks. The IMR applies to realized gains and losses attributable to changing market interest rates.

Because the AVR does not reflect interest-related changes, its importance is limited to the asset quality of included investments. It is therefore addressed as one of the principal provisions of the developing risk-based capital requirements discussed below. Upon enactment of risk-based capital statutes, the redundancy may be resolved by elimination and incorporation of the AVR into risk based capital ratios.

The IMR applies to all types of fixed income investments and is designed to capture realized capital gains and losses resulting from changes in the overall level of interest rates. The IMR amortizes the gains or losses into income over the remaining life of the investment, and thus it affects a company's net gain from operations, rather than being reflected in net income after net gain from operations.[21]

•*Special reserves* are sometimes established by insurers for general contingencies such as epidemics or other unexpected claims or liabilities when no reserve is required by statute. Some insurers choose to establish special reserves, while others will instead designate *special surplus* for the same purposes. For example, some insurers have established special reserves in anticipation of the higher mortality likely to arise as a result of AIDS-related claims.

---

[21]James F. Reiskytl, "Asset Valuation Reserve and the Interest Maintenance Reserve Executive Summary," presentation to the Investment Section Meeting of the 1991 Annual Meeting of the American Council of Life Insurance.

•*Post-Retirement Benefits*. Under GAAP accounting, employers are required by Financial Accounting Standard 106 to recognize a balance sheet liability for the cost of providing post-retirement benefits (other than retirement income benefits) to retirees. The most substantial post-retirement benefit is retiree health care. A statutory equivalent of FAS 106 was adopted by the NAIC.

•*Federal income taxes* under statutory accounting represent only the current year tax payable under tax basis accounting rules. Because of nonconcurrent tax basis rules, determinable amounts of tax liability may be deferred beyond the current SAP or GAAP reporting period. GAAP requires recognition of the future tax liability on the insurer's balance sheet.

**Capital Stock and Surplus**. The excess of a company's assets over its liabilities represents its **capital stock and surplus**. In other commercial companies, this excess may be known as **capital** or **net worth**.

•*Capital stock* represents the par value of all common and preferred shares issued and not owned by the insurer.

•*Contributed surplus* represents the excess, if any, paid to the corporation for shares that exceed par value.

•*Special surplus funds* are voluntarily earmarked surplus designated to meet general contingencies; they serve the same purpose as special reserves.

•*Unassigned surplus* consists of all other surplus amounts and represents the corporation's "free" capital. It is not legally earmarked for any particular purpose and may be used for distributions to policyowners or shareholders in the form of dividends or for the expansion or diversification of the insurer's operations.

Table 32-2 (assets, liabilities, surplus and other finds) presents the balance sheet, in SAP format, of a hypothetical life insurance company.

## SUMMARY OF OPERATIONS

The summary of operations represents an **income statement** for the reported year, providing a summary of the insurer's income, disposition of income, and a reconciliation of beginning and ending surplus. The summary of operations is an aggregated total of operations reported for each of the insurer's insurance products in the **analysis of operations by line of business**.

**Income**. The income of a life company consists of life and health insurance premiums and investment income. Premiums for annuities and supplementary contracts and deposits, together with miscellaneous income, complete the sources of income. When policy benefits are left with the company under dividend or settlement options, the amount is treated simultaneously as a disbursement to the policyowner or beneficiary and as income to the company.

•*Premium* income consists of regular policy premiums and annuity considerations, together with dividends used to purchase additional insurance and policy proceeds left with the company under settlement options having life contingencies.

•*Considerations for supplementary contracts and deposits* are funds left with the company under settlement or policy dividend options without life contingencies.

•*Investment income* is comprised primarily of interest, dividends, and rents derived from the insurer's investment bonds, loans, and property. Under GAAP, realized capital gains and losses are recognized in the income statement as part of operating income. Investment income also includes an accounting entry for rent paid by the company to itself for the use of owned and occupied real estate, in order to reflect an appropriate yield on investment in corporate real estate.

•*Miscellaneous income* is typically not significant in relation to total income, and would include revenue arising from administrative service contracts and other consulting fees as well as other noninsurance operating items.

***Disposition of Income***. A life company's income is devoted to the cost of doing an insurance business, including benefits and the maintenance of reserves. Any excess income is transferred to company surplus.

•*Benefits* include regular death, endowment, health, and annuity benefits, as well as waiver of premium and disability income payments. Benefits also include payment of cash surrender values, dividends, and amounts due under supplementary contracts without life contingencies.

•*Operating expenses and taxes* include all expenditures paid in the course of doing business, such as rents, salaries, and agent commissions. Both federal income taxes and state premium taxes may be substantial amounts. As noted above, there is a significant difference in SAP and GAAP treatment of first-year policy acquisition expenses.

•*Increases in required policy reserves* is usually a significant item in the disposition of income. Increased reserves are established whenever the current-year valuation requires reserves that exceed those of the previous year. If a company's insurance in force is declining, required policy reserves may decrease. Policy reserves are not actually entered on corporate accounting books, but are determined annually at the time of the actuarial valuation. The net increase or decrease is determined by reference to and reconciliation with the previous year's valuation.

•*Transfers to surplus*, a balancing item, represents the excess of income over the above disposition items. If an insurer is growing rapidly, substantial reserve increases and acquisition expenses may cause surplus

TABLE 32-2a STATUTORY ANNUAL STATEMENT — BALANCE SHEET

## ASSETS

| | | Year t | Year t-1 |
|---|---|---:|---:|
| 1. | Bonds (less $0 liability for asset transfers with put options) | 2,022,375,602 | 1,937,997,256 |
| 2. | Stocks: | | |
| | 2.1 Preferred stocks | 3,287,500 | 3,387,500 |
| | 2.2 Common stocks | 56,603,173 | 81,252,404 |
| 3. | Mortgage loans on real estate | 566,238,891 | 534,650,809 |
| 4. | Real estate: | | |
| | 4.1 Properties occupied by the company (less $0 encumbrances) | 10,758,693 | 10,737,382 |
| | 4.2 Properties acquired in satisfaction of debt (less $0 encumbrances) | 1,636,499 | 703,383 |
| | 4.3 Investment real estate (less $0 encumbrances) | 14,928,857 | 15,124,016 |
| 5. | Policy loans | 161,630,531 | 160,310,082 |
| 6. | Premium notes, including $0 for first year premiums | 0 | 0 |
| 7. | Collateral loans | 0 | 0 |
| 8.1 | Cash on hand and on deposit | 6,011,071 | 4,092,745 |
| 8.2 | Short-term investments | 101,504,537 | 145,234,525 |
| 9. | Other invested assets | 17,729,176 | 4,850,498 |
| 10. | Aggregate write-ins for invested assets | 0 | 0 |
| 10A. | Subtotals, cash and invested assets (Items 1 to 10) | 2,962,704,530 | 2,898,340,600 |
| 11. | Reinsurance ceded: | | |
| | 11.1 Amounts recoverable from reinsurers | 769,512 | 363,227 |
| | 11.2 Commissions and expense allowances due | 7,261 | 0 |
| | 11.3 Experience rating and other refunds due | 0 | 10,261 |

| | | |
|---|---:|---:|
| 12. Electronic data processing equipment | 3,126,407 | 2,569,856 |
| 13. Federal income tax recoverable | 14,653,411 | 2,137,550 |
| 14. Life insurance premiums and annuity considerations deferred and uncollected | 9,719,168 | 10,749,859 |
| 15. Accident and health premiums due and unpaid | 665,879 | 766,510 |
| 16. Investment income due and accrued | 40,297,652 | 39,682,686 |
| 17. Net adjustment in assets and liabilities due to foreign exchange rates | 0 | 0 |
| 18. Receivable from parent, subsidiaries and affiliates | 1,941,315 | 1,793,853 |
| 19. Amounts receivable relating to uninsured accident and health plans | 0 | 0 |
| 21. Aggregate write-ins for other than invested assets | 1,827,992 | 2,089,097 |
| 22. Total assets excluding Separate Accounts business (Items 10A to 21) | 3,035,713,127 | 2,958,503,499 |
| 23. From Separate Accounts Statement | 172,119,618 | 117,070,976 |
| 24. Totals (Items 22 and 23) | 3,207,832,745 | 3,075,574,475 |
| **DETAILS OF WRITE-INS AGGREGATED AT ITEM 10 FOR INVESTED ASSETS** | | |
| 1001. | | |
| 1002. | | |
| 1003. | | |
| 1004. | | |
| 1005. | | |
| 1098. Summary of remaining write-ins for Item 10 from overflow page | 0 | 0 |
| 1099. Totals (Items 1001 thru 1005 plus 1098) (Page 2, Item 10) | 0 | 0 |
| **DETAILS OF WRITE-INS AGGREGATED AT ITEM 21 FOR OTHER THAN INVESTED ASSETS** | | |
| 2101. Pension plan service fees due and uncollected | 927,443 | 746,997 |
| 2102. Guaranty association assessments recoverable | 872,871 | 663,824 |
| 2103. Prepaid insurance and taxes on mortgage loans | 15,912 | 86,195 |
| 2104. Premium and other taxes receivable | 11,766 | 297,569 |
| 2105. Receivable on investment real estate | 0 | 215,842 |
| 2198. Summary of remaining write-ins for Item 21 from overflow page | 0 | 78,670 |
| 2199. Totals (Items 2101 thru 2105 plus 2198) (Page 2, Item 21) | 1,827,992 | 2,089,097 |

TABLE 32-2a (continued) STATUTORY ANNUAL STATEMENT— BALANCE SHEET

# TABLE 32-2b STATUTORY ANNUAL STATEMENT — BALANCE SHEET

## LIABILITIES, SURPLUS AND OTHER FUNDS

| | Year t | Year t-1 |
|---|---|---|
| 1. Aggregate reserve for life policies and contracts $1,134,178,447 (Exh. 8, Line N) less $0 included in Item 7.3 | 1,134,178,447 | 1,082,326,021 |
| 2. Aggregate reserve for accident and health policies (Exhibit 9, Line C, Col. 1) | 92,867,179 | 73,596,599 |
| 3. Supplementary contracts without life contingencies (Exhibit 10, Part A, Line 2.3, Col. 1) | 59,135,487 | 54,380,081 |
| 4. Policy and contract claims: | | |
| 4.1 Life (Exhibit 11, Part 1, Line 4d, Column 1 less sum of Columns 9, 10 and 11) | 16,061,038 | 18,225,247 |
| 4.2 Accident and health (Exhibit 11, Part 1, Line 4d, sum of Columns 9, 10 and 11) | 2,249,891 | 1,904,612 |
| 5. Policyholders' dividend and coupon" accumulations (Exhibit 10, Part A, Line 3 plus Line 4, Col. 1) | 5,947,628 | 6,025,741 |
| 6. Policyholders' dividends $94,816 and coupons $0 due and unpaid (Exhibit 7, Item 10) | 94,816 | 318,680 |
| 7. Provision for policyholders' dividends and coupons payable in following calendar year — estimated amounts: | | |
| 7.1 Dividends apportioned for payment to ... December 31 ... , 1992 | 15,695,511 | 15,898,286 |
| 7.2 Dividends not yet apportioned | 0 | 0 |
| 7.3 Coupons and similar benefits | 0 | 0 |
| 8. Amount provisionally held for deferred dividend policies not included in Item 7 | 0 | 0 |
| 9. Premiums and annuity considerations received in advance less $177,521 accident and health premiums $0 discount; including (Exhibit 1, Part 1, Col. 1, sum of Lines 4 and 14) | 354,361 | 218,904 |
| 10. Liability for premium and other deposit funds: | | |
| 10.1 Policyholder premiums, including $0 deferred annuity liability (Exhibit 10, Part A, Line 1.1, Col. 1) | 776,686 | 816,091 |
| 10.2 Guaranteed interest contracts, including $22,228,473 deferred annuity liability (Exhibit 10, Part A, Line 1.2, Col. 1) | 22,228,473 | 42,991,719 |
| 10.3 Other contract deposit funds, including $1,453,491,975 deferred annuity liability (Exhibit 10, Part A, Line 1.3, Col. 1) | 1,453,491,975 | 1,450,541,512 |
| 11. Policy and contract liabilities not included elsewhere: | | |
| 11.1 Surrender values on cancelled policies | 0 | 0 |
| 11.2 Provision for experience rating refunds | 0 | 0 |
| 11.3 Other amounts payable on reinsurance assumed | 0 | 0 |
| 12. Commissions to agents due or accrued — life and annuity $3,269 accident and health $162,210 | 165,479 | 273,156 |
| 12A. Commissions and expense allowances payable on reinsurance assumed | 148,978 | 169,078 |
| 13. General expenses due or accrued (Exhibit 5, Line 12, Col. 5) | 4,529,560 | 5,978,106 |
| 13A. Transfers to Separate Accounts due or accrued (net) | 86,840 | |
| 14. Taxes, licenses and fees due or accrued, excluding federal income taxes (Exhibit 6, Line 9, Col. 5) | 2,385,935 | 2,658,746 |
| 14A. Federal income taxes due or accrued, including $0 on capital gains (excluding deferred taxes) | 0 | 0 |
| 15. "Cost of collection" on premiums and annuity considerations deferred and uncollected in excess of total loading thereon | 0 | 0 |
| 16. Unearned investment income (Exhibit 3, Line 10, Col. 2) | 103,787 | 211,803 |
| 17. Amounts withheld or retained by company as agent or trustee | 2,150,126 | 1,487,688 |
| 18. Amounts held for agents' account, including $0 agents' credit balances | 2,621,341 | 1,928,072 |
| 19. Remittances and items not allocated | 6,614,352 | 8,218,800 |
| 20. Net adjustment in assets and liabilities due to foreign exchange rates | 0 | 0 |
| 21. Liability for benefits for employees and agents if not included above | 0 | 0 |
| 22. Borrowed money $0 and interest thereon | 0 | 0 |
| 23. Dividends to stockholders declared and unpaid | 0 | 0 |

| | | | |
|---|---|---:|---:|
| 24. | Miscellaneous liabilities: | | |
| | 24.1 Mandatory securities valuation reserve (Page 29A, final Item) | 30,295,368 | 29,860,967 |
| | 24.2 Reinsurance in unauthorized companies | 0 | 0 |
| | 24.3 Funds held under reinsurance treaties with unauthorized reinsurers | 0 | 0 |
| | 24.4 Payable to parent, subsidiaries and affiliates | 250,000 | 0 |
| | 24.5 Drafts outstanding | 9,873,243 | 10,725,294 |
| | 24.6 Liability for amounts held under uninsured accident and health plans | 0 | 0 |
| 25. | Aggregate write-ins for liabilities | 12,202,664 | 15,147,869 |
| 26. | Total Liabilities excluding Separate Accounts business (Items 1 to 25) | 2,874,422,346 | 2,823,989,914 |
| 27. | From Separate Accounts Statement | 172,119,618 | 117,070,976 |
| 28. | Total Liabilities (Items 26 and 27) | 3,046,541,964 | 2,941,060,889 |
| 29. | Common capital stock | 0 | 0 |
| 30. | Preferred capital stock | 0 | 0 |
| 31. | Aggregate write-ins for other than special surplus funds | 0 | 0 |
| 32. | Gross paid in and contributed surplus (Page 3, Item 32. Col. 2 plus Page 4, Item 44a, Col. 1) | 0 | 0 |
| 33. | Aggregate write-ins for special surplus funds | 14,761,000 | 13,000,000 |
| 34. | Unassigned funds (surplus) | 146,529,781 | 121,513,586 |
| 35. | Less treasury stock, at cost: | | |
| | (1) 0 shares common (value included in Item 29  $0 ) | 0 | 0 |
| | (2) 0 shares preferred (value included in Item 30  $0 ) | 0 | 0 |
| 36 | Surplus (total Items 31 + 32 + 33 + 34 − 35) | 161,290,781 | 134,513,586 |
| 37. | Totals of Items 29, 30 and 36 (Page 4, Item 48) | 161,290,781 | 134,513,586 |
| 38. | Totals of Items 28 and 37 (Page 2, Item 24) | 3,207,832,745 | 3,075,574,475 |

*DETAILS OF WRITE-INS AGGREGATED AT ITEM 25 FOR LIABILITIES*

| | | | |
|---|---|---:|---:|
| 2501. | Deferred income taxes | 5,728,094 | 4,800,094 |
| 2502. | Reserve for deferred compensation plan | 2,768,601 | 2,444,057 |
| 2503. | Due to reinsuring company (reserve amount) | 2,285,767 | 2,910,956 |
| 2504. | Amounts held for benefit of group life policyholders | 1,000,700 | 1,323,700 |
| 2505. | Accounts Payable — purchase of securities | 0 | 2,078,546 |
| 2598. | Summary of remaining write-ins for Item 25 from overflow page | 419,502 | 1,550,515 |
| 2599. | Totals (Items 2501 thru 2505 plus 2598) (Page 3, Item 25) | 12,202,664 | 15,147,869 |

*DETAILS OF WRITE-INS AGGREGATED AT ITEM 31 FOR OTHER THAN SPECIAL SURPLUS FUNDS*

| | | | |
|---|---|---:|---:|
| 3101. | | | |
| 3102. | | | |
| 3103. | | | |
| 3104. | | | |
| 3105. | | | |
| 3198. | Summary of remaining write-ins for Item 31 from overflow page | 0 | 0 |
| 3199. | Totals (Items 3101 thru 3105 plus 3198) (Page 3, Item 31) | 0 | 0 |

*DETAILS OF WRITE-INS AGGREGATED AT ITEM 33 FOR SPECIAL SURPLUS FUNDS*

| | | | |
|---|---|---:|---:|
| 3301. | Reserve for asset fluctuations and other contingencies | 0 | 156,456 |
| 3302. | Reserve for group life insurance | 13,611,000 | 12,093,544 |
| 3303. | Reserve for Separate Accounts | 750,000 | 750,000 |
| 3304. | Reserve for guaranty fund — State of Colorado | 400,000 | 0 |
| 3305. | | | |
| 3398. | Summary of remaining write-ins for Item 33 from overflow page | 0 | 0 |
| 3399. | Totals (Items 3301 thru 3305 plus 3398) (Page 3, Item 33) | 14,761,000 | 13,000,000 |

TABLE 32-2b (continued) STATUTORY BALANCE SHEET

strain when the total disposition of income exceeds sources of income.[22] The surplus strain phenomenon is far less evident or nonexistent under GAAP rules, since (1) the majority of first-year acquisition expenses are capitalized and deferred, and (2) reserve calculations are typically based on more liberal assumptions.

*Changes in Surplus Account*. The difference in income and disposition of income is determined in the summary of operations. This net gain or loss from operations is a primary source of surplus change. There are also direct sources of surplus change:

•*Capital gains and losses* directly affect surplus if they are (a) realized during the reporting year through sale or other disposition or if they are (b) realized through a change in the admitted value of assets.

•Changes in the AVR and IMR (and formerly the MSVR) flow directly to the surplus account, without being reflected in the summary of operations.

•*Dividends paid to shareholders* are a distribution of surplus, unlike policyowner dividends, which are reflected in the summary of operations.

Table 32-3 presents the Summary of Operations and Reconciliation of Capital and Surplus Account for a hypothetical life insurance company.

## CASH FLOW STATEMENT

The NAIC requires a cash flow statement to be included in the annual report. As discussed earlier in this chapter and in Chapter 30, the balance sheet focus of statutory accounting does not adequately account for short-term cash flow activity. The cash flow statement reports an insurer's cash activities and may reveal potential liquidity problems in responding to potential disintermediation or other cash flow problems.

The cash flow statement reports the sources and uses of all insurer cash for a given reporting period both for insurance operations and investment activity, and it reconciles the cash and short-term investment holdings from period to period. Table 32-4 presents the cash flow statement for a hypothetical life insurance company.

## SUPPLEMENTARY SCHEDULES AND EXHIBITS

In general, the subsidiary exhibits and schedules required by statutory reporting requirements provide breakdowns, or further details, in regard to some of the items that appear only in total in the primary financial statements. Among the **Exhibits**, the more important are those that furnish details or classified information about (1) premium income; (2) investment income; (3) capital gains and losses; (4) expenses; (5) taxes; (6) policy reserves; (7) policy and contract claims; (8) life insurance issued, terminated, and in force (the "policy exhibit");

[22] See Chap. 2.

and (9) annuities issued, terminated, and in force (the "annuity exhibit"). General interrogatories and footnotes follow the exhibits.

The most important **Schedules** found in the NAIC statement are those relating to real estate, mortgage loans, and securities (bonds and stocks). The schedules for real estate and securities show, in considerable detail, the amounts owned at the end of the year and the purchases and sales during the year. Somewhat similar information is given for mortgage loans, but with less detail. Other important schedules show detailed information regarding (1) individual bank balances, month by month; (2) resisted claims; (3) expenses incurred in connection with legal matters or appearances before legislative bodies, and so on; and (4) proceedings of the last annual election of directors.

A statement of the company's business in the state in which the report is being filed is shown at the end of the statement, following the schedules. The statement shows the numbers and amounts of policies issued, terminated, and in force, together with a statement of premiums collected and policy dividends and benefits paid in the state. Naturally, the necessity of furnishing this information by state requires that the insurance company to maintain its records in such a way as to be able to report its business by state.

The NAIC statement is intended to provide technical information required for proper supervision by the state insurance department of all the financial operations and activities of the company. The nature, detail, and quantity of data required for regulatory purposes make the NAIC statement a complex and lengthy report.

## MANAGERIAL ACCOUNTING

In addition to using them for financial reporting systems, insurer management requires accounting tools for managerial purposes. Budget accounting is used for business planning purposes; cost accounting is used to identify the cost of creating, marketing, and operating discrete aspects of a company's business; and audit and control procedures are applied to minimize the possibility of accounting mistakes and irregularities.

### BUDGET ACCOUNTING

Financial reporting systems account for the historical financial performance of a company. Management also requires projections of future financial results for planning purposes. **Budget accounting** becomes central to the planning process by detailing expected income and expense over a specified period of time for a company or department. Planning can be characterized as operational or strategic.

**Operational planning** is short term in nature—typically two to five

# TABLE 32-3 STATUTORY ANNUAL STATEMENT —
## SUMMARY OF OPERATIONS

| | | Year t | Year t-1 |
|---|---|---:|---:|
| 1. | Premiums and annuity considerations (Exhibit 1, Part 1, Line 20d, Col. 1, less Col. 11) | 284,372,906 | 239,558,135 |
| 1A. | Annuity and other fund deposits | 189,039,766 | 183,680,444 |
| 2. | Considerations for supplementary contracts with life contingencies (Exhibit 12, Line 3) | 1,655,257 | 1,680,413 |
| 3. | Considerations for supplementary contracts without life contingencies and dividend accumulations (Exhibit 12, Lines 4 and 5) | 60,510,940 | 51,938,215 |
| 3A. | Coupons left to accumulate at interest (Exhibit 12, Line 5A) | 0 | 0 |
| 4. | Net investment income (includes $0 equity in undistributed income or loss of subsidiaries) (Exhibit 2, Line 7) | 252,959,266 | 248,165,829 |
| 5. | Commissions and expense allowances on reinsurance ceded (Exhibit 1, Part 2, Line 26a, Col. 1) | 3,731,649 | 4,130,262 |
| 5A. | Reserve adjustments on reinsurance ceded (Exhibit 12, Line 9A) | (57,596,597) | (14,250,301) |
| 6. | Aggregate write-ins for miscellaneous income | 11,817,116 | 10,592,691 |
| 7. | Totals (Items 1 to 6) | 746,490,304 | 725,495,688 |
| 8. | Death benefits | 63,501,552 | 59,033,426 |
| 9. | Matured endowments (excluding guaranteed annual pure endowments) | 1,757,212 | 1,627,491 |
| 10. | Annuity benefits (Exhibit 11, Part 2, Line 6d, Cols. 4 + 8) | 37,365,703 | 39,553,757 |
| 11. | Disability benefits and benefits under accident and health policies | 15,482,399 | 9,802,286 |
| 11A. | Coupons, guaranteed annual pure endowments and similar benefits (Exhibit 7, Line 15, Cols. 3 + 4) | 0 | 0 |
| 12. | Surrender benefits and other fund withdrawals | 346,208,936 | 365,506,090 |
| 13. | Group conversions | 23,360 | 8,348 |
| 14. | Interest on policy or contract funds | 1,185,878 | 1,100,912 |
| 15. | Payments on supplementary contracts with life contingencies (Exhibit 12, Line 20.1) | 2,957,416 | 2,944,826 |
| 16. | Payments on supplementary contracts without life contingencies and of dividend accumulations (Exhibit 12, Lines 20.2 & 21) | 59,581,600 | 46,338,455 |
| 16A. | Accumulated coupon payments (Exhibit 12, Line 21A) | 0 | 0 |
| 17. | Increase in aggregate reserves for life and accident and health policies and contracts | 71,123,006 | 68,491,664 |
| 17A. | Increase in liability for premium and other deposit funds | (17,852,188) | (56,277,596) |
| 18. | Increase in reserve for supplementary contracts without life contingencies and for dividend and coupon accumulations | 4,677,293 | 12,136,013 |
| 19. | Totals (Items 8 to 18) | 566,012,167 | 550,265,671 |
| 20. | Commissions on premiums and annuity considerations (direct business only) (Exhibit 1, Part 2, Line 30, Col. 1) | 26,935,447 | 27,637,575 |
| 21. | Commissions and expense allowances on reinsurance assumed (Exhibit 1, Part 2, Line 26b, less Col. 11) | 1,948,880 | 2,319,687 |
| 22. | General insurance expenses (Exhibit 5, Line 10, Cols. 1 + 2 + 3) | 69,566,107 | 74,635,344 |
| 23. | Insurance taxes, licenses and fees, excluding federal income taxes (Exhibit 6, Line 7, Cols. 1 + 2 + 3) | 8,915,689 | 9,395,367 |
| 24. | Increase in loading on and cost of collection in excess of loading on deferred and uncollected premiums | 559,712 | 655,360 |
| 24A. | Net transfers to or (from) Separate Accounts | 20,037,892 | 30,837,345 |
| 25. | Aggregate write-ins for deductions | 530,601 | (69,407) |
| 26. | Totals (Items 19 to 25) | 714,506,494 | 695,676,941 |

| | | |
|---|---:|---:|
| 27. Net gain from operations before dividends to policyholders and federal income taxes (Item 7 minus Item 26) | 31,983,810 | 29,818,748 |
| 28. Dividends to policyholders (Exhibit 7, Line 15, Cols. 1 and 2) | 15,525,456 | 15,061,138 |
| 29. Net gain from operations after dividends to policyholders and before federal income taxes (Item 27 minus Item 28) | 16,458,354 | 14,757,610 |
| 30. Federal income taxes incurred (excluding tax on capital gains) | 2,831,000 | 310,000 |
| 31. Net gain from operations after dividends to policyholders and federal income taxes and before realized capital gains or (losses) (Item 29 minus Item 30) | 13,627,354 | 14,447,610 |
| 32. Net realized capital gains or (losses) less capital gains tax of $1,245,000 | 2,415,596 | 190,292 |
| 33. Net income (Item 31 plus Item 32) | 16,042,951 | 14,637,902 |
| **CAPITAL AND SURPLUS ACCOUNT** | | |
| 34. Capital and surplus, December 31, previous year (Page 3, Item 37, Col. 2) | 134,513,586 | 120,291,105 |
| 35. Net income (Item 33) | 16,042,951 | 14,637,902 |
| 36. Change in net unrealized capital gains or (losses) | 1,530,410 | 4,822,546 |
| 37. Change in nonadmitted assets and related items (Exhibit 14, Item 13, Col. 3) | (152,733) | 49,747 |
| 38. Change in liability for reinsurance in unauthorized companies, (increase) or decrease (Page 3, Item 24.2, Col. 1 minus 2) | 0 | 0 |
| 39. Change in reserve on account of change in valuation basis, (increase) or decrease (Exh. 8A, Line D, Col. 4) | 0 | 0 |
| 40. Change in mandatory securities valuation reserve, (increase) or decrease (Page 3, Item 24.1, Col. 1 minus 2) | (434,401) | (4,229,020) |
| 41. Change in treasury stock, (increase) or decrease (Page 3, Items 35 (1) & (2), Col. 1 minus 2) | 0 | 0 |
| 42. Change in surplus in Separate Accounts Statement | 0 | 0 |
| 43. Capital changes: | | |
| (a) Paid in | 0 | 0 |
| (b) Transferred from surplus (Stock Dividend) | 0 | 0 |
| (c) Transferred to surplus (Exhibit 12, Line 24) | 0 | 0 |
| 44. Surplus adjustments: | | |
| (a) Paid in | 0 | 0 |
| (b) Transferred to capital (Stock Dividend) (Exhibit 12, Line 25, inside amount for stock $) | 0 | 0 |
| (c) Transferred from capital (Exhibit 12, Line 24) | 0 | 0 |
| 45. Dividends to stockholders | 0 | 0 |
| 46. Aggregate write-ins for gains and losses in surplus | 9,790,970 | (1,058,695) |
| 47. Net change in capital and surplus for the year (Items 35 through 46) | 26,777,195 | 14,222,481 |
| 48. Capital and surplus, December 31, current year (Items 34 + 47) (Page 3, Item 37) | 161,290,781 | 134,513,586 |

**TABLE 32-3 (continued) STATUTORY ANNUAL STATEMENT —**
**RECONCILIATION OF CAPITAL AND SURPLUS ACCOUNT**

TABLE 32-4    STATUTORY ANNUAL STATEMENT — CASH FLOW STATEMENT

## CASH FLOW

| | | Year t | Year t-1 |
|---|---|---|---|
| 1. | Premiums and annuity considerations | 285,079,993 | 240,685,425 |
| 2. | Annuity and other fund deposits | 189,039,766 | 183,680,444 |
| 3. | Other premiums, considerations and deposits | 62,166,198 | 53,618,627 |
| 4. | Allowances and reserve adjustments received on reinsurance ceded | (53,872,209) | (10,118,241) |
| 5. | Investment income received (excluding realized gains/losses and net of investment expenses) | 249,297,390 | 246,527,820 |
| 6. | Other income received | 7,993,116 | 10,592,691 |
| 7. | Total (Items 1 to 6) | 739,704,254 | 724,986,767 |
| 8. | Life and accident and health claims paid | 82,987,536 | 72,772,383 |
| 9. | Surrender benefits and other fund withdrawals paid | 346,198,675 | 365,512,461 |
| 10. | Other benefits to policyholders paid | 101,080,609 | 90,427,192 |
| 11. | Total (Items 8 to 10) | 530,266,820 | 528,712,036 |
| 12. | Commissions, other expenses and taxes paid (excluding FIT) | 106,670,253 | 111,047,784 |
| 13. | Net transfers to or (from) Separate Accounts (operational items only) | 20,037,892 | 30,837,345 |
| 14. | Total (Items 12 to 13) | 126,708,145 | 141,885,129 |
| 15. | Dividends to policyholders paid | 15,952,094 | 15,807,847 |
| 16. | Federal income taxes paid (excluding tax on capital gains) | 6,303,861 | 491,030 |
| 17. | Net increase or (decrease) in policy loans and premium notes | 1,320,449 | 1,765,333 |
| 18. | Other operating expenses paid | 4,239,985 | 5,011,746 |
| 19. | Total (Items 15 to 18) | 27,816,390 | 23,075,956 |
| 20. | Net cash from operations (Item 7 minus Item 11 minus Item 14 minus Item 19) | 54,912,900 | 31,313,645 |
| 21. | Proceeds from investments sold, matured or repaid: | | |
| | 21.1 Bonds | 726,601,807 | 422,718,738 |
| | 21.2 Stocks | 68,452,395 | 63,800,000 |
| | 21.3 Mortgage loans | 19,704,948 | 5,401,776 |
| | 21.4 Real estate | 0 | 0 |
| | 21.5 Collateral loans | 0 | 0 |
| | 21.6 Other invested assets | 400 | 0 |
| | 21.7 Net gains or (losses) on cash and short-term investments | 2,911 | (818) |
| | 21.8 Miscellaneous proceeds | 30,303 | 333,376 |
| | 21.9 Total investment proceeds (Items 21.1 to 21.8) | 814,792,762 | 492,253,072 |
| 22. | Tax on capital gains | 0 | 0 |

| | | |
|---|---:|---:|
| 23. Total (Item 21.9 minus Item 22) | 814,792,762 | 492,253,072 |
| 24. Other cash provided: | | |
| 24.1 Capital and surplus paid in | 0 | 0 |
| 24.2 Borrowed money $0 less amounts repaid $0 | 0 | 0 |
| 24.3 Other sources | 3,284,358 | 0 |
| 24.4 Total other cash provided (Items 24.1 to 24.3) | 3,284,358 | 0 |
| 25. Total (Item 20 plus Item 24.4) | 872,990,020 | 523,566,718 |
| 26. Cost of investments acquired (long-term only): | | |
| 26.1 Bonds | 799,645,561 | 340,798,110 |
| 26.2 Stocks | 42,450,683 | 64,821,601 |
| 26.3 Mortgage loans | 55,432,043 | 159,555,000 |
| 26.4 Real estate | 809,768 | 1,553,153 |
| 26.5 Collateral loans | 0 | 0 |
| 26.6 Other invested assets | 13,364,878 | 0 |
| 26.7 Miscellaneous applications | 1,750,846 | 672,520 |
| 26.8 Total investments acquired (Items 26.1 to 26.7) | 913,453,779 | 567,400,384 |
| 27. Other cash applied: | | |
| 27.1 Dividends to stockholders paid | 0 | 0 |
| 27.2 Other applications (net) | 1,347,904 | 1,186,605 |
| 27.3 Total other cash applied (Items 27.1 and 27.2) | 1,347,904 | 1,186,605 |
| 28. Total (Items 26.8 and 27.3) | 914,801,683 | 568,586,990 |
| 29. Net change in cash and short-term investments (Item 25 minus Item 28) | (41,811,663) | (45,020,272) |
| **RECONCILIATION** | | |
| 30. Cash and short-term investments: | | |
| 30.1 Beginning of year | 149,327,270 | 194,347,542 |
| 30.2 End of year (Item 29 plus Item 30.1) | 107,515,608 | 149,327,270 |

**TABLE 32-4 (continued) STATUTORY ANNUAL STATEMENT— CASH FLOW STATEMENT**

years—and focuses on the day-to-day financial activities of a company. Operating budgets are primarily concerned with income and expense statements for specified periods, and they can be presented by department or on an aggregate, companywide basis.

By contrast, **strategic planning** is more long term in nature, and it often involves fixed assets, capital expenditures, and long-term sources of capital. Strategic planning has been called capital budgeting on a grand scale, and it is essential for determining whether a company's capital will be invested efficiently.[23]

Differing approaches to budget preparation include top-down budgeting, bottom-up budgeting, and zero-base budgeting. **Top-down budgeting** is prepared by senior management based on past experience and current objectives, with little input from middle management and employees. This approach ensures that budgets reflect management wishes and can be prepared relatively easily, but it may not enjoy the full support of nonparticipating managers and employees.

**Bottom-up budgeting** is prepared with significant contributions from employees and middle managers and most likely maximizes their support. This approach typically generates high-quality management information, but is relatively time consuming. **Zero-base budgeting** begins with the assumption that past expenditures are not a measure of future expenditures and that each department's expected outlays must be justified in full.

## COST ACCOUNTING

The primary purpose of **cost accounting** is to identify the cost of creating, marketing, and operating discrete aspects of an insurer's business. The ability to distinguish costs among different products, services, and operations is necessary for effectively supporting the pricing of products and the analysis of budgets and capital investments.

With reliable cost information, management is better able to make informed operations decisions, such as:

•Identifying less productive areas of insurer operations for the purposes of cost control.

•Budgeting insurer resources to hold, expand, or contract market share where appropriate.

•Determining premium and dividend scales.

•Evaluating and controlling operations by checking procedures and personnel.

Cost accounting is conducted on both a marginal and functional cost

---

[23]See "Economic Value Analysis" below.

basis. **Marginal cost accounting** measures the additional expense of producing one additional product or service unit, and it is helpful because marginal cost and initial cost usually differ. Marginal costs will be less than initial costs because of the nonrecurring nature of many start-up expenditures. Understanding the marginal cost of a particular action reveals the true monetary effect that can be expected and is helpful in determining the prudence of proceeding or not proceeding with an action.

**Functional cost accounting** involves the identification of the cost associated with a series of operations that often cross departmental lines. As pointed out earlier, the actuarial department plays an important functional role in a number of areas within the insurer. For example, new product development may be basically an actuarial responsibility, but a new product necessarily involves marketing, investments, underwriting, systems, and other areas within the insurer. Functional cost accounting further refines the cost analysis procedure, and it is necessary to prepare the allocations by line of business, as is required for the statutory annual statement.

## AUDIT AND CONTROL

Internal control and audit procedures are concerned with limiting the risk of loss associated with mistakes and irregularities in the processing of transactions and the handling of assets. To ensure that records are kept appropriately, audit and control personnel should work independently of regular accounting personnel and have access to both senior management and the board's audit committee.

*Accounting control* is intended to promote the following objectives:

- •Transactions should be executed in accordance with the general or specific authorization of management.

- •Transactions should be recorded in a way that permits preparation of financial statements that conform to GAAP, SAP, and other necessary criteria.

- •Transactions should be recorded in a way that permits the proper monitoring of company assets.

- •Access to assets should be permitted only under authorized circumstances.

- •The company's record of its assets should be compared with existing assets at regular intervals in order to identify discrepancies.

*Accounting audits* provide confirmation to interested parties that financial results as reported are accurate. External audits are performed by accounting firms for the benefit of interested third parties such as shareholders, regulators,[24] and the IRS. These audits are conducted in accordance with generally accepted auditing standards. The primary objective of the audits is to certify, with reasonable assurance, that a company's financial statements are free of material misstatements and that the statements are in accord with GAAP or SAP, depending on the purpose of the audit. The audit is conducted on a risk-based sample that reflects the state of the company's internal controls and the identified critical and significant areas that represent the most important areas of exposure. Internal audits may be performed by company personnel for the benefit of management and directors. Where appropriate control procedures are utilized, the audit should substantially confirm the company's regular financial reports.

## ECONOMIC VALUE ANALYSIS

As discussed earlier in this chapter, both SAP and GAAP accounting exhibit significant limitations in describing certain aspects of life insurer financial condition. In order to measure adequately the long-term financial impact of current-year management decisions, it is necessary to avoid these limitations to the extent possible. Specifically, these are the goals of management-oriented measurement:

- It should not distort the long-term results of surrenders (lost future profits) and new sales (additional profits).

- It should recognize anticipated future profits on future business.

- It should recognize the long-term value resulting from current investment in distribution systems.

- It should recognize the unrealized capital gains and losses associated with active investment management programs.

As discussed in Chapter 29, the primary management objective for virtually every life insurer is to create value for shareholders, and in mutual companies, for policyowners. Performance measurement systems based on the creation of value are increasingly being adopted by life insurers as a standard for judging the effectiveness of management activity.

The two most important of these are the value-added and return on equity methods. Students of investment analysis will recognize these methods as derivations of net present value analysis and internal rate of return analysis, respectively.

---

[24]External audits by public accounting firms are required in all states.

## VALUE-ADDED ANALYSIS

**Value-added** for a given planning or analysis period is defined as follows:

|  | Ending net worth |
|---|---|
| Less: | Beginning net worth |
| Plus: | Stock and policyowner dividends paid |
| Less: | Capital infusions |
| Equals: | Value added for the period |

Net worth is defined as statutory surplus and statutory earnings for the period, plus the present value of future statutory earnings on existing business, plus the present value of future statutory earnings on future business.

Statutory earnings, rather than GAAP earnings or cash flow, are probably best used as profit measures, since statutory earnings represent the only source of capital for the payment of dividends or increases to surplus. Present values are calculated by discounting cash flows at the insurer's hurdle rate, or **cost of capital**.

Adjustments to the discount rate may be made to reflect the different risk properties of different products and ventures. For example, a higher discount rate would most likely be appropriate for discounting future profits on future business relative to future profits on existing business.

The value-added method, by incorporating future statutory earnings, recognizes the long-term value that can be expected to develop from current-year management actions. Value-added analysis can be applied to individual product lines, as well as to insurer net worth in the aggregate. Whenever the present value of future cash flows exceeds the investment under analysis, management is creating value for shareholders or policyowners.

## RETURN ON EQUITY ANALYSIS

**Return on equity** methods are used to calculate profitability as a return on an insurer's investment in a product line or other venture. Return on equity is the implicit internal rate of return associated with the cash flows or statutory profits of a product line or other venture.

When return on equity exceeds the insurer's cost of capital, value is created for shareholders or policyowners. As with the value-added method, the incorporation of future earnings recognizes the long-term value of current-year management actions.

A more sophisticated form of return on equity analysis is used by some companies. The level return on equity method attempts to account better for the special risk-taking nature of life insurance by incorporating the idea that equity includes not only cash invested in reserves and expenses for a product line, but also reflects some part of an insurer's surplus that supports the product line.

The idea of **benchmark surplus**, discussed in Chapter 30, is central to recognizing the risk-taking nature of insurance in the measurement of financial performance. Management practice dictates that statutory reserves are not sufficient in and of themselves to support a particular product line. Some level of statutory surplus is required to protect against unforeseen contingencies, and to satisfy the requirements of regulators, rating agencies, policyowners, shareholders, and other outside evaluators of life insurers.

While the mathematical and conceptual complexity of level return on equity makes a full discussion beyond the scope of this text (and has limited its implementation to relatively few insurers), the method is intended to recognize that the equity devoted to a particular product line is not limited to cash outlays for expenses and reserves, but also includes the benchmark surplus that effectively supports the product line. It is consistent with this recognition that after-tax earnings on benchmark surplus are combined with product earnings to calculate the implicit internal rate of return associated with the product, and the incidence of profit recognition is in part determined by periodically redetermined benchmark surplus requirements.[25]

## REGULATORY DEVELOPMENTS IN FINANCIAL REPORTING

### THE VALUATION ACTUARY

Regulators historically examined the statutory statement to evaluate an insurer's current and future solvency. As discussed above, the statutory statement is a static, nondynamic view of an insurer's financial position.

The statutory statement also suffers from rules that value assets and liabilities independently. Bonds not in default are valued at amortized cost, without regard to current market values, yields, or scheduled maturities. Liabilities are valued on the premise of interest and mortality assumptions permitted or required at the time of issue, without regard to current experience or asset values. As a result of the inherent cash flow nature of the life insurance business and the vulnerability of its pricing and reserving assumptions to changing market interest rates (both discussed in Chapter 30), and artificially stabilizing asset valuation conventions (discussed earlier in this chapter), the statutory statement has been an inadequate tool for fully evaluating company solvency.

---

[25]For a detailed discussion of level return on equity, see Donald R. Songergeld, "Earnings and the Internal Rate of Return Measurement of Profit," *Transactions of the Society of Actuaries*, Vol. 26 (1975), pp. 617–632.

In 1985 a joint committee of the American Academy of Actuaries and the Society of Actuaries recommended that each life company appoint a "valuation actuary" who would issue a "statement of actuarial opinion" on an annual basis, certifying a company's expected solvency under a variety of possible economic scenarios that recognize the interdependence of asset and liability cash flows. The stated opinion certifies as follows:

(1) Reserves, premiums, and investment cash flow are sufficient to satisfy a company's obligations in the event of *reasonable* deviations from expected assumptions, and

(2) Reserves, premiums, and investment cash flows, together with surplus, are sufficient to satisfy a company's obligations in the event of *plausible* deviations from expected assumptions.[26]

In 1990 the NAIC adopted amendments to the Standard Valuation Law (SVL) to provide a basis for establishing the integrity of the statutory balance sheet for life insurers with respect to policyowner liabilities. A qualified valuation actuary is defined as an **appointed actuary** in the amendments. For most insurers, appointed actuaries will be required to provide an opinion that addresses two questions:

(1) Does the statutory statement comply with the law?

(2) Given an accepted level of conservatism and an ongoing business assumption, what level of assets is needed to support the reported statement of liabilities?

The major change in the SVL is the addition of a new Section 3 which develops the actuarial opinion concepts. Other changes are made to implement the provisions of this new section, titled "Actuarial Analysis Opinion of Reserves and of Assets Supporting such Reserves." It becomes operative at the end of the first full calendar year following a state's adoption of the new model law.[27]

These changes in the SVL provide a significantly different role for actuaries in valuation. The appointed actuary is responsible by *law* for the liability reserves. The responsibility includes asset consideration and an asset adequacy opinion. The Actuarial Standards Board (ASB) provides the *professional base* for the appointed actuary's work.

In 1991 the NAIC adopted a model regulation regarding implementation of the new valuation opinion, and the ASB is developing standards of practice for the appointed actuary. Maintaining a balance between adequate regulation in the

---

[26]What constitutes *reasonable* and *plausible* deviations remains to be legally determined.

[27]In 1986 New York State issued Regulation 126, becoming the first state to require economic scenario testing in its solvency considerations. Canada, the United Kingdom, and other countries rely on similar actuarial certifications.

public interest and the insurer's need for investment management flexibility to compete effectively is an ongoing process. What has become clear, however, is the need for increased awareness at both the regulatory and insurer level of the interplay between investment, marketing, and valuation process.

## RISK-BASED CAPITAL REQUIREMENTS

Historically, regulators have not given detailed attention to the nature of particular risks assumed by insurers. Reserving requirements for broad classes of business were established, which, together with minimum admission and valuation requirements for assets, were intended to promote insurer solvency. Minimum capital requirements have been fixed-dollar in nature, and for most insurers they represent nominal amounts.

The NAIC has developed a risk-based capital formula establishing target surplus amounts that will be required above reserve requirements, and that would reflect the risk inherent in an insurer's contractual obligations and asset portfolio. The required amounts of capital are classified into the four major categories discussed in Chapter 30:  asset default risk (C-1), insurance pricing risk (C-2), asset/liability risk (C-3), and miscellaneous business risks (C-4).

The asset default risk component is intended to support all risks associated with losses related to assets. Insurance pricing requirements apply to both mortality and morbidity risks. Requirements attributable to mortality are based on the relative weight of group and individual business, as well as the relationship of insurance in force to the number of policies or lives insured. Morbidity requirements likewise are based on the mix of group and individual business, as well as the nature of coverages provided.

Asset/liability capital requirements depend on classification by the nature of the risk characteristics of individual product lines, as well as their withdrawal provisions. Miscellaneous risk capital requirements include amounts derived from an insurer's risk exposure with respect to guaranty fund assessability, its AVR and voluntary investment reserves established for real estate and mortgages, and dividend liabilities. The requirements also provide for a reduction in capital requirements where risks may be off-setting.

Implementation of the risk-based capital requirements, together with the IMR and the AVR, will likely reduce overall levels of reported surplus in the industry and lead to a significant increase in industry capital needs. As insurers manage their operations to develop a favorable risk-based capital profile, policyowners may expect generally increasing asset quality, while industry investors may expect generally declining return on equity results.

Although there is no consensus as to the effect, analysts have noted the nonconcurrence in emerging risk-based capital requirements between insurers and depository financial institutions (banks and thrifts). If differing regulations tend to impart a competitive advantage to one industry or the other, relative market shares of consumer savings may begin to reflect such an advantage.[28]

[28]See Peter Duran and Mark Olson, "A Tale of Two Industries," *Ernst & Young Insurance Executive Report* (Winter 1992), p. 2.

# Chapter 33

# MARKETING LIFE AND HEALTH INSURANCE

The degree to which a life insurance company succeeds reflects the consolidated effort of all the activities of the organization. As pointed out in Chapter 29, these activities may be arranged into three major functional classifications—marketing, investments, and administration. Of these three areas, marketing is the largest in terms of both personnel requirements and costs, and it is critically important to the success of any organization. Life insurers historically considered marketing to be synonymous with selling, and they considered their customers to be their agents. Insurers and agents alike were said often to sell to consumers while having little regard for consumers' wants, needs, or desires. As Adam Smith wrote in 1776:

> Consumption is the sole end and purpose of all production, and the interest of the producers ought to be attended to only so far as it may be necessary for promoting that of the consumer.[1]

In the 1950s a new philosophy, reflecting Adam Smith's words, began to emerge in business generally. The idea was that producers should analyze the needs of potential customers and then make decisions designed to satisfy these needs. As this marketing concept was adopted by more and more companies, it began to spread to the services industry generally and the life insurance industry specifically. It is now

---

[1] Adam Smith, *Wealth of Nations*, Book IV (New York: Modern Library, 1973), p. 625.

generally agreed that this marketing concept is essential to long-term success in market economies such as the United States. The concept involves:

- focusing on consumer needs,

- integrating all activities of the organization, including production, to satisfy these needs, and

- achieving long-term profits through satisfaction of consumer needs.[2]

While life insurers were late in adopting this concept, the intense competition of the 1980s within the life insurance business and the growing competition from other financial service organizations substantially heightened the importance of the marketing concept to the industry. Today a life insurer, to be successful over the long term, must create a satisfied customer and then turn that customer into a client.[3] Historically, this was done by the exclusive agent, whose relationship with customers was the basis of their satisfaction with the services provided. Today insurers cannot rely exclusively on agents to build a commitment to a particular insurer. The current emphasis on customer service and quality programs reflects this reality.[4]

Effective marketing—that is, the provision of appropriate products to consumers through an effective distribution system—is critical to the well-being of a life insurance company. It assures an adequate volume of new business at reasonable cost.

If an insurer's effort is to be successful, however, management must ensure that a proper relationship exists among all home office functions. Each home office executive who is responsible for a particular functional department must understand the role of his or her department in the marketing process and its contribution to the objectives of marketing as overall company goals.

## DEVELOPING AND MAINTAINING A MARKETING PROGRAM

The development and maintenance of a realistic marketing program is the primary responsibility of senior marketing executives. Each insurer has its own unique definition of desired markets, distribution systems, and products. The elements of a marketing program include an analysis of the markets available to or desired by the insurer, identification of the nature of the perceived competition, and determination of the distribution techniques to be used. A marketing plan must also include the design of a sales compensation system, a basic pricing strategy, and the special administrative systems and support needed

[2]Thomas C. Kinnear and Kenneth L. Bernhardt, *Principles of Marketing*, 3rd ed. (Glenview, Ill.: Scott, Foresman/Little, Brown Higher Education, 1990), p. 11.

[3]James H. Donnelly, Jr., Leonard L. Berry, and Thomas W. Thompson, *Marketing Financial Services: A Strategic Vision* (Homewood, Ill.: Dow Jones-Irwin, 1985), p. 3.

[4]Walter H. Zultowski, "Developing Long-Term Client Relationships: Will We Miss the Mark?" *MarketFacts* (July/Aug. 1991), pp. 24-26.

by particular market segments or products. For example, universal life and variable life are computer-intensive products that demand systems development far beyond normal administrative systems. The marketing plan is then utilized to develop a product portfolio and project future production by product and amount.

Once the insurer's marketing plan is initially documented, management must evaluate its basic goals with respect to growth and profit, and the capabilities of the home office and marketing operations. If there were no limit to the availability of capital, manpower, and expertise, then management could simply decide what to achieve and proceed to do it. In reality, however, the marketing plan must reflect the realistic growth and profit objectives of the company, the capital base that is available to permit the acceptance of risk and the capabilities of the home office and marketing support organizations. The marketing plan should reflect a realistic assessment of the particular strengths and weaknesses of the organization in relation to the factors considered critical to the success of the marketing plan. It is this assessment that leads to broad or narrow product portfolios, different distribution system structures, geographic concentration, and so on—the search for competitive advantages. It also should be noted that with the competitive emphasis on rates of return for interest-sensitive products and for separate-account business like variable life and annuities, a close coordination with the investment function is essential.[5]

The results of this planning and development activity will be a quantification of what the company wants to achieve, reflecting a balance between long-term and short-term goals. With priorities established, specific goals set down, and a product portfolio established, the stage is set, theoretically, for selecting and utilizing one or more distribution systems to deliver the products developed. Typically, however, the distribution system comes first, and the tentative decisions regarding distribution systems significantly influence the process of developing a product portfolio.

The management of the distribution system(s) selected (or already in place) traditionally has constituted the major operational responsibility of senior marketing management. In some large insurers today, however, the distribution and manufacturing functions are separated, with each run as a profit center under a senior marketing officer.

Most students of the industry agree that marketing systems utilizing career agents have been responsible for the widespread acceptance of life insurance in the United States.[6] Career agents in the United States are full-time commissioned sales personnel who hold an agency contract with at least one life insurance company. These career agents have been and are a vital force in the development of the industry. Per capita coverages in various countries suggest that those that

---

[5]The matching of assets and liabilities is a critical element of the investment process today (see Chap. 30).

[6]J. O. Stalson, *Marketing Life Insurance: Its History in America* (Cambridge, Mass.: Harvard University Press, 1942).

have emphasized career agent systems have been quite successful,[7] although it appears that success in several Asian countries can be achieved with part-time agents. For example, Japan and Korea, with high per capita premium expenditures, utilize very large part-time sales forces, predominantly made up of housewives.

In part because of the success of the systems utilizing career agents, other competing systems have developed. In fact, a number of systems might not be viable unless the basic career agency system survives and flourishes. Some systems serve special markets or provide special products. Others provide portfolios to almost everyone. Indeed, there are many systems for distributing life and health insurance—surprisingly many. Before examining the distribution management process, it might be helpful to review the various distribution systems in use in the U.S. life insurance industry today.

## DISTRIBUTION SYSTEMS

The individual life and health insurance business in the United States has two distinct distribution systems: (1) direct response and (2) agency.[8] Figure 33-1 shows these two systems, along with their various sub-systems.

**Direct response** marketing is a broad term for the practice of contacting potential customers without the use of a salesperson. In a direct response sale, no commissions are paid to an agent, since the buyer responds directly to the company because of solicitation via mail, broadcast media, coupons, and so on.[9] Although direct response marketing is growing rapidly, it is still estimated to account for less then 2 percent of new life insurance premiums and a slightly greater proportion of new health insurance premiums.

The **agency system** may be viewed as comprising two types: (1) agency-building and (2) nonagency-building. It includes the following classes of agents:

1. Those who sell only life and health insurance, either exclusively for a single insurer or for several insurers.

2. Those who sell both life and health insurance and property/liability insurance, either exclusively for one family of insurers or for several insurers.

3. Other entities that utilize client relationships to sell life insurance–related products (e.g., real estate agency offering mortgage protection insurance, automobile dealer offering credit life and health insurance, or a stock brokerage firm or bank offering annuity or life products).

Independent life insurance agents, independent property and liability agents, stockbrokers, realtors, and similar producers are commonly known as brokers.

---

[7]See Chap. 3

[8]This section draws on Archer L. Edgar, "Distribution Systems," *Marketing for Actuaries: Individual Life and Health Insurance, SOA Part 9 Study Note* (Hartford, Conn.: LIMRA, 1986), pp. viii-1 to viii-6. See also Dennis W. Goodman, *Life and Health Insurance Marketing* (Atlanta, Ga.: LOMA, 1989).

[9]In certain states, under existing countersignature laws, an agent is involved in direct response insurance transactions.

**FIGURE 33-1**

**INDIVIDUAL LIFE AND HEALTH DISTRIBUTION SYSTEMS IN THE UNITED STATES**

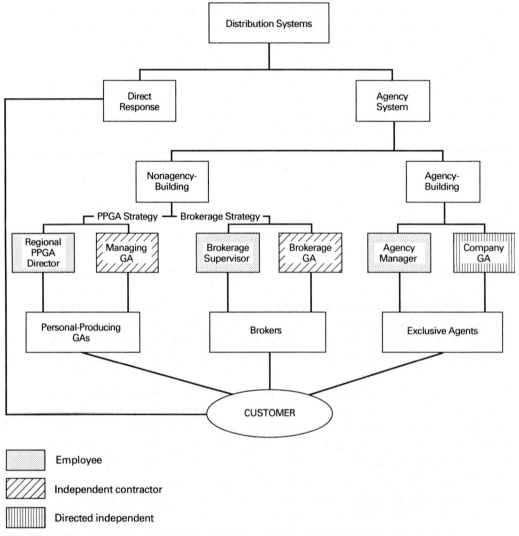

PPGA DENOTES PERSONAL-PRODUCING GENERAL AGENT AND GA DENOTES GENERAL AGENT

*Source*: *Marketing for Actuaries—Individual Life and Health* (Hartford, Conn.: LIMRA, 1986), p. viii-2

The term **broker**, as it is loosely used in the U.S. lexicon of life insurance distribution, describes a relationship between the producers and the insurer, and not the producer-client relationship as in nonlife insurance, in which the broker usually represents the client rather than any insurer. In other countries, the term *broker* in life insurance refers to a full-time intermediary who offers policies from several, if not all, licensed life insurers in the market.[10]

[10]See *Consumers and Life Insurance* (Paris: Organization for Economic Cooperation and Development, 1987).

Within each of the primary distribution systems, a variety of selling techniques is employed. For example, insurers have attempted to reach large numbers of prospects at the workplace through payroll deduction plans. More recently, experiments designed to make the agent more accessible—such as having their offices located in supermarkets and retail stores—have attempted to capture walk-in trade. Similarly, a number of insurers have made arrangements to offer their products at banking locations. In all of these cases, a salesperson of some kind, compensated either by salary or by commissions, is involved in the sale. In the United States, over 98 percent of new individual life premiums are generated by agents. The amount of life insurance sold has consistently been directly related to the size of the field force.

A given insurer's distribution strategy may involve direct response, agency system, or both. Within the agency system, the insurer may distribute its products through producers with whom it has an exclusive selling agreement, or it may offer its products through any available producers without their being required to represent that insurer exclusively.[11]

In theory, companies that use the agency-building strategy (also referred to as exclusive-agent or career-agent companies) recruit, finance, train, and house agents to represent them generally on an exclusive basis. Those that use nonagency-building strategies usually do not finance, train, or house the agents who represent them. Instead, they provide products to round out the portfolios of other insurers' exclusive agents and of other independent producing outlets.

Actual experience is not quite so clear-cut. For example, agency-building insurers may pay allowances instead of providing housing; some nonagency-building insurers try hard to provide a fairly complete portfolio of products to their producers and to capture most of their business. Nevertheless, in general, marketing strategy in nonagency-building companies involves gaining access to and maintaining relationships with producers whose primary affiliations and sometimes occupations are with others.

## AGENCY-BUILDING DISTRIBUTION SYSTEMS

Two well-organized marketing structures are used within the agency-building system: general agencies and branch offices. General agencies are headed by individuals referred to as general agents (GAs), who are appointed by the insurer and have a status akin to that of independent contractors. Usually, they receive expense allowances to cover such items as rent, clerical help, travel, postage, and telephone, and they are responsible for the financial management of the agency. Under the branch office structure, agencies are headed by agency managers—employees who carry out the assignments of the insurer and are directly supervised by the home office in the financial management of the agency.

---

[11]Producers known as **exclusive agents** in the United States are often referred to as **tied agents** in other markets.

*The General Agency System.* The **general-agency system,** which in its pure form is only theoretical today, is the oldest of the systems and aims at accomplishing through general agents what the managerial system is designed to do through branch offices. The company-appointed general agent represented the company within a designated territory over which he or she was given control, and, by contract, the insurer agreed to pay the agency a stipulated commission on the first year's premiums, plus a renewal on subsequent premiums. In return, the general agent agreed to build the company's business in a given territory. The general agent might pay his or her agents all of the agency's first year's commission, plus a somewhat smaller renewal commission than the one he or she received from the insurer; or the general agent might pay all of the commission of the first year's premium and retain the renewals; or again, he or she might retain a portion of the commission on both the first year's premium and the renewals. The difference between what the general agent received from the insurer and the amount paid to agents was (and still is) known as an **override** or **overriding commission.**

Although this was formerly the case, today most general agents are no longer directly responsible for the collection of premiums and interest on loans, the receipt of loan applications and proofs of loss, and other clerical work that arises naturally in connection with insurance sold in their territory. Routine matters of this nature usually are handled by a separate group of persons, who are located in the general agent's office or in separate offices throughout the country and are directly responsible to the home office. An arrangement of this nature relieves the general agent of details not directly related to production, and at the same time it offers the advantages that accrue from close contacts with such matters. It also is now common for the insurer to pay the office rent directly. This is done to discourage the closing of the office, which would leave the insurer without representation. In addition, companies now make payment of substantial nonvouchered amounts that are titled expense reimbursements allowances. These and other changes discussed below have led to GAs being called directed independents.

Formerly, individual agents' contracts were made with the general agent and not with the insurer. This also is no longer the case. Even in the pure general agency contract— in which the insurer, theoretically, has no control over the appointment of agents—the insurer usually specifies the form of contract to be used and reserves the right to reject agency appointments.

There are two classes of general agencies: (1) those in which the general agent relies chiefly upon personal business for his or her main profit and considers the income derived from subagents of minor importance[12] and (2) those in which the general agent subordinates his or her personal business and aims to develop a large force of subagents, with a view to deriving his or her chief profit

---

[12]This type of arrangement has evolved into a separate, significant marketing system: the personal-producing general agent, a nonagency-building strategy.

from the commission overrides on the business of these agents. In the first class, the general agent considers personal business of greatest importance and selects only prospective applicants that he or she can handle with minimal supervision and support. Needless to say, such an agency may not be as advantageous to subagents as the second class, since in this situation, although the general agent may obtain some personal business, he or she nevertheless promotes the welfare of his or her agents in preference to personal business.

*The Managerial System.* Many of the largest insurers use the managerial system instead of the general agency system. In this system the insurer has branch offices in various locations, each headed by an agency manager. The agency manager, who is a company employee, usually is selected because of his or her success as an agent, and is charged with the responsibility of securing and directing agents within a given territory and instructing and otherwise helping and encouraging them in their work as solicitors.

As in the case of home office employees, the agency manager and support staff at the branch office are paid by salary. The agency manager's compensation is composed of a base salary, which usually is relatively small, and an incentive element based on his or her performance. Much of the incentive portion is related to the amount of new production; there are additional payments (bonuses) for desirable performance such as increasing the volume of business through his or her office, adding to the number of productive agents, maintaining good persistency, or operating in a cost-effective manner.

Agency managers may be assisted by assistant managers, supervisors, specialist unit managers, or district managers. Assistants are responsible for specific functions or for units of agents, or they may provide overall assistance to the head of the agency.

The office manager is particularly important in the branch office system. He or she is expected to keep all office records; look after all correspondence in connection with applications and policies; assist in filing proofs of loss, applications for policy loans, and payment of cash values on surrenders; answer all communications from policyowners not sufficiently important to be referred to the home office; and supervise the clerical staff.

Agency-building systems (either general agency or managerial ones) also are used by *fraternal* organizations that offer life and health insurance to their members. The agents of these religious and social groups offer individual policies to the members of the association.

Two additional subsets of the agency-building system are multiple-line exclusive agent and combination operations. Agents in **multiple-line exclusive** operations sell only the life and health and property and liability insurance products of one group of affiliated insurers. Historically, most of these companies were rural operations that grew out of state farm bureaus. As contrasted with other career systems, agencies within this system normally are one-person operations with only clerical support that supplements the agent's personal sales effort.

*Combination* or *home service systems* have also been known as industrial and debit operations.[13] The unique characteristic of this operation is the assignment of a geographic territory to agents. At one time, agents also collected renewal premiums on business in force in the territory but the collection aspect has been deemphasized by many companies.

Originally, much of this business consisted of industrial insurance, with weekly home collections of premiums. Today almost all of the new sales consist of ordinary insurance, with premiums payable on a monthly or sometimes weekly basis. The assigned territory is becoming a sales region, since less of the business requires collection of premiums by the agent.

## NONAGENCY-BUILDING DISTRIBUTION SYSTEMS

The two most common subsets of the nonagency building subsystems are (1) brokerage and (2) personal-producing general agents (PPGAs).[14] As pointed out above, insurers that market through nonexclusive-agent strategies provide products or services to agents who are already engaged in life insurance selling. Thus the key to this strategy is to gain access to the producer. Retaining the producer's loyalty is accomplished by service, compensation, and personal relationships. The method of access to the producer, compensation agreements, and marketing philosophy of the brokerage companies differ from those of the PPGA companies.

*Brokerage.* Brokerage insurers gain access to producers through a company employee, a **brokerage supervisor,** who acts as a sort of "manufacturer's representative" or through an independent **brokerage general agent,** who performs the same function. Both of these individuals are authorized to appoint brokers on behalf of the insurer. Direct contracting in response to trade press advertising also is used.

Brokerage has many variations, depending on the insurer's orientation. Some life companies seek surplus or rated business from the agents of other companies; some find product niches; others seek life business from independent life producers. Some life affiliates of property and liability companies sell life insurance through independent insurance agencies that are associated with the property and liability parent. Still others sell through financial institutions, stockbrokers, lawyers, accountants, realtors, automobile dealers, and financial consultants. Since all of these producers may represent several insurers, the sale to the producing agency precedes the product sale. Here the insurer's brokerage supervisor plays a key role.

[13]See Bruce C. Dalzell, "Home Service: Myth and Fact," *Probe* (Sept. 21, 1990), p. 3.

[14]Paul H. McClain, "MGAs and Marketing Organizations: Are They the Right Distribution Opportunities for You?" *MarketFacts* (Jan./Feb. 1991), pp. 5-7.

At one time, insurers that utilized a brokerage strategy and sold through independent life agents and representatives of other companies specialized in term and substandard business. Today the range of products for which companies using the brokerage strategy compete has broadened to include almost all lines of insurance. Innovative products, pricing, commissions, and service are the competitive tools involved.

This full-product-line orientation has encouraged a separation between **manufacturing** and **distribution,** and it has spawned a variation of brokerage in which an exclusive-agent insurer formally acts as distributor for a product of another company, the manufacturer.[15] In this home-office-to-home-office arrangement, the distributing insurer acts as a brokerage general agent, and its agents act as brokers for the manufacturing insurer in product lines in which the distributing company may either be noncompetitive or simply may not wish to offer a particular product.

Another variation of this strategy has been the development of the noncompany affiliated **marketing organization** that is both independent and virtually totally self-supporting. Under its contracts, it receives maximum compensation with virtually no market support services. The marketing organization focuses on specific market segments or sales systems and methods, and provides the necessary sales and marketing support systems to the producer for a specific market segment. The marketing organization may consider a producer to be a business organization such as a bank or a credit union. The producer, however, may also be an individual or group of producers working with a particular sales concept such as executive bonus plans.

The marketing organization typically provides training, administration, illustration services, presubmission underwriting, and case management (after submission) to the producer. It also provides market-specific or sales-concept support for corporate-owned life insurance (COLI) and pension administration, prospecting or market access services, work-site selling (payroll deduction) support, and even turnkey sales and marketing systems such as the sale of insurance products by banks to their customers.

Typically, agents are contracted to the marketing organization and licensed through individual companies. All commissions are paid to the marketing organization, which, in turn, pays the agent.

Conversely, in **managing general agent** (MGA) and **brokerage general agent** (BGA) organizations, agents are contracted and licensed with each insurer represented. Commissions are paid directly to agents by the companies. MGAs and BGAs receive override compensation from the insurers they represent, based on agent/producer production. Thus under the marketing organization concept, the entire distribution function is delegated.

---

[15]For an excellent summary of this development, see Paul D. Laporte and Ross Trim, "The Future Looks Bright for Manufacturer-Distributor Agreements," *MarketFacts* (May/June 1990), pp. 34-36, 52.

**Wholesaling** is another practice in which an insurer produces a basic product to which the producer adds fees or commissions. Companies that utilize this concept attempt to serve the needs of financial planners and other financial advisors, who may work on a fee basis, such as accountants.[16]

*Personal-Producing General Agent.* PPGA insurers gain access to producers through an organizational structure that is similar to the one in brokerage insurers: (1) company-employed regional directors of PPGAs, (2) independent contractors—managing general agents, and (3) direct contracting with individuals identified through trade press advertising. Both regional directors and managing general agents are authorized to appoint PPGAs.

The PPGA strategy has gained importance in recent years. In the more traditional regional director approach, experienced life agents are hired under contracts that provide both direct and overriding commissions plus some type of expense allowance. For this the PPGAs supply their own office facilities and receive technical assistance in the form of computer services and advanced sales support. Personal-producing general agents usually have contracts with more than one insurer. The managing general agent approach typically specializes in single products, such as universal life or disability income, and it is essentially franchised to appoint PPGAs for the company in a territory.

Although there are philosophical differences in approach, the clear difference at the producer level between the independent contractor brokerage strategy and the independent contractor PPGA strategy is in the commission schedule. The former resembles an agent contract and the latter has elements of a general agent contract. Both strategies can operate simultaneously in the same insurer, along with others.

## DIRECT RESPONSE SYSTEM

A growing proportion of life and health insurance sales is made without the use of an agent—that is, using a **direct response marketing** arrangement. Although aggregate sales are still relatively small, interest in this strategy remains strong. Few insurance companies market their products solely by direct response methods, but many utilize both the agency marketing system and the direct response marketing system. These insurers may offer some of the same coverages through both marketing systems. The principal difference to the consumer for certain products can be one of cost and service. The same level of coverage sold through an agent may sometimes cost more than when sold through an efficient direct response marketing program, but, of course, the potential exists for greater personal service if an agent is involved in the transaction.

The life and health insurance sold by direct response marketing usually is

---

[16]See David F. West, "CPAs in the 1990s: What Role Will They Play in Marketing Insurance and Other Financial Products?" *Managers Magazine* (Mar. 1990), pp. 16-21.

not sold as basic coverage, but essentially is supplemental in nature (i.e., it helps to fill the gaps in basic coverages). The products are simple. They normally are easy to understand, require relatively small premium outlays, and are serviced through the economies of computerized solicitation, issuance, and administration. Comprehensive life and health insurance protection, annuities, estate planning, and other products do not readily lend themselves to direct response marketing methods; generally they require the services of a professional agent or other advisor. Where direct response marketing effort is directed to a select group of consumers under a **sponsored arrangement,** however, it can offer a broader range of relatively complex products. At least one successful insurer group sells automobile insurance, cash-value life insurance, and even tax shelters to its customer base in this manner, and does it effectively.

Regardless of how the sale has been completed—by an agent or by direct response marketing—from that point on the client frequently deals with the insurer on a direct basis. Premium notices are sent by mail. Premiums are paid by mail, and, at times, claims often are filed and benefit checks delivered by mail. In this sense, the direct response concept—whereby the insurer deals directly with the consumer—is not restricted to a few direct response specialty companies, but is a concept that is common to all elements of the insurance business.

**Direct mail** is the oldest method of direct response marketing. It is dependent on the availability of mailing lists that may be rented from a large number of sources. Today with the aid of technology, lists can be created that are specific as to the demographics and other characteristics of the individuals who make up the lists.

**Newspapers, magazine,** and **broadcast** (radio/TV) advertising reach large numbers of consumers, but only on a broad basis. In terms of total numbers reached, broadcast advertising surpasses all other media. The direct response marketing use of television, utilizing well-known personalities as sponsors,[17] is popular for two reasons. First, the size of the audience is staggering in its potential. Second, direct response specialists have learned how to efficiently reach specialized groups of viewers. Despite this interface, however, no insurer yet has systems in place that permit an application to be completed and the sales transaction finalized entirely electronically.

A knowledge of the specialized advertising techniques used is the key to understanding the direct response system of marketing. The National Association of Insurance Commissioners (NAIC) identified three broad types or categories of advertisements: (1) institutional advertisement, (2) invitation to inquire, and (3) invitation to contract. The NAIC advertising rules and regulations provide

---

[17]The use of such "stars" to sell insurance products has come under increasing attack. Opponents claim that the material often is misleading and the products high in price.

detailed stipulations as to the content of the advertisements, particularly those that are invitations to contract. Limitations and exclusions must be clearly set forth, and deceptive words or phrases may not be used. Some states require approval of every advertisement prior to its use.

The prevalent direct response media in use today (direct mail, print, and broadcast) have begun to be combined with **telemarketing**—the use of the telephone to improve life and health insurance sales. The importance of this approach is evidenced by the proliferation of toll-free numbers. Telemarketing is a high unit-cost medium, but justification for this higher cost is found in relatively high response rates. Telemarketing also is personal once a consumer makes the initial phone call. Personalization and mass marketing are combined in telemarketing, thus improving marketing effectiveness.

Advocates of direct response marketing believe that direct response insurance marketing and the traditional agency system are compatible. They point out that they complement each other by making available a maximum amount of insurance coverage to a maximum number of persons. Each system tends to concentrate on different segments of the marketplace: direct response reaches essentially the supplemental market and agents serve the basic needs as well as the more complex markets.

## GROUP INSURANCE DISTRIBUTION

The group department of a typical insurer markets its products through its general agencies or branch offices and through brokers and employee benefit consultants. The sales department is headed by an executive officer (group sales vice president) who is responsible for the sale and service of the product. Although some group insurance (usually the smaller-sized cases) is sold by an insurer's own career agents, group sales more commonly follow the brokerage model, with group representatives calling on independent benefit consultants, national brokerage houses, independent property and liability agencies, and agents of other insurers. Sales to the larger-case employer-employee and association markets tend to be made through specialized brokers or, in some instances, written directly with the employer. Many of the recent developments in distribution systems reflect a continuing effort to find more effective ways to deliver insurance products to larger numbers of customers.

In addition to group insurance as such, various forms of **mass marketing** have developed, frequently involving an agent. Association group, credit card solicitations, and payroll deduction efforts are examples. Although association group and credit card solicitations are direct response techniques, generally an agent is involved in the association group business. Supplementary coverage such as payroll deduction (salary allotment) is a form of mass marketing, sponsored by the employer. Just as innovations in products continue (leveraged by the financial environment and changing technology), marketing distribution systems will respond interactively to all present and evolving systems. This process should become even more innovative to the extent that distribution is separated from manufacturing and made a specific profit center.[18]

As the above discussion makes clear, U.S. distribution networks are organizationally diverse. Banks have long sought to participate in the U.S. insurance market. Historically, banks have been prohibited from doing so, but this is changing. U.S. banks generally appear to be gaining ground in their argument that globalization of financial services requires large sized, financially diversified firms. Proposals for major reforms of the U.S. financial system would permit considerably greater banking participation in the U.S. insurance markets. Although legislation to date has not passed, many observers believe banks ultimately will be permitted to participate fully in the U.S. insurance market.

## NON-U.S. DISTRIBUTION[19]

Distribution concerns are driving the insurance markets within the European Community (EC) and Western Europe. Banks already have excellent distribution networks. There has been a great deal of merger and acquisition activity among banks and insurance companies within the EC.

Insurance distribution methods differ from country to country in Europe. The Netherlands, for example, relies almost exclusively on independent agents, and 95 percent of the British premiums flow through brokers and other independent intermediaries. By contrast, Switzerland and Germany operate predominantly (more than 85 percent) through tied (exclusive) agents and company salespersons. In these markets, it is difficult for a new entrant to gain a significant market presence, because there are no established independent distribution networks. This has led to an acceleration in the number of mega-mergers and acquisitions within Europe among insurance companies domiciled in different EC member states, as well as among insurance companies and banks. Banking and insurance linkups have become so common that the French now talk of *bancassurance* and the Germans refer to *allfinanz*.

Japanese life insurance companies (as well as insurers in other Far Eastern markets such as Korea) are known for the hundreds of thousands of housewives and others whom they employ part-time to sell policies to friends, neighbors, and regular customers. In these markets, this distribution system, combined with a relatively high savings rate among individual citizens, has been very successful.

Distribution is the key to an insurer entering new markets, whether at home or abroad. Distribution networks take a great amount of time and resources to develop and administer.

---

[18]Susan R. Duncan, "Group Distribution: Systems of the Future," *MarketFacts* (Nov./Dec. 1991), pp. 53-56. See chaps. 26 and 27 for a comprehensive discussion of group insurance.

[19]This section draws on *Industry Trade Summary—Insurance* (Washington, DC: U.S. International Trade Commission, 1991).

## AGENCY MANAGEMENT[20]

As pointed out earlier, the agency system is the most widely used distribution system and accounts for the bulk of the premium income generated by the insurance industry. There are distribution outlets in at least all of the major cities in the states in which an insurer operates. These outlets, headed by an agency manager (general agent or branch manager), represent the life insurance industry's main contact with consumers. Effective field management is essential to the systems that employ an agency force.

### THE AGENCY MANAGER

An agency head's basic responsibility is to manage resources to achieve the common objectives of the agency and the company. In terms of activities, the duties of the agency head consist of (1) manpower development, including product and sales skills training; (2) supervision of the field force; (3) motivation of agents and staff; (4) business management activities (e.g., office duties, public relations activities, interpreting insurer policy, and expense management); and (5) personal production.

Personal production by the agency head has a low priority in agency-building companies. Although it is usually permitted, the need for growth and the design of the agency manager's compensation formula both militate against significant activity of this type.

*Agency Development.* Recruiting is the process by which the number of full-time career agents in the individual agencies is not only maintained but expanded. It is not one activity but a process, the steps of which include (1) finding sources of prospective agents, (2) determining acceptable qualifications, (3) approaching prospective agents, (4) using selection tools, (5) interviewing the candidate, and (6) contracting with qualified individuals. The manager usually attempts to locate a number (three to five) of prospective agents at one time. Since there is always fallout in the selection process, the group techniques usually allow some recruits to be added to the agency from each recruiting effort. Recruiting a group rather than one agent at a time also is a more efficient use of a field manager's time.

Considerable effort has been made in raising the standards for new agents and in increasing their productivity. One strategy that has proven effective in raising the standards for new agent selection is called precontract or preappointment training. It refers to what is usually a period of time before the prospective agent is contracted, during which licensing, training, and field work may take place. Only after this period is a full-time contract offered. Most

---

[20]This section draws on Dennis W. Goodwin, *Life and Health Insurance Marketing* (Atlanta, Ga.: LOMA, 1989).

insurers have become increasingly careful in their selection of new agents. They also devote much attention to the training of their agents in the nature and uses of life and health insurance and sales methods.

In view of the broad range of interest-sensitive and traditional products on the market today, the agency manager faces a significant challenge in adequately training an agency force. Agency managers do, however, have access to a wealth of training materials. In addition to those made available by the agency manager's own company, a wide array of material is available from industry associations and commercial publishers. The agency manager also must maintain an appropriate and effective continuing education program for all agents, those recently established as well as experienced professionals. Almost one-half the states require that agents pursue some form of continuing education to maintain their licenses.

*Supervision of the Agency Force.* The level of supervision provided for agents is a function of the agent's experience and length of service. Close supervision is particularly helpful to a new agent until he or she develops good work habits and feels comfortable in the working relationship with the supervisor. Experience has shown that agents react positively to supervision in which they (1) are told what to expect at the outset, (2) view the supervision as helpful in improving their performance, and (3) help set the objectives against which they will be measured. Most agency managers have a practice of having some form of communication with each of their agents every day. The relationship that develops between an agent and the manager (supervisor) is an important factor in the success or failure of a new agent.

In the sales management process, an agency manager provides the stimulus to make an agent feel motivated to take action that results in sales and related goals. Agency managers demonstrate personal interest in each agent, use formal in-depth reviews and group meetings, encourage attendance at industry organization meetings, provide special office privileges, and conduct sales contests, all to create an environment in which agents will feel motivated. Each of these motivational activities is intended to demonstrate to each agent the concern of the agency manager for his or her welfare and thus stimulate the agent to higher production.

*Business Management.* In addition to these basic activities, the agency manager also must carry out a number of normal business management activities, including expense management, running the office, public relations activities, and interpreting company policy. Whether the agency is a "scratch" agency or an established one, the agency manager must be or must quickly become a highly organized person, because the job is so unstructured. As the agency grows, the agency manager must develop second-line management and must delegate the functions for which his or her personal involvement is not essential. Otherwise, the agency manager will be unable to give adequate personal attention to matters that are critical to the success of the agency.

## MANAGEMENT COMPENSATION

*Basic Approach.* The agency manager is compensated for services according to the terms and conditions of a written compensation contract. In general agency insurers, the typical agreement provides for a scale of commissions (sometimes called first-year override) based on the first-year premiums for new business and a separate scale or scales to be applied to premiums paid in the second and subsequent policy years (a renewal override). In addition, the general agent receives expense allowances based on first-year commissions or premiums and, in many cases, a renewal expense allowance. Bonuses are paid for a variety of reasons—persistency, growth, agent retention and productivity, and low loan activity—that are not too different in motivational purpose from those seen in managerial company contracts.

In managerial companies, the compensation typically is an annual salary based on an incentive compensation formula applied to the previous (sometimes current) year's agency production. Most insurers design their formula to achieve specific objectives. Thus for example, some companies pay extra compensation to the agency manager based on the production of each new career agent for that agent's first two or three years; others pay a bonus for new gains in manpower. Some companies pay a bonus when annual production exceeds that of the previous years. Still others offer bonuses based on persistency targets or improvements in agency persistency. Regardless of the particular contract that an insurer may offer to an agency manager, the job of building a "career shop" is such that the contracts differ only in the emphasis that is placed on individual elements of the job. Expense experience is often reflected specifically as an aspect of managerial compensation.

*Current Developments.*[21] A number of interesting developments are taking place in management compensation. First, a minimum agency size, or the ability to attain some optimum or cost-effective stage, is becoming a standard requirement. This is vital to a successful agency operation, but arriving at that effective stage depends on a number of unrelated events. It is important to recognize, however, that size by itself will not ensure agency success. An adequate amount of production per agent, regardless of agency size, is critical. Sufficient capitalization and sound business judgment and management also are major facets of business life today.

The margins available to provide management compensation and expense absorption are shrinking. The per-unit payment on products delivered has been

---

[21]This section draws on John M. Wellborn, "Compensation Trends for the 1990s," *MarketFacts* (Mar./Apr. 1991), pp. 18-23.

steadily declining, and this can be offset only by increasing agent productivity. There also is a need to invest in technological advances to improve cost performance and provide needed agent support. High utilization is essential to permit recovery of technology costs. An agency must be able to afford to purchase technology and must be large enough to make its use profitable.

Managerial insurers often control expenses through an expense management formula. This formula credits or charges the manager, based on the relationship between actual costs and a standard tied to production and sometimes additional factors, such as the number of agents, mix of business, and business in force. These are often capped or limited, but the net impact on the manager's income can be significant. Some insurers try to link compensation directly to agency profitability (e.g., they penalize agency head compensation for poor persistency or for excessive loans on in-force business).

Traditionally, a distinguishing characteristic of a general agency operation has been the value of future renewal commissions built up as deferred compensation either as a retirement program or as a factor contributing toward a retirement program. This feature of a general agent's contract has been almost sacred, but it is now being reconsidered in light of changing conditions. Renewals can be wiped out by the replacement of existing business either now, with newer products paying less or nothing, or later, when nothing can be done to offset their disappearance. In the long run, the answer may well be a formal retirement program.

Since the field office administers a broader range of financial products, the agency head must provide increasing management support and expertise. The traditional line organization is being replaced by a functional emphasis. Thus an agency might have a brokerage specialist, specialists in various product lines, or technical support persons in specialized areas. This development meets a number of current needs, but, if carried too far, it creates problems for the agency and the insurer, as explained below.

A functional manager can be effective and can provide a return on investment more quickly than a line supervisor. The training time is virtually nonexistent, since the individual is employed because expertise is already present. In addition, functional managers are less likely to be sought after by other companies and thus are less likely to want to leave. Functional specialists are also significant in view of the increasing importance of investment-based or wealth accumulation products.

Functional management does, however, create company problems. Functional management is specialization management. Insurers need a pool of potential managers for future growth, and functional management does not produce additional first-line supervisors and agency managers. The transition from specialization to generalization is needed to satisfy the insurer's need for new, additional managers; this need is relatively more difficult to fill than in the typical line organization.

## AGENT COMPENSATION

*Basic Approach.* Agents are hired and compensated by the insurer. A significant portion of the agent's contract is devoted to the compensation he or she is to receive.[22] Agents' compensation usually is on a commission basis, and it calls for a high commission on the first year's premium and a smaller commission on future premiums. Most contracts provide for the **vesting** of renewal commissions if the agent achieves certain levels of production or completes a minimum period of service, such as 5, 10, 15, or perhaps 20 years.[23]

In recognition of the service an agent is called on to give long after the renewal commissions have expired, many companies pay a service fee that commences after renewals stop and continues as long as the agent remains with the company and the policy stays in force. The service fee is a small percentage, usually 2 or 3 percent, and almost never vests in the agent.

Many insurers also pay additional commissions or bonuses based on satisfactory production (commission, premiums, volume or number of lives sold) or persistency, or a combination of both. The presence and nature of this additional compensation varies widely and is a function of the insurer's philosophy. In addition to direct compensation, fringe benefits such as retirement, life, health, and disability insurance benefits are provided by many insurers.

Typically, life insurance companies that are licensed to do business in New York State pay agents' compensation equal to the present value of 55 percent the first year and 5 percent in years 2 to 10 of a level annual premium. The renewals may be equal in amount or concentrated into three or four unequal installments. If the insurer does not conduct business in New York State, agents' commission rates usually are larger.[24]

Under a straight-commission contract, the agent earns nothing until he or she makes sales. As a result, a new agent has to draw on another source of income until his or her commissions build to a reasonable level. Insurers commonly finance a new agent's first months or years in the business.[25] Financing plans differ widely but may be illustrated in general terms. For example, the **drawing-account approach** simply means that the new agent is extended credit by the insurer on a stipulated weekly or monthly basis, or as he or she needs it. In most cases, the agent must pay the money back as he or she is

[22]The Life Insurance Marketing and Research Association conducts research relating to field compensation.

[23]**Vesting** refers to the ownership of the renewals. From a practical standpoint, vested renewals mean that the agent's renewals will continue to be paid even if he or she terminated his or her connection with the insurer. Not all insurers' contracts provide for vesting of renewal commissions.

[24]For a variety of reasons, agents in New York operating companies tend to have higher productivity and better persistency, leading to equal or higher dollar earnings.

[25]Losses are usually shared to varying degrees by the insurer and the general agent or manager. See Paul D. Laporte, "Financing the New Agent," *Marketing for Actuaries—Individual Life and Health Insurance, SOA Study Note Part 9* (Hartford, Conn.: LIMRA, 1986), pp. xii-1 to xii-11.

able, and usually even if he or she terminated his or her contract. In some contracts, however, part of the advance is considered a training allowance.[26]

Many insurers agree to provide a stipulated salary against which any commissions earned are credited. Subject, usually, to certain minimum production or validation requirements, the agent may continue under this plan for a period of up to, say, three years. In most companies, he or she may go off the plan at any time he or she chooses. If the agent leaves the insurer, he or she usually is not responsible for any debit balance outstanding. Other financing plans provide decreasing salary and pay part or all of the commissions from the beginning. The variations are almost infinite. In any case, an agent must sell life insurance to make a living selling life insurance, regardless of the financing plan.

The agent's contract may contain provisions regulating the territory in which the agent must operate (usually only in combination or home service companies); his or her duties in the collection of premiums; his or her authority to alter or change the insurance contract; the maintenance and ownership of books or records; and numerous other provisions relating to the various things that might arise while the agent is devoting time and energy to the sale of life and health insurance.

*Current Developments.* Compensation plans increasingly include minimum production components. Today neither the insurer nor the individual agency can afford to provide support and service to producers who do not sell enough business. There is increasing recognition that the rising costs of the traditional support areas plus the significant price of new technology needed to deliver today's products require acceptable production levels. Small agencies and small producers often cannot be supported in light of current competitive conditions and the cost of benefit programs.

More and more insurers are imposing minimum production requirements as a requisite to receiving certain defined supports, such as housing or clerical assistance or even retention of the contract itself with attendant benefit programs. Some companies are even correlating the benefits available to the level of production.

Life insurance companies and agency managers recognize an obligation to provide reasonably competitive products if they are to expect an agent to place all or most of his or her business through the agency and with the company. High levels of individual performance make a producer very profitable to the insurer. This profit can be—and increasingly is—shared with successful producers through **bonus arrangements.** There are restraints on bonuses, especially for insurers operating in New York State, but significant, meaningful bonuses can be developed even within New York regulatory limitations.

Another area of current interest in agent compensation is the **leveling of**

---

[26]There is a trend toward using a variable training allowance. Some insurers pay a percentage of commissions earned in the prior three months as a training allowance, plus the commissions earned. Under this plan, financing becomes a variable cost determined by production.

**commissions**. The use of this approach can minimize the loss incurred on business not in force for a long enough period of time to recover the initial expenses. Level commissions also can compensate the agent in a way that is more in line with long-term service requirements of new types of products. A gradual increase in the use of level or partially leveled commissions is anticipated, especially with some of the newer products.

In connection with the use of level commissions, ongoing service requirements cause two concerns. First, there is the need, with attendant cost, to provide for transferability of the level renewals (or part of them) to a new, assigned agent. Ongoing service is considered a key requirement for some newer products. Second, there is increasing discussion of separating policy service and client service. There are no clear definitions of what these functions mean to the agent and, more important, to the client. This whole area is acknowledged to be a difficult administrative problem.

Work done by three major Canadian companies has confirmed that the levelized approach will support both higher agent incomes and income stability. The primary issue concerns transition to this system. Agents cannot be expected to finance such a change. The trend toward levelized commissions is well under way in Canada, and interest in it is growing rapidly around the world. The major constraint in the U.S. market relates to New York State's strict limitations on the manner in which commissions can be paid, as well as other expense limitations.

**Agent financing plans** are used to augment the early earnings shortfall in the compensation system. Level commission plans could materially increase financing subsidies. This situation can be compounded by an inability with flexible products to arrive at any meaningfully acceptable measure of net annualized commissions, a traditional financing plan measurement. Still another factor influencing the length of the financing period is the growing emphasis on financial counseling. There is a real question as to how a company can accomplish the necessary training and development in the face of the high financing validation requirements that are necessary to attract individuals required to sell current products and services.

Despite the significant investment by an insurer, an agent, once financed and trained, tends to feel that he or she is free to operate independently. Given the extremely high developmental cost and the potential that the successful agent may "go to the highest bidder," some thought is being given to an amortization of developmental costs as a contractual obligation of the agent. Naturally, this is a sensitive issue, but the realities of the situation may cause insurers to insist that something be done to deal with the cost question.

Still another development of current interest is the establishment of agent-owned reinsurance companies. Some insurers have helped establish such facilities to provide an incentive for high-volume agents to place a large proportion of their best-quality business with the sponsoring insurer, so the agents will then participate in the good experience of their quality production.

Essentially, it is a joint venture between an insurer and outstanding producers, with the result that both the direct writing company and the agent-owned reinsurer make additional profits. Agents' increased profits flow from their ownership of the reinsurance company where reinsurance on the business is placed by the direct writing company.

There has been considerable experimentation with **fees for services**. For agencies specializing in financial counseling, there appears to be some opportunity in selling services and advice as well as products. The industry has experience in the pension field, in which pension services for fees are provided to clients. There are major differences, however, between the marketing of pensions and the marketing of individual life and health insurance.

Support to an agent who does financial counseling for a fee is crucial. Shifting from a commission-based system to one employing fees for services is a major change, with significant implications for cost, individuals, and organizations. The entire area of compensation design is in a state of flux.

## COMPENSATION OF BROKERS AND INDEPENDENT AGENTS

*Brokers.* Since, from a legal standpoint, most brokers are agents, the commissions offered to these individuals vary as greatly as they do for agents.[27] If the brokering agent in question is not a general agent or is not entitled to override commissions, compensation will be paid as provided for in the agent contract. If the brokering agent is also a general agent, overrides and expense allowances equal to an additional 30 or 40 percent may be paid. Companies also pay overrides on renewal commissions. In addition to these commission renewals and overrides, general agents also may be eligible for production bonuses.

A wide range of employee benefits and other rewards for production are paid to brokers. It is necessary to examine the form of contract under which the brokering agent works. If the amount of business placed with a given insurer is large, the broker will participate in all bonuses offered by the company. A general agent who acts as a broker for an insurer usually receives the same fringe benefits and bonus arrangement that are available to full-time general agents of that insurer. If individual agents of the general agent provide a large volume of business to a particular company, those particular agents usually will receive extra bonuses and be invited to special sales conferences as a reward.

It is common practice in the life insurance industry to annualize first-year commission payments. Regardless of the mode of payment chosen by the applicant, the insurer assumes that all (or most) of the year's premium is received at the time the policy is issued. If a 55 percent commission rate is assumed, then 55 percent of the full year's premium will be paid to the agent as

---

[27]Most states require individuals selling life and health insurance to be licensed as an agent, regardless of the number of insurers with which they place business.

soon as the policy is issued. In many cases, brokerage companies do not have the close relationship that normally exists with exclusive agents. As a result, some do not annualize commissions, since it is sometimes difficult to retrieve unearned commissions when contracts lapse. Brokers who infrequently do business with a given company receive few extra benefits or bonuses. On the other hand, large brokerage producers tend to be treated as well as exclusive agents, and this treatment can even include a full range of employee benefits. Although there are exceptions, most agents receive no service fee allowance on brokered business.

*Independent Agents.* The intense competition for the life production of independent property and liability (P&L) agents has caused the total compensation package typically made available to independent agents to be similar to that granted career life agents. Comparable commission rates and expense allowances generally are included in the total package. In addition, the independent agent normally is provided the opportunity to qualify for sales contests, trips, awards, and other special prizes. The agreement between the company and the agent or agency may also provide for persistency and production bonuses (or both), fully vested renewal commissions, service fees payable after expiration of renewal commissions, and commission overrides if the agency possesses a general agent (usually PPGA) contract. A significant difference between the contracts offered to independent P&L agents and those offered to exclusive life agents pertains to agent financing plans, which are not made available to independent P&L agents. A major reason for this is that P&L agents usually begin their careers with a book of P&L business.

## PRODUCT DEVELOPMENT[28]

### THE PROCESS

Product development in a life insurance company must reflect and integrate many related elements. Products are created to facilitate the achievement of the life insurer's goals, and the product line will ultimately reflect the company's character, its culture, and its long-range strategic plans. Obviously, the insurer's goals must be built around its perception of the needs of the marketplace—that is, the consumers. In addition, products must be designed and developed with concern for the needs of the marketing personnel, shareholders, and the public.

Product development is a continuous process. It includes the evolution of an idea, its refinement, and ultimately the implementation of a marketable product. Even then, the process is incomplete until the actual experience in marketing and

[28]This section draws on Robert D. Shapiro, "The Process of Premium Formulation," *SOA Part 7 Study Note* (Itasca, Ill.: Society of Actuaries, 1982). See also Allen D. Booth and Robert D. Shapiro, "The Product Development Program for Insurance Companies," *SOA Part 9L Study Note* (Itasca, Ill.: Society of Actuaries, 1982).

managing the product has been reviewed and analyzed so that any necessary modifications can be made in a timely manner. This monitoring and analysis may lead to revisions of existing products or to other new products or marketing concepts.

Product development typically is organized by project. Such projects may range from the establishment of a new line of business to the creation of a portfolio of products, or to the design of a single product to augment an existing product line. When developing any product or group of products, the company must give careful attention to the integration of the ultimate product array, so that it properly and consistently serves the needs of the market in which the insurer operates.

The product development process includes both product design and product implementation. Constraints imposed on development or activities from either inside or outside of the company must be recognized and either eliminated or managed. **Product design** includes the generation and evaluation of a product idea, the clarification of the idea, and the assessment of its marketability. **Product implementation** includes the final determination of rates, values and dividends, the design of policy and application forms, the filing of these forms with regulatory authorities, the creation of supporting marketing materials and administrative systems that facilitate effective distribution and administration of the product, and the actual introduction of the product.

Approximate evaluations of profitability, equity, and contributions to surplus are made periodically throughout the product development process. A fine-tuning of design and pricing takes place during the implementation phase. The schematic presented in Figure 33-2 provides a visual overview of the concepts involved in the product development process.

Only after a life and health insurance company has developed a marketing plan should it consider the products it will develop to meet the needs of the markets it has chosen to address. In practice, of course, this order—define a target market, determine products, and then consider how best to market them— is often reversed. In any case, products play a critical role in the company's efforts to achieve market penetration. In the case of established companies, the process of constantly evaluating and upgrading the product portfolio is necessary, to respond to a changing external environment and revised company objectives.

## THE EXTERNAL ENVIRONMENT

Product development, of necessity, must reflect the changing social, economic, legal, and competitive environment. Ideally, an insurer's market research function will monitor the external environment continuously and forecast trends, so that the company can develop products to take advantage of new opportunities and respond to needed adjustments to its current portfolio.

**FIGURE 33-2**

**THE PRODUCT DEVELOPMENT PROCESS**

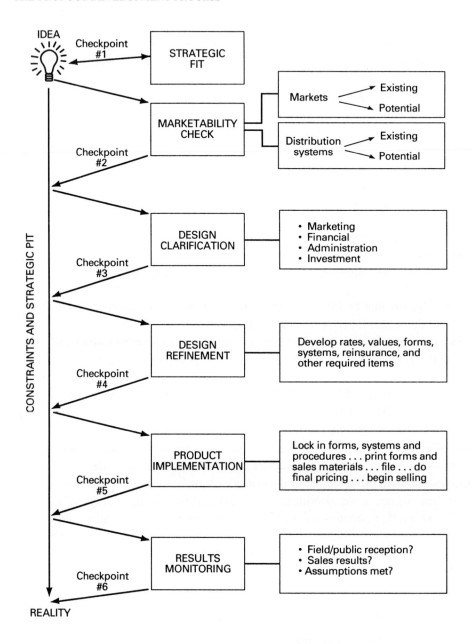

*Source*: Allen D. Booth and Robert D. Shapiro, "The Product Development Program for Insurance Companies," *SOA Part 9L Study Note* (Itasca; IL: Society of Actuaries, 1982), p.3.

Competition in life and health insurance comes from both other insurance companies and other industries.[29] Competition from other insurers can have a significant impact on product design. It may relate to competition for agents and brokers, or to price, product design, underwriting, or policyowner service. An insurer must respond to the actions of its major competitors when they develop a product that threatens its market share. Pressure on product designers also is created when a competitor develops an exciting new product, thus creating an innovative image for itself. An insurer's sales force may demand a similar product, and the product designers may have to respond with a product so that the insurer does not appear to be falling behind.

One critical management decision in product development has to do with evaluating whether to respond quickly to competition or wait to see how the market will respond to a competitor's new product. In particular, when high start-up costs or development expenses for administrative systems are involved, an insurer may decide to wait and assess the response to a competitor's product before committing resources to such a product.

Some major insurers have a specific philosophy of always staying just behind the leading edge on any new product. They let another company introduce a new product, obtain regulatory approval, and educate agents and the public about the virtues of the new product. In cases where the product is successful, these insurers then move to bring out an improved version of it as quickly as possible. This strategy is feasible since insurers cannot patent or copyright their new ideas.

The external environment provides a complex, difficult array of influences. Many factors in that environment interact and are synergistic, but all impinge on the product design process. Despite the uncertainties and the complexity of monitoring the environment and forecasting trends, the process of product design is critically dependent on the quality of this effort.

## THE PRODUCT DESIGN PROCESS

Once a marketing strategy has been established that is consistent with the company's corporate objectives and its perception of the external environment, then the broad guidelines are in place for the product design process to begin and decisions about the product portfolio to be made. The insurer's marketing strategy usually will be developed by the senior marketing officers and then approved by senior management. Establishing product design objectives that are consistent with the marketing strategy is a joint effort of the marketing department and the product design actuaries.

The product design function usually is handled as a staff function. Changes in the product mix may be essential if the insurer is to survive. Particular lines of

[29]E. J. Moorhead, "Competition," *Marketing for Actuaries—Individual Life and Health Insurance, SOA Part 9 Study Note* (Hartford, Conn.: LIMRA, 1986), pp. v-1 to v-9.

business may have to be eliminated because they are no longer growing and profitable. These decisions are best initiated by staff who have no vested interest (as line personnel might have) in continuing to offer unprofitable, existing products. In addition, the design of innovative products usually requires extensive research, which is best performed as a staff function. Agent involvement is essential to the product development process.

## THE PRICING PROCESS

The premium formulation function can have meaning only in the context of the insurance company strategic plans. In practice, premium rates cannot be set simply by building in profit along with the other assumptions as to mortality, morbidity, persistency, expenses, and other expected characteristics of the business. Instead, premium rates must be established to balance the various, often conflicting, requirements of management, stockholders, and policyowners (both present and future), within the overall constraints resulting from the need to preserve company solvency.

Sophisticated forward planning is a critical element of the premium formulation process. The nature of the business environment demands the ability to react quickly to changes and new opportunities. Actuaries, as managers of the pricing process, must develop detailed forecasts and evaluate anticipated and future scenarios, while at the same time work with values that are difficult to predict with accuracy. Although the particular procedural details of premium formulation may vary from company to company and from one line of business to another, the general **pricing process** includes (1) defining a pricing plan, (2) establishing actuarial assumptions, (3) determining products and prices, and (4) operating and managing results.

The process of premium formulation is a continuous and circular process; the experience from one round of product development is used as the basis for the next round of product development.

Most companies develop their rates on best-estimate actuarial assumptions, building in a specific desired margin for profit. By developing the premium scale utilizing realistic actuarial assumptions (including an explicit profit margin), the management of the results is made easier. The assumptions underlying the asset share studies can then function as performance standards for the company. The development of projections based on realistic gross premium assumptions provides a base against which to monitor future experience, thus facilitating decision-making.

Price management requires systematic comparison of actual with expected results, and the taking of action to rectify any significant deviations from expected results. Thus a rate increase on an individual health block of business, a revision in a dividend scale, or a new ratebook might be indicated. The projections described above provide a basis for creating the expected results. A good price management system also will include a periodic comparison of these results with the emerging actual experience.

When significant deviations occur, the reason for the deviations must be determined. Additional studies often are needed. When changes are indicated, they cannot be made without creating other unacceptable results (e.g., required premium increase could price the insurer out of particular critical markets), and therefore there may be a need for complete reassessment of the insurer's basic pricing plan.

Once the deviations have been defined and appropriate corrective action has been implemented, the process can continue to its next sequence. It is a dynamic circle of planning, product review and experience analysis. Findings may suggest that existing products or services have entered into the maturity or even decline stages of the product life cycle (see below).

## MARKETING IMPLICATIONS OF NEW PRODUCTS

In marketing theory, the **product life cycle** is a theoretical construct that attempts to describe the key turning points and stages in the life of a product, from introduction to decline. Like any generalization, it does not perfectly describe every product's life; however, it does represent a powerful analytical tool that marketers use to set strategy.[30]

The four stages of the product life cycle are introduction, growth, maturity, and decline. These stages are represented in Figure 33-3, a graph that displays the values of hypothetical sales and profits throughout the four stages.

During the **introduction stage** for a new product, sales are low and profits

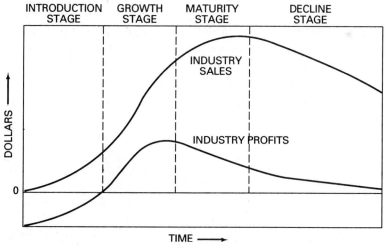

**FIGURE 33-3**

**PRODUCT LIFE CYCLE**

*Source*: Robert L. Posnak and Charles Carroll, "Overview of Non-Traditional Products: Definition, Terminology, Basics," *1983 Financial and Accounting Aspects of Non-traditional Products—Selected Proceedings* (Atlanta, GA: LOMA, 1983).

[30]This discussion draws on Robert L. Posnak and Charles Carroll, "Overview of Nontraditional Products: Definition, Terminology, Basics," *1983 Financial and Accounting Aspects of Nontraditional Products—Selected Proceedings* (Atlanta, Ga.: LOMA, 1983).

are negative because of the investment in start-up costs. In this stage, the typical promotion strategy is to convince consumers of the utility and value of the product itself rather than focusing on a particular brand or make. Since there are usually few competitors, pricing is not a major concern at this stage.

As the product moves into the **growth stage,** sales and profits increase dramatically. Eventually, profit per unit sold declines. This is because new competitors enter the market and some of these new entrants may use price-cutting as a strategy to increase market share and catch up to already established competitors. Promotion focuses on distinguishing the advantages of one brand over another.

In the **maturity stage,** sales level off and total profits begin to decline. There are few new entrants because existing competitors keep profit margins low. Some competitors may even withdraw because of the limited profit potential.

In the **decline stage,** sales and profits continue to slide. There is a general shakeout of the market. Unprofitable distribution channels are eliminated. Competitors generally sacrifice market share to maintain profit margins.

The product life cycle is a useful concept, because it can help predict how the market is likely to work in different phases. For example, a company entering the market during the growth stage would be well advised to build unique, valuable features into its version of the product because consumers will begin to make choices based on individual features once the value of the generic product is well established.

With a couple of key additions, the product life cycle can be adapted as a useful tool for describing the evolution of many life insurance products. One key addition is the regulatory environment for the new product. Another key addition is tax law. Because many products are so dependent on tax efficiencies for their marketability, changes in tax rulings and laws can have a major impact on their development.

## MARKETING TRENDS

The marketing scene in the United States continues to change at an unprecedented rate. The financial services evolution has masked the remarkable changes taking place in the provision of insurance services themselves. Distribution systems and product development both were influenced significantly by the economic, social, and competitive environment of the 1980s.

## DISTRIBUTION SYSTEMS

Table 33-1 indicates the market shares of 1984, 1987, 1989, and 1990 life insurance premiums that were developed through full-time career agents, brokerage, personal-producing general agents, multiple-line exclusive agents, combination insurers, and direct response marketing systems. Direct response marketing still accounts for only a small proportion of total premiums generated. The agency-building systems account for over one-half of the life and health insurance premiums. Information for use in splitting the nonagency producer premiums between brokerage and personal-producing general agents is not available. Brokerage is a significant factor, but most brokerage business is written by agents in the agency-building systems.

New agents remain the most important source of future growth in the insurance industry. Each year insurance companies spend large amounts of money to recruit, finance, train and support new agents. In a new agent's early years, expenditures exceed revenue; the difference is the company's investment. In the later years, when revenue is expected to exceed expenditures, the insurer hopes to recover the investment.

The size of the company's investment in new agents and the period of time to recover it depend on several factors. A LIMRA study demonstrated how improvement in certain performance factors can significantly reduce the cost of an insurer's future growth.[31]  Thus:

•Three years after contracting 100 new agents, a company with moderate
agent retention and high productivity will have 25 of its recruits remaining,
at a net investment of about $120,000 each.

TABLE 33-1    **1983, 1987, 1989, AND 1990 MARKET SHARE OF LIFE PREMIUMS BY DISTRIBUTION SYSTEM IN THE UNITED STATES**

| System | 1984 (%) | 1986 (%) | 1989* (%) | 1990 (%) |
|---|---|---|---|---|
| Ordinary | 42 | 38 | 40 | 41 |
| Combination | 15 | 13 | 5 | 5 |
| MLEA | 5 | 5 | 11 | 11 |
| Brokerage & PPGA | 36 | 43 | 43 | 42 |
| Direct Response | 2 | 1 | 1 | 1 |

| | |
|---|---|
| ORDINARY FULL-TIME: | Agents who sell for one primary company and work in a multiperson agency |
| BROKERAGE: | Brokers and independent agents |
| PPGA: | Personal-Producing General Agents who usually sell in one-person organizations |
| COMBINATION: | Agents who sell both ordinary and industrial life insurance |
| MLEA: | Multiple-Line Exclusive Agents who sell for one company that also provides property-casualty products |
| DIRECT RESPONSE: | A sale in which no agent is involved |

*In 1989, reclassification of Prudential of America's home service division to multiple-line exclusive agent and of John Hancock Mutual Life's home service division to ordinary should be considered when interpreting distribution system differences between 1989 and prior years.

Source: The 1990 Census of Life Insurance Sales Personnel, *LIMRA's Market Trends 1992* (Hartford, Connecticut: Life Insurance Marketing Research Association, 1992), p.2.

[31]LIMRA, *Investing in New Agents: A Cost Blueprint,* I/R Code 33.32, 1985.

•For a company with low agent retention, the net investment per recruit remaining increases by 60 percent.

•For a company with high agent retention, the net investment decreases by 25 percent.

•The time period for recovering these investments ranges from 9 years for high retention to 21 years for low retention.

The study concluded that the size of an insurer's investment in new agents and the period of time for recovering it depend on several factors, including productivity, persistency, inflation, and, most important, retention. The study clearly demonstrated that while improving agent retention may be far more difficult than improving persistency or productivity, capital spent in this area has the potential for much higher returns.

The agency system came under question during the early 1980s, and this questioning resulted in experimentation with alternative distribution systems during the mid-eighties. At the end of the decade, there was a recommitment to the agency system. As the industry moves through the 1990s and beyond, there is currently no evidence of any significant breakthroughs in the basic economic fundamentals of agency system management. With lower product profit margins, there is a serious question as to whether a growing field force can be supported in the long run at current performance levels in terms of productivity, retention, persistency, and expense control. Some industry observers wonder if the industry will not once again investigate whether distribution cannot be accomplished more efficiently through banks, supermarkets, and other nontraditional sources.[32] Although deregulation, in and of itself, may not have a large direct effect on life and health insurance distribution, an indirect impact of deregulation on distribution can arise from its legitimizing the utilization of alternative distribution systems.

## THE LIFE AND HEALTH INSURANCE MARKET OF THE FUTURE

The primary mission of the life insurance industry is changing. The focus of support, and thus customer service, has shifted from the insured's heirs to policyowners themselves. Instead of providing support for the heirs, life insurers are increasingly being called on to support an aging customer. For insurers who are in the health care field, quality of life issues have become important as well. The relatively recent practice of early payment of death benefits to those with terminal diseases underlines how much the focus has shifted.

It is clear that the U.S. public's evolving security needs differ structurally from those of previous decades. There is a clear trend toward increasing growth in spending to guard against the risks associated with poor health and, as

---

[32]Walter H. Zultowski, "Responding to the Marketplace of the 1990s," Society of Actuaries, 1990 spring meeting, June 4, 1990.

suggested in Chapter 14, outliving one's assets in retirement, in contrast to protection against premature death.

Since the 1970s, private spending (i.e., individual product purchases and spending by employers on behalf of employees) for personal economic security has become relatively more important than public sources (i.e., spending through tax-supported public programs). As concerns for retirement security, health, and long-term care continue to grow in the future, continuing government financing burdens in the United States and worldwide can be expected to exert increasing pressure for financial security needs to be met through private sector spending.

The U.S. public continues to believe that life insurance is the most appropriate vehicle for the protection of the family in the event of the breadwinner's death. Life insurance, however, has lost ground in terms of its recognition by the public as a suitable means of accumulating funds for children's education and for retirement.[33] Many life insurers have responded to these shifts in public perceptions and preferences by establishing broker/dealers to facilitate their marketing of investment products such as mutual funds, variable annuities, variable life, and variable universal life products. In 1991, approximately 75,000 licensed registered representatives were affiliated with life insurers.[34]

The life insurance industry's natural market remains solid and is expected to grow because a natural set of consumer needs remains unfulfilled. In fact, there are several reasons why the real rate of growth in market potential is expected to increase:

1. The federal government's reduced inclination to assume full responsibility for individual security has caused individuals to become more concerned about providing independently for their personal financial security.

2. Growing proportions of the U.S. population will be senior citizens. They are the most security-conscious demographic segment.

3. Corporations will continue to be more active in assisting employees in achieving a measure of financial security at the employee's expense. One reason for this is that corporations will continue to seek ways to scale back their own fringe benefit cost increases.

In the context of a growing market, there are reasons why the providers of services could change, either in identity or in methodology. First, the U.S. insurance industry is considered by many to be inefficient in its delivery of products. Many insurers have spent large sums to retool administrative systems, but they have not been pricing in support of those costs. When agent

[33] *1990 MAP Survey* (Washington, DC: American Council of Life Insurance, 1990), pp. 13, 53-54.
[34] LIMRA, *1991 U.S. Investment Products: The Year in Review*, I/R Code 30.00.

productivity and agent retention are low, the agency system is expensive. This system is driven by the theory that insurance must be sold and will not be demanded independently of agent initiatives.

Second, because of basic inefficiencies, new products with small margins, and competition, industry profit margins are believed by many to be inadequate, at least by historical standards. Third, many companies have focused their efforts on the so-called upscale markets. These markets may be oversold while unmet needs exist in less upscale areas.

As a result, it is likely that the successful insurer of the future will be larger, more market-focused, and more efficient. This means it is likely that some middle-tier insurers will rise to the top via growth coupled with merger or acquisitions; that many fringe companies will disappear; and that traditional agency insurers can remain competitive only in defined niches.

With respect to the U.S. upscale market—with its focus on planning and tax (income, estate, and inheritance tax) implications—relatively little change is expected to occur in terms of the nature of services it will demand. This market will remain an agent-served market, and it will continue to use a range of life insurance and other financial products. Its growth rate probably will not change materially (unless taxed away).

The size of the U.S. mid-scale market will probably grow materially for many of the reasons indicated. Successful competitors will focus on needs and will supplement and support their field forces effectively, using telemarketing, other financial institutions, and other third-party intermediaries. Current assumption and variable products should be featured, along with basic term insurance and cash-value products with traditional guarantees. Annuities supported by continued favorable tax treatment could constitute a major new market.

Downscale markets will probably be served by simple security products, work site marketing, possibly multiple-line exclusive agents, and government programs. The home service business will probably survive the next ten-year period, but it will be in a continuing, although not rapid, state of contraction. Direct response marketing should continue to play an important role, at least to the extent that it does today, and perhaps more so.

It is believed that corporate markets will grow at a rate exceeded only by that of the mid-scale market. Small businesses still have unmet needs. Large corporations can be served directly by insurers. Their experience with cost-plus or administrative-services-only group plans taught them that direct contact is possible and cost-effective. An extension of direct corporate purchase or corporate-owned life insurance could be the negotiation of rates and products for distribution directly to corporate employees. Most of these buyers will come from the mid-scale segment. Advisors and consultants could play a new, important role because of this major trend.

## MULTINATIONAL INSURERS[35]

As a world economy emerged over the years, the relative stability of the U.S. economy and growth of the U.S. financial markets made them attractive to international investors. For some time, international insurers (mostly European companies) have had significant investments in the U.S. life/health industry. In view of the size of the U.S. market (which represents about 40 percent of world life/health premiums), an insurer cannot be a true multinational insurer without a U.S. presence. U.S. markets are relatively easy to enter, and interest in doing so has intensified recently. In recent years, there have been several times when currency exchange rates have created attractive opportunities for international investors.

International insurers may choose to enter the U.S. market by acquiring a company directly, through a joint venture, or as a reinsurer. Entering the U.S. market as a reinsurer is not attractive to many non-U.S. firms because of the virtual absence of a capacity problem for the life/health insurance industry. Although there have been a few examples of mutual insurers being acquired, acquisition of a stock insurer is generally much more feasible. There are many more stock insurers than mutuals, and unless the buyer is also a mutual company that can offer a merger, acquiring a U.S. mutual means demutualization and purchase.

Generally, a holding company is used to acquire a U.S. stock insurer. This approach provides the buyer with greater flexibility, especially if the purchase price involves debt financing. The holding company structure also is well suited for acquiring additional U.S. insurance (or noninsurance) operations.

It is widely agreed that many small and middle-size U.S. insurers will not be able to survive, given their capitalization, the competitive U.S. environment, and current economic conditions. It seems reasonable to assume that international insurers will continue to find a supply of available companies and that interest in entering the U.S. market will continue.

Only a handful of U.S. (life and nonlife) insurers are truly multinational. Currently, there may be no more than 200 U.S. insurance companies (out of over 5,000) with any type of international operation at all. Furthermore, participation in the Canadian insurance market would account for the great majority of these companies' international market involvement..

The primary reason many U.S. insurers are not participating in international markets is that U.S. insurers have long enjoyed a large, expanding domestic market, so that relatively few companies have felt a need to establish a presence abroad. Other reasons may include the centralized management

[35]This section draws on *Strategic Opportunities in the U.S. Insurance Market from the Perspective of Overseas Investors* (Tillinghast 1990 Update) and *Industry Trade Summary—Insurance* (Washington, DC: U.S. International Trade Commission, 1991).

organization of many large U.S. insurers (e.g., resistance to granting the necessary autonomy for local executives to make on-the-spot major financial commitments), a lack of capital, and the tendency of U.S. companies generally to be overly concerned with short-term results. Recently, several major life insurers have established operations in Europe and the Far East, but the move of U.S. insurers into world markets is expected to continue to be limited to a relative handful of insurers.

# Chapter 34

# REGULATION AND TAXATION OF LIFE INSURANCE IN THE U.S.

Governments throughout the world are involved in insurance. The degree of involvement varies with each country's sociocultural and economic circumstances and its government's prevailing political philosophy. Thus almost every government, even those that are strongly committed to a capitalist, market-driven philosophy, acknowledge the need for some level of government-provided social insurance protection. This protection usually includes some type of survivor benefit (life insurance), retirement benefit, and health insurance.[1] In many (although a diminishing number of) countries, insurance of all types is supplied exclusively by government-owned insurance monopolies; no competition is permitted.[2]

The hand of government is also evident in nonmonopolistic insurance markets through its regulatory role. Although the degree varies, regulation of insurance is universal. To those who believe that overall social welfare is enhanced through private competition unfettered by governmental involvement, the question immediately arises as to *why* regulation of the insurance business is pervasive and *whether* it is necessary.[3]

---

[1] See Chap. 25 and *Social Security Programs throughout the World* (Washington, D.C.: U.S. Social Security Administration, periodically).

[2] Monopolistic insurers were the rule in the former socialist countries of central and eastern Europe. Several Asian and African countries retain monopoly insurance markets, although the trend is toward permitting competition.

[3] For an excellent treatment of regulation from an economic perspective, see Alfred E. Kahn, *The Economics of Regulation: Principles and Institutions* (Cambridge, Mass.: The MIT Press, 1989).

# THE RATIONALE FOR INSURANCE REGULATION

## MARKETPLACE IMPERFECTIONS

The economic objective that society has for the life insurance industry is the same as it has for other industries—an efficient allocation of resources. This objective is most likely to be achieved through reliance on competitive market forces. Underlying faith in the benefits of competition are assumptions that (1) there exists a sufficiently large number of identical buyers and sellers such that no one buyer or seller nor any group of them can influence the market, (2) sellers have complete freedom of entry into and exit from the market, (3) the sellers' products are identical, and (4) buyers and sellers are well informed about products. If these idealized conditions exist, it can be proven that all sellers will charge and all buyers will pay the same product price.[4]

Obviously, no industry fully meets these conditions. Fortunately, an industry can meet these conditions only partially and still realize substantial benefits.[5] The more removed an industry is from these ideal conditions, the more imperfect the resulting competition and the poorer the industry performance and attendant consumer value and choice. Variations of actual market structure from the ideal are referred to as **marketplace imperfections** or **market failures**. A legitimate role of government is to ameliorate market failures (imperfections) and, thereby, recoup some of the otherwise lost advantages of a competitive system. Of course, there is no guarantee that government intervention will, in fact, rectify the imperfection. Indeed, government regulation could make matters worse. Just as there is no perfect competition, there is no perfect regulation.

Do competitive forces in the U.S. life insurance industry function sufficiently well such that no (or only minor) government intervention is warranted? The answer to the question is explored here through an examination of the four idealized market conditions.

*Sufficient Number of Competitors.* Within the United States, the life insurance market is not overly concentrated and there appears to be a sufficiently large number of buyers and sellers, with perhaps 1,000 substantive life insurers.[6] The health insurance area seems reasonably competitive, with perhaps 200 to 300 meaningful competitors.

[4]See, generally, Jack Hirschleifer, *Price Theory and Applications*, 4th ed. (Englewood Cliffs, N.J.: Prentice Hall, Inc., 1988), chaps. 2, 7.

[5]Such real-world situations are referred to as **workable competition** as contrasted with **pure competition**. See Travis Pritchett and Ronald P. Wilder, *Stock Life Insurance Company Profitability and Workable Competition* (Philadelphia: S. S. Huebner Foundation for Insurance Education, 1986).

[6]Pritchett and Wilder (1986). Not all of the over 2,300 U.S. domestic life insurers are meaningful competitors in the market. Many, for example, are captive credit life and health insurers, and others are inactive.

The number of U.S. insurers and the national concentration ratio are not completely satisfactory measures of competitive potential. Some researchers have argued that the relevant measure is the concentration within state markets. See J. David Cummins, Herbert S. Denenberg, and William C. Scheel, "Concentration in the U.S. Life Insurance Industry," *The Journal of Risk and Insurance*, Vol. 39 (June 1972).

Sellers are assumed also to be identical. Clearly, no two life insurers are identical, but within a given target market, dozens of similar insurers typically compete.

A monopoly exists when an industry is composed of a single firm. Because of its complete market dominance, an unregulated monopoly produces less and charges more. Economists and regulators are concerned about two kinds of monopolies. There is a tendency toward a **natural monopoly** when economies of scale are present throughout an industry's relevant output range.[7] Where this tendency exists, society conserves resources by allowing only a single supplier. Government does not want to discourage this tendency, but it will regulate the monopoly, typically as to price.

Other monopolies can evolve through abuses of market power, although increasing returns to scale may not exist. Governments typically forbid the creation of such monopolies by prohibitions on mergers and on other activities that tend to create them.[8]

Available evidence does not suggest that the life insurance industry exhibits natural monopoly traits. Some evidence of increasing returns to scale has been found, but results are not determinative.[9] Even so, the U.S. regulatory response has been, in effect, to presume that a tendency toward a natural monopoly exists, or at least to guard against unreasonable accumulations of economic power.[10]

*Ease of Entry/Exit.* Entry into and exit from the U.S. life and health insurance market do not appear to be unreasonably difficult. As discussed later in this chapter, there are entry barriers in the form of licensing requirements and minimum capital and surplus requirements, but they are not particularly onerous.[11] No formal barriers to exit exist, but state governments are known to exert pressure to discourage domestic life insurers from attempting to redomesticate to other states. ·

Freedom of entry does not exist in many of the world's life insurance markets. Several countries prohibit or severely limit the creation of new

---

[7]Local and national monopolies are common in public utilities. These government-sanctioned monopolies often are natural monopolies (see Hirshleifer, Chap. 8).

[8]Of course, degrees of competition exist between the purely competitive and monopoly models. In an **oligopoly**, for example, there is competition among only a few firms within an industry. The proper regulatory response to an oligopoly varies depending on such factors as the similarity of products (if they are dissimilar, price competition will be less effective), the number of competitors (if it is a small number, collusion is more likely), and the characteristics of the buyers (if they are not well informed and numerous, product value will be less). Oligopolistic conditions do not seem to be prevalent in life and health insurance. (See Pritchett and Wilder, and Hirshleifer, Chap. 10).

[9]A recent study of the 300 largest U.S. life insurers found evidence of some scale economies, and this implies that the industry could become more efficient through mergers. See Martin M. Grace and Stephen M. Timme, "An Examination of Cost Economics in the U.S. Life Insurance Industry," *The Journal of Risk and Insurance*, Vol 59 (Mar. 1992), pp. 72–103. See also Lisa A. Gardner's "An Analysis of Cost Inefficiencies in U.S. Life Insurance Companies: Sources and Measurement," unpublished Ph.D. dissertation (Georgia State University, 1992), for a recent study and a review of relevant research on the question.

[10]For example, a state insurance regulator can prohibit a merger if, in his or her judgment, it tends to create a monopoly.

[11]See Pritchett and Wilder, Chap. 2.

domestic life insurers, and many erect substantial entry barriers to foreign insurers.[12] By contrast, international insurers encounter relatively few barriers in entering the U.S. market.[13]

*Homogeneous Products.* The third assumption within the competitive model is that firms' products are identical. If they are identical, the actual seller of the product becomes irrelevant. Although many insurance products are similar, there are substantial differences. To promote greater uniformity and, thereby, render comparisons easier, legislatures have given insurance regulators powers to review and approve policy forms and to regulate insurer advertisements. Certain minimum policy provisions are required, and, in some cases, policies permitted to be sold are specified by law (e.g., Medicare supplement policies) and others are prohibited.

The U.S. life insurance industry seems to exhibit traits of **monopolistic competition** characterized by numerous sellers, each of which has some market power to set price. With monopolistic competition, firms attempt to differentiate their products from those of competitors so that the firm can gain some limited monopoly power. This **product differentiation strategy** can lead to the development of complex-seeming products that do not lend themselves easily to comparison shopping. This practice provides firms with the ability to set price, within limits. In general, cash-value life products and disability income products naturally lend themselves better to product differentiation than do term, annuity, and group-based products.[14] As a consequence, a case can be made for different levels of regulatory intervention among products.

*Knowledgeable Buyers and Sellers.* The final assumption of the competitive model is that buyers and sellers are well informed. Informed buyers make wise purchase decisions. Informed sellers know what buyers want and what their competitors are doing. Together, they ensure marketplace efficiency.

In fact, consumers are not well informed about life and health insurance products, nor about the quality of the insurers and agents selling the products. Sellers, by contrast, are reasonably well informed. Thus there is a lack of information symmetry between insurance buyers and sellers.[15] Most government intervention into the life and health insurance business is rationalized because of this market failure.

---

[12]See Harold D. Skipper, Jr., "Protectionism in the Provision of International Insurance Services," *The Journal of Risk and Insurance*, Vol. 54 (Mar. 1987), pp. 55-85.

[13]The U.S. insurance market, one of the most open in the world, generally operates on the **national treatment principle**—that is, other nations' insurers operating in the United States receive the same treatment as do U.S. insurers. Nonetheless, there are some market access problems. For example, some states refuse to license government-owned insurers. Also, the European Community and others have complained that the U.S. system of state-by-state licensing and regulation is itself a market access impediment. See Harold D. Skipper, Jr., and Lisa A. Gardner, "Some Implications of a GATT Services Agreement for U.S. Insurance Regulation and Taxation," *The Geneva Papers on Risk and Insurance* (Apr. 1992), pp. 215–231.

[14]See Pritchett and Wilder, Chap. 3.

[15]In economic terms, there are substantial **informational asymmetries**.

The nature of the insurance transaction involves the utilization of a technical-legal document that makes a present promise of future performance upon the occurrence of stipulated events. Although much has been done to simplify insurance contracts and to enhance their readability, life and health insurance contracts remain technical, complex documents. In a nontechnical sense, the insurance product is purchased in good faith. Individuals rely on the integrity of the insurance company and those who act as its representatives.

Despite the widespread belief in the need for life and health insurance, and its vital importance to those who purchase it, few persons attempt to become acquainted with the management, business policy, and practices of the insurers backing their contracts. Even assuming that a considerable portion of policyowners could be induced to take an interest in the condition of their insurers, few would be sufficiently knowledgeable about insurance matters to ascertain intelligently the true state of affairs. Life insurance and health insurance are necessarily technical, complicated subjects, and, as pointed out in preceding chapters, the true financial condition of an insurance company can be determined only by expert examination. Government intervention seeks to rectify this unequal bargaining position.

## SPECIAL NATURE OF LIFE INSURANCE

A further argument for insurance regulation, which is said to go beyond market failure reasons, flows from its special nature.[16] Life and health insurance contracts may be in force for periods of 20, 30, or even 50 years or longer. Consumers' reliance on insurer integrity could easily be abused by the unscrupulous, who, by exploiting the complexity of the insurance business and attendant consumer ignorance, could collect premiums today for an ephemeral future promise.

The courts agree that the insurance business is special. They have characterized it as being "affected with a public interest." Unlike most other products and services, insurance bears directly on an individual's or a family's economic security. The mission of insurance is security. Millions of persons rely on it for protection against the financial deprivation caused by death, disability, retirement, and the expense of medical care.

Additionally, because high reserve liabilities are created as a by-product of the products they sell, insurers are an important source of funds for the capital market. Their activities can have broad fiscal and social implications for an economy.

---

[16]Kenneth J. Meier, *The Political Economy of Regulation: The Case of Insurance* (Albany, N.Y.: State University of New York Press, 1988), p. 46.

## PUBLIC VERSUS PRIVATE INTERESTS

Thus regulation of life and health insurers is justified because of market failures, because of the vital role insurers play in individual economic security, and because of their role as financial intermediaries.[17] This case for insurance regulation thus flows from the **public interest theory** for regulation—its purpose is to protect the public from abuse. This idyllic theory has its detractors. The premise that government can correct market failures presumes that government will function for the overall public good, and that it will be indifferent to conflicts of interest and special interest groups.[18]

What might be termed the **private interest theory** of regulation argues that interest groups other than the public ultimately benefit from regulation. Thus Stigler's **capture theory** holds that "as a rule, regulation is acquired by the [regulated] industry and is designed and operated primarily for its benefit."[19] Stigler and others note that special interest groups, with well-organized and well-financed lobbies, influence legislation and regulation for their own benefit.[20] Special interest groups in insurance could include, among others, bankers, agents, and insurers themselves, perhaps subdivided by line of insurance, state of domicile, size, and so on. Consumers, being widely dispersed, ill organized, poorly financed, and, on a given issue, not as well informed as their special interest group competitors, may be ineffective by comparison.

Regulation based on the private interest theory could be reasonably expected to relate to:

- Restricting entry of foreign and domestic competitors through licensure and other means

- Suppressing price competition

- Controlling interindustry competition from those selling similar or complementary products.[21]

Each of these phenomena is found in all life insurance markets to varying degrees, and, under appropriate conditions, can be justified under the public interest theory.

There is little research to confirm or refute whether life insurance regulation has been meaningfully shaped in accordance with private interest theory. According to the conclusions of one researcher, "the overall impression . . . is that

---

[17]Although regulation is economically justified, its appropriate quality and quantity are not immediately obvious.

[18]See Lutgart van den Berghe, "(De)Regulation of Insurance Markets," in Henri Louberghe, ed., *Risk, Information and Insurance* (Boston: Kluwer Academic Publishers, 1990), Chap. 10.

[19]George J. Stigler, "The Theory of Economic Regulation," *Bell Journal of Economics* (Spring 1971), p. 3.

[20]See Sam Peltzman, "Toward a More General Theory of Regulation," *Journal of Law and Economics,* Vol. 19, No. 2 (1976), pp. 211–240, and George Becker, "A Theory of Competition among Pressure Groups for Political Influence," *Quarterly Journal of Economics,* Vol. 98, No. 3 (1983), pp. 371–400.

[21]Van den Berghe, p. 211.

the insurance industry does not dominate the regulatory process."[22] Another researcher found evidence of the capture theory in one element of Canadian insurance regulation that could apply equally to U.S. regulation.[23] Thus, although complaints persist about the prominence of insurance industry personnel in the halls of federal and state governments and about the historical industry dominance on the advisory committees of the National Association of Insurance Commissioners (NAIC—see below), the limited available evidence does not suggest that U.S. insurance regulation has been "captured" by the insurance industry.[24]

Irrespective of one's views as to the efficiency of and rationale for insurance regulation, the heavy regulation of life insurers in the United States (and most other countries) is a fact. Regulation focuses on measures related to (1) the quality of insurance products, (2) the manner in which they are sold, and (3) the ability of insurers to meet their obligations.

## BACKGROUND OF U.S. INSURANCE REGULATION

In the United States, people have created governmental bodies to serve them and have vested powers in these bodies. The people granted broad general powers to their state governments. In creating a federal government, the people delegated to it certain specific limited authority to act on matters affecting the welfare of the entire nation. Since no provision of the U.S. Constitution specifically limits the authority of the states to legislate on matters over which the federal government was given specific authority, both governments may exercise power in these areas. Any conflict in legislation or regulation, however, must be resolved by considering the fact that the delegation of a specific power to the federal government limits a general state power. The power of the federal government to act on matters over which it has specific authority is supreme.

The framers of the U.S. Constitution, recognizing that the economic welfare and the safety of the nation would be jeopardized by trade barriers restricting the free flow of trade among the states, gave the Congress the exclusive power to regulate commerce with other nations and among the states.

[22]Meier, p. 166. In his study of the property/liability (P/L) insurance industry, D'Arcy concluded that none of the popular theories of regulation adequately explained P/L regulation. See Stephen P. D'Arcy, "Application of Economic Theories of Regulation to the Property-Liability Insurance Industry," *Journal of Insurance Regulation* (Sept. 1988), pp. 19–51.

[23]See G. F. Mathewson and R. A. Winter, "The Economics of Life Insurance Regulation: Valuation Constraints," in *The Economics of Insurance Regulation: A Cross-National Study*, Jörg Finsinger and Mark V. Pauly, eds. (London: The Macmillan Press, 1986), pp. 257–290.

[24]Regulators and industry personnel claim that because of the often technical nature of the NAIC advisory committees' tasks, the pool of qualified, nonindustry-affiliated persons is small. The NAIC has, nonetheless, announced its intention to abolish industry advisory committees and to seek more consumer input into their deliberations.

The right to regulate *intrastate* commerce was reserved to the states.[25] As the specifically delegated powers of Congress are supreme to the states' general powers, no state may restrict or impede interstate commerce where Congress has taken action. No state laws are valid that contradict or contravene federal law regarding interstate commerce or matters affecting interstate commerce. Yet, traditionally, insurance has been regulated exclusively by the states. Some background on this issue will be helpful.

## PAUL VERSUS VIRGINIA

In 1868, in *Paul v. Virginia*, the Supreme Court refused to declare an insurance contract an instrumentality of commerce, and, as the following quote shows, it asserted the doctrine that a state clearly had the power to prohibit foreign insurance companies from doing business within its limits:

> Issuing a policy of insurance is not a transaction of commerce. . . . These contracts are not articles of commerce in any proper meaning of the word. They are not subject to the trade and barter. . . . They are like other personal contracts between parties which are completed by their signature and the transfer of the consideration. Such contracts are not interstate transactions, though the parties may be domiciled in different states. . . . They are, then, local transactions, and governed by the local law. They do not constitute a part of the commerce between the states.[26]

## SOUTH-EASTERN UNDERWRITERS CASE

For three-quarters of a century following *Paul v. Virginia*, it was accepted practice to regard the general supervision of all forms of insurance as falling solely within state government jurisdiction. The Supreme Court repeatedly reasserted this view. In 1944, however, the Supreme Court, in *United States v. South-Eastern Underwriters Association, et al.*, abandoned this view.[27] It held that insurance was commerce and therefore the proper subject of federal regulation under the terms of the commerce clause of the U.S. Constitution. In holding that insurance was commerce—interstate commerce for the most part—the Court swept away the foundation on which the structure of state regulation of insurance had been built. It appeared that insurance was subject to any regulations Congress desired to impose, as well as several existing federal laws that could be construed as applying to the insurance business.

---

[25]Regulation of intrastate commerce can affect interstate commerce and it may thereby be found illegal or unconstitutional as an interference in interstate commerce.

[26](1868) Wall. (U.S.) 168. See also *New York Life Insurance Co. v. Deer Lodge County (1913), 231 U.S. 495.*

[27]322 U.S. 533 (1944).

## THE MCCARRAN-FERGUSON ACT

On the theory that it had the power to redefine the distribution of authority over interstate commerce, and consistent with the granting to other industries of complete or partial protection from antitrust laws, Congress, in 1945, passed the **McCarran-Ferguson Act**. The purpose of this act may be found in its title:

> An Act to Express the Intent of the Congress with Reference to the Regulation of the Business of Insurance.

In this act, Congress redefined the authority of states and established a plan for cooperative regulation. In retrospect, it seems clear that Congress desired that there be some amount of collaboration between federal and state governments in a complete system of regulation.

According to the terms of the McCarran-Ferguson Act, the federal government retains exclusive or primary control over certain matters that it deems national in character—that is, matters in which regulation is (or should be) uniform throughout the states. Employer-employee relations (National Labor Relations Act) and fair labor standards (Fair Labor Standards Act), as well as agreements on or acts of boycott, coercion, and intimidation (Sherman Act) are deemed by the McCarran-Ferguson Act to be matters of national character and thus subject to the exclusive control of Congress.

Furthermore, Congress may expand its area of insurance control by relating an act specifically to insurance. Such a federal law would be applicable to the business of insurance and would supersede all state statutes in conflict with it. Prior to 1964, the principal acts relating specifically to insurance were limited in application to the District of Columbia. In 1964 the Securities and Exchange Act of 1934 was amended to relate specifically to the business of insurance. Since then, other measures have been enacted that assert federal jurisdiction over and even federal operation of selected aspects of the insurance business, such as flood insurance, crop insurance, and Medicare. Employee retirement plans were declared a matter for federal jurisdiction by the 1974 Employee Retirement Income Security Act.

Although the McCarran-Ferguson Act declares that the continued regulation of insurance by the states is in the public interest, the law states that certain existing federal statutes (the Sherman Act, the Clayton Act, and the Federal Trade Commission Act), which are general in nature and do not deal with insurance specifically, are made specific to the business of insurance to the extent that "such business is not regulated by state laws." Hence a basic purpose of McCarran-Ferguson was to encourage improved, more uniform state regulation of insurance in the public interest.

## STATE VERSUS FEDERAL REGULATION

In the years following enactment of the McCarran-Ferguson Act, the NAIC (see below), together with representatives of the insurance industry, drafted model legislation intended to place the regulation of insurance among the several states on a more uniform and adequate basis—that is, to meet the challenge of the proviso clause of the act.

Today the states retain primary responsibility for the regulation of the insurance industry. Congress, however, retains oversight responsibility of state insurance regulation. In recent years, the adequacy of state insurance regulation has come under increasing scrutiny. Particular attention has been given to the continued validity of the antitrust exemption now afforded to the insurance business and to the effectiveness of the states' solvency regulation.

The question of whether the public interest would be better served by an alternative insurance regulatory regime within the United States arises periodically, typically following some new insurance-related difficulty. The latest difficulty stems from the combination of (1) the recent high failure rates of U.S. savings and loan (S&L) associations and, to a lesser extent, the failure of banks, and (2) an increasing number of insurer failures, especially a few large insurers. Although the S&L and bank difficulties are acknowledged to be far more severe than those experienced by or anticipated for the insurance industry, concern persists that state insurance regulators may not be up to the task of overseeing what is a more complex, national and even international business.[28] Several U.S. Congressional committees have held hearings on the issue and more hearings are anticipated.[29]

Departing from their historical positions in support of exclusive state regulation, some major insurers and at least one major property/liability trade association have supported reform. A U.S. General Accounting Office report concluded that the NAIC was incapable of coordinating effective U.S. insurance regulation and called for reform.[30] Mindful of the criticism of state regulation and of its role within that system, the NAIC has undertaken several measures, the intent of which is to strengthen the existing system (see below).

The debate as to whether the public interest is best served by federal regulation or state regulation is an old one. The controversy could result in (1) the states continuing to be the primary regulators of insurance,[31] (2) the federal

[28]See Robert E. Litan, *Back to Basics: Solvency as the Primary Object of Insurance Industry Regulation* (Jan. 1992).

[29]See, especially, U.S. House of Representatives, Committee on Energy and Commerce, Subcommittee on Oversight and Investigations, *Failed Promises: Insurance Company Insolvencies* (Washington, D.C.: GPO, 1990).

[30]U.S. General Accounting Office, *Insurance Regulation: States' Handling of Financially Troubled Property/Casualty Insurers* (Washington, D.C.: U.S. GPO, 1991).

[31]The states could continue their primacy role, yet alter aspects of the system in an effort to be more efficient and effective. Under one proposal, the states would enter into a regulatory interstate compact. An interstate commission would be established with authority to promulgate statutes, regulations, and rules that would bind competing states. There is concern about state sovereignty, but many proponents see this as a vehicle for promoting greater regulatory uniformity while retaining the best aspects of state regulation. See James M. Jackson, "Commerce, Compacts, and Congressional Consent: Federal and State Insurance Regulation," *Journal of Insurance Regulation*, Vol. 10 (Fall 1991), pp. 23-49.

The state regulators have undertaken activities to strengthen the regulatory oversight role of the NAIC itself and to enhance programs in education and training, financial services, research, and other areas. See *Services to NAIC Members* (NAIC, 1992).

government becoming the primary regulator of insurance, or (3) some system of dual regulation.[32]

Although a full discussion of the state-versus-federal regulation issue is beyond this chapter's scope, the following lists provide an idea of the issue's complexity. Some of the arguments made for continuing state regulation include:

- State regulation already exists.

- Decentralization of government is a virtue in itself.

- States can be more responsive than the federal government to local needs.

- There is no reason to believe that federal regulation would be more effective or efficient than state regulation, especially given the unsatisfactory federal S&L and banking regulatory experience.

- Whatever uniformity is necessary can be achieved through the NAIC.

- Effects of ill-advised insurance legislation are localized.

- States serve as laboratories for insurance regulation.

Arguments advanced in favor of federal regulation include:

- The expense of having to file financial reports in and deal with each jurisdiction's insurance department is high and leads to insurer inflexibility, ultimately hindering U.S. domestic insurers in their competition with international insurers.

- Ill-advised legislation can be passed easily in states where legislators cannot devote resources to studying legislation, as can the United States Congress

- The political nature of the appointment or election of state insurance commissioners may produce poorly qualified regulators.

- Insurance commissioners and state legislatures are sometimes overly responsive to domestic insurance companies' pressures, to the point of placing extra burdens on nondomestic companies (e.g., discriminatory premium taxes).

- Conflicts arise between standard federal regulations and state rulings, that adversely affect insurer operations.

- States find it increasingly difficult to solve regulatory problems involving non-U.S. insurers.

- Whereas U.S. insurers wishing to do business in other nations typically need to deal with only one national regulator, non-U.S. insurers wishing to do business in the United States must deal with dozens of regulators.

[32]Under one proposal, a two-tier insurance regulatory system would allow insurers to choose state or federal regulation. Insurers that elected federal regulation would be exempt from most state regulation. Insurers could elect to remain under state supervision, but state regulation itself would be subject to minimum federal solvency standards. Large insurers could be expected to be drawn to federal oversight whereas smaller insurers could be expected to choose the state option.

## AREAS OF FEDERAL INSURANCE REGULATION

Although insurance regulation in the United States remains the primary province of the states, the federal government plays a significant regulatory role in selected areas. Before exploring state insurance regulation in detail, a brief overview of federal involvement in insurance regulation is presented.

Committees of both the U.S. House of Representatives and the Senate periodically conduct investigations and conduct hearings on important contemporary insurance issues. An express or implied threat of corrective federal legislation often follows. State regulators are thereby spurred into developing a state-based solution to the perceived problem to preclude a possible federal solution. This process has been repeated time and again over the years. It is through this nonstatutory mechanism that the federal government exercises its greatest influence over insurance regulation.[33] In addition to this indirect approach, federal involvement also has more tangible avenues.

The *Internal Revenue Service* (IRS), especially through its enforcement authority, exercises substantial influence over life insurance policy design and value (see Chapter 13). Additionally, through taxation of insurers themselves, the IRS influences the levels of insurers' reserves, the types of investments they acquire, the form in which they operate (mutual or stock company), and the products they sell.

The impact on insurance product design and operation of the *Employee Retirement Income Security Act* (ERISA) has been made clear earlier (see Chapter 28). The 1974 enactment of ERISA probably has had a greater influence on insurers' employee benefit plan operations than any contemporary federal or state activity.

The *Securities and Exchange Commission* (SEC) is involved in regulatory oversight of the design, operations, and sales of variable life and annuity products (see Chapter 7), and of publicly owned insurers themselves. Publicly owned insurers must file certain forms with the SEC wherein detailed financial, personnel, and other information must be disclosed. The SEC is charged with protecting investors via mandated disclosures and enforcing laws prohibiting fraud and manipulative security practices (see Chapter 5).

The *Federal Trade Commission* (FTC) has, from time to time, exerted various degrees of regulation over insurance activities, and it remains involved in the oversight of direct mail insurance solicitations. Its 1979 report on life insurance disclosure caused substantial controversy within the business (see Chapter 10).

Other agencies of the federal government are involved in insurance activities by virtue of their role in international trade and commerce. Thus the

---

[33]Although it has no regulatory responsibilities, the U.S. *General Accounting Office* (GAO) has had an effect on insurance regulation. The GAO has conducted studies on various insurance issues for the U.S. Congress and other branches of the federal government. These studies, generally respected for their attempts at unbiasedness, often form the basis upon which federal or state regulatory action is taken.

Department of Commerce, the Department of State, and the U.S. Trade Representative's office all have been involved in trade negotiations and other actions, the effects of which can be felt directly by U.S. insurers. Other countries' insurance markets may be more or less open to U.S. insurers depending on negotiations undertaken by these agencies. Their activities can also influence domestic regulation. For example, the proposed North American Free Trade Agreement (NAFTA) among Canada, Mexico, and the United States would permit insurers of each country relatively free access to the others' markets and would prohibit discrimination between national and nonnational insurers.

Finally, the federal government, primarily through the Bank Holding Company Act, controls the extent to which banks may become involved in insurance. Currently, nationally chartered banks, most state-chartered banks, and bank holding companies generally are prohibited from selling or underwriting insurance except in limited circumstances.[34] Banks have long sought to enter the U.S. insurance market, but concerns persist about undue concentration of economic power and competition. Most within the life insurance business, especially agents, oppose bank involvement in insurance.[35] Changes in federal law permitting such involvement could have a major impact on U.S. insurance distribution and operations.

---

[34]National banks are permitted to act as brokers to sell annuities for insurance companies. These banks have been able to act as insurance agents in towns with populations of less than 5,000, although the validity of this exception has been struck down by one court. In connection with extensions of credit, the Office of the Comptroller of the Currency has permitted national banks to act as brokers to sell and also to underwrite credit life, accident, and health insurance. Bank holding companies are more restricted in their insurance activities. A bank holding company may underwrite and sell credit life, accident, and health insurance related to extensions of credit by the bank holding company or any of its subsidiaries. State law governs the operation of state-chartered banks and state-licensed branches and agencies. Many states allow banks to act as insurance agents.

[35]Insurance agents and industry trade associations assert that banks selling insurance present the following dangers:

- Banks would charge unreasonably high premiums or coerce customers into buying insurance as a condition for receiving loans.
- Banks would give preferential treatment to their insurance subsidiaries and affiliates and would deny credit to competing insurance sellers.
- Inexperienced banks selling insurance could incur losses and endanger the safety and soundness of the banking system.

In contrast, banks and many consumer groups assert that bank expansion into insurance would yield the following advantages:

- Banks' lower costs would result in lower insurance premiums.
- Increased competition between insurance sellers would also lower insurance premiums and improve service quality.
- Diversification into insurance sales would reduce risk and increase bank profits, thereby protecting bank safety and soundness.
- Financial service firms of the United States would be better able to compete with those of other countries, where such financial service integration is already a fact.

A GAO report concluded that (1) consumers may benefit from banks selling insurance, but they may also need protection from potential abuse, and (2) increased competition would result, but at no risk to banking safety or soundness. See U.S. GAO, *Bank Powers: Issues Related to Banks Selling Insurance* (Washington, D.C.: U.S. GPO, 1990).

## THE MECHANISM OF STATE REGULATION

State regulation of the insurance business is conducted by three agencies of government—the courts, the legislature, and the insurance commissioner or other administrative official. In addition, the NAIC performs an increasingly vital role in the development of model regulations and laws and in the coordination of legislative activities and of state commissioners.

The judiciary has a threefold role in state insurance regulation. Most obvious to the average insured is its function of deciding cases of conflict between insurers and policyowners. The courts further protect insurers and insureds by enforcing criminal penalties against those who violate insurance law. Finally, insurance companies and their agents occasionally resort to the courts to overturn arbitrary or unconstitutional statutes or administrative regulations or orders promulgated by the insurance department.

The role of the court in the regulatory process, although important to individual and corporate rights, is relatively less so when compared with the role played by the legislature and the insurance commissioner. Within constitutional limitations and with the permission of Congress, the state legislatures have the ultimate power to make and amend insurance law. **Insurance codes** establish each state's broad legal framework and prescribe the general standards governing the activities of the administrative agencies.

The law of a particular jurisdiction usually relates to the requirements, procedures, and standards for (1) the organization and operation of the state insurance department, (2) the formation and licensing of the various types of insurers for the various classes of insurance and reinsurance, (3) the licensing of agents and brokers, (4) the filing and sometimes approval of property and liability insurance rates, (5) the filing and approval of policy forms, (6) unauthorized insurers and unfair trade practices, (7) insurer financial requirements, (8) periodic reporting and examination of insurers, (9) complaint handling, (10) the liquidation and rehabilitation of insurers, and (11) guaranty funds. Most jurisdictions also incorporate into their insurance law certain standards for the insurance contract, with specific standards for certain lines of insurance—individual life and health insurance, group life and health insurance, industrial insurance, and fire insurance, among others. In addition, the code usually prescribes penalties for insurance law violations.

### ADMINISTRATIVE OFFICIALS

Generally, courts are not equipped to give protection in matters on which only experts are informed; and legislatures, in addition to their lack of experience, find it impractical to pass laws involving every phase of a highly technical and rapidly changing industry that might need regulation. Thus state departments or agencies were created with broad administrative, quasi-legislative, and quasi-judicial powers over the insurance business.

These state insurance departments usually are under the direction of a chief official who may have the title of commissioner, superintendent, or director. In a few states, the responsibility of direction is placed in a commission or board, which, in turn, selects an individual commissioner to carry out established policy. In 12 states, commissioners are elected; in the remainder of the states, they are appointed, usually by the governor.[36] In many states, the state official who has this responsibility also has other duties, such as state auditor, comptroller, or treasurer; or the department of insurance is associated with some other department, such as the department of banking or securities.

Since the right to conduct the insurance business, to represent an insurer in doing insurance business, or to represent the public in placing insurance is considered to be a privilege, it is limited to those who qualify by obtaining a license. Thus insurance is brought under the control and supervision of the insurance commissioner by means of the licensing function.

In granting a license, the state has the power to prescribe numerous conditions and limitations that must be observed by insurers as a condition precedent to exercising the privilege of doing business within the state. In implementing these various standards, the insurance commissioner is given numerous powers and duties, as discussed below.

## NATIONAL ASSOCIATION OF INSURANCE COMMISSIONERS

***Structure and Operation***. The NAIC is a voluntary association of the chief insurance regulatory officials of the 50 states, the District of Columbia, American Samoa, Guam, Puerto Rico, and the Virgin Islands. The NAIC (formerly the National Insurance Convention) was formed in 1871 to address issues concerning the supervision of interstate insurers within a state regulatory framework. The association has as its objectives (1) the maintenance and improvement of state regulation of insurance in a responsive and efficient manner; (2) ensuring reliability of the insurance institution as to financial solidity and guaranty against loss; and (3) fair, just, and equitable treatment of policyowners and claimants.

The association operates through a committee structure wherein tasks are assigned by line of business (e.g., life, health, property/liability) and activity. Committees are composed of selected state regulators, who historically have appointed **advisory committees** to assist them in their work. These advisory committees, composed mostly or exclusively of insurance industry representatives, have prepared background papers, conducted research, and drafted tentative model bills and regulations. (The NAIC, in response to criticism

---

[36]The 12 states are California, Delaware, Florida, Georgia, Kansas, Louisiana, Mississippi, Montana, North Carolina, North Dakota, Oklahoma, and Washington.

about this structure, recently announced that it will no longer utilize industry advisory committees.) Model bills and regulations are those agreed upon by the NAIC as being worthy of state adoption for purposes of addressing some regulatory issue or problem. The models themselves have no authority. They only have force when enacted by a state.

The NAIC has been successful in several respects and has served as a unifying and harmonizing force. Some of its more significant accomplishments include (1) the adoption by all states of a uniform blank for insurers' annual financial reports; (2) the acceptance by most states of a certificate of solvency by an insurer's home state, thus eliminating much duplication and expense; (3) the acceptance by most states of the principle that a deposit of securities should be required only in a company's home state; (4) the adoption of uniform rules for valuation of securities; (5) the development of the zone system of insurer examination; (6) the preparation of new standard mortality tables; (7) the preparation of standard valuation and nonforfeiture laws; (8) the creation of a state certification program to help strengthen and harmonize state solvency regulation; (9) the drafting of many other model laws and regulations in the fields of life and health insurance; and (10) the coordination of liaison activity with the federal government on insurance matters and with other state government associations.

There can be no question of the important role the NAIC has played in state regulation of the insurance industry. In recent years, there appears to have been even more interest in increased cooperative action among the states. The NAIC has adopted more than 215 model laws, regulations, and guidelines applicable to virtually all aspects of insurance regulation. In addition, the NAIC has undertaken a number of major research projects and expanded its services to members.[37]

*The NAIC State Accreditation Program.* No state is bound to follow the recommendations of the NAIC. Although the NAIC has no enforcement power, its **state accreditation program** suggests that the NAIC's role is evolving from a purely deliberative/consultative body to one attempting to instigate change.[38] The accreditation program has as its premise that any system of effective regulation has certain basic components. It requires that regulators have adequate statutory and administrative authority to regulate an insurer's corporate and financial affairs. It also requires that regulators be provided with the necessary resources to carry out that authority. Finally, it requires that insurance departments have in place organizational and personnel practices designed for effective regulation.

To guide state legislatures and state insurance departments in the development of effective regulation, particularly as it relates to solvency, the NAIC adopted a set of Financial Regulation Standards in 1989. These standards

[37]See *Services to NAIC Members* (NAIC, 1992).

[38]See *State Actions to Improve Insurance Solvency Regulation* (NAIC, 1990) and *The NAIC Solvency Policing Agenda: An Update* (NAIC, 1991).

establish what the NAIC believes to be minimum requirements for an effective regulatory regime. To provide guidance to the states regarding these minimum standards and as an incentive to put them into place, the accreditation program was adopted in 1990. Under this plan, each state's insurance department is to be reviewed by an independent review team whose job it is to assess that department's compliance with the NAIC's Financial Regulation Standards. Departments meeting the NAIC standards are *accredited* and the department publicly acknowledged. Departments not in compliance are given guidance by the NAIC on how to bring the department into compliance. It is intended that, beginning in 1994, accredited states generally will not accept examination reports prepared by nonaccredited states on those states' domestic insurers. Companies domiciled in nonaccredited states presumably would be required to obtain a second examination from an accredited state. This sanction is expected to pressure nonaccredited states into becoming accredited. The NAIC has not yet set out its longer-term view of the program.[39] Although the program has been praised, it also has its critics who contend it will prove ineffective.[40]

## AREAS OF STATE REGULATION

Because of the peculiar nature of the insurance business and the position of public trust that it holds, the authority of the state over the activities of insurance companies is exerted from their birth to their death. The insurance enterprise must meet certain requirements to be organized and to obtain a license in the various jurisdictions in which it wishes to do business. Its agents and brokers must be licensed, its contract forms approved, and, in some instances in the case of health insurance, rates may be scrutinized. Advertising and sales practices are considered and standards of fair competition established. Insurer expenses may be regulated. Deposits may be required in various jurisdictions as a guaranty of the willingness of the insurer to comply with state statutes and to discharge obligations under its contracts.

Insurer solvency is a matter of particular interest. Limitations may exist on the size of risk that may be accepted. Specific requirements are established for

---

[39]Many observers believe that the program could be made more effective if accredited states refused to license insurers domiciled in nonaccredited states. The legal and political problems of such a position are acknowledged. Also, state licensing could be streamlined if insurers licensed in an accredited state were accorded a presumption of financial solidity for purposes of obtaining licenses in other states. Reciprocal licensing recognition could follow, thus resulting in a European Community-type, home-state central system of supervision and licensing.

[40]The U.S. General Accounting Office found that the program suffers three problems: (1) the standards are too general and have been interpreted permissively; (2) the program focuses too little on actual state implementation of the standards; and (3) documentation of accreditation decisions has not always supported decisions to accredit states. See *Insurance Regulation: The Financial Regulation Standards and Accreditation Program of the National Association of Insurance Commissioners*, GAO/T-GGD-92-27 (1992). The NAIC counters that the program continues to evolve and criticisms at this early stage of its evolution are premature.

reserve liabilities, the minimum size of capital and surplus, and investments and their proper valuation. Finally, the state presides over the conservation or liquidation of companies whose solvency is in danger.

## ORGANIZATION AND LICENSING OF INSURERS

Although the organization of insurance companies is governed to some extent by the law applicable to the organization of general corporations, states have supplanted most of their general corporation law with special acts pertaining only to insurance companies. State insurance laws describe specifically the requirements for the organization of a life company. Health insurance may be written by a life, a casualty, or a monoline specialty company. When health insurance is written by a life company, the requirements for organization and licensing of a life company usually apply. Generally, a monoline health company may organize under either the life or casualty sections of the law.

State insurance codes require the drafting of a charter that specifically describes the insurer's name and location, the lines of insurance it plans to write, the powers of the organization, and its officers. Frequently, the method of internal organization must be specified. Minimum amounts of paid-in capital and surplus for stock companies are stated, varying from a few hundred thousand to $2 million and more of capital, plus an initial surplus varying from 50 to 200 percent of the minimum paid-in capital for each line of insurance (life and health) to be written. Minimum surplus and participation requirements for mutual insurers also are specified, with minimum surplus requirements that are similar to the minimum capital and surplus requirements for stock insurers.[41]

Before issuing the certificate of incorporation, a responsible state official investigates the character of the incorporators of the new firm, its proposed plan of operation and its marketing and financial projections. After meeting these and other requirements, the company is prepared to seek a license to conduct the insurance business.

For purposes of establishing an insurer's domicile, the state recognizes three types of insurers. A **domestic insurer** is one domiciled in the concerned state. A **foreign insurer** is an insurer domiciled in another U.S. jurisdiction. An **alien insurer** is domiciled in another country.[42]

The requirements for licensing foreign and alien insurers may be similar to those for licensing domestic companies (i.e., they are accorded national treatment), but sometimes they are more stringent. All insurers (domestic, foreign, and alien) are required to maintain a substantial deposit of securities of a specified quality in trust with the state. To meet this requirement, foreign insurers

---

[41]Risk-based capital requirements, in effect, augment fixed capital and surplus requirements (see Chap. 32 and discussion later in this chapter).

[42]In other countries, the term *foreign insurer* is reserved for nonnational firms—*alien insurer* in U.S. terminology.

may substitute a certificate from the insurance commissioner of another state in which they are licensed, to the effect that a deposit is being maintained in trust in that state for the purpose of protecting policyowners and creditors.

The deposit in trust for alien insurers operating through branch offices is usually substantial and must be equal in value to its liabilities in the United States, plus there must be a surplus at least equal to the minimum capital and surplus required for a domestic insurer licensed to transact the same kinds of business. In addition, several states require that there be a security deposit with the treasurer of the state for the purpose of protecting the state's policyowners. Also, a foreign or alien insurer generally must appoint a resident of the state in which it wants to do business as its attorney for purposes of serving a legal process.

## UNAUTHORIZED INSURANCE

One of the more vexatious problems confronting state insurance regulation involves the question of control over the activities of unauthorized insurance companies. By refusing to apply for a license, the unauthorized insurer may attempt to escape regulation in all states except its state or country of domicile, on the basis that it has no representatives within the state and consequently it is not legally "doing business" there. Unauthorized insurers generally make no reports to the state insurance department. They are not subject to examination, and their policy forms are not subject to state approval. Since their business often is conducted through the mail, and since interstate mail advertising is not subject to state control, the state commissioner may be handicapped in rendering any service to the policyowner in the adjustment of claims.

At present, seven principal types of regulation are utilized by the states in an effort to control the operations of unauthorized insurers:

> 1. Under the NAIC Unauthorized Insurers Model Statute, as adopted by most states, no person may (a) represent an unauthorized insurer in the solicitation, negotiation, or effectuation of insurance, or in any other manner in the transaction of insurance with respect to the subjects of insurance in the state involved; or (b) represent any person in the procuring of insurance from such an unauthorized insurer.

> 2. Although states' unauthorized insurers' acts generally exclude from their scope group life and health policies delivered in other states, the NAIC has recommended that mass-marketed life and health insurance offered by direct-response solicitation be subject to state advertising and claims settlement practices laws and be required to meet minimum-loss-ratio guidelines that states may have in effect.

> 3. Several states make such contracts legally voidable by the insured, unless, during the life of the contract, the insurer becomes licensed to transact the class of insurance involved (i.e., life or health insurance).

4. Advertising originating outside the state and designed to solicit insurance from persons located within the state may be prohibited. Usually, this prohibition is aimed at the publisher, radio station, and so on, as well as the insurer.

5. Under the NAIC Uniform Unauthorized Insurers Service of Process Act, as adopted by many jurisdictions, the insured may bring a legal action involving a claim against an unauthorized out-of-state insurer by serving process on the insurance commissioner of his or her home state.

6. The NAIC Nonadmitted Insurers Information Office—a central clearinghouse for the collection of information about nonadmitted foreign and alien insurers—may be used by individual states.

7. A significant number of states have enacted provisions of an NAIC model assuming jurisdiction of plans providing health care benefits. The purpose of this legislation is to assert jurisdiction over uninsured or partially insured multiple employer trusts or other trusts.

Despite the existence of laws of this type, numerous regulatory problems persist. They arise because the state of domicile does not adequately control the market practices and financial solvency of these insurers. Additionally, with multiple employer welfare arrangements (MEWAs), states have had difficulty enforcing existing laws because they cannot always identify MEWAs operating within their boundaries, as well as because of other problems.[43]

## INSURANCE POLICY OVERSIGHT

Once an insurance company is organized and licensed to transact business in the state, almost every phase of its operation is subject to state supervision. This section covers the policy form and rate oversight role of the regulator.

*Policy Forms*. In most lines of insurance—including life and health insurance—policy forms are subjected to some regulation in an effort to protect insureds, policyowners, and beneficiaries against unfair and deceptive provisions and practices.[44] Contract regulation involves (1) the requirement that a policy form may not be used until it is filed with and approved by the state insurance department, and (2) the various requirements or standards for policy form approval.[45]

[43]See *States Need Labor's Help Regulating Multiple Employer Welfare Arrangements* (Washington, D.C.: GAO, 1992).

[44]The definition of approval varies by jurisdiction. Many jurisdictions require approval of a form prior to its utilization, with the added provision that the form is approved by default at the end of 30 (or 45) days if the commissioner has not taken action.

[45]Much contract regulation actually arises because of undesirable claims, advertising, and other practices surrounding the use of the contract by a few insurers.

The insurance commissioner utilizes both general and specific legal standards as a guide to determine the appropriateness of forms in the public interest. Much of this statutory and administrative law is based on NAIC recommendations. Since the application of general standards creates problems for both the commissioners and the industry, the NAIC has developed specific standards designed to implement the general standard.

Every jurisdiction requires (or will accept) life insurance contract forms that contain, in substance, certain provisions as prescribed in the laws of most of the states. These statutory provisions, as recommended by the NAIC, include clauses related to the grace period, premium payment, incontestability, entire contract, misstatement of age, annual apportionment of dividends, surrender values and options, policy loans, settlement options, and reinstatement.[46] The required provisions for group life insurance contracts and certificates are treated separately.

In 1946, following the South-Eastern Underwriters decision and the passage of the McCarran-Ferguson Act, the NAIC and the All-Industry Committee recommended to the states the enactment of an Accident and Health Regulatory Law. In addition to establishing the requirement that contract forms, classifications, rates, and endorsements must be filed and that forms and endorsements must be approved, this law established the general standard that contracts must not be unjust, ambiguous, unfair, misleading, or encourage misrepresentation. Furthermore, the model law states (although this provision was omitted by some jurisdictions) that forms may be disapproved if "benefits are unreasonable in relation to the premium charged" (see below).

All jurisdictions have adopted the NAIC Uniform Individual Accident and Sickness Policy Provisions Law or a similar statute. This law includes specific language for both required and optional provisions and policy readability tests. As regards both the required and optional standard provisions, the insurer may use wording of its own choosing provided it is no less favorable to the insured or beneficiary than the law's provisions.[47]

The insurance commissioner of each jurisdiction has developed (in addition to the specific language contained in the law) specific guidelines by administrative regulation. Requirements are established for the clear labeling of limited policies. Certain types of provisions are prohibited or restricted, and certain practices with respect to the policy contract are controlled.

Increasingly, regulation of health insurance policies is built upon minimum benefit and disclosure requirements. The NAIC, for example, in 1973 adopted an Individual Accident and Sickness Insurance Minimum Standards Act as well as a regulation to implement the act. These regulatory measures separate accident and sickness coverages into nine categories, each of which is subject to particular minimum benefit standards and disclosure rules. This classification of policies,

[46]See Chaps. 8 and 9.
[47]See Chap. 16.

and the public demands for coverages that may be compared in the marketplace, has led to increased pressure for policy standardization.

Insurers wishing to sell Medicare supplemental policies must model their policies after one or more of ten standardized policies promulgated by the NAIC. These ten policies were developed by the NAIC in response to stipulations in the 1990 Omnibus Budget Reconciliation Act authorizing the NAIC to do so. (Failure to act by the NAIC would have resulted in the federal government doing so.)[48] This requirement was in response to what was perceived as a bewildering variety of policies formerly available and a lack of standards.[49]

*Rates*. In many lines of insurance, the supervision of the product involves the regulation of rates—the product price. The various states regulate rates in most of the property/liability insurance lines. Life (occasionally) and health insurance rates must be filed with the contract forms to which they apply. Generally, they are not subject to approval (see below). They are filed principally to make them a matter of public record for the benefit of persons who come under the misstatement-of-age provision and other provisions involving an age proration of premium.

*1. Life Insurance.* Life insurance rates for individual insurance are regulated only in a most indirect sense. Competition is believed to be an adequate regulator over any tendencies to rate excessiveness. As a practical matter, rate adequacy may be a problem, and it is believed that minimum reserve requirements (see below) and expense limitations are an adequate safeguard. The states of New York and Wisconsin have complex laws limiting the amount of expenses that can be incurred in the production of new business and the maintenance of old business in force.

The laws of most jurisdictions assume that, for stock insurers issuing nonparticipating contracts, competition is an adequate guarantor of rate equity among the different classes and generations of insureds. Mutual insurance companies often are prohibited from issuing nonparticipating policies. Where premiums prove to be redundant, equity demands that the excess be returned in the form of a dividend to each class or generation of insureds in proportion to their contributions to the surplus. Most states require that dividends be apportioned and paid annually. A few states limit the amount of aggregate surplus that may be accumulated by a mutual insurer. Although announced specific standards do not exist, some commissioners review dividend apportionment formulas from time to time—generally at the time of company examination.

Stock insurance companies issuing participating contracts may be required to limit the amount of dividends payable to stockholders in the interest of fairness

---

[48]See Chap. 16.

[49]In economic terms, insurers were believed to be practicing monopolistic competition via product differentiation to the point where they could extract excessive marketplace rents.

to insureds under these contracts. (These types of provisions are common in many other countries.)

Although life insurance rates are not directly regulated, in recent years there has been widespread state regulation activity designed to improve the quality of information provided to life insurance policyowners and applicants. The most significant price-related development is a requirement in the NAIC Life Insurance Disclosure Model Regulation (in force in some 40 states) that interest-adjusted cost comparison and other information be provided to consumers.[50]

*2. Health Insurance.* One of the general standards for the approval of health insurance contract forms is basically an attempt to regulate the benefit provisions. It attempts that task by relating the ratio of benefits to premiums. Thus forms must not be approved (or approval must be withdrawn) if "benefits are unreasonable in relation to the premium charged." This standard, found in the laws of a number of jurisdictions, is general in nature.

Although the distinction is somewhat tenuous, the law appears more nearly to establish standards for the approval of policy forms than for rates. Technically, it is the policy form that is subject to being disapproved—not the rates—if there is a question about the reasonableness of benefits.

Loss-ratio guidelines have been the focus of renewed interest within the regulatory community as a means for monitoring and controlling pricing activities of health insurers. The NAIC adopted guidelines for the filing of rates for individual health insurance forms. The guidelines establish loss-ratio requirements for medical expense and loss of income coverages, depending on terms of renewal. It is anticipated that heightened regulatory interest in health insurance pricing will continue in the coming years.[51]

## MARKETING PRACTICES

Broadly interpreted, state regulation of marketing practices includes control over the licensing of agents and brokers and over unfair trade practices.

*Licensing of Agents and Brokers*. The statutes of all U.S. jurisdictions contain provisions for the licensing of resident and nonresident agents and brokers. A few jurisdictions license counselors—fee-paid advisors. No person may act as agent, broker, or counselor within the jurisdiction without first obtaining a license. No insurer may issue a contract through or remunerate any person (other than on renewal business or other deferred compensation where the agent has ceased to participate in new business development), unless the person holds a valid license.

[50]See Chap. 10.
[51]See Chap. 16.

The procedure that must be followed in obtaining a license is similar for all lines. In addition to the filing of the application by the licensee (in which the licensee must give information regarding his or her character, experience, and general competence), each insurer for which he or she is to be licensed must submit a notice of appointment (or intention of appointment), together with a certificate of trustworthiness and competence signed by an officer of the insurer. In many states, the new applicant (usually defined as a person who has not held a license in the recent past; e.g., two years ) may receive a temporary license, with a permanent license being issued following the successful completion of a test of competency in the line for which he or she is seeking a license.[52] Several states require new licensees to undertake a certain minimum number of hours (e.g., 40) of formal training in insurance before they can sit for the state examination. In addition to establishing a minimum standard of competency, these examinations serve to reduce turnover and thus contribute further to the general upgrading of insurance representatives.

The agent's license may be perpetual until it is revoked or it may be subject to renewal at stipulated intervals. Licenses must be renewed through the payment of license or appointment fees. The license may be refused, revoked, or suspended by the commissioner, after notice and hearing, on the grounds that the agent willfully violated the law in his or her capacity as an agent, was guilty of fraudulent or dishonest practices, proved untrustworthy or incompetent, or made a material misrepresentation in the application for his or her license. In addition, the license is terminated by death or termination of the agent's appointment by the insurance company. In states making provision for brokers, the requirements and procedures for obtaining a broker's license are similar to those already discussed.

Several states also require agents and brokers annually to undertake specific continuing education in their field. The individual must either demonstrate that he or she has met the minimum number of hours' requirement or face nonrenewal of his or her license.

Many other countries do not require insurance agents to be licensed. Instead the regulatory officials rely on the insurer's selection and oversight responsibility to ensure appropriate knowledge and behavior.

*Unfair Trade Practices*. Although states have long exercised control over certain unfair practices—especially misrepresentation, twisting, rebating, and unfair discrimination—the impact of the SEUA decision and the McCarran-Ferguson Act led substantially all jurisdictions to adopt the NAIC Model Unfair Trade Practices Act. Although differing in philosophy, the Act was designed to be sufficiently comprehensive to oust the Federal Trade Commission from jurisdiction over these matters. All these acts identify and define certain trade practices as unfair. Usually, they give the commissioner the power to investigate and examine and, after notice and hearing, to issue cease and desist orders, with penalties for violations. The acts are designed to prevent numerous activities deemed to be unfair, some of which are discussed below.

---

[52]Controversy over the use of these temporary licenses has resulted in a decrease of their use.

**Rebating** is the practice by an agent (or insurer) of returning a portion of the premium (e.g., the agent's commission) to an insurance applicant. Rebating historically has been illegal. Antirebating statutes evolved decades ago in response to perceived marketplace abuses. Traditional arguments against rebating have focused on concerns about insurer solvency, about unfair discrimination, and about the unique nature of insurance.[53] Critics of antirebating statutes claim that the prohibition unfairly prevents buyers from negotiating fully with sellers—a result that is offensive in a competitive system. In the states of Florida and California, rebating is not illegal. Some other states' antirebating laws are being challenged on constitutional grounds.

**Twisting** refers to the practice by an agent of inducing a policyowner through misrepresentation to discontinue an existing life insurance policy in order to purchase a new one. In contrast to simple **replacement**—discontinuing one policy to purchase another—twisting is illegal. The purchase of a life insurance policy, although in itself not an overly complicated transaction, may involve a complex array of financial data. The consumer easily could be misled, either intentionally or unintentionally, by an agent. In recognition of this fact, several states have promulgated versions of the NAIC Model Replacement Regulations, which require the disclosure of certain information considered pertinent to the proposed replacement decision.[54]

Agents often handle large amounts of their policyowners' money in the form of premium payments, dividend checks, and surrender and loan funds. **Misappropriation** or misuse of these funds even on a temporary basis is illegal. Related to misappropriation is the practice of **commingling** of funds. Agents are not to combine monies belonging to policyowners with their own funds.

During the last few years, the NAIC has developed model regulations to deal with life insurance replacements, sex discrimination, discrimination on the basis of blindness, and discrimination on the basis of physical or mental handicaps. The NAIC also is focusing on the broader subject of classification of risks and on sex-based rate differentials in health insurance.

*Unfair Advertising Practices.* The Federal Trade Commission's Trade Practices Rules Relating to the Advertising of Mail Order Insurance, promulgated in 1950, represented the first attempt of the commission to regulate the practice of insurance companies (other than actions regarding boycott, coercion, and intimidation) under the proviso clause of the McCarran-Ferguson Act. To strengthen its contention that advertising was adequately regulated by the states, the NAIC developed for state adoption the Rules Governing Advertisements of Accident and Sickness Insurance with Interpretive Guidelines in 1955 and revised them in 1974. These rules are composed of standards designed to guide commissioners in the implementation of the general advertising standards contained in the model Uniform Trade Practices Act.

---

[53]See Dave Goodwin, "The Case for Rebating," *Best's Review* L/H ed (May 1990), pp. 36-45.
[54]See Chap. 10.

The NAIC's Model Life Insurance Advertising Regulation has been adopted in many states, with others devising similar rules to regulate life advertising. Some states' (e.g., Virginia) regulations have considerably expanded the scope of the NAIC model. The rules recommended by the NAIC regulate the form and content of advertisements, set forth minimum disclosure requirements, and provide for enforcement procedures.

## Solvency Surveillance

State insurance regulators are charged with the protection of the public interest by ensuring a financially healthy insurance industry. As with any other industry in which a fiduciary interest is involved, this entails a careful balancing of the goal of insolvency prevention with the goal of available, affordable insurance products. It is possible to design a regulatory system for insurance so restrictive that insolvency would be virtually impossible, but coverage would be expensive or simply unavailable for many consumers. The objective must be to establish the proper incentives for efficient as well as safe operation and to institute safeguards that keep insurer failures to an acceptable minimum. This entails early detection of financially troubled companies, taking corrective action to restore them to financial health when possible, and minimizing the negative effects of the financial difficulties that do occur. Financial failures are a natural economic consequence of the competitive environment that exists in the U.S. insurance industry and are to be expected.

State insurance solvency regulation has been continually challenged to meet the demands of a dynamic industry. The number of life insurer insolvencies during the late 1980s and early 1990s averaged about 0.5 to 1.0 percent of the total number of life insurers per year (some 10 to 30 per year). Most insolvencies have been of relatively small companies, but some have entailed large insurers. Indeed, congressional concern over insurer solvency has led to calls for a change in the way insurers are regulated, as discussed earlier in this chapter.

This section sets out the policies and procedures that states have adopted to regulate life insurer solvency. Solvency surveillance is accomplished primarily through four mechanisms: (1) financial statement filing requirements, (2) the Insurance Regulatory Information System, (3) examinations, and (4) enforcement and market surveillance.

***Financial Statement Filings***. Each state requires that all licensed insurers file financial statements detailing their financial condition and operation. Statements must be filed at least annually and more frequently if financial problems are suspected. As of 1992, insurers have had to file a supplement to the annual statement entitled "Management's Discussion and Analysis." This supplement must include material events known to management that would cause the insurer's reported financial information not to be indicative of future operating results or of its future financial position.

Insurance supervisory authorities require that insurance companies maintain at all times assets that are at least equal to their currently due and prospectively estimated liabilities plus the required minimum capital and surplus levels. Furthermore, in order that the relationship between assets and liabilities will have some meaning, a large body of law has been enacted that specifically relates to these items.

*1. Asset Limitations and Valuation.* Although there is a decided lack of uniformity in the insurance codes of the various states as they pertain to insurer assets, all jurisdictions are concerned with the types of investments that are permitted and the techniques of asset valuation. (Chapter 31 presented a discussion of the principal aspects of life insurer investment regulation.)

Nearly all jurisdictions distinguish between (1) capital and surplus and (2) reserve investments. New York follows the traditional pattern: It requires that funds equivalent to the minimum capital and surplus required by law for the line or lines of insurance being transacted be invested in certain secure types of assets (cash, government bonds, and mortgages). Life insurance companies may invest all remaining funds in "reserve investments"—that is, "capital investments" plus other permitted investments of second quality.

The law in most jurisdictions requires that no insurance company make any investment or loan unless it is authorized or approved by the company's board of directors, or by a committee authorized by the board and charged with the supervision or making of such investments. The law further requires that the minutes of any such committee shall be recorded, and that regular reports of the committee shall be submitted to the board of directors. The directors and officers must not have a personal interest in the investments or in their sale to the insurance company.

The valuation of the assets held by an insurer for annual-statement purposes is a complicated and detailed procedure. Most insurance statutes state that the commissioner may specify the rules for determining the value of securities, subject (in some cases) to the limitation that these rules shall not be inconsistent with those established by the NAIC.[55] Through its Securities Valuation Office (SVO), the NAIC values on a uniform basis the securities held in the portfolios of virtually every insurance company in the United States.

Investments in obligations or equities issued by non-U.S. governments and businesses have been severely limited by state investment laws for many years. Regulatory concerns about these investments relate to exchange rate fluctuations,

---

[55]See Chap. 32 for a discussion of the valuation of assets.

expropriations, wars, and the difficulties of monitoring such investments.[56] The state of New York permits an insurer to hold up to 10 percent of its assets in Canadian investments, while no more than 3 percent may be invested in securities from other countries.

The NAIC Model Regulation on Investments in Medium- and Lower-Quality Obligations establishes an aggregate cap of 20 percent on below-investment grade bonds, with a graded system of subcaps based on the quality of the bonds. The purpose of the regulation is to protect against insurer overinvestment in medium- to lower-grade bonds, while allowing some insurer flexibility. The regulation, adopted by the NAIC in 1991, is expected to be enacted by many states.

*2. Liability Valuation.* The principal liabilities on insurers' balance sheets are policy reserves. Policy reserves are balance sheet accounts established to reflect actual and potential liabilities under outstanding contracts.

Life insurers are required by law to establish minimum reserves as a liability. In this regard, the NAIC's Standard Valuation Law has been enacted or otherwise made effective in all jurisdictions. Its provisions are applicable, in general, to all policies issued since its enactment or amendment. (The valuation of life insurance reserves was discussed in Chapters 2 and 20.)

Annual-statement health insurance reserves include the unearned premium reserve; the additional reserve (active-life reserve) for policies in which the insurer's right of termination is restricted by the terms of the contract or company practice; the reserve for future contingent benefits; the reserve for the present value of amounts not yet due on approved claims; the reserve for claims in the course of settlement; the reserve for incurred but unreported claims; and the claim-expense reserve.

Although the continued financial soundness of an insurer depends on proper investments, together with the correct valuation of all assets, the establishment and proper valuation of reserves is just as important and, in the health insurance line, a much more difficult task. In most jurisdictions, the standards utilized in measuring the adequacy of the various health insurance reserves are left to individual insurer determination, with many companies making this determination in consultation with the actuaries of the respective state insurance departments.[57]

The replacement of the mandatory securities valuation reserve (MSVR) with the asset valuation reserve (AVR) and the interest maintenance reserve (IMR) is expected to cause larger reserves to be established. Unlike the MSVR, the AVR applies to all major investment classes (see Chapter 32). The IMR requires that interest-related realized capital gains and losses be deferred in the IMR and amortized to income over the remaining maturity of bonds sold.

---

[56]Kenneth M. Wright, *The Life Insurance Industry in the United States: An Analysis of Economic and Regulatory Issues* (The World Bank, 1992), p. 21.

[57]See Chaps. 22 and 32.

As discussed in Chapter 20, jurisdictions increasingly require the filing of a report by the insurer's appointed actuary wherein he or she explains results of certain mandated cash flow testing. This requirement, coupled with the NAIC annual-statement instruction that insurers annually must file an audit by a certified public accountant (CPA), means that regulators will receive a more complete view of insurers' operations.[58]

*3. Minimum Capital and Surplus.* State capital and surplus minimums were discussed earlier in the chapter. For ongoing insurers, regulators often establish internal minimums, which are greater than the statutorily prescribed minimums, against which they assess insurer solvency. These minimums may take into consideration some or all of the following factors:

- The insurer's size

- The lines of insurance written and their riskiness

- The nature and extent of the insurer's reinsurance program

- The quality, diversification, and liquidity of the insurer's investments

- Reserve adequacy

- The insurer's surplus trends and the surplus levels of comparable insurers

An important new component of life insurer solvency regulation was added by the NAIC through its 1992 adoption of the **Risk-Based Capital for Life and/or Health Insurers Model Act** and of a risk based capital formula and reporting requirements. These actions promise to alter the means by which minimally acceptable capital and surplus levels are defined and applied within the United States.

*4. Risk-Based Capital Requirements* The risk-based capital concept and requirements were discussed in Chapter 32. Briefly, according to the concept, minimum required capital and surplus should reflect the differences in insurer risk characteristics. Risk characteristics are a function of insurer size, asset quality, lines of business written, and other factors. To determine an insurer's risk-based capital ratio, an insurer's **total adjusted capital** (TAC) is compared with the risk-based capital obtained from the risk-based capital formula. TAC equals statutory capital and surplus plus the AVR, any voluntary reserves, and one-half of any policyowner dividend liability. If TAC is below the formula amount, one of three levels of regulatory authority would be triggered, depending on the extent of the deficiency.

Figure 34-1 provides a stylized illustration of how risk-based capital requirements affect insurers. Insurers with capital and surplus below the threshold level would be subject to various levels of regulatory attention.

[58]See Chap. 11.

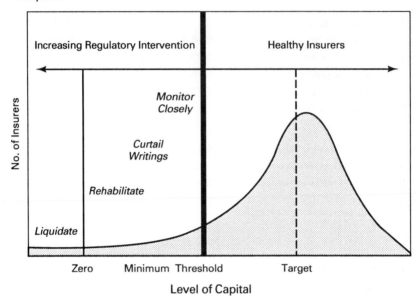

**FIGURE 34-1**

**HOW A RISK-BASED CAPITAL THRESHOLD WILL AFFECT INSURERS**

*Source*: Tillinghast

Historically, U.S. minimum capital and surplus requirements have largely ignored insurer risk. With this change, life insurers on average can be expected to be required to maintain greater levels of surplus.

The Model Act defines four levels of concern between threshold RBC levels and the TAC. Affected insurers and regulators would be required to take specific actions as the insurer's TAC passes these levels.

As of their 1993 annual statement filings, insurers are required to report their TAC and their **authorized control level** (ACL) RBC. The ACL is derived by a formula that reflects the insurer's particular asset risks (C1), insurance risks (C2), interest rate risks (C3), and business risks (C4). The riskier the element, the larger is the weighting for the factor and, hence, the larger the insurers ACL, *ceteris paribus*. Thus two insurers with the same TAC can have different ACLs, with the riskier insurer having a higher ACL.

The four RBC trigger points and accompanying required regulatory responses are:

| RBC Level | Trigger Point (as % of ACL) | Required Regulatory Action |
|---|---|---|
| Company Action Level | 200 to 150 | RBC Plan required. |
| Regulatory Action Level | 150 to 100 | RBC Plan and examination required, plus corrective action order. |
| Authorized Control Level | 100 to 70 | Insurer may be placed under regulatory control. |
| Mandatory Control Level | Below 70 | Insurer must be placed under regulatory control. |

Thus if an insurer's ACL were $100 million and its TAC were $200 million or more, the insurer would be above the company action level and, therefore, no special regulatory or company action ordinarily would be required. If the insurer's TAC were between $200 and $150 million, the company must file an *RBC Plan* with the commissioner of its domiciliary state. The plan is to describe the cause of the threat to the insurer's solvency, proposals to correct the situation, five years of financial projections, and other information. This is referred to as the *Company Action Level* as the company is required to take action.

If the insurer's TAC were between $150 and $100 million, an RBC plan would be required to be submitted and the regulator must perform appropriate analysis and examinations and may issue Corrective Orders—hence the name *Regulatory Action Level.*

TAC between $100 and $70 million—the *Authorized Control Level*—would subject the insurer to regulatory seizure. TAC below $70 million—the *Mandatory Control Level*—would *require* regulatory seizure.

The RBC requirements were developed to aid regulators in identifying financially troubled insurers while time remained for corrective action. The formula is not intended to be used by competitors or others to rate or rank companies. In an apparent effort to ensure that RBC calculations are not used in this way, the model act would prohibit agents and insurers from disseminating such figures. The act would also exempt certain other RBC information from public disclosure.

The adoption by the NAIC and ultimately by the states of risk-based capital standards represents a potentially important evolution in solvency surveillance. The approach, because of its necessarily broad nature, renders only gross approximations for insurers' "true" risk-based capital. This is the reason for regulatory concern over use of the results in competition. Nonetheless, it is difficult to envision that the NAIC's attempts to suppress the results will prove useful or effective.

*The Insurance Regulatory Information System* (IRIS). The data contained in insurers' annual statements are captured by the NAIC and serve as inputs for its IRIS program. This system plays an important role in the solvency surveillance process. The system prioritizes insurance companies for further regulatory review. As discussed in Chapter 11, IRIS consists of two phases. The first is a statistical phase that employs 12 financial ratios to flag companies that show unusual results. This is followed by an analytical phase, in which a team of financial examiners, on loan from state insurance departments, analyzes the annual statements and ratio results of the flagged companies. Upon more detailed analysis, insurers may be prioritized for further regulatory review by the domiciliary state. The NAIC also has begun work on an enhanced quarterly financial database and solvency surveillance system that can be used by the states to more quickly detect adverse trends in insurer financial condition. The actual ratios and their use are discussed in Chapter 11.[59]

*Examinations*. On-site financial examinations of insurers are useful regulatory tools. State laws require that the insurance regulator examine domestic insurers at least once every three to five years, depending on the state. These examinations involve a detailed review of all important aspects of operations. Investments are confirmed and their correct valuation checked. Liabilities are verified, as are income and expense items. Recent criticisms led to an NAIC study of the examination process and to revamping of certain procedures.

Targeted exams can be and are conducted more frequently, if circumstances dictate them. A targeted exam typically focuses on only certain aspects of an insurer's financial operations, such as reserves, investments, capital changes and so on. The objective of these examinations is to focus resources on the insurers that are most in need of review. The call for a targeted examination could be based on a CPA audit report, analysts' work papers, annual or quarterly statement filings, or IRIS results. Ideally, the frequency of examinations should not be based on the amount of time lapsed, but rather on the need for review.

*Enforcement and Surveillance*. State insurance regulators address potentially fraudulent activities and problem individuals and insurers operating in their state through the use of administrative sanctions or civil actions, usually in the form of agency or company license revocations, cease and desist orders, or injunctions. An indication or evidence of criminal activity is referred to local, state, or federal law enforcement authorities.

Currently, the Federal Racketeer-Influenced and Corrupt Organizations (RICO) Act is one of the most useful tools available to aid insurance regulators' enforcement activity. Civil rights actions routinely filed by insurance regulators and receivers—especially those containing RICO charges—have proven to have a deterrent impact on the future activities of problem individuals in the industry.

Although an informal network has always existed among states for the exchange of information on problem individuals, the NAIC also provides a formal method of information exchange. It publishes a bimonthly newsletter, available to insurance regulators only, that alerts insurance departments to current fraudulent or questionable activities, companies, and individuals. The newsletter provides information on potentially fraudulent schemes that affect the industry, tracks the activities of problem individuals, and alerts regulators about problem alien and offshore insurers that operate in the United States.

---

[59]The system has been criticized for being less effective than desirable and for flagging sound insurers. See *The Insurance Regulatory System Needs Improvement* (Washington, D.C.: GAO, 1990), and Inbum Cheong, *An Analysis of Solvency Regulation and Failure Prediction in the U.S. Life Insurance Industry* (unpublished Ph.D. dissertation, Georgia State University, 1991). For other approaches to modeling insurer solvency, see J. D. Cummins and R. A. Derrig, *Financial Models of Insurance Solvency* (Boston: Kluwer Academic Publisher, 1989).

Additionally, the NAIC has implemented a **Special Activities Database** (SAD) to expand the information available to insurance regulators and to provide a formalized vehicle for states to exchange information and inquire into the activities of companies and individuals of insurance regulatory concern, including persons who may be involved in fraudulent activities. This new database complements the **Regulatory Information Retrieval System** (RIRS), which is a computerized database containing information on regulatory actions taken against insurers and individuals.

## MERGERS AND ACQUISITIONS

Merger and acquisition activity continues at high levels within the U.S. life insurance industry as companies seek a competitive edge. Generally, regulatory approval is required for any change of insurer structure or ownership. Almost all state laws regarding mergers and acquisitions are patterned after the NAIC **Model Insurance Holding Company System Regulatory Act** or its predecessors. If control of an insurer is sought, the prospective acquirer must file a detailed disclosure statement—called a Form A—with the state insurance regulator. This Form A filing includes disclosure of the following types of information:

- The identity and background of the acquiring individuals or entities

- The source, nature, and amount of the consideration involved in the transaction

- Audited financial information concerning earnings and financial condition of each acquiring party

- The acquiring party's intentions as to material changes in the insurer's operations, assets, corporate structure, or management

- A full disclosure of the terms and conditions of the proposed acquisition

- Current ownership and recent purchase of the insurer's securities by the acquirer

- A description of any recommendations to purchase the insurer's securities, a copy of all tender offers and solicitation materials and terms of any broker-dealer agreements.

The insurance commissioner is accorded broad discovery powers in connection with the transaction. After review of the filings, the commissioner holds a hearing on the issue, and then, after due consideration of the information, renders a decision as to whether the transaction is acceptable. Grounds for disapproval include such circumstances as the following:

- The domestic insurer, after the change, would be unable to qualify for a license.

- The merger or acquisition would substantially lessen competition or tend to create a monopoly within the state.

- The acquirer's financial condition might jeopardize the insurer's financial stability or prejudice policyowners' interests.

- Any plans of the acquirer to liquidate, sell assets, or make other material changes in the insurer are unfair and unreasonable to policyowners and not in the public interest.

- The competence, experience and integrity of persons seeking control are such that the acquisition would not be in policyowners' and the public's interest.

- The acquisition is likely to be hazardous or prejudicial to the insurance-buying public.

"Control" is defined as the power to direct management and is presumed to exist if the transaction involves 10 percent or more of an insurer's voting shares.

## REHABILITATION AND LIQUIDATION

A regulator's typical first responses to a troubled insurer are informal. The regulator may attempt to work with management to identify and deal with the sources of difficulty. A friendly merger or acquisition might be arranged.

States also take formal actions—often in the form of so-called **corrective orders**—against financially troubled licensed insurers. Formal actions vary by state but ordinarily they consist of written directives requiring an insurer to (1) obtain state approval before undertaking certain transactions, (2) limit or cease its new business writings, (3) infuse capital, or (4) cease certain business practices. The regulator also may revoke an insurer's license. All these actions are subject to court review.

When, regardless of other regulatory efforts, an insurer is in serious financial difficulty or other type of difficulty, the state insurance department in most jurisdictions has the further responsibility of assuming control over its assets and management, in the case of domestic and alien insurers (if the largest amounts of the U.S. assets of the alien insurer are located within the state), or over its assets, in the case of foreign insurers located within the state. The usual procedure requires that when he or she deems it necessary, the commissioner petitions the proper court for an order appointing him or her (in his or her official capacity) receiver for the purpose of rehabilitation, conservation, or liquidation.

If the commissioner determines that reorganization, consolidation, conversion, reinsurance, merger, or other transformation is appropriate, a specific plan of rehabilitation may be prepared. Under an order of **rehabilitation**, the commissioner is granted title to the domestic insurance company's assets and is given the authority to carry on its business until the insurer either is returned to private management after the grounds for issuing the order have been removed or is liquidated.[60] Among the statutory grounds under which the commissioner may apply for a rehabilitation order are (1) a finding that further transaction of business would be financially hazardous to policyowners, creditors, or the public; (2) a determination that the insurer's officers or directors are guilty of certain acts or omissions; and (3) where a substantial transfer of assets, merger, or consolidation is attempted without the prior written consent of the commissioner.

**Liquidation** of a domestic insurer is the ultimate power of the commissioner. When it is found not advisable to attempt rehabilitation, or if rehabilitation becomes impracticable, the commissioner must petition the proper court for a liquidation order. Grounds for liquidation include those listed for rehabilitation and the additional ground that the insurer is insolvent. Under liquidation proceedings, the commissioner is given title to all assets of the insurer and is directed to take possession of them as soon as possible. Notice is required to be given to other insurance commissioners, guaranty funds, insurance agents, and all persons known or reasonably expected to have claims against the insurer. Priorities for distribution of assets are established, with the cost of administration, employee salaries, and policyowner claims receiving highest priorities. Irrespective of whether ancillary receiverships have been established, the distribution of assets in nondomiciliary states will be controlled by the statutes of the domiciliary state.

In a technical sense, the statutes of several jurisdictions use the term **conservation order** to refer to the court order directing the commissioner to act as receiver for the conservation of assets of a foreign or alien insurance company within the jurisdiction. The grounds forming the basis for the insurance commissioner's request are similar to those for liquidation and rehabilitation. Usually, prior to or concurrent with being named receiver under an order of conservation, the commissioner revokes or suspends the insurer's license to do business within the state.

The procedure of naming the insurance commissioner (rather than another person) as receiver was developed to reduce the delay and expense associated with the ordinary receivership procedure, the hope being that it would speed the return of a larger payment to the insurer's creditors and policyowners. In some cases, it makes possible the rehabilitation or merger of a company, with little or no loss to those involved. Some jurisdictions still apply the usual procedures utilized in the liquidation of a business firm—that is, the commissioner must petition the proper court for the appointment of a receiver (other than the commissioner), who then liquidates the insurer under the direction of the court. Under these circumstances, the possibility of rehabilitation may not exist because of delay, lack of technical ability, and so on.

[60]To avoid publicity and a possible mass withdrawal of business, many state regulators use rehabilitation as an intermediate step before moving insolvent insurers into liquidation.

# LIFE AND HEALTH INSURANCE GUARANTY ASSOCIATIONS[61]

Every state has some type of insolvency guaranty law. These laws have assumed even greater importance after several recent insolvencies. Generally, the laws provide for the indemnification of losses suffered by policyowners of insolvent insurers through an association that derives funds for this purpose from assessments against solvent insurers doing business in the state. In the case of life and health insurance guaranty laws, indemnification may be by payment of claims or cash values or by continuation of the insolvent insurer's policies.

*History*. The concept underlying guaranty laws first appeared in the early 1900s in state laws (all ultimately repealed) in the field of bank regulation. The first continuing laws that embody the concept are found at the federal level of bank regulation in the 1933 Federal Deposit Insurance Corporation Act which guarantees, up to specified limits, deposits in banks that fail.

Through the early 1940s, the concept spread in scattered enactments in the field of workers' compensation insurance and public motor vehicle liability insurance. The life and health guaranty association mechanism can be traced to 1941, when the first life and health guaranty law was enacted in New York. This law created the Life Insurance Guaranty Corporation which guaranteed the insurance contracts of all domestic New York life insurers in full and without regard to the residence of the insureds. New York continued to be the only state with such a mechanism until 1969.

Several bills were introduced in 1969 into the U.S. Senate to create a federal guaranty mechanism for property-liability insurance companies. In response to the possibility of federal intervention, the NAIC adopted a Postassessment Property and Liability Insurance Guaranty Association Model Act. In the following year, the NAIC Life and Health Insurance Guaranty Association Model Act was adopted. These model acts were used by the states as a basis for enacting their owns laws.

Since the 1970 Model Act, the life insurance industry has seen more competition and, therefore, greater risk. Pricing has been more competitive and interest rates have been more volatile. There have been more life insurance company insolvencies. As a result of these conditions and the practical experiences gained from dealing with these insolvencies, the Guaranty Association Model Act has been revised several times since 1970. The most recent model act is the 1987 amended version of the 1985 Model Act.

*Delinquency Proceedings*. If an insurer's financial problems cannot be resolved, some form of delinquency proceeding is started by the state regulator.

---

[61]This section draws on Lew H. Nathan, copyright © 1990, LOMA *Life and Health Guaranty Associations and Insurer Solvency* (Atlanta, Ga.: Life Office Management Association, 1990). Adapted with permission.

Generally, the company is categorized either as insolvent or impaired. As a last resort, when it is clear that the troubled company cannot be revived, the company is liquidated, as discussed earlier.

An insurer is **insolvent**, as noted in the model act, when it is placed under an order of liquidation by a court of competent jurisdiction with a finding of insolvency. Generally, this occurs when the assets of an insurer are inadequate to meet its liabilities. Typically, it is not practical for another company to take over an insolvent insurer with only the assets that the insolvent insurer has available.

An **impaired** insurer is an insurer that is not insolvent, but rather is either found by the commissioner to be potentially unable to fulfill its contractual obligations or is placed under an order of rehabilitation or conservation by a court of competent jurisdiction. The finding by the commissioner that an insurer is impaired, although not subject to a court proceeding, serves as a triggering mechanism that enables the guaranty association to act.

Companies that appear to have sufficient equity but are found by the insurance commissioner to be impaired may be placed under the direct supervision of the commissioner. The supervision process differs from rehabilitation in that under **supervision** the commissioner is working with the insurer's management to solve the company's problems and, in rehabilitation, the commissioner is in charge of the insurer. During the period of supervision, certain insurer actions may be restricted (such as transferring property) and require the approval of the commissioner. Some states provide that no public announcement is necessary for insurers placed under supervision.

*The NAIC Life and Health Insurance Guaranty Association Model Act.* The most recent NAIC Life and Health Insurance Guaranty Association Model Act was adopted by the NAIC in 1985 and amended in 1987. This model act creates a nonprofit legal entity called the (state) Life and Health Insurance Guaranty Association.

Highlights of the model act are listed below. (There are substantial differences among the states' actual guaranty association laws.)

- All insurers, as a condition of their being licensed to transact any type of insurance covered by the act in the state, must be members of the guaranty association.[62]

- The guaranty association is generally under the immediate supervision of the insurance commissioner and is subject to the applicable provisions of the insurance laws of the state.

---

[62]Entities not covered under the model act include nonprofit hospital or medical services organizations, Health Maintenance Organizations (HMOs), fraternal benefit societies, mandatory state pooling plans, mutual assessment companies, insurance exchanges, and any similar entities.

In some, but not all states, Blue Cross and Blue Shield plans and HMOs are covered under a guaranty association mechanism (whether separate or part of the Life and Health Guaranty Association law). The NAIC has been reviewing whether a guaranty association mechanism is appropriate for HMOs, and if so, how such a mechanism should work.

- The guaranty association exercises its duties through a board of directors, involving executives from five to nine member insurers. The insurance commissioner must approve each board member and the board's plan of operations.

- An assessment mechanism is specified for general administrative costs and for costs associated with settling the claims resulting from insolvent or impaired insurers.

- The act is primarily intended to cover the owners of insurance contracts who are residents of the state when the member insurer is determined to be insolvent or impaired. Beneficiaries are covered regardless of where they reside.

- The coverage under this act does not apply where any guaranty protection is provided to residents of the state by the laws of the domiciliary state.

- Coverage is limited to a maximum amount. No more than $300,000 will be paid to any one individual. There are also separate limits for life, health, and annuity coverages for any one individual:

  - $300,000 in life insurance benefits, but not more than $100,000 in net cash surrender values,

  - $100,000 in health insurance benefits, including any net cash surrender values, and

  - $100,000 in the present value of annuities, including any net cash surrender values.

  - The limit for unallocated annuity contracts is $5 million in benefits, irrespective of the number of such policies held by the policyowner.

- Advertising the guaranty association and its statutory obligations is prohibited;[63] however, the model act does provide for a disclosure to the purchasers of policies that coverage may be available from the guaranty association. Not all states have enacted this disclosure provision.

Most states permit a tax offset for any assessments paid by a member insurer. This offset can be applied to the premium tax, franchise tax, or income tax liability. The tax liability of the member insurer for each of the following five calendar years can be reduced by 20 percent of any assessment paid. Assessments can be carried on the insurer's books as a statutory asset until they are written off as a tax offset.

The costs of an insolvency go beyond the immediate financial outlay. The insolvent insurer may have underpriced its business relative to other insurers in the market, discouraging them from writing business at a reasonable price. Any

---

[63]The theory is that if advertising of the guaranty association were permitted, some insurers could take inappropriate risks while being able to assure the public that additional protections were available.

resulting insolvency cost is borne by the remaining solvent insurers and the state.[64] Furthermore, the insolvent insurer is exempted from assessments for other insolvencies occurring at the same time.

*The Assessment Process.* Two kinds of assessments are possible under the 1987 version of the Guaranty Association Model Act. Class A, the first type of assessment, is made for administrative costs, legal costs, examination costs where member insurers believed to be impaired or insolvent are reviewed, and other expenses. Class B, the second kind of assessment, is made to cover the costs associated with insolvent or impaired insurers. The latter assessment is undertaken after an insolvency or impairment.

Class B assessments are made of member insurers in the proportion that their state premium writings bear to the total writings for the relevant line of insurance. In total, for each calendar year, all assessments cannot exceed 2 percent of the member insurer's average premium received in the state on covered business during the three years preceding the year of impairment or insolvency. The assessment of any member can be abated or deferred if payment would be harmful to the member insurer in fulfilling its contractual obligations.

The current guaranty association structure has weaknesses. Coverage is not uniform among states. As a result, two individuals having identical insurance with the same failed insurer can receive substantially different payments, depending on their states of residence. Each state's association can act independently from the other associations, although the National Organization of Life and Health Insurance Guaranty Associations (NOLHGA) helps to achieve uniformity of the guaranty association process across the country.[65] Another problem is the potential for a very large insolvency or series of insolvencies that might overwhelm the assessment ability of each state's guaranty association to provide immediate indemnification.

## THE REGULATION OF LIFE INSURANCE INTERNATIONALLY[66]

As noted at the beginning of this chapter, life insurance regulation is universal. This section presents a survey of regulatory differences within selected large

[64]Although the cost is first met by the insurer, the actual costs of insolvency were found to be borne broadly by the population in their roles as insurance consumers, taxpayers, and owners of capital. See James Barrese and Jack M. Nelson, *The Consequences of Insurance Insolvencies* (unpublished paper, the College of Insurance, 1991).

[65]NOLHGA is a clearinghouse of information for most associations. It helps coordinate individual state association liabilities during an insolvency.

[66] This section draws on R. M. Hammond, "Life Insurance Regulation in Canada," *Canadian Journal of Life Insurance*, Vol. 9, No. 54 (1991), pp. 23-27; Mike Lombardi, "A New Era for Financial Services," *Emphasis*, No. 1 (1992), pp. 20-22; and *Industry and Trade Summary: Insurance* (Washington, D.C.: U.S. International Trade Commission, 1991).

markets worldwide.[67] Particular attention is accorded Canada because of its close proximity and importance to the U.S. market. Regulatory philosophies and practices can have a profound effect on the structure and operation of a nation's life insurance industry. Government determines who can sell insurance and the conditions under which and in some cases the prices at which it can be sold, and it also sets rules for reserves and insurer financial condition.

At one end of the international regulatory spectrum, some governments only lightly regulate insurance—their primary emphasis being on insurer solvency. Competition is encouraged and relied upon as the primary consumer-protection force. Hong Kong, the United Kingdom, Ireland, and the Netherlands are examples of this approach.

At the other extreme, government regulatory involvement can be extensive, covering not only solvency but also policy content and pricing. Germany, Japan, and Korea are traditional examples. Such heavy regulation is rationalized as being conducive to a more orderly, stable market. Many markets, including those of the United States and Canada, fall between the two extremes.

## Insurance Regulation in Canada

*Overview*. Supervision of insurance companies in Canada is shared by the federal and provincial governments. A life insurer may choose to incorporate and be regulated at the federal or the provincial level. The federal government is responsible for the solvency supervision of all non-Canadian companies operating in Canada on a branch basis and all federally incorporated insurers. These companies account for about 90 percent of the life insurance business in Canada. The Office of the Superintendent of Financial Institutions (OSFI) is the federal supervisory agency for insurance companies, banks, and other deposit-taking institutions. Provincial governments are responsible for the solvency supervision of all provincially incorporated insurers. In addition, provincial governments have exclusive jurisdiction over all insurers' marketing practices such as contract wording and its interpretation, licensing of agents and premium rates.

Mutual life insurance companies play a significant role in Canada. Fourteen life insurance companies account for about 75 percent of the business in Canada by premium volume; nine of these companies are mutual. Several Canadian life insurers have significant operations in the United States, the United Kingdom, and other countries.

In recent years, Canadian life insurance companies have aggressively competed with deposit-taking institutions for savings through the issuance of deferred annuities. The main deposit-taking institutions in Canada are banks and

---

[67]For empirical studies of various countries' insurance regulation, see Finsinger and Pauly.

trust and loan companies (similar to savings and loan associations in the United States). The six Canadian-controlled banks dominate the scene with an extensive system of branch offices across the country. The largest Canadian bank has assets that are equal to approximately 90 percent of the total assets of all Canadian life insurance companies combined.

*Control of Entry*. The approach to supervising federally incorporated insurers and the Canadian branch operations of foreign companies is basically the same. The main difference is that Canadian branch operations of foreign companies must maintain sufficient assets to cover their Canadian liabilities, plus any required capital margins, under the control of Canadian supervisory authorities.

Incorporation of a new federal insurance company requires at least $10 million of capital, an acceptable business plan, and reputable owners and managers. Foreign insurers can choose to operate in Canada either by establishing a branch operation or by incorporating a new federal insurer. Companies wishing to establish a branch operation in Canada must have at least $200 million in assets, adequate capital, and a track record of successful operations.

*Financial Regulation*. All federally incorporated insurance companies must submit an annual financial statement in a prescribed format, accompanied by an opinion from an auditor. All Canadian branch operations must also submit an annual financial statement in a prescribed format, but an auditor's opinion is not required. The possibility of requiring an auditor's opinion is being considered. On-site financial examinations by OSFI examiners are carried out every two years, and more frequently if needed.

Subject to certain concentration limits and limits on real estate and share investments, previous quantitative tests for investment have been replaced by the prudent portfolio approach. Under this approach, the onus is on companies to develop prudent investment policies and implement appropriate control procedures.

Life insurance companies may report bonds and mortgages at amortized values unless they are in default. A special reserve must be established that is equal to the larger of 1/3 percent of book value or 10 percent of the market deficiency.

Traded equity shares held by life insurance companies are reported at cost and are written up or down each year by 15 percent of the excess or deficiency of market value over cost. Realized capital gains and losses are recognized as adjustments to the amount written up or down. A similar approach, using a 10 percent rate, is used for real estate. The objective of these approaches is to promote equity between generations of participating policyowners by reflecting some portion of unrealized gains and losses in income. Another motivation is to encourage the making of investment decisions for investment reasons rather than income-reporting reasons.

The valuation actuary concept has been replaced by an appointed actuary concept, similar to the one in the United Kingdom. Appointment is made and terminated by the board of directors and the appointed actuary has access to the board. In addition to having the responsibility for determining the appropriateness of the actuarial reserves, the appointed actuary is responsible for reporting to the board at least yearly on the insurer's financial prospects. Also, if the appointed actuary becomes aware of any circumstances that may have a material impact on the insurer's ability to meet its obligations, he or she must bring the matter to the attention of management and the board. If, in the opinion of the appointed actuary, satisfactory action is not taken within a reasonable time period, he or she has a statutory obligation to make the superintendent aware of the situation.

***Recent Legislative Changes***. Recent legislative reforms are expected to produce major changes in the Canadian financial services business. Insurers and banks were given new and expanded powers. The law also created new corporate governance rules and gave the actuary a more responsible role in insurer operations. One of the government's objectives in sponsoring these changes was to establish a new framework for competition in the financial sector by removing many of the remaining restrictions on financial institutions fully competing with one another. As a result, under the new legislation, banks, trust and loan companies, and insurance companies have the opportunity to offer a similar range of products either directly or through subsidiaries.

Widely held financial institutions, such as mutual life companies, can own banks. Banks and trust and loan companies can own insurance companies as subsidiaries. Deposit-taking institutions, however, are prevented from retailing insurance in their deposit-taking branches except for credit life and accident and sickness policies in connection with loans. Also, deposit-taking institutions are prohibited from providing their insurance companies or brokers with detailed information about their clients, such as their age, marital status, financial position, and so on.[68]

To provide greater access to capital, life insurance companies, including mutual life insurance companies, will now be able to issue preferred shares and debentures to the extent that they meet the criteria of qualifying as capital under the capital adequacy rules.

A new reserving method permits a better measure of income, thereby enabling better monitoring of profitability of different classes and generations of business. The new method is based on generally accepted accounting principles. Consequently, one financial statement can be used for both regulatory and general financial reporting purposes.

---

[68]Canada's large banks are national banks and have thousands of offices. Such a vast, ready-made distribution system, coupled with extensive credit and personal information on bank customers, may provide banks with a formidable competitive advantage. Many observers believe that banks ultimately will obtain full retailing privileges (see Lombardi, p. 21).

## INSURANCE REGULATION IN THE EUROPEAN COMMUNITY

The national European Community (EC) insurance markets historically have been fragmented in terms of market accessibility, size, and regulation. The community has about 4,400 insurance companies.[69]

There are considerable differences in insurance regulatory philosophy among EC states. The United Kingdom, The Netherlands, and Ireland regulate their industries lightly, focusing chiefly on insurer solvency. They largely leave it to consumers to compare policies and the prices paid for them. The other EC member states have varying degrees of more intense regulation. Germany is perhaps the strictest; it reviews each new insurance product before it can be sold, judging how that product fits into the insurance company's business plan submitted previously to the regulators, and, in many cases, setting the price band that an insurer may charge for a given insurance product. Some German insurers assert that German consumers insist on this level of regulation and protection.[70] Others see signs of a growing consumer movement in which individuals more readily compare policies and prices on their own, without the guidance of the state.[71]

The EC market is said to be ahead of the legislators in rather comprehensively restructuring how insurance is bought and which companies might dominate certain markets. Indeed, as mentioned in the previous chapter, banking and insurance company linkups have become so common that the French now speak of *Bancassurance* and the Germans refer to *Allfinanz*.

The EC member states are undergoing a major internal trade liberalization—the single market integration program. When the currently proposed insurance directives are enacted fully, an EC-domiciled insurer obtaining a license in one EC nation will be able to underwrite and sell insurance in all member states.[72] Insurers will be regulated, moreover, only by their country of domicile (home-country control).

In Western Europe, any previous restrictive trade practices in insurance (as they apply among EC states) have recently been or are being abolished because of the market integration program. For example, restricting the investment of funds by insurance companies, which was a common practice in several EC nations, was abolished when the EC directive to fully liberalize capital movements took effect for most countries in 1990. Non-EC insurance companies already incorporated in at least one EC nation are unlikely to confront new nontariff barriers. They are established as European companies and presumably will be treated the same as other European-incorporated companies—that is, they

[69]European Community, *Panorama of EC Industry* (1990), pp. 26-35.

[70]*Industry and Trade Summary: Insurance*, p. 12.

[71]*Ibid.*

[72]In the case of foreign companies, these provisions will apply to subsidiary companies only, not to branch operations of non-EC companies.

will be accorded national treatment.[73] Many provisions of the directives are unlikely to be fully effective throughout the Community perhaps until the year 2000.

Distribution concerns are driving the insurance market within the European Community and Western Europe. Banks already have excellent distribution networks. Several EC member states permit universal banking, which includes the sale and sometimes the underwriting of insurance. This combination of factors has led to a great deal of merger and acquisition activity among banks and insurance companies within the European Community. One of the primary motivations behind this trend is the desire to quickly obtain an insurance distribution network that will compete effectively when all of the single market directives take effect.

## INSURANCE REGULATION IN JAPAN

The Japanese life insurance market is the world's second largest. The industry is characterized by a small number of very large companies. The Japanese Ministry of Finance (MOF) regulates both insurance and banking. The insurance sector reports to the banking division within the MOF. The system favors insurer financial stability over other factors. Limited competition and circumscribed insurance products are said to be preferred, even though this may result in higher insurance premiums for consumers and lower dividends for stockholders.[74]

Premium rates charged by life insurance companies are the same for all insurers, although dividends paid to policyowners may differ, if the MOF agrees. In marketing their products, insurers are legally restricted from telling consumers their relative market or investment performance—that is, no comparisons are permitted. The MOF has strict guidelines for the investment portfolios of insurance companies.

The Japanese Ministry of Finance is undertaking a gradual liberalization of the nation's financial community, breaking down the walls that traditionally separated banking, securities, and insurance. Each of these sectors increasingly offers overlapping products, and this trend is expected to continue. Competition among sectors is rising.

---

[73]There remains a lingering concern, however, over whether later insurance companies wishing to enter the EC market will enjoy the same benefits. The uncertainty stems from the possible future interpretation of the "reciprocity" ("third nation") clause of EC insurance directives, which provides for national treatment and effective market access for EC companies wishing to enter foreign markets. Some U.S. government and industry sources are concerned, for example, that current U.S. restrictions relating to the separation of insurance and banking might be judged to be a denial of effective market access for EC insurance companies wishing to enter the U.S. insurance market. These restrictions do not exist in Europe. If such a judgment were made, U.S. insurers wishing to enter the EC market could be denied entry until an accommodation between the United States and the European Community could be reached.

[74]*Industry and Trade Summary: Insurance*, p. 16.

## INSURANCE REGULATION IN OTHER COUNTRIES

Some 95 percent of the global life insurance market is accounted for by the United States, Canada, the European Community, and Japan.[75] Other life insurance markets, especially in Asia (e.g., Korea and Taiwan) are growing rapidly, and insurance regulation continues to evolve with the growth. With significant exceptions, many of the national insurance markets of South and Southeast Asia, the Middle East, Latin America, Central and Eastern Europe, and Africa have, in past decades, been dominated by state-owned insurers— often with monopoly power.

Heading toward the twenty-first century, these countries have largely recognized the benefits of a competitive market. The dramatic changes within the former Soviet Union and the Eastern European countries have highlighted these benefits. Most developing countries' life insurance regulatory regimes remain rigid, even with liberalization and limited deregulation. The challenge for them remains to balance the problems of imperfect competition with those of imperfect regulation.

## TAXATION OF U.S. LIFE AND HEALTH INSURERS

U.S. life and health insurers are taxed by the federal and state governments. Federal taxation is based on insurers' net income, whereas states continue to tax insurers primarily on premium income. Before covering the essential elements of federal and state taxation, an overview of desirable goals of a tax system is presented.

## DESIRABLE GOALS OF A TAX SYSTEM[76]

Ideally, tax systems should be:

- Simple

- Equitable

- Neutral

A tax system can be considered *simple* if it is not complex administratively, it is not easily evaded, and it is transparent in its functioning. Ideally, a tax system should be easily understood and explained by its enforcement authorities, and it should not appear bewilderingly complex to taxpayers.

---

[75]*Sigma,* Swiss Re (Feb. 1991).

[76]This section draws on Harold D. Skipper, Jr., "State Taxation of Insurance Companies: Time for a Change," *Journal of Insurance Regulation* (Dec. 1987), pp. 121-137.

The concept of *equity* in taxation poses theoretical and practical difficulties for tax-system designers. The intent is that each taxpayer should contribute his, her, or its fair share in taxes. Determining what is the "fair share" is the difficult part. For businesses and individuals in the United States, net income has generally been adopted as an appropriate measure of the taxpayer's ability to pay, and therefore the basis for calculation of the fair share. Equity in taxation in some situations also has meant taxing those who benefit from a government-provided product or service in some direct proportion to the extent of that benefit. Fuel taxes are examples.

A tax system, ideally, should be economically *neutral*. This concept is exceedingly important if the tax system is to avoid unintentionally creating incentives or disincentives with respect to economic and social behavior. In the absence of an overriding economic or social goal to be served by the tax system, the system should minimize interference with the economic and behavioral decisions of individual citizens, businesses, and other taxpaying entities.

The concept of economic neutrality suggests also that the tax system (1) should not benefit one industry grouping at the expense of another and (2), within a single industry grouping, should not disadvantage one set of competitors relative to other competitors—again, in the absence of overriding economic or social goals.

Finally, the concept of economic neutrality connotes that market forces, not the tax system, should drive business decisions. Thus, within a single business entity and in the absence of overriding social or economic goals, government should not establish tax incentives that would encourage a company to produce or market one kind of service or product in preference to others. The decision as to the product or service a company might wish to produce and market should remain with the company. In the absence of overriding social or economic considerations, government in a private enterprise economy should not attempt to influence this decision.

In reviewing insurer taxation, the preceding ideal characteristics should be kept in mind. As will be obvious, the goals are sometimes conflicting.

## STATE TAXATION[77]

States subject insurance companies to one or more of several types of taxes. The common types are discussed below.

***Premium Taxation***. All states in the United States impose a premium tax of some sort. Ordinarily, the premium tax takes the place of other state income or related taxation. A complete premium tax system is defined by the premium tax

---

[77]This section draws on Skipper, "State Taxation of Insurance Companies."

base, the premium tax rates, and any special deductions, credits, or exemptions provided for in the law.

Under the typical state premium tax structure, the tax base is the simple total of the insurer's premium revenue from the state, with certain alterations. Premiums received from assumed reinsurance are usually excluded from the tax base, since the original insurer that wrote the business would have already been subjected to premium tax for the direct premiums. Most states permit a deduction from the tax base for dividends paid to policyowners. The premium tax base may include premiums received for accident and health insurance, or such premiums may be taxed separately. Insurers' investment income is not included in the tax base.

Most states do not levy any premium tax on either domestic or out-of-state annuity considerations paid to insurers. Even the states that tax annuity considerations typically exempt federally qualified annuity plans (e.g., individual retirement annuities, tax-deferred annuities, and so on) from premium taxation. States that tax annuities place life insurers at a competitive disadvantage with banks and other savings media.

The tax rates on out-of-state insurers range from a low of 0.75 percent to a high of 4.2824 percent. Tax rates on domestic insurers vary from 0 percent to 4 percent. Some states tax health insurance premiums at a higher rate than that for life insurance premiums, while others do the opposite.

Selected forms of insuring organizations enjoy preferential treatment in many states. Both domestic and out-of-state fraternal life insurers are typically exempt from premium taxation. Blue Cross/Blue Shield organizations and other nonprofit health care service plans, until recently, were exempt from premium taxation in almost all states. The trend is toward taxing them, as with any other health insurer. Self-insurance arrangements by commercial enterprises for health and other employee benefit coverages are generally exempted from premium taxation—a fact that encourages self-insurance compared to group insurance.

Several states provide preferential tax treatment for their domestic insurers, although, since 1980, at least a dozen states have changed their laws to eliminate some or all of their discriminatory elements.[78]

Several states provide tax concessions if companies maintain certain proportions of their assets in the state. Many of these requirements are unrealistic in that the proportion of an insurer's total assets that is required to be invested in order to receive the concession is so large as either to benefit only domestic insurers or to be ignored by out-of-state insurers.

---

[78]The Supreme Court in *Metropolitan v. Ward*, 105 S. Ct. 1676 (1985), ruled that the two purposes proffered by the state in support of discriminatory taxation were not legitimate state purposes when fostered by discriminatory taxation. The Court remanded the case to the state court for further proceedings on other possible state purposes. Thus, according to some persons, the *Ward* decision did not provide an unequivocal indictment of discriminatory premium tax laws. The result is that many states have chosen not to materially alter the discriminatory aspects of their laws.

*Income Taxation*. Nine states subject out-of-state insurers to state income taxation. Three of these states provide that the income tax can be offset against the premium tax, and five provide that the premium tax can be offset against the income tax. New York provides that both income and premium taxes are to be paid by out-of-state insurers, up to a maximum amount.

Fourteen states subject their domestic insurers to state income taxation. Six of these states exempt domestic insurers from premium taxation and, in essence, tax insurers as they do any other domestic corporation, with recognition for their special characteristics. Five permit offsetting premium taxes paid by domestic insurers against the state income tax obligation. Two states permit offsetting the income tax against the premium tax due, and New York provides that domestic insurers must pay both premium taxes and income taxes up to a stated maximum.

*Retaliatory Taxation*. Retaliatory tax laws are intended to promote the interstate business of domestic insurers by discouraging other states from imposing excess or discriminatory taxes. These laws have been held to be constitutionally valid.[79] All states except Hawaii have retaliatory tax laws.[80] Retaliatory laws usually provide that when the laws of another state or country create a greater burden on a state's domestic insurers than the state's domestic laws impose on similar foreign insurers, the insurance commissioner of the state of domicile may impose similar obligations on foreign insurers seeking to do business in his or her state.

*Other Taxation*. States levy various other forms of taxes, fees, and assessments on insurers. These might include ad valorem taxes on real estate, personal property taxes, license fees, franchise taxes, and other taxes. Also, a few states permit their political subdivisions (e.g., cities, counties, and so on) to levy premium taxes on insurers. This taxation places disproportionate administrative burdens on insurers, and these approaches are universally and appropriately decried. Alternative revenue-sharing means of accomplishing the same purpose are far more efficient.

*Evaluation of Premium Taxation*. The premium tax system has both desirable and undesirable attributes. A system of taxation based on an insurance company's premium income is a simple approach to taxation. It is easy to administer by both insurers and tax authorities. Compliance verification is not

---

[79]*Western and Southern Life Insurance Company v. State Board of Equalization*, 451 U.S. 648 (1981).

[80]The effectiveness of retaliatory tax laws has been questioned. In one study, the researcher concluded: "They [retaliatory tax laws] have not been the historical cause of low tax rates for life insurers. Neither have they helped promote uniformity of state premium rates. However, there does exist a potential for retaliatory provisions to be used against the domestic insurers they were enacted to protect." See J. J. Bodily, "The Effects of Retaliation on the State Taxation of Life Insurers," *The Journal of Risk and Insurance*, Vol. 44 (Mar. 1977).

particularly difficult. This taxation produces a steady and usually increasing revenue flow to the state. Another possible positive attribute of the premium tax system is that it already exists. Insurers and state (and some local) governments are accustomed to it.

U.S. insurance companies have been subjected to premium taxation for over 150 years. This method of taxation arose at a time when governmental administration and tax units needed great simplicity and ease in administration. As a United Nations study pointed out, however, "Its simplicity is the source of potentially great inequity."[81]

The premium tax has been the object of criticism on the grounds that (1) it constitutes a direct tax on savings that is applicable only to insurers, (2) it is regressive in that it hits lower-income persons who purchase life insurance relatively harder than higher-income persons, (3) it discriminates unfairly against higher-premium (and cash-value) forms of life insurance, since it is levied on the premium, (4) it discriminates unfairly against those who must pay higher premium rates, such as the elderly and those who are rated substandard, and (5) it must be paid irrespective of insurer profitability.[82]

A premium tax that is higher for out-of-state insurers than it is for domestic insurers is an interstate trade barrier that, were it not for the McCarran-Ferguson Act, would almost certainly be unconstitutional.[83] Such discriminatory taxation has the same negative effects on trade as tariffs, and it has been condemned by the NAIC for distorting competition and ignoring the national character of the U.S. market.[84]

Tax rates in the 1 to 4 percent range may seem low. While the rate is low, it is applied to a large tax base and few tax concessions are provided. More particularly, no deductions are permitted for reasonable insurer expenses or even for claims payments to policyowners and beneficiaries. The net result, therefore, is a low tax rate but a high effective tax burden. Studies have found that the effective tax burden on insurers arising from premium taxation is consistently higher than that on other financial and nonfinancial institutions.[85]

With increasing competitiveness within the financial services community, economically neutral tax systems become more critical. As currently structured, the premium tax system can be defended only on the grounds of needed revenue and ease of collection.

[81]*Establishing Life Insurance Tax Policy in Developing Countries,* United Nations Conference on Trade and Development, Doc. No. TD/B/C.3/177 (1982).

[82]See Skipper, "State Taxation of Insurance Companies."

[83]See Martin F. Grace and Harold D. Skipper, Jr., "The Illinois Discriminatory Premium Tax: Time for Repeal?" *Southern Illinois University Law Review* (Spring 1990), pp. 345-399.

[84]"NAIC Statement of Policy on Insurance Taxation," 1 *NAIC Proceeding* (1971), pp. 58, 70.

[85]See Skipper, "State Taxation of Insurance Companies."

## FEDERAL INCOME TAXATION[86]

Since the advent of federal income taxation, life insurance company tax formulas have undergone frequent revisions designed to make them acceptable to all segments of the industry and, at the same time, to produce the revenues expected by Congress. To be equitable, a tax formula to be applied to life insurance companies should (1) recognize the long-term nature of the life insurance contract and the difficulty in determining the operating gain in any one year, (2) tax both mutual and stock companies fairly, without disrupting the existing competitive balance, and (3) provide an acceptable method for determining the deduction for interest required to maintain policyowner reserves.

From 1913 through 1920, U.S. life insurance companies were taxed on their total income under the provisions generally applicable to all business corporations. From 1921 until 1958, life insurance companies were taxed at ordinary corporate rates, but only on their net investment income. The Life Insurance Company Tax Act of 1959 changed this yet again by imposing a tax (at ordinary corporate rates) on a life insurance company's total income.

The manner in which the 1959 Act derived this total income base, however, was relatively complex and widely misunderstood. The 1959 Act tax base consisted of three parts—an investment income element, an underwriting gain element (which, for many insurers, was only partially taxed on a current basis), and a deferred underwriting gain base—and thus was said to constitute a three-phase approach to life insurance company taxation.

In the Deficit Reduction Act of 1984, Congress rewrote the 1959 Act in an effort to correct a number of inadequacies and to provide total tax revenue of a preestablished amount. These perceived inadequacies related, in part, to the changing nature of life insurance products; to fluctuating interest rates, as contrasted with the low and stable interest rates of the 1959 era; to a concern about the overstatement of reserve liabilities and of certain special deductions; and to the partial deferral of tax on underwriting gain. As a result, in the 1984 Act, Congress mandated a conceptually simple tax base that still encompasses a life insurance company's total income, but that does so on a single-phase basis.

*Taxable Income*. The 1984 Act defines **life insurance company taxable income** (LICTI) as gross income less applicable deductions. This general approach is the same as that of other corporations, but many of the details necessarily differ, as discussed below.

---

[86]This section draws on William B. Harman, "The Structure of Life Insurance Company Taxation: The New Pattern under the 1984 Act—Parts I and II," *Journal of the American Society of CLU*, Vol. 39 (Mar. 1985) and (May 1985).

1.    *Gross Income.* Gross income of a life insurance company can be divided into five categories:

1.    Premiums

2.    Investment income

3.    Capital gains

4.    Decreases in reserves

5.    All other items of gross income

Figure 34-2 illustrates the changing sources and magnitudes of U.S. life insurance companies' income.

Thus Internal Revenue Code (IRC) Section 803(a)(1) includes as income all *premiums and other considerations* received on insurance and annuity contracts. According to section 803(b), these receipt items include fees, deposits, assessments, advance or prepaid premiums, reinsurance premiums, and the amount of any policyowner dividends reimbursable to the insurer by a reinsurer. Also included are premiums or deposits on supplementary contracts or policy proceeds left with the company. An insurer may reduce its premium receipts includable in gross income by the amount of any returned premiums (e.g.,

**FIGURE 34-2**

**DISTRIBUTION OF TOTAL INCOME FOR U.S. LIFE INSURERS**

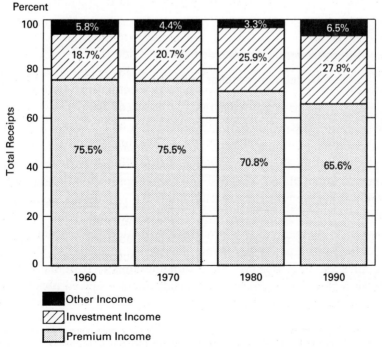

*Source*: ACLI

premiums returned because of policy cancellations or errors in determining the premium) and premiums paid to other insurers under reinsurance agreements. Approximately 60 to 80 percent of a typical life insurance company's gross income is included under this section.

The other principal source of income of a life insurance company is its *investment* activities. The investment earnings of an insurer consist primarily of interest, dividends, rents, and royalties. Approximately 20 to 40 percent of a typical life insurance company's gross income consists of investment earnings.

Life insurance companies are taxed on capital gains in the same manner as are other corporate taxpayers. Prior to 1987, there was an alternative tax at a 28 percent rate on any net capital gain (the excess of net long-term capital gains over net short-term capital losses) incurred by corporations. Corporations are currently taxed at a 34 percent rate on taxable income, including capital gains.

Any net *decrease in certain insurance reserves* produces an income item. The reserves in question are those peculiar to life insurance companies (see below). Life insurers are allowed tax deductions when net additions are made to these reserves. Thus when the reserves are no longer needed and released, their release or decrease produces an income item for the company.

Finally, the law contains a provision that encompasses all items of gross income not included under any of the other four categories discussed above. The sum of the five categories described above produces life insurance gross income.

2.    *Deductions.* The items of deduction allowed a life insurance company under current law can be divided into three categories:[87]

1.    General corporate deductions

2.    Deductions peculiar to the insurance business

3.    The small life insurance company deduction

*First*, life insurers are permitted all deductions allowable to other corporate taxpayers, with certain technical modification.[88] *Second*, life insurers are permitted certain deductions that are *peculiar to the insurance business*. Thus a deduction is allowed for all claims, benefits, and losses incurred on insurance and annuity contracts. These payments are analogous to income tax deductions permitted for the cost to a manufacturing organization of raw materials.

A life insurance company also is granted a deduction for any net annual additions to specified insurance reserves that it must maintain for its insurance and annuity contracts. This reserve deduction includes two items: (1) the "savings" element included in premiums or considerations received plus (2) the

---

[87]The 1984 act created a fourth deduction category—a special life insurer deduction equal to 20 percent of taxable income. This deduction was repealed by the Tax Reform Act of 1986.

[88]See Harmon (Mar. 1985), p. 61, for details.

interest assumed to be credited each year to the insurer's reserve to render it sufficient to meet its future obligations. The deductible net increase in reserves is computed by subtracting the opening balance of the reserves (January 1) from the closing balance of the reserves (December 31).

The six insurance reserves taken into account under the 1984 Act are:

1.  Life insurance policy reserves

2.  Unearned premiums and unpaid losses included in "total reserves"

3.  Discounted liabilities for insurance or annuity contracts not currently involving life, accident, or health contingencies

4.  Dividend accumulations and other amounts held at interest under insurance or annuity contracts

5.  Advance premiums and premium deposit fund liabilities

6.  Reasonable special contingency reserves under group contracts for retired lives and premium stabilization

Under the 1959 Act, the amounts of a life insurance company's reserves at the end of the taxable year generally were the amounts shown on the company's statutory annual statement. The 1984 Act substantially changed the rules for determining life insurance reserves, generally resulting in a considerable decrease in these reserves as compared to 1959 Act reserves, particularly in the early years of a policy. The rule under current law is that the life insurance reserve for any contract shall be the greater of (1) the net cash surrender value of the contract or (2) the reserve for the contract as computed under federally prescribed standards. In no event, however, is this amount permitted to exceed the annual statement figure.

The reserve computed under federal standards is an amount determined in accordance with the methods and assumptions used in calculating the life insurance reserves shown on the insurer's annual statement, but modified to take account of the following five federal standards.

1.  A prescribed tax reserve method. This is the Commissioners' Reserve Valuation Method for life insurance contracts.[89]

2.  A minimum valuation interest rate that is equal to the greater of (1) the applicable federal interest rate[90] for the year in which the contract was issued or (2) the prevailing state interest rate, defined as the highest assumed interest rate that at least 26 states permit to be used in computing reserves for the particular insurance or annuity contract.[91]

[89]See Chap. 20.

[90]The federal interest rate is computed as the average of the yields of midterm government bonds over the previous five years.

[91]See Chap. 20.

3.    The prevailing commissioners' standard tables. These are the most recent standard tables for mortality and morbidity prescribed by the National Association of Insurance Commissioners that at least 26 states permit to be used in computing reserves for the type of contract involved at the time of issue.[92]

4.    The elimination from the reserves of any amount in respect of deferred and uncollected premiums (unless the gross amount of these premiums is included in gross income).

5.    The elimination of any reserve in respect of "excess interest" (i.e., interest exceeding the prevailing state assumed interest rate) guaranteed beyond the end of the taxable year.

Another deduction peculiar to the life insurance business is that permitted for policyowner dividends.[93] This term is defined by Section 808 as any dividend paid or payable to a policyowner in his or her capacity as such, and it includes any distribution to a policyowner that is economically equivalent to a dividend. Accordingly, it includes excess interest, premium adjustments, and experience-rated refunds, as well as any amount paid or credited to policyowners (including an increase in benefits) where the amount is not fixed in the contract but depends on the insurer's experience or the discretion of management.

A stock life insurance company is allowed an unlimited deduction for policyowner dividends paid or accrued during the taxable year. A mutual life insurer, however, may be subject to a limitation on the deductibility of its policyowner dividends (see below).

The *third* major deduction allowed is the so-called *small life insurance company deduction*. This deduction, which was included primarily for political reasons and is consistent with the general congressional policy of encouraging small business, equals 60 percent of the tentative LICTI, up to a maximum of $3,000,000. Thus the small company deduction can never exceed $1,800,000 (i.e., 60% × $3,000,000). If a life insurance company's tentative LICTI exceeds $3,000,000, the amount of the small company deduction is phased out by an amount equal to 15 percent of tentative LICTI in excess of $3,000,000. Thus, for an insurer with tentative LICTI of $15,000,000 or more, no small company deduction is allowed.

For example, if a small life insurance company had tentative LICTI of $2,000,000, its small life insurance company deduction would be $1,200,000 (60% × $2,000,000). If, however, the insurer's tentative LICTI were $5,000,000,

---

[92]See Chap. 20.

[93]Two other potentially important deductions relate to deductions for assumption reinsurance and for policyowner dividends paid by a reinsurer to the ceding company. See Harmon (Mar. 1985), pp. 62-63.

its small life insurance company deduction would be $1,500,000, determined as follows:

1.  60% × $3,000,000 =   $1,800,000

2.  Reduced by 15% ×
    ($5,000,000 −
    $3,000,000)                          300,000
                                       $1,500,000

***Mutual Company Dividend Treatment***. According to current tax-law theory, distributions to customers should be fully deductible by a corporation, whereas distributions to owners of the enterprise should not be deductible. In the case of mutual organizations, however, the customers are also effectively the owners.

Mutual insurers often charge relatively higher-than-necessary premiums and return unneeded excess premiums as dividends to policyowners. This excess generally is conceded to be properly deductible at the corporate level. Also included in policyowner dividends, however, are some distribution of investment and underwriting earnings of the mutual company (since the policyowner is effectively an owner of the company, as well as a purchaser of its services). Many believe that, in contrast with the return of excess premiums, these earnings are properly taxable at the corporate level.

Intertwined with the dividend deductibility issue faced by Congress in crafting the 1984 Act was the amount of revenue to be raised from the industry and its apportionment between stock and mutual companies. For example, a 100 percent policyowner dividend deduction would have permitted mutual insurers to pay only a small amount of tax (or perhaps none at all) if they decided to distribute all or substantially all of their earnings to policyowners. On the other hand, if no deductions were permitted, then legitimate payments to policyowners as customers (rather than as owners), which should be deductible under general tax principles, would be denied to mutuals—an unfair result since it would have overtaxed those companies. Thus it was (and is) crucial to impose appropriate relative tax burdens on each—stock and mutual segment, so that the federal income tax does not favor one segment over the other. Accordingly, in an effort to treat the stock and mutual segments equitably and to raise appropriate revenues from the industry, it was judged necessary to limit the dividend deduction for mutual companies.

The objectives of the 1984 Act's dividend deduction limitation were twofold. First, it was designed to ensure that mutual life insurers did not, through a combination of policyowner dividend distributions and other deductions, reduce their gain from operations after dividends to an amount below a minimum, imputed return on equity. Second, it was desired to achieve a revenue balance between the stock and mutual segments of the industry. This segment balance was set at 55/45 percent but it could shift in future years, depending upon the relative earnings of each segment.

The assumption underlying the segment balance was that an appropriate guide to the profitability of mutual life insurers is the profitability on equity of stock life insurers. The mechanics of the limitation on the deductibility of policyowner dividends by a mutual insurer involve the determination of a differential earnings rate on "equity" between stock and mutual companies. The imputed earnings rate on equity for stock insurers was assumed to be higher than that for mutual insurers, and this difference was assumed to represent a return to policyowners in mutual companies on their ownership interests in the companies. As such, this amount must be excluded by the mutual company from its dividend deduction (i.e., it is not deductible). The differential earnings rate is recalculated each year.[94]

***The 1990 DAC Tax.***[95] The Revenue Reconciliation Act of 1990 added a new provision to life insurer tax law that purports to defer (capitalize and amortize) acquisition costs of life insurance and annuity contracts. This provision is known as the **DAC** (deferred acquisition costs) **tax.**

The theory is that certain insurance company expenses—commissions, underwriting expenses, agency expenses, and other costs of acquiring and retaining business—should be capitalized and amortized to produce a better matching of deductions with revenues. Such a capitalization is done under generally accepted accounting principles but not under statutory accounting principles.

The DAC provision came about because the Treasury Department and Congress believed the life insurance business should pay more in federal income taxes. The DAC provision was invented to produce a revenue estimate for the provision of $8 billion for the five-year estimation period. Given the tax level of the industry in recent years, this amounted to roughly a 50 percent increase in industry tax.

In form, the provision is a proxy for true deferral, which was seen as inadministrable. For each year, the amount of the insurer's general deductions to be capitalized is the sum of specified percentages of premiums by line of business:

- 1.75 percent of annuity contract premiums

- 2.05 percent of group life insurance premiums

- 7.70 percent of other life and noncancelable accident and health insurance premiums

---

[94]The differential earnings rate is calculated annually by the Treasury Department from tax return information. It has generally fallen within the 2 to 3 percent range. This rate is applied to a mutual insurer's equity base as defined in the law. The resulting **differential earnings amount** is subtracted from a mutual insurer's policyowner dividend payments to yield the deductible dividend amount. The procedure results, in effect, in a tax on mutual insurer surplus.

[95]This section draws on Wayne E. Bergquist, Nicholas Bauer, and Douglas N. Hutz, "Principles of Taxation," *SOA Course 200 Study Note* (Itasca, Ill.: Society of Actuaries, 1992).

In forming the amount to be capitalized, premiums on pension plan contracts are not included, nor are imputed premiums (e.g., where dividends are applied to reduce premiums). Generally, reinsurance ceded reduces premiums and reinsurance assumed increases them.

The capitalized amounts are to be amortized in a straight-line fashion over a ten-year period starting at the middle of the year of capitalization. It is of interest to smaller companies that the amortization period for the first $5 million capitalized in any year is five years. This $5 million amount is phased out as the capitalized amount moves from $10 million to $15 million, so large insurers obtain no benefit.

The DAC tax substantially raised the life insurance industry's federal income taxes. In turn, life insurers must make appropriate adjustments in existing and new product pricing to account for this increase. Interest rate credits, dividends, and other nonguaranteed benefits can be expected to be lower than they otherwise would have been.

# Index

Employers' response to rising health care costs, 749–50
Employment
    life insurance demand and, 347
    loss of, 8
    unemployment insurance, 711–12
Endorsement split–dollar plan, 467
Endorsement system, 462–63, 464
Endowment–at–age–100 policies. *See* Whole life insurance
Endowment insurance, 82, 95–97
    calculating net single premiums for, 544–46
    gift of proceeds from, 405
    matured endowment, tax treatments of, 382
    modified endowment contract, 379, 381
    pure, 95–96, 544–45
Enemy aliens, contract with, 182
Enforcement by regulators, 1004–5
England
    Friendly Societies in, 49
    guilds in, 48
    mutual assurance companies in, 49–50
    *See also* United Kingdom, insurance in
Enhanced ordinary life (EOL), 118–19, 144
    flexible (FEOL), 124, 144–45
Enhancements (persistency bonuses), 137–38
Entire contract clause, 200
Entity approach to partnership buy–and–sell agreement, 446
Entry–age normal method, 805
Entry/exit
    control of entry in Canada, 1013
    ease of, 977–78
Environment, 340–50
    cultural, 349–50
    demographic, 341–46
    economic, 346–47
    establishing investment policy and, 881
    health care, in U.S., 746–56
    insurer reactions to, 79–81
    political, 348–49
    product development and external, 963–65
    product innovation and, 74–79
    for retirement planning, 427–34
    significant changes in, program reevaluation and, 364
EPOs, 777–78
Equal outlay method (EOM), 242–46, 256–57, 261
Equitable Life Assurance Society of the United States, 54, 55, 56, 114, 201, 831
Equity
    concepts of, 572–74
    individual, 694
    among insureds, 644–45
    rate, 21, 22–23
    in taxation, 1018
Equity capital, demutualization to obtain access to, 832–33
Equity split–dollar plans, 464–65, 470
Equivalent level annual dividend (ELAD), 241, 266, 274
Equivalent level death benefit, 273
ERISA. *See* Employee Retirement Income Security Act (ERISA)
Estate, preservation of, 71
Estate planning, 15, 407–27
    impediments to well–planned estate, 407–10
    life insurance and generation–skipping transfer tax, 405–6, 421, 425–27

life insurance for estate liquidity, 424–25
process of, 410
team for, 410–11
tools for, 412–23
    gifts, 413–16
    joint ownership of property, 416–17
    living wills, 413
    trusts, 417–23
    wills, 408, 412–13
Estate tax, federal, 353, 388–402, 408–9, 442
    federal estate tax owed, 389, 397–99
    gross estate, 389, 390–95, 442, 448, 468
    illustration of, 399–402
    on nonqualified deferred compensation payments, 459
    overview of, 389–90
    on partnership buy–and–sell agreement, 448
    on split–dollar life insurance plans, 467–69
    taxable estate, 389, 395–96
    tentative federal estate tax, 389, 397
    tentative tax base, 389, 396–97
Estoppel, doctrine of, 190, 194, 197
Ethical responsibilities of advisor, 278
European Community (EC), 63, 64–66, 850, 953, 978n, 1015–16
European Economic Area, 66
European Free Trade Association (EFTA), 66
European life insurers, early, 52
Evaluation
    of insurance advisor, 276–78
    of insurer. *See* under Insurers
    program, 363–64
    *See also* Cost analysis
Evidence, parol (oral), 197
Excess–of–loss reinsurance, 690–91
Excess–of–time (extended elimination) reinsurance, 690–91
Exchanges, policy, 123, 381–82
Exclusion, gift tax, 403
Exclusion carve–out, 773
Exclusion provisions
    accidental death, 174
    hazard restriction clauses and, 208–9
    in health insurance contract, 493–94, 669–70
    New York law on, 179n
    preexisting conditions, 484, 493, 497, 670
Exclusion ratio, 388
Exclusive–agent companies. *See* Agency–building distribution system
Exclusive provider organizations (EPOs), 777–78
Executive committee, 839
Executive officers, 840
Exemption statutes, state, 232–33, 234
Exempt property in bankruptcy, 231
Exhaustive events, 513
Exhibit 8 of annual statement, 267–68
Exhibits, 927–29
Expectations
    consumer, 75–76
    reasonable, doctrine of, 197–98, 199
Expected return on annuity, 388
Expected value, 535, 536, 540n
    present, 540
Expense liabilities, health insurance, 632, 636
Expense management formula, 957
Expense rates, unit, 588–89
Expenses
    asset–share calculation sensitivity to increase in, 600